# WEBSTER'S NEW WORLD

D0286887

## 575+ German Verbs

# WEBSTER'S NEW WORLD™

# 575+ German Verbs

by Edward Swick

WILEY

Wiley Publishing, Inc.

Webster's New World® 575+ German Verbs

Copyright © 2006 by Wiley, Hoboken, NJ

Published by Wiley, Hoboken, NJ
Published simultaneously in Canada

No part of this publication may be reproduced, stored in a retrieval system, or transmitted in any form or by any means, electronic, mechanical, photocopying, recording, scanning, or otherwise, except as permitted under Sections 107 or 108 of the 1976 United States Copyright Act, without either the prior written permission of the Publisher, or authorization through payment of the appropriate per-copy fee to the Copyright Clearance Center, 222 Rosewood Drive, Danvers, MA 01923, 978-750-8400, fax 978-646-8600, or on the web at www.copyright.com. Requests to the Publisher for permission should be addressed to the Legal Department, Wiley Publishing, Inc., 10475 Crosspoint Blvd., Indianapolis, IN 46256, 317-572-3447, fax 317-572-4355, or online at http://www.wiley.com/go/permissions.

The publisher and the author make no representations or warranties with respect to the accuracy or completeness of the contents of this work and specifically disclaim all warranties, including without limitation warranties of fitness for a particular purpose. No warranty may be created or extended by sales or promotional materials. The advice and strategies contained herein may not be suitable for every situation. This work is sold with the understanding that the publisher is not engaged in rendering legal, accounting, or other professional services. If professional assistance is required, the services of a competent professional person should be sought. Neither the publisher nor the author shall be liable for damages arising herefrom. The fact that an organization or Website is referred to in this work as a citation and/or a potential source of further information does not mean that the author or the publisher endorses the information the organization or Website may provide or recommendations it may make. Further, readers should be aware that Internet Websites listed in this work may have changed or disappeared between when this work was written and when it is read.

**Trademarks:** Wiley, the Wiley Publishing logo, Webster's New World, the Webster's New World logo, and all related trademarks, logos, and trade dress are trademarks or registered trademarks of John Wiley & Sons, Inc. and/or its affiliates. All other trademarks are the property of their respective owners. Wiley Publishing, Inc. is not associated with any product or vendor mentioned in this book.

For general information on our other products and services or to obtain technical support, please contact our Customer Care Department within the U.S. at 800-762-2974, outside the U.S. at 317-572-3993, or fax 317-572-4002.

Wiley also publishes its books in a variety of electronic formats. Some content that appears in print may not be available in electronic books. For more information about Wiley products, please visit our web site at www.wiley.com.

**Library of Congress Cataloging-in-Publication Data:**

Swick, Edward.
Webster's new world 575+ German verbs / by Edward Swick.
p. cm.
Includes bibliographical references and index.
ISBN-13: 978-0-7645-9915-6 (pbk.)
ISBN-10: 0-7645-9915-1
1. German language--Verb. 2. German language--Self-instruction. I. Title.
PF3271.S933 2006
438.2'421--dc22
2005031023

ISBN-13: 978-0-7645-9915-6

ISBN-10: 0-7645-9915-1

Manufactured in the United States

10 9 8 7 6 5 4 3 2 1

# ACKNOWLEDGMENTS

With much gratitude to Sabine McNulty for all her help and suggestions.

# TABLE OF CONTENTS

**Introduction** . . . . . **1**

**Verb Usage Review** . . . . . **5**

A . . . . . 43

B . . . . . 69

D . . . . . 121

E . . . . . 137

F . . . . . 173

G . . . . . 205

H . . . . . 235

J . . . . . 257

K . . . . . 261

L . . . . . 293

M . . . . . 317

N . . . . . 335

O . . . . . 341

P . . . . . 343

Q . . . . . 361

R . . . . . 365

S . . . . . 393

T . . . . . 515

U . . . . . 537

V . . . . . 551

W . . . . . 581

Z . . . . . 602

**Appendix of Additional Verbs** . . . . . **618**

**Appendix of Irregular Verb Forms** . . . . . **663**

**English-German Verb Index** . . . . . **677**

# INTRODUCTION

German verbs, like English verbs, provide the action of a sentence as well as the number, tense, and mood of that action. In other words, verbs play a very significant role in language. This book is designed to give you quick access to the conjugations and functions of verbs and is a complete reference to the 575 most commonly used German verbs. Each of these verbs is conjugated in all the persons (first-person singular and plural, second-person singular and plural, and third-person singular and plural) in the three moods (indicative, subjunctive, and imperative), and in all the tenses (present, past, present perfect, past perfect, future, and future perfect). The verbs are presented in alphabetical order in 575 charts followed by examples and idiomatic uses of the verbs. There is also a Verb Usage Review, an appendix of 1,500 other verbs that are cross-referenced to the charts, an appendix of irregular verb forms as a quick reference, and an index of English and German verbs.

## Verb Usage Review

In this section, you'll find a review of German verbs and their tenses, moods, and conjugations. The verb charts give you the complete conjugation of each verb, but the Verb Usage Review shows you how and when to use the various moods and tenses.

First, you'll encounter the German subject pronouns and their English counterparts. German and English differ in that, in the present tense, English has only one conjugational ending that is different and is used in the third-person singular. That ending is *–s* (see third person singular below).

| | ***Singular*** | ***Plural*** |
|---|---|---|
| First person | I talk | we talk |
| Second person | you talk | you talk |
| Third person | he talks | they talk |

In the German present tense, each person has a unique ending that must be used with all regular verbs and, in some cases, there are alternatives to these endings with irregular verbs.

I also identify the principal parts of the verbs for you. The principal parts are particularly important with irregular verbs, which often break the patterns that exist with regular verbs. Fortunately for English speakers, relating to the irregularities of German verbs is often relatively simple, because English and German are brother and sister languages and frequently have the same kind of irregularities. For example:

| | | | |
|---|---|---|---|
| English | sing | sang | sung |
| German | singen | sang | gesungen |

You'll also encounter irregular verbs that are completely different from English verbs, as well as tense forms and usages that are unique to German.

Although German and English have the same tenses, German often applies them in ways that are different from English. Understanding these differences is important in understanding German verbs. This is particularly true when looking at the subjunctive mood, because English is moving away from using this mood, while the subjunctive mood still functions as a critical aspect of verbs in the German language. Take this into consideration when using the verb charts.

The indicative mood is the first of the three moods that I present. It is used to provide facts and information in the form of statements or questions. The indicative mood can occur in any of the tenses: present, past, present perfect, past perfect, future, or future perfect. You'll see how each tense in the indicative mood is formed, so when you refer to one of the verb charts, you'll understand the kinds of conjugations presented there.

The subjunctive mood is used extensively in German. You'll find that it has a function that does not exist in English: indirect discourse. This is the retelling of a statement made or a question posed by someone else. *Direct discourse* is the quote of someone's words:

> Mary said, "John found ten dollars."

*Indirect discourse* occurs when another speaker says what was stated in direct discourse:

> Mary said that John found ten dollars.

In German, indirect discourse requires a special subjunctive conjugation. The subjunctive is also used in conditional statements and in statements of wish or desire.

The imperative mood is a command. Unlike English, which has one command form, German has three forms of the imperative: one for the second-person singular informal *(du)*, one for the second-person plural informal *(ihr)*, and one for the second-person formal *(Sie)*.

Participles occur in German. They are both present and past participles. But you'll discover that English and German use present participles quite differently. German has no progressive tense and, therefore, does not use a participle in that kind of verbal expression. Present participles tend to be used as modifiers. But past participles have a similar function in both languages.

# Verb Charts

The verb charts, which make up the bulk of this book, consist of 575 fully conjugated verbs in alphabetical order by their infinitive. The sample verb chart below shows the infinitive and its meaning, the past participle, followed by the complete conjugation in all the tenses. If the verb is reflexive, it is identified as such by the reflexive pronoun *sich* in the infinitive. I chose the verbs for these charts because of their high-frequency usage in the language. Some of the verbs have no prefix; others have inseparable prefixes *(be–, er–, emp–, ent–, ge–, ver–,* and *zer–);* and still others have separable prefixes (for example, *an–, auf–, ein–, vor–,* and *zu–).*

**anwenden**
to employ, to use, to apply to
**Auxiliary verb:** haben **Past participle:** angewandt
**Imperative:** Wende an! Wendet an! Wenden Sie an!

| Mode | Simple Tenses | | Compound Tenses | |
|---|---|---|---|---|
| | *Singular* | *Plural* | *Singular* | *Plural* |
| Indicative | **Present** | | **Present Perfect** | |
| | wende an<br>wendest an<br>wendet an | wenden an<br>wendet an<br>wenden an | habe angewandt<br>hast angewandt<br>hat angewandt | haben angewandt<br>habt angewandt<br>haben angewandt |
| | **Past** | | **Past Perfect** | |
| | wandte an<br>wandtest an<br>wandte an | wandten an<br>wandtet an<br>wandten an | hatte angewandt<br>hattest angewandt<br>hatte angewandt | hatten angewandt<br>hattet angewandt<br>hatten angewandt |
| | **Future** | | **Future Perfect** | |
| | werde anwenden<br>wirst anwenden<br>wird anwenden | werden anwenden<br>werdet anwenden<br>werden anwenden | werde angewandt haben<br>wirst angewandt haben<br>wird angewandt haben | werden angewandt haben<br>werdet angewandt haben<br>werden angewandt haben |
| Subjunctive | **Present** | | **Present Perfect** | |
| | wende an<br>wendest an<br>wende an | wenden an<br>wendet an<br>wenden an | habe angewandt<br>habest angewandt<br>habe angewandt | haben angewandt<br>habet angewandt<br>haben angewandt |
| | **Past** | | **Past Perfect** | |
| | wendete an<br>wendetest an<br>wendete an | wendeten an<br>wendetet an<br>wendeten an | hätte angewandt<br>hättest angewandt<br>hätte angewandt | hätten angewandt<br>hättet angewandt<br>hätten angewandt |
| | **Future** | | **Future Perfect** | |
| | werde anwenden<br>werdest anwenden<br>werde anwenden | werden anwenden<br>werdet anwenden<br>werden anwenden | werde angewandt haben<br>werdest angewandt haben<br>werde angewandt haben | werden angewandt haben<br>werdet angewandt haben<br>werden angewandt haben |
| | **Present and Future Conditional** | | **Past Conditional** | |
| | würde anwenden<br>würdest anwenden<br>würde anwenden | würden anwenden<br>würdet anwenden<br>würden anwenden | würde angewandt haben<br>würdest angewandt haben<br>würde angewandt haben | würden angewandt haben<br>würdet angewandt haben<br>würden angewandt haben |

**Note:** This verb also has a regular conjugation. Its principal parts without a prefix are *wendet, wendete, hat gewendet. Wenden* means "turn" or "turn over."

The auxiliary verb *haben* or *sein* depends upon the kind of verb—transitive or verb of motion.

The past participle is used to form the perfect tenses with the verb *haben* It can also be used as an adjective.

The imperative mood is used for giving orders, commands, or requests. It can be expressed formally or informally.

The indicative mood presents facts that are happening, did happen, or will happen.

The subjunctive is used to express emotions, wishes, desires, and conditions.

A note points out differences that occur with the illustrated verb when there is a change of prefix, when the verb has two forms (regular and irregular) and when both auxiliaries *haben* and *sein* can be used. It also explains how a verb directed to the chart relates to the one illustrated in the chart.

## EXAMPLES

Hier muss man diese Formel anwenden.
Hast du das Desinfektionsmittel richtig angewandt?

Here you have to use this formula.
Did you apply the disinfectant correctly?

All the verb charts end with example sentences in German, translated into English. These sentences demonstrate the meaning and function of the verb in the chart. The verbs are conjugated in various tenses and moods and are sometimes shown in high-frequency idioms.

# Appendix of Additional Verbs

The Appendix of Additional Verbs contains 1,500 German verbs with a quick reference to a fully conjugated verb in the verb charts that has an equivalent conjugation. For example, the German verb *kosten* (to cost) will refer to *arbeiten* (to work), because it has an equivalent conjugation. In this way, you'll learn many other verbs instead of being referred to the same pattern verb over and over again.

# Appendix of Irregular Verb Forms

The Appendix of Irregular Verb Forms helps you locate the infinitive to which the irregular verb form belongs. It shows the spelling changes that occur in the present tense, past tense, and participle, as well as the infinitive from which those verbs were derived. This appendix will direct you to the fully conjugated verb. For example, *fährt* will direct you to *fahren*.

# English-German Verb Index

This index lists, in alphabetical order, the English verbs found in this book with their German translation. A reference to the fully conjugated verb or equivalent verb is also given.

# VERB USAGE REVIEW

This section presents the conjugations of German verbs in an easy-to-understand format. It will help you learn how the tenses are formed and how they relate to English tenses. It will also help you understand why some changes are necessary in the conjugations of certain German verbs, and why other changes have to be memorized. You should read this section first. It will give you a strong foundation on the conjugation of the different types of German verbs, making the conjugations in the verb charts more logical and easier to learn. In order to conjugate a verb, you need to know the subject pronouns, so let's start with a review of these.

## Subject Pronouns

A **noun** is a word used to name a person, thing, place, quality, or idea. For example:

> Max plays soccer.
> The new restaurant across the street is quite good.

A **subject pronoun** takes the place of a subject noun in order to avoid the repetition of the noun. For example:

> He plays soccer.
> It is quite good.

Before you can use verbs, you need to know the subject pronouns, because subject pronouns always signal how to conjugate a verb. For example:

> I play.
> She plays.

In German, the subject pronouns are singular or plural and identify a person, an object, or an idea.

Because nouns have to be in the nominative case to be the subject of a sentence, pronouns must also be in the nominative case when they are the subject of a sentence. Table 1 shows the German subject pronouns in the nominative case and their corresponding English subject pronouns.

**Table 1 German Subject Pronouns and Their Corresponding English Subject Pronouns**

| | *Singular* | | *Plural* | |
|---|---|---|---|---|
| | ***German*** | ***English*** | ***German*** | ***English*** |
| First person | *ich* | I | *wir* | we |
| Second person | *du* | you | *ihr* | you |
| | *Sie* | you | *Sie* | you |
| Third person | *er* | he | *sie* | they |
| | *sie* | she | | |
| | *es* | it | | |

German has three forms of the word "you": *du, ihr,* and *Sie*. Use informal *du* with children, family members, and close friends. The pronoun *ihr* is also informal and is the plural of *du*. Formal *Sie* is always capitalized and is used with people with whom you are on a formal basis: adults unfamiliar to you, your doctor, a new neighbor, the clerk at the store, and so on.

The three third-person singular pronouns—*er, sie,* and *es*—are, respectively, masculine, feminine, and neuter. But they do not just replace nouns that refer to males, females, and inanimate objects. Many masculine and feminine nouns refer to inanimate objects and are, therefore, replaced by the appropriate subject pronoun *er* or *sie*. And some neuter nouns refer to living things and must be replaced by *es*. For example:

| ***Masculine Nouns*** | ***Appropriate Pronoun Replacement*** |
|---|---|
| *der Mann* (the man) | *er* (he) |
| *der Tisch* (the table) | *er* (it) |
| *der Wagen* (the car) | *er* (it) |

| ***Feminine Nouns*** | ***Appropriate Pronoun Replacement*** |
|---|---|
| *die Frau* (the woman) | *sie* (she) |
| *die Zeitung* (the newspaper) | *sie* (it) |
| *die Lampe* (the lamp) | *sie* (it) |

| ***Neuter Nouns*** | ***Appropriate Pronoun Replacement*** |
|---|---|
| *das Haus* (the house) | *es* (it) |
| *das Kind* (the child) | *es* (he/she) |
| *das Pferd* (the horse) | *es* (he/she/it) |

In the plural, gender is not considered, and all nouns whether masculine, feminine, or neuter are replaced by plural *sie*.

The third-person singular pronoun *man* is used where "one" or "you" would be said in English. English uses the pronoun "one" in formal statements. The pronoun "you" is informal or casual. But both English pronouns are translated into German as *man*. On occasion, *man* is said in German where "they" or "people" are used.

| | |
|---|---|
| *Das sagt man nicht laut.* | One doesn't say that out loud.<br>You don't say that out loud.<br>People don't say that out loud. |
| *Man kann das Wasser hier nicht trinken.* | One can't drink the water here.<br>You can't drink the water here. |
| *Man fährt in Deutschland oft mit dem Fahrrad.* | One often goes by bicycle in Germany.<br>People often go by bicycle in Germany. |
| *Man hat gesagt, dass der Fluss viel Land überschwemmt habe.* | They said that the river flooded a lot of land. |

Be aware that *man* is only used in the nominative case. In the other cases, use the respective forms of *ein–* (for example, *einem, einen,* and so on).

# The Basics on Verbs

The verb is the main element of speech and expresses existence (for example, to be), action (to work), feeling (to laugh), movement (to go), or process (to build). It is part of the sentence that commands, emphasizes, declares, denies, or questions something. It is also the part of the sentence that requires a variety of ending changes—the conjugations. In German, the verb has to agree with the subject in number (singular or plural) and person (first, second, or third), and it also expresses time (present, past, or future) and mood (indicative, subjunctive, or imperative). The time of the verb, or the *tense,* tells when the action takes place, but the mood of the verb tells us about the attitude or disposition of the speaker, which can be considered as real (indicative); doubtful, conditional, or wished for (subjunctive); or an order (imperative).

In English, the infinitive form of a verb is most often expressed by the particle word "to" plus the verb (for example, "to talk" or "to see"). Sometimes the infinitive is expressed without the particle word "to" in certain kinds of sentences. Compare the following pair of sentences and the kind of infinitive used:

I ran <u>to open</u> the door for Tom.
I should <u>open</u> the door for Tom.

In German, infinitives will end in *–n, –eln, –ern,* or *–en*. For example:

| | |
|---|---|
| *–n* | *sein* (to be) |
| *–eln* | *basteln* (to do handicraft) |
| *–ern* | *hämmern* (to hammer) |
| *–en* | *kaufen* (to buy) |

When conjugational endings are added to the stem of an infinitive, they define the person, number, tense, and mood of the verb. Those endings tell you when the action takes place, who is doing the action, and what the mood or attitude of the speaker is. When looking up a verb in the dictionary, you will always find it listed under its infinitive form.

As in English, German verbs are classified as either regular or irregular (or weak or strong). In the conjugation of a **regular verb,** the stem does not change. **Irregular verbs** undergo changes in the stem when conjugated. Sometimes, irregular verbs may also have changes in their endings—that is, their conjugations do not follow the pattern suggested by the form of the infinitive. Fortunately for English speakers learning German, English and German are brother and sister languages—they often share the same pattern of irregularity. Compare the present, past, and present perfect tense of a regular verb and an irregular verb in the two languages.

| Regular Verb | | Irregular Verb | |
|---|---|---|---|
| **English** | **German** | **English** | **German** |
| he learns | *er lernt* | he drinks | *er trinkt* |
| he learned | *er lernte* | he drank | *er trank* |
| he has learned | *er hat gelernt* | he has drunk | *er hat getrunken* |

## Participles

In English, participles are verb forms that are used with the auxiliary verbs "be" and "have" to form the progressive and perfect tenses and the passive voice. The present participle in English ends in "–ing" (for example, "going" and "seeing") and is used with a form of "to be" to form the present and past progressive tenses. For example:

> They are running a marathon.
> The boy was crying.

But present participles can also be used as adjectives and modify nouns.

> I hear the sound of running water.
> He tried to calm the crying boy.

The English past participle is used to form the compound or perfect tenses and, for regular verbs, ends in *–ed* (talked, listened). Past participles of irregular verbs have a variety of forms but many end in *–en* ("spoken" from "speak, "seen" from "see"). For example:

> Have you talked with Dad about it yet?
> She has spoken for over an hour.

## German Present Participle

In German, the present participle is formed quite simply. Just add *–d* to the end of an infinitive (for example, *laufen* becomes *laufend, singen* becomes *singend*). But this verb form is not used in a progressive tense like English present participles. German present participles are used as modifiers and require the appropriate adjective endings for gender, number, and case like other adjectives. For example:

| | |
|---|---|
| *Kennst du den schlafenden Mann?* | Do you know the sleeping man? |
| *„Der fliegende Holländer" ist eine Oper.* | "The Flying Dutchman" is an opera. |

## German Past Participle

The past participle in German is used far more extensively than the present participle. It's needed to form the compound or perfect tenses. It's also used to form the passive voice with *werden* and can be used as an adjective as well. If a past participle is used as an adjective, it must agree in gender, case, and number with the noun it modifies. The German past participle of regular verbs is formed by adding the prefix *ge–* and the suffix *–t* to the stem of the infinitive. The stem is the infinitive minus the ending *–en*. So *stellen* becomes ***ge**stell**t***, and *suchen* becomes ***ge**such**t***. For example:

| | |
|---|---|
| *Wohin hast du den Eimer* ***gestellt****?* | Where did you put the pail? |
| *Wir haben den Hund* ***gesucht****.* | We have looked for the dog. |

There is a large group of verbs, most of which come to German from foreign sources. These verbs end in *–ieren*. Their conjugation is regular, but they do not require a *ge–* prefix when formed as past participles. For example:

| ***Present Tense*** | ***Present Pefect Tense*** |
|---|---|
| *er studiert* (he studies) | *er hat studiert* (he has studied) |
| *er arrangiert* (he arranges) | *er hat arrangiert* (he has arranged) |
| *er marschiert* (he marches) | *er ist marschiert* (he has marched) |

Don't confuse verbs that end in *–ieren* with true German verbs that appear to have the same ending, for example *verlieren*. This German verb is treated like other verbs. In the case of *verlieren*, the verb is irregular.

| ***Present Tense*** | ***Present Perfect Tense*** |
|---|---|
| *er verliert* (he loses) | *er hat verloren* (he has lost) |

Past participles can act as modifiers. When they are adjectives modifying a noun, they must show the appropriate adjective ending for gender, number, and case. For example:

| | |
|---|---|
| *Er ist ein* ***gelehrter*** *Mann.* | He's an educated man. |
| *Die* ***gerettete*** *Frau war ihre Mutter.* | The rescued woman was her mother. |

Some German verbs form irregular past participles. The past participle is formed by adding the prefix *ge–* and the suffix *–en* to the stem of many irregular verbs. Often there is also a vowel change in the stem of the verb. The following list shows some commonly used verbs that form irregular past participles.

| ***Infinitive*** | ***Irregular Past Participle*** |
|---|---|
| *bieten* | *geboten* |
| *bleiben* | *geblieben* |
| *brechen* | *gebrochen* |
| *singen* | *gesungen* |
| *stehlen* | *gestohlen* |
| *nennen* | *genannt* |

Here are some example sentences with irregular past participles.

| | |
|---|---|
| *Wer hat diesen Brief geschrieben?* | Who has written this letter? |
| *Karl hat mir geholfen.* | Karl has helped me. |

# The German Tenses

German has six tenses, and they are very similar in makeup and use to the English tenses. The main difference between tense usage in the two languages is that German has no progressive tenses (I am going, we were helping). In the perfect tenses,

English uses the auxiliary verb "to have" with a past participle. German, however, has two auxiliaries for the perfect tenses: *haben* and *sein*.

First, look at Table 2, which shows the verb *fragen* (to ask) in the six tenses with its English counterparts. This verb uses *haben* as its auxiliary.

**Table 2 The Six German Tenses with *fragen***

| *Tense* | *German* | *English* | |
|---|---|---|---|
| Present Indicative | *ich frage* | I ask | I am asking |
| | *du fragst* | you ask | you are asking |
| | *er fragt* | he asks | he is asking |
| | *wir fragen* | we ask | we are asking |
| | *ihr fragt* | you ask | you are asking |
| | *sie fragen* | they ask | they are asking |
| Past Indicative | *ich fragte* | I asked | I was asking |
| | *du fragtest* | you asked | you were asking |
| | *er fragte* | he asked | he was asking |
| | *wir fragten* | we asked | we were asking |
| | *ihr fragtet* | you asked | you were asking |
| | *sie fragten* | they asked | they were asking |
| Present Perfect Indicative | *ich habe gefragt* | I have asked | I have been asking |
| | *du hast gefragt* | you have asked | you have been asking |
| | *er hat gefragt* | he has asked | he has been asking |
| | *wir haben gefragt* | we have asked | we have been asking |
| | *ihr habt gefragt* | you have asked | you have been asking |
| | *sie haben gefragt* | they have asked | they have been asking |
| Past Perfect Indicative | *ich hatte gefragt* | I had asked | I had been asking |
| | *du hattest gefragt* | you had asked | you had been asking |
| | *er hatte gefragt* | he had asked | he has been asking |
| | *wir hatten gefragt* | we had asked | we had been asking |
| | *ihr hattet gefragt* | you had asked | you had been asking |
| | *sie hatten gefragt* | they had asked | they had been asking |
| Future Indicative | *ich werde fragen* | I will ask | I will be asking |
| | *du wirst fragen* | you will ask | you will be asking |
| | *er wird fragen* | he will ask | he will be asking |
| | *wir werden fragen* | we will ask | we will be asking |
| | *ihr werdet fragen* | you will ask | you will be asking |
| | *sie werden fragen* | they will ask | they will be asking |
| Future Perfect Indicative | *ich werde gefragt haben* | I will have asked | I will have been asking |
| | *du wirst gefragt haben* | you will have asked | you will have been asking |
| | *er wird gefragt haben* | he will have asked | he will have been asking |
| | *wir werden gefragt haben* | we will have asked | we will have been asking |
| | *ihr werdet gefragt haben* | you will have asked | you will have been asking |
| | *sie werden gefragt haben* | they will have asked | they will have been asking |

Each of those tense forms can also appear in the subjunctive mood. The German subjunctive mood consists of the **present subjunctive** (or subjunctive I) and the **past subjunctive** (or subjunctive II). The present subjunctive is frequently used in indirect discourse when retelling what someone else has stated. The past subjunctive is used to express a wish, a desire, or a condition. In Table 3, you will find the verb *fragen* in its various subjunctive tenses.

**Table 3 The German Subjunctive Tenses with *fragen***

| *Tense* | *German* | *English* | |
|---|---|---|---|
| Present Subjunctive | *ich frage* | I ask | I am asking |
| | *du fragest* | you ask | you are asking |
| | *er frage* | he asks | he is asking |
| | *wir fragen* | we ask | we are asking |
| | *ihr fraget* | you ask | you are asking |
| | *sie fragen* | they ask | they are asking |
| Past Subjunctive | *ich fragte* | (if) I asked | (if) I were asking |
| | *du fragtest* | you asked | you were asking |
| | *er fragte* | he asked | he were asking |
| | *wir fragten* | we asked | we were asking |
| | *ihr fragtet* | you asked | you were asking |
| | *sie fragten* | they asked | they were asking |
| Present Perfect Subjunctive | *ich habe gefragt* | I have asked | I have been asking |
| | *du habest gefragt* | you have asked | you have been asking |
| | *er habe gefragt* | he has asked | he has been asking |
| | *wir haben gefragt* | we have asked | we have been asking |
| | *ihr habet gefragt* | you have asked | you have been asking |
| | *sie haben gefragt* | they have asked | they have been asking |
| Past Perfect Subjunctive | *ich hätte gefragt* | I had asked | I had been asking |
| | *du hättest gefragt* | you had asked | you had been asking |
| | *er hättet gefragt* | he had asked | he has been asking |
| | *wir hätten gefragt* | we had asked | we had been asking |
| | *ihr hättet gefragt* | you had asked | you had been asking |
| | *sie hätten gefragt* | they had asked | they had been asking |
| Future Subjunctive | *ich werde fragen* | I will ask | I will be asking |
| | *du werdest fragen* | you will ask | you will be asking |
| | *er werde fragen* | he will ask | he will be asking |
| | *wir werden fragen* | we will ask | we will be asking |
| | *ihr werdet fragen* | you will ask | you will be asking |
| | *sie werden fragen* | they will ask | they will be asking |
| Future Perfect Subjunctive | *ich werde gefragt haben* | I will have asked | I will have been asking |
| | *du werdest gefragt haben* | you will have asked | you will have been asking |
| | *er werde gefragt haben* | he will have asked | he will have been asking |
| | *wir werden gefragt haben* | we will have asked | we will have been asking |
| | *ihr werdet gefragt haben* | you will have asked | you will have been asking |
| | *sie werden gefragt haben* | they will have asked | they will have been asking |
| Present Conditional | *ich würde fragen* | I would ask | I would be asking |
| | *du würdest fragen* | you would ask | you would be asking |
| | *er würde fragen* | he would ask | he would be asking |
| | *wir würden fragen* | we would ask | we would be asking |
| | *ihr würdet fragen* | you would ask | you would be asking |
| | *sie würden fragen* | they would ask | they would be asking |
| Past Conditional | *ich würde gefragt haben* | I would have asked | I would have been asking |
| | *du würdest gefragt haben* | you would have asked | you would have been asking |
| | *er würde gefragt haben* | he would have asked | he would have been asking |
| | *wir würden gefragt haben* | we would have asked | we would have been asking |
| | *ihr würdet gefragt haben* | you would have asked | you would have been asking |
| | *sie würden gefragt haben* | they would have asked | they would have been asking |

Now look at Tables 4 and 5, which provide all the conjugational forms with the verb *reisen* (to travel). This verb uses *sein* as its auxiliary in the perfect tenses.

**Table 4 The Six German Tenses with *reisen***

| *Tense* | *German* | *English* | |
|---|---|---|---|
| Present Indicative | *ich reise* | I travel | I am traveling |
| | *du reist* | you travel | you are traveling |
| | *er reist* | he travels | he is traveling |
| | *wir reisen* | we travel | we are traveling |
| | *ihr reist* | you travel | you are traveling |
| | *sie reisen* | they travel | they are traveling |
| Past Indicative | *ich reiste* | I traveled | I was traveling |
| | *du reistest* | you traveled | you were traveling |
| | *er reiste* | he traveled | he was traveling |
| | *wir reisten* | we traveled | we were traveling |
| | *ihr reistet* | you traveled | you were traveling |
| | *sie reisten* | they traveled | they were traveling |
| Present Perfect Indicative | *ich bin gereist* | I have traveled | I have been traveling |
| | *du bist gereist* | you have traveled | you have been traveling |
| | *er ist gereist* | he has traveled | he has been traveling |
| | *wir sind gereist* | we have traveled | we have been traveling |
| | *ihr seid gereist* | you have traveled | you have been traveling |
| | *sie sind gereist* | they have traveled | they have been traveling |
| Past Perfect Indicative | *ich war gereist* | I had traveled | I had been traveling |
| | *du warst gereist* | you had traveled | you had been traveling |
| | *er war gereist* | he had traveled | he has been traveling |
| | *wir waren gereist* | we had traveled | we had been traveling |
| | *ihr wart gereist* | you had traveled | you had been traveling |
| | *sie waren gereist* | they had traveled | they had been traveling |
| Future Indicative | *ich werde reisen* | I will travel | I will be traveling |
| | *du wirst reisen* | you will travel | you will be traveling |
| | *er wird reisen* | he will travel | he will be traveling |
| | *wir werden reisen* | we will travel | we will be traveling |
| | *ihr werdet reisen* | you will travel | you will be traveling |
| | *sie werden reisen* | they will travel | they will be traveling |
| Future Perfect Indicative | *ich werde gereist sein* | I will have traveled | I will have been traveling |
| | *du wirst gereist sein* | you will have traveled | you will have been traveling |
| | *er wird gereist sein* | he will have traveled | he will have been traveling |
| | *wir werden gereist sein* | we will have traveled | we will have been traveling |
| | *ihr werdet gereist sein* | you will have traveled | you will have been traveling |
| | *sie werden gereist sein* | they will have traveled | they will have been traveling |

In Table 5, you will find the verb *reisen* in its various subjunctive tenses.

**Table 5 The German Subjunctive Tenses with *reisen***

| *Tense* | *German* | *English* | |
|---|---|---|---|
| Present Subjunctive | *ich reise* | I travel | I am traveling |
| | *du reisest* | you travel | you are traveling |
| | *er reise* | he travels | he is traveling |
| | *wir reisen* | we travel | we are traveling |
| | *ihr reiset* | you travel | you are traveling |
| | *sie reisen* | they travel | they are traveling |
| Past Subjunctive | *ich reiste* | (if) I traveled | (if) I were traveling |
| | *du reistest* | you traveled | you were traveling |
| | *er reiste* | he traveled | he were traveling |
| | *wir reisten* | we traveled | we were traveling |
| | *ihr reistet* | you traveled | you were traveling |
| | *sie reisten* | they traveled | they were traveling |
| Present Perfect Subjunctive | *ich sei gereist* | I have traveled | I have been traveling |
| | *du seiest gereist* | you have traveled | you have been traveling |
| | *er sei gereist* | he has traveled | he has been traveling |
| | *wir seien gereist* | we have traveled | we have been traveling |
| | *ihr seiet gereist* | you have traveled | you have been traveling |
| | *sie seien gereist* | they have traveled | they have been traveling |
| Past Perfect Subjunctive | *ich wäre gereist* | I had traveled | I had been traveling |
| | *du wärest gereist* | you had traveled | you had been traveling |
| | *er wäre gereist* | he had traveled | he has been traveling |
| | *wir wären gereist* | we had traveled | we had been traveling |
| | *ihr wäret gereist* | you had traveled | you had been traveling |
| | *sie wären gereist* | they had traveled | they had been traveling |
| Future Subjunctive | *ich werde reisen* | I will travel | I will be traveling |
| | *du werdest reisen* | you will travel | you will be traveling |
| | *er werde reisen* | he will travel | he will be traveling |
| | *wir werden reisen* | we will travel | we will be traveling |
| | *ihr werdet reisen* | you will travel | you will be traveling |
| | *sie werden reisen* | they will travel | they will be traveling |
| Present Conditional | *ich würde reisen* | I would travel | I would be traveling |
| | *du würdest reisen* | you would travel | you would be traveling |
| | *er würde reisen* | he would travel | he would be traveling |
| | *wir würden reisen* | we would travel | we would be traveling |
| | *ihr würdet reisen* | you would travel | you would be traveling |
| | *sie würden reisen* | they would travel | they would be traveling |
| Future Perfect Subjunctive | *ich werde gereist sein* | I will have traveled | I will have been traveling |
| | *du werdest gereist sein* | you will have traveled | you will have been traveling |
| | *er werde gereist sein* | he will have traveled | he will have been traveling |
| | *wir werden gereist sein* | we will have traveled | we will have been traveling |
| | *ihr werdet gereist sein* | you will have traveled | you will have been traveling |
| | *sie werden gereist sein* | they will have traveled | they will have been traveling |

*continues*

**Table 5 *(continued)***

| *Tense* | *German* | *English* | |
|---|---|---|---|
| Present Conditional | *ich würde reisen* | I would travel | I would be traveling |
| | *du würdest reisen* | you would travel | you would be traveling |
| | *er würde reisen* | he would travel | he would be traveling |
| | *wir würden reisen* | we would travel | we would be traveling |
| | *ihr würdet reisen* | you would travel | you would be traveling |
| | *sie würden reisen* | they would travel | they would be traveling |
| Past Conditional | *ich würde gereist sein* | I would have traveled | I would have been traveling |
| | *du würdest gereist sein* | you would have traveled | you would have been traveling |
| | *er würde gereist sein* | he would have traveled | he would have been traveling |
| | *wir würden gereist sein* | we would have traveled | we would have been traveling |
| | *ihr würdet gereist sein* | you would have traveled | you would have been traveling |
| | *sie würden gereist sein* | they would have traveled | they would have been traveling |

**Note:** Infinitives that end in *–ern* and *–eln* can break the conjugational pattern in the present tense in the spoken, colloquial language. In the first-person singular, the vowel *e* before the letters *r* and *l* is often omitted:

| ***Present-Tense Conjugation*** | ***Conjugation in the Spoken Language*** |
|---|---|
| *ich hämmere* | *ich hämmre* |
| *ich wechsele* | *ich wechsle* |

The verb charts provide the full present-tense conjugation. The conjugation for the spoken, colloquial language is not shown.

# The Indicative Mood

The indicative mood states real facts indicating something that happened, is happening, or will happen. It is the mood that we use the most. For example:

I speak German.
We worked in Berlin.
They will travel to Switzerland.

In German, as in English, the indicative tenses state real facts in the past, present, or future. For example:

| | |
|---|---|
| *Ich spreche Deutsch.* | I speak German |
| *Wir arbeiteten in Berlin.* | We worked in Berlin. |
| *Sie werden in die Schweiz fahren.* | They will travel to Switzerland. |

In German, the six tenses are present, past, present perfect, past perfect, future, and future perfect.

# Indicative Present Tense

The German present tense expresses:

- General activities going on in the present time:

  *Ich liebe klassische Musik.* — I love classical music.

- Habits or habitual activities:

  *Jeden Tag spielen wir Schach.* — Every day we play chess.

- The English progressive tense:

  *Wir fahren nach Hause.* — We're driving home.

- The future tense if the future is understood by context or by an adverb indicating the future tense:

  *Morgen kommt Oma zu Besuch.* — Tomorrow granny is coming for a visit.

# Present Tense of Regular Verbs

Infinitives of regular verbs end in *–eln, –ern,* or *–en.* The present-tense conjugation of such infinitives is identical in each type with only a small variation made to make pronunciation easier. The present-tense endings are exemplified in the following chart.

| **Nominative Pronouns** | **basteln (do handicrafts)** | **hämmern (hammer)** | **spielen (play)** |
|---|---|---|---|
| *ich* | *bastele* | *hämmere* | *spiele* |
| *du* | *bastelst* | *hämmerst* | *spielst* |
| *er, sie, es* | *bastelt* | *hämmert* | *spielt* |
| *wir* | *basteln* | *hämmern* | *spielen* |
| *ihr* | *bastelt* | *hämmert* | *spielt* |
| *sie, Sie* | *basteln* | *hämmern* | *spielen* |

Other regular verbs with infinitives formed like the examples in the preceding chart follow this conjugational pattern in the present tense.

When a verb stem ends in *–s, –ss, –ß, –z,* or *–tz,* the second-person singular conjugation is formed by adding only *–t.* For example:

| | | |
|---|---|---|
| *heizen* | *du heizt* | heat |
| *passen* | *du passt* | fit |
| *putzen* | *du putzt* | polish |
| *reisen* | *du reist* | travel |
| *schließen* | *du schließt* | close |

And when a verb stem ends in *–d* or *–t,* add the vowel *–e* before the conjugational ending in the second-person singular and third-person singular.

| | | |
|---|---|---|
| *entscheiden* | *du entscheidest, er entscheidet* | decide |
| *bitten* | *du bittest, er bittet* | request |

## Irregularities in the Present Tense: Vowel Change

Although the conjugational endings of the present tense do not change, the vowel *e* in the stem of the verb sometimes shifts to *i* or *ie*. The following examples are of commonly used verbs. Notice that the vowel change only occurs in the second- and third-person singular.

| ***Nominative Pronouns*** | ***geben (go)*** | ***brechen (break)*** | ***sehen (see)*** | ***stehlen (steal)*** |
|---|---|---|---|---|
| *ich* | *gebe* | *breche* | *sehe* | *stehle* |
| *du* | ***gibst*** | ***brichst*** | ***siehst*** | ***stiehlst*** |
| *er, sie, es* | ***gibt*** | ***bricht*** | ***sieht*** | ***stiehlt*** |
| *wir* | *geben* | *brechen* | *sehen* | *stehlen* |
| *ihr* | *gebt* | *brecht* | *seht* | *stehlt* |
| *sie, Sie* | *geben* | *brechen* | *sehen* | *stehlen* |

## Irregularities in the Present Tense: Addition of the *Umlaut*

Once again, the conjugational endings of the present tense do not change. Instead of a vowel change, another present-tense irregularity is the addition of an umlaut over the vowel *a* and in one instance the vowel *o*. Notice again that these changes occur only in the second- and third-person singular.

| ***Nominative Pronouns*** | ***fahren (drive)*** | ***schlafen (sleep)*** | ***braten (roast)*** | ***stoßen (push)*** |
|---|---|---|---|---|
| *ich* | *fahre* | *schlafe* | *brate* | *stoße* |
| *du* | ***fährst*** | ***schläfst*** | ***brätst*** | ***stößt*** |
| *er, sie, es* | ***fährt*** | ***schläft*** | ***brät*** | ***stößt*** |
| *wir* | *fahren* | *schlafen* | *braten* | *stoßen* |
| *ihr* | *fahrt* | *schlaft* | *bratet* | *stoßt* |
| *sie, Sie* | *fahren* | *schlafen* | *braten* | *stoßen* |

## Modal Auxiliaries in the Present Tense

The modal auxiliaries have a unique conjugation in the present tense: The singular and plural conjugations are formed differently.

| ***Nominative Pronouns*** | ***dürfen (may)*** | ***müssen (must)*** | ***können (can)*** |
|---|---|---|---|
| *ich* | *darf* | *muss* | *kann* |
| *du* | *darfst* | *musst* | *kannst* |
| *er, sie, es* | *darf* | *muss* | *kann* |
| *wir* | *dürfen* | *müssen* | *können* |
| *ihr* | *dürft* | *müsst* | *könnt* |
| *sie, Sie* | *dürfen* | *müssen* | *können* |

| Nominative Pronouns | wollen (want) | sollen (should) | mögen (like) |
|---|---|---|---|
| ich | will | soll | mag |
| du | willst | sollst | magst |
| er, sie, es | will | soll | mag |
| wir | wollen | sollen | mögen |
| ihr | wollt | sollt | mögt |
| sie, Sie | wollen | sollen | mögen |

The modal auxiliaries are normally used with another verb (an infinitive) in a sentence:

| | |
|---|---|
| *Ich will nach Hause gehen.* | I want to go home. |
| *Kannst du mir helfen?* | Can you help me? |

## Three Important Verbs in the Present Tense

The verbs *haben, sein,* and *werden* have a special place in the German system of conjugations. They are the building blocks of various tenses and are the auxiliaries of all other verbs. Their present-tense conjugations are irregular.

| Nominative Pronouns | haben (have) | sein (be) | werden (will become) |
|---|---|---|---|
| ich | habe | bin | werde |
| du | hast | bist | wirst |
| er, sie, es | hat | ist | wird |
| wir | haben | sind | werden |
| ihr | habt | seid | werdet |
| sie, Sie | haben | sind | werden |

Note that when *werden* is used alone in a sentence it means "to become" or "to get." For example:

| | |
|---|---|
| *Er wird wieder gesund.* | He's getting well again. |

## The Regular Past Tense

The regular past tense is formed from the stem of a verb plus the suffix *–te* and the appropriate conjugational ending. Notice in the past tense that the first-person singular *(ich)* and the third-person singular *(er, sie, es)* are always the same. Some examples of the regular past-tense follow:

| Nominative Pronouns | lernen (learn) | machen (make) | besuchen (visit) |
|---|---|---|---|
| ich | lernte | machte | besuchte |
| du | lerntest | machtest | besuchtest |
| er, sie, es | lernte | machte | besuchte |
| wir | lernten | machten | besuchten |
| ihr | lerntet | machtet | besuchtet |
| sie, Sie | lernten | machten | besuchten |

Such past-tense verbs are used in sentences in much the same way as they are in English:

*Ich lernte das Gedicht auswendig.* I learned the poem by heart.

But in German there is a tendency to use the simple past tense for narratives, so the simple past tense is found most frequently in the written language. Spoken German tends to use the present perfect tense to express actions in the past.

## The Irregular Past Tense

Past-tense irregularities occur from vowel changes. In addition, most verbs do not use the *–te* suffix as part of the conjugation. Consider the following examples and take note of the vowel change from the infinitive to the past tense.

| **Nominative Pronouns** | **sehen (see)** | **fahren (drive)** | **bleiben (stay)** | **fangen (catch)** |
|---|---|---|---|---|
| *ich* | *sah* | *fuhr* | *blieb* | *fing* |
| *du* | *sahst* | *fuhrst* | *bliebst* | *fingst* |
| *er, sie, es* | *sah* | *fuhr* | *blieb* | *fing* |
| *wir* | *sahen* | *fuhren* | *blieben* | *fingen* |
| *ihr* | *saht* | *fuhrt* | *bliebt* | *fingt* |
| *sie, Sie* | *sahen* | *fuhren* | *blieben* | *fingen* |

A few verbs add the suffix *–te* as part of their past-tense irregular conjugation, thereby mixing regular and irregular features.

| **Nominative Pronouns** | **denken (think)** | **nennen (name)** | **senden (send)** | **kennen (know)** |
|---|---|---|---|---|
| *ich* | *dachte* | *nannte* | *sandte* | *kannte* |
| *du* | *dachtest* | *nanntest* | *sandtest* | *kanntest* |
| *er, sie, es* | *dachte* | *nannte* | *sandte* | *kannte* |
| *wir* | *dachten* | *nannten* | *sandten* | *kannten* |
| *ihr* | *dachtet* | *nanntet* | *sandtet* | *kanntet* |
| *sie, Sie* | *dachten* | *nannten* | *sandten* | *kannten* |

The modal auxiliaries follow a similar pattern in the past tense. Notice that the modal auxiliaries do not have an umlaut in the past-tense conjugation.

| **Nominative Pronouns** | **dürfen (may)** | **müssen (must)** | **können (can)** |
|---|---|---|---|
| *ich* | *durfte* | *musste* | *konnte* |
| *du* | *durftest* | *musstest* | *konntest* |
| *er, sie, es* | *durfte* | *musste* | *konnte* |
| *wir* | *durften* | *mussten* | *konnten* |
| *ihr* | *durftet* | *musstet* | *konntet* |
| *sie, Sie* | *durften* | *mussten* | *konnten* |

| Nominative Pronouns | wollen (want) | sollen (should) | mögen (like) |
|---|---|---|---|
| *ich* | *wollte* | *sollte* | *mochte* |
| *du* | *wolltest* | *solltest* | *mochtest* |
| *er, sie, es* | *wollte* | *sollte* | *mochte* |
| *wir* | *wollten* | *sollten* | *mochten* |
| *ihr* | *wolltet* | *solltet* | *mochtet* |
| *sie, Sie* | *wollten* | *sollten* | *mochten* |

The irregular past tense functions in sentences the same way as the regular past tense:

| | |
|---|---|
| *Er blieb an der Ecke stehen.* | He remained standing on the corner. |
| *Kannten Sie den Lehrer?* | Did you know the teacher? |
| *Ich konnte es nicht verstehen.* | I couldn't understand it. |

## The Future Tense

There are no irregularities in the future tense beyond the conjugation of *werden*. The verb *werden* is conjugated in the present tense, and an infinitive is placed at the end of the sentence. Now the sentence has a future-tense meaning.

| | |
|---|---|
| Ich werde es kaufen. | I will buy it. |
| Wirst du in die Schweiz reisen? | Will you travel to Switzerland? |
| Er wird mir helfen. | He will help me. |
| Wir werden zu Hause bleiben. | We will stay home. |
| Was werdet ihr tun? | What will you do? |
| Sie werden Onkel Peter besuchen. | They will visit Uncle Peter. |

This pattern for the future tense can be repeated with innumerable infinitives. The future tense describes an action taking place in the future.

## The Present Perfect Tense: Regular Participles

The present perfect tense consists of a present-tense conjugation of *haben* or *sein* and a past participle placed at the end of the sentence. The verb *haben* is the auxiliary for **transitive verbs** (verbs that have a direct object), and *sein* is the auxiliary for **verbs of motion,** verbs that describe a state or a radical change out of the control of the speaker (to be, to become, to die, and so on.). This tense describes an action begun in the past and completed in the present.

Regular participles of verbs that have no prefix (*machen, stellen,* and so on) are formed by adding the prefix *ge–* and the suffix *–t* to the stem of the verb. For example:

| | |
|---|---|
| *machen* (make) | *ge + mach + t = gemacht* |
| *suchen* (seek) | *ge + such + t = gesucht* |
| *hassen* (hate) | *ge + hass + t = gehasst* |

If the infinitive has an inseparable prefix (*be–, er–, emp–, ent–, ge–, ver–, zer–*), the addition of the prefix *ge–* is avoided.

| | |
|---|---|
| *besuchen* (visit) | *besuch + t = besucht* |
| *verlernen* (unlearn) | *verlern + t = verlernt* |
| *zerstören* (destroy) | *zerstör + t = zerstört* |

If the infinitive has a separable prefix (for example, *ab–, an–, fort–, mit–, weg–, zu–,* and so on), the prefix *ge–* is placed between the separable prefix and the stem of the verb:

| | |
|---|---|
| *anlegen* (lay on) | *an + ge + leg + t = angelegt* |
| *aufregen* (excite) | *auf + ge + reg + t = aufgeregt* |
| *zumachen* (close) | *zu + ge + mach + t = zugemacht* |

Look at the present perfect tense conjugation of the following transitive verb, which requires the auxiliary *haben,* and the accompanying verb of motion, which requires the auxiliary *sein.*

| ***kaufen (to buy)*** | ***reisen (to travel)*** |
|---|---|
| *ich habe gekauft* | *ich bin gereist* |
| *du hast gekauft* | *du bist gereist* |
| *er hat gekauft* | *er ist gereist* |
| *wir haben gekauft* | *wir sind gereist* |
| *ihr habt gekauft* | *ihr seid gereist* |
| *sie haben gekauft* | *sie sind gereist* |

# The Present Perfect Tense: Irregular Participles

Most irregular participles are formed by the addition of the prefix *ge–* and the suffix *–en.* In many cases, the vowel in the stem of the verb changes. Look at the variety of irregular participles in the examples that follow.

| ***Infinitive*** | ***Irregular Participle*** |
|---|---|
| *beißen* (bite) | *gebissen* |
| *bleiben* (stay) | *geblieben* |
| *finden* (find) | *gefunden* |
| *gehen* (go) | *gegangen* |
| *sprechen* (speak) | *gesprochen* |

Some irregular participles end in *–t.*

| ***Infinitive*** | ***Irregular Participle*** |
|---|---|
| *bringen* (bring) | *gebracht* |
| *denken* (think) | *gedacht* |
| *kennen* (know) | *gekannt* |
| *nennen* (name) | *genannt* |
| *senden* (send) | *gesandt* |

Just like regular participles, irregular participles can have an inseparable or a separable prefix.

| ***Infinitive*** | ***Irregular Participle*** |
|---|---|
| *sprechen* (speak) | *gesprochen* |
| *versprechen* (promise) | *versprochen* |
| *aussprechen* (pronounce) | *ausgesprochen* |

And, depending upon their meaning and usage, irregular participles can require either *haben* or *sein* as their auxiliary.

| ***schlagen (to hit)*** | ***kommen (to come)*** |
|---|---|
| *ich habe geschlagen* | *ich bin gekommen* |
| *du hast geschlagen* | *du bist gekommen* |
| *er hat geschlagen* | *er ist gekommen* |
| *wir haben geschlagen* | *wir sind gekommen* |
| *ihr habt geschlagen* | *ihr seid gekommen* |
| *sie haben geschlagen* | *sie sind gekommen* |

# The Past Perfect Tense

The past perfect tense is identical to the present perfect tense in structure, except that the auxiliaries (*haben* and *sein)* are conjugated in the past tense. The past perfect tense describes an action begun and completed in the past.

| ***denken (to think)*** | ***ankommen (to arrive)*** |
|---|---|
| *ich hatte gedacht* | *ich war angekommen* |
| *du hattest gedacht* | *du warst angekommen* |
| *er hatte gedacht* | *er war angekommen* |
| *wir hatten gedacht* | *wir waren angekommen* |
| *ihr hattet gedacht* | *ihr wart angekommen* |
| *sie hatten gedacht* | *sie waren angekommen* |

# The Future Perfect Tense

The German future perfect tense describes an action that will begin and will be completed in the future. It is formed from a present tense conjugation of *werden* and a past participle followed directly by either *haben* or *sein* and placed at the end of the sentence. Here are some examples:

| | |
|---|---|
| *Bis morgen werde ich den Roman fertiggelesen haben.* | By tomorrow I will have finished reading the novel. |
| *Wenn wir uns wieder treffen, wirst du Arzt geworden sein.* | When we meet again, you'll have become a physician. |

# Haben, Sein, and Werden

Having a firm grasp of these three verbs is important: They are the essentials for forming the perfect and future tenses. Look at their formations in the various tenses in the third-person singular.

| ***haben*** | ***sein*** | ***werden*** |
|---|---|---|
| *er hat* | *er ist* | *er wird* |
| *er hatte* | *er war* | *er wurde* |
| *er hat gehabt* | *er ist gewesen* | *er ist geworden* |
| *er hatte gehabt* | *er war gewesen* | *er war geworden* |
| *er wird haben* | *er wird sein* | *er wird werden* |
| *er wird gehabt haben* | *er wird gewesen sein* | *er wird geworden sein* |

Now let's look at how the indicative mood will look in the verb charts. The example is given with the verb *kaufen* (to buy). It requires the auxiliary *haben.*

| **Mode** | **Simple Tenses** | | **Compound Tenses** | |
|---|---|---|---|---|
| | ***Singular*** | ***Plural*** | ***Singular*** | ***Plural*** |
| Indicative | **Present** | | **Present Perfect** | |
| | kaufe | kaufen | habe gekauft | haben gekauft |
| | kaufst | kauft | hast gekauft | habt gekauft |
| | kauft | kaufen | hat gekauft | haben gekauft |
| | **Past** | | **Past Perfect** | |
| | kaufte | kauften | hatte gekauft | hatten gekauft |
| | kauftest | kauftet | hattest gekauft | hattet gekauft |
| | kaufte | kauften | hatte gekauft | hatten gekauft |
| | **Future** | | **Future Perfect** | |
| | werde kaufen | werden kaufen | werde gekauft haben | werden gekauft haben |
| | wirst kaufen | werdet kaufen | wirst gekauft haben | werdet gekauft haben |
| | wird kaufen | werden kaufen | wird gekauft haben | werden gekauft haben |

Compare that chart with the following verb chart for the verb *kommen,* which requires *sein* as its auxiliary.

| **Mode** | **Simple Tenses** | | **Compound Tenses** | |
|---|---|---|---|---|
| | ***Singular*** | ***Plural*** | ***Singular*** | ***Plural*** |
| Indicative | **Present** | | **Present Perfect** | |
| | komme | kommen | bin gekommen | sind gekommen |
| | kommst | kommt | bist gekommen | seid gekommen |
| | kommt | kommen | ist gekommen | sind gekommen |
| | **Past** | | **Past Perfect** | |
| | kam | kamen | war gekommen | waren gekommen |
| | kamst | kamt | warst gekommen | wart gekommen |
| | kam | kamen | war gekommen | waren gekommen |
| | **Future** | | **Future Perfect** | |
| | werde kommen | werden kommen | werde gekommen sein | werden gekommen sein |
| | wirst kommen | werdet kommen | wirst gekommen sein | werdet gekommen sein |
| | wird kommen | werden kommen | wird gekommen sein | werden gekommen sein |

# The Passive Voice

Some style manuals say that the passive voice is a structure to be avoided. But despite that warning, it continues to occur frequently in English and has an important function.

It is formed from a conjugation of "to be" and a past participle and is especially helpful when you want to avoid "placing the blame" for an action on someone or something. In the active voice, the person who carries out an action is quite apparent.

John hit Bill in the nose.
Mr. Miller fired all the salespeople.

But if the passive is used, the guilty parties for the action (John and Mr. Miller) can be omitted.

Bill was hit in the nose.
All the salespeople were fired.

Of course, the guilty parties can be included in a prepositional phrase if desired.

Bill was hit in the nose by John.
All the salespeople were fired by Mr. Miller.

The same thing occurs in the German passive voice.

The German passive voice is formed from a conjugation of *werden* plus a past participle of a transitive verb. The transitive verb is important, because a transitive verb can have a direct object, and direct objects become the subject of passive-voice sentences. Look at the following active-voice sentences and take note of the direct object (the accusative case).

| | |
|---|---|
| *Karl besucht den alten Professor.* | Karl visits the old professor. |

When you change this active sentence to the passive voice, *Professor* becomes the subject and is, therefore, in the nominative case, and the verb *besucht* becomes a past participle. Karl becomes the object of the dative preposition *von*.

| | |
|---|---|
| *Der alte Professor wird von Karl besucht.* | The old professor is visited by Karl. |

This example sentence is in the present tense. Let's look at the same sentence in all the tenses.

**Present:** *Der alte Professor wird von Karl besucht.*
**Past:** *Der alte Professor wurde von Karl besucht.*
**Present Perfect:** *Der alte Professor ist von Karl besucht worden.*
**Past Perfect:** *Der alte Professor war von Karl besucht worden.*
**Future:** *Der alte Professor wird von Karl besucht werden.*
**Future Perfect:** *Der alte Professor wird von Karl besucht worden sein.*

The past participle in such a structure can be any transitive verb, but the conjugation of *werden* is static. For example, in the third-person singular: *wird* + past participle, *wurde* + past participle, *ist* + past participle + *worden, war* + past participle + *worden, wird* + past participle + *werden,* and *wird* + past participle + *worden sein.*

If you change a present-tense active sentence to the passive voice, the passive-voice sentence should be in the present tense. If you change a past-tense active sentence to the passive voice, the passive-voice sentence should be in the past tense. The same is true of the other tenses. Here are some examples:

| | |
|---|---|
| **Active:** *Ich küsste seine Schwester.* | I kissed his sister. |
| **Passive:** *Seine Schwester wurde von mir geküsst.* | His sister was kissed by me. |
| **Active:** *Er hat das Auto gekauft.* | He has bought the car. |
| **Passive:** *Das Auto ist von ihm gekauft worden.* | The car has been bought by him. |
| **Active:** *Sie wird das Geld stehlen.* | She will steal the money. |
| **Passive:** *Das Geld wird von ihr gestohlen werden.* | The money will be stolen by her. |

German transitive verbs can have accusative-case objects. But there are also dative-case objects. They occur with dative verbs. When an active sentence with a dative object is made passive, the dative object remains in the dative case. The other parts of the passive-voice sentence are formed normally. Here are some examples:

| | |
|---|---|
| **Active:** *Sie dankten* ***ihm*** *für die Geschenke.* | They thanked him for the gifts. |
| **Passive:** ***Ihm*** *wurde für die Geschenke gedankt.* | He was thanked for the gifts. |

# Dative Verbs

German has a concept that does not exist in English. Certain objects of verbs are in the dative case instead of the accusative case, because the verbs are *dative verbs.* You need to use care when using dative verbs, because their objects in sentences appear as direct objects when translated into English. For example:

| | |
|---|---|
| *Ich habe meinem Onkel dafür gedankt.* | I thanked my uncle for it. |

In the German sentence, *meinem Onkel* is in the dative case, but in the English sentence, *my uncle* is a direct object. And direct objects in German are expressed in the accusative case. Therefore, distinguishing dative verbs from transitive verbs that require an accusative direct object is essential.

Some of the most commonly used dative verbs are:

| | |
|---|---|
| *begegnen* | to encounter |
| *danken* | to thank |
| *dienen* | to serve |
| *drohen* | to threaten |

| | |
|---|---|
| *entfliehen* | to flee from |
| *entlaufen* | to run away |
| *folgen* | to follow |
| *gefallen* | to please, to like |
| *gehorchen* | to obey |
| *gehören* | to belong to |
| *glauben* | to believe |
| *gleichen* | to resemble, to equal |
| *gratulieren* | to congratulate |
| *helfen* | to help |
| *imponieren* | to impress |
| *nähern (sich)* | to approach |
| *nützen* | to be useful |
| *raten* | to advise |
| *schaden* | to harm |
| *schmeicheln* | to flatter |
| *vertrauen* | to trust |
| *widersprechen* | to contradict |
| *zusehen* | to watch |
| *zutrauen* | to entrust |

No matter the form of a sentence (statement or question), and no matter the tense of the sentence, a dative verb will require a dative object. For example:

| | |
|---|---|
| **Present:** *Er hilft seinem Bruder.* | He helps his brother. |
| **Past:** *Er half seinem Bruder.* | He helped his brother. |
| **Present Perfect:** *Er hat seinem Bruder geholfen.* | He has helped his brother. |
| **Past Perfect:** *Er hatte seinem Bruder geholfen.* | He had helped his brother. |
| **Future:** *Er wird seinem Bruder helfen.* | He will help his brother. |
| **Future Perfect:** *Er wird seinem Bruder geholfen haben.* | He will have helped his brother. |

Even when a dative verb is used together in a sentence with a modal auxiliary, a dative verb will still require a dative object. Let's look at a few examples.

| | |
|---|---|
| *Ich kann dir damit helfen.* | I can help you with that. |
| *Sie wollte ihm glauben.* | She wanted to believe him. |
| *Er hat dem Fremden folgen müssen.* | He had to follow the stranger. |

Compare some example sentences with dative indirect objects and dative objects caused by a dative verb.

| | |
|---|---|
| **Indirect object:** *Erik gab **seiner Freundin** eine Rose.* | Erik gave his girlfriend a rose. |
| **Dative object:** *Erik glaubte **seiner Freundin** nicht.* | Erik didn't believe his girlfriend. |

| | |
|---|---|
| **Indirect object:** *Ich zeige **dir** die Bilder.* | I show you the pictures. |
| **Dative object:** *Ich helfe **dir** arbeiten.* | I help you work. |

# Accusative Reflexive Pronouns

A *reflexive pronoun* in English is the object of a verb or a preposition and is the same number and gender as the subject of the sentence. For example:

> **I** enjoyed **myself** at your party.

The subject, "I," and the reflexive pronoun, "myself," refer to the same person. You do not use a reflexive pronoun if the subject is a different person from the object. Compare the following two sentences:

> **We** bought **them** some flowers. (Different people are involved in this action.)
> **We** bought **ourselves** some flowers. (The same people are involved in this action.)

Compare the English and German reflexive pronouns in the following list.

| ***English*** | | ***German*** | |
|---|---|---|---|
| ***Subject Pronoun*** | ***Reflexive*** | ***Subject Pronoun*** | ***Accusative Reflexive*** |
| I | myself | *ich* | *mich* |
| you | yourself | *du* | *dich* |
| he | himself | *er* | *sich* |
| she | herself | *sie* | *sich* |
| it | itself | *es* | *sich* |
| we | ourselves | *wir* | *uns* |
| you | yourselves | *ihr* | *euch* |
| you | yourself/yourselves | *Sie* | *sich* |
| they | themselves | *sie* | *sich* |

If a German verb requires an accusative-case object (a direct object), the accusative-case reflexive pronouns listed in the preceding chart can be used when the subject and object are the same person. Notice how the reflexive pronoun changes in the following example sentences:

| | |
|---|---|
| *Ich benehme mich schlecht.* | I behave myself badly. |
| *Du benimmst dich schlecht.* | You behave yourself badly. |
| *Er benimmt sich schlecht.* | He behaves himself badly. |
| *Wir benehmen uns schlecht.* | We behave ourselves badly. |
| *Ihr benehmt euch schlecht.* | You behave yourselves badly. |
| *Sie benehmen sich schlecht.* | They behave themselves badly. |

As the tenses change, the reflexive pronoun remains directly after the present- or past-tense form of the verb and in the other tenses behind the auxiliary *(haben* or *werden),* and the conjugations occur normally.

| | |
|---|---|
| *Er wäscht sich.* | He washes himself. |
| *Er wusch sich.* | He washed himself. |
| *Er hat sich gewaschen.* | He has washed himself. |
| *Er hatte sich gewaschen.* | He had washed himself. |
| *Er wird sich waschen.* | He will wash himself. |
| *Er wird sich gewaschen haben.* | He will have washed himself. |

All verbs that have an accusative reflexive pronoun will use *haben* as their auxiliary.

In some cases, German reflexive verbs do not have matching English reflexive verbs, and the translation will therefore not include a reflexive. For example:

| | |
|---|---|
| *Wir beeilen uns.* | We hurry. |
| *Ich freue mich.* | I'm glad. |
| *Sie erinnert sich an ihn.* | She remembers him. |

# Dative Reflexive Pronouns

Some German verbs are so-called **dative verbs,** because they require a dative object instead of an accusative object. The dative case also is used for indirect objects. Here are just a few examples of German verbs that require a dative object in sentences:

| | |
|---|---|
| *Ich helfe dem Mann.* | I help the man. |
| *Hast du deiner Tante gedankt?* | Did you thank your aunt? |
| *Ich zeigte ihm den neuen Computer.* | I showed him the new computer. |

When the subject and dative object are the same person, a dative reflexive pronoun is used. Compare the English and German reflexive pronouns in the following chart.

| ***English*** | | ***German*** | |
|---|---|---|---|
| ***Subject Pronoun*** | ***Reflexive*** | ***Subject Pronoun*** | ***Dative Reflexive*** |
| I | myself | *ich* | *mir* |
| you | yourself | *du* | *dir* |
| he | himself | *er* | *sich* |
| she | herself | *sie* | *sich* |
| it | itself | *es* | *sich* |
| we | ourselves | *wir* | *uns* |
| you | yourselves | *ihr* | *euch* |
| you | yourself/yourselves | *Sie* | *sich* |
| they | themselves | *sie* | *sich* |

Consider the following pairs of sentences, which show a dative object pronoun that is not the same person as the subject and a dative reflexive pronoun that is the same person as the subject.

***Different Persons***

*Er hat* ***ihr*** *widersprochen.* (He contradicted her.)
*Ich helfe* ***ihm****, so gut ich kann.* (I help him as well as I can.)
*Du verzeihst* ***uns*** *diese Dummheit nicht.* (You don't forgive us for this stupidity.)
*Wir bestellen* ***ihnen*** *Suppe und Brot.* (We order soup and bread for them.)

***Same Person***

*Er hat* ***sich*** *widersprochen.* (He contradicted himself.)
*Ich helfe* ***mir****, so gut ich kann.* (I help mself as well as I can.)
*Du verzeihst* ***dir*** *diese Dummheit nicht.* (You don't forgive yourself for this stupidity.)
*Wir bestellen* ***uns*** *Suppe und Brot.* (We order soup and bread for ourselves.)

The dative reflexive pronouns follow the present or past tense form of the verb and in the other tenses stand behind the auxiliary *(haben* or *werden),* and the conjugations occur normally:

| | |
|---|---|
| *Ich kaufe mir einen Schlips.* | I buy myself a tie. |
| *Ich kaufte mir einen Schlips.* | I bought myself a tie. |
| *Ich habe mir einen Schlips gekauft.* | I have bought myself a tie. |
| *Ich hatte mir einen Schlips gekauft.* | I had bought myself a tie. |
| *Ich werde mir einen Schlips kaufen.* | I will buy myself a tie. |
| *Ich werde mir einen Schlips gekauft haben.* | I will have bought myself a tie. |

In the verb charts, reflexive verbs are identified, but the reflexive pronouns are not shown in the conjugations of the tenses. If the verb in question is used primarily with a reflexive pronoun, the reflexive pronoun *sich* will precede the infinitive:

*sich beeilen*

If the verb is used more often without a reflexive pronoun but has an occasional reflexive usage, the reflexive pronoun *sich* will be in parentheses and follow the infinitive:

*stützen (sich)*

## Impersonal Expressions

In addition to the dative verbs, there are a few impersonal verbal expressions that often begin with the pronoun *es* and that require the use of the dative case:

| | |
|---|---|
| *es fällt dir ein* | it occurs to you |
| *es gefällt dem Mann* | the man likes it |
| *es geht Ihnen gut* | you feel well |
| *es gelingt mir* | I succeed, I manage to do something |
| *es genügt der Dame* | the lady is satisfied with something |
| *es glückt ihm* | he prospers, he succeeds |
| *es kommt ihr vor* | it appears to her |
| *es kommt mir darauf an* | it is important to me |
| *es passt mir gut* | it fits me well |
| *es scheint ihr* | it seems to her |
| *es schmeckt mir* | it tastes good to me |
| *es steht ihnen gut* | they look good in it |

Although the impersonal expressions most frequently appear in this form, they are not used exclusively with the pronoun *es.* Most any noun that makes sense can be used as the subject of these verbs.

| | |
|---|---|
| *Dieses Restaurant hat mir sehr gut gefallen.* | I liked this restaurant a lot. |
| *Dieses Hemd passt dir nicht.* | This shirt doesn't fit you. |

These expressions cannot always be translated word-for-word into English. You have to know two things: how the German expression is used and what it means in English. Compare the following impersonal expressions in German with their English meaning:

| | |
|---|---|
| *Es gelang mir nicht, meine Hausarbeit rechtzeitig zu beendigen.* | I didn't succeed in finishing my homework on time. |
| *Es fiel ihm ein, dass es schon zu spät war.* | It occurred to him that it was already too late. |

# Double Infinitives

Double-infinitive structures occur in the present-perfect, past-perfect, future, and future-perfect tenses. They occur with modal auxiliaries and with the verbs *helfen, hören, lassen, sehen, gehen,* and *lernen*. In the present and past tenses, the double infinitive does not occur.

When using a modal auxiliary or *helfen, hören, lassen, sehen, gehen,* and *lernen*, there is often a second verbal element at the end of the sentence—an infinitive.

| | |
|---|---|
| *Ich muss der armen Frau helfen.* | I have to help the poor woman. |
| *Gudrun lernte Geige spielen.* | Gudrun learned to play the violin. |

When such sentences are stated in the perfect or future tenses, the final element becomes a **double infinitive,** so named because two infinitives stand next to one another. In the perfect tenses, a participle is normally required. But with the modal auxiliaries and with *helfen, hören, lassen, sehen, gehen,* and *lernen,* the verbs appear as infinitives. Look at these examples in the future tense:

| | |
|---|---|
| *Er wird es nicht verstehen können.* | He won't be able to understand it. |
| *Ich werde den Wagen reparieren lassen.* | I'll have the car repaired. |

Now look at the use of the double-infinitive structure in the present-perfect tense:

| | |
|---|---|
| *Wir haben es nicht tun wollen.* | We haven't wanted to do it. |
| *Hast du sie singen hören?* | Have you heard her sing? |

Although a past participle is normally used in the perfect tenses, a double-infinitive structure is used in its place with the modal auxiliaries and *helfen, hören, lassen, sehen, gehen,* and *lernen*. Compare the following sentences in all the tenses.

| ***No Modal Auxiliary Used*** | ***Modal Auxiliary wollen*** |
|---|---|
| *Wir reisen nach Spanien.* (We travel to Spain.) | *Wir wollen nach Spanien reisen.* (We want to travel to Spain.) |
| *Wir reisten nach Spanien.* | *Wir wollten nach Spanien reisen.* (We wanted to travel to Spain.) |
| *Wir sind nach Spanien gereist.* | *Wir haben nach Spanien reisen wollen.* (We have wanted to travel to Spain.) |
| *Wir waren nach Spanien gereist.* | *Wir hatten nach Spanien reisen wollen.* (We had wanted to travel to Spain.) |
| *Wir werden nach Spanien reisen.* | *Wir werden nach Spanien reisen wollen.* (We will want to travel to Spain.) |
| *Wir werden nach Spanien gereist sein.* | *Wir werden nach Spanien haben reisen wollen.* (We will have wanted to travel to Spain.) |

Notice that when a modal auxiliary or *helfen, hören, lassen, sehen, gehen,* or *lernen* are used in such sentences, the auxiliary verb is always *haben* in the perfect tenses.

If a modal auxiliary and another verb are used in the same sentence with *helfen, hören, lassen, sehen, gehen,* or *lernen,* a double infinitive will occur in the present and past tenses. For example:

| | |
|---|---|
| *Ich kann die Kinder singen hören.* | I can hear the children singing. |
| *Ich konnte die Kinder singen hören.* | I could hear the children singing. |

# The Subjunctive Mood

The conjugation of the subjunctive mood always has the same endings with the notable exception of the verb *sein* in the present subjunctive. Compare the subjunctive endings with *sein.*

| ***Subjunctive Endings*** | | | | ***sein*** | |
|---|---|---|---|---|---|
| *ich* | *–e* | *wir* | *–en* | *ich sei* | *wir seien* |
| *du* | *–est* | *ihr* | *–et* | *du seiest* | *ihr seiet* |
| *er* | *–e* | *sie* | *–en* | *er sei* | *sie seien* |

The present subjunctive (subjunctive I) is formed from the stem of the infinitive followed by the subjunctive endings shown in the preceding chart. There is no difference between regular and irregular verbs in this conjugation.

| ***Regular Verb machen (make, do)*** | ***Irregular Verb sehen (see)*** |
|---|---|
| *ich mache* | *sehe* |
| *du machest* | *sehest* |
| *er mache* | *sehe* |
| *wir machen* | *sehen* |
| *ihr machet* | *sehet* |
| *sie machen* | *sehen* |

Modal auxiliaries follow the same pattern: They add the subjunctive endings to the stem of the infinitive.

| ***müssen (must)*** | ***können (can)*** | ***wollen (want)*** |
|---|---|---|
| *ich müsse* | *könne* | *wolle* |
| *du müssest* | *könnest* | *wollest* |
| *er müsse* | *könne* | *wolle* |
| *wir müssen* | *können* | *wollen* |
| *ihr müsset* | *könnet* | *wollet* |
| *sie müssen* | *können* | *wollen* |

The past subjunctive (subjunctive II) is formed from the past tense of the verb followed by the subjunctive endings shown in the preceding chart. Regular verbs in subjunctive II are identical to the regular past tense.

| ***Regular Verb machen (make, do)*** | ***Regular Verb bestellen (order)*** |
|---|---|
| *ich machte* | *bestellte* |
| *du machtest* | *bestelltest* |
| *er machte* | *bestellte* |

| | |
|---|---|
| *wir machten* | *bestellten* |
| *ihr machtet* | *bestelltet* |
| *sie machten* | *bestellten* |

Irregular verbs in subjunctive II add the subjunctive endings to the irregular past-tense stem. If the verb has a vowel that can be given an umlaut (*a, o, u*), an umlaut is added to the verb.

| ***Irregular Verb gehen (go)*** | ***Irregular Verb sprechen (speak)*** |
|---|---|
| *ich ginge* | *spräche* |
| *du gingest* | *sprächest* |
| *er ginge* | *spräche* |
| *wir gingen* | *sprächen* |
| *ihr ginget* | *sprächet* |
| *sie gingen* | *sprächen* |

Those irregular verbs that require the *–te* suffix (*nennen, brennen, kennen,* and so on) change the vowel *a* of the irregular past tense stem to the vowel *e* in subjunctive II.

| ***nennen (name)*** | ***brennen (burn)*** | ***senden (send)*** |
|---|---|---|
| *ich nennte* | *brennte* | *sendete* |
| *du nenntest* | *brenntest* | *sendetest* |
| *er nennte* | *brennte* | *sendete* |
| *wir nennten* | *brennten* | *sendeten* |
| *ihr nenntet* | *brenntet* | *sendetet* |
| *sie nennten* | *brennten* | *sendeten* |

The modal auxiliaries in the subjunctive II conjugation resemble the past tense. However, the modal auxiliary infinitives that contain an umlaut keep the umlaut in the subjunctive II conjugation.

| ***müssen (must)*** | ***können (can)*** | ***wollen (want)*** |
|---|---|---|
| *ich müsste* | *könnte* | *wollte* |
| *du müsstest* | *könntest* | *wolltest* |
| *er müsste* | *könnte* | *wollte* |
| *wir müssten* | *könnten* | *wollten* |
| *ihr müsstet* | *könntet* | *wolltet* |
| *sie müssten* | *könnten* | *wollten* |

*Haben, sein,* and *werden* are three important verbs. Let's look at their conjugations in both the present (I) and past (II) subjunctive.

| ***haben*** | | ***sein*** | | ***werden*** | |
|---|---|---|---|---|---|
| ***I*** | ***II*** | ***I*** | ***II*** | ***I*** | ***II*** |
| *habe* | *hätte* | *sei* | *wäre* | *werde* | *würde* |
| *habest* | *hättest* | *seiest* | *wärest* | *werdest* | *würdest* |
| *habe* | *hätte* | *sei* | *wäre* | *werde* | *würde* |
| *haben* | *hätten* | *seien* | *wären* | *werden* | *würden* |
| *habet* | *hättet* | *seiet* | *wäret* | *werdet* | *würdet* |
| *haben* | *hätten* | *seien* | *wären* | *werden* | *würden* |

Now let's look at the transitive verb *kaufen* (to buy) in all the subjunctive tenses. This verb requires *haben* as its auxiliary in the perfect tenses.

| | | | | |
|---|---|---|---|---|
| Subjunctive | **Present** | | **Present Perfect** | |
| | kaufe | kaufen | habe gekauft | haben gekauft |
| | kaufest | kaufet | habest gekauft | habet gekauft |
| | kaufe | kaufen | habe gekauft | haben gekauft |
| | **Past** | | **Past Perfect** | |
| | kaufte | kauften | hätte gekauft | hätten gekauft |
| | kauftest | kauftet | hättest gekauft | hättet gekauft |
| | kaufte | kauften | hätte gekauft | hätten gekauft |
| | **Future** | | **Future Perfect** | |
| | werde kaufen | werden kaufen | werde gekauft haben | werden gekauft haben |
| | werdest kaufen | werdet kaufen | werdest gekauft haben | werdet gekauft haben |
| | werde kaufen | werden kaufen | werde gekauft haben | werden gekauft haben |
| | **Present and Future Conditional** | | **Past Conditional** | |
| | würde kaufen | würden kaufen | würde gekauft haben | würden gekauft haben |
| | würdest kaufen | würdet kaufen | würdest gekauft haben | würdet gekauft haben |
| | würde kaufen | würden kaufen | würde gekauft haben | würde gekauft haben |

The following example is the verb of motion *kommen* (to come) in all the subjunctive tenses. This verb requires *sein* as its auxiliary in the perfect tenses.

| | | | | |
|---|---|---|---|---|
| Subjunctive | **Present** | | **Present Perfect** | |
| | komme | kommen | sei gekommen | seien gekommen |
| | kommest | kommet | seiest gekommen | seiet gekommen |
| | komme | kommen | sei gekommen | seien gekommen |
| | **Past** | | **Past Perfect** | |
| | käme | kämen | wäre gekommen | wären gekommen |
| | kämest | kämet | wärest gekommen | wäret gekommen |
| | käme | kämen | wäre gekommen | wären gekommen |
| | **Future** | | **Future Perfect** | |
| | werde kommen | werden kommen | werde gekommen sein | werden gekommen sein |
| | werdest kommen | werdet kommen | werdest gekommen sein | werdet gekommen sein |
| | werde kommen | werden kommen | werde gekommen sein | werden gekommen sein |
| | **Present and Future Conditional** | | **Past Conditional** | |
| | würde kommen | würden kommen | würde gekommen sein | würden gekommen sein |
| | würdest kommen | würdet kommen | würdest gekommen sein | würdet gekommen sein |
| | würde kommen | würden kommen | würde gekommen sein | würden gekommen sein |

## Subjunctive and Indirect Discourse

**Indirect discourse** is a statement that tells what someone else has said. **Direct discourse** is a quote. Indirect discourse is the reporting of that quote. For example:

> **Direct discourse:** Tom has a cold today.
> **Indirect discourse:** Mary told me that Tom has a cold today.

In German indirect discourse, the verb is usually conjugated in the present subjunctive (I). If the present subjunctive is identical to the indicative conjugation, a switch is made to the past subjunctive (II) conjugation. You will discover with experience that the present subjunctive (I) is found primarily in the written language with indirect discourse. In the spoken language, it is common to use the past subjunctive (II) in indirect discourse. Let's look at some examples.

> **Direct discourse:** *Ich habe keine Zeit.* (I don't have any time.)
> **Indirect discourse:** *Frau Bauer sagte, dass sie keine Zeit* ***habe.*** (Mrs. Bauer said that she doesn't have any time.)

> **Direct discourse:** *Er schreibt Onkel Peter einen Brief.* (He writes Uncle Peter a letter.)
> **Indirect discourse:** *Er sagte, dass er Onkel Peter einen Brief* ***schreibe.*** (He said that he is writing Uncle Peter a letter.)

If the quote is a question, it will appear as an indirect question:

> **Direct question:** *Wer singt so schlecht?* (Who is singing so badly?)
> **Indirect question:** *Karl fragte, wer so schlecht* ***singe.*** (Karl asked who is singing so badly.)

If there is no interrogative word (*wer, was, warum,* and so on) in the question, the question is reported following the conjunction *ob* (whether, if):

> **Direct question:** *Kann der Junge es verstehen?* (Can the boy understand it?)
> **Indirect question:** *Der Lehrer fragte, ob der Junge es verstehen* ***könne.*** (The teacher asked whether the boy can understand it.)

When the present subjunctive (I) is identical to the indicative conjugation, you should use the past subjunctive (II) conjugation in its place. For example:

| | |
|---|---|
| *Er sagte, dass sie kein Deutsch sprechen.* | He said that they don't speak German. |

The subjunctive I conjugation *sie sprechen* is identical to the indicative present-tense conjugation *sie sprechen.* In such a case, change to *sie sprachen:*

> *Er sagte, dass sie kein Deutsch sprächen.*

If the verb in the direct quote is in the past, present-perfect, or past-perfect tense, state the verb in indirect discourse in the present-perfect or past-perfect subjunctive. For example:

> **Direct discourse:** *Sie* ***waren*** *gestern in der Stadt.* (They were in the city yesterday.)
> **Indirect discourse:** *Der Vater sagte, dass sie gestern in der Stadt* ***gewesen seien.*** (The father said that they were in the city yesterday.)

Now compare the same statement as it would appear in written form and as it would be stated in the spoken language.

> **Written:** *Der Rechtsanwalt sagte, dass der Mann unschuldig sei.* (The lawyer said that the man is innocent.)
> **Spoken:** *Der Rechtsanwalt sagte, dass der Mann unschuldig wäre.* (The lawyer said that the man is innocent.)

## Subjunctive with *als ob (als wenn)*

*Als ob* means "as if." The clause that follows *als ob* (or *als wenn*) requires the conjugated verb in that clause to be in the past subjunctive (II). This conjunction, like *dass,* causes the verb to be placed at the end of the clause. Let's look at some examples:

| | |
|---|---|
| *Sie tat so, als ob sie eine Schönheitskönigin wäre.* | She acted as if she were a beauty queen. |
| *Der Lehrer lachte, als ob die Schülerin eine Dummheit gesagt hätte.* | The teacher laughed as if the pupil had said something stupid. |
| *Der neue Angestelle arbeitete, als ob er viel Zeit hätte.* | The new employee worked as if he had a lot of time. |

## Subjunctive with *wenn*

The past-subjunctive (II) conjugation is used with *wenn* when it means "if." *Wenn* can be used in a single clause that expresses feeling or an emotional idea, and the verb in the sentence must then be in the past subjunctive (II). For example:

| | |
|---|---|
| *Wenn du doch wieder zu Hause wärest!* | If only you were back home again. |
| *Wenn er doch seine Frau nie verlassen hätte!* | If only he had never left his wife! |

The same conjunction is used to combine two sentences into one. The *if* clause sets a condition, and the second clause reports the result. Look at an example in English:

If you had come on time, you would have met Mr. Jones.
**Condition:** If you had come on time, . . .
**Result: . . .** you would have met Mr. Jones.

This idea of condition and result also occurs in German. But the conjugated verb in each of the two clauses is conjugated in the past subjunctive (II). The clause that expresses the result is often formed with *würden* (would) and an infinitive. When there is more than one verb in the clause (such as with modal auxiliaries), the verb *würden* can be avoided. For example:

| | |
|---|---|
| *Wenn die Hauptstadt nicht so weit wäre, <u>würden</u> wir dorthin fahren.* | If the capital weren't so far, we'd drive there. |
| *Wenn sie Zeit hätte, <u>würde</u> sie wahrscheinlich mitkommen.* | If she had time, she would probably come along. |
| *Ich <u>würde</u> den Artikel lesen, wenn er interessanter wäre.* | I'd read the article if it were more interesting. |
| *Wenn ich mehr Geld hätte, <u>könnte</u> ich einen neuen Wagen kaufen.* | If I had more money, I could buy a new car. |

Also, if the verbs are structured in the past-perfect tense, the verb *würde* can be avoided:

| | |
|---|---|
| *Wenn sie schneller gelaufen wären, hätten sie den Bus nicht verpasst.* | If they had run faster, they wouldn't have missed the bus. |

# The Imperative Mood

Imperatives are commands or requests. In German, commands are given in three ways: one way for each of the pronouns that means "you." *Du* is informal and singular. *Ihr* is informal and plural. And *Sie* is formal and can be singular or plural. The relationship you have with a person determines which form of "you" to use, and that form of "you" also determines the kind of imperative that should be used when giving a command to someone.

With children, family members, and close friends, use the *du* imperative. For most verbs, it is formed from the stem of the infinitive with the ending *–e*. (It is very common to omit that ending, particularly in the everyday colloquial language.) For example:

| | |
|---|---|
| *Komme mit!* | Come along. |
| *Trinke!* | Drink. |
| *Verkaufe den Wagen!* | Sell the car! |

or

*Komm mit!*
*Trink!*
*Verkauf den Wagen!*

In the case of verbs that make a vowel change in the present tense (*sehen* becomes *sieht, geben* becomes *gibt*), that same vowel change occurs in the *du* imperative. But the *–e* ending is not added. For example:

| | |
|---|---|
| *Sprich Deutsch!* | Speak German. |
| *Gib mir das Buch!* | Give me the book. |
| *Hilf ihm!* | Help him. |

Notice that German imperative statements end with an exclamation mark.

In the *ihr* imperative, the present-tense conjugation with the pronoun *ihr* is, in most cases, the command form:

| | |
|---|---|
| *Sprecht lauter!* | Speak louder. |
| *Lacht nicht!* | Don't laugh. |
| *Steigt ein!* | Get on. |

In the *Sie* imperative, the verb is conjugated for *Sie* and followed by the pronoun *Sie:*

| | |
|---|---|
| *Stehen Sie auf!* | Stand up. |
| *Kommen Sie mit!* | Come along. |
| *Hören Sie zu!* | Listen. |

If the verb has an inseparable prefix, the prefix remains in position in the imperative. Separable prefixes, however, separate as they do in the present-tense conjugation. Look at these examples for the three forms of imperative.

| ***Imperative*** | ***Inseparable Prefix*** | ***Separable Prefix*** |
|---|---|---|
| *du* | *Besuche ihn!* | *Höre damit auf!* |
| *ihr* | *Besucht ihn!* | *Hört damit auf!* |
| *Sie* | *Besuchen Sie ihn!* | *Hören Sie damit auf!* |

The verbs *haben, sein,* and *werden* always require a special look. Some examples in the imperative:

| | | | |
|---|---|---|---|
| *du* | *Habe!* | *Sei!* | *Werde!* |
| *ihr* | *Habt!* | *Seid!* | *Werdet!* |
| *Sie* | *Haben Sie!* | *Seien Sie!* | *Werden Sie!* |

The omission of the final *–e* of the *du* imperative occurs with certain irregular verbs as illustrated earlier and with many regular verbs as well. Regular verbs that do not end in *–eln, –ern, –nen, –igen,* or *–men* can omit the final *–e.* Consider the following examples:

| | | |
|---|---|---|
| *fragen* | *Frage!* or *Frag!* | ask |
| *lachen* | *Lache!* or *Lach!* | laugh |

but

| | | |
|---|---|---|
| *lächeln* | *Lächele!* | smile |
| *kümmern* | *Kümmere!* | worry |
| *öffnen* | *Öffne!* | open |
| *reinigen* | *Reinige!* | clean |
| *atmen* | *Atme!* | breathe |

It is very common to omit the medial *–e–* in the imperative of verbs ending in *–eln* and *–ern*: *Lächle! Kümmre!* In the verb charts, you will encounter such verbs in their full form.

Another very impersonal imperative is formed from the infinitive of a verb. It is used most often on signs or by an official or person of authority who is giving a general command to a group or crowd. For example, the conductor on the platform says the following when a train is pulling into the station:

| | |
|---|---|
| *Zurückbleiben!* | Keep back. |

Or you might see the following message on a sign in a bank:

| | |
|---|---|
| *Bitte von links anstellen!* | Please form a line on the left. |

And the following is the sign you hang on the doorknob of the door to your hotel room:

| | |
|---|---|
| *Bitte nicht stören!* | Please do not disturb. |

Some commands include the person who gives the command. In English, they begin with "let's" and are followed by an infinitive.

Let's go home now.
Let's make a reservation for dinner tonight.

The German counterpart of this kind of imperative is the conjugation of a verb with the pronoun *wir,* but the verb and the pronoun switch places.

| ***Present-Tense Conjugation*** | ***"Let's" as an Imperative*** |
|---|---|
| *wir gehen* | *Gehen wir!* (Let's go.) |
| *wir singen* | *Singen wir!* (Let's sing.) |

A similar expression is formed with the verb *lassen.* But when you use *lassen* in an imperative, you have to consider the relationship you have with the person(s) to whom you are giving the command:

| | |
|---|---|
| *du* | *Lass!* |
| *ihr* | *Lasst!* |
| *Sie* | *Lassen Sie!* |

When you include the accusative pronoun *uns* in such a command, you have another way of saying "let's." For example:

| | | |
|---|---|---|
| *du* | *Lass uns sofort gehen!* | Let's go immediately. |
| *ihr* | *Lasst uns darüber sprechen!* | Let's talk about that. |

# Prefixes and Verbs

Prefixes play an important role in German conjugations and particularly in the change or nuance of meaning of verbs. This occurs to a lesser degree in English. For example:

to come, to become, to overcome
to press, to repress, to impress
to cover, to recover, to discover

German prefixes belong to three types: inseparable prefixes, separable prefixes, and a few prefixes that serve as both inseparable and separable.

## Inseparable Prefixes

The inseparable prefixes are *be–, er–, emp–, ent–, ver–,* and *zer–.* They are called inseparable quite simply because they are not removed from their position at the beginning of a verb during conjugation. Let's look at a few verbs in the various tenses to illustrate this concept.

| ***bekommen (receive)*** | ***erwarten (expect)*** | ***verstehen (understand)*** |
|---|---|---|
| *er bekommt* | *erwartet* | *versteht* |
| *er bekam* | *erwartete* | *verstand* |
| *er hat bekommen* | *hat erwartet* | *hat verstanden* |
| *er hatte bekommen* | *hatte erwartet* | *hatte verstanden* |
| *er wird bekommen* | *wird erwarten* | *wird verstehen* |
| *er wird bekommen haben* | *wird erwartet haben* | *wird verstanden haben* |

## Separable Prefixes

The list of separable prefixes is long, because they come from various adverbs and prepositions but act, of course, as prefixes. A few commonly used separable prefixes are: *ab–, an–, auf–, aus–, bei–, heraus–, mit–, vor–, weg–,* and *zu–*. Except when a verb with a separable prefix is in infinitive form, the prefix is separated from the infinitive. In the present and past tenses, the prefix detaches and is placed at the end of the sentence. In participles, the prefix is separated from the participle by *ge* and the combination of those elements is written as one word.

Let's look at a few verbs in the various tenses to illustrate this concept.

| ***ankommen (arrive)*** | ***vorstellen (introduce)*** | ***zumachen (close)*** |
|---|---|---|
| *er kommt an* | *stellt vor* | *macht zu* |
| *er kam an* | *stellte vor* | *machte zu* |
| *er ist angekommen* | *hat vorgestellt* | *hat zugemacht* |
| *er war angekommen* | *hatte vorgestellt* | *hatte zugemacht* |
| *er wird ankommen* | *wird vorstellen* | *wird zumachen* |
| *er wird angekommen sein* | *wird vorgestellt haben* | *wird zugemacht haben* |

Notice that the stress is on the prefix of a verb with a separable prefix. But the stress is on the stem of the verb with an inseparable prefix, as in the following:

*ánkommen* *bekómmen*

## Separable-Inseparable Prefixes

There is a small list of prefixes that are primarily separable prefixes. But in a few instances they act like inseparable prefixes. You can identify how they are used by the stressed syllable of the verb as noted earlier. These prefixes are: *durch–, hinter–, über–, um–, unter–, voll–, wider–, and wieder–*. A list of example verbs where these prefixes are inseparable follows:

*durchdríngen* (to penetrate)
*unterbréchen* (to interrupt)
*hinterfrágen* (to question)
*vollénden* (to complete)
*überráschen* (to surprise)

*widerspréchen* (to contradict)
*umármen* (to embrace)
*wiederhólen* (to repeat)

In the verb charts, you'll find an accent mark on the stem of such infinitives to help you identify them as having an inseparable prefix, as in *widerspréchen.*

## Verbs with More Than One Prefix

Many German verbs have more than one prefix attached to the verb. The first prefix in the combination is the one that determines whether the verb should be conjugated as a verb with a separable prefix or as a verb with an inseparable prefix. For example, *veranlassen* (to cause) has two prefixes: *ver–* and *an–*. Because *ver–* is the first prefix in the combination, the verb is conjugated as a verb with an inseparable prefix with the following principal parts: *veranlasst, veranlasste, hat veranlasst.*

The verb *vorbereiten* (to prepare) has two prefixes: *vor–* and *be–*. Because *vor–* is a separable prefix in the combination, the verb is conjugated as a verb with a separable prefix with the following principal parts: *bereitet vor, bereitete vor, hat vorbereitet.* Note that the inclusion of the inseparable prefix *be–* means that *ge–* is not needed in the participle.

## Prefixes and the Verb Charts

In Appendix A, you'll find an extensive list of verbs that are not fully illustrated in all the tenses. But the appendix will direct you to the page of a verb that has an "equivalent conjugation." That means that the way the verb in Appendix A changes in each tense is the same as the one in the chart. For example, you'll find the verb *achten* in the verb charts. In Appendix A, one of the many additional verbs is *deuten.* If you want to know the conjugation of *deuten* in all the tenses, you'll be directed to the page where *achten* is shown, because *deuten* has a conjugation that is like the one illustrated for *achten.* Let's look at these two verbs in the third-person singular indicative to see how they compare.

| ***achten (pay attention, respect)*** | ***deuten (point, interpret)*** |
|---|---|
| *achtet* | *deutet* |
| *achtete* | *deutete* |
| *hat geachtet* | *hat gedeutet* |
| *hatte geachtet* | *hatte gedeutet* |
| *wird achten* | *wird deuten* |
| *wird geachtet haben* | *wird gedeutet haben* |

Of course, the charts also provide the various tenses in the subjunctive. In both the indicative and subjunctive, *deuten* follows the same conjugational patterns as *achten.*

In some cases, you'll be directed to a verb that has the equivalent conjugation of another verb that you've found in Appendix A, but the equivalent verb may have a prefix—an inseparable or a separable prefix. Knowing the rules of prefixes will help you to identify the conjugational forms without being confused by the prefixes.

For example, if you want to know the conjugation of the verbs *betrachten* and *hindeuten,* you'll once again be directed to the page where *achten* is located. Compare the conjugation of *achten* with that of *betrachten* (with an inseparable prefix) and *hindeuten* (with a separable prefix).

| ***achten*** ***(pay attention)*** | ***betrachten*** ***(consider)*** | ***hindeuten*** ***(hint at)*** |
|---|---|---|
| *achtet* | *betrachtet* | *deutet hin* |
| *achtete* | *betrachtete* | *deutete hin* |
| *hat geachtet* | *hat betrachtet* | *hat hingedeutet* |
| *hatte geachtet* | *hatte betrachtet* | *hatte hingedeutet* |
| *wird achten* | *wird betrachten* | *wird hindeuten* |
| *wird geachtet haben* | *wird betrachtet haben* | *wird hingedeutet haben* |

The three verbs follow the same conjugational patterns, and the inseparable and separable prefixes act in their own prescribed way. Knowing how the prefixes function will help you to use the charts effectively.

# The Personal Pronouns: Subjects in the Nominative Case

You're certainly quite familiar with the personal pronouns: *ich, du, er, sie, es, wir, ihr, sie,* and *Sie.* They've been used in the illustrations and examples of this section of the book. In the charts, however, the pronouns will not be shown, but the order of the conjugated verbs will always be the same. Compare the order of the subject pronouns with the order of the conjugations in the verb charts.

| ***Order of the Pronouns*** | | ***Order of the Conjugation*** | |
|---|---|---|---|
| ***Singular*** | ***Plural*** | ***Singular*** | ***Plural*** |
| *ich* (first person) | *wir* (first person) | *(ich) gehe* | *(wir) gehen* |
| *du* (second person) | *ihr* (second person) | *(du) gehst* | *(ihr) geht* |
| *er* (third person) | *sie* (third person) | *(er) geht* | *(sie) gehen* |

The third-person singular *er* is also the conjugation required for *sie* singular and *es,* as well as for all singular nouns and the impersonal pronoun *man.* The third-person plural *sie* is also the conjugation required for *Sie* formal as well as for all plural nouns. In the verb charts, the pronouns do not appear. The present-tense conjugation of *gehen* will look like this:

| ***Singular*** | ***Plural*** |
|---|---|
| *gehe* | *gehen* |
| *gehst* | *geht* |
| *geht* | *gehen* |

# VERB CHARTS

The charts in this section identify the German infinitive, its English meaning(s), the appropriate auxiliary (*haben* or *sein*) for the past participle, the past participle, and the imperative forms where applicable. All charts are followed by a series of example sentences in German and English that show the different usages and meanings of the specific verb.

**abspülen**
to rinse off, to wash off
**Auxiliary verb:** haben **Past participle:** abgespült
**Imperative:** Spüle ab! Spült ab! Spülen Sie ab!

| Mode | Simple Tenses | | Compound Tenses | |
|---|---|---|---|---|
| | *Singular* | *Plural* | *Singular* | *Plural* |
| Indicative | **Present** | | **Present Perfect** | |
| | spüle ab<br>spülst ab<br>spült ab | spülen ab<br>spült ab<br>spülen ab | habe abgespült<br>hast abgespült<br>hat abgespült | haben abgespült<br>habt abgespült<br>haben abgespült |
| | **Past** | | **Past Perfect** | |
| | spülte ab<br>spültest ab<br>spülte ab | spülten ab<br>spültet ab<br>spülten ab | hatte abgespült<br>hattest abgespült<br>hatte abgespült | hatten abgespült<br>hattet abgespült<br>hatten abgespült |
| | **Future** | | **Future Perfect** | |
| | werde abspülen<br>wirst abspülen<br>wird abspülen | werden abspülen<br>werdet abspülen<br>werden abspülen | werde abgespült haben<br>wirst abgespült haben<br>wird abgespült haben | werden abgespült haben<br>werdet abgespült haben<br>werden abgespült haben |
| Subjunctive | **Present** | | **Present Perfect** | |
| | spüle ab<br>spülest ab<br>spüle ab | spülen ab<br>spület ab<br>spülen ab | habe abgespült<br>habest abgespült<br>habe abgespült | haben abgespült<br>habet abgespült<br>haben abgespült |
| | **Past** | | **Past Perfect** | |
| | spülte ab<br>spültest ab<br>spülte ab | spülten ab<br>spültet ab<br>spülten ab | hätte abgespült<br>hättest abgespült<br>hätte abgespült | hätten abgespült<br>hättet abgespült<br>hätten abgespült |
| | **Future** | | **Future Perfect** | |
| | werde abspülen<br>werdest abspülen<br>werde abspülen | werden abspülen<br>werdet abspülen<br>werden abspülen | werde abgespült haben<br>werdest abgespült haben<br>werde abgespült haben | werden abgespült haben<br>werdet abgespült haben<br>werden abgespült haben |
| | **Present and Future Conditional** | | **Past Conditional** | |
| | würde abspülen<br>würdest abspülen<br>würde abspülen | würden abspülen<br>würdet abspülen<br>würden abspülen | würde abgespült haben<br>würdest abgespült haben<br>würde abgespült haben | würden abgespült haben<br>würdet abgespült haben<br>würden abgespült haben |

## EXAMPLES

Ich werde die Teller abspülen. — I'll rinse off the plates.
Werner hat die Tassen schon abgespült. — Werner already washed the cups.

**achten**

to pay attention, to regard, to respect

**Auxiliary verb:** haben **Past participle:** geachtet

**Imperative:** Achte! Achtet! Achten Sie!

| Mode | Simple Tenses | | Compound Tenses | |
|---|---|---|---|---|
| | *Singular* | *Plural* | *Singular* | *Plural* |
| Indicative | **Present** | | **Present Perfect** | |
| | achte<br>achtest<br>achtet | achten<br>achtet<br>achten | habe geachtet<br>hast geachtet<br>hat geachtet | haben geachtet<br>habt geachtet<br>haben geachtet |
| | **Past** | | **Past Perfect** | |
| | achtete<br>achtetest<br>achtete | achteten<br>achtetet<br>achteten | hatte geachtet<br>hattest geachtet<br>hatte geachtet | hatten geachtet<br>hattet geachtet<br>hatten geachtet |
| | **Future** | | **Future Perfect** | |
| | werde achten<br>wirst achten<br>wird achten | werden achten<br>werdet achten<br>werden geachtet haben | werde geachtet haben<br>wirst geachtet haben<br>wird geachtet haben | werden geachtet haben<br>werdet geachtet haben<br>werden geachtet haben |
| Subjunctive | **Present** | | **Present Perfect** | |
| | achte<br>achtest<br>achte | achten<br>achtet<br>achten | habe geachtet<br>habest geachtet<br>habe geachtet | haben geachtet<br>habet geachtet<br>haben geachtet |
| | **Past** | | **Past Perfect** | |
| | achtete<br>achtetest<br>achtete | achteten<br>achtetet<br>achteten | hätte geachtet<br>hättest geachtet<br>hätte geachtet | hätten geachtet<br>hättet geachtet<br>hätten geachtet |
| | **Future** | | **Future Perfect** | |
| | werde achten<br>werdest achten<br>werde achten | werden achten<br>werdet achten<br>werden achten | werde achten<br>werdest achten<br>werde achten | werden achten<br>werdet achten<br>werden achten |
| | **Present and Future Conditional** | | **Past Conditional** | |
| | würde achten<br>würdest achten<br>würde achten | würden achten<br>würdet achten<br>würden achten | würde geachtet haben<br>würdest geachtet haben<br>würde geachtet haben | würden geachtet haben<br>würdet geachtet haben<br>würden geachtet haben |

## EXAMPLES

Achten Sie darauf, niemand zu beleidigen!
Pay attention not to insult anyone.

Sie hat nicht auf die Regeln der neuen Rechtschreibung geachtet.
She didn't heed the rules for the new orthography.

**ahnen**
to surmise, to suspect, to have a feeling
**Auxiliary verb:** haben **Past participle:** geahnt
**Imperative:** Ahne! Ahnt! Ahnen Sie!

| Mode | Simple Tenses | | Compound Tenses | |
|---|---|---|---|---|
| | *Singular* | *Plural* | *Singular* | *Plural* |
| Indicative | **Present** | | **Present Perfect** | |
| | ahne<br>ahnst<br>ahnt | ahnen<br>ahnt<br>ahnen | habe geahnt<br>hast geahnt<br>hat geahnt | haben geahnt<br>habt geahnt<br>haben geahnt |
| | **Past** | | **Past Perfect** | |
| | ahnte<br>ahntest<br>ahnte | ahnten<br>ahntet<br>ahnten | hatte geahnt<br>hattest geahnt<br>hatte geahnt | hatten geahnt<br>hattet geahnt<br>hatten geahnt |
| | **Future** | | **Future Perfect** | |
| | werde ahnen<br>wirst ahnen<br>wird ahnen | werden ahnen<br>werdet ahnen<br>werden geahnt haben | werde geahnt haben<br>wirst geahnt haben<br>wird geahnt haben | werden geahnt haben<br>werdet geahnt haben<br>werden geahnt haben |
| Subjunctive | **Present** | | **Present Perfect** | |
| | ahne<br>ahnest<br>ahne | ahnen<br>ahnet<br>ahnen | habe geahnt<br>habest geahnt<br>habe geahnt | haben geahnt<br>habet geahnt<br>haben geahnt |
| | **Past** | | **Past Perfect** | |
| | ahnte<br>ahntest<br>ahnte | ahnten<br>ahntet<br>ahnten | hätte geahnt<br>hättest geahnt<br>hätte geahnt | hätten geahnt<br>hättet geahnt<br>hätten geahnt |
| | **Future** | | **Future Perfect** | |
| | werde ahnen<br>werdest ahnen<br>werde ahnen | werden ahnen<br>werdet ahnen<br>werden ahnen | werde ahnen<br>werdest ahnen<br>werde ahnen | werden ahnen<br>werdet ahnen<br>werden ahnen |
| | **Present and Future Conditional** | | **Past Conditional** | |
| | würde ahnen<br>würdest ahnen<br>würde ahnen | würden ahnen<br>würdet ahnen<br>würden ahnen | würde geahnt haben<br>würdest geahnt haben<br>würde geahnt haben | würden geahnt haben<br>würdet geahnt haben<br>würden geahnt haben |

## EXAMPLES

Ich ahnte nichts Gutes. — I had a foreboding of something bad.
Das habe ich bereits im Voraus geahnt. — I had a feeling about it from the start.

**anbieten**
to offer
**Auxiliary verb:** haben **Past participle:** angeboten
**Imperative:** Biete an! Bietet an! Bieten Sie an!

| Mode | Simple Tenses | | Compound Tenses | |
|---|---|---|---|---|
| | *Singular* | *Plural* | *Singular* | *Plural* |
| Indicative | **Present** | | **Present Perfect** | |
| | biete an<br>bietest an<br>bietet an | bieten an<br>bietet an<br>bieten an | habe angeboten<br>hast angeboten<br>hat angeboten | haben angeboten<br>habt angeboten<br>haben angeboten |
| | **Past** | | **Past Perfect** | |
| | bot an<br>botest an<br>bot an | boten an<br>botet an<br>boten an | hatte angeboten<br>hattest angeboten<br>hatte angeboten | hatten angeboten<br>hattet angeboten<br>hatten angeboten |
| | **Future** | | **Future Perfect** | |
| | werde anbieten<br>wirst anbieten<br>wird anbieten | werden anbieten<br>werdet anbieten<br>werden anbieten | werde angeboten haben<br>wirst angeboten haben<br>wird angeboten haben | werden angeboten haben<br>werdet angeboten haben<br>werden angeboten haben |
| Subjunctive | **Present** | | **Present Perfect** | |
| | biete an<br>bietest an<br>biete an | bieten an<br>bietet an<br>bieten an | habe angeboten<br>habest angeboten<br>habe angeboten | haben angeboten<br>habet angeboten<br>haben angeboten |
| | **Past** | | **Past Perfect** | |
| | böte an<br>bötest an<br>böte an | böten an<br>bötet an<br>böten an | hätte angeboten<br>hättest angeboten<br>hätte angeboten | hätten angeboten<br>hättet angeboten<br>hätten angeboten |
| | **Future** | | **Future Perfect** | |
| | werde anbieten<br>werdest anbieten<br>werde anbieten | werden anbieten<br>werdet anbieten<br>werden anbieten | werde angeboten haben<br>werdest angeboten haben<br>werde angeboten haben | werden angeboten haben<br>werdet angeboten haben<br>werden angeboten haben |
| | **Present and Future Conditional** | | **Past Conditional** | |
| | würde anbieten<br>würdest anbieten<br>würde anbieten | würden anbieten<br>würdet anbieten<br>würden anbieten | würde angeboten haben<br>würdest angeboten haben<br>würde angeboten haben | würden angeboten haben<br>würdet angeboten haben<br>würden angeboten haben |

## EXAMPLES

Sie bot mir einen neuen Plan an. — She offered me a new plan.
Eine gute Gelegenheit hat sich angeboten. — A good opportunity was in the offing.

**ändern (sich)**
to change, to alter, to amend
**Auxiliary verb:** haben **Past participle:** geändert
**Imperative:** Ändere! Ändert! Ändern Sie!

| Mode | Simple Tenses | | Compound Tenses | |
|---|---|---|---|---|
| | *Singular* | *Plural* | *Singular* | *Plural* |
| Indicative | **Present** | | **Present Perfect** | |
| | ändere<br>änderst<br>ändert | ändern<br>ändert<br>ändern | habe geändert<br>hast geändert<br>hat geändert | haben geändert<br>habt geändert<br>haben geändert |
| | **Past** | | **Past Perfect** | |
| | änderte<br>ändertest<br>änderte | änderten<br>ändertet<br>änderten | hatte geändert<br>hattest geändert<br>hatte geändert | hatten geändert<br>hattet geändert<br>hatten geändert |
| | **Future** | | **Future Perfect** | |
| | werde ändern<br>wirst ändern<br>wird ändern | werden ändern<br>werdet ändern<br>werden geändert haben | werde geändert haben<br>wirst geändert haben<br>wird geändert haben | werden geändert haben<br>werdet geändert haben<br>werden geändert haben |
| Subjunctive | **Present** | | **Present Perfect** | |
| | ändere<br>änderst<br>ändere | ändern<br>ändert<br>ändern | habe geändert<br>habest geändert<br>habe geändert | haben geändert<br>habet geändert<br>haben geändert |
| | **Past** | | **Past Perfect** | |
| | änderte<br>ändertest<br>änderte | änderten<br>ändertet<br>änderten | hätte geändert<br>hättest geändert<br>hätte geändert | hätten geändert<br>hättet geändert<br>hätten geändert |
| | **Future** | | **Future Perfect** | |
| | werde ändern<br>werdest ändern<br>werde ändern | werden ändern<br>werdet ändern<br>werden ändern | werde ändern<br>werdest ändern<br>werde ändern | werden ändern<br>werdet ändern<br>werden ändern |
| | **Present and Future Conditional** | | **Past Conditional** | |
| | würde ändern<br>würdest ändern<br>würde ändern | würden ändern<br>würdet ändern<br>würden ändern | würde geändert haben<br>würdest geändert haben<br>würde geändert haben | würden geändert haben<br>würdet geändert haben<br>würden geändert haben |

## EXAMPLES

Das lässt sich leider nicht ändern. — Unfortunately, it can't be changed.
Martin hat seine Meinung wieder geändert. — Martin changed his mind again.

**anfangen**
to begin, to start
**Auxiliary verb:** haben **Past participle:** angefangen
**Imperative:** Fange an! Fangt an! Fangen Sie an!

| Mode | Simple Tenses | | Compound Tenses | |
|---|---|---|---|---|
| | *Singular* | *Plural* | *Singular* | *Plural* |
| Indicative | **Present** | | **Present Perfect** | |
| | fange an<br>fängst an<br>fängt an | fangen an<br>fangt an<br>fangen an | habe angefangen<br>hast angefangen<br>hat angefangen | haben angefangen<br>habt angefangen<br>haben angefangen |
| | **Past** | | **Past Perfect** | |
| | fing an<br>fingst an<br>fing an | fingen an<br>fingt an<br>fingen an | hatte angefangen<br>hattest angefangen<br>hatte angefangen | hatten angefangen<br>hattet angefangen<br>hatten angefangen |
| | **Future** | | **Future Perfect** | |
| | werde anfangen<br>wirst anfangen<br>wird anfangen | werden anfangen<br>werdet anfangen<br>werden anfangen | werde angefangen haben<br>wirst angefangen haben<br>wird angefangen haben | werden angefangen haben<br>werdet angefangen haben<br>werden angefangen haben |
| Subjunctive | **Present** | | **Present Perfect** | |
| | fange an<br>fangest an<br>fange an | fangen an<br>fanget an<br>fangen an | habe angefangen<br>habest angefangen<br>habe angefangen | haben angefangen<br>habet angefangen<br>haben angefangen |
| | **Past** | | **Past Perfect** | |
| | finge an<br>fingest an<br>finge an | fingen an<br>finget an<br>fingen an | hätte angefangen<br>hättest angefangen<br>hätte angefangen | hätten angefangen<br>hättet angefangen<br>hätten angefangen |
| | **Future** | | **Future Perfect** | |
| | werde anfangen<br>werdest anfangen<br>werde anfangen | werden anfangen<br>werdet anfangen<br>werden anfangen | werde angefangen haben<br>werdest angefangen haben<br>werde angefangen haben | werden angefangen haben<br>werdet angefangen haben<br>werden angefangen haben |
| | **Present and Future Conditional** | | **Past Conditional** | |
| | würde anfangen<br>würdest anfangen<br>würde anfangen | würden anfangen<br>würdet anfangen<br>würden anfangen | würde angefangen haben<br>würdest angefangen haben<br>würde angefangen haben | würden angefangen haben<br>würdet angefangen haben<br>würden angefangen haben |

## EXAMPLES

Wann fangt ihr mit dem neuen Plan an? — When are you starting with the new plan?
Morgen fangen sie damit an. — They're starting with it tomorrow.
Hast du noch nicht angefangen? — Haven't you started yet?

**ankommen**
to arrive, to approach
**Auxiliary verb:** sein **Past participle:** angekommen
**Imperative:** Komme an! Kommt an! Kommen Sie an!

| Mode | Simple Tenses | | Compound Tenses | |
|---|---|---|---|---|
| | *Singular* | *Plural* | *Singular* | *Plural* |
| Indicative | **Present** | | **Present Perfect** | |
| | komme an<br>kommst an<br>kommt an | kommen an<br>kommt an<br>kommen an | bin angekommen<br>bist angekommen<br>ist angekommen | sind angekommen<br>seid angekommen<br>sind angekommen |
| | **Past** | | **Past Perfect** | |
| | kam an<br>kamst an<br>kam an | kamen an<br>kamt an<br>kamen an | war angekommen<br>warst angekommen<br>war angekommen | waren angekommen<br>wart angekommen<br>waren angekommen |
| | **Future** | | **Future Perfect** | |
| | werde ankommen<br>wirst ankommen<br>wird ankommen | werden ankommen<br>werdet ankommen<br>werden ankommen | werde angekommen sein<br>wirst angekommen sein<br>wird angekommen sein | werden angekommen sein<br>werdet angekommen sein<br>werden angekommen sein |
| Subjunctive | **Present** | | **Present Perfect** | |
| | komme an<br>kommest an<br>komme an | kommen an<br>kommet an<br>kommen an | sei angekommen<br>seiest angekommen<br>sei angekommen | seien angekommen<br>seiet angekommen<br>seien angekommen |
| | **Past** | | **Past Perfect** | |
| | käme an<br>kämest an<br>käme an | kämen an<br>kämet an<br>kämen an | wäre angekommen<br>wärest angekommen<br>wäre angekommen | wären angekommen<br>wäret angekommen<br>wären angekommen |
| | **Future** | | **Future Perfect** | |
| | werde ankommen<br>werdest ankommen<br>werde ankommen | werden ankommen<br>werdet ankommen<br>werden ankommen | werde angekommen sein<br>werdest angekommen sein<br>werde angekommen sein | werden angekommen sein<br>werdet angekommen sein<br>werden angekommen sein |
| | **Present and Future Conditional** | | **Past Conditional** | |
| | würde ankommen<br>würdest ankommen<br>würde ankommen | würden ankommen<br>würdet ankommen<br>würden ankommen | würde angekommen sein<br>würdest angekommen sein<br>würde angekommen sein | würden angekommen sein<br>würdet angekommen sein<br>würden angekommen sein |

## EXAMPLES

Papa kommt morgen um sechs an. — Dad arrives at six tomorrow.
Der Gast ist noch nicht angekommen. — The guest hasn't arrived yet.
Wann kommt der Zug an? — When does the train arrive?

**anrufen**
to call, to telephone
**Auxiliary verb:** haben **Past participle:** angerufen
**Imperative:** Rufe an! Ruft an! Rufen Sie an!

| Mode | Simple Tenses | | Compound Tenses | |
|---|---|---|---|---|
| | *Singular* | *Plural* | *Singular* | *Plural* |
| Indicative | **Present** | | **Present Perfect** | |
| | rufe an<br>rufst an<br>ruft an | rufen an<br>ruft an<br>rufen an | habe angerufen<br>hast angerufen<br>hat angerufen | haben angerufen<br>habt angerufen<br>haben angerufen |
| | **Past** | | **Past Perfect** | |
| | rief an<br>riefst an<br>rief an | riefen an<br>rieft an<br>riefen an | hatte angerufen<br>hattest angerufen<br>hatte angerufen | hatten angerufen<br>hattet angerufen<br>hatten angerufen |
| | **Future** | | **Future Perfect** | |
| | werde anrufen<br>wirst anrufen<br>wird anrufen | werden anrufen<br>werdet anrufen<br>werden anrufen | werde angerufen haben<br>wirst angerufen haben<br>wird angerufen haben | werden angerufen haben<br>werdet angerufen haben<br>werden angerufen haben |
| Subjunctive | **Present** | | **Present Perfect** | |
| | rufe an<br>rufest an<br>rufe an | rufen an<br>rufet an<br>rufen an | habe angerufen<br>habest angerufen<br>habe angerufen | haben angerufen<br>habet angerufen<br>haben angerufen |
| | **Past** | | **Past Perfect** | |
| | riefe an<br>riefest an<br>riefe an | riefen an<br>riefet an<br>riefen an | hätte angerufen<br>hättest angerufen<br>hätte angerufen | hätten angerufen<br>hättet angerufen<br>hätten angerufen |
| | **Future** | | **Future Perfect** | |
| | werde anrufen<br>werdest anrufen<br>werde anrufen | werden anrufen<br>werdet anrufen<br>werden anrufen | werde angerufen haben<br>werdest angerufen haben<br>werde angerufen haben | werden angerufen haben<br>werdet angerufen haben<br>werden angerufen haben |
| | **Present and Future Conditional** | | **Past Conditional** | |
| | würde anrufen<br>würdest anrufen<br>würde anrufen | würden anrufen<br>würdet anrufen<br>würden anrufen | würde angerufen haben<br>würdest angerufen haben<br>würde angerufen haben | würden angerufen haben<br>würdet angerufen haben<br>würden angerufen haben |

## EXAMPLES

| | |
|---|---|
| Oma hat um zehn Uhr angerufen. | Granny phoned at ten o'clock. |
| Er wird mich morgen anrufen. | He'll call me up tomorrow. |
| Rufen Sie an, wenn Sie Zeit haben. | Give me a call when you have time. |

**antasten**
to touch, to handle, to question
**Auxiliary verb:** haben **Past participle:** angetastet
**Imperative:** Taste an! Tastet an! Tasten Sie an!

| Mode | Simple Tenses | | Compound Tenses | |
|---|---|---|---|---|
| | *Singular* | *Plural* | *Singular* | *Plural* |
| Indicative | **Present** | | **Present Perfect** | |
| | taste an<br>tastest an<br>tastet an | tasten an<br>tastet an<br>tasten an | habe angetastet<br>hast angetastet<br>hat angetastet | haben angetastet<br>habt angetastet<br>haben angetastet |
| | **Past** | | **Past Perfect** | |
| | tastete an<br>tastetest an<br>tastete an | tasteten an<br>tastetet an<br>tasteten an | hatte angetastet<br>hattest angetastet<br>hatte angetastet | hatten angetastet<br>hattet angetastet<br>hatten angetastet |
| | **Future** | | **Future Perfect** | |
| | werde antasten<br>wirst antasten<br>wird antasten | werden antasten<br>werdet antasten<br>werden antasten | werde angetastet haben<br>wirst angetastet haben<br>wird angetastet haben | werden angetastet haben<br>werdet angetastet haben<br>werden angetastet haben |
| Subjunctive | **Present** | | **Present Perfect** | |
| | taste an<br>tastest an<br>taste an | tasten an<br>tastet an<br>tasten an | habe angetastet<br>habest angetastet<br>habe angetastet | haben angetastet<br>habet angetastet<br>haben angetastet |
| | **Past** | | **Past Perfect** | |
| | tastete an<br>tastetest an<br>tastete an | tasteten an<br>tastetet an<br>tasteten an | hätte angetastet<br>hättest angetastet<br>hätte angetastet | hätten angetastet<br>hättet angetastet<br>hätten angetastet |
| | **Future** | | **Future Perfect** | |
| | werde antasten<br>werdest antasten<br>werde antasten | werden antasten<br>werdet antasten<br>werden antasten | werde angetastet haben<br>werdest angetastet haben<br>werde angetastet haben | werden angetastet haben<br>werdet angetastet haben<br>werden angetastet haben |
| | **Present and Future Conditional** | | **Past Conditional** | |
| | würde antasten<br>würdest antasten<br>würde antasten | würden antasten<br>würdet antasten<br>würden antasten | würde angetastet haben<br>würdest angetastet haben<br>würde angetastet haben | würden angetastet haben<br>würdet angetastet haben<br>würden angetastet haben |

## EXAMPLES

Der Artikel tastete den guten Ruf des Politkers an.
The article questioned the good reputation of the politician.

Dieses Bankkonto darf nicht angetastet werden.
This bank account may not be touched.

**antworten**
to answer, to reply
**Auxiliary verb:** haben **Past participle:** geantwortet
**Imperative:** Antworte! Antwortet! Antworten Sie!

| Mode | Simple Tenses | | Compound Tenses | |
|---|---|---|---|---|
| | *Singular* | *Plural* | *Singular* | *Plural* |
| Indicative | **Present** | | **Present Perfect** | |
| | antworte<br>antwortest<br>antwortet | antworten<br>antwortet<br>antworten | habe geantwortet<br>hast geantwortet<br>hat geantwortet | haben geantwortet<br>habt geantwortet<br>haben geantwortet |
| | **Past** | | **Past Perfect** | |
| | antwortete<br>antwortetest<br>antwortete | antworteten<br>antwortetet<br>antworteten | hatte geantwortet<br>hattest geantwortet<br>hatte geantwortet | hatten geantwortet<br>hattet geantwortet<br>hatten geantwortet |
| | **Future** | | **Future Perfect** | |
| | werde antworten<br>wirst antworten<br>wird antworten | werden antworten<br>werdet antworten<br>werden antworten | werde geantwortet haben<br>wirst geantwortet haben<br>wird geantwortet haben | werden geantwortet haben<br>werdet geantwortet haben<br>werden geantwortet haben |
| Subjunctive | **Present** | | **Present Perfect** | |
| | antworte<br>antwortest<br>antworte | antworten<br>antwortet<br>antworten | habe geantwortet<br>habest geantwortet<br>habe geantwortet | haben geantwortet<br>habet geantwortet<br>haben geantwortet |
| | **Past** | | **Past Perfect** | |
| | antwortete<br>antwortetest<br>antwortete | antworteten<br>antwortetet<br>antworteten | hätte geantwortet<br>hättest geantwortet<br>hätte geantwortet | hätten geantwortet<br>hättet geantwortet<br>hätten geantwortet |
| | **Future** | | **Future Perfect** | |
| | werde antworten<br>werdest antworten<br>werde antworten | werden antworten<br>werdet antworten<br>werden antworten | werde antworten<br>werdest antworten<br>werde antworten | werden antworten<br>werdet antworten<br>werden antworten |
| | **Present and Future Conditional** | | **Past Conditional** | |
| | würde antworten<br>würdest antworten<br>würde antworten | würden antworten<br>würdet antworten<br>würden antworten | würde geantwortet haben<br>würdest geantwortet haben<br>würde geantwortet haben | würden geantwortet haben<br>würdet geantwortet haben<br>würden geantwortet haben |

## EXAMPLES

Es wäre gut, wenn du mir sofort antworten könntest.
It would be good if you could answer me right away.

Antworten Sie auf deutsch!
Answer in German.

**anwenden**
to employ, to use, to apply to
**Auxiliary verb:** haben **Past participle:** angewandt
**Imperative:** Wende an! Wendet an! Wenden Sie an!

| Mode | Simple Tenses | | Compound Tenses | |
|---|---|---|---|---|
| | *Singular* | *Plural* | *Singular* | *Plural* |
| Indicative | **Present** | | **Present Perfect** | |
| | wende an<br>wendest an<br>wendet an | wenden an<br>wendet an<br>wenden an | habe angewandt<br>hast angewandt<br>hat angewandt | haben angewandt<br>habt angewandt<br>haben angewandt |
| | **Past** | | **Past Perfect** | |
| | wandte an<br>wandtest an<br>wandte an | wandten an<br>wandtet an<br>wandten an | hatte angewandt<br>hattest angewandt<br>hatte angewandt | hatten angewandt<br>hattet angewandt<br>hatten angewandt |
| | **Future** | | **Future Perfect** | |
| | werde anwenden<br>wirst anwenden<br>wird anwenden | werden anwenden<br>werdet anwenden<br>werden anwenden | werde angewandt haben<br>wirst angewandt haben<br>wird angewandt haben | werden angewandt haben<br>werdet angewandt haben<br>werden angewandt haben |
| Subjunctive | **Present** | | **Present Perfect** | |
| | wende an<br>wendest an<br>wende an | wenden an<br>wendet an<br>wenden an | habe angewandt<br>habest angewandt<br>habe angewandt | haben angewandt<br>habet angewandt<br>haben angewandt |
| | **Past** | | **Past Perfect** | |
| | wendete an<br>wendetest an<br>wendete an | wendeten an<br>wendetet an<br>wendeten an | hätte angewandt<br>hättest angewandt<br>hätte angewandt | hätten angewandt<br>hättet angewandt<br>hätten angewandt |
| | **Future** | | **Future Perfect** | |
| | werde anwenden<br>werdest anwenden<br>werde anwenden | werden anwenden<br>werdet anwenden<br>werden anwenden | werde angewandt haben<br>werdest angewandt haben<br>werde angewandt haben | werden angewandt haben<br>werdet angewandt haben<br>werden angewandt haben |
| | **Present and Future Conditional** | | **Past Conditional** | |
| | würde anwenden<br>würdest anwenden<br>würde anwenden | würden anwenden<br>würdet anwenden<br>würden anwenden | würde angewandt haben<br>würdest angewandt haben<br>würde angewandt haben | würden angewandt haben<br>würdet angewandt haben<br>würden angewandt haben |

**Note:** This verb also has a regular conjugation. Its principal parts without a prefix are *wendet, wendete, hat gewendet. Wenden* means "turn" or "turn over."

## EXAMPLES

Hier muss man diese Formel anwenden.
Here you have to use this formula.

Hast du das Desinfektionsmittel richtig angewandt?
Did you apply the disinfectant correctly?

**anziehen (sich)**
to dress, to put on (clothes)
**Auxiliary verb:** haben **Past participle:** angezogen
**Imperative:** Ziehe an! Zieht an! Ziehen Sie an!

| Mode | Simple Tenses | | Compound Tenses | |
|---|---|---|---|---|
| | *Singular* | *Plural* | *Singular* | *Plural* |
| Indicative | **Present** | | **Present Perfect** | |
| | ziehe an<br>ziehst an<br>zieht an | ziehen an<br>zieht an<br>ziehen an | habe angezogen<br>hast angezogen<br>hat angezogen | haben angezogen<br>habt angezogen<br>haben angezogen |
| | **Past** | | **Past Perfect** | |
| | zog an<br>zogst an<br>zog an | zogen an<br>zogt an<br>zogen an | hatte angezogen<br>hattest angezogen<br>hatte angezogen | hatten angezogen<br>hattet angezogen<br>hatten angezogen |
| | **Future** | | **Future Perfect** | |
| | werde anziehen<br>wirst anziehen<br>wird anziehen | werden anziehen<br>werdet anziehen<br>werden anziehen | werde angezogen haben<br>wirst angezogen haben<br>wird angezogen haben | werden angezogen haben<br>werdet angezogen haben<br>werden angezogen haben |
| Subjunctive | **Present** | | **Present Perfect** | |
| | ziehe an<br>ziehest an<br>ziehe an | ziehen an<br>ziehet an<br>ziehen an | habe angezogen<br>habest angezogen<br>habe angezogen | haben angezogen<br>habet angezogen<br>haben angezogen |
| | **Past** | | **Past Perfect** | |
| | zöge an<br>zögest an<br>zöge an | zögen an<br>zöget an<br>zögen an | hätte angezogen<br>hättest angezogen<br>hätte angezogen | hätten angezogen<br>hättet angezogen<br>hätten angezogen |
| | **Future** | | **Future Perfect** | |
| | werde anziehen<br>werdest anziehen<br>werde anziehen | werden anziehen<br>werdet anziehen<br>werden anziehen | werde angezogen haben<br>werdest angezogen haben<br>werde angezogen haben | werden angezogen haben<br>werdet angezogen haben<br>werden angezogen haben |
| | **Present and Future Conditional** | | **Past Conditional** | |
| | würde anziehen<br>würdest anziehen<br>würde anziehen | würden anziehen<br>würdet anziehen<br>würden anziehen | würde angezogen haben<br>würdest angezogen haben<br>würde angezogen haben | würden angezogen haben<br>würdet angezogen haben<br>würden angezogen haben |

## EXAMPLES

Papa soll seinen Regenmantel anziehen. — Dad should put on his raincoat.
Hast du dich noch nicht angezogen? — Haven't you gotten dressed yet?

**arbeiten**
to work
**Auxiliary verb:** haben **Past participle:** gearbeitet
**Imperative:** Arbeite! Arbeitet! Arbeiten Sie!

| Mode | Simple Tenses | | Compound Tenses | |
|---|---|---|---|---|
| | *Singular* | *Plural* | *Singular* | *Plural* |
| Indicative | **Present** | | **Present Perfect** | |
| | arbeite<br>arbeitest<br>arbeitet | arbeiten<br>arbeitet<br>arbeiten | habe gearbeitet<br>hast gearbeitet<br>hat gearbeitet | haben gearbeitet<br>habt gearbeitet<br>haben gearbeitet |
| | **Past** | | **Past Perfect** | |
| | arbeitete<br>arbeitetest<br>arbeitete | arbeiteten<br>arbeitetet<br>arbeiteten | hatte gearbeitet<br>hattest gearbeitet<br>hatte gearbeitet | hatten gearbeitet<br>hattet gearbeitet<br>hatten gearbeitet |
| | **Future** | | **Future Perfect** | |
| | werde arbeiten<br>wirst arbeiten<br>wird arbeiten | werden arbeiten<br>werdet arbeiten<br>werden arbeiten | werde gearbeitet haben<br>wirst gearbeitet haben<br>wird gearbeitet haben | werden gearbeitet haben<br>werdet gearbeitet haben<br>werden gearbeitet haben |
| Subjunctive | **Present** | | **Present Perfect** | |
| | arbeite<br>arbeitest<br>arbeite | arbeiten<br>arbeitet<br>arbeiten | habe gearbeitet<br>habest gearbeitet<br>habe gearbeitet | haben gearbeitet<br>habet gearbeitet<br>haben gearbeitet |
| | **Past** | | **Past Perfect** | |
| | arbeitete<br>arbeitetest<br>arbeitete | arbeiteten<br>arbeitetet<br>arbeiteten | hätte gearbeitet<br>hättest gearbeitet<br>hätte gearbeitet | hätten gearbeitet<br>hättet gearbeitet<br>hätten gearbeitet |
| | **Future** | | **Future Perfect** | |
| | werde arbeiten<br>werdest arbeiten<br>werde arbeiten | werden arbeiten<br>werdet arbeiten<br>werden arbeiten | werde arbeiten<br>werdest arbeiten<br>werde arbeiten | werden arbeiten<br>werdet arbeiten<br>werden arbeiten |
| | **Present and Future Conditional** | | **Past Conditional** | |
| | würde arbeiten<br>würdest arbeiten<br>würde arbeiten | würden arbeiten<br>würdet arbeiten<br>würden arbeiten | würde gearbeitet haben<br>würdest gearbeitet haben<br>würde gearbeitet haben | würden gearbeitet haben<br>würdet gearbeitet haben<br>würden gearbeitet haben |

## EXAMPLES

Onkel Heinz arbeitet in der Hauptstadt.
Mit wem haben Sie gearbeitet?
Wo wirst du arbeiten?

Uncle Heinz works in the capital.
With whom did you work?
Where will you work?

**ärgern (sich)**
to annoy, to irritate, to vex
**Auxiliary verb:** haben **Past participle:** geärgert
**Imperative:** Ärgere! Ärgert! Ärgern Sie!

| Mode | Simple Tenses | | Compound Tenses | |
|---|---|---|---|---|
| | *Singular* | *Plural* | *Singular* | *Plural* |
| Indicative | **Present** | | **Present Perfect** | |
| | ärgere<br>ärgerst<br>ärgert | ärgern<br>ärgert<br>ärgern | habe geärgert<br>hast geärgert<br>hat geärgert | haben geärgert<br>habt geärgert<br>haben geärgert |
| | **Past** | | **Past Perfect** | |
| | ärgerte<br>ärgertest<br>ärgerte | ärgerten<br>ärgertet<br>ärgerten | hatte geärgert<br>hattest geärgert<br>hatte geärgert | hatten geärgert<br>hattet geärgert<br>hatten geärgert |
| | **Future** | | **Future Perfect** | |
| | werde ärgern<br>wirst ärgern<br>wird ärgern | werden ärgern<br>werdet ärgern<br>werden ärgern | werde geärgert haben<br>wirst geärgert haben<br>wird geärgert haben | werden geärgert haben<br>werdet geärgert haben<br>werden geärgert haben |
| Subjunctive | **Present** | | **Present Perfect** | |
| | ärgere<br>ärgerst<br>ärgere | ärgern<br>ärgert<br>ärgern | habe geärgert<br>habest geärgert<br>habe geärgert | haben geärgert<br>habet geärgert<br>haben geärgert |
| | **Past** | | **Past Perfect** | |
| | ärgerte<br>ärgertest<br>ärgerte | ärgerten<br>ärgertet<br>ärgerten | hätte geärgert<br>hättest geärgert<br>hätte geärgert | hätten geärgert<br>hättet geärgert<br>hätten geärgert |
| | **Future** | | **Future Perfect** | |
| | werde ärgern<br>werdest ärgern<br>werde ärgern | werden ärgern<br>werdet ärgern<br>werden ärgern | werde ärgern<br>werdest ärgern<br>werde ärgern | werden ärgern<br>werdet ärgern<br>werden ärgern |
| | **Present and Future Conditional** | | **Past Conditional** | |
| | würde ärgern<br>würdest ärgern<br>würde ärgern | würden ärgern<br>würdet ärgern<br>würden ärgern | würde geärgert haben<br>würdest geärgert haben<br>würde geärgert haben | würden geärgert haben<br>würdet geärgert haben<br>würden geärgert haben |

## EXAMPLES

Ärgere dich nicht darüber! Don't get annoyed over it.
Sie hat uns mit ihrem schlechten Benehmen geärgert. She irritated us with her bad behavior.

**arrangieren**
to arrange
**Auxiliary verb:** haben **Past participle:** arrangiert
**Imperative:** Arrangiere! Arrangiert! Arrangieren Sie!

| Mode | Simple Tenses | | Compound Tenses | |
|---|---|---|---|---|
| | *Singular* | *Plural* | *Singular* | *Plural* |
| Indicative | **Present** | | **Present Perfect** | |
| | arrangiere<br>arrangierst<br>arrangiert | arrangieren<br>arrangiert<br>arrangieren | habe arrangiert<br>hast arrangiert<br>hat arrangiert | haben arrangiert<br>habt arrangiert<br>haben arrangiert |
| | **Past** | | **Past Perfect** | |
| | arrangierte<br>arrangiertest<br>arrangierte | arrangierten<br>arrangiertet<br>arrangierten | hatte arrangiert<br>hattest arrangiert<br>hatte arrangiert | hatten arrangiert<br>hattet arrangiert<br>hatten arrangiert |
| | **Future** | | **Future Perfect** | |
| | werde arrangieren<br>wirst arrangieren<br>wird arrangieren | werden arrangieren<br>werdet arrangieren<br>werden arrangieren | werde arrangiert haben<br>wirst arrangiert haben<br>wird arrangiert haben | werden arrangiert haben<br>werdet arrangiert haben<br>werden arrangiert haben |
| Subjunctive | **Present** | | **Present Perfect** | |
| | arrangiere<br>arrangierest<br>arrangiere | arrangieren<br>arrangieret<br>arrangieren | habe arrangiert<br>habest arrangiert<br>habe arrangiert | haben arrangiert<br>habet arrangiert<br>haben arrangiert |
| | **Past** | | **Past Perfect** | |
| | arrangierte<br>arrangiertest<br>arrangierte | arrangierten<br>arrangiertet<br>arrangierten | hätte arrangiert<br>hättest arrangiert<br>hätte arrangiert | hätten arrangiert<br>hättet arrangiert<br>hätten arrangiert |
| | **Future** | | **Future Perfect** | |
| | werde arrangieren<br>werdest arrangieren<br>werde arrangieren | werden arrangieren<br>werdet arrangieren<br>werden arrangieren | werde arrangieren<br>werdest arrangieren<br>werde arrangieren | werden arrangieren<br>werdet arrangieren<br>werden arrangieren |
| | **Present and Future Conditional** | | **Past Conditional** | |
| | würde arrangieren<br>würdest arrangieren<br>würde arrangieren | würden arrangieren<br>würdet arrangieren<br>würden arrangieren | würde arrangiert haben<br>würdest arrangiert haben<br>würde arrangiert haben | würden arrangiert haben<br>würdet arrangiert haben<br>würden arrangiert haben |

**Note:** Infinitives that end in *–ieren* do not require a *ge–* prefix on the past participle.

## EXAMPLES

| | |
|---|---|
| Wer hat diesen interessanten Ausflug arrangiert? | Who arranged this interesting excursion? |
| Klaus arrangierte ein Treffen mit dem Bürgermeister. | Klaus arranged a meeting with the mayor. |

**atmen**
to breathe
**Auxiliary verb:** haben **Past participle:** geatmet
**Imperative:** Atme! Atmet! Atmen Sie!

| Mode | Simple Tenses | | Compound Tenses | |
|---|---|---|---|---|
| | *Singular* | *Plural* | *Singular* | *Plural* |
| Indicative | **Present** | | **Present Perfect** | |
| | atme<br>atmest<br>atmet | atmen<br>atmet<br>atmen | habe geatmet<br>hast geatmet<br>hat geatmet | haben geatmet<br>habt geatmet<br>haben geatmet |
| | **Past** | | **Past Perfect** | |
| | atmete<br>atmetest<br>atmete | atmeten<br>atmetet<br>atmeten | hatte geatmet<br>hattest geatmet<br>hatte geatmet | hatten geatmet<br>hattet geatmet<br>hatten geatmet |
| | **Future** | | **Future Perfect** | |
| | werde atmen<br>wirst atmen<br>wird atmen | werden atmen<br>werdet atmen<br>werden atmen | werde geatmet haben<br>wirst geatmet haben<br>wird geatmet haben | werden geatmet haben<br>werdet geatmet haben<br>werden geatmet haben |
| Subjunctive | **Present** | | **Present Perfect** | |
| | atme<br>atmest<br>atme | atmen<br>atmet<br>atmen | habe geatmet<br>habest geatmet<br>habe geatmet | haben geatmet<br>habet geatmet<br>haben geatmet |
| | **Past** | | **Past Perfect** | |
| | atmete<br>atmetest<br>atmete | atmeten<br>atmetet<br>atmeten | hätte geatmet<br>hättest geatmet<br>hätte geatmet | hätten geatmet<br>hättet geatmet<br>hätten geatmet |
| | **Future** | | **Future Perfect** | |
| | werde atmen<br>werdest atmen<br>werde atmen | werden atmen<br>werdet atmen<br>werden atmen | werde atmen<br>werdest atmen<br>werde atmen | werden atmen<br>werdet atmen<br>werden atmen |
| | **Present and Future Conditional** | | **Past Conditional** | |
| | würde atmen<br>würdest atmen<br>würde atmen | würden atmen<br>würdet atmen<br>würden atmen | würde geatmet haben<br>würdest geatmet haben<br>würde geatmet haben | würden geatmet haben<br>würdet geatmet haben<br>würden geatmet haben |

## EXAMPLES

Kannst du jetzt durch die Nase atmen?
Der Kranke hat leichter geatmet.

Can you breathe through your nose now?
The patient breathed easier.

**aufräumen**
to tidy up, to put in order, to clear away
**Auxiliary verb:** haben **Past participle:** aufgeräumt
**Imperative:** Räume auf! Räumt auf! Räumen Sie auf!

| Mode | Simple Tenses | | Compound Tenses | |
|---|---|---|---|---|
| | *Singular* | *Plural* | *Singular* | *Plural* |
| Indicative | **Present** | | **Present Perfect** | |
| | räume auf<br>räumst auf<br>räumt auf | räumen auf<br>räumt auf<br>räumen auf | habe aufgeräumt<br>hast aufgeräumt<br>hat aufgeräumt | haben aufgeräumt<br>habt aufgeräumt<br>haben aufgeräumt |
| | **Past** | | **Past Perfect** | |
| | räumte auf<br>räumtest auf<br>räumte auf | räumten auf<br>räumtet auf<br>räumten auf | hatte aufgeräumt<br>hattest aufgeräumt<br>hatte aufgeräumt | hatten aufgeräumt<br>hattet aufgeräumt<br>hatten aufgeräumt |
| | **Future** | | **Future Perfect** | |
| | werde aufräumen<br>wirst aufräumen<br>wird aufräumen | werden aufräumen<br>werdet aufräumen<br>werden aufräumen | werde aufgeräumt haben<br>wirst aufgeräumt haben<br>wird aufgeräumt haben | werden aufgeräumt haben<br>werdet aufgeräumt haben<br>werden aufgeräumt haben |
| Subjunctive | **Present** | | **Present Perfect** | |
| | räume auf<br>räumest auf<br>räume auf | räumen auf<br>räumet auf<br>räumen auf | habe aufgeräumt<br>habest aufgeräumt<br>habe aufgeräumt | haben aufgeräumt<br>habet aufgeräumt<br>haben aufgeräumt |
| | **Past** | | **Past Perfect** | |
| | räumte auf<br>räumtest auf<br>räumte auf | räumten auf<br>räumtet auf<br>räumten auf | hätte aufgeräumt<br>hättest aufgeräumt<br>hätte aufgeräumt | hätten aufgeräumt<br>hättet aufgeräumt<br>hätten aufgeräumt |
| | **Future** | | **Future Perfect** | |
| | werde aufräumen<br>werdest aufräumen<br>werde aufräumen | werden aufräumen<br>werdet aufräumen<br>werden aufräumen | werde aufgeräumt haben<br>werdest aufgeräumt haben<br>werde aufgeräumt haben | werden aufgeräumt haben<br>werdet aufgeräumt haben<br>werden aufgeräumt haben |
| | **Present and Future Conditional** | | **Past Conditional** | |
| | würde aufräumen<br>würdest aufräumen<br>würde aufräumen | würden aufräumen<br>würdet aufräumen<br>würden aufräumen | würde aufgeräumt haben<br>würdest aufgeräumt haben<br>würde aufgeräumt haben | würden aufgeräumt haben<br>würdet aufgeräumt haben<br>würden aufgeräumt haben |

## EXAMPLES

Räumt bitte euer Spielzeug auf! — Put away your toys, please.
Martin hat sein Zimmer aufgeräumt. — Martin tidied up his room.

**aufregen (sich)**
to stir up, to rouse, to excite
**Auxiliary verb:** haben **Past participle:** aufgeregt
**Imperative:** Rege auf! Regt auf! Regen Sie auf!

| Mode | Simple Tenses | | Compound Tenses | |
|---|---|---|---|---|
| | *Singular* | *Plural* | *Singular* | *Plural* |
| Indicative | **Present** | | **Present Perfect** | |
| | rege auf<br>regst auf<br>regt auf | regen auf<br>regt auf<br>regen auf | habe aufgeregt<br>hast aufgeregt<br>hat aufgeregt | haben aufgeregt<br>habt aufgeregt<br>haben aufgeregt |
| | **Past** | | **Past Perfect** | |
| | regte auf<br>regtest auf<br>regte auf | regten auf<br>regtet auf<br>regten auf | hatte aufgeregt<br>hattest aufgeregt<br>hatte aufgeregt | hatten aufgeregt<br>hattet aufgeregt<br>hatten aufgeregt |
| | **Future** | | **Future Perfect** | |
| | werde aufregen<br>wirst aufregen<br>wird aufregen | werden aufregen<br>werdet aufregen<br>werden aufregen | werde aufgeregt haben<br>wirst aufgeregt haben<br>wird aufgeregt haben | werden aufgeregt haben<br>werdet aufgeregt haben<br>werden aufgeregt haben |
| Subjunctive | **Present** | | **Present Perfect** | |
| | rege auf<br>regest auf<br>rege auf | regen auf<br>reget auf<br>regen auf | habe aufgeregt<br>habest aufgeregt<br>habe aufgeregt | haben aufgeregt<br>habet aufgeregt<br>haben aufgeregt |
| | **Past** | | **Past Perfect** | |
| | regte auf<br>regtest auf<br>regte auf | regten auf<br>regtet auf<br>regten auf | hätte aufgeregt<br>hättest aufgeregt<br>hätte aufgeregt | hätten aufgeregt<br>hättet aufgeregt<br>hätten aufgeregt |
| | **Future** | | **Future Perfect** | |
| | werde aufregen<br>werdest aufregen<br>werde aufregen | werden aufregen<br>werdet aufregen<br>werden aufregen | werde aufgeregt haben<br>werdest aufgeregt haben<br>werde aufgeregt haben | werden aufgeregt haben<br>werdet aufgeregt haben<br>werden aufgeregt haben |
| | **Present and Future Conditional** | | **Past Conditional** | |
| | würde aufregen<br>würdest aufregen<br>würde aufregen | würden aufregen<br>würdet aufregen<br>würden aufregen | würde aufgeregt haben<br>würdest aufgeregt haben<br>würde aufgeregt haben | würden aufgeregt haben<br>würdet aufgeregt haben<br>würden aufgeregt haben |

**Note:** This verb is often expressed with a reflexive pronoun. Look at the first example below.

## EXAMPLES

Regen Sie sich nicht auf! — Don't get mad.

Die Wissenschaftler machten eine aufregende Entdeckung. — The scientists made an exciting discovery.

**aufwachen**
to wake up, to awaken
**Auxiliary verb:** sein **Past participle:** aufgewacht
**Imperative:** Wache auf! Wacht auf! Wachen Sie auf!

| Mode | Simple Tenses | | Compound Tenses | |
|---|---|---|---|---|
| | *Singular* | *Plural* | *Singular* | *Plural* |
| Indicative | **Present** | | **Present Perfect** | |
| | wache auf<br>wachst auf<br>wacht auf | wachen auf<br>wacht auf<br>wachen auf | bin aufgewacht<br>bist aufgewacht<br>ist aufgewacht | sind aufgewacht<br>seid aufgewacht<br>sind aufgewacht |
| | **Past** | | **Past Perfect** | |
| | wachte auf<br>wachtest auf<br>wachte auf | wachten auf<br>wachtet auf<br>wachten auf | war aufgewacht<br>warst aufgewacht<br>war aufgewacht | waren aufgewacht<br>wart aufgewacht<br>waren aufgewacht |
| | **Future** | | **Future Perfect** | |
| | werde aufwachen<br>wirst aufwachen<br>wird aufwachen | werden aufwachen<br>werdet aufwachen<br>werden aufwachen | werde aufgewacht sein<br>wirst aufgewacht sein<br>wird aufgewacht sein | werden aufgewacht sein<br>werdet aufgewacht sein<br>werden aufgewacht sein |
| Subjunctive | **Present** | | **Present Perfect** | |
| | wache auf<br>wachest auf<br>wache auf | wachen auf<br>wachet auf<br>wachen auf | sei aufgewacht<br>seiest aufgewacht<br>sei aufgewacht | seien aufgewacht<br>seiet aufgewacht<br>seien aufgewacht |
| | **Past** | | **Past Perfect** | |
| | wachte auf<br>wachtest auf<br>wachte auf | wachten auf<br>wachtet auf<br>wachten auf | wäre aufgewacht<br>wärest aufgewacht<br>wäre aufgewacht | wären aufgewacht<br>wäret aufgewacht<br>wären aufgewacht |
| | **Future** | | **Future Perfect** | |
| | werde aufwachen<br>werdest aufwachen<br>werde aufwachen | werden aufwachen<br>werdet aufwachen<br>werden aufwachen | werde aufgewacht sein<br>werdest aufgewacht sein<br>werde aufgewacht sein | werden aufgewacht sein<br>werdet aufgewacht sein<br>werden aufgewacht sein |
| | **Present and Future Conditional** | | **Past Conditional** | |
| | würde aufwachen<br>würdest aufwachen<br>würde aufwachen | würden aufwachen<br>würdet aufwachen<br>würden aufwachen | würde aufgewacht sein<br>würdest aufgewacht sein<br>würde aufgewacht sein | würden aufgewacht sein<br>würdet aufgewacht sein<br>würden aufgewacht sein |

## EXAMPLES

Kinder, wacht auf! Es ist schon zehn.
Children, get up. It's already ten.

Onkel Heinz ist noch nicht aufgewacht.
Uncle Heinz hasn't woken up yet.

**ausfüllen**
to fill out, to fill up, to complete
**Auxiliary verb:** haben **Past participle:** ausgefüllt
**Imperative:** Fülle aus! Füllt aus! Füllen Sie aus!

| Mode | Simple Tenses | | Compound Tenses | |
|---|---|---|---|---|
| | *Singular* | *Plural* | *Singular* | *Plural* |
| Indicative | **Present** | | **Present Perfect** | |
| | fülle aus<br>füllst aus<br>füllt aus | füllen aus<br>füllt aus<br>füllen aus | habe ausgefüllt<br>hast ausgefüllt<br>hat ausgefüllt | haben ausgefüllt<br>habt ausgefüllt<br>haben ausgefüllt |
| | **Past** | | **Past Perfect** | |
| | füllte aus<br>fülltest aus<br>füllte aus | füllten aus<br>fülltet aus<br>füllten aus | hatte ausgefüllt<br>hattest ausgefüllt<br>hatte ausgefüllt | hatten ausgefüllt<br>hattet ausgefüllt<br>hatten ausgefüllt |
| | **Future** | | **Future Perfect** | |
| | werde ausfüllen<br>wirst ausfüllen<br>wird ausfüllen | werden ausfüllen<br>werdet ausfüllen<br>werden ausfüllen | werde ausgefüllt haben<br>wirst ausgefüllt haben<br>wird ausgefüllt haben | werden ausgefüllt haben<br>werdet ausgefüllt haben<br>werden ausgefüllt haben |
| Subjunctive | **Present** | | **Present Perfect** | |
| | fülle aus<br>füllest aus<br>fülle aus | füllen aus<br>füllet aus<br>füllen aus | habe ausgefüllt<br>habest ausgefüllt<br>habe ausgefüllt | haben ausgefüllt<br>habet ausgefüllt<br>haben ausgefüllt |
| | **Past** | | **Past Perfect** | |
| | füllte aus<br>fülltest aus<br>füllte aus | füllten aus<br>fülltet aus<br>füllten aus | hätte ausgefüllt<br>hättest ausgefüllt<br>hätte ausgefüllt | hätten ausgefüllt<br>hättet ausgefüllt<br>hätten ausgefüllt |
| | **Future** | | **Future Perfect** | |
| | werde ausfüllen<br>werdest ausfüllen<br>werde ausfüllen | werden ausfüllen<br>werdet ausfüllen<br>werden ausfüllen | werde ausgefüllt haben<br>werdest ausgefüllt haben<br>werde ausgefüllt haben | werden ausgefüllt haben<br>werdet ausgefüllt haben<br>werden ausgefüllt haben |
| | **Present and Future Conditional** | | **Past Conditional** | |
| | würde ausfüllen<br>würdest ausfüllen<br>würde ausfüllen | würden ausfüllen<br>würdet ausfüllen<br>würden ausfüllen | würde ausgefüllt haben<br>würdest ausgefüllt haben<br>würde ausgefüllt haben | würden ausgefüllt haben<br>würdet ausgefüllt haben<br>würden ausgefüllt haben |

## EXAMPLES

Ich musste ein langes Formular ausfüllen. — I had to fill out a long form.
Füllen Sie bitte diesen Fragebogen aus. — Please fill out this questionnaire.

**ausgeben**
to spend, to give out, to distribute
**Auxiliary verb:** haben **Past participle:** ausgegeben
**Imperative:** Gib aus! Gebt aus! Geben Sie aus!

| Mode | Simple Tenses | | Compound Tenses | |
|---|---|---|---|---|
| | *Singular* | *Plural* | *Singular* | *Plural* |
| Indicative | **Present** | | **Present Perfect** | |
| | gebe aus<br>gibst aus<br>gibt aus | geben aus<br>gebt aus<br>geben aus | habe ausgegeben<br>hast ausgegeben<br>hat ausgegeben | haben ausgegeben<br>habt ausgegeben<br>haben ausgegeben |
| | **Past** | | **Past Perfect** | |
| | gab aus<br>gabst aus<br>gab aus | gaben aus<br>gabt aus<br>gaben aus | hatte ausgegeben<br>hattest ausgegeben<br>hatte ausgegeben | hatten ausgegeben<br>hattet ausgegeben<br>hatten ausgegeben |
| | **Future** | | **Future Perfect** | |
| | werde ausgeben<br>wirst ausgeben<br>wird ausgeben | werden ausgeben<br>werdet ausgeben<br>werden ausgeben | werde ausgegeben haben<br>wirst ausgegeben haben<br>wird ausgegeben haben | werden ausgegeben haben<br>werdet ausgegeben haben<br>werden ausgegeben haben |
| Subjunctive | **Present** | | **Present Perfect** | |
| | gebe aus<br>gebest aus<br>gebe aus | geben aus<br>gebet aus<br>geben aus | habe ausgegeben<br>habest ausgegeben<br>habe ausgegeben | haben ausgegeben<br>habet ausgegeben<br>haben ausgegeben |
| | **Past** | | **Past Perfect** | |
| | gäbe aus<br>gäbest aus<br>gäbe aus | gäben aus<br>gäbet aus<br>gäben aus | hätte ausgegeben<br>hättest ausgegeben<br>hätte ausgegeben | hätten ausgegeben<br>hättet ausgegeben<br>hätten ausgegeben |
| | **Future** | | **Future Perfect** | |
| | werde ausgeben<br>werdest ausgeben<br>werde ausgeben | werden ausgeben<br>werdet ausgeben<br>werden ausgeben | werde ausgegeben haben<br>werdest ausgegeben haben<br>werde ausgegeben haben | werden ausgegeben haben<br>werdet ausgegeben haben<br>werden ausgegeben haben |
| | **Present and Future Conditional** | | **Past Conditional** | |
| | würde ausgeben<br>würdest ausgeben<br>würde ausgeben | würden ausgeben<br>würdet ausgeben<br>würden ausgeben | würde ausgegeben haben<br>würdest ausgegeben haben<br>würde ausgegeben haben | würden ausgegeben haben<br>würdet ausgegeben haben<br>würden ausgegeben haben |

## EXAMPLES

| | |
|---|---|
| Ich habe mehr als zwanzig Euro ausgegeben. | I spent more than twenty euros. |
| Werden Sie wirklich soviel dafür ausgeben? | Will you really spend so much for it? |

**auslüften**

to air out, to ventilate

**Auxiliary verb:** haben **Past participle:** ausgelüftet

**Imperative:** Lüfte aus! Lüftet aus! Lüften Sie aus!

| Mode | Simple Tenses | | Compound Tenses | |
|---|---|---|---|---|
| | *Singular* | *Plural* | *Singular* | *Plural* |
| Indicative | **Present** | | **Present Perfect** | |
| | lüfte aus<br>lüftest aus<br>lüftet aus | lüften aus<br>lüftet aus<br>lüften aus | habe ausgelüftet<br>hast ausgelüftet<br>hat ausgelüftet | haben ausgelüftet<br>habt ausgelüftet<br>haben ausgelüftet |
| | **Past** | | **Past Perfect** | |
| | lüftete aus<br>lüftetest aus<br>lüftete aus | lüfteten aus<br>lüftetet aus<br>lüfteten aus | hatte ausgelüftet<br>hattest ausgelüftet<br>hatte ausgelüftet | hatten ausgelüftet<br>hattet ausgelüftet<br>hatten ausgelüftet |
| | **Future** | | **Future Perfect** | |
| | werde auslüften<br>wirst auslüften<br>wird auslüften | werden auslüften<br>werdet auslüften<br>werden auslüften | werde ausgelüftet haben<br>wirst ausgelüftet haben<br>wird ausgelüftet haben | werden ausgelüftet haben<br>werdet ausgelüftet haben<br>werden ausgelüftet haben |
| Subjunctive | **Present** | | **Present Perfect** | |
| | lüfte aus<br>lüftest aus<br>lüfte aus | lüften aus<br>lüftet aus<br>lüften aus | habe ausgelüftet<br>habest ausgelüftet<br>habe ausgelüftet | haben ausgelüftet<br>habet ausgelüftet<br>haben ausgelüftet |
| | **Past** | | **Past Perfect** | |
| | lüftete aus<br>lüftetest aus<br>lüftete aus | lüfteten aus<br>lüftetet aus<br>lüfteten aus | hätte ausgelüftet<br>hättest ausgelüftet<br>hätte ausgelüftet | hätten ausgelüftet<br>hättet ausgelüftet<br>hätten ausgelüftet |
| | **Future** | | **Future Perfect** | |
| | werde auslüften<br>werdest auslüften<br>werde auslüften | werden auslüften<br>werdet auslüften<br>werden auslüften | werde ausgelüftet haben<br>werdest ausgelüftet haben<br>werde ausgelüftet haben | werden ausgelüftet haben<br>werdet ausgelüftet haben<br>werden ausgelüftet haben |
| | **Present and Future Conditional** | | **Past Conditional** | |
| | würde auslüften<br>würdest auslüften<br>würde auslüften | würden auslüften<br>würdet auslüften<br>würden auslüften | würde ausgelüftet haben<br>würdest ausgelüftet haben<br>würde ausgelüftet haben | würden ausgelüftet haben<br>würdet ausgelüftet haben<br>würden ausgelüftet haben |

**Note:** Without the prefix *aus–*, the principal parts of this verb are *lüftet, lüftete, hat gelüftet.*

## EXAMPLES

Mach die Fenster auf! Wir müssen dieses Zimmer auslüften.

Open the windows. We have to air out this room.

Das Raucherabteil muss besser gelüftet werden.

The smoking compartment has to be better ventilated.

**ausrüsten**
to outfit, to equip
**Auxiliary verb:** haben **Past participle:** ausgerüstet
**Imperative:** Rüste aus! Rüstet aus! Rüsten Sie aus!

| Mode | Simple Tenses | | Compound Tenses | |
|---|---|---|---|---|
| | *Singular* | *Plural* | *Singular* | *Plural* |
| Indicative | **Present** | | **Present Perfect** | |
| | rüste aus<br>rüstest aus<br>rüstet aus | rüsten aus<br>rüstet aus<br>rüsten aus | habe ausgerüstet<br>hast ausgerüstet<br>hat ausgerüstet | haben ausgerüstet<br>habt ausgerüstet<br>haben ausgerüstet |
| | **Past** | | **Past Perfect** | |
| | rüstete aus<br>rüstetest aus<br>rüstete aus | rüsteten aus<br>rüstetet aus<br>rüsteten aus | hatte ausgerüstet<br>hattest ausgerüstet<br>hatte ausgerüstet | hatten ausgerüstet<br>hattet ausgerüstet<br>hatten ausgerüstet |
| | **Future** | | **Future Perfect** | |
| | werde ausrüsten<br>wirst ausrüsten<br>wird ausrüsten | werden ausrüsten<br>werdet ausrüsten<br>werden ausrüsten | werde ausgerüstet haben<br>wirst ausgerüstet haben<br>wird ausgerüstet haben | werden ausgerüstet haben<br>werdet ausgerüstet haben<br>werden ausgerüstet haben |
| Subjunctive | **Present** | | **Present Perfect** | |
| | rüste aus<br>rüstest aus<br>rüste aus | rüsten aus<br>rüstet aus<br>rüsten aus | habe ausgerüstet<br>habest ausgerüstet<br>habe ausgerüstet | haben ausgerüstet<br>habet ausgerüstet<br>haben ausgerüstet |
| | **Past** | | **Past Perfect** | |
| | rüstete aus<br>rüstetest aus<br>rüstete aus | rüsteten aus<br>rüstetet aus<br>rüsteten aus | hätte ausgerüstet<br>hättest ausgerüstet<br>hätte ausgerüstet | hätten ausgerüstet<br>hättet ausgerüstet<br>hätten ausgerüstet |
| | **Future** | | **Future Perfect** | |
| | werde ausrüsten<br>werdest ausrüsten<br>werde ausrüsten | werden ausrüsten<br>werdet ausrüsten<br>werden ausrüsten | werde ausgerüstet haben<br>werdest ausgerüstet haben<br>werde ausgerüstet haben | werden ausgerüstet haben<br>werdet ausgerüstet haben<br>werden ausgerüstet haben |
| | **Present and Future Conditional** | | **Past Conditional** | |
| | würde ausrüsten<br>würdest ausrüsten<br>würde ausrüsten | würden ausrüsten<br>würdet ausrüsten<br>würden ausrüsten | würde ausgerüstet haben<br>würdest ausgerüstet haben<br>würde ausgerüstet haben | würden ausgerüstet haben<br>würdet ausgerüstet haben<br>würden ausgerüstet haben |

## EXAMPLES

Man will die Soldaten besser ausrüsten.
They want to equip the soldiers better.

Dieser Laden hat uns für unsere Reise ausgerüstet.
This store fitted us out for our trip.

**aussehen**
to look like
**Auxiliary verb:** haben **Past participle:** ausgesehen
**Imperative:** Sieh aus! Seht aus! Sehen Sie aus!

| Mode | Simple Tenses | | Compound Tenses | |
|---|---|---|---|---|
| | *Singular* | *Plural* | *Singular* | *Plural* |
| Indicative | **Present** | | **Present Perfect** | |
| | sehe aus<br>siehst aus<br>sieht aus | sehen aus<br>seht aus<br>sehen aus | habe ausgesehen<br>hast ausgesehen<br>hat ausgesehen | haben ausgesehen<br>habt ausgesehen<br>haben ausgesehen |
| | **Past** | | **Past Perfect** | |
| | sah aus<br>sahst aus<br>sah aus | sahen aus<br>saht aus<br>sahen aus | hatte ausgesehen<br>hattest ausgesehen<br>hatte ausgesehen | hatten ausgesehen<br>hattet ausgesehen<br>hatten ausgesehen |
| | **Future** | | **Future Perfect** | |
| | werde aussehen<br>wirst aussehen<br>wird aussehen | werden aussehen<br>werdet aussehen<br>werden aussehen | werde ausgesehen haben<br>wirst ausgesehen haben<br>wird ausgesehen haben | werden ausgesehen haben<br>werdet ausgesehen haben<br>werden ausgesehen haben |
| Subjunctive | **Present** | | **Present Perfect** | |
| | sehe aus<br>sehest aus<br>sehe aus | sehen aus<br>sehet aus<br>sehen aus | habe ausgesehen<br>habest ausgesehen<br>habe ausgesehen | haben ausgesehen<br>habet ausgesehen<br>haben ausgesehen |
| | **Past** | | **Past Perfect** | |
| | sähe aus<br>sähest aus<br>sähe aus | sähen aus<br>sähet aus<br>sähen aus | hätte ausgesehen<br>hättest ausgesehen<br>hätte ausgesehen | hätten ausgesehen<br>hättet ausgesehen<br>hätten ausgesehen |
| | **Future** | | **Future Perfect** | |
| | werde aussehen<br>werdest aussehen<br>werde aussehen | werden aussehen<br>werdet aussehen<br>werden aussehen | werde ausgesehen haben<br>werdest ausgesehen haben<br>werde ausgesehen haben | werden ausgesehen haben<br>werdet ausgesehen haben<br>werden ausgesehen haben |
| | **Present and Future Conditional** | | **Past Conditional** | |
| | würde aussehen<br>würdest aussehen<br>würde aussehen | würden aussehen<br>würdet aussehen<br>würden aussehen | würde ausgesehen haben<br>würdest ausgesehen haben<br>würde ausgesehen haben | würden ausgesehen haben<br>würdet ausgesehen haben<br>würden ausgesehen haben |

## EXAMPLES

Die alte Frau sieht krank aus.
The old woman looks sick.

Er hat immer stark ausgesehen.
He always looked strong.

**aussteigen**
to get out, to get off, to alight
**Auxiliary verb:** sein **Past participle:** ausgestiegen
**Imperative:** Steige aus! Steigt aus! Steigen Sie aus!

| Mode | Simple Tenses | | Compound Tenses | |
|---|---|---|---|---|
| | *Singular* | *Plural* | *Singular* | *Plural* |
| Indicative | **Present** | | **Present Perfect** | |
| | steige aus<br>steigst aus<br>steigt aus | steigen aus<br>steigt aus<br>steigen aus | bin ausgestiegen<br>bist ausgestiegen<br>ist ausgestiegen | sind ausgestiegen<br>seid ausgestiegen<br>sind ausgestiegen |
| | **Past** | | **Past Perfect** | |
| | stieg aus<br>stiegst aus<br>stieg aus | stiegen aus<br>stiegt aus<br>stiegen aus | war ausgestiegen<br>warst ausgestiegen<br>war ausgestiegen | waren ausgestiegen<br>wart ausgestiegen<br>waren ausgestiegen |
| | **Future** | | **Future Perfect** | |
| | werde aussteigen<br>wirst aussteigen<br>wird aussteigen | werden aussteigen<br>werdet aussteigen<br>werden aussteigen | werde ausgestiegen sein<br>wirst ausgestiegen sein<br>wird ausgestiegen sein | werden ausgestiegen sein<br>werdet ausgestiegen sein<br>werden ausgestiegen sein |
| Subjunctive | **Present** | | **Present Perfect** | |
| | steige aus<br>steigest aus<br>steige aus | steigen aus<br>steiget aus<br>steigen aus | sei ausgestiegen<br>seiest ausgestiegen<br>sei ausgestiegen | seien ausgestiegen<br>seiet ausgestiegen<br>seien ausgestiegen |
| | **Past** | | **Past Perfect** | |
| | stiege aus<br>stiegest aus<br>stiege aus | stiegen aus<br>stieget aus<br>stiegen aus | wäre ausgestiegen<br>wärest ausgestiegen<br>wäre ausgestiegen | wären ausgestiegen<br>wäret ausgestiegen<br>wären ausgestiegen |
| | **Future** | | **Future Perfect** | |
| | werde aussteigen<br>werdest aussteigen<br>werde aussteigen | werden aussteigen<br>werdet aussteigen<br>werden aussteigen | werde ausgestiegen sein<br>werdest ausgestiegen sein<br>werde ausgestiegen sein | werden ausgestiegen sein<br>werdet ausgestiegen sein<br>werden ausgestiegen sein |
| | **Present and Future Conditional** | | **Past Conditional** | |
| | würde aussteigen<br>würdest aussteigen<br>würde aussteigen | würden aussteigen<br>würdet aussteigen<br>würden aussteigen | würde ausgestiegen sein<br>würdest ausgestiegen sein<br>würde ausgestiegen sein | würden ausgestiegen sein<br>würdet ausgestiegen sein<br>würden ausgestiegen sein |

## EXAMPLES

Wir steigen in der Marktstraße aus.
We'll get off on Market Street.

Sagen Sie mir Bescheid, wo ich aussteigen soll.
Let me know where I should get out.

**austauschen**
to exchange, to change
**Auxiliary verb:** haben **Past participle:** ausgetauscht
**Imperative:** Tausche aus! Tauscht aus! Tauschen Sie aus!

| Mode | Simple Tenses | | Compound Tenses | |
|---|---|---|---|---|
| | *Singular* | *Plural* | *Singular* | *Plural* |
| Indicative | **Present** | | **Present Perfect** | |
| | tausche aus<br>tauschst aus<br>tauscht aus | tauschen aus<br>tauscht aus<br>tauschen aus | habe ausgetauscht<br>hast ausgetauscht<br>hat ausgetauscht | haben ausgetauscht<br>habt ausgetauscht<br>haben ausgetauscht |
| | **Past** | | **Past Perfect** | |
| | tauschte aus<br>tauschtest aus<br>tauschte aus | tauschten aus<br>tauschtet aus<br>tauschten aus | hatte ausgetauscht<br>hattest ausgetauscht<br>hatte ausgetauscht | hatten ausgetauscht<br>hattet ausgetauscht<br>hatten ausgetauscht |
| | **Future** | | **Future Perfect** | |
| | werde austauschen<br>wirst austauschen<br>wird austauschen | werden austauschen<br>werdet austauschen<br>werden austauschen | werde ausgetauscht haben<br>wirst ausgetauscht haben<br>wird ausgetauscht haben | werden ausgetauscht haben<br>werdet ausgetauscht haben<br>werden ausgetauscht haben |
| Subjunctive | **Present** | | **Present Perfect** | |
| | tausche aus<br>tauschest aus<br>tausche aus | tauschen aus<br>tauschet aus<br>tauschen aus | habe ausgetauscht<br>habest ausgetauscht<br>habe ausgetauscht | haben ausgetauscht<br>habet ausgetauscht<br>haben ausgetauscht |
| | **Past** | | **Past Perfect** | |
| | tauschte aus<br>tauschtest aus<br>tauschte aus | tauschten aus<br>tauschtet aus<br>tauschten aus | hätte ausgetauscht<br>hättest ausgetauscht<br>hätte ausgetauscht | hätten ausgetauscht<br>hättet ausgetauscht<br>hätten ausgetauscht |
| | **Future** | | **Future Perfect** | |
| | werde austauschen<br>werdest austauschen<br>werde austauschen | werden austauschen<br>werdet austauschen<br>werden austauschen | werde ausgetauscht haben<br>werdest ausgetauscht haben<br>werde ausgetauscht haben | werden ausgetauscht haben<br>werdet ausgetauscht haben<br>werden ausgetauscht haben |
| | **Present and Future Conditional** | | **Past Conditional** | |
| | würde austauschen<br>würdest austauschen<br>würde austauschen | würden austauschen<br>würdet austauschen<br>würden austauschen | würde ausgetauscht haben<br>würdest ausgetauscht haben<br>würde ausgetauscht haben | würden ausgetauscht haben<br>würdet ausgetauscht haben<br>würden ausgetauscht haben |

## EXAMPLE

Die Professoren haben ihre Gedanken ausgetauscht.

The professors exchanged ideas.

**backen**
to bake
**Auxiliary verb:** haben **Past participle:** gebacken
**Imperative:** Backe! Backt! Backen Sie!

| Mode | Simple Tenses | | Compound Tenses | |
|---|---|---|---|---|
| | *Singular* | *Plural* | *Singular* | *Plural* |
| Indicative | **Present** | | **Present Perfect** | |
| | backe<br>bäckst<br>bäckt | backen<br>backt<br>backen | habe gebacken<br>hast gebacken<br>hat gebacken | haben gebacken<br>habt gebacken<br>haben gebacken |
| | **Past** | | **Past Perfect** | |
| | buk<br>bukst<br>buk | buken<br>bukt<br>buken | hatte gebacken<br>hattest gebacken<br>hatte gebacken | hatten gebacken<br>hattet gebacken<br>hatten gebacken |
| | **Future** | | **Future Perfect** | |
| | werde backen<br>wirst backen<br>wird backen | werden backen<br>werdet backen<br>werden backen | werde gebacken haben<br>wirst gebacken haben<br>wird gebacken haben | werden gebacken haben<br>werdet gebacken haben<br>werden gebacken haben |
| Subjunctive | **Present** | | **Present Perfect** | |
| | backe<br>backest<br>backe | backen<br>backet<br>backen | habe gebacken<br>habest gebacken<br>habe gebacken | haben gebacken<br>habet gebacken<br>haben gebacken |
| | **Past** | | **Past Perfect** | |
| | büke<br>bükest<br>büke | büken<br>büket<br>büken | hätte gebacken<br>hättest gebacken<br>hätte gebacken | hätten gebacken<br>hättet gebacken<br>hätten gebacken |
| | **Future** | | **Future Perfect** | |
| | werde backen<br>werdest backen<br>werde backen | werden backen<br>werdet backen<br>werden backen | werde gebacken haben<br>werdest gebacken haben<br>werde gebacken haben | werden gebacken haben<br>werdet gebacken haben<br>werden gebacken haben |
| | **Present and Future Conditional** | | **Past Conditional** | |
| | würde backen<br>würdest backen<br>würde backen | würden backen<br>würdet backen<br>würden backen | würde gebacken haben<br>würdest gebacken haben<br>würde gebacken haben | würden gebacken haben<br>würdet gebacken haben<br>würden gebacken haben |

**Note:** In the past-tense indicative and subjunctive, this verb often appears as *backte, backtest, backte, backten, backtet, backten.*

## EXAMPLES

Morgen wird Oma eine schöne Torte backen. — Tomorrow grandma is going to bake a nice cream cake.

Wer hat diesen Schokoladenkuchen gebacken? — Who baked this chocolate cake?

**baden**
to bathe
**Auxiliary verb:** haben **Past participle:** gebadet
**Imperative:** Bade! Badet! Baden Sie!

| Mode | Simple Tenses | | Compound Tenses | |
|---|---|---|---|---|
| | *Singular* | *Plural* | *Singular* | *Plural* |
| Indicative | **Present** | | **Present Perfect** | |
| | bade<br>badest<br>badet | baden<br>badet<br>baden | habe gebadet<br>hast gebadet<br>hat gebadet | haben gebadet<br>habt gebadet<br>haben gebadet |
| | **Past** | | **Past Perfect** | |
| | badete<br>badetest<br>badete | badeten<br>badetet<br>badeten | hatte gebadet<br>hattest gebadet<br>hatte gebadet | hatten gebadet<br>hattet gebadet<br>hatten gebadet |
| | **Future** | | **Future Perfect** | |
| | werde baden<br>wirst baden<br>wird baden | werden baden<br>werdet baden<br>werden baden | werde gebadet haben<br>wirst gebadet haben<br>wird gebadet haben | werden gebadet haben<br>werdet gebadet haben<br>werden gebadet haben |
| Subjunctive | **Present** | | **Present Perfect** | |
| | bade<br>badest<br>bade | baden<br>badet<br>baden | habe gebadet<br>habest gebadet<br>habe gebadet | haben gebadet<br>habet gebadet<br>haben gebadet |
| | **Past** | | **Past Perfect** | |
| | badete<br>badetest<br>badete | badeten<br>badetet<br>badeten | hätte gebadet<br>hättest gebadet<br>hätte gebadet | hätten gebadet<br>hättet gebadet<br>hätten gebadet |
| | **Future** | | **Future Perfect** | |
| | werde baden<br>werdest baden<br>werde baden | werden baden<br>werdet baden<br>werden baden | werde gebadet haben<br>werdest gebadet haben<br>werde gebadet haben | werden gebadet haben<br>werdet gebadet haben<br>werden gebadet haben |
| | **Present and Future Conditional** | | **Past Conditional** | |
| | würde baden<br>würdest baden<br>würde baden | würden baden<br>würdet baden<br>würden baden | würde gebadet haben<br>würde gebadet haben<br>würde gebadet haben | würde gebadet haben<br>würde gebadet haben<br>würde gebadet haben |

## EXAMPLES

Karl badet sich jeden Tag. — Karl bathes every day.
Gestern haben wir im See gebadet. — Yesterday we bathed in the lake.

**basteln**
to work on a handicraft, to tinker
**Auxiliary verb:** haben **Past participle:** gebastelt
**Imperative:** Bastele! Bastelt! Basteln Sie!

| Mode | Simple Tenses | | Compound Tenses | |
|---|---|---|---|---|
| | *Singular* | *Plural* | *Singular* | *Plural* |
| Indicative | **Present** | | **Present Perfect** | |
| | bastele<br>bastelst<br>bastelt | basteln<br>bastelt<br>basteln | habe gebastelt<br>hast gebastelt<br>hat gebastelt | haben gebastelt<br>habt gebastelt<br>haben gebastelt |
| | **Past** | | **Past Perfect** | |
| | bastelte<br>basteltest<br>bastelte | bastelten<br>basteltet<br>bastelten | hatte gebastelt<br>hattest gebastelt<br>hatte gebastelt | hatten gebastelt<br>hattet gebastelt<br>hatten gebastelt |
| | **Future** | | **Future Perfect** | |
| | werde basteln<br>wirst basteln<br>wird basteln | werden basteln<br>werdet basteln<br>werden basteln | werde gebastelt haben<br>wirst gebastelt haben<br>wird gebastelt haben | werden gebastelt haben<br>werdet gebastelt haben<br>werden gebastelt haben |
| Subjunctive | **Present** | | **Present Perfect** | |
| | bastele<br>bastelst<br>bastele | basteln<br>bastelt<br>basteln | habe gebastelt<br>habest gebastelt<br>habe gebastelt | haben gebastelt<br>habet gebastelt<br>haben gebastelt |
| | **Past** | | **Past Perfect** | |
| | bastelte<br>basteltest<br>bastelte | bastelten<br>basteltet<br>bastelten | hätte gebastelt<br>hättest gebastelt<br>hätte gebastelt | hätten gebastelt<br>hättet gebastelt<br>hätten gebastelt |
| | **Future** | | **Future Perfect** | |
| | werde basteln<br>werdest basteln<br>werde basteln | werden basteln<br>werdet basteln<br>werden basteln | werde gebastelt haben<br>werdest gebastelt haben<br>werde gebastelt haben | werden gebastelt haben<br>werdet gebastelt haben<br>werden gebastelt haben |
| | **Present and Future Conditional** | | **Past Conditional** | |
| | würde basteln<br>würdest basteln<br>würde basteln | würden basteln<br>würdet basteln<br>würden basteln | würde gebastelt haben<br>würdest gebastelt haben<br>würde gebastelt haben | würden gebastelt haben<br>würdet gebastelt haben<br>würden gebastelt haben |

## EXAMPLES

Mein kleiner Bruder bastelt gern Modellflugzeuge.
In meiner Freizeit bastele ich an einem alten Auto.

My little brother likes to build model airplanes.
In my spare time I tinker around with an old car.

**bauen**
to build
**Auxiliary verb:** haben **Past participle:** gebaut
**Imperative:** Baue! Baut! Bauen Sie!

| Mode | Simple Tenses | | Compound Tenses | |
|---|---|---|---|---|
| | *Singular* | *Plural* | *Singular* | *Plural* |
| Indicative | **Present** | | **Present Perfect** | |
| | baue<br>baust<br>baut | bauen<br>baut<br>bauen | habe gebaut<br>hast gebaut<br>hat gebaut | haben gebaut<br>habt gebaut<br>haben gebaut |
| | **Past** | | **Past Perfect** | |
| | baute<br>bautest<br>baute | bauten<br>bautet<br>bauten | hatte gebaut<br>hattest gebaut<br>hatte gebaut | hatten gebaut<br>hattet gebaut<br>hatten gebaut |
| | **Future** | | **Future Perfect** | |
| | werde bauen<br>wirst bauen<br>wird bauen | werden bauen<br>werdet bauen<br>werden bauen | werde gebaut haben<br>wirst gebaut haben<br>wird gebaut haben | werden gebaut haben<br>werdet gebaut haben<br>werden gebaut haben |
| Subjunctive | **Present** | | **Present Perfect** | |
| | baue<br>bauest<br>baue | bauen<br>bauet<br>bauen | habe gebaut<br>habest gebaut<br>habe gebaut | haben gebaut<br>habet gebaut<br>haben gebaut |
| | **Past** | | **Past Perfect** | |
| | baute<br>bautest<br>böte an | bauten<br>bautet<br>bauten | hätte gebaut<br>hättest gebaut<br>hätte gebaut | hätten gebaut<br>hättet gebaut<br>hätten gebaut |
| | **Future** | | **Future Perfect** | |
| | werde bauen<br>werdest bauen<br>werde bauen | werden bauen<br>werdet bauen<br>werden bauen | werde gebaut haben<br>werdest gebaut haben<br>werde gebaut haben | werden gebaut haben<br>werdet gebaut haben<br>werden gebaut haben |
| | **Present and Future Conditional** | | **Past Conditional** | |
| | würde bauen<br>würdest bauen<br>würde bauen | würden bauen<br>würdet bauen<br>würden bauen | würde gebaut haben<br>würdest gebaut haben<br>würde gebaut haben | würden gebaut haben<br>würdet gebaut haben<br>würden gebaut haben |

## EXAMPLES

Ein kleines Haus wird in der Schillerstraße gebaut.
A little house is being built on Schiller Street.

Meine Eltern wollen ein neues Haus bauen.
My parents want to build a new house.

**sich beeilen**
to hurry, to hasten
**Auxiliary verb:** haben **Past participle:** beeilt
**Imperative:** Beeile dich! Beeilt euch! Beeilen Sie sich!

| Mode | Simple Tenses | | Compound Tenses | |
|---|---|---|---|---|
| | *Singular* | *Plural* | *Singular* | *Plural* |
| Indicative | **Present** | | **Present Perfect** | |
| | beeile<br>beeilst<br>beeilt | beeilen<br>beeilt<br>beeilen | habe beeilt<br>hast beeilt<br>hat beeilt | haben beeilt<br>habt beeilt<br>haben beeilt |
| | **Past** | | **Past Perfect** | |
| | beeilte<br>beeiltest<br>beeilte | beeilten<br>beeiltet<br>beeilten | hatte beeilt<br>hattest beeilt<br>hatte beeilt | hatten beeilt<br>hattet beeilt<br>hatten beeilt |
| | **Future** | | **Future Perfect** | |
| | werde beeilen<br>wirst beeilen<br>wird beeilen | werden beeilen<br>werdet beeilen<br>werden beeilen | werde beeilt haben<br>wirst beeilt haben<br>wird beeilt haben | werden beeilt haben<br>werdet beeilt haben<br>werden beeilt haben |
| Subjunctive | **Present** | | **Present Perfect** | |
| | beeile<br>beeilest<br>beeile | beeilen<br>beeilet<br>beeilen | habe beeilt<br>habest beeilt<br>habe beeilt | haben beeilt<br>habet beeilt<br>haben beeilt |
| | **Past** | | **Past Perfect** | |
| | beeilte<br>beeiltest<br>beeilte | beeilten<br>beeiltet<br>beeilten | hätte beeilt<br>hättest beeilt<br>hätte beeilt | hätten beeilt<br>hättet beeilt<br>hätten beeilt |
| | **Future** | | **Future Perfect** | |
| | werde beeilen<br>werdest beeilen<br>werde beeilen | werden beeilen<br>werdet beeilen<br>werden beeilen | werde beeilt haben<br>werdest beeilt haben<br>werde beeilt haben | werden beeilt haben<br>werdet beeilt haben<br>werden beeilt haben |
| | **Present and Future Conditional** | | **Past Conditional** | |
| | würde beeilen<br>würdest beeilen<br>würde beeilen | würden beeilen<br>würdet beeilen<br>würden beeilen | würde beeilt haben<br>würdest beeilt haben<br>würde beeilt haben | würden beeilt haben<br>würdet beeilt haben<br>würden beeilt haben |

**Note:** This verb is used with a reflexive pronoun to say that someone is in a hurry.

## EXAMPLES

Wir müssen uns beeilen. Der Zug fährt in zehn Minuten ab.
We have to hurry. The train leaves in ten minutes.

Ich beeilte mich, um pünktlich zur Arbeit zu kommen.
I hurried to get to work on time.

**beenden**

to end, to finish, to conclude

**Auxiliary verb:** haben **Past participle:** beendet

**Imperative:** Beende! Beendet! Beenden Sie!

| Mode | Simple Tenses | | Compound Tenses | |
|---|---|---|---|---|
| | *Singular* | *Plural* | *Singular* | *Plural* |
| Indicative | **Present** | | **Present Perfect** | |
| | beende<br>beendest<br>beendet | beenden<br>beendet<br>beenden | habe beendet<br>hast beendet<br>hat beendet | haben beendet<br>habt beendet<br>haben beendet |
| | **Past** | | **Past Perfect** | |
| | beendete<br>beendetest<br>beendete | beendeten<br>beendetet<br>beendeten | hatte beendet<br>hattest beendet<br>hatte beendet | hatten beendet<br>hattet beendet<br>hatten beendet |
| | **Future** | | **Future Perfect** | |
| | werde beenden<br>wirst beenden<br>wird beenden | werden beenden<br>werdet beenden<br>werden beenden | werde beendet haben<br>wirst beendet haben<br>wird beendet haben | werden beendet haben<br>werdet beendet haben<br>werden beendet haben |
| Subjunctive | **Present** | | **Present Perfect** | |
| | beende<br>beendest<br>beende | beenden<br>beendet<br>beenden | habe beendet<br>habest beendet<br>habe beendet | haben beendet<br>habet beendet<br>haben beendet |
| | **Past** | | **Past Perfect** | |
| | beendete<br>beendetest<br>beendete | beendeten<br>beendetet<br>beendeten | hätte beendet<br>hättest beendet<br>hätte beendet | hätten beendet<br>hättet beendet<br>hätten beendet |
| | **Future** | | **Future Perfect** | |
| | werde beenden<br>werdest beenden<br>werde beenden | werden beenden<br>werdet beenden<br>werden beenden | werde beendet haben<br>werdest beendet haben<br>werde beendet haben | werden beendet haben<br>werdet beendet haben<br>werden beendet haben |
| | **Present and Future Conditional** | | **Past Conditional** | |
| | würde beenden<br>würdest beenden<br>würde beenden | würden beenden<br>würdet beenden<br>würden beenden | würde beendet haben<br>würdest beendet haben<br>würde beendet haben | würden beendet haben<br>würdet beendet haben<br>würden beendet haben |

**Note:** With the prefix *ver– (verenden),* this verb requires the auxiliary *sein* in the perfect tenses.

## EXAMPLES

| | |
|---|---|
| Jetzt sollten wir unser Gespräch beenden. | We should end our conversation now. |
| Der Professor hat die Vorlesung früh beendet. | The professor ended the lecture early. |

**befehlen**
to order, to command
**Auxiliary verb:** haben **Past participle:** befohlen
**Imperative:** Befiehl! Befehlt! Befehlen Sie!

| Mode | Simple Tenses | | Compound Tenses | |
|---|---|---|---|---|
| | *Singular* | *Plural* | *Singular* | *Plural* |
| Indicative | **Present** | | **Present Perfect** | |
| | befehle<br>befiehlst<br>befiehlt | befehlen<br>befehlt<br>befehlen | habe befohlen<br>hast befohlen<br>hat befohlen | haben befohlen<br>habt befohlen<br>haben befohlen |
| | **Past** | | **Past Perfect** | |
| | befahl<br>befahlst<br>befahl | befahlen<br>befahlt<br>befahlen | hatte befohlen<br>hattest befohlen<br>hatte befohlen | hatten befohlen<br>hattet befohlen<br>hatten befohlen |
| | **Future** | | **Future Perfect** | |
| | werde befehlen<br>wirst befehlen<br>wird befehlen | werden befehlen<br>werdet befehlen<br>werden befehlen | werde befohlen haben<br>wirst befohlen haben<br>wird befohlen haben | werden befohlen haben<br>werdet befohlen haben<br>werden befohlen haben |
| Subjunctive | **Present** | | **Present Perfect** | |
| | befehle<br>befehlest<br>befehle | befehlen<br>befehlet<br>befehlen | habe befohlen<br>habest befohlen<br>habe befohlen | haben befohlen<br>habet befohlen<br>haben befohlen |
| | **Past** | | **Past Perfect** | |
| | beföhle<br>beföhlest<br>beföhle | beföhlen<br>beföhlet<br>beföhlen | hätte befohlen<br>hättest befohlen<br>hätte befohlen | hätten befohlen<br>hättet befohlen<br>hätten befohlen |
| | **Future** | | **Future Perfect** | |
| | werde befehlen<br>werdest befehlen<br>werde befehlen | werden befehlen<br>werdet befehlen<br>werden befehlen | werde befohlen haben<br>werdest befohlen haben<br>werde befohlen haben | werden befohlen haben<br>werdet befohlen haben<br>werden befohlen haben |
| | **Present and Future Conditional** | | **Past Conditional** | |
| | würde befehlen<br>würdest befehlen<br>würde befehlen | würden befehlen<br>würdet befehlen<br>würden befehlen | würde befohlen haben<br>würdest befohlen haben<br>würde befohlen haben | würden befohlen haben<br>würdet befohlen haben<br>würden befohlen haben |

## EXAMPLES

Der Hauptmann befiehlt den Soldaten den Gegner anzugreifen.
The captain orders the soldiers to attack the enemy.

Der König befahl dem Ritter den Drachen zu töten.
The king ordered the knight to kill the dragon.

**befestigen**
to attach, to fasten, to fix
**Auxiliary verb:** haben **Past participle:** befestigt
**Imperative:** Befestige! Befestigt! Befestigen Sie!

| Mode | Simple Tenses | | Compound Tenses | |
|---|---|---|---|---|
| | *Singular* | *Plural* | *Singular* | *Plural* |
| Indicative | **Present** | | **Present Perfect** | |
| | befestige<br>befestigst<br>befestigt | befestigen<br>befestigt<br>befestigen | habe befestigt<br>hast befestigt<br>hat befestigt | haben befestigt<br>habt befestigt<br>haben befestigt |
| | **Past** | | **Past Perfect** | |
| | befestigte<br>befestigtest<br>befestigte | befestigten<br>befestigtet<br>befestigten | hatte befestigt<br>hattest befestigt<br>hatte befestigt | hatten befestigt<br>hattet befestigt<br>hatten befestigt |
| | **Future** | | **Future Perfect** | |
| | werde befestigen<br>wirst befestigen<br>wird befestigen | werden befestigen<br>werdet befestigen<br>werden befestigen | werde befestigt haben<br>wirst befestigt haben<br>wird befestigt haben | werden befestigt haben<br>werdet befestigt haben<br>werden befestigt haben |
| Subjunctive | **Present** | | **Present Perfect** | |
| | befestige<br>befestigest<br>befestige | befestigen<br>befestiget<br>befestigen | habe befestigt<br>habest befestigt<br>habe befestigt | haben befestigt<br>habet befestigt<br>haben befestigt |
| | **Past** | | **Past Perfect** | |
| | befestigte<br>befestigtest<br>befestigte | befestigten<br>befestigtet<br>befestigten | hätte befestigt<br>hättest befestigt<br>hätte befestigt | hätten befestigt<br>hättet befestigt<br>hätten befestigt |
| | **Future** | | **Future Perfect** | |
| | werde befestigen<br>werdest befestigen<br>werde befestigen | werden befestigen<br>werdet befestigen<br>werden befestigen | werde befestigt haben<br>werdest befestigt haben<br>werde befestigt haben | werden befestigt haben<br>werdet befestigt haben<br>werden befestigt haben |
| | **Present and Future Conditional** | | **Past Conditional** | |
| | würde befestigen<br>würdest befestigen<br>würde befestigen | würden befestigen<br>würdet befestigen<br>würden befestigen | würde befestigt haben<br>würdest befestigt haben<br>würde befestigt haben | würden befestigt haben<br>würdet befestigt haben<br>würden befestigt haben |

## EXAMPLES

Das neue Dach wurde mit Nägeln befestigt. — The new roof was fastened with nails.
Diese Mauern müssen befestigt werden. — These walls must be fortified.

**begegnen**
to meet, to encounter, to happen upon
**Auxiliary verb:** sein **Past participle:** begegnet
**Imperative:** Begegne! Begegnet! Begegnen Sie!

| Mode | Simple Tenses | | Compound Tenses | |
|---|---|---|---|---|
| | *Singular* | *Plural* | *Singular* | *Plural* |
| Indicative | **Present** | | **Present Perfect** | |
| | begegne<br>begegnest<br>begegnet | begegnen<br>begegnet<br>begegnen | bin begegnet<br>bist begegnet<br>ist begegnet | sind begegnet<br>seid begegnet<br>sind begegnet |
| | **Past** | | **Past Perfect** | |
| | begegnete<br>begegnetest<br>begegnete | begegneten<br>begegnetet<br>begegneten | war begegnet<br>warst begegnet<br>war begegnet | waren begegnet<br>wart begegnet<br>waren begegnet |
| | **Future** | | **Future Perfect** | |
| | werde begegnen<br>wirst begegnen<br>wird begegnen | werden begegnen<br>werdet begegnen<br>werden begegnen | werde begegnet sein<br>wirst begegnet sein<br>wird begegnet sein | werden begegnet sein<br>werdet begegnet sein<br>werden begegnet sein |
| Subjunctive | **Present** | | **Present Perfect** | |
| | begegne<br>begegnest<br>begegne | begegnen<br>begegnet<br>begegnen | sei begegnet<br>seiest begegnet<br>sei begegnet | seien begegnet<br>seiet begegnet<br>seien begegnet |
| | **Past** | | **Past Perfect** | |
| | begegnete<br>begegnetest<br>begegnete | begegneten<br>begegnetet<br>begegneten | wäre begegnet<br>wärest begegnet<br>wäre begegnet | wären begegnet<br>wäret begegnet<br>wären begegnet |
| | **Future** | | **Future Perfect** | |
| | werde begegnen<br>werdest begegnen<br>werde begegnen | werden begegnen<br>werdet begegnen<br>werden begegnen | werde begegnet sein<br>werdest begegnet sein<br>werde begegnet sein | werden begegnet sein<br>werdet begegnet sein<br>werden begegnet sein |
| | **Present and Future Conditional** | | **Past Conditional** | |
| | würde begegnen<br>würdest begegnen<br>würde begegnen | würden begegnen<br>würdet begegnen<br>würden begegnen | würde begegnet sein<br>würdest begegnet sein<br>würde begegnet sein | würden begegnet sein<br>würdet begegnet sein<br>würden begegnet sein |

**Note:** *Begegnen* is a dative verb and requires a dative object.

## EXAMPLES

Ich bin Herrn Bauer im Stadtpark begegnet. — I met Mr. Bauer in the city park.
Wir begegneten ständig unserem Lehrer. — We kept on running into our teacher.

**beginnen**
to begin, to start
**Auxiliary verb:** haben **Past participle:** begonnen
**Imperative:** Beginne! Beginnt! Beginnen Sie!

| Mode | Simple Tenses | | Compound Tenses | |
|---|---|---|---|---|
| | *Singular* | *Plural* | *Singular* | *Plural* |
| Indicative | **Present** | | **Present Perfect** | |
| | beginne<br>beginnst<br>beginnt | beginnen<br>beginnt<br>beginnen | habe begonnen<br>hast begonnen<br>hat begonnen | haben begonnen<br>habt begonnen<br>haben begonnen |
| | **Past** | | **Past Perfect** | |
| | begann<br>begannst<br>begann | begannen<br>begannt<br>begannen | hatte begonnen<br>hattest begonnen<br>hatte begonnen | hatten begonnen<br>hattet begonnen<br>hatten begonnen |
| | **Future** | | **Future Perfect** | |
| | werde beginnen<br>wirst beginnen<br>wird beginnen | werden beginnen<br>werdet beginnen<br>werden beginnen | werde begonnen haben<br>wirst begonnen haben<br>wird begonnen haben | werden begonnen haben<br>werdet begonnen haben<br>werden begonnen haben |
| Subjunctive | **Present** | | **Present Perfect** | |
| | beginne<br>beginnest<br>beginne | beginnen<br>beginnet<br>beginnen | habe begonnen<br>habest begonnen<br>habe begonnen | haben begonnen<br>habet begonnen<br>haben begonnen |
| | **Past** | | **Past Perfect** | |
| | begönne<br>begönnest<br>begönne | begönnen<br>begönnet<br>begönnen | hätte begonnen<br>hättest begonnen<br>hätte begonnen | hätten begonnen<br>hättet begonnen<br>hätten begonnen |
| | **Future** | | **Future Perfect** | |
| | werde beginnen<br>werdest beginnen<br>werde beginnen | werden beginnen<br>werdet beginnen<br>werden beginnen | werde begonnen haben<br>werdest begonnen haben<br>werde begonnen haben | werden begonnen haben<br>werdet begonnen haben<br>werden begonnen haben |
| | **Present and Future Conditional** | | **Past Conditional** | |
| | würde beginnen<br>würdest beginnen<br>würde beginnen | würden beginnen<br>würdet beginnen<br>würden beginnen | würde begonnen haben<br>würdest begonnen haben<br>würde begonnen haben | würden begonnen haben<br>würdet begonnen haben<br>würden begonnen haben |

**Note:** The dialectical form of the past subjunctive *begänne* is also common.

## EXAMPLES

| | |
|---|---|
| Wann beginnt die nächste Vorstellung? | When does the next show start? |
| Martin hatte begonnen ein Lied vorzusingen. | Martin had begun to sing a song. |

**begleiten**
to accompany, to escort
**Auxiliary verb:** haben **Past participle:** begleitet
**Imperative:** Begleite! Begleitet! Begleiten Sie!

| Mode | Simple Tenses | | Compound Tenses | |
|---|---|---|---|---|
| | *Singular* | *Plural* | *Singular* | *Plural* |
| Indicative | **Present** | | **Present Perfect** | |
| | begleite<br>begleitest<br>begleitet | begleiten<br>begleitet<br>begleiten | habe begleitet<br>hast begleitet<br>hat begleitet | haben begleitet<br>habt begleitet<br>haben begleitet |
| | **Past** | | **Past Perfect** | |
| | begleitete<br>begleitetest<br>begleitete | begleiteten<br>begleitetet<br>begleiteten | hatte begleitet<br>hattest begleitet<br>hatte begleitet | hatten begleitet<br>hattet begleitet<br>hatten begleitet |
| | **Future** | | **Future Perfect** | |
| | werde begleiten<br>wirst begleiten<br>wird begleiten | werden begleiten<br>werdet begleiten<br>werden begleiten | werde begleitet haben<br>wirst begleitet haben<br>wird begleitet haben | werden begleitet haben<br>werdet begleitet haben<br>werden begleitet haben |
| Subjunctive | **Present** | | **Present Perfect** | |
| | begleite<br>begleitest<br>begleite | begleiten<br>begleitet<br>begleiten | habe begleitet<br>habest begleitet<br>habe begleitet | haben begleitet<br>habet begleitet<br>haben begleitet |
| | **Past** | | **Past Perfect** | |
| | begleitete<br>begleitetest<br>begleitete | begleiteten<br>begleitetet<br>begleiteten | hätte begleitet<br>hättest begleitet<br>hätte begleitet | hätten begleitet<br>hättet begleitet<br>hätten begleitet |
| | **Future** | | **Future Perfect** | |
| | werde begleiten<br>werdest begleiten<br>werde begleiten | werden begleiten<br>werdet begleiten<br>werden begleiten | werde begleitet haben<br>werdest begleitet haben<br>werde begleitet haben | werden begleitet haben<br>werdet begleitet haben<br>werden begleitet haben |
| | **Present and Future Conditional** | | **Past Conditional** | |
| | würde begleiten<br>würdest begleiten<br>würde begleiten | würden begleiten<br>würdet begleiten<br>würden begleiten | würde begleitet haben<br>würdest begleitet haben<br>würde begleitet haben | würden begleitet haben<br>würdet begleitet haben<br>würden begleitet haben |

**Note:** Do not confuse this verb with the irregular verb *gleiten (gleitet, glitt, geglitten).*

## EXAMPLES

Karl hat die alte Dame nach Hause begleitet. — Karl escorted the old lady home.

Die Königin lässt sich immer zur Kirche begleiten. — The queen always has someone accompany her to church.

**behalten**
to keep, to retain
**Auxiliary verb:** haben **Past participle:** behalten
**Imperative:** Behalte! Behaltet! Behalten Sie!

| Mode | Simple Tenses | | Compound Tenses | |
|---|---|---|---|---|
| | *Singular* | *Plural* | *Singular* | *Plural* |
| Indicative | **Present** | | **Present Perfect** | |
| | behalte<br>behältst<br>behält | behalten<br>behaltet<br>behalten | habe behalten<br>hast behalten<br>hat behalten | haben behalten<br>habt behalten<br>haben behalten |
| | **Past** | | **Past Perfect** | |
| | behielt<br>behieltst<br>behielt | behielten<br>behieltet<br>behielten | hatte behalten<br>hattest behalten<br>hatte behalten | hatten behalten<br>hattet behalten<br>hatten behalten |
| | **Future** | | **Future Perfect** | |
| | werde behalten<br>wirst behalten<br>wird behalten | werden behalten<br>werdet behalten<br>werden behalten | werde behalten haben<br>wirst behalten haben<br>wird behalten haben | werden behalten haben<br>werdet behalten haben<br>werden behalten haben |
| Subjunctive | **Present** | | **Present Perfect** | |
| | behalte<br>behaltest<br>behalte | behalten<br>behaltet<br>behalten | habe behalten<br>habest behalten<br>habe behalten | haben behalten<br>habet behalten<br>haben behalten |
| | **Past** | | **Past Perfect** | |
| | behielte<br>behieltest<br>behielte | behielten<br>behieltet<br>behielten | hätte behalten<br>hättest behalten<br>hätte behalten | hätten behalten<br>hättet behalten<br>hätten behalten |
| | **Future** | | **Future Perfect** | |
| | werde behalten<br>werdest behalten<br>werde behalten | werden behalten<br>werdet behalten<br>werden behalten | werde behalten haben<br>werdest behalten haben<br>werde behalten haben | werden behalten haben<br>werdet behalten haben<br>werden behalten haben |
| | **Present and Future Conditional** | | **Past Conditional** | |
| | würde behalten<br>würdest behalten<br>würde behalten | würden behalten<br>würdet behalten<br>würden behalten | würde behalten haben<br>würdest behalten haben<br>würde behalten haben | würden behalten haben<br>würdet behalten haben<br>würden behalten haben |

## EXAMPLES

Du musst deine Fassung behalten. — You have to keep your composure.

Thomas behielt die 50 Euro, die er gefunden hatte. — Thomas kept the 50 euros that he found.

**behandeln**
to handle, to treat, to manage
**Auxiliary verb:** haben **Past participle:** behandelt
**Imperative:** Behandele! Behandelt! Behandeln Sie!

| Mode | Simple Tenses | | Compound Tenses | |
|---|---|---|---|---|
| | *Singular* | *Plural* | *Singular* | *Plural* |
| Indicative | **Present** | | **Present Perfect** | |
| | behandele<br>behandelst<br>behandelt | behandeln<br>behandelt<br>behandeln | habe behandelt<br>hast behandelt<br>hat behandelt | haben behandelt<br>habt behandelt<br>haben behandelt |
| | **Past** | | **Past Perfect** | |
| | behandelte<br>behandeltest<br>behandelte | behandelten<br>behandeltet<br>behandelten | hatte behandelt<br>hattest behandelt<br>hatte behandelt | hatten behandelt<br>hattet behandelt<br>hatten behandelt |
| | **Future** | | **Future Perfect** | |
| | werde behandeln<br>wirst behandeln<br>wird behandeln | werden behandeln<br>werdet behandeln<br>werden behandeln | werde behandelt haben<br>wirst behandelt haben<br>wird behandelt haben | werden behandelt haben<br>werdet behandelt haben<br>werden behandelt haben |
| Subjunctive | **Present** | | **Present Perfect** | |
| | behandele<br>behandelst<br>behandele | behandeln<br>behandelt<br>behandeln | habe behandelt<br>habest behandelt<br>habe behandelt | haben behandelt<br>habet behandelt<br>haben behandelt |
| | **Past** | | **Past Perfect** | |
| | behandelte<br>behandeltest<br>behandelte | behandelten<br>behandeltet<br>behandelten | hätte behandelt<br>hättest behandelt<br>hätte behandelt | hätten behandelt<br>hättet behandelt<br>hätten behandelt |
| | **Future** | | **Future Perfect** | |
| | werde behandeln<br>werdest behandeln<br>werde behandeln | werden behandeln<br>werdet behandeln<br>werden behandeln | werde behandelt haben<br>werdest behandelt haben<br>werde behandelt haben | werden behandelt haben<br>werdet behandelt haben<br>werden behandelt haben |
| | **Present and Future Conditional** | | **Past Conditional** | |
| | würde behandeln<br>würdest behandeln<br>würde behandeln | würden behandeln<br>würdet behandeln<br>würden behandeln | würde behandelt haben<br>würdest behandelt haben<br>würde behandelt haben | würden behandelt haben<br>würdet behandelt haben<br>würden behandelt haben |

## EXAMPLES

Warum behandelst du mich wie ein kleines Kind? — Why do you treat me like a little child?
Doktor Meyer hat uns beide behandelt. — Dr. Meyer treated us both.

**beißen**

to bite, to sting, to smart

**Auxiliary verb:** haben **Past participle:** gebissen

**Imperative:** Beiße! Beißt! Beißen Sie!

| Mode | Simple Tenses | | Compound Tenses | |
|---|---|---|---|---|
| | *Singular* | *Plural* | *Singular* | *Plural* |
| Indicative | **Present** | | **Present Perfect** | |
| | beiße<br>beißt<br>beißt | beißen<br>beißt<br>beißen | habe gebissen<br>hast gebissen<br>hat gebissen | haben gebissen<br>habt gebissen<br>haben gebissen |
| | **Past** | | **Past Perfect** | |
| | biss<br>bissest<br>biss | bissen<br>bisst<br>bissen | hatte gebissen<br>hattest gebissen<br>hatte gebissen | hatten gebissen<br>hattet gebissen<br>hatten gebissen |
| | **Future** | | **Future Perfect** | |
| | werde beißen<br>wirst beißen<br>wird beißen | werden beißen<br>werdet beißen<br>werden beißen | werde gebissen haben<br>wirst gebissen haben<br>wird gebissen haben | werden gebissen haben<br>werdet gebissen haben<br>werden gebissen haben |
| Subjunctive | **Present** | | **Present Perfect** | |
| | beiße<br>beißest<br>beiße | beißen<br>beißet<br>beißen | habe gebissen<br>habest gebissen<br>habe gebissen | haben gebissen<br>habet gebissen<br>haben gebissen |
| | **Past** | | **Past Perfect** | |
| | bisse<br>bissest<br>bisse | bissen<br>bisset<br>bissen | hätte gebissen<br>hättest gebissen<br>hätte gebissen | hätten gebissen<br>hättet gebissen<br>hätten gebissen |
| | **Future** | | **Future Perfect** | |
| | werde beißen<br>werdest beißen<br>werde beißen | werden beißen<br>werdet beißen<br>werden beißen | werde gebissen haben<br>werdest gebissen haben<br>werde gebissen haben | werden gebissen haben<br>werdet gebissen haben<br>werden gebissen haben |
| | **Present and Future Conditional** | | **Past Conditional** | |
| | würde beißen<br>würdest beißen<br>würde beißen | würden beißen<br>würdet beißen<br>würden beißen | würde gebissen haben<br>würdest gebissen haben<br>würde gebissen haben | würden gebissen haben<br>würdet gebissen haben<br>würden gebissen haben |

## EXAMPLES

| | |
|---|---|
| Manchmal muss man in den sauren Apfel beißen. | Sometimes you have to swallow a bitter pill. |
| Vorsicht! Das ist ein bissiger Hund! | Careful! That dog bites! |

**bekommen**
to receive, to get
**Auxiliary verb:** haben **Past participle:** bekommen
**Imperative:** Bekomme! Bekommt! Bekommen Sie!

| Mode | Simple Tenses | | Compound Tenses | |
|---|---|---|---|---|
| | *Singular* | *Plural* | *Singular* | *Plural* |
| Indicative | **Present** | | **Present Perfect** | |
| | bekomme<br>bekommst<br>bekommt | bekommen<br>bekommt<br>bekommen | habe bekommen<br>hast bekommen<br>hat bekommen | haben bekommen<br>habt bekommen<br>haben bekommen |
| | **Past** | | **Past Perfect** | |
| | bekam<br>bekamst<br>bekam | bekamen<br>bekamt<br>bekamen | hatte bekommen<br>hattest bekommen<br>hatte bekommen | hatten bekommen<br>hattet bekommen<br>hatten bekommen |
| | **Future** | | **Future Perfect** | |
| | werde bekommen<br>wirst bekommen<br>wird bekommen | werden bekommen<br>werdet bekommen<br>werden bekommen | werde bekommen haben<br>wirst bekommen haben<br>wird bekommen haben | werden bekommen haben<br>werdet bekommen haben<br>werden bekommen haben |
| Subjunctive | **Present** | | **Present Perfect** | |
| | bekomme<br>bekommest<br>bekomme | bekommen<br>bekommet<br>bekommen | habe bekommen<br>habest bekommen<br>habe bekommen | haben bekommen<br>habet bekommen<br>haben bekommen |
| | **Past** | | **Past Perfect** | |
| | bekäme<br>bekämest<br>bekäme | bekämen<br>bekämet<br>bekämen | hätte bekommen<br>hättest bekommen<br>hätte bekommen | hätten bekommen<br>hättet bekommen<br>hätten bekommen |
| | **Future** | | **Future Perfect** | |
| | werde bekommen<br>werdest bekommen<br>werde bekommen | werden bekommen<br>werdet bekommen<br>werden bekommen | werde bekommen haben<br>werdest bekommen haben<br>werde bekommen haben | werden bekommen haben<br>werdet bekommen haben<br>werden bekommen haben |
| | **Present and Future Conditional** | | **Past Conditional** | |
| | würde bekommen<br>würdest bekommen<br>würde bekommen | würden bekommen<br>würdet bekommen<br>würden bekommen | würde bekommen haben<br>würdest bekommen haben<br>würde bekommen haben | würden bekommen haben<br>würdet bekommen haben<br>würden bekommen haben |

## EXAMPLES

Kann ich ein Zimmer bekommen? — Can I have a room?
Gestern haben wir einen Brief von ihm bekommen. — Yesterday we got a letter from him.

**bellen**
to bark
**Auxiliary verb:** haben **Past participle:** gebellt
**Imperative:** Belle! Bellt! Bellen Sie!

| Mode | Simple Tenses | | Compound Tenses | |
|---|---|---|---|---|
| | *Singular* | *Plural* | *Singular* | *Plural* |
| Indicative | **Present** | | **Present Perfect** | |
| | belle<br>bellst<br>bellt | bellen<br>bellt<br>bellen | habe gebellt<br>hast gebellt<br>hat gebellt | haben gebellt<br>habt gebellt<br>haben gebellt |
| | **Past** | | **Past Perfect** | |
| | bellte<br>belltest<br>bellte | bellten<br>belltet<br>bellten | hatte gebellt<br>hattest gebellt<br>hatte gebellt | hatten gebellt<br>hattet gebellt<br>hatten gebellt |
| | **Future** | | **Future Perfect** | |
| | werde bellen<br>wirst bellen<br>wird bellen | werden bellen<br>werdet bellen<br>werden bellen | werde gebellt haben<br>wirst gebellt haben<br>wird gebellt haben | werden gebellt haben<br>werdet gebellt haben<br>werden gebellt haben |
| Subjunctive | **Present** | | **Present Perfect** | |
| | belle<br>bellest<br>belle | bellen<br>bellet<br>bellen | habe gebellt<br>habest gebellt<br>habe gebellt | haben gebellt<br>habet gebellt<br>haben gebellt |
| | **Past** | | **Past Perfect** | |
| | bellte<br>belltest<br>bellte | bellten<br>belltet<br>bellten | hätte gebellt<br>hättest gebellt<br>hätte gebellt | hätten gebellt<br>hättet gebellt<br>hätten gebellt |
| | **Future** | | **Future Perfect** | |
| | werde bellen<br>werdest bellen<br>werde bellen | werden bellen<br>werdet bellen<br>werden bellen | werde gebellt haben<br>werdest gebellt haben<br>werde gebellt haben | werden gebellt haben<br>werdet gebellt haben<br>werden gebellt haben |
| | **Present and Future Conditional** | | **Past Conditional** | |
| | würde bellen<br>würdest bellen<br>würde bellen | würden bellen<br>würdet bellen<br>würden bellen | würde gebellt haben<br>würdest gebellt haben<br>würde gebellt haben | würden gebellt haben<br>würdet gebellt haben<br>würden gebellt haben |

## EXAMPLES

Warum bellen die Hunde so?
Der alte Hund sah den Fremden an der Tür aber konnte nicht bellen.

Why are the dogs barking like that?
The old dog saw the stranger at the door but couldn't bark.

**belohnen**
to reward
**Auxiliary verb:** haben **Past participle:** belohnt
**Imperative:** Belohne! Belohnt! Belohnen Sie!

| Mode | Simple Tenses | | Compound Tenses | |
|---|---|---|---|---|
| | *Singular* | *Plural* | *Singular* | *Plural* |
| Indicative | **Present** | | **Present Perfect** | |
| | belohne<br>belohnst<br>belohnt | belohnen<br>belohnt<br>belohnen | habe belohnt<br>hast belohnt<br>hat belohnt | haben belohnt<br>habt belohnt<br>haben belohnt |
| | **Past** | | **Past Perfect** | |
| | belohnte<br>belohntest<br>belohnte | belohnten<br>belohntet<br>belohnten | hatte belohnt<br>hattest belohnt<br>hatte belohnt | hatten belohnt<br>hattet belohnt<br>hatten belohnt |
| | **Future** | | **Future Perfect** | |
| | werde belohnen<br>wirst belohnen<br>wird belohnen | werden belohnen<br>werdet belohnen<br>werden belohnen | werde belohnt haben<br>wirst belohnt haben<br>wird belohnt haben | werden belohnt haben<br>werdet belohnt haben<br>werden belohnt haben |
| Subjunctive | **Present** | | **Present Perfect** | |
| | belohne<br>belohnest<br>belohne | belohnen<br>belohnet<br>belohnen | habe belohnt<br>habest belohnt<br>habe belohnt | haben belohnt<br>habet belohnt<br>haben belohnt |
| | **Past** | | **Past Perfect** | |
| | belohnte<br>belohntest<br>belohnte | belohnten<br>belohntet<br>belohnten | hätte belohnt<br>hättest belohnt<br>hätte belohnt | hätten belohnt<br>hättet belohnt<br>hätten belohnt |
| | **Future** | | **Future Perfect** | |
| | werde belohnen<br>werdest belohnen<br>werde belohnen | werden belohnen<br>werdet belohnen<br>werden belohnen | werde belohnt haben<br>werdest belohnt haben<br>werde belohnt haben | werden belohnt haben<br>werdet belohnt haben<br>werden belohnt haben |
| | **Present and Future Conditional** | | **Past Conditional** | |
| | würde belohnen<br>würdest belohnen<br>würde belohnen | würden belohnen<br>würdet belohnen<br>würden belohnen | würde belohnt haben<br>würdest belohnt haben<br>würde belohnt haben | würden belohnt haben<br>würdet belohnt haben<br>würden belohnt haben |

## EXAMPLES

Herr Weidner belohnte den Finder seiner Schlüssel mit 50 Euro.
Mr. Weidner gave the man who found his keys a reward of 50 euros.

Lukas wurde für sein gutes Benehmen belohnt.
Lukas was rewarded for his good behavior.

**bemerken**

to notice, to observe, to remark

**Auxiliary verb:** haben **Past participle:** bemerkt

**Imperative:** Bemerke! Bemerkt! Bemerken Sie!

| Mode | Simple Tenses | | Compound Tenses | |
|---|---|---|---|---|
| | *Singular* | *Plural* | *Singular* | *Plural* |
| Indicative | **Present** | | **Present Perfect** | |
| | bemerke<br>bemerkst<br>bemerkt | bemerken<br>bemerkt<br>bemerken | habe bemerkt<br>hast bemerkt<br>hat bemerkt | haben bemerkt<br>habt bemerkt<br>haben bemerkt |
| | **Past** | | **Past Perfect** | |
| | bemerkte<br>bemerktest<br>bemerkte | bemerkten<br>bemerktet<br>bemerkten | hatte bemerkt<br>hattest bemerkt<br>hatte bemerkt | hatten bemerkt<br>hattet bemerkt<br>hatten bemerkt |
| | **Future** | | **Future Perfect** | |
| | werde bemerken<br>wirst bemerken<br>wird bemerken | werden bemerken<br>werdet bemerken<br>werden bemerken | werde bemerkt haben<br>wirst bemerkt haben<br>wird bemerkt haben | werden bemerkt haben<br>werdet bemerkt haben<br>werden bemerkt haben |
| Subjunctive | **Present** | | **Present Perfect** | |
| | bemerke<br>bemerkest<br>bemerke | bemerken<br>bemerket<br>bemerken | habe bemerkt<br>habest bemerkt<br>habe bemerkt | haben bemerkt<br>habet bemerkt<br>haben bemerkt |
| | **Past** | | **Past Perfect** | |
| | bemerkte<br>bemerktest<br>bemerkte | bemerkten<br>bemerktet<br>bemerkten | hätte bemerkt<br>hättest bemerkt<br>hätte bemerkt | hätten bemerkt<br>hättet bemerkt<br>hätten bemerkt |
| | **Future** | | **Future Perfect** | |
| | werde bemerken<br>werdest bemerken<br>werde bemerken | werden bemerken<br>werdet bemerken<br>werden bemerken | werde bemerkt haben<br>werdest bemerkt haben<br>werde bemerkt haben | werden bemerkt haben<br>werdet bemerkt haben<br>werden bemerkt haben |
| | **Present and Future Conditional** | | **Past Conditional** | |
| | würde bemerken<br>würdest bemerken<br>würde bemerken | würden bemerken<br>würdet bemerken<br>würden bemerken | würde bemerkt haben<br>würdest bemerkt haben<br>würde bemerkt haben | würden bemerkt haben<br>würdet bemerkt haben<br>würden bemerkt haben |

## EXAMPLES

Niemand hat den Diebstahl bemerkt. — No one noticed the theft.

Er tat, als ob er mich nicht bemerkte. — He acted as if he didn't notice me.

**beneiden**
to envy
**Auxiliary verb:** haben **Past participle:** beneidet
**Imperative:** Beneide! Beneidet! Beneiden Sie!

| Mode | Simple Tenses | | Compound Tenses | |
|---|---|---|---|---|
| | *Singular* | *Plural* | *Singular* | *Plural* |
| Indicative | **Present** | | **Present Perfect** | |
| | beneide<br>beneidest<br>beneidet | beneiden<br>beneidet<br>beneiden | habe beneidet<br>hast beneidet<br>hat beneidet | haben beneidet<br>habt beneidet<br>haben beneidet |
| | **Past** | | **Past Perfect** | |
| | beneidete<br>beneidetest<br>beneidete | beneideten<br>beneidetet<br>beneideten | hatte beneidet<br>hattest beneidet<br>hatte beneidet | hatten beneidet<br>hattet beneidet<br>hatten beneidet |
| | **Future** | | **Future Perfect** | |
| | werde beneiden<br>wirst beneiden<br>wird beneiden | werden beneiden<br>werdet beneiden<br>werden beneiden | werde beneidet haben<br>wirst beneidet haben<br>wird beneidet haben | werden beneidet haben<br>werdet beneidet haben<br>werden beneidet haben |
| Subjunctive | **Present** | | **Present Perfect** | |
| | beneide<br>beneidest<br>beneide | beneiden<br>beneidet<br>beneiden | habe beneidet<br>habest beneidet<br>habe beneidet | haben beneidet<br>habet beneidet<br>haben beneidet |
| | **Past** | | **Past Perfect** | |
| | beneidete<br>beneidetest<br>beneidete | beneideten<br>beneidetet<br>beneideten | hätte beneidet<br>hättest beneidet<br>hätte beneidet | hätten beneidet<br>hättet beneidet<br>hätten beneidet |
| | **Future** | | **Future Perfect** | |
| | werde beneiden<br>werdest beneiden<br>werde beneiden | werden beneiden<br>werdet beneiden<br>werden beneiden | werde beneidet haben<br>werdest beneidet haben<br>werde beneidet haben | werden beneidet haben<br>werdet beneidet haben<br>werden beneidet haben |
| | **Present and Future Conditional** | | **Past Conditional** | |
| | würde beneiden<br>würdest beneiden<br>würde beneiden | würden beneiden<br>würdet beneiden<br>würden beneiden | würde beneidet haben<br>würdest beneidet haben<br>würde beneidet haben | würden beneidet haben<br>würdet beneidet haben<br>würden beneidet haben |

## EXAMPLES

Alle beneiden ihn. — Everyone envies him.
Sonja hat sie um ihre Stelle beneidet. — Sonja envied her for her job.

**benutzen**

to use, to employ

**Auxiliary verb:** haben **Past participle:** benutzt

**Imperative:** Benutze! Benutzt! Benutzen Sie!

| Mode | Simple Tenses | | Compound Tenses | |
|---|---|---|---|---|
| | *Singular* | *Plural* | *Singular* | *Plural* |
| Indicative | **Present** | | **Present Perfect** | |
| | benutze<br>benutzt<br>benutzt | benutzen<br>benutzt<br>benutzen | habe benutzt<br>hast benutzt<br>hat benutzt | haben benutzt<br>habt benutzt<br>haben benutzt |
| | **Past** | | **Past Perfect** | |
| | benutzte<br>benutztest<br>benutzte | benutzten<br>benutztet<br>benutzten | hatte benutzt<br>hattest benutzt<br>hatte benutzt | hatten benutzt<br>hattet benutzt<br>hatten benutzt |
| | **Future** | | **Future Perfect** | |
| | werde benutzen<br>wirst benutzen<br>wird benutzen | werden benutzen<br>werdet benutzen<br>werden benutzen | werde benutzt haben<br>wirst benutzt haben<br>wird benutzt haben | werden benutzt haben<br>werdet benutzt haben<br>werden benutzt haben |
| Subjunctive | **Present** | | **Present Perfect** | |
| | benutze<br>benutzest<br>benutze | benutzen<br>benutzet<br>benutzen | habe benutzt<br>habest benutzt<br>habe benutzt | haben benutzt<br>habet benutzt<br>haben benutzt |
| | **Past** | | **Past Perfect** | |
| | benutzte<br>benutztest<br>benutzte | benutzten<br>benutztet<br>benutzten | hätte benutzt<br>hättest benutzt<br>hätte benutzt | hätten benutzt<br>hättet benutzt<br>hätten benutzt |
| | **Future** | | **Future Perfect** | |
| | werde benutzen<br>werdest benutzen<br>werde benutzen | werden benutzen<br>werdet benutzen<br>werden benutzen | werde benutzt haben<br>werdest benutzt haben<br>werde benutzt haben | werden benutzt haben<br>werdet benutzt haben<br>werden benutzt haben |
| | **Present and Future Conditional** | | **Past Conditional** | |
| | würde benutzen<br>würdest benutzen<br>würde benutzen | würden benutzen<br>würdet benutzen<br>würden benutzen | würde benutzt haben<br>würdest benutzt haben<br>würde benutzt haben | würden benutzt haben<br>würdet benutzt haben<br>würden benutzt haben |

**Note:** This verb is also commonly spelled with an *umlaut: benützen.*

## EXAMPLES

| | |
|---|---|
| In Deutschland habe ich oft den Bus benutzt. | In Germany I often used the bus. |
| Wir benützen nur umweltfreundliche Produkte. | We only use environmentally-friendly products. |

**beschäftigen (sich)**
to occupy (oneself), to keep busy
**Auxiliary verb:** haben **Past participle:** beschäftigt
**Imperative:** Beschäftige dich! Beschäftigt euch! Beschäftigen Sie sich!

| Mode | Simple Tenses | | Compound Tenses | |
|---|---|---|---|---|
| | *Singular* | *Plural* | *Singular* | *Plural* |
| Indicative | **Present** | | **Present Perfect** | |
| | beschäftige<br>beschäftigst<br>beschäftigt | beschäftigen<br>beschäftigt<br>beschäftigen | habe beschäftigt<br>hast beschäftigt<br>hat beschäftigt | haben beschäftigt<br>habt beschäftigt<br>haben beschäftigt |
| | **Past** | | **Past Perfect** | |
| | beschäftigte<br>beschäftigtest<br>beschäftigte | beschäftigten<br>beschäftigtet<br>beschäftigten | hatte beschäftigt<br>hattest beschäftigt<br>hatte beschäftigt | hatten beschäftigt<br>hattet beschäftigt<br>hatten beschäftigt |
| | **Future** | | **Future Perfect** | |
| | werde beschäftigen<br>wirst beschäftigen<br>wird beschäftigen | werden beschäftigen<br>werdet beschäftigen<br>werden beschäftigen | werde beschäftigt haben<br>wirst beschäftigt haben<br>wird beschäftigt haben | werden beschäftigt haben<br>werdet beschäftigt haben<br>werden beschäftigt haben |
| Subjunctive | **Present** | | **Present Perfect** | |
| | beschäftige<br>beschäftigest<br>beschäftige | beschäftigen<br>beschäftiget<br>beschäftigen | habe beschäftigt<br>habest beschäftigt<br>habe beschäftigt | haben beschäftigt<br>habet beschäftigt<br>haben beschäftigt |
| | **Past** | | **Past Perfect** | |
| | beschäftigte<br>beschäftigtest<br>beschäftigte | beschäftigten<br>beschäftigtet<br>beschäftigten | hätte beschäftigt<br>hättest beschäftigt<br>hätte beschäftigt | hätten beschäftigt<br>hättet beschäftigt<br>hätten beschäftigt |
| | **Future** | | **Future Perfect** | |
| | werde beschäftigen<br>werdest beschäftigen<br>werde beschäftigen | werden beschäftigen<br>werdet beschäftigen<br>werden beschäftigen | werde beschäftigt haben<br>werdest beschäftigt haben<br>werde beschäftigt haben | werden beschäftigt haben<br>werdet beschäftigt haben<br>werden beschäftigt haben |
| | **Present and Future Conditional** | | **Past Conditional** | |
| | würde beschäftigen<br>würdest beschäftigen<br>würde beschäftigen | würden beschäftigen<br>würdet beschäftigen<br>würden beschäftigen | würde beschäftigt haben<br>würdest beschäftigt haben<br>würde beschäftigt haben | würden beschäftigt haben<br>würdet beschäftigt haben<br>würden beschäftigt haben |

## EXAMPLES

Ich beschäftige mich zur Zeit mit einem wichtigen Projekt.
Er ist noch sehr beschäftigt damit.

I'm currently occupied with an important project.
He's still very busy with it.

**beschreiben**
to describe
**Auxiliary verb:** haben **Past participle:** beschrieben
**Imperative:** Beschreibe! Beschreibt! Beschreiben Sie!

| Mode | Simple Tenses | | Compound Tenses | |
|---|---|---|---|---|
| | *Singular* | *Plural* | *Singular* | *Plural* |
| Indicative | **Present** | | **Present Perfect** | |
| | beschreibe<br>beschreibst<br>beschreibt | beschreiben<br>beschreibt<br>beschreiben | habe beschrieben<br>hast beschrieben<br>hat beschrieben | haben beschrieben<br>habt beschrieben<br>haben beschrieben |
| | **Past** | | **Past Perfect** | |
| | beschrieb<br>beschriebst<br>beschrieb | beschrieben<br>beschriebt<br>beschrieben | hatte beschrieben<br>hattest beschrieben<br>hatte beschrieben | hatten beschrieben<br>hattet beschrieben<br>hatten beschrieben |
| | **Future** | | **Future Perfect** | |
| | werde beschreiben<br>wirst beschreiben<br>wird beschreiben | werden beschreiben<br>werdet beschreiben<br>werden beschreiben | werde beschrieben haben<br>wirst beschrieben haben<br>wird beschrieben haben | werden beschrieben haben<br>werdet beschrieben haben<br>werden beschrieben haben |
| Subjunctive | **Present** | | **Present Perfect** | |
| | beschreibe<br>beschreibest<br>beschreibe | beschreiben<br>beschreibet<br>beschreiben | habe beschrieben<br>habest beschrieben<br>habe beschrieben | haben beschrieben<br>habet beschrieben<br>haben beschrieben |
| | **Past** | | **Past Perfect** | |
| | beschriebe<br>beschriebest<br>beschriebe | beschrieben<br>beschriebet<br>beschrieben | hätte beschrieben<br>hättest beschrieben<br>hätte beschrieben | hätten beschrieben<br>hättet beschrieben<br>hätten beschrieben |
| | **Future** | | **Future Perfect** | |
| | werde beschreiben<br>werdest beschreiben<br>werde beschreiben | werden beschreiben<br>werdet beschreiben<br>werden beschreiben | werde beschrieben haben<br>werdest beschrieben haben<br>werde beschrieben haben | werden beschrieben haben<br>werdet beschrieben haben<br>werden beschrieben haben |
| | **Present and Future Conditional** | | **Past Conditional** | |
| | würde beschreiben<br>würdest beschreiben<br>würde beschreiben | würden beschreiben<br>würdet beschreiben<br>würden beschreiben | würde beschrieben haben<br>würdest beschrieben haben<br>würde beschrieben haben | würden beschrieben haben<br>würdet beschrieben haben<br>würden beschrieben haben |

## EXAMPLES

Kannst du das Alltagsleben in Berlin beschreiben? — Can you describe daily life in Berlin?
Die Zeugen haben den Dieb beschrieben. — The witnesses described the thief.

**besichtigen**
to inspect, to view, to go sightseeing
**Auxiliary verb:** haben **Past participle:** besichtigt
**Imperative:** Besichtige! Besichtigt! Besichtigen Sie!

| Mode | Simple Tenses | | Compound Tenses | |
|---|---|---|---|---|
| | *Singular* | *Plural* | *Singular* | *Plural* |
| Indicative | **Present** | | **Present Perfect** | |
| | besichtige<br>besichtigst<br>besichtigt | besichtigen<br>besichtigt<br>besichtigen | habe besichtigt<br>hast besichtigt<br>hat besichtigt | haben besichtigt<br>habt besichtigt<br>haben besichtigt |
| | **Past** | | **Past Perfect** | |
| | besichtigte<br>besichtigtest<br>besichtigte | besichtigten<br>besichtigtet<br>besichtigten | hatte besichtigt<br>hattest besichtigt<br>hatte besichtigt | hatten besichtigt<br>hattet besichtigt<br>hatten besichtigt |
| | **Future** | | **Future Perfect** | |
| | werde besichtigen<br>wirst besichtigen<br>wird besichtigen | werden besichtigen<br>werdet besichtigen<br>werden besichtigen | werde besichtigt haben<br>wirst besichtigt haben<br>wird besichtigt haben | werden besichtigt haben<br>werdet besichtigt haben<br>werden besichtigt haben |
| Subjunctive | **Present** | | **Present Perfect** | |
| | besichtige<br>besichtigest<br>besichtige | besichtigen<br>besichtiget<br>besichtigen | habe besichtigt<br>habest besichtigt<br>habe besichtigt | haben besichtigt<br>habet besichtigt<br>haben besichtigt |
| | **Past** | | **Past Perfect** | |
| | besichtigte<br>besichtigtest<br>besichtigte | besichtigten<br>besichtigtet<br>besichtigten | hätte besichtigt<br>hättest besichtigt<br>hätte besichtigt | hätten besichtigt<br>hättet besichtigt<br>hätten besichtigt |
| | **Future** | | **Future Perfect** | |
| | werde besichtigen<br>werdest besichtigen<br>werde besichtigen | werden besichtigen<br>werdet besichtigen<br>werden besichtigen | werde besichtigt haben<br>werdest besichtigt haben<br>werde besichtigt haben | werden besichtigt haben<br>werdet besichtigt haben<br>werden besichtigt haben |
| | **Present and Future Conditional** | | **Past Conditional** | |
| | würde besichtigen<br>würdest besichtigen<br>würde besichtigen | würden besichtigen<br>würdet besichtigen<br>würden besichtigen | würde besichtigt haben<br>würdest besichtigt haben<br>würde besichtigt haben | würden besichtigt haben<br>würdet besichtigt haben<br>würden besichtigt haben |

## EXAMPLE

Morgen werden sie das alte Rathaus besichtigen. Tomorrow they're going to take a tour of the old city hall.

**besiegen**
to conquer, to defeat
**Auxiliary verb:** haben **Past participle:** besiegt
**Imperative:** Besiege! Besiegt! Besiegen Sie!

| Mode | Simple Tenses | | Compound Tenses | |
|---|---|---|---|---|
| | *Singular* | *Plural* | *Singular* | *Plural* |
| Indicative | **Present** | | **Present Perfect** | |
| | besiege<br>besiegst<br>besiegt | besiegen<br>besiegt<br>besiegen | habe besiegt<br>hast besiegt<br>hat besiegt | haben besiegt<br>habt besiegt<br>haben besiegt |
| | **Past** | | **Past Perfect** | |
| | besiegte<br>besiegtest<br>besiegte | besiegten<br>besiegtet<br>besiegten | hatte besiegt<br>hattest besiegt<br>hatte besiegt | hatten besiegt<br>hattet besiegt<br>hatten besiegt |
| | **Future** | | **Future Perfect** | |
| | werde besiegen<br>wirst besiegen<br>wird besiegen | werden besiegen<br>werdet besiegen<br>werden besiegen | werde besiegt haben<br>wirst besiegt haben<br>wird besiegt haben | werden besiegt haben<br>werdet besiegt haben<br>werden besiegt haben |
| Subjunctive | **Present** | | **Present Perfect** | |
| | besiege<br>besiegest<br>besiege | besiegen<br>besieget<br>besiegen | habe besiegt<br>habest besiegt<br>habe besiegt | haben besiegt<br>habet besiegt<br>haben besiegt |
| | **Past** | | **Past Perfect** | |
| | besiegte<br>besiegtest<br>besiegte | besiegten<br>besiegtet<br>besiegten | hätte besiegt<br>hättest besiegt<br>hätte besiegt | hätten besiegt<br>hättet besiegt<br>hätten besiegt |
| | **Future** | | **Future Perfect** | |
| | werde besiegen<br>werdest besiegen<br>werde besiegen | werden besiegen<br>werdet besiegen<br>werden besiegen | werde besiegt haben<br>werdest besiegt haben<br>werde besiegt haben | werden besiegt haben<br>werdet besiegt haben<br>werden besiegt haben |
| | **Present and Future Conditional** | | **Past Conditional** | |
| | würde besiegen<br>würdest besiegen<br>würde besiegen | würden besiegen<br>würdet besiegen<br>würden besiegen | würde besiegt haben<br>würdest besiegt haben<br>würde besiegt haben | würden besiegt haben<br>würdet besiegt haben<br>würden besiegt haben |

## EXAMPLES

Warum konnten sie den Gegner nicht besiegen? — Why couldn't they defeat the opponent?
Der Feind ist endlich besiegt worden. — The enemy has finally been conquered.

**sich besinnen**
to recollect, to call to mind, to think of
**Auxiliary verb:** haben **Past participle:** besonnen
**Imperative:** Besinne dich! Besinnt euch! Besinnen Sie sich!

| Mode | Simple Tenses | | Compound Tenses | |
|---|---|---|---|---|
| | *Singular* | *Plural* | *Singular* | *Plural* |
| Indicative | **Present** | | **Present Perfect** | |
| | besinne<br>besinnst<br>besinnt | besinnen<br>besinnt<br>besinnen | habe besonnen<br>hast besonnen<br>hat besonnen | haben besonnen<br>habt besonnen<br>haben besonnen |
| | **Past** | | **Past Perfect** | |
| | besann<br>besannst<br>besann | besannen<br>besannt<br>besannen | hatte besonnen<br>hattest besonnen<br>hatte besonnen | hatten besonnen<br>hattet besonnen<br>hatten besonnen |
| | **Future** | | **Future Perfect** | |
| | werde besinnen<br>wirst besinnen<br>wird besinnen | werden besinnen<br>werdet besinnen<br>werden besinnen | werde besonnen haben<br>wirst besonnen haben<br>wird besonnen haben | werden besonnen haben<br>werdet besonnen haben<br>werden besonnen haben |
| Subjunctive | **Present** | | **Present Perfect** | |
| | besinne<br>besinnest<br>besinne | besinnen<br>besinnet<br>besinnen | habe besonnen<br>habest besonnen<br>habe besonnen | haben besonnen<br>habet besonnen<br>haben besonnen |
| | **Past** | | **Past Perfect** | |
| | besänne<br>besännest<br>besänne | besännen<br>besännet<br>besännen | hätte besonnen<br>hättest besonnen<br>hätte besonnen | hätten besonnen<br>hättet besonnen<br>hätten besonnen |
| | **Future** | | **Future Perfect** | |
| | werde besinnen<br>werdest besinnen<br>werde besinnen | werden besinnen<br>werdet besinnen<br>werden besinnen | werde besonnen haben<br>werdest besonnen haben<br>werde besonnen haben | werden besonnen haben<br>werdet besonnen haben<br>werden besonnen haben |
| | **Present and Future Conditional** | | **Past Conditional** | |
| | würde besinnen<br>würdest besinnen<br>würde besinnen | würden besinnen<br>würdet besinnen<br>würden besinnen | würde besonnen haben<br>würdest besonnen haben<br>würde besonnen haben | würden besonnen haben<br>würdet besonnen haben<br>würden besonnen haben |

## EXAMPLES

Er lief ins brennende Haus, ohne sich zu besinnen.
He ran into the burning house without thinking.

Ich besann mich auf meine Stärken.
I remembered what my strengths were.

**bestellen**
to order
**Auxiliary verb:** haben **Past participle:** bestellt
**Imperative:** Bestelle! Bestellt! Bestellen Sie!

| Mode | Simple Tenses | | Compound Tenses | |
|---|---|---|---|---|
| | *Singular* | *Plural* | *Singular* | *Plural* |
| Indicative | **Present** | | **Present Perfect** | |
| | bestelle<br>bestellst<br>bestellt | bestellen<br>bestellt<br>bestellen | habe bestellt<br>hast bestellt<br>hat bestellt | haben bestellt<br>habt bestellt<br>haben bestellt |
| | **Past** | | **Past Perfect** | |
| | bestellte<br>bestelltest<br>bestellte | bestellten<br>bestelltet<br>bestellten | hatte bestellt<br>hattest bestellt<br>hatte bestellt | hatten bestellt<br>hattet bestellt<br>hatten bestellt |
| | **Future** | | **Future Perfect** | |
| | werde bestellen<br>wirst bestellen<br>wird bestellen | werden bestellen<br>werdet bestellen<br>werden bestellen | werde bestellt haben<br>wirst bestellt haben<br>wird bestellt haben | werden bestellt haben<br>werdet bestellt haben<br>werden bestellt haben |
| Subjunctive | **Present** | | **Present Perfect** | |
| | bestelle<br>bestellest<br>bestelle | bestellen<br>bestellet<br>bestellen | habe bestellt<br>habest bestellt<br>habe bestellt | haben bestellt<br>habet bestellt<br>haben bestellt |
| | **Past** | | **Past Perfect** | |
| | bestellte<br>bestelltest<br>bestellte | bestellten<br>bestelltet<br>bestellten | hätte bestellt<br>hättest bestellt<br>hätte bestellt | hätten bestellt<br>hättet bestellt<br>hätten bestellt |
| | **Future** | | **Future Perfect** | |
| | werde bestellen<br>werdest bestellen<br>werde bestellen | werden bestellen<br>werdet bestellen<br>werden bestellen | werde bestellt haben<br>werdest bestellt haben<br>werde bestellt haben | werden bestellt haben<br>werdet bestellt haben<br>werden bestellt haben |
| | **Present and Future Conditional** | | **Past Conditional** | |
| | würde bestellen<br>würdest bestellen<br>würde bestellen | würden bestellen<br>würdet bestellen<br>würden bestellen | würde bestellt haben<br>würdest bestellt haben<br>würde bestellt haben | würden bestellt haben<br>würdet bestellt haben<br>würden bestellt haben |

**Note:** The verb *verhallen* has a regular conjugation like the one illustrated above but requires *sein* as its auxiliary in the perfect tenses.

## EXAMPLES

Herr Schmidt hat die teure Ware nicht bestellen wollen.
Mr. Schmidt didn't want to order the expensive goods.

Ich habe eine Bratwurst und ein Bier bestellt.
I ordered a sausage and a beer.

**bestimmen**
to decide, to determine
**Auxiliary verb:** haben **Past participle:** bestimmt
**Imperative:** Bestimme! Bestimmt! Bestimmen Sie!

| Mode | Simple Tenses | | Compound Tenses | |
|---|---|---|---|---|
| | *Singular* | *Plural* | *Singular* | *Plural* |
| Indicative | **Present** | | **Present Perfect** | |
| | bestimme<br>bestimmst<br>bestimmt | bestimmen<br>bestimmt<br>bestimmen | habe bestimmt<br>hast bestimmt<br>hat bestimmt | haben bestimmt<br>habt bestimmt<br>haben bestimmt |
| | **Past** | | **Past Perfect** | |
| | bestimmte<br>bestimmtest<br>bestimmte | bestimmten<br>bestimmtet<br>bestimmten | hatte bestimmt<br>hattest bestimmt<br>hatte bestimmt | hatten bestimmt<br>hattet bestimmt<br>hatten bestimmt |
| | **Future** | | **Future Perfect** | |
| | werde bestimmen<br>wirst bestimmen<br>wird bestimmen | werden bestimmen<br>werdet bestimmen<br>werden bestimmen | werde bestimmt haben<br>wirst bestimmt haben<br>wird bestimmt haben | werden bestimmt haben<br>werdet bestimmt haben<br>werden bestimmt haben |
| Subjunctive | **Present** | | **Present Perfect** | |
| | bestimme<br>bestimmest<br>bestimme | bestimmen<br>bestimmet<br>bestimmen | habe bestimmt<br>habest bestimmt<br>habe bestimmt | haben bestimmt<br>habet bestimmt<br>haben bestimmt |
| | **Past** | | **Past Perfect** | |
| | bestimmte<br>bestimmtest<br>bestimmte | bestimmten<br>bestimmtet<br>bestimmten | hätte bestimmt<br>hättest bestimmt<br>hätte bestimmt | hätten bestimmt<br>hättet bestimmt<br>hätten bestimmt |
| | **Future** | | **Future Perfect** | |
| | werde bestimmen<br>werdest bestimmen<br>werde bestimmen | werden bestimmen<br>werdet bestimmen<br>werden bestimmen | werde bestimmt haben<br>werdest bestimmt haben<br>werde bestimmt haben | werden bestimmt haben<br>werdet bestimmt haben<br>werden bestimmt haben |
| | **Present and Future Conditional** | | **Past Conditional** | |
| | würde bestimmen<br>würdest bestimmen<br>würde bestimmen | würden bestimmen<br>würdet bestimmen<br>würden bestimmen | würde bestimmt haben<br>würdest bestimmt haben<br>würde bestimmt haben | würden bestimmt haben<br>würdet bestimmt haben<br>würden bestimmt haben |

## EXAMPLES

Sie hat das Geld für mich bestimmt.
She intended the money for me.

Der Richter bestimmt, wann er aus dem Gefängnis entlassen werden kann.
The judge will decide when he can be released from prison.

**besuchen**
to visit, to attend
**Auxiliary verb:** haben **Past participle:** besucht
**Imperative:** Besuche! Besucht! Besuchen Sie!

| Mode | Simple Tenses | | Compound Tenses | |
|---|---|---|---|---|
| | *Singular* | *Plural* | *Singular* | *Plural* |
| Indicative | **Present** | | **Present Perfect** | |
| | besuche<br>besuchst<br>besucht | besuchen<br>besucht<br>besuchen | habe besucht<br>hast besucht<br>hat besucht | haben besucht<br>habt besucht<br>haben besucht |
| | **Past** | | **Past Perfect** | |
| | besuchte<br>besuchtest<br>besuchte | besuchten<br>besuchtet<br>besuchten | hatte besucht<br>hattest besucht<br>hatte besucht | hatten besucht<br>hattet besucht<br>hatten besucht |
| | **Future** | | **Future Perfect** | |
| | werde besuchen<br>wirst besuchen<br>wird besuchen | werden besuchen<br>werdet besuchen<br>werden besuchen | werde besucht haben<br>wirst besucht haben<br>wird besucht haben | werden besucht haben<br>werdet besucht haben<br>werden besucht haben |
| Subjunctive | **Present** | | **Present Perfect** | |
| | besuche<br>besuchest<br>besuche | besuchen<br>besuchet<br>besuchen | habe besucht<br>habest besucht<br>habe besucht | haben besucht<br>habet besucht<br>haben besucht |
| | **Past** | | **Past Perfect** | |
| | besuchte<br>besuchtest<br>besuchte | besuchten<br>besuchtet<br>besuchten | hätte besucht<br>hättest besucht<br>hätte besucht | hätten besucht<br>hättet besucht<br>hätten besucht |
| | **Future** | | **Future Perfect** | |
| | werde besuchen<br>werdest besuchen<br>werde besuchen | werden besuchen<br>werdet besuchen<br>werden besuchen | werde besucht haben<br>werdest besucht haben<br>werde besucht haben | werden besucht haben<br>werdet besucht haben<br>werden besucht haben |
| | **Present and Future Conditional** | | **Past Conditional** | |
| | würde besuchen<br>würdest besuchen<br>würde besuchen | würden besuchen<br>würdet besuchen<br>würden besuchen | würde besucht haben<br>würdest besucht haben<br>würde besucht haben | würden besucht haben<br>würdet besucht haben<br>würden besucht haben |

## EXAMPLES

Ich werde Onkel Heinrich im Krankenhaus besuchen.
I'm going to visit Uncle Heinrich in the hospital.

Sie besucht eine Schule in Rahlstedt.
She attends a school in Rahlstedt.

**beten**
to pray, to say in prayer
**Auxiliary verb:** haben **Past participle:** gebetet
**Imperative:** Bete! Betet! Beten Sie!

| Mode | Simple Tenses | | Compound Tenses | |
|---|---|---|---|---|
| | *Singular* | *Plural* | *Singular* | *Plural* |
| Indicative | **Present** | | **Present Perfect** | |
| | bete<br>betest<br>betet | beten<br>betet<br>beten | habe gebetet<br>hast gebetet<br>hat gebetet | haben gebetet<br>habt gebetet<br>haben gebetet |
| | **Past** | | **Past Perfect** | |
| | betete<br>betetest<br>betete | beteten<br>betetet<br>beteten | hatte gebetet<br>hattest gebetet<br>hatte gebetet | hatten gebetet<br>hattet gebetet<br>hatten gebetet |
| | **Future** | | **Future Perfect** | |
| | werde beten<br>wirst beten<br>wird beten | werden beten<br>werdet beten<br>werden beten | werde gebetet haben<br>wirst gebetet haben<br>wird gebetet haben | werden gebetet haben<br>werdet gebetet haben<br>werden gebetet haben |
| Subjunctive | **Present** | | **Present Perfect** | |
| | bete<br>betest<br>bete | beten<br>betet<br>beten | habe gebetet<br>habest gebetet<br>habe gebetet | haben gebetet<br>habet gebetet<br>haben gebetet |
| | **Past** | | **Past Perfect** | |
| | betete<br>betetest<br>betete | beteten<br>betetet<br>beteten | hätte gebetet<br>hättest gebetet<br>hätte gebetet | hätten gebetet<br>hättet gebetet<br>hätten gebetet |
| | **Future** | | **Future Perfect** | |
| | werde beten<br>werdest beten<br>werde beten | werden beten<br>werdet beten<br>werden beten | werde gebetet haben<br>werdest gebetet haben<br>werde gebetet haben | werden gebetet haben<br>werdet gebetet haben<br>werden gebetet haben |
| | **Present and Future Conditional** | | **Past Conditional** | |
| | würde beten<br>würdest beten<br>würde beten | würden beten<br>würdet beten<br>würden beten | würde gebetet haben<br>würdest gebetet haben<br>würde gebetet haben | würden gebetet haben<br>würdet gebetet haben<br>würden gebetet haben |

## EXAMPLES

Die arme Familie betet um Hilfe. — The poor family prays for help.
Die Kinder beten, bevor sie ins Bett gehen. — The children pray before going to bed.

**betrügen**
to cheat, to deceive
**Auxiliary verb:** haben **Past participle:** betrogen
**Imperative:** Betrüge! Betrügt! Betrügen Sie!

| Mode | Simple Tenses | | Compound Tenses | |
|---|---|---|---|---|
| | *Singular* | *Plural* | *Singular* | *Plural* |
| Indicative | **Present** | | **Present Perfect** | |
| | betrüge<br>betrügst<br>betrügt | betrügen<br>betrügt<br>betrügen | habe betrogen<br>hast betrogen<br>hat betrogen | haben betrogen<br>habt betrogen<br>haben betrogen |
| | **Past** | | **Past Perfect** | |
| | betrog<br>betrogst<br>betrog | betrogen<br>betrogt<br>betrogen | hatte betrogen<br>hattest betrogen<br>hatte betrogen | hatten betrogen<br>hattet betrogen<br>hatten betrogen |
| | **Future** | | **Future Perfect** | |
| | werde betrügen<br>wirst betrügen<br>wird betrügen | werden betrügen<br>werdet betrügen<br>werden betrügen | werde betrogen haben<br>wirst betrogen haben<br>wird betrogen haben | werden betrogen haben<br>werdet betrogen haben<br>werden betrogen haben |
| Subjunctive | **Present** | | **Present Perfect** | |
| | betrüge<br>betrügest<br>betrüge | betrügen<br>betrüget<br>betrügen | habe betrogen<br>habest betrogen<br>habe betrogen | haben betrogen<br>habet betrogen<br>haben betrogen |
| | **Past** | | **Past Perfect** | |
| | betröge<br>betrögest<br>betröge | betrögen<br>betröget<br>betrögen | hätte betrogen<br>hättest betrogen<br>hätte betrogen | hätten betrogen<br>hättet betrogen<br>hätten betrogen |
| | **Future** | | **Future Perfect** | |
| | werde betrügen<br>werdest betrügen<br>werde betrügen | werden betrügen<br>werdet betrügen<br>werden betrügen | werde betrogen haben<br>werdest betrogen haben<br>werde betrogen haben | werden betrogen haben<br>werdet betrogen haben<br>werden betrogen haben |
| | **Present and Future Conditional** | | **Past Conditional** | |
| | würde betrügen<br>würdest betrügen<br>würde betrügen | würden betrügen<br>würdet betrügen<br>würden betrügen | würde betrogen haben<br>würdest betrogen haben<br>würde betrogen haben | würden betrogen haben<br>würdet betrogen haben<br>würden betrogen haben |

## EXAMPLES

Der Wirt ist um 50 Euro betrogen worden.
The innkeeper was cheated out of 50 euros.

Der Student betrog in seiner Prüfung.
The student cheated on his exam.

**betteln**
to beg
**Auxiliary verb:** haben **Past participle:** gebettelt
**Imperative:** Bettele! Bettelt! Betteln Sie!

| Mode | Simple Tenses | | Compound Tenses | |
|---|---|---|---|---|
| | *Singular* | *Plural* | *Singular* | *Plural* |
| Indicative | **Present** | | **Present Perfect** | |
| | bettele<br>bettelst<br>bettelt | betteln<br>bettelt<br>betteln | habe gebettelt<br>hast gebettelt<br>hat gebettelt | haben gebettelt<br>habt gebettelt<br>haben gebettelt |
| | **Past** | | **Past Perfect** | |
| | bettelte<br>betteltest<br>bettelte | bettelten<br>betteltet<br>bettelten | hatte gebettelt<br>hattest gebettelt<br>hatte gebettelt | hatten gebettelt<br>hattet gebettelt<br>hatten gebettelt |
| | **Future** | | **Future Perfect** | |
| | werde betteln<br>wirst betteln<br>wird betteln | werden betteln<br>werdet betteln<br>werden betteln | werde gebettelt haben<br>wirst gebettelt haben<br>wird gebettelt haben | werden gebettelt haben<br>werdet gebettelt haben<br>werden gebettelt haben |
| Subjunctive | **Present** | | **Present Perfect** | |
| | bettele<br>bettlest<br>bettele | betteln<br>bettelt<br>betteln | habe gebettelt<br>habest gebettelt<br>habe gebettelt | haben gebettelt<br>habet gebettelt<br>haben gebettelt |
| | **Past** | | **Past Perfect** | |
| | bettelte<br>betteltest<br>bettelte | bettelten<br>betteltet<br>bettelten | hätte gebettelt<br>hättest gebettelt<br>hätte gebettelt | hätten gebettelt<br>hättet gebettelt<br>hätten gebettelt |
| | **Future** | | **Future Perfect** | |
| | werde betteln<br>werdest betteln<br>werde betteln | werden betteln<br>werdet betteln<br>werden betteln | werde gebettelt haben<br>werdest gebettelt haben<br>werde gebettelt haben | werden gebettelt haben<br>werdet gebettelt haben<br>werden gebettelt haben |
| | **Present and Future Conditional** | | **Past Conditional** | |
| | würde betteln<br>würdest betteln<br>würde betteln | würden betteln<br>würdet betteln<br>würden betteln | würde gebettelt haben<br>würdest gebettelt haben<br>würde gebettelt haben | würden gebettelt haben<br>würdet gebettelt haben<br>würden gebettelt haben |

## EXAMPLES

Der Hund bettelte um ein Stückchen von meiner Schokolade.
The dog begged for a little piece of my chocolate.

Betteln ist verboten.
Begging is not allowed.

**beugen (sich)**
to bend
**Auxiliary verb:** haben **Past participle:** gebeugt
**Imperative:** Beuge! Beugt! Beugen Sie!

| Mode | Simple Tenses | | Compound Tenses | |
|---|---|---|---|---|
| | *Singular* | *Plural* | *Singular* | *Plural* |
| Indicative | **Present** | | **Present Perfect** | |
| | beuge<br>beugst<br>beugt | beugen<br>beugt<br>beugen | habe gebeugt<br>hast gebeugt<br>hat gebeugt | haben gebeugt<br>habt gebeugt<br>haben gebeugt |
| | **Past** | | **Past Perfect** | |
| | beugte<br>beugtest<br>beugte | beugten<br>beugtet<br>beugten | hatte gebeugt<br>hattest gebeugt<br>hatte gebeugt | hatten gebeugt<br>hattet gebeugt<br>hatten gebeugt |
| | **Future** | | **Future Perfect** | |
| | werde beugen<br>wirst beugen<br>wird beugen | werden beugen<br>werdet beugen<br>werden beugen | werde gebeugt haben<br>wirst gebeugt haben<br>wird gebeugt haben | werden gebeugt haben<br>werdet gebeugt haben<br>werden gebeugt haben |
| Subjunctive | **Present** | | **Present Perfect** | |
| | beuge<br>beugest<br>beuge | beugen<br>beuget<br>beugen | habe gebeugt<br>habest gebeugt<br>habe gebeugt | haben gebeugt<br>habet gebeugt<br>haben gebeugt |
| | **Past** | | **Past Perfect** | |
| | beugte<br>beugtest<br>beugte | beugten<br>beugtet<br>beugten | hätte gebeugt<br>hättest gebeugt<br>hätte gebeugt | hätten gebeugt<br>hättet gebeugt<br>hätten gebeugt |
| | **Future** | | **Future Perfect** | |
| | werde beugen<br>werdest beugen<br>werde beugen | werden beugen<br>werdet beugen<br>werden beugen | werde gebeugt haben<br>werdest gebeugt haben<br>werde gebeugt haben | werden gebeugt haben<br>werdet gebeugt haben<br>werden gebeugt haben |
| | **Present and Future Conditional** | | **Past Conditional** | |
| | würde beugen<br>würdest beugen<br>würde beugen | würden beugen<br>würdet beugen<br>würden beugen | würde gebeugt haben<br>würdest gebeugt haben<br>würde gebeugt haben | würden gebeugt haben<br>würdet gebeugt haben<br>würden gebeugt haben |

## EXAMPLES

Beuge dich nicht aus dem Fenster! — Don't lean out the window.
Die Bäume beugten sich im Wind. — The trees bent in the wind.

**beurteilen**
to judge, to criticize
**Auxiliary verb:** haben **Past participle:** beurteilt
**Imperative:** Beurteile! Beurteilt! Beurteilen Sie!

| Mode | Simple Tenses | | Compound Tenses | |
|---|---|---|---|---|
| | *Singular* | *Plural* | *Singular* | *Plural* |
| Indicative | **Present** | | **Present Perfect** | |
| | beurteile<br>beurteilst<br>beurteilt | beurteilen<br>beurteilt<br>beurteilen | habe beurteilt<br>hast beurteilt<br>hat beurteilt | haben beurteilt<br>habt beurteilt<br>haben beurteilt |
| | **Past** | | **Past Perfect** | |
| | beurteilte<br>beurteiltest<br>beurteilte | beurteilten<br>beurteiltet<br>beurteilten | hatte beurteilt<br>hattest beurteilt<br>hatte beurteilt | hatten beurteilt<br>hattet beurteilt<br>hatten beurteilt |
| | **Future** | | **Future Perfect** | |
| | werde beurteilen<br>wirst beurteilen<br>wird beurteilen | werden beurteilen<br>werdet beurteilen<br>werden beurteilen | werde beurteilt haben<br>wirst beurteilt haben<br>wird beurteilt haben | werden beurteilt haben<br>werdet beurteilt haben<br>werden beurteilt haben |
| Subjunctive | **Present** | | **Present Perfect** | |
| | beurteile<br>beurteilest<br>beurteile | beurteilen<br>beurteilet<br>beurteilen | habe beurteilt<br>habest beurteilt<br>habe beurteilt | haben beurteilt<br>habet beurteilt<br>haben beurteilt |
| | **Past** | | **Past Perfect** | |
| | beurteilte<br>beurteiltest<br>beurteilte | beurteilten<br>beurteiltet<br>beurteilten | hätte beurteilt<br>hättest beurteilt<br>hätte beurteilt | hätten beurteilt<br>hättet beurteilt<br>hätten beurteilt |
| | **Future** | | **Future Perfect** | |
| | werde beurteilen<br>werdest beurteilen<br>werde beurteilen | werden beurteilen<br>werdet beurteilen<br>werden beurteilen | werde beurteilt haben<br>werdest beurteilt haben<br>werde beurteilt haben | werden beurteilt haben<br>werdet beurteilt haben<br>werden beurteilt haben |
| | **Present and Future Conditional** | | **Past Conditional** | |
| | würde beurteilen<br>würdest beurteilen<br>würde beurteilen | würden beurteilen<br>würdet beurteilen<br>würden beurteilen | würde beurteilt haben<br>würdest beurteilt haben<br>würde beurteilt haben | würden beurteilt haben<br>würdet beurteilt haben<br>würden beurteilt haben |

## EXAMPLES

Wie hat er die Situation beurteilt?
Der Rechtsanwalt beurteilte die Lage als hoffnungslos.

How did he judge the situation?
The lawyer judged the circumstances as hopeless.

**bewegen (sich) [1]**
to move, to budge
**Auxiliary verb:** haben **Past participle:** bewegt
**Imperative:** Bewege! Bewegt! Bewegen Sie!

| Mode | Simple Tenses | | Compound Tenses | |
|---|---|---|---|---|
| | *Singular* | *Plural* | *Singular* | *Plural* |
| Indicative | **Present** | | **Present Perfect** | |
| | bewege<br>bewegst<br>bewegt | bewegen<br>bewegt<br>bewegen | habe bewegt<br>hast bewegt<br>hat bewegt | haben bewegt<br>habt bewegt<br>haben bewegt |
| | **Past** | | **Past Perfect** | |
| | bewegte<br>bewegtest<br>bewegte | bewegten<br>bewegtet<br>bewegten | hatte bewegt<br>hattest bewegt<br>hatte bewegt | hatten bewegt<br>hattet bewegt<br>hatten bewegt |
| | **Future** | | **Future Perfect** | |
| | werde bewegen<br>wirst bewegen<br>wird bewegen | werden bewegen<br>werdet bewegen<br>werden bewegen | werde bewegt haben<br>wirst bewegt haben<br>wird bewegt haben | werden bewegt haben<br>werdet bewegt haben<br>werden bewegt haben |
| Subjunctive | **Present** | | **Present Perfect** | |
| | bewege<br>bewegest<br>bewege | bewegen<br>beweget<br>bewegen | habe bewegt<br>habest bewegt<br>habe bewegt | haben bewegt<br>habet bewegt<br>haben bewegt |
| | **Past** | | **Past Perfect** | |
| | bewegte<br>bewegtest<br>bewegte | bewegten<br>bewegtet<br>bewegten | hätte bewegt<br>hättest bewegt<br>hätte bewegt | hätten bewegt<br>hättet bewegt<br>hätten bewegt |
| | **Future** | | **Future Perfect** | |
| | werde bewegen<br>werdest bewegen<br>werde bewegen | werden bewegen<br>werdet bewegen<br>werden bewegen | werde bewegt haben<br>werdest bewegt haben<br>werde bewegt haben | werden bewegt haben<br>werdet bewegt haben<br>werden bewegt haben |
| | **Present and Future Conditional** | | **Past Conditional** | |
| | würde bewegen<br>würdest bewegen<br>würde bewegen | würden bewegen<br>würdet bewegen<br>würden bewegen | würde bewegt haben<br>würdest bewegt haben<br>würde bewegt haben | würden bewegt haben<br>würdet bewegt haben<br>würden bewegt haben |

**Note:** Do not confuse this verb with the one that follows. Both have the infinitive *bewegen*. This verb has a regular conjugation.

## EXAMPLES

Der verwundete Mann versucht sich zu bewegen. — The wounded man tries to move.
Der Tisch ließ sich einfach nicht bewegen. — The table simply wouldn't budge.

**bewegen [2]**
to prompt, to induce
**Auxiliary verb:** haben **Past participle:** bewogen
**Imperative:** Bewege! Bewegt! Bewegen Sie!

| Mode | Simple Tenses | | Compound Tenses | |
|---|---|---|---|---|
| | *Singular* | *Plural* | *Singular* | *Plural* |
| Indicative | **Present** | | **Present Perfect** | |
| | bewege<br>bewegst<br>bewegt | bewegen<br>bewegt<br>bewegen | habe bewogen<br>hast bewogen<br>hat bewogen | haben bewogen<br>habt bewogen<br>haben bewogen |
| | **Past** | | **Past Perfect** | |
| | bewog<br>bewogst<br>bewog | bewogen<br>bewogt<br>bewogen | hatte bewogen<br>hattest bewogen<br>hatte bewogen | hatten bewogen<br>hattet bewogen<br>hatten bewogen |
| | **Future** | | **Future Perfect** | |
| | werde bewegen<br>wirst bewegen<br>wird bewegen | werden bewegen<br>werdet bewegen<br>werden bewegen | werde bewogen haben<br>wirst bewogen haben<br>wird bewogen haben | werden bewogen haben<br>werdet bewogen haben<br>werden bewogen haben |
| Subjunctive | **Present** | | **Present Perfect** | |
| | bewege<br>bewegest<br>bewege | bewegen<br>beweget<br>bewegen | habe bewogen<br>habest bewogen<br>habe bewogen | haben bewogen<br>habet bewogen<br>haben bewogen |
| | **Past** | | **Past Perfect** | |
| | bewöge<br>bewögest<br>bewöge | bewögen<br>bewöget<br>bewögen | hätte bewogen<br>hättest bewogen<br>hätte bewogen | hätten bewogen<br>hättet bewogen<br>hätten bewogen |
| | **Future** | | **Future Perfect** | |
| | werde bewegen<br>werdest bewegen<br>werde bewegen | werden bewegen<br>werdet bewegen<br>werden bewegen | werde bewogen haben<br>werdest bewogen haben<br>werde bewogen haben | werden bewogen haben<br>werdet bewogen haben<br>werden bewogen haben |
| | **Present and Future Conditional** | | **Past Conditional** | |
| | würde bewegen<br>würdest bewegen<br>würde bewegen | würden bewegen<br>würdet bewegen<br>würden bewegen | würde bewogen haben<br>würdest bewogen haben<br>würde bewogen haben | würden bewogen haben<br>würdet bewogen haben<br>würden bewogen haben |

**Note:** Do not confuse this verb with the preceding one. Both have the infinitive *bewegen*. This verb has an irregular conjugation.

## EXAMPLE

Was hat dich dazu bewogen? — What prompted you to do that?

**beweisen**

to prove

**Auxiliary verb:** haben **Past participle:** bewiesen

**Imperative:** Beweise! Beweist! Beweisen Sie!

| Mode | Simple Tenses | | Compound Tenses | |
|---|---|---|---|---|
| | *Singular* | *Plural* | *Singular* | *Plural* |
| Indicative | **Present** | | **Present Perfect** | |
| | beweise<br>beweist<br>beweist | beweisen<br>beweist<br>beweisen | habe bewiesen<br>hast bewiesen<br>hat bewiesen | haben bewiesen<br>habt bewiesen<br>haben bewiesen |
| | **Past** | | **Past Perfect** | |
| | bewies<br>bewiesest<br>bewies | bewiesen<br>bewiest<br>bewiesen | hatte bewiesen<br>hattest bewiesen<br>hatte bewiesen | hatten bewiesen<br>hattet bewiesen<br>hatten bewiesen |
| | **Future** | | **Future Perfect** | |
| | werde beweisen<br>wirst beweisen<br>wird beweisen | werden beweisen<br>werdet beweisen<br>werden beweisen | werde bewiesen haben<br>wirst bewiesen haben<br>wird bewiesen haben | werden bewiesen haben<br>werdet bewiesen haben<br>werden bewiesen haben |
| Subjunctive | **Present** | | **Present Perfect** | |
| | beweise<br>beweisest<br>beweise | beweisen<br>beweiset<br>beweisen | habe bewiesen<br>habest bewiesen<br>habe bewiesen | haben bewiesen<br>habet bewiesen<br>haben bewiesen |
| | **Past** | | **Past Perfect** | |
| | bewiese<br>bewiesest<br>bewiese | bewiesen<br>bewieset<br>bewiesen | hätte bewiesen<br>hättest bewiesen<br>hätte bewiesen | hätten bewiesen<br>hättet bewiesen<br>hätten bewiesen |
| | **Future** | | **Future Perfect** | |
| | werde beweisen<br>werdest beweisen<br>werde beweisen | werden beweisen<br>werdet beweisen<br>werden beweisen | werde bewiesen haben<br>werdest bewiesen haben<br>werde bewiesen haben | werden bewiesen haben<br>werdet bewiesen haben<br>werden bewiesen haben |
| | **Present and Future Conditional** | | **Past Conditional** | |
| | würde beweisen<br>würdest beweisen<br>würde beweisen | würden beweisen<br>würdet beweisen<br>würden beweisen | würde bewiesen haben<br>würdest bewiesen haben<br>würde bewiesen haben | würden bewiesen haben<br>würdet bewiesen haben<br>würden bewiesen haben |

## EXAMPLES

| | |
|---|---|
| Ihre Schuld muss vor Gericht bewiesen werden. | Your guilt has to be proven in court. |
| Wie können Sie so eine merkwürdige Theorie beweisen? | How can you prove such a strange theory? |

**bezahlen**
to pay
**Auxiliary verb:** haben **Past participle:** bezahlt
**Imperative:** Bezahle! Bezahlt! Bezahlen Sie!

| Mode | Simple Tenses | | Compound Tenses | |
|---|---|---|---|---|
| | *Singular* | *Plural* | *Singular* | *Plural* |
| Indicative | **Present** | | **Present Perfect** | |
| | bezahle<br>bezahlst<br>bezahlt | bezahlen<br>bezahlt<br>bezahlen | habe bezahlt<br>hast bezahlt<br>hat bezahlt | haben bezahlt<br>habt bezahlt<br>haben bezahlt |
| | **Past** | | **Past Perfect** | |
| | bezahlte<br>bezahltest<br>bezahlte | bezahlten<br>bezahltet<br>bezahlten | hatte bezahlt<br>hattest bezahlt<br>hatte bezahlt | hatten bezahlt<br>hattet bezahlt<br>hatten bezahlt |
| | **Future** | | **Future Perfect** | |
| | werde bezahlen<br>wirst bezahlen<br>wird bezahlen | werden bezahlen<br>werdet bezahlen<br>werden bezahlen | werde bezahlt haben<br>wirst bezahlt haben<br>wird bezahlt haben | werden bezahlt haben<br>werdet bezahlt haben<br>werden bezahlt haben |
| Subjunctive | **Present** | | **Present Perfect** | |
| | bezahle<br>bezahlest<br>bezahle | bezahlen<br>bezahlet<br>bezahlen | habe bezahlt<br>habest bezahlt<br>habe bezahlt | haben bezahlt<br>habet bezahlt<br>haben bezahlt |
| | **Past** | | **Past Perfect** | |
| | bezahlte<br>bezahltest<br>bezahlte | bezahlten<br>bezahltet<br>bezahlten | hätte bezahlt<br>hättest bezahlt<br>hätte bezahlt | hätten bezahlt<br>hättet bezahlt<br>hätten bezahlt |
| | **Future** | | **Future Perfect** | |
| | werde bezahlen<br>werdest bezahlen<br>werde bezahlen | werden bezahlen<br>werdet bezahlen<br>werden bezahlen | werde bezahlt haben<br>werdest bezahlt haben<br>werde bezahlt haben | werden bezahlt haben<br>werdet bezahlt haben<br>werden bezahlt haben |
| | **Present and Future Conditional** | | **Past Conditional** | |
| | würde bezahlen<br>würdest bezahlen<br>würde bezahlen | würden bezahlen<br>würdet bezahlen<br>würden bezahlen | würde bezahlt haben<br>würdest bezahlt haben<br>würde bezahlt haben | würden bezahlt haben<br>würdet bezahlt haben<br>würden bezahlt haben |

## EXAMPLES

Wo kann ich diese Sachen bezahlen?
Er hat schon im Voraus bezahlt.

Where can I pay for these things?
He already paid in advance.

**biegen**
to bend, to curve
**Auxiliary verb:** haben **Past participle:** gebogen
**Imperative:** Biege! Biegt! Biegen Sie!

| Mode | Simple Tenses | | Compound Tenses | |
|---|---|---|---|---|
| | *Singular* | *Plural* | *Singular* | *Plural* |
| Indicative | **Present** | | **Present Perfect** | |
| | biege<br>biegst<br>biegt | biegen<br>biegt<br>biegen | habe gebogen<br>hast gebogen<br>hat gebogen | haben gebogen<br>habt gebogen<br>haben gebogen |
| | **Past** | | **Past Perfect** | |
| | bog<br>bogst<br>bog | bogen<br>bogt<br>bogen | hatte gebogen<br>hattest gebogen<br>hatte gebogen | hatten gebogen<br>hattet gebogen<br>hatten gebogen |
| | **Future** | | **Future Perfect** | |
| | werde biegen<br>wirst biegen<br>wird biegen | werden biegen<br>werdet biegen<br>werden biegen | werde gebogen haben<br>wirst gebogen haben<br>wird gebogen haben | werden gebogen haben<br>werdet gebogen haben<br>werden gebogen haben |
| Subjunctive | **Present** | | **Present Perfect** | |
| | biege<br>biegest<br>biege | biegen<br>bieget<br>biegen | habe gebogen<br>habest gebogen<br>habe gebogen | haben gebogen<br>habet gebogen<br>haben gebogen |
| | **Past** | | **Past Perfect** | |
| | böge<br>bögest<br>böge | bögen<br>böget<br>bögen | hätte gebogen<br>hättest gebogen<br>hätte gebogen | hätten gebogen<br>hättet gebogen<br>hätten gebogen |
| | **Future** | | **Future Perfect** | |
| | werde biegen<br>werdest biegen<br>werde biegen | werden biegen<br>werdet biegen<br>werden biegen | werde gebogen haben<br>werdest gebogen haben<br>werde gebogen haben | werden gebogen haben<br>werdet gebogen haben<br>werden gebogen haben |
| | **Present and Future Conditional** | | **Past Conditional** | |
| | würde biegen<br>würdest biegen<br>würde biegen | würden biegen<br>würdet biegen<br>würden biegen | würde gebogen haben<br>würdest gebogen haben<br>würde gebogen haben | würden gebogen haben<br>würdet gebogen haben<br>würden gebogen haben |

## EXAMPLES

Die eiserne Stange ließ sich nicht biegen. — The iron post couldn't be bent.
Das Auto bog langsam um die Ecke. — The car slowly turned the corner.

**bieten**
to offer
**Auxiliary verb:** haben **Past participle:** geboten
**Imperative:** Biete! Bietet! Bieten Sie!

| Mode | Simple Tenses | | Compound Tenses | |
|---|---|---|---|---|
| | *Singular* | *Plural* | *Singular* | *Plural* |
| Indicative | **Present** | | **Present Perfect** | |
| | biete<br>bietest<br>bietet | bieten<br>bietet<br>bieten | habe geboten<br>hast geboten<br>hat geboten | haben geboten<br>habt geboten<br>haben geboten |
| | **Past** | | **Past Perfect** | |
| | bot<br>botest<br>bot | boten<br>botet<br>boten | hatte geboten<br>hattest geboten<br>hatte geboten | hatten geboten<br>hattet geboten<br>hatten geboten |
| | **Future** | | **Future Perfect** | |
| | werde bieten<br>wirst bieten<br>wird bieten | werden bieten<br>werdet bieten<br>werden bieten | werde geboten haben<br>wirst geboten haben<br>wird geboten haben | werden geboten haben<br>werdet geboten haben<br>werden geboten haben |
| Subjunctive | **Present** | | **Present Perfect** | |
| | biete<br>bietest<br>biete | bieten<br>bietet<br>bieten | habe geboten<br>habest geboten<br>habe geboten | haben geboten<br>habet geboten<br>haben geboten |
| | **Past** | | **Past Perfect** | |
| | böte<br>bötest<br>böte | böten<br>bötet<br>boten | hätte geboten<br>hättest geboten<br>hätte geboten | hätten geboten<br>hättet geboten<br>hätten geboten |
| | **Future** | | **Future Perfect** | |
| | werde bieten<br>werdest bieten<br>werde bieten | werden bieten<br>werdet bieten<br>werden bieten | werde geboten haben<br>werdest geboten haben<br>werde geboten haben | werden geboten haben<br>werdet geboten haben<br>werden geboten haben |
| | **Present and Future Conditional** | | **Past Conditional** | |
| | würde bieten<br>würdest bieten<br>würde bieten | würden bieten<br>würdet bieten<br>würden bieten | würde geboten haben<br>würdest geboten haben<br>würde geboten haben | würden geboten haben<br>würdet geboten haben<br>würden geboten haben |

**Note:** With inseparable prefixes, the principal parts of this verb are, for example, *gebietet, gebot, hat geboten.* With separable prefixes, the principal parts are, for example, *bietet an, bot an, hat angeboten.* The verb *triefen* has a similar conjugation and the following principal parts: *trieft, troff, ist getroffen* (sometimes *getrieft*).

## EXAMPLES

| | |
|---|---|
| Ich muss bereit sein, wenn sich eine Gelegenheit bietet. | I have to be ready if an opportunity arises. |
| Das Leben in diesem Dorf bietet nichts. | Life in this village offers nothing. |

**bilden**

to form, to shape, to model

**Auxiliary verb:** haben **Past participle:** gebildet

**Imperative:** Bilde! Bildet! Bilden Sie!

| Mode | Simple Tenses | | Compound Tenses | |
|---|---|---|---|---|
| | *Singular* | *Plural* | *Singular* | *Plural* |
| Indicative | **Present** | | **Present Perfect** | |
| | bilde<br>bildest<br>bildet | bilden<br>bildet<br>bilden | habe gebildet<br>hast gebildet<br>hat gebildet | haben gebildet<br>habt gebildet<br>haben gebildet |
| | **Past** | | **Past Perfect** | |
| | bildete<br>bildetest<br>bildete | bildeten<br>bildetet<br>bildeten | hatte gebildet<br>hattest gebildet<br>hatte gebildet | hatten gebildet<br>hattet gebildet<br>hatten gebildet |
| | **Future** | | **Future Perfect** | |
| | werde bilden<br>wirst bilden<br>wird bilden | werden bilden<br>werdet bilden<br>werden bilden | werde gebildet haben<br>wirst gebildet haben<br>wird gebildet haben | werden gebildet haben<br>werdet gebildet haben<br>werden gebildet haben |
| Subjunctive | **Present** | | **Present Perfect** | |
| | bilde<br>bildest<br>bilde | bilden<br>bildet<br>bilden | habe gebildet<br>habest gebildet<br>habe gebildet | haben gebildet<br>habet gebildet<br>haben gebildet |
| | **Past** | | **Past Perfect** | |
| | bildete<br>bildetest<br>bildete | bildeten<br>bildetet<br>bildeten | hätte gebildet<br>hättest gebildet<br>hätte gebildet | hätten gebildet<br>hättet gebildet<br>hätten gebildet |
| | **Future** | | **Future Perfect** | |
| | werde bilden<br>werdest bilden<br>werde bilden | werden bilden<br>werdet bilden<br>werden bilden | werde gebildet haben<br>werdest gebildet haben<br>werde gebildet haben | werden gebildet haben<br>werdet gebildet haben<br>werden gebildet haben |
| | **Present and Future Conditional** | | **Past Conditional** | |
| | würde bilden<br>würdest bilden<br>würde bilden | würden bilden<br>würdet bilden<br>würden bilden | würde gebildet haben<br>würdest gebildet haben<br>würde gebildet haben | würden gebildet haben<br>würdet gebildet haben<br>würden gebildet haben |

## EXAMPLES

| | |
|---|---|
| Im Garten haben die Kinder einen Kreis gebildet. | The children formed a circle in the garden. |
| Zuerst bildet der Bildhauer eine Figur aus Wachs. | First the sculptor forms a figure out of wax. |

**binden**
to tie, to bind
**Auxiliary verb:** haben **Past participle:** gebunden
**Imperative:** Binde! Bindet! Binden Sie!

| Mode | Simple Tenses | | Compound Tenses | |
|---|---|---|---|---|
| | *Singular* | *Plural* | *Singular* | *Plural* |
| Indicative | **Present** | | **Present Perfect** | |
| | binde<br>bindest<br>bindet | binden<br>bindet<br>binden | habe gebunden<br>hast gebunden<br>hat gebunden | haben gebunden<br>habt gebunden<br>haben gebunden |
| | **Past** | | **Past Perfect** | |
| | band<br>bandest<br>band | banden<br>bandet<br>banden | hatte gebunden<br>hattest gebunden<br>hatte gebunden | hatten gebunden<br>hattet gebunden<br>hatten gebunden |
| | **Future** | | **Future Perfect** | |
| | werde binden<br>wirst binden<br>wird binden | werden binden<br>werdet binden<br>werden binden | werde gebunden haben<br>wirst gebunden haben<br>wird gebunden haben | werden gebunden haben<br>werdet gebunden haben<br>werden gebunden haben |
| Subjunctive | **Present** | | **Present Perfect** | |
| | binde<br>bindest<br>binde | binden<br>bindet<br>binden | habe gebunden<br>habest gebunden<br>habe gebunden | haben gebunden<br>habet gebunden<br>haben gebunden |
| | **Past** | | **Past Perfect** | |
| | bände<br>bändest<br>bände | bänden<br>bändet<br>bänden | hätte gebunden<br>hättest gebunden<br>hätte gebunden | hätten gebunden<br>hättet gebunden<br>hätten gebunden |
| | **Future** | | **Future Perfect** | |
| | werde binden<br>werdest binden<br>werde binden | werden binden<br>werdet binden<br>werden binden | werde gebunden haben<br>werdest gebunden haben<br>werde gebunden haben | werden gebunden haben<br>werdet gebunden haben<br>werden gebunden haben |
| | **Present and Future Conditional** | | **Past Conditional** | |
| | würde binden<br>würdest binden<br>würde binden | würden binden<br>würdet binden<br>würden binden | würde gebunden haben<br>würdest gebunden haben<br>würde gebunden haben | würden gebunden haben<br>würdet gebunden haben<br>würden gebunden haben |

## EXAMPLES

Kannst du mir helfen, diesen Schlips zu binden?
Mein Ehrenwort ist bindend.
Ich fühle mich an mein Versprechen gebunden.

Can you help me tie this tie?
My word of honor is binding.
I feel bound to my promise.

**bitten**

to ask, to request, to beg

**Auxiliary verb:** haben **Past participle:** gebeten

**Imperative:** Bitte! Bittet! Bitten Sie!

| Mode | Simple Tenses | | Compound Tenses | |
|---|---|---|---|---|
| | *Singular* | *Plural* | *Singular* | *Plural* |
| Indicative | **Present** | | **Present Perfect** | |
| | bitte<br>bittest<br>bittet | biten<br>bittet<br>bitten | habe gebeten<br>hast gebeten<br>hat gebeten | haben gebeten<br>habt gebeten<br>haben gebeten |
| | **Past** | | **Past Perfect** | |
| | bat<br>batest<br>bat | baten<br>batet<br>baten | hatte gebeten<br>hattest gebeten<br>hatte gebeten | hatten gebeten<br>hattet gebeten<br>hatten gebeten |
| | **Future** | | **Future Perfect** | |
| | werde bitten<br>wirst bitten<br>wird bitten | werden bitten<br>werdet bitten<br>werden bitten | werde gebeten haben<br>wirst gebeten haben<br>wird gebeten haben | werden gebeten haben<br>werdet gebeten haben<br>werden gebeten haben |
| Subjunctive | **Present** | | **Present Perfect** | |
| | bitte<br>bittest<br>bitte | bitten<br>bittet<br>bitten | habe gebeten<br>habest gebeten<br>habe gebeten | haben gebeten<br>habet gebeten<br>haben gebeten |
| | **Past** | | **Past Perfect** | |
| | bäte<br>bätest<br>bäte | bäten<br>bätet<br>bäten | hätte gebeten<br>hättest gebeten<br>hätte gebeten | hätten gebeten<br>hättet gebeten<br>hätten gebeten |
| | **Future** | | **Future Perfect** | |
| | werde bitten<br>werdest bitten<br>werde bitten | werden bitten<br>werdet bitten<br>werden bitten | werde gebeten haben<br>werdest gebeten haben<br>werde gebeten haben | werden gebeten haben<br>werdet gebeten haben<br>werden gebeten haben |
| | **Present and Future Conditional** | | **Past Conditional** | |
| | würde bitten<br>würdest bitten<br>würde bitten | würden bitten<br>würdet bitten<br>würden bitten | würde gebeten haben<br>würdest gebeten haben<br>würde gebeten haben | würden gebeten haben<br>würdet gebeten haben<br>würden gebeten haben |

## EXAMPLES

Ich bitte dich um Verzeihung.
I beg your pardon.

Mein Freund hat mich gebeten ihn um acht abzuholen.
My friend asked me to pick him up at eight.

**blasen**
to blow
**Auxiliary verb:** haben **Past participle:** geblasen
**Imperative:** Blase! Blast! Blasen Sie!

| Mode | Simple Tenses | | Compound Tenses | |
|---|---|---|---|---|
| | *Singular* | *Plural* | *Singular* | *Plural* |
| Indicative | **Present** | | **Present Perfect** | |
| | blase<br>bläst<br>bläst | blasen<br>blast<br>blasen | habe geblasen<br>hast geblasen<br>hat geblasen | haben geblasen<br>habt geblasen<br>haben geblasen |
| | **Past** | | **Past Perfect** | |
| | blies<br>bliesest<br>blies | bliesen<br>bliest<br>bliesen | hatte geblasen<br>hattest geblasen<br>hatte geblasen | hatten geblasen<br>hattet geblasen<br>hatten geblasen |
| | **Future** | | **Future Perfect** | |
| | werde blasen<br>wirst blasen<br>wird blasen | werden blasen<br>werdet blasen<br>werden blasen | werde geblasen haben<br>wirst geblasen haben<br>wird geblasen haben | werden geblasen haben<br>werdet geblasen haben<br>werden geblasen haben |
| Subjunctive | **Present** | | **Present Perfect** | |
| | blase<br>blasest<br>blase | blasen<br>blaset<br>blasen | habe geblasen<br>habest geblasen<br>habe geblasen | haben geblasen<br>habet geblasen<br>haben geblasen |
| | **Past** | | **Past Perfect** | |
| | bliese<br>bliesest<br>bliese | bliesen<br>blieset<br>bliesen | hätte geblasen<br>hättest geblasen<br>hätte geblasen | hätten geblasen<br>hättet geblasen<br>hätten geblasen |
| | **Future** | | **Future Perfect** | |
| | werde blasen<br>werdest blasen<br>werde blasen | werden blasen<br>werdet blasen<br>werden blasen | werde geblasen haben<br>werdest geblasen haben<br>werde geblasen haben | werden geblasen haben<br>werdet geblasen haben<br>werden geblasen haben |
| | **Present and Future Conditional** | | **Past Conditional** | |
| | würde blasen<br>würdest blasen<br>würde blasen | würden blasen<br>würdet blasen<br>würden blasen | würde geblasen haben<br>würdest geblasen haben<br>würde geblasen haben | würden geblasen haben<br>würdet geblasen haben<br>würden geblasen haben |

## EXAMPLES

Der Wind bläst heute heftiger als gestern.
The wind is blowing harder today than yesterday.

Der Jäger blies ins Horn.
The hunter blew his horn.

**bleiben**

to remain, to stay

**Auxiliary verb:** sein **Past participle:** geblieben

**Imperative:** Bleibe! Bleibt! Bleiben Sie!

| Mode | Simple Tenses | | Compound Tenses | |
|---|---|---|---|---|
| | *Singular* | *Plural* | *Singular* | *Plural* |
| Indicative | **Present** | | **Present Perfect** | |
| | bleibe<br>bleibst<br>bleibt | bleiben<br>bleibt<br>bleiben | bin geblieben<br>bist geblieben<br>ist geblieben | sind geblieben<br>seid geblieben<br>sind geblieben |
| | **Past** | | **Past Perfect** | |
| | blieb<br>bliebst<br>blieb | blieben<br>bliebt<br>blieben | war geblieben<br>warst geblieben<br>war geblieben | waren geblieben<br>wart geblieben<br>waren geblieben |
| | **Future** | | **Future Perfect** | |
| | werde bleiben<br>wirst bleiben<br>wird bleiben | werden bleiben<br>werdet bleiben<br>werden bleiben | werde geblieben sein<br>wirst geblieben sein<br>wird geblieben sein | werden geblieben sein<br>werdet geblieben sein<br>werden geblieben sein |
| Subjunctive | **Present** | | **Present Perfect** | |
| | bleibe<br>bleibest<br>bleibe | bleiben<br>bleibet<br>bleiben | sei geblieben<br>seiest geblieben<br>sei geblieben | seien geblieben<br>seiet geblieben<br>seien geblieben |
| | **Past** | | **Past Perfect** | |
| | bliebe<br>bliebest<br>bliebe | blieben<br>bliebet<br>blieben | wäre geblieben<br>wärest geblieben<br>wäre geblieben | wären geblieben<br>wäret geblieben<br>wären geblieben |
| | **Future** | | **Future Perfect** | |
| | werde bleiben<br>werdest bleiben<br>werde bleiben | werden bleiben<br>werdet bleiben<br>werden bleiben | werde geblieben sein<br>werdest geblieben sein<br>werde geblieben sein | werden geblieben sein<br>werdet geblieben sein<br>werden geblieben sein |
| | **Present and Future Conditional** | | **Past Conditional** | |
| | würde bleiben<br>würdest bleiben<br>würde bleiben | würden bleiben<br>würdet bleiben<br>würden bleiben | würde geblieben sein<br>würdest geblieben sein<br>würde geblieben sein | würden geblieben sein<br>würdet geblieben sein<br>würden geblieben sein |

**Note:** With inseparable prefixes, the principal parts are, for example, *verbleibt, verblieb, ist verblieben.* With separable prefixes, the principal parts are, for example, *bleibt weg, blieb weg, ist weggeblieben.*

## EXAMPLES

| | |
|---|---|
| Der Chef bleibt bei seiner Meinung. | The boss persists in his opinion. |
| Wo ist Ihr Vetter geblieben? | What's become of your cousin? |

**blitzen**

to flash lightning, to take pictures with a flash

**Auxiliary verb:** haben **Past participle:** geblitzt

**Imperative:** Blitze! Blitzt! Blitzen Sie!

| Mode | Simple Tenses | | Compound Tenses | |
|---|---|---|---|---|
| | *Singular* | *Plural* | *Singular* | *Plural* |
| Indicative | **Present** | | **Present Perfect** | |
| | blitze<br>blitzt<br>blitzt | blitzen<br>blitzt<br>blitzen | habe geblitzt<br>hast geblitzt<br>hat geblitzt | haben geblitzt<br>habt geblitzt<br>haben geblitzt |
| | **Past** | | **Past Perfect** | |
| | blitzte<br>blitztest<br>blitzte | blitzten<br>blitztet<br>blitzten | hatte geblitzt<br>hattest geblitzt<br>hatte geblitzt | hatten geblitzt<br>hattet geblitzt<br>hatten geblitzt |
| | **Future** | | **Future Perfect** | |
| | werde blitzen<br>wirst blitzen<br>wird blitzen | werden blitzen<br>werdet blitzen<br>werden blitzen | werde geblitzt haben<br>wirst geblitzt haben<br>wird geblitzt haben | werden geblitzt haben<br>werdet geblitzt haben<br>werden geblitzt haben |
| Subjunctive | **Present** | | **Present Perfect** | |
| | blitze<br>blitzest<br>blitze | blitzen<br>blitzet<br>blitzen | habe geblitzt<br>habest geblitzt<br>habe geblitzt | haben geblitzt<br>habet geblitzt<br>haben geblitzt |
| | **Past** | | **Past Perfect** | |
| | blitzte<br>blitztest<br>blitzte | blitzten<br>blitztet<br>blitzten | hätte geblitzt<br>hättest geblitzt<br>hätte geblitzt | hätten geblitzt<br>hättet geblitzt<br>hätten geblitzt |
| | **Future** | | **Future Perfect** | |
| | werde blitzen<br>werdest blitzen<br>werde blitzen | werden blitzen<br>werdet blitzen<br>werden blitzen | werde geblitzt haben<br>werdest geblitzt haben<br>werde geblitzt haben | werden geblitzt haben<br>werdet geblitzt haben<br>werden geblitzt haben |
| | **Present and Future Conditional** | | **Past Conditional** | |
| | würde blitzen<br>würdest blitzen<br>würde blitzen | würden blitzen<br>würdet blitzen<br>würden blitzen | würde geblitzt haben<br>würdest geblitzt haben<br>würde geblitzt haben | würden geblitzt haben<br>würdet geblitzt haben<br>würden geblitzt haben |

**Note:** This verb is most commonly used with the third-person singular pronoun *es*.

## EXAMPLE

Es blitzt. Lightning is flashing.

**blühen**
to bloom, to flower
**Auxiliary verb:** haben **Past participle:** geblüht
**Imperative:** Blühe! Blüht! Blühen Sie!

| Mode | Simple Tenses | | Compound Tenses | |
|---|---|---|---|---|
| | *Singular* | *Plural* | *Singular* | *Plural* |
| Indicative | **Present** | | **Present Perfect** | |
| | blühe<br>blühst<br>blüht | blühen<br>blüht<br>blühen | habe geblüht<br>hast geblüht<br>hat geblüht | haben geblüht<br>habt geblüht<br>haben geblüht |
| | **Past** | | **Past Perfect** | |
| | blühte<br>blühtest<br>blühte | blühten<br>blühtet<br>blühten | hatte geblüht<br>hattest geblüht<br>hatte geblüht | hatten geblüht<br>hattet geblüht<br>hatten geblüht |
| | **Future** | | **Future Perfect** | |
| | werde blühen<br>wirst blühen<br>wird blühen | werden blühen<br>werdet blühen<br>werden blühen | werde geblüht haben<br>wirst geblüht haben<br>wird geblüht haben | werden geblüht haben<br>werdet geblüht haben<br>werden geblüht haben |
| Subjunctive | **Present** | | **Present Perfect** | |
| | blühe<br>blühest<br>blühe | blühen<br>blühet<br>blühen | habe geblüht<br>habest geblüht<br>habe geblüht | haben geblüht<br>habet geblüht<br>haben geblüht |
| | **Past** | | **Past Perfect** | |
| | blühte<br>blühtest<br>blühte | blühten<br>blühtet<br>blühten | hätte geblüht<br>hättest geblüht<br>hätte geblüht | hätten geblüht<br>hättet geblüht<br>hätten geblüht |
| | **Future** | | **Future Perfect** | |
| | werde blühen<br>werdest blühen<br>werde blühen | werden blühen<br>werdet blühen<br>werden blühen | werde geblüht haben<br>werdest geblüht haben<br>werde geblüht haben | werden geblüht haben<br>werdet geblüht haben<br>werden geblüht haben |
| | **Present and Future Conditional** | | **Past Conditional** | |
| | würde blühen<br>würdest blühen<br>würde blühen | würden blühen<br>würdet blühen<br>würden blühen | würde geblüht haben<br>würdest geblüht haben<br>würde geblüht haben | würden geblüht haben<br>würdet geblüht haben<br>würden geblüht haben |

## EXAMPLES

Endlich blüht das neue Geschäft.
The new business is finally prospering.

In unserem Garten werden Nelken und Rosen blühen.
Carnations and roses will bloom in our garden.

**borgen**
to borrow, to lend
**Auxiliary verb:** haben **Past participle:** geborgt
**Imperative:** Borge! Borgt! Borgen Sie!

| Mode | Simple Tenses | | Compound Tenses | |
|---|---|---|---|---|
| | *Singular* | *Plural* | *Singular* | *Plural* |
| Indicative | **Present** | | **Present Perfect** | |
| | borge<br>borgst<br>borgt | borgen<br>borgt<br>borgen | habe geborgt<br>hast geborgt<br>hat geborgt | haben geborgt<br>habt geborgt<br>haben geborgt |
| | **Past** | | **Past Perfect** | |
| | borgte<br>borgtest<br>borgte | borgten<br>borgtet<br>borgten | hatte geborgt<br>hattest geborgt<br>hatte geborgt | hatten geborgt<br>hattet geborgt<br>hatten geborgt |
| | **Future** | | **Future Perfect** | |
| | werde borgen<br>wirst borgen<br>wird borgen | werden borgen<br>werdet borgen<br>werden borgen | werde geborgt haben<br>wirst geborgt haben<br>wird geborgt haben | werden geborgt haben<br>werdet geborgt haben<br>werden geborgt haben |
| Subjunctive | **Present** | | **Present Perfect** | |
| | borge<br>borgest<br>borge | borgen<br>borget<br>borgen | habe geborgt<br>habest geborgt<br>habe geborgt | haben geborgt<br>habet geborgt<br>haben geborgt |
| | **Past** | | **Past Perfect** | |
| | borgte<br>borgtest<br>borgte | borgten<br>borgtet<br>borgten | hätte geborgt<br>hättest geborgt<br>hätte geborgt | hätten geborgt<br>hättet geborgt<br>hätten geborgt |
| | **Future** | | **Future Perfect** | |
| | werde borgen<br>werdest borgen<br>werde borgen | werden borgen<br>werdet borgen<br>werden borgen | werde geborgt haben<br>werdest geborgt haben<br>werde geborgt haben | werden geborgt haben<br>werdet geborgt haben<br>werden geborgt haben |
| | **Present and Future Conditional** | | **Past Conditional** | |
| | würde borgen<br>würdest borgen<br>würde borgen | würden borgen<br>würdet borgen<br>würden borgen | würde geborgt haben<br>würdest geborgt haben<br>würde geborgt haben | würden geborgt haben<br>würdet geborgt haben<br>würden geborgt haben |

## EXAMPLES

Mein Bruder hat sich den Sportwagen nur geborgt.
My brother only borrowed the sports car.

Darf ich deinen Regenschirm borgen?
May I borrow your umbrella?

**braten**

to roast, to fry

**Auxiliary verb:** haben **Past participle:** gebraten

**Imperative:** Brate! Bratet! Braten Sie!

| Mode | Simple Tenses | | Compound Tenses | |
|---|---|---|---|---|
| | *Singular* | *Plural* | *Singular* | *Plural* |
| Indicative | **Present** | | **Present Perfect** | |
| | brate<br>brätst<br>brät | braten<br>bratet<br>braten | habe gebraten<br>hast gebraten<br>hat gebraten | haben gebraten<br>habt gebraten<br>haben gebraten |
| | **Past** | | **Past Perfect** | |
| | briet<br>brietst<br>briet | brieten<br>brietet<br>brieten | hatte gebraten<br>hattest gebraten<br>hatte gebraten | hatten gebraten<br>hattet gebraten<br>hatten gebraten |
| | **Future** | | **Future Perfect** | |
| | werde braten<br>wirst braten<br>wird braten | werden braten<br>werdet braten<br>werden braten | werde gebraten haben<br>wirst gebraten haben<br>wird gebraten haben | werden gebraten haben<br>werdet gebraten haben<br>werden gebraten haben |
| Subjunctive | **Present** | | **Present Perfect** | |
| | brate<br>bratest<br>brate | braten<br>bratet<br>braten | habe gebraten<br>habest gebraten<br>habe gebraten | haben gebraten<br>habet gebraten<br>haben gebraten |
| | **Past** | | **Past Perfect** | |
| | briete<br>brietest<br>briete | brieten<br>brietet<br>brieten | hätte gebraten<br>hättest gebraten<br>hätte gebraten | hätten gebraten<br>hättet gebraten<br>hätten gebraten |
| | **Future** | | **Future Perfect** | |
| | werde braten<br>werdest braten<br>werde braten | werden braten<br>werdet braten<br>werden braten | werde gebraten haben<br>werdest gebraten haben<br>werde gebraten haben | werden gebraten haben<br>werdet gebraten haben<br>werden gebraten haben |
| | **Present and Future Conditional** | | **Past Conditional** | |
| | würde braten<br>würdest braten<br>würde braten | würden braten<br>würdet braten<br>würden braten | würde gebraten haben<br>würdest gebraten haben<br>würde gebraten haben | würden gebraten haben<br>würdet gebraten haben<br>würden gebraten haben |

## EXAMPLES

Dieses Schweinefleisch ist zu wenig gebraten. — This pork is underdone.

Onkel Heinz brät die Würstchen in Öl. — Uncle Heinz fries the sausages in oil.

Ich habe das Fleisch nur kurz gebraten. — I fried the meat only briefly.

**brauchen**
to need
**Auxiliary verb:** haben **Past participle:** gebraucht
**Imperative:** Brauche! Braucht! Brauchen Sie!

| Mode | Simple Tenses | | Compound Tenses | |
|---|---|---|---|---|
| | *Singular* | *Plural* | *Singular* | *Plural* |
| Indicative | **Present** | | **Present Perfect** | |
| | brauche<br>brauchst<br>braucht | brauchen<br>braucht<br>brauchen | habe gebraucht<br>hast gebraucht<br>hat gebraucht | haben gebraucht<br>habt gebraucht<br>haben gebraucht |
| | **Past** | | **Past Perfect** | |
| | brauchte<br>brauchtest<br>brauchte | brauchten<br>brauchtet<br>brauchten | hatte gebraucht<br>hattest gebraucht<br>hatte gebraucht | hatten gebraucht<br>hattet gebraucht<br>hatten gebraucht |
| | **Future** | | **Future Perfect** | |
| | werde brauchen<br>wirst brauchen<br>wird brauchen | werden brauchen<br>werdet brauchen<br>werden brauchen | werde gebraucht haben<br>wirst gebraucht haben<br>wird gebraucht haben | werden gebraucht haben<br>werdet gebraucht haben<br>werden gebraucht haben |
| Subjunctive | **Present** | | **Present Perfect** | |
| | brauche<br>brauchest<br>brauche | brauchen<br>brauchet<br>brauchen | habe gebraucht<br>habest gebraucht<br>habe gebraucht | haben gebraucht<br>habet gebraucht<br>haben gebraucht |
| | **Past** | | **Past Perfect** | |
| | brauchte<br>brauchtest<br>brauchte | brauchten<br>brauchtet<br>brauchten | hätte gebraucht<br>hättest gebraucht<br>hätte gebraucht | hätten gebraucht<br>hättet gebraucht<br>hätten gebraucht |
| | **Future** | | **Future Perfect** | |
| | werde brauchen<br>werdest brauchen<br>werde brauchen | werden brauchen<br>werdet brauchen<br>werden brauchen | werde gebraucht haben<br>werdest gebraucht haben<br>werde gebraucht haben | werden gebraucht haben<br>werdet gebraucht haben<br>werden gebraucht haben |
| | **Present and Future Conditional** | | **Past Conditional** | |
| | würde brauchen<br>würdest brauchen<br>würde brauchen | würden brauchen<br>würdet brauchen<br>würden brauchen | würde gebraucht haben<br>würdest gebraucht haben<br>würde gebraucht haben | würden gebraucht haben<br>würdet gebraucht haben<br>würden gebraucht haben |

## EXAMPLES

Du brauchst es nur zu sagen. — You only need to mention it.

Sie dürfen nicht nach Hause gehen. Der Chef braucht Sie noch. — You can't go home. The boss still needs you.

**brechen**
to break, to vomit
**Auxiliary verb:** haben **Past participle:** gebrochen
**Imperative:** Brich! Brecht! Brechen Sie!

| Mode | Simple Tenses | | Compound Tenses | |
|---|---|---|---|---|
| | *Singular* | *Plural* | *Singular* | *Plural* |
| Indicative | **Present** | | **Present Perfect** | |
| | breche<br>brichst<br>bricht | brechen<br>brecht<br>brechen | habe gebrochen<br>hast gebrochen<br>hat gebrochen | haben gebrochen<br>habt gebrochen<br>haben gebrochen |
| | **Past** | | **Past Perfect** | |
| | brach<br>brachst<br>brach | brachen<br>bracht<br>brachen | hatte gebrochen<br>hattest gebrochen<br>hatte gebrochen | hatten gebrochen<br>hattet gebrochen<br>hatten gebrochen |
| | **Future** | | **Future Perfect** | |
| | werde brechen<br>wirst brechen<br>wird brechen | werden brechen<br>werdet brechen<br>werden brechen | werde gebrochen haben<br>wirst gebrochen haben<br>wird gebrochen haben | werden gebrochen haben<br>werdet gebrochen haben<br>werden gebrochen haben |
| Subjunctive | **Present** | | **Present Perfect** | |
| | breche<br>brechest<br>breche | brechen<br>brechet<br>brechen | habe gebrochen<br>habest gebrochen<br>habe gebrochen | haben gebrochen<br>habet gebrochen<br>haben gebrochen |
| | **Past** | | **Past Perfect** | |
| | bräche<br>brächest<br>bräche | brächen<br>brächet<br>brächen | hätte gebrochen<br>hättest gebrochen<br>hätte gebrochen | hätten gebrochen<br>hättet gebrochen<br>hätten gebrochen |
| | **Future** | | **Future Perfect** | |
| | werde brechen<br>werdest brechen<br>werde brechen | werden brechen<br>werdet brechen<br>werden brechen | werde gebrochen haben<br>werdest gebrochen haben<br>werde gebrochen haben | werden gebrochen haben<br>werdet gebrochen haben<br>werden gebrochen haben |
| | **Present and Future Conditional** | | **Past Conditional** | |
| | würde brechen<br>würdest brechen<br>würde brechen | würden brechen<br>würdet brechen<br>würden brechen | würde gebrochen haben<br>würdest gebrochen haben<br>würde gebrochen haben | würden gebrochen haben<br>würdet gebrochen haben<br>würden gebrochen haben |

**Note:** With inseparable prefixes, the principal parts are, for example, *verbricht, verbrach, hat verbrochen.* With separable prefixes, the principal parts are, for example, *bricht durch, brach durch, ist durchgebrochen.*

## EXAMPLES

| | |
|---|---|
| Der Junge hat sich den Arm gebrochen. | The boy broke his arm. |
| Der kranke Mann hat oft brechen müssen. | The sick man had to vomit often. |

**brennen**
to burn
**Auxiliary verb:** haben **Past participle:** gebrannt
**Imperative:** Brenne! Brennt! Brennen Sie!

| Mode | Simple Tenses | | Compound Tenses | |
|---|---|---|---|---|
| | *Singular* | *Plural* | *Singular* | *Plural* |
| Indicative | **Present** | | **Present Perfect** | |
| | brenne<br>brennst<br>brennt | brennen<br>brennt<br>brennen | habe gebrannt<br>hast gebrannt<br>hat gebrannt | haben gebrannt<br>habt gebrannt<br>haben gebrannt |
| | **Past** | | **Past Perfect** | |
| | brannte<br>branntest<br>brannte | brannten<br>branntet<br>brannten | hatte gebrannt<br>hattest gebrannt<br>hatte gebrannt | hatten gebrannt<br>hattet gebrannt<br>hatten gebrannt |
| | **Future** | | **Future Perfect** | |
| | werde brennen<br>wirst brennen<br>wird brennen | werden brennen<br>werdet brennen<br>werden brennen | werde gebrannt haben<br>wirst gebrannt haben<br>wird gebrannt haben | werden gebrannt haben<br>werdet gebrannt haben<br>werden gebrannt haben |
| Subjunctive | **Present** | | **Present Perfect** | |
| | brenne<br>brennest<br>brenne | brennen<br>brennet<br>brennen | habe gebrannt<br>habest gebrannt<br>habe gebrannt | haben gebrannt<br>habet gebrannt<br>haben gebrannt |
| | **Past** | | **Past Perfect** | |
| | brennte<br>brenntest<br>brennte | brennten<br>brenntet<br>brennten | hätte gebrannt<br>hättest gebrannt<br>hätte gebrannt | hätten gebrannt<br>hättet gebrannt<br>hätten gebrannt |
| | **Future** | | **Future Perfect** | |
| | werde brennen<br>werdest brennen<br>werde brennen | werden brennen<br>werdet brennen<br>werden brennen | werde gebrannt haben<br>werdest gebrannt haben<br>werde gebrannt haben | werden gebrannt haben<br>werdet gebrannt haben<br>werden gebrannt haben |
| | **Present and Future Conditional** | | **Past Conditional** | |
| | würde brennen<br>würdest brennen<br>würde brennen | würden brennen<br>würdet brennen<br>würden brennen | würde gebrannt haben<br>würdest gebrannt haben<br>würde gebrannt haben | würden gebrannt haben<br>würdet gebrannt haben<br>würden gebrannt haben |

## EXAMPLES

Mir haben die Augen gebrannt. — My eyes were burning.
Es brennt im Stadtzentrum. — There's a fire downtown.

**bringen**
to bring
**Auxiliary verb:** haben **Past participle:** gebracht
**Imperative:** Bringe! Bringt! Bringen Sie!

| Mode | Simple Tenses | | Compound Tenses | |
|---|---|---|---|---|
| | *Singular* | *Plural* | *Singular* | *Plural* |
| Indicative | **Present** | | **Present Perfect** | |
| | bringe<br>bringst<br>bringt | bringen<br>bringt<br>bringen | habe gebracht<br>hast gebracht<br>hat gebracht | haben gebracht<br>habt gebracht<br>haben gebracht |
| | **Past** | | **Past Perfect** | |
| | brachte<br>brachtest<br>brachte | brachten<br>brachtet<br>brachten | hatte gebracht<br>hattest gebracht<br>hatte gebracht | hatten gebracht<br>hattet gebracht<br>hatten gebracht |
| | **Future** | | **Future Perfect** | |
| | werde bringen<br>wirst bringen<br>wird bringen | werden bringen<br>werdet bringen<br>werden bringen | werde gebracht haben<br>wirst gebracht haben<br>wird gebracht haben | werden gebracht haben<br>werdet gebracht haben<br>werden gebracht haben |
| Subjunctive | **Present** | | **Present Perfect** | |
| | bringe<br>bringest<br>bringe | bringen<br>bringet<br>bringen | habe gebracht<br>habest gebracht<br>habe gebracht | haben gebracht<br>habet gebracht<br>haben gebracht |
| | **Past** | | **Past Perfect** | |
| | brächte<br>brächtest<br>brächte | brächten<br>brächtet<br>brächten | hätte gebracht<br>hättest gebracht<br>hätte gebracht | hätten gebracht<br>hättet gebracht<br>hätten gebracht |
| | **Future** | | **Future Perfect** | |
| | werde bringen<br>werdest bringen<br>werde bringen | werden bringen<br>werdet bringen<br>werden bringen | werde gebracht haben<br>werdest gebracht haben<br>werde gebracht haben | werden gebracht haben<br>werdet gebracht haben<br>werden gebracht haben |
| | **Present and Future Conditional** | | **Past Conditional** | |
| | würde bringen<br>würdest bringen<br>würde bringen | würden bringen<br>würdet bringen<br>würden bringen | würde gebracht haben<br>würdest gebracht haben<br>würde gebracht haben | würden gebracht haben<br>würdet gebracht haben<br>würden gebracht haben |

**Note:** With inseparable prefixes, the principal parts are, for example, *verbringt, verbrachte, hat verbracht.* With separable prefixes, the principal parts are, for example, *bringt um, brachte um, hat umgebracht.*

## EXAMPLES

Um vierzehn Uhr werde ich meine Tante zum Bahnhof bringen.

At two p.m. I'll take my aunt to the railroad station.

**danken**
to thank
**Auxiliary verb:** haben **Past participle:** gedankt
**Imperative:** Danke! Dankt! Danken Sie!

| Mode | Simple Tenses | | Compound Tenses | |
|---|---|---|---|---|
| | *Singular* | *Plural* | *Singular* | *Plural* |
| Indicative | **Present** | | **Present Perfect** | |
| | danke<br>dankst<br>dankt | danken<br>dankt<br>danken | habe gedankt<br>hast gedankt<br>hat gedankt | haben gedankt<br>habt gedankt<br>haben gedankt |
| | **Past** | | **Past Perfect** | |
| | dankte<br>danktest<br>dankte | dankten<br>danktet<br>dankten | hatte gedankt<br>hattest gedankt<br>hatte gedankt | hatten gedankt<br>hattet gedankt<br>hatten gedankt |
| | **Future** | | **Future Perfect** | |
| | werde danken<br>wirst danken<br>wird danken | werden danken<br>werdet danken<br>werden danken | werde gedankt haben<br>wirst gedankt haben<br>wird gedankt haben | werden gedankt haben<br>werdet gedankt haben<br>werden gedankt haben |
| Subjunctive | **Present** | | **Present Perfect** | |
| | danke<br>dankest<br>danke | danken<br>danket<br>danken | habe gedankt<br>habest gedankt<br>habe gedankt | haben gedankt<br>habet gedankt<br>haben gedankt |
| | **Past** | | **Past Perfect** | |
| | dankte<br>danktest<br>dankte | dankten<br>danktet<br>dankten | hätte gedankt<br>hättest gedankt<br>hätte gedankt | hätten gedankt<br>hättet gedankt<br>hätten gedankt |
| | **Future** | | **Future Perfect** | |
| | werde danken<br>werdest danken<br>werde danken | werden danken<br>werdet danken<br>werden danken | werde gedankt haben<br>werdest gedankt haben<br>werde gedankt haben | werden gedankt haben<br>werdet gedankt haben<br>werden gedankt haben |
| | **Present and Future Conditional** | | **Past Conditional** | |
| | würde danken<br>würdest danken<br>würde danken | würden danken<br>würdet danken<br>würden danken | würde gedankt haben<br>würdest gedankt haben<br>würde gedankt haben | würden gedankt haben<br>würdet gedankt haben<br>würden gedankt haben |

## EXAMPLES

Paul soll seinem Onkel für den neuen Schlips danken.

Paul should thank his uncle for the new tie.

„Danke schön," sagte Gudrun, als sie das Geschenk bekam.

"Thank you," Gudrun said when she received the gift.

**darstellen**

to represent, to state, to portray

**Auxiliary verb:** haben **Past participle:** dargestellt

**Imperative:** Stelle dar! Stellt dar! Stellen Sie dar!

| Mode | Simple Tenses | | Compound Tenses | |
|---|---|---|---|---|
| | *Singular* | *Plural* | *Singular* | *Plural* |
| Indicative | **Present** | | **Present Perfect** | |
| | stelle dar<br>stellst dar<br>stellt dar | stellen dar<br>stellt dar<br>stellen dar | habe dargestellt<br>hast dargestellt<br>hat dargestellt | haben dargestellt<br>habt dargestellt<br>haben dargestellt |
| | **Past** | | **Past Perfect** | |
| | stellte dar<br>stelltest dar<br>stellte dar | stellten dar<br>stelltet dar<br>stellten dar | hatte dargestellt<br>hattest dargestellt<br>hatte dargestellt | hatten dargestellt<br>hattet dargestellt<br>hatten dargestellt |
| | **Future** | | **Future Perfect** | |
| | werde darstellen<br>wirst darstellen<br>wird darstellen | werden darstellen<br>werdet darstellen<br>werden darstellen | werde dargestellt haben<br>wirst dargestellt haben<br>wird dargestellt haben | werden dargestellt haben<br>werdet dargestellt haben<br>werden dargestellt haben |
| Subjunctive | **Present** | | **Present Perfect** | |
| | stelle dar<br>stellest dar<br>stelle dar | stellen dar<br>stellet dar<br>stellen dar | habe dargestellt<br>habest dargestellt<br>habe dargestellt | haben dargestellt<br>habet dargestellt<br>haben dargestellt |
| | **Past** | | **Past Perfect** | |
| | stellte dar<br>stelltest dar<br>stellte dar | stellten dar<br>stelltet dar<br>stellten dar | hätte dargestellt<br>hättest dargestellt<br>hätte dargestellt | hätten dargestellt<br>hättet dargestellt<br>hätten dargestellt |
| | **Future** | | **Future Perfect** | |
| | werde darstellen<br>werdest darstellen<br>werde darstellen | werden darstellen<br>werdet darstellen<br>werden darstellen | werde dargestellt haben<br>werdest dargestellt haben<br>werde dargestellt haben | werden dargestellt haben<br>werdet dargestellt haben<br>werden dargestellt haben |
| | **Present and Future Conditional** | | **Past Conditional** | |
| | würde darstellen<br>würdest darstellen<br>würde darstellen | würden darstellen<br>würdet darstellen<br>würden darstellen | würde dargestellt haben<br>würdest dargestellt haben<br>würde dargestellt haben | würden dargestellt haben<br>würdet dargestellt haben<br>würden dargestellt haben |

## EXAMPLES

Sie haben diesen Fall falsch dargestellt. — You've misrepresented this case.

Das Bild stellt Mozart als Kind dar. — The painting portrays Mozart as a child.

**dauern**
to last, to continue
**Auxiliary verb:** haben **Past participle:** gedauert
**Imperative:** N/A

| Mode | Simple Tenses | | Compound Tenses | |
|---|---|---|---|---|
| | *Singular* | *Plural* | *Singular* | *Plural* |
| Indicative | **Present** | | **Present Perfect** | |
| | dauert | dauern | hat gedauert | haben gedauert |
| | **Past** | | **Past Perfect** | |
| | dauerte | dauerten | hatte gedauert | hatten gedauert |
| | **Future** | | **Future Perfect** | |
| | wird dauern | werden dauern | wird gedauert haben | werden gedauert haben |
| Subjunctive | **Present** | | **Present Perfect** | |
| | dauere | dauern | habe gedauert | haben gedauert |
| | **Past** | | **Past Perfect** | |
| | dauerte | dauerten | hätte gedauert | hätten gedauert |
| | **Future** | | **Future Perfect** | |
| | werde dauern | werden dauern | werde gedauert haben | werden gedauert haben |
| | **Present and Future Conditional** | | **Past Conditional** | |
| | würde dauern | würden dauern | würde gedauert haben | würden gedauert haben |

**Note:** This verb is ordinarily used in the third person.

## EXAMPLES

| | |
|---|---|
| Das Schauspiel hat mehr als vier Stunden gedauert. | The play lasted more than four hours. |
| Wie lange dauert der Film? | How long does the movie last? |

**decken**

to cover

**Auxiliary verb:** haben **Past participle:** gedeckt

**Imperative:** Decke! Deckt! Decken Sie!

| Mode | Simple Tenses | | Compound Tenses | |
|---|---|---|---|---|
| | *Singular* | *Plural* | *Singular* | *Plural* |
| Indicative | **Present** | | **Present Perfect** | |
| | decke<br>deckst<br>deckt | decken<br>deckt<br>decken | habe gedeckt<br>hast gedeckt<br>hat gedeckt | haben gedeckt<br>habt gedeckt<br>haben gedeckt |
| | **Past** | | **Past Perfect** | |
| | deckte<br>decktest<br>deckte | deckten<br>decktet<br>deckten | hatte gedeckt<br>hattest gedeckt<br>hatte gedeckt | hatten gedeckt<br>hattet gedeckt<br>hatten gedeckt |
| | **Future** | | **Future Perfect** | |
| | werde decken<br>wirst decken<br>wird decken | werden decken<br>werdet decken<br>werden decken | werde gedeckt haben<br>wirst gedeckt haben<br>wird gedeckt haben | werden gedeckt haben<br>werdet gedeckt haben<br>werden gedeckt haben |
| Subjunctive | **Present** | | **Present Perfect** | |
| | decke<br>deckest<br>decke | decken<br>decket<br>decken | habe gedeckt<br>habest gedeckt<br>habe gedeckt | haben gedeckt<br>habet gedeckt<br>haben gedeckt |
| | **Past** | | **Past Perfect** | |
| | deckte<br>decktest<br>deckte | deckten<br>decktet<br>deckten | hätte gedeckt<br>hättest gedeckt<br>hätte gedeckt | hätten gedeckt<br>hättet gedeckt<br>hätten gedeckt |
| | **Future** | | **Future Perfect** | |
| | werde decken<br>werdest decken<br>werde decken | werden decken<br>werdet decken<br>werden decken | werde gedeckt haben<br>werdest gedeckt haben<br>werde gedeckt haben | werden gedeckt haben<br>werdet gedeckt haben<br>werden gedeckt haben |
| | **Present and Future Conditional** | | **Past Conditional** | |
| | würde decken<br>würdest decken<br>würde decken | würden decken<br>würdet decken<br>würden decken | würde gedeckt haben<br>würdest gedeckt haben<br>würde gedeckt haben | würden gedeckt haben<br>würdet gedeckt haben<br>würden gedeckt haben |

## EXAMPLES

Der große Tisch im Esszimmer ist schon gedeckt.

The large table in the dining room is already set.

Du kannst das Kind mit meinem Mantel zudecken.

You can cover the child with my coat.

**denken**
to think
**Auxiliary verb:** haben **Past participle:** gedacht
**Imperative:** Denke! Denkt! Denken Sie!

| Mode | Simple Tenses | | Compound Tenses | |
|---|---|---|---|---|
| | *Singular* | *Plural* | *Singular* | *Plural* |
| Indicative | **Present** | | **Present Perfect** | |
| | denke<br>denkst<br>denkt | denken<br>denkt<br>denken | habe gedacht<br>hast gedacht<br>hat gedacht | haben gedacht<br>habt gedacht<br>haben gedacht |
| | **Past** | | **Past Perfect** | |
| | dachte<br>dachtest<br>dachte | dachten<br>dachtet<br>dachten | hatte gedacht<br>hattest gedacht<br>hatte gedacht | hatten gedacht<br>hattet gedacht<br>hatten gedacht |
| | **Future** | | **Future Perfect** | |
| | werde denken<br>wirst denken<br>wird denken | werden denken<br>werdet denken<br>werden denken | werde gedacht haben<br>wirst gedacht haben<br>wird gedacht haben | werden gedacht haben<br>werdet gedacht haben<br>werden gedacht haben |
| Subjunctive | **Present** | | **Present Perfect** | |
| | denke<br>denkest<br>denke | denken<br>denket<br>denken | habe gedacht<br>habest gedacht<br>habe gedacht | haben gedacht<br>habet gedacht<br>haben gedacht |
| | **Past** | | **Past Perfect** | |
| | dächte<br>dächtest<br>dächte | dächten<br>dächtet<br>dächten | hätte gedacht<br>hättest gedacht<br>hätte gedacht | hätten gedacht<br>hättet gedacht<br>hätten gedacht |
| | **Future** | | **Future Perfect** | |
| | werde denken<br>werdest denken<br>werde denken | werden denken<br>werdet denken<br>werden denken | werde gedacht haben<br>werdest gedacht haben<br>werde gedacht haben | werden gedacht haben<br>werdet gedacht haben<br>werden gedacht haben |
| | **Present and Future Conditional** | | **Past Conditional** | |
| | würde denken<br>würdest denken<br>würde denken | würden denken<br>würdet denken<br>würden denken | würde gedacht haben<br>würdest gedacht haben<br>würde gedacht haben | würden gedacht haben<br>würdet gedacht haben<br>würden gedacht haben |

## EXAMPLES

Ich habe oft an Großmutter gedacht.
Denk nicht mehr daran!

I have often thought of grandmother.
Don't think about it anymore.

**dichten**

to compose poetry

**Auxiliary verb:** haben **Past participle:** gedichtet

**Imperative:** Dichte! Dichtet! Dichten Sie!

| Mode | Simple Tenses | | Compound Tenses | |
|---|---|---|---|---|
| | *Singular* | *Plural* | *Singular* | *Plural* |
| Indicative | **Present** | | **Present Perfect** | |
| | dichte<br>dichtest<br>dichtet | dichten<br>dichtet<br>dichten | habe gedichtet<br>hast gedichtet<br>hat gedichtet | haben gedichtet<br>habt gedichtet<br>haben gedichtet |
| | **Past** | | **Past Perfect** | |
| | dichtete<br>dichtetest<br>dichtete | dichteten<br>dichtetet<br>dichteten | hatte gedichtet<br>hattest gedichtet<br>hatte gedichtet | hatten gedichtet<br>hattet gedichtet<br>hatten gedichtet |
| | **Future** | | **Future Perfect** | |
| | werde dichten<br>wirst dichten<br>wird dichten | werden dichten<br>werdet dichten<br>werden dichten | werde gedichtet haben<br>wirst gedichtet haben<br>wird gedichtet haben | werden gedichtet haben<br>werdet gedichtet haben<br>werden gedichtet haben |
| Subjunctive | **Present** | | **Present Perfect** | |
| | dichte<br>dichtest<br>dichte | dichten<br>dichtet<br>dichten | habe gedichtet<br>habest gedichtet<br>habe gedichtet | haben gedichtet<br>habet gedichtet<br>haben gedichtet |
| | **Past** | | **Past Perfect** | |
| | dichtete<br>dichtetest<br>dichtete | dichteten<br>dichtetet<br>dichteten | hätte gedichtet<br>hättest gedichtet<br>hätte gedichtet | hätten gedichtet<br>hättet gedichtet<br>hätten gedichtet |
| | **Future** | | **Future Perfect** | |
| | werde dichten<br>werdest dichten<br>werde dichten | werden dichten<br>werdet dichten<br>werden dichten | werde gedichtet haben<br>werdest gedichtet haben<br>werde gedichtet haben | werden gedichtet haben<br>werdet gedichtet haben<br>werden gedichtet haben |
| | **Present and Future Conditional** | | **Past Conditional** | |
| | würde dichten<br>würdest dichten<br>würde dichten | würden dichten<br>würdet dichten<br>würden dichten | würde gedichtet haben<br>würdest gedichtet haben<br>würde gedichtet haben | würden gedichtet haben<br>würdet gedichtet haben<br>würden gedichtet haben |

## EXAMPLES

Goethe hat als junger Mann zu dichten angefangen.

Goethe began writing poetry as a young man.

Deutschland ist das Land der Dichter und Denker.

Germany is the land of poets and philosophers.

**dienen**
to serve
**Auxiliary verb:** haben **Past participle:** gedient
**Imperative:** Diene! Dient! Dienen Sie!

| Mode | Simple Tenses | | Compound Tenses | |
|---|---|---|---|---|
| | *Singular* | *Plural* | *Singular* | *Plural* |
| Indicative | **Present** | | **Present Perfect** | |
| | diene<br>dienst<br>dient | dienen<br>dient<br>dienen | habe gedient<br>hast gedient<br>hat gedient | haben gedient<br>habt gedient<br>haben gedient |
| | **Past** | | **Past Perfect** | |
| | diente<br>dientest<br>diente | dienten<br>dientet<br>dienten | hatte gedient<br>hattest gedient<br>hatte gedient | hatten gedient<br>hattet gedient<br>hatten gedient |
| | **Future** | | **Future Perfect** | |
| | werde dienen<br>wirst dienen<br>wird dienen | werden dienen<br>werdet dienen<br>werden dienen | werde gedient haben<br>wirst gedient haben<br>wird gedient haben | werden gedient haben<br>werdet gedient haben<br>werden gedient haben |
| Subjunctive | **Present** | | **Present Perfect** | |
| | diene<br>dienest<br>diene | dienen<br>dienet<br>dienen | habe gedient<br>habest gedient<br>habe gedient | haben gedient<br>habet gedient<br>haben gedient |
| | **Past** | | **Past Perfect** | |
| | diente<br>dientest<br>diente | dienten<br>dientet<br>dienten | hätte gedient<br>hättest gedient<br>hätte gedient | hätten gedient<br>hättet gedient<br>hätten gedient |
| | **Future** | | **Future Perfect** | |
| | werde dienen<br>werdest dienen<br>werde dienen | werden dienen<br>werdet dienen<br>werden dienen | werde gedient haben<br>werdest gedient haben<br>werde gedient haben | werden gedient haben<br>werdet gedient haben<br>werden gedient haben |
| | **Present and Future Conditional** | | **Past Conditional** | |
| | würde dienen<br>würdest dienen<br>würde dienen | würden dienen<br>würdet dienen<br>würden dienen | würde gedient haben<br>würdest gedient haben<br>würde gedient haben | würden gedient haben<br>würdet gedient haben<br>würden gedient haben |

**Note:** The verb *dienen* is a dative verb.

## EXAMPLES

Die Hauptfigur des Romans dient bei einer reichen Dame.
The main character in the novel is in the service of a rich lady.

Wie kann ich Ihnen dienen?
How can I serve you?

**donnern**
to thunder
**Auxiliary verb:** haben **Past participle:** gedonnert
**Imperative:** N/A

| Mode | Simple Tenses | | Compound Tenses | |
|---|---|---|---|---|
| | *Singular* | *Plural* | *Singular* | *Plural* |
| Indicative | **Present** | | **Present Perfect** | |
| | donnert | | hat gedonnert | |
| | **Past** | | **Past Perfect** | |
| | donnerte | | hatte gedonnert | |
| | **Future** | | **Future Perfect** | |
| | wird donnern | | wird gedonnert haben | |
| Subjunctive | **Present** | | **Present Perfect** | |
| | donnere | | habe gedonnert | |
| | **Past** | | **Past Perfect** | |
| | donnerte | | hätte gedonnert | |
| | **Future** | | **Future Perfect** | |
| | werde donnern | | werde gedonnert haben | |
| | **Present and Future Conditional** | | **Past Conditional** | |
| | würde donnern | | würde gedonnert haben | |

**Note:** This verb is used primarily in the third-person singular with the pronoun *es*. It is an impersonal expression. The verb can be used with other persons in a figurative sense.

## EXAMPLE

Es blitzt und donnert. — There's lightning and thunder.

**drängen**
to shove, to press, to urge
**Auxiliary verb:** haben **Past participle:** gedrängt
**Imperative:** Dränge! Drängt! Drängen Sie!

| Mode | Simple Tenses | | Compound Tenses | |
|---|---|---|---|---|
| | *Singular* | *Plural* | *Singular* | *Plural* |
| Indicative | **Present** | | **Present Perfect** | |
| | dränge<br>drängst<br>drängt | drängen<br>drängt<br>drängen | habe gedrängt<br>hast gedrängt<br>hat gedrängt | haben gedrängt<br>habt gedrängt<br>haben gedrängt |
| | **Past** | | **Past Perfect** | |
| | drängte<br>drängtest<br>drängte | drängten<br>drängtet<br>drängten | hatte gedrängt<br>hattest gedrängt<br>hatte gedrängt | hatten gedrängt<br>hattet gedrängt<br>hatten gedrängt |
| | **Future** | | **Future Perfect** | |
| | werde drängen<br>wirst drängen<br>wird drängen | werden drängen<br>werdet drängen<br>werden drängen | werde gedrängt haben<br>wirst gedrängt haben<br>wird gedrängt haben | werden gedrängt haben<br>werdet gedrängt haben<br>werden gedrängt haben |
| Subjunctive | **Present** | | **Present Perfect** | |
| | dränge<br>drängest<br>dränge | drängen<br>dränget<br>drängen | habe gedrängt<br>habest gedrängt<br>habe gedrängt | haben gedrängt<br>habet gedrängt<br>haben gedrängt |
| | **Past** | | **Past Perfect** | |
| | drängte<br>drängtest<br>drängte | drängten<br>drängtet<br>drängten | hätte gedrängt<br>hättest gedrängt<br>hätte gedrängt | hätten gedrängt<br>hättet gedrängt<br>hätten gedrängt |
| | **Future** | | **Future Perfect** | |
| | werde drängen<br>werdest drängen<br>werde drängen | werden drängen<br>werdet drängen<br>werden drängen | werde gedrängt haben<br>werdest gedrängt haben<br>werde gedrängt haben | werden gedrängt haben<br>werdet gedrängt haben<br>werden gedrängt haben |
| | **Present and Future Conditional** | | **Past Conditional** | |
| | würde drängen<br>würdest drängen<br>würde drängen | würden drängen<br>würdet drängen<br>würden drängen | würde gedrängt haben<br>würdest gedrängt haben<br>würde gedrängt haben | würden gedrängt haben<br>würdet gedrängt haben<br>würden gedrängt haben |

## EXAMPLES

Die Zuschauer drängten auf die Bühne.
The spectators rushed onto the stage.

Felix wurde von seinen Eltern dazu gedrängt, in die Armee einzutreten.
Felix was pressured by his parents to go into the army.

**dringen**

to urge, to press forward

**Auxiliary verb:** haben **Past participle:** gedrungen

**Imperative:** Dringe! Dringt! Dringen Sie!

| Mode | Simple Tenses | | Compound Tenses | |
|---|---|---|---|---|
| | *Singular* | *Plural* | *Singular* | *Plural* |
| Indicative | **Present** | | **Present Perfect** | |
| | dringe<br>dringst<br>dringt | dringen<br>dringt<br>dringen | habe gedrungen<br>hast gedrungen<br>hat gedrungen | haben gedrungen<br>habt gedrungen<br>haben gedrungen |
| | **Past** | | **Past Perfect** | |
| | drang<br>drangst<br>drang | drangen<br>drangt<br>drangen | hatte gedrungen<br>hattest gedrungen<br>hatte gedrungen | hatten gedrungen<br>hattet gedrungen<br>hatten gedrungen |
| | **Future** | | **Future Perfect** | |
| | werde dringen<br>wirst dringen<br>wird dringen | werden dringen<br>werdet dringen<br>werden dringen | werde gedrungen haben<br>wirst gedrungen haben<br>wird gedrungen haben | werden gedrungen haben<br>werdet gedrungen haben<br>werden gedrungen haben |
| Subjunctive | **Present** | | **Present Perfect** | |
| | dringe<br>dringest<br>dringe | dringen<br>dringet<br>dringen | habe gedrungen<br>habest gedrungen<br>habe gedrungen | haben gedrungen<br>habet gedrungen<br>haben gedrungen |
| | **Past** | | **Past Perfect** | |
| | dränge<br>drängest<br>dränge | drängen<br>dränget<br>drängen | hätte gedrungen<br>hättest gedrungen<br>hätte gedrungen | hätten gedrungen<br>hättet gedrungen<br>hätten gedrungen |
| | **Future** | | **Future Perfect** | |
| | werde dringen<br>werdest dringen<br>werde dringen | werden dringen<br>werdet dringen<br>werden dringen | werde gedrungen haben<br>werdest gedrungen haben<br>werde gedrungen haben | werden gedrungen haben<br>werdet gedrungen haben<br>werden gedrungen haben |
| | **Present and Future Conditional** | | **Past Conditional** | |
| | würde dringen<br>würdest dringen<br>würde dringen | würden dringen<br>würdet dringen<br>würden dringen | würde gedrungen haben<br>würdest gedrungen haben<br>würde gedrungen haben | würden gedrungen haben<br>würdet gedrungen haben<br>würden gedrungen haben |

## EXAMPLES

Wir müssen durch diese dichte Menge dringen.
We have to force our way through this dense crowd.

Es ist dringend.
It's urgent.

Das Sonnenlicht drang ins Zimmer.
The sunlight streamed into the room.

**drohen**
to threaten, to menace
**Auxiliary verb:** haben **Past participle:** gedroht
**Imperative:** Drohe! Droht! Drohen Sie!

| Mode | Simple Tenses | | Compound Tenses | |
|---|---|---|---|---|
| | *Singular* | *Plural* | *Singular* | *Plural* |
| Indicative | **Present** | | **Present Perfect** | |
| | drohe<br>drohst<br>droht | drohen<br>droht<br>drohen | habe gedroht<br>hast gedroht<br>hat gedroht | haben gedroht<br>habt gedroht<br>haben gedroht |
| | **Past** | | **Past Perfect** | |
| | drohte<br>drohtest<br>drohte | drohten<br>drohtet<br>drohten | hatte gedroht<br>hattest gedroht<br>hatte gedroht | hatten gedroht<br>hattet gedroht<br>hatten gedroht |
| | **Future** | | **Future Perfect** | |
| | werde drohen<br>wirst drohen<br>wird drohen | werden drohen<br>werdet drohen<br>werden drohen | werde gedroht haben<br>wirst gedroht haben<br>wird gedroht haben | werden gedroht haben<br>werdet gedroht haben<br>werden gedroht haben |
| Subjunctive | **Present** | | **Present Perfect** | |
| | drohe<br>drohest<br>drohe | drohen<br>drohet<br>drohen | habe gedroht<br>habest gedroht<br>habe gedroht | haben gedroht<br>habet gedroht<br>haben gedroht |
| | **Past** | | **Past Perfect** | |
| | drohte<br>drohtest<br>drohte | drohten<br>drohtet<br>drohten | hätte gedroht<br>hättest gedroht<br>hätte gedroht | hätten gedroht<br>hättet gedroht<br>hätten gedroht |
| | **Future** | | **Future Perfect** | |
| | werde drohen<br>werdest drohen<br>werde drohen | werden drohen<br>werdet drohen<br>werden drohen | werde gedroht haben<br>werdest gedroht haben<br>werde gedroht haben | werden gedroht haben<br>werdet gedroht haben<br>werden gedroht haben |
| | **Present and Future Conditional** | | **Past Conditional** | |
| | würde drohen<br>würdest drohen<br>würde drohen | würden drohen<br>würdet drohen<br>würden drohen | würde gedroht haben<br>würdest gedroht haben<br>würde gedroht haben | würden gedroht haben<br>würdet gedroht haben<br>würden gedroht haben |

## EXAMPLES

Der Politiker drohte damit, die Zeitung zu verklagen.
The politician threatened to bring a suit against the newspaper.

Der Richter hat ihm mit dem Todesurteil gedroht.
The judge threatened him with the death penalty.

**drucken**
to print, to impress
**Auxiliary verb:** haben **Past participle:** gedruckt
**Imperative:** Drucke! Druckt! Drucken Sie!

| Mode | Simple Tenses | | Compound Tenses | |
|---|---|---|---|---|
| | *Singular* | *Plural* | *Singular* | *Plural* |
| Indicative | **Present** | | **Present Perfect** | |
| | drucke<br>druckst<br>druckt | drucken<br>druckt<br>drucken | habe gedruckt<br>hast gedruckt<br>hat gedruckt | haben gedruckt<br>habt gedruckt<br>haben gedruckt |
| | **Past** | | **Past Perfect** | |
| | druckte<br>drucktest<br>druckte | druckten<br>drucktet<br>druckten | hatte gedruckt<br>hattest gedruckt<br>hatte gedruckt | hatten gedruckt<br>hattet gedruckt<br>hatten gedruckt |
| | **Future** | | **Future Perfect** | |
| | werde drucken<br>wirst drucken<br>wird drucken | werden drucken<br>werdet drucken<br>werden drucken | werde gedruckt haben<br>wirst gedruckt haben<br>wird gedruckt haben | werden gedruckt haben<br>werdet gedruckt haben<br>werden gedruckt haben |
| Subjunctive | **Present** | | **Present Perfect** | |
| | drucke<br>druckest<br>drucke | drucken<br>drucket<br>drucken | habe gedruckt<br>habest gedruckt<br>habe gedruckt | haben gedruckt<br>habet gedruckt<br>haben gedruckt |
| | **Past** | | **Past Perfect** | |
| | druckte<br>drucktest<br>druckte | druckten<br>drucktet<br>druckten | hätte gedruckt<br>hättest gedruckt<br>hätte gedruckt | hätten gedruckt<br>hättet gedruckt<br>hätten gedruckt |
| | **Future** | | **Future Perfect** | |
| | werde drucken<br>werdest drucken<br>werde drucken | werden drucken<br>werdet drucken<br>werden drucken | werde gedruckt haben<br>werdest gedruckt haben<br>werde gedruckt haben | werden gedruckt haben<br>werdet gedruckt haben<br>werden gedruckt haben |
| | **Present and Future Conditional** | | **Past Conditional** | |
| | würde drucken<br>würdest drucken<br>würde drucken | würden drucken<br>würdet drucken<br>würden drucken | würde gedruckt haben<br>würdest gedruckt haben<br>würde gedruckt haben | würden gedruckt haben<br>würdet gedruckt haben<br>würden gedruckt haben |

## EXAMPLES

Der Dieb lügt wie gedruckt.
The thief is a bald-faced liar.

Gutenberg druckte die erste Bibel.
Gutenberg printed the first Bible.

Ihre Bücher sind gewöhnlich in Deutschland gedruckt worden.
Her books were usually printed in Germany.

**drücken**

to press, to squeeze, to oppress

**Auxiliary verb:** haben **Past participle:** gedrückt

**Imperative:** Drücke! Drückt! Drücken Sie!

| Mode | Simple Tenses | | Compound Tenses | |
|---|---|---|---|---|
| | *Singular* | *Plural* | *Singular* | *Plural* |
| Indicative | **Present** | | **Present Perfect** | |
| | drücke<br>drückst<br>drückt | drücken<br>drückt<br>drücken | habe gedrückt<br>hast gedrückt<br>hat gedrückt | haben gedrückt<br>habt gedrückt<br>haben gedrückt |
| | **Past** | | **Past Perfect** | |
| | drückte<br>drücktest<br>drückte | drückten<br>drücktet<br>drückten | hatte gedrückt<br>hattest gedrückt<br>hatte gedrückt | hatten gedrückt<br>hattet gedrückt<br>hatten gedrückt |
| | **Future** | | **Future Perfect** | |
| | werde drücken<br>wirst drücken<br>wird drücken | werden drücken<br>werdet drücken<br>werden drücken | werde gedrückt haben<br>wirst gedrückt haben<br>wird gedrückt haben | werden gedrückt haben<br>werdet gedrückt haben<br>werden gedrückt haben |
| Subjunctive | **Present** | | **Present Perfect** | |
| | drücke<br>drückest<br>drücke | drücken<br>drücket<br>drücken | habe gedrückt<br>habest gedrückt<br>habe gedrückt | haben gedrückt<br>habet gedrückt<br>haben gedrückt |
| | **Past** | | **Past Perfect** | |
| | drückte<br>drücktest<br>drückte | drückten<br>drücktet<br>drückten | hätte gedrückt<br>hättest gedrückt<br>hätte gedrückt | hätten gedrückt<br>hättet gedrückt<br>hätten gedrückt |
| | **Future** | | **Future Perfect** | |
| | werde drücken<br>werdest drücken<br>werde drücken | werden drücken<br>werdet drücken<br>werden drücken | werde gedrückt haben<br>werdest gedrückt haben<br>werde gedrückt haben | werden gedrückt haben<br>werdet gedrückt haben<br>werden gedrückt haben |
| | **Present and Future Conditional** | | **Past Conditional** | |
| | würde drücken<br>würdest drücken<br>würde drücken | würden drücken<br>würdet drücken<br>würden drücken | würde gedrückt haben<br>würdest gedrückt haben<br>würde gedrückt haben | würden gedrückt haben<br>würdet gedrückt haben<br>würden gedrückt haben |

## EXAMPLES

Er drückte mir ein bisschen Geld in die Hand.

He put some money in my hand.

Man muss diese Taste drücken, um den Computer anzustellen.

You have to press this button to turn on the computer.

**dulden**

to endure, to bear, to tolerate

**Auxiliary verb:** haben **Past participle:** geduldet

**Imperative:** Dulde! Duldet! Dulden Sie!

| Mode | Simple Tenses | | Compound Tenses | |
|---|---|---|---|---|
| | *Singular* | *Plural* | *Singular* | *Plural* |
| Indicative | **Present** | | **Present Perfect** | |
| | dulde<br>duldest<br>duldet | dulden<br>duldet<br>dulden | habe geduldet<br>hast geduldet<br>hat geduldet | haben geduldet<br>habt geduldet<br>haben geduldet |
| | **Past** | | **Past Perfect** | |
| | duldete<br>duldetest<br>duldete | duldeten<br>duldetet<br>duldeten | hatte geduldet<br>hattest geduldet<br>hatte geduldet | hatten geduldet<br>hattet geduldet<br>hatten geduldet |
| | **Future** | | **Future Perfect** | |
| | werde dulden<br>wirst dulden<br>wird dulden | werden dulden<br>werdet dulden<br>werden dulden | werde geduldet haben<br>wirst geduldet haben<br>wird geduldet haben | werden geduldet haben<br>werdet geduldet haben<br>werden geduldet haben |
| Subjunctive | **Present** | | **Present Perfect** | |
| | dulde<br>duldest<br>dulde | dulden<br>duldet<br>dulden | habe geduldet<br>habest geduldet<br>habe geduldet | haben geduldet<br>habet geduldet<br>haben geduldet |
| | **Past** | | **Past Perfect** | |
| | duldete<br>duldetest<br>duldete | duldeten<br>duldetet<br>duldeten | hätte geduldet<br>hättest geduldet<br>hätte geduldet | hätten geduldet<br>hättet geduldet<br>hätten geduldet |
| | **Future** | | **Future Perfect** | |
| | werde dulden<br>werdest dulden<br>werde dulden | werden dulden<br>werdet dulden<br>werden dulden | werde geduldet haben<br>werdest geduldet haben<br>werde geduldet haben | werden geduldet haben<br>werdet geduldet haben<br>werden geduldet haben |
| | **Present and Future Conditional** | | **Past Conditional** | |
| | würde dulden<br>würdest dulden<br>würde dulden | würden dulden<br>würdet dulden<br>würden dulden | würde geduldet haben<br>würdest geduldet haben<br>würde geduldet haben | würden geduldet haben<br>würdet geduldet haben<br>würden geduldet haben |

## EXAMPLES

Ich dulde es nicht, dass du meinen Fotoapparat benutzt.

I won't put up with your using my camera.

Mutter kann sein schlechtes Benehmen nicht mehr dulden.

Mother can't tolerate his bad behavior any longer.

**dürfen**
to be allowed, may
**Auxiliary verb:** haben **Past participle:** gedurft
**Imperative:** N/A

| Mode | Simple Tenses | | Compound Tenses | |
|---|---|---|---|---|
| | *Singular* | *Plural* | *Singular* | *Plural* |
| Indicative | **Present** | | **Present Perfect** | |
| | darf<br>darfst<br>darf | dürfen<br>dürft<br>dürfen | habe gedurft<br>hast gedurft<br>hat gedurft | haben gedurft<br>habt gedurft<br>haben gedurft |
| | **Past** | | **Past Perfect** | |
| | durfte<br>durftest<br>durfte | durften<br>durftet<br>durften | hatte gedurft<br>hattest gedurft<br>hatte gedurft | hatten gedurft<br>hattet gedurft<br>hatten gedurft |
| | **Future** | | **Future Perfect** | |
| | werde dürfen<br>wirst dürfen<br>wird dürfen | werden dürfen<br>werdet dürfen<br>werden dürfen | werde gedurft haben<br>wirst gedurft haben<br>wird gedurft haben | werden gedurft haben<br>werdet gedurft haben<br>werden gedurft haben |
| Subjunctive | **Present** | | **Present Perfect** | |
| | dürfe<br>dürfest<br>dürfe | dürfen<br>dürfet<br>dürfen | habe gedurft<br>habest gedurft<br>habe gedurft | haben gedurft<br>habet gedurft<br>haben gedurft |
| | **Past** | | **Past Perfect** | |
| | dürfte<br>dürftest<br>dürfte | dürften<br>dürftet<br>dürften | hätte gedurft<br>hättest gedurft<br>hätte gedurft | hätten gedurft<br>hättet gedurft<br>hätten gedurft |
| | **Future** | | **Future Perfect** | |
| | werde dürfen<br>werdest dürfen<br>werde dürfen | werden dürfen<br>werdet dürfen<br>werden dürfen | werde gedurft haben<br>werdest gedurft haben<br>werde gedurft haben | werden gedurft haben<br>werdet gedurft haben<br>werden gedurft haben |
| | **Present and Future Conditional** | | **Past Conditional** | |
| | würde dürfen<br>würdest dürfen<br>würde dürfen | würden dürfen<br>würdet dürfen<br>würden dürfen | würde gedurft haben<br>würdest gedurft haben<br>würde gedurft haben | würden gedurft haben<br>würdet gedurft haben<br>würden gedurft haben |

**Note:** This verb is a modal auxiliary. In the perfect and future tenses, when there is a second verb in the sentence, a double-infinitive structure is required: *Haben Sie mit ihm sprechen dürfen?* ("Were you allowed to speak with him?").

## EXAMPLES

| | |
|---|---|
| Darf ich bitten? | May I have this dance? |
| Sie dürfen nicht alles sagen, was Sie wollen. | You may not say everything you want. |

**duzen (sich)**
to address a person informally with *du*
**Auxiliary verb:** haben **Past participle:** geduzt
**Imperative:** Duze! Duzt! Duzen Sie!

| Mode | Simple Tenses | | Compound Tenses | |
|---|---|---|---|---|
| | *Singular* | *Plural* | *Singular* | *Plural* |
| Indicative | **Present** | | **Present Perfect** | |
| | duze<br>duzt<br>duzt | duzen<br>duzt<br>duzen | habe geduzt<br>hast geduzt<br>hat geduzt | haben geduzt<br>habt geduzt<br>haben geduzt |
| | **Past** | | **Past Perfect** | |
| | duzte<br>duztest<br>duzte | duzten<br>duztet<br>duzten | hatte geduzt<br>hattest geduzt<br>hatte geduzt | hatten geduzt<br>hattet geduzt<br>hatten geduzt |
| | **Future** | | **Future Perfect** | |
| | werde duzen<br>wirst duzen<br>wird duzen | werden duzen<br>werdet duzen<br>werden duzen | werde geduzt haben<br>wirst geduzt haben<br>wird geduzt haben | werden geduzt haben<br>werdet geduzt haben<br>werden geduzt haben |
| Subjunctive | **Present** | | **Present Perfect** | |
| | duze<br>duzest<br>duze | duzen<br>duzet<br>duzen | habe geduzt<br>habest geduzt<br>habe geduzt | haben geduzt<br>habet geduzt<br>haben geduzt |
| | **Past** | | **Past Perfect** | |
| | duzte<br>duztest<br>duzte | duzten<br>duztet<br>duzten | hätte geduzt<br>hättest geduzt<br>hätte geduzt | hätten geduzt<br>hättet geduzt<br>hätten geduzt |
| | **Future** | | **Future Perfect** | |
| | werde duzen<br>werdest duzen<br>werde duzen | werden duzen<br>werdet duzen<br>werden duzen | werde geduzt haben<br>werdest geduzt haben<br>werde geduzt haben | werden geduzt haben<br>werdet geduzt haben<br>werden geduzt haben |
| | **Present and Future Conditional** | | **Past Conditional** | |
| | würde duzen<br>würdest duzen<br>würde duzen | würden duzen<br>würdet duzen<br>würden duzen | würde geduzt haben<br>würdest geduzt haben<br>würde geduzt haben | würden geduzt haben<br>würdet geduzt haben<br>würden geduzt haben |

## EXAMPLE

Man darf alle Kinder duzen.

You can say *du* to all children.

**einfallen**
to fall in, to occur to, to invade
**Auxiliary verb:** sein **Past participle:** eingefallen
**Imperative:** Falle ein! Fallt ein! Fallen Sie ein!

| Mode | Simple Tenses | | Compound Tenses | |
|---|---|---|---|---|
| | *Singular* | *Plural* | *Singular* | *Plural* |
| Indicative | **Present** | | **Present Perfect** | |
| | falle ein<br>fällst ein<br>fällt ein | fallen ein<br>fallt ein<br>fallen ein | bin eingefallen<br>bist eingefallen<br>ist eingefallen | sind eingefallen<br>seid eingefallen<br>sind eingefallen |
| | **Past** | | **Past Perfect** | |
| | fiel ein<br>fielst ein<br>fiel ein | fielen ein<br>fielt ein<br>fielen ein | war eingefallen<br>warst eingefallen<br>war eingefallen | waren eingefallen<br>wart eingefallen<br>waren eingefallen |
| | **Future** | | **Future Perfect** | |
| | werde einfallen<br>wirst einfallen<br>wird einfallen | werden einfallen<br>werdet einfallen<br>werden einfallen | werde eingefallen sein<br>wirst eingefallen sein<br>wird eingefallen sein | werden eingefallen sein<br>werdet eingefallen sein<br>werden eingefallen sein |
| Subjunctive | **Present** | | **Present Perfect** | |
| | falle ein<br>fallest ein<br>falle ein | fallen ein<br>fallet ein<br>fallen ein | sei eingefallen<br>seiest eingefallen<br>sei eingefallen | seien eingefallen<br>seiet eingefallen<br>seien eingefallen |
| | **Past** | | **Past Perfect** | |
| | fiele ein<br>fielest ein<br>fiele ein | fielen ein<br>fielet ein<br>fielen ein | wäre eingefallen<br>wärest eingefallen<br>wäre eingefallen | wären eingefallen<br>wäret eingefallen<br>wären eingefallen |
| | **Future** | | **Future Perfect** | |
| | werde einfallen<br>werdest einfallen<br>werde einfallen | werden einfallen<br>werdet einfallen<br>werden einfallen | werde eingefallen sein<br>werdest eingefallen sein<br>werde eingefallen sein | werden eingefallen sein<br>werdet eingefallen sein<br>werden eingefallen sein |
| | **Present and Future Conditional** | | **Past Conditional** | |
| | würde einfallen<br>würdest einfallen<br>würde einfallen | würden einfallen<br>würdet einfallen<br>würden einfallen | würde eingefallen sein<br>würdest eingefallen sein<br>würde eingefallen sein | würden eingefallen sein<br>würdet eingefallen sein<br>würden eingefallen sein |

## EXAMPLES

| | |
|---|---|
| Nach dem Erdbeben ist unser Haus eingefallen. | After the earthquake our house collapsed. |
| Ist dir der Name des Schauspielers nicht eingefallen? | Didn't you recall the name of the actor? |
| Die Armee droht in die Stadt einzufallen. | The army is threatening to invade the city. |

**einladen**
to invite
**Auxiliary verb:** haben **Past participle:** eingeladen
**Imperative:** Lade ein! Ladet ein! Laden Sie ein!

| Mode | Simple Tenses | | Compound Tenses | |
|---|---|---|---|---|
| | *Singular* | *Plural* | *Singular* | *Plural* |
| Indicative | **Present** | | **Present Perfect** | |
| | lade ein<br>lädst ein<br>lädt ein | laden ein<br>ladet ein<br>laden ein | habe eingeladen<br>hast eingeladen<br>hat eingeladen | haben eingeladen<br>habt eingeladen<br>haben eingeladen |
| | **Past** | | **Past Perfect** | |
| | lud ein<br>ludst ein<br>lud ein | luden ein<br>ludet ein<br>luden ein | hatte eingeladen<br>hattest eingeladen<br>hatte eingeladen | hatten eingeladen<br>hattet eingeladen<br>hatten eingeladen |
| | **Future** | | **Future Perfect** | |
| | werde einladen<br>wirst einladen<br>wird einladen | werden einladen<br>werdet einladen<br>werden einladen | werde eingeladen haben<br>wirst eingeladen haben<br>wird eingeladen haben | werden eingeladen haben<br>werdet eingeladen haben<br>werden eingeladen haben |
| Subjunctive | **Present** | | **Present Perfect** | |
| | lade ein<br>ladest ein<br>lade ein | laden ein<br>ladet ein<br>laden ein | habe eingeladen<br>habest eingeladen<br>habe eingeladen | haben eingeladen<br>habet eingeladen<br>haben eingeladen |
| | **Past** | | **Past Perfect** | |
| | lüde ein<br>lüdest ein<br>lüde ein | lüden ein<br>lüdet ein<br>lüden ein | hätte eingeladen<br>hättest eingeladen<br>hätte eingeladen | hätten eingeladen<br>hättet eingeladen<br>hätten eingeladen |
| | **Future** | | **Future Perfect** | |
| | werde einladen<br>werdest einladen<br>werde einladen | werden einladen<br>werdet einladen<br>werden einladen | werde eingeladen haben<br>werdest eingeladen haben<br>werde eingeladen haben | werden eingeladen haben<br>werdet eingeladen haben<br>werden eingeladen haben |
| | **Present and Future Conditional** | | **Past Conditional** | |
| | würde einladen<br>würdest einladen<br>würde einladen | würden einladen<br>würdet einladen<br>würden einladen | würde eingeladen haben<br>würdest eingeladen haben<br>würde eingeladen haben | würden eingeladen haben<br>würdet eingeladen haben<br>würden eingeladen haben |

## EXAMPLES

Der Rechtsanwalt hat uns zum Mittagessen eingeladen. — The lawyer invited us to lunch.

Wen lädst du zum Tanz ein? — Whom are you asking to the dance?

**einschlafen**
to fall asleep
**Auxiliary verb:** sein **Past participle:** eingeschlafen
**Imperative:** Schlafe ein! Schlaft ein! Schlafen Sie ein!

| Mode | Simple Tenses | | Compound Tenses | |
|---|---|---|---|---|
| | *Singular* | *Plural* | *Singular* | *Plural* |
| Indicative | **Present** | | **Present Perfect** | |
| | schlafe ein<br>schläfst ein<br>schläft ein | schlafen ein<br>schlaft ein<br>schlafen ein | bin eingeschlafen<br>bist eingeschlafen<br>ist eingeschlafen | sind eingeschlafen<br>seid eingeschlafen<br>sind eingeschlafen |
| | **Past** | | **Past Perfect** | |
| | schlief ein<br>schliefst ein<br>schlief ein | schliefen ein<br>schlieft ein<br>schliefen ein | war eingeschlafen<br>warst eingeschlafen<br>war eingeschlafen | waren eingeschlafen<br>wart eingeschlafen<br>waren eingeschlafen |
| | **Future** | | **Future Perfect** | |
| | werde einschlafen<br>wirst einschlafen<br>wird einschlafen | werden einschlafen<br>werdet einschlafen<br>werden einschlafen | werde eingeschlafen sein<br>wirst eingeschlafen sein<br>wird eingeschlafen sein | werden eingeschlafen sein<br>werdet eingeschlafen sein<br>werden eingeschlafen sein |
| Subjunctive | **Present** | | **Present Perfect** | |
| | schlafe ein<br>schlafest ein<br>schlafe ein | schlafen ein<br>schlafet ein<br>schlafen ein | sei eingeschlafen<br>seiest eingeschlafen<br>sei eingeschlafen | seien eingeschlafen<br>seiet eingeschlafen<br>seien eingeschlafen |
| | **Past** | | **Past Perfect** | |
| | schliefe ein<br>schliefest ein<br>schliefe ein | schliefen ein<br>schliefet ein<br>schliefen ein | wäre eingeschlafen<br>wärest eingeschlafen<br>wäre eingeschlafen | wären eingeschlafen<br>wäret eingeschlafen<br>wären eingeschlafen |
| | **Future** | | **Future Perfect** | |
| | werde einschlafen<br>werdest einschlafen<br>werde einschlafen | werden einschlafen<br>werdet einschlafen<br>werden einschlafen | werde eingeschlafen sein<br>werdest eingeschlafen sein<br>werde eingeschlafen sein | werden eingeschlafen sein<br>werdet eingeschlafen sein<br>werden eingeschlafen sein |
| | **Present and Future Conditional** | | **Past Conditional** | |
| | würde einschlafen<br>würdest einschlafen<br>würde einschlafen | würden einschlafen<br>würdet einschlafen<br>würden einschlafen | würde eingeschlafen sein<br>würdest eingeschlafen sein<br>würde eingeschlafen sein | würden eingeschlafen sein<br>würdet eingeschlafen sein<br>würden eingeschlafen sein |

## EXAMPLES

Großvater schläft immer im Kino ein.
Grandfather always falls asleep at the movies.

Meine Füße sind eingeschlafen.
My feet fell asleep.

**einsteigen**
to get on (a vehicle), to board
**Auxiliary verb:** sein **Past participle:** eingestiegen
**Imperative:** Steige ein! Steigt ein! Steigen Sie ein!

| Mode | Simple Tenses | | Compound Tenses | |
|---|---|---|---|---|
| | *Singular* | *Plural* | *Singular* | *Plural* |
| Indicative | **Present** | | **Present Perfect** | |
| | steige ein<br>steigst ein<br>steigt ein | steigen ein<br>steigt ein<br>steigen ein | bin eingestiegen<br>bist eingestiegen<br>ist eingestiegen | sind eingestiegen<br>seid eingestiegen<br>sind eingestiegen |
| | **Past** | | **Past Perfect** | |
| | stieg ein<br>stiegst ein<br>stieg ein | stiegen ein<br>stiegt ein<br>stiegen ein | war eingestiegen<br>warst eingestiegen<br>war eingestiegen | waren eingestiegen<br>wart eingestiegen<br>waren eingestiegen |
| | **Future** | | **Future Perfect** | |
| | werde einsteigen<br>wirst einsteigen<br>wird einsteigen | werden einsteigen<br>werdet einsteigen<br>werden einsteigen | werde eingestiegen sein<br>wirst eingestiegen sein<br>wird eingestiegen sein | werden eingestiegen sein<br>werdet eingestiegen sein<br>werden eingestiegen sein |
| Subjunctive | **Present** | | **Present Perfect** | |
| | steige ein<br>steigest ein<br>steige ein | steigen ein<br>steiget ein<br>steigen ein | sei eingestiegen<br>seiest eingestiegen<br>sei eingestiegen | seien eingestiegen<br>seiet eingestiegen<br>seien eingestiegen |
| | **Past** | | **Past Perfect** | |
| | stiege ein<br>stiegest ein<br>stiege ein | stiegen ein<br>stieget ein<br>stiegen ein | wäre eingestiegen<br>wärest eingestiegen<br>wäre eingestiegen | wären eingestiegen<br>wäret eingestiegen<br>wären eingestiegen |
| | **Future** | | **Future Perfect** | |
| | werde einsteigen<br>werdest einsteigen<br>werde einsteigen | werden einsteigen<br>werdet einsteigen<br>werden einsteigen | werde eingestiegen sein<br>werdest eingestiegen sein<br>werde eingestiegen sein | werden eingestiegen sein<br>werdet eingestiegen sein<br>werden eingestiegen sein |
| | **Present and Future Conditional** | | **Past Conditional** | |
| | würde einsteigen<br>würdest einsteigen<br>würde einsteigen | würden einsteigen<br>würdet einsteigen<br>würden einsteigen | würde eingestiegen sein<br>würdest eingestiegen sein<br>würde eingestiegen sein | würden eingestiegen sein<br>würdet eingestiegen sein<br>würden eingestiegen sein |

## EXAMPLES

Sagen Sie mir bitte, wo ich in die U-Bahn einsteigen kann.
Please tell me where I can get on the subway.

Steigen wir in diesen Bus ein!
Let's get on this bus.

**entdecken**
to discover, to find out
**Auxiliary verb:** haben **Past participle:** entdeckt
**Imperative:** Entdecke! Entdeckt! Entdecken Sie!

| Mode | Simple Tenses | | Compound Tenses | |
|---|---|---|---|---|
| | *Singular* | *Plural* | *Singular* | *Plural* |
| Indicative | **Present** | | **Present Perfect** | |
| | entdecke<br>entdeckst<br>entdeckt | entdecken<br>entdeckt<br>entdecken | habe entdeckt<br>hast entdeckt<br>hat entdeckt | haben entdeckt<br>habt entdeckt<br>haben entdeckt |
| | **Past** | | **Past Perfect** | |
| | entdeckte<br>entdecktest<br>entdeckte | entdeckten<br>entdecktet<br>entdeckten | hatte entdeckt<br>hattest entdeckt<br>hatte entdeckt | hatten entdeckt<br>hattet entdeckt<br>hatten entdeckt |
| | **Future** | | **Future Perfect** | |
| | werde entdecken<br>wirst entdecken<br>wird entdecken | werden entdecken<br>werdet entdecken<br>werden entdecken | werde entdeckt haben<br>wirst entdeckt haben<br>wird entdeckt haben | werden entdeckt haben<br>werdet entdeckt haben<br>werden entdeckt haben |
| Subjunctive | **Present** | | **Present Perfect** | |
| | entdecke<br>entdeckest<br>entdecke | entdecken<br>entdecket<br>entdecken | habe entdeckt<br>habest entdeckt<br>habe entdeckt | haben entdeckt<br>habet entdeckt<br>haben entdeckt |
| | **Past** | | **Past Perfect** | |
| | entdeckte<br>entdecktest<br>entdeckte | entdeckten<br>entdecktet<br>entdeckten | hätte entdeckt<br>hättest entdeckt<br>hätte entdeckt | hätten entdeckt<br>hättet entdeckt<br>hätten entdeckt |
| | **Future** | | **Future Perfect** | |
| | werde entdecken<br>werdest entdecken<br>werde entdecken | werden entdecken<br>werdet entdecken<br>werden entdecken | werde entdeckt haben<br>werdest entdeckt haben<br>werde entdeckt haben | werden entdeckt haben<br>werdet entdeckt haben<br>werden entdeckt haben |
| | **Present and Future Conditional** | | **Past Conditional** | |
| | würde entdecken<br>würdest entdecken<br>würde entdecken | würden entdecken<br>würdet entdecken<br>würden entdecken | würde entdeckt haben<br>würdest entdeckt haben<br>würde entdeckt haben | würden entdeckt haben<br>würdet entdeckt haben<br>würden entdeckt haben |

## EXAMPLES

Haben Kolumbus oder die Skandinavier Amerika entdeckt?
Did Columbus or the Scandinavians discover America?

Ich entdeckte ein paar Fehler in Ihrer Arbeit.
I discovered a couple of errors in your work.

**entfernen**
to remove, to take away
**Auxiliary verb:** haben **Past participle:** entfernt
**Imperative:** Entferne! Entfernt! Entfernen Sie!

| Mode | Simple Tenses | | Compound Tenses | |
|---|---|---|---|---|
| | *Singular* | *Plural* | *Singular* | *Plural* |
| Indicative | **Present** | | **Present Perfect** | |
| | entferne<br>entfernst<br>entfernt | entfernen<br>entfernt<br>entfernen | habe entfernt<br>hast entfernt<br>hat entfernt | haben entfernt<br>habt entfernt<br>haben entfernt |
| | **Past** | | **Past Perfect** | |
| | entfernte<br>entferntest<br>entfernte | entfernten<br>entferntet<br>entfernten | hatte entfernt<br>hattest entfernt<br>hatte entfernt | hatten entfernt<br>hattet entfernt<br>hatten entfernt |
| | **Future** | | **Future Perfect** | |
| | werde entfernen<br>wirst entfernen<br>wird entfernen | werden entfernen<br>werdet entfernen<br>werden entfernen | werde entfernt haben<br>wirst entfernt haben<br>wird entfernt haben | werden entfernt haben<br>werdet entfernt haben<br>werden entfernt haben |
| Subjunctive | **Present** | | **Present Perfect** | |
| | entferne<br>entfernest<br>entferne | entfernen<br>entfernet<br>entfernen | habe entfernt<br>habest entfernt<br>habe entfernt | haben entfernt<br>habet entfernt<br>haben entfernt |
| | **Past** | | **Past Perfect** | |
| | entfernte<br>entferntest<br>entfernte | entfernten<br>entferntet<br>entfernten | hätte entfernt<br>hättest entfernt<br>hätte entfernt | hätten entfernt<br>hättet entfernt<br>hätten entfernt |
| | **Future** | | **Future Perfect** | |
| | werde entfernen<br>werdest entfernen<br>werde entfernen | werden entfernen<br>werdet entfernen<br>werden entfernen | werde entfernt haben<br>werdest entfernt haben<br>werde entfernt haben | werden entfernt haben<br>werdet entfernt haben<br>werden entfernt haben |
| | **Present and Future Conditional** | | **Past Conditional** | |
| | würde entfernen<br>würdest entfernen<br>würde entfernen | würden entfernen<br>würdet entfernen<br>würden entfernen | würde entfernt haben<br>würdest entfernt haben<br>würde entfernt haben | würden entfernt haben<br>würdet entfernt haben<br>würden entfernt haben |

## EXAMPLES

Können diese Flecke aus meiner Bluse entfernt werden?
Das ist leider eine entfernte Möglichkeit.
Bitte entferne dich nicht von der Gruppe!

Can these spots be removed from my blouse?
Unfortunately, that's a remote possibility.
Please don't wander away from the group.

**entfliehen**
to flee from, to escape
**Auxiliary verb:** sein **Past participle:** entflohen
**Imperative:** Entfliehe! Entflieht! Entfliehen Sie!

| Mode | Simple Tenses | | Compound Tenses | |
|---|---|---|---|---|
| | *Singular* | *Plural* | *Singular* | *Plural* |
| Indicative | **Present** | | **Present Perfect** | |
| | entfliehe<br>entfliehst<br>entflieht | entfliehen<br>entflieht<br>entfliehen | bin entflohen<br>bist entflohen<br>ist entflohen | sind entflohen<br>seid entflohen<br>sind entflohen |
| | **Past** | | **Past Perfect** | |
| | entfloh<br>entflohst<br>entfloh | entflohen<br>entfloht<br>entflohen | war entflohen<br>warst entflohen<br>war entflohen | waren entflohen<br>wart entflohen<br>waren entflohen |
| | **Future** | | **Future Perfect** | |
| | werde entfliehen<br>wirst entfliehen<br>wird entfliehen | werden entfliehen<br>werdet entfliehen<br>werden entfliehen | werde entflohen sein<br>wirst entflohen sein<br>wird entflohen sein | werden entflohen sein<br>werdet entflohen sein<br>werden entflohen sein |
| Subjunctive | **Present** | | **Present Perfect** | |
| | entfliehe<br>entfliehest<br>entfliehe | entfliehen<br>entfliehet<br>entfliehen | sei entflohen<br>seiest entflohen<br>sei entflohen | seien entflohen<br>seiet entflohen<br>seien entflohen |
| | **Past** | | **Past Perfect** | |
| | entflöhe<br>entflöhest<br>entflöhe | entflöhen<br>entflöhet<br>entflöhen | wäre entflohen<br>wärest entflohen<br>wäre entflohen | wären entflohen<br>wäret entflohen<br>wären entflohen |
| | **Future** | | **Future Perfect** | |
| | werde entfliehen<br>werdest entfliehen<br>werde entfliehen | werden entfliehen<br>werdet entfliehen<br>werden entfliehen | werde entflohen sein<br>werdest entflohen sein<br>werde entflohen sein | werden entflohen sein<br>werdet entflohen sein<br>werden entflohen sein |
| | **Present and Future Conditional** | | **Past Conditional** | |
| | würde entfliehen<br>würdest entfliehen<br>würde entfliehen | würden entfliehen<br>würdet entfliehen<br>würden entfliehen | würde entflohen sein<br>würdest entflohen sein<br>würde entflohen sein | würden entflohen sein<br>würdet entflohen sein<br>würden entflohen sein |

## EXAMPLES

Der verhaftete Mann ist aus dem Gefängnis entflohen.

The arrested man has escaped from the prison.

Deutsche Touristen entfliehen dem Winter gern in Spanien.

German tourists like to escape to Spain in the winter.

**entfremden (sich)**
to estrange, to alienate
**Auxiliary verb:** haben **Past participle:** entfremdet
**Imperative:** Entfremde! Entfremdet! Entfremden Sie!

| Mode | Simple Tenses | | Compound Tenses | |
|---|---|---|---|---|
| | *Singular* | *Plural* | *Singular* | *Plural* |
| Indicative | **Present** | | **Present Perfect** | |
| | entfremde<br>entfremdest<br>entfremdet | entfremden<br>entfremdet<br>entfremden | habe entfremdet<br>hast entfremdet<br>hat entfremdet | haben entfremdet<br>habt entfremdet<br>haben entfremdet |
| | **Past** | | **Past Perfect** | |
| | enttremdete<br>entfremdetest<br>entfremdete | enttremdeten<br>entfremdetet<br>entfremdeten | hatte entfremdet<br>hattest entfremdet<br>hatte entfremdet | hatten entfremdet<br>hattet entfremdet<br>hatten entfremdet |
| | **Future** | | **Future Perfect** | |
| | werde entfremden<br>wirst entfremden<br>wird entfremden | werden entfremden<br>werdet entfremden<br>werden entfremden | werde entfremdet haben<br>wirst entfremdet haben<br>wird entfremdet haben | werden entfremdet haben<br>werdet entfremdet haben<br>werden entfremdet haben |
| Subjunctive | **Present** | | **Present Perfect** | |
| | entfremde<br>entfremdest<br>entfremde | entfremden<br>entfremdet<br>entfremden | habe entfremdet<br>habest entfremdet<br>habe entfremdet | haben entfremdet<br>habet entfremdet<br>haben entfremdet |
| | **Past** | | **Past Perfect** | |
| | entfremdete<br>entfremdetest<br>entfremdete | entfremdeten<br>entfremdetet<br>entfremdeten | hätte entfremdet<br>hättest entfremdet<br>hätte entfremdet | hätten entfremdet<br>hättet entfremdet<br>hätten entfremdet |
| | **Future** | | **Future Perfect** | |
| | werde entfremden<br>werdest entfremden<br>werde entfremden | werden entfremden<br>werdet entfremden<br>werden entfremden | werde entfremdet haben<br>werdest entfremdet haben<br>werde entfremdet haben | werden entfremdet haben<br>werdet entfremdet haben<br>werden entfremdet haben |
| | **Present and Future Conditional** | | **Past Conditional** | |
| | würde entfremden<br>würdest entfremden<br>würde entfremden | würden entfremden<br>würdet entfremden<br>würden entfremden | würde entfremdet haben<br>würdest entfremdet haben<br>würde entfremdet haben | würden entfremdet haben<br>würdet entfremdet haben<br>würden entfremdet haben |

## EXAMPLES

Niemand versteht, warum er sich von seinen Freunden entfremdet hat.
No one understands why he alienated himself from his friends.

Angelika hat sich von ihrem Mann entfremdet.
Angelika has been feeling estranged from her husband.

**enthaupten**
to behead
**Auxiliary verb:** haben **Past participle:** enthauptet
**Imperative:** Enthaupte! Enthauptet! Enthaupten Sie!

| Mode | Simple Tenses | | Compound Tenses | |
|---|---|---|---|---|
| | *Singular* | *Plural* | *Singular* | *Plural* |
| Indicative | **Present** | | **Present Perfect** | |
| | enthaupte<br>enthauptest<br>enthauptet | enthaupten<br>enthauptet<br>enthaupten | habe enthauptet<br>hast enthauptet<br>hat enthauptet | haben enthauptet<br>habt enthauptet<br>haben enthauptet |
| | **Past** | | **Past Perfect** | |
| | enthauptete<br>enthauptetest<br>enthauptete | enthaupteten<br>enthauptetet<br>enthaupteten | hatte enthauptet<br>hattest enthauptet<br>hatte enthauptet | hatten enthauptet<br>hattet enthauptet<br>hatten enthauptet |
| | **Future** | | **Future Perfect** | |
| | werde enthaupten<br>wirst enthaupten<br>wird enthaupten | werden enthaupten<br>werdet enthaupten<br>werden enthaupten | werde enthauptet haben<br>wirst enthauptet haben<br>wird enthauptet haben | werden enthauptet haben<br>werdet enthauptet haben<br>werden enthauptet haben |
| Subjunctive | **Present** | | **Present Perfect** | |
| | enthaupte<br>enthauptest<br>enthaupte | enthaupten<br>enthauptet<br>enthaupten | habe enthauptet<br>habest enthauptet<br>habe enthauptet | haben enthauptet<br>habet enthauptet<br>haben enthauptet |
| | **Past** | | **Past Perfect** | |
| | enthauptete<br>enthauptetest<br>enthauptete | enthaupteten<br>enthauptetet<br>enthaupteten | hätte enthauptet<br>hättest enthauptet<br>hätte enthauptet | hätten enthauptet<br>hättet enthauptet<br>hätten enthauptet |
| | **Future** | | **Future Perfect** | |
| | werde enthaupten<br>werdest enthaupten<br>werde enthaupten | werden enthaupten<br>werdet enthaupten<br>werden enthaupten | werde enthauptet haben<br>werdest enthauptet haben<br>werde enthauptet haben | werden enthauptet haben<br>werdet enthauptet haben<br>werden enthauptet haben |
| | **Present and Future Conditional** | | **Past Conditional** | |
| | würde enthaupten<br>würdest enthaupten<br>würde enthaupten | würden enthaupten<br>würdet enthaupten<br>würden enthaupten | würde enthauptet haben<br>würdest enthauptet haben<br>würde enthauptet haben | würden enthauptet haben<br>würdet enthauptet haben<br>würden enthauptet haben |

## EXAMPLES

Die Rebellen haben den alten König enthauptet.
The rebel troops have beheaded the old king.

Enthauptung ist heutzutage ungesetzlich.
Beheading is illegal nowadays.

**entrüsten (sich)**
to feel enraged
**Auxiliary verb:** haben **Past participle:** entrüstet
**Imperative:** Entrüste! Entrüstet! Entrüsten Sie!

| Mode | Simple Tenses | | Compound Tenses | |
|---|---|---|---|---|
| | *Singular* | *Plural* | *Singular* | *Plural* |
| Indicative | **Present** | | **Present Perfect** | |
| | entrüste<br>entrüstest<br>entrüstet | entrüsten<br>entrüstet<br>entrüsten | habe entrüstet<br>hast entrüstet<br>hat entrüstet | haben entrüstet<br>habt entrüstet<br>haben entrüstet |
| | **Past** | | **Past Perfect** | |
| | entrüstete<br>entrüstetest<br>entrüstete | entrüsteten<br>entrüstetet<br>entrüsteten | hatte entrüstet<br>hattest entrüstet<br>hatte entrüstet | hatten entrüstet<br>hattet entrüstet<br>hatten entrüstet |
| | **Future** | | **Future Perfect** | |
| | werde entrüsten<br>wirst entrüsten<br>wird entrüsten | werden entrüsten<br>werdet entrüsten<br>werden entrüsten | werde entrüstet haben<br>wirst entrüstet haben<br>wird entrüstet haben | werden entrüstet haben<br>werdet entrüstet haben<br>werden entrüstet haben |
| Subjunctive | **Present** | | **Present Perfect** | |
| | entrüste<br>entrüstest<br>entrüste | entrüsten<br>entrüstet<br>entrüsten | habe entrüstet<br>habest entrüstet<br>habe entrüstet | haben entrüstet<br>habet entrüstet<br>haben entrüstet |
| | **Past** | | **Past Perfect** | |
| | entrüstete<br>entrüstetest<br>entrüstete | entrüsteten<br>entrüstetet<br>entrüsteten | hätte entrüstet<br>hättest entrüstet<br>hätte entrüstet | hätten entrüstet<br>hättet entrüstet<br>hätten entrüstet |
| | **Future** | | **Future Perfect** | |
| | werde entrüsten<br>werdest entrüsten<br>werde entrüsten | werden entrüsten<br>werdet entrüsten<br>werden entrüsten | werde entrüstet haben<br>werdest entrüstet haben<br>werde entrüstet haben | werden entrüstet haben<br>werdet entrüstet haben<br>werden entrüstet haben |
| | **Present and Future Conditional** | | **Past Conditional** | |
| | würde entrüsten<br>würdest entrüsten<br>würde entrüsten | würden entrüsten<br>würdet entrüsten<br>würden entrüsten | würde entrüstet haben<br>würdest entrüstet haben<br>würde entrüstet haben | würden entrüstet haben<br>würdet entrüstet haben<br>würden entrüstet haben |

## EXAMPLES

Der unerwartete Angriff hat die ganze Nation entrüstet.
The unexpected attack enraged the whole nation.

Er entrüstete sich über den hohen Preis.
He expressed his anger at the high price.

**entscheiden (sich)**
to decide
**Auxiliary verb:** haben **Past participle:** entschieden
**Imperative:** Entscheide! Entscheidet! Entscheiden Sie!

| Mode | Simple Tenses | | Compound Tenses | |
|---|---|---|---|---|
| | *Singular* | *Plural* | *Singular* | *Plural* |
| Indicative | **Present** | | **Present Perfect** | |
| | entscheide<br>entscheidest<br>entscheidet | entscheiden<br>entscheidet<br>entscheiden | habe entschieden<br>hast entschieden<br>hat entschieden | haben entschieden<br>habt entschieden<br>haben entschieden |
| | **Past** | | **Past Perfect** | |
| | entschied<br>entschiedest<br>entschied | entschieden<br>entschiedet<br>entschieden | hatte entschieden<br>hattest entschieden<br>hatte entschieden | hatten entschieden<br>hattet entschieden<br>hatten entschieden |
| | **Future** | | **Future Perfect** | |
| | werde entscheiden<br>wirst entscheiden<br>wird entscheiden | werden entscheiden<br>werdet entscheiden<br>werden entscheiden | werde entschieden haben<br>wirst entschieden haben<br>wird entschieden haben | werden entschieden haben<br>werdet entschieden haben<br>werden entschieden haben |
| Subjunctive | **Present** | | **Present Perfect** | |
| | entscheide<br>entscheidest<br>entscheide | entscheiden<br>entscheidet<br>entscheiden | habe entschieden<br>habest entschieden<br>habe entschieden | haben entschieden<br>habet entschieden<br>haben entschieden |
| | **Past** | | **Past Perfect** | |
| | entschiede<br>entschiedest<br>entschiede | entschieden<br>entschiedet<br>entschieden | hätte entschieden<br>hättest entschieden<br>hätte entschieden | hätten entschieden<br>hättet entschieden<br>hätten entschieden |
| | **Future** | | **Future Perfect** | |
| | werde entscheiden<br>werdest entscheiden<br>werde entscheiden | werden entscheiden<br>werdet entscheiden<br>werden entscheiden | werde entschieden haben<br>werdest entschieden haben<br>werde entschieden haben | werden entschieden haben<br>werdet entschieden haben<br>werden entschieden haben |
| | **Present and Future Conditional** | | **Past Conditional** | |
| | würde entscheiden<br>würdest entscheiden<br>würde entscheiden | würden entscheiden<br>würdet entscheiden<br>würden entscheiden | würde entschieden haben<br>würdest entschieden haben<br>würde entschieden haben | würden entschieden haben<br>würdet entschieden haben<br>würden entschieden haben |

## EXAMPLES

Ich habe mich für das rote Kleid entschieden.
I decided in favor of the red dress.

Der Bauingenieur entscheidet über den Bau der Brücke.
The engineer will decide about the construction of the bridge.

**entschuldigen (sich)**
to excuse
**Auxiliary verb:** haben **Past participle:** entschuldigt
**Imperative:** Entschuldige! Entschuldigt! Entschuldigen Sie!

| Mode | Simple Tenses | | Compound Tenses | |
|---|---|---|---|---|
| | *Singular* | *Plural* | *Singular* | *Plural* |
| Indicative | **Present** | | **Present Perfect** | |
| | entschuldige<br>entschuldigst<br>entschuldigt | entschuldigen<br>entschuldigt<br>entschuldigen | habe entschuldigt<br>hast entschuldigt<br>hat entschuldigt | haben entschuldigt<br>habt entschuldigt<br>haben entschuldigt |
| | **Past** | | **Past Perfect** | |
| | entschuldigte<br>entschuldigtest<br>entschuldigte | entschuldigten<br>entschuldigtet<br>entschuldigten | hatte entschuldigt<br>hattest entschuldigt<br>hatte entschuldigt | hatten entschuldigt<br>hattet entschuldigt<br>hatten entschuldigt |
| | **Future** | | **Future Perfect** | |
| | werde entschuldigen<br>wirst entschuldigen<br>wird entschuldigen | werden entschuldigen<br>werdet entschuldigen<br>werden entschuldigen | werde entschuldigt haben<br>wirst entschuldigt haben<br>wird entschuldigt haben | werden entschuldigt haben<br>werdet entschuldigt haben<br>werden entschuldigt haben |
| Subjunctive | **Present** | | **Present Perfect** | |
| | entschuldige<br>entschuldigest<br>entschuldige | entschuldigen<br>entschuldiget<br>entschuldigen | habe entschuldigt<br>habest entschuldigt<br>habe entschuldigt | haben entschuldigt<br>habet entschuldigt<br>haben entschuldigt |
| | **Past** | | **Past Perfect** | |
| | entschuldigte<br>entschuldigtest<br>entschuldigte | entschuldigten<br>entschuldigtet<br>entschuldigten | hätte entschuldigt<br>hättest entschuldigt<br>hätte entschuldigt | hätten entschuldigt<br>hättet entschuldigt<br>hätten entschuldigt |
| | **Future** | | **Future Perfect** | |
| | werde entschuldigen<br>werdest entschuldigen<br>werde entschuldigen | werden entschuldigen<br>werdet entschuldigen<br>werden entschuldigen | werde entschuldigt haben<br>werdest entschuldigt haben<br>werde entschuldigt haben | werden entschuldigt haben<br>werdet entschuldigt haben<br>werden entschuldigt haben |
| | **Present and Future Conditional** | | **Past Conditional** | |
| | würde entschuldigen<br>würdest entschuldigen<br>würde entschuldigen | würden entschuldigen<br>würdet entschuldigen<br>würden entschuldigen | würde entschuldigt haben<br>würdest entschuldigt haben<br>würde entschuldigt haben | würden entschuldigt haben<br>würdet entschuldigt haben<br>würden entschuldigt haben |

## EXAMPLES

| | |
|---|---|
| Er will sich bei Ihnen entschuldigen. | He wants to apologize to you. |
| Das lässt sich nicht entschuldigen. | There's no excuse for that. |
| Bitte entschuldigen Sie die Störung. | Please pardon the interruption. |

**entspannen (sich)**
to relax
**Auxiliary verb:** haben **Past participle:** entspannt
**Imperative:** Entspanne! Entspannt! Entspannen Sie!

| Mode | Simple Tenses | | Compound Tenses | |
|---|---|---|---|---|
| | *Singular* | *Plural* | *Singular* | *Plural* |
| Indicative | **Present** | | **Present Perfect** | |
| | entspanne<br>entspannst<br>entspannt | entspannen<br>entspannt<br>entspannen | habe entspannt<br>hast entspannt<br>hat entspannt | haben entspannt<br>habt entspannt<br>haben entspannt |
| | **Past** | | **Past Perfect** | |
| | entspannte<br>entspanntest<br>entspannte | entspannten<br>entspanntet<br>entspannten | hatte entspannt<br>hattest entspannt<br>hatte entspannt | hatten entspannt<br>hattet entspannt<br>hatten entspannt |
| | **Future** | | **Future Perfect** | |
| | werde entspannen<br>wirst entspannen<br>wird entspannen | werden entspannen<br>werdet entspannen<br>werden entspannen | werde entspannt haben<br>wirst entspannt haben<br>wird entspannt haben | werden entspannt haben<br>werdet entspannt haben<br>werden entspannt haben |
| Subjunctive | **Present** | | **Present Perfect** | |
| | entspanne<br>entspannest<br>entspanne | entspannen<br>entspannet<br>entspannen | habe entspannt<br>habest entspannt<br>habe entspannt | haben entspannt<br>habet entspannt<br>haben entspannt |
| | **Past** | | **Past Perfect** | |
| | entspannte<br>entspanntest<br>entspannte | entspannten<br>entspanntet<br>entspannten | hätte entspannt<br>hättest entspannt<br>hätte entspannt | hätten entspannt<br>hättet entspannt<br>hätten entspannt |
| | **Future** | | **Future Perfect** | |
| | werde entspannen<br>werdest entspannen<br>werde entspannen | werden entspannen<br>werdet entspannen<br>werden entspannen | werde entspannt haben<br>werdest entspannt haben<br>werde entspannt haben | werden entspannt haben<br>werdet entspannt haben<br>werden entspannt haben |
| | **Present and Future Conditional** | | **Past Conditional** | |
| | würde entspannen<br>würdest entspannen<br>würde entspannen | würden entspannen<br>würdet entspannen<br>würden entspannen | würde entspannt haben<br>würdest entspannt haben<br>würde entspannt haben | würden entspannt haben<br>würdet entspannt haben<br>würden entspannt haben |

## EXAMPLES

Entspanne dich erst einmal!
Relax for a moment.

Nach so viel Arbeit muss ich mich wirklich entspannen.
After so much work I really have to relax.

**entwickeln (sich)**
to develop, to unfold
**Auxiliary verb:** haben **Past participle:** entwickelt
**Imperative:** Entwickele! Entwickelt! Entwickeln Sie!

| Mode | Simple Tenses | | Compound Tenses | |
|---|---|---|---|---|
| | *Singular* | *Plural* | *Singular* | *Plural* |
| Indicative | **Present** | | **Present Perfect** | |
| | entwickele<br>entwickelst<br>entwickelt | entwickeln<br>entwickelt<br>entwickeln | habe entwickelt<br>hast entwickelt<br>hat entwickelt | haben entwickelt<br>habt entwickelt<br>haben entwickelt |
| | **Past** | | **Past Perfect** | |
| | entwickelte<br>entwickeltest<br>entwickelte | entwickelten<br>entwickeltet<br>entwickelten | hatte entwickelt<br>hattest entwickelt<br>hatte entwickelt | hatten entwickelt<br>hattet entwickelt<br>hatten entwickelt |
| | **Future** | | **Future Perfect** | |
| | werde entwickeln<br>wirst entwickeln<br>wird entwickeln | werden entwickeln<br>werdet entwickeln<br>werden entwickeln | werde entwickelt haben<br>wirst entwickelt haben<br>wird entwickelt haben | werden entwickelt haben<br>werdet entwickelt haben<br>werden entwickelt haben |
| Subjunctive | **Present** | | **Present Perfect** | |
| | entwickele<br>entwickelst<br>entwickele | entwickeln<br>entwickelt<br>entwickeln | habe entwickelt<br>habest entwickelt<br>habe entwickelt | haben entwickelt<br>habet entwickelt<br>haben entwickelt |
| | **Past** | | **Past Perfect** | |
| | entwickelte<br>entwickeltest<br>entwickelte | entwickelten<br>entwickeltet<br>entwickelten | hätte entwickelt<br>hättest entwickelt<br>hätte entwickelt | hätten entwickelt<br>hättet entwickelt<br>hätten entwickelt |
| | **Future** | | **Future Perfect** | |
| | werde entwickeln<br>werdest entwickeln<br>werde entwickeln | werden entwickeln<br>werdet entwickeln<br>werden entwickeln | werde entwickelt haben<br>werdest entwickelt haben<br>werde entwickelt haben | werden entwickelt haben<br>werdet entwickelt haben<br>werden entwickelt haben |
| | **Present and Future Conditional** | | **Past Conditional** | |
| | würde entwickeln<br>würdest entwickeln<br>würde entwickeln | würden entwickeln<br>würdet entwickeln<br>würden entwickeln | würde entwickelt haben<br>würdest entwickelt haben<br>würde entwickelt haben | würden entwickelt haben<br>würdet entwickelt haben<br>würden entwickelt haben |

**Note:** With separable prefixes the principal parts of this verb are, for example, *wickelt aus, wickelte aus, hat ausgewickelt.*

## EXAMPLES

Es entwickelt sich gut. — Things are turning out well.
Ich möchte diese Filme entwickeln lassen. — I'd like to have this film developed.

**erben**
to inherit
**Auxiliary verb:** haben **Past participle:** geerbt
**Imperative:** Erbe! Erbt! Erben Sie!

| Mode | Simple Tenses | | Compound Tenses | |
|---|---|---|---|---|
| | *Singular* | *Plural* | *Singular* | *Plural* |
| Indicative | **Present** | | **Present Perfect** | |
| | erbe<br>erbst<br>erbt | erben<br>erbt<br>erben | habe geerbt<br>hast geerbt<br>hat geerbt | haben geerbt<br>habt geerbt<br>haben geerbt |
| | **Past** | | **Past Perfect** | |
| | erbte<br>erbtest<br>erbte | erbten<br>erbtet<br>erbten | hatte geerbt<br>hattest geerbt<br>hatte geerbt | hatten geerbt<br>hattet geerbt<br>hatten geerbt |
| | **Future** | | **Future Perfect** | |
| | werde erben<br>wirst erben<br>wird erben | werden erben<br>werdet erben<br>werden erben | werde geerbt haben<br>wirst geerbt haben<br>wird geerbt haben | werden geerbt haben<br>werdet geerbt haben<br>werden geerbt haben |
| Subjunctive | **Present** | | **Present Perfect** | |
| | erbe<br>erbest<br>erbe | erben<br>erbet<br>erben | habe geerbt<br>habest geerbt<br>habe geerbt | haben geerbt<br>habet geerbt<br>haben geerbt |
| | **Past** | | **Past Perfect** | |
| | erbte<br>erbtest<br>erbte | erbten<br>erbtet<br>erbten | hätte geerbt<br>hättest geerbt<br>hätte geerbt | hätten geerbt<br>hättet geerbt<br>hätten geerbt |
| | **Future** | | **Future Perfect** | |
| | werde erben<br>werdest erben<br>werde erben | werden erben<br>werdet erben<br>werden erben | werde geerbt haben<br>werdest geerbt haben<br>werde geerbt haben | werden geerbt haben<br>werdet geerbt haben<br>werden geerbt haben |
| | **Present and Future Conditional** | | **Past Conditional** | |
| | würde erben<br>würdest erben<br>würde erben | würden erben<br>würdet erben<br>würden erben | würde geerbt haben<br>würdest geerbt haben<br>würde geerbt haben | würden geerbt haben<br>würdet geerbt haben<br>würden geerbt haben |

## EXAMPLES

Sie hat alles von ihrem Vater geerbt.
Wer wird ihr ganzes Vermögen erben?

She inherited everything from her father.
Who will inherit her entire estate?

**erfinden**
to invent, to discover
**Auxiliary verb:** haben **Past participle:** erfunden
**Imperative:** Erfinde! Erfindet! Erfinden Sie!

| Mode | Simple Tenses | | Compound Tenses | |
|---|---|---|---|---|
| | *Singular* | *Plural* | *Singular* | *Plural* |
| Indicative | **Present** | | **Present Perfect** | |
| | erfinde<br>erfindest<br>erfindet | erfinden<br>erfindet<br>erfinden | habe erfunden<br>hast erfunden<br>hat erfunden | haben erfunden<br>habt erfunden<br>haben erfunden |
| | **Past** | | **Past Perfect** | |
| | erfand<br>erfandest<br>erfand | erfanden<br>erfandet<br>erfanden | hatte erfunden<br>hattest erfunden<br>hatte erfunden | hatten erfunden<br>hattet erfunden<br>hatten erfunden |
| | **Future** | | **Future Perfect** | |
| | werde erfinden<br>wirst erfinden<br>wird erfinden | werden erfinden<br>werdet erfinden<br>werden erfinden | werde erfunden haben<br>wirst erfunden haben<br>wird erfunden haben | werden erfunden haben<br>werdet erfunden haben<br>werden erfunden haben |
| Subjunctive | **Present** | | **Present Perfect** | |
| | erfinde<br>erfindest<br>erfinde | erfinden<br>erfindet<br>erfinden | habe erfunden<br>habest erfunden<br>habe erfunden | haben erfunden<br>habet erfunden<br>haben erfunden |
| | **Past** | | **Past Perfect** | |
| | erfände<br>erfändest<br>erfände | erfänden<br>erfändet<br>erfänden | hätte erfunden<br>hättest erfunden<br>hätte erfunden | hätten erfunden<br>hättet erfunden<br>hätten erfunden |
| | **Future** | | **Future Perfect** | |
| | werde erfinden<br>werdest erfinden<br>werde erfinden | werden erfinden<br>werdet erfinden<br>werden erfinden | werde erfunden haben<br>werdest erfunden haben<br>werde erfunden haben | werden erfunden haben<br>werdet erfunden haben<br>werden erfunden haben |
| | **Present and Future Conditional** | | **Past Conditional** | |
| | würde erfinden<br>würdest erfinden<br>würde erfinden | würden erfinden<br>würdet erfinden<br>würden erfinden | würde erfunden haben<br>würdest erfunden haben<br>würde erfunden haben | würden erfunden haben<br>würdet erfunden haben<br>würden erfunden haben |

## EXAMPLES

Wer hat den ersten Fernsehapparat erfunden?
Who invented the first television set?

Diese Firma erfindet umweltfreundliche Produkte.
This company is inventing environmentally-friendly products.

**erfrischen (sich)**
to refresh
**Auxiliary verb:** haben **Past participle:** erfrischt
**Imperative:** Erfrische! Erfrischt! Erfrischen Sie!

| Mode | Simple Tenses | | Compound Tenses | |
|---|---|---|---|---|
| | *Singular* | *Plural* | *Singular* | *Plural* |
| Indicative | **Present** | | **Present Perfect** | |
| | erfrische<br>erfrischst<br>erfrischt | erfrischen<br>erfrischt<br>erfrischen | habe erfrischt<br>hast erfrischt<br>hat erfrischt | haben erfrischt<br>habt erfrischt<br>haben erfrischt |
| | **Past** | | **Past Perfect** | |
| | erfrischte<br>erfrischtest<br>erfrischte | erfrischten<br>erfrischtet<br>erfrischten | hatte erfrischt<br>hattest erfrischt<br>hatte erfrischt | hatten erfrischt<br>hattet erfrischt<br>hatten erfrischt |
| | **Future** | | **Future Perfect** | |
| | werde erfrischen<br>wirst erfrischen<br>wird erfrischen | werden erfrischen<br>werdet erfrischen<br>werden erfrischen | werde erfrischt haben<br>wirst erfrischt haben<br>wird erfrischt haben | werden erfrischt haben<br>werdet erfrischt haben<br>werden erfrischt haben |
| Subjunctive | **Present** | | **Present Perfect** | |
| | erfrische<br>erfrischest<br>erfrische | erfrischen<br>erfrischet<br>erfrischen | habe erfrischt<br>habest erfrischt<br>habe erfrischt | haben erfrischt<br>habet erfrischt<br>haben erfrischt |
| | **Past** | | **Past Perfect** | |
| | erfrischte<br>erfrischtest<br>erfrischte | erfrischten<br>erfrischtet<br>erfrischten | hätte erfrischt<br>hättest erfrischt<br>hätte erfrischt | hätten erfrischt<br>hättet erfrischt<br>hätten erfrischt |
| | **Future** | | **Future Perfect** | |
| | werde erfrischen<br>werdest erfrischen<br>werde erfrischen | werden erfrischen<br>werdet erfrischen<br>werden erfrischen | werde erfrischt haben<br>werdest erfrischt haben<br>werde erfrischt haben | werden erfrischt haben<br>werdet erfrischt haben<br>werden erfrischt haben |
| | **Present and Future Conditional** | | **Past Conditional** | |
| | würde erfrischen<br>würdest erfrischen<br>würde erfrischen | würden erfrischen<br>würdet erfrischen<br>würden erfrischen | würde erfrischt haben<br>würdest erfrischt haben<br>würde erfrischt haben | würden erfrischt haben<br>würdet erfrischt haben<br>würden erfrischt haben |

## EXAMPLES

Er erfrischt sich unter einer kühlen Dusche.
Dieses Getränk ist sehr erfrischend.

He refreshes himself under a cool shower.
This drink is very refreshing.

**ergänzen**
to complete, to replenish, to fill in
**Auxiliary verb:** haben **Past participle:** ergänzt
**Imperative:** Ergänze! Ergänzt! Ergänzen Sie!

| Mode | Simple Tenses | | Compound Tenses | |
|---|---|---|---|---|
| | *Singular* | *Plural* | *Singular* | *Plural* |
| Indicative | **Present** | | **Present Perfect** | |
| | ergänze<br>ergänzt<br>ergänzt | ergänzen<br>ergänzt<br>ergänzen | habe ergänzt<br>hast ergänzt<br>hat ergänzt | haben ergänzt<br>habt ergänzt<br>haben ergänzt |
| | **Past** | | **Past Perfect** | |
| | ergänzte<br>ergänztest<br>ergänzte | ergänzten<br>ergänztet<br>ergänzten | hatte ergänzt<br>hattest ergänzt<br>hatte ergänzt | hatten ergänzt<br>hattet ergänzt<br>hatten ergänzt |
| | **Future** | | **Future Perfect** | |
| | werde ergänzen<br>wirst ergänzen<br>wird ergänzen | werden ergänzen<br>werdet ergänzen<br>werden ergänzen | werde ergänzt haben<br>wirst ergänzt haben<br>wird ergänzt haben | werden ergänzt haben<br>werdet ergänzt haben<br>werden ergänzt haben |
| Subjunctive | **Present** | | **Present Perfect** | |
| | ergänze<br>ergänzest<br>ergänze | ergänzen<br>ergänzet<br>ergänzen | habe ergänzt<br>habest ergänzt<br>habe ergänzt | haben ergänzt<br>habet ergänzt<br>haben ergänzt |
| | **Past** | | **Past Perfect** | |
| | ergänzte<br>ergänztest<br>ergänzte | ergänzten<br>ergänztet<br>ergänzten | hätte ergänzt<br>hättest ergänzt<br>hätte ergänzt | hätten ergänzt<br>hättet ergänzt<br>hätten ergänzt |
| | **Future** | | **Future Perfect** | |
| | werde ergänzen<br>werdest ergänzen<br>werde ergänzen | werden ergänzen<br>werdet ergänzen<br>werden ergänzen | werde ergänzt haben<br>werdest ergänzt haben<br>werde ergänzt haben | werden ergänzt haben<br>werdet ergänzt haben<br>werden ergänzt haben |
| | **Present and Future Conditional** | | **Past Conditional** | |
| | würde ergänzen<br>würdest ergänzen<br>würde ergänzen | würden ergänzen<br>würdet ergänzen<br>würden ergänzen | würde ergänzt haben<br>würdest ergänzt haben<br>würde ergänzt haben | würden ergänzt haben<br>würdet ergänzt haben<br>würden ergänzt haben |

# EXAMPLES

Die Studenten müssen hier die Verben ergänzen.
The students have to fill in the verbs here.

Ich möchte meine Sammlung ergänzen und habe deshalb noch zwei neue Briefmarken dazu gekauft.
I want to complete my collection, and therefore bought two more stamps.

**erinnern (sich)**
to remember, to remind
**Auxiliary verb:** haben **Past participle:** erinnert
**Imperative:** Erinnere! Erinnert! Erinnern Sie!

| Mode | Simple Tenses | | Compound Tenses | |
|---|---|---|---|---|
| | *Singular* | *Plural* | *Singular* | *Plural* |
| Indicative | **Present** | | **Present Perfect** | |
| | erinnere<br>erinnerst<br>erinnert | erinnern<br>erinnert<br>erinnern | habe erinnert<br>hast erinnert<br>hat erinnert | haben erinnert<br>habt erinnert<br>haben erinnert |
| | **Past** | | **Past Perfect** | |
| | erinnerte<br>erinnertest<br>erinnerte | erinnerten<br>erinnertet<br>erinnerten | hatte erinnert<br>hattest erinnert<br>hatte erinnert | hatten erinnert<br>hattet erinnert<br>hatten erinnert |
| | **Future** | | **Future Perfect** | |
| | werde erinnern<br>wirst erinnern<br>wird erinnern | werden erinnern<br>werdet erinnern<br>werden erinnern | werde erinnert haben<br>wirst erinnert haben<br>wird erinnert haben | werden erinnert haben<br>werdet erinnert haben<br>werden erinnert haben |
| Subjunctive | **Present** | | **Present Perfect** | |
| | erinnere<br>erinnerst<br>erinnere | erinnern<br>erinnert<br>erinnern | habe erinnert<br>habest erinnert<br>habe erinnert | haben erinnert<br>habet erinnert<br>haben erinnert |
| | **Past** | | **Past Perfect** | |
| | erinnerte<br>erinnertest<br>erinnerte | erinnerten<br>erinnertet<br>erinnerten | hätte erinnert<br>hättest erinnert<br>hätte erinnert | hätten erinnert<br>hättet erinnert<br>hätten erinnert |
| | **Future** | | **Future Perfect** | |
| | werde erinnern<br>werdest erinnern<br>werde erinnern | werden erinnern<br>werdet erinnern<br>werden erinnern | werde erinnert haben<br>werdest erinnert haben<br>werde erinnert haben | werden erinnert haben<br>werdet erinnert haben<br>werden erinnert haben |
| | **Present and Future Conditional** | | **Past Conditional** | |
| | würde erinnern<br>würdest erinnern<br>würde erinnern | würden erinnern<br>würdet erinnern<br>würden erinnern | würde erinnert haben<br>würdest erinnert haben<br>würde erinnert haben | würden erinnert haben<br>würdet erinnert haben<br>würden erinnert haben |

## EXAMPLES

Wenn ich mich recht erinnere, wohnst du noch bei deinen Eltern.
If I remember correctly, you still live with your parents.

Erinnern Sie mich bitte daran, dass ich Herrn Vogt anrufe.
Please remind me to call Mr. Vogt.

**erkälten (sich)**
to cool, to catch cold
**Auxiliary verb:** haben **Past participle:** erkältet
**Imperative:** Erkälte! Erkältet! Erkälten Sie!

| Mode | Simple Tenses | | Compound Tenses | |
|---|---|---|---|---|
| | *Singular* | *Plural* | *Singular* | *Plural* |
| Indicative | **Present** | | **Present Perfect** | |
| | erkälte<br>erkältest<br>erkältet | erkälten<br>erkältet<br>erkälten | habe erkältet<br>hast erkältet<br>hat erkältet | haben erkältet<br>habt erkältet<br>haben erkältet |
| | **Past** | | **Past Perfect** | |
| | erkältete<br>erkältetest<br>erkältete | erkälteten<br>erkältetet<br>erkälteten | hatte erkältet<br>hattest erkältet<br>hatte erkältet | hatten erkältet<br>hattet erkältet<br>hatten erkältet |
| | **Future** | | **Future Perfect** | |
| | werde erkälten<br>wirst erkälten<br>wird erkälten | werden erkälten<br>werdet erkälten<br>werden erkälten | werde erkältet haben<br>wirst erkältet haben<br>wird erkältet haben | werden erkältet haben<br>werdet erkältet haben<br>werden erkältet haben |
| Subjunctive | **Present** | | **Present Perfect** | |
| | erkälte<br>erkältest<br>erkälte | erkälten<br>erkältet<br>erkälten | habe erkältet<br>habest erkältet<br>habe erkältet | haben erkältet<br>habet erkältet<br>haben erkältet |
| | **Past** | | **Past Perfect** | |
| | erkältete<br>erkältetest<br>erkältete | erkälteten<br>erkältetet<br>erkälteten | hätte erkältet<br>hättest erkältet<br>hätte erkältet | hätten erkältet<br>hättet erkältet<br>hätten erkältet |
| | **Future** | | **Future Perfect** | |
| | werde erkälten<br>werdest erkälten<br>werde erkälten | werden erkälten<br>werdet erkälten<br>werden erkälten | werde erkältet haben<br>werdest erkältet haben<br>werde erkältet haben | werden erkältet haben<br>werdet erkältet haben<br>werden erkältet haben |
| | **Present and Future Conditional** | | **Past Conditional** | |
| | würde erkälten<br>würdest erkälten<br>würde erkälten | würden erkälten<br>würdet erkälten<br>würden erkälten | würde erkältet haben<br>würdest erkältet haben<br>würde erkältet haben | würden erkältet haben<br>würdet erkältet haben<br>würden erkältet haben |

## EXAMPLES

Werner ist wieder stark erkältet.
Werner has a bad cold again.

Du hast dich wahrscheinlich beim Schwimmen erkältet.
You probably caught a cold swimming.

**erklären**
to explain, to declare
**Auxiliary verb:** haben **Past participle:** erklärt
**Imperative:** Erkläre! Erklärt! Erklären Sie!

| Mode | Simple Tenses | | Compound Tenses | |
|---|---|---|---|---|
| | *Singular* | *Plural* | *Singular* | *Plural* |
| Indicative | **Present** | | **Present Perfect** | |
| | erkläre<br>erklärst<br>erklärt | erklären<br>erklärt<br>erklären | habe erklärt<br>hast erklärt<br>hat erklärt | haben erklärt<br>habt erklärt<br>haben erklärt |
| | **Past** | | **Past Perfect** | |
| | erklärte<br>erklärtest<br>erklärte | erklärten<br>erklärtet<br>erklärten | hatte erklärt<br>hattest erklärt<br>hatte erklärt | hatten erklärt<br>hattet erklärt<br>hatten erklärt |
| | **Future** | | **Future Perfect** | |
| | werde erklären<br>wirst erklären<br>wird erklären | werden erklären<br>werdet erklären<br>werden erklären | werde erklärt haben<br>wirst erklärt haben<br>wird erklärt haben | werden erklärt haben<br>werdet erklärt haben<br>werden erklärt haben |
| Subjunctive | **Present** | | **Present Perfect** | |
| | erkläre<br>erklärest<br>erkläre | erklären<br>erkläret<br>erklären | habe erklärt<br>habest erklärt<br>habe erklärt | haben erklärt<br>habet erklärt<br>haben erklärt |
| | **Past** | | **Past Perfect** | |
| | erklärte<br>erklärtest<br>erklärte | erklärten<br>erklärtet<br>erklärten | hätte erklärt<br>hättest erklärt<br>hätte erklärt | hätten erklärt<br>hättet erklärt<br>hätten erklärt |
| | **Future** | | **Future Perfect** | |
| | werde erklären<br>werdest erklären<br>werde erklären | werden erklären<br>werdet erklären<br>werden erklären | werde erklärt haben<br>werdest erklärt haben<br>werde erklärt haben | werden erklärt haben<br>werdet erklärt haben<br>werden erklärt haben |
| | **Present and Future Conditional** | | **Past Conditional** | |
| | würde erklären<br>würdest erklären<br>würde erklären | würden erklären<br>würdet erklären<br>würden erklären | würde erklärt haben<br>würdest erklärt haben<br>würde erklärt haben | würden erklärt haben<br>würdet erklärt haben<br>würden erklärt haben |

## EXAMPLES

Sie werden den Krieg erklären.
They're going to declare war.

Kannst du mir erklären, wie diese Maschine funktioniert?
Can you explain to me how this machine works?

**erlauben**
to allow, to permit
**Auxiliary verb:** haben **Past participle:** erlaubt
**Imperative:** Erlaube! Erlaubt! Erlauben Sie!

| Mode | Simple Tenses | | Compound Tenses | |
|---|---|---|---|---|
| | *Singular* | *Plural* | *Singular* | *Plural* |
| Indicative | **Present** | | **Present Perfect** | |
| | erlaube<br>erlaubst<br>erlaubt | erlauben<br>erlaubt<br>erlauben | habe erlaubt<br>hast erlaubt<br>hat erlaubt | haben erlaubt<br>habt erlaubt<br>haben erlaubt |
| | **Past** | | **Past Perfect** | |
| | erlaubte<br>erlaubtest<br>erlaubte | erlaubten<br>erlaubtet<br>erlaubten | hatte erlaubt<br>hattest erlaubt<br>hatte erlaubt | hatten erlaubt<br>hattet erlaubt<br>hatten erlaubt |
| | **Future** | | **Future Perfect** | |
| | werde erlauben<br>wirst erlauben<br>wird erlauben | werden erlauben<br>werdet erlauben<br>werden erlauben | werde erlaubt haben<br>wirst erlaubt haben<br>wird erlaubt haben | werden erlaubt haben<br>werdet erlaubt haben<br>werden erlaubt haben |
| Subjunctive | **Present** | | **Present Perfect** | |
| | erlaube<br>erlaubest<br>erlaube | erlauben<br>erlaubet<br>erlauben | habe erlaubt<br>habest erlaubt<br>habe erlaubt | haben erlaubt<br>habet erlaubt<br>haben erlaubt |
| | **Past** | | **Past Perfect** | |
| | erlaubte<br>erlaubtest<br>erlaubte | erlaubten<br>erlaubtet<br>erlaubten | hätte erlaubt<br>hättest erlaubt<br>hätte erlaubt | hätten erlaubt<br>hättet erlaubt<br>hätten erlaubt |
| | **Future** | | **Future Perfect** | |
| | werde erlauben<br>werdest erlauben<br>werde erlauben | werden erlauben<br>werdet erlauben<br>werden erlauben | werde erlaubt haben<br>werdest erlaubt haben<br>werde erlaubt haben | werden erlaubt haben<br>werdet erlaubt haben<br>werden erlaubt haben |
| | **Present and Future Conditional** | | **Past Conditional** | |
| | würde erlauben<br>würdest erlauben<br>würde erlauben | würden erlauben<br>würdet erlauben<br>würden erlauben | würde erlaubt haben<br>würdest erlaubt haben<br>würde erlaubt haben | würden erlaubt haben<br>würdet erlaubt haben<br>würden erlaubt haben |

## EXAMPLES

Das kannst du dir erlauben.
You can afford it.

Vater wird mir erlauben morgen einkaufen zu gehen.
Father will allow me to go shopping tomorrow.

**erledigen**
to bring to a conclusion, to settle
**Auxiliary verb:** haben **Past participle:** erledigt
**Imperative:** Erledige! Erledigt! Erledigen Sie!

| Mode | Simple Tenses | | Compound Tenses | |
|---|---|---|---|---|
| | *Singular* | *Plural* | *Singular* | *Plural* |
| Indicative | **Present** | | **Present Perfect** | |
| | erledige<br>erledigst<br>erledigt | erledigen<br>erledigt<br>erledigen | habe erledigt<br>hast erledigt<br>hat erledigt | haben erledigt<br>habt erledigt<br>haben erledigt |
| | **Past** | | **Past Perfect** | |
| | erledigte<br>erledigtest<br>erledigte | erledigten<br>erledigtet<br>erledigten | hatte erledigt<br>hattest erledigt<br>hatte erledigt | hatten erledigt<br>hattet erledigt<br>hatten erledigt |
| | **Future** | | **Future Perfect** | |
| | werde erledigen<br>wirst erledigen<br>wird erledigen | werden erledigen<br>werdet erledigen<br>werden erledigen | werde erledigt haben<br>wirst erledigt haben<br>wird erledigt haben | werden erledigt haben<br>werdet erledigt haben<br>werden erledigt haben |
| Subjunctive | **Present** | | **Present Perfect** | |
| | erledige<br>erledigest<br>erledige | erledigen<br>erlediget<br>erledigen | habe erledigt<br>habest erledigt<br>habe erledigt | haben erledigt<br>habet erledigt<br>haben erledigt |
| | **Past** | | **Past Perfect** | |
| | erledigte<br>erledigtest<br>erledigte | erledigten<br>erledigtet<br>erledigten | hätte erledigt<br>hättest erledigt<br>hätte erledigt | hätten erledigt<br>hättet erledigt<br>hätten erledigt |
| | **Future** | | **Future Perfect** | |
| | werde erledigen<br>werdest erledigen<br>werde erledigen | werden erledigen<br>werdet erledigen<br>werden erledigen | werde erledigt haben<br>werdest erledigt haben<br>werde erledigt haben | werden erledigt haben<br>werdet erledigt haben<br>werden erledigt haben |
| | **Present and Future Conditional** | | **Past Conditional** | |
| | würde erledigen<br>würdest erledigen<br>würde erledigen | würden erledigen<br>würdet erledigen<br>würden erledigen | würde erledigt haben<br>würdest erledigt haben<br>würde erledigt haben | würden erledigt haben<br>würdet erledigt haben<br>würden erledigt haben |

## EXAMPLES

Für heute haben wir unsere Arbeit erledigt.
Die Sache erledigt sich hiermit.

We've concluded our work for today.
The matter is herewith concluded.

**erleichtern**
to ease, to lighten
**Auxiliary verb:** haben **Past participle:** erleichtert
**Imperative:** Erleichtere! Erleichtert! Erleichtern Sie!

| Mode | Simple Tenses | | Compound Tenses | |
|---|---|---|---|---|
| | *Singular* | *Plural* | *Singular* | *Plural* |
| Indicative | **Present** | | **Present Perfect** | |
| | erleichtere<br>erleichterst<br>erleichtert | erleichtere<br>erleichtert<br>erleichtern | habe erleichtert<br>hast erleichtert<br>hat erleichtert | haben erleichtert<br>habt erleichtert<br>haben erleichtert |
| | **Past** | | **Past Perfect** | |
| | erleichterte<br>erleichtertest<br>erleichterte | erleichterten<br>erleichtertet<br>erleichterten | hatte erleichtert<br>hattest erleichtert<br>hatte erleichtert | hatten erleichtert<br>hattet erleichtert<br>hatten erleichtert |
| | **Future** | | **Future Perfect** | |
| | werde erleichtern<br>wirst erleichtern<br>wird erleichtern | werden erleichtern<br>werdet erleichtern<br>werden erleichtern | werde erleichtert haben<br>wirst erleichtert haben<br>wird erleichtert haben | werden erleichtert haben<br>werdet erleichtert haben<br>werden erleichtert haben |
| Subjunctive | **Present** | | **Present Perfect** | |
| | erleichtere<br>erleichterst<br>erleichtere | erleichtern<br>erleichtert<br>erleichtern | habe erleichtert<br>habest erleichtert<br>habe erleichtert | haben erleichtert<br>habet erleichtert<br>haben erleichtert |
| | **Past** | | **Past Perfect** | |
| | erleichterte<br>erleichtertest<br>erleichterte | erleichterten<br>erleichtertet<br>erleichterten | hätte erleichtert<br>hättest erleichtert<br>hätte erleichtert | hätten erleichtert<br>hättet erleichtert<br>hätten erleichtert |
| | **Future** | | **Future Perfect** | |
| | werde erleichtern<br>werdest erleichtern<br>werde erleichtern | werden erleichtern<br>werdet erleichtern<br>werden erleichtern | werde erleichtert haben<br>werdest erleichtert haben<br>werde erleichtert haben | werden erleichtert haben<br>werdet erleichtert haben<br>werden erleichtert haben |
| | **Present and Future Conditional** | | **Past Conditional** | |
| | würde erleichtern<br>würdest erleichtern<br>würde erleichtern | würden erleichtern<br>würdet erleichtern<br>würden erleichtern | würde erleichtert haben<br>würdest erleichtert haben<br>würde erleichtert haben | würden erleichtert haben<br>würdet erleichtert haben<br>würden erleichtert haben |

## EXAMPLES

| | |
|---|---|
| Der Arzt versuchte ihre Schmerzen zu erleichtern. | The doctor tried to ease her pain. |
| Die gute Nachricht hat uns sehr erleichtert. | We were very relieved by the good news. |

**ernähren (sich)**
to nourish, to feed, to subsist
**Auxiliary verb:** haben **Past participle:** ernährt
**Imperative:** Ernähre! Ernährt! Ernähren Sie!

| Mode | Simple Tenses | | Compound Tenses | |
|---|---|---|---|---|
| | *Singular* | *Plural* | *Singular* | *Plural* |
| Indicative | **Present** | | **Present Perfect** | |
| | ernähre<br>ernährst<br>ernährt | ernähren<br>ernährt<br>ernähren | habe ernährt<br>hast ernährt<br>hat ernährt | haben ernährt<br>habt ernährt<br>haben ernährt |
| | **Past** | | **Past Perfect** | |
| | ernährte<br>ernährtest<br>ernährte | ernährten<br>ernährtet<br>ernährten | hatte ernährt<br>hattest ernährt<br>hatte ernährt | hatten ernährt<br>hattet ernährt<br>hatten ernährt |
| | **Future** | | **Future Perfect** | |
| | werde ernähren<br>wirst ernähren<br>wird ernähren | werden ernähren<br>werdet ernähren<br>werden ernähren | werde ernährt haben<br>wirst ernährt haben<br>wird ernährt haben | werden ernährt haben<br>werdet ernährt haben<br>werden ernährt haben |
| Subjunctive | **Present** | | **Present Perfect** | |
| | ernähre<br>ernährest<br>ernähre | ernähren<br>ernähret<br>ernähren | habe ernährt<br>habest ernährt<br>habe ernährt | haben ernährt<br>habet ernährt<br>haben ernährt |
| | **Past** | | **Past Perfect** | |
| | ernährte<br>ernährtest<br>ernährte | ernährten<br>ernährtet<br>ernährten | hätte ernährt<br>hättest ernährt<br>hätte ernährt | hätten ernährt<br>hättet ernährt<br>hätten ernährt |
| | **Future** | | **Future Perfect** | |
| | werde ernähren<br>werdest ernähren<br>werde ernähren | werden ernähren<br>werdet ernähren<br>werden ernähren | werde ernährt haben<br>werdest ernährt haben<br>werde ernährt haben | werden ernährt haben<br>werdet ernährt haben<br>werden ernährt haben |
| | **Present and Future Conditional** | | **Past Conditional** | |
| | würde ernähren<br>würdest ernähren<br>würde ernähren | würden ernähren<br>würdet ernähren<br>würden ernähren | würde ernährt haben<br>würdest ernährt haben<br>würde ernährt haben | würden ernährt haben<br>würdet ernährt haben<br>würden ernährt haben |

## EXAMPLES

Der Sportler ernährte sich nur von Gemüse und Fleisch.
The athlete ate only vegetables and meat.

Wie können wir so viele Flüchtlinge ernähren?
How can we feed so many refugees?

**eröffnen**

to open, to inaugurate

**Auxiliary verb:** haben **Past participle:** eröffnet

**Imperative:** Eröffne! Eröffnet! Eröffnen Sie!

| Mode | Simple Tenses | | Compound Tenses | |
|---|---|---|---|---|
| | *Singular* | *Plural* | *Singular* | *Plural* |
| Indicative | **Present** | | **Present Perfect** | |
| | eröffne<br>eröffnest<br>eröffnet | eröffnen<br>eröffnet<br>eröffnen | habe eröffnet<br>hast eröffnet<br>hat eröffnet | haben eröffnet<br>habt eröffnet<br>haben eröffnet |
| | **Past** | | **Past Perfect** | |
| | eröffnete<br>eröffnetest<br>eröffnete | eröffneten<br>eröffnete<br>eröffneten | hatte eröffnet<br>hattest eröffnet<br>hatte eröffnet | hatten eröffnet<br>hattet eröffnet<br>hatten eröffnet |
| | **Future** | | **Future Perfect** | |
| | werde eröffnen<br>wirst eröffnen<br>wird eröffnen | werden eröffnen<br>werdet eröffnen<br>werden eröffnen | werde eröffnet haben<br>wirst eröffnet haben<br>wird eröffnet haben | werden eröffnet haben<br>werdet eröffnet haben<br>werden eröffnet haben |
| Subjunctive | **Present** | | **Present Perfect** | |
| | eröffne<br>eröffnest<br>eröffne | eröffnen<br>eröffnet<br>eröffnen | habe eröffnet<br>habest eröffnet<br>habe eröffnet | haben eröffnet<br>habet eröffnet<br>haben eröffnet |
| | **Past** | | **Past Perfect** | |
| | eröffnete<br>eröffnetest<br>eröffnete | eröffneten<br>eröffnete<br>eröffneten | hätte eröffnet<br>hättest eröffnet<br>hätte eröffnet | hätten eröffnet<br>hättet eröffnet<br>hätten eröffnet |
| | **Future** | | **Future Perfect** | |
| | werde eröffnen<br>werdest eröffnen<br>werde eröffnen | werden eröffnen<br>werdet eröffnen<br>werden eröffnen | werde eröffnet haben<br>werdest eröffnet haben<br>werde eröffnet haben | werden eröffnet haben<br>werdet eröffnet haben<br>werden eröffnet haben |
| | **Present and Future Conditional** | | **Past Conditional** | |
| | würde eröffnen<br>würdest eröffnen<br>würde eröffnen | würden eröffnen<br>würdet eröffnen<br>würden eröffnen | würde eröffnet haben<br>würdest eröffnet haben<br>würde eröffnet haben | würden eröffnet haben<br>würdet eröffnet haben<br>würden eröffnet haben |

## EXAMPLES

In der Nähe des Rathauses ist ein neues Kaufhaus eröffnet worden.

A new department store opened in the vicinity of city hall.

Die Ausstellung wurde schon letzte Woche eröffnet.

The exhibition was opened last week.

**erröten**
to blush, to redden
**Auxiliary verb:** sein **Past participle:** errötet
**Imperative:** Erröte! Errötet! Erröten Sie!

| Mode | Simple Tenses | | Compound Tenses | |
|---|---|---|---|---|
| | *Singular* | *Plural* | *Singular* | *Plural* |
| Indicative | **Present** | | **Present Perfect** | |
| | erröte<br>errötest<br>errötet | erröten<br>errötet<br>erröten | bin errötet<br>bist errötet<br>ist errötet | sind errötet<br>seid errötet<br>sind errötet |
| | **Past** | | **Past Perfect** | |
| | errötete<br>errötetest<br>errötete | erröteten<br>errötetet<br>erröteten | war errötet<br>warst errötet<br>war errötet | waren errötet<br>wart errötet<br>waren errötet |
| | **Future** | | **Future Perfect** | |
| | werde erröten<br>wirst erröten<br>wird erröten | werden erröten<br>werdet erröten<br>werden erröten | werde errötet sein<br>wirst errötet sein<br>wird errötet sein | werden errötet sein<br>werdet errötet sein<br>werden errötet sein |
| Subjunctive | **Present** | | **Present Perfect** | |
| | erröte<br>errötest<br>erröte | erröten<br>errötet<br>erröten | sei errötet<br>seiest errötet<br>sei errötet | seien errötet<br>seiet errötet<br>seien errötet |
| | **Past** | | **Past Perfect** | |
| | errötete<br>errötetest<br>errötete | erröteten<br>errötetet<br>erröteten | wäre errötet<br>wärest errötet<br>wäre errötet | wären errötet<br>wäret errötet<br>wären errötet |
| | **Future** | | **Future Perfect** | |
| | werde erröten<br>werdest erröten<br>werde erröten | werden erröten<br>werdet erröten<br>werden erröten | werde errötet sein<br>werdest errötet sein<br>werde errötet sein | werden errötet sein<br>werdet errötet sein<br>werden errötet sein |
| | **Present and Future Conditional** | | **Past Conditional** | |
| | würde erröten<br>würdest erröten<br>würde erröten | würden erröten<br>würdet erröten<br>würden erröten | würde errötet sein<br>würdest errötet sein<br>würde errötet sein | würden errötet sein<br>würdet errötet sein<br>würden errötet sein |

## EXAMPLES

Erröten macht die Hässlichen schön.
Blushing gives beauty to the plainest.

Warum errötet sie?
Why is she blushing?

**erscheinen**

to appear, to be published

**Auxiliary verb:** sein **Past participle:** erschienen

**Imperative:** Erscheine! Erscheint! Erscheinen Sie!

| Mode | Simple Tenses | | Compound Tenses | |
|---|---|---|---|---|
| | *Singular* | *Plural* | *Singular* | *Plural* |
| Indicative | **Present** | | **Present Perfect** | |
| | erscheine<br>erscheinst<br>erscheint | erscheinen<br>erscheint<br>erscheinen | bin erschienen<br>bist erschienen<br>ist erschienen | sind erschienen<br>seid erschienen<br>sind erschienen |
| | **Past** | | **Past Perfect** | |
| | erschien<br>erschienst<br>erschien | erschienen<br>erschient<br>erschienen | war erschienen<br>warst erschienen<br>war erschienen | waren erschienen<br>wart erschienen<br>waren erschienen |
| | **Future** | | **Future Perfect** | |
| | werde erscheinen<br>wirst erscheinen<br>wird erscheinen | werden erscheinen<br>werdet erscheinen<br>werden erscheinen | werde erschienen sein<br>wirst erschienen sein<br>wird erschienen sein | werden erschienen sein<br>werdet erschienen sein<br>werden erschienen sein |
| Subjunctive | **Present** | | **Present Perfect** | |
| | erscheine<br>erscheinest<br>erscheine | erscheinen<br>erscheinet<br>erscheinen | sei erschienen<br>seiest erschienen<br>sei erschienen | seien erschienen<br>seiet erschienen<br>seien erschienen |
| | **Past** | | **Past Perfect** | |
| | erschiene<br>erschienest<br>erschiene | erschienen<br>erschienet<br>erschienen | wäre erschienen<br>wärest erschienen<br>wäre erschienen | wären erschienen<br>wäret erschienen<br>wären erschienen |
| | **Future** | | **Future Perfect** | |
| | werde erscheinen<br>werdest erscheinen<br>werde erscheinen | werden erscheinen<br>werdet erscheinen<br>werden erscheinen | werde erschienen sein<br>werdest erschienen sein<br>werde erschienen sein | werden erschienen sein<br>werdet erschienen sein<br>werden erschienen sein |
| | **Present and Future Conditional** | | **Past Conditional** | |
| | würde erscheinen<br>würdest erscheinen<br>würde erscheinen | würden erscheinen<br>würdet erscheinen<br>würden erscheinen | würde erschienen sein<br>würdest erschienen sein<br>würde erschienen sein | würden erschienen sein<br>würdet erschienen sein<br>würden erschienen sein |

## EXAMPLES

Sein nächster Roman wird am Montag erscheinen. — His next novel is coming out on Monday.

Diese Idee erscheint mir ausgezeichnet. — This idea seems excellent to me.

**erschöpfen**
to exhaust
**Auxiliary verb:** haben **Past participle:** erschöpft
**Imperative:** Erschöpfe! Erschöpft! Erschöpfen Sie!

| Mode | Simple Tenses | | Compound Tenses | |
|---|---|---|---|---|
| | *Singular* | *Plural* | *Singular* | *Plural* |
| Indicative | **Present** | | **Present Perfect** | |
| | erschöpfe<br>erschöpfst<br>erschöpft | erschöpfen<br>erschöpft<br>erschöpfen | habe erschöpft<br>hast erschöpft<br>hat erschöpft | haben erschöpft<br>habt erschöpft<br>haben erschöpft |
| | **Past** | | **Past Perfect** | |
| | erschöpfte<br>erschöpftest<br>erschöpfte | erschöpften<br>erschöpftet<br>erschöpften | hatte erschöpft<br>hattest erschöpft<br>hatte erschöpft | hatten erschöpft<br>hattet erschöpft<br>hatten erschöpft |
| | **Future** | | **Future Perfect** | |
| | werde erschöpfen<br>wirst erschöpfen<br>wird erschöpfen | werden erschöpfen<br>werdet erschöpfen<br>werden erschöpfen | werde erschöpft haben<br>wirst erschöpft haben<br>wird erschöpft haben | werden erschöpft haben<br>werdet erschöpft haben<br>werden erschöpft haben |
| Subjunctive | **Present** | | **Present Perfect** | |
| | erschöpfe<br>erschöpfest<br>erschöpfe | erschöpfen<br>erschöpfet<br>erschöpfen | habe erschöpft<br>habest erschöpft<br>habe erschöpft | haben erschöpft<br>habet erschöpft<br>haben erschöpft |
| | **Past** | | **Past Perfect** | |
| | erschöpfte<br>erschöpftest<br>erschöpfte | erschöpften<br>erschöpftet<br>erschöpften | hätte erschöpft<br>hättest erschöpft<br>hätte erschöpft | hätten erschöpft<br>hättet erschöpft<br>hätten erschöpft |
| | **Future** | | **Future Perfect** | |
| | werde erschöpfen<br>werdest erschöpfen<br>werde erschöpfen | werden erschöpfen<br>werdet erschöpfen<br>werden erschöpfen | werde erschöpft haben<br>werdest erschöpft haben<br>werde erschöpft haben | werden erschöpft haben<br>werdet erschöpft haben<br>werden erschöpft haben |
| | **Present and Future Conditional** | | **Past Conditional** | |
| | würde erschöpfen<br>würdest erschöpfen<br>würde erschöpfen | würden erschöpfen<br>würdet erschöpfen<br>würden erschöpfen | würde erschöpft haben<br>würdest erschöpft haben<br>würde erschöpft haben | würden erschöpft haben<br>würdet erschöpft haben<br>würden erschöpft haben |

## EXAMPLES

Meine Geduld ist endlich erschöpft. — My patience is finally exhausted.

Das kalte Wetter wird die Arbeiter erschöpfen. — The cold weather is going to exhaust the workers.

**erschrecken**
to be frightened, to be shocked
**Auxiliary verb:** sein **Past participle:** erschrocken
**Imperative:** Erschrick! Erschreckt! Erschrecken Sie!

| Mode | Simple Tenses | | Compound Tenses | |
|---|---|---|---|---|
| | *Singular* | *Plural* | *Singular* | *Plural* |
| Indicative | **Present** | | **Present Perfect** | |
| | erschrecke<br>erschrickst<br>erschrickt | erschrecken<br>erschreckt<br>erschrecken | bin erschrocken<br>bist erschrocken<br>ist erschrocken | sind erschrocken<br>seid erschrocken<br>sind erschrocken |
| | **Past** | | **Past Perfect** | |
| | erschrak<br>erschrakst<br>erschrak | erschraken<br>erschrakt<br>erschraken | war erschrocken<br>warst erschrocken<br>war erschrocken | waren erschrocken<br>wart erschrocken<br>waren erschrocken |
| | **Future** | | **Future Perfect** | |
| | werde erschrecken<br>wirst erschrecken<br>wird erschrecken | werden erschrecken<br>werdet erschrecken<br>werden erschrecken | werde erschrocken sein<br>wirst erschrocken sein<br>wird erschrocken sein | werden erschrocken sein<br>werdet erschrocken sein<br>werden erschrocken sein |
| Subjunctive | **Present** | | **Present Perfect** | |
| | erschrecke<br>erschreckest<br>erschrecke | erschrecken<br>erschrecket<br>erschrecken | sei erschrocken<br>seiest erschrocken<br>sei erschrocken | seien erschrocken<br>seiet erschrocken<br>seien erschrocken |
| | **Past** | | **Past Perfect** | |
| | erschräke<br>erschräkest<br>erschräke | erschräken<br>erschräket<br>erschräken | wäre erschrocken<br>wärest erschrocken<br>wäre erschrocken | wären erschrocken<br>wäret erschrocken<br>wären erschrocken |
| | **Future** | | **Future Perfect** | |
| | werde erschrecken<br>werdest erschrecken<br>werde erschrecken | werden erschrecken<br>werdet erschrecken<br>werden erschrecken | werde erschrocken sein<br>werdest erschrocken sein<br>werde erschrocken sein | werden erschrocken sein<br>werdet erschrocken sein<br>werden erschrocken sein |
| | **Present and Future Conditional** | | **Past Conditional** | |
| | würde erschrecken<br>würdest erschrecken<br>würde erschrecken | würden erschrecken<br>würdet erschrecken<br>würden erschrecken | würde erschrocken sein<br>würdest erschrocken sein<br>würde erschrocken sein | würden erschrocken sein<br>würdet erschrocken sein<br>würden erschrocken sein |

**Note:** The same infinitive, *erschrecken,* is conjugated as a regular verb (like *entdecken*) with the auxiliary *haben* when it means "to frighten" or "to startle."

## EXAMPLES

Sie ist plötzlich erschrocken, als sie ein Geräusch aus der Küche hörte.
Ich erschrak, als ich den Zustand des Patienten sah.

She was suddenly frightened when she heard a noise in the kitchen.
I was shocked when I saw the condition of the patient.

**ertragen**
to bear, to suffer, to tolerate
**Auxiliary verb:** haben **Past participle:** ertragen
**Imperative:** Ertrage! Ertragt! Ertragen Sie!

| Mode | Simple Tenses | | Compound Tenses | |
|---|---|---|---|---|
| | *Singular* | *Plural* | *Singular* | *Plural* |
| Indicative | **Present** | | **Present Perfect** | |
| | ertrage<br>erträgst<br>erträgt | ertragen<br>ertragt<br>ertragen | habe ertragen<br>hast ertragen<br>hat ertragen | haben ertragen<br>habt ertragen<br>haben ertragen |
| | **Past** | | **Past Perfect** | |
| | ertrug<br>ertrugst<br>ertrug | ertrugen<br>ertrugt<br>ertrugen | hatte ertragen<br>hattest ertragen<br>hatte ertragen | hatten ertragen<br>hattet ertragen<br>hatten ertragen |
| | **Future** | | **Future Perfect** | |
| | werde ertragen<br>wirst ertragen<br>wird ertragen | werden ertragen<br>werdet ertragen<br>werden ertragen | werde ertragen haben<br>wirst ertragen haben<br>wird ertragen haben | werden ertragen haben<br>werdet ertragen haben<br>werden ertragen haben |
| Subjunctive | **Present** | | **Present Perfect** | |
| | ertrage<br>ertragest<br>ertrage | ertragen<br>ertraget<br>ertragen | habe ertragen<br>habest ertragen<br>habe ertragen | haben ertragen<br>habet ertragen<br>haben ertragen |
| | **Past** | | **Past Perfect** | |
| | ertrüge<br>ertrügest<br>ertrüge | ertrügen<br>ertrüget<br>ertrügen | hätte ertragen<br>hättest ertragen<br>hätte ertragen | hätten ertragen<br>hättet ertragen<br>hätten ertragen |
| | **Future** | | **Future Perfect** | |
| | werde ertragen<br>werdest ertragen<br>werde ertragen | werden ertragen<br>werdet ertragen<br>werden ertragen | werde ertragen haben<br>werdest ertragen haben<br>werde ertragen haben | werden ertragen haben<br>werdet ertragen haben<br>werden ertragen haben |
| | **Present and Future Conditional** | | **Past Conditional** | |
| | würde ertragen<br>würdest ertragen<br>würde ertragen | würden ertragen<br>würdet ertragen<br>würden ertragen | würde ertragen haben<br>würdest ertragen haben<br>würde ertragen haben | würden ertragen haben<br>würdet ertragen haben<br>würden ertragen haben |

## EXAMPLES

Ich werde das nicht länger ertragen.
I won't put up with this any longer.

Er konnte es noch nie ertragen, wenn jemand unhöflich ist.
He could never bear people who are impolite.

**ertrinken**
to drown
**Auxiliary verb:** sein **Past participle:** ertrunken
**Imperative:** Ertrinke! Ertrinkt! Ertrinken Sie!

| Mode | Simple Tenses | | Compound Tenses | |
|---|---|---|---|---|
| | *Singular* | *Plural* | *Singular* | *Plural* |
| Indicative | **Present** | | **Present Perfect** | |
| | ertrinke<br>ertrinkst<br>ertrinkt | ertrinken<br>ertrinkt<br>ertrinken | bin ertrunken<br>bist ertrunken<br>ist ertrunken | sind ertrunken<br>seid ertrunken<br>sind ertrunken |
| | **Past** | | **Past Perfect** | |
| | ertrank<br>ertrankst<br>ertrank | ertranken<br>ertrankt<br>ertranken | war ertrunken<br>warst ertrunken<br>war ertrunken | waren ertrunken<br>wart ertrunken<br>waren ertrunken |
| | **Future** | | **Future Perfect** | |
| | werde ertrinken<br>wirst ertrinken<br>wird ertrinken | werden ertrinken<br>werdet ertrinken<br>werden ertrinken | werde ertrunken sein<br>wirst ertrunken sein<br>wird ertrunken sein | werden ertrunken sein<br>werdet ertrunken sein<br>werden ertrunken sein |
| Subjunctive | **Present** | | **Present Perfect** | |
| | ertrinke<br>ertrinkest<br>ertrinke | ertrinken<br>ertrinket<br>ertrinken | sei ertrunken<br>seiest ertrunken<br>sei ertrunken | seien ertrunken<br>seiet ertrunken<br>seien ertrunken |
| | **Past** | | **Past Perfect** | |
| | ertränke<br>ertränkest<br>ertränke | ertränken<br>ertränket<br>ertränken | wäre ertrunken<br>wärest ertrunken<br>wäre ertrunken | wären ertrunken<br>wäret ertrunken<br>wären ertrunken |
| | **Future** | | **Future Perfect** | |
| | werde ertrinken<br>werdest ertrinken<br>werde ertrinken | werden ertrinken<br>werdet ertrinken<br>werden ertrinken | werde ertrunken sein<br>werdest ertrunken sein<br>werde ertrunken sein | werden ertrunken sein<br>werdet ertrunken sein<br>werden ertrunken sein |
| | **Present and Future Conditional** | | **Past Conditional** | |
| | würde ertrinken<br>würdest ertrinken<br>würde ertrinken | würden ertrinken<br>würdet ertrinken<br>würden ertrinken | würde ertrunken sein<br>würdest ertrunken sein<br>würde ertrunken sein | würden ertrunken sein<br>würdet ertrunken sein<br>würden ertrunken sein |

## EXAMPLES

Der Polizist hat den Ertrunkenen am Strand gefunden.
The policeman found the drowned man on the beach.

Der arme Kerl ist beim Schwimmen ertrunken.
The poor fellow drowned while swimming.

**erwarten**
to expect, to await
**Auxiliary verb:** haben **Past participle:** erwartet
**Imperative:** Erwarte! Erwartet! Erwarten Sie!

| Mode | Simple Tenses | | Compound Tenses | |
|---|---|---|---|---|
| | *Singular* | *Plural* | *Singular* | *Plural* |
| Indicative | **Present** | | **Present Perfect** | |
| | erwarte<br>erwartest<br>erwartet | erwarten<br>erwartet<br>erwarten | habe erwartet<br>hast erwartet<br>hat erwartet | haben erwartet<br>habt erwartet<br>haben erwartet |
| | **Past** | | **Past Perfect** | |
| | erwartete<br>erwartetest<br>erwartete | erwarteten<br>erwartetet<br>erwarteten | hatte erwartet<br>hattest erwartet<br>hatte erwartet | hatten erwartet<br>hattet erwartet<br>hatten erwartet |
| | **Future** | | **Future Perfect** | |
| | werde erwarten<br>wirst erwarten<br>wird erwarten | werden erwarten<br>werdet erwarten<br>werden erwarten | werde erwartet haben<br>wirst erwartet haben<br>wird erwartet haben | werden erwartet haben<br>werdet erwartet haben<br>werden erwartet haben |
| Subjunctive | **Present** | | **Present Perfect** | |
| | erwarte<br>erwartest<br>erwarte | erwarten<br>erwartet<br>erwarten | habe erwartet<br>habest erwartet<br>habe erwartet | haben erwartet<br>habet erwartet<br>haben erwartet |
| | **Past** | | **Past Perfect** | |
| | erwartete<br>erwartetest<br>erwartete | erwarteten<br>erwartetet<br>erwarteten | hätte erwartet<br>hättest erwartet<br>hätte erwartet | hätten erwartet<br>hättet erwartet<br>hätten erwartet |
| | **Future** | | **Future Perfect** | |
| | werde erwarten<br>werdest erwarten<br>werde erwarten | werden erwarten<br>werdet erwarten<br>werden erwarten | werde erwartet haben<br>werdest erwartet haben<br>werde erwartet haben | werden erwartet haben<br>werdet erwartet haben<br>werden erwartet haben |
| | **Present and Future Conditional** | | **Past Conditional** | |
| | würde erwarten<br>würdest erwarten<br>würde erwarten | würden erwarten<br>würdet erwarten<br>würden erwarten | würde erwartet haben<br>würdest erwartet haben<br>würde erwartet haben | würden erwartet haben<br>würdet erwartet haben<br>würden erwartet haben |

## EXAMPLES

Das lässt sich kaum erwarten. — You can hardly expect that.

Wir erwarten von euch, dass ihr euch besser benehmt. — We expect that you will be behaving better.

**erzählen**

to tell, to relate

**Auxiliary verb:** haben **Past participle:** erzählt

**Imperative:** Erzähle! Erzählt! Erzählen Sie!

| Mode | Simple Tenses | | Compound Tenses | |
|---|---|---|---|---|
| | *Singular* | *Plural* | *Singular* | *Plural* |
| Indicative | **Present** | | **Present Perfect** | |
| | erzähle<br>erzählst<br>erzählt | erzählen<br>erzählt<br>erzählen | habe erzählt<br>hast erzählt<br>hat erzählt | haben erzählt<br>habt erzählt<br>haben erzählt |
| | **Past** | | **Past Perfect** | |
| | erzählte<br>erzähltest<br>erzählte | erzählten<br>erzähltet<br>erzählten | hatte erzählt<br>hattest erzählt<br>hatte erzählt | hatten erzählt<br>hattet erzählt<br>hatten erzählt |
| | **Future** | | **Future Perfect** | |
| | werde erzählen<br>wirst erzählen<br>wird erzählen | werden erzählen<br>werdet erzählen<br>werden erzählen | werde erzählt haben<br>wirst erzählt haben<br>wird erzählt haben | werden erzählt haben<br>werdet erzählt haben<br>werden erzählt haben |
| Subjunctive | **Present** | | **Present Perfect** | |
| | erzähle<br>erzählest<br>erzähle | erzählen<br>erzählet<br>erzählen | habe erzählt<br>habest erzählt<br>habe erzählt | haben erzählt<br>habet erzählt<br>haben erzählt |
| | **Past** | | **Past Perfect** | |
| | erzählte<br>erzähltest<br>erzählte | erzählten<br>erzähltet<br>erzählten | hätte erzählt<br>hättest erzählt<br>hätte erzählt | hätten erzählt<br>hättet erzählt<br>hätten erzählt |
| | **Future** | | **Future Perfect** | |
| | werde erzählen<br>werdest erzählen<br>werde erzählen | werden erzählen<br>werdet erzählen<br>werden erzählen | werde erzählt haben<br>werdest erzählt haben<br>werde erzählt haben | werden erzählt haben<br>werdet erzählt haben<br>werden erzählt haben |
| | **Present and Future Conditional** | | **Past Conditional** | |
| | würde erzählen<br>würdest erzählen<br>würde erzählen | würden erzählen<br>würdet erzählen<br>würden erzählen | würde erzählt haben<br>würdest erzählt haben<br>würde erzählt haben | würden erzählt haben<br>würdet erzählt haben<br>würden erzählt haben |

## EXAMPLES

Erzählen Sie bitte etwas über Ihre Reise!
Please tell something about your trip.

Tante Gerda hat den Kindern einige Märchen erzählt.
Aunt Gerda told the children a few fairy tales.

**erziehen**
to bring up, to raise, to educate
**Auxiliary verb:** haben **Past participle:** erzogen
**Imperative:** Erziehe! Erzieht! Erziehen Sie!

| Mode | Simple Tenses | | Compound Tenses | |
|---|---|---|---|---|
| | *Singular* | *Plural* | *Singular* | *Plural* |
| Indicative | **Present** | | **Present Perfect** | |
| | erziehe<br>erziehst<br>erzieht | erziehen<br>erzieht<br>erziehen | habe erzogen<br>hast erzogen<br>hat erzogen | haben erzogen<br>habt erzogen<br>haben erzogen |
| | **Past** | | **Past Perfect** | |
| | erzog<br>erzogst<br>erzog | erzogen<br>erzogt<br>erzogen | hatte erzogen<br>hattest erzogen<br>hatte erzogen | hatten erzogen<br>hattet erzogen<br>hatten erzogen |
| | **Future** | | **Future Perfect** | |
| | werde erziehen<br>wirst erziehen<br>wird erziehen | werden erziehen<br>werdet erziehen<br>werden erziehen | werde erzogen haben<br>wirst erzogen haben<br>wird erzogen haben | werden erzogen haben<br>werdet erzogen haben<br>werden erzogen haben |
| Subjunctive | **Present** | | **Present Perfect** | |
| | erziehe<br>erziehest<br>erziehe | erziehen<br>erziehet<br>erziehen | habe erzogen<br>habest erzogen<br>habe erzogen | haben erzogen<br>habet erzogen<br>haben erzogen |
| | **Past** | | **Past Perfect** | |
| | erzöge<br>erzögest<br>erzöge | erzögen<br>erzöget<br>erzögen | hätte erzogen<br>hättest erzogen<br>hätte erzogen | hätten erzogen<br>hättet erzogen<br>hätten erzogen |
| | **Future** | | **Future Perfect** | |
| | werde erziehen<br>werdest erziehen<br>werde erziehen | werden erziehen<br>werdet erziehen<br>werden erziehen | werde erzogen haben<br>werdest erzogen haben<br>werde erzogen haben | werden erzogen haben<br>werdet erzogen haben<br>werden erzogen haben |
| | **Present and Future Conditional** | | **Past Conditional** | |
| | würde erziehen<br>würdest erziehen<br>würde erziehen | würden erziehen<br>würdet erziehen<br>würden erziehen | würde erzogen haben<br>würdest erzogen haben<br>würde erzogen haben | würden erzogen haben<br>würdet erzogen haben<br>würden erzogen haben |

## EXAMPLES

Ihre Kinder sind gut erzogen. — Their children have been raised well.
Herr Bauer muss seinen Sohn allein erziehen. — Mr. Bauer has to raise his son alone.

**essen**

to eat

**Auxiliary verb:** haben **Past participle:** gegessen

**Imperative:** Iss! Esst! Essen Sie!

| Mode | Simple Tenses | | Compound Tenses | |
|---|---|---|---|---|
| | *Singular* | *Plural* | *Singular* | *Plural* |
| Indicative | **Present** | | **Present Perfect** | |
| | esse<br>isst<br>isst | essen<br>esst<br>essen | habe gegessen<br>hast gegessen<br>hat gegessen | haben gegessen<br>habt gegessen<br>haben gegessen |
| | **Past** | | **Past Perfect** | |
| | aß<br>aßt<br>aß | aßen<br>aßt<br>aßen | hatte gegessen<br>hattest gegessen<br>hatte gegessen | hatten gegessen<br>hattet gegessen<br>hatten gegessen |
| | **Future** | | **Future Perfect** | |
| | werde essen<br>wirst essen<br>wird essen | werden essen<br>werdet essen<br>werden essen | werde gegessen haben<br>wirst gegessen haben<br>wird gegessen haben | werden gegessen haben<br>werdet gegessen haben<br>werden gegessen haben |
| Subjunctive | **Present** | | **Present Perfect** | |
| | esse<br>essest<br>esse | essen<br>esset<br>essen | habe gegessen<br>habest gegessen<br>habe gegessen | haben gegessen<br>habet gegessen<br>haben gegessen |
| | **Past** | | **Past Perfect** | |
| | äße<br>äßest<br>äße | äßen<br>äßet<br>äßen | hätte gegessen<br>hättest gegessen<br>hätte gegessen | hätten gegessen<br>hättet gegessen<br>hätten gegessen |
| | **Future** | | **Future Perfect** | |
| | werde essen<br>werdest essen<br>werde essen | werden essen<br>werdet essen<br>werden essen | werde gegessen haben<br>werdest gegessen haben<br>werde gegessen haben | werden gegessen haben<br>werdet gegessen haben<br>werden gegessen haben |
| | **Present and Future Conditional** | | **Past Conditional** | |
| | würde essen<br>würdest essen<br>würde essen | würden essen<br>würdet essen<br>würden essen | würde gegessen haben<br>würdest gegessen haben<br>würde gegessen haben | würden gegessen haben<br>würdet gegessen haben<br>würden gegessen haben |

## EXAMPLE

Was gibt's heute zu essen? — What do we have to eat today?

**fahren**
to drive, to travel
**Auxiliary verb:** sein **Past participle:** gefahren
**Imperative:** Fahre! Fahrt! Fahren Sie!

| Mode | Simple Tenses | | Compound Tenses | |
|---|---|---|---|---|
| | *Singular* | *Plural* | *Singular* | *Plural* |
| Indicative | **Present** | | **Present Perfect** | |
| | fahre<br>fährst<br>fährt | fahren<br>fahrt<br>fahren | bin gefahren<br>bist gefahren<br>ist gefahren | sind gefahren<br>seid gefahren<br>sind gefahren |
| | **Past** | | **Past Perfect** | |
| | fuhr<br>fuhrst<br>fuhr | fuhren<br>fuhrt<br>fuhren | war gefahren<br>warst gefahren<br>war gefahren | waren gefahren<br>wart gefahren<br>waren gefahren |
| | **Future** | | **Future Perfect** | |
| | werde fahren<br>wirst fahren<br>wird fahren | werden fahren<br>werdet fahren<br>werden fahren | werde gefahren sein<br>wirst gefahren sein<br>wird gefahren sein | werden gefahren sein<br>werdet gefahren sein<br>werden gefahren sein |
| Subjunctive | **Present** | | **Present Perfect** | |
| | fahre<br>fahrest<br>fahre | fahren<br>fahret<br>fahren | sei gefahren<br>seiest gefahren<br>sei gefahren | seien gefahren<br>seiet gefahren<br>seien gefahren |
| | **Past** | | **Past Perfect** | |
| | führe<br>führest<br>führe | führen<br>führet<br>führen | wäre gefahren<br>wärest gefahren<br>wäre gefahren | wären gefahren<br>wäret gefahren<br>wären gefahren |
| | **Future** | | **Future Perfect** | |
| | werde fahren<br>werdest fahren<br>werde fahren | werden fahren<br>werdet fahren<br>werden fahren | werde gefahren sein<br>werdest gefahren sein<br>werde gefahren sein | werden gefahren sein<br>werdet gefahren sein<br>werden gefahren sein |
| | **Present and Future Conditional** | | **Past Conditional** | |
| | würde fahren<br>würdest fahren<br>würde fahren | würden fahren<br>würdet fahren<br>würden fahren | würde gefahren sein<br>würdest gefahren sein<br>würde gefahren sein | würden gefahren sein<br>würdet gefahren sein<br>würden gefahren sein |

**Note:** With inseparable prefixes, the principal parts of this verb are, for example, *verfährt, verfuhr, ist verfahren*. With separable prefixes, the principal parts are, for example, *fährt ab, fuhr ab, ist abgefahren*. With the inseparable prefix *er–* this verb becomes transitive and requires the auxiliary *haben* in the perfect tenses. It then means "to experience": *Er ist ein erfahrener Mann* ("He's an experienced man"). When *über– (überfáhren)* is an inseparable prefix, the verb means "to run over" and requires *haben* as its auxiliary.

## EXAMPLES

| | |
|---|---|
| Wir sind mit der Eisenbahn dorthin gefahren. | We traveled there by train. |
| Im Sommer fahren wir nach Dänemark. | In summer we're going to Denmark. |

**fallen**
to fall, to drop
**Auxiliary verb:** sein **Past participle:** gefallen
**Imperative:** Falle! Fallt! Fallen Sie!

| Mode | Simple Tenses | | Compound Tenses | |
|---|---|---|---|---|
| | *Singular* | *Plural* | *Singular* | *Plural* |
| Indicative | **Present** | | **Present Perfect** | |
| | falle<br>fällst<br>fällt | fallen<br>fallt<br>fallen | bin gefallen<br>bist gefallen<br>ist gefallen | sind gefallen<br>seid gefallen<br>sind gefallen |
| | **Past** | | **Past Perfect** | |
| | fiel<br>fielst<br>fiel | fielen<br>fielt<br>fielen | war gefallen<br>warst gefallen<br>war gefallen | waren gefallen<br>wart gefallen<br>waren gefallen |
| | **Future** | | **Future Perfect** | |
| | werde fallen<br>wirst fallen<br>wird fallen | werden fallen<br>werdet fallen<br>werden fallen | werde gefallen sein<br>wirst gefallen sein<br>wird gefallen sein | werden gefallen sein<br>werdet gefallen sein<br>werden gefallen sein |
| Subjunctive | **Present** | | **Present Perfect** | |
| | falle<br>fallest<br>falle | fallen<br>fallet<br>fallen | sei gefallen<br>seiest gefallen<br>sei gefallen | seien gefallen<br>seiet gefallen<br>seien gefallen |
| | **Past** | | **Past Perfect** | |
| | fiele<br>fielest<br>fiele | fielen<br>fielet<br>fielen | wäre gefallen<br>wärest gefallen<br>wäre gefallen | wären gefallen<br>wäret gefallen<br>wären gefallen |
| | **Future** | | **Future Perfect** | |
| | werde fallen<br>werdest fallen<br>werde fallen | werden fallen<br>werdet fallen<br>werden fallen | werde gefallen sein<br>werdest gefallen sein<br>werde gefallen sein | werden gefallen sein<br>werdet gefallen sein<br>werden gefallen sein |
| | **Present and Future Conditional** | | **Past Conditional** | |
| | würde fallen<br>würdest fallen<br>würde fallen | würden fallen<br>würdet fallen<br>würden fallen | würde gefallen sein<br>würdest gefallen sein<br>würde gefallen sein | würden gefallen sein<br>würdet gefallen sein<br>würden gefallen sein |

**Note:** With inseparable prefixes, the principal parts are, for example, *verfällt, verfiel, ist verfallen.* With the prefix *be–,* this verb becomes transitive. The principal parts are *befällt, befiel, hat befallen.* With separable prefixes, the principal parts are, for example, *fällt aus, fiel aus, ist ausgefallen.*

## EXAMPLES

Die ganze Erbschaft fiel an seinen jüngsten Bruder.
The entire inheritance fell to his youngest brother.

Passt auf, dass ihr die Teller nicht fallen lasst.
Be careful not to drop the plates.

**falten**
to fold
**Auxiliary verb:** haben **Past participle:** gefaltet
**Imperative:** Falte! Faltet! Falten Sie!

| Mode | Simple Tenses | | Compound Tenses | |
|---|---|---|---|---|
| | *Singular* | *Plural* | *Singular* | *Plural* |
| Indicative | **Present** | | **Present Perfect** | |
| | falte<br>faltest<br>faltet | falten<br>faltet<br>falten | habe gefaltet<br>hast gefaltet<br>hat gefaltet | haben gefaltet<br>habt gefaltet<br>haben gefaltet |
| | **Past** | | **Past Perfect** | |
| | faltete<br>faltetest<br>faltete | falteten<br>faltetet<br>falteten | hatte gefaltet<br>hattest gefaltet<br>hatte gefaltet | hatten gefaltet<br>hattet gefaltet<br>hatten gefaltet |
| | **Future** | | **Future Perfect** | |
| | werde falten<br>wirst falten<br>wird falten | werden falten<br>werdet falten<br>werden falten | werde gefaltet haben<br>wirst gefaltet haben<br>wird gefaltet haben | werden gefaltet haben<br>werdet gefaltet haben<br>werden gefaltet haben |
| Subjunctive | **Present** | | **Present Perfect** | |
| | falte<br>faltest<br>falte | falten<br>faltet<br>falten | habe gefaltet<br>habest gefaltet<br>habe gefaltet | haben gefaltet<br>habet gefaltet<br>haben gefaltet |
| | **Past** | | **Past Perfect** | |
| | faltete<br>faltetest<br>faltete | falteten<br>faltetet<br>falteten | hätte gefaltet<br>hättest gefaltet<br>hätte gefaltet | hätten gefaltet<br>hättet gefaltet<br>hätten gefaltet |
| | **Future** | | **Future Perfect** | |
| | werde falten<br>werdest falten<br>werde falten | werden falten<br>werdet falten<br>werden falten | werde gefaltet haben<br>werdest gefaltet haben<br>werde gefaltet haben | werden gefaltet haben<br>werdet gefaltet haben<br>werden gefaltet haben |
| | **Present and Future Conditional** | | **Past Conditional** | |
| | würde falten<br>würdest falten<br>würde falten | würden falten<br>würdet falten<br>würden falten | würde gefaltet haben<br>würdest gefaltet haben<br>würde gefaltet haben | würden gefaltet haben<br>würdet gefaltet haben<br>würden gefaltet haben |

## EXAMPLES

Der fromme Mann faltet die Hände. — The pious man folds his hands.
Die Handtücher müssen noch gefaltet werden. — The towels still have to be folded.

**fangen**
to catch, to capture
**Auxiliary verb:** haben **Past participle:** gefangen
**Imperative:** Fange! Fangt! Fangen Sie!

| Mode | Simple Tenses | | Compound Tenses | |
|---|---|---|---|---|
| | *Singular* | *Plural* | *Singular* | *Plural* |
| Indicative | **Present** | | **Present Perfect** | |
| | fange<br>fängst<br>fängt | fangen<br>fangt<br>fangen | habe gefangen<br>hast gefangen<br>hat gefangen | haben gefangen<br>habt gefangen<br>haben gefangen |
| | **Past** | | **Past Perfect** | |
| | fing<br>fingst<br>fing | fingen<br>fingt<br>fingen | hatte gefangen<br>hattest gefangen<br>hatte gefangen | hatten gefangen<br>hattet gefangen<br>hatten gefangen |
| | **Future** | | **Future Perfect** | |
| | werde fangen<br>wirst fangen<br>wird fangen | werden fangen<br>werdet fangen<br>werden fangen | werde gefangen haben<br>wirst gefangen haben<br>wird gefangen haben | werden gefangen haben<br>werdet gefangen haben<br>werden gefangen haben |
| Subjunctive | **Present** | | **Present Perfect** | |
| | fange<br>fangest<br>fange | fangen<br>fanget<br>fangen | habe gefangen<br>habest gefangen<br>habe gefangen | haben gefangen<br>habet gefangen<br>haben gefangen |
| | **Past** | | **Past Perfect** | |
| | finge<br>fingest<br>finge | fingen<br>finget<br>fingen | hätte gefangen<br>hättest gefangen<br>hätte gefangen | hätten gefangen<br>hättet gefangen<br>hätten gefangen |
| | **Future** | | **Future Perfect** | |
| | werde fangen<br>werdest fangen<br>werde fangen | werden fangen<br>werdet fangen<br>werden fangen | werde gefangen haben<br>werdest gefangen haben<br>werde gefangen haben | werden gefangen haben<br>werdet gefangen haben<br>werden gefangen haben |
| | **Present and Future Conditional** | | **Past Conditional** | |
| | würde fangen<br>würdest fangen<br>würde fangen | würden fangen<br>würdet fangen<br>würden fangen | würde gefangen haben<br>würdest gefangen haben<br>würde gefangen haben | würden gefangen haben<br>würdet gefangen haben<br>würden gefangen haben |

## EXAMPLES

| | |
|---|---|
| Unsere Katze hat gestern eine Maus gefangen. | Our cat caught a mouse yesterday. |
| Der Torwart fängt den Ball auf der Torlinie. | The goalie catches the ball on the goal line. |

**färben**
to color, to dye
**Auxiliary verb:** haben **Past participle:** gefärbt
**Imperative:** Färbe! Färbt! Färben Sie!

| Mode | Simple Tenses | | Compound Tenses | |
|---|---|---|---|---|
| | *Singular* | *Plural* | *Singular* | *Plural* |
| Indicative | **Present** | | **Present Perfect** | |
| | färbe<br>färbst<br>färbt | färben<br>färbt<br>färben | habe gefärbt<br>hast gefärbt<br>hat gefärbt | haben gefärbt<br>habt gefärbt<br>haben gefärbt |
| | **Past** | | **Past Perfect** | |
| | färbte<br>färbtest<br>färbte | färbten<br>färbtet<br>färbten | hatte gefärbt<br>hattest gefärbt<br>hatte gefärbt | hatten gefärbt<br>hattet gefärbt<br>hatten gefärbt |
| | **Future** | | **Future Perfect** | |
| | werde färben<br>wirst färben<br>wird färben | werden färben<br>werdet färben<br>werden färben | werde gefärbt haben<br>wirst gefärbt haben<br>wird gefärbt haben | werden gefärbt haben<br>werdet gefärbt haben<br>werden gefärbt haben |
| Subjunctive | **Present** | | **Present Perfect** | |
| | färbe<br>färbest<br>färbe | färben<br>färbet<br>färben | habe gefärbt<br>habest gefärbt<br>habe gefärbt | haben gefärbt<br>habet gefärbt<br>haben gefärbt |
| | **Past** | | **Past Perfect** | |
| | färbte<br>färbtest<br>färbte | färbten<br>färbtet<br>färbten | hätte gefärbt<br>hättest gefärbt<br>hätte gefärbt | hätten gefärbt<br>hättet gefärbt<br>hatten gefärbt |
| | **Future** | | **Future Perfect** | |
| | werde färben<br>werdest färben<br>werde färben | werden färben<br>werdet färben<br>werden färben | werde gefärbt haben<br>werdest gefärbt haben<br>werde gefärbt haben | werden gefärbt haben<br>werdet gefärbt haben<br>werden gefärbt haben |
| | **Present and Future Conditional** | | **Past Conditional** | |
| | würde färben<br>würdest färben<br>würde färben | würden färben<br>würdet färben<br>würden färben | würde gefärbt haben<br>würdest gefärbt haben<br>würde gefärbt haben | würden gefärbt haben<br>würdet gefärbt haben<br>würden gefärbt haben |

## EXAMPLES

Meine Tante will ihr Haar schwarz färben.
Hast du deine Augenbrauen gefärbt?

My aunt wants to color her hair black.
Did you dye your eyebrows?

**fassen**

to grasp, to seize

**Auxiliary verb:** haben **Past participle:** gefasst

**Imperative:** Fasse! Fasst! Fassen Sie!

| Mode | Simple Tenses | | Compound Tenses | |
|---|---|---|---|---|
| | *Singular* | *Plural* | *Singular* | *Plural* |
| Indicative | **Present** | | **Present Perfect** | |
| | fasse<br>fasst<br>fasst | fassen<br>fasst<br>fassen | habe gefasst<br>hast gefasst<br>hat gefasst | haben gefasst<br>habt gefasst<br>haben gefasst |
| | **Past** | | **Past Perfect** | |
| | fasste<br>fasstest<br>fasste | fassten<br>fasstet<br>fassten | hatte gefasst<br>hattest gefasst<br>hatte gefasst | hatten gefasst<br>hattet gefasst<br>hatten gefasst |
| | **Future** | | **Future Perfect** | |
| | werde fassen<br>wirst fassen<br>wird fassen | werden fassen<br>werdet fassen<br>werden fassen | werde gefasst haben<br>wirst gefasst haben<br>wird gefasst haben | werden gefasst haben<br>werdet gefasst haben<br>werden gefasst haben |
| Subjunctive | **Present** | | **Present Perfect** | |
| | fasse<br>fassest<br>fasse | fassen<br>fasset<br>fassen | habe gefasst<br>habest gefasst<br>habe gefasst | haben gefasst<br>habet gefasst<br>haben gefasst |
| | **Past** | | **Past Perfect** | |
| | fasste<br>fasstest<br>fasste | fassten<br>fasstet<br>fassten | hätte gefasst<br>hättest gefasst<br>hätte gefasst | hätten gefasst<br>hättet gefasst<br>hätten gefasst |
| | **Future** | | **Future Perfect** | |
| | werde fassen<br>werdest fassen<br>werde fassen | werden fassen<br>werdet fassen<br>werden fassen | werde gefasst haben<br>werdest gefasst haben<br>werde gefasst haben | werden gefasst haben<br>werdet gefasst haben<br>werden gefasst haben |
| | **Present and Future Conditional** | | **Past Conditional** | |
| | würde fassen<br>würdest fassen<br>würde fassen | würden fassen<br>würdet fassen<br>würden fassen | würde gefasst haben<br>würdest gefasst haben<br>würde gefasst haben | würden gefasst haben<br>würdet gefasst haben<br>würden gefasst haben |

## EXAMPLES

Ich konnte es nicht fassen, dass meine Freunde ohne mich gegangen waren.

I couldn't believe that my friends had gone without me.

Der Dieb wurde endlich von der Polizei gefasst.

The thief was finally seized by the police.

**fasten**
to fast
**Auxiliary verb:** haben **Past participle:** gefastet
**Imperative:** Faste! Fastet! Fasten Sie!

| Mode | Simple Tenses | | Compound Tenses | |
|---|---|---|---|---|
| | *Singular* | *Plural* | *Singular* | *Plural* |
| Indicative | **Present** | | **Present Perfect** | |
| | faste<br>fastest<br>fastet | fasten<br>fastet<br>fasten | habe gefastet<br>hast gefastet<br>hat gefastet | haben gefastet<br>habt gefastet<br>haben gefastet |
| | **Past** | | **Past Perfect** | |
| | fastete<br>fastetest<br>fastete | fasteten<br>fastetet<br>fasteten | hatte gefastet<br>hattest gefastet<br>hatte gefastet | hatten gefastet<br>hattet gefastet<br>hatten gefastet |
| | **Future** | | **Future Perfect** | |
| | werde fasten<br>wirst fasten<br>wird fasten | werden fasten<br>werdet fasten<br>werden fasten | werde gefastet haben<br>wirst gefastet haben<br>wird gefastet haben | werden gefastet haben<br>werdet gefastet haben<br>werden gefastet haben |
| Subjunctive | **Present** | | **Present Perfect** | |
| | faste<br>fastest<br>faste | fasten<br>fastet<br>fasten | habe gefastet<br>habest gefastet<br>habe gefastet | haben gefastet<br>habet gefastet<br>haben gefastet |
| | **Past** | | **Past Perfect** | |
| | fastete<br>fastetest<br>fastete | fasteten<br>fastetet<br>fasteten | hätte gefastet<br>hättest gefastet<br>hätte gefastet | hätten gefastet<br>hättet gefastet<br>hätten gefastet |
| | **Future** | | **Future Perfect** | |
| | werde fasten<br>werdest fasten<br>werde fasten | werden fasten<br>werdet fasten<br>werden fasten | werde gefastet haben<br>werdest gefastet haben<br>werde gefastet haben | werden gefastet haben<br>werdet gefastet haben<br>werden gefastet haben |
| | **Present and Future Conditional** | | **Past Conditional** | |
| | würde fasten<br>würdest fasten<br>würde fasten | würden fasten<br>würdet fasten<br>würden fasten | würde gefastet haben<br>würdest gefastet haben<br>würde gefastet haben | würden gefastet haben<br>würdet gefastet haben<br>würden gefastet haben |

## EXAMPLES

Jeden Frühling fasten die Leute in diesem Stamm eine Woche lang.
The people in this tribe fast for one week every spring.

Er fastet aus religiösen Gründen.
He fasts for religious reasons.

**fechten**

to fence

**Auxiliary verb:** haben **Past participle:** gefochten

**Imperative:** Ficht! Fechtet! Fechten Sie!

| Mode | Simple Tenses | | Compound Tenses | |
|---|---|---|---|---|
| | *Singular* | *Plural* | *Singular* | *Plural* |
| Indicative | **Present** | | **Present Perfect** | |
| | fechte<br>fichtst<br>ficht | fechten<br>fechtet<br>fechten | habe gefochten<br>hast gefochten<br>hat gefochten | haben gefochten<br>habt gefochten<br>haben gefochten |
| | **Past** | | **Past Perfect** | |
| | focht<br>fochtest<br>focht | fochten<br>fochtet<br>fochten | hatte gefochten<br>hattest gefochten<br>hatte gefochten | hatten gefochten<br>hattet gefochten<br>hatten gefochten |
| | **Future** | | **Future Perfect** | |
| | werde fechten<br>wirst fechten<br>wird fechten | werden fechten<br>werdet fechten<br>werden fechten | werde gefochten haben<br>wirst gefochten haben<br>wird gefochten haben | werden gefochten haben<br>werdet gefochten haben<br>werden gefochten haben |
| Subjunctive | **Present** | | **Present Perfect** | |
| | fechte<br>fechtest<br>fechte | fechten<br>fechtet<br>fechten | habe gefochten<br>habest gefochten<br>habe gefochten | haben gefochten<br>habet gefochten<br>haben gefochten |
| | **Past** | | **Past Perfect** | |
| | föchte<br>föchtest<br>föchte | föchten<br>föchtet<br>föchten | hätte gefochten<br>hättest gefochten<br>hätte gefochten | hätten gefochten<br>hättet gefochten<br>hätten gefochten |
| | **Future** | | **Future Perfect** | |
| | werde fechten<br>werdest fechten<br>werde fechten | werden fechten<br>werdet fechten<br>werden fechten | werde gefochten haben<br>werdest gefochten haben<br>werde gefochten haben | werden gefochten haben<br>werdet gefochten haben<br>werden gefochten haben |
| | **Present and Future Conditional** | | **Past Conditional** | |
| | würde fechten<br>würdest fechten<br>würde fechten | würden fechten<br>würdet fechten<br>würden fechten | würde gefochten haben<br>würdest gefochten haben<br>würde gefochten haben | würden gefochten haben<br>würdet gefochten haben<br>würden gefochten haben |

## EXAMPLES

Er wurde beim Fechten verwundet. — He was wounded fencing.

Ich kenne wenige Leute, die fechten können. — I know few people who know how to fence.

**fehlen**
to miss, to be absent
**Auxiliary verb:** haben **Past participle:** gefehlt
**Imperative:** Fehle! Fehlt! Fehlen Sie!

| Mode | Simple Tenses | | Compound Tenses | |
|---|---|---|---|---|
| | *Singular* | *Plural* | *Singular* | *Plural* |
| Indicative | **Present** | | **Present Perfect** | |
| | fehle<br>fehlst<br>fehlt | fehlen<br>fehlt<br>fehlen | habe gefehlt<br>hast gefehlt<br>hat gefehlt | haben gefehlt<br>habt gefehlt<br>haben gefehlt |
| | **Past** | | **Past Perfect** | |
| | fehlte<br>fehltest<br>fehlte | fehlten<br>fehltet<br>fehlten | hatte gefehlt<br>hattest gefehlt<br>hatte gefehlt | hatten gefehlt<br>hattet gefehlt<br>hatten gefehlt |
| | **Future** | | **Future Perfect** | |
| | werde fehlen<br>wirst fehlen<br>wird fehlen | werden fehlen<br>werdet fehlen<br>werden fehlen | werde gefehlt haben<br>wirst gefehlt haben<br>wird gefehlt haben | werden gefehlt haben<br>werdet gefehlt haben<br>werden gefehlt haben |
| Subjunctive | **Present** | | **Present Perfect** | |
| | fehle<br>fehlest<br>fehle | fehlen<br>fehlet<br>fehlen | habe gefehlt<br>habest gefehlt<br>habe gefehlt | haben gefehlt<br>habet gefehlt<br>haben gefehlt |
| | **Past** | | **Past Perfect** | |
| | fehlte<br>fehltest<br>fehlte | fehlten<br>fehltet<br>fehlten | hätte gefehlt<br>hättest gefehlt<br>hätte gefehlt | hätten gefehlt<br>hättet gefehlt<br>hätten gefehlt |
| | **Future** | | **Future Perfect** | |
| | werde fehlen<br>werdest fehlen<br>werde fehlen | werden fehlen<br>werdet fehlen<br>werden fehlen | werde gefehlt haben<br>werdest gefehlt haben<br>werde gefehlt haben | werden gefehlt haben<br>werdet gefehlt haben<br>werden gefehlt haben |
| | **Present and Future Conditional** | | **Past Conditional** | |
| | würde fehlen<br>würdest fehlen<br>würde fehlen | würden fehlen<br>würdet fehlen<br>würden fehlen | würde gefehlt haben<br>würdest gefehlt haben<br>würde gefehlt haben | würden gefehlt haben<br>würdet gefehlt haben<br>würden gefehlt haben |

## EXAMPLES

Dieser Zeitschrift fehlen die ersten zehn Seiten. — This magazine is missing the first ten pages.

Wer fehlt heute? — Who's absent today?

**feiern**
to celebrate
**Auxiliary verb:** haben **Past participle:** gefeiert
**Imperative:** Feiere! Feiert! Feiern Sie!

| Mode | Simple Tenses | | Compound Tenses | |
|---|---|---|---|---|
| | *Singular* | *Plural* | *Singular* | *Plural* |
| Indicative | **Present** | | **Present Perfect** | |
| | feiere<br>feierst<br>feiert | feiern<br>feiert<br>feiern | habe gefeiert<br>hast gefeiert<br>hat gefeiert | haben gefeiert<br>habt gefeiert<br>haben gefeiert |
| | **Past** | | **Past Perfect** | |
| | feierte<br>feiertest<br>feierte | feierten<br>feiertet<br>feierten | hatte gefeiert<br>hattest gefeiert<br>hatte gefeiert | hatten gefeiert<br>hattet gefeiert<br>hatten gefeiert |
| | **Future** | | **Future Perfect** | |
| | werde feiern<br>wirst feiern<br>wird feiern | werden feiern<br>werdet feiern<br>werden feiern | werde gefeiert haben<br>wirst gefeiert haben<br>wird gefeiert haben | werden gefeiert haben<br>werdet gefeiert haben<br>werden gefeiert haben |
| Subjunctive | **Present** | | **Present Perfect** | |
| | feiere<br>feierst<br>feiere | feiern<br>feiert<br>feiern | habe gefeiert<br>habest gefeiert<br>habe gefeiert | haben gefeiert<br>habet gefeiert<br>haben gefeiert |
| | **Past** | | **Past Perfect** | |
| | feierte<br>feiertest<br>feierte | feierten<br>feiertet<br>feierten | hätte gefeiert<br>hättest gefeiert<br>hätte gefeiert | hätten gefeiert<br>hättet gefeiert<br>hätten gefeiert |
| | **Future** | | **Future Perfect** | |
| | werde feiern<br>werdest feiern<br>werde feiern | werden feiern<br>werdet feiern<br>werden feiern | werde gefeiert haben<br>werdest gefeiert haben<br>werde gefeiert haben | werden gefeiert haben<br>werdet gefeiert haben<br>werden gefeiert haben |
| | **Present and Future Conditional** | | **Past Conditional** | |
| | würde feiern<br>würdest feiern<br>würde feiern | würden feiern<br>würdet feiern<br>würden feiern | würde gefeiert haben<br>würdest gefeiert haben<br>würde gefeiert haben | würden gefeiert haben<br>würdet gefeiert haben<br>würden gefeiert haben |

## EXAMPLES

Das junge Ehepaar hat seine Hochzeit im Hotel Adler gefeiert.
The young couple celebrated their wedding at Hotel Adler.

Die Deutschen feiern am 24. Dezember Weihnachten.
Germans celebrate Christmas on December 24.

**feststellen**
to ascertain, to determine, to establish
**Auxiliary verb:** haben **Past participle:** festgestellt
**Imperative:** Stelle fest! Stellt fest! Stellen Sie fest!

| Mode | Simple Tenses | | Compound Tenses | |
|---|---|---|---|---|
| | *Singular* | *Plural* | *Singular* | *Plural* |
| Indicative | **Present** | | **Present Perfect** | |
| | stelle fest<br>stellst fest<br>stellt fest | stellen fest<br>stellt fest<br>stellen fest | habe festgestellt<br>hast festgestellt<br>hat festgestellt | haben festgestellt<br>habt festgestellt<br>haben festgestellt |
| | **Past** | | **Past Perfect** | |
| | stellte fest<br>stelltest fest<br>stellte fest | stellten fest<br>stelltet fest<br>stellten fest | hatte festgestellt<br>hattest festgestellt<br>hatte festgestellt | hatten festgestellt<br>hattet festgestellt<br>hatten festgestellt |
| | **Future** | | **Future Perfect** | |
| | werde feststellen<br>wirst feststellen<br>wird feststellen | werden feststellen<br>werdet feststellen<br>werden feststellen | werde festgestellt haben<br>wirst festgestellt haben<br>wird festgestellt haben | werden festgestellt haben<br>werdet festgestellt haben<br>werden festgestellt haben |
| Subjunctive | **Present** | | **Present Perfect** | |
| | stelle fest<br>stellest fest<br>stelle fest | stellen fest<br>stellet fest<br>stellen fest | habe festgestellt<br>habest festgestellt<br>habe festgestellt | haben festgestellt<br>habet festgestellt<br>haben festgestellt |
| | **Past** | | **Past Perfect** | |
| | stellte fest<br>stelltest fest<br>stellte fest | stellten fest<br>stelltet fest<br>stellten fest | hätte festgestellt<br>hättest festgestellt<br>hätte festgestellt | hätten festgestellt<br>hättet festgestellt<br>hätten festgestellt |
| | **Future** | | **Future Perfect** | |
| | werde feststellen<br>werdest feststellen<br>werde feststellen | werden feststellen<br>werdet feststellen<br>werden feststellen | werde festgestellt haben<br>werdest festgestellt haben<br>werde festgestellt haben | werden festgestellt haben<br>werdet festgestellt haben<br>werden festgestellt haben |
| | **Present and Future Conditional** | | **Past Conditional** | |
| | würde feststellen<br>würdest feststellen<br>würde feststellen | würden feststellen<br>würdet feststellen<br>würden feststellen | würde festgestellt haben<br>würdest festgestellt haben<br>würde festgestellt haben | würden festgestellt haben<br>würdet festgestellt haben<br>würden festgestellt haben |

## EXAMPLES

Haben sie den Täter noch nicht festgestellt? — Haven't they determined who the culprit is yet?

Er stellte fest, dass die Theorie richtig ist. — He established that the theory is correct.

**finden**
to find
**Auxiliary verb:** haben **Past participle:** gefunden
**Imperative:** Finde! Findet! Finden Sie!

| Mode | Simple Tenses | | Compound Tenses | |
|---|---|---|---|---|
| | *Singular* | *Plural* | *Singular* | *Plural* |
| Indicative | **Present** | | **Present Perfect** | |
| | finde<br>findest<br>findet | finden<br>findet<br>finden | habe gefunden<br>hast gefunden<br>hat gefunden | haben gefunden<br>habt gefunden<br>haben gefunden |
| | **Past** | | **Past Perfect** | |
| | fand<br>fandest<br>fand | fanden<br>fandet<br>fanden | hatte gefunden<br>hattest gefunden<br>hatte gefunden | hatten gefunden<br>hattet gefunden<br>hatten gefunden |
| | **Future** | | **Future Perfect** | |
| | werde finden<br>wirst finden<br>wird finden | werden finden<br>werdet finden<br>werden finden | werde gefunden haben<br>wirst gefunden haben<br>wird gefunden haben | werden gefunden haben<br>werdet gefunden haben<br>werden gefunden haben |
| Subjunctive | **Present** | | **Present Perfect** | |
| | finde<br>findest<br>finde | finden<br>findet<br>finden | habe gefunden<br>habest gefunden<br>habe gefunden | haben gefunden<br>habet gefunden<br>haben gefunden |
| | **Past** | | **Past Perfect** | |
| | fände<br>fändest<br>fände | fänden<br>fändet<br>fänden | hätte gefunden<br>hättest gefunden<br>hätte gefunden | hätten gefunden<br>hättet gefunden<br>hätten gefunden |
| | **Future** | | **Future Perfect** | |
| | werde finden<br>werdest finden<br>werde finden | werden finden<br>werdet finden<br>werden finden | werde gefunden haben<br>werdest gefunden haben<br>werde gefunden haben | werden gefunden haben<br>werdet gefunden haben<br>werden gefunden haben |
| | **Present and Future Conditional** | | **Past Conditional** | |
| | würde finden<br>würdest finden<br>würde finden | würden finden<br>würdet finden<br>würden finden | würde gefunden haben<br>würdest gefunden haben<br>würde gefunden haben | würden gefunden haben<br>würdet gefunden haben<br>würden gefunden haben |

**Note:** With inseparable prefixes, the principal parts are, for example, *erfindet, erfand, hat erfunden.* With separable prefixes, the principal parts are, for example, *findet statt, fand statt, hat stattgefunden.*

## EXAMPLES

| | |
|---|---|
| Ich finde diesen Wein ausgezeichnet. | I think this wine is excellent. |
| Die Kinder können ihre Handschuhe nicht finden. | The children can't find their gloves. |

**fletschen**
to show one's teeth, to snarl
**Auxiliary verb:** haben **Past participle:** gefletscht
**Imperative:** Fletsche! Fletscht! Fletschen Sie!

| Mode | Simple Tenses | | Compound Tenses | |
|---|---|---|---|---|
| | *Singular* | *Plural* | *Singular* | *Plural* |
| Indicative | **Present** | | **Present Perfect** | |
| | fletsche<br>fletschst<br>fletscht | fletschen<br>fletscht<br>fletschen | habe gefletscht<br>hast gefletscht<br>hat gefletscht | haben gefletscht<br>habt gefletscht<br>haben gefletscht |
| | **Past** | | **Past Perfect** | |
| | fletschte<br>fletschtest<br>fletschte | fletschten<br>fletschtet<br>fletschten | hatte gefletscht<br>hattest gefletscht<br>hatte gefletscht | hatten gefletscht<br>hattet gefletscht<br>hatten gefletscht |
| | **Future** | | **Future Perfect** | |
| | werde fletschen<br>wirst fletschen<br>wird fletschen | werden fletschen<br>werdet fletschen<br>werden fletschen | werde gefletscht haben<br>wirst gefletscht haben<br>wird gefletscht haben | werden gefletscht haben<br>werdet gefletscht haben<br>werden gefletscht haben |
| Subjunctive | **Present** | | **Present Perfect** | |
| | fletsche<br>fletschest<br>fletsche | fletschen<br>fletschet<br>fletschen | habe gefletscht<br>habest gefletscht<br>habe gefletscht | haben gefletscht<br>habet gefletscht<br>haben gefletscht |
| | **Past** | | **Past Perfect** | |
| | fletschte<br>fletschtest<br>fletschte | fletschten<br>fletschtet<br>fletschten | hätte gefletscht<br>hättest gefletscht<br>hätte gefletscht | hätten gefletscht<br>hättet gefletscht<br>hätten gefletscht |
| | **Future** | | **Future Perfect** | |
| | werde fletschen<br>werdest fletschen<br>werde fletschen | werden fletschen<br>werdet fletschen<br>werden fletschen | werde gefletscht haben<br>werdest gefletscht haben<br>werde gefletscht haben | werden gefletscht haben<br>werdet gefletscht haben<br>werden gefletscht haben |
| | **Present and Future Conditional** | | **Past Conditional** | |
| | würde fletschen<br>würdest fletschen<br>würde fletschen | würden fletschen<br>würdet fletschen<br>würden fletschen | würde gefletscht haben<br>würdest gefletscht haben<br>würde gefletscht haben | würden gefletscht haben<br>würdet gefletscht haben<br>würden gefletscht haben |

## EXAMPLE

Der bissige Hund hat die Zähne gefletscht. The mean dog snarled.

**fliegen**
to fly
**Auxiliary verb:** sein **Past participle:** geflogen
**Imperative:** Fliege! Fliegt! Fliegen Sie!

| Mode | Simple Tenses | | Compound Tenses | |
|---|---|---|---|---|
| | *Singular* | *Plural* | *Singular* | *Plural* |
| Indicative | **Present** | | **Present Perfect** | |
| | fliege<br>fliegst<br>fliegt | fliegen<br>fliegt<br>fliegen | bin geflogen<br>bist geflogen<br>ist geflogen | sind geflogen<br>seid geflogen<br>sind geflogen |
| | **Past** | | **Past Perfect** | |
| | flog<br>flogst<br>flog | flogen<br>flogt<br>flogen | war geflogen<br>warst geflogen<br>war geflogen | waren geflogen<br>wart geflogen<br>waren geflogen |
| | **Future** | | **Future Perfect** | |
| | werde fliegen<br>wirst fliegen<br>wird fliegen | werden fliegen<br>werdet fliegen<br>werden fliegen | werde geflogen sein<br>wirst geflogen sein<br>wird geflogen sein | werden geflogen sein<br>werdet geflogen sein<br>werden geflogen sein |
| Subjunctive | **Present** | | **Present Perfect** | |
| | fliege<br>fliegest<br>fliege | fliegen<br>flieget<br>fliegen | sei geflogen<br>seiest geflogen<br>sei geflogen | seien geflogen<br>seiet geflogen<br>seien geflogen |
| | **Past** | | **Past Perfect** | |
| | flöge<br>flögest<br>flöge | flögen<br>flöget<br>flögen | wäre geflogen<br>wärest geflogen<br>wäre geflogen | wären geflogen<br>wäret geflogen<br>wären geflogen |
| | **Future** | | **Future Perfect** | |
| | werde fliegen<br>werdest fliegen<br>werde fliegen | werden fliegen<br>werdet fliegen<br>werden fliegen | werde geflogen sein<br>werdest geflogen sein<br>werde geflogen sein | werden geflogen sein<br>werdet geflogen sein<br>werden geflogen sein |
| | **Present and Future Conditional** | | **Past Conditional** | |
| | würde fliegen<br>würdest fliegen<br>würde fliegen | würden fliegen<br>würdet fliegen<br>würden fliegen | würde geflogen sein<br>würdest geflogen sein<br>würde geflogen sein | würden geflogen sein<br>würdet geflogen sein<br>würden geflogen sein |

**Note:** If *fliegen* is used as a transitive verb, its auxiliary in the perfect tenses will be *haben* (see the second example below). With separable prefixes, the principal parts are, for example, *fliegt aus, flog aus, ist ausgeflogen.*

## EXAMPLES

Die Touristen werden mit einer deutschen Fluggesellschaft nach Berlin fliegen.
The tourists will fly to Berlin on a German airline.

Der junge Pilot hat zum ersten Mal einen Düsenjäger geflogen.
The young pilot flew a jet fighter for the first time.

**fliehen**
to flee, to escape
**Auxiliary verb:** sein **Past participle:** geflohen
**Imperative:** Fliehe! Flieht! Fliehen Sie!

| Mode | Simple Tenses | | Compound Tenses | |
|---|---|---|---|---|
| | *Singular* | *Plural* | *Singular* | *Plural* |
| Indicative | **Present** | | **Present Perfect** | |
| | fliehe<br>fliehst<br>flieht | fliehen<br>flieht<br>fliehen | bin geflohen<br>bist geflohen<br>ist geflohen | sind geflohen<br>seid geflohen<br>sind geflohen |
| | **Past** | | **Past Perfect** | |
| | floh<br>flohst<br>floh | flohen<br>floht<br>flohen | war geflohen<br>warst geflohen<br>war geflohen | waren geflohen<br>wart geflohen<br>waren geflohen |
| | **Future** | | **Future Perfect** | |
| | werde fliehen<br>wirst fliehen<br>wird fliehen | werden fliehen<br>werdet fliehen<br>werden fliehen | werde geflohen sein<br>wirst geflohen sein<br>wird geflohen sein | werden geflohen sein<br>werdet geflohen sein<br>werden geflohen sein |
| Subjunctive | **Present** | | **Present Perfect** | |
| | fliehe<br>fliehest<br>fliehe | fliehen<br>fliehet<br>fliehen | sei geflohen<br>seiest geflohen<br>sei geflohen | seien geflohen<br>seiet geflohen<br>seien geflohen |
| | **Past** | | **Past Perfect** | |
| | flöhe<br>flöhest<br>flöhe | flöhen<br>flöhet<br>flöhen | wäre geflohen<br>wärest geflohen<br>wäre geflohen | wären geflohen<br>wäret geflohen<br>wären geflohen |
| | **Future** | | **Future Perfect** | |
| | werde fliehen<br>werdest fliehen<br>werde fliehen | werden fliehen<br>werdet fliehen<br>werden fliehen | werde geflohen sein<br>werdest geflohen sein<br>werde geflohen sein | werden geflohen sein<br>werdet geflohen sein<br>werden geflohen sein |
| | **Present and Future Conditional** | | **Past Conditional** | |
| | würde fliehen<br>würdest fliehen<br>würde fliehen | würden fliehen<br>würdet fliehen<br>würden fliehen | würde geflohen sein<br>würdest geflohen sein<br>würde geflohen sein | würden geflohen sein<br>würdet geflohen sein<br>würden geflohen sein |

## EXAMPLES

Die Bevölkerung ist vor der angreifenden Armee geflohen.
The population fled from the attacking army.

Die Flüchtlinge versuchen in den Wald zu fliehen.
The refugees try to flee into the woods.

**fließen**

to flow, to run

**Auxiliary verb:** sein **Past participle:** geflossen

**Imperative:** Fließe! Fließt! Fließen Sie!

| Mode | Simple Tenses | | Compound Tenses | |
|---|---|---|---|---|
| | *Singular* | *Plural* | *Singular* | *Plural* |
| Indicative | **Present** | | **Present Perfect** | |
| | fließe<br>fließt<br>fließt | fließen<br>fließt<br>fließen | bin geflossen<br>bist geflossen<br>ist geflossen | sind geflossen<br>seid geflossen<br>sind geflossen |
| | **Past** | | **Past Perfect** | |
| | floss<br>flossest<br>floss | flossen<br>flosst<br>flossen | war geflossen<br>warst geflossen<br>war geflossen | waren geflossen<br>wart geflossen<br>waren geflossen |
| | **Future** | | **Future Perfect** | |
| | werde fließen<br>wirst fließen<br>wird fließen | werden fließen<br>werdet fließen<br>werden fließen | werde geflossen sein<br>wirst geflossen sein<br>wird geflossen sein | werden geflossen sein<br>werdet geflossen sein<br>werden geflossen sein |
| Subjunctive | **Present** | | **Present Perfect** | |
| | fließe<br>fließest<br>fließe | fließen<br>fließet<br>fließen | sei geflossen<br>seiest geflossen<br>sei geflossen | seien geflossen<br>seiet geflossen<br>seien geflossen |
| | **Past** | | **Past Perfect** | |
| | flösse<br>flössest<br>flösse | flössen<br>flösset<br>flössen | wäre geflossen<br>wärest geflossen<br>wäre geflossen | wären geflossen<br>wäret geflossen<br>wären geflossen |
| | **Future** | | **Future Perfect** | |
| | werde fließen<br>werdest fließen<br>werde fließen | werden fließen<br>werdet fließen<br>werden fließen | werde geflossen sein<br>werdest geflossen sein<br>werde geflossen sein | werden geflossen sein<br>werdet geflossen sein<br>werden geflossen sein |
| | **Present and Future Conditional** | | **Past Conditional** | |
| | würde fließen<br>würdest fließen<br>würde fließen | würden fließen<br>würdet fließen<br>würden fließen | würde geflossen sein<br>würdest geflossen sein<br>würde geflossen sein | würden geflossen sein<br>würdet geflossen sein<br>würden geflossen sein |

## EXAMPLES

In welche Richtung fließt die Oder?
Die Flüsse fließen in die Nordsee.

In what direction does the Oder flow?
The rivers flow into the North Sea.

**fluchen**
to curse, to swear
**Auxiliary verb:** haben **Past participle:** geflucht
**Imperative:** Fluche! Flucht! Fluchen Sie!

| Mode | Simple Tenses | | Compound Tenses | |
|---|---|---|---|---|
| | *Singular* | *Plural* | *Singular* | *Plural* |
| Indicative | **Present** | | **Present Perfect** | |
| | fluche<br>fluchst<br>flucht | fluchen<br>flucht<br>fluchen | habe geflucht<br>hast geflucht<br>hat geflucht | haben geflucht<br>habt geflucht<br>haben geflucht |
| | **Past** | | **Past Perfect** | |
| | fluchte<br>fluchtest<br>fluchte | fluchten<br>fluchtet<br>fluchten | hatte geflucht<br>hattest geflucht<br>hatte geflucht | hatten geflucht<br>hattet geflucht<br>hatten geflucht |
| | **Future** | | **Future Perfect** | |
| | werde fluchen<br>wirst fluchen<br>wird fluchen | werden fluchen<br>werdet fluchen<br>werden fluchen | werde geflucht haben<br>wirst geflucht haben<br>wird geflucht haben | werden geflucht haben<br>werdet geflucht haben<br>werden geflucht haben |
| Subjunctive | **Present** | | **Present Perfect** | |
| | fluche<br>fluchest<br>fluche | fluchen<br>fluchet<br>fluchen | habe geflucht<br>habest geflucht<br>habe geflucht | haben geflucht<br>habet geflucht<br>haben geflucht |
| | **Past** | | **Past Perfect** | |
| | fluchte<br>fluchtest<br>fluchte | fluchten<br>fluchtet<br>fluchten | hätte geflucht<br>hättest geflucht<br>hätte geflucht | hätten geflucht<br>hättet geflucht<br>hätten geflucht |
| | **Future** | | **Future Perfect** | |
| | werde fluchen<br>werdest fluchen<br>werde fluchen | werden fluchen<br>werdet fluchen<br>werden fluchen | werde geflucht haben<br>werdest geflucht haben<br>werde geflucht haben | werden geflucht haben<br>werdet geflucht haben<br>werden geflucht haben |
| | **Present and Future Conditional** | | **Past Conditional** | |
| | würde fluchen<br>würdest fluchen<br>würde fluchen | würden fluchen<br>würdet fluchen<br>würden fluchen | würde geflucht haben<br>würdest geflucht haben<br>würde geflucht haben | würden geflucht haben<br>würdet geflucht haben<br>würden geflucht haben |

## EXAMPLES

Ich hörte sie über ihre Schulden fluchen. — I heard them cursing their debts.
Großvater kann nicht sprechen, ohne zu fluchen. — Grandfather can't talk without cursing.

**flüchten**
to flee, to escape
**Auxiliary verb:** sein **Past participle:** geflüchtet
**Imperative:** Flüchte! Flüchtet! Flüchten Sie!

| Mode | Simple Tenses | | Compound Tenses | |
|---|---|---|---|---|
| | *Singular* | *Plural* | *Singular* | *Plural* |
| Indicative | **Present** | | **Present Perfect** | |
| | flüchte<br>flüchtest<br>flüchtet | flüchten<br>flüchtet<br>flüchten | bin geflüchtet<br>bist geflüchtet<br>ist geflüchtet | sind geflüchtet<br>seid geflüchtet<br>sind geflüchtet |
| | **Past** | | **Past Perfect** | |
| | flüchtete<br>flüchtetest<br>flüchtete | flüchteten<br>flüchtetet<br>flüchteten | war geflüchtet<br>warst geflüchtet<br>war geflüchtet | waren geflüchtet<br>wart geflüchtet<br>waren geflüchtet |
| | **Future** | | **Future Perfect** | |
| | werde flüchten<br>wirst flüchten<br>wird flüchten | werden flüchten<br>werdet flüchten<br>werden flüchten | werde geflüchtet sein<br>wirst geflüchtet sein<br>wird geflüchtet sein | werden geflüchtet sein<br>werdet geflüchtet sein<br>werden geflüchtet sein |
| Subjunctive | **Present** | | **Present Perfect** | |
| | flüchte<br>flüchtest<br>flüchte | flüchten<br>flüchtet<br>flüchten | sei geflüchtet<br>seiest geflüchtet<br>sei geflüchtet | seien geflüchtet<br>seiet geflüchtet<br>seien geflüchtet |
| | **Past** | | **Past Perfect** | |
| | flüchtete<br>flüchtetest<br>flüchtete | flüchteten<br>flüchtetet<br>flüchteten | wäre geflüchtet<br>wärest geflüchtet<br>wäre geflüchtet | wären geflüchtet<br>wäret geflüchtet<br>wären geflüchtet |
| | **Future** | | **Future Perfect** | |
| | werde flüchten<br>werdest flüchten<br>werde flüchten | werden flüchten<br>werdet flüchten<br>werden flüchten | werde geflüchtet sein<br>werdest geflüchtet sein<br>werde geflüchtet sein | werden geflüchtet sein<br>werdet geflüchtet sein<br>werden geflüchtet sein |
| | **Present and Future Conditional** | | **Past Conditional** | |
| | würde flüchten<br>würdest flüchten<br>würde flüchten | würden flüchten<br>würdet flüchten<br>würden flüchten | würde geflüchtet sein<br>würdest geflüchtet sein<br>würde geflüchtet sein | würden geflüchtet sein<br>würdet geflüchtet sein<br>würden geflüchtet sein |

## EXAMPLES

| | |
|---|---|
| Der Angeklagte versuchte nach Kanada zu fliehen. | The defendant tried to escape to Canada. |
| Die Gefangenen sind geflüchtet. | The prisoners fled. |

**flüstern**
to whisper
**Auxiliary verb:** haben **Past participle:** geflüstert
**Imperative:** Flüstere! Flüstert! Flüstern Sie!

| Mode | Simple Tenses | | Compound Tenses | |
|---|---|---|---|---|
| | *Singular* | *Plural* | *Singular* | *Plural* |
| Indicative | **Present** | | **Present Perfect** | |
| | flüstere<br>flüsterst<br>flüstert | flüstern<br>flüstert<br>flüstern | habe geflüstert<br>hast geflüstert<br>hat geflüstert | haben geflüstert<br>habt geflüstert<br>haben geflüstert |
| | **Past** | | **Past Perfect** | |
| | flüsterte<br>flüstertest<br>flüsterte | flüsterten<br>flüstertet<br>flüsterten | hatte geflüstert<br>hattest geflüstert<br>hatte geflüstert | hatten geflüstert<br>hattet geflüstert<br>hatten geflüstert |
| | **Future** | | **Future Perfect** | |
| | werde flüstern<br>wirst flüstern<br>wird flüstern | werden flüstern<br>werdet flüstern<br>werden flüstern | werde geflüstert haben<br>wirst geflüstert haben<br>wird geflüstert haben | werden geflüstert haben<br>werdet geflüstert haben<br>werden geflüstert haben |
| Subjunctive | **Present** | | **Present Perfect** | |
| | flüstere<br>flüsterst<br>flüstere | flüstern<br>flüstert<br>flüstern | habe geflüstert<br>habest geflüstert<br>habe geflüstert | haben geflüstert<br>habet geflüstert<br>haben geflüstert |
| | **Past** | | **Past Perfect** | |
| | flüsterte<br>flüstertest<br>flüsterte | flüsterten<br>flüstertet<br>flüsterten | hätte geflüstert<br>hättest geflüstert<br>hätte geflüstert | hätten geflüstert<br>hättet geflüstert<br>hätten geflüstert |
| | **Future** | | **Future Perfect** | |
| | werde flüstern<br>werdest flüstern<br>werde flüstern | werden flüstern<br>werdet flüstern<br>werden flüstern | werde geflüstert haben<br>werdest geflüstert haben<br>werde geflüstert haben | werden geflüstert haben<br>werdet geflüstert haben<br>werden geflüstert haben |
| | **Present and Future Conditional** | | **Past Conditional** | |
| | würde flüstern<br>würdest flüstern<br>würde flüstern | würden flüstern<br>würdet flüstern<br>würden flüstern | würde geflüstert haben<br>würdest geflüstert haben<br>würde geflüstert haben | würden geflüstert haben<br>würdet geflüstert haben<br>würden geflüstert haben |

## EXAMPLES

Die Jungen stehen an der Ecke und flüstern. — The boys stand on the corner and whisper.
Kennst du den alten Film *Bettgeflüster?* — Do you know the old movie *Pillow Talk?*

**folgen**
to follow
**Auxiliary verb:** sein **Past participle:** gefolgt
**Imperative:** Folge! Folgt! Folgen Sie!

| Mode | Simple Tenses | | Compound Tenses | |
|---|---|---|---|---|
| | *Singular* | *Plural* | *Singular* | *Plural* |
| Indicative | **Present** | | **Present Perfect** | |
| | folge<br>folgst<br>folgt | folgen<br>folgt<br>folgen | bin gefolgt<br>bist gefolgt<br>ist gefolgt | sind gefolgt<br>seid gefolgt<br>sind gefolgt |
| | **Past** | | **Past Perfect** | |
| | folgte<br>folgtest<br>folgte | folgten<br>folgtet<br>folgten | war gefolgt<br>warst gefolgt<br>war gefolgt | waren gefolgt<br>wart gefolgt<br>waren gefolgt |
| | **Future** | | **Future Perfect** | |
| | werde folgen<br>wirst folgen<br>wird folgen | werden folgen<br>werdet folgen<br>werden folgen | werde gefolgt sein<br>wirst gefolgt sein<br>wird gefolgt sein | werden gefolgt sein<br>werdet gefolgt sein<br>werden gefolgt sein |
| Subjunctive | **Present** | | **Present Perfect** | |
| | folge<br>folgest<br>folge | folgen<br>folget<br>folgen | sei gefolgt<br>seiest gefolgt<br>sei gefolgt | seien gefolgt<br>seiet gefolgt<br>seien gefolgt |
| | **Past** | | **Past Perfect** | |
| | folgte<br>folgtest<br>folgte | folgten<br>folgtet<br>folgten | wäre gefolgt<br>wärest gefolgt<br>wäre gefolgt | wären gefolgt<br>wäret gefolgt<br>wären gefolgt |
| | **Future** | | **Future Perfect** | |
| | werde folgen<br>werdest folgen<br>werde folgen | werden folgen<br>werdet folgen<br>werden folgen | werde gefolgt sein<br>werdest gefolgt sein<br>werde gefolgt sein | werden gefolgt sein<br>werdet gefolgt sein<br>werden gefolgt sein |
| | **Present and Future Conditional** | | **Past Conditional** | |
| | würde folgen<br>würdest folgen<br>würde folgen | würden folgen<br>würdet folgen<br>würden folgen | würde gefolgt sein<br>würdest gefolgt sein<br>würde gefolgt sein | würden gefolgt sein<br>würdet gefolgt sein<br>würden gefolgt sein |

**Note:** When this verb means "to obey" or "to listen to," it requires the auxiliary *haben* in the perfect tenses: *Er hat seinem Vater gefolgt* ("He listened to his father"). *Folgen* is a dative verb.

## EXAMPLES

| | |
|---|---|
| Wir sind dem Fremden in den Wald gefolgt. | We followed the stranger into the woods. |
| Der alte Hund folgte seinem Herrn. | The old dog followed his master. |

**fordern**
to demand, to ask
**Auxiliary verb:** haben **Past participle:** gefordert
**Imperative:** Fordere! Fordert! Fordern Sie!

| Mode | Simple Tenses | | Compound Tenses | |
|---|---|---|---|---|
| | *Singular* | *Plural* | *Singular* | *Plural* |
| Indicative | **Present** | | **Present Perfect** | |
| | fordere<br>forderst<br>fordert | fordern<br>fordert<br>fordern | habe gefordert<br>hast gefordert<br>hat gefordert | haben gefordert<br>habt gefordert<br>haben gefordert |
| | **Past** | | **Past Perfect** | |
| | forderte<br>fordertest<br>forderte | forderten<br>fordertet<br>forderten | hatte gefordert<br>hattest gefordert<br>hatte gefordert | hatten gefordert<br>hattet gefordert<br>hatten gefordert |
| | **Future** | | **Future Perfect** | |
| | werde fordern<br>wirst fordern<br>wird fordern | werden fordern<br>werdet fordern<br>werden fordern | werde gefordert haben<br>wirst gefordert haben<br>wird gefordert haben | werden gefordert haben<br>werdet gefordert haben<br>werden gefordert haben |
| Subjunctive | **Present** | | **Present Perfect** | |
| | fordere<br>forderst<br>fordere | fordern<br>fordert<br>fordern | habe gefordert<br>habest gefordert<br>habe gefordert | haben gefordert<br>habet gefordert<br>haben gefordert |
| | **Past** | | **Past Perfect** | |
| | forderte<br>fordertest<br>forderte | forderten<br>fordertet<br>forderten | hätte gefordert<br>hättest gefordert<br>hätte gefordert | hätten gefordert<br>hättet gefordert<br>hätten gefordert |
| | **Future** | | **Future Perfect** | |
| | werde fordern<br>werdest fordern<br>werde fordern | werden fordern<br>werdet fordern<br>werden fordern | werde gefordert haben<br>werdest gefordert haben<br>werde gefordert haben | werden gefordert haben<br>werdet gefordert haben<br>werden gefordert haben |
| | **Present and Future Conditional** | | **Past Conditional** | |
| | würde fordern<br>würdest fordern<br>würde fordern | würden fordern<br>würdet fordern<br>würden fordern | würde gefordert haben<br>würdest gefordert haben<br>würde gefordert haben | würden gefordert haben<br>würdet gefordert haben<br>würden gefordert haben |

## EXAMPLES

Die Entführer forderten 2 Millionen Euro.
Er hat für seine Arbeit einen höheren Lohn gefordert.

The kidnappers demanded 2 million euros.
He demanded a higher wage for his work.

**fördern**

to further, to promote

**Auxiliary verb:** haben **Past participle:** gefördert

**Imperative:** Fördere! Fördert! Fördern Sie!

| Mode | Simple Tenses | | Compound Tenses | |
|---|---|---|---|---|
| | *Singular* | *Plural* | *Singular* | *Plural* |
| Indicative | **Present** | | **Present Perfect** | |
| | fördere<br>förderst<br>fördert | fördern<br>fördert<br>fördern | habe gefördert<br>hast gefördert<br>hat gefördert | haben gefördert<br>habt gefördert<br>haben gefördert |
| | **Past** | | **Past Perfect** | |
| | förderte<br>fördertest<br>förderte | förderten<br>fördertet<br>förderten | hatte gefördert<br>hattest gefördert<br>hatte gefördert | hatten gefördert<br>hattet gefördert<br>hatten gefördert |
| | **Future** | | **Future Perfect** | |
| | werde fördern<br>wirst fördern<br>wird fördern | werden fördern<br>werdet fördern<br>werden fördern | werde gefördert haben<br>wirst gefördert haben<br>wird gefördert haben | werden gefördert haben<br>werdet gefördert haben<br>werden gefördert haben |
| Subjunctive | **Present** | | **Present Perfect** | |
| | fördere<br>förderst<br>fördere | fördern<br>fördert<br>fördern | habe gefördert<br>habest gefördert<br>habe gefördert | haben gefördert<br>habet gefördert<br>haben gefördert |
| | **Past** | | **Past Perfect** | |
| | förderte<br>fördertest<br>förderte | förderten<br>fördertet<br>förderten | hätte gefördert<br>hättest gefördert<br>hätte gefördert | hätten gefördert<br>hättet gefördert<br>hätten gefördert |
| | **Future** | | **Future Perfect** | |
| | werde fördern<br>werdest fördern<br>werde fördern | werden fördern<br>werdet fördern<br>werden fördern | werde gefördert haben<br>werdest gefördert haben<br>werde gefördert haben | werden gefördert haben<br>werdet gefördert haben<br>werden gefördert haben |
| | **Present and Future Conditional** | | **Past Conditional** | |
| | würde fördern<br>würdest fördern<br>würde fördern | würden fördern<br>würdet fördern<br>würden fördern | würde gefördert haben<br>würdest gefördert haben<br>würde gefördert haben | würden gefördert haben<br>würdet gefördert haben<br>würden gefördert haben |

## EXAMPLES

Sie haben die neue Rechtschreibung gefördert.
Die Universität möchte den jungen Pianisten fördern.

They promoted the new orthography.
The university would like to promote the young pianist.

**forschen**
to search, to investigate, to do research
**Auxiliary verb:** haben **Past participle:** geforscht
**Imperative:** Forsche! Forscht! Forschen Sie!

| Mode | Simple Tenses | | Compound Tenses | |
|---|---|---|---|---|
| | *Singular* | *Plural* | *Singular* | *Plural* |
| Indicative | **Present** | | **Present Perfect** | |
| | forsche<br>forschst<br>forscht | forschen<br>forscht<br>forschen | habe geforscht<br>hast geforscht<br>hat geforscht | haben geforscht<br>habt geforscht<br>haben geforscht |
| | **Past** | | **Past Perfect** | |
| | forschte<br>forschtest<br>forschte | forschten<br>forschtet<br>forschten | hatte geforscht<br>hattest geforscht<br>hatte geforscht | hatten geforscht<br>hattet geforscht<br>hatten geforscht |
| | **Future** | | **Future Perfect** | |
| | werde forschen<br>wirst forschen<br>wird forschen | werden forschen<br>werdet forschen<br>werden forschen | werde geforscht haben<br>wirst geforscht haben<br>wird geforscht haben | werden geforscht haben<br>werdet geforscht haben<br>werden geforscht haben |
| Subjunctive | **Present** | | **Present Perfect** | |
| | forsche<br>forschest<br>forsche | forschen<br>forschet<br>forschen | habe geforscht<br>habest geforscht<br>habe geforscht | haben geforscht<br>habet geforscht<br>haben geforscht |
| | **Past** | | **Past Perfect** | |
| | forschte<br>forschtest<br>forschte | forschten<br>forschtet<br>forschten | hätte geforscht<br>hättest geforscht<br>hätte geforscht | hätten geforscht<br>hättet geforscht<br>hätten geforscht |
| | **Future** | | **Future Perfect** | |
| | werde forschen<br>werdest forschen<br>werde forschen | werden forschen<br>werdet forschen<br>werden forschen | werde geforscht haben<br>werdest geforscht haben<br>werde geforscht haben | werden geforscht haben<br>werdet geforscht haben<br>werden geforscht haben |
| | **Present and Future Conditional** | | **Past Conditional** | |
| | würde forschen<br>würdest forschen<br>würde forschen | würden forschen<br>würdet forschen<br>würden forschen | würde geforscht haben<br>würdest geforscht haben<br>würde geforscht haben | würden geforscht haben<br>würdet geforscht haben<br>würden geforscht haben |

## EXAMPLES

Ein Philosoph forscht nach Wahrheit.
A philosopher seeks truth.

Die Wissenschaftler haben lange nach einem Heilmittel geforscht.
The scientists searched long for a cure.

**fortsetzen**

to carry on, to continue

**Auxiliary verb:** haben **Past participle:** fortgesetzt

**Imperative:** Setze fort! Setzt fort! Setzen Sie fort!

| Mode | Simple Tenses | | Compound Tenses | |
|---|---|---|---|---|
| | *Singular* | *Plural* | *Singular* | *Plural* |
| Indicative | **Present** | | **Present Perfect** | |
| | setze fort<br>setzt fort<br>setzt fort | setzen fort<br>setzt fort<br>setzen fort | habe fortgesetzt<br>hast fortgesetzt<br>hat fortgesetzt | haben fortgesetzt<br>habt fortgesetzt<br>haben fortgesetzt |
| | **Past** | | **Past Perfect** | |
| | setzte fort<br>setztest fort<br>setzte fort | setzten fort<br>setztet fort<br>setzten fort | hatte fortgesetzt<br>hattest fortgesetzt<br>hatte fortgesetzt | hatten fortgesetzt<br>hattet fortgesetzt<br>hatten fortgesetzt |
| | **Future** | | **Future Perfect** | |
| | werde fortsetzen<br>wirst fortsetzen<br>wird fortsetzen | werden fortsetzen<br>werdet fortsetzen<br>werden fortsetzen | werde fortgesetzt haben<br>wirst fortgesetzt haben<br>wird fortgesetzt haben | werden fortgesetzt haben<br>werdet fortgesetzt haben<br>werden fortgesetzt haben |
| Subjunctive | **Present** | | **Present Perfect** | |
| | setze fort<br>setzest fort<br>setze fort | setzen fort<br>setzet fort<br>setzen fort | habe fortgesetzt<br>habest fortgesetzt<br>habe fortgesetzt | haben fortgesetzt<br>habet fortgesetzt<br>haben fortgesetzt |
| | **Past** | | **Past Perfect** | |
| | setzte fort<br>setztest fort<br>setzte fort | setzten fort<br>setztet fort<br>setzten fort | hätte fortgesetzt<br>hättest fortgesetzt<br>hätte fortgesetzt | hätten fortgesetzt<br>hättet fortgesetzt<br>hätten fortgesetzt |
| | **Future** | | **Future Perfect** | |
| | werde fortsetzen<br>werdest fortsetzen<br>werde fortsetzen | werden fortsetzen<br>werdet fortsetzen<br>werden fortsetzen | werde fortgesetzt haben<br>werdest fortgesetzt haben<br>werde fortgesetzt haben | werden fortgesetzt haben<br>werdet fortgesetzt haben<br>werden fortgesetzt haben |
| | **Present and Future Conditional** | | **Past Conditional** | |
| | würde fortsetzen<br>würdest fortsetzen<br>würde fortsetzen | würden fortsetzen<br>würdet fortsetzen<br>würden fortsetzen | würde fortgesetzt haben<br>würdest fortgesetzt haben<br>würde fortgesetzt haben | würden fortgesetzt haben<br>würdet fortgesetzt haben<br>würden fortgesetzt haben |

## EXAMPLES

Wir müssen diese wichtigen Experimente fortsetzen.
We have to continue these important experiments.

Sie hat die Forschung fortgesetzt.
She has resumed the research.

**fragen**
to ask
**Auxiliary verb:** haben **Past participle:** gefragt
**Imperative:** Frage! Fragt! Fragen Sie!

| Mode | Simple Tenses | | Compound Tenses | |
|---|---|---|---|---|
| | *Singular* | *Plural* | *Singular* | *Plural* |
| Indicative | **Present** | | **Present Perfect** | |
| | frage<br>fragst<br>fragt | fragen<br>fragt<br>fragen | habe gefragt<br>hast gefragt<br>hat gefragt | haben gefragt<br>habt gefragt<br>haben gefragt |
| | **Past** | | **Past Perfect** | |
| | fragte<br>fragtest<br>fragte | fragten<br>fragtet<br>fragten | hatte gefragt<br>hattest gefragt<br>hatte gefragt | hatten gefragt<br>hattet gefragt<br>hatten gefragt |
| | **Future** | | **Future Perfect** | |
| | werde fragen<br>wirst fragen<br>wird fragen | werden fragen<br>werdet fragen<br>werden fragen | werde gefragt haben<br>wirst gefragt haben<br>wird gefragt haben | werden gefragt haben<br>werdet gefragt haben<br>werden gefragt haben |
| Subjunctive | **Present** | | **Present Perfect** | |
| | frage<br>fragest<br>frage | fragen<br>fraget<br>fragen | habe gefragt<br>habest gefragt<br>habe gefragt | haben gefragt<br>habet gefragt<br>haben gefragt |
| | **Past** | | **Past Perfect** | |
| | fragte<br>fragtest<br>fragte | fragten<br>fragtet<br>fragten | hätte gefragt<br>hättest gefragt<br>hätte gefragt | hätten gefragt<br>hättet gefragt<br>hätten gefragt |
| | **Future** | | **Future Perfect** | |
| | werde fragen<br>werdest fragen<br>werde fragen | werden fragen<br>werdet fragen<br>werden fragen | werde gefragt haben<br>werdest gefragt haben<br>werde gefragt haben | werden gefragt haben<br>werdet gefragt haben<br>werden gefragt haben |
| | **Present and Future Conditional** | | **Past Conditional** | |
| | würde fragen<br>würdest fragen<br>würde fragen | würden fragen<br>würdet fragen<br>würden fragen | würde gefragt haben<br>würdest gefragt haben<br>würde gefragt haben | würden gefragt haben<br>würdet gefragt haben<br>würden gefragt haben |

## EXAMPLES

Hat jemand nach uns gefragt? — Did anyone ask about us?
Erdöl ist sehr gefragt. — Oil is in much demand.

**fressen**

to eat, to feed (animals)

**Auxiliary verb:** haben **Past participle:** gefressen

**Imperative:** Friss! Fresst! Fressen Sie!

| Mode | Simple Tenses | | Compound Tenses | |
|---|---|---|---|---|
| | *Singular* | *Plural* | *Singular* | *Plural* |
| Indicative | **Present** | | **Present Perfect** | |
| | fresse<br>frisst<br>frisst | fressen<br>fresst<br>fressen | habe gefressen<br>hast gefressen<br>hat gefressen | haben gefressen<br>habt gefressen<br>haben gefressen |
| | **Past** | | **Past Perfect** | |
| | fraß<br>fraßest<br>fraß | fraßen<br>fraßt<br>fraßen | hatte gefressen<br>hattest gefressen<br>hatte gefressen | hatten gefressen<br>hattet gefressen<br>hatten gefressen |
| | **Future** | | **Future Perfect** | |
| | werde fressen<br>wirst fressen<br>wird fressen | werden fressen<br>werdet fressen<br>werden fressen | werde gefressen haben<br>wirst gefressen haben<br>wird gefressen haben | werden gefressen haben<br>werdet gefressen haben<br>werden gefressen haben |
| Subjunctive | **Present** | | **Present Perfect** | |
| | fresse<br>fressest<br>fresse | fressen<br>fresset<br>fressen | habe gefressen<br>habest gefressen<br>habe gefressen | haben gefressen<br>habet gefressen<br>haben gefressen |
| | **Past** | | **Past Perfect** | |
| | fräße<br>fräßest<br>fräße | fräßen<br>fräßet<br>fräßen | hätte gefressen<br>hättest gefressen<br>hätte gefressen | hätten gefressen<br>hättet gefressen<br>hätten gefressen |
| | **Future** | | **Future Perfect** | |
| | werde fressen<br>werdest fressen<br>werde fressen | werden fressen<br>werdet fressen<br>werden fressen | werde gefressen haben<br>werdest gefressen haben<br>werde gefressen haben | werden gefressen haben<br>werdet gefressen haben<br>werden gefressen haben |
| | **Present and Future Conditional** | | **Past Conditional** | |
| | würde fressen<br>würdest fressen<br>würde fressen | würden fressen<br>würdet fressen<br>würden fressen | würde gefressen haben<br>würdest gefressen haben<br>würde gefressen haben | würden gefressen haben<br>würdet gefressen haben<br>würden gefressen haben |

## EXAMPLES

Hat der Hund deute schon zu fressen bekommen?
Das sind fleischfressende Tiere.

Did the dog already get fed today?
Those animals are carnivores.

**freuen (sich)**
to be glad, to be happy
**Auxiliary verb:** haben **Past participle:** gefreut
**Imperative:** Freue! Freut! Freuen Sie!

| Mode | Simple Tenses | | Compound Tenses | |
|---|---|---|---|---|
| | *Singular* | *Plural* | *Singular* | *Plural* |
| Indicative | **Present** | | **Present Perfect** | |
| | freue<br>freust<br>freut | freuen<br>freut<br>freuen | habe gefreut<br>hast gefreut<br>hat gefreut | haben gefreut<br>habt gefreut<br>haben gefreut |
| | **Past** | | **Past Perfect** | |
| | freute<br>freutest<br>freute | freuten<br>freutet<br>freuten | hatte gefreut<br>hattest gefreut<br>hatte gefreut | hatten gefreut<br>hattet gefreut<br>hatten gefreut |
| | **Future** | | **Future Perfect** | |
| | werde freuen<br>wirst freuen<br>wird freuen | werden freuen<br>werdet freuen<br>werden freuen | werde gefreut haben<br>wirst gefreut haben<br>wird gefreut haben | werden gefreut haben<br>werdet gefreut haben<br>werden gefreut haben |
| Subjunctive | **Present** | | **Present Perfect** | |
| | freue<br>freuest<br>freue | freuen<br>freuet<br>freuen | habe gefreut<br>habest gefreut<br>habe gefreut | haben gefreut<br>habet gefreut<br>haben gefreut |
| | **Past** | | **Past Perfect** | |
| | freute<br>freutest<br>freute | freuten<br>freutet<br>freuten | hätte gefreut<br>hättest gefreut<br>hätte gefreut | hätten gefreut<br>hättet gefreut<br>hätten gefreut |
| | **Future** | | **Future Perfect** | |
| | werde freuen<br>werdest freuen<br>werde freuen | werden freuen<br>werdet freuen<br>werden freuen | werde gefreut haben<br>werdest gefreut haben<br>werde gefreut haben | werden gefreut haben<br>werdet gefreut haben<br>werden gefreut haben |
| | **Present and Future Conditional** | | **Past Conditional** | |
| | würde freuen<br>würdest freuen<br>würde freuen | würden freuen<br>würdet freuen<br>würden freuen | würde gefreut haben<br>würdest gefreut haben<br>würde gefreut haben | würden gefreut haben<br>würdet gefreut haben<br>würden gefreut haben |

**Note:** When not reflexive, this verb is usually used as a third-person impersonal expression with the pronoun *es: Es freut mich Sie kennenzulernen* ("I'm pleased to meet you").

## EXAMPLES

Wir freuen uns über deinen Besuch.
We're happy about your visit.

Er freut sich schon darauf, eine Reise nach Spanien zu machen.
He's already looking forward to his trip to Spain.

**frieren**
to freeze
**Auxiliary verb:** haben **Past participle:** gefroren
**Imperative:** Friere! Friert! Frieren Sie!

| Mode | Simple Tenses | | Compound Tenses | |
|---|---|---|---|---|
| | *Singular* | *Plural* | *Singular* | *Plural* |
| Indicative | **Present** | | **Present Perfect** | |
| | friere<br>frierst<br>friert | frieren<br>friert<br>frieren | habe gefroren<br>hast gefroren<br>hat gefroren | haben gefroren<br>habt gefroren<br>haben gefroren |
| | **Past** | | **Past Perfect** | |
| | fror<br>frorst<br>fror | froren<br>frort<br>froren | hatte gefroren<br>hattest gefroren<br>hatte gefroren | hatten gefroren<br>hattet gefroren<br>hatten gefroren |
| | **Future** | | **Future Perfect** | |
| | werde frieren<br>wirst frieren<br>wird frieren | werden frieren<br>werdet frieren<br>werden frieren | werde gefroren haben<br>wirst gefroren haben<br>wird gefroren haben | werden gefroren haben<br>werdet gefroren haben<br>werden gefroren haben |
| Subjunctive | **Present** | | **Present Perfect** | |
| | friere<br>frierest<br>friere | frieren<br>frieret<br>frieren | habe gefroren<br>habest gefroren<br>habe gefroren | haben gefroren<br>habet gefroren<br>haben gefroren |
| | **Past** | | **Past Perfect** | |
| | fröre<br>frörest<br>fröre | frören<br>fröret<br>frören | hätte gefroren<br>hättest gefroren<br>hätte gefroren | hätten gefroren<br>hättet gefroren<br>hätten gefroren |
| | **Future** | | **Future Perfect** | |
| | werde frieren<br>werdest frieren<br>werde frieren | werden frieren<br>werdet frieren<br>werden frieren | werde gefroren haben<br>werdest gefroren haben<br>werde gefroren haben | werden gefroren haben<br>werdet gefroren haben<br>werden gefroren haben |
| | **Present and Future Conditional** | | **Past Conditional** | |
| | würde frieren<br>würdest frieren<br>würde frieren | würden frieren<br>würdet frieren<br>würden frieren | würde gefroren haben<br>würdest gefroren haben<br>würde gefroren haben | würden gefroren haben<br>würdet gefroren haben<br>würden gefroren haben |

**Note:** With the prefix *er–*, this verb requires *sein* as its auxiliary in the perfect tenses: *ist erfroren.*

## EXAMPLES

Heute morgen hat es gefroren. — There was a freeze this morning.
Ich friere. Mach bitte das Fenster zu! — I'm freezing. Please close the window.

**frühstücken**
to have breakfast
**Auxiliary verb:** haben **Past participle:** gefrühstückt
**Imperative:** Frühstücke! Frühstückt! Frühstücken Sie!

| Mode | Simple Tenses | | Compound Tenses | |
|---|---|---|---|---|
| | *Singular* | *Plural* | *Singular* | *Plural* |
| Indicative | **Present** | | **Present Perfect** | |
| | frühstücke<br>frühstückst<br>frühstückt | frühstücken<br>frühstückt<br>frühstücken | habe gefrühstückt<br>hast gefrühstückt<br>hat gefrühstückt | haben gefrühstückt<br>habt gefrühstückt<br>haben gefrühstückt |
| | **Past** | | **Past Perfect** | |
| | frühstückte<br>frühstücktest<br>frühstückte | frühstückten<br>frühstücktet<br>frühstückten | hatte gefrühstückt<br>hattest gefrühstückt<br>hatte gefrühstückt | hatten gefrühstückt<br>hattet gefrühstückt<br>hatten gefrühstückt |
| | **Future** | | **Future Perfect** | |
| | werde frühstücken<br>wirst frühstücken<br>wird frühstücken | werden frühstücken<br>werdet frühstücken<br>werden frühstücken | werde gefrühstückt haben<br>wirst gefrühstückt haben<br>wird gefrühstückt haben | werden gefrühstückt haben<br>werdet gefrühstückt haben<br>werden gefrühstückt haben |
| Subjunctive | **Present** | | **Present Perfect** | |
| | frühstücke<br>frühstückest<br>frühstücke | frühstücken<br>frühstücket<br>frühstücken | habe gefrühstückt<br>habest gefrühstückt<br>habe gefrühstückt | haben gefrühstückt<br>habet gefrühstückt<br>haben gefrühstückt |
| | **Past** | | **Past Perfect** | |
| | frühstückte<br>frühstücktest<br>frühstückte | frühstückten<br>frühstücktet<br>frühstückten | hätte gefrühstückt<br>hättest gefrühstückt<br>hätte gefrühstückt | hätten gefrühstückt<br>hättet gefrühstückt<br>hätten gefrühstückt |
| | **Future** | | **Future Perfect** | |
| | werde frühstücken<br>werdest frühstücken<br>werde frühstücken | werden frühstücken<br>werdet frühstücken<br>werden frühstücken | werde gefrühstückt haben<br>werdest gefrühstückt haben<br>werde gefrühstückt haben | werden gefrühstückt haben<br>werdet gefrühstückt haben<br>werden gefrühstückt haben |
| | **Present and Future Conditional** | | **Past Conditional** | |
| | würde frühstücken<br>würdest frühstücken<br>würde frühstücken | würden frühstücken<br>würdet frühstücken<br>würden frühstücken | würde gefrühstückt haben<br>würdest gefrühstückt haben<br>würde gefrühstückt haben | würden gefrühstückt haben<br>würdet gefrühstückt haben<br>würden gefrühstückt haben |

## EXAMPLES

Um wieviel Uhr frühstückt ihr?
Die Kinder haben noch nicht gefrühstückt.

At what time do you have breakfast?
The children haven't eaten breakfast yet.

**fühlen (sich)**
to feel, to perceive
**Auxiliary verb:** haben **Past participle:** gefühlt
**Imperative:** Fühle! Fühlt! Fühlen Sie!

| Mode | Simple Tenses | | Compound Tenses | |
|---|---|---|---|---|
| | *Singular* | *Plural* | *Singular* | *Plural* |
| Indicative | **Present** | | **Present Perfect** | |
| | fühle<br>fühlst<br>fühlt | fühlen<br>fühlt<br>fühlen | habe gefühlt<br>hast gefühlt<br>hat gefühlt | haben gefühlt<br>habt gefühlt<br>haben gefühlt |
| | **Past** | | **Past Perfect** | |
| | fühlte<br>fühltest<br>fühlte | fühlten<br>fühltet<br>fühlten | hatte gefühlt<br>hattest gefühlt<br>hatte gefühlt | hatten gefühlt<br>hattet gefühlt<br>hatten gefühlt |
| | **Future** | | **Future Perfect** | |
| | werde fühlen<br>wirst fühlen<br>wird fühlen | werden fühlen<br>werdet fühlen<br>werden fühlen | werde gefühlt haben<br>wirst gefühlt haben<br>wird gefühlt haben | werden gefühlt haben<br>werdet gefühlt haben<br>werden gefühlt haben |
| Subjunctive | **Present** | | **Present Perfect** | |
| | fühle<br>fühlest<br>fühle | fühlen<br>fühlet<br>fühlen | habe gefühlt<br>habest gefühlt<br>habe gefühlt | haben gefühlt<br>habet gefühlt<br>haben gefühlt |
| | **Past** | | **Past Perfect** | |
| | fühlte<br>fühltest<br>fühlte | fühlten<br>fühltet<br>fühlten | hätte gefühlt<br>hättest gefühlt<br>hätte gefühlt | hätten gefühlt<br>hättet gefühlt<br>hätten gefühlt |
| | **Future** | | **Future Perfect** | |
| | werde fühlen<br>werdest fühlen<br>werde fühlen | werden fühlen<br>werdet fühlen<br>werden fühlen | werde gefühlt haben<br>werdest gefühlt haben<br>werde gefühlt haben | werden gefühlt haben<br>werdet gefühlt haben<br>werden gefühlt haben |
| | **Present and Future Conditional** | | **Past Conditional** | |
| | würde fühlen<br>würdest fühlen<br>würde fühlen | würden fühlen<br>würdet fühlen<br>würden fühlen | würde gefühlt haben<br>würdest gefühlt haben<br>würde gefühlt haben | würden gefühlt haben<br>würdet gefühlt haben<br>würden gefühlt haben |

## EXAMPLES

| | |
|---|---|
| Die Krankenschwester hat dem Patienten den Puls gefühlt. | The nurse felt the patient's pulse. |
| Tante Luise fühlt sich müde. | Aunt Luise feels tired. |

**führen**
to lead, to conduct, to guide
**Auxiliary verb:** haben **Past participle:** geführt
**Imperative:** Führe! Führt! Führen Sie!

| Mode | Simple Tenses | | Compound Tenses | |
|---|---|---|---|---|
| | *Singular* | *Plural* | *Singular* | *Plural* |
| Indicative | **Present** | | **Present Perfect** | |
| | führe<br>führst<br>führt | führen<br>führt<br>führen | habe geführt<br>hast geführt<br>hat geführt | haben geführt<br>habt geführt<br>haben geführt |
| | **Past** | | **Past Perfect** | |
| | führte<br>führtest<br>führte | führten<br>führtet<br>führten | hatte geführt<br>hattest geführt<br>hatte geführt | hatten geführt<br>hattet geführt<br>hatten geführt |
| | **Future** | | **Future Perfect** | |
| | werde führen<br>wirst führen<br>wird führen | werden führen<br>werdet führen<br>werden führen | werde geführt haben<br>wirst geführt haben<br>wird geführt haben | werden geführt haben<br>werdet geführt haben<br>werden geführt haben |
| Subjunctive | **Present** | | **Present Perfect** | |
| | führe<br>führest<br>führe | führen<br>führet<br>führen | habe geführt<br>habest geführt<br>habe geführt | haben geführt<br>habet geführt<br>haben geführt |
| | **Past** | | **Past Perfect** | |
| | führte<br>führtest<br>führte | führten<br>führtet<br>führten | hätte geführt<br>hättest geführt<br>hätte geführt | hätten geführt<br>hättet geführt<br>hätten geführt |
| | **Future** | | **Future Perfect** | |
| | werde führen<br>werdest führen<br>werde führen | werden führen<br>werdet führen<br>werden führen | werde geführt haben<br>werdest geführt haben<br>werde geführt haben | werden geführt haben<br>werdet geführt haben<br>werden geführt haben |
| | **Present and Future Conditional** | | **Past Conditional** | |
| | würde führen<br>würdest führen<br>würde führen | würden führen<br>würdet führen<br>würden führen | würde geführt haben<br>würdest geführt haben<br>würde geführt haben | würden geführt haben<br>würdet geführt haben<br>würden geführt haben |

## EXAMPLES

Wir haben ein Gespräch mit dem neuen Bundeskanzler geführt.
We had a conversation with the new federal chancellor.

Wohin führt dieser Weg?
Where does this path lead?

**füttern**
to feed
**Auxiliary verb:** haben **Past participle:** gefüttert
**Imperative:** Füttere! Füttert! Füttern Sie!

| Mode | Simple Tenses | | Compound Tenses | |
|---|---|---|---|---|
| | *Singular* | *Plural* | *Singular* | *Plural* |
| Indicative | **Present** | | **Present Perfect** | |
| | füttere<br>fütterst<br>füttert | füttern<br>füttert<br>füttern | habe gefüttert<br>hast gefüttert<br>hat gefüttert | haben gefüttert<br>habt gefüttert<br>haben gefüttert |
| | **Past** | | **Past Perfect** | |
| | fütterte<br>füttertest<br>fütterte | fütterten<br>füttertet<br>fütterten | hatte gefüttert<br>hattest gefüttert<br>hatte gefüttert | hatten gefüttert<br>hattet gefüttert<br>hatten gefüttert |
| | **Future** | | **Future Perfect** | |
| | werde füttern<br>wirst füttern<br>wird füttern | werden füttern<br>werdet füttern<br>werden füttern | werde gefüttert haben<br>wirst gefüttert haben<br>wird gefüttert haben | werden gefüttert haben<br>werdet gefüttert haben<br>werden gefüttert haben |
| Subjunctive | **Present** | | **Present Perfect** | |
| | füttere<br>fütterst<br>füttere | füttern<br>füttert<br>füttern | habe gefüttert<br>habest gefüttert<br>habe gefüttert | haben gefüttert<br>habet gefüttert<br>haben gefüttert |
| | **Past** | | **Past Perfect** | |
| | fütterte<br>füttertest<br>fütterte | fütterten<br>füttertet<br>fütterten | hätte gefüttert<br>hättest gefüttert<br>hätte gefüttert | hätten gefüttert<br>hättet gefüttert<br>hätten gefüttert |
| | **Future** | | **Future Perfect** | |
| | werde füttern<br>werdest füttern<br>werde füttern | werden füttern<br>werdet füttern<br>werden füttern | werde gefüttert haben<br>werdest gefüttert haben<br>werde gefüttert haben | werden gefüttert haben<br>werdet gefüttert haben<br>werden gefüttert haben |
| | **Present and Future Conditional** | | **Past Conditional** | |
| | würde füttern<br>würdest füttern<br>würde füttern | würden füttern<br>würdet füttern<br>würden füttern | würde gefüttert haben<br>würdest gefüttert haben<br>würde gefüttert haben | würden gefüttert haben<br>würdet gefüttert haben<br>würden gefüttert haben |

## EXAMPLE

Karl musste ihm die Kühe und Schweine füttern helfen.

Karl had to help him feed the cows and pigs.

**gähnen**
to yawn, to gape
**Auxiliary verb:** haben **Past participle:** gegähnt
**Imperative:** Gähne! Gähnt! Gähnen Sie!

| Mode | Simple Tenses | | Compound Tenses | |
|---|---|---|---|---|
| | *Singular* | *Plural* | *Singular* | *Plural* |
| Indicative | **Present** | | **Present Perfect** | |
| | gähne<br>gähnst<br>gähnt | gähnen<br>gähnt<br>gähnen | habe gegähnt<br>hast gegähnt<br>hat gegähnt | haben gegähnt<br>habt gegähnt<br>haben gegähnt |
| | **Past** | | **Past Perfect** | |
| | gähnte<br>gähntest<br>gähnte | gähnten<br>gähntet<br>gähnten | hatte gegähnt<br>hattest gegähnt<br>hatte gegähnt | hatten gegähnt<br>hattet gegähnt<br>hatten gegähnt |
| | **Future** | | **Future Perfect** | |
| | werde gähnen<br>wirst gähnen<br>wird gähnen | werden gähnen<br>werdet gähnen<br>werden gähnen | werde gegähnt haben<br>wirst gegähnt haben<br>wird gegähnt haben | werden gegähnt haben<br>werdet gegähnt haben<br>werden gegähnt haben |
| Subjunctive | **Present** | | **Present Perfect** | |
| | gähne<br>gähnest<br>gähne | gähnen<br>gähnet<br>gähnen | habe gegähnt<br>habest gegähnt<br>habe gegähnt | haben gegähnt<br>habet gegähnt<br>haben gegähnt |
| | **Past** | | **Past Perfect** | |
| | gähnte<br>gähntest<br>gähnte | gähnten<br>gähntet<br>gähnten | hätte gegähnt<br>hättest gegähnt<br>hätte gegähnt | hätten gegähnt<br>hättet gegähnt<br>hätten gegähnt |
| | **Future** | | **Future Perfect** | |
| | werde gähnen<br>werdest gähnen<br>werde gähnen | werden gähnen<br>werdet gähnen<br>werden gähnen | werde gegähnt haben<br>werdest gegähnt haben<br>werde gegähnt haben | werden gegähnt haben<br>werdet gegähnt haben<br>werden gegähnt haben |
| | **Present and Future Conditional** | | **Past Conditional** | |
| | würde gähnen<br>würdest gähnen<br>würde gähnen | würden gähnen<br>würdet gähnen<br>würden gähnen | würde gegähnt haben<br>würdest gegähnt haben<br>würde gegähnt haben | würden gegähnt haben<br>würdet gegähnt haben<br>würden gegähnt haben |

## EXAMPLES

Warum muss Onkel Peter so laut gähnen?
Am Ende des Weges sahen sie einen gähnenden Abgrund.

Why must Uncle Peter yawn so loudly?
At the end of the path, they saw a gaping chasm.

**gebären**

to bear, to give birth to

**Auxiliary verb:** haben **Past participle:** geboren

**Imperative:** Gebäre! Gebärt! Gebären Sie!

| Mode | Simple Tenses | | Compound Tenses | |
|---|---|---|---|---|
| | *Singular* | *Plural* | *Singular* | *Plural* |
| Indicative | **Present** | | **Present Perfect** | |
| | gebäre<br>gebärst / gebierst<br>gebärt / gebiert | gebären<br>gebärt<br>gebären | habe geboren<br>hast geboren<br>hat geboren | haben geboren<br>habt geboren<br>haben geboren |
| | **Past** | | **Past Perfect** | |
| | gebar<br>gebarst<br>gebar | gebaren<br>gebart<br>gebaren | hatte geboren<br>hattest geboren<br>hatte geboren | hatten geboren<br>hattet geboren<br>hatten geboren |
| | **Future** | | **Future Perfect** | |
| | werde gebären<br>wirst gebären<br>wird gebären | werden gebären<br>werdet gebären<br>werden gebären | werde geboren haben<br>wirst geboren haben<br>wird geboren haben | werden geboren haben<br>werdet geboren haben<br>werden geboren haben |
| Subjunctive | **Present** | | **Present Perfect** | |
| | gebäre<br>gebärest<br>gebäre | gebären<br>gebäret<br>gebären | habe geboren<br>habest geboren<br>habe geboren | haben geboren<br>habet geboren<br>haben geboren |
| | **Past** | | **Past Perfect** | |
| | gebäre<br>gebärest<br>gebäre | gebären<br>gebäret<br>gebären | hätte geboren<br>hättest geboren<br>hätte geboren | hätten geboren<br>hättet geboren<br>hätten geboren |
| | **Future** | | **Future Perfect** | |
| | werde gebären<br>werdest gebären<br>werde gebären | werden gebären<br>werdet gebären<br>werden gebären | werde geboren haben<br>werdest geboren haben<br>werde geboren haben | werden geboren haben<br>werdet geboren haben<br>werden geboren haben |
| | **Present and Future Conditional** | | **Past Conditional** | |
| | würde gebären<br>würdest gebären<br>würde gebären | würden gebären<br>würdet gebären<br>würden gebären | würde geboren haben<br>würdest geboren haben<br>würde geboren haben | würden geboren haben<br>würdet geboren haben<br>würden geboren haben |

## EXAMPLES

Wolfgang Amadeus Mozart wurde in Österreich geboren.
Wolfgang Amadeus Mozart was born in Austria.

Maria hat Zwillinge geboren.
Maria had twins.

**geben**
to give
**Auxiliary verb:** haben **Past participle:** gegeben
**Imperative:** Gib! Gebt! Geben Sie!

| Mode | Simple Tenses | | Compound Tenses | |
|---|---|---|---|---|
| | *Singular* | *Plural* | *Singular* | *Plural* |
| Indicative | **Present** | | **Present Perfect** | |
| | gebe<br>gibst<br>gibt | geben<br>gebt<br>geben | habe gegeben<br>hast gegeben<br>hat gegeben | haben gegeben<br>habt gegeben<br>haben gegeben |
| | **Past** | | **Past Perfect** | |
| | gab<br>gabst<br>gab | gaben<br>gabt<br>gaben | hatte gegeben<br>hattest gegeben<br>hatte gegeben | hatten gegeben<br>hattet gegeben<br>hatten gegeben |
| | **Future** | | **Future Perfect** | |
| | werde geben<br>wirst geben<br>wird geben | werden geben<br>werdet geben<br>werden geben | werde gegeben haben<br>wirst gegeben haben<br>wird gegeben haben | werden gegeben haben<br>werdet gegeben haben<br>werden gegeben haben |
| Subjunctive | **Present** | | **Present Perfect** | |
| | gebe<br>gebest<br>gebe | geben<br>gebet<br>geben | habe gegeben<br>habest gegeben<br>habe gegeben | haben gegeben<br>habet gegeben<br>haben gegeben |
| | **Past** | | **Past Perfect** | |
| | gäbe<br>gäbest<br>gäbe | gäben<br>gäbet<br>gäben | hätte gegeben<br>hättest gegeben<br>hätte gegeben | hatten gegeben<br>hättet gegeben<br>hätten gegeben |
| | **Future** | | **Future Perfect** | |
| | werde geben<br>werdest geben<br>werde geben | werden geben<br>werdet geben<br>werden geben | werde gegeben haben<br>werdest gegeben haben<br>werde gegeben haben | werden gegeben haben<br>werdet gegeben haben<br>werden gegeben haben |
| | **Present and Future Conditional** | | **Past Conditional** | |
| | würde geben<br>würdest geben<br>würde geben | würden geben<br>würdet geben<br>würden geben | würde gegeben haben<br>würdest gegeben haben<br>würde gegeben haben | würden gegeben haben<br>würdet gegeben haben<br>würden gegeben haben |

**Note:** The phrase *es gibt* means "there is." Its subject is always the pronoun *es*, and its principal parts are *es gibt, es gab, es hat gegeben.* With inseparable prefixes, the principal parts of this verb are, for example, *vergibt, vergab, hat vergeben.* With separable prefixes, the principal parts are, for example, *gibt aus, gab aus, hat ausgegeben.*

## EXAMPLES

| | |
|---|---|
| Der Schauspieler hat gestern vier Interviews gegeben. | The actor gave four interviews yesterday. |
| Zur Zeit gibt es auf dem Markt kein frisches Gemüse. | At the moment, there are no fresh vegetables at the market. |

**gebrauchen**
to use, to employ
**Auxiliary verb:** haben **Past participle:** gebraucht
**Imperative:** Gebrauche! Gebraucht! Gebrauchen Sie!

| Mode | Simple Tenses | | Compound Tenses | |
|---|---|---|---|---|
| | *Singular* | *Plural* | *Singular* | *Plural* |
| Indicative | **Present** | | **Present Perfect** | |
| | gebrauche<br>gebrauchst<br>gebraucht | gebrauchen<br>gebraucht<br>gebrauchen | habe gebraucht<br>hast gebraucht<br>hat gebraucht | haben gebraucht<br>habt gebraucht<br>haben gebraucht |
| | **Past** | | **Past Perfect** | |
| | gebrauchte<br>gebrauchtest<br>gebrauchte | gebrauchten<br>gebrauchtet<br>gebrauchten | hatte gebraucht<br>hattest gebraucht<br>hatte gebraucht | hatten gebraucht<br>hattet gebraucht<br>hatten gebraucht |
| | **Future** | | **Future Perfect** | |
| | werde gebrauchen<br>wirst gebrauchen<br>wird gebrauchen | werden gebrauchen<br>werdet gebrauchen<br>werden gebrauchen | werde gebraucht haben<br>wirst gebraucht haben<br>wird gebraucht haben | werden gebraucht haben<br>werdet gebraucht haben<br>werden gebraucht haben |
| Subjunctive | **Present** | | **Present Perfect** | |
| | gebrauche<br>gebrauchest<br>gebrauche | gebrauchen<br>gebrauchet<br>gebrauchen | habe gebraucht<br>habest gebraucht<br>habe gebraucht | haben gebraucht<br>habet gebraucht<br>haben gebraucht |
| | **Past** | | **Past Perfect** | |
| | gebrauchte<br>gebrauchtest<br>gebrauchte | gebrauchten<br>gebrauchtet<br>gebrauchten | hätte gebraucht<br>hättest gebraucht<br>hätte gebraucht | hätten gebraucht<br>hättet gebraucht<br>hätten gebraucht |
| | **Future** | | **Future Perfect** | |
| | werde gebrauchen<br>werdest gebrauchen<br>werde gebrauchen | werden gebrauchen<br>werdet gebrauchen<br>werden gebrauchen | werde gebraucht haben<br>werdest gebraucht haben<br>werde gebraucht haben | werden gebraucht haben<br>werdet gebraucht haben<br>werden gebraucht haben |
| | **Present and Future Conditional** | | **Past Conditional** | |
| | würde gebrauchen<br>würdest gebrauchen<br>würde gebrauchen | würden gebrauchen<br>würdet gebrauchen<br>würden gebrauchen | würde gebraucht haben<br>würdest gebraucht haben<br>würde gebraucht haben | würden gebraucht haben<br>würdet gebraucht haben<br>würden gebraucht haben |

## EXAMPLES

Dieser Entwurf ist nicht zu gebrauchen.
This design is of no use.

Den Anrufbeantworter können wir gut gebrauchen.
We can make good use of the answering machine.

**gefallen**
to please, to like
**Auxiliary verb:** haben **Past participle:** gefallen
**Imperative:** Gefalle! Gefallt! Gefallen Sie!

| Mode | Simple Tenses | | Compound Tenses | |
|---|---|---|---|---|
| | *Singular* | *Plural* | *Singular* | *Plural* |
| Indicative | **Present** | | **Present Perfect** | |
| | gefalle<br>gefällst<br>gefällt | gefallen<br>gefallt<br>gefallen | habe gefallen<br>hast gefallen<br>hat gefallen | haben gefallen<br>habt gefallen<br>haben gefallen |
| | **Past** | | **Past Perfect** | |
| | gefiel<br>gefielst<br>gefiel | gefielen<br>gefielt<br>gefielen | hatte gefallen<br>hattest gefallen<br>hatte gefallen | hatten gefallen<br>hattet gefallen<br>hatten gefallen |
| | **Future** | | **Future Perfect** | |
| | werde gefallen<br>wirst gefallen<br>wird gefallen | werden gefallen<br>werdet gefallen<br>werden gefallen | werde gefallen haben<br>wirst gefallen haben<br>wird gefallen haben | werden gefallen haben<br>werdet gefallen haben<br>werden gefallen haben |
| Subjunctive | **Present** | | **Present Perfect** | |
| | gefalle<br>gefallest<br>gefalle | gefallen<br>gefallet<br>gefallen | habe gefallen<br>habest gefallen<br>habe gefallen | haben gefallen<br>habet gefallen<br>haben gefallen |
| | **Past** | | **Past Perfect** | |
| | gefiele<br>gefielest<br>gefiele | gefielen<br>gefielet<br>gefielen | hätte gefallen<br>hättest gefallen<br>hatte gefallen | hätten gefallen<br>hättet gefallen<br>hätten gefallen |
| | **Future** | | **Future Perfect** | |
| | werde gefallen<br>werdest gefallen<br>werde gefallen | werden gefallen<br>werdet gefallen<br>werden gefallen | werde gefallen haben<br>werdest gefallen haben<br>werde gefallen haben | werden gefallen haben<br>werdet gefallen haben<br>werden gefallen haben |
| | **Present and Future Conditional** | | **Past Conditional** | |
| | würde gefallen<br>würdest gefallen<br>würde gefallen | würden gefallen<br>würdet gefallen<br>würden gefallen | würde gefallen haben<br>würdest gefallen haben<br>würde gefallen haben | würden gefallen haben<br>würdet gefallen haben<br>würden gefallen haben |

**Note:** *Gefallen* is a dative verb.

## EXAMPLES

Wie gefällt Ihnen dieser Hut? — How do you like this hat?
Das werde ich mir nicht gefallen lassen. — I won't put up with that.

**gehen**

to go

**Auxiliary verb:** sein **Past participle:** gegangen

**Imperative:** Gehe! Geht! Gehen Sie!

| Mode | Simple Tenses | | Compound Tenses | |
|---|---|---|---|---|
| | *Singular* | *Plural* | *Singular* | *Plural* |
| Indicative | **Present** | | **Present Perfect** | |
| | gehe<br>gehst<br>geht | gehen<br>geht<br>gehen | bin gegangen<br>bist gegangen<br>ist gegangen | sind gegangen<br>seid gegangen<br>sind gegangen |
| | **Past** | | **Past Perfect** | |
| | ging<br>gingst<br>ging | gingen<br>gingt<br>gingen | war gegangen<br>warst gegangen<br>war gegangen | waren gegangen<br>wart gegangen<br>waren gegangen |
| | **Future** | | **Future Perfect** | |
| | werde gehen<br>wirst gehen<br>wird gehen | werden gehen<br>werdet gehen<br>werden gehen | werde gegangen sein<br>wirst gegangen sein<br>wird gegangen sein | werden gegangen sein<br>werdet gegangen sein<br>werden gegangen sein |
| Subjunctive | **Present** | | **Present Perfect** | |
| | gehe<br>gehest<br>gehe | gehen<br>gehet<br>gehen | sei gegangen<br>seiest gegangen<br>sei gegangen | seien gegangen<br>seiet gegangen<br>seien gegangen |
| | **Past** | | **Past Perfect** | |
| | ginge<br>gingest<br>ginge | gingen<br>ginget<br>gingen | wäre gegangen<br>wärest gegangen<br>wäre gegangen | wären gegangen<br>wäret gegangen<br>wären gegangen |
| | **Future** | | **Future Perfect** | |
| | werde gehen<br>werdest gehen<br>werde gehen | werden gehen<br>werdet gehen<br>werden gehen | werde gegangen sein<br>werdest gegangen sein<br>werde gegangen sein | werden gegangen sein<br>werdet gegangen sein<br>werden gegangen sein |
| | **Present and Future Conditional** | | **Past Conditional** | |
| | würde gehen<br>würdest gehen<br>würde gehen | würden gehen<br>würdet gehen<br>würden gehen | würde gegangen sein<br>würdest gegangen sein<br>würde gegangen sein | würden gegangen sein<br>würdet gegangen sein<br>würden gegangen sein |

**Note:** With the prefix *be–* the verb *gehen* becomes transitive and means "to commit." The auxiliary for *begehen* is *haben: Er hat ein Verbrechen begangen* ("He committed a crime"). With separable prefixes, the principal parts of this verb are, for example, *geht weg, ging weg, ist weggegangen.*

## EXAMPLES

| | |
|---|---|
| Nächstes Jahr gehen die Kinder zur Schule. | Next year the children are going to school. |
| Wie geht es Ihnen? | How are you? |

**gehorchen**
to obey
**Auxiliary verb:** haben **Past participle:** gehorcht
**Imperative:** Gehorche! Gehorcht! Gehorchen Sie!

| Mode | Simple Tenses | | Compound Tenses | |
|---|---|---|---|---|
| | *Singular* | *Plural* | *Singular* | *Plural* |
| Indicative | **Present** | | **Present Perfect** | |
| | gehorche<br>gehorchst<br>gehorcht | gehorchen<br>gehorcht<br>gehorchen | habe gehorcht<br>hast gehorcht<br>hat gehorcht | haben gehorcht<br>habt gehorcht<br>haben gehorcht |
| | **Past** | | **Past Perfect** | |
| | gehorchte<br>gehorchtest<br>gehorchte | gehorchten<br>gehorchtet<br>gehorchten | hatte gehorcht<br>hattest gehorcht<br>hatte gehorcht | hatten gehorcht<br>hattet gehorcht<br>hatten gehorcht |
| | **Future** | | **Future Perfect** | |
| | werde gehorchen<br>wirst gehorchen<br>wird gehorchen | werden gehorchen<br>werdet gehorchen<br>werden gehorchen | werde gehorcht haben<br>wirst gehorcht haben<br>wird gehorcht haben | werden gehorcht haben<br>werdet gehorcht haben<br>werden gehorcht haben |
| Subjunctive | **Present** | | **Present Perfect** | |
| | gehorche<br>gehorchest<br>gehorche | gehorchen<br>gehorchet<br>gehorchen | habe gehorcht<br>habest gehorcht<br>habe gehorcht | haben gehorcht<br>habet gehorcht<br>haben gehorcht |
| | **Past** | | **Past Perfect** | |
| | gehorchte<br>gehorchtest<br>gehorchte | gehorchten<br>gehorchtet<br>gehorchten | hätte gehorcht<br>hättest gehorcht<br>hätte gehorcht | hätten gehorcht<br>hättet gehorcht<br>hätten gehorcht |
| | **Future** | | **Future Perfect** | |
| | werde gehorchen<br>werdest gehorchen<br>werde gehorchen | werden gehorchen<br>werdet gehorchen<br>werden gehorchen | werde gehorcht haben<br>werdest gehorcht haben<br>werde gehorcht haben | werden gehorcht haben<br>werdet gehorcht haben<br>werden gehorcht haben |
| | **Present and Future Conditional** | | **Past Conditional** | |
| | würde gehorchen<br>würdest gehorchen<br>würde gehorchen | würden gehorchen<br>würdet gehorchen<br>würden gehorchen | würde gehorcht haben<br>würdest gehorcht haben<br>würde gehorcht haben | würden gehorcht haben<br>würdet gehorcht haben<br>würden gehorcht haben |

## EXAMPLES

Die Schüler gehorchten dem Lehrer nicht.
Er hat seinem Vater nie gehorcht.

The pupils did not obey the teacher.
He never obeyed his father.

**gehören**
to belong to
**Auxiliary verb:** haben **Past participle:** gehört
**Imperative:** Gehöre! Gehört! Gehören Sie!

| Mode | Simple Tenses | | Compound Tenses | |
|---|---|---|---|---|
| | *Singular* | *Plural* | *Singular* | *Plural* |
| Indicative | **Present** | | **Present Perfect** | |
| | gehöre<br>gehörst<br>gehört | gehören<br>gehört<br>gehören | habe gehört<br>hast gehört<br>hat gehört | haben gehört<br>habt gehört<br>haben gehört |
| | **Past** | | **Past Perfect** | |
| | gehörte<br>gehörtest<br>gehörte | gehörten<br>gehörtet<br>gehörten | hatte gehört<br>hattest gehört<br>hatte gehört | hatten gehört<br>hattet gehört<br>hatten gehört |
| | **Future** | | **Future Perfect** | |
| | werde gehören<br>wirst gehören<br>wird gehören | werden gehören<br>werdet gehören<br>werden gehören | werde gehört haben<br>wirst gehört haben<br>wird gehört haben | werden gehört haben<br>werdet gehört haben<br>werden gehört haben |
| Subjunctive | **Present** | | **Present Perfect** | |
| | gehöre<br>gehörest<br>gehöre | gehören<br>gehöret<br>gehören | habe gehört<br>habest gehört<br>habe gehört | haben gehört<br>habet gehört<br>haben gehört |
| | **Past** | | **Past Perfect** | |
| | gehörte<br>gehörtest<br>gehörte | gehörten<br>gehörtet<br>gehörten | hätte gehört<br>hättest gehört<br>hätte gehört | hätten gehört<br>hättet gehört<br>hätten gehört |
| | **Future** | | **Future Perfect** | |
| | werde gehören<br>werdest gehören<br>werde gehören | werden gehören<br>werdet gehören<br>werden gehören | werde gehört haben<br>werdest gehört haben<br>werde gehört haben | werden gehört haben<br>werdet gehört haben<br>werden gehört haben |
| | **Present and Future Conditional** | | **Past Conditional** | |
| | würde gehören<br>würdest gehören<br>würde gehören | würden gehören<br>würdet gehören<br>würden gehören | würde gehört haben<br>würdest gehört haben<br>würde gehört haben | würden gehört haben<br>würdet gehört haben<br>würden gehört haben |

**Note:** *Gehören* is a dative verb.

## EXAMPLES

Wem gehören diese Handschuhe?
To whom do these gloves belong?

Dieser Wagen hat einmal einem reichen Amerikaner gehört.
This car once belonged to a rich American.

**gelingen**
to succeed, to manage to do
**Auxiliary verb:** sein **Past participle:** gelungen
**Imperative:** N/A

| Mode | Simple Tenses | | Compound Tenses | |
|---|---|---|---|---|
| | *Singular* | *Plural* | *Singular* | *Plural* |
| Indicative | **Present** | | **Present Perfect** | |
| | gelingt | | ist gelungen | |
| | **Past** | | **Past Perfect** | |
| | gelang | | war gelungen | |
| | **Future** | | **Future Perfect** | |
| | wird gelingen | | wird gelungen sein | |
| Subjunctive | **Present** | | **Present Perfect** | |
| | gelinge | | sei gelungen | |
| | **Past** | | **Past Perfect** | |
| | gelänge | | wäre gelungen | |
| | **Future** | | **Future Perfect** | |
| | werde gelingen | | würde gelungen sein | |
| | **Present and Future Conditional** | | **Past Conditional** | |
| | würde gelingen | | würde gelungen sein | |

**Note:** This verb is used as a third-person impersonal expression with the pronoun *es*. The object of the verb must be in the dative case: *Es gelingt mir* ("I succeed") or *Es gelang uns nicht* ("We didn't manage to do it").

## EXAMPLES

| | |
|---|---|
| Die Experimente sind ihm nicht gelungen. | His experiments didn't succeed. |
| Hoffentlich gelingt es mir einen neuen Wagen zu kaufen. | I hope I succeed in buying a new car. |

**gelten**
to be valid, to be worth
**Auxiliary verb:** haben **Past participle:** gegolten
**Imperative:** Gilt! Geltet! Gelten Sie!

| Mode | Simple Tenses | | Compound Tenses | |
|---|---|---|---|---|
| | *Singular* | *Plural* | *Singular* | *Plural* |
| Indicative | **Present** | | **Present Perfect** | |
| | gelte<br>giltst<br>gilt | gelten<br>geltet<br>gelten | habe gegolten<br>hast gegolten<br>hat gegolten | haben gegolten<br>habt gegolten<br>haben gegolten |
| | **Past** | | **Past Perfect** | |
| | galt<br>galtest<br>galt | galten<br>galtet<br>galten | hatte gegolten<br>hattest gegolten<br>hatte gegolten | hatten gegolten<br>hattet gegolten<br>hatten gegolten |
| | **Future** | | **Future Perfect** | |
| | werde gelten<br>wirst gelten<br>wird gelten | werden gelten<br>werdet gelten<br>werden gelten | werde gegolten haben<br>wirst gegolten haben<br>wird gegolten haben | werden gegolten haben<br>werdet gegolten haben<br>werden gegolten haben |
| Subjunctive | **Present** | | **Present Perfect** | |
| | gelte<br>geltest<br>gelte | gelten<br>geltet<br>gelten | habe gegolten<br>habest gegolten<br>habe gegolten | haben gegolten<br>habet gegolten<br>haben gegolten |
| | **Past** | | **Past Perfect** | |
| | gälte<br>gältest<br>gälte | gälten<br>gältet<br>gälten | hätte gegolten<br>hättest gegolten<br>hätte gegolten | hätten gegolten<br>hättet gegolten<br>hätten gegolten |
| | **Future** | | **Future Perfect** | |
| | werde gelten<br>werdest gelten<br>werde gelten | werden gelten<br>werdet gelten<br>werden gelten | werde gegolten haben<br>werdest gegolten haben<br>werde gegolten haben | werden gegolten haben<br>werdet gegolten haben<br>werden gegolten haben |
| | **Present and Future Conditional** | | **Past Conditional** | |
| | würde gelten<br>würdest gelten<br>würde gelten | würden gelten<br>würdet gelten<br>würden gelten | würde gegolten haben<br>würdest gegolten haben<br>würde gegolten haben | würden gegolten haben<br>würdet gegolten haben<br>würden gegolten haben |

**Note:** The past subjunctive is also commonly expressed as *gölte, göltest, gölte, gölten, göltet, gölten.*

## EXAMPLES

Der junge Professor galt als intelligent, aber er verstand seine Studenten nicht.
The young professor was considered intelligent, but he didn't understand his students.

Ihr Visum gilt nicht mehr.
Your visa isn't valid anymore.

**genesen**
to get well, to recover
**Auxiliary verb:** sein **Past participle:** genesen
**Imperative:** Genese! Genest! Genesen Sie!

| Mode | Simple Tenses | | Compound Tenses | |
|---|---|---|---|---|
| | *Singular* | *Plural* | *Singular* | *Plural* |
| Indicative | **Present** | | **Present Perfect** | |
| | genese<br>genest<br>genest | genesen<br>genest<br>genesen | bin genesen<br>bist genesen<br>ist genesen | sind genesen<br>seid genesen<br>sind genesen |
| | **Past** | | **Past Perfect** | |
| | genas<br>genasest<br>genas | genasen<br>genast<br>genasen | war genesen<br>warst genesen<br>war genesen | waren genesen<br>wart genesen<br>waren genesen |
| | **Future** | | **Future Perfect** | |
| | werde genesen<br>wirst genesen<br>wird genesen | werden genesen<br>werdet genesen<br>werden genesen | werde genesen sein<br>wirst genesen sein<br>wird genesen sein | werden genesen sein<br>werdet genesen sein<br>werden genesen sein |
| Subjunctive | **Present** | | **Present Perfect** | |
| | genese<br>genesest<br>genese | genesen<br>geneset<br>genesen | sei genesen<br>seiest genesen<br>sei genesen | seien genesen<br>seiet genesen<br>seien genesen |
| | **Past** | | **Past Perfect** | |
| | genäse<br>genäsest<br>genäse | genäsen<br>genäset<br>genäsen | wäre genesen<br>wärest genesen<br>wäre genesen | wären genesen<br>wäret genesen<br>wären genesen |
| | **Future** | | **Future Perfect** | |
| | werde genesen<br>werdest genesen<br>werde genesen | werden genesen<br>werdet genesen<br>werden genesen | werde genesen sein<br>werdest genesen sein<br>werde genesen sein | werden genesen sein<br>werdet genesen sein<br>werden genesen sein |
| | **Present and Future Conditional** | | **Past Conditional** | |
| | würde genesen<br>würdest genesen<br>würde genesen | würden genesen<br>würdet genesen<br>würden genesen | würde genesen sein<br>würdest genesen sein<br>würde genesen sein | würden genesen sein<br>würdet genesen sein<br>würden genesen sein |

## EXAMPLES

Die alte Frau wird bald genesen sein.
The old woman will soon be well.

Nach drei Wochen war Frau Helsberg völlig von ihrer Krankheit genesen.
In three weeks Mrs. Helsberg was completely recovered from her illness.

**genießen**
to enjoy
**Auxiliary verb:** haben **Past participle:** genossen
**Imperative:** Genieße! Genießt! Genießen Sie!

| Mode | Simple Tenses | | Compound Tenses | |
|---|---|---|---|---|
| | *Singular* | *Plural* | *Singular* | *Plural* |
| Indicative | **Present** | | **Present Perfect** | |
| | genieße<br>genießt<br>genießt | genießen<br>genießt<br>genießen | habe genossen<br>hast genossen<br>hat genossen | haben genossen<br>habt genossen<br>haben genossen |
| | **Past** | | **Past Perfect** | |
| | genoss<br>genossest<br>genoss | genossen<br>genosst<br>genossen | hatte genossen<br>hattest genossen<br>hatte genossen | hatten genossen<br>hattet genossen<br>hatten genossen |
| | **Future** | | **Future Perfect** | |
| | werde genießen<br>wirst genießen<br>wird genießen | werden genießen<br>werdet genießen<br>werden genießen | werde genossen haben<br>wirst genossen haben<br>wird genossen haben | werden genossen haben<br>werdet genossen haben<br>werden genossen haben |
| Subjunctive | **Present** | | **Present Perfect** | |
| | genieße<br>genießest<br>genieße | genießen<br>genießet<br>genießen | habe genossen<br>habest genossen<br>habe genossen | haben genossen<br>habet genossen<br>haben genossen |
| | **Past** | | **Past Perfect** | |
| | genösse<br>genössest<br>genösse | genössen<br>genösset<br>genössen | hätte genossen<br>hättest genossen<br>hätte genossen | hätten genossen<br>hättet genossen<br>hätten genossen |
| | **Future** | | **Future Perfect** | |
| | werde genießen<br>werdest genießen<br>werde genießen | werden genießen<br>werdet genießen<br>werden genießen | werde genossen haben<br>werdest genossen haben<br>werde genossen haben | werden genossen haben<br>werdet genossen haben<br>werden genossen haben |
| | **Present and Future Conditional** | | **Past Conditional** | |
| | würde genießen<br>würdest genießen<br>würde genießen | würden genießen<br>würdet genießen<br>würden genießen | würde genossen haben<br>würdest genossen haben<br>würde genossen haben | würden genossen haben<br>würdet genossen haben<br>würden genossen haben |

## EXAMPLES

Das warme Bier ist nicht zu genießen.
You can't enjoy warm beer.

Im Park haben wir die Sonne und frische Luft genossen.
We enjoyed the sun and fresh air in the park.

**genügen**
to suffice, to be enough
**Auxiliary verb:** haben **Past participle:** genügt
**Imperative:** Genüge! Genügt! Genügen Sie!

| Mode | Simple Tenses | | Compound Tenses | |
|---|---|---|---|---|
| | *Singular* | *Plural* | *Singular* | *Plural* |
| Indicative | **Present** | | **Present Perfect** | |
| | genüge<br>genügst<br>genügt | genügen<br>genügt<br>genügen | habe genügt<br>hast genügt<br>hat genügt | haben genügt<br>habt genügt<br>haben genügt |
| | **Past** | | **Past Perfect** | |
| | genügte<br>genügtest<br>genügte | genügten<br>genügtet<br>genügten | hatte genügt<br>hattest genügt<br>hatte genügt | hatten genügt<br>hattet genügt<br>hatten genügt |
| | **Future** | | **Future Perfect** | |
| | werde genügen<br>wirst genügen<br>wird genügen | werden genügen<br>werdet genügen<br>werden genügen | werde genügt haben<br>wirst genügt haben<br>wird genügt haben | werden genügt haben<br>werdet genügt haben<br>werden genügt haben |
| Subjunctive | **Present** | | **Present Perfect** | |
| | genüge<br>genügest<br>genüge | genügen<br>genüget<br>genügen | habe genügt<br>habest genügt<br>habe genügt | haben genügt<br>habet genügt<br>haben genügt |
| | **Past** | | **Past Perfect** | |
| | genügte<br>genügtest<br>genügte | genügten<br>genügtet<br>genügten | hätte genügt<br>hättest genügt<br>hätte genügt | hätten genügt<br>hättet genügt<br>hätten genügt |
| | **Future** | | **Future Perfect** | |
| | werde genügen<br>werdest genügen<br>werde genügen | werden genügen<br>werdet genügen<br>werden genügen | werde genügt haben<br>werdest genügt haben<br>werde genügt haben | werden genügt haben<br>werdet genügt haben<br>werden genügt haben |
| | **Present and Future Conditional** | | **Past Conditional** | |
| | würde genügen<br>würdest genügen<br>würde genügen | würden genügen<br>würdet genügen<br>würden genügen | würde genügt haben<br>würdest genügt haben<br>würde genügt haben | würden genügt haben<br>würdet genügt haben<br>würden genügt haben |

## EXAMPLES

Das genügt für unsere Zwecke. — That's enough for our purposes.

Die Bewerber genügten seinen Ansprüchen nicht. — The applicants didn't fulfill his requirements.

**geschehen**
to happen, to occur
**Auxiliary verb:** sein **Past participle:** geschehen
**Imperative:** N/A

| Mode | Simple Tenses | | Compound Tenses | |
|---|---|---|---|---|
| | *Singular* | *Plural* | *Singular* | *Plural* |
| Indicative | **Present** | | **Present Perfect** | |
| | geschieht | geschehen | ist geschehen | sind geschehen |
| | **Past** | | **Past Perfect** | |
| | geschah | geschahen | war geschehen | waren geschehen |
| | **Future** | | **Future Perfect** | |
| | wird geschehen | werden geschehen | wird geschehen sein | werden geschehen sein |
| Subjunctive | **Present** | | **Present Perfect** | |
| | geschehe | geschehen | sei geschehen | seien geschehen |
| | **Past** | | **Past Perfect** | |
| | geschähe | geschähen | wäre geschehen | wären geschehen |
| | **Future** | | **Future Perfect** | |
| | werde geschehen | werden geschehen | werde geschehen sein | werden geschehen sein |
| | **Present and Future Conditional** | | **Past Conditional** | |
| | würde geschehen | würden geschehen | würde geschehen sein | würden geschehen sein |

**Note:** This verb is used in the third person.

## EXAMPLES

Das wird nicht ohne große Kosten für die Firma geschehen.
That will not happen without great expense to the company.

Das Verbrechen ist am 10. August geschehen.
The crime occurred on the tenth of August.

**gestalten**
to form, to shape
**Auxiliary verb:** haben **Past participle:** gestaltet
**Imperative:** Gestalte! Gestaltet! Gestalten Sie!

| Mode | Simple Tenses | | Compound Tenses | |
|---|---|---|---|---|
| | *Singular* | *Plural* | *Singular* | *Plural* |
| Indicative | **Present** | | **Present Perfect** | |
| | gestalte<br>gestaltest<br>gestaltet | gestalten<br>gestaltet<br>gestalten | habe gestaltet<br>hast gestaltet<br>hat gestaltet | haben gestaltet<br>habt gestaltet<br>haben gestaltet |
| | **Past** | | **Past Perfect** | |
| | gestaltete<br>gestaltetest<br>gestaltete | gestalteten<br>gestaltetet<br>gestalteten | hatte gestaltet<br>hattest gestaltet<br>hatte gestaltet | hatten gestaltet<br>hattet gestaltet<br>hatten gestaltet |
| | **Future** | | **Future Perfect** | |
| | werde gestalten<br>wirst gestalten<br>wird gestalten | werden gestalten<br>werdet gestalten<br>werden gestalten | werde gestaltet haben<br>wirst gestaltet haben<br>wird gestaltet haben | werden gestaltet haben<br>werdet gestaltet haben<br>werden gestaltet haben |
| Subjunctive | **Present** | | **Present Perfect** | |
| | gestalte<br>gestaltest<br>gestalte | gestalten<br>gestaltet<br>gestalten | habe gestaltet<br>habest gestaltet<br>habe gestaltet | haben gestaltet<br>habet gestaltet<br>haben gestaltet |
| | **Past** | | **Past Perfect** | |
| | gestaltete<br>gestaltetest<br>gestaltete | gestalteten<br>gestaltetet<br>gestalteten | hätte gestaltet<br>hättest gestaltet<br>hätte gestaltet | hätten gestaltet<br>hättet gestaltet<br>hätten gestaltet |
| | **Future** | | **Future Perfect** | |
| | werde gestalten<br>werdest gestalten<br>werde gestalten | werden gestalten<br>werdet gestalten<br>werden gestalten | werde gestaltet haben<br>werdest gestaltet haben<br>werde gestaltet haben | werden gestaltet haben<br>werdet gestaltet haben<br>werden gestaltet haben |
| | **Present and Future Conditional** | | **Past Conditional** | |
| | würde gestalten<br>würdest gestalten<br>würde gestalten | würden gestalten<br>würdet gestalten<br>würden gestalten | würde gestaltet haben<br>würdest gestaltet haben<br>würde gestaltet haben | würden gestaltet haben<br>würdet gestaltet haben<br>würden gestaltet haben |

## EXAMPLES

Die Schüler gestalteten ein Poster über die Photosynthese.
The students designed a poster about photosynthesis.

Am Schluss gestaltete es sich zu seinem Besten.
In the end, it turned out to be to his advantage.

**gestatten**
to permit, to consent to
**Auxiliary verb:** haben **Past participle:** gestattet
**Imperative:** Gestatte! Gestattet! Gestatten Sie!

| Mode | Simple Tenses | | Compound Tenses | |
|---|---|---|---|---|
| | *Singular* | *Plural* | *Singular* | *Plural* |
| Indicative | **Present** | | **Present Perfect** | |
| | gestatte<br>gestattest<br>gestattet | gestatten<br>gestattet<br>gestatten | habe gestattet<br>hast gestattet<br>hat gestattet | haben gestattet<br>habt gestattet<br>haben gestattet |
| | **Past** | | **Past Perfect** | |
| | gestattete<br>gestattetest<br>gestattete | gestatteten<br>gestattetet<br>gestatteten | hatte gestattet<br>hattest gestattet<br>hatte gestattet | hatten gestattet<br>hattet gestattet<br>hatten gestattet |
| | **Future** | | **Future Perfect** | |
| | werde gestatten<br>wirst gestatten<br>wird gestatten | werden gestatten<br>werdet gestatten<br>werden gestatten | werde gestattet haben<br>wirst gestattet haben<br>wird gestattet haben | werden gestattet haben<br>werdet gestattet haben<br>werden gestattet haben |
| Subjunctive | **Present** | | **Present Perfect** | |
| | gestatte<br>gestattest<br>gestatte | gestatten<br>gestattet<br>gestatten | habe gestattet<br>habest gestattet<br>habe gestattet | haben gestattet<br>habet gestattet<br>haben gestattet |
| | **Past** | | **Past Perfect** | |
| | gestattete<br>gestattetest<br>gestattete | gestatteten<br>gestattetet<br>gestatteten | hätte gestattet<br>hättest gestattet<br>hätte gestattet | hätten gestattet<br>hättet gestattet<br>hätten gestattet |
| | **Future** | | **Future Perfect** | |
| | werde gestatten<br>werdest gestatten<br>werde gestatten | werden gestatten<br>werdet gestatten<br>werden gestatten | werde gestattet haben<br>werdest gestattet haben<br>werde gestattet haben | werden gestattet haben<br>werdet gestattet haben<br>werden gestattet haben |
| | **Present and Future Conditional** | | **Past Conditional** | |
| | würde gestatten<br>würdest gestatten<br>würde gestatten | würden gestatten<br>würdet gestatten<br>würden gestatten | würde gestattet haben<br>würdest gestattet haben<br>würde gestattet haben | würden gestattet haben<br>würdet gestattet haben<br>würden gestattet haben |

## EXAMPLES

Gestatten Sie!
May I get by? (Pardon me.)

Der Präsident gestattet nicht, dass wir eintreten.
The president doesn't consent to our coming in.

**gestehen**
to admit
**Auxiliary verb:** haben **Past participle:** gestanden
**Imperative:** Gestehe! Gesteht! Gestehen Sie!

| Mode | Simple Tenses | | Compound Tenses | |
|---|---|---|---|---|
| | *Singular* | *Plural* | *Singular* | *Plural* |
| Indicative | **Present** | | **Present Perfect** | |
| | gestehe<br>gestehst<br>gesteht | gestehen<br>gesteht<br>gestehen | habe gestanden<br>hast gestanden<br>hat gestanden | haben gestanden<br>habt gestanden<br>haben gestanden |
| | **Past** | | **Past Perfect** | |
| | gestand<br>gestandest<br>gestand | gestanden<br>gestandet<br>gestanden | hatte gestanden<br>hattest gestanden<br>hatte gestanden | hatten gestanden<br>hattet gestanden<br>hatten gestanden |
| | **Future** | | **Future Perfect** | |
| | werde gestehen<br>wirst gestehen<br>wird gestehen | werden gestehen<br>werdet gestehen<br>werden gestehen | werde gestanden haben<br>wirst gestanden haben<br>wird gestanden haben | werden gestanden haben<br>werdet gestanden haben<br>werden gestanden haben |
| Subjunctive | **Present** | | **Present Perfect** | |
| | gestehe<br>gestehest<br>gestehe | gestehen<br>gestehet<br>gestehen | habe gestanden<br>habest gestanden<br>habe gestanden | haben gestanden<br>habet gestanden<br>haben gestanden |
| | **Past** | | **Past Perfect** | |
| | gestände<br>geständest<br>gestände | geständen<br>geständet<br>geständen | hätte gestanden<br>hättest gestanden<br>hätte gestanden | hätten gestanden<br>hättet gestanden<br>hätten gestanden |
| | **Future** | | **Future Perfect** | |
| | werde gestehen<br>werdest gestehen<br>werde gestehen | werden gestehen<br>werdet gestehen<br>werden gestehen | werde gestanden haben<br>werdest gestanden haben<br>werde gestanden haben | werden gestanden haben<br>werdet gestanden haben<br>werden gestanden haben |
| | **Present and Future Conditional** | | **Past Conditional** | |
| | würde gestehen<br>würdest gestehen<br>würde gestehen | würden gestehen<br>würdet gestehen<br>würden gestehen | würde gestanden haben<br>würdest gestanden haben<br>würde gestanden haben | würden gestanden haben<br>würdet gestanden haben<br>würden gestanden haben |

## EXAMPLES

Sie hat mir gestern gestanden, dass sie jetzt Paul liebt.
She admitted to me yesterday that she now loves Paul.

Gestehen Sie, dass Sie gelogen haben!
Admit that you lied.

**gewinnen**
to win, to gain
**Auxiliary verb:** haben **Past participle:** gewonnen
**Imperative:** Gewinne! Gewinnt! Gewinnen Sie!

| Mode | Simple Tenses | | Compound Tenses | |
|---|---|---|---|---|
| | *Singular* | *Plural* | *Singular* | *Plural* |
| Indicative | **Present** | | **Present Perfect** | |
| | gewinne<br>gewinnst<br>gewinnt | gewinnen<br>gewinnt<br>gewinnen | habe gewonnen<br>hast gewonnen<br>hat gewonnen | haben gewonnen<br>habt gewonnen<br>haben gewonnen |
| | **Past** | | **Past Perfect** | |
| | gewann<br>gewannst<br>gewann | gewannen<br>gewannt<br>gewannen | hatte gewonnen<br>hattest gewonnen<br>hatte gewonnen | hatten gewonnen<br>hattet gewonnen<br>hatten gewonnen |
| | **Future** | | **Future Perfect** | |
| | werde gewinnen<br>wirst gewinnen<br>wird gewinnen | werden gewinnen<br>werdet gewinnen<br>werden gewinnen | werde gewonnen haben<br>wirst gewonnen haben<br>wird gewonnen haben | werden gewonnen haben<br>werdet gewonnen haben<br>werden gewonnen haben |
| Subjunctive | **Present** | | **Present Perfect** | |
| | gewinne<br>gewinnest<br>gewinne | gewinnen<br>gewinnet<br>gewinnen | habe gewonnen<br>habest gewonnen<br>habe gewonnen | haben gewonnen<br>habet gewonnen<br>haben gewonnen |
| | **Past** | | **Past Perfect** | |
| | gewänne<br>gewännest<br>gewänne | gewännen<br>gewännet<br>gewännen | hätte gewonnen<br>hättest gewonnen<br>hätte gewonnen | hätten gewonnen<br>hättet gewonnen<br>hätten gewonnen |
| | **Future** | | **Future Perfect** | |
| | werde gewinnen<br>werdest gewinnen<br>werde gewinnen | werden gewinnen<br>werdet gewinnen<br>werden gewinnen | werde gewonnen haben<br>werdest gewonnen haben<br>werde gewonnen haben | werden gewonnen haben<br>werdet gewonnen haben<br>werden gewonnen haben |
| | **Present and Future Conditional** | | **Past Conditional** | |
| | würde gewinnen<br>würdest gewinnen<br>würde gewinnen | würden gewinnen<br>würdet gewinnen<br>würden gewinnen | würde gewonnen haben<br>würdest gewonnen haben<br>würde gewonnen haben | würden gewonnen haben<br>würdet gewonnen haben<br>würden gewonnen haben |

**Note:** The past subjunctive is also said as *gewönne.*

## EXAMPLES

Der Feind hat wieder Boden gewonnen.
Sie hat aber ein gewinnendes Lächeln.
Denkst du, dass unsere Mannschaft gewinnen kann?

The enemy has gained ground again.
She really has a winning smile.
Do you think that our team can win?

**gewöhnen (sich)**
to accustom, to become accustomed
**Auxiliary verb:** haben **Past participle:** gewöhnt
**Imperative:** Gewöhne! Gewöhnt! Gewöhnen Sie!

| Mode | Simple Tenses | | Compound Tenses | |
|---|---|---|---|---|
| | *Singular* | *Plural* | *Singular* | *Plural* |
| Indicative | **Present** | | **Present Perfect** | |
| | gewöhne<br>gewöhnst<br>gewöhnt | gewöhnen<br>gewöhnt<br>gewöhnen | habe gewöhnt<br>hast gewöhnt<br>hat gewöhnt | haben gewöhnt<br>habt gewöhnt<br>haben gewöhnt |
| | **Past** | | **Past Perfect** | |
| | gewöhnte<br>gewöhntest<br>gewöhnte | gewöhnten<br>gewöhntet<br>gewöhnten | hatte gewöhnt<br>hattest gewöhnt<br>hatte gewöhnt | hatten gewöhnt<br>hattet gewöhnt<br>hatten gewöhnt |
| | **Future** | | **Future Perfect** | |
| | werde gewöhnen<br>wirst gewöhnen<br>wird gewöhnen | werden gewöhnen<br>werdet gewöhnen<br>werden gewöhnen | werde gewöhnt haben<br>wirst gewöhnt haben<br>wird gewöhnt haben | werden gewöhnt haben<br>werdet gewöhnt haben<br>werden gewöhnt haben |
| Subjunctive | **Present** | | **Present Perfect** | |
| | gewöhne<br>gewöhnest<br>gewöhne | gewöhnen<br>gewöhnet<br>gewöhnen | habe gewöhnt<br>habest gewöhnt<br>habe gewöhnt | haben gewöhnt<br>habet gewöhnt<br>haben gewöhnt |
| | **Past** | | **Past Perfect** | |
| | gewöhnte<br>gewöhntest<br>gewöhnte | gewöhnten<br>gewöhntet<br>gewöhnten | hätte gewöhnt<br>hättest gewöhnt<br>hätte gewöhnt | hätten gewöhnt<br>hättet gewöhnt<br>hätten gewöhnt |
| | **Future** | | **Future Perfect** | |
| | werde gewöhnen<br>werdest gewöhnen<br>werde gewöhnen | werden gewöhnen<br>werdet gewöhnen<br>werden gewöhnen | werde gewöhnt haben<br>werdest gewöhnt haben<br>werde gewöhnt haben | werden gewöhnt haben<br>werdet gewöhnt haben<br>werden gewöhnt haben |
| | **Present and Future Conditional** | | **Past Conditional** | |
| | würde gewöhnen<br>würdest gewöhnen<br>würde gewöhnen | würden gewöhnen<br>würdet gewöhnen<br>würden gewöhnen | würde gewöhnt haben<br>würdest gewöhnt haben<br>würde gewöhnt haben | würden gewöhnt haben<br>würdet gewöhnt haben<br>würden gewöhnt haben |

## EXAMPLES

Wir müssen unseren Hund langsam an die Leine gewöhnen.
We have to slowly accustom our dog to being on a leash.

Gudrun hat sich noch nicht an die Großstadt gewöhnt.
Gudrun still hasn't gotten used to life in the big city.

**gießen**

to water, to pour

**Auxiliary verb:** haben **Past participle:** gegossen

**Imperative:** Gieße! Gießt! Gießen Sie!

| Mode | Simple Tenses | | Compound Tenses | |
|---|---|---|---|---|
| | *Singular* | *Plural* | *Singular* | *Plural* |
| Indicative | **Present** | | **Present Perfect** | |
| | gieße<br>gießt<br>gießt | gießen<br>gießt<br>gießen | habe gegossen<br>hast gegossen<br>hat gegossen | haben gegossen<br>habt gegossen<br>haben gegossen |
| | **Past** | | **Past Perfect** | |
| | goss<br>gossest<br>goss | gossen<br>gosst<br>gossen | hatte gegossen<br>hattest gegossen<br>hatte gegossen | hatten gegossen<br>hattet gegossen<br>hatten gegossen |
| | **Future** | | **Future Perfect** | |
| | werde gießen<br>wirst gießen<br>wird gießen | werden gießen<br>werdet gießen<br>werden gießen | werde gegossen haben<br>wirst gegossen haben<br>wird gegossen haben | werden gegossen haben<br>werdet gegossen haben<br>werden gegossen haben |
| Subjunctive | **Present** | | **Present Perfect** | |
| | gieße<br>gießest<br>gieße | gießen<br>gießet<br>gießen | habe gegossen<br>habest gegossen<br>habe gegossen | haben gegossen<br>habet gegossen<br>haben gegossen |
| | **Past** | | **Past Perfect** | |
| | gösse<br>gössest<br>gösse | gössen<br>gösset<br>gössen | hätte gegossen<br>hättest gegossen<br>hätte gegossen | hätten gegossen<br>hättet gegossen<br>hätten gegossen |
| | **Future** | | **Future Perfect** | |
| | werde gießen<br>werdest gießen<br>werde gießen | werden gießen<br>werdet gießen<br>werden gießen | werde gegossen haben<br>werdest gegossen haben<br>werde gegossen haben | werden gegossen haben<br>werdet gegossen haben<br>werden gegossen haben |
| | **Present and Future Conditional** | | **Past Conditional** | |
| | würde gießen<br>würdest gießen<br>würde gießen | würden gießen<br>würdet gießen<br>würden gießen | würde gegossen haben<br>würdest gegossen haben<br>würde gegossen haben | würden gegossen haben<br>würdet gegossen haben<br>würden gegossen haben |

**Note:** The verb *sprießen* follows the same conjugational pattern as the verb illustrated above, but it requires *sein* as its auxiliary in the perfect tenses.

## EXAMPLES

| | |
|---|---|
| Der Gärtner hat die Tulpen schon gegossen. | The gardener already watered the tulips. |
| Was für ein Unwetter! Es gießt! | What terrible weather. It's pouring. |

**glänzen**
to gleam, to glitter, to shine
**Auxiliary verb:** haben **Past participle:** geglänzt
**Imperative:** Glänze! Glänzt! Glänzen Sie!

| Mode | Simple Tenses | | Compound Tenses | |
|---|---|---|---|---|
| | *Singular* | *Plural* | *Singular* | *Plural* |
| Indicative | **Present** | | **Present Perfect** | |
| | glänze<br>glänzt<br>glänzt | glänzen<br>glänzt<br>glänzen | habe geglänzt<br>hast geglänzt<br>hat geglänzt | haben geglänzt<br>habt geglänzt<br>haben geglänzt |
| | **Past** | | **Past Perfect** | |
| | glänzte<br>glänztest<br>glänzte | glänzten<br>glänztet<br>glänzten | hatte geglänzt<br>hattest geglänzt<br>hatte geglänzt | hatten geglänzt<br>hattet geglänzt<br>hatten geglänzt |
| | **Future** | | **Future Perfect** | |
| | werde glänzen<br>wirst glänzen<br>wird glänzen | werden glänzen<br>werdet glänzen<br>werden glänzen | werde geglänzt haben<br>wirst geglänzt haben<br>wird geglänzt haben | werden geglänzt haben<br>werdet geglänzt haben<br>werden geglänzt haben |
| Subjunctive | **Present** | | **Present Perfect** | |
| | glänze<br>glänzest<br>glänze | glänzen<br>glänzet<br>glänzen | habe geglänzt<br>habest geglänzt<br>habe geglänzt | haben geglänzt<br>habet geglänzt<br>haben geglänzt |
| | **Past** | | **Past Perfect** | |
| | glänzte<br>glänztest<br>glänzte | glänzten<br>glänztet<br>glänzten | hätte geglänzt<br>hättest geglänzt<br>hätte geglänzt | hätten geglänzt<br>hättet geglänzt<br>hätten geglänzt |
| | **Future** | | **Future Perfect** | |
| | werde glänzen<br>werdest glänzen<br>werde glänzen | werden glänzen<br>werdet glänzen<br>werden glänzen | werde geglänzt haben<br>werdest geglänzt haben<br>werde geglänzt haben | werden geglänzt haben<br>werdet geglänzt haben<br>werden geglänzt haben |
| | **Present and Future Conditional** | | **Past Conditional** | |
| | würde glänzen<br>würdest glänzen<br>würde glänzen | würden glänzen<br>würdet glänzen<br>würden glänzen | würde geglänzt haben<br>würdest geglänzt haben<br>würde geglänzt haben | würden geglänzt haben<br>würdet geglänzt haben<br>würden geglänzt haben |

## EXAMPLES

Die Edelsteine glänzten im Licht. — The gems gleamed in the light.
Ihre Aufführung war glänzend. — Her performance was brilliant.

**glauben**
to believe
**Auxiliary verb:** haben **Past participle:** geglaubt
**Imperative:** Glaube! Glaubt! Glauben Sie!

| Mode | Simple Tenses | | Compound Tenses | |
|---|---|---|---|---|
| | *Singular* | *Plural* | *Singular* | *Plural* |
| Indicative | **Present** | | **Present Perfect** | |
| | glaube<br>glaubst<br>glaubt | glauben<br>glaubt<br>glauben | habe geglaubt<br>hast geglaubt<br>hat geglaubt | haben geglaubt<br>habt geglaubt<br>haben geglaubt |
| | **Past** | | **Past Perfect** | |
| | glaubte<br>glaubtest<br>glaubte | glaubten<br>glaubtet<br>glaubten | hatte geglaubt<br>hattest geglaubt<br>hatte geglaubt | hatten geglaubt<br>hattet geglaubt<br>hatten geglaubt |
| | **Future** | | **Future Perfect** | |
| | werde glauben<br>wirst glauben<br>wird glauben | werden glauben<br>werdet glauben<br>werden glauben | werde geglaubt haben<br>wirst geglaubt haben<br>wird geglaubt haben | werden geglaubt haben<br>werdet geglaubt haben<br>werden geglaubt haben |
| Subjunctive | **Present** | | **Present Perfect** | |
| | glaube<br>glaubest<br>glaube | glauben<br>glaubet<br>glauben | habe geglaubt<br>habest geglaubt<br>habe geglaubt | haben geglaubt<br>habet geglaubt<br>haben geglaubt |
| | **Past** | | **Past Perfect** | |
| | glaubte<br>glaubtest<br>glaubte | glaubten<br>glaubtet<br>glaubten | hätte geglaubt<br>hättest geglaubt<br>hätte geglaubt | hätten geglaubt<br>hättet geglaubt<br>hätten geglaubt |
| | **Future** | | **Future Perfect** | |
| | werde glauben<br>werdest glauben<br>werde glauben | werden glauben<br>werdet glauben<br>werden glauben | werde geglaubt haben<br>werdest geglaubt haben<br>werde geglaubt haben | werden geglaubt haben<br>werdet geglaubt haben<br>werden geglaubt haben |
| | **Present and Future Conditional** | | **Past Conditional** | |
| | würde glauben<br>würdest glauben<br>würde glauben | würden glauben<br>würdet glauben<br>würden glauben | würde geglaubt haben<br>würdest geglaubt haben<br>würde geglaubt haben | würden geglaubt haben<br>würdet geglaubt haben<br>würden geglaubt haben |

## EXAMPLES

Wir glauben dir aufs Wort. — We take your word for it.
Ich kann überhaupt nicht mehr an Sie glauben. — I can't believe in you anymore.

**gleichen**
to equal, to resemble, to look like
**Auxiliary verb:** haben **Past participle:** geglichen
**Imperative:** N/A

| Mode | Simple Tenses | | Compound Tenses | |
|---|---|---|---|---|
| | *Singular* | *Plural* | *Singular* | *Plural* |
| Indicative | **Present** | | **Present Perfect** | |
| | gleiche<br>gleichst<br>gleicht | gleichen<br>gleicht<br>gleichen | habe geglichen<br>hast geglichen<br>hat geglichen | haben geglichen<br>habt geglichen<br>haben geglichen |
| | **Past** | | **Past Perfect** | |
| | glich<br>glichst<br>glich | glichen<br>glicht<br>glichen | hatte geglichen<br>hattest geglichen<br>hatte geglichen | hatten geglichen<br>hattet geglichen<br>hatten geglichen |
| | **Future** | | **Future Perfect** | |
| | werde gleichen<br>wirst gleichen<br>wird gleichen | werden gleichen<br>werdet gleichen<br>werden gleichen | werde geglichen haben<br>wirst geglichen haben<br>wird geglichen haben | werden geglichen haben<br>werdet geglichen haben<br>werden geglichen haben |
| Subjunctive | **Present** | | **Present Perfect** | |
| | gleiche<br>gleichest<br>gleiche | gleichen<br>gleichet<br>gleichen | habe geglichen<br>habest geglichen<br>habe geglichen | haben geglichen<br>habet geglichen<br>haben geglichen |
| | **Past** | | **Past Perfect** | |
| | gliche<br>glichest<br>gliche | glichen<br>glichet<br>glichen | hätte geglichen<br>hättest geglichen<br>hätte geglichen | hätten geglichen<br>hättet geglichen<br>hatten geglichen |
| | **Future** | | **Future Perfect** | |
| | werde gleichen<br>werdest gleichen<br>werde gleichen | werden gleichen<br>werdet gleichen<br>werden gleichen | werde geglichen haben<br>werdest geglichen haben<br>werde geglichen haben | werden geglichen haben<br>werdet geglichen haben<br>werden geglichen haben |
| | **Present and Future Conditional** | | **Past Conditional** | |
| | würde gleichen<br>würdest gleichen<br>würde gleichen | würden gleichen<br>würdet gleichen<br>würden gleichen | würde geglichen haben<br>würdest geglichen haben<br>würde geglichen haben | würden geglichen haben<br>würdet geglichen haben<br>würden geglichen haben |

## EXAMPLES

Man sagt, die Brüder hätten einander wie Zwillinge geglichen.

Karl gleicht seinem Onkel mehr als seinem Vater.

They say the brothers resemble each other like twins.

Karl looks more like his uncle than his father.

**graben**
to dig
**Auxiliary verb:** haben **Past participle:** gegraben
**Imperative:** Grabe! Grabt! Graben Sie!

| Mode | Simple Tenses | | Compound Tenses | |
|---|---|---|---|---|
| | *Singular* | *Plural* | *Singular* | *Plural* |
| Indicative | **Present** | | **Present Perfect** | |
| | grabe<br>gräbst<br>gräbt | graben<br>grabt<br>graben | habe gegraben<br>hast gegraben<br>hat gegraben | haben gegraben<br>habt gegraben<br>haben gegraben |
| | **Past** | | **Past Perfect** | |
| | grub<br>grubst<br>grub | gruben<br>grubt<br>gruben | hatte gegraben<br>hattest gegraben<br>hatte gegraben | hatten gegraben<br>hattet gegraben<br>hatten gegraben |
| | **Future** | | **Future Perfect** | |
| | werde graben<br>wirst graben<br>wird graben | werden graben<br>werdet graben<br>werden graben | werde gegraben haben<br>wirst gegraben haben<br>wird gegraben haben | werden gegraben haben<br>werdet gegraben haben<br>werden gegraben haben |
| Subjunctive | **Present** | | **Present Perfect** | |
| | grabe<br>grabest<br>grabe | graben<br>grabet<br>graben | habe gegraben<br>habest gegraben<br>habe gegraben | haben gegraben<br>habet gegraben<br>haben gegraben |
| | **Past** | | **Past Perfect** | |
| | grübe<br>grübest<br>grübe | grüben<br>grübet<br>grüben | hätte gegraben<br>hättest gegraben<br>hätte gegraben | hätten gegraben<br>hättet gegraben<br>hätten gegraben |
| | **Future** | | **Future Perfect** | |
| | werde graben<br>werdest graben<br>werde graben | werden graben<br>werdet graben<br>werden graben | werde gegraben haben<br>werdest gegraben haben<br>werde gegraben haben | werden gegraben haben<br>werdet gegraben haben<br>werden gegraben haben |
| | **Present and Future Conditional** | | **Past Conditional** | |
| | würde graben<br>würdest graben<br>würde graben | würden graben<br>würdet graben<br>würden graben | würde gegraben haben<br>würdest gegraben haben<br>würde gegraben haben | würden gegraben haben<br>würdet gegraben haben<br>würden gegraben haben |

## EXAMPLES

| | |
|---|---|
| Die Kinder haben am Strand ein tiefes Loch gegraben. | The children dug a deep hole on the beach. |
| Er weiß nicht, dass er sich sein eigenes Grab gräbt. | He doesn't know that he's digging his own grave. |

**grauen**
to have an aversion to, to dread
**Auxiliary verb:** haben **Past participle:** gegraut
**Imperative:** Graue! Graut! Grauen Sie!

| Mode | Simple Tenses | | Compound Tenses | |
|---|---|---|---|---|
| | *Singular* | *Plural* | *Singular* | *Plural* |
| Indicative | **Present** | | **Present Perfect** | |
| | graue<br>graust<br>graut | grauen<br>graut<br>grauen | habe gegraut<br>hast gegraut<br>hat gegraut | haben gegraut<br>habt gegraut<br>haben gegraut |
| | **Past** | | **Past Perfect** | |
| | graute<br>grautest<br>graute | grauten<br>grautet<br>grauten | hatte gegraut<br>hattest gegraut<br>hatte gegraut | hatten gegraut<br>hattet gegraut<br>hatten gegraut |
| | **Future** | | **Future Perfect** | |
| | werde grauen<br>wirst grauen<br>wird grauen | werden grauen<br>werdet grauen<br>werden grauen | werde gegraut haben<br>wirst gegraut haben<br>wird gegraut haben | werden gegraut haben<br>werdet gegraut haben<br>werden gegraut haben |
| Subjunctive | **Present** | | **Present Perfect** | |
| | graue<br>grauest<br>graue | grauen<br>grauet<br>grauen | habe gegraut<br>habest gegraut<br>habe gegraut | haben gegraut<br>habet gegraut<br>haben gegraut |
| | **Past** | | **Past Perfect** | |
| | graute<br>grautest<br>graute | grauten<br>grautet<br>grauten | hätte gegraut<br>hättest gegraut<br>hätte gegraut | hätten gegraut<br>hättet gegraut<br>hätten gegraut |
| | **Future** | | **Future Perfect** | |
| | werde grauen<br>werdest grauen<br>werde grauen | werden grauen<br>werdet grauen<br>werden grauen | werde gegraut haben<br>werdest gegraut haben<br>werde gegraut haben | werden gegraut haben<br>werdet gegraut haben<br>werden gegraut haben |
| | **Present and Future Conditional** | | **Past Conditional** | |
| | würde grauen<br>würdest grauen<br>würde grauen | würden grauen<br>würdet grauen<br>würden grauen | würde gegraut haben<br>würdest gegraut haben<br>würde gegraut haben | würden gegraut haben<br>würdet gegraut haben<br>würden gegraut haben |

**Note:** This verb is commonly used as a third-person impersonal expression with the pronoun *es*.

## EXAMPLES

Ihm graut vor Gespenstern.
He's afraid of ghosts.

Es graut mir, wenn ich an das Ungeheuer denke.
I feel scared just thinking of that monster.

**greifen**
to seize, to grasp
**Auxiliary verb:** haben **Past participle:** gegriffen
**Imperative:** Greife! Greift! Greifen Sie!

| Mode | Simple Tenses | | Compound Tenses | |
|---|---|---|---|---|
| | *Singular* | *Plural* | *Singular* | *Plural* |
| Indicative | **Present** | | **Present Perfect** | |
| | greife<br>greifst<br>greift | greifen<br>greift<br>greifen | habe gegriffen<br>hast gegriffen<br>hat gegriffen | haben gegriffen<br>habt gegriffen<br>haben gegriffen |
| | **Past** | | **Past Perfect** | |
| | griff<br>griffst<br>griff | griffen<br>grifft<br>griffen | hatte gegriffen<br>hattest gegriffen<br>hatte gegriffen | hatten gegriffen<br>hattet gegriffen<br>hatten gegriffen |
| | **Future** | | **Future Perfect** | |
| | werde greifen<br>wirst greifen<br>wird greifen | werden greifen<br>werdet greifen<br>werden greifen | werde gegriffen haben<br>wirst gegriffen haben<br>wird gegriffen haben | werden gegriffen haben<br>werdet gegriffen haben<br>werden gegriffen haben |
| Subjunctive | **Present** | | **Present Perfect** | |
| | greife<br>greifest<br>greife | greifen<br>greifet<br>greifen | habe gegriffen<br>habest gegriffen<br>habe gegriffen | haben gegriffen<br>habet gegriffen<br>haben gegriffen |
| | **Past** | | **Past Perfect** | |
| | griffe<br>griffest<br>griffe | griffen<br>griffet<br>griffen | hätte gegriffen<br>hättest gegriffen<br>hätte gegriffen | hätten gegriffen<br>hättet gegriffen<br>hätten gegriffen |
| | **Future** | | **Future Perfect** | |
| | werde greifen<br>werdest greifen<br>werde greifen | werden greifen<br>werdet greifen<br>werden greifen | werde gegriffen haben<br>werdest gegriffen haben<br>werde gegriffen haben | werden gegriffen haben<br>werdet gegriffen haben<br>werden gegriffen haben |
| | **Present and Future Conditional** | | **Past Conditional** | |
| | würde greifen<br>würdest greifen<br>würde greifen | würden greifen<br>würdet greifen<br>würden greifen | würde gegriffen haben<br>würdest gegriffen haben<br>würde gegriffen haben | würden gegriffen haben<br>würdet gegriffen haben<br>würden gegriffen haben |

**Note:** With inseparable prefixes, the principal parts of this verb are, for example, *begreift, begriff, hat begriffen.* With separable prefixes, the principal parts are, for example, *greift an, griff an, hat angegriffen.*

## EXAMPLES

| | |
|---|---|
| Das ist völlig aus der Luft gegriffen. | You plucked that idea out of thin air. |
| Die Fotografin griff nach ihrem Fotoapparat. | The photographer reached for her camera. |

**gründen**
to found, to establish
**Auxiliary verb:** haben **Past participle:** gegründet
**Imperative:** Gründe! Gründet! Gründen Sie!

| Mode | Simple Tenses | | Compound Tenses | |
|---|---|---|---|---|
| | *Singular* | *Plural* | *Singular* | *Plural* |
| Indicative | **Present** | | **Present Perfect** | |
| | gründe<br>gründest<br>gründet | gründen<br>gründet<br>gründen | habe gegründet<br>hast gegründet<br>hat gegründet | haben gegründet<br>habt gegründet<br>haben gegründet |
| | **Past** | | **Past Perfect** | |
| | gründete<br>gründetest<br>gründete | gründeten<br>gründetet<br>gründeten | hatte gegründet<br>hattest gegründet<br>hatte gegründet | hatten gegründet<br>hattet gegründet<br>hatten gegründet |
| | **Future** | | **Future Perfect** | |
| | werde gründen<br>wirst gründen<br>wird gründen | werden gründen<br>werdet gründen<br>werden gründen | werde gegründet haben<br>wirst gegründet haben<br>wird gegründet haben | werden gegründet haben<br>werdet gegründet haben<br>werden gegründet haben |
| Subjunctive | **Present** | | **Present Perfect** | |
| | gründe<br>gründest<br>gründe | gründen<br>gründet<br>gründen | habe gegründet<br>habest gegründet<br>habe gegründet | haben gegründet<br>habet gegründet<br>haben gegründet |
| | **Past** | | **Past Perfect** | |
| | gründete<br>gründetest<br>gründete | gründeten<br>gründetet<br>gründeten | hätte gegründet<br>hättest gegründet<br>hätte gegründet | hätten gegründet<br>hättet gegründet<br>hätten gegründet |
| | **Future** | | **Future Perfect** | |
| | werde gründen<br>werdest gründen<br>werde gründen | werden gründen<br>werdet gründen<br>werden gründen | werde gegründet haben<br>werdest gegründet haben<br>werde gegründet haben | werden gegründet haben<br>werdet gegründet haben<br>werden gegründet haben |
| | **Present and Future Conditional** | | **Past Conditional** | |
| | würde gründen<br>würdest gründen<br>würde gründen | würden gründen<br>würdet gründen<br>würden gründen | würde gegründet haben<br>würdest gegründet haben<br>würde gegründet haben | würden gegründet haben<br>würdet gegründet haben<br>würden gegründet haben |

## EXAMPLES

Vier Freunde versuchen eine neue Firma zu gründen.
Four friends are trying to start up a new company.

In welchem Jahr ist die Stadt gegründet worden?
In what year was the city founded?

**grunzen**
to grunt
**Auxiliary verb:** haben **Past participle:** gegrunzt
**Imperative:** Grunze! Grunzt! Grunzen Sie!

| Mode | Simple Tenses | | Compound Tenses | |
|---|---|---|---|---|
| | *Singular* | *Plural* | *Singular* | *Plural* |
| Indicative | **Present** | | **Present Perfect** | |
| | grunze<br>grunzt<br>grunzt | grunzen<br>grunzt<br>grunzen | habe gegrunzt<br>hast gegrunzt<br>hat gegrunzt | haben gegrunzt<br>habt gegrunzt<br>haben gegrunzt |
| | **Past** | | **Past Perfect** | |
| | grunzte<br>grunztest<br>grunzte | grunzten<br>grunztet<br>grunzten | hatte gegrunzt<br>hattest gegrunzt<br>hatte gegrunzt | hatten gegrunzt<br>hattet gegrunzt<br>hatten gegrunzt |
| | **Future** | | **Future Perfect** | |
| | werde grunzen<br>wirst grunzen<br>wird grunzen | werden grunzen<br>werdet grunzen<br>werden grunzen | werde gegrunzt haben<br>wirst gegrunzt haben<br>wird gegrunzt haben | werden gegrunzt haben<br>werdet gegrunzt haben<br>werden gegrunzt haben |
| Subjunctive | **Present** | | **Present Perfect** | |
| | grunze<br>grunzest<br>grunze | grunzen<br>grunzet<br>grunzen | habe gegrunzt<br>habest gegrunzt<br>habe gegrunzt | haben gegrunzt<br>habet gegrunzt<br>haben gegrunzt |
| | **Past** | | **Past Perfect** | |
| | grunzte<br>grunztest<br>grunzte | grunzten<br>grunztet<br>grunzten | hätte gegrunzt<br>hättest gegrunzt<br>hätte gegrunzt | hätten gegrunzt<br>hättet gegrunzt<br>hätten gegrunzt |
| | **Future** | | **Future Perfect** | |
| | werde grunzen<br>werdest grunzen<br>werde grunzen | werden grunzen<br>werdet grunzen<br>werden grunzen | werde gegrunzt haben<br>werdest gegrunzt haben<br>werde gegrunzt haben | werden gegrunzt haben<br>werdet gegrunzt haben<br>werden gegrunzt haben |
| | **Present and Future Conditional** | | **Past Conditional** | |
| | würde grunzen<br>würdest grunzen<br>würde grunzen | würden grunzen<br>würdet grunzen<br>würden grunzen | würde gegrunzt haben<br>würdest gegrunzt haben<br>würde gegrunzt haben | würden gegrunzt haben<br>würdet gegrunzt haben<br>würden gegrunzt haben |

## EXAMPLES

Die Ferkel grunzten im Schlamm.
Mensch, hör auf zu grunzen!

The piglets grunted in the mud.
Man, stop grunting!

**grüßen**
to greet
**Auxiliary verb:** haben **Past participle:** gegrüßt
**Imperative:** Grüße! Grüßt! Grüßen Sie!

| Mode | Simple Tenses | | Compound Tenses | |
|---|---|---|---|---|
| | *Singular* | *Plural* | *Singular* | *Plural* |
| Indicative | **Present** | | **Present Perfect** | |
| | grüße<br>grüßt<br>grüßt | grüßen<br>grüßt<br>grüßen | habe gegrüßt<br>hast gegrüßt<br>hat gegrüßt | haben gegrüßt<br>habt gegrüßt<br>haben gegrüßt |
| | **Past** | | **Past Perfect** | |
| | grüßte<br>grüßtest<br>grüßte | grüßten<br>grüßtet<br>grüßten | hatte gegrüßt<br>hattest gegrüßt<br>hatte gegrüßt | hatten gegrüßt<br>hattet gegrüßt<br>hatten gegrüßt |
| | **Future** | | **Future Perfect** | |
| | werde grüßen<br>wirst grüßen<br>wird grüßen | werden grüßen<br>werdet grüßen<br>werden grüßen | werde gegrüßt haben<br>wirst gegrüßt haben<br>wird gegrüßt haben | werden gegrüßt haben<br>werdet gegrüßt haben<br>werden gegrüßt haben |
| Subjunctive | **Present** | | **Present Perfect** | |
| | grüße<br>grüßest<br>grüße | grüßen<br>grüßet<br>grüßen | habe gegrüßt<br>habest gegrüßt<br>habe gegrüßt | haben gegrüßt<br>habet gegrüßt<br>haben gegrüßt |
| | **Past** | | **Past Perfect** | |
| | grüßte<br>grüßtest<br>grüßte | grüßten<br>grüßtet<br>grüßten | hätte gegrüßt<br>hättest gegrüßt<br>hätte gegrüßt | hätten gegrüßt<br>hättet gegrüßt<br>hätten gegrüßt |
| | **Future** | | **Future Perfect** | |
| | werde grüßen<br>werdest grüßen<br>werde grüßen | werden grüßen<br>werdet grüßen<br>werden grüßen | werde gegrüßt haben<br>werdest gegrüßt haben<br>werde gegrüßt haben | werden gegrüßt haben<br>werdet gegrüßt haben<br>werden gegrüßt haben |
| | **Present and Future Conditional** | | **Past Conditional** | |
| | würde grüßen<br>würdest grüßen<br>würde grüßen | würden grüßen<br>würdet grüßen<br>würden grüßen | würde gegrüßt haben<br>würdest gegrüßt haben<br>würde gegrüßt haben | würden gegrüßt haben<br>würdet gegrüßt haben<br>würden gegrüßt haben |

## EXAMPLES

Bitte grüßen Sie Ihren Bruder von mir!
Please say hello to your brother from me.

Tante Gerda lässt dich grüßen.
Aunt Gerda gives you her regards.

**gucken**
to look, to peer
**Auxiliary verb:** haben **Past participle:** geguckt
**Imperative:** Gucke! Guckt! Gucken Sie!

| Mode | Simple Tenses | | Compound Tenses | |
|---|---|---|---|---|
| | *Singular* | *Plural* | *Singular* | *Plural* |
| Indicative | **Present** | | **Present Perfect** | |
| | gucke<br>guckst<br>guckt | gucken<br>guckt<br>gucken | habe geguckt<br>hast geguckt<br>hat geguckt | haben geguckt<br>habt geguckt<br>haben geguckt |
| | **Past** | | **Past Perfect** | |
| | guckte<br>gucktest<br>guckte | guckten<br>gucktet<br>guckten | hatte geguckt<br>hattest geguckt<br>hatte geguckt | hatten geguckt<br>hattet geguckt<br>hatten geguckt |
| | **Future** | | **Future Perfect** | |
| | werde gucken<br>wirst gucken<br>wird gucken | werden gucken<br>werdet gucken<br>werden gucken | werde geguckt haben<br>wirst geguckt haben<br>wird geguckt haben | werden geguckt haben<br>werdet geguckt haben<br>werden geguckt haben |
| Subjunctive | **Present** | | **Present Perfect** | |
| | gucke<br>guckest<br>gucke | gucken<br>gucket<br>gucken | habe geguckt<br>habest geguckt<br>habe geguckt | haben geguckt<br>habet geguckt<br>haben geguckt |
| | **Past** | | **Past Perfect** | |
| | guckte<br>gucktest<br>guckte | guckten<br>gucktet<br>guckten | hätte geguckt<br>hättest geguckt<br>hätte geguckt | hätten geguckt<br>hättet geguckt<br>hätten geguckt |
| | **Future** | | **Future Perfect** | |
| | werde gucken<br>werdest gucken<br>werde gucken | werden gucken<br>werdet gucken<br>werden gucken | werde geguckt haben<br>werdest geguckt haben<br>werde geguckt haben | werden geguckt haben<br>werdet geguckt haben<br>werden geguckt haben |
| | **Present and Future Conditional** | | **Past Conditional** | |
| | würde gucken<br>würdest gucken<br>würde gucken | würden gucken<br>würdet gucken<br>würden gucken | würde geguckt haben<br>würdest geguckt haben<br>würde geguckt haben | würden geguckt haben<br>würdet geguckt haben<br>würden geguckt haben |

**Note:** This verb is used colloquially, often in place of *sehen* or *schauen*.

## EXAMPLE

Guck mal, was der Mann dort drüben tut! Look what the man over there is doing.

**haben**
to have
**Auxiliary verb:** haben **Past participle:** gehabt
**Imperative:** Habe! Habt! Haben Sie!

| Mode | Simple Tenses | | Compound Tenses | |
|---|---|---|---|---|
| | *Singular* | *Plural* | *Singular* | *Plural* |
| Indicative | **Present** | | **Present Perfect** | |
| | habe<br>hast<br>hat | haben<br>habt<br>haben | habe gehabt<br>hast gehabt<br>hat gehabt | haben gehabt<br>habt gehabt<br>haben gehabt |
| | **Past** | | **Past Perfect** | |
| | hatte<br>hattest<br>hatte | hatten<br>hattet<br>hatten | hatte gehabt<br>hattest gehabt<br>hatte gehabt | hatten gehabt<br>hattet gehabt<br>hatten gehabt |
| | **Future** | | **Future Perfect** | |
| | werde haben<br>wirst haben<br>wird haben | werden haben<br>werdet haben<br>werden haben | werde gehabt haben<br>wirst gehabt haben<br>wird gehabt haben | werden gehabt haben<br>werdet gehabt haben<br>werden gehabt haben |
| Subjunctive | **Present** | | **Present Perfect** | |
| | habe<br>habest<br>habe | haben<br>habet<br>haben | habe gehabt<br>habest gehabt<br>habe gehabt | haben gehabt<br>habet gehabt<br>haben gehabt |
| | **Past** | | **Past Perfect** | |
| | hätte<br>hättest<br>hätte | hätten<br>hättet<br>hätten | hätte gehabt<br>hättest gehabt<br>hätte gehabt | hätten gehabt<br>hättet gehabt<br>hätten gehabt |
| | **Future** | | **Future Perfect** | |
| | werde haben<br>werdest haben<br>werde haben | werden haben<br>werdet haben<br>werden haben | werde gehabt haben<br>werdest gehabt haben<br>werde gehabt haben | werden gehabt haben<br>werdet gehabt haben<br>werden gehabt haben |
| | **Present and Future Conditional** | | **Past Conditional** | |
| | würde haben<br>würdest haben<br>würde haben | würden haben<br>würdet haben<br>würden haben | würde gehabt haben<br>würdest gehabt haben<br>würde gehabt haben | würden gehabt haben<br>würdet gehabt haben<br>würden gehabt haben |

## EXAMPLES

Hast du mein neues Wörterbuch?
Do you have my new dictionary?

Der Geschäftsmann hat keine Zeit dazu gehabt.
The businessman didn't have any time for that.

**halten**

to hold, to keep, to stop

**Auxiliary verb:** haben **Past participle:** gehalten

**Imperative:** Halte! Haltet! Halten Sie!

| Mode | Simple Tenses | | Compound Tenses | |
|---|---|---|---|---|
| | *Singular* | *Plural* | *Singular* | *Plural* |
| Indicative | **Present** | | **Present Perfect** | |
| | halte<br>hältst<br>hält | halten<br>haltet<br>halten | habe gehalten<br>hast gehalten<br>hat gehalten | haben gehalten<br>habt gehalten<br>haben gehalten |
| | **Past** | | **Past Perfect** | |
| | hielt<br>hieltest<br>hielt | hielten<br>hieltet<br>hielten | hatte gehalten<br>hattest gehalten<br>hatte gehalten | hatten gehalten<br>hattet gehalten<br>hatten gehalten |
| | **Future** | | **Future Perfect** | |
| | werde halten<br>wirst halten<br>wird halten | werden halten<br>werdet halten<br>werden halten | werde gehalten haben<br>wirst gehalten haben<br>wird gehalten haben | werden gehalten haben<br>werdet gehalten haben<br>werden gehalten haben |
| Subjunctive | **Present** | | **Present Perfect** | |
| | halte<br>haltest<br>halte | halten<br>haltet<br>halten | habe gehalten<br>habest gehalten<br>habe gehalten | haben gehalten<br>habet gehalten<br>haben gehalten |
| | **Past** | | **Past Perfect** | |
| | hielte<br>hieltest<br>hielte | hielten<br>hieltet<br>hielten | hätte gehalten<br>hättest gehalten<br>hätte gehalten | hätten gehalten<br>hättet gehalten<br>hätten gehalten |
| | **Future** | | **Future Perfect** | |
| | werde halten<br>werdest halten<br>werde halten | werden halten<br>werdet halten<br>werden halten | werde gehalten haben<br>werdest gehalten haben<br>werde gehalten haben | werden gehalten haben<br>werdet gehalten haben<br>werden gehalten haben |
| | **Present and Future Conditional** | | **Past Conditional** | |
| | würde halten<br>würdest halten<br>würde halten | würden halten<br>würdet halten<br>würden halten | würde gehalten haben<br>würdest gehalten haben<br>würde gehalten haben | würden gehalten haben<br>würdet gehalten haben<br>würden gehalten haben |

**Note:** With inseparable prefixes, the principal parts of this verb are, for example, *enthält, enthielt, hat enthalten.* With separable prefixes, the principal parts are, for example, *hält aus, hielt aus, hat ausgehalten.*

## EXAMPLES

| | |
|---|---|
| Hält diese Straßenbahn in der Nähe des Rathauses? | Does this streetcar stop near city hall? |
| In diesem Mietshaus darf man keine Haustiere halten. | In this apartment building you can't have pets. |

**hämmern**
to hammer
**Auxiliary verb:** haben **Past participle:** gehämmert
**Imperative:** Hämmere! Hämmert! Hämmern Sie!

| Mode | Simple Tenses | | Compound Tenses | |
|---|---|---|---|---|
| | *Singular* | *Plural* | *Singular* | *Plural* |
| Indicative | **Present** | | **Present Perfect** | |
| | hämmere<br>hämmerst<br>hämmert | hämmern<br>hämmert<br>hämmern | habe gehämmert<br>hast gehämmert<br>hat gehämmert | haben gehämmert<br>habt gehämmert<br>haben gehämmert |
| | **Past** | | **Past Perfect** | |
| | hämmerte<br>hämmertest<br>hämmerte | hämmerten<br>hämmertet<br>hämmerten | hatte gehämmert<br>hattest gehämmert<br>hatte gehämmert | hatten gehämmert<br>hattet gehämmert<br>hatten gehämmert |
| | **Future** | | **Future Perfect** | |
| | werde hämmern<br>wirst hämmern<br>wird hämmern | werden hämmern<br>werdet hämmern<br>werden hämmern | werde gehämmert haben<br>wirst gehämmert haben<br>wird gehämmert haben | werden gehämmert haben<br>werdet gehämmert haben<br>werden gehämmert haben |
| Subjunctive | **Present** | | **Present Perfect** | |
| | hämmere<br>hämmerst<br>hämmere | hämmern<br>hämmert<br>hämmern | habe gehämmert<br>habest gehämmert<br>habe gehämmert | haben gehämmert<br>habet gehämmert<br>haben gehämmert |
| | **Past** | | **Past Perfect** | |
| | hämmerte<br>hämmertest<br>hämmerte | hämmerten<br>hämmertet<br>hämmerten | hätte gehämmert<br>hättest gehämmert<br>hätte gehämmert | hätten gehämmert<br>hättet gehämmert<br>hätten gehämmert |
| | **Future** | | **Future Perfect** | |
| | werde hämmern<br>werdest hämmern<br>werde hämmern | werden hämmern<br>werdet hämmern<br>werden hämmern | werde gehämmert haben<br>werdest gehämmert haben<br>werde gehämmert haben | werden gehämmert haben<br>werdet gehämmert haben<br>werden gehämmert haben |
| | **Present and Future Conditional** | | **Past Conditional** | |
| | würde hämmern<br>würdest hämmern<br>würde hämmern | würden hämmern<br>würdet hämmern<br>würden hämmern | würde gehämmert haben<br>würdest gehämmert haben<br>würde gehämmert haben | würden gehämmert haben<br>würdet gehämmert haben<br>würden gehämmert haben |

## EXAMPLES

Er scheint den ganzen Tag zu hämmern, ohne etwas gebaut zu haben.
He seems to hammer all day long without building anything.

Der Nachbar hämmerte mit der Faust gegen die Tür.
The neighbor banged on the door with his fist.

**hängen**

to hang, to suspend

**Auxiliary verb:** haben **Past participle:** gehangen

**Imperative:** Hänge! Hängt! Hängen Sie!

| Mode | Simple Tenses | | Compound Tenses | |
|---|---|---|---|---|
| | *Singular* | *Plural* | *Singular* | *Plural* |
| Indicative | **Present** | | **Present Perfect** | |
| | hänge<br>hängst<br>hängt | hängen<br>hängt<br>hängen | habe gehangen<br>hast gehangen<br>hat gehangen | haben gehangen<br>habt gehangen<br>haben gehangen |
| | **Past** | | **Past Perfect** | |
| | hing<br>hingst<br>hing | hingen<br>hingt<br>hingen | hatte gehangen<br>hattest gehangen<br>hatte gehangen | hatten gehangen<br>hattet gehangen<br>hatten gehangen |
| | **Future** | | **Future Perfect** | |
| | werde hängen<br>wirst hängen<br>wird hängen | werden hängen<br>werdet hängen<br>werden hängen | werde gehangen haben<br>wirst gehangen haben<br>wird gehangen haben | werden gehangen haben<br>werdet gehangen haben<br>werden gehangen haben |
| Subjunctive | **Present** | | **Present Perfect** | |
| | hänge<br>hängest<br>hänge | hängen<br>hänget<br>hängen | habe gehangen<br>habest gehangen<br>habe gehangen | haben gehangen<br>habet gehangen<br>haben gehangen |
| | **Past** | | **Past Perfect** | |
| | hinge<br>hingest<br>hinge | hingen<br>hinget<br>hingen | hätte gehangen<br>hättest gehangen<br>hätte gehangen | hätten gehangen<br>hättet gehangen<br>hätten gehangen |
| | **Future** | | **Future Perfect** | |
| | werde hängen<br>werdest hängen<br>werde hängen | werden hängen<br>werdet hängen<br>werden hängen | werde gehangen haben<br>werdest gehangen haben<br>werde gehangen haben | werden gehangen haben<br>werdet gehangen haben<br>werden gehangen haben |
| | **Present and Future Conditional** | | **Past Conditional** | |
| | würde hängen<br>würdest hängen<br>würde hängen | würden hängen<br>würdet hängen<br>würden hängen | würde gehangen haben<br>würdest gehangen haben<br>würde gehangen haben | würden gehangen haben<br>würdet gehangen haben<br>würden gehangen haben |

**Note:** When this verb is used as a transitive verb, its conjugation is regular: *hängt, hängte, hat gehängt.* This is also the case with the verbs *abhängen* and *aufhängen.*

## EXAMPLES

| | |
|---|---|
| Der neue Spiegel hing schief. | The new mirror was hanging crooked. |
| Vater hängte ein Bild über den Schrank. | Father hung a picture over the cabinet. |

**hassen**
to hate
**Auxiliary verb:** haben **Past participle:** gehasst
**Imperative:** Hasse! Hasst! Hassen Sie!

| Mode | Simple Tenses | | Compound Tenses | |
|---|---|---|---|---|
| | *Singular* | *Plural* | *Singular* | *Plural* |
| Indicative | **Present** | | **Present Perfect** | |
| | hasse<br>hasst<br>hasst | hassen<br>hasst<br>hassen | habe gehasst<br>hast gehasst<br>hat gehasst | haben gehasst<br>habt gehasst<br>haben gehasst |
| | **Past** | | **Past Perfect** | |
| | hasste<br>hasstest<br>hasste | hassten<br>hasstet<br>hassten | hatte gehasst<br>hattest gehasst<br>hatte gehasst | hatten gehasst<br>hattet gehasst<br>hatten gehasst |
| | **Future** | | **Future Perfect** | |
| | werde hassen<br>wirst hassen<br>wird hassen | werden hassen<br>werdet hassen<br>werden hassen | werde gehasst haben<br>wirst gehasst haben<br>wird gehasst haben | werden gehasst haben<br>werdet gehasst haben<br>werden gehasst haben |
| Subjunctive | **Present** | | **Present Perfect** | |
| | hasse<br>hassest<br>hasse | hassen<br>hasset<br>hassen | habe gehasst<br>habest gehasst<br>habe gehasst | haben gehasst<br>habet gehasst<br>haben gehasst |
| | **Past** | | **Past Perfect** | |
| | hasste<br>hasstest<br>hasste | hassten<br>hasstet<br>hassten | hätte gehasst<br>hättest gehasst<br>hätte gehasst | hätten gehasst<br>hättet gehasst<br>hätten gehasst |
| | **Future** | | **Future Perfect** | |
| | werde hassen<br>werdest hassen<br>werde hassen | werden hassen<br>werdet hassen<br>werden hassen | werde gehasst haben<br>werdest gehasst haben<br>werde gehasst haben | werden gehasst haben<br>werdet gehasst haben<br>werden gehasst haben |
| | **Present and Future Conditional** | | **Past Conditional** | |
| | würde hassen<br>würdest hassen<br>würde hassen | würden hassen<br>würdet hassen<br>würden hassen | würde gehasst haben<br>würdest gehasst haben<br>würde gehasst haben | würden gehasst haben<br>würdet gehasst haben<br>würden gehasst haben |

## EXAMPLES

Wie kannst du deinen eigenen Bruder hassen? How can you hate your own brother?
Ich hasse Montage. I hate Mondays.

**hauen**

to chop, to hew, to hit

**Auxiliary verb:** haben **Past participle:** gehauen

**Imperative:** Haue! Haut! Hauen Sie!

| Mode | Simple Tenses | | Compound Tenses | |
|---|---|---|---|---|
| | *Singular* | *Plural* | *Singular* | *Plural* |
| Indicative | **Present** | | **Present Perfect** | |
| | haue<br>haust<br>haut | hauen<br>haut<br>hauen | habe gehauen<br>hast gehauen<br>hat gehauen | haben gehauen<br>habt gehauen<br>haben gehauen |
| | **Past** | | **Past Perfect** | |
| | hieb<br>hiebst<br>hieb | hieben<br>hiebt<br>hieben | hatte gehauen<br>hattest gehauen<br>hatte gehauen | hatten gehauen<br>hattet gehauen<br>hatten gehauen |
| | **Future** | | **Future Perfect** | |
| | werde hauen<br>wirst hauen<br>wird hauen | werden hauen<br>werdet hauen<br>werden hauen | werde gehauen haben<br>wirst gehauen haben<br>wird gehauen haben | werden gehauen haben<br>werdet gehauen haben<br>werden gehauen haben |
| Subjunctive | **Present** | | **Present Perfect** | |
| | haue<br>hauest<br>haue | hauen<br>hauet<br>hauen | habe gehauen<br>habest gehauen<br>habe gehauen | haben gehauen<br>habet gehauen<br>haben gehauen |
| | **Past** | | **Past Perfect** | |
| | hiebe<br>hiebest<br>hiebe | hieben<br>hiebet<br>hieben | hätte gehauen<br>hättest gehauen<br>hätte gehauen | hätten gehauen<br>hättet gehauen<br>hätten gehauen |
| | **Future** | | **Future Perfect** | |
| | werde hauen<br>werdest hauen<br>werde hauen | werden hauen<br>werdet hauen<br>werden hauen | werde gehauen haben<br>werdest gehauen haben<br>werde gehauen haben | werden gehauen haben<br>werdet gehauen haben<br>werden gehauen haben |
| | **Present and Future Conditional** | | **Past Conditional** | |
| | würde hauen<br>würdest hauen<br>würde hauen | würden hauen<br>würdet hauen<br>würden hauen | würde gehauen haben<br>würdest gehauen haben<br>würde gehauen haben | würden gehauen haben<br>würdet gehauen haben<br>würden gehauen haben |

**Note:** You will sometimes hear *haute* used in the past tense in place of *hieb*.

## EXAMPLES

Oma hat Karl hinter die Ohren gehauen. — Granny slapped Karl over the ears.

Thomas haut immer seinen Bruder. — Thomas always hits his brother.

**heben**
to lift, to raise
**Auxiliary verb:** haben **Past participle:** gehoben
**Imperative:** Hebe! Hebt! Heben Sie!

| Mode | Simple Tenses | | Compound Tenses | |
|---|---|---|---|---|
| | *Singular* | *Plural* | *Singular* | *Plural* |
| Indicative | **Present** | | **Present Perfect** | |
| | hebe<br>hebst<br>hebt | heben<br>hebt<br>heben | habe gehoben<br>hast gehoben<br>hat gehoben | haben gehoben<br>habt gehoben<br>haben gehoben |
| | **Past** | | **Past Perfect** | |
| | hob<br>hobst<br>hob | hoben<br>hobt<br>hoben | hatte gehoben<br>hattest gehoben<br>hatte gehoben | hatten gehoben<br>hattet gehoben<br>hatten gehoben |
| | **Future** | | **Future Perfect** | |
| | werde heben<br>wirst heben<br>wird heben | werden heben<br>werdet heben<br>werden heben | werde gehoben haben<br>wirst gehoben haben<br>wird gehoben haben | werden gehoben haben<br>werdet gehoben haben<br>werden gehoben haben |
| Subjunctive | **Present** | | **Present Perfect** | |
| | hebe<br>hebest<br>hebe | heben<br>hebet<br>heben | habe gehoben<br>habest gehoben<br>habe gehoben | haben gehoben<br>habet gehoben<br>haben gehoben |
| | **Past** | | **Past Perfect** | |
| | höbe<br>höbest<br>höbe | höben<br>höbet<br>höben | hätte gehoben<br>hättest gehoben<br>hätte gehoben | hätten gehoben<br>hättet gehoben<br>hätten gehoben |
| | **Future** | | **Future Perfect** | |
| | werde heben<br>werdest heben<br>werde heben | werden heben<br>werdet heben<br>werden heben | werde gehoben haben<br>werdest gehoben haben<br>werde gehoben haben | werden gehoben haben<br>werdet gehoben haben<br>werden gehoben haben |
| | **Present and Future Conditional** | | **Past Conditional** | |
| | würde heben<br>würdest heben<br>würde heben | würden heben<br>würdet heben<br>würden heben | würde gehoben haben<br>würdest gehoben haben<br>würde gehoben haben | würden gehoben haben<br>würdet gehoben haben<br>würden gehoben haben |

## EXAMPLES

Wir müssen die Tür aus den Angeln heben. — We have to take the door off its hinges.
Kannst du mir helfen diesen Sessel zu heben? — Can you help me lift this armchair?

**heilen**
to heal, to cure
**Auxiliary verb:** haben **Past participle:** geheilt
**Imperative:** Heile! Heilt! Heilen Sie!

| Mode | Simple Tenses | | Compound Tenses | |
|---|---|---|---|---|
| | *Singular* | *Plural* | *Singular* | *Plural* |
| Indicative | **Present** | | **Present Perfect** | |
| | heile<br>heilst<br>heilt | heilen<br>heilt<br>heilen | habe geheilt<br>hast geheilt<br>hat geheilt | haben geheilt<br>habt geheilt<br>haben geheilt |
| | **Past** | | **Past Perfect** | |
| | heilte<br>heiltest<br>heilte | heilten<br>heiltet<br>heilten | hatte geheilt<br>hattest geheilt<br>hatte geheilt | hatten geheilt<br>hattet geheilt<br>hatten geheilt |
| | **Future** | | **Future Perfect** | |
| | werde heilen<br>wirst heilen<br>wird heilen | werden heilen<br>werdet heilen<br>werden heilen | werde geheilt haben<br>wirst geheilt haben<br>wird geheilt haben | werden geheilt haben<br>werdet geheilt haben<br>werden geheilt haben |
| Subjunctive | **Present** | | **Present Perfect** | |
| | heile<br>heilest<br>heile | heilen<br>heilet<br>heilen | habe geheilt<br>habest geheilt<br>habe geheilt | haben geheilt<br>habet geheilt<br>haben geheilt |
| | **Past** | | **Past Perfect** | |
| | heilte<br>heiltest<br>heilte | heilten<br>heiltet<br>heilten | hätte geheilt<br>hättest geheilt<br>hätte geheilt | hätten geheilt<br>hättet geheilt<br>hätten geheilt |
| | **Future** | | **Future Perfect** | |
| | werde heilen<br>werdest heilen<br>werde heilen | werden heilen<br>werdet heilen<br>werden heilen | werde geheilt haben<br>werdest geheilt haben<br>werde geheilt haben | werden geheilt haben<br>werdet geheilt haben<br>werden geheilt haben |
| | **Present and Future Conditional** | | **Past Conditional** | |
| | würde heilen<br>würdest heilen<br>würde heilen | würden heilen<br>würdet heilen<br>würden heilen | würde geheilt haben<br>würdest geheilt haben<br>würde geheilt haben | würden geheilt haben<br>würdet geheilt haben<br>würden geheilt haben |

## EXAMPLES

Ihre Wunde wird von selbst heilen.
Your wound will heal without treatment.

Diese Krankheit kann in vielen Fällen geheilt werden.
In many cases, this disease can be cured.

**heiraten**
to marry, to wed
**Auxiliary verb:** haben **Past participle:** geheiratet
**Imperative:** Heirate! Heiratet! Heiraten Sie!

| Mode | Simple Tenses | | Compound Tenses | |
|---|---|---|---|---|
| | *Singular* | *Plural* | *Singular* | *Plural* |
| Indicative | **Present** | | **Present Perfect** | |
| | heirate<br>heiratest<br>heiratet | heiraten<br>heiratet<br>heiraten | habe geheiratet<br>hast geheiratet<br>hat geheiratet | haben geheiratet<br>habt geheiratet<br>haben geheiratet |
| | **Past** | | **Past Perfect** | |
| | heiratete<br>heiratetest<br>heiratete | heirateten<br>heiratetet<br>heirateten | hatte geheiratet<br>hattest geheiratet<br>hatte geheiratet | hatten geheiratet<br>hattet geheiratet<br>hatten geheiratet |
| | **Future** | | **Future Perfect** | |
| | werde heiraten<br>wirst heiraten<br>wird heiraten | werden heiraten<br>werdet heiraten<br>werden heiraten | werde geheiratet haben<br>wirst geheiratet haben<br>wird geheiratet haben | werden geheiratet haben<br>werdet geheiratet haben<br>werden geheiratet haben |
| Subjunctive | **Present** | | **Present Perfect** | |
| | heirate<br>heiratest<br>heirate | heiraten<br>heiratet<br>heiraten | habe geheiratet<br>habest geheiratet<br>habe geheiratet | haben geheiratet<br>habet geheiratet<br>haben geheiratet |
| | **Past** | | **Past Perfect** | |
| | heiratete<br>heiratetest<br>heiratete | heirateten<br>heiratetet<br>heirateten | hätte geheiratet<br>hättest geheiratet<br>hätte geheiratet | hätten geheiratet<br>hättet geheiratet<br>hätten geheiratet |
| | **Future** | | **Future Perfect** | |
| | werde heiraten<br>werdest heiraten<br>werde heiraten | werden heiraten<br>werdet heiraten<br>werden heiraten | werde geheiratet haben<br>werdest geheiratet haben<br>werde geheiratet haben | werden geheiratet haben<br>werdet geheiratet haben<br>werden geheiratet haben |
| | **Present and Future Conditional** | | **Past Conditional** | |
| | würde heiraten<br>würdest heiraten<br>würde heiraten | würden heiraten<br>würdet heiraten<br>würden heiraten | würde geheiratet haben<br>würdest geheiratet haben<br>würde geheiratet haben | würden geheiratet haben<br>würdet geheiratet haben<br>würden geheiratet haben |

## EXAMPLES

Meine Tante wird zum vierten Mal heiraten. — My aunt's going to get married for the fourth time.

Wir haben vor sechs Monaten geheiratet. — We got married six months ago.

**heißen**

to name, to call

**Auxiliary verb:** haben **Past participle:** geheißen

**Imperative:** Heiße! Heißt! Heißen Sie!

| Mode | Simple Tenses | | Compound Tenses | |
|---|---|---|---|---|
| | *Singular* | *Plural* | *Singular* | *Plural* |
| Indicative | **Present** | | **Present Perfect** | |
| | heiße<br>heißt<br>heißt | heißen<br>heißt<br>heißen | habe geheißen<br>hast geheißen<br>hat geheißen | haben geheißen<br>habt geheißen<br>haben geheißen |
| | **Past** | | **Past Perfect** | |
| | hieß<br>hießest<br>hieß | hießen<br>hießt<br>hießen | hatte geheißen<br>hattest geheißen<br>hatte geheißen | hatten geheißen<br>hattet geheißen<br>hatten geheißen |
| | **Future** | | **Future Perfect** | |
| | werde heißen<br>wirst heißen<br>wird heißen | werden heißen<br>werdet heißen<br>werden heißen | werde geheißen haben<br>wirst geheißen haben<br>wird geheißen haben | werden geheißen haben<br>werdet geheißen haben<br>werden geheißen haben |
| Subjunctive | **Present** | | **Present Perfect** | |
| | heiße<br>heißest<br>heiße | heißen<br>heißet<br>heißen | habe geheißen<br>habest geheißen<br>habe geheißen | haben geheißen<br>habet geheißen<br>haben geheißen |
| | **Past** | | **Past Perfect** | |
| | hieße<br>hießest<br>hieße | hießen<br>hießet<br>hießen | hätte geheißen<br>hättest geheißen<br>hätte geheißen | hätten geheißen<br>hättet geheißen<br>hätten geheißen |
| | **Future** | | **Future Perfect** | |
| | werde heißen<br>werdest heißen<br>werde heißen | werden heißen<br>werdet heißen<br>werden heißen | werde geheißen haben<br>werdest geheißen haben<br>werde geheißen haben | werden geheißen haben<br>werdet geheißen haben<br>werden geheißen haben |
| | **Present and Future Conditional** | | **Past Conditional** | |
| | würde heißen<br>würdest heißen<br>würde heißen | würden heißen<br>würdet heißen<br>würden heißen | würde geheißen haben<br>würdest geheißen haben<br>würde geheißen haben | würden geheißen haben<br>würdet geheißen haben<br>würden geheißen haben |

**Note:** *Es heißt* is sometimes used to express "they say" or "it is known."

## EXAMPLES

Wie heißen Ihre Kinder?
What are your children's names?

Es heißt, Sie haben eine Reise um die Welt gemacht.
People say you took a trip around the world.

**heizen**
to heat
**Auxiliary verb:** haben **Past participle:** geheizt
**Imperative:** Heize! Heizt! Heizen Sie!

| Mode | Simple Tenses | | Compound Tenses | |
|---|---|---|---|---|
| | *Singular* | *Plural* | *Singular* | *Plural* |
| Indicative | **Present** | | **Present Perfect** | |
| | heize<br>heizt<br>heizt | heizen<br>heizt<br>heizen | habe geheizt<br>hast geheizt<br>hat geheizt | haben geheizt<br>habt geheizt<br>haben geheizt |
| | **Past** | | **Past Perfect** | |
| | heizte<br>heiztest<br>heizte | heizten<br>heiztet<br>heizten | hatte geheizt<br>hattest geheizt<br>hatte geheizt | hatten geheizt<br>hattet geheizt<br>hatten geheizt |
| | **Future** | | **Future Perfect** | |
| | werde heizen<br>wirst heizen<br>wird heizen | werden heizen<br>werdet heizen<br>werden heizen | werde geheizt haben<br>wirst geheizt haben<br>wird geheizt haben | werden geheizt haben<br>werdet geheizt haben<br>werden geheizt haben |
| Subjunctive | **Present** | | **Present Perfect** | |
| | heize<br>heizest<br>heize | heizen<br>heizet<br>heizen | habe geheizt<br>habest geheizt<br>habe geheizt | haben geheizt<br>habet geheizt<br>haben geheizt |
| | **Past** | | **Past Perfect** | |
| | heizte<br>heiztest<br>heizte | heizten<br>heiztet<br>heizten | hätte geheizt<br>hättest geheizt<br>hätte geheizt | hätten geheizt<br>hättet geheizt<br>hätten geheizt |
| | **Future** | | **Future Perfect** | |
| | werde heizen<br>werdest heizen<br>werde heizen | werden heizen<br>werdet heizen<br>werden heizen | werde geheizt haben<br>werdest geheizt haben<br>werde geheizt haben | werden geheizt haben<br>werdet geheizt haben<br>werden geheizt haben |
| | **Present and Future Conditional** | | **Past Conditional** | |
| | würde heizen<br>würdest heizen<br>würde heizen | würden heizen<br>würdet heizen<br>würden heizen | würde geheizt haben<br>würdest geheizt haben<br>würde geheizt haben | würden geheizt haben<br>würdet geheizt haben<br>würden geheizt haben |

## EXAMPLES

In der Berghütte heizen wir mit Holz.
We heat the mountain cabin by burning wood.

Es ist unmöglich so ein großes Haus zu heizen.
It is impossible to heat such a big house.

**helfen**
to help
**Auxiliary verb:** haben **Past participle:** geholfen
**Imperative:** Hilf! Helft! Helfen Sie!

| Mode | Simple Tenses | | Compound Tenses | |
|---|---|---|---|---|
| | *Singular* | *Plural* | *Singular* | *Plural* |
| Indicative | **Present** | | **Present Perfect** | |
| | helfe<br>hilfst<br>hilft | helfen<br>helft<br>helfen | habe geholfen<br>hast geholfen<br>hat geholfen | haben geholfen<br>habt geholfen<br>haben geholfen |
| | **Past** | | **Past Perfect** | |
| | half<br>halfst<br>half | halfen<br>halft<br>halfen | hatte geholfen<br>hattest geholfen<br>hatte geholfen | hatten geholfen<br>hattet geholfen<br>hatten geholfen |
| | **Future** | | **Future Perfect** | |
| | werde helfen<br>wirst helfen<br>wird helfen | werden helfen<br>werdet helfen<br>werden helfen | werde geholfen haben<br>wirst geholfen haben<br>wird geholfen haben | werden geholfen haben<br>werdet geholfen haben<br>werden geholfen haben |
| Subjunctive | **Present** | | **Present Perfect** | |
| | helfe<br>helfest<br>helfe | helfen<br>helfet<br>helfen | habe geholfen<br>habest geholfen<br>habe geholfen | haben geholfen<br>habet geholfen<br>haben geholfen |
| | **Past** | | **Past Perfect** | |
| | hülfe<br>hülfest<br>hülfe | hülfen<br>hülfet<br>hülfen | hätte geholfen<br>hättest geholfen<br>hätte geholfen | hätten geholfen<br>hättet geholfen<br>hätten geholfen |
| | **Future** | | **Future Perfect** | |
| | werde helfen<br>werdest helfen<br>werde helfen | werden helfen<br>werdet helfen<br>werden helfen | werde geholfen haben<br>werdest geholfen haben<br>werde geholfen haben | werden geholfen haben<br>werdet geholfen haben<br>werden geholfen haben |
| | **Present and Future Conditional** | | **Past Conditional** | |
| | würde helfen<br>würdest helfen<br>würde helfen | würden helfen<br>würdet helfen<br>würden helfen | würde geholfen haben<br>würdest geholfen haben<br>würde geholfen haben | würden geholfen haben<br>würdet geholfen haben<br>würden geholfen haben |

**Note:** With inseparable prefixes, the principal parts of this verb are, for example, *verhilft, verhalf, hat verholfen.* With separable prefixes, the principal parts are, for example, *hilft aus, half aus, hat ausgeholfen.*

## EXAMPLES

| | |
|---|---|
| Er hat mir damit nicht helfen wollen. | He didn't want to help me with it. |
| In den Ferien half ich auf einem Bauernhof. | During vacation, I helped out on a farm. |

**herrschen**
to rule, to reign
**Auxiliary verb:** haben **Past participle:** geherrscht
**Imperative:** Herrsche! Herrscht! Herrschen Sie!

| Mode | Simple Tenses | | Compound Tenses | |
|---|---|---|---|---|
| | *Singular* | *Plural* | *Singular* | *Plural* |
| Indicative | **Present** | | **Present Perfect** | |
| | herrsche<br>herrschst<br>herrscht | herrschen<br>herrscht<br>herrschen | habe geherrscht<br>hast geherrscht<br>hat geherrscht | haben geherrscht<br>habt geherrscht<br>haben geherrscht |
| | **Past** | | **Past Perfect** | |
| | herrschte<br>herrschtest<br>herrschte | herrschten<br>herrschtet<br>herrschten | hatte geherrscht<br>hattest geherrscht<br>hatte geherrscht | hatten geherrscht<br>hattet geherrscht<br>hatten geherrscht |
| | **Future** | | **Future Perfect** | |
| | werde herrschen<br>wirst herrschen<br>wird herrschen | werden herrschen<br>werdet herrschen<br>werden herrschen | werde geherrscht haben<br>wirst geherrscht haben<br>wird geherrscht haben | werden geherrscht haben<br>werdet geherrscht haben<br>werden geherrscht haben |
| Subjunctive | **Present** | | **Present Perfect** | |
| | herrsche<br>herrschest<br>herrsche | herrschen<br>herrschet<br>herrschen | habe geherrscht<br>habest geherrscht<br>habe geherrscht | haben geherrscht<br>habet geherrscht<br>haben geherrscht |
| | **Past** | | **Past Perfect** | |
| | herrschte<br>herrschtest<br>herrschte | herrschten<br>herrschtet<br>herrschten | hätte geherrscht<br>hättest geherrscht<br>hätte geherrscht | hätten geherrscht<br>hättet geherrscht<br>hätten geherrscht |
| | **Future** | | **Future Perfect** | |
| | werde herrschen<br>werdest herrschen<br>werde herrschen | werden herrschen<br>werdet herrschen<br>werden herrschen | werde geherrscht haben<br>werdest geherrscht haben<br>werde geherrscht haben | werden geherrscht haben<br>werdet geherrscht haben<br>werden geherrscht haben |
| | **Present and Future Conditional** | | **Past Conditional** | |
| | würde herrschen<br>würdest herrschen<br>würde herrschen | würden herrschen<br>würdet herrschen<br>würden herrschen | würde geherrscht haben<br>würdest geherrscht haben<br>würde geherrscht haben | würden geherrscht haben<br>würdet geherrscht haben<br>würden geherrscht haben |

## EXAMPLES

Vor der Prüfung herrschte ein ängstliches Schweigen. — Before the test, a fearful silence reigned.

Damals herrschten noch die Hohenzollern. — Back then the Hohenzollerns still reigned.

**heulen**
to howl, to cry
**Auxiliary verb:** haben **Past participle:** geheult
**Imperative:** Heule! Heult! Heulen Sie!

| Mode | Simple Tenses | | Compound Tenses | |
|---|---|---|---|---|
| | *Singular* | *Plural* | *Singular* | *Plural* |
| Indicative | **Present** | | **Present Perfect** | |
| | heule<br>heulst<br>heult | heulen<br>heult<br>heulen | habe geheult<br>hast geheult<br>hat geheult | haben geheult<br>habt geheult<br>haben geheult |
| | **Past** | | **Past Perfect** | |
| | heulte<br>heultest<br>heulte | heulten<br>heultet<br>heulten | hatte geheult<br>hattest geheult<br>hatte geheult | hatten geheult<br>hattet geheult<br>hatten geheult |
| | **Future** | | **Future Perfect** | |
| | werde heulen<br>wirst heulen<br>wird heulen | werden heulen<br>werdet heulen<br>werden heulen | werde geheult haben<br>wirst geheult haben<br>wird geheult haben | werden geheult haben<br>werdet geheult haben<br>werden geheult haben |
| Subjunctive | **Present** | | **Present Perfect** | |
| | heule<br>heulest<br>heule | heulen<br>heulet<br>heulen | habe geheult<br>habest geheult<br>habe geheult | haben geheult<br>habet geheult<br>haben geheult |
| | **Past** | | **Past Perfect** | |
| | heulte<br>heultest<br>heulte | heulten<br>heultet<br>heulten | hätte geheult<br>hättest geheult<br>hätte geheult | hätten geheult<br>hättet geheult<br>hätten geheult |
| | **Future** | | **Future Perfect** | |
| | werde heulen<br>werdest heulen<br>werde heulen | werden heulen<br>werdet heulen<br>werden heulen | werde geheult haben<br>werdest geheult haben<br>werde geheult haben | werden geheult haben<br>werdet geheult haben<br>werden geheult haben |
| | **Present and Future Conditional** | | **Past Conditional** | |
| | würde heulen<br>würdest heulen<br>würde heulen | würden heulen<br>würdet heulen<br>würden heulen | würde geheult haben<br>würdest geheult haben<br>würde geheult haben | würden geheult haben<br>würdet geheult haben<br>würden geheult haben |

## EXAMPLES

| | |
|---|---|
| Das Nachbarskind heulte gestern pausenlos. | The neighbors' child cried for hours yesterday. |
| Man muss mit den Wölfen heulen. | When in Rome, do as the Romans do. |

**hinken**
to limp, to hobble
**Auxiliary verb:** sein **Past participle:** gehinkt
**Imperative:** Hinke! Hinkt! Hinken Sie!

| Mode | Simple Tenses | | Compound Tenses | |
|---|---|---|---|---|
| | *Singular* | *Plural* | *Singular* | *Plural* |
| Indicative | **Present** | | **Present Perfect** | |
| | hinke<br>hinkst<br>hinkt | hinken<br>hinkt<br>hinken | bin gehinkt<br>bist gehinkt<br>ist gehinkt | sind gehinkt<br>seid gehinkt<br>sind gehinkt |
| | **Past** | | **Past Perfect** | |
| | hinkte<br>hinktest<br>hinkte | hinkten<br>hinktet<br>hinkten | war gehinkt<br>warst gehinkt<br>war gehinkt | waren gehinkt<br>wart gehinkt<br>waren gehinkt |
| | **Future** | | **Future Perfect** | |
| | werde hinken<br>wirst hinken<br>wird hinken | werden hinken<br>werdet hinken<br>werden hinken | werde gehinkt sein<br>wirst gehinkt sein<br>wird gehinkt sein | werden gehinkt sein<br>werdet gehinkt sein<br>werden gehinkt sein |
| Subjunctive | **Present** | | **Present Perfect** | |
| | hinke<br>hinkest<br>hinke | hinken<br>hinket<br>hinken | sei gehinkt<br>seiest gehinkt<br>sei gehinkt | seien gehinkt<br>seiet gehinkt<br>seien gehinkt |
| | **Past** | | **Past Perfect** | |
| | hinkte<br>hinktest<br>hinkte | hinkten<br>hinktet<br>hinkten | wäre gehinkt<br>wärest gehinkt<br>wäre gehinkt | wären gehinkt<br>wäret gehinkt<br>wären gehinkt |
| | **Future** | | **Future Perfect** | |
| | werde hinken<br>werdest hinken<br>werde hinken | werden hinken<br>werdet hinken<br>werden hinken | werde gehinkt sein<br>werdest gehinkt sein<br>werde gehinkt sein | werden gehinkt sein<br>werdet gehinkt sein<br>werden gehinkt sein |
| | **Present and Future Conditional** | | **Past Conditional** | |
| | würde hinken<br>würdest hinken<br>würde hinken | würden hinken<br>würdet hinken<br>würden hinken | würde gehinkt sein<br>würdest gehinkt sein<br>würde gehinkt sein | würden gehinkt sein<br>würdet gehinkt sein<br>würden gehinkt sein |

## EXAMPLES

Nach dem Unfall bin ich noch drei Wochen gehinkt.
After the accident, I limped for three weeks.

Ohne einen Stock hinke ich.
Without a cane I limp.

**hinzufügen**
to add to
**Auxiliary verb:** haben **Past participle:** hinzugefügt
**Imperative:** Füge hinzu! Fügt hinzu! Fügen Sie hinzu!

| Mode | Simple Tenses | | Compound Tenses | |
|---|---|---|---|---|
| | *Singular* | *Plural* | *Singular* | *Plural* |
| Indicative | **Present** | | **Present Perfect** | |
| | füge hinzu<br>fügst hinzu<br>fügt hinzu | fügen hinzu<br>fügt hinzu<br>fügen hinzu | habe hinzugefügt<br>hast hinzugefügt<br>hat hinzugefügt | haben hinzugefügt<br>habt hinzugefügt<br>haben hinzugefügt |
| | **Past** | | **Past Perfect** | |
| | fügte hinzu<br>fügtest hinzu<br>fügte hinzu | fügten hinzu<br>fügtet hinzu<br>fügten hinzu | hatte hinzugefügt<br>hattest hinzugefügt<br>hatte hinzugefügt | hatten hinzugefügt<br>hattet hinzugefügt<br>hatten hinzugefügt |
| | **Future** | | **Future Perfect** | |
| | werde hinzufügen<br>wirst hinzufügen<br>wird hinzufügen | werden hinzufügen<br>werdet hinzufügen<br>werden hinzufügen | werde hinzugefügt haben<br>wirst hinzugefügt haben<br>wird hinzugefügt haben | werden hinzugefügt haben<br>werdet hinzugefügt haben<br>werden hinzugefügt haben |
| Subjunctive | **Present** | | **Present Perfect** | |
| | füge hinzu<br>fügest hinzu<br>füge hinzu | fügen hinzu<br>füget hinzu<br>fügen hinzu | habe hinzugefügt<br>habest hinzugefügt<br>habe hinzugefügt | haben hinzugefügt<br>habet hinzugefügt<br>haben hinzugefügt |
| | **Past** | | **Past Perfect** | |
| | fügte hinzu<br>fügtest hinzu<br>fügte hinzu | fügten hinzu<br>fügtet hinzu<br>fügten hinzu | hätte hinzugefügt<br>hättest hinzugefügt<br>hätte hinzugefügt | hätten hinzugefügt<br>hättet hinzugefügt<br>hätten hinzugefügt |
| | **Future** | | **Future Perfect** | |
| | werde hinzufügen<br>werdest hinzufügen<br>werde hinzufügen | werden hinzufügen<br>werdet hinzufügen<br>werden hinzufügen | werde hinzugefügt haben<br>werdest hinzugefügt haben<br>werde hinzugefügt haben | werden hinzugefügt haben<br>werdet hinzugefügt haben<br>werden hinzugefügt haben |
| | **Present and Future Conditional** | | **Past Conditional** | |
| | würde hinzufügen<br>würdest hinzufügen<br>würde hinzufügen | würden hinzufügen<br>würdet hinzufügen<br>würden hinzufügen | würde hinzugefügt haben<br>würdest hinzugefügt haben<br>würde hinzugefügt haben | würden hinzugefügt haben<br>würdet hinzugefügt haben<br>würden hinzugefügt haben |

## EXAMPLES

Er fügt hinzu, dass er nie verhaftet worden ist. — He adds that he has never been arrested.

Die meisten Jungen hatten viel zu sagen, aber Christian hat nichts hinzugefügt. — Most of the boys had a lot to say, but Christian added nothing.

**hocken**
to crouch, to squat
**Auxiliary verb:** haben **Past participle:** gehockt
**Imperative:** Hocke! Hockt! Hocken Sie!

| Mode | Simple Tenses | | Compound Tenses | |
|---|---|---|---|---|
| | *Singular* | *Plural* | *Singular* | *Plural* |
| Indicative | **Present** | | **Present Perfect** | |
| | hocke<br>hockst<br>hockt | hocken<br>hockt<br>hocken | habe gehockt<br>hast gehockt<br>hat gehockt | haben gehockt<br>habt gehockt<br>haben gehockt |
| | **Past** | | **Past Perfect** | |
| | hockte<br>hocktest<br>hockte | hockten<br>hocktet<br>hockten | hatte gehockt<br>hattest gehockt<br>hatte gehockt | hatten gehockt<br>hattet gehockt<br>hatten gehockt |
| | **Future** | | **Future Perfect** | |
| | werde hocken<br>wirst hocken<br>wird hocken | werden hocken<br>werdet hocken<br>werden hocken | werde gehockt haben<br>wirst gehockt haben<br>wird gehockt haben | werden gehockt haben<br>werdet gehockt haben<br>werden gehockt haben |
| Subjunctive | **Present** | | **Present Perfect** | |
| | hocke<br>hockest<br>hocke | hocken<br>hocket<br>hocken | habe gehockt<br>habest gehockt<br>habe gehockt | haben gehockt<br>habet gehockt<br>haben gehockt |
| | **Past** | | **Past Perfect** | |
| | hockte<br>hocktest<br>hockte | hockten<br>hocktet<br>hockten | hätte gehockt<br>hättest gehockt<br>hätte gehockt | hätten gehockt<br>hättet gehockt<br>hätten gehockt |
| | **Future** | | **Future Perfect** | |
| | werde hocken<br>werdest hocken<br>werde hocken | werden hocken<br>werdet hocken<br>werden hocken | werde gehockt haben<br>werdest gehockt haben<br>werde gehockt haben | werden gehockt haben<br>werdet gehockt haben<br>werden gehockt haben |
| | **Present and Future Conditional** | | **Past Conditional** | |
| | würde hocken<br>würdest hocken<br>würde hocken | würden hocken<br>würdet hocken<br>würden hocken | würde gehockt haben<br>würdest gehockt haben<br>würde gehockt haben | würden gehockt haben<br>würdet gehockt haben<br>würden gehockt haben |

## EXAMPLES

Karin war immer eine Stubenhockerin.
Der Knabe hockte neben seinem Vater.

Karin was always a real home-body.
The little boy crouched next to his father.

**hoffen**
to hope
**Auxiliary verb:** haben **Past participle:** gehofft
**Imperative:** Hoffe! Hofft! Hoffen Sie!

| Mode | Simple Tenses | | Compound Tenses | |
|---|---|---|---|---|
| | *Singular* | *Plural* | *Singular* | *Plural* |
| Indicative | **Present** | | **Present Perfect** | |
| | hoffe<br>hoffst<br>hofft | hoffen<br>hofft<br>hoffen | habe gehofft<br>hast gehofft<br>hat gehofft | haben gehofft<br>habt gehofft<br>haben gehofft |
| | **Past** | | **Past Perfect** | |
| | hoffte<br>hofftest<br>hoffte | hofften<br>hofftet<br>hofften | hatte gehofft<br>hattest gehofft<br>hatte gehofft | hatten gehofft<br>hattet gehofft<br>hatten gehofft |
| | **Future** | | **Future Perfect** | |
| | werde hoffen<br>wirst hoffen<br>wird hoffen | werden hoffen<br>werdet hoffen<br>werden hoffen | werde gehofft haben<br>wirst gehofft haben<br>wird gehofft haben | werden gehofft haben<br>werdet gehofft haben<br>werden gehofft haben |
| Subjunctive | **Present** | | **Present Perfect** | |
| | hoffe<br>hoffest<br>hoffe | hoffen<br>hoffet<br>hoffen | habe gehofft<br>habest gehofft<br>habe gehofft | haben gehofft<br>habet gehofft<br>haben gehofft |
| | **Past** | | **Past Perfect** | |
| | hoffte<br>hofftest<br>hoffte | hofften<br>hofftet<br>hofften | hätte gehofft<br>hättest gehofft<br>hätte gehofft | hätten gehofft<br>hättet gehofft<br>hätten gehofft |
| | **Future** | | **Future Perfect** | |
| | werde hoffen<br>werdest hoffen<br>werde hoffen | werden hoffen<br>werdet hoffen<br>werden hoffen | werde gehofft haben<br>werdest gehofft haben<br>werde gehofft haben | werden gehofft haben<br>werdet gehofft haben<br>werden gehofft haben |
| | **Present and Future Conditional** | | **Past Conditional** | |
| | würde hoffen<br>würdest hoffen<br>würde hoffen | würden hoffen<br>würdet hoffen<br>würden hoffen | würde gehofft haben<br>würdest gehofft haben<br>würde gehofft haben | würden gehofft haben<br>würdet gehofft haben<br>würden gehofft haben |

## EXAMPLES

Ich hoffe, dass wir uns bald wiedersehen. — I hope we see one another again soon.
Der Kranke hofft auf eine baldige Genesung. — The patient is hoping for a speedy recovery.

**holen**
to fetch, to go for, to get
**Auxiliary verb:** haben **Past participle:** geholt
**Imperative:** Hole! Holt! Holen Sie!

| Mode | Simple Tenses | | Compound Tenses | |
|---|---|---|---|---|
| | *Singular* | *Plural* | *Singular* | *Plural* |
| Indicative | **Present** | | **Present Perfect** | |
| | hole<br>holst<br>holt | holen<br>holt<br>holen | habe geholt<br>hast geholt<br>hat geholt | haben geholt<br>habt geholt<br>haben geholt |
| | **Past** | | **Past Perfect** | |
| | holte<br>holtest<br>holte | holten<br>holtet<br>holten | hatte geholt<br>hattest geholt<br>hatte geholt | hatten geholt<br>hattet geholt<br>hatten geholt |
| | **Future** | | **Future Perfect** | |
| | werde holen<br>wirst holen<br>wird holen | werden holen<br>werdet holen<br>werden holen | werde geholt haben<br>wirst geholt haben<br>wird geholt haben | werden geholt haben<br>werdet geholt haben<br>werden geholt haben |
| Subjunctive | **Present** | | **Present Perfect** | |
| | hole<br>holest<br>hole | holen<br>holet<br>holen | habe geholt<br>habest geholt<br>habe geholt | haben geholt<br>habet geholt<br>haben geholt |
| | **Past** | | **Past Perfect** | |
| | holte<br>holtest<br>holte | holten<br>holtet<br>holten | hätte geholt<br>hättest geholt<br>hätte geholt | hätten geholt<br>hättet geholt<br>hätten geholt |
| | **Future** | | **Future Perfect** | |
| | werde holen<br>werdest holen<br>werde holen | werden holen<br>werdet holen<br>werden holen | werde geholt haben<br>werdest geholt haben<br>werde geholt haben | werden geholt haben<br>werdet geholt haben<br>werden geholt haben |
| | **Present and Future Conditional** | | **Past Conditional** | |
| | würde holen<br>würdest holen<br>würde holen | würden holen<br>würdet holen<br>würden holen | würde geholt haben<br>würdest geholt haben<br>würde geholt haben | würden geholt haben<br>würdet geholt haben<br>würden geholt haben |

## EXAMPLES

Martin holte eine Flasche Bier aus dem Kühlschrank.
Martin got a bottle of beer out of the refrigerator.

Holen Sie bitte sofort einen Arzt!
Please get a doctor right away.

**horchen**
to listen attentively, to eavesdrop
**Auxiliary verb:** haben **Past participle:** gehorcht
**Imperative:** Horche! Horcht! Horchen Sie!

| Mode | Simple Tenses | | Compound Tenses | |
|---|---|---|---|---|
| | *Singular* | *Plural* | *Singular* | *Plural* |
| Indicative | **Present** | | **Present Perfect** | |
| | horche<br>horchst<br>horcht | horchen<br>horcht<br>horchen | habe gehorcht<br>hast gehorcht<br>hat gehorcht | haben gehorcht<br>habt gehorcht<br>haben gehorcht |
| | **Past** | | **Past Perfect** | |
| | horchte<br>horchtest<br>horchte | horchten<br>horchtet<br>horchten | hatte gehorcht<br>hattest gehorcht<br>hatte gehorcht | hatten gehorcht<br>hattet gehorcht<br>hatten gehorcht |
| | **Future** | | **Future Perfect** | |
| | werde horchen<br>wirst horchen<br>wird horchen | werden horchen<br>werdet horchen<br>werden horchen | werde gehorcht haben<br>wirst gehorcht haben<br>wird gehorcht haben | werden gehorcht haben<br>werdet gehorcht haben<br>werden gehorcht haben |
| Subjunctive | **Present** | | **Present Perfect** | |
| | horche<br>horchest<br>horche | horchen<br>horchet<br>horchen | habe gehorcht<br>habest gehorcht<br>habe gehorcht | haben gehorcht<br>habet gehorcht<br>haben gehorcht |
| | **Past** | | **Past Perfect** | |
| | horchte<br>horchtest<br>horchte | horchten<br>horchtet<br>horchten | hätte gehorcht<br>hättest gehorcht<br>hätte gehorcht | hätten gehorcht<br>hättet gehorcht<br>hätten gehorcht |
| | **Future** | | **Future Perfect** | |
| | werde horchen<br>werdest horchen<br>werde horchen | werden horchen<br>werdet horchen<br>werden horchen | werde gehorcht haben<br>werdest gehorcht haben<br>werde gehorcht haben | werden gehorcht haben<br>werdet gehorcht haben<br>werden gehorcht haben |
| | **Present and Future Conditional** | | **Past Conditional** | |
| | würde horchen<br>würdest horchen<br>würde horchen | würden horchen<br>würdet horchen<br>würden horchen | würde gehorcht haben<br>würdest gehorcht haben<br>würde gehorcht haben | würden gehorcht haben<br>würdet gehorcht haben<br>würden gehorcht haben |

## EXAMPLES

Jemand horcht an der Tür. — Someone is listening at the door.
Ich horche auf jedes Wort. — I pay attention to every word.

**hören**
to hear
**Auxiliary verb:** haben **Past participle:** gehört
**Imperative:** Höre! Hört! Hören Sie!

| Mode | Simple Tenses | | Compound Tenses | |
|---|---|---|---|---|
| | *Singular* | *Plural* | *Singular* | *Plural* |
| Indicative | **Present** | | **Present Perfect** | |
| | höre<br>hörst<br>hört | hören<br>hört<br>hören | habe gehört<br>hast gehört<br>hat gehört | haben gehört<br>habt gehört<br>haben gehört |
| | **Past** | | **Past Perfect** | |
| | hörte<br>hörtest<br>hörte | hörten<br>hörtet<br>hörten | hatte gehört<br>hattest gehört<br>hatte gehört | hatten gehört<br>hattet gehört<br>hatten gehört |
| | **Future** | | **Future Perfect** | |
| | werde hören<br>wirst hören<br>wird hören | werden hören<br>werdet hören<br>werden hören | werde gehört haben<br>wirst gehört haben<br>wird gehört haben | werden gehört haben<br>werdet gehört haben<br>werden gehört haben |
| Subjunctive | **Present** | | **Present Perfect** | |
| | höre<br>hörest<br>höre | hören<br>höret<br>hören | habe gehört<br>habest gehört<br>habe gehört | haben gehört<br>habet gehört<br>haben gehört |
| | **Past** | | **Past Perfect** | |
| | hörte<br>hörtest<br>hörte | hörten<br>hörtet<br>hörten | hätte gehört<br>hättest gehört<br>hätte gehört | hätten gehört<br>hättet gehört<br>hätten gehört |
| | **Future** | | **Future Perfect** | |
| | werde hören<br>werdest hören<br>werde hören | werden hören<br>werdet hören<br>werden hören | werde gehört haben<br>werdest gehört haben<br>werde gehört haben | werden gehört haben<br>werdet gehört haben<br>werden gehört haben |
| | **Present and Future Conditional** | | **Past Conditional** | |
| | würde hören<br>würdest hören<br>würde hören | würden hören<br>würdet hören<br>würden hören | würde gehört haben<br>würdest gehört haben<br>würde gehört haben | würden gehört haben<br>würdet gehört haben<br>würden gehört haben |

## EXAMPLES

Von hier aus kann man die Kirchglocken hören.
From here you can hear the church bells.

Hast du gehört, dass Frau Bauer wieder schwanger ist?
Did you hear that Mrs. Bauer is pregnant again?

**husten**

to cough

**Auxiliary verb:** haben **Past participle:** gehustet

**Imperative:** Huste! Hustet! Husten Sie!

| Mode | Simple Tenses | | Compound Tenses | |
|---|---|---|---|---|
| | *Singular* | *Plural* | *Singular* | *Plural* |
| Indicative | **Present** | | **Present Perfect** | |
| | huste<br>hustest<br>hustet | husten<br>hustet<br>husten | habe gehustet<br>hast gehustet<br>hat gehustet | haben gehustet<br>habt gehustet<br>haben gehustet |
| | **Past** | | **Past Perfect** | |
| | hustete<br>hustetest<br>hustete | husteten<br>hustetet<br>husteten | hatte gehustet<br>hattest gehustet<br>hatte gehustet | hatten gehustet<br>hattet gehustet<br>hatten gehustet |
| | **Future** | | **Future Perfect** | |
| | werde husten<br>wirst husten<br>wird husten | werden husten<br>werdet husten<br>werden husten | werde gehustet haben<br>wirst gehustet haben<br>wird gehustet haben | werden gehustet haben<br>werdet gehustet haben<br>werden gehustet haben |
| Subjunctive | **Present** | | **Present Perfect** | |
| | huste<br>hustest<br>huste | husten<br>hustet<br>husten | habe gehustet<br>habest gehustet<br>habe gehustet | haben gehustet<br>habet gehustet<br>haben gehustet |
| | **Past** | | **Past Perfect** | |
| | hustete<br>hustetest<br>hustete | husteten<br>hustetet<br>husteten | hätte gehustet<br>hättest gehustet<br>hätte gehustet | hätten gehustet<br>hättet gehustet<br>hätten gehustet |
| | **Future** | | **Future Perfect** | |
| | werde husten<br>werdest husten<br>werde husten | werden husten<br>werdet husten<br>werden husten | werde gehustet haben<br>werdest gehustet haben<br>werde gehustet haben | werden gehustet haben<br>werdet gehustet haben<br>werden gehustet haben |
| | **Present and Future Conditional** | | **Past Conditional** | |
| | würde husten<br>würdest husten<br>würde husten | würden husten<br>würdet husten<br>würden husten | würde gehustet haben<br>würdest gehustet haben<br>würde gehustet haben | würden gehustet haben<br>würdet gehustet haben<br>würden gehustet haben |

## EXAMPLE

Der kranke Junge hat die ganze Nacht durch gehustet. — The sick boy coughed throughout the night.

**jagen**
to chase, to hunt
**Auxiliary verb:** haben **Past participle:** gejagt
**Imperative:** Jage! Jagt! Jagen Sie!

| Mode | Simple Tenses | | Compound Tenses | |
|---|---|---|---|---|
| | *Singular* | *Plural* | *Singular* | *Plural* |
| Indicative | **Present** | | **Present Perfect** | |
| | jage<br>jagst<br>jagt | jagen<br>jagt<br>jagen | habe gejagt<br>hast gejagt<br>hat gejagt | haben gejagt<br>habt gejagt<br>haben gejagt |
| | **Past** | | **Past Perfect** | |
| | jagte<br>jagtest<br>jagte | jagten<br>jagtet<br>jagten | hatte gejagt<br>hattest gejagt<br>hatte gejagt | hatten gejagt<br>hattet gejagt<br>hatten gejagt |
| | **Future** | | **Future Perfect** | |
| | werde jagen<br>wirst jagen<br>wird jagen | werden jagen<br>werdet jagen<br>werden jagen | werde gejagt haben<br>wirst gejagt haben<br>wird gejagt haben | werden gejagt haben<br>werdet gejagt haben<br>werden gejagt haben |
| Subjunctive | **Present** | | **Present Perfect** | |
| | jage<br>jagest<br>jage | jagen<br>jaget<br>jagen | habe gejagt<br>habest gejagt<br>habe gejagt | haben gejagt<br>habet gejagt<br>haben gejagt |
| | **Past** | | **Past Perfect** | |
| | jagte<br>jagtest<br>jagte | jagten<br>jagtet<br>jagten | hätte gejagt<br>hättest gejagt<br>hätte gejagt | hätten gejagt<br>hättet gejagt<br>hätten gejagt |
| | **Future** | | **Future Perfect** | |
| | werde jagen<br>werdest jagen<br>werde jagen | werden jagen<br>werdet jagen<br>werden jagen | werde gejagt haben<br>werdest gejagt haben<br>werde gejagt haben | werden gejagt haben<br>werdet gejagt haben<br>werden gejagt haben |
| | **Present and Future Conditional** | | **Past Conditional** | |
| | würde jagen<br>würdest jagen<br>würde jagen | würden jagen<br>würdet jagen<br>würden jagen | würde gejagt haben<br>würdest gejagt haben<br>würde gejagt haben | würden gejagt haben<br>würdet gejagt haben<br>würden gejagt haben |

## EXAMPLES

Die Katze jagte die Maus durch den Garten. — The cat chased the mouse through the garden.

Im Winter gehen die drei Brüder oft jagen. — The three brothers often go hunting in winter.

**jodeln**
to yodel
**Auxiliary verb:** haben **Past participle:** gejodelt
**Imperative:** Jodele! Jodelt! Jodeln Sie!

| Mode | Simple Tenses | | Compound Tenses | |
|---|---|---|---|---|
| | *Singular* | *Plural* | *Singular* | *Plural* |
| Indicative | **Present** | | **Present Perfect** | |
| | jodele<br>jodelst<br>jodelt | jodeln<br>jodelt<br>jodeln | habe gejodelt<br>hast gejodelt<br>hat gejodelt | haben gejodelt<br>habt gejodelt<br>haben gejodelt |
| | **Past** | | **Past Perfect** | |
| | jodelte<br>jodeltest<br>jodelte | jodelten<br>jodeltet<br>jodelten | hatte gejodelt<br>hattest gejodelt<br>hatte gejodelt | hatten gejodelt<br>hattet gejodelt<br>hatten gejodelt |
| | **Future** | | **Future Perfect** | |
| | werde jodeln<br>wirst jodeln<br>wird jodeln | werden jodeln<br>werdet jodeln<br>werden jodeln | werde gejodelt haben<br>wirst gejodelt haben<br>wird gejodelt haben | werden gejodelt haben<br>werdet gejodelt haben<br>werden gejodelt haben |
| Subjunctive | **Present** | | **Present Perfect** | |
| | jodele<br>jodelst<br>jodele | jodeln<br>jodelt<br>jodeln | habe gejodelt<br>habest gejodelt<br>habe gejodelt | haben gejodelt<br>habet gejodelt<br>haben gejodelt |
| | **Past** | | **Past Perfect** | |
| | jodelte<br>jodeltest<br>jodelte | jodelten<br>jodeltet<br>jodelten | hätte gejodelt<br>hättest gejodelt<br>hätte gejodelt | hätten gejodelt<br>hättet gejodelt<br>hätten gejodelt |
| | **Future** | | **Future Perfect** | |
| | werde jodeln<br>werdest jodeln<br>werde jodeln | werden jodeln<br>werdet jodeln<br>werden jodeln | werde gejodelt haben<br>werdest gejodelt haben<br>werde gejodelt haben | werden gejodelt haben<br>werdet gejodelt haben<br>werden gejodelt haben |
| | **Present and Future Conditional** | | **Past Conditional** | |
| | würde jodeln<br>würdest jodeln<br>würde jodeln | würden jodeln<br>würdet jodeln<br>würden jodeln | würde gejodelt haben<br>würdest gejodelt haben<br>würde gejodelt haben | würden gejodelt haben<br>würdet gejodelt haben<br>würden gejodelt haben |

## EXAMPLES

Mein Vetter versucht zu jodeln. Aber er krächzt nur.
My cousin tries to yodel. But he only sounds like a crow.

In der Volksmusik der Alpen hört man oft Jodeln.
You often hear yodeling in folk music from the Alps.

**jubeln**
to rejoice, to shout with joy
**Auxiliary verb:** haben **Past participle:** gejubelt
**Imperative:** Jubele! Jubelt! Jubeln Sie!

| Mode | Simple Tenses | | Compound Tenses | |
|---|---|---|---|---|
| | *Singular* | *Plural* | *Singular* | *Plural* |
| Indicative | **Present** | | **Present Perfect** | |
| | jubele<br>jubelst<br>jubelt | jubeln<br>jubelt<br>jubeln | habe gejubelt<br>hast gejubelt<br>hat gejubelt | haben gejubelt<br>habt gejubelt<br>haben gejubelt |
| | **Past** | | **Past Perfect** | |
| | jubelte<br>jubeltest<br>jubelte | jubelten<br>jubeltet<br>jubelten | hatte gejubelt<br>hattest gejubelt<br>hatte gejubelt | hatten gejubelt<br>hattet gejubelt<br>hatten gejubelt |
| | **Future** | | **Future Perfect** | |
| | werde jubeln<br>wirst jubeln<br>wird jubeln | werden jubeln<br>werdet jubeln<br>werden jubeln | werde gejubelt haben<br>wirst gejubelt haben<br>wird gejubelt haben | werden gejubelt haben<br>werdet gejubelt haben<br>werden gejubelt haben |
| Subjunctive | **Present** | | **Present Perfect** | |
| | jubele<br>jubelst<br>jubele | jubeln<br>jubelt<br>jubeln | habe gejubelt<br>habest gejubelt<br>habe gejubelt | haben gejubelt<br>habet gejubelt<br>haben gejubelt |
| | **Past** | | **Past Perfect** | |
| | jubelte<br>jubeltest<br>jubelte | jubelten<br>jubeltet<br>jubelten | hätte gejubelt<br>hättest gejubelt<br>hätte gejubelt | hätten gejubelt<br>hättet gejubelt<br>hätten gejubelt |
| | **Future** | | **Future Perfect** | |
| | werde jubeln<br>werdest jubeln<br>werde jubeln | werden jubeln<br>werdet jubeln<br>werden jubeln | werde gejubelt haben<br>werdest gejubelt haben<br>werde gejubelt haben | werden gejubelt haben<br>werdet gejubelt haben<br>werden gejubelt haben |
| | **Present and Future Conditional** | | **Past Conditional** | |
| | würde jubeln<br>würdest jubeln<br>würde jubeln | würden jubeln<br>würdet jubeln<br>würden jubeln | würde gejubelt haben<br>würdest gejubelt haben<br>würde gejubelt haben | würden gejubelt haben<br>würdet gejubelt haben<br>würden gejubelt haben |

## EXAMPLES

Die ganze Stadt jubelte, als die siegreiche Armee in die Stadt marschierte.
The whole city rejoiced, when the victorious army marched into the city.

Die Zuschauer jubelten, als Schmidt das entscheidende Tor schoss.
The crowd cheered when Schmidt shot the winning goal.

**jucken**
to itch, to irritate
**Auxiliary verb:** haben **Past participle:** gejuckt
**Imperative:** Jucke! Juckt! Jucken Sie!

| Mode | Simple Tenses | | Compound Tenses | |
|---|---|---|---|---|
| | *Singular* | *Plural* | *Singular* | *Plural* |
| Indicative | **Present** | | **Present Perfect** | |
| | jucke<br>juckst<br>juckt | jucken<br>juckt<br>jucken | habe gejuckt<br>hast gejuckt<br>hat gejuckt | haben gejuckt<br>habt gejuckt<br>haben gejuckt |
| | **Past** | | **Past Perfect** | |
| | juckte<br>jucktest<br>juckte | juckten<br>jucktet<br>juckten | hatte gejuckt<br>hattest gejuckt<br>hatte gejuckt | hatten gejuckt<br>hattet gejuckt<br>hatten gejuckt |
| | **Future** | | **Future Perfect** | |
| | werde jucken<br>wirst jucken<br>wird jucken | werden jucken<br>werdet jucken<br>werden jucken | werde gejuckt haben<br>wirst gejuckt haben<br>wird gejuckt haben | werden gejuckt haben<br>werdet gejuckt haben<br>werden gejuckt haben |
| Subjunctive | **Present** | | **Present Perfect** | |
| | jucke<br>juckest<br>jucke | jucken<br>jucket<br>jucken | habe gejuckt<br>habest gejuckt<br>habe gejuckt | haben gejuckt<br>habet gejuckt<br>haben gejuckt |
| | **Past** | | **Past Perfect** | |
| | juckte<br>jucktest<br>juckte | juckten<br>jucktet<br>juckten | hätte gejuckt<br>hättest gejuckt<br>hätte gejuckt | hätten gejuckt<br>hättet gejuckt<br>hätten gejuckt |
| | **Future** | | **Future Perfect** | |
| | werde jucken<br>werdest jucken<br>werde jucken | werden jucken<br>werdet jucken<br>werden jucken | werde gejuckt haben<br>werdest gejuckt haben<br>werde gejuckt haben | werden gejuckt haben<br>werdet gejuckt haben<br>werden gejuckt haben |
| | **Present and Future Conditional** | | **Past Conditional** | |
| | würde jucken<br>würdest jucken<br>würde jucken | würden jucken<br>würdet jucken<br>würden jucken | würde gejuckt haben<br>würdest gejuckt haben<br>würde gejuckt haben | würden gejuckt haben<br>würdet gejuckt haben<br>würden gejuckt haben |

## EXAMPLE

Mein Bein juckt. My leg itches.

**kämmen (sich)**
to comb
**Auxiliary verb:** haben **Past participle:** gekämmt
**Imperative:** Kämme! Kämmt! Kämmen Sie!

| Mode | Simple Tenses | | Compound Tenses | |
|---|---|---|---|---|
| | *Singular* | *Plural* | *Singular* | *Plural* |
| Indicative | **Present** | | **Present Perfect** | |
| | kämme<br>kämmst<br>kämmt | kämmen<br>kämmt<br>kämmen | habe gekämmt<br>hast gekämmt<br>hat gekämmt | haben gekämmt<br>habt gekämmt<br>haben gekämmt |
| | **Past** | | **Past Perfect** | |
| | kämmte<br>kämmtest<br>kämmte | kämmten<br>kämmtet<br>kämmten | hatte gekämmt<br>hattest gekämmt<br>hatte gekämmt | hatten gekämmt<br>hattet gekämmt<br>hatten gekämmt |
| | **Future** | | **Future Perfect** | |
| | werde kämmen<br>wirst kämmen<br>wird kämmen | werden kämmen<br>werdet kämmen<br>werden kämmen | werde gekämmt haben<br>wirst gekämmt haben<br>wird gekämmt haben | werden gekämmt haben<br>werdet gekämmt haben<br>werden gekämmt haben |
| Subjunctive | **Present** | | **Present Perfect** | |
| | kämme<br>kämmest<br>kämme | kämmen<br>kämmet<br>kämmen | habe gekämmt<br>habest gekämmt<br>habe gekämmt | haben gekämmt<br>habet gekämmt<br>haben gekämmt |
| | **Past** | | **Past Perfect** | |
| | kämmte<br>kämmtest<br>kämmte | kämmten<br>kämmtet<br>kämmten | hätte gekämmt<br>hättest gekämmt<br>hätte gekämmt | hätten gekämmt<br>hättet gekämmt<br>hätten gekämmt |
| | **Future** | | **Future Perfect** | |
| | werde kämmen<br>werdest kämmen<br>werde kämmen | werden kämmen<br>werdet kämmen<br>werden kämmen | werde gekämmt haben<br>werdest gekämmt haben<br>werde gekämmt haben | werden gekämmt haben<br>werdet gekämmt haben<br>werden gekämmt haben |
| | **Present and Future Conditional** | | **Past Conditional** | |
| | würde kämmen<br>würdest kämmen<br>würde kämmen | würden kämmen<br>würdet kämmen<br>würden kämmen | würde gekämmt haben<br>würdest gekämmt haben<br>würde gekämmt haben | würden gekämmt haben<br>würdet gekämmt haben<br>würden gekämmt haben |

**Note:** Use the reflexive when one combs one's own hair: *Der Vierjährige kann sich schon die Haare kämmen* (The four-year-old can already comb his hair).

## EXAMPLES

Mutti muss den Kindern die Haare kämmen. — Mom has to comb the children's hair.
Du sollst dich besser kämmen. — You should comb your hair better.

**kämpfen**
to struggle, to battle
**Auxiliary verb:** haben **Past participle:** gekämpft
**Imperative:** Kämpfe! Kämpft! Kämpfen Sie!

| Mode | Simple Tenses | | Compound Tenses | |
|---|---|---|---|---|
| | *Singular* | *Plural* | *Singular* | *Plural* |
| Indicative | **Present** | | **Present Perfect** | |
| | kämpfe<br>kämpfst<br>kämpft | kämpfen<br>kämpft<br>kämpfen | habe gekämpft<br>hast gekämpft<br>hat gekämpft | haben gekämpft<br>habt gekämpft<br>haben gekämpft |
| | **Past** | | **Past Perfect** | |
| | kämpfte<br>kämpftest<br>kämpfte | kämpften<br>kämpftet<br>kämpften | hatte gekämpft<br>hattest gekämpft<br>hatte gekämpft | hatten gekämpft<br>hattet gekämpft<br>hatten gekämpft |
| | **Future** | | **Future Perfect** | |
| | werde kämpfen<br>wirst kämpfen<br>wird kämpfen | werden kämpfen<br>werdet kämpfen<br>werden kämpfen | werde gekämpft haben<br>wirst gekämpft haben<br>wird gekämpft haben | werden gekämpft haben<br>werdet gekämpft haben<br>werden gekämpft haben |
| Subjunctive | **Present** | | **Present Perfect** | |
| | kämpfe<br>kämpfest<br>kämpfe | kämpfen<br>kämpfet<br>kämpfen | habe gekämpft<br>habest gekämpft<br>habe gekämpft | haben gekämpft<br>habet gekämpft<br>haben gekämpft |
| | **Past** | | **Past Perfect** | |
| | kämpfte<br>kämpftest<br>kämpfte | kämpften<br>kämpftet<br>kämpften | hätte gekämpft<br>hättest gekämpft<br>hätte gekämpft | hätten gekämpft<br>hättet gekämpft<br>hätten gekämpft |
| | **Future** | | **Future Perfect** | |
| | werde kämpfen<br>werdest kämpfen<br>werde kämpfen | werden kämpfen<br>werdet kämpfen<br>werden kämpfen | werde gekämpft haben<br>werdest gekämpft haben<br>werde gekämpft haben | werden gekämpft haben<br>werdet gekämpft haben<br>werden gekämpft haben |
| | **Present and Future Conditional** | | **Past Conditional** | |
| | würde kämpfen<br>würdest kämpfen<br>würde kämpfen | würden kämpfen<br>würdet kämpfen<br>würden kämpfen | würde gekämpft haben<br>würdest gekämpft haben<br>würde gekämpft haben | würden gekämpft haben<br>würdet gekämpft haben<br>würden gekämpft haben |

## EXAMPLES

Die Jungen kämpfen wieder um das Spielzeug.
The boys are fighting over the toys again.

Der Politiker hat um seine Wiederwahl gekämpft.
The politician was fighting for his reelection.

**kauen**
to chew
**Auxiliary verb:** haben **Past participle:** gekaut
**Imperative:** Kaue! Kaut! Kauen Sie!

| Mode | Simple Tenses | | Compound Tenses | |
|---|---|---|---|---|
| | *Singular* | *Plural* | *Singular* | *Plural* |
| Indicative | **Present** | | **Present Perfect** | |
| | kaue<br>kaust<br>kaut | kauen<br>kaut<br>kauen | habe gekaut<br>hast gekaut<br>hat gekaut | haben gekaut<br>habt gekaut<br>haben gekaut |
| | **Past** | | **Past Perfect** | |
| | kaute<br>kautest<br>kaute | kauten<br>kautet<br>kauten | hatte gekaut<br>hattest gekaut<br>hatte gekaut | hatten gekaut<br>hattet gekaut<br>hatten gekaut |
| | **Future** | | **Future Perfect** | |
| | werde kauen<br>wirst kauen<br>wird kauen | werden kauen<br>werdet kauen<br>werden kauen | werde gekaut haben<br>wirst gekaut haben<br>wird gekaut haben | werden gekaut haben<br>werdet gekaut haben<br>werden gekaut haben |
| Subjunctive | **Present** | | **Present Perfect** | |
| | kaue<br>kauest<br>kaue | kauen<br>kauet<br>kauen | habe gekaut<br>habest gekaut<br>habe gekaut | haben gekaut<br>habet gekaut<br>haben gekaut |
| | **Past** | | **Past Perfect** | |
| | kaute<br>kautest<br>kaute | kauten<br>kautet<br>kauten | hätte gekaut<br>hättest gekaut<br>hätte gekaut | hätten gekaut<br>hättet gekaut<br>hatten gekaut |
| | **Future** | | **Future Perfect** | |
| | werde kauen<br>werdest kauen<br>werde kauen | werden kauen<br>werdet kauen<br>werden kauen | werde gekaut haben<br>werdest gekaut haben<br>werde gekaut haben | werden gekaut haben<br>werdet gekaut haben<br>werden gekaut haben |
| | **Present and Future Conditional** | | **Past Conditional** | |
| | würde kauen<br>würdest kauen<br>würde kauen | würden kauen<br>würdet kauen<br>würden kauen | würde gekaut haben<br>würdest gekaut haben<br>würde gekaut haben | würden gekaut haben<br>würdet gekaut haben<br>würden gekaut haben |

## EXAMPLES

Lukas, warum kaust du immer an den Nägeln? — Lukas, why are you always chewing on your nails?

Wenn du kaust, sollst du nicht reden. — When you chew, you shouldn't talk.

**kauern**

to crouch, to cower

**Auxiliary verb:** sein **Past participle:** gekauert

**Imperative:** Kauere! Kauert! Kauern Sie!

| Mode | Simple Tenses | | Compound Tenses | |
|---|---|---|---|---|
| | *Singular* | *Plural* | *Singular* | *Plural* |
| Indicative | **Present** | | **Present Perfect** | |
| | kauere<br>kauerst<br>kauert | kauern<br>kauert<br>kauern | bin gekauert<br>bist gekauert<br>ist gekauert | sind gekauert<br>seid gekauert<br>sind gekauert |
| | **Past** | | **Past Perfect** | |
| | kauerte<br>kauertest<br>kauerte | kauerten<br>kauertet<br>kauerten | war gekauert<br>warst gekauert<br>war gekauert | waren gekauert<br>wart gekauert<br>waren gekauert |
| | **Future** | | **Future Perfect** | |
| | werde kauern<br>wirst kauern<br>wird kauern | werden kauern<br>werdet kauern<br>werden kauern | werde gekauert sein<br>wirst gekauert sein<br>wird gekauert sein | werden gekauert sein<br>werdet gekauert sein<br>werden gekauert sein |
| Subjunctive | **Present** | | **Present Perfect** | |
| | kauere<br>kauerst<br>kauere | kauern<br>kauert<br>kauern | sei gekauert<br>seiest gekauert<br>sei gekauert | seien gekauert<br>seiet gekauert<br>seien gekauert |
| | **Past** | | **Past Perfect** | |
| | kauerte<br>kauertest<br>kauerte | kauerten<br>kauertet<br>kauerten | wäre gekauert<br>wärest gekauert<br>wäre gekauert | wären gekauert<br>wäret gekauert<br>wären gekauert |
| | **Future** | | **Future Perfect** | |
| | werde kauern<br>werdest kauern<br>werde kauern | werden kauern<br>werdet kauern<br>werden kauern | werde gekauert sein<br>werdest gekauert sein<br>werde gekauert sein | werden gekauert sein<br>werdet gekauert sein<br>werden gekauert sein |
| | **Present and Future Conditional** | | **Past Conditional** | |
| | würde kauern<br>würdest kauern<br>würde kauern | würden kauern<br>würdet kauern<br>würden kauern | würde gekauert sein<br>würdest gekauert sein<br>würde gekauert sein | würden gekauert sein<br>würdet gekauert sein<br>würden gekauert sein |

## EXAMPLES

Der Gefangene kauert in einer dunklen Ecke.
The prisoner is cowering in a dark corner.

Der verängstigte Hund kauerte unter dem Stuhl.
The frightened dog cowered under the chair.

**kaufen**
to buy
**Auxiliary verb:** haben **Past participle:** gekauft
**Imperative:** Kaufe! Kauft! Kaufen Sie!

| Mode | Simple Tenses | | Compound Tenses | |
|---|---|---|---|---|
| | *Singular* | *Plural* | *Singular* | *Plural* |
| Indicative | **Present** | | **Present Perfect** | |
| | kaufe<br>kaufst<br>kauft | kaufen<br>kauft<br>kaufen | habe gekauft<br>hast gekauft<br>hat gekauft | haben gekauft<br>habt gekauft<br>haben gekauft |
| | **Past** | | **Past Perfect** | |
| | kaufte<br>kauftest<br>kaufte | kauften<br>kauftet<br>kauften | hatte gekauft<br>hattest gekauft<br>hatte gekauft | hatten gekauft<br>hattet gekauft<br>hatten gekauft |
| | **Future** | | **Future Perfect** | |
| | werde kaufen<br>wirst kaufen<br>wird kaufen | werden kaufen<br>werdet kaufen<br>werden kaufen | werde gekauft haben<br>wirst gekauft haben<br>wird gekauft haben | werden gekauft haben<br>werdet gekauft haben<br>werden gekauft haben |
| Subjunctive | **Present** | | **Present Perfect** | |
| | kaufe<br>kaufest<br>kaufe | kaufen<br>kaufet<br>kaufen | habe gekauft<br>habest gekauft<br>habe gekauft | haben gekauft<br>habet gekauft<br>haben gekauft |
| | **Past** | | **Past Perfect** | |
| | kaufte<br>kauftest<br>kaufte | kauften<br>kauftet<br>kauften | hätte gekauft<br>hättest gekauft<br>hätte gekauft | hätten gekauft<br>hättet gekauft<br>hätten gekauft |
| | **Future** | | **Future Perfect** | |
| | werde kaufen<br>werdest kaufen<br>werde kaufen | werden kaufen<br>werdet kaufen<br>werden kaufen | werde gekauft haben<br>werdest gekauft haben<br>werde gekauft haben | werden gekauft haben<br>werdet gekauft haben<br>werden gekauft haben |
| | **Present and Future Conditional** | | **Past Conditional** | |
| | würde kaufen<br>würdest kaufen<br>würde kaufen | würden kaufen<br>würdet kaufen<br>würden kaufen | würde gekauft haben<br>würdest gekauft haben<br>würde gekauft haben | würden gekauft haben<br>würdet gekauft haben<br>würden gekauft haben |

## EXAMPLES

Wo kauft ihr gewöhnlich euer Brot?
Ich habe nur Bier und Wurst gekauft.

Where do you usually buy your bread?
I only bought beer and sausage.

**kehren**

to sweep

**Auxiliary verb:** haben **Past participle:** gekehrt

**Imperative:** Kehre! Kehrt! Kehren Sie!

| Mode | Simple Tenses | | Compound Tenses | |
|---|---|---|---|---|
| | *Singular* | *Plural* | *Singular* | *Plural* |
| Indicative | **Present** | | **Present Perfect** | |
| | kehre<br>kehrst<br>kehrt | kehren<br>kehrt<br>kehren | habe gekehrt<br>hast gekehrt<br>hat gekehrt | haben gekehrt<br>habt gekehrt<br>haben gekehrt |
| | **Past** | | **Past Perfect** | |
| | kehrte<br>kehrtest<br>kehrte | kehrten<br>kehrtet<br>kehrten | hatte gekehrt<br>hattest gekehrt<br>hatte gekehrt | hatten gekehrt<br>hattet gekehrt<br>hatten gekehrt |
| | **Future** | | **Future Perfect** | |
| | werde kehren<br>wirst kehren<br>wird kehren | werden kehren<br>werdet kehren<br>werden kehren | werde gekehrt haben<br>wirst gekehrt haben<br>wird gekehrt haben | werden gekehrt haben<br>werdet gekehrt haben<br>werden gekehrt haben |
| Subjunctive | **Present** | | **Present Perfect** | |
| | kehre<br>kehrest<br>kehre | kehren<br>kehret<br>kehren | habe gekehrt<br>habest gekehrt<br>habe gekehrt | haben gekehrt<br>habet gekehrt<br>haben gekehrt |
| | **Past** | | **Past Perfect** | |
| | kehrte<br>kehrtest<br>kehrte | kehrten<br>kehrtet<br>kehrten | hätte gekehrt<br>hättest gekehrt<br>hätte gekehrt | hätten gekehrt<br>hättet gekehrt<br>hätten gekehrt |
| | **Future** | | **Future Perfect** | |
| | werde kehren<br>werdest kehren<br>werde kehren | werden kehren<br>werdet kehren<br>werden kehren | werde gekehrt haben<br>werdest gekehrt haben<br>werde gekehrt haben | werden gekehrt haben<br>werdet gekehrt haben<br>werden gekehrt haben |
| | **Present and Future Conditional** | | **Past Conditional** | |
| | würde kehren<br>würdest kehren<br>würde kehren | würden kehren<br>würdet kehren<br>würden kehren | würde gekehrt haben<br>würdest gekehrt haben<br>würde gekehrt haben | würden gekehrt haben<br>würdet gekehrt haben<br>würden gekehrt haben |

## EXAMPLES

Kehre vor deiner eigenen Tür!
Mind your own business.

Die Zwillinge wollen helfen die Küche zu kehren.
The twins want to help sweep the kitchen.

**kennen**
to know, to be acquainted
**Auxiliary verb:** haben **Past participle:** gekannt
**Imperative:** Kenne! Kennt! Kennen Sie!

| Mode | Simple Tenses | | Compound Tenses | |
|---|---|---|---|---|
| | *Singular* | *Plural* | *Singular* | *Plural* |
| Indicative | **Present** | | **Present Perfect** | |
| | kenne<br>kennst<br>kennt | kennen<br>kennt<br>kennen | habe gekannt<br>hast gekannt<br>hat gekannt | haben gekannt<br>habt gekannt<br>haben gekannt |
| | **Past** | | **Past Perfect** | |
| | kannte<br>kanntest<br>kannte | kannten<br>kanntet<br>kannten | hatte gekannt<br>hattest gekannt<br>hatte gekannt | hatten gekannt<br>hattet gekannt<br>hatten gekannt |
| | **Future** | | **Future Perfect** | |
| | werde kennen<br>wirst kennen<br>wird kennen | werden kennen<br>werdet kennen<br>werden kennen | werde gekannt haben<br>wirst gekannt haben<br>wird gekannt haben | werden gekannt haben<br>werdet gekannt haben<br>werden gekannt haben |
| Subjunctive | **Present** | | **Present Perfect** | |
| | kenne<br>kennest<br>kenne | kennen<br>kennet<br>kennen | habe gekannt<br>habest gekannt<br>habe gekannt | haben gekannt<br>habet gekannt<br>haben gekannt |
| | **Past** | | **Past Perfect** | |
| | kennte<br>kenntest<br>kennte | kennten<br>kenntet<br>kennten | hätte gekannt<br>hättest gekannt<br>hätte gekannt | hätten gekannt<br>hättet gekannt<br>hätten gekannt |
| | **Future** | | **Future Perfect** | |
| | werde kennen<br>werdest kennen<br>werde kennen | werden kennen<br>werdet kennen<br>werden kennen | werde gekannt haben<br>werdest gekannt haben<br>werde gekannt haben | werden gekannt haben<br>werdet gekannt haben<br>werden gekannt haben |
| | **Present and Future Conditional** | | **Past Conditional** | |
| | würde kennen<br>würdest kennen<br>würde kennen | würden kennen<br>würdet kennen<br>würden kennen | würde gekannt haben<br>würdest gekannt haben<br>würde gekannt haben | würden gekannt haben<br>würdet gekannt haben<br>würden gekannt haben |

## EXAMPLES

Wir kennen uns schon.
We already know one another.

Kennen Sie das schöne Mädchen neben Herrn Schmidt?
Do you know the pretty girl next to Mr. Schmidt?

**kippen**

to tip, to tilt

**Auxiliary verb:** haben **Past participle:** gekippt

**Imperative:** Kippe! Kippt! Kippen Sie!

| Mode | Simple Tenses | | Compound Tenses | |
|---|---|---|---|---|
| | *Singular* | *Plural* | *Singular* | *Plural* |
| Indicative | **Present** | | **Present Perfect** | |
| | kippe<br>kippst<br>kippt | kippen<br>kippt<br>kippen | habe gekippt<br>hast gekippt<br>hat gekippt | haben gekippt<br>habt gekippt<br>haben gekippt |
| | **Past** | | **Past Perfect** | |
| | kippte<br>kipptest<br>kippte | kippten<br>kipptet<br>kippten | hatte gekippt<br>hattest gekippt<br>hatte gekippt | hatten gekippt<br>hattet gekippt<br>hatten gekippt |
| | **Future** | | **Future Perfect** | |
| | werde kippen<br>wirst kippen<br>wird kippen | werden kippen<br>werdet kippen<br>werden kippen | werde gekippt haben<br>wirst gekippt haben<br>wird gekippt haben | werden gekippt haben<br>werdet gekippt haben<br>werden gekippt haben |
| Subjunctive | **Present** | | **Present Perfect** | |
| | kippe<br>kippest<br>kippe | kippen<br>kippet<br>kippen | habe gekippt<br>habest gekippt<br>habe gekippt | haben gekippt<br>habet gekippt<br>haben gekippt |
| | **Past** | | **Past Perfect** | |
| | kippte<br>kipptest<br>kippte | kippten<br>kipptet<br>kippten | hätte gekippt<br>hättest gekippt<br>hätte gekippt | hätten gekippt<br>hättet gekippt<br>hätten gekippt |
| | **Future** | | **Future Perfect** | |
| | werde kippen<br>werdest kippen<br>werde kippen | werden kippen<br>werdet kippen<br>werden kippen | werde gekippt haben<br>werdest gekippt haben<br>werde gekippt haben | werden gekippt haben<br>werdet gekippt haben<br>werden gekippt haben |
| | **Present and Future Conditional** | | **Past Conditional** | |
| | würde kippen<br>würdest kippen<br>würde kippen | würden kippen<br>würdet kippen<br>würden kippen | würde gekippt haben<br>würdest gekippt haben<br>würde gekippt haben | würden gekippt haben<br>würdet gekippt haben<br>würden gekippt haben |

**Note:** With the prefix *um–*, the verb means "to tip over." Its principal parts are *kippt um, kippte um, hat umgekippt.*

## EXAMPLES

| | |
|---|---|
| Vorsicht! Der Tisch kippt gleich. | Careful. The table is about to tip over. |
| Er hat ein Glas Wasser umgekippt. | He tipped over a glass of water. |

**klagen**
to complain, to bemoan
**Auxiliary verb:** haben **Past participle:** geklagt
**Imperative:** Klage! Klagt! Klagen Sie!

| Mode | Simple Tenses | | Compound Tenses | |
|---|---|---|---|---|
| | *Singular* | *Plural* | *Singular* | *Plural* |
| Indicative | **Present** | | **Present Perfect** | |
| | klage<br>klagst<br>klagt | klagen<br>klagt<br>klagen | habe geklagt<br>hast geklagt<br>hat geklagt | haben geklagt<br>habt geklagt<br>haben geklagt |
| | **Past** | | **Past Perfect** | |
| | klagte<br>klagtest<br>klagte | klagten<br>klagtet<br>klagten | hatte geklagt<br>hattest geklagt<br>hatte geklagt | hatten geklagt<br>hattet geklagt<br>hatten geklagt |
| | **Future** | | **Future Perfect** | |
| | werde klagen<br>wirst klagen<br>wird klagen | werden klagen<br>werdet klagen<br>werden klagen | werde geklagt haben<br>wirst geklagt haben<br>wird geklagt haben | werden geklagt haben<br>werdet geklagt haben<br>werden geklagt haben |
| Subjunctive | **Present** | | **Present Perfect** | |
| | klage<br>klagest<br>klage | klagen<br>klaget<br>klagen | habe geklagt<br>habest geklagt<br>habe geklagt | haben geklagt<br>habet geklagt<br>haben geklagt |
| | **Past** | | **Past Perfect** | |
| | klagte<br>klagtest<br>klagte | klagten<br>klagtet<br>klagten | hätte geklagt<br>hättest geklagt<br>hätte geklagt | hätten geklagt<br>hättet geklagt<br>hätten geklagt |
| | **Future** | | **Future Perfect** | |
| | werde klagen<br>werdest klagen<br>werde klagen | werden klagen<br>werdet klagen<br>werden klagen | werde geklagt haben<br>werdest geklagt haben<br>werde geklagt haben | werden geklagt haben<br>werdet geklagt haben<br>werden geklagt haben |
| | **Present and Future Conditional** | | **Past Conditional** | |
| | würde klagen<br>würdest klagen<br>würde klagen | würden klagen<br>würdet klagen<br>würden klagen | würde geklagt haben<br>würdest geklagt haben<br>würde geklagt haben | würden geklagt haben<br>würdet geklagt haben<br>würden geklagt haben |

## EXAMPLES

Ich kann nicht klagen. Mir geht's gut.
I can't complain. I'm fine.

Frau Bauer hat vor Gericht gegen einen ihrer Mieter geklagt.
Mrs. Bauer made a complaint in court against one of her tenants.

**klappen**

to work out well, to fold, to tilt

**Auxiliary verb:** haben **Past participle:** geklappt

**Imperative:** Klappe! Klappt! Klappen Sie!

| Mode | Simple Tenses | | Compound Tenses | |
|---|---|---|---|---|
| | *Singular* | *Plural* | *Singular* | *Plural* |
| Indicative | **Present** | | **Present Perfect** | |
| | klappe<br>klappst<br>klappt | klappen<br>klappt<br>klappen | habe geklappt<br>hast geklappt<br>hat geklappt | haben geklappt<br>habt geklappt<br>haben geklappt |
| | **Past** | | **Past Perfect** | |
| | klappte<br>klapptest<br>klappte | klapptcn<br>klapptet<br>klappten | hatto goklappt<br>hattest geklappt<br>hatte geklappt | hatten geklappt<br>hattet geklappt<br>hatten geklappt |
| | **Future** | | **Future Perfect** | |
| | werde klappen<br>wirst klappen<br>wird klappen | werden klappen<br>werdet klappen<br>werden klappen | werde geklappt haben<br>wirst geklappt haben<br>wird geklappt haben | werden geklappt haben<br>werdet geklappt haben<br>werden geklappt haben |
| Subjunctive | **Present** | | **Present Perfect** | |
| | klappe<br>klappest<br>klappe | klappen<br>klappet<br>klappen | habe geklappt<br>habest geklappt<br>habe geklappt | haben geklappt<br>habet geklappt<br>haben geklappt |
| | **Past** | | **Past Perfect** | |
| | klappte<br>klapptest<br>klappte | klappten<br>klapptet<br>klappten | hätte geklappt<br>hättest geklappt<br>hätte geklappt | hätten geklappt<br>hättet geklappt<br>hätten geklappt |
| | **Future** | | **Future Perfect** | |
| | werde klappen<br>werdest klappen<br>werde klappen | werden klappen<br>werdet klappen<br>werden klappen | werde geklappt haben<br>werdest geklappt haben<br>werde geklappt haben | werden geklappt haben<br>werdet geklappt haben<br>werden geklappt haben |
| | **Present and Future Conditional** | | **Past Conditional** | |
| | würde klappen<br>würdest klappen<br>würde klappen | würden klappen<br>würdet klappen<br>würden klappen | würde geklappt haben<br>würdest geklappt haben<br>würde geklappt haben | würden geklappt haben<br>würdet geklappt haben<br>würden geklappt haben |

**Note:** *Klappen* is only used with the third person when it means "to work out well."

## EXAMPLES

| | |
|---|---|
| Der Projekt hat gut geklappt. | The project worked out well. |
| Alles klappte großartig. | Everything turned out great. |
| Klapp den Sitz nach vorne! | Tilt the seat forward. |

**klatschen**
to clap, to applaud
**Auxiliary verb:** haben **Past participle:** geklatscht
**Imperative:** Klatsche! Klatscht! Klatschen Sie!

| Mode | Simple Tenses | | Compound Tenses | |
|---|---|---|---|---|
| | *Singular* | *Plural* | *Singular* | *Plural* |
| Indicative | **Present** | | **Present Perfect** | |
| | klatsche<br>klatschst<br>klatscht | klatschen<br>klatscht<br>klatschen | habe geklatscht<br>hast geklatscht<br>hat geklatscht | haben geklatscht<br>habt geklatscht<br>haben geklatscht |
| | **Past** | | **Past Perfect** | |
| | klatschte<br>klatschtest<br>klatschte | klatschten<br>klatschtet<br>klatschten | hatte geklatscht<br>hattest geklatscht<br>hatte geklatscht | hatten geklatscht<br>hattet geklatscht<br>hatten geklatscht |
| | **Future** | | **Future Perfect** | |
| | werde klatschen<br>wirst klatschen<br>wird klatschen | werden klatschen<br>werdet klatschen<br>werden klatschen | werde geklatscht haben<br>wirst geklatscht haben<br>wird geklatscht haben | werden geklatscht haben<br>werdet geklatscht haben<br>werden geklatscht haben |
| Subjunctive | **Present** | | **Present Perfect** | |
| | klatsche<br>klatschest<br>klatsche | klatschen<br>klatschet<br>klatschen | habe geklatscht<br>habest geklatscht<br>habe geklatscht | haben geklatscht<br>habet geklatscht<br>haben geklatscht |
| | **Past** | | **Past Perfect** | |
| | klatschte<br>klatschtest<br>klatschte | klatschten<br>klatschtet<br>klatschten | hätte geklatscht<br>hättest geklatscht<br>hätte geklatscht | hätten geklatscht<br>hättet geklatscht<br>hätten geklatscht |
| | **Future** | | **Future Perfect** | |
| | werde klatschen<br>werdest klatschen<br>werde klatschen | werden klatschen<br>werdet klatschen<br>werden klatschen | werde geklatscht haben<br>werdest geklatscht haben<br>werde geklatscht haben | werden geklatscht haben<br>werdet geklatscht haben<br>werden geklatscht haben |
| | **Present and Future Conditional** | | **Past Conditional** | |
| | würde klatschen<br>würdest klatschen<br>würde klatschen | würden klatschen<br>würdet klatschen<br>würden klatschen | würde geklatscht haben<br>würdest geklatscht haben<br>würde geklatscht haben | würden geklatscht haben<br>würdet geklatscht haben<br>würden geklatscht haben |

## EXAMPLE

Das Publikum ist vom Schauspiel begeistert und klatscht Beifall.
The audience enjoys the play a lot and applauds.

Die Kinder klatschen in die Hände und singen.
The children clap their hands and sing.

**kleben**

to glue, to paste, to stick

**Auxiliary verb:** haben **Past participle:** geklebt

**Imperative:** Klebe! Klebt! Kleben Sie!

| Mode | Simple Tenses | | Compound Tenses | |
|---|---|---|---|---|
| | *Singular* | *Plural* | *Singular* | *Plural* |
| Indicative | **Present** | | **Present Perfect** | |
| | klebe<br>klebst<br>klebt | kleben<br>klebt<br>kleben | habe geklebt<br>hast geklebt<br>hat geklebt | haben geklebt<br>habt geklebt<br>haben geklebt |
| | **Past** | | **Past Perfect** | |
| | klebte<br>klebtest<br>klebte | klebten<br>klebtet<br>klebten | hatte geklebt<br>hattest geklebt<br>hatte geklebt | hatten geklebt<br>hattet geklebt<br>hatten geklebt |
| | **Future** | | **Future Perfect** | |
| | werde kleben<br>wirst kleben<br>wird kleben | werden kleben<br>werdet kleben<br>werden kleben | werde geklebt haben<br>wirst geklebt haben<br>wird geklebt haben | werden geklebt haben<br>werdet geklebt haben<br>werden geklebt haben |
| Subjunctive | **Present** | | **Present Perfect** | |
| | klebe<br>klebest<br>klebe | kleben<br>klebet<br>kleben | habe geklebt<br>habest geklebt<br>habe geklebt | haben geklebt<br>habet geklebt<br>haben geklebt |
| | **Past** | | **Past Perfect** | |
| | klebte<br>klebtest<br>klebte | klebten<br>klebtet<br>klebten | hätte geklebt<br>hättest geklebt<br>hätte geklebt | hätten geklebt<br>hättet geklebt<br>hätten geklebt |
| | **Future** | | **Future Perfect** | |
| | werde kleben<br>werdest kleben<br>werde kleben | werden kleben<br>werdet kleben<br>werden kleben | werde geklebt haben<br>werdest geklebt haben<br>werde geklebt haben | werden geklebt haben<br>werdet geklebt haben<br>werden geklebt haben |
| | **Present and Future Conditional** | | **Past Conditional** | |
| | würde kleben<br>würdest kleben<br>würde kleben | würden kleben<br>würdet kleben<br>würden kleben | würde geklebt haben<br>würdest geklebt haben<br>würde geklebt haben | würden geklebt haben<br>würdet geklebt haben<br>würden geklebt haben |

## EXAMPLES

Sie haben nicht genug Briefmarken auf diesen Brief geklebt.

You haven't put enough stamps on this letter.

An deiner Jacke klebt Kaugummi.

There's chewing gum stuck on your jacket.

**kleiden (sich)**
to dress, to get dressed
**Auxiliary verb:** haben **Past participle:** gekleidet
**Imperative:** Kleide! Kleidet! Kleiden Sie!

| Mode | Simple Tenses | | Compound Tenses | |
|---|---|---|---|---|
| | *Singular* | *Plural* | *Singular* | *Plural* |
| Indicative | **Present** | | **Present Perfect** | |
| | kleide<br>kleidest<br>kleidet | kleiden<br>kleidet<br>kleiden | habe gekleidet<br>hast gekleidet<br>hat gekleidet | haben gekleidet<br>habt gekleidet<br>haben gekleidet |
| | **Past** | | **Past Perfect** | |
| | kleidete<br>kleidetest<br>kleidete | kleideten<br>kleidetet<br>kleideten | hatte gekleidet<br>hattest gekleidet<br>hatte gekleidet | hatten gekleidet<br>hattet gekleidet<br>hatten gekleidet |
| | **Future** | | **Future Perfect** | |
| | werde kleiden<br>wirst kleiden<br>wird kleiden | werden kleiden<br>werdet kleiden<br>werden kleiden | werde gekleidet haben<br>wirst gekleidet haben<br>wird gekleidet haben | werden gekleidet haben<br>werdet gekleidet haben<br>werden gekleidet haben |
| Subjunctive | **Present** | | **Present Perfect** | |
| | kleide<br>kleidest<br>kleide | kleiden<br>kleidet<br>kleiden | habe gekleidet<br>habest gekleidet<br>habe gekleidet | haben gekleidet<br>habet gekleidet<br>haben gekleidet |
| | **Past** | | **Past Perfect** | |
| | kleidete<br>kleidetest<br>kleidete | kleideten<br>kleidetet<br>kleideten | hätte gekleidet<br>hättest gekleidet<br>hätte gekleidet | hätten gekleidet<br>hättet gekleidet<br>hätten gekleidet |
| | **Future** | | **Future Perfect** | |
| | werde kleiden<br>werdest kleiden<br>werde kleiden | werden kleiden<br>werdet kleiden<br>werden kleiden | werde gekleidet haben<br>werdest gekleidet haben<br>werde gekleidet haben | werden gekleidet haben<br>werdet gekleidet haben<br>werden gekleidet haben |
| | **Present and Future Conditional** | | **Past Conditional** | |
| | würde kleiden<br>würdest kleiden<br>würde kleiden | würden kleiden<br>würdet kleiden<br>würden kleiden | würde gekleidet haben<br>würdest gekleidet haben<br>würde gekleidet haben | würden gekleidet haben<br>würdet gekleidet haben<br>würden gekleidet haben |

## EXAMPLES

Die Braut war traditionell gekleidet.
The bride was dressed in traditional garb.

Professor Schäfer kleidet sich immer gut.
Professor Schäfer always dresses well.

**klettern**
to climb
**Auxiliary verb:** sein **Past participle:** geklettert
**Imperative:** Klettere! Klettert! Klettern Sie!

| Mode | Simple Tenses | | Compound Tenses | |
|---|---|---|---|---|
| | *Singular* | *Plural* | *Singular* | *Plural* |
| Indicative | **Present** | | **Present Perfect** | |
| | klettere<br>kletterst<br>klettert | klettern<br>klettert<br>klettern | bin geklettert<br>bist geklettert<br>ist geklettert | sind geklettert<br>seid geklettert<br>sind geklettert |
| | **Past** | | **Past Perfect** | |
| | kletterte<br>klettertest<br>kletterte | kletterten<br>klettertet<br>kletterten | war geklettert<br>warst geklettert<br>war geklettert | waren geklettert<br>wart geklettert<br>waren geklettert |
| | **Future** | | **Future Perfect** | |
| | werde klettern<br>wirst klettern<br>wird klettern | werden klettern<br>werdet klettern<br>werden klettern | werde geklettert sein<br>wirst geklettert sein<br>wird geklettert sein | werden geklettert sein<br>werdet geklettert sein<br>werden geklettert sein |
| Subjunctive | **Present** | | **Present Perfect** | |
| | klettere<br>kletterst<br>klettere | klettern<br>klettert<br>klettern | sei geklettert<br>seiest geklettert<br>sei geklettert | seien geklettert<br>seiet geklettert<br>seien geklettert |
| | **Past** | | **Past Perfect** | |
| | kletterte<br>klettertest<br>kletterte | kletterten<br>klettertet<br>kletterten | wäre geklettert<br>wärest geklettert<br>wäre geklettert | wären geklettert<br>wäret geklettert<br>wären geklettert |
| | **Future** | | **Future Perfect** | |
| | werde klettern<br>werdest klettern<br>werde klettern | werden klettern<br>werdet klettern<br>werden klettern | werde geklettert sein<br>werdest geklettert sein<br>werde geklettert sein | werden geklettert sein<br>werdet geklettert sein<br>werden geklettert sein |
| | **Present and Future Conditional** | | **Past Conditional** | |
| | würde klettern<br>würdest klettern<br>würde klettern | würden klettern<br>würdet klettern<br>würden klettern | würde geklettert sein<br>würdest geklettert sein<br>würde geklettert sein | würden geklettert sein<br>würdet geklettert sein<br>würden geklettert sein |

## EXAMPLES

Die alte Katze ist auf einen hohen Baum geklettert. — The old cat climbed up a tall tree.
Ein Freund von mir ist beim Klettern abgestürzt. — A friend of mine fell while climbing.

**klingeln**
to ring, to tinkle
**Auxiliary verb:** haben **Past participle:** geklingelt
**Imperative:** Klingle! Klingelt! Klingeln Sie!

| Mode | Simple Tenses | | Compound Tenses | |
|---|---|---|---|---|
| | *Singular* | *Plural* | *Singular* | *Plural* |
| Indicative | **Present** | | **Present Perfect** | |
| | klingle<br>klingelst<br>klingelt | klingeln<br>klingelt<br>klingeln | habe geklingelt<br>hast geklingelt<br>hat geklingelt | haben geklingelt<br>habt geklingelt<br>haben geklingelt |
| | **Past** | | **Past Perfect** | |
| | klingelte<br>klingeltest<br>klingelte | klingelten<br>klingeltet<br>klingelten | hatte geklingelt<br>hattest geklingelt<br>hatte geklingelt | hatten geklingelt<br>hattet geklingelt<br>hatten geklingelt |
| | **Future** | | **Future Perfect** | |
| | werde klingeln<br>wirst klingeln<br>wird klingeln | werden klingeln<br>werdet klingeln<br>werden klingeln | werde geklingelt haben<br>wirst geklingelt haben<br>wird geklingelt haben | werden geklingelt haben<br>werdet geklingelt haben<br>werden geklingelt haben |
| Subjunctive | **Present** | | **Present Perfect** | |
| | klingele<br>klingelst<br>klingele | klingeln<br>klingelt<br>klingeln | habe geklingelt<br>habest geklingelt<br>habe geklingelt | haben geklingelt<br>habet geklingelt<br>haben geklingelt |
| | **Past** | | **Past Perfect** | |
| | klingelte<br>klingeltest<br>klingelte | klingelten<br>klingeltet<br>klingelten | hätte geklingelt<br>hättest geklingelt<br>hätte geklingelt | hätten geklingelt<br>hättet geklingelt<br>hätten geklingelt |
| | **Future** | | **Future Perfect** | |
| | werde klingeln<br>werdest klingeln<br>werde klingeln | werden klingeln<br>werdet klingeln<br>werden klingeln | werde geklingelt haben<br>werdest geklingelt haben<br>werde geklingelt haben | werden geklingelt haben<br>werdet geklingelt haben<br>werden geklingelt haben |
| | **Present and Future Conditional** | | **Past Conditional** | |
| | würde klingeln<br>würdest klingeln<br>würde klingeln | würden klingeln<br>würdet klingeln<br>würden klingeln | würde geklingelt haben<br>würdest geklingelt haben<br>würde geklingelt haben | würden geklingelt haben<br>würdet geklingelt haben<br>würden geklingelt haben |

## EXAMPLES

Während des Films klingelten ständig die Handys.
Cell phones kept ringing during the movie.

Es klingelt.
The doorbell's ringing.

**klingen**

to sound, to ring

**Auxiliary verb:** haben **Past participle:** geklungen

**Imperative:** Klinge! Klingt! Klingen Sie!

| Mode | Simple Tenses | | Compound Tenses | |
|---|---|---|---|---|
| | *Singular* | *Plural* | *Singular* | *Plural* |
| Indicative | **Present** | | **Present Perfect** | |
| | klinge<br>klingst<br>klingt | klingen<br>klingt<br>klingen | habe geklungen<br>hast geklungen<br>hat geklungen | haben geklungen<br>habt geklungen<br>haben geklungen |
| | **Past** | | **Past Perfect** | |
| | klang<br>klangst<br>klang | klangen<br>klangt<br>klangen | hatte geklungen<br>hattest geklungen<br>hatte geklungen | hatten geklungen<br>hattet geklungen<br>hatten geklungen |
| | **Future** | | **Future Perfect** | |
| | werde klingen<br>wirst klingen<br>wird klingen | werden klingen<br>werdet klingen<br>werden klingen | werde geklungen haben<br>wirst geklungen haben<br>wird geklungen haben | werden geklungen haben<br>werdet geklungen haben<br>werden geklungen haben |
| Subjunctive | **Present** | | **Present Perfect** | |
| | klinge<br>klingest<br>klinge | klingen<br>klinget<br>klingen | habe geklungen<br>habest geklungen<br>habe geklungen | haben geklungen<br>habet geklungen<br>haben geklungen |
| | **Past** | | **Past Perfect** | |
| | klänge<br>klängest<br>klänge | klängen<br>klänget<br>klängen | hätte geklungen<br>hättest geklungen<br>hätte geklungen | hätten geklungen<br>hättet geklungen<br>hätten geklungen |
| | **Future** | | **Future Perfect** | |
| | werde klingen<br>werdest klingen<br>werde klingen | werden klingen<br>werdet klingen<br>werden klingen | werde geklungen haben<br>werdest geklungen haben<br>werde geklungen haben | werden geklungen haben<br>werdet geklungen haben<br>werden geklungen haben |
| | **Present and Future Conditional** | | **Past Conditional** | |
| | würde klingen<br>würdest klingen<br>würde klingen | würden klingen<br>würdet klingen<br>würden klingen | würde geklungen haben<br>würdest geklungen haben<br>würde geklungen haben | würden geklungen haben<br>würdet geklungen haben<br>würden geklungen haben |

## EXAMPLES

Diese Band klingt ziemlich altmodisch.
This bands sounds rather old-fashioned.

Ihre Idee klingt merkwürdig.
Your idea sounds strange.

**klopfen**
to knock, to beat, to rap
**Auxiliary verb:** haben **Past participle:** geklopft
**Imperative:** Klopfe! Klopft! Klopfen Sie!

| Mode | Simple Tenses | | Compound Tenses | |
|---|---|---|---|---|
| | *Singular* | *Plural* | *Singular* | *Plural* |
| Indicative | **Present** | | **Present Perfect** | |
| | klopfe<br>klopfst<br>klopft | klopfen<br>klopft<br>klopfen | habe geklopft<br>hast geklopft<br>hat geklopft | haben geklopft<br>habt geklopft<br>haben geklopft |
| | **Past** | | **Past Perfect** | |
| | klopfte<br>klopftest<br>klopfte | klopften<br>klopftet<br>klopften | hatte geklopft<br>hattest geklopft<br>hatte geklopft | hatten geklopft<br>hattet geklopft<br>hatten geklopft |
| | **Future** | | **Future Perfect** | |
| | werde klopfen<br>wirst klopfen<br>wird klopfen | werden klopfen<br>werdet klopfen<br>werden klopfen | werde geklopft haben<br>wirst geklopft haben<br>wird geklopft haben | werden geklopft haben<br>werdet geklopft haben<br>werden geklopft haben |
| Subjunctive | **Present** | | **Present Perfect** | |
| | klopfe<br>klopfest<br>klopfe | klopfen<br>klopfet<br>klopfen | habe geklopft<br>habest geklopft<br>habe geklopft | haben geklopft<br>habet geklopft<br>haben geklopft |
| | **Past** | | **Past Perfect** | |
| | klopfte<br>klopftest<br>klopfte | klopften<br>klopftet<br>klopften | hätte geklopft<br>hättest geklopft<br>hätte geklopft | hätten geklopft<br>hättet geklopft<br>hätten geklopft |
| | **Future** | | **Future Perfect** | |
| | werde klopfen<br>werdest klopfen<br>werde klopfen | werden klopfen<br>werdet klopfen<br>werden klopfen | werde geklopft haben<br>werdest geklopft haben<br>werde geklopft haben | werden geklopft haben<br>werdet geklopft haben<br>werden geklopft haben |
| | **Present and Future Conditional** | | **Past Conditional** | |
| | würde klopfen<br>würdest klopfen<br>würde klopfen | würden klopfen<br>würdet klopfen<br>würden klopfen | würde geklopft haben<br>würdest geklopft haben<br>würde geklopft haben | würden geklopft haben<br>würdet geklopft haben<br>würden geklopft haben |

## EXAMPLES

Großmutter hat mir auf die Finger geklopft. — Grandmother rapped me over the knuckles.
Bitte klopfen! — Knock before entering.

**knattern**

to rattle, to clatter

**Auxiliary verb:** haben **Past participle:** geknattert

**Imperative:** Knattere! Knattert! Knattern Sie!

| Mode | Simple Tenses | | Compound Tenses | |
|---|---|---|---|---|
| | *Singular* | *Plural* | *Singular* | *Plural* |
| Indicative | **Present** | | **Present Perfect** | |
| | knattere<br>knatterst<br>knattert | knattern<br>knattert<br>knattern | habe geknattert<br>hast geknattert<br>hat geknattert | haben geknattert<br>habt geknattert<br>haben geknattert |
| | **Past** | | **Past Perfect** | |
| | knatterte<br>knattertest<br>knatterte | knatterten<br>knattertet<br>knatterten | hatte geknattert<br>hattest geknattert<br>hatte geknattert | hatten geknattert<br>hattet geknattert<br>hatten geknattert |
| | **Future** | | **Future Perfect** | |
| | werde knattern<br>wirst knattern<br>wird knattern | werden knattern<br>werdet knattern<br>werden knattern | werde geknattert haben<br>wirst geknattert haben<br>wird geknattert haben | werden geknattert haben<br>werdet geknattert haben<br>werden geknattert haben |
| Subjunctive | **Present** | | **Present Perfect** | |
| | knattere<br>knatterst<br>knattere | knattern<br>knattert<br>knattern | habe geknattert<br>habest geknattert<br>habe geknattert | haben geknattert<br>habet geknattert<br>haben geknattert |
| | **Past** | | **Past Perfect** | |
| | knatterte<br>knattertest<br>knatterte | knatterten<br>knattertet<br>knatterten | hätte geknattert<br>hättest geknattert<br>hätte geknattert | hätten geknattert<br>hättet geknattert<br>hätten geknattert |
| | **Future** | | **Future Perfect** | |
| | werde knattern<br>werdest knattern<br>werde knattern | werden knattern<br>werdet knattern<br>werden knattern | werde geknattert haben<br>werdest geknattert haben<br>werde geknattert haben | werden geknattert haben<br>werdet geknattert haben<br>werden geknattert haben |
| | **Present and Future Conditional** | | **Past Conditional** | |
| | würde knattern<br>würdest knattern<br>würde knattern | würden knattern<br>würdet knattern<br>würden knattern | würde geknattert haben<br>würdest geknattert haben<br>würde geknattert haben | würden geknattert haben<br>würdet geknattert haben<br>würden geknattert haben |

## EXAMPLES

In der Ferne hörten wir das Knattern der Motorräder.

In the distance, we heard the clattering of motorcycles.

Ein alter Wagen knatterte die Hauptstraße entlang.

An old car rattled down Main Street.

**knüpfen**
to fasten together, to join
**Auxiliary verb:** haben **Past participle:** geknüpft
**Imperative:** Knüpfe! Knüpft! Knüpfen Sie!

| Mode | Simple Tenses | | Compound Tenses | |
|---|---|---|---|---|
| | *Singular* | *Plural* | *Singular* | *Plural* |
| Indicative | **Present** | | **Present Perfect** | |
| | knüpfe<br>knüpfst<br>knüpft | knüpfen<br>knüpft<br>knüpfen | habe geknüpft<br>hast geknüpft<br>hat geknüpft | haben geknüpft<br>habt geknüpft<br>haben geknüpft |
| | **Past** | | **Past Perfect** | |
| | knüpfte<br>knüpftest<br>knüpfte | knüpften<br>knüpftet<br>knüpften | hatte geknüpft<br>hattest geknüpft<br>hatte geknüpft | hatten geknüpft<br>hattet geknüpft<br>hatten geknüpft |
| | **Future** | | **Future Perfect** | |
| | werde knüpfen<br>wirst knüpfen<br>wird knüpfen | werden knüpfen<br>werdet knüpfen<br>werden knüpfen | werde geknüpft haben<br>wirst geknüpft haben<br>wird geknüpft haben | werden geknüpft haben<br>werdet geknüpft haben<br>werden geknüpft haben |
| Subjunctive | **Present** | | **Present Perfect** | |
| | knüpfe<br>knüpfest<br>knüpfe | knüpfen<br>knüpfet<br>knüpfen | habe geknüpft<br>habest geknüpft<br>habe geknüpft | haben geknüpft<br>habet geknüpft<br>haben geknüpft |
| | **Past** | | **Past Perfect** | |
| | knüpfte<br>knüpftest<br>knüpfte | knüpften<br>knüpftet<br>knüpften | hätte geknüpft<br>hättest geknüpft<br>hätte geknüpft | hätten geknüpft<br>hättet geknüpft<br>hätten geknüpft |
| | **Future** | | **Future Perfect** | |
| | werde knüpfen<br>werdest knüpfen<br>werde knüpfen | werden knüpfen<br>werdet knüpfen<br>werden knüpfen | werde geknüpft haben<br>werdest geknüpft haben<br>werde geknüpft haben | werden geknüpft haben<br>werdet geknüpft haben<br>werden geknüpft haben |
| | **Present and Future Conditional** | | **Past Conditional** | |
| | würde knüpfen<br>würdest knüpfen<br>würde knüpfen | würden knüpfen<br>würdet knüpfen<br>würden knüpfen | würde geknüpft haben<br>würdest geknüpft haben<br>würde geknüpft haben | würden geknüpft haben<br>würdet geknüpft haben<br>würden geknüpft haben |

## EXAMPLES

Viele europäische Länder hatten ein Bündnis gegen Napoleon geknüpft.
Many European countries had formed an alliance against Napoleon.

Bei diesem Geschäftessen hat Herr Bauer viele neue Kontakte geknüpft.
At this business dinner Mr. Bauer made many new contacts.

**kochen**

to cook, to boil

**Auxiliary verb:** haben **Past participle:** gekocht

**Imperative:** Koche! Kocht! Kochen Sie!

| Mode | Simple Tenses | | Compound Tenses | |
|---|---|---|---|---|
| | *Singular* | *Plural* | *Singular* | *Plural* |
| Indicative | **Present** | | **Present Perfect** | |
| | koche<br>kochst<br>kocht | kochen<br>kocht<br>kochen | habe gekocht<br>hast gekocht<br>hat gekocht | haben gekocht<br>habt gekocht<br>haben gekocht |
| | **Past** | | **Past Perfect** | |
| | kochte<br>kochtest<br>kochte | kochten<br>kochtet<br>kochten | hatte gekocht<br>hattest gekocht<br>hatte gekocht | hatten gekocht<br>hattet gekocht<br>hatten gekocht |
| | **Future** | | **Future Perfect** | |
| | werde kochen<br>wirst kochen<br>wird kochen | werden kochen<br>werdet kochen<br>werden kochen | werde gekocht haben<br>wirst gekocht haben<br>wird gekocht haben | werden gekocht haben<br>werdet gekocht haben<br>werden gekocht haben |
| Subjunctive | **Present** | | **Present Perfect** | |
| | koche<br>kochest<br>koche | kochen<br>kochet<br>kochen | habe gekocht<br>habest gekocht<br>habe gekocht | haben gekocht<br>habet gekocht<br>haben gekocht |
| | **Past** | | **Past Perfect** | |
| | kochte<br>kochtest<br>kochte | kochten<br>kochtet<br>kochten | hätte gekocht<br>hättest gekocht<br>hätte gekocht | hätten gekocht<br>hättet gekocht<br>hätten gekocht |
| | **Future** | | **Future Perfect** | |
| | werde kochen<br>werdest kochen<br>werde kochen | werden kochen<br>werdet kochen<br>werden kochen | werde gekocht haben<br>werdest gekocht haben<br>werde gekocht haben | werden gekocht haben<br>werdet gekocht haben<br>werden gekocht haben |
| | **Present and Future Conditional** | | **Past Conditional** | |
| | würde kochen<br>würdest kochen<br>würde kochen | würden kochen<br>würdet kochen<br>würden kochen | würde gekocht haben<br>würdest gekocht haben<br>würde gekocht haben | würden gekocht haben<br>würdet gekocht haben<br>würden gekocht haben |

## EXAMPLES

Mein Mann kocht sehr gut.
My husband's a very good cook.

Zum Abendessen hat Simone etwas Besonderes gekocht.
Simone made something special for supper.

**kommen**
to come
**Auxiliary verb:** sein **Past participle:** gekommen
**Imperative:** Komme! Kommt! Kommen Sie!

| Mode | Simple Tenses | | Compound Tenses | |
|---|---|---|---|---|
| | *Singular* | *Plural* | *Singular* | *Plural* |
| Indicative | **Present** | | **Present Perfect** | |
| | komme<br>kommst<br>kommt | kommen<br>kommt<br>kommen | bin gekommen<br>bist gekommen<br>ist gekommen | sind gekommen<br>seid gekommen<br>sind gekommen |
| | **Past** | | **Past Perfect** | |
| | kam<br>kamst<br>kam | kamen<br>kamt<br>kamen | war gekommen<br>warst gekommen<br>war gekommen | waren gekommen<br>wart gekommen<br>waren gekommen |
| | **Future** | | **Future Perfect** | |
| | werde kommen<br>wirst kommen<br>wird kommen | werden kommen<br>werdet kommen<br>werden kommen | werde gekommen sein<br>wirst gekommen sein<br>wird gekommen sein | werden gekommen sein<br>werdet gekommen sein<br>werden gekommen sein |
| Subjunctive | **Present** | | **Present Perfect** | |
| | komme<br>kommest<br>komme | kommen<br>kommet<br>kommen | sei gekommen<br>seiest gekommen<br>sei gekommen | seien gekommen<br>seiet gekommen<br>seien gekommen |
| | **Past** | | **Past Perfect** | |
| | käme<br>kämest<br>käme | kämen<br>kämet<br>kämen | wäre gekommen<br>wärest gekommen<br>wäre gekommen | wären gekommen<br>wäret gekommen<br>wären gekommen |
| | **Future** | | **Future Perfect** | |
| | werde kommen<br>werdest kommen<br>werde kommen | werden kommen<br>werdet kommen<br>werden kommen | werde gekommen sein<br>werdest gekommen sein<br>werde gekommen sein | werden gekommen sein<br>werdet gekommen sein<br>werden gekommen sein |
| | **Present and Future Conditional** | | **Past Conditional** | |
| | würde kommen<br>würdoot kommen<br>würde kommen | wurden kommen<br>würdet kommen<br>würden kommen | würde gekommen sein<br>würdest gekommen sein<br>würde gekommen sein | würden gekommen sein<br>wurdet gekommen sein<br>würden gekommen sein |

**Note:** With inseparable prefixes, the principal parts of this verb are, for example, *entkommt, entkam, ist entkommen.* With the prefix *be–,* the verb becomes transitive and requires the auxiliary *haben* in the perfect tenses: *Er hat einen Brief bekommen* (He received a letter). With separable prefixes, the principal parts are, for example, *kommt an, kam an, ist angekommen.*

## EXAMPLES

Meine Verwandten kommen aus Italien. — My relatives come from Italy.
Um wieviel Uhr sind die Touristen gekommen? — At what time did the tourists come?

**können**

to be able to, can, to know a language

**Auxiliary verb:** haben **Past participle:** gekonnt

**Imperative:** N/A

| Mode | Simple Tenses | | Compound Tenses | |
|---|---|---|---|---|
| | *Singular* | *Plural* | *Singular* | *Plural* |
| Indicative | **Present** | | **Present Perfect** | |
| | kann<br>kannst<br>kann | können<br>könnt<br>können | habe gekonnt<br>hast gekonnt<br>hat gekonnt | haben gekonnt<br>habt gekonnt<br>haben gekonnt |
| | **Past** | | **Past Perfect** | |
| | konnte<br>konntest<br>konnte | konnten<br>konntet<br>konnten | hatte gekonnt<br>hattest gekonnt<br>hatte gekonnt | hatten gekonnt<br>hattet gekonnt<br>hatten gekonnt |
| | **Future** | | **Future Perfect** | |
| | werde können<br>wirst können<br>wird können | werden können<br>werdet können<br>werden können | werde gekonnt haben<br>wirst gekonnt haben<br>wird gekonnt haben | werden gekonnt haben<br>werdet gekonnt haben<br>werden gekonnt haben |
| Subjunctive | **Present** | | **Present Perfect** | |
| | könne<br>könnest<br>könne | können<br>könnet<br>können | habe gekonnt<br>habest gekonnt<br>habe gekonnt | haben gekonnt<br>habet gekonnt<br>haben gekonnt |
| | **Past** | | **Past Perfect** | |
| | könnte<br>könntest<br>könnte | könnten<br>könntet<br>könnten | hätte gekonnt<br>hättest gekonnt<br>hätte gekonnt | hätten gekonnt<br>hättet gekonnt<br>hätten gekonnt |
| | **Future** | | **Future Perfect** | |
| | werde können<br>werdest können<br>werde können | werden können<br>werdet können<br>werden können | werde gekonnt haben<br>werdest gekonnt haben<br>werde gekonnt haben | werden gekonnt haben<br>werdet gekonnt haben<br>werden gekonnt haben |
| | **Present and Future Conditional** | | **Past Conditional** | |
| | würde können<br>würdest können<br>würde können | würden können<br>würdet können<br>würden können | würde gekonnt haben<br>würdest gekonnt haben<br>würde gekonnt haben | würden gekonnt haben<br>würdet gekonnt haben<br>würden gekonnt haben |

***Note:*** This verb is a modal auxiliary. In the perfect and future tenses, when there is a second verb in the sentence, a double-infinitive structure is required: *Haben Sie mit ihm sprechen können?* (Were you able to speak with him?)

## EXAMPLES

| | |
|---|---|
| Die Studenten können die Vorlesung nicht verstehen. | The students cannot understand the lecture. |
| Ich kann Englisch und Deutsch. | I know English and German. |

**kosten**

to cost, to taste

**Auxiliary verb:** haben **Past participle:** gekostet

**Imperative:** Koste! Kostet! Kosten Sie!

| Mode | Simple Tenses | | Compound Tenses | |
|---|---|---|---|---|
| | *Singular* | *Plural* | *Singular* | *Plural* |
| Indicative | **Present** | | **Present Perfect** | |
| | koste<br>kostest<br>kostet | kosten<br>kostet<br>kosten | habe gekostet<br>hast gekostet<br>hat gekostet | haben gekostet<br>habt gekostet<br>haben gekostet |
| | **Past** | | **Past Perfect** | |
| | kostete<br>kostetest<br>kostete | kosteten<br>kostetet<br>kosteten | hatte gekostet<br>hattest gekostet<br>hatte gekostet | hatten gekostet<br>hattet gekostet<br>hatten gekostet |
| | **Future** | | **Future Perfect** | |
| | werde kosten<br>wirst kosten<br>wird kosten | werden kosten<br>werdet kosten<br>werden kosten | werde gekostet haben<br>wirst gekostet haben<br>wird gekostet haben | werden gekostet haben<br>werdet gekostet haben<br>werden gekostet haben |
| Subjunctive | **Present** | | **Present Perfect** | |
| | koste<br>kostest<br>koste | kosten<br>kostet<br>kosten | habe gekostet<br>habest gekostet<br>habe gekostet | haben gekostet<br>habet gekostet<br>haben gekostet |
| | **Past** | | **Past Perfect** | |
| | kostete<br>kostetest<br>kostete | kosteten<br>kostetet<br>kosteten | hätte gekostet<br>hättest gekostet<br>hätte gekostet | hätten gekostet<br>hättet gekostet<br>hätten gekostet |
| | **Future** | | **Future Perfect** | |
| | werde kosten<br>werdest kosten<br>werde kosten | werden kosten<br>werdet kosten<br>werden kosten | werde gekostet haben<br>werdest gekostet haben<br>werde gekostet haben | werden gekostet haben<br>werdet gekostet haben<br>werden gekostet haben |
| | **Present and Future Conditional** | | **Past Conditional** | |
| | würde kosten<br>würdest kosten<br>würde kosten | würden kosten<br>würdet kosten<br>würden kosten | würde gekostet haben<br>würdest gekostet haben<br>würde gekostet haben | würden gekostet haben<br>würdet gekostet haben<br>würden gekostet haben |

## EXAMPLES

Dieser Wagen kostet zu viel. — This car costs too much.

Ich will die Soße nicht kosten. — I don't want to taste the sauce.

**krächzen**

to caw, to croak

**Auxiliary verb:** haben **Past participle:** gekrächzt

**Imperative:** Krächze! Krächzt! Krächzen Sie!

| Mode | Simple Tenses | | Compound Tenses | |
|---|---|---|---|---|
| | *Singular* | *Plural* | *Singular* | *Plural* |
| Indicative | **Present** | | **Present Perfect** | |
| | krächze<br>krächzt<br>krächzt | krächzen<br>krächzt<br>krächzen | habe gekrächzt<br>hast gekrächzt<br>hat gekrächzt | haben gekrächzt<br>habt gekrächzt<br>haben gekrächzt |
| | **Past** | | **Past Perfect** | |
| | krächzte<br>krächztest<br>krächzte | krächzten<br>krächztet<br>krächzten | hatte gekrächzt<br>hattest gekrächzt<br>hatte gekrächzt | hatten gekrächzt<br>hattet gekrächzt<br>hatten gekrächzt |
| | **Future** | | **Future Perfect** | |
| | werde krächzen<br>wirst krächzen<br>wird krächzen | werden krächzen<br>werdet krächzen<br>werden krächzen | werde gekrächzt haben<br>wirst gekrächzt haben<br>wird gekrächzt haben | werden gekrächzt haben<br>werdet gekrächzt haben<br>werden gekrächzt haben |
| Subjunctive | **Present** | | **Present Perfect** | |
| | krächze<br>krächzest<br>krächze | krächzen<br>krächzet<br>krächzen | habe gekrächzt<br>habest gekrächzt<br>habe gekrächzt | haben gekrächzt<br>habet gekrächzt<br>haben gekrächzt |
| | **Past** | | **Past Perfect** | |
| | krächzte<br>krächztest<br>krächzte | krächzten<br>krächztet<br>krächzten | hätte gekrächzt<br>hättest gekrächzt<br>hätte gekrächzt | hätten gekrächzt<br>hättet gekrächzt<br>hätten gekrächzt |
| | **Future** | | **Future Perfect** | |
| | werde krächzen<br>werdest krächzen<br>werde krächzen | werden krächzen<br>werdet krächzen<br>werden krächzen | werde gekrächzt haben<br>werdest gekrächzt haben<br>werde gekrächzt haben | werden gekrächzt haben<br>werdet gekrächzt haben<br>werden gekrächzt haben |
| | **Present and Future Conditional** | | **Past Conditional** | |
| | würde krächzen<br>würdest krächzen<br>würde krächzen | würden krächzen<br>würdet krächzen<br>würden krächzen | würde gekrächzt haben<br>würdest gekrächzt haben<br>würde gekrächzt haben | würden gekrächzt haben<br>würdet gekrächzt haben<br>würden gekrächzt haben |

## EXAMPLES

Warum krächzen die Krähen so?
„Das Kind ist noch nicht fett genug," krächzte die hungrige Hexe.

Why are the crows cawing like that?
"The child isn't yet fat enough," crowed the hungry witch.

**kränkeln**
to be sickly
**Auxiliary verb:** haben **Past participle:** gekränkelt
**Imperative:** Kränkele! Kränkelt! Kränkeln Sie!

| Mode | Simple Tenses | | Compound Tenses | |
|---|---|---|---|---|
| | *Singular* | *Plural* | *Singular* | *Plural* |
| Indicative | **Present** | | **Present Perfect** | |
| | kränkele<br>kränkelst<br>kränkelt | kränkeln<br>kränkelt<br>kränkeln | habe gekränkelt<br>hast gekränkelt<br>hat gekränkelt | haben gekränkelt<br>habt gekränkelt<br>haben gekränkelt |
| | **Past** | | **Past Perfect** | |
| | kränkelte<br>kränkeltest<br>kränkelte | kränkelten<br>kränkeltet<br>kränkelten | hatte gekränkelt<br>hattest gekränkelt<br>hatte gekränkelt | hatten gekränkelt<br>hattet gekränkelt<br>hatten gekränkelt |
| | **Future** | | **Future Perfect** | |
| | werde kränkeln<br>wirst kränkeln<br>wird kränkeln | werden kränkeln<br>werdet kränkeln<br>werden kränkeln | werde gekränkelt haben<br>wirst gekränkelt haben<br>wird gekränkelt haben | werden gekränkelt haben<br>werdet gekränkelt haben<br>werden gekränkelt haben |
| Subjunctive | **Present** | | **Present Perfect** | |
| | kränkele<br>kränkelst<br>kränkele | kränkeln<br>kränkelt<br>kränkeln | habe gekränkelt<br>habest gekränkelt<br>habe gekränkelt | haben gekränkelt<br>habet gekränkelt<br>haben gekränkelt |
| | **Past** | | **Past Perfect** | |
| | kränkelte<br>kränkeltest<br>kränkelte | kränkelten<br>kränkeltet<br>kränkelten | hätte gekränkelt<br>hättest gekränkelt<br>hätte gekränkelt | hätten gekränkelt<br>hättet gekränkelt<br>hätten gekränkelt |
| | **Future** | | **Future Perfect** | |
| | werde kränkeln<br>werdest kränkeln<br>werde kränkeln | werden kränkeln<br>werdet kränkeln<br>werden kränkeln | werde gekränkelt haben<br>werdest gekränkelt haben<br>werde gekränkelt haben | werden gekränkelt haben<br>werdet gekränkelt haben<br>werden gekränkelt haben |
| | **Present and Future Conditional** | | **Past Conditional** | |
| | würde kränkeln<br>würdest kränkeln<br>würde kränkeln | würden kränkeln<br>würdet kränkeln<br>würden kränkeln | würde gekränkelt haben<br>würdest gekränkelt haben<br>würde gekränkelt haben | würden gekränkelt haben<br>würdet gekränkelt haben<br>würden gekränkelt haben |

## EXAMPLES

Das arme Kind hat sein ganzes Leben gekränkelt.
The poor child has been sickly his whole life.

Andreas kränkelt noch und muss zu Hause bleiben.
Andreas is still sickly and has to stay home.

**kratzen (sich)**
to scratch, to scrape
**Auxiliary verb:** haben **Past participle:** gekratzt
**Imperative:** Kratze! Kratzt! Kratzen Sie!

| Mode | Simple Tenses | | Compound Tenses | |
|---|---|---|---|---|
| | *Singular* | *Plural* | *Singular* | *Plural* |
| Indicative | **Present** | | **Present Perfect** | |
| | kratze<br>kratzt<br>kratzt | kratzen<br>kratzt<br>kratzen | habe gekratzt<br>hast gekratzt<br>hat gekratzt | haben gekratzt<br>habt gekratzt<br>haben gekratzt |
| | **Past** | | **Past Perfect** | |
| | kratzte<br>kratztest<br>kratzte | kratzten<br>kratztet<br>kratzten | hatte gekratzt<br>hattest gekratzt<br>hatte gekratzt | hatten gekratzt<br>hattet gekratzt<br>hatten gekratzt |
| | **Future** | | **Future Perfect** | |
| | werde kratzen<br>wirst kratzen<br>wird kratzen | werden kratzen<br>werdet kratzen<br>werden kratzen | werde gekratzt haben<br>wirst gekratzt haben<br>wird gekratzt haben | werden gekratzt haben<br>werdet gekratzt haben<br>werden gekratzt haben |
| Subjunctive | **Present** | | **Present Perfect** | |
| | kratze<br>kratzest<br>kratze | kratzen<br>kratzet<br>kratzen | habe gekratzt<br>habest gekratzt<br>habe gekratzt | haben gekratzt<br>habet gekratzt<br>haben gekratzt |
| | **Past** | | **Past Perfect** | |
| | kratzte<br>kratztest<br>kratzte | kratzten<br>kratztet<br>kratzten | hätte gekratzt<br>hättest gekratzt<br>hätte gekratzt | hätten gekratzt<br>hättet gekratzt<br>hätten gekratzt |
| | **Future** | | **Future Perfect** | |
| | werde kratzen<br>werdest kratzen<br>werde kratzen | werden kratzen<br>werdet kratzen<br>werden kratzen | werde gekratzt haben<br>werdest gekratzt haben<br>werde gekratzt haben | werden gekratzt haben<br>werdet gekratzt haben<br>werden gekratzt haben |
| | **Present and Future Conditional** | | **Past Conditional** | |
| | würde kratzen<br>würdest kratzen<br>würde kratzen | würden kratzen<br>würdet kratzen<br>würden kratzen | würde gekratzt haben<br>würdest gekratzt haben<br>würde gekratzt haben | würden gekratzt haben<br>würdet gekratzt haben<br>würden gekratzt haben |

## EXAMPLES

Der Rauch kratzte mir im Halse. — The smoke scratched my throat.
Paul hat sich am rechten Arm gekratzt. — Paul scratched his right arm.

**kriechen**
to creep, to crawl
**Auxiliary verb:** sein **Past participle:** gekrochen
**Imperative:** Krieche! Kriecht! Kriechen Sie!

| Mode | Simple Tenses | | Compound Tenses | |
|---|---|---|---|---|
| | *Singular* | *Plural* | *Singular* | *Plural* |
| Indicative | **Present** | | **Present Perfect** | |
| | krieche<br>kriechst<br>kriecht | kriechen<br>kriecht<br>kriechen | bin gekrochen<br>bist gekrochen<br>ist gekrochen | sind gekrochen<br>seid gekrochen<br>sind gekrochen |
| | **Past** | | **Past Perfect** | |
| | kroch<br>krochst<br>kroch | krochen<br>krocht<br>krochen | war gekrochen<br>warst gekrochen<br>war gekrochen | waren gekrochen<br>wart gekrochen<br>waren gekrochen |
| | **Future** | | **Future Perfect** | |
| | werde kriechen<br>wirst kriechen<br>wird kriechen | werden kriechen<br>werdet kriechen<br>werden kriechen | werde gekrochen sein<br>wirst gekrochen sein<br>wird gekrochen sein | werden gekrochen sein<br>werdet gekrochen sein<br>werden gekrochen sein |
| Subjunctive | **Present** | | **Present Perfect** | |
| | krieche<br>kriechest<br>krieche | kriechen<br>kriechet<br>kriechen | sei gekrochen<br>seiest gekrochen<br>sei gekrochen | seien gekrochen<br>seiet gekrochen<br>seien gekrochen |
| | **Past** | | **Past Perfect** | |
| | kröche<br>kröchest<br>kröche | kröchen<br>kröchet<br>kröchen | wäre gekrochen<br>wärest gekrochen<br>wäre gekrochen | wären gekrochen<br>wäret gekrochen<br>wären gekrochen |
| | **Future** | | **Future Perfect** | |
| | werde kriechen<br>werdest kriechen<br>werde kriechen | werden kriechen<br>werdet kriechen<br>werden kriechen | werde gekrochen sein<br>werdest gekrochen sein<br>werde gekrochen sein | werden gekrochen sein<br>werdet gekrochen sein<br>werden gekrochen sein |
| | **Present and Future Conditional** | | **Past Conditional** | |
| | würde kriechen<br>würdest kriechen<br>würde kriechen | würden kriechen<br>würdet kriechen<br>würden kriechen | würde gekrochen sein<br>würdest gekrochen sein<br>würde gekrochen sein | würden gekrochen sein<br>würdet gekrochen sein<br>würden gekrochen sein |

## EXAMPLES

Aus den Eiern kriechen kleine Schlangen.
Little snakes are hatched from the eggs.

Es war ekelhaft, wie die jüngsten Angestellten vor dem Chef krochen.
It was disgusting how the youngest employees tip-toed around the boss.

**kriegen**

to get, to receive, to obtain

**Auxiliary verb:** haben **Past participle:** gekriegt

**Imperative:** Kriege! Kriegt! Kriegen Sie!

| Mode | Simple Tenses | | Compound Tenses | |
|---|---|---|---|---|
| | *Singular* | *Plural* | *Singular* | *Plural* |
| Indicative | **Present** | | **Present Perfect** | |
| | kriege<br>kriegst<br>kriegt | kriegen<br>kriegt<br>kriegen | habe gekriegt<br>hast gekriegt<br>hat gekriegt | haben gekriegt<br>habt gekriegt<br>haben gekriegt |
| | **Past** | | **Past Perfect** | |
| | kriegte<br>kriegtest<br>kriegte | kriegten<br>kriegtet<br>kriegten | hatte gekriegt<br>hattest gekriegt<br>hatte gekriegt | hatten gekriegt<br>hattet gekriegt<br>hatten gekriegt |
| | **Future** | | **Future Perfect** | |
| | werde kriegen<br>wirst kriegen<br>wird kriegen | werden kriegen<br>werdet kriegen<br>werden kriegen | werde gekriegt haben<br>wirst gekriegt haben<br>wird gekriegt haben | werden gekriegt haben<br>werdet gekriegt haben<br>werden gekriegt haben |
| Subjunctive | **Present** | | **Present Perfect** | |
| | kriege<br>kriegest<br>kriege | kriegen<br>krieget<br>kriegen | habe gekriegt<br>habest gekriegt<br>habe gekriegt | haben gekriegt<br>habet gekriegt<br>haben gekriegt |
| | **Past** | | **Past Perfect** | |
| | kriegte<br>kriegtest<br>kriegte | kriegten<br>kriegtet<br>kriegten | hätte gekriegt<br>hättest gekriegt<br>hätte gekriegt | hätten gekriegt<br>hättet gekriegt<br>hätten gekriegt |
| | **Future** | | **Future Perfect** | |
| | werde kriegen<br>werdest kriegen<br>werde kriegen | werden kriegen<br>werdet kriegen<br>werden kriegen | werde gekriegt haben<br>werdest gekriegt haben<br>werde gekriegt haben | werden gekriegt haben<br>werdet gekriegt haben<br>werden gekriegt haben |
| | **Present and Future Conditional** | | **Past Conditional** | |
| | würde kriegen<br>würdest kriegen<br>würde kriegen | würden kriegen<br>würdet kriegen<br>würden kriegen | würde gekriegt haben<br>würdest gekriegt haben<br>würde gekriegt haben | würden gekriegt haben<br>würdet gekriegt haben<br>würden gekriegt haben |

## EXAMPLES

Ich habe ein bisschen Geld von meiner Tante gekriegt. — I got a little money from my aunt.

Meine Schwester kriegt ein Baby. — My sister is going to have a baby.

**kritzeln**
to scribble, to scrawl
**Auxiliary verb:** haben **Past participle:** gekritzelt
**Imperative:** Kritzele! Kritzelt! Kritzeln Sie!

| Mode | Simple Tenses | | Compound Tenses | |
|---|---|---|---|---|
| | *Singular* | *Plural* | *Singular* | *Plural* |
| Indicative | **Present** | | **Present Perfect** | |
| | kritzele<br>kritzelst<br>kritzelt | kritzeln<br>kritzelt<br>kritzeln | habe gekritzelt<br>hast gekritzelt<br>hat gekritzelt | haben gekritzelt<br>habt gekritzelt<br>haben gekritzelt |
| | **Past** | | **Past Perfect** | |
| | kritzelte<br>kritzeltest<br>kritzelte | kritzelten<br>kritzeltet<br>kritzelten | hatte gekritzelt<br>hattest gekritzelt<br>hatte gekritzelt | hatten gekritzelt<br>hattet gekritzelt<br>hatten gekritzelt |
| | **Future** | | **Future Perfect** | |
| | werde kritzeln<br>wirst kritzeln<br>wird kritzeln | werden kritzeln<br>werdet kritzeln<br>werden kritzeln | werde gekritzelt haben<br>wirst gekritzelt haben<br>wird gekritzelt haben | werden gekritzelt haben<br>werdet gekritzelt haben<br>werden gekritzelt haben |
| Subjunctive | **Present** | | **Present Perfect** | |
| | kritzele<br>kritzelst<br>kritzele | kritzeln<br>kritzelt<br>kritzeln | habe gekritzelt<br>habest gekritzelt<br>habe gekritzelt | haben gekritzelt<br>habet gekritzelt<br>haben gekritzelt |
| | **Past** | | **Past Perfect** | |
| | kritzelte<br>kritzeltest<br>kritzelte | kritzelten<br>kritzeltet<br>kritzelten | hätte gekritzelt<br>hättest gekritzelt<br>hätte gekritzelt | hätten gekritzelt<br>hättet gekritzelt<br>hätten gekritzelt |
| | **Future** | | **Future Perfect** | |
| | werde kritzeln<br>werdest kritzeln<br>werde kritzeln | werden kritzeln<br>werdet kritzeln<br>werden kritzeln | werde gekritzelt haben<br>werdest gekritzelt haben<br>werde gekritzelt haben | werden gekritzelt haben<br>werdet gekritzelt haben<br>werden gekritzelt haben |
| | **Present and Future Conditional** | | **Past Conditional** | |
| | würde kritzeln<br>würdest kritzeln<br>würde kritzeln | würden kritzeln<br>würdet kritzeln<br>würden kritzeln | würde gekritzelt haben<br>würdest gekritzelt haben<br>würde gekritzelt haben | würden gekritzelt haben<br>würdet gekritzelt haben<br>würden gekritzelt haben |

## EXAMPLES

Der betrunkene Mann kritzelte ein paar Worte auf ein Stück Papier.
The drunken man scribbled a few words on a piece of paper.

Der Schüler schreibt nicht. Er kritzelt.
The pupil doesn't write. He scribbles.

**krönen**

to crown

**Auxiliary verb:** haben **Past participle:** gekrönt

**Imperative:** Kröne! Krönt! Krönen Sie!

| Mode | Simple Tenses | | Compound Tenses | |
|---|---|---|---|---|
| | *Singular* | *Plural* | *Singular* | *Plural* |
| Indicative | **Present** | | **Present Perfect** | |
| | kröne<br>krönst<br>krönt | krönen<br>krönt<br>krönen | habe gekrönt<br>hast gekrönt<br>hat gekrönt | haben gekrönt<br>habt gekrönt<br>haben gekrönt |
| | **Past** | | **Past Perfect** | |
| | krönte<br>kröntest<br>krönte | krönten<br>kröntet<br>krönten | hatte gekrönt<br>hattest gekrönt<br>hatte gekrönt | hatten gekrönt<br>hattet gekrönt<br>hatten gekrönt |
| | **Future** | | **Future Perfect** | |
| | werde krönen<br>wirst krönen<br>wird krönen | werden krönen<br>werdet krönen<br>werden krönen | werde gekrönt haben<br>wirst gekrönt haben<br>wird gekrönt haben | werden gekrönt haben<br>werdet gekrönt haben<br>werden gekrönt haben |
| Subjunctive | **Present** | | **Present Perfect** | |
| | kröne<br>krönest<br>kröne | krönen<br>krönet<br>krönen | habe gekrönt<br>habest gekrönt<br>habe gekrönt | haben gekrönt<br>habet gekrönt<br>haben gekrönt |
| | **Past** | | **Past Perfect** | |
| | krönte<br>kröntest<br>krönte | krönten<br>kröntet<br>krönten | hätte gekrönt<br>hättest gekrönt<br>hätte gekrönt | hätten gekrönt<br>hättet gekrönt<br>hätten gekrönt |
| | **Future** | | **Future Perfect** | |
| | werde krönen<br>werdest krönen<br>werde krönen | werden krönen<br>werdet krönen<br>werden krönen | werde gekrönt haben<br>werdest gekrönt haben<br>werde gekrönt haben | werden gekrönt haben<br>werdet gekrönt haben<br>werden gekrönt haben |
| | **Present and Future Conditional** | | **Past Conditional** | |
| | würde krönen<br>würdest krönen<br>würde krönen | würden krönen<br>würdet krönen<br>würden krönen | würde gekrönt haben<br>würdest gekrönt haben<br>würde gekrönt haben | würden gekrönt haben<br>würdet gekrönt haben<br>würden gekrönt haben |

## EXAMPLES

Nach dem Tod seines Vaters wollte der Kronprinz nicht gekrönt werden.

After the death of his father, the crown prince did not want to be crowned.

Der krönende Abschluss der Reise war unser Berlinausflug.

The crowning end to our trip was our visit to Berlin.

**kuscheln**
to snuggle
**Auxiliary verb:** haben **Past participle:** gekuschelt
**Imperative:** Kuschele! Kuschelt! Kuscheln Sie!

| Mode | Simple Tenses | | Compound Tenses | |
|---|---|---|---|---|
| | *Singular* | *Plural* | *Singular* | *Plural* |
| Indicative | **Present** | | **Present Perfect** | |
| | kuschele<br>kuschelst<br>kuschelt | kuscheln<br>kuschelt<br>kuscheln | habe gekuschelt<br>hast gekuschelt<br>hat gekuschelt | haben gekuschelt<br>habt gekuschelt<br>haben gekuschelt |
| | **Past** | | **Past Perfect** | |
| | kuschelte<br>kuscheltest<br>kuschelte | kuschelten<br>kuscheltet<br>kuschelten | hatte gekuschelt<br>hattest gekuschelt<br>hatte gekuschelt | hatten gekuschelt<br>hattet gekuschelt<br>hatten gekuschelt |
| | **Future** | | **Future Perfect** | |
| | werde kuscheln<br>wirst kuscheln<br>wird kuscheln | werden kuscheln<br>werdet kuscheln<br>werden kuscheln | werde gekuschelt haben<br>wirst gekuschelt haben<br>wird gekuschelt haben | werden gekuschelt haben<br>werdet gekuschelt haben<br>werden gekuschelt haben |
| Subjunctive | **Present** | | **Present Perfect** | |
| | kuschele<br>kuschelst<br>kuschele | kuscheln<br>kuschelt<br>kuscheln | habe gekuschelt<br>habest gekuschelt<br>habe gekuschelt | haben gekuschelt<br>habet gekuschelt<br>haben gekuschelt |
| | **Past** | | **Past Perfect** | |
| | kuschelte<br>kuscheltest<br>kuschelte | kuschelten<br>kuscheltet<br>kuschelten | hätte gekuschelt<br>hättest gekuschelt<br>hätte gekuschelt | hätten gekuschelt<br>hättet gekuschelt<br>hätten gekuschelt |
| | **Future** | | **Future Perfect** | |
| | werde kuscheln<br>werdest kuscheln<br>werde kuscheln | werden kuscheln<br>werdet kuscheln<br>werden kuscheln | werde gekuschelt haben<br>werdest gekuschelt haben<br>werde gekuschelt haben | werden gekuschelt haben<br>werdet gekuschelt haben<br>werden gekuschelt haben |
| | **Present and Future Conditional** | | **Past Conditional** | |
| | würde kuscheln<br>würdest kuscheln<br>würde kuscheln | würden kuscheln<br>würdet kuscheln<br>würden kuscheln | würde gekuschelt haben<br>würdest gekuschelt haben<br>würde gekuschelt haben | würden gekuschelt haben<br>würdet gekuschelt haben<br>würden gekuschelt haben |

## EXAMPLES

Das junge Paar kuschelt in einer dunklen Ecke.
The young couple is snuggling in a dark corner.

Sie haben sich in der furchtbaren Kälte aneinander gekuschelt.
They snuggled up to one another in the terrible cold.

**küssen**

to kiss

**Auxiliary verb:** haben **Past participle:** geküsst

**Imperative:** Küsse! Küsst! Küssen Sie!

| Mode | Simple Tenses | | Compound Tenses | |
|---|---|---|---|---|
| | *Singular* | *Plural* | *Singular* | *Plural* |
| Indicative | **Present** | | **Present Perfect** | |
| | küsse<br>küsst<br>küsst | küssen<br>küsst<br>küssen | habe geküsst<br>hast geküsst<br>hat geküsst | haben geküsst<br>habt geküsst<br>haben geküsst |
| | **Past** | | **Past Perfect** | |
| | küsste<br>küsstest<br>küsste | küssten<br>küsstet<br>küssten | hatte geküsst<br>hattest geküsst<br>hatte geküsst | hatten geküsst<br>hattet geküsst<br>hatten geküsst |
| | **Future** | | **Future Perfect** | |
| | werde küssen<br>wirst küssen<br>wird küssen | werden küssen<br>werdet küssen<br>werden küssen | werde geküsst haben<br>wirst geküsst haben<br>wird geküsst haben | werden geküsst haben<br>werdet geküsst haben<br>werden geküsst haben |
| Subjunctive | **Present** | | **Present Perfect** | |
| | küsse<br>küssest<br>küsse | küssen<br>küsset<br>küssen | habe geküsst<br>habest geküsst<br>habe geküsst | haben geküsst<br>habet geküsst<br>haben geküsst |
| | **Past** | | **Past Perfect** | |
| | küsste<br>küsstest<br>küsste | küssten<br>küsstet<br>küssten | hätte geküsst<br>hättest geküsst<br>hätte geküsst | hätten geküsst<br>hättet geküsst<br>hätten geküsst |
| | **Future** | | **Future Perfect** | |
| | werde küssen<br>werdest küssen<br>werde küssen | werden küssen<br>werdet küssen<br>werden küssen | werde geküsst haben<br>werdest geküsst haben<br>werde geküsst haben | werden geküsst haben<br>werdet geküsst haben<br>werden geküsst haben |
| | **Present and Future Conditional** | | **Past Conditional** | |
| | würde küssen<br>würdest küssen<br>würde küssen | würden küssen<br>würdet küssen<br>würden küssen | würde geküsst haben<br>würdest geküsst haben<br>würde geküsst haben | würden geküsst haben<br>würdet geküsst haben<br>würden geküsst haben |

## EXAMPLE

Er nimmt sie in den Arm und küsst sie leidenschaftlich.

He takes her in his arms and kisses her passionately.

**lächeln**
to smile
**Auxiliary verb:** haben **Past participle:** gelächelt
**Imperative:** Lächele! Lächelt! Lächeln Sie!

| Mode | Simple Tenses | | Compound Tenses | |
|---|---|---|---|---|
| | *Singular* | *Plural* | *Singular* | *Plural* |
| Indicative | **Present** | | **Present Perfect** | |
| | lächele<br>lächelst<br>lächelt | lächeln<br>lächelt<br>lächeln | habe gelächelt<br>hast gelächelt<br>hat gelächelt | haben gelächelt<br>habt gelächelt<br>haben gelächelt |
| | **Past** | | **Past Perfect** | |
| | lächelte<br>lächeltest<br>lächelte | lächelten<br>lächeltet<br>lächelten | hatte gelächelt<br>hattest gelächelt<br>hatte gelächelt | hatten gelächelt<br>hattet gelächelt<br>hatten gelächelt |
| | **Future** | | **Future Perfect** | |
| | werde lächeln<br>wirst lächeln<br>wird lächeln | werden lächeln<br>werdet lächeln<br>werden lächeln | werde gelächelt haben<br>wirst gelächelt haben<br>wird gelächelt haben | werden gelächelt haben<br>werdet gelächelt haben<br>werden gelächelt haben |
| Subjunctive | **Present** | | **Present Perfect** | |
| | lächele<br>lächelst<br>lächele | lächeln<br>lächelt<br>lächeln | habe gelächelt<br>habest gelächelt<br>habe gelächelt | haben gelächelt<br>habet gelächelt<br>haben gelächelt |
| | **Past** | | **Past Perfect** | |
| | lächelte<br>lächeltest<br>lächelte | lächelten<br>lächeltet<br>lächelten | hätte gelächelt<br>hättest gelächelt<br>hätte gelächelt | hätten gelächelt<br>hättet gelächelt<br>hätten gelächelt |
| | **Future** | | **Future Perfect** | |
| | werde lächeln<br>werdest lächeln<br>werde lächeln | werden lächeln<br>werdet lächeln<br>werden lächeln | werde gelächelt haben<br>werdest gelächelt haben<br>werde gelächelt haben | werden gelächelt haben<br>werdet gelächelt haben<br>werden gelächelt haben |
| | **Present and Future Conditional** | | **Past Conditional** | |
| | würde lächeln<br>würdest lächeln<br>würde lächeln | würden lächeln<br>würdet lächeln<br>würden lächeln | würde gelächelt haben<br>würdest gelächelt haben<br>würde gelächelt haben | würden gelächelt haben<br>würdet gelächelt haben<br>würden gelächelt haben |

**Note:** With the prefix *zu–*, the principal parts of this verb are *lächelt zu, lächelte zu, hat zugelächelt.*

## EXAMPLES

Warum lächelt der alte Herr so?
Why is the old gentleman smiling that way?

Der hübsche Sportler hat meiner Schwester zugelächelt.
The handsome athlete smiled at my sister.

**lachen**
to laugh
**Auxiliary verb:** haben **Past participle:** gelacht
**Imperative:** Lache! Lacht! Lachen Sie!

| Mode | Simple Tenses | | Compound Tenses | |
|---|---|---|---|---|
| | *Singular* | *Plural* | *Singular* | *Plural* |
| Indicative | **Present** | | **Present Perfect** | |
| | lache<br>lachst<br>lacht | lachen<br>lacht<br>lachen | habe gelacht<br>hast gelacht<br>hat gelacht | haben gelacht<br>habt gelacht<br>haben gelacht |
| | **Past** | | **Past Perfect** | |
| | lachte<br>lachtest<br>lachte | lachten<br>lachtet<br>lachten | hatte gelacht<br>hattest gelacht<br>hatte gelacht | hatten gelacht<br>hattet gelacht<br>hatten gelacht |
| | **Future** | | **Future Perfect** | |
| | werde lachen<br>wirst lachen<br>wird lachen | werden lachen<br>werdet lachen<br>werden lachen | werde gelacht haben<br>wirst gelacht haben<br>wird gelacht haben | werden gelacht haben<br>werdet gelacht haben<br>werden gelacht haben |
| Subjunctive | **Present** | | **Present Perfect** | |
| | lache<br>lachest<br>lache | lachen<br>lachet<br>lachen | habe gelacht<br>habest gelacht<br>habe gelacht | haben gelacht<br>habet gelacht<br>haben gelacht |
| | **Past** | | **Past Perfect** | |
| | lachte<br>lachtest<br>lachte | lachten<br>lachtet<br>lachten | hätte gelacht<br>hättest gelacht<br>hätte gelacht | hätten gelacht<br>hättet gelacht<br>hätten gelacht |
| | **Future** | | **Future Perfect** | |
| | werde lachen<br>werdest lachen<br>werde lachen | werden lachen<br>werdet lachen<br>werden lachen | werde gelacht haben<br>werdest gelacht haben<br>werde gelacht haben | werden gelacht haben<br>werdet gelacht haben<br>werden gelacht haben |
| | **Present and Future Conditional** | | **Past Conditional** | |
| | würde lachen<br>würdest lachen<br>würde lachen | würden lachen<br>würdet lachen<br>würden lachen | würde gelacht haben<br>würdest gelacht haben<br>würde gelacht haben | würden gelacht haben<br>würdet gelacht haben<br>würden gelacht haben |

## EXAMPLES

Ihre Freunde lachten heimlich über ihre Haare.
Her friends were secretly laughing about her hair.

Ihr werdet über diesen Witz sehr lachen.
You're really going to get a good laugh out of this joke.

**lähmen**
to cripple, to disable
**Auxiliary verb:** haben **Past participle:** gelähmt
**Imperative:** Lähme! Lähmt! Lähmen Sie!

| Mode | Simple Tenses | | Compound Tenses | |
|---|---|---|---|---|
| | *Singular* | *Plural* | *Singular* | *Plural* |
| Indicative | **Present** | | **Present Perfect** | |
| | lähme<br>lähmst<br>lähmt | lähmen<br>lähmt<br>lähmen | habe gelähmt<br>hast gelähmt<br>hat gelähmt | haben gelähmt<br>habt gelähmt<br>haben gelähmt |
| | **Past** | | **Past Perfect** | |
| | lähmte<br>lähmtest<br>lähmte | lähmten<br>lähmtet<br>lähmten | hatte gelähmt<br>hattest gelähmt<br>hatte gelähmt | hatten gelähmt<br>hattet gelähmt<br>hatten gelähmt |
| | **Future** | | **Future Perfect** | |
| | werde lähmen<br>wirst lähmen<br>wird lähmen | werden lähmen<br>werdet lähmen<br>werden lähmen | werde gelähmt haben<br>wirst gelähmt haben<br>wird gelähmt haben | werden gelähmt haben<br>werdet gelähmt haben<br>werden gelähmt haben |
| Subjunctive | **Present** | | **Present Perfect** | |
| | lähme<br>lähmest<br>lähme | lähmen<br>lähmet<br>lähmen | habe gelähmt<br>habest gelähmt<br>habe gelähmt | haben gelähmt<br>habet gelähmt<br>haben gelähmt |
| | **Past** | | **Past Perfect** | |
| | lähmte<br>lähmtest<br>lähmte | lähmten<br>lähmtet<br>lähmten | hätte gelähmt<br>hättest gelähmt<br>hätte gelähmt | hätten gelähmt<br>hättet gelähmt<br>hätten gelähmt |
| | **Future** | | **Future Perfect** | |
| | werde lähmen<br>werdest lähmen<br>werde lähmen | werden lähmen<br>werdet lähmen<br>werden lähmen | werde gelähmt haben<br>werdest gelähmt haben<br>werde gelähmt haben | werden gelähmt haben<br>werdet gelähmt haben<br>werden gelähmt haben |
| | **Present and Future Conditional** | | **Past Conditional** | |
| | würde lähmen<br>würdest lähmen<br>würde lähmen | würden lähmen<br>würdet lähmen<br>würden lähmen | würde gelähmt haben<br>würdest gelähmt haben<br>würde gelähmt haben | würden gelähmt haben<br>würdet gelähmt haben<br>würden gelähmt haben |

## EXAMPLES

Mein Cousin ist seit seinem Motorradunfall gelähmt.
Ein Wasserrohrbruch lähmte heute den Verkehr in der Innenstadt.

Ever since his motorcycle accident, my cousin has been unable to walk.
A broken water main crippled traffic in the downtown area today.

**lassen**

to let, to leave, to have done

**Auxiliary verb:** haben **Past participle:** gelassen

**Imperative:** Lasse! Lasst! Lassen Sie!

| Mode | Simple Tenses | | Compound Tenses | |
|---|---|---|---|---|
| | *Singular* | *Plural* | *Singular* | *Plural* |
| Indicative | **Present** | | **Present Perfect** | |
| | lasse<br>lässt<br>lässt | lassen<br>lasst<br>lassen | habe gelassen<br>hast gelassen<br>hat gelassen | haben gelassen<br>habt gelassen<br>haben gelassen |
| | **Past** | | **Past Perfect** | |
| | ließ<br>ließest<br>ließ | ließen<br>ließt<br>ließen | hatte gelassen<br>hattest gelassen<br>hatte gelassen | hatten gelassen<br>hattet gelassen<br>hatten gelassen |
| | **Future** | | **Future Perfect** | |
| | werde lassen<br>wirst lassen<br>wird lassen | werden lassen<br>werdet lassen<br>werden lassen | werde gelassen haben<br>wirst gelassen haben<br>wird gelassen haben | werden gelassen haben<br>werdet gelassen haben<br>werden gelassen haben |
| Subjunctive | **Present** | | **Present Perfect** | |
| | lasse<br>lassest<br>lasse | lassen<br>lasset<br>lassen | habe gelassen<br>habest gelassen<br>habe gelassen | haben gelassen<br>habet gelassen<br>haben gelassen |
| | **Past** | | **Past Perfect** | |
| | ließe<br>ließest<br>ließe | ließen<br>ließet<br>ließen | hätte gelassen<br>hättest gelassen<br>hätte gelassen | hätten gelassen<br>hättet gelassen<br>hätten gelassen |
| | **Future** | | **Future Perfect** | |
| | werde lassen<br>werdest lassen<br>werde lassen | werden lassen<br>werdet lassen<br>werden lassen | werde gelassen haben<br>werdest gelassen haben<br>werde gelassen haben | werden gelassen haben<br>werdet gelassen haben<br>werden gelassen haben |
| | **Present and Future Conditional** | | **Past Conditional** | |
| | würde lassen<br>würdest lassen<br>würde lassen | würden lassen<br>würdet lassen<br>würden lassen | würde gelassen haben<br>würdest gelassen haben<br>würde gelassen haben | würden gelassen haben<br>würdet gelassen haben<br>würden gelassen haben |

**Note:** This verb can be used as a reflexive impersonal expression. It means "it can be": *Das lässt sich nicht machen* ("That can't be done").

## EXAMPLES

| | |
|---|---|
| Lass mich in Ruhe! | Leave me alone. |
| Du hättest die Hände davon lassen sollen. | You shouldn't have been meddling with that. |
| Er ließ den Wagen reparieren. | He had the car repaired. |

**lauern**
to lurk
**Auxiliary verb:** haben **Past participle:** gelauert
**Imperative:** Lauere! Lauert! Lauern Sie!

| Mode | Simple Tenses | | Compound Tenses | |
|---|---|---|---|---|
| | *Singular* | *Plural* | *Singular* | *Plural* |
| Indicative | **Present** | | **Present Perfect** | |
| | lauere<br>lauerst<br>lauert | lauern<br>lauert<br>lauern | habe gelauert<br>hast gelauert<br>hat gelauert | haben gelauert<br>habt gelauert<br>haben gelauert |
| | **Past** | | **Past Perfect** | |
| | lauerte<br>lauertest<br>lauerte | lauerten<br>lauertet<br>lauerten | hatte gelauert<br>hattest gelauert<br>hatte gelauert | hatten gelauert<br>hattet gelauert<br>hatten gelauert |
| | **Future** | | **Future Perfect** | |
| | werde lauern<br>wirst lauern<br>wird lauern | werden lauern<br>werdet lauern<br>werden lauern | werde gelauert haben<br>wirst gelauert haben<br>wird gelauert haben | werden gelauert haben<br>werdet gelauert haben<br>werden gelauert haben |
| Subjunctive | **Present** | | **Present Perfect** | |
| | lauere<br>lauerst<br>lauere | lauern<br>lauert<br>lauern | habe gelauert<br>habest gelauert<br>habe gelauert | haben gelauert<br>habet gelauert<br>haben gelauert |
| | **Past** | | **Past Perfect** | |
| | lauerte<br>lauertest<br>lauerte | lauerten<br>lauertet<br>lauerten | hätte gelauert<br>hättest gelauert<br>hätte gelauert | hätten gelauert<br>hättet gelauert<br>hätten gelauert |
| | **Future** | | **Future Perfect** | |
| | werde lauern<br>werdest lauern<br>werde lauern | werden lauern<br>werdet lauern<br>werden lauern | werde gelauert haben<br>werdest gelauert haben<br>werde gelauert haben | werden gelauert haben<br>werdet gelauert haben<br>werden gelauert haben |
| | **Present and Future Conditional** | | **Past Conditional** | |
| | würde lauern<br>würdest lauern<br>würde lauern | würden lauern<br>würdet lauern<br>würden lauern | würde gelauert haben<br>würdest gelauert haben<br>würde gelauert haben | würden gelauert haben<br>würdet gelauert haben<br>würden gelauert haben |

## EXAMPLES

Die Katze lauert seit Stunden vor dem Mauseloch.
The cat has been lurking in front of the mouse hole for hours.

Eine Hexe hat hinter dem Busch gelauert.
A witch was lurking behind the bush.

**laufen**

to run, to walk

**Auxiliary verb:** sein **Past participle:** gelaufen

**Imperative:** Laufe! Lauft! Laufen Sie!

| Mode | Simple Tenses | | Compound Tenses | |
|---|---|---|---|---|
| | *Singular* | *Plural* | *Singular* | *Plural* |
| Indicative | **Present** | | **Present Perfect** | |
| | laufe<br>läufst<br>läuft | laufen<br>lauft<br>laufen | bin gelaufen<br>bist gelaufen<br>ist gelaufen | sind gelaufen<br>seid gelaufen<br>sind gelaufen |
| | **Past** | | **Past Perfect** | |
| | lief<br>liefst<br>lief | liefen<br>lieft<br>liefen | war gelaufen<br>warst gelaufen<br>war gelaufen | waren gelaufen<br>wart gelaufen<br>waren gelaufen |
| | **Future** | | **Future Perfect** | |
| | werde laufen<br>wirst laufen<br>wird laufen | werden laufen<br>werdet laufen<br>werden laufen | werde gelaufen sein<br>wirst gelaufen sein<br>wird gelaufen sein | werden gelaufen sein<br>werdet gelaufen sein<br>werden gelaufen sein |
| Subjunctive | **Present** | | **Present Perfect** | |
| | laufe<br>laufest<br>laufe | laufen<br>laufet<br>laufen | sei gelaufen<br>seiest gelaufen<br>sei gelaufen | seien gelaufen<br>seiet gelaufen<br>seien gelaufen |
| | **Past** | | **Past Perfect** | |
| | liefe<br>liefest<br>liefe | liefen<br>liefet<br>liefen | wäre gelaufen<br>wärest gelaufen<br>wäre gelaufen | wären gelaufen<br>wäret gelaufen<br>wären gelaufen |
| | **Future** | | **Future Perfect** | |
| | werde laufen<br>werdest laufen<br>werde laufen | werden laufen<br>werdet laufen<br>werden laufen | werde gelaufen sein<br>werdest gelaufen sein<br>werde gelaufen sein | werden gelaufen sein<br>werdet gelaufen sein<br>werden gelaufen sein |
| | **Present and Future Conditional** | | **Past Conditional** | |
| | würde laufen<br>würdest laufen<br>würde laufen | würden laufen<br>würdet laufen<br>würden laufen | würde gelaufen sein<br>würdest gelaufen sein<br>würde gelaufen sein | würden gelaufen sein<br>würdet gelaufen sein<br>würden gelaufen sein |

**Note:** With inseparable prefixes, the principal parts of this verb are, for example, *verläuft, verlief, ist verlaufen.* With separable prefixes, the principal parts are, for example, *läuft weg, lief weg, ist weggelaufen.*

## EXAMPLES

| | |
|---|---|
| Das Theaterstück ist nur zwei Monate gelaufen. | The play ran for only two months. |
| Sie sind im Statdtzentrum viel zu Fuß gelaufen. | They did a lot of walking downtown. |

**leben**
to live
**Auxiliary verb:** haben **Past participle:** gelebt
**Imperative:** Lebe! Lebt! Leben Sie!

| Mode | Simple Tenses | | Compound Tenses | |
|---|---|---|---|---|
| | *Singular* | *Plural* | *Singular* | *Plural* |
| Indicative | **Present** | | **Present Perfect** | |
| | lebe<br>lebst<br>lebt | leben<br>lebt<br>leben | habe gelebt<br>hast gelebt<br>hat gelebt | haben gelebt<br>habt gelebt<br>haben gelebt |
| | **Past** | | **Past Perfect** | |
| | lebte<br>lebtest<br>lebte | lebten<br>lebtet<br>lebten | hatte gelebt<br>hattest gelebt<br>hatte gelebt | hatten gelebt<br>hattet gelebt<br>hatten gelebt |
| | **Future** | | **Future Perfect** | |
| | werde leben<br>wirst leben<br>wird leben | werden leben<br>werdet leben<br>werden leben | werde gelebt haben<br>wirst gelebt haben<br>wird gelebt haben | werden gelebt haben<br>werdet gelebt haben<br>werden gelebt haben |
| Subjunctive | **Present** | | **Present Perfect** | |
| | lebe<br>lebest<br>lebe | leben<br>lebet<br>leben | habe gelebt<br>habest gelebt<br>habe gelebt | haben gelebt<br>habet gelebt<br>haben gelebt |
| | **Past** | | **Past Perfect** | |
| | lebte<br>lebtest<br>lebte | lebten<br>lebtet<br>lebten | hätte gelebt<br>hättest gelebt<br>hätte gelebt | hätten gelebt<br>hättet gelebt<br>hätten gelebt |
| | **Future** | | **Future Perfect** | |
| | werde leben<br>werdest leben<br>werde leben | werden leben<br>werdet leben<br>werden leben | werde gelebt haben<br>werdest gelebt haben<br>werde gelebt haben | werden gelebt haben<br>werdet gelebt haben<br>werden gelebt haben |
| | **Present and Future Conditional** | | **Past Conditional** | |
| | würde leben<br>würdest leben<br>würde leben | würden leben<br>würdet leben<br>würden leben | würde gelebt haben<br>würdest gelebt haben<br>würde gelebt haben | würden gelebt haben<br>würdet gelebt haben<br>würden gelebt haben |

## EXAMPLES

Leben Sie noch in Leipzig?
Do you still live in Leipzig?

Er lebt in dem Glauben, dass alle Frauen ihn bewundern.
He's convinced that all women admire him.

**lecken**
to lick, to leak
**Auxiliary verb:** haben **Past participle:** geleckt
**Imperative:** Lecke! Leckt! Lecken Sie!

| Mode | Simple Tenses | | Compound Tenses | |
|---|---|---|---|---|
| | *Singular* | *Plural* | *Singular* | *Plural* |
| Indicative | **Present** | | **Present Perfect** | |
| | lecke<br>leckst<br>leckt | lecken<br>leckt<br>lecken | habe geleckt<br>hast geleckt<br>hat geleckt | haben geleckt<br>habt geleckt<br>haben geleckt |
| | **Past** | | **Past Perfect** | |
| | leckte<br>lecktest<br>leckte | leckten<br>lecktet<br>leckten | hatte geleckt<br>hattest geleckt<br>hatte geleckt | hatten geleckt<br>hattet geleckt<br>hatten geleckt |
| | **Future** | | **Future Perfect** | |
| | werde lecken<br>wirst lecken<br>wird lecken | werden lecken<br>werdet lecken<br>werden lecken | werde geleckt haben<br>wirst geleckt haben<br>wird geleckt haben | werden geleckt haben<br>werdet geleckt haben<br>werden geleckt haben |
| Subjunctive | **Present** | | **Present Perfect** | |
| | lecke<br>leckest<br>lecke | lecken<br>lecket<br>lecken | habe geleckt<br>habest geleckt<br>habe geleckt | haben geleckt<br>habet geleckt<br>haben geleckt |
| | **Past** | | **Past Perfect** | |
| | leckte<br>lecktest<br>leckte | leckten<br>lecktet<br>leckten | hätte geleckt<br>hättest geleckt<br>hätte geleckt | hätten geleckt<br>hättet geleckt<br>hätten geleckt |
| | **Future** | | **Future Perfect** | |
| | werde lecken<br>werdest lecken<br>werde lecken | werden lecken<br>werdet lecken<br>werden lecken | werde geleckt haben<br>werdest geleckt haben<br>werde geleckt haben | werden geleckt haben<br>werdet geleckt haben<br>werden geleckt haben |
| | **Present and Future Conditional** | | **Past Conditional** | |
| | würde lecken<br>würdest lecken<br>würde lecken | würden lecken<br>würdet lecken<br>würden lecken | würde geleckt haben<br>würdest geleckt haben<br>würde geleckt haben | würden geleckt haben<br>würdet geleckt haben<br>würden geleckt haben |

## EXAMPLES

Nach jedem Abendessen leckt er sich die Finger. — After every supper, he licks his fingers.
Unser Boot fing an zu lecken. — Our boat began to leak.

**legen**
to lay, to put
**Auxiliary verb:** haben **Past participle:** gelegt
**Imperative:** Lege! Legt! Legen Sie!

| Mode | Simple Tenses | | Compound Tenses | |
|---|---|---|---|---|
| | *Singular* | *Plural* | *Singular* | *Plural* |
| Indicative | **Present** | | **Present Perfect** | |
| | lege<br>legst<br>legt | legen<br>legt<br>legen | habe gelegt<br>hast gelegt<br>hat gelegt | haben gelegt<br>habt gelegt<br>haben gelegt |
| | **Past** | | **Past Perfect** | |
| | legte<br>legtest<br>legte | legten<br>legtet<br>legten | hatte gelegt<br>hattest gelegt<br>hatte gelegt | hatten gelegt<br>hattet gelegt<br>hatten gelegt |
| | **Future** | | **Future Perfect** | |
| | werde legen<br>wirst legen<br>wird legen | werden legen<br>werdet legen<br>werden legen | werde gelegt haben<br>wirst gelegt haben<br>wird gelegt haben | werden gelegt haben<br>werdet gelegt haben<br>werden gelegt haben |
| Subjunctive | **Present** | | **Present Perfect** | |
| | lege<br>legest<br>lege | legen<br>leget<br>legen | habe gelegt<br>habest gelegt<br>habe gelegt | haben gelegt<br>habet gelegt<br>haben gelegt |
| | **Past** | | **Past Perfect** | |
| | legte<br>legtest<br>legte | legten<br>legtet<br>legten | hätte gelegt<br>hättest gelegt<br>hätte gelegt | hätten gelegt<br>hättet gelegt<br>hätten gelegt |
| | **Future** | | **Future Perfect** | |
| | werde legen<br>werdest legen<br>werde legen | werden legen<br>werdet legen<br>werden legen | werde gelegt haben<br>werdest gelegt haben<br>werde gelegt haben | werden gelegt haben<br>werdet gelegt haben<br>werden gelegt haben |
| | **Present and Future Conditional** | | **Past Conditional** | |
| | würde legen<br>würdest legen<br>würde legen | würden legen<br>würdet legen<br>würden legen | würde gelegt haben<br>würdest gelegt haben<br>würde gelegt haben | würden gelegt haben<br>würdet gelegt haben<br>würden gelegt haben |

## EXAMPLES

Sie haben großen Wert auf diesen Plan gelegt.
They attached great importance to this plan.

Er legte die Zeitung auf das Klavier.
He laid the newspaper on the piano.

**lehren**
to teach
**Auxiliary verb:** haben **Past participle:** gelehrt
**Imperative:** Lehre! Lehrt! Lehren Sie!

| Mode | Simple Tenses | | Compound Tenses | |
|---|---|---|---|---|
| | *Singular* | *Plural* | *Singular* | *Plural* |
| Indicative | **Present** | | **Present Perfect** | |
| | lehre<br>lehrst<br>lehrt | lehren<br>lehrt<br>lehren | habe gelehrt<br>hast gelehrt<br>hat gelehrt | haben gelehrt<br>habt gelehrt<br>haben gelehrt |
| | **Past** | | **Past Perfect** | |
| | lehrte<br>lehrtest<br>lehrte | lehrten<br>lehrtet<br>lehrten | hatte gelehrt<br>hattest gelehrt<br>hatte gelehrt | hatten gelehrt<br>hattet gelehrt<br>hatten gelehrt |
| | **Future** | | **Future Perfect** | |
| | werde lehren<br>wirst lehren<br>wird lehren | werden lehren<br>werdet lehren<br>werden lehren | werde gelehrt haben<br>wirst gelehrt haben<br>wird gelehrt haben | werden gelehrt haben<br>werdet gelehrt haben<br>werden gelehrt haben |
| Subjunctive | **Present** | | **Present Perfect** | |
| | lehre<br>lehrest<br>lehre | lehren<br>lehret<br>lehren | habe gelehrt<br>habest gelehrt<br>habe gelehrt | haben gelehrt<br>habet gelehrt<br>haben gelehrt |
| | **Past** | | **Past Perfect** | |
| | lehrte<br>lehrtest<br>lehrte | lehrten<br>lehrtet<br>lehrten | hätte gelehrt<br>hättest gelehrt<br>hätte gelehrt | hätten gelehrt<br>hättet gelehrt<br>hätten gelehrt |
| | **Future** | | **Future Perfect** | |
| | werde lehren<br>werdest lehren<br>werde lehren | werden lehren<br>werdet lehren<br>werden lehren | werde gelehrt haben<br>werdest gelehrt haben<br>werde gelehrt haben | werden gelehrt haben<br>werdet gelehrt haben<br>werden gelehrt haben |
| | **Present and Future Conditional** | | **Past Conditional** | |
| | würde lehren<br>würdest lehren<br>würde lehren | würden lehren<br>würdet lehren<br>würden lehren | würde gelehrt haben<br>würdest gelehrt haben<br>würde gelehrt haben | würden gelehrt haben<br>würdet gelehrt haben<br>würden gelehrt haben |

## EXAMPLES

Frau Bauer lehrt Physik und Chemie. — Mrs. Bauer teaches physics and chemistry.
Sein Vater hat ihn die Zeichensprache gelehrt. — His father taught him sign language.

**leiden**
to suffer, to endure
**Auxiliary verb:** haben **Past participle:** gelitten
**Imperative:** Leide! Leidet! Leiden Sie!

| Mode | Simple Tenses | | Compound Tenses | |
|---|---|---|---|---|
| | *Singular* | *Plural* | *Singular* | *Plural* |
| Indicative | **Present** | | **Present Perfect** | |
| | leide<br>leidest<br>leidet | leiden<br>leidet<br>leiden | habe gelitten<br>hast gelitten<br>hat gelitten | haben gelitten<br>habt gelitten<br>haben gelitten |
| | **Past** | | **Past Perfect** | |
| | litt<br>littest<br>litt | litten<br>littet<br>litten | hatte gelitten<br>hattest gelitten<br>hatte gelitten | hatten gelitten<br>hattet gelitten<br>hatten gelitten |
| | **Future** | | **Future Perfect** | |
| | werde leiden<br>wirst leiden<br>wird leiden | werden leiden<br>werdet leiden<br>werden leiden | werde gelitten haben<br>wirst gelitten haben<br>wird gelitten haben | werden gelitten haben<br>werdet gelitten haben<br>werden gelitten haben |
| Subjunctive | **Present** | | **Present Perfect** | |
| | leide<br>leidest<br>leide | leiden<br>leidet<br>leiden | habe gelitten<br>habest gelitten<br>habe gelitten | haben gelitten<br>habet gelitten<br>haben gelitten |
| | **Past** | | **Past Perfect** | |
| | litte<br>littest<br>litte | litten<br>littet<br>litten | hätte gelitten<br>hättest gelitten<br>hätte gelitten | hätten gelitten<br>hättet gelitten<br>hätten gelitten |
| | **Future** | | **Future Perfect** | |
| | werde leiden<br>werdest leiden<br>werde leiden | werden leiden<br>werdet leiden<br>werden leiden | werde gelitten haben<br>werdest gelitten haben<br>werde gelitten haben | werden gelitten haben<br>werdet gelitten haben<br>werden gelitten haben |
| | **Present and Future Conditional** | | **Past Conditional** | |
| | würde leiden<br>würdest leiden<br>würde leiden | würden leiden<br>würdet leiden<br>würden leiden | würde gelitten haben<br>würdest gelitten haben<br>würde gelitten haben | würden gelitten haben<br>würdet gelitten haben<br>würden gelitten haben |

## EXAMPLES

Ich kann den neuen Chef nicht leiden.
I can't stand the new boss.

Meine Tante leidet schon lange an Krebs.
My aunt has suffered from cancer for a long time.

**leihen**

to lend, to loan

**Auxiliary verb:** haben **Past participle:** geliehen

**Imperative:** Leihe! Leiht! Leihen Sie!

| Mode | Simple Tenses | | Compound Tenses | |
|---|---|---|---|---|
| | *Singular* | *Plural* | *Singular* | *Plural* |
| Indicative | **Present** | | **Present Perfect** | |
| | leihe<br>leihst<br>leiht | leihen<br>leiht<br>leihen | habe geliehen<br>hast geliehen<br>hat geliehen | haben geliehen<br>habt geliehen<br>haben geliehen |
| | **Past** | | **Past Perfect** | |
| | lieh<br>liehst<br>lieh | liehen<br>lieht<br>liehen | hatte geliehen<br>hattest geliehen<br>hatte geliehen | hatten geliehen<br>hattet geliehen<br>hatten geliehen |
| | **Future** | | **Future Perfect** | |
| | werde leihen<br>wirst leihen<br>wird leihen | werden leihen<br>werdet leihen<br>werden leihen | werde geliehen haben<br>wirst geliehen haben<br>wird geliehen haben | werden geliehen haben<br>werdet geliehen haben<br>werden geliehen haben |
| Subjunctive | **Present** | | **Present Perfect** | |
| | leihe<br>leihest<br>leihe | leihen<br>leihet<br>leihen | habe geliehen<br>habest geliehen<br>habe geliehen | haben geliehen<br>habet geliehen<br>haben geliehen |
| | **Past** | | **Past Perfect** | |
| | liehe<br>liehest<br>liehe | liehen<br>liehet<br>liehen | hätte geliehen<br>hättest geliehen<br>hätte geliehen | hätten geliehen<br>hättet geliehen<br>hätten geliehen |
| | **Future** | | **Future Perfect** | |
| | werde leihen<br>werdest leihen<br>werde leihen | werden leihen<br>werdet leihen<br>werden leihen | werde geliehen haben<br>werdest geliehen haben<br>werde geliehen haben | werden geliehen haben<br>werdet geliehen haben<br>werden geliehen haben |
| | **Present and Future Conditional** | | **Past Conditional** | |
| | würde leihen<br>würdest leihen<br>würde leihen | würden leihen<br>würdet leihen<br>würden leihen | würde geliehen haben<br>würdest geliehen haben<br>würde geliehen haben | würden geliehen haben<br>würdet geliehen haben<br>würden geliehen haben |

## EXAMPLES

Martin hat mir seinen Regenschirm geliehen.
Martin loaned me his umbrella.

Wenn Sie wollen, kann er Ihnen ein paar Dollar leihen.
If you want, he can lend you a couple of dollars.

**leisten (sich)**
to fulfill, to accomplish, to afford
**Auxiliary verb:** haben **Past participle:** geleistet
**Imperative:** Leiste! Leistet! Leisten Sie!

| Mode | Simple Tenses | | Compound Tenses | |
|---|---|---|---|---|
| | *Singular* | *Plural* | *Singular* | *Plural* |
| Indicative | **Present** | | **Present Perfect** | |
| | leiste<br>leistest<br>leistet | leisten<br>leistet<br>leisten | habe geleistet<br>hast geleistet<br>hat geleistet | haben geleistet<br>habt geleistet<br>haben geleistet |
| | **Past** | | **Past Perfect** | |
| | leistete<br>leistetest<br>leistete | leisteten<br>leistetet<br>leisteten | hatte geleistet<br>hattest geleistet<br>hatte geleistet | hatten geleistet<br>hattet geleistet<br>hatten geleistet |
| | **Future** | | **Future Perfect** | |
| | werde leisten<br>wirst leisten<br>wird leisten | werden leisten<br>werdet leisten<br>werden leisten | werde geleistet haben<br>wirst geleistet haben<br>wird geleistet haben | werden geleistet haben<br>werdet geleistet haben<br>werden geleistet haben |
| Subjunctive | **Present** | | **Present Perfect** | |
| | leiste<br>leistest<br>leiste | leisten<br>leistet<br>leisten | habe geleistet<br>habest geleistet<br>habe geleistet | haben geleistet<br>habet geleistet<br>haben geleistet |
| | **Past** | | **Past Perfect** | |
| | leistete<br>leistetest<br>leistete | leisteten<br>leistetet<br>leisteten | hätte geleistet<br>hättest geleistet<br>hätte geleistet | hätten geleistet<br>hättet geleistet<br>hätten geleistet |
| | **Future** | | **Future Perfect** | |
| | werde leisten<br>werdest leisten<br>werde leisten | werden leisten<br>werdet leisten<br>werden leisten | werde geleistet haben<br>werdest geleistet haben<br>werde geleistet haben | werden geleistet haben<br>werdet geleistet haben<br>werden geleistet haben |
| | **Present and Future Conditional** | | **Past Conditional** | |
| | würde leisten<br>würdest leisten<br>würde leisten | würden leisten<br>würdet leisten<br>würden leisten | würde geleistet haben<br>würdest geleistet haben<br>würde geleistet haben | würden geleistet haben<br>würdet geleistet haben<br>würden geleistet haben |

## EXAMPLES

| | |
|---|---|
| Ich kann es mir nicht leisten so oft ins Kino zu gehen. | I can't afford to go to the movies so often. |
| Der Wissenschaftler hat in seinem Leben viel geleistet. | The scientist accomplished a lot in his life. |

**leiten**

to lead, to guide, to oversee

**Auxiliary verb:** haben **Past participle:** geleitet

**Imperative:** Leite! Leitet! Leiten Sie!

| Mode | Simple Tenses | | Compound Tenses | |
|---|---|---|---|---|
| | *Singular* | *Plural* | *Singular* | *Plural* |
| Indicative | **Present** | | **Present Perfect** | |
| | leite<br>leitest<br>leitet | leiten<br>leitet<br>leiten | habe geleitet<br>hast geleitet<br>hat geleitet | haben geleitet<br>habt geleitet<br>haben geleitet |
| | **Past** | | **Past Perfect** | |
| | leitete<br>leitetest<br>leitete | leiteten<br>leitetet<br>leiteten | hatte geleitet<br>hattest geleitet<br>hatte geleitet | hatten geleitet<br>hattet geleitet<br>hatten geleitet |
| | **Future** | | **Future Perfect** | |
| | werde leiten<br>wirst leiten<br>wird leiten | werden leiten<br>werdet leiten<br>werden leiten | werde geleitet haben<br>wirst geleitet haben<br>wird geleitet haben | werden geleitet haben<br>werdet geleitet haben<br>werden geleitet haben |
| Subjunctive | **Present** | | **Present Perfect** | |
| | leite<br>leitest<br>leite | leiten<br>leitet<br>leiten | habe geleitet<br>habest geleitet<br>habe geleitet | haben geleitet<br>habet geleitet<br>haben geleitet |
| | **Past** | | **Past Perfect** | |
| | leitete<br>leitetest<br>leitete | leiteten<br>leitetet<br>leiteten | hätte geleitet<br>hättest geleitet<br>hätte geleitet | hätten geleitet<br>hättet geleitet<br>hätten geleitet |
| | **Future** | | **Future Perfect** | |
| | werde leiten<br>werdest leiten<br>werde leiten | werden leiten<br>werdet leiten<br>werden leiten | werde geleitet haben<br>werdest geleitet haben<br>werde geleitet haben | werden geleitet haben<br>werdet geleitet haben<br>werden geleitet haben |
| | **Present and Future Conditional** | | **Past Conditional** | |
| | würde leiten<br>würdest leiten<br>würde leiten | würden leiten<br>würdet leiten<br>würden leiten | würde geleitet haben<br>würdest geleitet haben<br>würde geleitet haben | würden geleitet haben<br>würdet geleitet haben<br>würden geleitet haben |

## EXAMPLES

Könntest du heute die Diskussion leiten?
Could you lead the discussion today?

Doktor Schneider leitet diese Abteilung.
Doctor Schneider leads this department.

**lenken**
to turn, to navigate, to steer
**Auxiliary verb:** haben **Past participle:** gelenkt
**Imperative:** Lenke! Lenkt! Lenken Sie!

| Mode | Simple Tenses | | Compound Tenses | |
|---|---|---|---|---|
| | *Singular* | *Plural* | *Singular* | *Plural* |
| Indicative | **Present** | | **Present Perfect** | |
| | lenke<br>lenkst<br>lenkt | lenken<br>lenkt<br>lenken | habe gelenkt<br>hast gelenkt<br>hat gelenkt | haben gelenkt<br>habt gelenkt<br>haben gelenkt |
| | **Past** | | **Past Perfect** | |
| | lenkte<br>lenktest<br>lenkte | lenkten<br>lenktet<br>lenkten | hatte gelenkt<br>hattest gelenkt<br>hatte gelenkt | hatten gelenkt<br>hattet gelenkt<br>hatten gelenkt |
| | **Future** | | **Future Perfect** | |
| | werde lenken<br>wirst lenken<br>wird lenken | werden lenken<br>werdet lenken<br>werden lenken | werde gelenkt haben<br>wirst gelenkt haben<br>wird gelenkt haben | werden gelenkt haben<br>werdet gelenkt haben<br>werden gelenkt haben |
| Subjunctive | **Present** | | **Present Perfect** | |
| | lenke<br>lenkest<br>lenke | lenken<br>lenket<br>lenken | habe gelenkt<br>habest gelenkt<br>habe gelenkt | haben gelenkt<br>habet gelenkt<br>haben gelenkt |
| | **Past** | | **Past Perfect** | |
| | lenkte<br>lenktest<br>lenkte | lenkten<br>lenktet<br>lenkten | hätte gelenkt<br>hättest gelenkt<br>hätte gelenkt | hätten gelenkt<br>hättet gelenkt<br>hätten gelenkt |
| | **Future** | | **Future Perfect** | |
| | werde lenken<br>werdest lenken<br>werde lenken | werden lenken<br>werdet lenken<br>werden lenken | werde gelenkt haben<br>werdest gelenkt haben<br>werde gelenkt haben | werden gelenkt haben<br>werdet gelenkt haben<br>werden gelenkt haben |
| | **Present and Future Conditional** | | **Past Conditional** | |
| | würde lenken<br>würdest lenken<br>würde lenken | würden lenken<br>würdet lenken<br>würden lenken | würde gelenkt haben<br>würdest gelenkt haben<br>würde gelenkt haben | würden gelenkt haben<br>würdet gelenkt haben<br>würden gelenkt haben |

## EXAMPLES

Er versucht das Gespräch auf einen bestimmten Gegenstand zu lenken.
He tries to turn the conversation toward a specific topic.

Ohne meine Brille kann ich den Wagen nicht lenken.
Without my glasses, I can't steer the car.

**lernen**
to learn
**Auxiliary verb:** haben **Past participle:** gelernt
**Imperative:** Lerne! Lernt! Lernen Sie!

| Mode | Simple Tenses | | Compound Tenses | |
|---|---|---|---|---|
| | *Singular* | *Plural* | *Singular* | *Plural* |
| Indicative | **Present** | | **Present Perfect** | |
| | lerne<br>lernst<br>lernt | lernen<br>lernt<br>lernen | habe gelernt<br>hast gelernt<br>hat gelernt | haben gelernt<br>habt gelernt<br>haben gelernt |
| | **Past** | | **Past Perfect** | |
| | lernte<br>lerntest<br>lernte | lernten<br>lerntet<br>lernten | hatte gelernt<br>hattest gelernt<br>hatte gelernt | hatten gelernt<br>hattet gelernt<br>hatten gelernt |
| | **Future** | | **Future Perfect** | |
| | werde lernen<br>wirst lernen<br>wird lernen | werden lernen<br>werdet lernen<br>werden lernen | werde gelernt haben<br>wirst gelernt haben<br>wird gelernt haben | werden gelernt haben<br>werdet gelernt haben<br>werden gelernt haben |
| Subjunctive | **Present** | | **Present Perfect** | |
| | lerne<br>lernest<br>lerne | lernen<br>lernet<br>lernen | habe gelernt<br>habest gelernt<br>habe gelernt | haben gelernt<br>habet gelernt<br>haben gelernt |
| | **Past** | | **Past Perfect** | |
| | lernte<br>lerntest<br>lernte | lernten<br>lerntet<br>lernten | hätte gelernt<br>hättest gelernt<br>hätte gelernt | hätten gelernt<br>hättet gelernt<br>hätten gelernt |
| | **Future** | | **Future Perfect** | |
| | werde lernen<br>werdest lernen<br>werde lernen | werden lernen<br>werdet lernen<br>werden lernen | werde gelernt haben<br>werdest gelernt haben<br>werde gelernt haben | werden gelernt haben<br>werdet gelernt haben<br>werden gelernt haben |
| | **Present and Future Conditional** | | **Past Conditional** | |
| | würde lernen<br>würdest lernen<br>würde lernen | würden lernen<br>würdet lernen<br>würden lernen | würde gelernt haben<br>würdest gelernt haben<br>würde gelernt haben | würden gelernt haben<br>würdet gelernt haben<br>würden gelernt haben |

## EXAMPLES

Auf dieser Stufe lernen die Studenten programmieren.
On this level, the students learn programming.

„Was hast du heute gelernt?", fragte Onkel Johannes.
"What did you learn today?", Uncle Johannes asked.

**lesen**
to read
**Auxiliary verb:** haben **Past participle:** gelesen
**Imperative:** Lies! Lest! Lesen Sie!

| Mode | Simple Tenses | | Compound Tenses | |
|---|---|---|---|---|
| | *Singular* | *Plural* | *Singular* | *Plural* |
| Indicative | **Present** | | **Present Perfect** | |
| | lese<br>liest<br>liest | lesen<br>lest<br>lesen | habe gelesen<br>hast gelesen<br>hat gelesen | haben gelesen<br>habt gelesen<br>haben gelesen |
| | **Past** | | **Past Perfect** | |
| | las<br>lasest<br>las | lasen<br>last<br>lasen | hatte gelesen<br>hattest gelesen<br>hatte gelesen | hatten gelesen<br>hattet gelesen<br>hatten gelesen |
| | **Future** | | **Future Perfect** | |
| | werde lesen<br>wirst lesen<br>wird lesen | werden lesen<br>werdet lesen<br>werden lesen | werde gelesen haben<br>wirst gelesen haben<br>wird gelesen haben | werden gelesen haben<br>werdet gelesen haben<br>werden gelesen haben |
| Subjunctive | **Present** | | **Present Perfect** | |
| | lese<br>lesest<br>lese | lesen<br>leset<br>lesen | habe gelesen<br>habest gelesen<br>habe gelesen | haben gelesen<br>habet gelesen<br>haben gelesen |
| | **Past** | | **Past Perfect** | |
| | läse<br>läsest<br>läse | läsen<br>läset<br>läsen | hätte gelesen<br>hättest gelesen<br>hätte gelesen | hätten gelesen<br>hättet gelesen<br>hätten gelesen |
| | **Future** | | **Future Perfect** | |
| | werde lesen<br>werdest lesen<br>werde lesen | werden lesen<br>werdet lesen<br>werden lesen | werde gelesen haben<br>werdest gelesen haben<br>werde gelesen haben | werden gelesen haben<br>werdet gelesen haben<br>werden gelesen haben |
| | **Present and Future Conditional** | | **Past Conditional** | |
| | würde lesen<br>würdest lesen<br>würde lesen | würden lesen<br>würdet lesen<br>würden lesen | würde gelesen haben<br>würdest gelesen haben<br>würde gelesen haben | würden gelesen haben<br>würdet gelesen haben<br>würden gelesen haben |

**Note:** With inseparable prefixes, the principal parts of this verb are, for example, *verliest, verlas, hat verlesen.* With separable prefixes, the principal parts are, for example, *liest vor, las vor, hat vorgelesen.*

## EXAMPLES

In der ersten Klasse lernen die Kinder lesen und schreiben.
In the first grade, the children learn to read and write.

Ich habe den Text dreimal gelesen, aber ich verstehe ihn nicht.
I read the text three times, but I don't understand it.

**lieben**

to love, to like

**Auxiliary verb:** haben **Past participle:** geliebt

**Imperative:** Liebe! Liebt! Lieben Sie!

| Mode | Simple Tenses | | Compound Tenses | |
|---|---|---|---|---|
| | *Singular* | *Plural* | *Singular* | *Plural* |
| Indicative | **Present** | | **Present Perfect** | |
| | liebe<br>liebst<br>liebt | lieben<br>liebt<br>lieben | habe geliebt<br>hast geliebt<br>hat geliebt | haben geliebt<br>habt geliebt<br>haben geliebt |
| | **Past** | | **Past Perfect** | |
| | liebte<br>liebtest<br>liebte | liebten<br>liebtet<br>liebten | hatte geliebt<br>hattest geliebt<br>hatte geliebt | hatten geliebt<br>hattet geliebt<br>hatten geliebt |
| | **Future** | | **Future Perfect** | |
| | werde lieben<br>wirst lieben<br>wird lieben | werden lieben<br>werdet lieben<br>werden lieben | werde geliebt haben<br>wirst geliebt haben<br>wird geliebt haben | werden geliebt haben<br>werdet geliebt haben<br>werden geliebt haben |
| Subjunctive | **Present** | | **Present Perfect** | |
| | liebe<br>liebest<br>liebe | lieben<br>liebet<br>lieben | habe geliebt<br>habest geliebt<br>habe geliebt | haben geliebt<br>habet geliebt<br>haben geliebt |
| | **Past** | | **Past Perfect** | |
| | liebte<br>liebtest<br>liebte | liebten<br>liebtet<br>liebten | hätte geliebt<br>hättest geliebt<br>hätte geliebt | hätten geliebt<br>hättet geliebt<br>hätten geliebt |
| | **Future** | | **Future Perfect** | |
| | werde lieben<br>werdest lieben<br>werde lieben | werden lieben<br>werdet lieben<br>werden lieben | werde geliebt haben<br>werdest geliebt haben<br>werde geliebt haben | werden geliebt haben<br>werdet geliebt haben<br>werden geliebt haben |
| | **Present and Future Conditional** | | **Past Conditional** | |
| | würde lieben<br>würdest lieben<br>würde lieben | würden lieben<br>würdet lieben<br>würden lieben | würde geliebt haben<br>würdest geliebt haben<br>würde geliebt haben | würden geliebt haben<br>würdet geliebt haben<br>würden geliebt haben |

## EXAMPLES

Großvater liebte seine Enkelkinder über alles.

Grandfather loved his grandchildren more than anything.

„Ich liebe dich," flüsterte er ihr ins Ohr.

"I love you," he whispered in her ear.

**liegen**
to lie, to recline, to be situated
**Auxiliary verb:** haben **Past participle:** gelegen
**Imperative:** Liege! Liegt! Liegen Sie!

| Mode | Simple Tenses | | Compound Tenses | |
|---|---|---|---|---|
| | *Singular* | *Plural* | *Singular* | *Plural* |
| Indicative | **Present** | | **Present Perfect** | |
| | liege<br>liegst<br>liegt | liegen<br>liegt<br>liegen | habe gelegen<br>hast gelegen<br>hat gelegen | haben gelegen<br>habt gelegen<br>haben gelegen |
| | **Past** | | **Past Perfect** | |
| | lag<br>lagst<br>lag | lagen<br>lagt<br>lagen | hatte gelegen<br>hattest gelegen<br>hatte gelegen | hatten gelegen<br>hattet gelegen<br>hatten gelegen |
| | **Future** | | **Future Perfect** | |
| | werde liegen<br>wirst liegen<br>wird liegen | werden liegen<br>werdet liegen<br>werden liegen | werde gelegen haben<br>wirst gelegen haben<br>wird gelegen haben | werden gelegen haben<br>werdet gelegen haben<br>werden gelegen haben |
| Subjunctive | **Present** | | **Present Perfect** | |
| | liege<br>liegest<br>liege | liegen<br>lieget<br>liegen | habe gelegen<br>habest gelegen<br>habe gelegen | haben gelegen<br>habet gelegen<br>haben gelegen |
| | **Past** | | **Past Perfect** | |
| | läge<br>lägest<br>läge | lägen<br>läget<br>lägen | hätte gelegen<br>hättest gelegen<br>hätte gelegen | hätten gelegen<br>hättet gelegen<br>hätten gelegen |
| | **Future** | | **Future Perfect** | |
| | werde liegen<br>werdest liegen<br>werde liegen | werden liegen<br>werdet liegen<br>werden liegen | werde gelegen haben<br>werdest gelegen haben<br>werde gelegen haben | werden gelegen haben<br>werdet gelegen haben<br>werden gelegen haben |
| | **Present and Future Conditional** | | **Past Conditional** | |
| | würde liegen<br>würdest liegen<br>würde liegen | würden liegen<br>würdet liegen<br>würden liegen | würde gelegen haben<br>würdest gelegen haben<br>würde gelegen haben | würden gelegen haben<br>würdet gelegen haben<br>würden gelegen haben |

## EXAMPLES

Die Schuld liegt an dir.
It's your fault.

Wir haben den ganzen Tag neben dem Schwimmbecken in der Sonne gelegen.
We spent the whole day lying out in the sun next to the pool.

Hamburg liegt an der Elbe.
Hamburg is located on the Elbe River.

**loben**

to praise

**Auxiliary verb:** haben **Past participle:** gelobt

**Imperative:** Lobe! Lobt! Loben Sie!

| Mode | Simple Tenses | | Compound Tenses | |
|---|---|---|---|---|
| | *Singular* | *Plural* | *Singular* | *Plural* |
| Indicative | **Present** | | **Present Perfect** | |
| | lobe<br>lobst<br>lobt | loben<br>lobt<br>loben | habe gelobt<br>hast gelobt<br>hat gelobt | haben gelobt<br>habt gelobt<br>haben gelobt |
| | **Past** | | **Past Perfect** | |
| | lobte<br>lobtest<br>lobte | lobten<br>lobtet<br>lobten | hatte gelobt<br>hattest gelobt<br>hatte gelobt | hatten gelobt<br>hattet gelobt<br>hatten gelobt |
| | **Future** | | **Future Perfect** | |
| | werde loben<br>wirst loben<br>wird loben | werden loben<br>werdet loben<br>werden loben | werde gelobt haben<br>wirst gelobt haben<br>wird gelobt haben | werden gelobt haben<br>werdet gelobt haben<br>werden gelobt haben |
| Subjunctive | **Present** | | **Present Perfect** | |
| | lobe<br>lobest<br>lobe | loben<br>lobet<br>loben | habe gelobt<br>habest gelobt<br>habe gelobt | haben gelobt<br>habet gelobt<br>haben gelobt |
| | **Past** | | **Past Perfect** | |
| | lobte<br>lobtest<br>lobte | lobten<br>lobtet<br>lobten | hätte gelobt<br>hättest gelobt<br>hätte gelobt | hätten gelobt<br>hättet gelobt<br>hätten gelobt |
| | **Future** | | **Future Perfect** | |
| | werde loben<br>werdest loben<br>werde loben | werden loben<br>werdet loben<br>werden loben | werde gelobt haben<br>werdest gelobt haben<br>werde gelobt haben | werden gelobt haben<br>werdet gelobt haben<br>werden gelobt haben |
| | **Present and Future Conditional** | | **Past Conditional** | |
| | würde loben<br>würdest loben<br>würde loben | würden loben<br>würdet loben<br>würden loben | würde gelobt haben<br>würdest gelobt haben<br>würde gelobt haben | würden gelobt haben<br>würdet gelobt haben<br>würden gelobt haben |

## EXAMPLES

Du solltest deine Kinder öfter loben.
You should praise your children more often.

Sie ist von ihrem Professor wegen ihrer ausgezeichneten Dissertation gelobt worden.
She was praised by her professor for her excellent disseration.

**lohnen (sich)**
to be worth, to reward
**Auxiliary verb:** haben **Past participle:** gelohnt
**Imperative:** N/A

| Mode | Simple Tenses | | Compound Tenses | |
|---|---|---|---|---|
| | *Singular* | *Plural* | *Singular* | *Plural* |
| Indicative | **Present** | | **Present Perfect** | |
| | lohne<br>lohnst<br>lohnt | lohnen<br>lohnt<br>lohnen | habe gelohnt<br>hast gelohnt<br>hat gelohnt | haben gelohnt<br>habt gelohnt<br>haben gelohnt |
| | **Past** | | **Past Perfect** | |
| | lohnte<br>lohntest<br>lohnte | lohnten<br>lohntet<br>lohnten | hatte gelohnt<br>hattest gelohnt<br>hatte gelohnt | hatten gelohnt<br>hattet gelohnt<br>hatten gelohnt |
| | **Future** | | **Future Perfect** | |
| | werde lohnen<br>wirst lohnen<br>wird lohnen | werden lohnen<br>werdet lohnen<br>werden lohnen | werde gelohnt haben<br>wirst gelohnt haben<br>wird gelohnt haben | werden gelohnt haben<br>werdet gelohnt haben<br>werden gelohnt haben |
| Subjunctive | **Present** | | **Present Perfect** | |
| | lohne<br>lohnest<br>lohne | lohnen<br>lohnet<br>lohnen | habe gelohnt<br>habest gelohnt<br>habe gelohnt | haben gelohnt<br>habet gelohnt<br>haben gelohnt |
| | **Past** | | **Past Perfect** | |
| | lohnte<br>lohntest<br>lohnte | lohnten<br>lohntet<br>lohnten | hätte gelohnt<br>hättest gelohnt<br>hätte gelohnt | hätten gelohnt<br>hättet gelohnt<br>hätten gelohnt |
| | **Future** | | **Future Perfect** | |
| | werde lohnen<br>werdest lohnen<br>werde lohnen | werden lohnen<br>werdet lohnen<br>werden lohnen | werde gelohnt haben<br>werdest gelohnt haben<br>werde gelohnt haben | werden gelohnt haben<br>werdet gelohnt haben<br>werden gelohnt haben |
| | **Present and Future Conditional** | | **Past Conditional** | |
| | würde lohnen<br>würdest lohnen<br>würde lohnen | würden lohnen<br>würdet lohnen<br>würden lohnen | würde gelohnt haben<br>würdest gelohnt haben<br>würde gelohnt haben | würden gelohnt haben<br>würdet gelohnt haben<br>würden gelohnt haben |

## EXAMPLES

Es lohnt sich nicht.
It's not worth it.

Der eigennützige Mann hat seinem Retter mit Undank gelohnt.
The selfish man rewarded his rescuer with ingratitude.

**löschen**

to extinguish, to quench

**Auxiliary verb:** haben **Past participle:** gelöscht

**Imperative:** Lösche! Löscht! Löschen Sie!

| Mode | Simple Tenses | | Compound Tenses | |
|---|---|---|---|---|
| | *Singular* | *Plural* | *Singular* | *Plural* |
| Indicative | **Present** | | **Present Perfect** | |
| | lösche<br>löschst<br>löscht | löschen<br>löscht<br>löschen | habe gelöscht<br>hast gelöscht<br>hat gelöscht | haben gelöscht<br>habt gelöscht<br>haben gelöscht |
| | **Past** | | **Past Perfect** | |
| | löschte<br>löschtest<br>löschte | löschten<br>löschtet<br>löschten | hatte gelöscht<br>hattest gelöscht<br>hatte gelöscht | hatten gelöscht<br>hattet gelöscht<br>hatten gelöscht |
| | **Future** | | **Future Perfect** | |
| | werde löschen<br>wirst löschen<br>wird löschen | werden löschen<br>werdet löschen<br>werden löschen | werde gelöscht haben<br>wirst gelöscht haben<br>wird gelöscht haben | werden gelöscht haben<br>werdet gelöscht haben<br>werden gelöscht haben |
| Subjunctive | **Present** | | **Present Perfect** | |
| | lösche<br>löschest<br>lösche | löschen<br>löschet<br>löschen | habe gelöscht<br>habest gelöscht<br>habe gelöscht | haben gelöscht<br>habet gelöscht<br>haben gelöscht |
| | **Past** | | **Past Perfect** | |
| | löschte<br>löschtest<br>löschte | löschten<br>löschtet<br>löschten | hätte gelöscht<br>hättest gelöscht<br>hätte gelöscht | hätten gelöscht<br>hättet gelöscht<br>hätten gelöscht |
| | **Future** | | **Future Perfect** | |
| | werde löschen<br>werdest löschen<br>werde löschen | werden löschen<br>werdet löschen<br>werden löschen | werde gelöscht haben<br>werdest gelöscht haben<br>werde gelöscht haben | werden gelöscht haben<br>werdet gelöscht haben<br>werden gelöscht haben |
| | **Present and Future Conditional** | | **Past Conditional** | |
| | würde löschen<br>würdest löschen<br>würde löschen | würden löschen<br>würdet löschen<br>würden löschen | würde gelöscht haben<br>würdest gelöscht haben<br>würde gelöscht haben | würden gelöscht haben<br>würdet gelöscht haben<br>würden gelöscht haben |

**Note:** *Erlöschen* is intransitive. It requires the auxiliary *sein* in the perfect tenses and has the following principal parts: *erlöscht, erlosch, ist erloschen.*

## EXAMPLES

Das Mineralwasser löschte meinen Durst sofort.

The mineral water immediately quenched my thirst.

Trotz des starken Windes konnte die Feuerwehr das Feuer löschen.

In spite of the strong wind, the fire department was able to extinguish the fire.

**lösen**
to loosen, to solve, to dissolve
**Auxiliary verb:** haben **Past participle:** gelöst
**Imperative:** Löse! Löst! Lösen Sie!

| Mode | Simple Tenses | | Compound Tenses | |
|---|---|---|---|---|
| | *Singular* | *Plural* | *Singular* | *Plural* |
| Indicative | **Present** | | **Present Perfect** | |
| | löse<br>löst<br>löst | lösen<br>löst<br>lösen | habe gelöst<br>hast gelöst<br>hat gelöst | haben gelöst<br>habt gelöst<br>haben gelöst |
| | **Past** | | **Past Perfect** | |
| | löste<br>löstest<br>löste | lösten<br>löstet<br>lösten | hatte gelöst<br>hattest gelöst<br>hatte gelöst | hatten gelöst<br>hattet gelöst<br>hatten gelöst |
| | **Future** | | **Future Perfect** | |
| | werde lösen<br>wirst lösen<br>wird lösen | werden lösen<br>werdet lösen<br>werden lösen | werde gelöst haben<br>wirst gelöst haben<br>wird gelöst haben | werden gelöst haben<br>werdet gelöst haben<br>werden gelöst haben |
| Subjunctive | **Present** | | **Present Perfect** | |
| | löse<br>lösest<br>löse | lösen<br>löset<br>lösen | habe gelöst<br>habest gelöst<br>habe gelöst | haben gelöst<br>habet gelöst<br>haben gelöst |
| | **Past** | | **Past Perfect** | |
| | löste<br>löstest<br>löste | lösten<br>löstet<br>lösten | hätte gelöst<br>hättest gelöst<br>hätte gelöst | hätten gelöst<br>hättet gelöst<br>hätten gelöst |
| | **Future** | | **Future Perfect** | |
| | werde lösen<br>werdest lösen<br>werde lösen | werden lösen<br>werdet lösen<br>werden lösen | werde gelöst haben<br>werdest gelöst haben<br>werde gelöst haben | werden gelöst haben<br>werdet gelöst haben<br>werden gelöst haben |
| | **Present and Future Conditional** | | **Past Conditional** | |
| | würde lösen<br>würdest lösen<br>würde lösen | würden lösen<br>würdet lösen<br>würden lösen | würde gelöst haben<br>würdest gelöst haben<br>würde gelöst haben | würden gelöst haben<br>würdet gelöst haben<br>würden gelöst haben |

## EXAMPLES

Diese neue Arznei wird seinen Husten lösen. — This new medicine will loosen his cough.
Lisa hat das Rätsel nicht lösen können. — Lisa couldn't solve the riddle.

**lügen**
to lie, to fib
**Auxiliary verb:** haben **Past participle:** gelogen
**Imperative:** Lüge! Lügt! Lügen Sie!

| Mode | Simple Tenses | | Compound Tenses | |
|---|---|---|---|---|
| | *Singular* | *Plural* | *Singular* | *Plural* |
| Indicative | **Present** | | **Present Perfect** | |
| | lüge<br>lügst<br>lügt | lügen<br>lügt<br>lügen | habe gelogen<br>hast gelogen<br>hat gelogen | haben gelogen<br>habt gelogen<br>haben gelogen |
| | **Past** | | **Past Perfect** | |
| | log<br>logst<br>log | logen<br>logt<br>logen | hatte gelogen<br>hattest gelogen<br>hatte gelogen | hatten gelogen<br>hattet gelogen<br>hatten gelogen |
| | **Future** | | **Future Perfect** | |
| | werde lügen<br>wirst lügen<br>wird lügen | werden lügen<br>werdet lügen<br>werden lügen | werde gelogen haben<br>wirst gelogen haben<br>wird gelogen haben | werden gelogen haben<br>werdet gelogen haben<br>werden gelogen haben |
| Subjunctive | **Present** | | **Present Perfect** | |
| | lüge<br>lügest<br>lüge | lügen<br>lüget<br>lügen | habe gelogen<br>habest gelogen<br>habe gelogen | haben gelogen<br>habet gelogen<br>haben gelogen |
| | **Past** | | **Past Perfect** | |
| | löge<br>lögest<br>löge | lögen<br>löget<br>lögen | hätte gelogen<br>hättest gelogen<br>hätte gelogen | hätten gelogen<br>hättet gelogen<br>hätten gelogen |
| | **Future** | | **Future Perfect** | |
| | werde lügen<br>werdest lügen<br>werde lügen | werden lügen<br>werdet lügen<br>werden lügen | werde gelogen haben<br>werdest gelogen haben<br>werde gelogen haben | werden gelogen haben<br>werdet gelogen haben<br>werden gelogen haben |
| | **Present and Future Conditional** | | **Past Conditional** | |
| | würde lügen<br>würdest lügen<br>würde lügen | würden lügen<br>würdet lügen<br>würden lügen | würde gelogen haben<br>würdest gelogen haben<br>würde gelogen haben | würden gelogen haben<br>würdet gelogen haben<br>würden gelogen haben |

## EXAMPLE

Der unverschämte Junge lügt das Blaue vom Himmel herunter. — The shameless boy lies like a rug.

**machen**
to make, to do
**Auxiliary verb:** haben **Past participle:** gemacht
**Imperative:** Mache! Macht! Machen Sie!

| Mode | Simple Tenses | | Compound Tenses | |
|---|---|---|---|---|
| | *Singular* | *Plural* | *Singular* | *Plural* |
| Indicative | **Present** | | **Present Perfect** | |
| | mache<br>machst<br>macht | machen<br>macht<br>machen | habe gemacht<br>hast gemacht<br>hat gemacht | haben gemacht<br>habt gemacht<br>haben gemacht |
| | **Past** | | **Past Perfect** | |
| | machte<br>machtest<br>machte | machten<br>machtet<br>machten | hatte gemacht<br>hattest gemacht<br>hatte gemacht | hatten gemacht<br>hattet gemacht<br>hatten gemacht |
| | **Future** | | **Future Perfect** | |
| | werde machen<br>wirst machen<br>wird machen | werden machen<br>werdet machen<br>werden machen | werde gemacht haben<br>wirst gemacht haben<br>wird gemacht haben | werden gemacht haben<br>werdet gemacht haben<br>werden gemacht haben |
| Subjunctive | **Present** | | **Present Perfect** | |
| | mache<br>machest<br>mache | machen<br>machet<br>machen | habe gemacht<br>habest gemacht<br>habe gemacht | haben gemacht<br>habet gemacht<br>haben gemacht |
| | **Past** | | **Past Perfect** | |
| | machte<br>machtest<br>machte | machten<br>machtet<br>machten | hätte gemacht<br>hättest gemacht<br>hätte gemacht | hätten gemacht<br>hättet gemacht<br>hätten gemacht |
| | **Future** | | **Future Perfect** | |
| | werde machen<br>werdest machen<br>werde machen | werden machen<br>werdet machen<br>werden machen | werde gemacht haben<br>werdest gemacht haben<br>werde gemacht haben | werden gemacht haben<br>werdet gemacht haben<br>werden gemacht haben |
| | **Present and Future Conditional** | | **Past Conditional** | |
| | würde machen<br>würdest machen<br>würde machen | würden machen<br>würdet machen<br>würden machen | würde gemacht haben<br>würdest gemacht haben<br>würde gemacht haben | würden gemacht haben<br>würdet gemacht haben<br>würden gemacht haben |

## EXAMPLES

So macht es jeder. — Everybody does it like that.
Haben Sie diese Röcke selbst gemacht? — Did you make these skirts yourself?
Wir wollten ihm eine kleine Freude machen. — We wanted to do something nice for him.

**mähen**

to mow, to cut

**Auxiliary verb:** haben **Past participle:** gemäht

**Imperative:** Mähe! Mäht! Mähen Sie!

| Mode | Simple Tenses | | Compound Tenses | |
|---|---|---|---|---|
| | *Singular* | *Plural* | *Singular* | *Plural* |
| Indicative | **Present** | | **Present Perfect** | |
| | mähe<br>mähst<br>mäht | mähen<br>mäht<br>mähen | habe gemäht<br>hast gemäht<br>hat gemäht | haben gemäht<br>habt gemäht<br>haben gemäht |
| | **Past** | | **Past Perfect** | |
| | mähte<br>mähtest<br>mähte | mähten<br>mähtet<br>mähten | hatte gemäht<br>hattest gemäht<br>hatte gemäht | hatten gemäht<br>hattet gemäht<br>hatten gemäht |
| | **Future** | | **Future Perfect** | |
| | werde mähen<br>wirst mähen<br>wird mähen | werden mähen<br>werdet mähen<br>werden mähen | werde gemäht haben<br>wirst gemäht haben<br>wird gemäht haben | werden gemäht haben<br>werdet gemäht haben<br>werden gemäht haben |
| Subjunctive | **Present** | | **Present Perfect** | |
| | mähe<br>mähest<br>mähe | mähen<br>mähet<br>mähen | habe gemäht<br>habest gemäht<br>habe gemäht | haben gemäht<br>habet gemäht<br>haben gemäht |
| | **Past** | | **Past Perfect** | |
| | mähte<br>mähtest<br>mähte | mähten<br>mähtet<br>mähten | hätte gemäht<br>hättest gemäht<br>hätte gemäht | hätten gemäht<br>hättet gemäht<br>hätten gemäht |
| | **Future** | | **Future Perfect** | |
| | werde mähen<br>werdest mähen<br>werde mähen | werden mähen<br>werdet mähen<br>werden mähen | werde gemäht haben<br>werdest gemäht haben<br>werde gemäht haben | werden gemäht haben<br>werdet gemäht haben<br>werden gemäht haben |
| | **Present and Future Conditional** | | **Past Conditional** | |
| | würde mähen<br>würdest mähen<br>würde mähen | würden mähen<br>würdet mähen<br>würden mähen | würde gemäht haben<br>würdest gemäht haben<br>würde gemäht haben | würden gemäht haben<br>würdet gemäht haben<br>würden gemäht haben |

## EXAMPLES

Die Wiesen werden morgen gemäht.
The meadows will be mowed tomorrow.

Wann mähst du den Rasen?
When are you going to mow the lawn?

**mahlen**
to grind, to mill
**Auxiliary verb:** haben **Past participle:** gemahlen
**Imperative:** Mahle! Mahlt! Mahlen Sie!

| Mode | Simple Tenses | | Compound Tenses | |
|---|---|---|---|---|
| | *Singular* | *Plural* | *Singular* | *Plural* |
| Indicative | **Present** | | **Present Perfect** | |
| | mahle<br>mahlst<br>mahlt | mahlen<br>mahlt<br>mahlen | habe gemahlen<br>hast gemahlen<br>hat gemahlen | haben gemahlen<br>habt gemahlen<br>haben gemahlen |
| | **Past** | | **Past Perfect** | |
| | mahlte<br>mahltest<br>mahlte | mahlten<br>mahltet<br>mahlten | hatte gemahlen<br>hattest gemahlen<br>hatte gemahlen | hatten gemahlen<br>hattet gemahlen<br>hatten gemahlen |
| | **Future** | | **Future Perfect** | |
| | werde mahlen<br>wirst mahlen<br>wird mahlen | werden mahlen<br>werdet mahlen<br>werden mahlen | werde gemahlen haben<br>wirst gemahlen haben<br>wird gemahlen haben | werden gemahlen haben<br>werdet gemahlen haben<br>werden gemahlen haben |
| Subjunctive | **Present** | | **Present Perfect** | |
| | mahle<br>mahlest<br>mahle | mahlen<br>mahlet<br>mahlen | habe gemahlen<br>habest gemahlen<br>habe gemahlen | haben gemahlen<br>habet gemahlen<br>haben gemahlen |
| | **Past** | | **Past Perfect** | |
| | mahlte<br>mahltest<br>mahlte | mahlten<br>mahltet<br>mahlten | hätte gemahlen<br>hättest gemahlen<br>hätte gemahlen | hätten gemahlen<br>hättet gemahlen<br>hätten gemahlen |
| | **Future** | | **Future Perfect** | |
| | werde mahlen<br>werdest mahlen<br>werde mahlen | werden mahlen<br>werdet mahlen<br>werden mahlen | werde gemahlen haben<br>werdest gemahlen haben<br>werde gemahlen haben | werden gemahlen haben<br>werdet gemahlen haben<br>werden gemahlen haben |
| | **Present and Future Conditional** | | **Past Conditional** | |
| | würde mahlen<br>würdest mahlen<br>würde mahlen | würden mahlen<br>würdet mahlen<br>würden mahlen | würde gemahlen haben<br>würdest gemahlen haben<br>würde gemahlen haben | würden gemahlen haben<br>würdet gemahlen haben<br>würden gemahlen haben |

## EXAMPLES

Wo wird das gemahlene Korn gelagert? — Where will the milled grain be stored?
Die Bauern mahlen das Korn in der Mühle. — The farmers grind the grain at the mill.

**mahnen**
to remind, to admonish
**Auxiliary verb:** haben **Past participle:** gemahnt
**Imperative:** Mahne! Mahnt! Mahnen Sie!

| Mode | Simple Tenses | | Compound Tenses | |
|---|---|---|---|---|
| | *Singular* | *Plural* | *Singular* | *Plural* |
| Indicative | **Present** | | **Present Perfect** | |
| | mahne<br>mahnst<br>mahnt | mahnen<br>mahnt<br>mahnen | habe gemahnt<br>hast gemahnt<br>hat gemahnt | haben gemahnt<br>habt gemahnt<br>haben gemahnt |
| | **Past** | | **Past Perfect** | |
| | mahnte<br>mahntest<br>mahnte | mahnten<br>mahntet<br>mahnten | hatte gemahnt<br>hattest gemahnt<br>hatte gemahnt | hatten gemahnt<br>hattet gemahnt<br>hatten gemahnt |
| | **Future** | | **Future Perfect** | |
| | werde mahnen<br>wirst mahnen<br>wird mahnen | werden mahnen<br>werdet mahnen<br>werden mahnen | werde gemahnt haben<br>wirst gemahnt haben<br>wird gemahnt haben | werden gemahnt haben<br>werdet gemahnt haben<br>werden gemahnt haben |
| Subjunctive | **Present** | | **Present Perfect** | |
| | mahne<br>mahnest<br>mahne | mahnen<br>mahnet<br>mahnen | habe gemahnt<br>habest gemahnt<br>habe gemahnt | haben gemahnt<br>habet gemahnt<br>haben gemahnt |
| | **Past** | | **Past Perfect** | |
| | mahnte<br>mahntest<br>mahnte | mahnten<br>mahntet<br>mahnten | hätte gemahnt<br>hättest gemahnt<br>hätte gemahnt | hätten gemahnt<br>hättet gemahnt<br>hätten gemahnt |
| | **Future** | | **Future Perfect** | |
| | werde mahnen<br>werdest mahnen<br>werde mahnen | werden mahnen<br>werdet mahnen<br>werden mahnen | werde gemahnt haben<br>werdest gemahnt haben<br>werde gemahnt haben | werden gemahnt haben<br>werdet gemahnt haben<br>werden gemahnt haben |
| | **Present and Future Conditional** | | **Past Conditional** | |
| | würde mahnen<br>würdest mahnen<br>würde mahnen | würden mahnen<br>würdet mahnen<br>würden mahnen | würde gemahnt haben<br>würdest gemahnt haben<br>würde gemahnt haben | würden gemahnt haben<br>würdet gemahnt haben<br>würden gemahnt haben |

## EXAMPLES

Nach drei Wochen mahnte ihn die Bibliothek wegen des überfälligen Buches.
After three weeks the library sent him an overdue book notice.

Der geizige Mann hat sie wegen ihrer Schuld gemahnt.
The stingy man reminded her of her debt to him.

**malen**
to paint, to portray
**Auxiliary verb:** haben **Past participle:** gemalt
**Imperative:** Male! Malt! Malen Sie!

| Mode | Simple Tenses | | Compound Tenses | |
|---|---|---|---|---|
| | *Singular* | *Plural* | *Singular* | *Plural* |
| Indicative | **Present** | | **Present Perfect** | |
| | male<br>malst<br>malt | malen<br>malt<br>malen | habe gemalt<br>hast gemalt<br>hat gemalt | haben gemalt<br>habt gemalt<br>haben gemalt |
| | **Past** | | **Past Perfect** | |
| | malte<br>maltest<br>malte | malten<br>maltet<br>malten | hatte gemalt<br>hattest gemalt<br>hatte gemalt | hatten gemalt<br>hattet gemalt<br>hatten gemalt |
| | **Future** | | **Future Perfect** | |
| | werde malen<br>wirst malen<br>wird malen | werden malen<br>werdet malen<br>werden malen | werde gemalt haben<br>wirst gemalt haben<br>wird gemalt haben | werden gemalt haben<br>werdet gemalt haben<br>werden gemalt haben |
| Subjunctive | **Present** | | **Present Perfect** | |
| | male<br>malest<br>male | malen<br>malet<br>malen | habe gemalt<br>habest gemalt<br>habe gemalt | haben gemalt<br>habet gemalt<br>haben gemalt |
| | **Past** | | **Past Perfect** | |
| | malte<br>maltest<br>malte | malten<br>maltet<br>malten | hätte gemalt<br>hättest gemalt<br>hätte gemalt | hätten gemalt<br>hättet gemalt<br>hätten gemalt |
| | **Future** | | **Future Perfect** | |
| | werde malen<br>werdest malen<br>werde malen | werden malen<br>werdet malen<br>werden malen | werde gemalt haben<br>werdest gemalt haben<br>werde gemalt haben | werden gemalt haben<br>werdet gemalt haben<br>werden gemalt haben |
| | **Present and Future Conditional** | | **Past Conditional** | |
| | würde malen<br>würdest malen<br>würde malen | würden malen<br>würdet malen<br>würden malen | würde gemalt haben<br>würdest gemalt haben<br>würde gemalt haben | würden gemalt haben<br>würdet gemalt haben<br>würden gemalt haben |

## EXAMPLES

Meine Schwester hat in der Schule ein Selbstporträt gemalt.
My sister painted a self-portrait in school.

Was für Bilder hat der junge Künstler gemalt?
What kind of pictures did the young artist paint?

**meiden**
to avoid
**Auxiliary verb:** haben **Past participle:** gemieden
**Imperative:** Meide! Meidet! Meiden Sie!

| Mode | Simple Tenses | | Compound Tenses | |
|---|---|---|---|---|
| | *Singular* | *Plural* | *Singular* | *Plural* |
| Indicative | **Present** | | **Present Perfect** | |
| | meide<br>meidest<br>meidet | meiden<br>meidet<br>meiden | habe gemieden<br>hast gemieden<br>hat gemieden | haben gemieden<br>habt gemieden<br>haben gemieden |
| | **Past** | | **Past Perfect** | |
| | mied<br>miedest<br>mied | mieden<br>miedet<br>mieden | hatte gemieden<br>hattest gemieden<br>hatte gemieden | hatten gemieden<br>hattet gemieden<br>hatten gemieden |
| | **Future** | | **Future Perfect** | |
| | werde meiden<br>wirst meiden<br>wird meiden | werden meiden<br>werdet meiden<br>werden meiden | werde gemieden haben<br>wirst gemieden haben<br>wird gemieden haben | werden gemieden haben<br>werdet gemieden haben<br>werden gemieden haben |
| Subjunctive | **Present** | | **Present Perfect** | |
| | meide<br>meidest<br>meide | meiden<br>meidet<br>meiden | habe gemieden<br>habest gemieden<br>habe gemieden | haben gemieden<br>habet gemieden<br>haben gemieden |
| | **Past** | | **Past Perfect** | |
| | miede<br>miedest<br>miede | mieden<br>miedet<br>mieden | hätte gemieden<br>hättest gemieden<br>hätte gemieden | hätten gemieden<br>hättet gemieden<br>hätten gemieden |
| | **Future** | | **Future Perfect** | |
| | werde meiden<br>werdest meiden<br>werde meiden | werden meiden<br>werdet meiden<br>werden meiden | werde gemieden haben<br>werdest gemieden haben<br>werde gemieden haben | werden gemieden haben<br>werdet gemieden haben<br>werden gemieden haben |
| | **Present and Future Conditional** | | **Past Conditional** | |
| | würde meiden<br>würdest meiden<br>würde meiden | würden meiden<br>würdet meiden<br>würden meiden | würde gemieden haben<br>würdest gemieden haben<br>würde gemieden haben | würden gemieden haben<br>würdet gemieden haben<br>würden gemieden haben |

## EXAMPLES

Man kann nicht alle Probleme meiden.
You can't avoid all problems.

Die anderen Kinder haben das einsame Mädchen gemieden.
The other children shunned the lonely girl.

**meinen**
to have the opinion, to mean
**Auxiliary verb:** haben **Past participle:** gemeint
**Imperative:** Meine! Meint! Meinen Sie!

| Mode | Simple Tenses | | Compound Tenses | |
|---|---|---|---|---|
| | *Singular* | *Plural* | *Singular* | *Plural* |
| Indicative | **Present** | | **Present Perfect** | |
| | meine<br>meinst<br>meint | meinen<br>meint<br>meinen | habe gemeint<br>hast gemeint<br>hat gemeint | haben gemeint<br>habt gemeint<br>haben gemeint |
| | **Past** | | **Past Perfect** | |
| | meinte<br>meintest<br>meinte | meinten<br>meintet<br>meinten | hatte gemeint<br>hattest gemeint<br>hatte gemeint | hatten gemeint<br>hattet gemeint<br>hatten gemeint |
| | **Future** | | **Future Perfect** | |
| | werde meinen<br>wirst meinen<br>wird meinen | werden meinen<br>werdet meinen<br>werden meinen | werde gemeint haben<br>wirst gemeint haben<br>wird gemeint haben | werden gemeint haben<br>werdet gemeint haben<br>werden gemeint haben |
| Subjunctive | **Present** | | **Present Perfect** | |
| | meine<br>meinest<br>meine | meinen<br>meinet<br>meinen | habe gemeint<br>habest gemeint<br>habe gemeint | haben gemeint<br>habet gemeint<br>haben gemeint |
| | **Past** | | **Past Perfect** | |
| | meinte<br>meintest<br>meinte | meinten<br>meintet<br>meinten | hätte gemeint<br>hättest gemeint<br>hätte gemeint | hätten gemeint<br>hättet gemeint<br>hätten gemeint |
| | **Future** | | **Future Perfect** | |
| | werde meinen<br>werdest meinen<br>werde meinen | werden meinen<br>werdet meinen<br>werden meinen | werde gemeint haben<br>werdest gemeint haben<br>werde gemeint haben | werden gemeint haben<br>werdet gemeint haben<br>werden gemeint haben |
| | **Present and Future Conditional** | | **Past Conditional** | |
| | würde meinen<br>würdest meinen<br>würde meinen | würden meinen<br>würdet meinen<br>würden meinen | würde gemeint haben<br>würdest gemeint haben<br>würde gemeint haben | würden gemeint haben<br>würdet gemeint haben<br>würden gemeint haben |

## EXAMPLES

Was meinst du zu dieser Lage? — What do you think about this situation?
Das habe ich nicht so gemeint. — I didn't mean it like that.

**melden (sich)**

to inform, to report, to announce

**Auxiliary verb:** haben **Past participle:** gemeldet

**Imperative:** Melde! Meldet! Melden Sie!

| Mode | Simple Tenses | | Compound Tenses | |
|---|---|---|---|---|
| | *Singular* | *Plural* | *Singular* | *Plural* |
| Indicative | **Present** | | **Present Perfect** | |
| | melde<br>meldest<br>meldet | melden<br>meldet<br>melden | habe gemeldet<br>hast gemeldet<br>hat gemeldet | haben gemeldet<br>habt gemeldet<br>haben gemeldet |
| | **Past** | | **Past Perfect** | |
| | meldete<br>meldetest<br>meldete | meldeten<br>meldetet<br>meldeten | hatte gemeldet<br>hattest gemeldet<br>hatte gemeldet | hatten gemeldet<br>hattet gemeldet<br>hatten gemeldet |
| | **Future** | | **Future Perfect** | |
| | werde melden<br>wirst melden<br>wird melden | werden melden<br>werdet melden<br>werden melden | werde gemeldet haben<br>wirst gemeldet haben<br>wird gemeldet haben | werden gemeldet haben<br>werdet gemeldet haben<br>werden gemeldet haben |
| Subjunctive | **Present** | | **Present Perfect** | |
| | melde<br>meldest<br>melde | melden<br>meldet<br>melden | habe gemeldet<br>habest gemeldet<br>habe gemeldet | haben gemeldet<br>habet gemeldet<br>haben gemeldet |
| | **Past** | | **Past Perfect** | |
| | meldete<br>meldetest<br>meldete | meldeten<br>meldetet<br>meldeten | hätte gemeldet<br>hättest gemeldet<br>hätte gemeldet | hätten gemeldet<br>hättet gemeldet<br>hätten gemeldet |
| | **Future** | | **Future Perfect** | |
| | werde melden<br>werdest melden<br>werde melden | werden melden<br>werdet melden<br>werden melden | werde gemeldet haben<br>werdest gemeldet haben<br>werde gemeldet haben | werden gemeldet haben<br>werdet gemeldet haben<br>werden gemeldet haben |
| | **Present and Future Conditional** | | **Past Conditional** | |
| | würde melden<br>würdest melden<br>würde melden | würden melden<br>würdet melden<br>würden melden | würde gemeldet haben<br>würdest gemeldet haben<br>würde gemeldet haben | würden gemeldet haben<br>würdet gemeldet haben<br>würden gemeldet haben |

## EXAMPLES

Die alte Frau hat der Polizei den Einbruch gemeldet.

The old woman reported the burglary to the police.

Bitte melden Sie sich, wenn Sie wieder in Darmstadt sind!

Please let us know when you're in Darmstadt again!

**melken**
to milk
**Auxiliary verb:** haben **Past participle:** gemelkt
**Imperative:** Melke! Melkt! Melken Sie!

| Mode | Simple Tenses | | Compound Tenses | |
|---|---|---|---|---|
| | *Singular* | *Plural* | *Singular* | *Plural* |
| Indicative | **Present** | | **Present Perfect** | |
| | melke<br>melkst<br>melkt | melken<br>melkt<br>melken | habe gemelkt<br>hast gemelkt<br>hat gemelkt | haben gemelkt<br>habt gemelkt<br>haben gemelkt |
| | **Past** | | **Past Perfect** | |
| | melkte<br>melktest<br>melkte | melkten<br>melktet<br>melkten | hatte gemelkt<br>hattest gemelkt<br>hatte gemelkt | hatten gemelkt<br>hattet gemelkt<br>hatten gemelkt |
| | **Future** | | **Future Perfect** | |
| | werde melken<br>wirst melken<br>wird melken | werden melken<br>werdet melken<br>werden melken | werde gemelkt haben<br>wirst gemelkt haben<br>wird gemelkt haben | werden gemelkt haben<br>werdet gemelkt haben<br>werden gemelkt haben |
| Subjunctive | **Present** | | **Present Perfect** | |
| | melke<br>melkest<br>melke | melken<br>melket<br>melken | habe gemelkt<br>habest gemelkt<br>habe gemelkt | haben gemelkt<br>habet gemelkt<br>haben gemelkt |
| | **Past** | | **Past Perfect** | |
| | mölke<br>mölkest<br>mölke | mölken<br>mölke<br>mölken | hätte gemelkt<br>hättest gemelkt<br>hätte gemelkt | hätten gemelkt<br>hättet gemelkt<br>hätten gemelkt |
| | **Future** | | **Future Perfect** | |
| | werde melken<br>werdest melken<br>werde melken | werden melken<br>werdet melken<br>werden melken | werde gemelkt haben<br>werdest gemelkt haben<br>werde gemelkt haben | werden gemelkt haben<br>werdet gemelkt haben<br>werden gemelkt haben |
| | **Present and Future Conditional** | | **Past Conditional** | |
| | würde melken<br>würdest melken<br>würde melken | würden melken<br>würdet melken<br>würden melken | würde gemelkt haben<br>würdest gemelkt haben<br>würde gemelkt haben | würden gemelkt haben<br>würdet gemelkt haben<br>würden gemelkt haben |

**Note:** You will sometimes hear *du milkst* and *er milkt* in the present tense. *Gemelkt* is the past participle in the perfect tenses and *gemolken* serves as a participial adjective. The verb *verhehlen* (to conceal) does something similar. The present- and past-tense forms follow a regular conjugational pattern, but the participle is irregular: *verhehlt, verhehlte, hat verhohlen.*

## Examples

Wo kann man heutzutage frisch gemolkene Milch kaufen?
Where can you buy fresh milk straight from the cow nowadays?

Die Bauern melken früh am Morgen die Kühe.
The farmers milk the cows early in the morning.

**merken (sich)**

to note, to bear in mind, to remember

**Auxiliary verb:** haben **Past participle:** gemerkt

**Imperative:** Merke! Merkt! Merken Sie!

| Mode | Simple Tenses | | Compound Tenses | |
|---|---|---|---|---|
| | *Singular* | *Plural* | *Singular* | *Plural* |
| Indicative | **Present** | | **Present Perfect** | |
| | merke<br>merkst<br>merkt | merken<br>merkt<br>merken | habe gemerkt<br>hast gemerkt<br>hat gemerkt | haben gemerkt<br>habt gemerkt<br>haben gemerkt |
| | **Past** | | **Past Perfect** | |
| | merkte<br>merktest<br>merkte | merkten<br>merktet<br>merkten | hatte gemerkt<br>hattest gemerkt<br>hatte gemerkt | hatten gemerkt<br>hattet gemerkt<br>hatten gemerkt |
| | **Future** | | **Future Perfect** | |
| | werde merken<br>wirst merken<br>wird merken | werden merken<br>werdet merken<br>werden merken | werde gemerkt haben<br>wirst gemerkt haben<br>wird gemerkt haben | werden gemerkt haben<br>werdet gemerkt haben<br>werden gemerkt haben |
| Subjunctive | **Present** | | **Present Perfect** | |
| | merke<br>merkest<br>merke | merken<br>merket<br>merken | habe gemerkt<br>habest gemerkt<br>habe gemerkt | haben gemerkt<br>habet gemerkt<br>haben gemerkt |
| | **Past** | | **Past Perfect** | |
| | merkte<br>merktest<br>merkte | merkten<br>merktet<br>merkten | hätte gemerkt<br>hättest gemerkt<br>hätte gemerkt | hätten gemerkt<br>hättet gemerkt<br>hätten gemerkt |
| | **Future** | | **Future Perfect** | |
| | werde merken<br>werdest merken<br>werde merken | werden merken<br>werdet merken<br>werden merken | werde gemerkt haben<br>werdest gemerkt haben<br>werde gemerkt haben | werden gemerkt haben<br>werdet gemerkt haben<br>werden gemerkt haben |
| | **Present and Future Conditional** | | **Past Conditional** | |
| | würde merken<br>würdest merken<br>würde merken | würden merken<br>würdet merken<br>würden merken | würde gemerkt haben<br>würdest gemerkt haben<br>würde gemerkt haben | würden gemerkt haben<br>würdet gemerkt haben<br>würden gemerkt haben |

## EXAMPLES

Ich kann mir einfach keine Zahlen merken. — I simply can't remember numbers.

Hast du gemerkt, dass er sich noch einen neuen Anzug gekauft hat? — Did you notice that he bought another new suit?

**messen**
to measure
**Auxiliary verb:** haben **Past participle:** gemessen
**Imperative:** Miss! Messt! Messen Sie!

| Mode | Simple Tenses | | Compound Tenses | |
|---|---|---|---|---|
| | *Singular* | *Plural* | *Singular* | *Plural* |
| Indicative | **Present** | | **Present Perfect** | |
| | messe<br>misst<br>misst | messen<br>messt<br>messen | habe gemessen<br>hast gemessen<br>hat gemessen | haben gemessen<br>habt gemessen<br>haben gemessen |
| | **Past** | | **Past Perfect** | |
| | maß<br>maßest<br>maß | maßen<br>maßt<br>maßen | hatte gemessen<br>hattest gemessen<br>hatte gemessen | hatten gemessen<br>hattet gemessen<br>hatten gemessen |
| | **Future** | | **Future Perfect** | |
| | werde messen<br>wirst messen<br>wird messen | werden messen<br>werdet messen<br>werden messen | werde gemessen haben<br>wirst gemessen haben<br>wird gemessen haben | werden gemessen haben<br>werdet gemessen haben<br>werden gemessen haben |
| Subjunctive | **Present** | | **Present Perfect** | |
| | messe<br>messest<br>messe | messen<br>messet<br>messen | habe gemessen<br>habest gemessen<br>habe gemessen | haben gemessen<br>habet gemessen<br>haben gemessen |
| | **Past** | | **Past Perfect** | |
| | mäße<br>mäßest<br>mäße | mäßen<br>mäßet<br>mäßen | hätte gemessen<br>hättest gemessen<br>hätte gemessen | hätten gemessen<br>hättet gemessen<br>hätten gemessen |
| | **Future** | | **Future Perfect** | |
| | werde messen<br>werdest messen<br>werde messen | werden messen<br>werdet messen<br>werden messen | werde gemessen haben<br>werdest gemessen haben<br>werde gemessen haben | werden gemessen haben<br>werdet gemessen haben<br>werden gemessen haben |
| | **Present and Future Conditional** | | **Past Conditional** | |
| | würde messen<br>würdest messen<br>würde messen | würden messen<br>würdet messen<br>würden messen | würde gemessen haben<br>würdest gemessen haben<br>würde gemessen haben | würden gemessen haben<br>würdet gemessen haben<br>würden gemessen haben |

## EXAMPLES

An deinem älteren Bruder gemessen bist du noch sehr klein.
Measured against your older brother, you're still very little.

Wir messen die Temperatur des Kranken alle zwanzig Minuten.
We take the patient's temperature every twenty minutes.

**mieten**

to rent, to hire

**Auxiliary verb:** haben **Past participle:** gemietet

**Imperative:** Miete! Mietet! Mieten Sie!

| Mode | Simple Tenses | | Compound Tenses | |
|---|---|---|---|---|
| | *Singular* | *Plural* | *Singular* | *Plural* |
| Indicative | **Present** | | **Present Perfect** | |
| | miete<br>mietest<br>mietet | mieten<br>mietet<br>mieten | habe gemietet<br>hast gemietet<br>hat gemietet | haben gemietet<br>habt gemietet<br>haben gemietet |
| | **Past** | | **Past Perfect** | |
| | mietete<br>mietetest<br>mietete | mieteten<br>mietetet<br>mieteten | hatte gemietet<br>hattest gemietet<br>hatte gemietet | hatten gemietet<br>hattet gemietet<br>hatten gemietet |
| | **Future** | | **Future Perfect** | |
| | werde mieten<br>wirst mieten<br>wird mieten | werden mieten<br>werdet mieten<br>werden mieten | werde gemietet haben<br>wirst gemietet haben<br>wird gemietet haben | werden gemietet haben<br>werdet gemietet haben<br>werden gemietet haben |
| Subjunctive | **Present** | | **Present Perfect** | |
| | miete<br>mietest<br>miete | mieten<br>mietet<br>mieten | habe gemietet<br>habest gemietet<br>habe gemietet | haben gemietet<br>habet gemietet<br>haben gemietet |
| | **Past** | | **Past Perfect** | |
| | mietete<br>mietetest<br>mietete | mieteten<br>mietetet<br>mieteten | hätte gemietet<br>hättest gemietet<br>hätte gemietet | hätten gemietet<br>hättet gemietet<br>hätten gemietet |
| | **Future** | | **Future Perfect** | |
| | werde mieten<br>werdest mieten<br>werde mieten | werden mieten<br>werdet mieten<br>werden mieten | werde gemietet haben<br>werdest gemietet haben<br>werde gemietet haben | werden gemietet haben<br>werdet gemietet haben<br>werden gemietet haben |
| | **Present and Future Conditional** | | **Past Conditional** | |
| | würde mieten<br>würdest mieten<br>würde mieten | würden mieten<br>würdet mieten<br>würden mieten | würde gemietet haben<br>würdest gemietet haben<br>würde gemietet haben | würden gemietet haben<br>würdet gemietet haben<br>würden gemietet haben |

## EXAMPLES

Wo kann man in der Nähe einen Wagen mieten?

Where can you rent a car around here?

Der reiche Mann hat ein großes Haus in der Schillerstraße gemietet.

The rich man rented a big house on Schiller Street.

**mischen**
to mix, to combine
**Auxiliary verb:** haben **Past participle:** gemischt
**Imperative:** Mische! Mischt! Mischen Sie!

| Mode | Simple Tenses | | Compound Tenses | |
|---|---|---|---|---|
| | *Singular* | *Plural* | *Singular* | *Plural* |
| Indicative | **Present** | | **Present Perfect** | |
| | mische<br>mischst<br>mischt | mischen<br>mischt<br>mischen | habe gemischt<br>hast gemischt<br>hat gemischt | haben gemischt<br>habt gemischt<br>haben gemischt |
| | **Past** | | **Past Perfect** | |
| | mischte<br>mischtest<br>mischte | mischten<br>mischtet<br>mischten | hatte gemischt<br>hattest gemischt<br>hatte gemischt | hatten gemischt<br>hattet gemischt<br>hatten gemischt |
| | **Future** | | **Future Perfect** | |
| | werde mischen<br>wirst mischen<br>wird mischen | werden mischen<br>werdet mischen<br>werden mischen | werde gemischt haben<br>wirst gemischt haben<br>wird gemischt haben | werden gemischt haben<br>werdet gemischt haben<br>werden gemischt haben |
| Subjunctive | **Present** | | **Present Perfect** | |
| | mische<br>mischest<br>mische | mischen<br>mischet<br>mischen | habe gemischt<br>habest gemischt<br>habe gemischt | haben gemischt<br>habet gemischt<br>haben gemischt |
| | **Past** | | **Past Perfect** | |
| | mischte<br>mischtest<br>mischte | mischten<br>mischtet<br>mischten | hätte gemischt<br>hättest gemischt<br>hätte gemischt | hätten gemischt<br>hättet gemischt<br>hätten gemischt |
| | **Future** | | **Future Perfect** | |
| | werde mischen<br>werdest mischen<br>werde mischen | werden mischen<br>werdet mischen<br>werden mischen | werde gemischt haben<br>werdest gemischt haben<br>werde gemischt haben | werden gemischt haben<br>werdet gemischt haben<br>werden gemischt haben |
| | **Present and Future Conditional** | | **Past Conditional** | |
| | würde mischen<br>würdest mischen<br>würde mischen | würden mischen<br>würdet mischen<br>würden mischen | würde gemischt haben<br>würdest gemischt haben<br>würde gemischt haben | würden gemischt haben<br>würdet gemischt haben<br>würden gemischt haben |

## EXAMPLES

Du bist jetzt dran, die Karten zu mischen. — It's your turn to shuffle the cards.
Diese beiden Lösungen darf man nicht mischen. — You mustn't mix these two solutions.

**mitteilen**

to inform, to communicate

**Auxiliary verb:** haben **Past participle:** mitgeteilt

**Imperative:** Teile mit! Teilt mit! Teilen Sie mit!

| Mode | Simple Tenses | | Compound Tenses | |
|---|---|---|---|---|
| | *Singular* | *Plural* | *Singular* | *Plural* |
| Indicative | **Present** | | **Present Perfect** | |
| | teile mit<br>teilst mit<br>teilt mit | teilen mit<br>teilt mit<br>teilen mit | habe mitgeteilt<br>hast mitgeteilt<br>hat mitgeteilt | haben mitgeteilt<br>habt mitgeteilt<br>haben mitgeteilt |
| | **Past** | | **Past Perfect** | |
| | teilte mit<br>teiltest mit<br>teilte mit | teilten mit<br>teiltet mit<br>teilten mit | hatte mitgeteilt<br>hattest mitgeteilt<br>hatte mitgeteilt | hatten mitgeteilt<br>hattet mitgeteilt<br>hatten mitgeteilt |
| | **Future** | | **Future Perfect** | |
| | werde mitteilen<br>wirst mitteilen<br>wird mitteilen | werden mitteilen<br>werdet mitteilen<br>werden mitteilen | werde mitgeteilt haben<br>wirst mitgeteilt haben<br>wird mitgeteilt haben | werden mitgeteilt haben<br>werdet mitgeteilt haben<br>werden mitgeteilt haben |
| Subjunctive | **Present** | | **Present Perfect** | |
| | teile mit<br>teilest mit<br>teile mit | teilen mit<br>teilet mit<br>teilen mit | habe mitgeteilt<br>habest mitgeteilt<br>habe mitgeteilt | haben mitgeteilt<br>habet mitgeteilt<br>haben mitgeteilt |
| | **Past** | | **Past Perfect** | |
| | teilte mit<br>teiltest mit<br>teilte mit | teilten mit<br>teiltet mit<br>teilten mit | hätte mitgeteilt<br>hättest mitgeteilt<br>hätte mitgeteilt | hätten mitgeteilt<br>hättet mitgeteilt<br>hätten mitgeteilt |
| | **Future** | | **Future Perfect** | |
| | werde mitteilen<br>werdest mitteilen<br>werde mitteilen | werden mitteilen<br>werdet mitteilen<br>werden mitteilen | werde mitgeteilt haben<br>werdest mitgeteilt haben<br>werde mitgeteilt haben | werden mitgeteilt haben<br>werdet mitgeteilt haben<br>werden mitgeteilt haben |
| | **Present and Future Conditional** | | **Past Conditional** | |
| | würde mitteilen<br>würdest mitteilen<br>würde mitteilen | würden mitteilen<br>würdet mitteilen<br>würden mitteilen | würde mitgeteilt haben<br>würdest mitgeteilt haben<br>würde mitgeteilt haben | würden mitgeteilt haben<br>würdet mitgeteilt haben<br>würden mitgeteilt haben |

## EXAMPLES

Er hat mir mitgeteilt, dass es einen furchtbaren Unfall gegeben hat.

He informed me that there had been a terrible accident.

Karl wird uns die neuesten Nachrichten mitteilen.

Karl will inform us of the latest news.

**möblieren**
to furnish
**Auxiliary verb:** haben **Past participle:** möbliert
**Imperative:** Möbliere! Möbliert! Möblieren Sie!

| Mode | Simple Tenses | | Compound Tenses | |
|---|---|---|---|---|
| | *Singular* | *Plural* | *Singular* | *Plural* |
| Indicative | **Present** | | **Present Perfect** | |
| | möbliere<br>möblierst<br>möbliert | möblieren<br>möbliert<br>möblieren | habe möbliert<br>hast möbliert<br>hat möbliert | haben möbliert<br>habt möbliert<br>haben möbliert |
| | **Past** | | **Past Perfect** | |
| | möblierte<br>möbliertest<br>möblierte | möblierten<br>möbliertet<br>möblierten | hatte möbliert<br>hattest möbliert<br>hatte möbliert | hatten möbliert<br>hattet möbliert<br>hatten möbliert |
| | **Future** | | **Future Perfect** | |
| | werde möblieren<br>wirst möblieren<br>wird möblieren | werden möblieren<br>werdet möblieren<br>werden möblieren | werde möbliert haben<br>wirst möbliert haben<br>wird möbliert haben | werden möbliert haben<br>werdet möbliert haben<br>werden möbliert haben |
| Subjunctive | **Present** | | **Present Perfect** | |
| | möbliere<br>möblierest<br>möbliere | möblieren<br>möblieret<br>möblieren | habe möbliert<br>habest möbliert<br>habe möbliert | haben möbliert<br>habet möbliert<br>haben möbliert |
| | **Past** | | **Past Perfect** | |
| | möblierte<br>möbliertest<br>möblierte | möblierten<br>möbliertet<br>möblierten | hätte möbliert<br>hättest möbliert<br>hätte möbliert | hätten möbliert<br>hättet möbliert<br>hätten möbliert |
| | **Future** | | **Future Perfect** | |
| | werde möblieren<br>werdest möblieren<br>werde möblieren | werden möblieren<br>werdet möblieren<br>werden möblieren | werde möbliert haben<br>werdest möbliert haben<br>werde möbliert haben | werden möbliert haben<br>werdet möbliert haben<br>werden möbliert haben |
| | **Present and Future Conditional** | | **Past Conditional** | |
| | würde möblieren<br>würdest möblieren<br>würde möblieren | würden möblieren<br>würdet möblieren<br>würden möblieren | würde möbliert haben<br>würdest möbliert haben<br>würde möbliert haben | würden möbliert haben<br>würdet möbliert haben<br>würden möbliert haben |

## EXAMPLE

Ihre neue Wohnung ist sehr schön möbliert. Your new apartment is very nicely furnished.

**mögen**
to like, may, might
**Auxiliary verb:** haben **Past participle:** gemocht
**Imperative:** N/A

| Mode | Simple Tenses | | Compound Tenses | |
|---|---|---|---|---|
| | *Singular* | *Plural* | *Singular* | *Plural* |
| Indicative | **Present** | | **Present Perfect** | |
| | mag<br>magst<br>mag | mögen<br>mögt<br>mögen | habe gemocht<br>hast gemocht<br>hat gemocht | haben gemocht<br>habt gemocht<br>haben gemocht |
| | **Past** | | **Past Perfect** | |
| | mochte<br>mochtest<br>mochte | mochten<br>mochtet<br>mochten | hatte gemocht<br>hattest gemocht<br>hatte gemocht | hatten gemocht<br>hattet gemocht<br>hatten gemocht |
| | **Future** | | **Future Perfect** | |
| | werde mögen<br>wirst mögen<br>wird mögen | werden mögen<br>werdet mögen<br>werden mögen | werde gemocht haben<br>wirst gemocht haben<br>wird gemocht haben | werden gemocht haben<br>werdet gemocht haben<br>werden gemocht haben |
| Subjunctive | **Present** | | **Present Perfect** | |
| | möge<br>mögest<br>möge | mögen<br>möget<br>mögen | habe gemocht<br>habest gemocht<br>habe gemocht | haben gemocht<br>habet gemocht<br>haben gemocht |
| | **Past** | | **Past Perfect** | |
| | möchte<br>möchtest<br>möchte | möchten<br>möchtet<br>möchten | hätte gemocht<br>hättest gemocht<br>hätte gemocht | hätten gemocht<br>hättet gemocht<br>hätten gemocht |
| | **Future** | | **Future Perfect** | |
| | werde mögen<br>werdest mögen<br>werde mögen | werden mögen<br>werdet mögen<br>werden mögen | werde gemocht haben<br>werdest gemocht haben<br>werde gemocht haben | werden gemocht haben<br>werdet gemocht haben<br>werden gemocht haben |
| | **Present and Future Conditional** | | **Past Conditional** | |
| | würde mögen<br>würdest mögen<br>würde mögen | würden mögen<br>würdet mögen<br>würden mögen | würde gemocht haben<br>würdest gemocht haben<br>würde gemocht haben | würden gemocht haben<br>würdet gemocht haben<br>würden gemocht haben |

**Note:** There is frequent use of the subjunctive II *möchte* to mean "would like": *Ich möchte ein Stück Kuchen* (I'd like a piece of cake).

## EXAMPLES

| | |
|---|---|
| Das mag wohl sein. | That may well be. |
| Die Kinder mögen die Suppe nicht. | The children don't like the soup. |
| Wir möchten heute abend ins Kino gehen. | We'd like to go to the movies tonight. |

**münden**
to flow, to empty into
**Auxiliary verb:** haben **Past participle:** gemündet
**Imperative:** N/A

| Mode | Simple Tenses | | Compound Tenses | |
|---|---|---|---|---|
| | *Singular* | *Plural* | *Singular* | *Plural* |
| Indicative | **Present** | | **Present Perfect** | |
| | mündet | münden | hat gemündet | haben gemündet |
| | **Past** | | **Past Perfect** | |
| | mündete | mündeten | hatte gemündet | hatten gemündet |
| | **Future** | | **Future Perfect** | |
| | wird münden | werden münden | wird gemündet haben | werden gemündet haben |
| Subjunctive | **Present** | | **Present Perfect** | |
| | münde | münden | habe gemündet | haben gemündet |
| | **Past** | | **Past Perfect** | |
| | mündete | mündeten | hätte gemündet | hätten gemündet |
| | **Future** | | **Future Perfect** | |
| | werde münden | werden münden | würde münden | würden münden |
| | **Present and Future Conditional** | | **Past Conditional** | |
| | werde gemündet haben | werden gemündet haben | würde gemündet haben | würden gemündet haben |

**Note:** This verb is used primarily to describe a body of water that "empties" into another body of water.

## EXAMPLES

Die Elbe mündet in die Nordsee.
The Elbe empties into the North Sea.

Welche europäischen Flüsse münden ins Mittelmeer?
What European rivers flow into the Mediterranean Sea?

**müssen**
to have to, must
**Auxiliary verb:** haben **Past participle:** gemusst
**Imperative:** N/A

| Mode | Simple Tenses | | Compound Tenses | |
|---|---|---|---|---|
| | *Singular* | *Plural* | *Singular* | *Plural* |
| Indicative | **Present** | | **Present Perfect** | |
| | muss<br>musst<br>muss | müssen<br>müsst<br>müssen | habe gemusst<br>hast gemusst<br>hat gemusst | haben gemusst<br>habt gemusst<br>haben gemusst |
| | **Past** | | **Past Perfect** | |
| | mußte<br>musstest<br>musste | mußten<br>musstet<br>mussten | hatte gemusst<br>hattest gemusst<br>hatte gemusst | hatten gemusst<br>hattet gemusst<br>hatten gemusst |
| | **Future** | | **Future Perfect** | |
| | werde müssen<br>wirst müssen<br>wird müssen | werden müssen<br>werdet müssen<br>werden müssen | werde gemusst haben<br>wirst gemusst haben<br>wird gemusst haben | werden gemusst haben<br>werdet gemusst haben<br>werden gemusst haben |
| Subjunctive | **Present** | | **Present Perfect** | |
| | müsse<br>müssest<br>müsse | müssen<br>müsset<br>müssen | habe gemusst<br>habest gemusst<br>habe gemusst | haben gemusst<br>habet gemusst<br>haben gemusst |
| | **Past** | | **Past Perfect** | |
| | müsste<br>müsstest<br>müsste | müssten<br>müsstet<br>müssten | hätte gemusst<br>hättest gemusst<br>hätte gemusst | hätten gemusst<br>hättet gemusst<br>hätten gemusst |
| | **Future** | | **Future Perfect** | |
| | werde müssen<br>werdest müssen<br>werde müssen | werden müssen<br>werdet müssen<br>werden müssen | werde gemusst haben<br>werdest gemusst haben<br>werde gemusst haben | werden gemusst haben<br>werdet gemusst haben<br>werden gemusst haben |
| | **Present and Future Conditional** | | **Past Conditional** | |
| | würde müssen<br>würdest müssen<br>würde müssen | würden müssen<br>würdet müssen<br>würden müssen | würde gemusst haben<br>würdest gemusst haben<br>würde gemusst haben | würden gemusst haben<br>würdet gemusst haben<br>würden gemusst haben |

**Note:** This verb is a modal auxiliary. In the perfect and future tenses, when there is a second verb in the sentence, a double-infinitive structure is required: *Haben Sie mit ihm sprechen müssen?* (Did you have to speak with him?)

## EXAMPLES

Man muss nichts müssen. — There's nothing that a person has to do.
Es muss schon sehr spät sein. — It must already be very late.

**nähen**
to sew
**Auxiliary verb:** haben **Past participle:** genäht
**Imperative:** Nähe! Näht! Nähen Sie!

| Mode | Simple Tenses | | Compound Tenses | |
|---|---|---|---|---|
| | *Singular* | *Plural* | *Singular* | *Plural* |
| Indicative | **Present** | | **Present Perfect** | |
| | nähe<br>nähst<br>näht | nähen<br>näht<br>nähen | habe genäht<br>hast genäht<br>hat genäht | haben genäht<br>habt genäht<br>haben genäht |
| | **Past** | | **Past Perfect** | |
| | nähte<br>nähtest<br>nähte | nähten<br>nähtet<br>nähten | hatte genäht<br>hattest genäht<br>hatte genäht | hatten genäht<br>hattet genäht<br>hatten genäht |
| | **Future** | | **Future Perfect** | |
| | werde nähen<br>wirst nähen<br>wird nähen | werden nähen<br>werdet nähen<br>werden nähen | werde genäht haben<br>wirst genäht haben<br>wird genäht haben | werden genäht haben<br>werdet genäht haben<br>werden genäht haben |
| Subjunctive | **Present** | | **Present Perfect** | |
| | nähe<br>nähest<br>nähe | nähen<br>nähet<br>nähen | habe genäht<br>habest genäht<br>habe genäht | haben genäht<br>habet genäht<br>haben genäht |
| | **Past** | | **Past Perfect** | |
| | nähte<br>nähtest<br>nähte | nähten<br>nähtet<br>nähten | hätte genäht<br>hättest genäht<br>hätte genäht | hätten genäht<br>hättet genäht<br>hätten genäht |
| | **Future** | | **Future Perfect** | |
| | werde nähen<br>werdest nähen<br>werde nähen | werden nähen<br>werdet nähen<br>werden nähen | werde genäht haben<br>werdest genäht haben<br>werde genäht haben | werden genäht haben<br>werdet genäht haben<br>werden genäht haben |
| | **Present and Future Conditional** | | **Past Conditional** | |
| | würde nähen<br>würdest nähen<br>würde nähen | würden nähen<br>würdet nähen<br>würden nähen | würde genäht haben<br>würdest genäht haben<br>würde genäht haben | würden genäht haben<br>würdet genäht haben<br>würden genäht haben |

## EXAMPLES

Kannst du mir diesen Saum nähen?
Can you sew this hem for me?

Sie können sich bei Frau Neumann schöne Röcke und Kleider nähen lassen.
You can have nice skirts and dresses made in Mrs. Neumann's shop.

**necken**
to tease
**Auxiliary verb:** haben **Past participle:** geneckt
**Imperative:** Necke! Neckt! Necken Sie!

| Mode | Simple Tenses | | Compound Tenses | |
|---|---|---|---|---|
| | *Singular* | *Plural* | *Singular* | *Plural* |
| Indicative | **Present** | | **Present Perfect** | |
| | necke<br>neckst<br>neckt | necken<br>neckt<br>necken | habe geneckt<br>hast geneckt<br>hat geneckt | haben geneckt<br>habt geneckt<br>haben geneckt |
| | **Past** | | **Past Perfect** | |
| | neckte<br>necktest<br>neckte | neckten<br>necktet<br>neckten | hatte geneckt<br>hattest geneckt<br>hatte geneckt | hatten geneckt<br>hattet geneckt<br>hatten geneckt |
| | **Future** | | **Future Perfect** | |
| | werde necken<br>wirst necken<br>wird necken | werden necken<br>werdet necken<br>werden necken | werde geneckt haben<br>wirst geneckt haben<br>wird geneckt haben | werden geneckt haben<br>werdet geneckt haben<br>werden geneckt haben |
| Subjunctive | **Present** | | **Present Perfect** | |
| | necke<br>neckest<br>necke | necken<br>necket<br>necken | habe geneckt<br>habest geneckt<br>habe geneckt | haben geneckt<br>habet geneckt<br>haben geneckt |
| | **Past** | | **Past Perfect** | |
| | neckte<br>necktest<br>neckte | neckten<br>necktet<br>neckten | hätte geneckt<br>hättest geneckt<br>hätte geneckt | hätten geneckt<br>hättet geneckt<br>hätten geneckt |
| | **Future** | | **Future Perfect** | |
| | werde necken<br>werdest necken<br>werde necken | werden necken<br>werdet necken<br>werden necken | werde geneckt haben<br>werdest geneckt haben<br>werde geneckt haben | werden geneckt haben<br>werdet geneckt haben<br>werden geneckt haben |
| | **Present and Future Conditional** | | **Past Conditional** | |
| | würde necken<br>würdest necken<br>würde necken | würden necken<br>würdet necken<br>würden necken | würde geneckt haben<br>würdest geneckt haben<br>würde geneckt haben | würden geneckt haben<br>würdet geneckt haben<br>würden geneckt haben |

## EXAMPLES

Die Zwillinge necken einander erbarmungslos.
The twins tease one another mercilessly.

Karsten neckt Daniela, weil er sie gern hat.
Karsten teases Daniela, because he likes her.

**nehmen**
to take
**Auxiliary verb:** haben **Past participle:** genommen
**Imperative:** Nimm! Nehmt! Nehmen Sie!

| Mode | Simple Tenses | | Compound Tenses | |
|---|---|---|---|---|
| | *Singular* | *Plural* | *Singular* | *Plural* |
| Indicative | **Present** | | **Present Perfect** | |
| | nehme<br>nimmst<br>nimmt | nehmen<br>nehmt<br>nehmen | habe genommen<br>hast genommen<br>hat genommen | haben genommen<br>habt genommen<br>haben genommen |
| | **Past** | | **Past Perfect** | |
| | nahm<br>nahmst<br>nahm | nahmen<br>nahmt<br>nahmen | hatte genommen<br>hattest genommen<br>hatte genommen | hatten genommen<br>hattet genommen<br>hatten genommen |
| | **Future** | | **Future Perfect** | |
| | werde nehmen<br>wirst nehmen<br>wird nehmen | werden nehmen<br>werdet nehmen<br>werden nehmen | werde genommen haben<br>wirst genommen haben<br>wird genommen haben | werden genommen haben<br>werdet genommen haben<br>werden genommen haben |
| Subjunctive | **Present** | | **Present Perfect** | |
| | nehme<br>nehmest<br>nehme | nehmen<br>nehmet<br>nehmen | habe genommen<br>habest genommen<br>habe genommen | haben genommen<br>habet genommen<br>haben genommen |
| | **Past** | | **Past Perfect** | |
| | nähme<br>nähmest<br>nähme | nähmen<br>nähmet<br>nähmen | hätte genommen<br>hättest genommen<br>hätte genommen | hätten genommen<br>hättet genommen<br>hätten genommen |
| | **Future** | | **Future Perfect** | |
| | werde nehmen<br>werdest nehmen<br>werde nehmen | werden nehmen<br>werdet nehmen<br>werden nehmen | werde genommen haben<br>werdest genommen haben<br>werde genommen haben | werden genommen haben<br>werdet genommen haben<br>werden genommen haben |
| | **Present and Future Conditional** | | **Past Conditional** | |
| | würde nehmen<br>würdest nehmen<br>würde nehmen | würden nehmen<br>würdet nehmen<br>würden nehmen | würde genommen haben<br>würdest genommen haben<br>würde genommen haben | würden genommen haben<br>würdet genommen haben<br>würden genommen haben |

**Note:** With inseparable prefixes, the principal parts of this verb are, for example, *benimmt, benahm, hat benommen.* With separable prefixes, the principal parts are, for example, *nimmt ab, nahm ab, hat abgenommen.*

## EXAMPLES

| | |
|---|---|
| Meine Eltern haben die Verantwortung auf sich genommen. | My parents took the responsibility. |
| Er nimmt seinen Hut und Regenschirm und geht. | He takes his hat and umbrella and goes. |

**neigen (sich)**
to incline, to be inclined, to tend
**Auxiliary verb:** haben **Past participle:** geneigt
**Imperative:** Neige! Neigt! Neigen Sie!

| Mode | Simple Tenses | | Compound Tenses | |
|---|---|---|---|---|
| | *Singular* | *Plural* | *Singular* | *Plural* |
| Indicative | **Present** | | **Present Perfect** | |
| | neige<br>neigst<br>neigt | neigen<br>neigt<br>neigen | habe geneigt<br>hast geneigt<br>hat geneigt | haben geneigt<br>habt geneigt<br>haben geneigt |
| | **Past** | | **Past Perfect** | |
| | neigte<br>neigtest<br>neigte | neigten<br>neigtet<br>neigten | hatte geneigt<br>hattest geneigt<br>hatte geneigt | hatten geneigt<br>hattet geneigt<br>hatten geneigt |
| | **Future** | | **Future Perfect** | |
| | werde neigen<br>wirst neigen<br>wird neigen | werden neigen<br>werdet neigen<br>werden neigen | werde geneigt haben<br>wirst geneigt haben<br>wird geneigt haben | werden geneigt haben<br>werdet geneigt haben<br>werden geneigt haben |
| Subjunctive | **Present** | | **Present Perfect** | |
| | neige<br>neigest<br>neige | neigen<br>neiget<br>neigen | habe geneigt<br>habest geneigt<br>habe geneigt | haben geneigt<br>habet geneigt<br>haben geneigt |
| | **Past** | | **Past Perfect** | |
| | neigte<br>neigtest<br>neigte | neigten<br>neigtet<br>neigten | hätte geneigt<br>hättest geneigt<br>hätte geneigt | hätten geneigt<br>hättet geneigt<br>hätten geneigt |
| | **Future** | | **Future Perfect** | |
| | werde neigen<br>werdest neigen<br>werde neigen | werden neigen<br>werdet neigen<br>werden neigen | werde geneigt haben<br>werdest geneigt haben<br>werde geneigt haben | werden geneigt haben<br>werdet geneigt haben<br>werden geneigt haben |
| | **Present and Future Conditional** | | **Past Conditional** | |
| | würde neigen<br>würdest neigen<br>würde neigen | würden neigen<br>würdet neigen<br>würden neigen | würde geneigt haben<br>würdest geneigt haben<br>würde geneigt haben | würden geneigt haben<br>würdet geneigt haben<br>würden geneigt haben |

## EXAMPLES

Die Mutter fragt den Arzt, warum ihre Tochter zu Erkältungen neigt.
The mother asks the doctor why her daughter is inclined toward colds.

Er ist dazu geneigt, sich ein neues Auto zu kaufen.
He's leaning toward buying a new car.

**nennen**
to name, to call
**Auxiliary verb:** haben **Past participle:** genannt
**Imperative:** Nenne! Nennt! Nennen Sie!

| Mode | Simple Tenses | | Compound Tenses | |
|---|---|---|---|---|
| | *Singular* | *Plural* | *Singular* | *Plural* |
| Indicative | **Present** | | **Present Perfect** | |
| | nenne<br>nennst<br>nennt | nennen<br>nennt<br>nennen | habe genannt<br>hast genannt<br>hat genannt | haben genannt<br>habt genannt<br>haben genannt |
| | **Past** | | **Past Perfect** | |
| | nannte<br>nanntest<br>nannte | nannten<br>nanntet<br>nannten | hatte genannt<br>hattest genannt<br>hatte genannt | hatten genannt<br>hattet genannt<br>hatten genannt |
| | **Future** | | **Future Perfect** | |
| | werde nennen<br>wirst nennen<br>wird nennen | werden nennen<br>werdet nennen<br>werden nennen | werde genannt haben<br>wirst genannt haben<br>wird genannt haben | werden genannt haben<br>werdet genannt haben<br>werden genannt haben |
| Subjunctive | **Present** | | **Present Perfect** | |
| | nenne<br>nennest<br>nenne | nennen<br>nennet<br>nennen | habe genannt<br>habest genannt<br>habe genannt | haben genannt<br>habet genannt<br>haben genannt |
| | **Past** | | **Past Perfect** | |
| | nennte<br>nenntest<br>nennte | nennten<br>nenntet<br>nennten | hätte genannt<br>hättest genannt<br>hätte genannt | hätten genannt<br>hättet genannt<br>hätten genannt |
| | **Future** | | **Future Perfect** | |
| | werde nennen<br>werdest nennen<br>werde nennen | werden nennen<br>werdet nennen<br>werden nennen | werde genannt haben<br>werdest genannt haben<br>werde genannt haben | werden genannt haben<br>werdet genannt haben<br>werden genannt haben |
| | **Present and Future Conditional** | | **Past Conditional** | |
| | würde nennen<br>würdest nennen<br>würde nennen | würden nennen<br>würdet nennen<br>würden nennen | würde genannt haben<br>würdest genannt haben<br>würde genannt haben | würden genannt haben<br>würdet genannt haben<br>würden genannt haben |

## EXAMPLES

Das nenne ich einfach absurd. — That's what I call absurd.

Sie heißt Angelika, aber alle nennen sie Geli. — Her name is Angelika, but everyone calls her Geli.

**niesen**

to sneeze

**Auxiliary verb:** haben **Past participle:** geniest

**Imperative:** Niese! Niest! Niesen Sie!

| Mode | Simple Tenses | | Compound Tenses | |
|---|---|---|---|---|
| | *Singular* | *Plural* | *Singular* | *Plural* |
| Indicative | **Present** | | **Present Perfect** | |
| | niese<br>niest<br>niest | niesen<br>niest<br>niesen | habe geniest<br>hast geniest<br>hat geniest | haben geniest<br>habt geniest<br>haben geniest |
| | **Past** | | **Past Perfect** | |
| | nieste<br>niestest<br>nieste | niesten<br>niestet<br>niesten | hatte geniest<br>hattest geniest<br>hatte geniest | hatten geniest<br>hattet geniest<br>hatten geniest |
| | **Future** | | **Future Perfect** | |
| | werde niesen<br>wirst niesen<br>wird niesen | werden niesen<br>werdet niesen<br>werden niesen | werde geniest haben<br>wirst geniest haben<br>wird geniest haben | werden geniest haben<br>werdet geniest haben<br>werden geniest haben |
| Subjunctive | **Present** | | **Present Perfect** | |
| | niese<br>niesest<br>niese | niesen<br>nieset<br>niesen | habe geniest<br>habest geniest<br>habe geniest | haben geniest<br>habet geniest<br>haben geniest |
| | **Past** | | **Past Perfect** | |
| | nieste<br>niestest<br>nieste | niesten<br>niestet<br>niesten | hätte geniest<br>hättest geniest<br>hätte geniest | hätten geniest<br>hättet geniest<br>hätten geniest |
| | **Future** | | **Future Perfect** | |
| | werde niesen<br>werdest niesen<br>werde niesen | werden niesen<br>werdet niesen<br>werden niesen | werde geniest haben<br>werdest geniest haben<br>werde geniest haben | werden geniest haben<br>werdet geniest haben<br>werden geniest haben |
| | **Present and Future Conditional** | | **Past Conditional** | |
| | würde niesen<br>würdest niesen<br>würde niesen | würden niesen<br>würdet niesen<br>würden niesen | würde geniest haben<br>würdest geniest haben<br>würde geniest haben | würden geniest haben<br>würdet geniest haben<br>würden geniest haben |

## EXAMPLE

Im Frühling habe ich eine Allergie und niese viel.

In the spring, I have an allergy and sneeze a lot.

**öffnen**
to open
**Auxiliary verb:** haben **Past participle:** geöffnet
**Imperative:** Öffne! Öffnet! Öffnen Sie!

| Mode | Simple Tenses | | Compound Tenses | |
|---|---|---|---|---|
| | *Singular* | *Plural* | *Singular* | *Plural* |
| Indicative | **Present** | | **Present Perfect** | |
| | öffne<br>öffnest<br>öffnet | öffnen<br>öffnet<br>öffnen | habe geöffnet<br>hast geöffnet<br>hat geöffnet | haben geöffnet<br>habt geöffnet<br>haben geöffnet |
| | **Past** | | **Past Perfect** | |
| | öffnete<br>öffnetest<br>öffnete | öffneten<br>öffnetet<br>öffneten | hatte geöffnet<br>hattest geöffnet<br>hatte geöffnet | hatten geöffnet<br>hattet geöffnet<br>hatten geöffnet |
| | **Future** | | **Future Perfect** | |
| | werde öffnen<br>wirst öffnen<br>wird öffnen | werden öffnen<br>werdet öffnen<br>werden öffnen | werde geöffnet haben<br>wirst geöffnet haben<br>wird geöffnet haben | werden geöffnet haben<br>werdet geöffnet haben<br>werden geöffnet haben |
| Subjunctive | **Present** | | **Present Perfect** | |
| | öffne<br>öffnest<br>öffne | öffnen<br>öffnet<br>öffnen | habe geöffnet<br>habest geöffnet<br>habe geöffnet | haben geöffnet<br>habet geöffnet<br>haben geöffnet |
| | **Past** | | **Past Perfect** | |
| | öffnete<br>öffnetest<br>öffnete | öffneten<br>öffnetet<br>öffneten | hätte geöffnet<br>hättest geöffnet<br>hätte geöffnet | hätten geöffnet<br>hättet geöffnet<br>hätten geöffnet |
| | **Future** | | **Future Perfect** | |
| | werde öffnen<br>werdest öffnen<br>werde öffnen | werden öffnen<br>werdet öffnen<br>werden öffnen | werde geöffnet haben<br>werdest geöffnet haben<br>werde geöffnet haben | werden geöffnet haben<br>werdet geöffnet haben<br>werden geöffnet haben |
| | **Present and Future Conditional** | | **Past Conditional** | |
| | würde öffnen<br>würdest öffnen<br>würde öffnen | würden öffnen<br>würdet öffnen<br>würden öffnen | würde geöffnet haben<br>würdest geöffnet haben<br>würde geöffnet haben | würden geöffnet haben<br>würdet geöffnet haben<br>würden geöffnet haben |

## EXAMPLES

Der Tag ist warm und sonnig und sie öffnet alle Fenster.

The day is warm and sunny, and she opens all the windows.

Herr Bauer bekam ein unerwartetes Paket und öffnete es sofort.

Mr. Bauer received an unexpected package and opened it immediately.

**ordnen**

to arrange, to order

**Auxiliary verb:** haben **Past participle:** geordnet

**Imperative:** Ordne! Ordnet! Ordnen Sie!

| Mode | Simple Tenses | | Compound Tenses | |
|---|---|---|---|---|
| | *Singular* | *Plural* | *Singular* | *Plural* |
| Indicative | **Present** | | **Present Perfect** | |
| | ordne<br>ordnest<br>ordnet | ordnen<br>ordnet<br>ordnen | habe geordnet<br>hast geordnet<br>hat geordnet | haben geordnet<br>habt geordnet<br>haben geordnet |
| | **Past** | | **Past Perfect** | |
| | ordnete<br>ordnetest<br>ordnete | ordneten<br>ordnetet<br>ordneten | hatte geordnet<br>hattest geordnet<br>hatte geordnet | hatten geordnet<br>hattet geordnet<br>hatten geordnet |
| | **Future** | | **Future Perfect** | |
| | werde ordnen<br>wirst ordnen<br>wird ordnen | werden ordnen<br>werdet ordnen<br>werden ordnen | werde geordnet haben<br>wirst geordnet haben<br>wird geordnet haben | werden geordnet haben<br>werdet geordnet haben<br>werden geordnet haben |
| Subjunctive | **Present** | | **Present Perfect** | |
| | ordne<br>ordnest<br>ordne | ordnen<br>ordnet<br>ordnen | habe geordnet<br>habest geordnet<br>habe geordnet | haben geordnet<br>habet geordnet<br>haben geordnet |
| | **Past** | | **Past Perfect** | |
| | ordnete<br>ordnetest<br>ordnete | ordneten<br>ordnetet<br>ordneten | hätte geordnet<br>hättest geordnet<br>hätte geordnet | hätten geordnet<br>hättet geordnet<br>hätten geordnet |
| | **Future** | | **Future Perfect** | |
| | werde ordnen<br>werdest ordnen<br>werde ordnen | werden ordnen<br>werdet ordnen<br>werden ordnen | werde geordnet haben<br>werdest geordnet haben<br>werde geordnet haben | werden geordnet haben<br>werdet geordnet haben<br>werden geordnet haben |
| | **Present and Future Conditional** | | **Past Conditional** | |
| | würde ordnen<br>würdest ordnen<br>würde ordnen | würden ordnen<br>würdet ordnen<br>würden ordnen | würde geordnet haben<br>würdest geordnet haben<br>würde geordnet haben | würden geordnet haben<br>würdet geordnet haben<br>würden geordnet haben |

## EXAMPLE

Ich bin jetzt dabei meine Notizen zu ordnen. I'm working on putting my notes in order.

**pachten**
to lease, to rent real estate
**Auxiliary verb:** haben **Past participle:** gepachtet
**Imperative:** Pachte! Pachtet! Pachten Sie!

| Mode | Simple Tenses | | Compound Tenses | |
|---|---|---|---|---|
| | *Singular* | *Plural* | *Singular* | *Plural* |
| Indicative | **Present** | | **Present Perfect** | |
| | pachte<br>pachtest<br>pachtet | pachten<br>pachtet<br>pachten | habe gepachtet<br>hast gepachtet<br>hat gepachtet | haben gepachtet<br>habt gepachtet<br>haben gepachtet |
| | **Past** | | **Past Perfect** | |
| | pachtete<br>pachtetest<br>pachtete | pachteten<br>pachtetet<br>pachteten | hatte gepachtet<br>hattest gepachtet<br>hatte gepachtet | hatten gepachtet<br>hattet gepachtet<br>hatten gepachtet |
| | **Future** | | **Future Perfect** | |
| | werde pachten<br>wirst pachten<br>wird pachten | werden pachten<br>werdet pachten<br>werden pachten | werde gepachtet haben<br>wirst gepachtet haben<br>wird gepachtet haben | werden gepachtet haben<br>werdet gepachtet haben<br>werden gepachtet haben |
| Subjunctive | **Present** | | **Present Perfect** | |
| | pachte<br>pachtest<br>pachte | pachten<br>pachtet<br>pachten | habe gepachtet<br>habest gepachtet<br>habe gepachtet | haben gepachtet<br>habet gepachtet<br>haben gepachtet |
| | **Past** | | **Past Perfect** | |
| | pachtete<br>pachtetest<br>pachtete | pachteten<br>pachtetet<br>pachteten | hätte gepachtet<br>hättest gepachtet<br>hätte gepachtet | hätten gepachtet<br>hättet gepachtet<br>hätten gepachtet |
| | **Future** | | **Future Perfect** | |
| | werde pachten<br>werdest pachten<br>werde pachten | werden pachten<br>werdet pachten<br>werden pachten | werde gepachtet haben<br>werdest gepachtet haben<br>werde gepachtet haben | werden gepachtet haben<br>werdet gepachtet haben<br>werden gepachtet haben |
| | **Present and Future Conditional** | | **Past Conditional** | |
| | würde pachten<br>würdest pachten<br>würde pachten | würden pachten<br>würdet pachten<br>würden pachten | würde gepachtet haben<br>würdest gepachtet haben<br>würde gepachtet haben | würden gepachtet haben<br>würdet gepachtet haben<br>würden gepachtet haben |

## EXAMPLES

Sie haben einen Bauernhof in der Nähe von Oldenburg gepachtet.
They've leased a farm in the vicinity of Oldenburg.

Der junge Koch wird eine Gaststätte in der Stadt pachten.
The young cook is going to lease a cafe in the city.

**paddeln**

to paddle, to row

**Auxiliary verb:** haben **Past participle:** gepaddelt

**Imperative:** Paddele! Paddelt! Paddeln Sie!

| Mode | Simple Tenses | | Compound Tenses | |
|---|---|---|---|---|
| | *Singular* | *Plural* | *Singular* | *Plural* |
| Indicative | **Present** | | **Present Perfect** | |
| | paddele<br>paddelst<br>paddelt | paddeln<br>paddelt<br>paddeln | habe gepaddelt<br>hast gepaddelt<br>hat gepaddelt | haben gepaddelt<br>habt gepaddelt<br>haben gepaddelt |
| | **Past** | | **Past Perfect** | |
| | paddelte<br>paddeltest<br>paddelte | paddelten<br>paddeltet<br>paddelten | hatte gepaddelt<br>hattest gepaddelt<br>hatte gepaddelt | hatten gepaddelt<br>hattet gepaddelt<br>hatten gepaddelt |
| | **Future** | | **Future Perfect** | |
| | werde paddeln<br>wirst paddeln<br>wird paddeln | werden paddeln<br>werdet paddeln<br>werden paddeln | werde gepaddelt haben<br>wirst gepaddelt haben<br>wird gepaddelt haben | werden gepaddelt haben<br>werdet gepaddelt haben<br>werden gepaddelt haben |
| Subjunctive | **Present** | | **Present Perfect** | |
| | paddele<br>paddelst<br>paddele | paddeln<br>paddelt<br>paddeln | habe gepaddelt<br>habest gepaddelt<br>habe gepaddelt | haben gepaddelt<br>habet gepaddelt<br>haben gepaddelt |
| | **Past** | | **Past Perfect** | |
| | paddelte<br>paddeltest<br>paddelte | paddelten<br>paddeltet<br>paddelten | hätte gepaddelt<br>hättest gepaddelt<br>hätte gepaddelt | hätten gepaddelt<br>hättet gepaddelt<br>hätten gepaddelt |
| | **Future** | | **Future Perfect** | |
| | werde paddeln<br>werdest paddeln<br>werde paddeln | werden paddeln<br>werdet paddeln<br>werden paddeln | werde gepaddelt haben<br>werdest gepaddelt haben<br>werde gepaddelt haben | werden gepaddelt haben<br>werdet gepaddelt haben<br>werden gepaddelt haben |
| | **Present and Future Conditional** | | **Past Conditional** | |
| | würde paddeln<br>würdest paddeln<br>würde paddeln | würden paddeln<br>würdet paddeln<br>würden paddeln | würde gepaddelt haben<br>würdest gepaddelt haben<br>würde gepaddelt haben | würden gepaddelt haben<br>würdet gepaddelt haben<br>würden gepaddelt haben |

## EXAMPLES

Wir haben den ganzen Nachmittag gepaddelt und jetzt sind wir erschöpft.
We paddled all afternoon, and now we're exhausted.

Kannst du nicht paddeln helfen?
Can't you help row?

**parken**
to park
**Auxiliary verb:** haben **Past participle:** geparkt
**Imperative:** Parke! Parkt! Parken Sie!

| Mode | Simple Tenses | | Compound Tenses | |
|---|---|---|---|---|
| | *Singular* | *Plural* | *Singular* | *Plural* |
| Indicative | **Present** | | **Present Perfect** | |
| | parke<br>parkst<br>parkt | parken<br>parkt<br>parken | habe geparkt<br>hast geparkt<br>hat geparkt | haben geparkt<br>habt geparkt<br>haben geparkt |
| | **Past** | | **Past Perfect** | |
| | parkte<br>parktest<br>parkte | parkten<br>parktet<br>parkten | hatte geparkt<br>hattest geparkt<br>hatte geparkt | hatten geparkt<br>hattet geparkt<br>hatten geparkt |
| | **Future** | | **Future Perfect** | |
| | werde parken<br>wirst parken<br>wird parken | werden parken<br>werdet parken<br>werden parken | werde geparkt haben<br>wirst geparkt haben<br>wird geparkt haben | werden geparkt haben<br>werdet geparkt haben<br>werden geparkt haben |
| Subjunctive | **Present** | | **Present Perfect** | |
| | parke<br>parkest<br>parke | parken<br>parket<br>parken | habe geparkt<br>habest geparkt<br>habe geparkt | haben geparkt<br>habet geparkt<br>haben geparkt |
| | **Past** | | **Past Perfect** | |
| | parkte<br>parktest<br>parkte | parkten<br>parktet<br>parkten | hätte geparkt<br>hättest geparkt<br>hätte geparkt | hätten geparkt<br>hättet geparkt<br>hätten geparkt |
| | **Future** | | **Future Perfect** | |
| | werde parken<br>werdest parken<br>werde parken | werden parken<br>werdet parken<br>werden parken | werde geparkt haben<br>werdest geparkt haben<br>werde geparkt haben | werden geparkt haben<br>werdet geparkt haben<br>werden geparkt haben |
| | **Present and Future Conditional** | | **Past Conditional** | |
| | würde parken<br>würdest parken<br>würde parken | würden parken<br>würdet parken<br>würden parken | würde geparkt haben<br>würdest geparkt haben<br>würde geparkt haben | würden geparkt haben<br>würdet geparkt haben<br>würden geparkt haben |

## EXAMPLES

Hast du an einem Parkautomaten geparkt?
Es ist immer sehr schwierig in einer Großstadt zu parken.

Did you park at a parking meter?
It's always so difficult to park in a big city.

**passen**
to fit
**Auxiliary verb:** haben **Past participle:** gepasst
**Imperative:** Passe! Passt! Passen Sie!

| Mode | Simple Tenses | | Compound Tenses | |
|---|---|---|---|---|
| | *Singular* | *Plural* | *Singular* | *Plural* |
| Indicative | **Present** | | **Present Perfect** | |
| | passe<br>passt<br>passt | passen<br>passt<br>passen | habe gepasst<br>hast gepasst<br>hat gepasst | haben gepasst<br>habt gepasst<br>haben gepasst |
| | **Past** | | **Past Perfect** | |
| | passte<br>passtest<br>passte | passten<br>passtet<br>passten | hatte gepasst<br>hattest gepasst<br>hatte gepasst | hatten gepasst<br>hattet gepasst<br>hatten gepasst |
| | **Future** | | **Future Perfect** | |
| | werde passen<br>wirst passen<br>wird passen | werden passen<br>werdet passen<br>werden passen | werde gepasst haben<br>wirst gepasst haben<br>wird gepasst haben | werden gepasst haben<br>werdet gepasst haben<br>werden gepasst haben |
| Subjunctive | **Present** | | **Present Perfect** | |
| | passe<br>passest<br>passe | passen<br>passet<br>passen | habe gepasst<br>habest gepasst<br>habe gepasst | haben gepasst<br>habet gepasst<br>haben gepasst |
| | **Past** | | **Past Perfect** | |
| | passte<br>passtest<br>passte | passten<br>passtet<br>passten | hätte gepasst<br>hättest gepasst<br>hätte gepasst | hätten gepasst<br>hättet gepasst<br>hätten gepasst |
| | **Future** | | **Future Perfect** | |
| | werde passen<br>werdest passen<br>werde passen | werden passen<br>werdet passen<br>werden passen | werde gepasst haben<br>werdest gepasst haben<br>werde gepasst haben | werden gepasst haben<br>werdet gepasst haben<br>werden gepasst haben |
| | **Present and Future Conditional** | | **Past Conditional** | |
| | würde passen<br>würdest passen<br>würde passen | würden passen<br>würdet passen<br>würden passen | würde gepasst haben<br>würdest gepasst haben<br>würde gepasst haben | würden gepasst haben<br>würdet gepasst haben<br>würden gepasst haben |

## EXAMPLES

Das grössere Hemd passt mir besser.
The larger shirt fits me better.

Dieser Termin passt mir leider gar nicht.
Unfortunately, this appointment doesn't fit my schedule.

**passieren**
to happen, to pass, to travel through
**Auxiliary verb:** sein **Past participle:** passiert
**Imperative:** Passiere! Passiert! Passieren Sie!

| Mode | Simple Tenses | | Compound Tenses | |
|---|---|---|---|---|
| | *Singular* | *Plural* | *Singular* | *Plural* |
| Indicative | **Present** | | **Present Perfect** | |
| | passiere<br>passierst<br>passiert | passieren<br>passiert<br>passieren | bin passiert<br>bist passiert<br>ist passiert | sind passiert<br>seid passiert<br>sind passiert |
| | **Past** | | **Past Perfect** | |
| | passierte<br>passiertest<br>passierte | passierten<br>passiertet<br>passierten | war passiert<br>warst passiert<br>war passiert | waren passiert<br>wart passiert<br>waren passiert |
| | **Future** | | **Future Perfect** | |
| | werde passieren<br>wirst passieren<br>wird passieren | werden passieren<br>werdet passieren<br>werden passieren | werde passiert sein<br>wirst passiert sein<br>wird passiert sein | werden passiert sein<br>werdet passiert sein<br>werden passiert sein |
| Subjunctive | **Present** | | **Present Perfect** | |
| | passiere<br>passierest<br>passiere | passieren<br>passieret<br>passieren | sei passiert<br>seiest passiert<br>sei passiert | seien passiert<br>seiet passiert<br>seien passiert |
| | **Past** | | **Past Perfect** | |
| | passierte<br>passiertest<br>passierte | passierten<br>passiertet<br>passierten | wäre passiert<br>wärest passiert<br>wäre passiert | wären passiert<br>wäret passiert<br>wären passiert |
| | **Future** | | **Future Perfect** | |
| | werde passieren<br>werdest passieren<br>werde passieren | werden passieren<br>werdet passieren<br>werden passieren | werde passiert sein<br>werdest passiert sein<br>werde passiert sein | werden passiert sein<br>werdet passiert sein<br>werden passiert sein |
| | **Present and Future Conditional** | | **Past Conditional** | |
| | würde passieren<br>würdest passieren<br>würde passieren | würden passieren<br>würdet passieren<br>würden passieren | würde passiert sein<br>würdest passiert sein<br>würde passiert sein | würden passiert sein<br>würdet passiert sein<br>würden passiert sein |

**Note:** When *passieren* means "to pass," it is a transitive verb and requires *haben* as its auxiliary in the perfect tenses.

## EXAMPLES

| | |
|---|---|
| Was ist Ihnen passiert? | What has happened to you? |
| In der Nähe des Marktplatzes passierte ein schwerer Unfall. | A bad accident happened near the market square. |
| Der Bus passiert gerade die Kreuzung. | The bus is just now passing the intersection. |

**pfeifen**
to whistle
**Auxiliary verb:** haben **Past participle:** gepfiffen
**Imperative:** Pfeife! Pfeift! Pfeifen Sie!

| Mode | Simple Tenses | | Compound Tenses | |
|---|---|---|---|---|
| | *Singular* | *Plural* | *Singular* | *Plural* |
| Indicative | **Present** | | **Present Perfect** | |
| | pfeife<br>pfeifst<br>pfeift | pfeifen<br>pfeift<br>pfeifen | habe gepfiffen<br>hast gepfiffen<br>hat gepfiffen | haben gepfiffen<br>habt gepfiffen<br>haben gepfiffen |
| | **Past** | | **Past Perfect** | |
| | pfiff<br>pfiffst<br>pfiff | pfiffen<br>pfifft<br>pfiffen | hatte gepfiffen<br>hattest gepfiffen<br>hatte gepfiffen | hatten gepfiffen<br>hattet gepfiffen<br>hatten gepfiffen |
| | **Future** | | **Future Perfect** | |
| | werde pfeifen<br>wirst pfeifen<br>wird pfeifen | werden pfeifen<br>werdet pfeifen<br>werden pfeifen | werde gepfiffen haben<br>wirst gepfiffen haben<br>wird gepfiffen haben | werden gepfiffen haben<br>werdet gepfiffen haben<br>werden gepfiffen haben |
| Subjunctive | **Present** | | **Present Perfect** | |
| | pfeife<br>pfeifest<br>pfeife | pfeifen<br>pfeifet<br>pfeifen | habe gepfiffen<br>habest gepfiffen<br>habe gepfiffen | haben gepfiffen<br>habet gepfiffen<br>haben gepfiffen |
| | **Past** | | **Past Perfect** | |
| | pfiffe<br>pfiffest<br>pfiffe | pfiffen<br>pfiffet<br>pfiffen | hätte gepfiffen<br>hättest gepfiffen<br>hätte gepfiffen | hätten gepfiffen<br>hättet gepfiffen<br>hätten gepfiffen |
| | **Future** | | **Future Perfect** | |
| | werde pfeifen<br>werdest pfeifen<br>werde pfeifen | werden pfeifen<br>werdet pfeifen<br>werden pfeifen | werde gepfiffen haben<br>werdest gepfiffen haben<br>werde gepfiffen haben | werden gepfiffen haben<br>werdet gepfiffen haben<br>werden gepfiffen haben |
| | **Present and Future Conditional** | | **Past Conditional** | |
| | würde pfeifen<br>würdest pfeifen<br>würde pfeifen | würden pfeifen<br>würdet pfeifen<br>würden pfeifen | würde gepfiffen haben<br>würdest gepfiffen haben<br>würde gepfiffen haben | würden gepfiffen haben<br>würdet gepfiffen haben<br>würden gepfiffen haben |

## EXAMPLES

Ich fragte den Jungen, ob er pfeifen kann.
I asked the boy whether he could whistle.

Der Maler pfeift beim Arbeiten vor sich hin.
The painter whistles to himself while he works.

**pflanzen**
to plant
**Auxiliary verb:** haben **Past participle:** gepflanzt
**Imperative:** Pflanze! Pflanzt! Pflanzen Sie!

| Mode | Simple Tenses | | Compound Tenses | |
|---|---|---|---|---|
| | *Singular* | *Plural* | *Singular* | *Plural* |
| Indicative | **Present** | | **Present Perfect** | |
| | pflanze<br>pflanzt<br>pflanzt | pflanzen<br>pflanzt<br>pflanzen | habe gepflanzt<br>hast gepflanzt<br>hat gepflanzt | haben gepflanzt<br>habt gepflanzt<br>haben gepflanzt |
| | **Past** | | **Past Perfect** | |
| | pflanzte<br>pflanztest<br>pflanzte | pflanzten<br>pflanztet<br>pflanzten | hatte gepflanzt<br>hattest gepflanzt<br>hatte gepflanzt | hatten gepflanzt<br>hattet gepflanzt<br>hatten gepflanzt |
| | **Future** | | **Future Perfect** | |
| | werde pflanzen<br>wirst pflanzen<br>wird pflanzen | werden pflanzen<br>werdet pflanzen<br>werden pflanzen | werde gepflanzt haben<br>wirst gepflanzt haben<br>wird gepflanzt haben | werden gepflanzt haben<br>werdet gepflanzt haben<br>werden gepflanzt haben |
| Subjunctive | **Present** | | **Present Perfect** | |
| | pflanze<br>pflanzest<br>pflanze | pflanzen<br>pflanzet<br>pflanzen | habe gepflanzt<br>habest gepflanzt<br>habe gepflanzt | haben gepflanzt<br>habet gepflanzt<br>haben gepflanzt |
| | **Past** | | **Past Perfect** | |
| | pflanzte<br>pflanztest<br>pflanzte | pflanzten<br>pflanztet<br>pflanzten | hätte gepflanzt<br>hättest gepflanzt<br>hätte gepflanzt | hätten gepflanzt<br>hättet gepflanzt<br>hätten gepflanzt |
| | **Future** | | **Future Perfect** | |
| | werde pflanzen<br>werdest pflanzen<br>werde pflanzen | werden pflanzen<br>werdet pflanzen<br>werden pflanzen | werde gepflanzt haben<br>werdest gepflanzt haben<br>werde gepflanzt haben | werden gepflanzt haben<br>werdet gepflanzt haben<br>werden gepflanzt haben |
| | **Present and Future Conditional** | | **Past Conditional** | |
| | würde pflanzen<br>würdest pflanzen<br>würde pflanzen | würden pflanzen<br>würdet pflanzen<br>würden pflanzen | würde gepflanzt haben<br>würdest gepflanzt haben<br>würde gepflanzt haben | würden gepflanzt haben<br>würdet gepflanzt haben<br>würden gepflanzt haben |

## EXAMPLES

Ich möchte hier hunderte von Rosen pflanzen.
I want to plant hundreds of roses here.

Die Bäuerin hat im Garten Gemüse und ein paar Blumen gepflanzt.
The farm woman planted vegetables and a few flowers in her garden.

**pflegen**

to care for, to tend

**Auxiliary verb:** haben **Past participle:** gepflegt

**Imperative:** Pflege! Pflegt! Pflegen Sie!

| Mode | Simple Tenses | | Compound Tenses | |
|---|---|---|---|---|
| | *Singular* | *Plural* | *Singular* | *Plural* |
| Indicative | **Present** | | **Present Perfect** | |
| | pflege<br>pflegst<br>pflegt | pflegen<br>pflegt<br>pflegen | habe gepflegt<br>hast gepflegt<br>hat gepflegt | haben gepflegt<br>habt gepflegt<br>haben gepflegt |
| | **Past** | | **Past Perfect** | |
| | pflegte<br>pflegtest<br>pflegte | pflegten<br>pflegtet<br>pflegten | hatte gepflegt<br>hattest gepflegt<br>hatte gepflegt | hatten gepflegt<br>hattet gepflegt<br>hatten gepflegt |
| | **Future** | | **Future Perfect** | |
| | werde pflegen<br>wirst pflegen<br>wird pflegen | werden pflegen<br>werdet pflegen<br>werden pflegen | werde gepflegt haben<br>wirst gepflegt haben<br>wird gepflegt haben | werden gepflegt haben<br>werdet gepflegt haben<br>werden gepflegt haben |
| Subjunctive | **Present** | | **Present Perfect** | |
| | pflege<br>pflegest<br>pflege | pflegen<br>pfleget<br>pflegen | habe gepflegt<br>habest gepflegt<br>habe gepflegt | haben gepflegt<br>habet gepflegt<br>haben gepflegt |
| | **Past** | | **Past Perfect** | |
| | pflegte<br>pflegtest<br>pflegte | pflegten<br>pflegtet<br>pflegten | hätte gepflegt<br>hättest gepflegt<br>hätte gepflegt | hätten gepflegt<br>hättet gepflegt<br>hätten gepflegt |
| | **Future** | | **Future Perfect** | |
| | werde pflegen<br>werdest pflegen<br>werde pflegen | werden pflegen<br>werdet pflegen<br>werden pflegen | werde gepflegt haben<br>werdest gepflegt haben<br>werde gepflegt haben | werden gepflegt haben<br>werdet gepflegt haben<br>werden gepflegt haben |
| | **Present and Future Conditional** | | **Past Conditional** | |
| | würde pflegen<br>würdest pflegen<br>würde pflegen | würden pflegen<br>würdet pflegen<br>würden pflegen | würde gepflegt haben<br>würdest gepflegt haben<br>würde gepflegt haben | würden gepflegt haben<br>würdet gepflegt haben<br>würden gepflegt haben |

## EXAMPLES

Ich pflegte eine Freundschaft mit einem alten Schulkameraden.

I cultivated a friendship with an old school friend.

Der verletzte Mann wird von seiner Frau gepflegt.

The injured man is cared for by his wife.

**pflücken**
to pick, to pluck
**Auxiliary verb:** haben **Past participle:** gepflückt
**Imperative:** Pflücke! Pflückt! Pflücken Sie!

| Mode | Simple Tenses | | Compound Tenses | |
|---|---|---|---|---|
| | *Singular* | *Plural* | *Singular* | *Plural* |
| Indicative | **Present** | | **Present Perfect** | |
| | pflücke<br>pflückst<br>pflückt | pflücken<br>pflückt<br>pflücken | habe gepflückt<br>hast gepflückt<br>hat gepflückt | haben gepflückt<br>habt gepflückt<br>haben gepflückt |
| | **Past** | | **Past Perfect** | |
| | pflückte<br>pflücktest<br>pflückte | pflückten<br>pflücktet<br>pflückten | hatte gepflückt<br>hattest gepflückt<br>hatte gepflückt | hatten gepflückt<br>hattet gepflückt<br>hatten gepflückt |
| | **Future** | | **Future Perfect** | |
| | werde pflücken<br>wirst pflücken<br>wird pflücken | werden pflücken<br>werdet pflücken<br>werden pflücken | werde gepflückt haben<br>wirst gepflückt haben<br>wird gepflückt haben | werden gepflückt haben<br>werdet gepflückt haben<br>werden gepflückt haben |
| Subjunctive | **Present** | | **Present Perfect** | |
| | pflücke<br>pflückest<br>pflücke | pflücken<br>pflücket<br>pflücken | habe gepflückt<br>habest gepflückt<br>habe gepflückt | haben gepflückt<br>habet gepflückt<br>haben gepflückt |
| | **Past** | | **Past Perfect** | |
| | pflückte<br>pflücktest<br>pflückte | pflückten<br>pflücktet<br>pflückten | hätte gepflückt<br>hättest gepflückt<br>hätte gepflückt | hätten gepflückt<br>hättet gepflückt<br>hätten gepflückt |
| | **Future** | | **Future Perfect** | |
| | werde pflücken<br>werdest pflücken<br>werde pflücken | werden pflücken<br>werdet pflücken<br>werden pflücken | werde gepflückt haben<br>werdest gepflückt haben<br>werde gepflückt haben | werden gepflückt haben<br>werdet gepflückt haben<br>werden gepflückt haben |
| | **Present and Future Conditional** | | **Past Conditional** | |
| | würde pflücken<br>würdest pflücken<br>würde pflücken | würden pflücken<br>würdet pflücken<br>würden pflücken | würde gepflückt haben<br>würdest gepflückt haben<br>würde gepflückt haben | würden gepflückt haben<br>würdet gepflückt haben<br>würden gepflückt haben |

## EXAMPLES

Tante Luise ist im Garten und pflückt Tulpen.
Aunt Luise is in the garden picking tulips.

Wer hat so viele Blumen gepflückt?
Who picked so many flowers?

**plagen**
to plague, to annoy
**Auxiliary verb:** haben **Past participle:** geplagt
**Imperative:** Plage! Plagt! Plagen Sie!

| Mode | Simple Tenses | | Compound Tenses | |
|---|---|---|---|---|
| | *Singular* | *Plural* | *Singular* | *Plural* |
| Indicative | **Present** | | **Present Perfect** | |
| | plage<br>plagst<br>plagt | plagen<br>plagt<br>plagen | habe geplagt<br>hast geplagt<br>hat geplagt | haben geplagt<br>habt geplagt<br>haben geplagt |
| | **Past** | | **Past Perfect** | |
| | plagte<br>plagtest<br>plagte | plagten<br>plagtet<br>plagten | hatte geplagt<br>hattest geplagt<br>hatte geplagt | hatten geplagt<br>hattet geplagt<br>hatten geplagt |
| | **Future** | | **Future Perfect** | |
| | werde plagen<br>wirst plagen<br>wird plagen | werden plagen<br>werdet plagen<br>werden plagen | werde geplagt haben<br>wirst geplagt haben<br>wird geplagt haben | werden geplagt haben<br>werdet geplagt haben<br>werden geplagt haben |
| Subjunctive | **Present** | | **Present Perfect** | |
| | plage<br>plagest<br>plage | plagen<br>plaget<br>plagen | habe geplagt<br>habest geplagt<br>habe geplagt | haben geplagt<br>habet geplagt<br>haben geplagt |
| | **Past** | | **Past Perfect** | |
| | plagte<br>plagtest<br>plagte | plagten<br>plagtet<br>plagten | hätte geplagt<br>hättest geplagt<br>hätte geplagt | hätten geplagt<br>hättet geplagt<br>hätten geplagt |
| | **Future** | | **Future Perfect** | |
| | werde plagen<br>werdest plagen<br>werde plagen | werden plagen<br>werdet plagen<br>werden plagen | werde geplagt haben<br>werdest geplagt haben<br>werde geplagt haben | werden geplagt haben<br>werdet geplagt haben<br>werden geplagt haben |
| | **Present and Future Conditional** | | **Past Conditional** | |
| | würde plagen<br>würdest plagen<br>würde plagen | würden plagen<br>würdet plagen<br>würden plagen | würde geplagt haben<br>würdest geplagt haben<br>würde geplagt haben | würden geplagt haben<br>würdet geplagt haben<br>würden geplagt haben |

## EXAMPLES

Die Kinder plagen ihn mit Fragen.
The children annoy him with questions.

Mein Mann ist wieder von Kopfschmerzen geplagt.
My husband is plagued by headaches again.

**platzen**
to burst, to explode
**Auxiliary verb:** sein **Past participle:** geplatzt
**Imperative:** Platze! Platzt! Platzen Sie!

| Mode | Simple Tenses | | Compound Tenses | |
|---|---|---|---|---|
| | *Singular* | *Plural* | *Singular* | *Plural* |
| Indicative | **Present** | | **Present Perfect** | |
| | platze<br>platzt<br>platzt | platzen<br>platzt<br>platzen | bin geplatzt<br>bist geplatzt<br>ist geplatzt | sind geplatzt<br>seid geplatzt<br>sind geplatzt |
| | **Past** | | **Past Perfect** | |
| | platzte<br>platztest<br>platzte | platzten<br>platztet<br>platzten | war geplatzt<br>warst geplatzt<br>war geplatzt | waren geplatzt<br>wart geplatzt<br>waren geplatzt |
| | **Future** | | **Future Perfect** | |
| | werde platzen<br>wirst platzen<br>wird platzen | werden platzen<br>werdet platzen<br>werden platzen | werde geplatzt sein<br>wirst geplatzt sein<br>wird geplatzt sein | werden geplatzt sein<br>werdet geplatzt sein<br>werden geplatzt sein |
| Subjunctive | **Present** | | **Present Perfect** | |
| | platze<br>platzest<br>platze | platzen<br>platzet<br>platzen | sei geplatzt<br>seiest geplatzt<br>sei geplatzt | seien geplatzt<br>seiet geplatzt<br>seien geplatzt |
| | **Past** | | **Past Perfect** | |
| | platzte<br>platztest<br>platzte | platzten<br>platztet<br>platzten | wäre geplatzt<br>wärest geplatzt<br>wäre geplatzt | wären geplatzt<br>wäret geplatzt<br>wären geplatzt |
| | **Future** | | **Future Perfect** | |
| | werde platzen<br>werdest platzen<br>werde platzen | werden platzen<br>werdet platzen<br>werden platzen | werde geplatzt sein<br>werdest geplatzt sein<br>werde geplatzt sein | werden geplatzt sein<br>werdet geplatzt sein<br>werden geplatzt sein |
| | **Present and Future Conditional** | | **Past Conditional** | |
| | würde platzen<br>würdest platzen<br>würde platzen | würden platzen<br>würdet platzen<br>würden platzen | würde geplatzt sein<br>würdest geplatzt sein<br>würde geplatzt sein | würden geplatzt sein<br>würdet geplatzt sein<br>würden geplatzt sein |

## EXAMPLES

Mir platzt fast der Kopf von so viel Arbeit! — My head is about to explode from all this work!
Sie schrie, als ihr Ballon platzte. — She screamed when her balloon burst.

**plaudern**
to chat, to converse
**Auxiliary verb:** haben **Past participle:** geplaudert
**Imperative:** Plaudere! Plaudert! Plaudern Sie!

| Mode | Simple Tenses | | Compound Tenses | |
|---|---|---|---|---|
| | *Singular* | *Plural* | *Singular* | *Plural* |
| Indicative | **Present** | | **Present Perfect** | |
| | plaudere<br>plauderst<br>plaudert | plaudern<br>plaudert<br>plaudern | habe geplaudert<br>hast geplaudert<br>hat geplaudert | haben geplaudert<br>habt geplaudert<br>haben geplaudert |
| | **Past** | | **Past Perfect** | |
| | plauderte<br>plaudertest<br>plauderte | plauderten<br>plaudertet<br>plauderten | hatte geplaudert<br>hattest geplaudert<br>hatte geplaudert | hatten geplaudert<br>hattet geplaudert<br>hatten geplaudert |
| | **Future** | | **Future Perfect** | |
| | werde plaudern<br>wirst plaudern<br>wird plaudern | werden plaudern<br>werdet plaudern<br>werden plaudern | werde geplaudert haben<br>wirst geplaudert haben<br>wird geplaudert haben | werden geplaudert haben<br>werdet geplaudert haben<br>werden geplaudert haben |
| Subjunctive | **Present** | | **Present Perfect** | |
| | plaudere<br>plauderst<br>plaudere | plaudern<br>plaudert<br>plaudern | habe geplaudert<br>habest geplaudert<br>habe geplaudert | haben geplaudert<br>habet geplaudert<br>haben geplaudert |
| | **Past** | | **Past Perfect** | |
| | plauderte<br>plaudertest<br>plauderte | plauderten<br>plaudertet<br>plauderten | hätte geplaudert<br>hättest geplaudert<br>hätte geplaudert | hätten geplaudert<br>hättet geplaudert<br>hätten geplaudert |
| | **Future** | | **Future Perfect** | |
| | werde plaudern<br>werdest plaudern<br>werde plaudern | werden plaudern<br>werdet plaudern<br>werden plaudern | werde geplaudert haben<br>werdest geplaudert haben<br>werde geplaudert haben | werden geplaudert haben<br>werdet geplaudert haben<br>werden geplaudert haben |
| | **Present and Future Conditional** | | **Past Conditional** | |
| | würde plaudern<br>würdest plaudern<br>würde plaudern | würden plaudern<br>würdet plaudern<br>würden plaudern | würde geplaudert haben<br>würdest geplaudert haben<br>würde geplaudert haben | würden geplaudert haben<br>würdet geplaudert haben<br>würden geplaudert haben |

## EXAMPLES

| | |
|---|---|
| Es ist immer schön mit alten Bekannten zu plaudern. | It is always nice to chat with old acquaintances. |
| Ich habe lange mit einem alten Freund geplaudert. | I chatted with an old friend for a long time. |

**prägen**
to coin, to stamp
**Auxiliary verb:** haben **Past participle:** geprägt
**Imperative:** Präge! Prägt! Prägen Sie!

| Mode | Simple Tenses | | Compound Tenses | |
|---|---|---|---|---|
| | *Singular* | *Plural* | *Singular* | *Plural* |
| Indicative | **Present** | | **Present Perfect** | |
| | präge<br>prägst<br>prägt | prägen<br>prägt<br>prägen | habe geprägt<br>hast geprägt<br>hat geprägt | haben geprägt<br>habt geprägt<br>haben geprägt |
| | **Past** | | **Past Perfect** | |
| | prägte<br>prägtest<br>prägte | prägten<br>prägtet<br>prägten | hatte geprägt<br>hattest geprägt<br>hatte geprägt | hatten geprägt<br>hattet geprägt<br>hatten geprägt |
| | **Future** | | **Future Perfect** | |
| | werde prägen<br>wirst prägen<br>wird prägen | werden prägen<br>werdet prägen<br>werden prägen | werde geprägt haben<br>wirst geprägt haben<br>wird geprägt haben | werden geprägt haben<br>werdet geprägt haben<br>werden geprägt haben |
| Subjunctive | **Present** | | **Present Perfect** | |
| | präge<br>prägest<br>präge | prägen<br>präget<br>prägen | habe geprägt<br>habest geprägt<br>habe geprägt | haben geprägt<br>habet geprägt<br>haben geprägt |
| | **Past** | | **Past Perfect** | |
| | prägte<br>prägtest<br>prägte | prägten<br>prägtet<br>prägten | hätte geprägt<br>hättest geprägt<br>hätte geprägt | hätten geprägt<br>hättet geprägt<br>hatten geprägt |
| | **Future** | | **Future Perfect** | |
| | werde prägen<br>werdest prägen<br>werde prägen | werden prägen<br>werdet prägen<br>werden prägen | werde geprägt haben<br>werdest geprägt haben<br>werde geprägt haben | werden geprägt haben<br>werdet geprägt haben<br>werden geprägt haben |
| | **Present and Future Conditional** | | **Past Conditional** | |
| | würde prägen<br>würdest prägen<br>würde prägen | würden prägen<br>würdet prägen<br>würden prägen | würde geprägt haben<br>würdest geprägt haben<br>würde geprägt haben | würden geprägt haben<br>würdet geprägt haben<br>würden geprägt haben |

## EXAMPLES

Winston Churchill hat den Ausdruck „der Eiserne Vorhang" geprägt.
Winston Churchill coined the expression "the Iron Curtain."

In Denver werden viele Münzen geprägt.
Many coins are imprinted in Denver.

**prahlen**

to brag, to boast

**Auxiliary verb:** haben **Past participle:** geprahlt

**Imperative:** Prahle! Prahlt! Prahlen Sie!

| Mode | Simple Tenses | | Compound Tenses | |
|---|---|---|---|---|
| | *Singular* | *Plural* | *Singular* | *Plural* |
| Indicative | **Present** | | **Present Perfect** | |
| | prahle<br>prahlst<br>prahlt | prahlen<br>prahlt<br>prahlen | habe geprahlt<br>hast geprahlt<br>hat geprahlt | haben geprahlt<br>habt geprahlt<br>haben geprahlt |
| | **Past** | | **Past Perfect** | |
| | prahlte<br>prahltest<br>prahlte | prahlten<br>prahltet<br>prahlten | hatte geprahlt<br>hattest geprahlt<br>hatte geprahlt | hatten geprahlt<br>hattet geprahlt<br>hatten geprahlt |
| | **Future** | | **Future Perfect** | |
| | werde prahlen<br>wirst prahlen<br>wird prahlen | werden prahlen<br>werdet prahlen<br>werden prahlen | werde geprahlt haben<br>wirst geprahlt haben<br>wird geprahlt haben | werden geprahlt haben<br>werdet geprahlt haben<br>werden geprahlt haben |
| Subjunctive | **Present** | | **Present Perfect** | |
| | prahle<br>prahlest<br>prahle | prahlen<br>prahlet<br>prahlen | habe geprahlt<br>habest geprahlt<br>habe geprahlt | haben geprahlt<br>habet geprahlt<br>haben geprahlt |
| | **Past** | | **Past Perfect** | |
| | prahlte<br>prahltest<br>prahlte | prahlten<br>prahltet<br>prahlten | hätte geprahlt<br>hättest geprahlt<br>hätte geprahlt | hätten geprahlt<br>hättet geprahlt<br>hätten geprahlt |
| | **Future** | | **Future Perfect** | |
| | werde prahlen<br>werdest prahlen<br>werde prahlen | werden prahlen<br>werdet prahlen<br>werden prahlen | werde geprahlt haben<br>werdest geprahlt haben<br>werde geprahlt haben | werden geprahlt haben<br>werdet geprahlt haben<br>werden geprahlt haben |
| | **Present and Future Conditional** | | **Past Conditional** | |
| | würde prahlen<br>würdest prahlen<br>würde prahlen | würden prahlen<br>würdet prahlen<br>würden prahlen | würde geprahlt haben<br>würdest geprahlt haben<br>würde geprahlt haben | würden geprahlt haben<br>würdet geprahlt haben<br>würden geprahlt haben |

## EXAMPLES

Warum muss sie immer mit ihrem Einkommen prahlen?

Why does she always have to brag about her income?

Meine Cousine prahlt, dass sie die beste Studentin an der Uni ist.

My cousin brags that she's the best student at college.

**predigen**
to preach
**Auxiliary verb:** haben **Past participle:** gepredigt
**Imperative:** Predige! Predigt! Predigen Sie!

| Mode | Simple Tenses | | Compound Tenses | |
|---|---|---|---|---|
| | *Singular* | *Plural* | *Singular* | *Plural* |
| Indicative | **Present** | | **Present Perfect** | |
| | predige<br>predigst<br>predigt | predigen<br>predigt<br>predigen | habe gepredigt<br>hast gepredigt<br>hat gepredigt | haben gepredigt<br>habt gepredigt<br>haben gepredigt |
| | **Past** | | **Past Perfect** | |
| | predigte<br>predigtest<br>predigte | predigten<br>predigtet<br>predigten | hatte gepredigt<br>hattest gepredigt<br>hatte gepredigt | hatten gepredigt<br>hattet gepredigt<br>hatten gepredigt |
| | **Future** | | **Future Perfect** | |
| | werde predigen<br>wirst predigen<br>wird predigen | werden predigen<br>werdet predigen<br>werden predigen | werde gepredigt haben<br>wirst gepredigt haben<br>wird gepredigt haben | werden gepredigt haben<br>werdet gepredigt haben<br>werden gepredigt haben |
| Subjunctive | **Present** | | **Present Perfect** | |
| | predige<br>predigest<br>predige | predigen<br>prediget<br>predigen | habe gepredigt<br>habest gepredigt<br>habe gepredigt | haben gepredigt<br>habet gepredigt<br>haben gepredigt |
| | **Past** | | **Past Perfect** | |
| | predigte<br>predigtest<br>predigte | predigten<br>predigtet<br>predigten | hätte gepredigt<br>hättest gepredigt<br>hätte gepredigt | hätten gepredigt<br>hättet gepredigt<br>hätten gepredigt |
| | **Future** | | **Future Perfect** | |
| | werde predigen<br>werdest predigen<br>werde predigen | werden predigen<br>werdet predigen<br>werden predigen | werde gepredigt haben<br>werdest gepredigt haben<br>werde gepredigt haben | werden gepredigt haben<br>werdet gepredigt haben<br>werden gepredigt haben |
| | **Present and Future Conditional** | | **Past Conditional** | |
| | würde predigen<br>würdest predigen<br>würde predigen | würden predigen<br>würdet predigen<br>würden predigen | würde gepredigt haben<br>würdest gepredigt haben<br>würde gepredigt haben | würden gepredigt haben<br>würdet gepredigt haben<br>würden gepredigt haben |

## EXAMPLES

Der Pfarrer fing an mit leisen Worten zu predigen.
The minister began to preach with quiet words.

Der Vater predigte und die Kinder waren stumm.
The father preached, and the children were mute.

**prüfen**
to test, to inspect
**Auxiliary verb:** haben **Past participle:** geprüft
**Imperative:** Prüfe! Prüft! Prüfen Sie!

| Mode | Simple Tenses | | Compound Tenses | |
|---|---|---|---|---|
| | *Singular* | *Plural* | *Singular* | *Plural* |
| Indicative | **Present** | | **Present Perfect** | |
| | prüfe<br>prüfst<br>prüft | prüfen<br>prüft<br>prüfen | habe geprüft<br>hast geprüft<br>hat geprüft | haben geprüft<br>habt geprüft<br>haben geprüft |
| | **Past** | | **Past Perfect** | |
| | prüfte<br>prüftest<br>prüfte | prüften<br>prüftet<br>prüften | hatte geprüft<br>hattest geprüft<br>hatte geprüft | hatten geprüft<br>hattet geprüft<br>hatten geprüft |
| | **Future** | | **Future Perfect** | |
| | werde prüfen<br>wirst prüfen<br>wird prüfen | werden prüfen<br>werdet prüfen<br>werden prüfen | werde geprüft haben<br>wirst geprüft haben<br>wird geprüft haben | werden geprüft haben<br>werdet geprüft haben<br>werden geprüft haben |
| Subjunctive | **Present** | | **Present Perfect** | |
| | prüfe<br>prüfest<br>prüfe | prüfen<br>prüfet<br>prüfen | habe geprüft<br>habest geprüft<br>habe geprüft | haben geprüft<br>habet geprüft<br>haben geprüft |
| | **Past** | | **Past Perfect** | |
| | prüfte<br>prüftest<br>prüfte | prüften<br>prüftet<br>prüften | hätte geprüft<br>hättest geprüft<br>hätte geprüft | hätten geprüft<br>hättet geprüft<br>hätten geprüft |
| | **Future** | | **Future Perfect** | |
| | werde prüfen<br>werdest prüfen<br>werde prüfen | werden prüfen<br>werdet prüfen<br>werden prüfen | werde geprüft haben<br>werdest geprüft haben<br>werde geprüft haben | werden geprüft haben<br>werdet geprüft haben<br>werden geprüft haben |
| | **Present and Future Conditional** | | **Past Conditional** | |
| | würde prüfen<br>würdest prüfen<br>würde prüfen | würden prüfen<br>würdet prüfen<br>würden prüfen | würde geprüft haben<br>würdest geprüft haben<br>würde geprüft haben | würden geprüft haben<br>würdet geprüft haben<br>würden geprüft haben |

## EXAMPLES

Jeder Student muss am Ende des Semesters geprüft werden.
Each student has to be tested at the end of the semester.

Prüfen Sie bitte auch den Reifendruck!
Please also check the tire pressure.

**pudern**
to powder
**Auxiliary verb:** haben **Past participle:** gepudert
**Imperative:** Pudere! Pudert! Pudern Sie!

| Mode | Simple Tenses | | Compound Tenses | |
|---|---|---|---|---|
| | *Singular* | *Plural* | *Singular* | *Plural* |
| Indicative | **Present** | | **Present Perfect** | |
| | pudere<br>puderst<br>pudert | pudern<br>pudert<br>pudern | habe gepudert<br>hast gepudert<br>hat gepudert | haben gepudert<br>habt gepudert<br>haben gepudert |
| | **Past** | | **Past Perfect** | |
| | puderte<br>pudertest<br>puderte | puderten<br>pudertet<br>puderten | hatte gepudert<br>hattest gepudert<br>hatte gepudert | hatten gepudert<br>hattet gepudert<br>hatten gepudert |
| | **Future** | | **Future Perfect** | |
| | werde pudern<br>wirst pudern<br>wird pudern | werden pudern<br>werdet pudern<br>werden pudern | werde gepudert haben<br>wirst gepudert haben<br>wird gepudert haben | werden gepudert haben<br>werdet gepudert haben<br>werden gepudert haben |
| Subjunctive | **Present** | | **Present Perfect** | |
| | pudere<br>puderst<br>pudere | pudern<br>pudert<br>pudern | habe gepudert<br>habest gepudert<br>habe gepudert | haben gepudert<br>habet gepudert<br>haben gepudert |
| | **Past** | | **Past Perfect** | |
| | puderte<br>pudertest<br>puderte | puderten<br>pudertet<br>puderten | hätte gepudert<br>hättest gepudert<br>hätte gepudert | hätten gepudert<br>hättet gepudert<br>hätten gepudert |
| | **Future** | | **Future Perfect** | |
| | werde pudern<br>werdest pudern<br>werde pudern | werden pudern<br>werdet pudern<br>werden pudern | werde gepudert haben<br>werdest gepudert haben<br>werde gepudert haben | werden gepudert haben<br>werdet gepudert haben<br>werden gepudert haben |
| | **Present and Future Conditional** | | **Past Conditional** | |
| | würde pudern<br>würdest pudern<br>würde pudern | würden pudern<br>würdet pudern<br>würden pudern | würde gepudert haben<br>würdest gepudert haben<br>würde gepudert haben | würden gepudert haben<br>würdet gepudert haben<br>würden gepudert haben |

## EXAMPLES

Die Schauspielerin hatte sich noch nicht geschminkt und gepudert.
The actress hadn't yet put on her makeup or powder.

Damals trugen auch Männer gepuderte Perücken.
Back then, even men wore powdered wigs.

**putzen**
to clean, to scour
**Auxiliary verb:** haben **Past participle:** geputzt
**Imperative:** Putze! Putzt! Putzen Sie!

| Mode | Simple Tenses | | Compound Tenses | |
|---|---|---|---|---|
| | *Singular* | *Plural* | *Singular* | *Plural* |
| Indicative | **Present** | | **Present Perfect** | |
| | putze<br>putzt<br>putzt | putzen<br>putzt<br>putzen | habe geputzt<br>hast geputzt<br>hat geputzt | haben geputzt<br>habt geputzt<br>haben geputzt |
| | **Past** | | **Past Perfect** | |
| | putzte<br>putztest<br>putzte | putzten<br>putztet<br>putzten | hatte geputzt<br>hattest geputzt<br>hatte geputzt | hatten geputzt<br>hattet geputzt<br>hatten geputzt |
| | **Future** | | **Future Perfect** | |
| | werde putzen<br>wirst putzen<br>wird putzen | werden putzen<br>werdet putzen<br>werden putzen | werde geputzt haben<br>wirst geputzt haben<br>wird geputzt haben | werden geputzt haben<br>werdet geputzt haben<br>werden geputzt haben |
| Subjunctive | **Present** | | **Present Perfect** | |
| | putze<br>putzest<br>putze | putzen<br>putzet<br>putzen | habe geputzt<br>habest geputzt<br>habe geputzt | haben geputzt<br>habet geputzt<br>haben geputzt |
| | **Past** | | **Past Perfect** | |
| | putzte<br>putztest<br>putzte | putzten<br>putztet<br>putzten | hätte geputzt<br>hättest geputzt<br>hätte geputzt | hätten geputzt<br>hättet geputzt<br>hätten geputzt |
| | **Future** | | **Future Perfect** | |
| | werde putzen<br>werdest putzen<br>werde putzen | werden putzen<br>werdet putzen<br>werden putzen | werde geputzt haben<br>werdest geputzt haben<br>werde geputzt haben | werden geputzt haben<br>werdet geputzt haben<br>werden geputzt haben |
| | **Present and Future Conditional** | | **Past Conditional** | |
| | würde putzen<br>würdest putzen<br>würde putzen | würden putzen<br>würdet putzen<br>würden putzen | würde geputzt haben<br>würdest geputzt haben<br>würde geputzt haben | würden geputzt haben<br>würdet geputzt haben<br>würden geputzt haben |

## EXAMPLE

Der Küchenboden muss unbedingt geputzt werden.

The kitchen floor definitely has to be washed.

**quälen**
to torture, to torment
**Auxiliary verb:** haben **Past participle:** gequält
**Imperative:** Quäle! Quält! Quälen Sie!

| Mode | Simple Tenses | | Compound Tenses | |
|---|---|---|---|---|
| | *Singular* | *Plural* | *Singular* | *Plural* |
| Indicative | **Present** | | **Present Perfect** | |
| | quäle<br>quälst<br>quält | quälen<br>quält<br>quälen | habe gequält<br>hast gequält<br>hat gequält | haben gequält<br>habt gequält<br>haben gequält |
| | **Past** | | **Past Perfect** | |
| | quälte<br>quältest<br>quälte | quälten<br>quältet<br>quälten | hatte gequält<br>hattest gequält<br>hatte gequält | hatten gequält<br>hattet gequält<br>hatten gequält |
| | **Future** | | **Future Perfect** | |
| | werde quälen<br>wirst quälen<br>wird quälen | werden quälen<br>werdet quälen<br>werden quälen | werde gequält haben<br>wirst gequält haben<br>wird gequält haben | werden gequält haben<br>werdet gequält haben<br>werden gequält haben |
| Subjunctive | **Present** | | **Present Perfect** | |
| | quäle<br>quälest<br>quäle | quälen<br>quälet<br>quälen | habe gequält<br>habest gequält<br>habe gequält | haben gequält<br>habet gequält<br>haben gequält |
| | **Past** | | **Past Perfect** | |
| | quälte<br>quältest<br>quälte | quälten<br>quältet<br>quälten | hätte gequält<br>hättest gequält<br>hätte gequält | hätten gequält<br>hättet gequält<br>hätten gequält |
| | **Future** | | **Future Perfect** | |
| | werde quälen<br>werdest quälen<br>werde quälen | werden quälen<br>werdet quälen<br>werden quälen | werde gequält haben<br>werdest gequält haben<br>werde gequält haben | werden gequält haben<br>werdet gequält haben<br>werden gequält haben |
| | **Present and Future Conditional** | | **Past Conditional** | |
| | würde quälen<br>würdest quälen<br>würde quälen | würden quälen<br>würdet quälen<br>würden quälen | würde gequält haben<br>würdest gequält haben<br>würde gequält haben | würden gequält haben<br>würdet gequält haben<br>würden gequält haben |

## EXAMPLES

Warum quälst du ihn ständig mit diesen Geschichten?
Why do you keep torturing him with these stories?

Die Sorgen um meine Gesundheit quälen mich Tag und Nacht.
Worries about my health torment me day and night.

**qualifizieren**
to qualify
**Auxiliary verb:** haben **Past participle:** qualifiziert
**Imperative:** Qualifiziere! Qualifiziert! Qualifizieren Sie!

| Mode | Simple Tenses | | Compound Tenses | |
|---|---|---|---|---|
| | *Singular* | *Plural* | *Singular* | *Plural* |
| Indicative | **Present** | | **Present Perfect** | |
| | qualifiziere<br>qualifizierst<br>qualifiziert | qualifizieren<br>qualifiziert<br>qualifizieren | habe qualifiziert<br>hast qualifiziert<br>hat qualifiziert | haben qualifiziert<br>habt qualifiziert<br>haben qualifiziert |
| | **Past** | | **Past Perfect** | |
| | qualifizierte<br>qualifiziertest<br>qualifizierte | qualifizierten<br>qualifiziertet<br>qualifizierten | hatte qualifiziert<br>hattest qualifiziert<br>hatte qualifiziert | hatten qualifiziert<br>hattet qualifiziert<br>hatten qualifiziert |
| | **Future** | | **Future Perfect** | |
| | werde qualifizieren<br>wirst qualifizieren<br>wird qualifizieren | werden qualifizieren<br>werdet qualifizieren<br>werden qualifizieren | werde qualifiziert haben<br>wirst qualifiziert haben<br>wird qualifiziert haben | werden qualifiziert haben<br>werdet qualifiziert haben<br>werden qualifiziert haben |
| Subjunctive | **Present** | | **Present Perfect** | |
| | qualifiziere<br>qualifizierest<br>qualifiziere | qualifizieren<br>qualifizieret<br>qualifizieren | habe qualifiziert<br>habest qualifiziert<br>habe qualifiziert | haben qualifiziert<br>habet qualifiziert<br>haben qualifiziert |
| | **Past** | | **Past Perfect** | |
| | qualifizierte<br>qualifiziertest<br>qualifizierte | qualifizierten<br>qualifiziertet<br>qualifizierten | hätte qualifiziert<br>hättest qualifiziert<br>hätte qualifiziert | hätten qualifiziert<br>hättet qualifiziert<br>hätten qualifiziert |
| | **Future** | | **Future Perfect** | |
| | werde qualifizieren<br>werdest qualifizieren<br>werde qualifizieren | werden qualifizieren<br>werdet qualifizieren<br>werden qualifizieren | werde qualifiziert haben<br>werdest qualifiziert haben<br>werde qualifiziert haben | werden qualifiziert haben<br>werdet qualifiziert haben<br>werden qualifiziert haben |
| | **Present and Future Conditional** | | **Past Conditional** | |
| | würde qualifizieren<br>würdest qualifizieren<br>würde qualifizieren | würden qualifizieren<br>würdet qualifizieren<br>würden qualifizieren | würde qualifiziert haben<br>würdest qualifiziert haben<br>würde qualifiziert haben | würden qualifiziert haben<br>würdet qualifiziert haben<br>würden qualifiziert haben |

## EXAMPLES

| | |
|---|---|
| Erik will sich für den Marathonlauf qualifizieren. | Erik wants to qualify for the marathon. |
| Frau Berger ist für die Stellung höchst qualifiziert. | Ms. Berger is highly qualified for the job. |

**quatschen**
to talk nonsense, to chat
**Auxiliary verb:** haben **Past participle:** gequatscht
**Imperative:** Quatsche! Quatscht! Quatschen Sie!

| Mode | Simple Tenses | | Compound Tenses | |
|---|---|---|---|---|
| | *Singular* | *Plural* | *Singular* | *Plural* |
| Indicative | **Present** | | **Present Perfect** | |
| | quatsche<br>quatschst<br>quatscht | quatschen<br>quatscht<br>quatschen | habe gequatscht<br>hast gequatscht<br>hat gequatscht | haben gequatscht<br>habt gequatscht<br>haben gequatscht |
| | **Past** | | **Past Perfect** | |
| | quatschte<br>quatschtest<br>quatschte | quatschten<br>quatschtet<br>quatschten | hatte gequatscht<br>hattest gequatscht<br>hatte gequatscht | hatten gequatscht<br>hattet gequatscht<br>hatten gequatscht |
| | **Future** | | **Future Perfect** | |
| | werde quatschen<br>wirst quatschen<br>wird quatschen | werden quatschen<br>werdet quatschen<br>werden quatschen | werde gequatscht haben<br>wirst gequatscht haben<br>wird gequatscht haben | werden gequatscht haben<br>werdet gequatscht haben<br>werden gequatscht haben |
| Subjunctive | **Present** | | **Present Perfect** | |
| | quatsche<br>quatschest<br>quatsche | quatschen<br>quatschet<br>quatschen | habe gequatscht<br>habest gequatscht<br>habe gequatscht | haben gequatscht<br>habet gequatscht<br>haben gequatscht |
| | **Past** | | **Past Perfect** | |
| | quatschte<br>quatschtest<br>quatschte | quatschten<br>quatschtet<br>quatschten | hätte gequatscht<br>hättest gequatscht<br>hätte gequatscht | hätten gequatscht<br>hättet gequatscht<br>hätten gequatscht |
| | **Future** | | **Future Perfect** | |
| | werde quatschen<br>werdest quatschen<br>werde quatschen | werden quatschen<br>werdet quatschen<br>werden quatschen | werde gequatscht haben<br>werdest gequatscht haben<br>werde gequatscht haben | werden gequatscht haben<br>werdet gequatscht haben<br>werden gequatscht haben |
| | **Present and Future Conditional** | | **Past Conditional** | |
| | würde quatschen<br>würdest quatschen<br>würde quatschen | würden quatschen<br>würdet quatschen<br>würden quatschen | würde gequatscht haben<br>würdest gequatscht haben<br>würde gequatscht haben | würden gequatscht haben<br>würdet gequatscht haben<br>würden gequatscht haben |

## EXAMPLES

Paul hat nichts zu sagen. Er quatscht nur.
Paul has nothing to say. He's just talking nonsense.

Wir haben Karten gespielt und gequatscht.
We played cards and gabbed.

**quellen**

to gush, to well from, to be the source

**Auxiliary verb:** sein **Past participle:** gequollen

**Imperative:** N/A

| Mode | Simple Tenses | | Compound Tenses | |
|---|---|---|---|---|
| | *Singular* | *Plural* | *Singular* | *Plural* |
| Indicative | **Present** | | **Present Perfect** | |
| | quelle<br>quillst<br>quillt | quellen<br>quellt<br>quellen | bin gequollen<br>bist gequollen<br>ist gequollen | sind gequollen<br>seid gequollen<br>sind gequollen |
| | **Past** | | **Past Perfect** | |
| | quoll<br>quollst<br>quoll | quollen<br>quollt<br>quollen | war gequollen<br>warst gequollen<br>war gequollen | waren gequollen<br>wart gequollen<br>waren gequollen |
| | **Future** | | **Future Perfect** | |
| | werde quellen<br>wirst quellen<br>wird quellen | werden quellen<br>werdet quellen<br>werden quellen | werde gequollen sein<br>wirst gequollen sein<br>wird gequollen sein | werden gequollen sein<br>werdet gequollen sein<br>werden gequollen sein |
| Subjunctive | **Present** | | **Present Perfect** | |
| | quelle<br>quellest<br>quelle | quellen<br>quellet<br>quellen | sei gequollen<br>seiest gequollen<br>sei gequollen | seien gequollen<br>seiet gequollen<br>seien gequollen |
| | **Past** | | **Past Perfect** | |
| | quölle<br>quöllest<br>quölle | quöllen<br>quöllet<br>quöllen | wäre gequollen<br>wärest gequollen<br>wäre gequollen | wären gequollen<br>wäret gequollen<br>wären gequollen |
| | **Future** | | **Future Perfect** | |
| | werde quellen<br>werdest quellen<br>werde quellen | werden quellen<br>werdet quellen<br>werden quellen | werde gequollen sein<br>werdest gequollen sein<br>werde gequollen sein | werden gequollen sein<br>werdet gequollen sein<br>werden gequollen sein |
| | **Present and Future Conditional** | | **Past Conditional** | |
| | würde quellen<br>würdest quellen<br>würde quellen | würden quellen<br>würdet quellen<br>würden quellen | würde gequollen sein<br>würdest gequollen sein<br>würde gequollen sein | würden gequollen sein<br>würdet gequollen sein<br>würden gequollen sein |

## EXAMPLE

Dicke Tränen quollen ihr aus den Augen. — Heavy tears welled up in her eyes.

**rächen (sich)**
to avenge
**Auxiliary verb:** haben **Past participle:** gerächt
**Imperative:** Räche! Rächt! Rächen Sie!

| Mode | Simple Tenses | | Compound Tenses | |
|---|---|---|---|---|
| | *Singular* | *Plural* | *Singular* | *Plural* |
| Indicative | **Present** | | **Present Perfect** | |
| | räche<br>rächst<br>rächt | rächen<br>rächt<br>rächen | habe gerächt<br>hast gerächt<br>hat gerächt | haben gerächt<br>habt gerächt<br>haben gerächt |
| | **Past** | | **Past Perfect** | |
| | rächte<br>rächtest<br>rächte | rächten<br>rächtet<br>rächten | hatte gerächt<br>hattest gerächt<br>hatte gerächt | hatten gerächt<br>hattet gerächt<br>hatten gerächt |
| | **Future** | | **Future Perfect** | |
| | werde rächen<br>wirst rächen<br>wird rächen | werden rächen<br>werdet rächen<br>werden rächen | werde gerächt haben<br>wirst gerächt haben<br>wird gerächt haben | werden gerächt haben<br>werdet gerächt haben<br>werden gerächt haben |
| Subjunctive | **Present** | | **Present Perfect** | |
| | räche<br>rächest<br>räche | rächen<br>rächet<br>rächen | habe gerächt<br>habest gerächt<br>habe gerächt | haben gerächt<br>habet gerächt<br>haben gerächt |
| | **Past** | | **Past Perfect** | |
| | rächte<br>rächtest<br>rächte | rächten<br>rächtet<br>rächten | hätte gerächt<br>hättest gerächt<br>hätte gerächt | hätten gerächt<br>hättet gerächt<br>hätten gerächt |
| | **Future** | | **Future Perfect** | |
| | werde rächen<br>werdest rächen<br>werde rächen | werden rächen<br>werdet rächen<br>werden rächen | werde gerächt haben<br>werdest gerächt haben<br>werde gerächt haben | werden gerächt haben<br>werdet gerächt haben<br>werden gerächt haben |
| | **Present and Future Conditional** | | **Past Conditional** | |
| | würde rächen<br>würdest rächen<br>würde rächen | würden rächen<br>würdet rächen<br>würden rächen | würde gerächt haben<br>würdest gerächt haben<br>würde gerächt haben | würden gerächt haben<br>würdet gerächt haben<br>würden gerächt haben |

# EXAMPLES

Der Lehrer rächte sich für den Schülerstreich. — The teacher took revenge for the students' prank.

Diese Tat hat sich an ihm gerächt. — This deed has been brought home to him.

**rasen**

to speed, to rave, to be mad

**Auxiliary verb: sein** **Past participle:** gerast

**Imperative:** Rase! Rast! Rasen Sie!

| Mode | Simple Tenses | | Compound Tenses | |
|---|---|---|---|---|
| | *Singular* | *Plural* | *Singular* | *Plural* |
| Indicative | **Present** | | **Present Perfect** | |
| | rase<br>rast<br>rast | rasen<br>rast<br>rasen | bin gerast<br>bist gerast<br>ist gerast | sind gerast<br>seid gerast<br>sind gerast |
| | **Past** | | **Past Perfect** | |
| | raste<br>rastest<br>raste | rasten<br>rastet<br>rasten | war gerast<br>warst gerast<br>war gerast | waren gerast<br>wart gerast<br>waren gerast |
| | **Future** | | **Future Perfect** | |
| | werde rasen<br>wirst rasen<br>wird rasen | werden rasen<br>werdet rasen<br>werden rasen | werde gerast sein<br>wirst gerast sein<br>wird gerast sein | werden gerast sein<br>werdet gerast sein<br>werden gerast sein |
| Subjunctive | **Present** | | **Present Perfect** | |
| | rase<br>rasest<br>rase | rasen<br>raset<br>rasen | sei gerast<br>seiest gerast<br>sei gerast | seien gerast<br>seiet gerast<br>sind gerast |
| | **Past** | | **Past Perfect** | |
| | raste<br>rastest<br>raste | rasten<br>rastet<br>rasten | wäre gerast<br>wärest gerast<br>wäre gerast | wären gerast<br>wäret gerast<br>wären gerast |
| | **Future** | | **Future Perfect** | |
| | werde rasen<br>werdest rasen<br>werde rasen | werden rasen<br>werdet rasen<br>werden rasen | werde gerast sein<br>werdest gerast sein<br>werde gerast sein | werden gerast sein<br>werdet gerast sein<br>werden gerast sein |
| | **Present and Future Conditional** | | **Past Conditional** | |
| | würde rasen<br>würdest rasen<br>würde rasen | würden rasen<br>würdet rasen<br>würden rasen | würde gerast sein<br>würdest gerast sein<br>würde gerast sein | würden gerast sein<br>würdet gerast sein<br>würden gerast sein |

**Note:** *Rasen* is used with the auxiliary verb *sein* when it takes the meaning of "to speed," but it usually takes the auxiliary verb *haben* when it means "to be mad." The meaning "to be mad" is used much less frequently.

## EXAMPLES

| | |
|---|---|
| Warum muss Michael immer so rasen? | Why does Michael always have to speed like that? |
| Das ist zum Rasendwerden! | That's enough to drive you mad. |

**raten**

to guess, to advise, to counsel

**Auxiliary verb:** haben **Past participle:** geraten

**Imperative:** Rate! Ratet! Raten Sie!

| Mode | Simple Tenses | | Compound Tenses | |
|---|---|---|---|---|
| | *Singular* | *Plural* | *Singular* | *Plural* |
| Indicative | **Present** | | **Present Perfect** | |
| | rate<br>rätst<br>rät | raten<br>ratet<br>raten | habe geraten<br>hast geraten<br>hat geraten | haben geraten<br>habt geraten<br>haben geraten |
| | **Past** | | **Past Perfect** | |
| | riet<br>rietest<br>riet | rieten<br>rietet<br>rieten | hatte geraten<br>hattest geraten<br>hatte geraten | hatten geraten<br>hattet geraten<br>hatten geraten |
| | **Future** | | **Future Perfect** | |
| | werde raten<br>wirst raten<br>wird raten | werden raten<br>werdet raten<br>werden raten | werde geraten haben<br>wirst geraten haben<br>wird geraten haben | werden geraten haben<br>werdet geraten haben<br>werden geraten haben |
| Subjunctive | **Present** | | **Present Perfect** | |
| | rate<br>ratest<br>rate | raten<br>ratet<br>raten | habe geraten<br>habest geraten<br>habe geraten | haben geraten<br>habet geraten<br>haben geraten |
| | **Past** | | **Past Perfect** | |
| | riete<br>rietest<br>riete | rieten<br>rietet<br>rieten | hätte geraten<br>hättest geraten<br>hätte geraten | hätten geraten<br>hättet geraten<br>hätten geraten |
| | **Future** | | **Future Perfect** | |
| | werde raten<br>werdest raten<br>werde raten | werden raten<br>werdet raten<br>werden raten | werde geraten haben<br>werdest geraten haben<br>werde geraten haben | werden geraten haben<br>werdet geraten haben<br>werden geraten haben |
| | **Present and Future Conditional** | | **Past Conditional** | |
| | würde raten<br>wurdest raten<br>würde raten | würden raten<br>würdet raten<br>würden raten | würde geraten haben<br>würdest geraten haben<br>würde geraten haben | würden geraten haben<br>würdet geraten haben<br>würden geraten haben |

**Note:** When the inseparable prefix *ge–* is added to this verb, its auxiliary in the perfect tenses is *sein: gerät, geriet, ist geraten.*

## EXAMPLES

Können Sie raten, in welcher Hand der Ring ist?
Can you guess which hand the ring is in?

Ich habe meinem Bruder geraten entweder Arzt oder Professor zu werden.
I advised my brother to become a doctor or a professor.

**rauben**

to rob, to steal

**Auxiliary verb:** haben **Past participle:** geraubt

**Imperative:** Raube! Raubt! Rauben Sie!

| Mode | Simple Tenses | | Compound Tenses | |
|---|---|---|---|---|
| | *Singular* | *Plural* | *Singular* | *Plural* |
| Indicative | **Present** | | **Present Perfect** | |
| | raube<br>raubst<br>raubt | rauben<br>raubt<br>rauben | habe geraubt<br>hast geraubt<br>hat geraubt | haben geraubt<br>habt geraubt<br>haben geraubt |
| | **Past** | | **Past Perfect** | |
| | raubte<br>raubtest<br>raubte | raubten<br>raubtet<br>raubten | hatte geraubt<br>hattest geraubt<br>hatte geraubt | hatten geraubt<br>hattet geraubt<br>hatten geraubt |
| | **Future** | | **Future Perfect** | |
| | werde rauben<br>wirst rauben<br>wird rauben | werden rauben<br>werdet rauben<br>werden rauben | werde geraubt haben<br>wirst geraubt haben<br>wird geraubt haben | werden geraubt haben<br>werdet geraubt haben<br>werden geraubt haben |
| Subjunctive | **Present** | | **Present Perfect** | |
| | raube<br>raubest<br>raube | rauben<br>raubet<br>rauben | habe geraubt<br>habest geraubt<br>habe geraubt | haben geraubt<br>habet geraubt<br>haben geraubt |
| | **Past** | | **Past Perfect** | |
| | raubte<br>raubtest<br>raubte | raubten<br>raubtet<br>raubten | hätte geraubt<br>hättest geraubt<br>hätte geraubt | hätten geraubt<br>hättet geraubt<br>hätten geraubt |
| | **Future** | | **Future Perfect** | |
| | werde rauben<br>werdest rauben<br>werde rauben | werden rauben<br>werdet rauben<br>werden rauben | werde geraubt haben<br>werdest geraubt haben<br>werde geraubt haben | werden geraubt haben<br>werdet geraubt haben<br>werden geraubt haben |
| | **Present and Future Conditional** | | **Past Conditional** | |
| | würde rauben<br>würdest rauben<br>würde rauben | würden rauben<br>würdet rauben<br>würden rauben | würde geraubt haben<br>würdest geraubt haben<br>würde geraubt haben | würden geraubt haben<br>würdet geraubt haben<br>würden geraubt haben |

## EXAMPLES

| | |
|---|---|
| Diese Musik raubt mir noch den letzten Nerv! | This music is driving me crazy. |
| Ein Taschendieb versuchte mir die Armbanduhr zu rauben. | A pickpocket tried to rob me of my wristwatch. |

**rauchen**
to smoke
**Auxiliary verb:** haben **Past participle:** geraucht
**Imperative:** Rauche! Raucht! Rauchen Sie!

| Mode | Simple Tenses | | Compound Tenses | |
|---|---|---|---|---|
| | *Singular* | *Plural* | *Singular* | *Plural* |
| Indicative | **Present** | | **Present Perfect** | |
| | rauche<br>rauchst<br>raucht | rauchen<br>raucht<br>rauchen | habe geraucht<br>hast geraucht<br>hat geraucht | haben geraucht<br>habt geraucht<br>haben geraucht |
| | **Past** | | **Past Perfect** | |
| | rauchte<br>rauchtest<br>rauchte | rauchten<br>rauchtet<br>rauchten | hatte geraucht<br>hattest geraucht<br>hatte geraucht | hatten geraucht<br>hattet geraucht<br>hatten geraucht |
| | **Future** | | **Future Perfect** | |
| | werde rauchen<br>wirst rauchen<br>wird rauchen | werden rauchen<br>werdet rauchen<br>werden rauchen | werde geraucht haben<br>wirst geraucht haben<br>wird geraucht haben | werden geraucht haben<br>werdet geraucht haben<br>werden geraucht haben |
| Subjunctive | **Present** | | **Present Perfect** | |
| | rauche<br>rauchest<br>rauche | rauchen<br>rauchet<br>rauchen | habe geraucht<br>habest geraucht<br>habe geraucht | haben geraucht<br>habet geraucht<br>haben geraucht |
| | **Past** | | **Past Perfect** | |
| | rauchte<br>rauchtest<br>rauchte | rauchten<br>rauchtet<br>rauchten | hätte geraucht<br>hättest geraucht<br>hätte geraucht | hätten geraucht<br>hättet geraucht<br>hätten geraucht |
| | **Future** | | **Future Perfect** | |
| | werde rauchen<br>werdest rauchen<br>werde rauchen | werden rauchen<br>werdet rauchen<br>werden rauchen | werde geraucht haben<br>werdest geraucht haben<br>werde geraucht haben | werden geraucht haben<br>werdet geraucht haben<br>werden geraucht haben |
| | **Present and Future Conditional** | | **Past Conditional** | |
| | würde rauchen<br>würdest rauchen<br>würde rauchen | würden rauchen<br>würdet rauchen<br>würden rauchen | würde geraucht haben<br>würdest geraucht haben<br>würde geraucht haben | würden geraucht haben<br>würdet geraucht haben<br>würden geraucht haben |

## EXAMPLES

Rauchen verboten!
No smoking.

Onkel Johannes hat mehr als zwanzig Zigaretten pro Tag geraucht.
Uncle Johannes smoked more than twenty cigarettes per day.

**rechnen**

to count, to compute, to reckon

**Auxiliary verb:** haben **Past participle:** gerechnet

**Imperative:** Rechne! Rechnet! Rechnen Sie!

| Mode | Simple Tenses | | Compound Tenses | |
|---|---|---|---|---|
| | *Singular* | *Plural* | *Singular* | *Plural* |
| Indicative | **Present** | | **Present Perfect** | |
| | rechne<br>rechnest<br>rechnet | rechnen<br>rechnet<br>rechnen | habe gerechnet<br>hast gerechnet<br>hat gerechnet | haben gerechnet<br>habt gerechnet<br>haben gerechnet |
| | **Past** | | **Past Perfect** | |
| | rechnete<br>rechnetest<br>rechnete | rechneten<br>rechnetet<br>rechneten | hatte gerechnet<br>hattest gerechnet<br>hatte gerechnet | hatten gerechnet<br>hattet gerechnet<br>hatten gerechnet |
| | **Future** | | **Future Perfect** | |
| | werde rechnen<br>wirst rechnen<br>wird rechnen | werden rechnen<br>werdet rechnen<br>werden rechnen | werde gerechnet haben<br>wirst gerechnet haben<br>wird gerechnet haben | werden gerechnet haben<br>werdet gerechnet haben<br>werden gerechnet haben |
| Subjunctive | **Present** | | **Present Perfect** | |
| | rechne<br>rechnest<br>rechne | rechnen<br>rechnet<br>rechnen | habe gerechnet<br>habest gerechnet<br>habe gerechnet | haben gerechnet<br>habet gerechnet<br>haben gerechnet |
| | **Past** | | **Past Perfect** | |
| | rechnete<br>rechnetest<br>rechnete | rechneten<br>rechnetet<br>rechneten | hätte gerechnet<br>hättest gerechnet<br>hätte gerechnet | hätten gerechnet<br>hättet gerechnet<br>hätten gerechnet |
| | **Future** | | **Future Perfect** | |
| | werde rechnen<br>werdest rechnen<br>werde rechnen | werden rechnen<br>werdet rechnen<br>werden rechnen | werde gerechnet haben<br>werdest gerechnet haben<br>werde gerechnet haben | werden gerechnet haben<br>werdet gerechnet haben<br>werden gerechnet haben |
| | **Present and Future Conditional** | | **Past Conditional** | |
| | würde rechnen<br>würdest rechnen<br>würde rechnen | würden rechnen<br>würdet rechnen<br>würden rechnen | würde gerechnet haben<br>würdest gerechnet haben<br>würde gerechnet haben | würden gerechnet haben<br>würdet gerechnet haben<br>würden gerechnet haben |

## EXAMPLES

In dieser Situation haben Sie leider falsch gerechnet.
Unfortunately, you've calculated wrong in this situation.

Wir rechneten nicht damit, dass es Schnee geben würde.
We didn't count on there being snow.

**rechtfertigen (sich)**
to justify
**Auxiliary verb:** haben **Past participle:** gerechtfertigt
**Imperative:** Rechtfertige! Rechtfertigt! Rechtfertigen Sie!

| Mode | Simple Tenses | | Compound Tenses | |
|---|---|---|---|---|
| | *Singular* | *Plural* | *Singular* | *Plural* |
| Indicative | **Present** | | **Present Perfect** | |
| | rechtfertige<br>rechtfertigst<br>rechtfertigt | rechtfertigen<br>rechtfertigt<br>rechtfertigen | habe gerechtfertigt<br>hast gerechtfertigt<br>hat gerechtfertigt | haben gerechtfertigt<br>habt gerechtfertigt<br>haben gerechtfertigt |
| | **Past** | | **Past Perfect** | |
| | rechtfertigte<br>rechtfertigtest<br>rechtfertigte | rechtfertigten<br>rechtfertigtet<br>rechtfertigten | hatte gerechtfertigt<br>hattest gerechtfertigt<br>hatte gerechtfertigt | hatten gerechtfertigt<br>hattet gerechtfertigt<br>hatten gerechtfertigt |
| | **Future** | | **Future Perfect** | |
| | werde rechtfertigen<br>wirst rechtfertigen<br>wird rechtfertigen | werden rechtfertigen<br>werdet rechtfertigen<br>werden rechtfertigen | werde gerechtfertigt haben<br>wirst gerechtfertigt haben<br>wird gerechtfertigt haben | werden gerechtfertigt haben<br>werdet gerechtfertigt haben<br>werden gerechtfertigt haben |
| Subjunctive | **Present** | | **Present Perfect** | |
| | rechtfertige<br>rechtfertigest<br>rechtfertige | rechtfertigen<br>rechtfertiget<br>rechtfertigen | habe gerechtfertigt<br>habest gerechtfertigt<br>habe gerechtfertigt | haben gerechtfertigt<br>habet gerechtfertigt<br>haben gerechtfertigt |
| | **Past** | | **Past Perfect** | |
| | rechtfertigte<br>rechtfertigtest<br>rechtfertigte | rechtfertigten<br>rechtfertigtet<br>rechtfertigten | hätte gerechtfertigt<br>hättest gerechtfertigt<br>hätte gerechtfertigt | hätten gerechtfertigt<br>hättet gerechtfertigt<br>hätten gerechtfertigt |
| | **Future** | | **Future Perfect** | |
| | werde rechtfertigen<br>werdest rechtfertigen<br>werde rechtfertigen | werden rechtfertigen<br>werdet rechtfertigen<br>werden rechtfertigen | werde gerechtfertigt haben<br>werdest gerechtfertigt haben<br>werde gerechtfertigt haben | werden gerechtfertigt haben<br>werdet gerechtfertigt haben<br>werden gerechtfertigt haben |
| | **Present and Future Conditional** | | **Past Conditional** | |
| | würde rechtfertigen<br>würdest rechtfertigen<br>würde rechtfertigen | würden rechtfertigen<br>würdet rechtfertigen<br>würden rechtfertigen | würde gerechtfertigt haben<br>würdest gerechtfertigt haben<br>würde gerechtfertigt haben | würden gerechtfertigt haben<br>würdet gerechtfertigt haben<br>würden gerechtfertigt haben |

## EXAMPLES

Wie kannst du dein schlechtes Benehmen rechtfertigen?
How can you justify your bad behavior?

Der General hat den Angriff mit Lügen und Übertreibungen gerechtfertigt.
The general justified the attack with lies and exaggerations.

Du brauchst dich nicht bei mir zu rechtfertigen.
You don't have to justify yourself to me.

**reden**

to talk, to converse

**Auxiliary verb:** haben **Past participle:** geredet

**Imperative:** Rede! Redet! Reden Sie!

| Mode | Simple Tenses | | Compound Tenses | |
|---|---|---|---|---|
| | *Singular* | *Plural* | *Singular* | *Plural* |
| Indicative | **Present** | | **Present Perfect** | |
| | rede<br>redest<br>redet | reden<br>redet<br>reden | habe geredet<br>hast geredet<br>hat geredet | haben geredet<br>habt geredet<br>haben geredet |
| | **Past** | | **Past Perfect** | |
| | redete<br>redetest<br>redete | redeten<br>redetet<br>redeten | hatte geredet<br>hattest geredet<br>hatte geredet | hatten geredet<br>hattet geredet<br>hatten geredet |
| | **Future** | | **Future Perfect** | |
| | werde reden<br>wirst reden<br>wird reden | werden reden<br>werdet reden<br>werden reden | werde geredet haben<br>wirst geredet haben<br>wird geredet haben | werden geredet haben<br>werdet geredet haben<br>werden geredet haben |
| Subjunctive | **Present** | | **Present Perfect** | |
| | rede<br>redest<br>rede | reden<br>redet<br>reden | habe geredet<br>habest geredet<br>habe geredet | haben geredet<br>habet geredet<br>haben geredet |
| | **Past** | | **Past Perfect** | |
| | redete<br>redetest<br>redete | redeten<br>redetet<br>redeten | hätte geredet<br>hättest geredet<br>hätte geredet | hätten geredet<br>hättet geredet<br>hätten geredet |
| | **Future** | | **Future Perfect** | |
| | werde reden<br>werdest reden<br>werde reden | werden reden<br>werdet reden<br>werden reden | werde geredet haben<br>werdest geredet haben<br>werde geredet haben | werden geredet haben<br>werdet geredet haben<br>werden geredet haben |
| | **Present and Future Conditional** | | **Past Conditional** | |
| | würde reden<br>würdest reden<br>würde reden | würden reden<br>würdet reden<br>würden reden | würde geredet haben<br>würdest geredet haben<br>würde geredet haben | würden geredet haben<br>würdet geredet haben<br>würden geredet haben |

## EXAMPLES

Wir haben lange über ihre Pläne für die Zukunft geredet.

We talked long about her plans for the future.

Die jungen Künstler redeten über die Picasso-Ausstellung.

The young artists conversed about the Picasso exhibition.

**regieren**
to rule, to regulate
**Auxiliary verb:** haben **Past participle:** regiert
**Imperative:** Regiere! Regiert! Regieren Sie!

| Mode | Simple Tenses | | Compound Tenses | |
|---|---|---|---|---|
| | *Singular* | *Plural* | *Singular* | *Plural* |
| Indicative | **Present** | | **Present Perfect** | |
| | regiere<br>regierst<br>regiert | regieren<br>regiert<br>regieren | habe regiert<br>hast regiert<br>hat regiert | haben regiert<br>habt regiert<br>haben regiert |
| | **Past** | | **Past Perfect** | |
| | regierte<br>regiertest<br>regierte | regierten<br>regiertet<br>regierten | hatte regiert<br>hattest regiert<br>hatte regiert | hatten regiert<br>hattet regiert<br>hatten regiert |
| | **Future** | | **Future Perfect** | |
| | werde regieren<br>wirst regieren<br>wird regieren | werden regieren<br>werdet regieren<br>werden regieren | werde regiert haben<br>wirst regiert haben<br>wird regiert haben | werden regiert haben<br>werdet regiert haben<br>werden regiert haben |
| Subjunctive | **Present** | | **Present Perfect** | |
| | regiere<br>regierest<br>regiere | regieren<br>regieret<br>regieren | habe regiert<br>habest regiert<br>habe regiert | haben regiert<br>habet regiert<br>haben regiert |
| | **Past** | | **Past Perfect** | |
| | regierte<br>regiertest<br>regierte | regierten<br>regiertet<br>regierten | hätte regiert<br>hättest regiert<br>hätte regiert | hätten regiert<br>hättet regiert<br>hätten regiert |
| | **Future** | | **Future Perfect** | |
| | werde regieren<br>werdest regieren<br>werde regieren | werden regieren<br>werdet regieren<br>werden regieren | werde regiert haben<br>werdest regiert haben<br>werde regiert haben | werden regiert haben<br>werdet regiert haben<br>werden regiert haben |
| | **Present and Future Conditional** | | **Past Conditional** | |
| | würde regieren<br>würdest regieren<br>würde regieren | würden regieren<br>würdet regieren<br>würden regieren | würde regiert haben<br>würdest regiert haben<br>würde regiert haben | würden regiert haben<br>würdet regiert haben<br>würden regiert haben |

## EXAMPLES

Welche politische Partei regiert heute in Deutschland?
What political party is governing in Germany today?

Wann hat Kaiser Wilhelm II. regiert?
When did Kaiser Wilhelm II reign?

**regnen**
to rain
**Auxiliary verb:** haben **Past participle:** geregnet
**Imperative:** N/A

| Mode | Simple Tenses | | Compound Tenses | |
|---|---|---|---|---|
| | *Singular* | *Plural* | *Singular* | *Plural* |
| Indicative | **Present** | | **Present Perfect** | |
| | regnet | | hat geregnet | |
| | **Past** | | **Past Perfect** | |
| | regnete | | hatte geregnet | |
| | **Future** | | **Future Perfect** | |
| | wird regnen | | wird geregnet haben | |
| Subjunctive | **Present** | | **Present Perfect** | |
| | regne | | habe geregnet | |
| | **Past** | | **Past Perfect** | |
| | regnete | | hätte geregnet | |
| | **Future** | | **Future Perfect** | |
| | werde regnen | | werde geregnet haben | |
| | **Present and Future Conditional** | | **Past Conditional** | |
| | würde regnen | | würde geregnet haben | |

**Note:** This verb is used as a third-person impersonal expression with the pronoun *es*.

## EXAMPLES

Gestern hat es den ganzen Tag geregnet. — It rained the whole day yesterday.
Hat es noch nicht aufgehört zu regnen? — Hasn't it stopped raining yet?

**reiben**
to rub, to grate, to chafe
**Auxiliary verb:** haben **Past participle:** gerieben
**Imperative:** Reibe! Reibt! Reiben Sie!

| Mode | Simple Tenses | | Compound Tenses | |
|---|---|---|---|---|
| | *Singular* | *Plural* | *Singular* | *Plural* |
| Indicative | **Present** | | **Present Perfect** | |
| | reibe<br>reibst<br>reibt | reiben<br>reibt<br>reiben | habe gerieben<br>hast gerieben<br>hat gerieben | haben gerieben<br>habt gerieben<br>haben gerieben |
| | **Past** | | **Past Perfect** | |
| | rieb<br>riebst<br>rieb | rieben<br>riebt<br>rieben | hatte gerieben<br>hattest gerieben<br>hatte gerieben | hatten gerieben<br>hattet gerieben<br>hatten gerieben |
| | **Future** | | **Future Perfect** | |
| | werde reiben<br>wirst reiben<br>wird reiben | werden reiben<br>werdet reiben<br>werden reiben | werde gerieben haben<br>wirst gerieben haben<br>wird gerieben haben | werden gerieben haben<br>werdet gerieben haben<br>werden gerieben haben |
| Subjunctive | **Present** | | **Present Perfect** | |
| | reibe<br>reibest<br>reibe | reiben<br>reibet<br>reiben | habe gerieben<br>habest gerieben<br>habe gerieben | haben gerieben<br>habet gerieben<br>haben gerieben |
| | **Past** | | **Past Perfect** | |
| | riebe<br>riebest<br>riebe | rieben<br>riebet<br>rieben | hätte gerieben<br>hättest gerieben<br>hätte gerieben | hätten gerieben<br>hättet gerieben<br>hätten gerieben |
| | **Future** | | **Future Perfect** | |
| | werde reiben<br>werdest reiben<br>werde reiben | werden reiben<br>werdet reiben<br>werden reiben | werde gerieben haben<br>werdest gerieben haben<br>werde gerieben haben | werden gerieben haben<br>werdet gerieben haben<br>werden gerieben haben |
| | **Present and Future Conditional** | | **Past Conditional** | |
| | würde reiben<br>würdest reiben<br>würde reiben | würden reiben<br>würdet reiben<br>würden reiben | würde gerieben haben<br>würdest gerieben haben<br>würde gerieben haben | würden gerieben haben<br>würdet gerieben haben<br>würden gerieben haben |

## EXAMPLES

Der Junge war müde und rieb sich die Augen. — The boy was tired and rubbed his eyes.
Kannst du den Käse für die Pizza reiben? — Can you grate the cheese for the pizza?

**reichen**

to reach, to extend, to be enough

**Auxiliary verb:** haben **Past participle:** gereicht

**Imperative:** Reiche! Reicht! Reichen Sie!

| Mode | Simple Tenses | | Compound Tenses | |
|---|---|---|---|---|
| | *Singular* | *Plural* | *Singular* | *Plural* |
| Indicative | **Present** | | **Present Perfect** | |
| | reiche<br>reichst<br>reicht | reichen<br>reicht<br>reichen | habe gereicht<br>hast gereicht<br>hat gereicht | haben gereicht<br>habt gereicht<br>haben gereicht |
| | **Past** | | **Past Perfect** | |
| | reichte<br>reichtest<br>reichte | reichten<br>reichtet<br>reichten | hatte gereicht<br>hattest gereicht<br>hatte gereicht | hatten gereicht<br>hattet gereicht<br>hatten gereicht |
| | **Future** | | **Future Perfect** | |
| | werde reichen<br>wirst reichen<br>wird reichen | werden reichen<br>werdet reichen<br>werden reichen | werde gereicht haben<br>wirst gereicht haben<br>wird gereicht haben | werden gereicht haben<br>werdet gereicht haben<br>werden gereicht haben |
| Subjunctive | **Present** | | **Present Perfect** | |
| | reiche<br>reichest<br>reiche | reichen<br>reichet<br>reichen | habe gereicht<br>habest gereicht<br>habe gereicht | haben gereicht<br>habet gereicht<br>haben gereicht |
| | **Past** | | **Past Perfect** | |
| | reichte<br>reichtest<br>reichte | reichten<br>reichtet<br>reichten | hätte gereicht<br>hättest gereicht<br>hätte gereicht | hätten gereicht<br>hättet gereicht<br>hätten gereicht |
| | **Future** | | **Future Perfect** | |
| | werde reichen<br>werdest reichen<br>werde reichen | werden reichen<br>werdet reichen<br>werden reichen | werde gereicht haben<br>werdest gereicht haben<br>werde gereicht haben | werden gereicht haben<br>werdet gereicht haben<br>werden gereicht haben |
| | **Present and Future Conditional** | | **Past Conditional** | |
| | würde reichen<br>würdest reichen<br>würde reichen | würden reichen<br>würdet reichen<br>würden reichen | würde gereicht haben<br>würdest gereicht haben<br>würde gereicht haben | würden gereicht haben<br>würdet gereicht haben<br>würden gereicht haben |

## EXAMPLES

Als ich ihn erkannte, reichte ich ihm sofort die Hand.

When I recognized him, I immediately extended my hand to him.

Die Suppe hat nicht für sechs Leute gereicht.

There wasn't enough soup for six people.

**reinigen**
to clean, to purify, to clarify
**Auxiliary verb:** haben **Past participle:** gereinigt
**Imperative:** Reinige! Reinigt! Reinigen Sie!

| Mode | Simple Tenses | | Compound Tenses | |
|---|---|---|---|---|
| | *Singular* | *Plural* | *Singular* | *Plural* |
| Indicative | **Present** | | **Present Perfect** | |
| | reinige<br>reinigst<br>reinigt | reinigen<br>reinigt<br>reinigen | habe gereinigt<br>hast gereinigt<br>hat gereinigt | haben gereinigt<br>habt gereinigt<br>haben gereinigt |
| | **Past** | | **Past Perfect** | |
| | reinigte<br>reinigtest<br>reinigte | reinigten<br>reinigtet<br>reinigten | hatte gereinigt<br>hattest gereinigt<br>hatte gereinigt | hatten gereinigt<br>hattet gereinigt<br>hatten gereinigt |
| | **Future** | | **Future Perfect** | |
| | werde reinigen<br>wirst reinigen<br>wird reinigen | werden reinigen<br>werdet reinigen<br>werden reinigen | werde gereinigt haben<br>wirst gereinigt haben<br>wird gereinigt haben | werden gereinigt haben<br>werdet gereinigt haben<br>werden gereinigt haben |
| Subjunctive | **Present** | | **Present Perfect** | |
| | reinige<br>reinigest<br>reinige | reinigen<br>reiniget<br>reinigen | habe gereinigt<br>habest gereinigt<br>habe gereinigt | haben gereinigt<br>habet gereinigt<br>haben gereinigt |
| | **Past** | | **Past Perfect** | |
| | reinigte<br>reinigtest<br>reinigte | reinigten<br>reinigtet<br>reinigten | hätte gereinigt<br>hättest gereinigt<br>hätte gereinigt | hätten gereinigt<br>hättet gereinigt<br>hätten gereinigt |
| | **Future** | | **Future Perfect** | |
| | werde reinigen<br>werdest reinigen<br>werde reinigen | werden reinigen<br>werdet reinigen<br>werden reinigen | werde gereinigt haben<br>werdest gereinigt haben<br>werde gereinigt haben | werden gereinigt haben<br>werdet gereinigt haben<br>werden gereinigt haben |
| | **Present and Future Conditional** | | **Past Conditional** | |
| | würde reinigen<br>würdest reinigen<br>würde reinigen | würden reinigen<br>würdet reinigen<br>würden reinigen | würde gereinigt haben<br>würdest gereinigt haben<br>würde gereinigt haben | würden gereinigt haben<br>würdet gereinigt haben<br>würden gereinigt haben |

## EXAMPLES

Sie wollte sich von jedem Verdacht reinigen. — She wanted to clear her name of all suspicion.

Diese Anzüge müssen gereinigt werden. — These suits have to be dry-cleaned.

**reisen**

to travel, to journey

**Auxiliary verb:** sein **Past participle:** gereist

**Imperative:** Reise! Reist! Reisen Sie!

| Mode | Simple Tenses | | Compound Tenses | |
|---|---|---|---|---|
| | *Singular* | *Plural* | *Singular* | *Plural* |
| Indicative | **Present** | | **Present Perfect** | |
| | reise<br>reist<br>reist | reisen<br>reist<br>reisen | bin gereist<br>bist gereist<br>ist gereist | sind gereist<br>seid gereist<br>sind gereist |
| | **Past** | | **Past Perfect** | |
| | reiste<br>reistest<br>reiste | reisteen<br>reistet<br>reisteen | war gereist<br>warst gereist<br>war gereist | waren gereist<br>wart gereist<br>waren gereist |
| | **Future** | | **Future Perfect** | |
| | werde reisen<br>wirst reisen<br>wird reisen | werden reisen<br>werdet reisen<br>werden reisen | werde gereist sein<br>wirst gereist sein<br>wird gereist sein | werden gereist sein<br>werdet gereist sein<br>werden gereist sein |
| Subjunctive | **Present** | | **Present Perfect** | |
| | reise<br>reisest<br>reise | reisen<br>reiset<br>reisen | sei gereist<br>seiest gereist<br>sei gereist | seien gereist<br>seiet gereist<br>seien gereist |
| | **Past** | | **Past Perfect** | |
| | reiste<br>reistest<br>reiste | reisten<br>reistet<br>reisten | wäre gereist<br>wärest gereist<br>wäre gereist | wären gereist<br>wäret gereist<br>wären gereist |
| | **Future** | | **Future Perfect** | |
| | werde reisen<br>werdest reisen<br>werde reisen | werden reisen<br>werdet reisen<br>werden reisen | werde gereist sein<br>werdest gereist sein<br>werde gereist sein | werden gereist sein<br>werdet gereist sein<br>werden gereist sein |
| | **Present and Future Conditional** | | **Past Conditional** | |
| | würde reisen<br>würdest reisen<br>würde reisen | würden reisen<br>würdet reisen<br>würden reisen | würde gereist sein<br>würdest gereist sein<br>würde gereist sein | würden gereist sein<br>würdet gereist sein<br>würden gereist sein |

## EXAMPLES

| | |
|---|---|
| Im Winter reisen wir jedes Jahr nach Mexiko. | We travel to Mexico every winter. |
| Martin ist vor einigen Tagen nach Polen gereist. | Martin traveled to Poland a few days ago. |

**reißen**
to tear, to rip, to snatch
**Auxiliary verb:** haben **Past participle:** gerissen
**Imperative:** Reiße! Reißt! Reißen Sie!

| Mode | Simple Tenses | | Compound Tenses | |
|---|---|---|---|---|
| | *Singular* | *Plural* | *Singular* | *Plural* |
| Indicative | **Present** | | **Present Perfect** | |
| | reiße<br>reißt<br>reißt | reißen<br>reißt<br>reißen | habe gerissen<br>hast gerissen<br>hat gerissen | haben gerissen<br>habt gerissen<br>haben gerissen |
| | **Past** | | **Past Perfect** | |
| | riss<br>rissest<br>riss | rissen<br>risst<br>rissen | hatte gerissen<br>hattest gerissen<br>hatte gerissen | hatten gerissen<br>hattet gerissen<br>hatten gerissen |
| | **Future** | | **Future Perfect** | |
| | werde reißen<br>wirst reißen<br>wird reißen | werden reißen<br>werdet reißen<br>werden reißen | werde gerissen haben<br>wirst gerissen haben<br>wird gerissen haben | werden gerissen haben<br>werdet gerissen haben<br>werden gerissen haben |
| Subjunctive | **Present** | | **Present Perfect** | |
| | reiße<br>reißest<br>reiße | reißen<br>reißet<br>reißen | habe gerissen<br>habest gerissen<br>habe gerissen | haben gerissen<br>habet gerissen<br>haben gerissen |
| | **Past** | | **Past Perfect** | |
| | risse<br>rissest<br>risse | rissen<br>risset<br>rissen | hätte gerissen<br>hättest gerissen<br>hätte gerissen | hätten gerissen<br>hättet gerissen<br>hätten gerissen |
| | **Future** | | **Future Perfect** | |
| | werde reißen<br>werdest reißen<br>werde reißen | werden reißen<br>werdet reißen<br>werden reißen | werde gerissen haben<br>werdest gerissen haben<br>werde gerissen haben | werden gerissen haben<br>werdet gerissen haben<br>werden gerissen haben |
| | **Present and Future Conditional** | | **Past Conditional** | |
| | würde reißen<br>würdest reißen<br>würde reißen | würden reißen<br>würdet reißen<br>würden reißen | würde gerissen haben<br>würdest gerissen haben<br>würde gerissen haben | würden gerissen haben<br>würdet gerissen haben<br>würden gerissen haben |

**Note:** With the separable prefix *zer–*, the principal parts of this verb are: *zerreißt, zerriss, hat zerrissen.*

## EXAMPLES

Der erschrockene Vater riss seine Tochter aus der drohenden Gefahr.
The terrified father snatched his daughter from the threat of danger.

Das Seil ist zu dünn, es wird reißen.
The rope is too thin. It will break.

Ach, ich habe meine neue Hose zerrissen.
Oh, I've ripped my new pants.

**reiten**

to ride, to go horseback riding

**Auxiliary verb:** sein **Past participle:** geritten

**Imperative:** Reite! Reitet! Reiten Sie!

| Mode | Simple Tenses | | Compound Tenses | |
|---|---|---|---|---|
| | *Singular* | *Plural* | *Singular* | *Plural* |
| Indicative | **Present** | | **Present Perfect** | |
| | reite<br>reitest<br>reitet | reiten<br>reitet<br>reiten | bin geritten<br>bist geritten<br>ist geritten | sind geritten<br>seid geritten<br>sind geritten |
| | **Past** | | **Past Perfect** | |
| | ritt<br>rittest<br>ritt | ritten<br>rittet<br>ritten | war geritten<br>warst geritten<br>war geritten | waren geritten<br>wart geritten<br>waren geritten |
| | **Future** | | **Future Perfect** | |
| | werde reiten<br>wirst reiten<br>wird reiten | werden reiten<br>werdet reiten<br>werden reiten | werde geritten sein<br>wirst geritten sein<br>wird geritten sein | werden geritten sein<br>werdet geritten sein<br>werden geritten sein |
| Subjunctive | **Present** | | **Present Perfect** | |
| | reite<br>reitest<br>reite | reiten<br>reitet<br>reiten | sei geritten<br>seiest geritten<br>sei geritten | seien geritten<br>seiet geritten<br>seien geritten |
| | **Past** | | **Past Perfect** | |
| | ritte<br>rittest<br>ritte | ritten<br>rittet<br>ritten | wäre geritten<br>wärest geritten<br>wäre geritten | wären geritten<br>wäret geritten<br>wären geritten |
| | **Future** | | **Future Perfect** | |
| | werde reiten<br>werdest reiten<br>werde reiten | werden reiten<br>werdet reiten<br>werden reiten | werde geritten sein<br>werdest geritten sein<br>werde geritten sein | werden geritten sein<br>werdet geritten sein<br>werden geritten sein |
| | **Present and Future Conditional** | | **Past Conditional** | |
| | würde reiten<br>würdest reiten<br>würde reiten | würden reiten<br>würdet reiten<br>würden reiten | würde geritten sein<br>würdest geritten sein<br>würde geritten sein | würden geritten sein<br>würdet geritten sein<br>würden geritten sein |

## EXAMPLES

Der verwundete Prinz ist auf seinem Pferd in den Wald geritten.

The wounded prince rode his horse into the woods.

Könnt ihr reiten?

Can you ride a horse?

**rennen**
to run, to race
**Auxiliary verb:** sein **Past participle:** gerannt
**Imperative:** Renne! Rennt! Rennen Sie!

| Mode | Simple Tenses | | Compound Tenses | |
|---|---|---|---|---|
| | *Singular* | *Plural* | *Singular* | *Plural* |
| Indicative | **Present** | | **Present Perfect** | |
| | renne<br>rennst<br>rennt | rennen<br>rennt<br>rennen | bin gerannt<br>bist gerannt<br>ist gerannt | sind gerannt<br>seid gerannt<br>sind gerannt |
| | **Past** | | **Past Perfect** | |
| | rannte<br>ranntest<br>rannte | rannten<br>ranntet<br>rannten | war gerannt<br>warst gerannt<br>war gerannt | waren gerannt<br>wart gerannt<br>waren gerannt |
| | **Future** | | **Future Perfect** | |
| | werde rennen<br>wirst rennen<br>wird rennen | werden rennen<br>werdet rennen<br>werden rennen | werde gerannt sein<br>wirst gerannt sein<br>wird gerannt sein | werden gerannt sein<br>werdet gerannt sein<br>werden gerannt sein |
| Subjunctive | **Present** | | **Present Perfect** | |
| | renne<br>rennest<br>renne | rennen<br>rennet<br>rennen | sei gerannt<br>seiest gerannt<br>sei gerannt | seien gerannt<br>seiet gerannt<br>seien gerannt |
| | **Past** | | **Past Perfect** | |
| | rennte<br>renntest<br>rennte | rennten<br>renntet<br>rennten | wäre gerannt<br>wärest gerannt<br>wäre gerannt | wären gerannt<br>wäret gerannt<br>wären gerannt |
| | **Future** | | **Future Perfect** | |
| | werde rennen<br>werdest rennen<br>werde rennen | werden rennen<br>werdet rennen<br>werden rennen | werde gerannt sein<br>werdest gerannt sein<br>werde gerannt sein | werden gerannt sein<br>werdet gerannt sein<br>werden gerannt sein |
| | **Present and Future Conditional** | | **Past Conditional** | |
| | würde rennen<br>würdest rennen<br>würde rennen | würden rennen<br>würdet rennen<br>würden rennen | würde gerannt sein<br>würdest gerannt sein<br>würde gerannt sein | würden gerannt sein<br>würdet gerannt sein<br>würden gerannt sein |

## EXAMPLES

Ich kann viel schneller als mein älterer Bruder rennen.
I can run a lot faster than my older brother.

Sie kamen gleichzeitig ins Ziel. Es war ein unentschiedenes Rennen.
They came to the finish at the same time. It was a dead heat.

**retten**

to save, to rescue

**Auxiliary verb:** haben **Past participle:** gerettet

**Imperative:** Rette! Rettet! Retten Sie!

| Mode | Simple Tenses | | Compound Tenses | |
|---|---|---|---|---|
| | *Singular* | *Plural* | *Singular* | *Plural* |
| Indicative | **Present** | | **Present Perfect** | |
| | rette<br>rettest<br>rettet | retten<br>rettet<br>retten | habe gerettet<br>hast gerettet<br>hat gerettet | haben gerettet<br>habt gerettet<br>haben gerettet |
| | **Past** | | **Past Perfect** | |
| | rettete<br>rettetest<br>rettete | retteten<br>rettetet<br>retteten | hatte gerettet<br>hattest gerettet<br>hatte gerettet | hatten gerettet<br>hattet gerettet<br>hatten gerettet |
| | **Future** | | **Future Perfect** | |
| | werde retten<br>wirst retten<br>wird retten | werden retten<br>werdet retten<br>werden retten | werde gerettet haben<br>wirst gerettet haben<br>wird gerettet haben | werden gerettet haben<br>werdet gerettet haben<br>werden gerettet haben |
| Subjunctive | **Present** | | **Present Perfect** | |
| | rette<br>rettest<br>rette | retten<br>rettet<br>retten | habe gerettet<br>habest gerettet<br>habe gerettet | haben gerettet<br>habet gerettet<br>haben gerettet |
| | **Past** | | **Past Perfect** | |
| | rettete<br>rettetest<br>rettete | retteten<br>rettetet<br>retteten | hätte gerettet<br>hättest gerettet<br>hätte gerettet | hätten gerettet<br>hättet gerettet<br>hätten gerettet |
| | **Future** | | **Future Perfect** | |
| | werde retten<br>werdest retten<br>werde retten | werden retten<br>werdet retten<br>werden retten | werde gerettet haben<br>werdest gerettet haben<br>werde gerettet haben | werden gerettet haben<br>werdet gerettet haben<br>werden gerettet haben |
| | **Present and Future Conditional** | | **Past Conditional** | |
| | würde retten<br>würdest retten<br>würde retten | würden retten<br>würdet retten<br>würden retten | würde gerettet haben<br>würdest gerettet haben<br>würde gerettet haben | würden gerettet haben<br>würdet gerettet haben<br>würden gerettet haben |

## EXAMPLES

Rette sich wer kann! — Every man for himself!

Es konnten nur noch fünf Wale gerettet werden. — Only five more whales were able to be rescued.

**richten**
to set right, to direct
**Auxiliary verb:** haben **Past participle:** gerichtet
**Imperative:** Richte! Richtet! Richten Sie!

| Mode | Simple Tenses | | Compound Tenses | |
|---|---|---|---|---|
| | *Singular* | *Plural* | *Singular* | *Plural* |
| Indicative | **Present** | | **Present Perfect** | |
| | richte<br>richtest<br>richtet | richten<br>richtet<br>richten | habe gerichtet<br>hast gerichtet<br>hat gerichtet | haben gerichtet<br>habt gerichtet<br>haben gerichtet |
| | **Past** | | **Past Perfect** | |
| | richtete<br>richtetest<br>richtete | richteten<br>richtetet<br>richteten | hatte gerichtet<br>hattest gerichtet<br>hatte gerichtet | hatten gerichtet<br>hattet gerichtet<br>hatten gerichtet |
| | **Future** | | **Future Perfect** | |
| | werde richten<br>wirst richten<br>wird richten | werden richten<br>werdet richten<br>werden richten | werde gerichtet haben<br>wirst gerichtet haben<br>wird gerichtet haben | werden gerichtet haben<br>werdet gerichtet haben<br>werden gerichtet haben |
| Subjunctive | **Present** | | **Present Perfect** | |
| | richte<br>richtest<br>richte | richten<br>richtet<br>richten | habe gerichtet<br>habest gerichtet<br>habe gerichtet | haben gerichtet<br>habet gerichtet<br>haben gerichtet |
| | **Past** | | **Past Perfect** | |
| | richtete<br>richtetest<br>richtete | richteten<br>richtetet<br>richteten | hätte gerichtet<br>hättest gerichtet<br>hätte gerichtet | hätten gerichtet<br>hättet gerichtet<br>hätten gerichtet |
| | **Future** | | **Future Perfect** | |
| | werde richten<br>werdest richten<br>werde richten | werden richten<br>werdet richten<br>werden richten | werde gerichtet haben<br>werdest gerichtet haben<br>werde gerichtet haben | werden gerichtet haben<br>werdet gerichtet haben<br>werden gerichtet haben |
| | **Present and Future Conditional** | | **Past Conditional** | |
| | würde richten<br>würdest richten<br>würde richten | würden richten<br>würdet richten<br>würden richten | würde gerichtet haben<br>würdest gerichtet haben<br>würde gerichtet haben | würden gerichtet haben<br>würdet gerichtet haben<br>würden gerichtet haben |

## EXAMPLES

Ihre Vorwürfe richten sich gegen meine Familie. Her reproaches are meant for my family.
War das auf meine Frau gerichtet? Was that aimed at my wife?

**riechen**
to smell
**Auxiliary verb:** haben **Past participle:** gerochen
**Imperative:** Rieche! Riecht! Riechen Sie!

| Mode | Simple Tenses | | Compound Tenses | |
|---|---|---|---|---|
| | *Singular* | *Plural* | *Singular* | *Plural* |
| Indicative | **Present** | | **Present Perfect** | |
| | rieche<br>riechst<br>riecht | riechen<br>riecht<br>riechen | habe gerochen<br>hast gerochen<br>hat gerochen | haben gerochen<br>habt gerochen<br>haben gerochen |
| | **Past** | | **Past Perfect** | |
| | roch<br>rochst<br>roch | rochen<br>rocht<br>rochen | hatte gerochen<br>hattest gerochen<br>hatte gerochen | hatten gerochen<br>hattet gerochen<br>hatten gerochen |
| | **Future** | | **Future Perfect** | |
| | werde riechen<br>wirst riechen<br>wird riechen | werden riechen<br>werdet riechen<br>werden riechen | werde gerochen haben<br>wirst gerochen haben<br>wird gerochen haben | werden gerochen haben<br>werdet gerochen haben<br>werden gerochen haben |
| Subjunctive | **Present** | | **Present Perfect** | |
| | rieche<br>riechest<br>rieche | riechen<br>riechet<br>riechen | habe gerochen<br>habest gerochen<br>habe gerochen | haben gerochen<br>habet gerochen<br>haben gerochen |
| | **Past** | | **Past Perfect** | |
| | röche<br>röchest<br>röche | röchen<br>röchet<br>röchen | hätte gerochen<br>hättest gerochen<br>hätte gerochen | hätten gerochen<br>hättet gerochen<br>hätten gerochen |
| | **Future** | | **Future Perfect** | |
| | werde riechen<br>werdest riechen<br>werde riechen | werden riechen<br>werdet riechen<br>werden riechen | werde gerochen haben<br>werdest gerochen haben<br>werde gerochen haben | werden gerochen haben<br>werdet gerochen haben<br>werden gerochen haben |
| | **Present and Future Conditional** | | **Past Conditional** | |
| | würde riechen<br>würdest riechen<br>würde riechen | würden riechen<br>würdet riechen<br>würden riechen | würde gerochen haben<br>würdest gerochen haben<br>würde gerochen haben | würden gerochen haben<br>würdet gerochen haben<br>würden gerochen haben |

## EXAMPLES

Dieses Handtuch riecht nach Weichspüler. This towel smells of fabric softener.
Ich habe einen komischen Geruch gerochen. I smelled a strange odor.

**rudern**
to row
**Auxiliary verb:** haben **Past participle:** gerudert
**Imperative:** Rudere! Rudert! Rudern Sie!

| Mode | Simple Tenses | | Compound Tenses | |
|---|---|---|---|---|
| | *Singular* | *Plural* | *Singular* | *Plural* |
| Indicative | **Present** | | **Present Perfect** | |
| | rudere<br>ruderst<br>rudert | rudern<br>rudert<br>rudern | habe gerudert<br>hast gerudert<br>hat gerudert | haben gerudert<br>habt gerudert<br>haben gerudert |
| | **Past** | | **Past Perfect** | |
| | ruderte<br>rudertest<br>ruderte | ruderten<br>rudertet<br>ruderten | hatte gerudert<br>hattest gerudert<br>hatte gerudert | hatten gerudert<br>hattet gerudert<br>hatten gerudert |
| | **Future** | | **Future Perfect** | |
| | werde rudern<br>wirst rudern<br>wird rudern | werden rudern<br>werdet rudern<br>werden rudern | werde gerudert haben<br>wirst gerudert haben<br>wird gerudert haben | werden gerudert haben<br>werdet gerudert haben<br>werden gerudert haben |
| Subjunctive | **Present** | | **Present Perfect** | |
| | rudere<br>ruderst<br>rudere | rudern<br>rudert<br>rudern | habe gerudert<br>habest gerudert<br>habe gerudert | haben gerudert<br>habet gerudert<br>haben gerudert |
| | **Past** | | **Past Perfect** | |
| | ruderte<br>rudertest<br>ruderte | ruderten<br>rudertet<br>ruderten | hätte gerudert<br>hättest gerudert<br>hätte gerudert | hätten gerudert<br>hättet gerudert<br>hätten gerudert |
| | **Future** | | **Future Perfect** | |
| | werde rudern<br>werdest rudern<br>werde rudern | werden rudern<br>werdet rudern<br>werden rudern | werde gerudert haben<br>werdest gerudert haben<br>werde gerudert haben | werden gerudert haben<br>werdet gerudert haben<br>werden gerudert haben |
| | **Present and Future Conditional** | | **Past Conditional** | |
| | würde rudern<br>würdest rudern<br>würde rudern | würden rudern<br>würdet rudern<br>würden rudern | würde gerudert haben<br>würdest gerudert haben<br>würde gerudert haben | würden gerudert haben<br>würdet gerudert haben<br>würden gerudert haben |

**Note:** This verb also has a usage as a verb of motion, which requires its auxiliary in the perfect tenses to be *sein: Er ist über den Fluss gerudert* ("He rowed across the river").

## EXAMPLES

Wir versuchten über den breiten Fluss zu rudern.
We tried to row across the wide river.

Ich bin früher viel gerudert, aber jetzt spiele ich lieber Tennis.
I used to do a lot of rowing, but now I prefer to play tennis.

**rufen**
to call
**Auxiliary verb:** haben **Past participle:** gerufen
**Imperative:** Rufe! Ruft! Rufen Sie!

| Mode | Simple Tenses | | Compound Tenses | |
|---|---|---|---|---|
| | *Singular* | *Plural* | *Singular* | *Plural* |
| Indicative | **Present** | | **Present Perfect** | |
| | rufe<br>rufst<br>ruft | rufen<br>ruft<br>rufen | habe gerufen<br>hast gerufen<br>hat gerufen | haben gerufen<br>habt gerufen<br>haben gerufen |
| | **Past** | | **Past Perfect** | |
| | rief<br>riefst<br>rief | riefen<br>rieft<br>riefen | hatte gerufen<br>hattest gerufen<br>hatte gerufen | hatten gerufen<br>hattet gerufen<br>hatten gerufen |
| | **Future** | | **Future Perfect** | |
| | werde rufen<br>wirst rufen<br>wird rufen | werden rufen<br>werdet rufen<br>werden rufen | werde gerufen haben<br>wirst gerufen haben<br>wird gerufen haben | werden gerufen haben<br>werdet gerufen haben<br>werden gerufen haben |
| Subjunctive | **Present** | | **Present Perfect** | |
| | rufe<br>rufest<br>rufe | rufen<br>rufet<br>rufen | habe gerufen<br>habest gerufen<br>habe gerufen | haben gerufen<br>habet gerufen<br>haben gerufen |
| | **Past** | | **Past Perfect** | |
| | riefe<br>riefest<br>riefe | riefen<br>riefet<br>riefen | hätte gerufen<br>hättest gerufen<br>hätte gerufen | hätten gerufen<br>hättet gerufen<br>hätten gerufen |
| | **Future** | | **Future Perfect** | |
| | werde rufen<br>werdest rufen<br>werde rufen | werden rufen<br>werdet rufen<br>werden rufen | werde gerufen haben<br>werdest gerufen haben<br>werde gerufen haben | werden gerufen haben<br>werdet gerufen haben<br>werden gerufen haben |
| | **Present and Future Conditional** | | **Past Conditional** | |
| | würde rufen<br>würdest rufen<br>würde rufen | würden rufen<br>würdet rufen<br>würden rufen | würde gerufen haben<br>würdest gerufen haben<br>würde gerufen haben | würden gerufen haben<br>würdet gerufen haben<br>würden gerufen haben |

**Note:** With inseparable prefixes, the principal parts of this verb are, for example, *verruft, verrief, hat verrufen.* With separable prefixes, the principal parts are, for example, *ruft an, rief an, hat angerufen.*

## EXAMPLES

| | |
|---|---|
| Ruf mich an, wenn du ein Problem hast. Ich kann dir helfen. | If you have a problem, call me. I can help you. |
| Er hat sie viermal gerufen. | He called to her four times. |

**ruhen**
to rest, to pause
**Auxiliary verb:** haben **Past participle:** geruht
**Imperative:** Ruhe! Ruht! Ruhen Sie!

| Mode | Simple Tenses | | Compound Tenses | |
|---|---|---|---|---|
| | *Singular* | *Plural* | *Singular* | *Plural* |
| Indicative | **Present** | | **Present Perfect** | |
| | ruhe<br>ruhst<br>ruht | ruhen<br>ruht<br>ruhen | habe geruht<br>hast geruht<br>hat geruht | haben geruht<br>habt geruht<br>haben geruht |
| | **Past** | | **Past Perfect** | |
| | ruhte<br>ruhtest<br>ruhte | ruhten<br>ruhtet<br>ruhten | hatte geruht<br>hattest geruht<br>hatte geruht | hatten geruht<br>hattet geruht<br>hatten geruht |
| | **Future** | | **Future Perfect** | |
| | werde ruhen<br>wirst ruhen<br>wird ruhen | werden ruhen<br>werdet ruhen<br>werden ruhen | werde geruht haben<br>wirst geruht haben<br>wird geruht haben | werden geruht haben<br>werdet geruht haben<br>werden geruht haben |
| Subjunctive | **Present** | | **Present Perfect** | |
| | ruhe<br>ruhest<br>ruhe | ruhen<br>ruhet<br>ruhen | habe geruht<br>habest geruht<br>habe geruht | haben geruht<br>habet geruht<br>haben geruht |
| | **Past** | | **Past Perfect** | |
| | ruhte<br>ruhtest<br>ruhte | ruhten<br>ruhtet<br>ruhten | hätte geruht<br>hättest geruht<br>hätte geruht | hätten geruht<br>hättet geruht<br>hätten geruht |
| | **Future** | | **Future Perfect** | |
| | werde ruhen<br>werdest ruhen<br>werde ruhen | werden ruhen<br>werdet ruhen<br>werden ruhen | werde geruht haben<br>werdest geruht haben<br>werde geruht haben | werden geruht haben<br>werdet geruht haben<br>werden geruht haben |
| | **Present and Future Conditional** | | **Past Conditional** | |
| | würde ruhen<br>würdest ruhen<br>würde ruhen | würden ruhen<br>würdet ruhen<br>würden ruhen | würde geruht haben<br>würdest geruht haben<br>würde geruht haben | würden geruht haben<br>würdet geruht haben<br>würden geruht haben |

## EXAMPLES

Ich möchte die ganze Sache endlich ruhen lassen.
I'd finally like to put the whole matter to rest.

Hier ruht Johann Wolfgang von Goethe: Dichter, Denker, Genie.
Here lies Johann Wolfgang von Goethe: Poet, Philosopher, Genius.

**rühmen**

to praise, to extol

**Auxiliary verb:** haben **Past participle:** gerühmt

**Imperative:** Rühme! Rühmt! Rühmen Sie!

| Mode | Simple Tenses | | Compound Tenses | |
|---|---|---|---|---|
| | *Singular* | *Plural* | *Singular* | *Plural* |
| Indicative | **Present** | | **Present Perfect** | |
| | rühme<br>rühmst<br>rühmt | rühmen<br>rühmt<br>rühmen | habe gerühmt<br>hast gerühmt<br>hat gerühmt | haben gerühmt<br>habt gerühmt<br>haben gerühmt |
| | **Past** | | **Past Perfect** | |
| | rühmte<br>rühmtest<br>rühmte | rühmten<br>rühmtet<br>rühmten | hatte gerühmt<br>hattest gerühmt<br>hatte gerühmt | hatten gerühmt<br>hattet gerühmt<br>hatten gerühmt |
| | **Future** | | **Future Perfect** | |
| | werde rühmen<br>wirst rühmen<br>wird rühmen | werden rühmen<br>werdet rühmen<br>werden rühmen | werde gerühmt haben<br>wirst gerühmt haben<br>wird gerühmt haben | werden gerühmt haben<br>werdet gerühmt haben<br>werden gerühmt haben |
| Subjunctive | **Present** | | **Present Perfect** | |
| | rühme<br>rühmest<br>rühme | rühmen<br>rühmet<br>rühmen | habe gerühmt<br>habest gerühmt<br>habe gerühmt | haben gerühmt<br>habet gerühmt<br>haben gerühmt |
| | **Past** | | **Past Perfect** | |
| | rühmte<br>rühmtest<br>rühmte | rühmten<br>rühmtet<br>rühmten | hätte gerühmt<br>hättest gerühmt<br>hätte gerühmt | hätten gerühmt<br>hättet gerühmt<br>hätten gerühmt |
| | **Future** | | **Future Perfect** | |
| | werde rühmen<br>werdest rühmen<br>werde rühmen | werden rühmen<br>werdet rühmen<br>werden rühmen | werde gerühmt haben<br>werdest gerühmt haben<br>werde gerühmt haben | werden gerühmt haben<br>werdet gerühmt haben<br>werden gerühmt haben |
| | **Present and Future Conditional** | | **Past Conditional** | |
| | würde rühmen<br>würdest rühmen<br>würde rühmen | würden rühmen<br>würdet rühmen<br>würden rühmen | würde gerühmt haben<br>würdest gerühmt haben<br>würde gerühmt haben | würden gerühmt haben<br>würdet gerühmt haben<br>würden gerühmt haben |

## EXAMPLES

Alle rühmten ihn als ehrlich und treu.
Man rühmt ihren Schokoladenkuchen auf jeder Familienfeier.

Everyone praised him as honest and loyal.
Her chocolate cake is praised at every family gathering.

**rühren**
to touch, to stir
**Auxiliary verb:** haben **Past participle:** gerührt
**Imperative:** Rühre! Rührt! Rühren Sie!

| Mode | Simple Tenses | | Compound Tenses | |
|---|---|---|---|---|
| | *Singular* | *Plural* | *Singular* | *Plural* |
| Indicative | **Present** | | **Present Perfect** | |
| | rühre<br>rührst<br>rührt | rühren<br>rührt<br>rühren | habe gerührt<br>hast gerührt<br>hat gerührt | haben gerührt<br>habt gerührt<br>haben gerührt |
| | **Past** | | **Past Perfect** | |
| | rührte<br>rührtest<br>rührte | rührten<br>rührtet<br>rührten | hatte gerührt<br>hattest gerührt<br>hatte gerührt | hatten gerührt<br>hattet gerührt<br>hatten gerührt |
| | **Future** | | **Future Perfect** | |
| | werde rühren<br>wirst rühren<br>wird rühren | werden rühren<br>werdet rühren<br>werden rühren | werde gerührt haben<br>wirst gerührt haben<br>wird gerührt haben | werden gerührt haben<br>werdet gerührt haben<br>werden gerührt haben |
| Subjunctive | **Present** | | **Present Perfect** | |
| | rühre<br>rührest<br>rühre | rühren<br>rührет<br>rühren | habe gerührt<br>habest gerührt<br>habe gerührt | haben gerührt<br>habet gerührt<br>haben gerührt |
| | **Past** | | **Past Perfect** | |
| | rührte<br>rührtest<br>rührte | rührten<br>rührtet<br>rührten | hätte gerührt<br>hättest gerührt<br>hätte gerührt | hätten gerührt<br>hättet gerührt<br>hätten gerührt |
| | **Future** | | **Future Perfect** | |
| | werde rühren<br>werdest rühren<br>werde rühren | werden rühren<br>werdet rühren<br>werden rühren | werde gerührt haben<br>werdest gerührt haben<br>werde gerührt haben | werden gerührt haben<br>werdet gerührt haben<br>werden gerührt haben |
| | **Present and Future Conditional** | | **Past Conditional** | |
| | würde rühren<br>würdest rühren<br>würde rühren | würden rühren<br>würdet rühren<br>würden rühren | würde gerührt haben<br>würdest gerührt haben<br>würde gerührt haben | würden gerührt haben<br>würdet gerührt haben<br>würden gerührt haben |

## EXAMPLES

| | |
|---|---|
| Das traurige Schauspiel hat uns zu Tränen gerührt. | The sad play touched us to the point of tears. |
| „Rührt euch!" schreit der Feldwebel. | "At ease!" the sergeant shouts. |
| Man sollte diesen Teig nicht zu viel rühren. | You shouldn't stir this batter too much. |

**rülpsen**
to belch
**Auxiliary verb:** haben **Past participle:** gerülpst
**Imperative:** Rülpse! Rülpst! Rülpsen Sie!

| Mode | Simple Tenses | | Compound Tenses | |
|---|---|---|---|---|
| | *Singular* | *Plural* | *Singular* | *Plural* |
| Indicative | **Present** | | **Present Perfect** | |
| | rülpse<br>rülpst<br>rülpst | rülpsen<br>rülpst<br>rülpsen | habe gerülpst<br>hast gerülpst<br>hat gerülpst | haben gerülpst<br>habt gerülpst<br>haben gerülpst |
| | **Past** | | **Past Perfect** | |
| | rülpste<br>rülpstest<br>rülpste | rülpsten<br>rülpstet<br>rülpsten | hatte gerülpst<br>hattest gerülpst<br>hatte gerülpst | hatten gerülpst<br>hattet gerülpst<br>hatten gerülpst |
| | **Future** | | **Future Perfect** | |
| | werde rülpsen<br>wirst rülpsen<br>wird rülpsen | werden rülpsen<br>werdet rülpsen<br>werden rülpsen | werde gerülpst haben<br>wirst gerülpst haben<br>wird gerülpst haben | werden gerülpst haben<br>werdet gerülpst haben<br>werden gerülpst haben |
| Subjunctive | **Present** | | **Present Perfect** | |
| | rülpse<br>rülpsest<br>rülpse | rülpsen<br>rülpset<br>rülpsen | habe gerülpst<br>habest gerülpst<br>habe gerülpst | haben gerülpst<br>habet gerülpst<br>haben gerülpst |
| | **Past** | | **Past Perfect** | |
| | rülpste<br>rülpstest<br>rülpste | rülpsten<br>rülpstet<br>rülpsten | hätte gerülpst<br>hättest gerülpst<br>hätte gerülpst | hätten gerülpst<br>hättet gerülpst<br>hätten gerülpst |
| | **Future** | | **Future Perfect** | |
| | werde rülpsen<br>werdest rülpsen<br>werde rülpsen | werden rülpsen<br>werdet rülpsen<br>werden rülpsen | werde gerülpst haben<br>werdest gerülpst haben<br>werde gerülpst haben | werden gerülpst haben<br>werdet gerülpst haben<br>werden gerülpst haben |
| | **Present and Future Conditional** | | **Past Conditional** | |
| | würde rülpsen<br>würdest rülpsen<br>würde rülpsen | würden rülpsen<br>würdet rülpsen<br>würden rülpsen | würde gerülpst haben<br>würdest gerülpst haben<br>würde gerülpst haben | würden gerülpst haben<br>würdet gerülpst haben<br>würden gerülpst haben |

## EXAMPLES

Onkel Heinrich trank sein Bier und rülpste leise. Er war zufrieden.

„Rülpsen gehört zu einem guten Abendessen," hat unser Vater oft gesagt.

Vor Fremden sollte man nicht rülpsen.

Uncle Heinrich drank his beer and belched quietly. He was content.

"Belching is part of a good meal," our father often said.

You shouldn't belch in front of strangers.

**rupfen**
to pluck, to pull
**Auxiliary verb:** haben **Past participle:** gerupft
**Imperative:** Rupfe! Rupft! Rupfen Sie!

| Mode | Simple Tenses | | Compound Tenses | |
|---|---|---|---|---|
| | *Singular* | *Plural* | *Singular* | *Plural* |
| Indicative | **Present** | | **Present Perfect** | |
| | rupfe<br>rupfst<br>rupft | rupfen<br>rupft<br>rupfen | habe gerupft<br>hast gerupft<br>hat gerupft | haben gerupft<br>habt gerupft<br>haben gerupft |
| | **Past** | | **Past Perfect** | |
| | rupfte<br>rupftest<br>rupfte | rupften<br>rupftet<br>rupften | hatte gerupft<br>hattest gerupft<br>hatte gerupft | hatten gerupft<br>hattet gerupft<br>hatten gerupft |
| | **Future** | | **Future Perfect** | |
| | werde rupfen<br>wirst rupfen<br>wird rupfen | werden rupfen<br>werdet rupfen<br>werden rupfen | werde gerupft haben<br>wirst gerupft haben<br>wird gerupft haben | werden gerupft haben<br>werdet gerupft haben<br>werden gerupft haben |
| Subjunctive | **Present** | | **Present Perfect** | |
| | rupfe<br>rupfest<br>rupfe | rupfen<br>rupfet<br>rupfen | habe gerupft<br>habest gerupft<br>habe gerupft | haben gerupft<br>habet gerupft<br>haben gerupft |
| | **Past** | | **Past Perfect** | |
| | rupfte<br>rupftest<br>rupfte | rupften<br>rupftet<br>rupften | hätte gerupft<br>hättest gerupft<br>hätte gerupft | hätten gerupft<br>hättet gerupft<br>hätten gerupft |
| | **Future** | | **Future Perfect** | |
| | werde rupfen<br>werdest rupfen<br>werde rupfen | werden rupfen<br>werdet rupfen<br>werden rupfen | werde gerupft haben<br>werdest gerupft haben<br>werde gerupft haben | werden gerupft haben<br>werdet gerupft haben<br>werden gerupft haben |
| | **Present and Future Conditional** | | **Past Conditional** | |
| | würde rupfen<br>würdest rupfen<br>würde rupfen | würden rupfen<br>würdet rupfen<br>würden rupfen | würde gerupft haben<br>würdest gerupft haben<br>würde gerupft haben | würden gerupft haben<br>würdet gerupft haben<br>würden gerupft haben |

## EXAMPLES

Früher musste man seine Hühner selbst rupfen.
In the past people had to pluck their chickens themselves.

Ich habe ein Hühnchen mit dir zu rupfen.
I've got a bone to pick with you.

**rutschen**
to slide, to slip
**Auxiliary verb:** sein **Past participle:** gerutscht
**Imperative:** Rutsche! Rutscht! Rutschen Sie!

| Mode | Simple Tenses | | Compound Tenses | |
|---|---|---|---|---|
| | *Singular* | *Plural* | *Singular* | *Plural* |
| Indicative | **Present** | | **Present Perfect** | |
| | rutsche<br>rutschst<br>rutscht | rutschen<br>rutscht<br>rutschen | bin gerutscht<br>bist gerutscht<br>ist gerutscht | sind gerutscht<br>seid gerutscht<br>sind gerutscht |
| | **Past** | | **Past Perfect** | |
| | rutschte<br>rutschtest<br>rutschte | rutschten<br>rutschtet<br>rutschten | war gerutscht<br>wast gerutscht<br>war gerutscht | waren gerutscht<br>wart gerutscht<br>waren gerutscht |
| | **Future** | | **Future Perfect** | |
| | werde rutschen<br>wirst rutschen<br>wird rutschen | werden rutschen<br>werdet rutschen<br>werden rutschen | werde gerutscht sein<br>wirst gerutscht sein<br>wird gerutscht sein | werden gerutscht sein<br>werdet gerutscht sein<br>werden gerutscht sein |
| Subjunctive | **Present** | | **Present Perfect** | |
| | rutsche<br>rutschest<br>rutsche | rutschen<br>rutschet<br>rutschen | sei gerutscht<br>seiest gerutscht<br>sei gerutscht | seien gerutscht<br>seiet gerutscht<br>seien gerutscht |
| | **Past** | | **Past Perfect** | |
| | rutschte<br>rutschtest<br>rutschte | rutschten<br>rutschtet<br>rutschten | wäre gerutscht<br>wärest gerutscht<br>wäre gerutscht | wären gerutscht<br>wäret gerutscht<br>wären gerutscht |
| | **Future** | | **Future Perfect** | |
| | werde rutschen<br>werdest rutschen<br>werde rutschen | werden rutschen<br>werdet rutschen<br>werden rutschen | werde gerutscht sein<br>werdest gerutscht sein<br>werde gerutscht sein | werden gerutscht sein<br>werdet gerutscht sein<br>werden gerutscht sein |
| | **Present and Future Conditional** | | **Past Conditional** | |
| | würde rutschen<br>würdest rutschen<br>würde rutschen | würden rutschen<br>würdet rutschen<br>würden rutschen | würde gerutscht sein<br>würdest gerutscht sein<br>würde gerutscht sein | würden gerutscht sein<br>würdet gerutscht sein<br>würden gerutscht sein |

## EXAMPLE

Rutsch doch mal ein Stückchen! — Scoot over a bit.

**säen**

to sow

**Auxiliary verb:** haben **Past participle:** gesät

**Imperative:** Säe! Sät! Säen Sie!

| Mode | Simple Tenses | | Compound Tenses | |
|---|---|---|---|---|
| | *Singular* | *Plural* | *Singular* | *Plural* |
| Indicative | **Present** | | **Present Perfect** | |
| | säe<br>säst<br>sät | säen<br>sät<br>säen | habe gesät<br>hast gesät<br>hat gesät | haben gesät<br>habt gesät<br>haben gesät |
| | **Past** | | **Past Perfect** | |
| | säte<br>sätest<br>säte | säten<br>sätet<br>säten | hatte gesät<br>hattest gesät<br>hatte gesät | hatten gesät<br>hattet gesät<br>hatten gesät |
| | **Future** | | **Future Perfect** | |
| | werde säen<br>wirst säen<br>wird säen | werden säen<br>werdet säen<br>werden säen | werde gesät haben<br>wirst gesät haben<br>wird gesät haben | werden gesät haben<br>werdet gesät haben<br>werden gesät haben |
| Subjunctive | **Present** | | **Present Perfect** | |
| | säe<br>säest<br>säe | säen<br>säet<br>säen | habe gesät<br>habest gesät<br>habe gesät | haben gesät<br>habet gesät<br>haben gesät |
| | **Past** | | **Past Perfect** | |
| | säte<br>sätest<br>säte | säten<br>sätet<br>säten | hätte gesät<br>hättest gesät<br>hätte gesät | hätten gesät<br>hättet gesät<br>hätten gesät |
| | **Future** | | **Future Perfect** | |
| | werde säen<br>werdest säen<br>werde säen | werden säen<br>werdet säen<br>werden säen | werde gesät haben<br>werdest gesät haben<br>werde gesät haben | werden gesät haben<br>werdet gesät haben<br>werden gesät haben |
| | **Present and Future Conditional** | | **Past Conditional** | |
| | würde säen<br>würdest säen<br>würde säen | würden säen<br>würdet säen<br>würden säen | würde gesät haben<br>würdest gesät haben<br>würde gesät haben | würden gesät haben<br>würdet gesät haben<br>würden gesät haben |

## EXAMPLES

Das Korn muss Anfang April gesät werden.

The grain has to be sown in the beginning of April.

Man soll Sonnenblumen nicht zu eng säen.

You shouldn't sow sunflowers too closely together.

**sagen**
to say, to tell
**Auxiliary verb:** haben **Past participle:** gesagt
**Imperative:** Sage! Sagt! Sagen Sie!

| Mode | Simple Tenses | | Compound Tenses | |
|---|---|---|---|---|
| | *Singular* | *Plural* | *Singular* | *Plural* |
| Indicative | **Present** | | **Present Perfect** | |
| | sage<br>sagst<br>sagt | sagen<br>sagt<br>sagen | habe gesagt<br>hast gesagt<br>hat gesagt | haben gesagt<br>habt gesagt<br>haben gesagt |
| | **Past** | | **Past Perfect** | |
| | sagte<br>sagtest<br>sagte | sagten<br>sagtet<br>sagten | hatte gesagt<br>hattest gesagt<br>hatte gesagt | hatten gesagt<br>hattet gesagt<br>hatten gesagt |
| | **Future** | | **Future Perfect** | |
| | werde sagen<br>wirst sagen<br>wird sagen | werden sagen<br>werdet sagen<br>werden sagen | werde gesagt haben<br>wirst gesagt haben<br>wird gesagt haben | werden gesagt haben<br>werdet gesagt haben<br>werden gesagt haben |
| Subjunctive | **Present** | | **Present Perfect** | |
| | sage<br>sagest<br>sage | sagen<br>saget<br>sagen | habe gesagt<br>habest gesagt<br>habe gesagt | haben gesagt<br>habet gesagt<br>haben gesagt |
| | **Past** | | **Past Perfect** | |
| | sagte<br>sagtest<br>sagte | sagten<br>sagtet<br>sagten | hätte gesagt<br>hättest gesagt<br>hätte gesagt | hätten gesagt<br>hättet gesagt<br>hätten gesagt |
| | **Future** | | **Future Perfect** | |
| | werde sagen<br>werdest sagen<br>werde sagen | werden sagen<br>werdet sagen<br>werden sagen | werde gesagt haben<br>werdest gesagt haben<br>werde gesagt haben | werden gesagt haben<br>werdet gesagt haben<br>werden gesagt haben |
| | **Present and Future Conditional** | | **Past Conditional** | |
| | würde sagen<br>würdest sagen<br>würde sagen | würden sagen<br>würdet sagen<br>würden sagen | würde gesagt haben<br>würdest gesagt haben<br>würde gesagt haben | würden gesagt haben<br>würdet gesagt haben<br>würden gesagt haben |

## EXAMPLES

| | |
|---|---|
| Wenn ich etwas zu sagen hätte, würde ich meine Hand heben. | If I had something to say, I'd raise my hand. |
| Sagen Sie bitte, warum Sie Ihren Wagen verkaufen wollen! | Please tell me why you want to sell your car. |

**sammeln**
to collect, to gather
**Auxiliary verb:** haben **Past participle:** gesammelt
**Imperative:** Sammele! Sammelt! Sammeln Sie!

| Mode | Simple Tenses | | Compound Tenses | |
|---|---|---|---|---|
| | *Singular* | *Plural* | *Singular* | *Plural* |
| Indicative | **Present** | | **Present Perfect** | |
| | sammele<br>sammelst<br>sammelt | sammeln<br>sammelt<br>sammeln | habe gesammelt<br>hast gesammelt<br>hat gesammelt | haben gesammelt<br>habt gesammelt<br>haben gesammelt |
| | **Past** | | **Past Perfect** | |
| | sammelte<br>sammeltest<br>sammelte | sammelten<br>sammeltet<br>sammelten | hatte gesammelt<br>hattest gesammelt<br>hatte gesammelt | hatten gesammelt<br>hattet gesammelt<br>hatten gesammelt |
| | **Future** | | **Future Perfect** | |
| | werde sammeln<br>wirst sammeln<br>wird sammeln | werden sammeln<br>werdet sammeln<br>werden sammeln | werde gesammelt haben<br>wirst gesammelt haben<br>wird gesammelt haben | werden gesammelt haben<br>werdet gesammelt haben<br>werden gesammelt haben |
| Subjunctive | **Present** | | **Present Perfect** | |
| | sammele<br>sammelst<br>sammele | sammeln<br>sammelt<br>sammeln | habe gesammelt<br>habest gesammelt<br>habe gesammelt | haben gesammelt<br>habet gesammelt<br>haben gesammelt |
| | **Past** | | **Past Perfect** | |
| | sammelte<br>sammeltest<br>sammelte | sammelten<br>sammeltet<br>sammelten | hätte gesammelt<br>hättest gesammelt<br>hätte gesammelt | hätten gesammelt<br>hättet gesammelt<br>hätten gesammelt |
| | **Future** | | **Future Perfect** | |
| | werde sammeln<br>werdest sammeln<br>werde sammeln | werden sammeln<br>werdet sammeln<br>werden sammeln | werde gesammelt haben<br>werdest gesammelt haben<br>werde gesammelt haben | werden gesammelt haben<br>werdet gesammelt haben<br>werden gesammelt haben |
| | **Present and Future Conditional** | | **Past Conditional** | |
| | würde sammeln<br>würdest sammeln<br>würde sammeln | würden sammeln<br>würdet sammeln<br>würden sammeln | würde gesammelt haben<br>würdest gesammelt haben<br>würde gesammelt haben | würden gesammelt haben<br>würdet gesammelt haben<br>würden gesammelt haben |

## EXAMPLES

Meine Schwester sammelt Briefmarken. — My sister collects stamps.
Karl hat viele römische Münzen gesammelt. — Karl has collected a lot of Roman coins.

**sättigen**
to fill, to satisfy, to satiate
**Auxiliary verb:** haben **Past participle:** gesättigt
**Imperative:** Sättige! Sättigt! Sättigen Sie!

| Mode | Simple Tenses | | Compound Tenses | |
|---|---|---|---|---|
| | *Singular* | *Plural* | *Singular* | *Plural* |
| Indicative | **Present** | | **Present Perfect** | |
| | sättige<br>sättigst<br>sättigt | sättigen<br>sättigt<br>sättigen | habe gesättigt<br>hast gesättigt<br>hat gesättigt | haben gesättigt<br>habt gesättigt<br>haben gesättigt |
| | **Past** | | **Past Perfect** | |
| | sättigte<br>sättigtest<br>sättigte | sättigten<br>sättigtet<br>sättigten | hatte gesättigt<br>hattest gesättigt<br>hatte gesättigt | hatten gesättigt<br>hattet gesättigt<br>hatten gesättigt |
| | **Future** | | **Future Perfect** | |
| | werde sättigen<br>wirst sättigen<br>wird sättigen | werden sättigen<br>werdet sättigen<br>werden sättigen | werde gesättigt haben<br>wirst gesättigt haben<br>wird gesättigt haben | werden gesättigt haben<br>werdet gesättigt haben<br>werden gesättigt haben |
| Subjunctive | **Present** | | **Present Perfect** | |
| | sättige<br>sättigest<br>sättige | sättigen<br>sättiget<br>sättigen | habe gesättigt<br>habest gesättigt<br>habe gesättigt | haben gesättigt<br>habet gesättigt<br>haben gesättigt |
| | **Past** | | **Past Perfect** | |
| | sättigte<br>sättigtest<br>sättigte | sättigten<br>sättigtet<br>sättigten | hätte gesättigt<br>hättest gesättigt<br>hätte gesättigt | hätten gesättigt<br>hättet gesättigt<br>hätten gesättigt |
| | **Future** | | **Future Perfect** | |
| | werde sättigen<br>werdest sättigen<br>werde sättigen | werden sättigen<br>werdet sättigen<br>werden sättigen | werde gesättigt haben<br>werdest gesättigt haben<br>werde gesättigt haben | werden gesättigt haben<br>werdet gesättigt haben<br>werden gesättigt haben |
| | **Present and Future Conditional** | | **Past Conditional** | |
| | würde sättigen<br>würdest sättigen<br>würde sättigen | würden sättigen<br>würdet sättigen<br>würden sättigen | würde gesättigt haben<br>würdest gesättigt haben<br>würde gesättigt haben | würden gesättigt haben<br>würdet gesättigt haben<br>würden gesättigt haben |

## EXAMPLES

Die neue Diät sättigt kaum.
The new diet hardly makes you feel full.

Der Handymarkt ist seit einigen Jahren gesättigt.
The cellphone market has been saturated for a few years.

**saufen**

to drink (as of animals), to tipple, to booze

**Auxiliary verb:** haben **Past participle:** gesoffen

**Imperative:** Saufe! Sauft! Saufen Sie!

| Mode | Simple Tenses | | Compound Tenses | |
|---|---|---|---|---|
| | *Singular* | *Plural* | *Singular* | *Plural* |
| Indicative | **Present** | | **Present Perfect** | |
| | saufe<br>säufst<br>säuft | saufen<br>sauft<br>saufen | habe gesoffen<br>hast gesoffen<br>hat gesoffen | haben gesoffen<br>habt gesoffen<br>haben gesoffen |
| | **Past** | | **Past Perfect** | |
| | soff<br>soffst<br>soff | soffen<br>sofft<br>soffen | hatte gesoffen<br>hattest gesoffen<br>hatte gesoffen | hatten gesoffen<br>hattet gesoffen<br>hatten gesoffen |
| | **Future** | | **Future Perfect** | |
| | werde saufen<br>wirst saufen<br>wird saufen | werden saufen<br>werdet saufen<br>werden saufen | werde gesoffen haben<br>wirst gesoffen haben<br>wird gesoffen haben | werden gesoffen haben<br>werdet gesoffen haben<br>werden gesoffen haben |
| Subjunctive | **Present** | | **Present Perfect** | |
| | saufe<br>saufest<br>saufe | saufen<br>saufet<br>saufen | habe gesoffen<br>habest gesoffen<br>habe gesoffen | haben gesoffen<br>habet gesoffen<br>haben gesoffen |
| | **Past** | | **Past Perfect** | |
| | söffe<br>söffest<br>söffe | söffen<br>söffet<br>söffen | hätte gesoffen<br>hättest gesoffen<br>hätte gesoffen | hätten gesoffen<br>hättet gesoffen<br>hätten gesoffen |
| | **Future** | | **Future Perfect** | |
| | werde saufen<br>werdest saufen<br>werde saufen | werden saufen<br>werdet saufen<br>werden saufen | werde gesoffen haben<br>werdest gesoffen haben<br>werde gesoffen haben | werden gesoffen haben<br>werdet gesoffen haben<br>werden gesoffen haben |
| | **Present and Future Conditional** | | **Past Conditional** | |
| | würde saufen<br>würdest saufen<br>würde saufen | würden saufen<br>würdet saufen<br>würden saufen | würde gesoffen haben<br>würdest gesoffen haben<br>würde gesoffen haben | würden gesoffen haben<br>würdet gesoffen haben<br>würden gesoffen haben |

**Note:** This verb, when it refers to humans, is considered very colloquial or even rude.

## EXAMPLES

| | |
|---|---|
| Du sollst nicht so viel saufen. | You shouldn't drink so much. |
| Mein Onkel blieb im Lokal und soff. | My uncle remained at the bar and drank. |

**saugen**
to suck
**Auxiliary verb:** haben **Past participle:** gesogen
**Imperative:** Sauge! Saugt! Saugen Sie!

| Mode | Simple Tenses | | Compound Tenses | |
|---|---|---|---|---|
| | *Singular* | *Plural* | *Singular* | *Plural* |
| Indicative | **Present** | | **Present Perfect** | |
| | sauge<br>saugst<br>saugt | saugen<br>saugt<br>saugen | habe gesogen<br>hast gesogen<br>hat gesogen | haben gesogen<br>habt gesogen<br>haben gesogen |
| | **Past** | | **Past Perfect** | |
| | sog<br>sogst<br>sog | sogen<br>sogt<br>sogen | hatte gesogen<br>hattest gesogen<br>hatte gesogen | hatten gesogen<br>hattet gesogen<br>hatten gesogen |
| | **Future** | | **Future Perfect** | |
| | werde saugen<br>wirst saugen<br>wird saugen | werden saugen<br>werdet saugen<br>werden saugen | werde gesogen haben<br>wirst gesogen haben<br>wird gesogen haben | werden gesogen haben<br>werdet gesogen haben<br>werden gesogen haben |
| Subjunctive | **Present** | | **Present Perfect** | |
| | sauge<br>saugest<br>sauge | saugen<br>sauget<br>saugen | habe gesogen<br>habest gesogen<br>habe gesogen | haben gesogen<br>habet gesogen<br>haben gesogen |
| | **Past** | | **Past Perfect** | |
| | söge<br>sögest<br>söge | sögen<br>söget<br>sögen | hätte gesogen<br>hättest gesogen<br>hätte gesogen | hätten gesogen<br>hättet gesogen<br>hätten gesogen |
| | **Future** | | **Future Perfect** | |
| | werde saugen<br>werdest saugen<br>werde saugen | werden saugen<br>werdet saugen<br>werden saugen | werde gesogen haben<br>werdest gesogen haben<br>werde gesogen haben | werden gesogen haben<br>werdet gesogen haben<br>werden gesogen haben |
| | **Present and Future Conditional** | | **Past Conditional** | |
| | würde saugen<br>würdest saugen<br>würde saugen | würden saugen<br>würdet saugen<br>würden saugen | würde gesogen haben<br>würdest gesogen haben<br>würde gesogen haben | würden gesogen haben<br>würdet gesogen haben<br>würden gesogen haben |

**Note:** It is common to omit the word *Staub* from *staubsaugen,* which means "to vacuum." See the first example below. *Saugen* is often also used as a regular verb, with its principal parts then being *saugt, saugte, gesaugt.*

## EXAMPLES

Ludwig, bitte sauge die Böden im Wohnzimmer und Esszimmer!
Ludwig, please vacuum the floors in the living room and dining room.

Das schlafende Kind saugte an seinem Nuckel.
The sleeping child sucked on her pacifier.

**schaden**
to harm
**Auxiliary verb:** haben **Past participle:** geschadet
**Imperative:** Schade! Schadet! Schaden Sie!

| Mode | Simple Tenses | | Compound Tenses | |
|---|---|---|---|---|
| | *Singular* | *Plural* | *Singular* | *Plural* |
| Indicative | **Present** | | **Present Perfect** | |
| | schade<br>schadest<br>schadet | schaden<br>schadet<br>schaden | habe geschadet<br>hast geschadet<br>hat geschadet | haben geschadet<br>habt geschadet<br>haben geschadet |
| | **Past** | | **Past Perfect** | |
| | schadete<br>schadetest<br>schadete | schadeten<br>schadetet<br>schadeten | hatte geschadet<br>hattest geschadet<br>hatte geschadet | hatten geschadet<br>hattet geschadet<br>hatten geschadet |
| | **Future** | | **Future Perfect** | |
| | werde schaden<br>wirst schaden<br>wird schaden | werden schaden<br>werdet schaden<br>werden schaden | werde geschadet haben<br>wirst geschadet haben<br>wird geschadet haben | werden geschadet haben<br>werdet geschadet haben<br>werden geschadet haben |
| Subjunctive | **Present** | | **Present Perfect** | |
| | schade<br>schadest<br>schade | schaden<br>schadet<br>schaden | habe geschadet<br>habest geschadet<br>habe geschadet | haben geschadet<br>habet geschadet<br>haben geschadet |
| | **Past** | | **Past Perfect** | |
| | schadete<br>schadetest<br>schadete | schadeten<br>schadetet<br>schadeten | hätte geschadet<br>hättest geschadet<br>hätte geschadet | hätten geschadet<br>hättet geschadet<br>hätten geschadet |
| | **Future** | | **Future Perfect** | |
| | werde schaden<br>werdest schaden<br>werde schaden | werden schaden<br>werdet schaden<br>werden schaden | werde geschadet haben<br>werdest geschadet haben<br>werde geschadet haben | werden geschadet haben<br>werdet geschadet haben<br>werden geschadet haben |
| | **Present and Future Conditional** | | **Past Conditional** | |
| | wurde schaden<br>würdest schaden<br>würde schaden | würden schaden<br>würdet schaden<br>würden schaden | würde geschadet haben<br>würdest geschadet haben<br>würde geschadet haben | würden geschadet haben<br>würdet geschadet haben<br>würden geschadet haben |

**Note:** The word *schade* is used to mean "a pity"—for example, *Schade, dass es heute regnet* ("It's a pity that it's raining today").

## EXAMPLES

Zu viel Alkohol schadet dem Gehirn.
Das Rauchen hat ihm sehr geschadet.

Too much alcohol harms the brain.
Smoking has done a lot of harm to him.

**schaffen**

to create, to produce, to accomplish

**Auxiliary verb:** haben **Past participle:** geschaffen

**Imperative:** Schaffe! Schafft! Schaffen Sie!

| Mode | Simple Tenses | | Compound Tenses | |
|---|---|---|---|---|
| | *Singular* | *Plural* | *Singular* | *Plural* |
| Indicative | **Present** | | **Present Perfect** | |
| | schaffe<br>schaffst<br>schafft | schaffen<br>schafft<br>schaffen | habe geschaffen<br>hast geschaffen<br>hat geschaffen | haben geschaffen<br>habt geschaffen<br>haben geschaffen |
| | **Past** | | **Past Perfect** | |
| | schuf<br>schufst<br>schuf | schufen<br>schuft<br>schufen | hatte geschaffen<br>hattest geschaffen<br>hatte geschaffen | hatten geschaffen<br>hattet geschaffen<br>hatten geschaffen |
| | **Future** | | **Future Perfect** | |
| | werde schaffen<br>wirst schaffen<br>wird schaffen | werden schaffen<br>werdet schaffen<br>werden schaffen | werde geschaffen haben<br>wirst geschaffen haben<br>wird geschaffen haben | werden geschaffen haben<br>werdet geschaffen haben<br>werden geschaffen haben |
| Subjunctive | **Present** | | **Present Perfect** | |
| | schaffe<br>schaffest<br>schaffe | schaffen<br>schaffet<br>schaffen | habe geschaffen<br>habest geschaffen<br>habe geschaffen | haben geschaffen<br>habet geschaffen<br>haben geschaffen |
| | **Past** | | **Past Perfect** | |
| | schüfe<br>schüfest<br>schüfe | schüfen<br>schüfet<br>schüfen | hätte geschaffen<br>hättest geschaffen<br>hätte geschaffen | hätten geschaffen<br>hättet geschaffen<br>hätten geschaffen |
| | **Future** | | **Future Perfect** | |
| | werde schaffen<br>werdest schaffen<br>werde schaffen | werden schaffen<br>werdet schaffen<br>werden schaffen | werde geschaffen haben<br>werdest geschaffen haben<br>werde geschaffen haben | werden geschaffen haben<br>werdet geschaffen haben<br>werden geschaffen haben |
| | **Present and Future Conditional** | | **Past Conditional** | |
| | würde schaffen<br>würdest schaffen<br>würde schaffen | würden schaffen<br>würdet schaffen<br>würden schaffen | würde geschaffen haben<br>würdest geschaffen haben<br>würde geschaffen haben | würden geschaffen haben<br>würdet geschaffen haben<br>würden geschaffen haben |

**Note:** When this verb means "to accomplish," it has a regular conjugation and its principal parts are *schafft, schaffte, hat geschafft.*

## EXAMPLES

| | |
|---|---|
| Ein unbekannter Dichter hat diese Gedichte geschaffen. | An unknown poet created these poems. |
| Martin hat das Examen ohne Mühe geschafft. | Martin passed the exam without trying very hard. |

**schälen**
to peel, to pare
**Auxiliary verb:** haben **Past participle:** geschält
**Imperative:** Schäle! Schält! Schälen Sie!

| Mode | Simple Tenses | | Compound Tenses | |
|---|---|---|---|---|
| | *Singular* | *Plural* | *Singular* | *Plural* |
| Indicative | **Present** | | **Present Perfect** | |
| | schäle<br>schälst<br>schält | schälen<br>schält<br>schälen | habe geschält<br>hast geschält<br>hat geschält | haben geschält<br>habt geschält<br>haben geschält |
| | **Past** | | **Past Perfect** | |
| | schälte<br>schältest<br>schälte | schälten<br>schältet<br>schälten | hatte geschält<br>hattest geschält<br>hatte geschält | hatten geschält<br>hattet geschält<br>hatten geschält |
| | **Future** | | **Future Perfect** | |
| | werde schälen<br>wirst schälen<br>wird schälen | werden schälen<br>werdet schälen<br>werden schälen | werde geschält haben<br>wirst geschält haben<br>wird geschält haben | werden geschält haben<br>werdet geschält haben<br>werden geschält haben |
| Subjunctive | **Present** | | **Present Perfect** | |
| | schäle<br>schälest<br>schäle | schälen<br>schälet<br>schälen | habe geschält<br>habest geschält<br>habe geschält | haben geschält<br>habet geschält<br>haben geschält |
| | **Past** | | **Past Perfect** | |
| | schälte<br>schältest<br>schälte | schälten<br>schältet<br>schälten | hätte geschält<br>hättest geschält<br>hätte geschält | hätten geschält<br>hättet geschält<br>hätten geschält |
| | **Future** | | **Future Perfect** | |
| | werde schälen<br>werdest schälen<br>werde schälen | werden schälen<br>werdet schälen<br>werden schälen | werde geschält haben<br>werdest geschält haben<br>werde geschält haben | werden geschält haben<br>werdet geschält haben<br>werden geschält haben |
| | **Present and Future Conditional** | | **Past Conditional** | |
| | würde schälen<br>würdest schälen<br>würde schälen | würden schälen<br>würdet schälen<br>würden schälen | würde geschält haben<br>würdest geschält haben<br>würde geschält haben | würden geschält haben<br>würdet geschält haben<br>würden geschält haben |

## EXAMPLES

Angelika, kannst du mir Äpfel schälen helfen?
Die Kartoffeln brauchen für dieses Rezept nicht geschält zu werden.

Angelika, can you help me peel apples?
The potatoes don't have to be peeled for this recipe.

**schalten**

to switch, to change gears

**Auxiliary verb:** haben **Past participle:** geschaltet

**Imperative:** Schalte! Schaltet! Schalten Sie!

| Mode | Simple Tenses | | Compound Tenses | |
|---|---|---|---|---|
| | *Singular* | *Plural* | *Singular* | *Plural* |
| Indicative | **Present** | | **Present Perfect** | |
| | schalte<br>schaltest<br>schaltet | schalten<br>schaltet<br>schalten | habe geschaltet<br>hast geschaltet<br>hat geschaltet | haben geschaltet<br>habt geschaltet<br>haben geschaltet |
| | **Past** | | **Past Perfect** | |
| | schaltete<br>schaltetest<br>schaltete | schalteten<br>schaltetet<br>schalteten | hatte geschaltet<br>hattest geschaltet<br>hatte geschaltet | hatten geschaltet<br>hattet geschaltet<br>hatten geschaltet |
| | **Future** | | **Future Perfect** | |
| | werde schalten<br>wirst schalten<br>wird schalten | werden schalten<br>werdet schalten<br>werden schalten | werde geschaltet haben<br>wirst geschaltet haben<br>wird geschaltet haben | werden geschaltet haben<br>werdet geschaltet haben<br>werden geschaltet haben |
| Subjunctive | **Present** | | **Present Perfect** | |
| | schalte<br>schaltest<br>schalte | schalten<br>schaltet<br>schalten | habe geschaltet<br>habest geschaltet<br>habe geschaltet | haben geschaltet<br>habet geschaltet<br>haben geschaltet |
| | **Past** | | **Past Perfect** | |
| | schaltete<br>schaltetest<br>schaltete | schalteten<br>schaltetet<br>schalteten | hätte geschaltet<br>hättest geschaltet<br>hätte geschaltet | hätten geschaltet<br>hättet geschaltet<br>hätten geschaltet |
| | **Future** | | **Future Perfect** | |
| | werde schalten<br>werdest schalten<br>werde schalten | werden schalten<br>werdet schalten<br>werden schalten | werde geschaltet haben<br>werdest geschaltet haben<br>werde geschaltet haben | werden geschaltet haben<br>werdet geschaltet haben<br>werden geschaltet haben |
| | **Present and Future Conditional** | | **Past Conditional** | |
| | würde schalten<br>würdest schalten<br>würde schalten | würden schalten<br>würdet schalten<br>würden schalten | würde geschaltet haben<br>würdest geschaltet haben<br>würde geschaltet haben | würden geschaltet haben<br>würdet geschaltet haben<br>würden geschaltet haben |

**Note:** This verb is usually used with prefixes—*abschalten, ausschalten, einschalten* (to disconnect, to switch off, to switch on). See the third example below.

## EXAMPLES

| | |
|---|---|
| Hast du noch nicht vom ersten in den zweiten Gang geschaltet? | Haven't you shifted from first into second gear yet? |
| Wenn er frei schalten und walten könnte, würde er nach Amerika auswandern. | If he were his own master, he'd emigrate to America. |
| Hast du den Fernseher ausgeschaltet? | Did you switch off the TV? |

**sich schämen**
to be ashamed
**Auxiliary verb:** haben **Past participle:** geschämt
**Imperative:** Schäme dich! Schämt euch! Schämen Sie sich!

| Mode | Simple Tenses | | Compound Tenses | |
|---|---|---|---|---|
| | *Singular* | *Plural* | *Singular* | *Plural* |
| Indicative | **Present** | | **Present Perfect** | |
| | schäme<br>schämst<br>schämt | schämen<br>schämt<br>schämen | habe geschämt<br>hast geschämt<br>hat geschämt | haben geschämt<br>habt geschämt<br>haben geschämt |
| | **Past** | | **Past Perfect** | |
| | schämte<br>schämtest<br>schämte | schämten<br>schämtet<br>schämten | hatte geschämt<br>hattest geschämt<br>hatte geschämt | hatten geschämt<br>hattet geschämt<br>hatten geschämt |
| | **Future** | | **Future Perfect** | |
| | werde schämen<br>wirst schämen<br>wird schämen | werden schämen<br>werdet schämen<br>werden schämen | werde geschämt haben<br>wirst geschämt haben<br>wird geschämt haben | werden geschämt haben<br>werdet geschämt haben<br>werden geschämt haben |
| Subjunctive | **Present** | | **Present Perfect** | |
| | schäme<br>schämest<br>schäme | schämen<br>schämet<br>schämen | habe geschämt<br>habest geschämt<br>habe geschämt | haben geschämt<br>habet geschämt<br>haben geschämt |
| | **Past** | | **Past Perfect** | |
| | schämte<br>schämtest<br>schämte | schämten<br>schämtet<br>schämten | hätte geschämt<br>hättest geschämt<br>hätte geschämt | hätten geschämt<br>hättet geschämt<br>hätten geschämt |
| | **Future** | | **Future Perfect** | |
| | werde schämen<br>werdest schämen<br>werde schämen | werden schämen<br>werdet schämen<br>werden schämen | werde geschämt haben<br>werdest geschämt haben<br>werde geschämt haben | werden geschämt haben<br>werdet geschämt haben<br>werden geschämt haben |
| | **Present and Future Conditional** | | **Past Conditional** | |
| | würde schämen<br>würdest schämen<br>würde schämen | würden schämen<br>würdet schämen<br>würden schämen | würde geschämt haben<br>würdest geschämt haben<br>würde geschämt haben | würden geschämt haben<br>würdet geschämt haben<br>würden geschämt haben |

## EXAMPLES

Er schämt sich dafür, dass sein Anzug so alt und schmutzig ist.
He's ashamed that his suit is so old and dirty.

Ich schämte mich für die grausamen Worte meines Sohnes.
I was ashamed of my son's cruel words.

**schärfen**
to sharpen, to whet
**Auxiliary verb:** haben **Past participle:** geschärft
**Imperative:** Schärfe! Schärft! Schärfen Sie!

| Mode | Simple Tenses | | Compound Tenses | |
|---|---|---|---|---|
| | *Singular* | *Plural* | *Singular* | *Plural* |
| Indicative | **Present** | | **Present Perfect** | |
| | schärfe<br>schärfst<br>schärft | schärfen<br>schärft<br>schärfen | habe geschärft<br>hast geschärft<br>hat geschärft | haben geschärft<br>habt geschärft<br>haben geschärft |
| | **Past** | | **Past Perfect** | |
| | schärfte<br>schärftest<br>schärfte | schärften<br>schärftet<br>schärften | hatte geschärft<br>hattest geschärft<br>hatte geschärft | hatten geschärft<br>hattet geschärft<br>hatten geschärft |
| | **Future** | | **Future Perfect** | |
| | werde schärfen<br>wirst schärfen<br>wird schärfen | werden schärfen<br>werdet schärfen<br>werden schärfen | werde geschärft haben<br>wirst geschärft haben<br>wird geschärft haben | werden geschärft haben<br>werdet geschärft haben<br>werden geschärft haben |
| Subjunctive | **Present** | | **Present Perfect** | |
| | schärfe<br>schärfest<br>schärfe | schärfen<br>schärfet<br>schärfen | habe geschärft<br>habest geschärft<br>habe geschärft | haben geschärft<br>habet geschärft<br>haben geschärft |
| | **Past** | | **Past Perfect** | |
| | schärfte<br>schärftest<br>schärfte | schärften<br>schärftet<br>schärften | hätte geschärft<br>hättest geschärft<br>hätte geschärft | hätten geschärft<br>hättet geschärft<br>hätten geschärft |
| | **Future** | | **Future Perfect** | |
| | werde schärfen<br>werdest schärfen<br>werde schärfen | werden schärfen<br>werdet schärfen<br>werden schärfen | werde geschärft haben<br>werdest geschärft haben<br>werde geschärft haben | werden geschärft haben<br>werdet geschärft haben<br>werden geschärft haben |
| | **Present and Future Conditional** | | **Past Conditional** | |
| | würde schärfen<br>würdest schärfen<br>würde schärfen | würden schärfen<br>würdet schärfen<br>würden schärfen | würde geschärft haben<br>würdest geschärft haben<br>würde geschärft haben | würden geschärft haben<br>würdet geschärft haben<br>würden geschärft haben |

## EXAMPLES

| | |
|---|---|
| Mein Bruder versuchte die alten Klingen zu schärfen. | My brother tried to sharpen the old blades. |
| Diese Messer müssen geschärft werden. | These knives have to be sharpened. |
| Diese Kräuter sollen den Verstand schärfen. | These herbs are supposed to sharpen the mind. |

**schätzen**
to value, to esteem
**Auxiliary verb:** haben **Past participle:** geschätzt
**Imperative:** Schätze! Schätzt! Schätzen Sie!

| Mode | Simple Tenses | | Compound Tenses | |
|---|---|---|---|---|
| | *Singular* | *Plural* | *Singular* | *Plural* |
| Indicative | **Present** | | **Present Perfect** | |
| | schätze<br>schätzt<br>schätzt | schätzen<br>schätzt<br>schätzen | habe geschätzt<br>hast geschätzt<br>hat geschätzt | haben geschätzt<br>habt geschätzt<br>haben geschätzt |
| | **Past** | | **Past Perfect** | |
| | schätzte<br>schätztest<br>schätzte | schätzten<br>schätztet<br>schätzten | hatte geschätzt<br>hattest geschätzt<br>hatte geschätzt | hatten geschätzt<br>hattet geschätzt<br>hatten geschätzt |
| | **Future** | | **Future Perfect** | |
| | werde schätzen<br>wirst schätzen<br>wird schätzen | werden schätzen<br>werdet schätzen<br>werden schätzen | werde geschätzt haben<br>wirst geschätzt haben<br>wird geschätzt haben | werden geschätzt haben<br>werdet geschätzt haben<br>werden geschätzt haben |
| Subjunctive | **Present** | | **Present Perfect** | |
| | schätze<br>schätzest<br>schätze | schätzen<br>schätzet<br>schätzen | habe geschätzt<br>habest geschätzt<br>habe geschätzt | haben geschätzt<br>habet geschätzt<br>haben geschätzt |
| | **Past** | | **Past Perfect** | |
| | schätzte<br>schätztest<br>schätzte | schätzten<br>schätztet<br>schätzten | hätte geschätzt<br>hättest geschätzt<br>hätte geschätzt | hätten geschätzt<br>hättet geschätzt<br>hätten geschätzt |
| | **Future** | | **Future Perfect** | |
| | werde schätzen<br>werdest schätzen<br>werde schätzen | werden schätzen<br>werdet schätzen<br>werden schätzen | werde geschätzt haben<br>werdest geschätzt haben<br>werde geschätzt haben | werden geschätzt haben<br>werdet geschätzt haben<br>werden geschätzt haben |
| | **Present and Future Conditional** | | **Past Conditional** | |
| | würde schätzen<br>würdest schätzen<br>würde schätzen | würden schätzen<br>würdet schätzen<br>würden schätzen | würde geschätzt haben<br>würdest geschätzt haben<br>würde geschätzt haben | würden geschätzt haben<br>würdet geschätzt haben<br>würden geschätzt haben |

## EXAMPLES

Ich schätze mich glücklich, mit so guten Kollgen zusammen arbeiten zu dürfen.
I consider myself lucky to be able to work with such good colleagues.

Der Schaden vom Tornado wurde auf 10.000 Dollar geschätzt.
The damage from the tornado was estimated at $10,000.

**schauen**

to see, to look, to gaze

**Auxiliary verb:** haben **Past participle:** geschaut

**Imperative:** Schaue! Schaut! Schauen Sie!

| Mode | Simple Tenses | | Compound Tenses | |
|---|---|---|---|---|
| | *Singular* | *Plural* | *Singular* | *Plural* |
| Indicative | **Present** | | **Present Perfect** | |
| | schaue<br>schaust<br>schaut | schauen<br>schaut<br>schauen | habe geschaut<br>hast geschaut<br>hat geschaut | haben geschaut<br>habt geschaut<br>haben geschaut |
| | **Past** | | **Past Perfect** | |
| | schaute<br>schautest<br>schaute | schauten<br>schautet<br>schauten | hatte geschaut<br>hattest geschaut<br>hatte geschaut | hatten geschaut<br>hattet geschaut<br>hatten geschaut |
| | **Future** | | **Future Perfect** | |
| | werde schauen<br>wirst schauen<br>wird schauen | werden schauen<br>werdet schauen<br>werden schauen | werde geschaut haben<br>wirst geschaut haben<br>wird geschaut haben | werden geschaut haben<br>werdet geschaut haben<br>werden geschaut haben |
| Subjunctive | **Present** | | **Present Perfect** | |
| | schaue<br>schauest<br>schaue | schauen<br>schauet<br>schauen | habe geschaut<br>habest geschaut<br>habe geschaut | haben geschaut<br>habet geschaut<br>haben geschaut |
| | **Past** | | **Past Perfect** | |
| | schaute<br>schautest<br>schaute | schauten<br>schautet<br>schauten | hätte geschaut<br>hättest geschaut<br>hätte geschaut | hätten geschaut<br>hättet geschaut<br>hätten geschaut |
| | **Future** | | **Future Perfect** | |
| | werde schauen<br>werdest schauen<br>werde schauen | werden schauen<br>werdet schauen<br>werden schauen | werde geschaut haben<br>werdest geschaut haben<br>werde geschaut haben | werden geschaut haben<br>werdet geschaut haben<br>werden geschaut haben |
| | **Present and Future Conditional** | | **Past Conditional** | |
| | würde schauen<br>würdest schauen<br>würde schauen | würden schauen<br>würdet schauen<br>würden schauen | würde geschaut haben<br>würdest geschaut haben<br>würde geschaut haben | würden geschaut haben<br>würdet geschaut haben<br>würden geschaut haben |

## EXAMPLES

Niemand kann in die Zukunft schauen.
No one can look into the future.

Die Kinder schauten aus dem Fenster, um die Parade zu beobachten.
The children looked out the window to watch the parade.

**schaufeln**
to shovel, to dig
**Auxiliary verb:** haben **Past participle:** geschaufelt
**Imperative:** Schaufele! Schaufelt! Schaufeln Sie!

| Mode | Simple Tenses | | Compound Tenses | |
|---|---|---|---|---|
| | *Singular* | *Plural* | *Singular* | *Plural* |
| Indicative | **Present** | | **Present Perfect** | |
| | schaufele<br>schaufelst<br>schaufelt | schaufeln<br>schaufelt<br>schaufeln | habe geschaufelt<br>hast geschaufelt<br>hat geschaufelt | haben geschaufelt<br>habt geschaufelt<br>haben geschaufelt |
| | **Past** | | **Past Perfect** | |
| | schaufelte<br>schaufeltest<br>schaufelte | schaufelten<br>schaufeltet<br>schaufelten | hatte geschaufelt<br>hattest geschaufelt<br>hatte geschaufelt | hatten geschaufelt<br>hattet geschaufelt<br>hatten geschaufelt |
| | **Future** | | **Future Perfect** | |
| | werde schaufeln<br>wirst schaufeln<br>wird schaufeln | werden schaufeln<br>werdet schaufeln<br>werden schaufeln | werde geschaufelt haben<br>wirst geschaufelt haben<br>wird geschaufelt haben | werden geschaufelt haben<br>werdet geschaufelt haben<br>werden geschaufelt haben |
| Subjunctive | **Present** | | **Present Perfect** | |
| | schaufele<br>schaufelst<br>schaufele | schaufeln<br>schaufelt<br>schaufeln | habe geschaufelt<br>habest geschaufelt<br>habe geschaufelt | haben geschaufelt<br>habet geschaufelt<br>haben geschaufelt |
| | **Past** | | **Past Perfect** | |
| | schaufelte<br>schaufeltest<br>schaufelte | schaufelten<br>schaufeltet<br>schaufelten | hätte geschaufelt<br>hättest geschaufelt<br>hätte geschaufelt | hätten geschaufelt<br>hättet geschaufelt<br>hätten geschaufelt |
| | **Future** | | **Future Perfect** | |
| | werde schaufeln<br>werdest schaufeln<br>werde schaufeln | werden schaufeln<br>werdet schaufeln<br>werden schaufeln | werde geschaufelt haben<br>werdest geschaufelt haben<br>werde geschaufelt haben | werden geschaufelt haben<br>werdet geschaufelt haben<br>werden geschaufelt haben |
| | **Present and Future Conditional** | | **Past Conditional** | |
| | würde schaufeln<br>würdest schaufeln<br>würde schaufeln | würden schaufeln<br>würdet schaufeln<br>würden schaufeln | würde geschaufelt haben<br>würdest geschaufelt haben<br>würde geschaufelt haben | würden geschaufelt haben<br>würdet geschaufelt haben<br>würden geschaufelt haben |

## EXAMPLES

Die Kinder haben gern im Sandkasten geschaufelt.
The children liked shoveling in the sandbox.

Könnt ihr mir beim Schaufeln helfen?
Can you help me shovel?

**schaukeln**

to swing, to rock, to pitch

**Auxiliary verb:** haben **Past participle:** geschaukelt

**Imperative:** Schaukele! Schaukelt! Schaukeln Sie!

| Mode | Simple Tenses | | Compound Tenses | |
|---|---|---|---|---|
| | *Singular* | *Plural* | *Singular* | *Plural* |
| Indicative | **Present** | | **Present Perfect** | |
| | schaukele<br>schaukelst<br>schaukelt | schaukeln<br>schaukelt<br>schaukeln | habe geschaukelt<br>hast geschaukelt<br>hat geschaukelt | haben geschaukelt<br>habt geschaukelt<br>haben geschaukelt |
| | **Past** | | **Past Perfect** | |
| | schaukelte<br>schaukeltest<br>schaukelte | schaukelten<br>schaukeltet<br>schaukelten | hatte geschaukelt<br>hattest geschaukelt<br>hatte geschaukelt | hatten geschaukelt<br>hattet geschaukelt<br>hatten geschaukelt |
| | **Future** | | **Future Perfect** | |
| | werde schaukeln<br>wirst schaukeln<br>wird schaukeln | werden schaukeln<br>werdet schaukeln<br>werden schaukeln | werde geschaukelt haben<br>wirst geschaukelt haben<br>wird geschaukelt haben | werden geschaukelt haben<br>werdet geschaukelt haben<br>werden geschaukelt haben |
| Subjunctive | **Present** | | **Present Perfect** | |
| | schaukele<br>schaukelst<br>schaukele | schaukeln<br>schaukelt<br>schaukeln | habe geschaukelt<br>habest geschaukelt<br>habe geschaukelt | haben geschaukelt<br>habet geschaukelt<br>haben geschaukelt |
| | **Past** | | **Past Perfect** | |
| | schaukelte<br>schaukeltest<br>schaukelte | schaukelten<br>schaukeltet<br>schaukelten | hätte geschaukelt<br>hättest geschaukelt<br>hätte geschaukelt | hätten geschaukelt<br>hättet geschaukelt<br>hätten geschaukelt |
| | **Future** | | **Future Perfect** | |
| | werde schaukeln<br>werdest schaukeln<br>werde schaukeln | werden schaukeln<br>werdet schaukeln<br>werden schaukeln | werde geschaukelt haben<br>werdest geschaukelt haben<br>werde geschaukelt haben | werden geschaukelt haben<br>werdet geschaukelt haben<br>werden geschaukelt haben |
| | **Present and Future Conditional** | | **Past Conditional** | |
| | würde schaukeln<br>würdest schaukeln<br>würde schaukeln | würden schaukeln<br>würdet schaukeln<br>würden schaukeln | würde geschaukelt haben<br>würdest geschaukelt haben<br>würde geschaukelt haben | würden geschaukelt haben<br>würdet geschaukelt haben<br>würden geschaukelt haben |

## EXAMPLES

| | |
|---|---|
| Während des Sturmes hat das Schiff furchtbar geschaukelt. | During the storm, the ship pitched terribly. |
| Die Kinder wurden von meinem Neffen geschaukelt. | The children were swung by my nephew. |

**scheiden (sich)**
to separate, to part, to divorce
**Auxiliary verb:** haben **Past participle:** geschieden
**Imperative:** Scheide! Scheidet! Scheiden Sie!

| Mode | Simple Tenses | | Compound Tenses | |
|---|---|---|---|---|
| | *Singular* | *Plural* | *Singular* | *Plural* |
| Indicative | **Present** | | **Present Perfect** | |
| | scheide<br>scheidest<br>scheidet | scheiden<br>scheidet<br>scheiden | habe geschieden<br>hast geschieden<br>hat geschieden | haben geschieden<br>habt geschieden<br>haben geschieden |
| | **Past** | | **Past Perfect** | |
| | schied<br>schiedest<br>schied | schieden<br>schiedet<br>schieden | hatte geschieden<br>hattest geschieden<br>hatte geschieden | hatten geschieden<br>hattet geschieden<br>hatten geschieden |
| | **Future** | | **Future Perfect** | |
| | werde scheiden<br>wirst scheiden<br>wird scheiden | werden scheiden<br>werdet scheiden<br>werden scheiden | werde geschieden haben<br>wirst geschieden haben<br>wird geschieden haben | werden geschieden haben<br>werdet geschieden haben<br>werden geschieden haben |
| Subjunctive | **Present** | | **Present Perfect** | |
| | scheide<br>scheidest<br>scheide | scheiden<br>scheidet<br>scheiden | habe geschieden<br>habest geschieden<br>habe geschieden | haben geschieden<br>habet geschieden<br>haben geschieden |
| | **Past** | | **Past Perfect** | |
| | schiede<br>schiedest<br>schiede | schieden<br>schiedet<br>schieden | hätte geschieden<br>hättest geschieden<br>hätte geschieden | hätten geschieden<br>hättet geschieden<br>hätten geschieden |
| | **Future** | | **Future Perfect** | |
| | werde scheiden<br>werdest scheiden<br>werde scheiden | werden scheiden<br>werdet scheiden<br>werden scheiden | werde geschieden haben<br>werdest geschieden haben<br>werde geschieden haben | werden geschieden haben<br>werdet geschieden haben<br>werden geschieden haben |
| | **Present and Future Conditional** | | **Past Conditional** | |
| | würde scheiden<br>würdest scheiden<br>würde scheiden | würden scheiden<br>würdet scheiden<br>würden scheiden | würde geschieden haben<br>würdest geschieden haben<br>würde geschieden haben | würden geschieden haben<br>würdet geschieden haben<br>würden geschieden haben |

## EXAMPLES

Hier scheiden sich unsere Wege.
Our paths part here.

Meine Eltern denken daran, sich scheiden zu lassen.
My parents are thinking of getting a divorce.

**scheinen**

to shine, to appear, to seem

**Auxiliary verb:** haben **Past participle:** geschienen

**Imperative:** Scheine! Scheint! Scheinen Sie!

| Mode | Simple Tenses | | Compound Tenses | |
|---|---|---|---|---|
| | *Singular* | *Plural* | *Singular* | *Plural* |
| Indicative | **Present** | | **Present Perfect** | |
| | scheine<br>scheinst<br>scheint | scheinen<br>scheint<br>scheinen | habe geschienen<br>hast geschienen<br>hat geschienen | haben geschienen<br>habt geschienen<br>haben geschienen |
| | **Past** | | **Past Perfect** | |
| | schien<br>schienst<br>schien | schienen<br>schient<br>schienen | hatte geschienen<br>hattest geschienen<br>hatte geschienen | hatten geschienen<br>hattet geschienen<br>hatten geschienen |
| | **Future** | | **Future Perfect** | |
| | werde scheinen<br>wirst scheinen<br>wird scheinen | werden scheinen<br>werdet scheinen<br>werden scheinen | werde geschienen haben<br>wirst geschienen haben<br>wird geschienen haben | werden geschienen haben<br>werdet geschienen haben<br>werden geschienen haben |
| Subjunctive | **Present** | | **Present Perfect** | |
| | scheine<br>scheinest<br>scheine | scheinen<br>scheinet<br>scheinen | habe geschienen<br>habest geschienen<br>habe geschienen | haben geschienen<br>habet geschienen<br>haben geschienen |
| | **Past** | | **Past Perfect** | |
| | schiene<br>schienest<br>schiene | schienen<br>schienet<br>schienen | hätte geschienen<br>hättest geschienen<br>hätte geschienen | hätten geschienen<br>hättet geschienen<br>hätten geschienen |
| | **Future** | | **Future Perfect** | |
| | werde scheinen<br>werdest scheinen<br>werde scheinen | werden scheinen<br>werdet scheinen<br>werden scheinen | werde geschienen haben<br>werdest geschienen haben<br>werde geschienen haben | werden geschienen haben<br>werdet geschienen haben<br>werden geschienen haben |
| | **Present and Future Conditional** | | **Past Conditional** | |
| | würde scheinen<br>würdest scheinen<br>würde scheinen | würden scheinen<br>würdet scheinen<br>würden scheinen | würde geschienen haben<br>würdest geschienen haben<br>würde geschienen haben | würden geschienen haben<br>würdet geschienen haben<br>würden geschienen haben |

## EXAMPLES

| | |
|---|---|
| Heute scheint die Sonne. | The sun is shining today. |
| Diese Rechnung scheint nicht zu stimmen. | This bill seems to be wrong. |
| Der Mann schien sehr arm zu sein. | The man appeared to be very poor. |

**scheitern**
to fail, to run aground, to be wrecked
**Auxiliary verb:** sein **Past participle:** gescheitert
**Imperative:** Scheitere! Scheitert! Scheitern Sie!

| Mode | Simple Tenses | | Compound Tenses | |
|---|---|---|---|---|
| | *Singular* | *Plural* | *Singular* | *Plural* |
| Indicative | **Present** | | **Present Perfect** | |
| | scheitere<br>scheiterst<br>scheitert | scheitern<br>scheitert<br>scheitern | bin gescheitert<br>bist gescheitert<br>ist gescheitert | sind gescheitert<br>seid gescheitert<br>sind gescheitert |
| | **Past** | | **Past Perfect** | |
| | scheiterte<br>scheitertest<br>scheiterte | scheiterten<br>scheitertet<br>scheiterten | war gescheitert<br>warst gescheitert<br>war gescheitert | waren gescheitert<br>wart gescheitert<br>waren gescheitert |
| | **Future** | | **Future Perfect** | |
| | werde scheitern<br>wirst scheitern<br>wird scheitern | werden scheitern<br>werdet scheitern<br>werden scheitern | werde gescheitert sein<br>wirst gescheitert sein<br>wird gescheitert sein | werden gescheitert sein<br>werdet gescheitert sein<br>werden gescheitert sein |
| Subjunctive | **Present** | | **Present Perfect** | |
| | scheitere<br>scheiterst<br>scheitere | scheitern<br>scheitert<br>scheitern | sei gescheitert<br>seiest gescheitert<br>sei gescheitert | seien gescheitert<br>seiet gescheitert<br>seien gescheitert |
| | **Past** | | **Past Perfect** | |
| | scheiterte<br>scheitertest<br>scheiterte | scheiterten<br>scheitertet<br>scheiterten | wäre gescheitert<br>wärest gescheitert<br>wäre gescheitert | wären gescheitert<br>wäret gescheitert<br>wären gescheitert |
| | **Future** | | **Future Perfect** | |
| | werde scheitern<br>werdest scheitern<br>werde scheitern | werden scheitern<br>werdet scheitern<br>werden scheitern | werde gescheitert sein<br>werdest gescheitert sein<br>werde gescheitert sein | werden gescheitert sein<br>werdet gescheitert sein<br>werden gescheitert sein |
| | **Present and Future Conditional** | | **Past Conditional** | |
| | würde scheitern<br>würdest scheitern<br>würde scheitern | würden scheitern<br>würdet scheitern<br>würden scheitern | würde gescheitert sein<br>würdest gescheitert sein<br>würde gescheitert sein | würden gescheitert sein<br>würdet gescheitert sein<br>würden gescheitert sein |

## EXAMPLES

Erik scheiterte an der Aufnahmeprüfung für die Musikhochschule.
Erik failed the entrance exam for the school of music.

Bei diesem Unwetter wird das kleine Schiff auf jeden Fall scheitern.
The ship will surely be wrecked in such bad weather.

**schelten**
to scold, to reproach
**Auxiliary verb:** haben **Past participle:** gescholten
**Imperative:** Schilt! Scheltet! Schelten Sie!

| Mode | Simple Tenses | | Compound Tenses | |
|---|---|---|---|---|
| | *Singular* | *Plural* | *Singular* | *Plural* |
| Indicative | **Present** | | **Present Perfect** | |
| | schelte<br>schiltst<br>schilt | schelten<br>scheltet<br>schelten | habe gescholten<br>hast gescholten<br>hat gescholten | haben gescholten<br>habt gescholten<br>haben gescholten |
| | **Past** | | **Past Perfect** | |
| | schalt<br>schaltest<br>schalt | schalten<br>schaltet<br>schalten | hatte gescholten<br>hattest gescholten<br>hatte gescholten | hatten gescholten<br>hattet gescholten<br>hatten gescholten |
| | **Future** | | **Future Perfect** | |
| | werde schelten<br>wirst schelten<br>wird schelten | werden schelten<br>werdet schelten<br>werden schelten | werde gescholten haben<br>wirst gescholten haben<br>wird gescholten haben | werden gescholten haben<br>werdet gescholten haben<br>werden gescholten haben |
| Subjunctive | **Present** | | **Present Perfect** | |
| | schelte<br>scheltest<br>schelte | schelten<br>scheltet<br>schelten | habe gescholten<br>habest gescholten<br>habe gescholten | haben gescholten<br>habet gescholten<br>haben gescholten |
| | **Past** | | **Past Perfect** | |
| | schölte<br>schöltest<br>schölte | schölten<br>schöltet<br>schölten | hätte gescholten<br>hättest gescholten<br>hätte gescholten | hätten gescholten<br>hättet gescholten<br>hätten gescholten |
| | **Future** | | **Future Perfect** | |
| | werde schelten<br>werdest schelten<br>werde schelten | werden schelten<br>werdet schelten<br>werden schelten | werde gescholten haben<br>werdest gescholten haben<br>werde gescholten haben | werden gescholten haben<br>werdet gescholten haben<br>werden gescholten haben |
| | **Present and Future Conditional** | | **Past Conditional** | |
| | würde schelten<br>würdest schelten<br>würde schelten | würden schelten<br>würdet schelten<br>würden schelten | würde gescholten haben<br>würdest gescholten haben<br>würde gescholten haben | würden gescholten haben<br>würdet gescholten haben<br>würden gescholten haben |

## EXAMPLES

Als die böse Stiefmutter ihn schalt, fing der kleine Hans an zu weinen.
When the wicked stepmother scolded him, little Hans began to cry.

Der Graf schalt seinen Diener wegen der schmutzigen Kalesche.
The count scolded his servant because of the dirty coach.

**schenken**
to give, to present
**Auxiliary verb:** haben **Past participle:** geschenkt
**Imperative:** Schenke! Schenkt! Schenken Sie!

| Mode | Simple Tenses | | Compound Tenses | |
|---|---|---|---|---|
| | *Singular* | *Plural* | *Singular* | *Plural* |
| Indicative | **Present** | | **Present Perfect** | |
| | schenke<br>schenkst<br>schenkt | schenken<br>schenkt<br>schenken | habe geschenkt<br>hast geschenkt<br>hat geschenkt | haben geschenkt<br>habt geschenkt<br>haben geschenkt |
| | **Past** | | **Past Perfect** | |
| | schenkte<br>schenktest<br>schenkte | schenkten<br>schenktet<br>schenkten | hatte geschenkt<br>hattest geschenkt<br>hatte geschenkt | hatten geschenkt<br>hattet geschenkt<br>hatten geschenkt |
| | **Future** | | **Future Perfect** | |
| | werde schenken<br>wirst schenken<br>wird schenken | werden schenken<br>werdet schenken<br>werden schenken | werde geschenkt haben<br>wirst geschenkt haben<br>wird geschenkt haben | werden geschenkt haben<br>werdet geschenkt haben<br>werden geschenkt haben |
| Subjunctive | **Present** | | **Present Perfect** | |
| | schenke<br>schenkest<br>schenke | schenken<br>schenket<br>schenken | habe geschenkt<br>habest geschenkt<br>habe geschenkt | haben geschenkt<br>habet geschenkt<br>haben geschenkt |
| | **Past** | | **Past Perfect** | |
| | schenkte<br>schenktest<br>schenkte | schenkten<br>schenktet<br>schenkten | hätte geschenkt<br>hättest geschenkt<br>hätte geschenkt | hätten geschenkt<br>hättet geschenkt<br>hätten geschenkt |
| | **Future** | | **Future Perfect** | |
| | werde schenken<br>werdest schenken<br>werde schenken | werden schenken<br>werdet schenken<br>werden schenken | werde geschenkt haben<br>werdest geschenkt haben<br>werde geschenkt haben | werden geschenkt haben<br>werdet geschenkt haben<br>werden geschenkt haben |
| | **Present and Future Conditional** | | **Past Conditional** | |
| | würde schenken<br>würdest schenken<br>würde schenken | würden schenken<br>würdet schenken<br>würden schenken | würde geschenkt haben<br>würdest geschenkt haben<br>würde geschenkt haben | würden geschenkt haben<br>würdet geschenkt haben<br>würden geschenkt haben |

## EXAMPLES

Was wirst du Ingrid zum Geburtstag schenken?
What are you going to give Ingrid for her birthday?

Ich habe den Pullover beinahe geschenkt bekommen.
I got the sweater for a real bargain.

**scheren**
to shear, to shave, to clip
**Auxiliary verb:** haben **Past participle:** geschoren
**Imperative:** Schier! Schert! Scheren Sie!

| Mode | Simple Tenses | | Compound Tenses | |
|---|---|---|---|---|
| | *Singular* | *Plural* | *Singular* | *Plural* |
| Indicative | **Present** | | **Present Perfect** | |
| | schere<br>scherst<br>schert | scheren<br>schert<br>scheren | habe geschoren<br>hast geschoren<br>hat geschoren | haben geschoren<br>habt geschoren<br>haben geschoren |
| | **Past** | | **Past Perfect** | |
| | schor<br>schorst<br>schor | schoren<br>schort<br>schoren | hatte geschoren<br>hattest geschoren<br>hatte geschoren | hatten geschoren<br>hattet geschoren<br>hatten geschoren |
| | **Future** | | **Future Perfect** | |
| | werde scheren<br>wirst scheren<br>wird scheren | werden scheren<br>werdet scheren<br>werden scheren | werde geschoren haben<br>wirst geschoren haben<br>wird geschoren haben | werden geschoren haben<br>werdet geschoren haben<br>werden geschoren haben |
| Subjunctive | **Present** | | **Present Perfect** | |
| | schere<br>scherest<br>schere | scheren<br>scheret<br>scheren | habe geschoren<br>habest geschoren<br>habe geschoren | haben geschoren<br>habet geschoren<br>haben geschoren |
| | **Past** | | **Past Perfect** | |
| | schöre<br>schörest<br>schöre | schören<br>schöret<br>schören | hätte geschoren<br>hättest geschoren<br>hätte geschoren | hätten geschoren<br>hättet geschoren<br>hätten geschoren |
| | **Future** | | **Future Perfect** | |
| | werde scheren<br>werdest scheren<br>werde scheren | werden scheren<br>werdet scheren<br>werden scheren | werde geschoren haben<br>werdest geschoren haben<br>werde geschoren haben | werden geschoren haben<br>werdet geschoren haben<br>werden geschoren haben |
| | **Present and Future Conditional** | | **Past Conditional** | |
| | würde scheren<br>würdest scheren<br>würde scheren | würden scheren<br>würdet scheren<br>würden scheren | würde geschoren haben<br>würdest geschoren haben<br>würde geschoren haben | würden geschoren haben<br>würdet geschoren haben<br>würden geschoren haben |

## EXAMPLES

Wir werden Herrn Bauer beim Scheren der Schafe helfen.
We're going to help Mr. Bauer with the shearing of the sheep.

Manche Mönche müssen sich die Haare scheren lassen.
Some monks have to have their heads shaved.

**scherzen**
to joke, to have fun
**Auxiliary verb:** haben **Past participle:** gescherzt
**Imperative:** Scherze! Scherzt! Scherzen Sie!

| Mode | Simple Tenses | | Compound Tenses | |
|---|---|---|---|---|
| | *Singular* | *Plural* | *Singular* | *Plural* |
| Indicative | **Present** | | **Present Perfect** | |
| | scherze<br>scherzt<br>scherzt | scherzen<br>scherzt<br>scherzen | habe gescherzt<br>hast gescherzt<br>hat gescherzt | haben gescherzt<br>habt gescherzt<br>haben gescherzt |
| | **Past** | | **Past Perfect** | |
| | scherzte<br>scherztest<br>scherzte | scherzten<br>scherztet<br>scherzten | hatte gescherzt<br>hattest gescherzt<br>hatte gescherzt | hatten gescherzt<br>hattet gescherzt<br>hatten gescherzt |
| | **Future** | | **Future Perfect** | |
| | werde scherzen<br>wirst scherzen<br>wird scherzen | werden scherzen<br>werdet scherzen<br>werden scherzen | werde gescherzt haben<br>wirst gescherzt haben<br>wird gescherzt haben | werden gescherzt haben<br>werdet gescherzt haben<br>werden gescherzt haben |
| Subjunctive | **Present** | | **Present Perfect** | |
| | scherze<br>scherzest<br>scherze | scherzen<br>scherzet<br>scherzen | habe gescherzt<br>habest gescherzt<br>habe gescherzt | haben gescherzt<br>habet gescherzt<br>haben gescherzt |
| | **Past** | | **Past Perfect** | |
| | scherzte<br>scherztest<br>scherzte | scherzten<br>scherztet<br>scherzten | hätte gescherzt<br>hättest gescherzt<br>hätte gescherzt | hätten gescherzt<br>hättet gescherzt<br>hätten gescherzt |
| | **Future** | | **Future Perfect** | |
| | werde scherzen<br>werdest scherzen<br>werde scherzen | werden scherzen<br>werdet scherzen<br>werden scherzen | werde gescherzt haben<br>werdest gescherzt haben<br>werde gescherzt haben | werden gescherzt haben<br>werdet gescherzt haben<br>werden gescherzt haben |
| | **Present and Future Conditional** | | **Past Conditional** | |
| | würde scherzen<br>würdest scherzen<br>würde scherzen | würden scherzen<br>würdet scherzen<br>würden scherzen | würde gescherzt haben<br>würdest gescherzt haben<br>würde gescherzt haben | würden gescherzt haben<br>würdet gescherzt haben<br>würden gescherzt haben |

## EXAMPLES

Das ist aber nicht zum Scherzen.
That's really no joking matter.

Tante Gerda verstand nicht, dass er scherzte, und glaubte ihm aufs Wort.
Aunt Gerda didn't understand that he was joking and took him at his word.

**schicken**
to send
**Auxiliary verb:** haben **Past participle:** geschickt
**Imperative:** Schicke! Schickt! Schicken Sie!

| Mode | Simple Tenses | | Compound Tenses | |
|---|---|---|---|---|
| | *Singular* | *Plural* | *Singular* | *Plural* |
| Indicative | **Present** | | **Present Perfect** | |
| | schicke<br>schickst<br>schickt | schicken<br>schickt<br>schicken | habe geschickt<br>hast geschickt<br>hat geschickt | haben geschickt<br>habt geschickt<br>haben geschickt |
| | **Past** | | **Past Perfect** | |
| | schickte<br>schicktest<br>schickte | schickten<br>schicktet<br>schickten | hatte geschickt<br>hattest geschickt<br>hatte geschickt | hatten geschickt<br>hattet geschickt<br>hatten geschickt |
| | **Future** | | **Future Perfect** | |
| | werde schicken<br>wirst schicken<br>wird schicken | werden schicken<br>werdet schicken<br>werden schicken | werde geschickt haben<br>wirst geschickt haben<br>wird geschickt haben | werden geschickt haben<br>werdet geschickt haben<br>werden geschickt haben |
| Subjunctive | **Present** | | **Present Perfect** | |
| | schicke<br>schickest<br>schicke | schicken<br>schicket<br>schicken | habe geschickt<br>habest geschickt<br>habe geschickt | haben geschickt<br>habet geschickt<br>haben geschickt |
| | **Past** | | **Past Perfect** | |
| | schickte<br>schicktest<br>schickte | schickten<br>schicktet<br>schickten | hätte geschickt<br>hättest geschickt<br>hätte geschickt | hätten geschickt<br>hättet geschickt<br>hätten geschickt |
| | **Future** | | **Future Perfect** | |
| | werde schicken<br>werdest schicken<br>werde schicken | werden schicken<br>werdet schicken<br>werden schicken | werde geschickt haben<br>werdest geschickt haben<br>werde geschickt haben | werden geschickt haben<br>werdet geschickt haben<br>werden geschickt haben |
| | **Present and Future Conditional** | | **Past Conditional** | |
| | würde schicken<br>würdest schicken<br>würde schicken | würden schicken<br>würdet schicken<br>würden schicken | würde geschickt haben<br>würdest geschickt haben<br>würde geschickt haben | würden geschickt haben<br>würdet geschickt haben<br>würden geschickt haben |

## EXAMPLES

Meine Kusine in London hat mir ein Geschenk geschickt.
My cousin in London sent me a gift.

Meine Eltern wollen mich auf eine Privatschule schicken.
My parents want to send me to a private school.

**schieben**
to shove, to push, to move
**Auxiliary verb:** haben **Past participle:** geschoben
**Imperative:** Schiebe! Schiebt! Schieben Sie!

| Mode | Simple Tenses | | Compound Tenses | |
|---|---|---|---|---|
| | *Singular* | *Plural* | *Singular* | *Plural* |
| Indicative | **Present** | | **Present Perfect** | |
| | schiebe<br>schiebst<br>schiebt | schieben<br>schiebt<br>schieben | habe geschoben<br>hast geschoben<br>hat geschoben | haben geschoben<br>habt geschoben<br>haben geschoben |
| | **Past** | | **Past Perfect** | |
| | schob<br>schobst<br>schob | schoben<br>schobt<br>schoben | hatte geschoben<br>hattest geschoben<br>hatte geschoben | hatten geschoben<br>hattet geschoben<br>hatten geschoben |
| | **Future** | | **Future Perfect** | |
| | werde schieben<br>wirst schieben<br>wird schieben | werden schieben<br>werdet schieben<br>werden schieben | werde geschoben haben<br>wirst geschoben haben<br>wird geschoben haben | werden geschoben haben<br>werdet geschoben haben<br>werden geschoben haben |
| Subjunctive | **Present** | | **Present Perfect** | |
| | schiebe<br>schiebest<br>schiebe | schieben<br>schiebet<br>schieben | habe geschoben<br>habest geschoben<br>habe geschoben | haben geschoben<br>habet geschoben<br>haben geschoben |
| | **Past** | | **Past Perfect** | |
| | schöbe<br>schöbest<br>schöbe | schöben<br>schöbet<br>schöben | hätte geschoben<br>hättest geschoben<br>hätte geschoben | hätten geschoben<br>hättet geschoben<br>hätten geschoben |
| | **Future** | | **Future Perfect** | |
| | werde schieben<br>werdest schieben<br>werde schieben | werden schieben<br>werdet schieben<br>werden schieben | werde geschoben haben<br>werdest geschoben haben<br>werde geschoben haben | werden geschoben haben<br>werdet geschoben haben<br>werden geschoben haben |
| | **Present and Future Conditional** | | **Past Conditional** | |
| | würde schieben<br>würdest schieben<br>würde schieben | würden schieben<br>würdet schieben<br>würden schieben | würde geschoben haben<br>würdest geschoben haben<br>würde geschoben haben | würden geschoben haben<br>würdet geschoben haben<br>würden geschoben haben |

**Note:** With inseparable prefixes, the principal parts of this verb are, for example, *verschiebt, verschob, hat verschoben.* With separable prefixes, the principal parts are, for example, *schiebt vor, schob vor, hat vorgeschoben.*

## EXAMPLES

Niemand hilft uns den schweren Tisch an die Wand zu schieben.
No one helps us to push the heavy table against the wall.

Mein ältester Sohn muss immer ein bisschen geschoben werden.
My oldest son always has to be pushed a little (to get things done).

**schießen**
to shoot, to fire
**Auxiliary verb:** haben **Past participle:** geschossen
**Imperative:** Schieße! Schießt! Schießen Sie!

| Mode | Simple Tenses | | Compound Tenses | |
|---|---|---|---|---|
| | *Singular* | *Plural* | *Singular* | *Plural* |
| Indicative | **Present** | | **Present Perfect** | |
| | schieße<br>schießt<br>schießt | schießen<br>schießt<br>schießen | habe geschossen<br>hast geschossen<br>hat geschossen | haben geschossen<br>habt geschossen<br>haben geschossen |
| | **Past** | | **Past Perfect** | |
| | schoss<br>schossest<br>schoss | schossen<br>schosst<br>schossen | hatte geschossen<br>hattest geschossen<br>hatte geschossen | hatten geschossen<br>hattet geschossen<br>hatten geschossen |
| | **Future** | | **Future Perfect** | |
| | werde schießen<br>wirst schießen<br>wird schießen | werden schießen<br>werdet schießen<br>werden schießen | werde geschossen haben<br>wirst geschossen haben<br>wird geschossen haben | werden geschossen haben<br>werdet geschossen haben<br>werden geschossen haben |
| Subjunctive | **Present** | | **Present Perfect** | |
| | schieße<br>schießest<br>schieße | schießen<br>schießet<br>schießen | habe geschossen<br>habest geschossen<br>habe geschossen | haben geschossen<br>habet geschossen<br>haben geschossen |
| | **Past** | | **Past Perfect** | |
| | schösse<br>schössest<br>schösse | schössen<br>schösset<br>schössen | hätte geschossen<br>hättest geschossen<br>hätte geschossen | hätten geschossen<br>hättet geschossen<br>hätten geschossen |
| | **Future** | | **Future Perfect** | |
| | werde schießen<br>werdest schießen<br>werde schießen | werden schießen<br>werdet schießen<br>werden schießen | werde geschossen haben<br>werdest geschossen haben<br>werde geschossen haben | werden geschossen haben<br>werdet geschossen haben<br>werden geschossen haben |
| | **Present and Future Conditional** | | **Past Conditional** | |
| | würde schießen<br>würdest schießen<br>würde schießen | würden schießen<br>würdet schießen<br>würden schießen | würde geschossen haben<br>würdest geschossen haben<br>würde geschossen haben | würden geschossen haben<br>würdet geschossen haben<br>würden geschossen haben |

**Note:** With inseparable prefixes, the principal parts of this verb are, for example, *beschießt, beschoss, hat beschossen.* With separable prefixes, the principal parts are, for example, *schießt nieder, schoss nieder, hat niedergeschossen.*

## EXAMPLES

Der neue Stürmer schoss schon in seinem ersten Spiel ein Tor.
The new forward scored a goal in his very first game.

Als es hell wurde, wurde wieder geschossen.
When it became light, shots were fired once again.

**schildern**
to delineate, to depict, to portray
**Auxiliary verb:** haben **Past participle:** geschildert
**Imperative:** Schildere! Schildert! Schildern Sie!

| Mode | Simple Tenses | | Compound Tenses | |
|---|---|---|---|---|
| | *Singular* | *Plural* | *Singular* | *Plural* |
| Indicative | **Present** | | **Present Perfect** | |
| | schildere<br>schilderst<br>schildert | schildern<br>schildert<br>schildern | habe geschildert<br>hast geschildert<br>hat geschildert | haben geschildert<br>habt geschildert<br>haben geschildert |
| | **Past** | | **Past Perfect** | |
| | schilderte<br>schildertest<br>schilderte | schilderten<br>schildertet<br>schilderten | hatte geschildert<br>hattest geschildert<br>hatte geschildert | hatten geschildert<br>hattet geschildert<br>hatten geschildert |
| | **Future** | | **Future Perfect** | |
| | werde schildern<br>wirst schildern<br>wird schildern | werden schildern<br>werdet schildern<br>werden schildern | werde geschildert haben<br>wirst geschildert haben<br>wird geschildert haben | werden geschildert haben<br>werdet geschildert haben<br>werden geschildert haben |
| Subjunctive | **Present** | | **Present Perfect** | |
| | schildere<br>schilderst<br>schildere | schildern<br>schildert<br>schildern | habe geschildert<br>habest geschildert<br>habe geschildert | haben geschildert<br>habet geschildert<br>haben geschildert |
| | **Past** | | **Past Perfect** | |
| | schilderte<br>schildertest<br>schilderte | schilderten<br>schildertet<br>schilderten | hätte geschildert<br>hättest geschildert<br>hätte geschildert | hätten geschildert<br>hättet geschildert<br>hätten geschildert |
| | **Future** | | **Future Perfect** | |
| | werde schildern<br>werdest schildern<br>werde schildern | werden schildern<br>werdet schildern<br>werden schildern | werde geschildert haben<br>werdest geschildert haben<br>werde geschildert haben | werden geschildert haben<br>werdet geschildert haben<br>werden geschildert haben |
| | **Present and Future Conditional** | | **Past Conditional** | |
| | würde schildern<br>würdest schildern<br>würde schildern | würden schildern<br>würdet schildern<br>würden schildern | würde geschildert haben<br>würdest geschildert haben<br>würde geschildert haben | würden geschildert haben<br>würdet geschildert haben<br>würden geschildert haben |

## EXAMPLES

Er hat Gretchen als eine schwache Frau geschildert.
He portrayed Gretchen as a weak woman.

Der Artikel schilderte den Hergang des Unfalls.
The article described the events that led up to the accident.

**schimmern**
to glitter, to glisten
**Auxiliary verb:** haben **Past participle:** geschimmert
**Imperative:** Schimmere! Schimmert! Schimmern Sie!

| Mode | Simple Tenses | | Compound Tenses | |
|---|---|---|---|---|
| | *Singular* | *Plural* | *Singular* | *Plural* |
| Indicative | **Present** | | **Present Perfect** | |
| | schimmere<br>schimmerst<br>schimmert | schimmern<br>schimmert<br>schimmern | habe geschimmert<br>hast geschimmert<br>hat geschimmert | haben geschimmert<br>habt geschimmert<br>haben geschimmert |
| | **Past** | | **Past Perfect** | |
| | schimmerte<br>schimmertest<br>schimmerte | schimmerten<br>schimmertet<br>schimmerten | hatte geschimmert<br>hattest geschimmert<br>hatte geschimmert | hatten geschimmert<br>hattet geschimmert<br>hatten geschimmert |
| | **Future** | | **Future Perfect** | |
| | werde schimmern<br>wirst schimmern<br>wird schimmern | werden schimmern<br>werdet schimmern<br>werden schimmern | werde geschimmert haben<br>wirst geschimmert haben<br>wird geschimmert haben | werden geschimmert haben<br>werdet geschimmert haben<br>werden geschimmert haben |
| Subjunctive | **Present** | | **Present Perfect** | |
| | schimmere<br>schimmerst<br>schimmere | schimmern<br>schimmert<br>schimmern | habe geschimmert<br>habest geschimmert<br>habe geschimmert | haben geschimmert<br>habet geschimmert<br>haben geschimmert |
| | **Past** | | **Past Perfect** | |
| | schimmerte<br>schimmertest<br>schimmerte | schimmerten<br>schimmertet<br>schimmerten | hätte geschimmert<br>hättest geschimmert<br>hätte geschimmert | hätten geschimmert<br>hättet geschimmert<br>hätten geschimmert |
| | **Future** | | **Future Perfect** | |
| | werde schimmern<br>werdest schimmern<br>werde schimmern | werden schimmern<br>werdet schimmern<br>werden schimmern | werde geschimmert haben<br>werdest geschimmert haben<br>werde geschimmert haben | werden geschimmert haben<br>werdet geschimmert haben<br>werden geschimmert haben |
| | **Present and Future Conditional** | | **Past Conditional** | |
| | würde schimmern<br>würdest schimmern<br>würde schimmern | würden schimmern<br>würdet schimmern<br>würden schimmern | würde geschimmert haben<br>würdest geschimmert haben<br>würde geschimmert haben | würden geschimmert haben<br>würdet geschimmert haben<br>würden geschimmert haben |

## EXAMPLES

| | |
|---|---|
| Im Mondschein schimmerte der See wie Kristall. | In the moonlight, the lake glistened like crystal. |
| Oben sehen wir endlose, schimmernde Sterne. | Overhead, we see endless glistening stars. |

**schimpfen**
to scold, to complain
**Auxiliary verb:** haben **Past participle:** geschimpft
**Imperative:** Schimpfe! Schimpft! Schimpfen Sie!

| Mode | Simple Tenses | | Compound Tenses | |
|---|---|---|---|---|
| | *Singular* | *Plural* | *Singular* | *Plural* |
| Indicative | **Present** | | **Present Perfect** | |
| | schimpfe<br>schimpfst<br>schimpft | schimpfen<br>schimpft<br>schimpfen | habe geschimpft<br>hast geschimpft<br>hat geschimpft | haben geschimpft<br>habt geschimpft<br>haben geschimpft |
| | **Past** | | **Past Perfect** | |
| | schimpfte<br>schimpftest<br>schimpfte | schimpften<br>schimpftet<br>schimpften | hatte geschimpft<br>hattest geschimpft<br>hatte geschimpft | hatten geschimpft<br>hattet geschimpft<br>hatten geschimpft |
| | **Future** | | **Future Perfect** | |
| | werde schimpfen<br>wirst schimpfen<br>wird schimpfen | werden schimpfen<br>werdet schimpfen<br>werden schimpfen | werde geschimpft haben<br>wirst geschimpft haben<br>wird geschimpft haben | werden geschimpft haben<br>werdet geschimpft haben<br>werden geschimpft haben |
| Subjunctive | **Present** | | **Present Perfect** | |
| | schimpfe<br>schimpfest<br>schimpfe | schimpfen<br>schimpfet<br>schimpfen | habe geschimpft<br>habest geschimpft<br>habe geschimpft | haben geschimpft<br>habet geschimpft<br>haben geschimpft |
| | **Past** | | **Past Perfect** | |
| | schimpfte<br>schimpftest<br>schimpfte | schimpften<br>schimpftet<br>schimpften | hätte geschimpft<br>hättest geschimpft<br>hätte geschimpft | hätten geschimpft<br>hättet geschimpft<br>hätten geschimpft |
| | **Future** | | **Future Perfect** | |
| | werde schimpfen<br>werdest schimpfen<br>werde schimpfen | werden schimpfen<br>werdet schimpfen<br>werden schimpfen | werde geschimpft haben<br>werdest geschimpft haben<br>werde geschimpft haben | werden geschimpft haben<br>werdet geschimpft haben<br>werden geschimpft haben |
| | **Present and Future Conditional** | | **Past Conditional** | |
| | würde schimpfen<br>würdest schimpfen<br>würde schimpfen | würden schimpfen<br>würdet schimpfen<br>würden schimpfen | würde geschimpft haben<br>würdest geschimpft haben<br>würde geschimpft haben | würden geschimpft haben<br>würdet geschimpft haben<br>würden geschimpft haben |

## EXAMPLES

Viele Leute schimpften über den neuen Chef.
A lot of people complained about the new boss.

Raffael ist ein artiger Junge und sein Vater muss selten mit ihm schimpfen.
Raffael is a good boy, and his father rarely has to scold him.

**schinden (sich)**
to flay, to torture, to work extremely hard
**Auxiliary verb:** haben **Past participle:** geschunden
**Imperative:** Schinde! Schindet! Schinden Sie!

| Mode | Simple Tenses | | Compound Tenses | |
|---|---|---|---|---|
| | *Singular* | *Plural* | *Singular* | *Plural* |
| Indicative | **Present** | | **Present Perfect** | |
| | schinde<br>schindest<br>schindet | schinden<br>schindet<br>schinden | habe geschunden<br>hast geschunden<br>hat geschunden | haben geschunden<br>habt geschunden<br>haben geschunden |
| | **Past** | | **Past Perfect** | |
| | schund<br>schundest<br>schund | schunden<br>schundet<br>schunden | hatte geschunden<br>hattest geschunden<br>hatte geschunden | hatten geschunden<br>hattet geschunden<br>hatten geschunden |
| | **Future** | | **Future Perfect** | |
| | werde schinden<br>wirst schinden<br>wird schinden | werden schinden<br>werdet schinden<br>werden schinden | werde geschunden haben<br>wirst geschunden haben<br>wird geschunden haben | werden geschunden haben<br>werdet geschunden haben<br>werden geschunden haben |
| Subjunctive | **Present** | | **Present Perfect** | |
| | schinde<br>schindest<br>schinde | schinden<br>schindet<br>schinden | habe geschunden<br>habest geschunden<br>habe geschunden | haben geschunden<br>habet geschunden<br>haben geschunden |
| | **Past** | | **Past Perfect** | |
| | schünde<br>schündest<br>schünde | schünden<br>schündet<br>schünden | hätte geschunden<br>hättest geschunden<br>hätte geschunden | hätten geschunden<br>hättet geschunden<br>hätten geschunden |
| | **Future** | | **Future Perfect** | |
| | werde schinden<br>werdest schinden<br>werde schinden | werden schinden<br>werdet schinden<br>werden schinden | werde geschunden haben<br>werdest geschunden haben<br>werde geschunden haben | werden geschunden haben<br>werdet geschunden haben<br>werden geschunden haben |
| | **Present and Future Conditional** | | **Past Conditional** | |
| | würde schinden<br>würdest schinden<br>würde schinden | würden schinden<br>würdet schinden<br>würden schinden | würde geschunden haben<br>würdest geschunden haben<br>würde geschunden haben | würden geschunden haben<br>würdet geschunden haben<br>würden geschunden haben |

## EXAMPLES

Die Ochsen wurden bis aufs Blut geschunden. — The oxen were made to work until they bled.

Manche Mädchen schinden sich für ihre schlanke Linie. — Some girls go through torture to be thin.

**schlachten**
to slaughter, to massacre
**Auxiliary verb:** haben **Past participle:** geschlachtet
**Imperative:** Schlachte! Schlachtet! Schlachten Sie!

| Mode | Simple Tenses | | Compound Tenses | |
|---|---|---|---|---|
| | *Singular* | *Plural* | *Singular* | *Plural* |
| Indicative | **Present** | | **Present Perfect** | |
| | schlachte<br>schlachtest<br>schlachtet | schlachten<br>schlachtet<br>schlachten | habe geschlachtet<br>hast geschlachtet<br>hat geschlachtet | haben geschlachtet<br>habt geschlachtet<br>haben geschlachtet |
| | **Past** | | **Past Perfect** | |
| | schlachtete<br>schlachtetest<br>schlachtete | schlachteten<br>schlachtetet<br>schlachteten | hatte geschlachtet<br>hattest geschlachtet<br>hatte geschlachtet | hatten geschlachtet<br>hattet geschlachtet<br>hatten geschlachtet |
| | **Future** | | **Future Perfect** | |
| | werde schlachten<br>wirst schlachten<br>wird schlachten | werden schlachten<br>werdet schlachten<br>werden schlachten | werde geschlachtet haben<br>wirst geschlachtet haben<br>wird geschlachtet haben | werden geschlachtet haben<br>werdet geschlachtet haben<br>werden geschlachtet haben |
| Subjunctive | **Present** | | **Present Perfect** | |
| | schlachte<br>schlachtest<br>schlachte | schlachten<br>schlachtet<br>schlachten | habe geschlachtet<br>habest geschlachtet<br>habe geschlachtet | haben geschlachtet<br>habet geschlachtet<br>haben geschlachtet |
| | **Past** | | **Past Perfect** | |
| | schlachtete<br>schlachtetest<br>schlachtete | schlachteten<br>schlachtetet<br>schlachteten | hätte geschlachtet<br>hättest geschlachtet<br>hätte geschlachtet | hätten geschlachtet<br>hättet geschlachtet<br>hätten geschlachtet |
| | **Future** | | **Future Perfect** | |
| | werde schlachten<br>werdest schlachten<br>werde schlachten | werden schlachten<br>werdet schlachten<br>werden schlachten | werde geschlachtet haben<br>werdest geschlachtet haben<br>werde geschlachtet haben | werden geschlachtet haben<br>werdet geschlachtet haben<br>werden geschlachtet haben |
| | **Present and Future Conditional** | | **Past Conditional** | |
| | würde schlachten<br>würdest schlachten<br>würde schlachten | würden schlachten<br>würdet schlachten<br>würden schlachten | würde geschlachtet haben<br>würdest geschlachtet haben<br>würde geschlachtet haben | würden geschlachtet haben<br>würdet geschlachtet haben<br>würden geschlachtet haben |

## EXAMPLES

Zu Silvester hat mein Opa immer einen Karpfen geschlachtet und gekocht.
For New Year's Eve my grandpa always killed and cooked a carp.

Herr Bauer wird zwei Schweine und eine Kuh schlachten.
Mr. Bauer is going to slaughter two pigs and a cow.

**schlafen**
to sleep
**Auxiliary verb:** haben **Past participle:** geschlafen
**Imperative:** Schlafe! Schlaft! Schlafen Sie!

| Mode | Simple Tenses | | Compound Tenses | |
|---|---|---|---|---|
| | *Singular* | *Plural* | *Singular* | *Plural* |
| Indicative | **Present** | | **Present Perfect** | |
| | schlafe<br>schläfst<br>schläft | schlafen<br>schlaft<br>schlafen | habe geschlafen<br>hast geschlafen<br>hat geschlafen | haben geschlafen<br>habt geschlafen<br>haben geschlafen |
| | **Past** | | **Past Perfect** | |
| | schlief<br>schliefst<br>schlief | schliefen<br>schlieft<br>schliefen | hatte geschlafen<br>hattest geschlafen<br>hatte geschlafen | hatten geschlafen<br>hattet geschlafen<br>hatten geschlafen |
| | **Future** | | **Future Perfect** | |
| | werde schlafen<br>wirst schlafen<br>wird schlafen | werden schlafen<br>werdet schlafen<br>werden schlafen | werde geschlafen haben<br>wirst geschlafen haben<br>wird geschlafen haben | werden geschlafen haben<br>werdet geschlafen haben<br>werden geschlafen haben |
| Subjunctive | **Present** | | **Present Perfect** | |
| | schlafe<br>schlafest<br>schlafe | schlafen<br>schlafet<br>schlafen | habe geschlafen<br>habest geschlafen<br>habe geschlafen | haben geschlafen<br>habet geschlafen<br>haben geschlafen |
| | **Past** | | **Past Perfect** | |
| | schliefe<br>schliefest<br>schliefe | schliefen<br>schliefet<br>schliefen | hätte geschlafen<br>hättest geschlafen<br>hätte geschlafen | hätten geschlafen<br>hättet geschlafen<br>hätten geschlafen |
| | **Future** | | **Future Perfect** | |
| | werde schlafen<br>werdest schlafen<br>werde schlafen | werden schlafen<br>werdet schlafen<br>werden schlafen | werde geschlafen haben<br>werdest geschlafen haben<br>werde geschlafen haben | werden geschlafen haben<br>werdet geschlafen haben<br>werden geschlafen haben |
| | **Present and Future Conditional** | | **Past Conditional** | |
| | würde schlafen<br>würdest schlafen<br>würde schlafen | würden schlafen<br>würdet schlafen<br>würden schlafen | würde geschlafen haben<br>würdest geschlafen haben<br>würde geschlafen haben | würden geschlafen haben<br>würdet geschlafen haben<br>würden geschlafen haben |

**Note:** With separable prefixes, the principal parts of this verb are, for example, *schläft aus, schlief aus, hat ausgeschlafen.*

# EXAMPLES

| | |
|---|---|
| Vier Töchter haben in einem kleinen Schlafzimmer geschlafen. | Four daughters slept in a little bedroom. |
| Es regnet noch. Du kannst bei uns schlafen. | It's still raining. You can sleep at our house. |

**schlagen**
to beat, to strike
**Auxiliary verb:** haben **Past participle:** geschlagen
**Imperative:** Schlage! Schlagt! Schlagen Sie!

| Mode | Simple Tenses | | Compound Tenses | |
|---|---|---|---|---|
| | *Singular* | *Plural* | *Singular* | *Plural* |
| Indicative | **Present** | | **Present Perfect** | |
| | schlage<br>schlägst<br>schlägt | schlagen<br>schlagt<br>schlagen | habe geschlagen<br>hast geschlagen<br>hat geschlagen | haben geschlagen<br>habt geschlagen<br>haben geschlagen |
| | **Past** | | **Past Perfect** | |
| | schlug<br>schlugst<br>schlug | schlugen<br>schlugt<br>schlugen | hatte geschlagen<br>hattest geschlagen<br>hatte geschlagen | hatten geschlagen<br>hattet geschlagen<br>hatten geschlagen |
| | **Future** | | **Future Perfect** | |
| | werde schlagen<br>wirst schlagen<br>wird schlagen | werden schlagen<br>werdet schlagen<br>werden schlagen | werde geschlagen haben<br>wirst geschlagen haben<br>wird geschlagen haben | werden geschlagen haben<br>werdet geschlagen haben<br>werden geschlagen haben |
| Subjunctive | **Present** | | **Present Perfect** | |
| | schlage<br>schlagest<br>schlage | schlagen<br>schlaget<br>schlagen | habe geschlagen<br>habest geschlagen<br>habe geschlagen | haben geschlagen<br>habet geschlagen<br>haben geschlagen |
| | **Past** | | **Past Perfect** | |
| | schlüge<br>schlügest<br>schlüge | schlügen<br>schlüget<br>schlügen | hätte geschlagen<br>hättest geschlagen<br>hätte geschlagen | hätten geschlagen<br>hättet geschlagen<br>hätten geschlagen |
| | **Future** | | **Future Perfect** | |
| | werde schlagen<br>werdest schlagen<br>werde schlagen | werden schlagen<br>werdet schlagen<br>werden schlagen | werde geschlagen haben<br>werdest geschlagen haben<br>werde geschlagen haben | werden geschlagen haben<br>werdet geschlagen haben<br>werden geschlagen haben |
| | **Present and Future Conditional** | | **Past Conditional** | |
| | würde schlagen<br>würdest schlagen<br>würde schlagen | würden schlagen<br>würdet schlagen<br>würden schlagen | würde geschlagen haben<br>würdest geschlagen haben<br>würde geschlagen haben | würden geschlagen haben<br>würdet geschlagen haben<br>würden geschlagen haben |

**Note:** With inseparable prefixes, the principal parts of this verb are, for example, *erschlägt, erschlug, hat erschlagen.* With separable prefixes, the principal parts are, for example, *schlägt nieder, schlug nieder, hat niedergeschlagen.*

## EXAMPLES

| | |
|---|---|
| Sie hat dem Dieb den Revolver aus der Hand geschlagen. | She knocked the revolver out of the thief's hand. |
| Herr Keller schlug seine Kinder selten. | Mr. Keller seldom beat his children. |

**sich schlängeln**
to twist, to wind
**Auxiliary verb:** haben **Past participle:** geschlängelt
**Imperative:** Schlängele! Schlängelt! Schlängeln Sie!

| Mode | Simple Tenses | | Compound Tenses | |
|---|---|---|---|---|
| | *Singular* | *Plural* | *Singular* | *Plural* |
| Indicative | **Present** | | **Present Perfect** | |
| | schlängele<br>schlängelst<br>schlängelt | schlängeln<br>schlängelt<br>schlängeln | habe geschlängelt<br>hast geschlängelt<br>hat geschlängelt | haben geschlängelt<br>habt geschlängelt<br>haben geschlängelt |
| | **Past** | | **Past Perfect** | |
| | schlängelte<br>schlängeltest<br>schlängelte | schlängelten<br>schlängeltet<br>schlängelten | hatte geschlängelt<br>hattest geschlängelt<br>hatte geschlängelt | hatten geschlängelt<br>hattet geschlangelt<br>hatten geschlängelt |
| | **Future** | | **Future Perfect** | |
| | werde schlängeln<br>wirst schlängeln<br>wird schlängeln | werden schlängeln<br>werdet schlängeln<br>werden schlängeln | werde geschlängelt haben<br>wirst geschlängelt haben<br>wird geschlängelt haben | werden geschlängelt haben<br>werdet geschlängelt haben<br>werden geschlängelt haben |
| Subjunctive | **Present** | | **Present Perfect** | |
| | schlängele<br>schlängelst<br>schlängele | schlängeln<br>schlängelt<br>schlängeln | habe geschlängelt<br>habest geschlängelt<br>habe geschlängelt | haben geschlängelt<br>habet geschlängelt<br>haben geschlängelt |
| | **Past** | | **Past Perfect** | |
| | schlängelte<br>schlängeltest<br>schlängelte | schlängelten<br>schlängeltet<br>schlängelten | hätte geschlängelt<br>hättest geschlängelt<br>hätte geschlängelt | hätten geschlängelt<br>hättet geschlängelt<br>hätten geschlängelt |
| | **Future** | | **Future Perfect** | |
| | werde schlängeln<br>werdest schlängeln<br>werde schlängeln | werden schlängeln<br>werdet schlängeln<br>werden schlängeln | werde geschlängelt haben<br>werdest geschlängelt haben<br>werde geschlängelt haben | werden geschlängelt haben<br>werdet geschlängelt haben<br>werden geschlängelt haben |
| | **Present and Future Conditional** | | **Past Conditional** | |
| | würde schlängeln<br>würdest schlängeln<br>würde schlängeln | würden schlängeln<br>würdet schlängeln<br>würden schlängeln | würde geschlängelt haben<br>würdest geschlängelt haben<br>würde geschlängelt haben | würden geschlängelt haben<br>würdet geschlängelt haben<br>würden geschlängelt haben |

## EXAMPLES

Zwischen Neudorf und unserem Bauernhof gibt es nur einen gefährlichen, sich schlängelnden Weg.
There's only a dangerous, winding path between Neudorf and our farm.

Luise schlängelte sich durch die Konzertbesucher.
Luise was weaving her way through the concert-goers.

**schleichen**
to creep, to sneak, to crawl
**Auxiliary verb:** sein **Past participle:** geschlichen
**Imperative:** Schleiche! Schleicht! Schleichen Sie!

| Mode | Simple Tenses | | Compound Tenses | |
|---|---|---|---|---|
| | *Singular* | *Plural* | *Singular* | *Plural* |
| Indicative | **Present** | | **Present Perfect** | |
| | schleiche<br>schleichst<br>schleicht | schleichen<br>schleicht<br>schleichen | bin geschlichen<br>bist geschlichen<br>ist geschlichen | sind geschlichen<br>seid geschlichen<br>sind geschlichen |
| | **Past** | | **Past Perfect** | |
| | schlich<br>schlichst<br>schlich | schlichen<br>schlicht<br>schlichen | war geschlichen<br>warst geschlichen<br>war geschlichen | waren geschlichen<br>wart geschlichen<br>waren geschlichen |
| | **Future** | | **Future Perfect** | |
| | werde schleichen<br>wirst schleichen<br>wird schleichen | werden schleichen<br>werdet schleichen<br>werden schleichen | werde geschlichen sein<br>wirst geschlichen sein<br>wird geschlichen sein | werden geschlichen sein<br>werdet geschlichen sein<br>werden geschlichen sein |
| Subjunctive | **Present** | | **Present Perfect** | |
| | schleiche<br>schleichest<br>schleiche | schleichen<br>schleichet<br>schleichen | sei geschlichen<br>seiest geschlichen<br>sei geschlichen | seien geschlichen<br>seiet geschlichen<br>seien geschlichen |
| | **Past** | | **Past Perfect** | |
| | schliche<br>schlichest<br>schliche | schlichen<br>schlichet<br>schlichen | wäre geschlichen<br>wärest geschlichen<br>wäre geschlichen | wären geschlichen<br>wäret geschlichen<br>wären geschlichen |
| | **Future** | | **Future Perfect** | |
| | werde schleichen<br>werdest schleichen<br>werde schleichen | werden schleichen<br>werdet schleichen<br>werden schleichen | werde geschlichen sein<br>werdest geschlichen sein<br>werde geschlichen sein | werden geschlichen sein<br>werdet geschlichen sein<br>werden geschlichen sein |
| | **Present and Future Conditional** | | **Past Conditional** | |
| | würde schleichen<br>würdest schleichen<br>würde schleichen | würden schleichen<br>würdet schleichen<br>würden schleichen | würde geschlichen sein<br>würdest geschlichen sein<br>würde geschlichen sein | würden geschlichen sein<br>würdet geschlichen sein<br>würden geschlichen sein |

## EXAMPLES

Um Mitternacht ist der Junge aus dem Haus geschlichen.
Er schlich die Treppe hinunter.

At midnight, the boy sneaked out of the house.
He crept down the stairs.

**schleifen**
to grind, to polish, to drag
**Auxiliary verb:** haben **Past participle:** geschliffen
**Imperative:** Schleife! Schleift! Schleifen Sie!

| Mode | Simple Tenses | | Compound Tenses | |
|---|---|---|---|---|
| | *Singular* | *Plural* | *Singular* | *Plural* |
| Indicative | **Present** | | **Present Perfect** | |
| | schleife<br>schleifst<br>schleift | schleifen<br>schleift<br>schleifen | habe geschliffen<br>hast geschliffen<br>hat geschliffen | haben geschliffen<br>habt geschliffen<br>haben geschliffen |
| | **Past** | | **Past Perfect** | |
| | schliff<br>schliffst<br>schliff | schliffen<br>schlifft<br>schliffen | hatte geschliffen<br>hattest geschliffen<br>hatte geschliffen | hatten geschliffen<br>hattet geschliffen<br>hatten geschliffen |
| | **Future** | | **Future Perfect** | |
| | werde schleifen<br>wirst schleifen<br>wird schleifen | werden schleifen<br>werdet schleifen<br>werden schleifen | werde geschliffen haben<br>wirst geschliffen haben<br>wird geschliffen haben | werden geschliffen haben<br>werdet geschliffen haben<br>werden geschliffen haben |
| Subjunctive | **Present** | | **Present Perfect** | |
| | schleife<br>schleifest<br>schleife | schleifen<br>schleifet<br>schleifen | habe geschliffen<br>habest geschliffen<br>habe geschliffen | haben geschliffen<br>habet geschliffen<br>haben geschliffen |
| | **Past** | | **Past Perfect** | |
| | schliffe<br>schliffest<br>schliffe | schliffen<br>schliffet<br>schliffen | hätte geschliffen<br>hättest geschliffen<br>hätte geschliffen | hätten geschliffen<br>hättet geschliffen<br>hätten geschliffen |
| | **Future** | | **Future Perfect** | |
| | werde schleifen<br>werdest schleifen<br>werde schleifen | werden schleifen<br>werdet schleifen<br>werden schleifen | werde geschliffen haben<br>werdest geschliffen haben<br>werde geschliffen haben | werden geschliffen haben<br>werdet geschliffen haben<br>werden geschliffen haben |
| | **Present and Future Conditional** | | **Past Conditional** | |
| | würde schleifen<br>würdest schleifen<br>würde schleifen | würden schleifen<br>würdet schleifen<br>würden schleifen | würde geschliffen haben<br>würdest geschliffen haben<br>würde geschliffen haben | würden geschliffen haben<br>würdet geschliffen haben<br>würden geschliffen haben |

## EXAMPLES

Die neue Vase auf dem Klavier ist aus geschliffenem Glas.
The new vase on the piano is made of cut glass.

Meine Schwester schleift mich bestimmt wieder durch die Diskos.
My sister will probably drag me around the clubs again.

**schleppen (sich)**
to carry, to drag, to trail
**Auxiliary verb:** haben **Past participle:** geschleppt
**Imperative:** Schleppe! Schleppt! Schleppen Sie!

| Mode | Simple Tenses | | Compound Tenses | |
|---|---|---|---|---|
| | *Singular* | *Plural* | *Singular* | *Plural* |
| Indicative | **Present** | | **Present Perfect** | |
| | schleppe<br>schleppst<br>schleppt | schleppen<br>schleppt<br>schleppen | habe geschleppt<br>hast geschleppt<br>hat geschleppt | haben geschleppt<br>habt geschleppt<br>haben geschleppt |
| | **Past** | | **Past Perfect** | |
| | schleppte<br>schlepptest<br>schleppte | schleppten<br>schlepptet<br>schleppten | hatte geschleppt<br>hattest geschleppt<br>hatte geschleppt | hatten geschleppt<br>hattet geschleppt<br>hatten geschleppt |
| | **Future** | | **Future Perfect** | |
| | werde schleppen<br>wirst schleppen<br>wird schleppen | werden schleppen<br>werdet schleppen<br>werden schleppen | werde geschleppt haben<br>wirst geschleppt haben<br>wird geschleppt haben | werden geschleppt haben<br>werdet geschleppt haben<br>werden geschleppt haben |
| Subjunctive | **Present** | | **Present Perfect** | |
| | schleppe<br>schleppest<br>schleppe | schleppen<br>schleppet<br>schleppen | habe geschleppt<br>habest geschleppt<br>habe geschleppt | haben geschleppt<br>habet geschleppt<br>haben geschleppt |
| | **Past** | | **Past Perfect** | |
| | schleppte<br>schlepptest<br>schleppte | schleppten<br>schlepptet<br>schleppten | hätte geschleppt<br>hättest geschleppt<br>hätte geschleppt | hätten geschleppt<br>hättet geschleppt<br>hätten geschleppt |
| | **Future** | | **Future Perfect** | |
| | werde schleppen<br>werdest schleppen<br>werde schleppen | werden schleppen<br>werdet schleppen<br>werden schleppen | werde geschleppt haben<br>werdest geschleppt haben<br>werde geschleppt haben | werden geschleppt haben<br>werdet geschleppt haben<br>werden geschleppt haben |
| | **Present and Future Conditional** | | **Past Conditional** | |
| | würde schleppen<br>würdest schleppen<br>würde schleppen | würden schleppen<br>würdet schleppen<br>würden schleppen | würde geschleppt haben<br>würdest geschleppt haben<br>würde geschleppt haben | würden geschleppt haben<br>würdet geschleppt haben<br>würden geschleppt haben |

## EXAMPLES

Wie lange müssen wir diese schweren Koffer noch schleppen?
How much longer do we have to lug these heavy suitcases?

Erich hat einen Kater und schleppt sich langsam vom Schlafzimmer in die Küche.
Erich has a hangover and slowly drags himself from the bedroom to the kitchen.

**schließen**

to shut, to close, to lock

**Auxiliary verb:** haben **Past participle:** geschlossen

**Imperative:** Schließe! Schließt! Schließen Sie!

| Mode | Simple Tenses | | Compound Tenses | |
|---|---|---|---|---|
| | *Singular* | *Plural* | *Singular* | *Plural* |
| Indicative | **Present** | | **Present Perfect** | |
| | schließe<br>schließt<br>schließt | schließen<br>schließt<br>schließen | habe geschlossen<br>hast geschlossen<br>hat geschlossen | haben geschlossen<br>habt geschlossen<br>haben geschlossen |
| | **Past** | | **Past Perfect** | |
| | schloss<br>schlossest<br>schloss | schlossen<br>schlosst<br>schlossen | hatte geschlossen<br>hattest geschlossen<br>hatte geschlossen | hatten geschlossen<br>hattet geschlossen<br>hatten geschlossen |
| | **Future** | | **Future Perfect** | |
| | werde schließen<br>wirst schließen<br>wird schließen | werden schließen<br>werdet schließen<br>werden schließen | werde geschlossen haben<br>wirst geschlossen haben<br>wird geschlossen haben | werden geschlossen haben<br>werdet geschlossen haben<br>werden geschlossen haben |
| Subjunctive | **Present** | | **Present Perfect** | |
| | schließe<br>schließest<br>schließe | schließen<br>schließet<br>schließen | habe geschlossen<br>habest geschlossen<br>habe geschlossen | haben geschlossen<br>habet geschlossen<br>haben geschlossen |
| | **Past** | | **Past Perfect** | |
| | schlösse<br>schlössest<br>schlösse | schlössen<br>schlösset<br>schlössen | hätte geschlossen<br>hättest geschlossen<br>hätte geschlossen | hätten geschlossen<br>hättet geschlossen<br>hätten geschlossen |
| | **Future** | | **Future Perfect** | |
| | werde schließen<br>werdest schließen<br>werde schließen | werden schließen<br>werdet schließen<br>werden schließen | werde geschlossen haben<br>werdest geschlossen haben<br>werde geschlossen haben | werden geschlossen haben<br>werdet geschlossen haben<br>werden geschlossen haben |
| | **Present and Future Conditional** | | **Past Conditional** | |
| | würde schließen<br>würdest schließen<br>würde schließen | würden schließen<br>würdet schließen<br>würden schließen | würde geschlossen haben<br>würdest geschlossen haben<br>würde geschlossen haben | würden geschlossen haben<br>würdet geschlossen haben<br>würden geschlossen haben |

**Note:** With inseparable prefixes, the principal parts of this verb are, for example, *entschließt, entschloss, hat entschlossen.* With separable prefixes, the principal parts are, for example, *schließt auf, schloss auf, hat aufgeschlossen.*

## EXAMPLES

| | |
|---|---|
| Die zwei Feinde haben endlich Frieden geschlossen. | The two enemies finally made peace. |
| Herr Schäfer hat eine dritte Ehe geschlossen. Seine neue Frau ist eine reiche Witwe. | Mr. Schäfer has gone into his third marriage. His new wife is a rich widow. |
| Schließen Sie bitte die Tür! | Close the door please. |

**schlüpfen**

to hatch, to slip, to slide, to glide

**Auxiliary verb:** sein **Past participle:** geschlüpft

**Imperative:** Schlüpfe! Schlüpft! Schlüpfen Sie!

| Mode | Simple Tenses | | Compound Tenses | |
|---|---|---|---|---|
| | *Singular* | *Plural* | *Singular* | *Plural* |
| Indicative | **Present** | | **Present Perfect** | |
| | schlüpfe<br>schlüpfst<br>schlüpft | schlüpfen<br>schlüpft<br>schlüpfen | bin geschlüpft<br>bist geschlüpft<br>ist geschlüpft | sind geschlüpft<br>seid geschlüpft<br>sind geschlüpft |
| | **Past** | | **Past Perfect** | |
| | schlüpfte<br>schlüpftest<br>schlüpfte | schlüpften<br>schlüpftet<br>schlüpften | war geschlüpft<br>warst geschlüpft<br>war geschlüpft | waren geschlüpft<br>wart geschlüpft<br>waren geschlüpft |
| | **Future** | | **Future Perfect** | |
| | werde schlüpfen<br>wirst schlüpfen<br>wird schlüpfen | werden schlüpfen<br>werdet schlüpfen<br>werden schlüpfen | werde geschlüpft sein<br>wirst geschlüpft sein<br>wird geschlüpft sein | werden geschlüpft sein<br>werdet geschlüpft sein<br>werden geschlüpft sein |
| Subjunctive | **Present** | | **Present Perfect** | |
| | schlüpfe<br>schlüpfest<br>schlüpfe | schlüpfen<br>schlüpfet<br>schlüpfen | sei geschlüpft<br>seiest geschlüpft<br>sei geschlüpft | seien geschlüpft<br>seiet geschlüpft<br>seien geschlüpft |
| | **Past** | | **Past Perfect** | |
| | schlüpfte<br>schlüpftest<br>schlüpfte | schlüpften<br>schlüpftet<br>schlüpften | wäre geschlüpft<br>wärest geschlüpft<br>wäre geschlüpft | wären geschlüpft<br>wäret geschlüpft<br>wären geschlüpft |
| | **Future** | | **Future Perfect** | |
| | werde schlüpfen<br>werdest schlüpfen<br>werde schlüpfen | werden schlüpfen<br>werdet schlüpfen<br>werden schlüpfen | werde geschlüpft sein<br>werdest geschlüpft sein<br>werde geschlüpft sein | werden geschlüpft sein<br>werdet geschlüpft sein<br>werden geschlüpft sein |
| | **Present and Future Conditional** | | **Past Conditional** | |
| | würde schlüpfen<br>würdest schlüpfen<br>würde schlüpfen | würden schlüpfen<br>würdet schlüpfen<br>würden schlüpfen | würde geschlüpft sein<br>würdest geschlüpft sein<br>würde geschlüpft sein | würden geschlüpft sein<br>würdet geschlüpft sein<br>würden geschlüpft sein |

## EXAMPLES

Er kroch leise aus dem Bett und schlüpfte in seine Kleider.

He crawled quietly out of bed and slipped into his clothes.

Die Zwillinge schlüpfen unter das Federbett und schlafen ein.

The twins slip under the featherbed and fall asleep.

Mama, die Küken sind geschlüpft!

Mom, the chicks have hatched.

**schmähen**

to abuse, to belittle, to insult

**Auxiliary verb:** haben **Past participle:** geschmäht

**Imperative:** Schmähe! Schmäht! Schmähen Sie!

| Mode | Simple Tenses | | Compound Tenses | |
|---|---|---|---|---|
| | *Singular* | *Plural* | *Singular* | *Plural* |
| Indicative | **Present** | | **Present Perfect** | |
| | schmähe<br>schmähst<br>schmäht | schmähen<br>schmäht<br>schmähen | habe geschmäht<br>hast geschmäht<br>hat geschmäht | haben geschmäht<br>habt geschmäht<br>haben geschmäht |
| | **Past** | | **Past Perfect** | |
| | schmähte<br>schmähtest<br>schmähte | schmähten<br>schmähtet<br>schmähten | hatte geschmäht<br>hattest geschmäht<br>hatte geschmäht | hatten geschmäht<br>hattet geschmäht<br>hatten geschmäht |
| | **Future** | | **Future Perfect** | |
| | werde schmähen<br>wirst schmähen<br>wird schmähen | werden schmähen<br>werdet schmähen<br>werden schmähen | werde geschmäht haben<br>wirst geschmäht haben<br>wird geschmäht haben | werden geschmäht haben<br>werdet geschmäht haben<br>werden geschmäht haben |
| Subjunctive | **Present** | | **Present Perfect** | |
| | schmähe<br>schmähest<br>schmähe | schmähen<br>schmähet<br>schmähen | habe geschmäht<br>habest geschmäht<br>habe geschmäht | haben geschmäht<br>habet geschmäht<br>haben geschmäht |
| | **Past** | | **Past Perfect** | |
| | schmähte<br>schmähtest<br>schmähte | schmähten<br>schmähtet<br>schmähten | hätte geschmäht<br>hättest geschmäht<br>hätte geschmäht | hätten geschmäht<br>hättet geschmäht<br>hätten geschmäht |
| | **Future** | | **Future Perfect** | |
| | werde schmähen<br>werdest schmähen<br>werde schmähen | werden schmähen<br>werdet schmähen<br>werden schmähen | werde geschmäht haben<br>werdest geschmäht haben<br>werde geschmäht haben | werden geschmäht haben<br>werdet geschmäht haben<br>werden geschmäht haben |
| | **Present and Future Conditional** | | **Past Conditional** | |
| | würde schmähen<br>würdest schmähen<br>würde schmähen | würden schmähen<br>würdet schmähen<br>würden schmähen | würde geschmäht haben<br>würdest geschmäht haben<br>würde geschmäht haben | würden geschmäht haben<br>würdet geschmäht haben<br>würden geschmäht haben |

**Note:** With an inseperable prefix, the principal parts of this verb are, for example, *verschmäht, verschmähte, hat verschmäht.*

## EXAMPLES

Die Demonstranten schmähten den Poliker als Mörder und Verbrecher.

The demonstrators vilified the politician as a murderer and criminal.

Man sollte guten Rat nie verschmähen.

You should never scorn good advice.

**schmecken**
to taste
**Auxiliary verb:** haben **Past participle:** geschmeckt
**Imperative:** Schmecke! Schmeckt! Schmecken Sie!

| Mode | Simple Tenses | | Compound Tenses | |
|---|---|---|---|---|
| | *Singular* | *Plural* | *Singular* | *Plural* |
| Indicative | **Present** | | **Present Perfect** | |
| | schmecke<br>schmeckst<br>schmeckt | schmecken<br>schmeckt<br>schmecken | habe geschmeckt<br>hast geschmeckt<br>hat geschmeckt | haben geschmeckt<br>habt geschmeckt<br>haben geschmeckt |
| | **Past** | | **Past Perfect** | |
| | schmeckte<br>schmecktest<br>schmeckte | schmeckten<br>schmecktet<br>schmeckten | hatte geschmeckt<br>hattest geschmeckt<br>hatte geschmeckt | hatten geschmeckt<br>hattet geschmeckt<br>hatten geschmeckt |
| | **Future** | | **Future Perfect** | |
| | werde schmecken<br>wirst schmecken<br>wird schmecken | werden schmecken<br>werdet schmecken<br>werden schmecken | werde geschmeckt haben<br>wirst geschmeckt haben<br>wird geschmeckt haben | werden geschmeckt haben<br>werdet geschmeckt haben<br>werden geschmeckt haben |
| Subjunctive | **Present** | | **Present Perfect** | |
| | schmecke<br>schmeckest<br>schmecke | schmecken<br>schmecket<br>schmecken | habe geschmeckt<br>habest geschmeckt<br>habe geschmeckt | haben geschmeckt<br>habet geschmeckt<br>haben geschmeckt |
| | **Past** | | **Past Perfect** | |
| | schmeckte<br>schmecktest<br>schmeckte | schmeckten<br>schmecktet<br>schmeckten | hätte geschmeckt<br>hättest geschmeckt<br>hätte geschmeckt | hätten geschmeckt<br>hättet geschmeckt<br>hätten geschmeckt |
| | **Future** | | **Future Perfect** | |
| | werde schmecken<br>werdest schmecken<br>werde schmecken | werden schmecken<br>werdet schmecken<br>werden schmecken | werde geschmeckt haben<br>werdest geschmeckt haben<br>werde geschmeckt haben | werden geschmeckt haben<br>werdet geschmeckt haben<br>werden geschmeckt haben |
| | **Present and Future Conditional** | | **Past Conditional** | |
| | würde schmecken<br>würdest schmecken<br>würde schmecken | würden schmecken<br>würdet schmecken<br>würden schmecken | würde geschmeckt haben<br>würdest geschmeckt haben<br>würde geschmeckt haben | würden geschmeckt haben<br>würdet geschmeckt haben<br>würden geschmeckt haben |

## EXAMPLES

Wie hat dir die Hühnersuppe geschmeckt? — How did you like the chicken soup?
Dieser Rotwein schmeckt nach Essig. — This red wine tastes like vinegar.

**schmeicheln**
to flatter
**Auxiliary verb:** haben **Past participle:** geschmeichelt
**Imperative:** Schmeichele! Schmeichelt! Schmeicheln Sie!

| Mode | Simple Tenses | | Compound Tenses | |
|---|---|---|---|---|
| | *Singular* | *Plural* | *Singular* | *Plural* |
| Indicative | **Present** | | **Present Perfect** | |
| | schmeichele<br>schmeichelst<br>schmeichelt | schmeicheln<br>schmeichelt<br>schmeicheln | habe geschmeichelt<br>hast geschmeichelt<br>hat geschmeichelt | haben geschmeichelt<br>habt geschmeichelt<br>haben geschmeichelt |
| | **Past** | | **Past Perfect** | |
| | schmeichelte<br>schmeicheltest<br>schmeichelte | schmeichelten<br>schmeicheltet<br>schmeichelten | hatte geschmeichelt<br>hattest geschmeichelt<br>hatte geschmeichelt | hatten geschmeichelt<br>hattet geschmeichelt<br>hatten geschmeichelt |
| | **Future** | | **Future Perfect** | |
| | werde schmeicheln<br>wirst schmeicheln<br>wird schmeicheln | werden schmeicheln<br>werdet schmeicheln<br>werden schmeicheln | werde geschmeichelt haben<br>wirst geschmeichelt haben<br>wird geschmeichelt haben | werden geschmeichelt haben<br>werdet geschmeichelt haben<br>werden geschmeichelt haben |
| Subjunctive | **Present** | | **Present Perfect** | |
| | schmeichele<br>schmeichelst<br>schmeichele | schmeicheln<br>schmeichelt<br>schmeicheln | habe geschmeichelt<br>habest geschmeichelt<br>habe geschmeichelt | haben geschmeichelt<br>habet geschmeichelt<br>haben geschmeichelt |
| | **Past** | | **Past Perfect** | |
| | schmeichelte<br>schmeicheltest<br>schmeichelte | schmeichelten<br>schmeicheltet<br>schmeichelten | hätte geschmeichelt<br>hättest geschmeichelt<br>hätte geschmeichelt | hätten geschmeichelt<br>hättet geschmeichelt<br>hätten geschmeichelt |
| | **Future** | | **Future Perfect** | |
| | werde schmeicheln<br>werdest schmeicheln<br>werde schmeicheln | werden schmeicheln<br>werdet schmeicheln<br>werden schmeicheln | werde geschmeichelt haben<br>werdest geschmeichelt haben<br>werde geschmeichelt haben | werden geschmeichelt haben<br>werdet geschmeichelt haben<br>werden geschmeichelt haben |
| | **Present and Future Conditional** | | **Past Conditional** | |
| | würde schmeicheln<br>würdest schmeicheln<br>würde schmeicheln | würden schmeicheln<br>würdet schmeicheln<br>würden schmeicheln | würde geschmeichelt haben<br>würdest geschmeichelt haben<br>würde geschmeichelt haben | würden geschmeichelt haben<br>würdet geschmeichelt haben<br>würden geschmeichelt haben |

# EXAMPLES

| | |
|---|---|
| Der Artikel schmeichelte der Schauspielerin sehr. | The article flattered the actress very much. |
| Der reiche Herr versuchte dem naiven Mädchen zu schmeicheln. | The rich gentleman tried to flatter the naive girl. |

**schmeißen**
to fling, to dash, to slam
**Auxiliary verb:** haben **Past participle:** geschmissen
**Imperative:** Schmeiße! Schmeißt! Schmeißen Sie!

| Mode | Simple Tenses | | Compound Tenses | |
|---|---|---|---|---|
| | *Singular* | *Plural* | *Singular* | *Plural* |
| Indicative | **Present** | | **Present Perfect** | |
| | schmeiße<br>schmeißt<br>schmeißt | schmeißen<br>schmeißt<br>schmeißen | habe geschmissen<br>hast geschmissen<br>hat geschmissen | haben geschmissen<br>habt geschmissen<br>haben geschmissen |
| | **Past** | | **Past Perfect** | |
| | schmiss<br>schmissest<br>schmiss | schmissen<br>schmisst<br>schmissen | hatte geschmissen<br>hattest geschmissen<br>hatte geschmissen | hatten geschmissen<br>hattet geschmissen<br>hatten geschmissen |
| | **Future** | | **Future Perfect** | |
| | werde schmeißen<br>wirst schmeißen<br>wird schmeißen | werden schmeißen<br>werdet schmeißen<br>werden schmeißen | werde geschmissen haben<br>wirst geschmissen haben<br>wird geschmissen haben | werden geschmissen haben<br>werdet geschmissen haben<br>werden geschmissen haben |
| Subjunctive | **Present** | | **Present Perfect** | |
| | schmeiße<br>schmeißest<br>schmeiße | schmeißen<br>schmeißet<br>schmeißen | habe geschmissen<br>habest geschmissen<br>habe geschmissen | haben geschmissen<br>habet geschmissen<br>haben geschmissen |
| | **Past** | | **Past Perfect** | |
| | schmisse<br>schmissest<br>schmisse | schmissen<br>schmisset<br>schmissen | hätte geschmissen<br>hättest geschmissen<br>hätte geschmissen | hätten geschmissen<br>hättet geschmissen<br>hätten geschmissen |
| | **Future** | | **Future Perfect** | |
| | werde schmeißen<br>werdest schmeißen<br>werde schmeißen | werden schmeißen<br>werdet schmeißen<br>werden schmeißen | werde geschmissen haben<br>werdest geschmissen haben<br>werde geschmissen haben | werden geschmissen haben<br>werdet geschmissen haben<br>werden geschmissen haben |
| | **Present and Future Conditional** | | **Past Conditional** | |
| | würde schmeißen<br>würdest schmeißen<br>würde schmeißen | würden schmeißen<br>würdet schmeißen<br>würden schmeißen | würde geschmissen haben<br>würdest geschmissen haben<br>würde geschmissen haben | würden geschmissen haben<br>würdet geschmissen haben<br>würden geschmissen haben |

## EXAMPLES

Warum hast du die Vase gegen die Wand geschmissen?
Why did you throw the vase against the wall?

Er schmeißt mit Geld um sich, als ob er reich wäre.
He throws money around as if he were rich.

**schmelzen**
to melt
**Auxiliary verb:** sein **Past participle:** geschmolzen
**Imperative:** Schmilz! Schmelzt! Schmelzen Sie!

| Mode | Simple Tenses | | Compound Tenses | |
|---|---|---|---|---|
| | *Singular* | *Plural* | *Singular* | *Plural* |
| Indicative | **Present** | | **Present Perfect** | |
| | schmelze<br>schmilzt<br>schmilzt | schmelzen<br>schmelzt<br>schmelzen | bin geschmolzen<br>bist geschmolzen<br>ist geschmolzen | sind geschmolzen<br>seid geschmolzen<br>sind geschmolzen |
| | **Past** | | **Past Perfect** | |
| | schmolz<br>schmolzest<br>schmolz | schmolzen<br>schmolzt<br>schmolzen | war geschmolzen<br>warst geschmolzen<br>war geschmolzen | waren geschmolzen<br>wart geschmolzen<br>waren geschmolzen |
| | **Future** | | **Future Perfect** | |
| | werde schmelzen<br>wirst schmelzen<br>wird schmelzen | werden schmelzen<br>werdet schmelzen<br>werden schmelzen | werde geschmolzen sein<br>wirst geschmolzen sein<br>wird geschmolzen sein | werden geschmolzen sein<br>werdet geschmolzen sein<br>werden geschmolzen sein |
| Subjunctive | **Present** | | **Present Perfect** | |
| | schmelze<br>schmelzest<br>schmelze | schmelzen<br>schmelzet<br>schmelzen | sei geschmolzen<br>seiest geschmolzen<br>sei geschmolzen | seien geschmolzen<br>seiet geschmolzen<br>seien geschmolzen |
| | **Past** | | **Past Perfect** | |
| | schmölze<br>schmölzest<br>schmölze | schmölzen<br>schmölzet<br>schmölzen | wäre geschmolzen<br>wärest geschmolzen<br>wäre geschmolzen | wären geschmolzen<br>wäret geschmolzen<br>wären geschmolzen |
| | **Future** | | **Future Perfect** | |
| | werde schmelzen<br>werdest schmelzen<br>werde schmelzen | werden schmelzen<br>werdet schmelzen<br>werden schmelzen | werde geschmolzen sein<br>werdest geschmolzen sein<br>werde geschmolzen sein | werden geschmolzen sein<br>werdet geschmolzen sein<br>werden geschmolzen sein |
| | **Present and Future Conditional** | | **Past Conditional** | |
| | würde schmelzen<br>würdest schmelzen<br>würde schmelzen | würden schmelzen<br>würdet schmelzen<br>würden schmelzen | würde geschmolzen sein<br>würdest geschmolzen sein<br>würde geschmolzen sein | würden geschmolzen sein<br>würdet geschmolzen sein<br>würden geschmolzen sein |

**Note:** When used as a transitive verb, the auxiliary verb is *haben*.

## EXAMPLES

Mein Eis ist schon geschmolzen. — My ice cream has already melted.
Der gefrorene See fängt erst an zu schmelzen. — The frozen lake is just now starting to melt.
Die Köchin hat Schweizer Käse für das Fondue geschmolzen. — The cook melted Swiss cheese for the fondue.

**schmerzen**
to pain, to hurt
**Auxiliary verb:** haben **Past participle:** geschmerzt
**Imperative:** Schmerze! Schmerzt! Schmerzen Sie!

| Mode | Simple Tenses | | Compound Tenses | |
|---|---|---|---|---|
| | *Singular* | *Plural* | *Singular* | *Plural* |
| Indicative | **Present** | | **Present Perfect** | |
| | schmerze<br>schmerzt<br>schmerzt | schmerzen<br>schmerzt<br>schmerzen | habe geschmerzt<br>hast geschmerzt<br>hat geschmerzt | haben geschmerzt<br>habt geschmerzt<br>haben geschmerzt |
| | **Past** | | **Past Perfect** | |
| | schmerzte<br>schmerztest<br>schmerzte | schmerzten<br>schmerztet<br>schmerzten | hatte geschmerzt<br>hattest geschmerzt<br>hatte geschmerzt | hatten geschmerzt<br>hattet geschmerzt<br>hatten geschmerzt |
| | **Future** | | **Future Perfect** | |
| | werde schmerzen<br>wirst schmerzen<br>wird schmerzen | werden schmerzen<br>werdet schmerzen<br>werden schmerzen | werde geschmerzt haben<br>wirst geschmerzt haben<br>wird geschmerzt haben | werden geschmerzt haben<br>werdet geschmerzt haben<br>werden geschmerzt haben |
| Subjunctive | **Present** | | **Present Perfect** | |
| | schmerze<br>schmerzest<br>schmerze | schmerzen<br>schmerzet<br>schmerzen | habe geschmerzt<br>habest geschmerzt<br>habe geschmerzt | haben geschmerzt<br>habet geschmerzt<br>haben geschmerzt |
| | **Past** | | **Past Perfect** | |
| | schmerzte<br>schmerztest<br>schmerzte | schmerzten<br>schmerztet<br>schmerzten | hätte geschmerzt<br>hättest geschmerzt<br>hätte geschmerzt | hätten geschmerzt<br>hättet geschmerzt<br>hätten geschmerzt |
| | **Future** | | **Future Perfect** | |
| | werde schmerzen<br>werdest schmerzen<br>werde schmerzen | werden schmerzen<br>werdet schmerzen<br>werden schmerzen | werde geschmerzt haben<br>werdest geschmerzt haben<br>werde geschmerzt haben | werden geschmerzt haben<br>werdet geschmerzt haben<br>werden geschmerzt haben |
| | **Present and Future Conditional** | | **Past Conditional** | |
| | würde schmerzen<br>würdest schmerzen<br>würde schmerzen | würden schmerzen<br>würdet schmerzen<br>würden schmerzen | würde geschmerzt haben<br>würdest geschmerzt haben<br>würde geschmerzt haben | würden geschmerzt haben<br>würdet geschmerzt haben<br>würden geschmerzt haben |

## EXAMPLES

Es schmerzte mich zu sagen, dass ich eine andere Frau liebte.
It pained me to say that I loved another woman.

Ihm schmerzen die Beine.
His legs hurt.

**schmieren**

to grease, to lubricate, to smear

**Auxiliary verb:** haben **Past participle:** geschmiert

**Imperative:** Schmiere! Schmiert! Schmieren Sie!

| Mode | Simple Tenses | | Compound Tenses | |
|---|---|---|---|---|
| | *Singular* | *Plural* | *Singular* | *Plural* |
| Indicative | **Present** | | **Present Perfect** | |
| | schmiere<br>schmierst<br>schmiert | schmieren<br>schmiert<br>schmieren | habe geschmiert<br>hast geschmiert<br>hat geschmiert | haben geschmiert<br>habt geschmiert<br>haben geschmiert |
| | **Past** | | **Past Perfect** | |
| | schmierte<br>schmiertest<br>schmierte | schmierten<br>schmiertet<br>schmierten | hatte geschmiert<br>hattest geschmiert<br>hatte geschmiert | hatten geschmiert<br>hattet geschmiert<br>hatten geschmiert |
| | **Future** | | **Future Perfect** | |
| | werde schmieren<br>wirst schmieren<br>wird schmieren | werden schmieren<br>werdet schmieren<br>werden schmieren | werde geschmiert haben<br>wirst geschmiert haben<br>wird geschmiert haben | werden geschmiert haben<br>werdet geschmiert haben<br>werden geschmiert haben |
| Subjunctive | **Present** | | **Present Perfect** | |
| | schmiere<br>schmierest<br>schmiere | schmieren<br>schmieret<br>schmieren | habe geschmiert<br>habest geschmiert<br>habe geschmiert | haben geschmiert<br>habet geschmiert<br>haben geschmiert |
| | **Past** | | **Past Perfect** | |
| | schmierte<br>schmiertest<br>schmierte | schmierten<br>schmiertet<br>schmierten | hätte geschmiert<br>hättest geschmiert<br>hätte geschmiert | hätten geschmiert<br>hättet geschmiert<br>hätten geschmiert |
| | **Future** | | **Future Perfect** | |
| | werde schmieren<br>werdest schmieren<br>werde schmieren | werden schmieren<br>werdet schmieren<br>werden schmieren | werde geschmiert haben<br>werdest geschmiert haben<br>werde geschmiert haben | werden geschmiert haben<br>werdet geschmiert haben<br>werden geschmiert haben |
| | **Present and Future Conditional** | | **Past Conditional** | |
| | würde schmieren<br>würdest schmieren<br>würde schmieren | würden schmieren<br>würdet schmieren<br>würden schmieren | würde geschmiert haben<br>würdest geschmiert haben<br>würde geschmiert haben | würden geschmiert haben<br>würdet geschmiert haben<br>würden geschmiert haben |

**Note:** In the colloquial language *schmieren* can mean "to bribe."

## EXAMPLES

| | |
|---|---|
| Alles in unserer Ehe läuft wie geschmiert. | Everything in our marriage is going smoothly. |
| Als er versuchte den Beamten zu schmieren, wurde er verhaftet. | When he tried to bribe the official, he was arrested. |
| Schmier doch nicht so viel Butter auf dein Brot! | Don't put so much butter on your bread. |

**schminken (sich)**
to put on make-up
**Auxiliary verb:** haben **Past participle:** geschminkt
**Imperative:** Schminke! Schminkt! Schminken Sie!

| Mode | Simple Tenses | | Compound Tenses | |
|---|---|---|---|---|
| | *Singular* | *Plural* | *Singular* | *Plural* |
| Indicative | **Present** | | **Present Perfect** | |
| | schminke<br>schminkst<br>schminkt | schminken<br>schminkt<br>schminken | habe geschminkt<br>hast geschminkt<br>hat geschminkt | haben geschminkt<br>habt geschminkt<br>haben geschminkt |
| | **Past** | | **Past Perfect** | |
| | schminkte<br>schminktest<br>schminkte | schminkten<br>schminktet<br>schminkten | hatte geschminkt<br>hattest geschminkt<br>hatte geschminkt | hatten geschminkt<br>hattet geschminkt<br>hatten geschminkt |
| | **Future** | | **Future Perfect** | |
| | werde schminken<br>wirst schminken<br>wird schminken | werden schminken<br>werdet schminken<br>werden schminken | werde geschminkt haben<br>wirst geschminkt haben<br>wird geschminkt haben | werden geschminkt haben<br>werdet geschminkt haben<br>werden geschminkt haben |
| Subjunctive | **Present** | | **Present Perfect** | |
| | schminke<br>schminkest<br>schminke | schminken<br>schminket<br>schminken | habe geschminkt<br>habest geschminkt<br>habe geschminkt | haben geschminkt<br>habet geschminkt<br>haben geschminkt |
| | **Past** | | **Past Perfect** | |
| | schminkte<br>schminktest<br>schminkte | schminkten<br>schminktet<br>schminkten | hätte geschminkt<br>hättest geschminkt<br>hätte geschminkt | hätten geschminkt<br>hättet geschminkt<br>hätten geschminkt |
| | **Future** | | **Future Perfect** | |
| | werde schminken<br>werdest schminken<br>werde schminken | werden schminken<br>werdet schminken<br>werden schminken | werde geschminkt haben<br>werdest geschminkt haben<br>werde geschminkt haben | werden geschminkt haben<br>werdet geschminkt haben<br>werden geschminkt haben |
| | **Present and Future Conditional** | | **Past Conditional** | |
| | würde schminken<br>würdest schminken<br>würde schminken | würden schminken<br>würdet schminken<br>würden schminken | würde geschminkt haben<br>würdest geschminkt haben<br>würde geschminkt haben | würden geschminkt haben<br>würdet geschminkt haben<br>würden geschminkt haben |

## EXAMPLES

Meine Mutter schminkt sich nie.
My mother never uses make-up.

Klaudia, du bist viel zu jung, um dich zu schminken.
Klaudia, you're much too young to put on make-up.

**schmollen**

to pout

**Auxiliary verb:** haben **Past participle:** geschmollt

**Imperative:** Schmolle! Schmollt! Schmollen Sie!

| Mode | Simple Tenses | | Compound Tenses | |
|---|---|---|---|---|
| | *Singular* | *Plural* | *Singular* | *Plural* |
| Indicative | **Present** | | **Present Perfect** | |
| | schmolle<br>schmollst<br>schmollt | schmollen<br>schmollt<br>schmollen | habe geschmollt<br>hast geschmollt<br>hat geschmollt | haben geschmollt<br>habt geschmollt<br>haben geschmollt |
| | **Past** | | **Past Perfect** | |
| | schmollte<br>schmolltest<br>schmollte | schmollten<br>schmolltet<br>schmollten | hatte geschmollt<br>hattest geschmollt<br>hatte geschmollt | hatten geschmollt<br>hattet geschmollt<br>hatten geschmollt |
| | **Future** | | **Future Perfect** | |
| | werde schmollen<br>wirst schmollen<br>wird schmollen | werden schmollen<br>werdet schmollen<br>werden schmollen | werde geschmollt haben<br>wirst geschmollt haben<br>wird geschmollt haben | werden geschmollt haben<br>werdet geschmollt haben<br>werden geschmollt haben |
| Subjunctive | **Present** | | **Present Perfect** | |
| | schmolle<br>schmollest<br>schmolle | schmollen<br>schmollet<br>schmollen | habe geschmollt<br>habest geschmollt<br>habe geschmollt | haben geschmollt<br>habet geschmollt<br>haben geschmollt |
| | **Past** | | **Past Perfect** | |
| | schmollte<br>schmolltest<br>schmollte | schmollten<br>schmolltet<br>schmollten | hätte geschmollt<br>hättest geschmollt<br>hätte geschmollt | hätten geschmollt<br>hättet geschmollt<br>hätten geschmollt |
| | **Future** | | **Future Perfect** | |
| | werde schmollen<br>werdest schmollen<br>werde schmollen | werden schmollen<br>werdet schmollen<br>werden schmollen | werde geschmollt haben<br>werdest geschmollt haben<br>werde geschmollt haben | werden geschmollt haben<br>werdet geschmollt haben<br>werden geschmollt haben |
| | **Present and Future Conditional** | | **Past Conditional** | |
| | würde schmollen<br>würdest schmollen<br>würde schmollen | würden schmollen<br>würdet schmollen<br>würden schmollen | würde geschmollt haben<br>würdest geschmollt haben<br>würde geschmollt haben | würden geschmollt haben<br>würdet geschmollt haben<br>würden geschmollt haben |

## EXAMPLES

Manchmal schmollt mein Mann, als ob er ein kleiner Junge wäre.
Sometimes my husband pouts as if he were a little boy.

Viktoria, du bist zu alt, um so viel zu schmollen.
Viktoria, you're too old to pout so much.

**schmuggeln**
to smuggle
**Auxiliary verb:** haben **Past participle:** geschmuggelt
**Imperative:** Schmuggele! Schmuggelt! Schmuggeln Sie!

| Mode | Simple Tenses | | Compound Tenses | |
|---|---|---|---|---|
| | *Singular* | *Plural* | *Singular* | *Plural* |
| Indicative | **Present** | | **Present Perfect** | |
| | schmuggele<br>schmuggelst<br>schmuggelt | schmuggeln<br>schmuggelt<br>schmuggeln | habe geschmuggelt<br>hast geschmuggelt<br>hat geschmuggelt | haben geschmuggelt<br>habt geschmuggelt<br>haben geschmuggelt |
| | **Past** | | **Past Perfect** | |
| | schmuggelte<br>schmuggeltest<br>schmuggelte | schmuggelten<br>schmuggeltet<br>schmuggelten | hatte geschmuggelt<br>hattest geschmuggelt<br>hatte geschmuggelt | hatten geschmuggelt<br>hattet geschmuggelt<br>hatten geschmuggelt |
| | **Future** | | **Future Perfect** | |
| | werde schmuggeln<br>wirst schmuggeln<br>wird schmuggeln | werden schmuggeln<br>werdet schmuggeln<br>werden schmuggeln | werde geschmuggelt haben<br>wirst geschmuggelt haben<br>wird geschmuggelt haben | werden geschmuggelt haben<br>werdet geschmuggelt haben<br>werden geschmuggelt haben |
| Subjunctive | **Present** | | **Present Perfect** | |
| | schmuggele<br>schmuggelst<br>schmuggele | schmuggeln<br>schmuggelt<br>schmuggeln | habe geschmuggelt<br>habest geschmuggelt<br>habe geschmuggelt | haben geschmuggelt<br>habet geschmuggelt<br>haben geschmuggelt |
| | **Past** | | **Past Perfect** | |
| | schmuggelte<br>schmuggeltest<br>schmuggelte | schmuggelten<br>schmuggeltet<br>schmuggelten | hätte geschmuggelt<br>hättest geschmuggelt<br>hätte geschmuggelt | hätten geschmuggelt<br>hättet geschmuggelt<br>hätten geschmuggelt |
| | **Future** | | **Future Perfect** | |
| | werde schmuggeln<br>werdest schmuggeln<br>werde schmuggeln | werden schmuggeln<br>werdet schmuggeln<br>werden schmuggeln | werde geschmuggelt haben<br>werdest geschmuggelt haben<br>werde geschmuggelt haben | werden geschmuggelt haben<br>werdet geschmuggelt haben<br>werden geschmuggelt haben |
| | **Present and Future Conditional** | | **Past Conditional** | |
| | würde schmuggeln<br>würdest schmuggeln<br>würde schmuggeln | würden schmuggeln<br>würdet schmuggeln<br>würden schmuggeln | würde geschmuggelt haben<br>würdest geschmuggelt haben<br>würde geschmuggelt haben | würden geschmuggelt haben<br>würdet geschmuggelt haben<br>würden geschmuggelt haben |

## EXAMPLES

Die Bande hat Drogen nach Europa geschmuggelt.
The gang smuggled drugs to Europe.

Es ist albern, Rotwein nach Frankreich zu schmuggeln.
It's absurd to smuggle red wine into France.

**schnarchen**

to snore

**Auxiliary verb:** haben **Past participle:** geschnarcht

**Imperative:** Schnarche! Schnarcht! Schnarchen Sie!

| Mode | Simple Tenses | | Compound Tenses | |
|---|---|---|---|---|
| | *Singular* | *Plural* | *Singular* | *Plural* |
| Indicative | **Present** | | **Present Perfect** | |
| | schnarche<br>schnarchst<br>schnarcht | schnarchen<br>schnarcht<br>schnarchen | habe geschnarcht<br>hast geschnarcht<br>hat geschnarcht | haben geschnarcht<br>habt geschnarcht<br>haben geschnarcht |
| | **Past** | | **Past Perfect** | |
| | schnarchte<br>schnarchtest<br>schnarchte | schnarchten<br>schnarchtet<br>schnarchten | hatte geschnarcht<br>hattest geschnarcht<br>hatte geschnarcht | hatten geschnarcht<br>hattet geschnarcht<br>hatten geschnarcht |
| | **Future** | | **Future Perfect** | |
| | werde schnarchen<br>wirst schnarchen<br>wird schnarchen | werden schnarchen<br>werdet schnarchen<br>werden schnarchen | werde geschnarcht haben<br>wirst geschnarcht haben<br>wird geschnarcht haben | werden geschnarcht haben<br>werdet geschnarcht haben<br>werden geschnarcht haben |
| Subjunctive | **Present** | | **Present Perfect** | |
| | schnarche<br>schnarchest<br>schnarche | schnarchen<br>schnarchet<br>schnarchen | habe geschnarcht<br>habest geschnarcht<br>habe geschnarcht | haben geschnarcht<br>habet geschnarcht<br>haben geschnarcht |
| | **Past** | | **Past Perfect** | |
| | schnarchte<br>schnarchtest<br>schnarchte | schnarchten<br>schnarchtet<br>schnarchten | hätte geschnarcht<br>hättest geschnarcht<br>hätte geschnarcht | hätten geschnarcht<br>hättet geschnarcht<br>hätten geschnarcht |
| | **Future** | | **Future Perfect** | |
| | werde schnarchen<br>werdest schnarchen<br>werde schnarchen | werden schnarchen<br>werdet schnarchen<br>werden schnarchen | werde geschnarcht haben<br>werdest geschnarcht haben<br>werde geschnarcht haben | werden geschnarcht haben<br>werdet geschnarcht haben<br>werden geschnarcht haben |
| | **Present and Future Conditional** | | **Past Conditional** | |
| | würde schnarchen<br>würdest schnarchen<br>würde schnarchen | würden schnarchen<br>würdet schnarchen<br>würden schnarchen | würde geschnarcht haben<br>würdest geschnarcht haben<br>würde geschnarcht haben | würden geschnarcht haben<br>würdet geschnarcht haben<br>würden geschnarcht haben |

## EXAMPLES

Mein Mann schläft sehr gut, aber er schnarcht. Wegen meiner Allergie schnarche ich seit meiner Kindheit.

My husband sleeps well, but he snores. Because of my allergy, I've snored since childhood.

**schneiden**
to cut
**Auxiliary verb:** haben **Past participle:** geschnitten
**Imperative:** Schneide! Schneidet! Schneiden Sie!

| Mode | Simple Tenses | | Compound Tenses | |
|---|---|---|---|---|
| | *Singular* | *Plural* | *Singular* | *Plural* |
| Indicative | **Present** | | **Present Perfect** | |
| | schneide<br>schneidest<br>schneidet | schneiden<br>schneidet<br>schneiden | habe geschnitten<br>hast geschnitten<br>hat geschnitten | haben geschnitten<br>habt geschnitten<br>haben geschnitten |
| | **Past** | | **Past Perfect** | |
| | schnitt<br>schnittest<br>schnitt | schnitten<br>schnittet<br>schnitten | hatte geschnitten<br>hattest geschnitten<br>hatte geschnitten | hatten geschnitten<br>hattet geschnitten<br>hatten geschnitten |
| | **Future** | | **Future Perfect** | |
| | werde schneiden<br>wirst schneiden<br>wird schneiden | werden schneiden<br>werdet schneiden<br>werden schneiden | werde geschnitten haben<br>wirst geschnitten haben<br>wird geschnitten haben | werden geschnitten haben<br>werdet geschnitten haben<br>werden geschnitten haben |
| Subjunctive | **Present** | | **Present Perfect** | |
| | schneide<br>schneidest<br>schneide | schneiden<br>schneidet<br>schneiden | habe geschnitten<br>habest geschnitten<br>habe geschnitten | haben geschnitten<br>habet geschnitten<br>haben geschnitten |
| | **Past** | | **Past Perfect** | |
| | schnitte<br>schnittest<br>schnitte | schnitten<br>schnittet<br>schnitten | hätte geschnitten<br>hättest geschnitten<br>hätte geschnitten | hätten geschnitten<br>hättet geschnitten<br>hätten geschnitten |
| | **Future** | | **Future Perfect** | |
| | werde schneiden<br>werdest schneiden<br>werde schneiden | werden schneiden<br>werdet schneiden<br>werden schneiden | werde geschnitten haben<br>werdest geschnitten haben<br>werde geschnitten haben | werden geschnitten haben<br>werdet geschnitten haben<br>werden geschnitten haben |
| | **Present and Future Conditional** | | **Past Conditional** | |
| | würde schneiden<br>würdest schneiden<br>würde schneiden | würden schneiden<br>würdet schneiden<br>würden schneiden | würde geschnitten haben<br>würdest geschnitten haben<br>würde geschnitten haben | würden geschnitten haben<br>würdet geschnitten haben<br>würden geschnitten haben |

**Note:** With separable prefixes, the principal parts of this verb are, for example, *schneidet durch, schnitt durch, hat durchgeschnitten.*

## EXAMPLES

| | |
|---|---|
| Karl, ich habe zu tun. Bitte schneide das Fleisch. | Karl, I have things to do. Please carve the meat. |
| Er will sich die Haare ein bisschen kürzer schneiden lassen. | He wants to have his hair cut a little shorter. |

**schneien**

to snow

**Auxiliary verb:** haben **Past participle:** geschneit

**Imperative:** N/A

| Mode | Simple Tenses | | Compound Tenses | |
|---|---|---|---|---|
| | *Singular* | *Plural* | *Singular* | *Plural* |
| Indicative | **Present** | | **Present Perfect** | |
| | schneit | | hat geschneit | |
| | **Past** | | **Past Perfect** | |
| | schneite | | hatte geschneit | |
| | **Future** | | **Future Perfect** | |
| | wird schneien | | wird geschneit haben | |
| Subjunctive | **Present** | | **Present Perfect** | |
| | schneie | | habe geschneit | |
| | **Past** | | **Past Perfect** | |
| | schneite | | hätte geschneit | |
| | **Future** | | **Future Perfect** | |
| | werde schneien | | werde geschneit haben | |
| | **Present and Future Conditional** | | **Past Conditional** | |
| | würde schneien | | würde geschneit haben | |

**Note:** This verb is used primarily as a third-person impersonal expression with the pronoun *es*.

## EXAMPLES

Die Kinder freuen sich darüber, dass es schneit. — The children are glad that it's snowing.

Es hat schon angefangen zu schneien. — It's already started to snow.

**schnüren**
to tie, to tighten up
**Auxiliary verb:** haben **Past participle:** geschnürt
**Imperative:** Schnüre! Schnürt! Schnüren Sie!

| Mode | Simple Tenses | | Compound Tenses | |
|---|---|---|---|---|
| | *Singular* | *Plural* | *Singular* | *Plural* |
| Indicative | **Present** | | **Present Perfect** | |
| | schnüre<br>schnürst<br>schnürt | schnüren<br>schnürt<br>schnüren | habe geschnürt<br>hast geschnürt<br>hat geschnürt | haben geschnürt<br>habt geschnürt<br>haben geschnürt |
| | **Past** | | **Past Perfect** | |
| | schnürte<br>schnürtest<br>schnürte | schnürten<br>schnürtet<br>schnürten | hatte geschnürt<br>hattest geschnürt<br>hatte geschnürt | hatten geschnürt<br>hattet geschnürt<br>hatten geschnürt |
| | **Future** | | **Future Perfect** | |
| | werde schnüren<br>wirst schnüren<br>wird schnüren | werden schnüren<br>werdet schnüren<br>werden schnüren | werde geschnürt haben<br>wirst geschnürt haben<br>wird geschnürt haben | werden geschnürt haben<br>werdet geschnürt haben<br>werden geschnürt haben |
| Subjunctive | **Present** | | **Present Perfect** | |
| | schnüre<br>schnürest<br>schnüre | schnüren<br>schnüret<br>schnüren | habe geschnürt<br>habest geschnürt<br>habe geschnürt | haben geschnürt<br>habet geschnürt<br>haben geschnürt |
| | **Past** | | **Past Perfect** | |
| | schnürte<br>schnürtest<br>schnürte | schnürten<br>schnürtet<br>schnürten | hätte geschnürt<br>hättest geschnürt<br>hätte geschnürt | hätten geschnürt<br>hättet geschnürt<br>hätten geschnürt |
| | **Future** | | **Future Perfect** | |
| | werde schnüren<br>werdest schnüren<br>werde schnüren | werden schnüren<br>werdet schnüren<br>werden schnüren | werde geschnürt haben<br>werdest geschnürt haben<br>werde geschnürt haben | werden geschnürt haben<br>werdet geschnürt haben<br>werden geschnürt haben |
| | **Present and Future Conditional** | | **Past Conditional** | |
| | würde schnüren<br>würdest schnüren<br>würde schnüren | würden schnüren<br>würdet schnüren<br>würden schnüren | würde geschnürt haben<br>würdest geschnürt haben<br>würde geschnürt haben | würden geschnürt haben<br>würdet geschnürt haben<br>würden geschnürt haben |

## EXAMPLES

Ich habe endlich das letzte Päckchen geschnürt.
I finally tied up the last package.

Die kleine Hannah muss noch lernen, sich die Schuhe zu schnüren.
Little Hannah still has to learn how to tie her shoes.

**schonen**

to spare, to show consideration

**Auxiliary verb:** haben **Past participle:** geschont

**Imperative:** Schone! Schont! Schonen Sie!

| Mode | Simple Tenses | | Compound Tenses | |
|---|---|---|---|---|
| | *Singular* | *Plural* | *Singular* | *Plural* |
| Indicative | **Present** | | **Present Perfect** | |
| | schone<br>schonst<br>schont | schonen<br>schont<br>schonen | habe geschont<br>hast geschont<br>hat geschont | haben geschont<br>habt geschont<br>haben geschont |
| | **Past** | | **Past Perfect** | |
| | schonte<br>schontest<br>schonte | schonten<br>schontet<br>schonten | hatte geschont<br>hattest geschont<br>hatte geschont | hatten geschont<br>hattet geschont<br>hatten geschont |
| | **Future** | | **Future Perfect** | |
| | werde schonen<br>wirst schonen<br>wird schonen | werden schonen<br>werdet schonen<br>werden schonen | werde geschont haben<br>wirst geschont haben<br>wird geschont haben | werden geschont haben<br>werdet geschont haben<br>werden geschont haben |
| Subjunctive | **Present** | | **Present Perfect** | |
| | schone<br>schonest<br>schone | schonen<br>schonet<br>schonen | habe geschont<br>habest geschont<br>habe geschont | haben geschont<br>habet geschont<br>haben geschont |
| | **Past** | | **Past Perfect** | |
| | schonte<br>schontest<br>schonte | schonten<br>schontet<br>schonten | hätte geschont<br>hättest geschont<br>hätte geschont | hätten geschont<br>hättet geschont<br>hätten geschont |
| | **Future** | | **Future Perfect** | |
| | werde schonen<br>werdest schonen<br>werde schonen | werden schonen<br>werdet schonen<br>werden schonen | werde geschont haben<br>werdest geschont haben<br>werde geschont haben | werden geschont haben<br>werdet geschont haben<br>werden geschont haben |
| | **Present and Future Conditional** | | **Past Conditional** | |
| | würde schonen<br>würdest schonen<br>würde schonen | würden schonen<br>würdet schonen<br>würden schonen | würde geschont haben<br>würdest geschont haben<br>würde geschont haben | würden geschont haben<br>würdet geschont haben<br>würden geschont haben |

## EXAMPLES

Die Lehrerin schont sich nicht, wenn es um ihre Schüler geht.

The teacher doesn't spare herself when it comes to her pupils.

Der König versuchte die armen Familien im Dorf zu schonen.

The king tried to be considerate of the poor families in the village.

**schöpfen**
to draw, to ladle, to scoop out
**Auxiliary verb:** haben **Past participle:** geschöpft
**Imperative:** Schöpfe! Schöpft! Schöpfen Sie!

| Mode | Simple Tenses | | Compound Tenses | |
|---|---|---|---|---|
| | *Singular* | *Plural* | *Singular* | *Plural* |
| Indicative | **Present** | | **Present Perfect** | |
| | schöpfe<br>schöpfst<br>schöpft | schöpfen<br>schöpft<br>schöpfen | habe geschöpft<br>hast geschöpft<br>hat geschöpft | haben geschöpft<br>habt geschöpft<br>haben geschöpft |
| | **Past** | | **Past Perfect** | |
| | schöpfte<br>schöpftest<br>schöpfte | schöpften<br>schöpftet<br>schöpften | hatte geschöpft<br>hattest geschöpft<br>hatte geschöpft | hatten geschöpft<br>hattet geschöpft<br>hatten geschöpft |
| | **Future** | | **Future Perfect** | |
| | werde schöpfen<br>wirst schöpfen<br>wird schöpfen | werden schöpfen<br>werdet schöpfen<br>werden schöpfen | werde geschöpft haben<br>wirst geschöpft haben<br>wird geschöpft haben | werden geschöpft haben<br>werdet geschöpft haben<br>werden geschöpft haben |
| Subjunctive | **Present** | | **Present Perfect** | |
| | schöpfe<br>schöpfest<br>schöpfe | schöpfen<br>schöpfet<br>schöpfen | habe geschöpft<br>habest geschöpft<br>habe geschöpft | haben geschöpft<br>habet geschöpft<br>haben geschöpft |
| | **Past** | | **Past Perfect** | |
| | schöpfte<br>schöpftest<br>schöpfte | schöpften<br>schöpftet<br>schöpften | hätte geschöpft<br>hättest geschöpft<br>hätte geschöpft | hätten geschöpft<br>hättet geschöpft<br>hätten geschöpft |
| | **Future** | | **Future Perfect** | |
| | werde schöpfen<br>werdest schöpfen<br>werde schöpfen | werden schöpfen<br>werdet schöpfen<br>werden schöpfen | werde geschöpft haben<br>werdest geschöpft haben<br>werde geschöpft haben | werden geschöpft haben<br>werdet geschöpft haben<br>werden geschöpft haben |
| | **Present and Future Conditional** | | **Past Conditional** | |
| | würde schöpfen<br>würdest schöpfen<br>würde schöpfen | würden schöpfen<br>würdet schöpfen<br>würden schöpfen | würde geschöpft haben<br>würdest geschöpft haben<br>würde geschöpft haben | würden geschöpft haben<br>würdet geschöpft haben<br>würden geschöpft haben |

**Note:** With inseparable prefixes, the principal parts of this verb are, for example, *erschöpft, erschöpfte, hat erschöpft.*

## EXAMPLES

Das Boot war alt und er musste alle paar Minuten Wasser schöpfen.
The boat was old, and he had to bail out water every few minutes.

Ich kann kaum Atem schöpfen.
I can scarcely take a breath.

**schrauben**

to screw

**Auxiliary verb:** haben **Past participle:** geschraubt

**Imperative:** Schraube! Schraubt! Schrauben Sie!

| Mode | Simple Tenses | | Compound Tenses | |
|---|---|---|---|---|
| | *Singular* | *Plural* | *Singular* | *Plural* |
| Indicative | **Present** | | **Present Perfect** | |
| | schraube<br>schraubst<br>schraubt | schrauben<br>schraubt<br>schrauben | habe geschraubt<br>hast geschraubt<br>hat geschraubt | haben geschraubt<br>habt geschraubt<br>haben geschraubt |
| | **Past** | | **Past Perfect** | |
| | schraubte<br>schraubtest<br>schraubte | schraubten<br>schraubtet<br>schraubten | hatte geschraubt<br>hattest geschraubt<br>hatte geschraubt | hatten geschraubt<br>hattet geschraubt<br>hatten geschraubt |
| | **Future** | | **Future Perfect** | |
| | werde schrauben<br>wirst schrauben<br>wird schrauben | werden schrauben<br>werdet schrauben<br>werden schrauben | werde geschraubt haben<br>wirst geschraubt haben<br>wird geschraubt haben | werden geschraubt haben<br>werdet geschraubt haben<br>werden geschraubt haben |
| Subjunctive | **Present** | | **Present Perfect** | |
| | schraube<br>schraubest<br>schraube | schrauben<br>schraubet<br>schrauben | habe geschraubt<br>habest geschraubt<br>habe geschraubt | haben geschraubt<br>habet geschraubt<br>haben geschraubt |
| | **Past** | | **Past Perfect** | |
| | schraubte<br>schraubtest<br>schraubte | schraubten<br>schraubtet<br>schraubten | hätte geschraubt<br>hättest geschraubt<br>hätte geschraubt | hätten geschraubt<br>hättet geschraubt<br>hätten geschraubt |
| | **Future** | | **Future Perfect** | |
| | werde schrauben<br>werdest schrauben<br>werde schrauben | werden schrauben<br>werdet schrauben<br>werden schrauben | werde geschraubt haben<br>werdest geschraubt haben<br>werde geschraubt haben | werden geschraubt haben<br>werdet geschraubt haben<br>werden geschraubt haben |
| | **Present and Future Conditional** | | **Past Conditional** | |
| | würde schrauben<br>würdest schrauben<br>würde schrauben | würden schrauben<br>würdet schrauben<br>würden schrauben | würde geschraubt haben<br>würdest geschraubt haben<br>würde geschraubt haben | würden geschraubt haben<br>würdet geschraubt haben<br>würden geschraubt haben |

## EXAMPLES

Das ist eines der ersten Schraubenboote.
This is one of the first boats with a screw drive.

Kannst du hier einen Haken in die Wand schrauben?
Can you screw a hook into the wall here?

**schreiben**
to write
**Auxiliary verb:** haben **Past participle:** geschrieben
**Imperative:** Schreibe! Schreibt! Schreiben Sie!

| Mode | Simple Tenses | | Compound Tenses | |
|---|---|---|---|---|
| | *Singular* | *Plural* | *Singular* | *Plural* |
| Indicative | **Present** | | **Present Perfect** | |
| | schreibe<br>schreibst<br>schreibt | schreiben<br>schreibt<br>schreiben | habe geschrieben<br>hast geschrieben<br>hat geschrieben | haben geschrieben<br>habt geschrieben<br>haben geschrieben |
| | **Past** | | **Past Perfect** | |
| | schrieb<br>schriebst<br>schrieb | schrieben<br>schriebt<br>schrieben | hatte geschrieben<br>hattest geschrieben<br>hatte geschrieben | hatten geschrieben<br>hattet geschrieben<br>hatten geschrieben |
| | **Future** | | **Future Perfect** | |
| | werde schreiben<br>wirst schreiben<br>wird schreiben | werden schreiben<br>werdet schreiben<br>werden schreiben | werde geschrieben haben<br>wirst geschrieben haben<br>wird geschrieben haben | werden geschrieben haben<br>werdet geschrieben haben<br>werden geschrieben haben |
| Subjunctive | **Present** | | **Present Perfect** | |
| | schreibe<br>schreibest<br>schreibe | schreiben<br>schreibet<br>schreiben | habe geschrieben<br>habest geschrieben<br>habe geschrieben | haben geschrieben<br>habet geschrieben<br>haben geschrieben |
| | **Past** | | **Past Perfect** | |
| | schriebe<br>schriebest<br>schriebe | schrieben<br>schriebet<br>schrieben | hätte geschrieben<br>hättest geschrieben<br>hätte geschrieben | hätten geschrieben<br>hättet geschrieben<br>hätten geschrieben |
| | **Future** | | **Future Perfect** | |
| | werde schreiben<br>werdest schreiben<br>werde schreiben | werden schreiben<br>werdet schreiben<br>werden schreiben | werde geschrieben haben<br>werdest geschrieben haben<br>werde geschrieben haben | werden geschrieben haben<br>werdet geschrieben haben<br>werden geschrieben haben |
| | **Present and Future Conditional** | | **Past Conditional** | |
| | würde schreiben<br>würdest schreiben<br>würde schreiben | würden schreiben<br>würdet schreiben<br>würden schreiben | würde geschrieben haben<br>würdest geschrieben haben<br>würde geschrieben haben | würden geschrieben haben<br>würdet geschrieben haben<br>würden geschrieben haben |

**Note:** With inseparable prefixes, the principal parts of this verb are, for example, *beschreibt, beschrieb, hat beschrieben.* With separable prefixes, the principal parts are, for example, *schreibt an, schrieb an, hat angeschrieben.*

## EXAMPLES

In der Grundschule lernen die Kinder lesen und schreiben.
In elementary school, the children learn to read and write.

Wer hat dieses schöne Gedicht geschrieben?
Who wrote this beautiful poem?

**schreien**
to scream, to shout
**Auxiliary verb:** haben **Past participle:** geschrien
**Imperative:** Schreie! Schreit! Schreien Sie!

| Mode | Simple Tenses | | Compound Tenses | |
|---|---|---|---|---|
| | *Singular* | *Plural* | *Singular* | *Plural* |
| Indicative | **Present** | | **Present Perfect** | |
| | schreie<br>schreist<br>schreit | schreien<br>schreit<br>schreien | habe geschrien<br>hast geschrien<br>hat geschrien | haben geschrien<br>habt geschrien<br>haben geschrien |
| | **Past** | | **Past Perfect** | |
| | schrie<br>schriest<br>schrie | schrien<br>schriet<br>schrien | hatte geschrien<br>hattest geschrien<br>hatte geschrien | hatten geschrien<br>hattet geschrien<br>hatten geschrien |
| | **Future** | | **Future Perfect** | |
| | werde schreien<br>wirst schreien<br>wird schreien | werden schreien<br>werdet schreien<br>werden schreien | werde geschrien haben<br>wirst geschrien haben<br>wird geschrien haben | werden geschrien haben<br>werdet geschrien haben<br>werden geschrien haben |
| Subjunctive | **Present** | | **Present Perfect** | |
| | schreie<br>schreiest<br>schreie | schreien<br>schreiet<br>schreien | habe geschrien<br>habest geschrien<br>habe geschrien | haben geschrien<br>habet geschrien<br>haben geschrien |
| | **Past** | | **Past Perfect** | |
| | schriee<br>schrieest<br>schriee | schrieen<br>schrieet<br>schrieen | hätte geschrien<br>hättest geschrien<br>hätte geschrien | hätten geschrien<br>hättet geschrien<br>hätten geschrien |
| | **Future** | | **Future Perfect** | |
| | werde schreien<br>werdest schreien<br>werde schreien | werden schreien<br>werdet schreien<br>werden schreien | werde geschrien haben<br>werdest geschrien haben<br>werde geschrien haben | werden geschrien haben<br>werdet geschrien haben<br>werden geschrien haben |
| | **Present and Future Conditional** | | **Past Conditional** | |
| | würde schreien<br>würdest schreien<br>würde schreien | würden schreien<br>würdet schreien<br>würden schreien | würde geschrien haben<br>würdest geschrien haben<br>würde geschrien haben | würden geschrien haben<br>würdet geschrien haben<br>würden geschrien haben |

## EXAMPLES

Schreie nicht so! Ich höre dich schon. — Don't shout like that. I hear you.
Der kleine Junge schreit nach seinen Eltern. — The little boy screams for his parents.

**schreiten**
to step, to stride
**Auxiliary verb:** sein **Past participle:** geschritten
**Imperative:** Schreite! Schreitet! Schreiten Sie!

| Mode | Simple Tenses | | Compound Tenses | |
|---|---|---|---|---|
| | *Singular* | *Plural* | *Singular* | *Plural* |
| Indicative | **Present** | | **Present Perfect** | |
| | schreite<br>schreitest<br>schreitet | schreiten<br>schreitet<br>schreiten | bin geschritten<br>bist geschritten<br>ist geschritten | sind geschritten<br>seid geschritten<br>sind geschritten |
| | **Past** | | **Past Perfect** | |
| | schritt<br>schrittest<br>schritt | schritten<br>schrittet<br>schritten | war geschritten<br>warst geschritten<br>war geschritten | waren geschritten<br>wart geschritten<br>waren geschritten |
| | **Future** | | **Future Perfect** | |
| | werde schreiten<br>wirst schreiten<br>wird schreiten | werden schreiten<br>werdet schreiten<br>werden schreiten | werde geschritten sein<br>wirst geschritten sein<br>wird geschritten sein | werden geschritten sein<br>werdet geschritten sein<br>werden geschritten sein |
| Subjunctive | **Present** | | **Present Perfect** | |
| | schreite<br>schreitest<br>schreite | schreiten<br>schreitet<br>schreiten | sei geschritten<br>seiest geschritten<br>sei geschritten | seien geschritten<br>seiet geschritten<br>seien geschritten |
| | **Past** | | **Past Perfect** | |
| | schritte<br>schrittest<br>schritte | schritten<br>schrittet<br>schritten | wäre geschritten<br>wärest geschritten<br>wäre geschritten | wären geschritten<br>wäret geschritten<br>wären geschritten |
| | **Future** | | **Future Perfect** | |
| | werde schreiten<br>werdest schreiten<br>werde schreiten | werden schreiten<br>werdet schreiten<br>werden schreiten | werde geschritten sein<br>werdest geschritten sein<br>werde geschritten sein | werden geschritten sein<br>werdet geschritten sein<br>werden geschritten sein |
| | **Present and Future Conditional** | | **Past Conditional** | |
| | würde schreiten<br>würdest schreiten<br>würde schreiten | würden schreiten<br>würdet schreiten<br>würden schreiten | würde geschritten sein<br>würdest geschritten sein<br>würde geschritten sein | würden geschritten sein<br>würdet geschritten sein<br>würden geschritten sein |

## EXAMPLES

Die Jungen schreiten nebeneinander und versuchen wie Soldaten zu marschieren.
The boys stride next to one another and try to march like soldiers.

Die Braut schritt langsam zum Altar.
The bride stepped slowly toward the altar.

**schulden**

to owe, to be indebted

**Auxiliary verb:** haben **Past participle:** geschuldet

**Imperative:** Schulde! Schuldet! Schulden Sie!

| Mode | Simple Tenses | | Compound Tenses | |
|---|---|---|---|---|
| | *Singular* | *Plural* | *Singular* | *Plural* |
| Indicative | **Present** | | **Present Perfect** | |
| | schulde<br>schuldest<br>schuldet | schulden<br>schuldet<br>schulden | habe geschuldet<br>hast geschuldet<br>hat geschuldet | haben geschuldet<br>habt geschuldet<br>haben geschuldet |
| | **Past** | | **Past Perfect** | |
| | schuldete<br>schuldetest<br>schuldete | schuldeten<br>schuldetet<br>schuldeten | hatte geschuldet<br>hattest geschuldet<br>hatte geschuldet | hatten geschuldet<br>hattet geschuldet<br>hatten geschuldet |
| | **Future** | | **Future Perfect** | |
| | werde schulden<br>wirst schulden<br>wird schulden | werden schulden<br>werdet schulden<br>werden schulden | werde geschuldet haben<br>wirst geschuldet haben<br>wird geschuldet haben | werden geschuldet haben<br>werdet geschuldet haben<br>werden geschuldet haben |
| Subjunctive | **Present** | | **Present Perfect** | |
| | schulde<br>schuldest<br>schulde | schulden<br>schuldet<br>schulden | habe geschuldet<br>habest geschuldet<br>habe geschuldet | haben geschuldet<br>habet geschuldet<br>haben geschuldet |
| | **Past** | | **Past Perfect** | |
| | schuldete<br>schuldetest<br>schuldete | schuldeten<br>schuldetet<br>schuldeten | hätte geschuldet<br>hättest geschuldet<br>hätte geschuldet | hätten geschuldet<br>hättet geschuldet<br>hätten geschuldet |
| | **Future** | | **Future Perfect** | |
| | werde schulden<br>werdest schulden<br>werde schulden | werden schulden<br>werdet schulden<br>werden schulden | werde geschuldet haben<br>werdest geschuldet haben<br>werde geschuldet haben | werden geschuldet haben<br>werdet geschuldet haben<br>werden geschuldet haben |
| | **Present and Future Conditional** | | **Past Conditional** | |
| | würde schulden<br>würdest schulden<br>würde schulden | würden schulden<br>würdet schulden<br>würden schulden | würde geschuldet haben<br>würdest geschuldet haben<br>würde geschuldet haben | würden geschuldet haben<br>würdet geschuldet haben<br>würdne geschuldet haben |

## EXAMPLES

Heinrich schuldet mir fünfzig Euro.
Heinrich owes me fifty euros.

Ich habe nie jemandem Geld geschuldet.
I have never owed anyone money.

**schütteln**
to shake, to agitate
**Auxiliary verb:** haben **Past participle:** geschüttelt
**Imperative:** Schüttele! Schüttelt! Schütteln Sie!

| Mode | Simple Tenses | | Compound Tenses | |
|---|---|---|---|---|
| | *Singular* | *Plural* | *Singular* | *Plural* |
| Indicative | **Present** | | **Present Perfect** | |
| | schüttele<br>schüttelst<br>schüttelt | schütteln<br>schüttelt<br>schütteln | habe geschüttelt<br>hast geschüttelt<br>hat geschüttelt | haben geschüttelt<br>habt geschüttelt<br>haben geschüttelt |
| | **Past** | | **Past Perfect** | |
| | schüttelte<br>schütteltest<br>schüttelte | schüttelten<br>schüttelteet<br>schüttelten | hatte geschüttelt<br>hattest geschüttelt<br>hatte geschüttelt | hatten geschüttelt<br>hattet geschüttelt<br>hatten geschüttelt |
| | **Future** | | **Future Perfect** | |
| | werde schütteln<br>wirst schütteln<br>wird schütteln | werden schütteln<br>werdet schütteln<br>werden schütteln | werde geschüttelt haben<br>wirst geschüttelt haben<br>wird geschüttelt haben | werden geschüttelt haben<br>werdet geschüttelt haben<br>werden geschüttelt haben |
| Subjunctive | **Present** | | **Present Perfect** | |
| | schüttele<br>schüttelst<br>schüttele | schütteln<br>schüttelt<br>schütteln | habe geschüttelt<br>habest geschüttelt<br>habe geschüttelt | haben geschüttelt<br>habet geschüttelt<br>haben geschüttelt |
| | **Past** | | **Past Perfect** | |
| | schüttelte<br>schütteltest<br>schüttelte | schüttelten<br>schüttelteet<br>schüttelten | hätte geschüttelt<br>hättest geschüttelt<br>hätte geschüttelt | hätten geschüttelt<br>hättet geschüttelt<br>hätten geschüttelt |
| | **Future** | | **Future Perfect** | |
| | werde schütteln<br>werdest schütteln<br>werde schütteln | werden schütteln<br>werdet schütteln<br>werden schütteln | werde geschüttelt haben<br>werdest geschüttelt haben<br>werde geschüttelt haben | werden geschüttelt haben<br>werdet geschüttelt haben<br>werden geschüttelt haben |
| | **Present and Future Conditional** | | **Past Conditional** | |
| | würde schütteln<br>würdest schütteln<br>würde schütteln | würden schütteln<br>würdet schütteln<br>würden schütteln | würde geschüttelt haben<br>würdest geschüttelt haben<br>würde geschüttelt haben | würden geschüttelt haben<br>würdet geschüttelt haben<br>würden geschüttelt haben |

## EXAMPLES

| | |
|---|---|
| Er konnte es nicht glauben und schüttelte den Kopf. | He couldn't believe it and shook his head. |
| Als Gudrun mir ihren Mann vorstellte, schüttelte ich ihm die Hand. | When Gudrun introduced her husband, I shook his hand. |

**schützen**

to protect, to guard

**Auxiliary verb:** haben **Past participle:** geschützt

**Imperative:** Schütze! Schützt! Schützen Sie!

| Mode | Simple Tenses | | Compound Tenses | |
|---|---|---|---|---|
| | *Singular* | *Plural* | *Singular* | *Plural* |
| Indicative | **Present** | | **Present Perfect** | |
| | schütze<br>schützt<br>schützt | schützen<br>schützt<br>schützen | habe geschützt<br>hast geschützt<br>hat geschützt | haben geschützt<br>habt geschützt<br>haben geschützt |
| | **Past** | | **Past Perfect** | |
| | schützte<br>schütztest<br>schützte | schützten<br>schütztet<br>schützten | hatte geschützt<br>hattest geschützt<br>hatte geschützt | hatten geschützt<br>hattet geschützt<br>hatten geschützt |
| | **Future** | | **Future Perfect** | |
| | werde schützen<br>wirst schützen<br>wird schützen | werden schützen<br>werdet schützen<br>werden schützen | werde geschützt haben<br>wirst geschützt haben<br>wird geschützt haben | werden geschützt haben<br>werdet geschützt haben<br>werden geschützt haben |
| Subjunctive | **Present** | | **Present Perfect** | |
| | schütze<br>schützest<br>schütze | schützen<br>schützet<br>schützen | habe geschützt<br>habest geschützt<br>habe geschützt | haben geschützt<br>habet geschützt<br>haben geschützt |
| | **Past** | | **Past Perfect** | |
| | schützte<br>schütztest<br>schützte | schützten<br>schütztet<br>schützten | hätte geschützt<br>hättest geschützt<br>hätte geschützt | hätten geschützt<br>hättet geschützt<br>hätten geschützt |
| | **Future** | | **Future Perfect** | |
| | werde schützen<br>werdest schützen<br>werde schützen | werden schützen<br>werdet schützen<br>werden schützen | werde geschützt haben<br>werdest geschützt haben<br>werde geschützt haben | werden geschützt haben<br>werdet geschützt haben<br>werden geschützt haben |
| | **Present and Future Conditional** | | **Past Conditional** | |
| | würde schützen<br>würdest schützen<br>würde schützen | würden schützen<br>würdet schützen<br>würden schützen | würde geschützt haben<br>würdest geschützt haben<br>würde geschützt haben | würden geschützt haben<br>würdet geschützt haben<br>würdne geschützt haben |

## EXAMPLES

Der Wind war eiskalt und die Mutter versuchte irh Baby davor zu schützen.

The wind was ice-cold and the mother tried to protect her baby from it.

In der U-Bahn muss man sich vor Taschendieben schützen.

On the subway, you have to guard against pickpockets.

**schwänzen**
to cut class
**Auxiliary verb:** haben **Past participle:** geschwänzt
**Imperative:** Schwänze! Schwänzt! Schwänzen Sie!

| Mode | Simple Tenses | | Compound Tenses | |
|---|---|---|---|---|
| | *Singular* | *Plural* | *Singular* | *Plural* |
| Indicative | **Present** | | **Present Perfect** | |
| | schwänze<br>schwänzt<br>schwänzt | schwänzen<br>schwänzt<br>schwänzen | habe geschwänzt<br>hast geschwänzt<br>hat geschwänzt | haben geschwänzt<br>habt geschwänzt<br>haben geschwänzt |
| | **Past** | | **Past Perfect** | |
| | schwänzte<br>schwänztest<br>schwänzte | schwänzten<br>schwänztet<br>schwänzten | hatte geschwänzt<br>hattest geschwänzt<br>hatte geschwänzt | hatten geschwänzt<br>hattet geschwänzt<br>hatten geschwänzt |
| | **Future** | | **Future Perfect** | |
| | werde schwänzen<br>wirst schwänzen<br>wird schwänzen | werden schwänzen<br>werdet schwänzen<br>werden schwänzen | werde geschwänzt haben<br>wirst geschwänzt haben<br>wird geschwänzt haben | werden geschwänzt haben<br>werdet geschwänzt haben<br>werden geschwänzt haben |
| Subjunctive | **Present** | | **Present Perfect** | |
| | schwänze<br>schwänzest<br>schwänze | schwänzen<br>schwänzet<br>schwänzen | habe geschwänzt<br>habest geschwänzt<br>habe geschwänzt | haben geschwänzt<br>habet geschwänzt<br>haben geschwänzt |
| | **Past** | | **Past Perfect** | |
| | schwänzte<br>schwänztest<br>schwänzte | schwänzten<br>schwänztet<br>schwänzten | hätte geschwänzt<br>hättest geschwänzt<br>hätte geschwänzt | hätten geschwänzt<br>hättet geschwänzt<br>hätten geschwänzt |
| | **Future** | | **Future Perfect** | |
| | werde schwänzen<br>werdest schwänzen<br>werde schwänzen | werden schwänzen<br>werdet schwänzen<br>werden schwänzen | werde geschwänzt haben<br>werdest geschwänzt haben<br>werde geschwänzt haben | werden geschwänzt haben<br>werdet geschwänzt haben<br>werden geschwänzt haben |
| | **Present and Future Conditional** | | **Past Conditional** | |
| | würde schwänzen<br>würdest schwänzen<br>würde schwänzen | würden schwänzen<br>würdet schwänzen<br>würden schwänzen | würde geschwänzt haben<br>würdest geschwänzt haben<br>würde geschwänzt haben | würden geschwänzt haben<br>würdet geschwänzt haben<br>würden geschwänzt haben |

## EXAMPLES

Zwei Jungen und ein Mädchen aus der elften Klasse haben die Schule geschwänzt.
Two boys and a girl from the eleventh grade cut school.

Er schwänzt zu oft und wird bei der Prüfung durchfallen.
He cuts classes too often and will fail the exam.

**schweben**
to hover, to soar
**Auxiliary verb:** haben **Past participle:** geschwebt
**Imperative:** Schwebe! Schwebt! Schweben Sie!

| Mode | Simple Tenses | | Compound Tenses | |
|---|---|---|---|---|
| | *Singular* | *Plural* | *Singular* | *Plural* |
| Indicative | **Present** | | **Present Perfect** | |
| | schwebe<br>schwebst<br>schwebt | schweben<br>schwebt<br>schweben | habe geschwebt<br>hast geschwebt<br>hat geschwebt | haben geschwebt<br>habt geschwebt<br>haben geschwebt |
| | **Past** | | **Past Perfect** | |
| | schwebte<br>schwebtest<br>schwebte | schwebten<br>schwebtet<br>schwebten | hatte geschwebt<br>hattest geschwebt<br>hatte geschwebt | hatten geschwebt<br>hattet geschwebt<br>hatten geschwebt |
| | **Future** | | **Future Perfect** | |
| | werde schweben<br>wirst schweben<br>wird schweben | werden schweben<br>werdet schweben<br>werden schweben | werde geschwebt haben<br>wirst geschwebt haben<br>wird geschwebt haben | werden geschwebt haben<br>werdet geschwebt haben<br>werden geschwebt haben |
| Subjunctive | **Present** | | **Present Perfect** | |
| | schwebe<br>schwebest<br>schwebe | schweben<br>schwebet<br>schweben | habe geschwebt<br>habest geschwebt<br>habe geschwebt | haben geschwebt<br>habet geschwebt<br>haben geschwebt |
| | **Past** | | **Past Perfect** | |
| | schwebte<br>schwebtest<br>schwebte | schwebten<br>schwebtet<br>schwebten | hätte geschwebt<br>hättest geschwebt<br>hätte geschwebt | hätten geschwebt<br>hättet geschwebt<br>hätten geschwebt |
| | **Future** | | **Future Perfect** | |
| | werde schweben<br>werdest schweben<br>werde schweben | werden schweben<br>werdet schweben<br>werden schweben | werde geschwebt haben<br>werdest geschwebt haben<br>werde geschwebt haben | werden geschwebt haben<br>werdet geschwebt haben<br>werden geschwebt haben |
| | **Present and Future Conditional** | | **Past Conditional** | |
| | würde schweben<br>würdest schweben<br>würde schweben | würden schweben<br>würdet schweben<br>würden schweben | würde geschwebt haben<br>würdest geschwebt haben<br>würde geschwebt haben | würden geschwebt haben<br>würdet geschwebt haben<br>würden geschwebt haben |

**Note:** *Schweben* is also used with the auxiliary verb *sein.*

## EXAMPLES

Onkel Johannes schwebt noch zwischen Leben und Tod.
Uncle Johannes still hovers between life and death.

Dichter Nebel schwebte über dem Wasser.
Thick fog hung over the water.

**schweigen**
to be silent
**Auxiliary verb:** haben **Past participle:** geschwiegen
**Imperative:** Schweige! Schweigt! Schweigen Sie!

| Mode | Simple Tenses | | Compound Tenses | |
|---|---|---|---|---|
| | *Singular* | *Plural* | *Singular* | *Plural* |
| Indicative | **Present** | | **Present Perfect** | |
| | schweige<br>schweigst<br>schweigt | schweigen<br>schweigt<br>schweigen | habe geschwiegen<br>hast geschwiegen<br>hat geschwiegen | haben geschwiegen<br>habt geschwiegen<br>haben geschwiegen |
| | **Past** | | **Past Perfect** | |
| | schwieg<br>schwiegst<br>schwieg | schwiegen<br>schwiegt<br>schwiegen | hatte geschwiegen<br>hattest geschwiegen<br>hatte geschwiegen | hatten geschwiegen<br>hattet geschwiegen<br>hatten geschwiegen |
| | **Future** | | **Future Perfect** | |
| | werde schweigen<br>wirst schweigen<br>wird schweigen | werden schweigen<br>werdet schweigen<br>werden schweigen | werde geschwiegen haben<br>wirst geschwiegen haben<br>wird geschwiegen haben | werden geschwiegen haben<br>werdet geschwiegen haben<br>werden geschwiegen haben |
| Subjunctive | **Present** | | **Present Perfect** | |
| | schweige<br>schweigest<br>schweige | schweigen<br>schweiget<br>schweigen | habe geschwiegen<br>habest geschwiegen<br>habe geschwiegen | haben geschwiegen<br>habet geschwiegen<br>haben geschwiegen |
| | **Past** | | **Past Perfect** | |
| | schwiege<br>schwiegest<br>schwiege | schwiegen<br>schwieget<br>schwiegen | hätte geschwiegen<br>hättest geschwiegen<br>hätte geschwiegen | hätten geschwiegen<br>hättet geschwiegen<br>hätten geschwiegen |
| | **Future** | | **Future Perfect** | |
| | werde schweigen<br>werdest schweigen<br>werde schweigen | werden schweigen<br>werdet schweigen<br>werden schweigen | werde geschwiegen haben<br>werdest geschwiegen haben<br>werde geschwiegen haben | werden geschwiegen haben<br>werdet geschwiegen haben<br>werden geschwiegen haben |
| | **Present and Future Conditional** | | **Past Conditional** | |
| | würde schweigen<br>würdest schweigen<br>würde schweigen | würden schweigen<br>würdet schweigen<br>würden schweigen | würde geschwiegen haben<br>würdest geschwiegen haben<br>würde geschwiegen haben | würden geschwiegen haben<br>würdet geschwiegen haben<br>würden geschwiegen haben |

## EXAMPLES

Die Presse konnte nicht länger schweigen. — The press could remain silent no longer.
Der Angeklagte schwieg. — The defendant remained silent.

**schwellen**

to swell, to rise, to increase

**Auxiliary verb:** sein **Past participle:** geschwollen

**Imperative:** Schwill! Schwellt! Schwellen Sie!

| Mode | Simple Tenses | | Compound Tenses | |
|---|---|---|---|---|
| | *Singular* | *Plural* | *Singular* | *Plural* |
| Indicative | **Present** | | **Present Perfect** | |
| | schwelle<br>schwillst<br>schwillt | schwellen<br>schwellt<br>schwellen | bin geschwollen<br>bist geschwollen<br>ist geschwollen | sind geschwollen<br>seid geschwollen<br>sind geschwollen |
| | **Past** | | **Past Perfect** | |
| | schwoll<br>schwollst<br>schwoll | schwollen<br>schwollt<br>schwollen | war geschwollen<br>warst geschwollen<br>war geschwollen | waren geschwollen<br>wart geschwollen<br>waren geschwollen |
| | **Future** | | **Future Perfect** | |
| | werde schwellen<br>wirst schwellen<br>wird schwellen | werden schwellen<br>werdet schwellen<br>werden schwellen | werde geschwollen sein<br>wirst geschwollen sein<br>wird geschwollen sein | werden geschwollen sein<br>werdet geschwollen sein<br>werden geschwollen sein |
| Subjunctive | **Present** | | **Present Perfect** | |
| | schwelle<br>schwellest<br>schwelle | schwellen<br>schwellet<br>schwellen | sei geschwollen<br>seiest geschwollen<br>sei geschwollen | seien geschwollen<br>seiet geschwollen<br>seien geschwollen |
| | **Past** | | **Past Perfect** | |
| | schwölle<br>schwöllest<br>schwölle | schwöllen<br>schwöllet<br>schwöllen | wäre geschwollen<br>wärest geschwollen<br>wäre geschwollen | wären geschwollen<br>wäret geschwollen<br>wären geschwollen |
| | **Future** | | **Future Perfect** | |
| | werde schwellen<br>werdest schwellen<br>werde schwellen | werden schwellen<br>werdet schwellen<br>werden schwellen | werde geschwollen sein<br>werdest geschwollen sein<br>werde geschwollen sein | werden geschwollen sein<br>werdet geschwollen sein<br>werden geschwollen sein |
| | **Present and Future Conditional** | | **Past Conditional** | |
| | würde schwellen<br>würdest schwellen<br>würde schwellen | würden schwellen<br>würdet schwellen<br>würden schwellen | würde geschwollen sein<br>würdest geschwollen sein<br>würde geschwollen sein | würden geschwollen sein<br>würdet geschwollen sein<br>würden geschwollen sein |

## EXAMPLES

| | |
|---|---|
| Der Bienenstich schwoll immer mehr und tat sehr weh. | The bee sting kept swelling and hurt a lot. |
| Es schwoll ihm der Mut. | His courage increased. |
| Nach dem Unfall war seine rechte Hand geschwollen. | After the accident, his right hand was swollen. |

**schwimmen**
to swim, to float
**Auxiliary verb:** sein **Past participle:** geschwommen
**Imperative:** Schwimme! Schwimmt! Schwimmen Sie!

| Mode | Simple Tenses | | Compound Tenses | |
|---|---|---|---|---|
| | *Singular* | *Plural* | *Singular* | *Plural* |
| Indicative | **Present** | | **Present Perfect** | |
| | schwimme<br>schwimmst<br>schwimmt | schwimmen<br>schwimmt<br>schwimmen | bin geschwommen<br>bist geschwommen<br>ist geschwommen | sind geschwommen<br>seid geschwommen<br>sind geschwommen |
| | **Past** | | **Past Perfect** | |
| | schwamm<br>schwammst<br>schwamm | schwammen<br>schwammt<br>schwammen | war geschwommen<br>warst geschwommen<br>war geschwommen | waren geschwommen<br>wart geschwommen<br>waren geschwommen |
| | **Future** | | **Future Perfect** | |
| | werde schwimmen<br>wirst schwimmen<br>wird schwimmen | werden schwimmen<br>werdet schwimmen<br>werden schwimmen | werde geschwommen sein<br>wirst geschwommen sein<br>wird geschwommen sein | werden geschwommen sein<br>werdet geschwommen sein<br>werden geschwommen sein |
| Subjunctive | **Present** | | **Present Perfect** | |
| | schwimme<br>schwimmest<br>schwimme | schwimmen<br>schwimmet<br>schwimmen | sei geschwommen<br>seiest geschwommen<br>sei geschwommen | seien geschwommen<br>seiet geschwommen<br>seien geschwommen |
| | **Past** | | **Past Perfect** | |
| | schwömme<br>schwömmest<br>schwömme | schwömmen<br>schwömmet<br>schwömmen | wäre geschwommen<br>wärest geschwommen<br>wäre geschwommen | wären geschwommen<br>wäret geschwommen<br>wären geschwommen |
| | **Future** | | **Future Perfect** | |
| | werde schwimmen<br>werdest schwimmen<br>werde schwimmen | werden schwimmen<br>werdet schwimmen<br>werden schwimmen | werde geschwommen sein<br>werdest geschwommen sein<br>werde geschwommen sein | werden geschwommen sein<br>werdet geschwommen sein<br>werden geschwommen sein |
| | **Present and Future Conditional** | | **Past Conditional** | |
| | würde schwimmen<br>würdest schwimmen<br>würde schwimmen | würden schwimmen<br>würdet schwimmen<br>würden schwimmen | würde geschwommen sein<br>würdest geschwommen sein<br>würde geschwommen sein | würden geschwommen sein<br>würdet geschwommen sein<br>würden geschwommen sein |

## EXAMPLES

Mein Vetter wird versuchen über den ganzen See zu schwimmen.
My cousin is going to try to swim across the entire lake.

Als ich in Italien war, bin ich im Mittelmeer geschwommen.
When I was in Italy, I went swimming in the Mediterranean Sea.

**schwitzen**

to sweat

**Auxiliary verb:** haben **Past participle:** geschwitzt

**Imperative:** Schwitze! Schwitzt! Schwitzen Sie!

| Mode | Simple Tenses | | Compound Tenses | |
|---|---|---|---|---|
| | *Singular* | *Plural* | *Singular* | *Plural* |
| Indicative | **Present** | | **Present Perfect** | |
| | schwitze<br>schwitzt<br>schwitzt | schwitzen<br>schwitzt<br>schwitzen | habe geschwitzt<br>hast geschwitzt<br>hat geschwitzt | haben geschwitzt<br>habt geschwitzt<br>haben geschwitzt |
| | **Past** | | **Past Perfect** | |
| | schwitzte<br>schwitztest<br>schwitzte | schwitzten<br>schwitztet<br>schwitzten | hatte geschwitzt<br>hattest geschwitzt<br>hatte geschwitzt | hatten geschwitzt<br>hattet geschwitzt<br>hatten geschwitzt |
| | **Future** | | **Future Perfect** | |
| | werde schwitzen<br>wirst schwitzen<br>wird schwitzen | werden schwitzen<br>werdet schwitzen<br>werden schwitzen | werde geschwitzt haben<br>wirst geschwitzt haben<br>wird geschwitzt haben | werden geschwitzt haben<br>werdet geschwitzt haben<br>werden geschwitzt haben |
| Subjunctive | **Present** | | **Present Perfect** | |
| | schwitze<br>schwitzest<br>schwitze | schwitzen<br>schwitzet<br>schwitzen | habe geschwitzt<br>habest geschwitzt<br>habe geschwitzt | haben geschwitzt<br>habet geschwitzt<br>haben geschwitzt |
| | **Past** | | **Past Perfect** | |
| | schwitzte<br>schwitztest<br>schwitzte | schwitzten<br>schwitztet<br>schwitzten | hätte geschwitzt<br>hättest geschwitzt<br>hätte geschwitzt | hätten geschwitzt<br>hättet geschwitzt<br>hätten geschwitzt |
| | **Future** | | **Future Perfect** | |
| | werde schwitzen<br>werdest schwitzen<br>werde schwitzen | werden schwitzen<br>werdet schwitzen<br>werden schwitzen | werde geschwitzt haben<br>werdest geschwitzt haben<br>werde geschwitzt haben | werden geschwitzt haben<br>werdet geschwitzt haben<br>werden geschwitzt haben |
| | **Present and Future Conditional** | | **Past Conditional** | |
| | würde schwitzen<br>würdest schwitzen<br>würde schwitzen | würden schwitzen<br>würdet schwitzen<br>würden schwitzen | würde geschwitzt haben<br>würdest geschwitzt haben<br>würde geschwitzt haben | würden geschwitzt haben<br>würdet geschwitzt haben<br>würden geschwitzt haben |

## EXAMPLES

Während der Hitzewelle bin ich leicht ins Schwitzen gekommen.

During the heat wave, it was easy for me to break into a sweat.

Wenn wir arbeiten, schwitzen wir viel.

When we work, we sweat a lot.

**schwören**
to swear, to curse
**Auxiliary verb:** haben **Past participle:** geschworen
**Imperative:** Schwöre! Schwört! Schwören Sie!

| Mode | Simple Tenses | | Compound Tenses | |
|---|---|---|---|---|
| | *Singular* | *Plural* | *Singular* | *Plural* |
| Indicative | **Present** | | **Present Perfect** | |
| | schwöre<br>schwörst<br>schwört | schwören<br>schwört<br>schwören | habe geschworen<br>hast geschworen<br>hat geschworen | haben geschworen<br>habt geschworen<br>haben geschworen |
| | **Past** | | **Past Perfect** | |
| | schwur<br>schwurst<br>schwur | schwuren<br>schwurt<br>schwuren | hatte geschworen<br>hattest geschworen<br>hatte geschworen | hatten geschworen<br>hattet geschworen<br>hatten geschworen |
| | **Future** | | **Future Perfect** | |
| | werde schwören<br>wirst schwören<br>wird schwören | werden schwören<br>werdet schwören<br>werden schwören | werde geschworen haben<br>wirst geschworen haben<br>wird geschworen haben | werden geschworen haben<br>werdet geschworen haben<br>werden geschworen haben |
| Subjunctive | **Present** | | **Present Perfect** | |
| | schwöre<br>schwörest<br>schwöre | schwören<br>schwöret<br>schwören | habe geschworen<br>habest geschworen<br>habe geschworen | haben geschworen<br>habet geschworen<br>haben geschworen |
| | **Past** | | **Past Perfect** | |
| | schwüre<br>schwürest<br>schwüre | schwüren<br>schwüret<br>schwüren | hätte geschworen<br>hättest geschworen<br>hätte geschworen | hätten geschworen<br>hättet geschworen<br>hätten geschworen |
| | **Future** | | **Future Perfect** | |
| | werde schwören<br>werdest schwören<br>werde schwören | werden schwören<br>werdet schwören<br>werden schwören | werde geschworen haben<br>werdest geschworen haben<br>werde geschworen haben | werden geschworen haben<br>werdet geschworen haben<br>werden geschworen haben |
| | **Present and Future Conditional** | | **Past Conditional** | |
| | würde schwören<br>würdest schwören<br>würde schwören | würden schwören<br>würdet schwören<br>würden schwören | würde geschworen haben<br>würdest geschworen haben<br>würde geschworen haben | würden geschworen haben<br>würdet geschworen haben<br>würden geschworen haben |

## EXAMPLES

Die Ritter mussten der neuen Königin einen Treueid schwören.
The knights had to swear an oath of loyalty to the new queen.

Ich schwöre auf meinen alten Freund.
I have total confidence in my old friend.

**segeln**
to sail
**Auxiliary verb:** sein **Past participle:** gesegelt
**Imperative:** Segele! Segelt! Segeln Sie!

| Mode | Simple Tenses | | Compound Tenses | |
|---|---|---|---|---|
| | *Singular* | *Plural* | *Singular* | *Plural* |
| Indicative | **Present** | | **Present Perfect** | |
| | segele<br>segelst<br>segelt | segeln<br>segelt<br>segeln | bin gesegelt<br>bist gesegelt<br>ist gesegelt | sind gesegelt<br>seid gesegelt<br>sind gesegelt |
| | **Past** | | **Past Perfect** | |
| | segelte<br>segeltest<br>segelte | segelten<br>segeltet<br>segelten | war gesegelt<br>warst gesegelt<br>war gesegelt | waren gesegelt<br>wart gesegelt<br>waren gesegelt |
| | **Future** | | **Future Perfect** | |
| | werde segeln<br>wirst segeln<br>wird segeln | werden segeln<br>werdet segeln<br>werden segeln | werde gesegelt sein<br>wirst gesegelt sein<br>wird gesegelt sein | werden gesegelt sein<br>werdet gesegelt sein<br>werden gesegelt sein |
| Subjunctive | **Present** | | **Present Perfect** | |
| | segele<br>segelst<br>segele | segeln<br>segelt<br>segeln | sei gesegelt<br>seiest gesegelt<br>sei gesegelt | seien gesegelt<br>seiet gesegelt<br>seien gesegelt |
| | **Past** | | **Past Perfect** | |
| | segelte<br>segeltest<br>segelte | segelten<br>segeltet<br>segelten | wäre gesegelt<br>wärest gesegelt<br>wäre gesegelt | wären gesegelt<br>wäret gesegelt<br>wären gesegelt |
| | **Future** | | **Future Perfect** | |
| | werde segeln<br>werdest segeln<br>werde segeln | werden segeln<br>werdet segeln<br>werden segeln | werde gesegelt sein<br>werdest gesegelt sein<br>werde gesegelt sein | werden gesegelt sein<br>werdet gesegelt sein<br>werden gesegelt sein |
| | **Present and Future Conditional** | | **Past Conditional** | |
| | würde segeln<br>würdest segeln<br>würde segeln | würden segeln<br>würdet segeln<br>würden segeln | würde gesegelt sein<br>würdest gesegelt sein<br>würde gesegelt sein | würden gesegelt sein<br>würdet gesegelt sein<br>würden gesegelt sein |

**Note:** When the noun form *Segel* is attached to the verb *fliegen,* it means "flying" or "piloting a glider."

## EXAMPLES

Im 15. Jahrhundert musste man mutig sein, um übers Meer zu segeln.
In the 15th century, you had to be brave to sail across the sea.

Meine Schwester geht gern Segelfliegen.
My sister likes to go flying on a glider.

**segnen**
to bless
**Auxiliary verb:** haben **Past participle:** gesegnet
**Imperative:** Segne! Segnet! Segnen Sie!

| Mode | Simple Tenses | | Compound Tenses | |
|---|---|---|---|---|
| | *Singular* | *Plural* | *Singular* | *Plural* |
| Indicative | **Present** | | **Present Perfect** | |
| | segne<br>segnest<br>segnet | segnen<br>segnet<br>segnen | habe gesegnet<br>hast gesegnet<br>hat gesegnet | haben gesegnet<br>habt gesegnet<br>haben gesegnet |
| | **Past** | | **Past Perfect** | |
| | segnete<br>segnetest<br>segnete | segneten<br>segnetet<br>segneten | hatte gesegnet<br>hattest gesegnet<br>hatte gesegnet | hatten gesegnet<br>hattet gesegnet<br>hatten gesegnet |
| | **Future** | | **Future Perfect** | |
| | werde segnen<br>wirst segnen<br>wird segnen | werden segnen<br>werdet segnen<br>werden segnen | werde gesegnet haben<br>wirst gesegnet haben<br>wird gesegnet haben | werden gesegnet haben<br>werdet gesegnet haben<br>werden gesegnet haben |
| Subjunctive | **Present** | | **Present Perfect** | |
| | segne<br>segnest<br>segne | segnen<br>segnet<br>segnen | habe gesegnet<br>habest gesegnet<br>habe gesegnet | haben gesegnet<br>habet gesegnet<br>haben gesegnet |
| | **Past** | | **Past Perfect** | |
| | segnete<br>segnetest<br>segnete | segneten<br>segnetet<br>segneten | hätte gesegnet<br>hättest gesegnet<br>hätte gesegnet | hätten gesegnet<br>hättet gesegnet<br>hätten gesegnet |
| | **Future** | | **Future Perfect** | |
| | werde segnen<br>werdest segnen<br>werde segnen | werden segnen<br>werdet segnen<br>werden segnen | werde gesegnet haben<br>werdest gesegnet haben<br>werde gesegnet haben | werden gesegnet haben<br>werdet gesegnet haben<br>werden gesegnet haben |
| | **Present and Future Conditional** | | **Past Conditional** | |
| | würde segnen<br>würdest segnen<br>würde segnen | würden segnen<br>würdet segnen<br>würden segnen | würde gesegnet haben<br>würdest gesegnet haben<br>würde gesegnet haben | würden gesegnet haben<br>würdet gesegnet haben<br>würden gesegnet haben |

## EXAMPLES

Der Pfarrer segnete die Gemeinde und fing an zu beten.
The minister blessed the congregation and began to pray.

Der Priester hat den sterbenden Mann gesegnet.
The priest blessed the dying man.

**sehen**

to see

**Auxiliary verb:** haben **Past participle:** gesehen

**Imperative:** Sieh! Seht! Sehen Sie!

| Mode | Simple Tenses | | Compound Tenses | |
|---|---|---|---|---|
| | *Singular* | *Plural* | *Singular* | *Plural* |
| Indicative | **Present** | | **Present Perfect** | |
| | sehe<br>siehst<br>sieht | sehen<br>seht<br>sehen | habe gesehen<br>hast gesehen<br>hat gesehen | haben gesehen<br>habt gesehen<br>haben gesehen |
| | **Past** | | **Past Perfect** | |
| | sah<br>sahst<br>sah | sahen<br>saht<br>sahen | hatte gesehen<br>hattest gesehen<br>hatte gesehen | hatten gesehen<br>hattet gesehen<br>hatten gesehen |
| | **Future** | | **Future Perfect** | |
| | werde sehen<br>wirst sehen<br>wird sehen | werden sehen<br>werdet sehen<br>werden sehen | werde gesehen haben<br>wirst gesehen haben<br>wird gesehen haben | werden gesehen haben<br>werdet gesehen haben<br>werden gesehen haben |
| Subjunctive | **Present** | | **Present Perfect** | |
| | sehe<br>sehest<br>sehe | sehen<br>sehet<br>sehen | habe gesehen<br>habest gesehen<br>habe gesehen | haben gesehen<br>habet gesehen<br>haben gesehen |
| | **Past** | | **Past Perfect** | |
| | sähe<br>sähest<br>sähe | sähen<br>sähet<br>sähen | hätte gesehen<br>hättest gesehen<br>hätte gesehen | hätten gesehen<br>hättet gesehen<br>hätten gesehen |
| | **Future** | | **Future Perfect** | |
| | werde sehen<br>werdest sehen<br>werde sehen | werden sehen<br>werdet sehen<br>werden sehen | werde gesehen haben<br>werdest gesehen haben<br>werde gesehen haben | werden gesehen haben<br>werdet gesehen haben<br>werden gesehen haben |
| | **Present and Future Conditional** | | **Past Conditional** | |
| | würde sehen<br>würdest sehen<br>würde sehen | würden sehen<br>würdet sehen<br>würden sehen | würde gesehen haben<br>würdest gesehen haben<br>würde gesehen haben | würden gesehen haben<br>würdet gesehen haben<br>würden gesehen haben |

**Note:** With inseparable prefixes, the principal parts of this verb are, for example, *versieht, versah, hat versehen.* With separable prefixes, the principal parts are, for example, *sieht an, sah an, hat angesehen.*

## EXAMPLES

| | |
|---|---|
| Ich sehe schon, dass Sie keine Zeit haben mich zu besuchen. | I see that you have no time to visit me. |
| Ohne seine Brille kann er nichts sehen. | He can't see anything without his glasses. |

**sich sehnen**
to yearn, to long for
**Auxiliary verb:** haben **Past participle:** gesehnt
**Imperative:** Sehne! Sehnt! Sehnen Sie!

| Mode | Simple Tenses | | Compound Tenses | |
|---|---|---|---|---|
| | *Singular* | *Plural* | *Singular* | *Plural* |
| Indicative | **Present** | | **Present Perfect** | |
| | sehne<br>sehnst<br>sehnt | sehnen<br>sehnt<br>sehnen | habe gesehnt<br>hast gesehnt<br>hat gesehnt | haben gesehnt<br>habt gesehnt<br>haben gesehnt |
| | **Past** | | **Past Perfect** | |
| | sehnte<br>sehntest<br>sehnte | sehnten<br>sehntet<br>sehnten | hatte gesehnt<br>hattest gesehnt<br>hatte gesehnt | hatten gesehnt<br>hattet gesehnt<br>hatten gesehnt |
| | **Future** | | **Future Perfect** | |
| | werde sehnen<br>wirst sehnen<br>wird sehnen | werden sehnen<br>werdet sehnen<br>werden sehnen | werde gesehnt haben<br>wirst gesehnt haben<br>wird gesehnt haben | werden gesehnt haben<br>werdet gesehnt haben<br>werden gesehnt haben |
| Subjunctive | **Present** | | **Present Perfect** | |
| | sehne<br>sehnest<br>sehne | sehnen<br>sehnet<br>sehnen | habe gesehnt<br>habest gesehnt<br>habe gesehnt | haben gesehnt<br>habet gesehnt<br>haben gesehnt |
| | **Past** | | **Past Perfect** | |
| | sehnte<br>sehntest<br>sehnte | sehnten<br>sehntet<br>sehnten | hätte gesehnt<br>hättest gesehnt<br>hätte gesehnt | hätten gesehnt<br>hättet gesehnt<br>hätten gesehnt |
| | **Future** | | **Future Perfect** | |
| | werde sehnen<br>werdest sehnen<br>werde sehnen | werden sehnen<br>werdet sehnen<br>werden sehnen | werde gesehnt haben<br>werdest gesehnt haben<br>werde gesehnt haben | werden gesehnt haben<br>werdet gesehnt haben<br>werden gesehnt haben |
| | **Present and Future Conditional** | | **Past Conditional** | |
| | würde sehnen<br>würdest sehnen<br>würde sehnen | würden sehnen<br>würdet sehnen<br>würden sehnen | würde gesehnt haben<br>würdest gesehnt haben<br>würde gesehnt haben | würden gesehnt haben<br>würdet gesehnt haben<br>würden gesehnt haben |

## EXAMPLES

Wir sehnen uns danach noch einmal nach Deutschland zu reisen.
We long to travel to Germany once again.

Ich sehnte mich so nach euch.
I missed you so very much.

**sein**

to be

**Auxiliary verb:** sein **Past participle:** gewesen

**Imperative:** Sei! Seid! Seien Sie!

| Mode | Simple Tenses | | Compound Tenses | |
|---|---|---|---|---|
| | *Singular* | *Plural* | *Singular* | *Plural* |
| Indicative | **Present** | | **Present Perfect** | |
| | bin<br>bist<br>ist | sind<br>seid<br>sind | bin gewesen<br>bist gewesen<br>ist gewesen | sind gewesen<br>seid gewesen<br>sind gewesen |
| | **Past** | | **Past Perfect** | |
| | war<br>warst<br>war | waren<br>wart<br>waren | war gewesen<br>warst gewesen<br>war gewesen | waren gewesen<br>wart gewesen<br>waren gewesen |
| | **Future** | | **Future Perfect** | |
| | werde sein<br>wirst sein<br>wird sein | werden sein<br>werdet sein<br>werden sein | werde gewesen sein<br>wirst gewesen sein<br>wird gewesen sein | werden gewesen sein<br>werdet gewesen sein<br>werden gewesen sein |
| Subjunctive | **Present** | | **Present Perfect** | |
| | sei<br>seiest<br>sei | seien<br>seiet<br>seien | sei gewesen<br>seiest gewesen<br>sei gewesen | seien gewesen<br>seiet gewesen<br>seien gewesen |
| | **Past** | | **Past Perfect** | |
| | wäre<br>wärest<br>wäre | wären<br>wäret<br>wären | wäre gewesen<br>wärest gewesen<br>wäre gewesen | wären gewesen<br>wäret gewesen<br>wären gewesen |
| | **Future** | | **Future Perfect** | |
| | werde sein<br>werdest sein<br>werde sein | werden sein<br>werdet sein<br>werden sein | werde gewesen sein<br>werdest gewesen sein<br>werde gewesen sein | werden gewesen sein<br>werdet gewesen sein<br>werden gewesen sein |
| | **Present and Future Conditional** | | **Past Conditional** | |
| | würde sein<br>würdest sein<br>würde sein | würden sein<br>würdet sein<br>würden sein | würde gewesen sein<br>würdest gewesen sein<br>würde gewesen sein | würden gewesen sein<br>würdet gewesen sein<br>würden gewesen sein |

## EXAMPLES

| | |
|---|---|
| Klemens ist mein Cousin und mein bester Freund. | Klemens is my cousin and my best friend. |
| Vor einer Woche waren wir noch in China. | A week ago, we were still in China. |

**senden**
to send, to broadcast
**Auxiliary verb:** haben **Past participle:** gesandt
**Imperative:** Sende! Sendet! Senden Sie!

| Mode | Simple Tenses | | Compound Tenses | |
|---|---|---|---|---|
| | *Singular* | *Plural* | *Singular* | *Plural* |
| Indicative | **Present** | | **Present Perfect** | |
| | sende<br>sendest<br>sendet | senden<br>sendet<br>senden | habe gesandt<br>hast gesandt<br>hat gesandt | haben gesandt<br>habt gesandt<br>haben gesandt |
| | **Past** | | **Past Perfect** | |
| | sandte<br>sandtest<br>sandte | sandten<br>sandtet<br>sandten | hatte gesandt<br>hattest gesandt<br>hatte gesandt | hatten gesandt<br>hattet gesandt<br>hatten gesandt |
| | **Future** | | **Future Perfect** | |
| | werde senden<br>wirst senden<br>wird senden | werden senden<br>werdet senden<br>werden senden | werde gesandt haben<br>wirst gesandt haben<br>wird gesandt haben | werden gesandt haben<br>werdet gesandt haben<br>werden gesandt haben |
| Subjunctive | **Present** | | **Present Perfect** | |
| | sende<br>sendest<br>sende | senden<br>sendet<br>senden | habe gesandt<br>habest gesandt<br>habe gesandt | haben gesandt<br>habet gesandt<br>haben gesandt |
| | **Past** | | **Past Perfect** | |
| | sendete<br>sendetest<br>sendete | sendeten<br>sendetet<br>sendeten | hätte gesandt<br>hättest gesandt<br>hätte gesandt | hätten gesandt<br>hättet gesandt<br>hätten gesandt |
| | **Future** | | **Future Perfect** | |
| | werde senden<br>werdest senden<br>werde senden | werden senden<br>werdet senden<br>werden senden | werde gesandt haben<br>werdest gesandt haben<br>werde gesandt haben | werden gesandt haben<br>werdet gesandt haben<br>werden gesandt haben |
| | **Present and Future Conditional** | | **Past Conditional** | |
| | würde senden<br>würdest senden<br>würde senden | würden senden<br>würdet senden<br>würden senden | würde gesandt haben<br>würdest gesandt haben<br>würde gesandt haben | würden gesandt haben<br>würdet gesandt haben<br>würden gesandt haben |

**Note:** When *senden* means "to broadcast," it is a regular verb: *sendet, sendete, hat gesendet.* With separable prefixes, the principal parts of this verb are, for example, *sendet nach, sandte nach, hat nachgesandt.*

## EXAMPLES

Sie bittet ihren Bruder den Brief sofort an ihre Mutter zu senden.
She asks her brother to send the letter to their mother immediately.

Der Bericht über den Unfall wird in den Nachrichten gesendet werden.
The report about the accident will be broadcast on the news.

**setzen (sich)**

to set, to place, to put, to be seated

**Auxiliary verb:** haben **Past participle:** gesetzt

**Imperative:** Setze! Setzt! Setzen Sie!

| Mode | Simple Tenses | | Compound Tenses | |
|---|---|---|---|---|
| | *Singular* | *Plural* | *Singular* | *Plural* |
| Indicative | **Present** | | **Present Perfect** | |
| | setze<br>setzt<br>setzt | setzen<br>setzt<br>setzen | habe gesetzt<br>hast gesetzt<br>hat gesetzt | haben gesetzt<br>habt gesetzt<br>haben gesetzt |
| | **Past** | | **Past Perfect** | |
| | setzte<br>setztest<br>setzte | setzten<br>setztet<br>setzten | hatte gesetzt<br>hattest gesetzt<br>hatte gesetzt | hatten gesetzt<br>hattet gesetzt<br>hatten gesetzt |
| | **Future** | | **Future Perfect** | |
| | werde setzen<br>wirst setzen<br>wird setzen | werden setzen<br>werdet setzen<br>werden setzen | werde gesetzt haben<br>wirst gesetzt haben<br>wird gesetzt haben | werden gesetzt haben<br>werdet gesetzt haben<br>werden gesetzt haben |
| Subjunctive | **Present** | | **Present Perfect** | |
| | setze<br>setzest<br>setze | setzen<br>setzet<br>setzen | habe gesetzt<br>habest gesetzt<br>habe gesetzt | haben gesetzt<br>habet gesetzt<br>haben gesetzt |
| | **Past** | | **Past Perfect** | |
| | setzte<br>setztest<br>setzte | setzten<br>setztet<br>setzten | hätte gesetzt<br>hättest gesetzt<br>hätte gesetzt | hätten gesetzt<br>hättet gesetzt<br>hätten gesetzt |
| | **Future** | | **Future Perfect** | |
| | werde setzen<br>werdest setzen<br>werde setzen | werden setzen<br>werdet setzen<br>werden setzen | werde gesetzt haben<br>werdest gesetzt haben<br>werde gesetzt haben | werden gesetzt haben<br>werdet gesetzt haben<br>werden gesetzt haben |
| | **Present and Future Conditional** | | **Past Conditional** | |
| | würde setzen<br>würdest setzen<br>würde setzen | würden setzen<br>würdet setzen<br>würden setzen | würde gesetzt haben<br>würdest gesetzt haben<br>würde gesetzt haben | würden gesetzt haben<br>würdet gesetzt haben<br>würden gesetzt haben |

## EXAMPLES

| | |
|---|---|
| Er hat sein ganzes Vermögen auf eine Karte gesetzt. | He placed his entire fortune on one card. |
| Bitte setzen Sie sich! | Please sit down. |

**seufzen**
to sigh
**Auxiliary verb:** haben **Past participle:** geseufzt
**Imperative:** Seufze! Seufzt! Seufzen Sie!

| Mode | Simple Tenses | | Compound Tenses | |
|---|---|---|---|---|
| | *Singular* | *Plural* | *Singular* | *Plural* |
| Indicative | **Present** | | **Present Perfect** | |
| | seufze<br>seufzt<br>seufzt | seufzen<br>seufzt<br>seufzen | habe geseufzt<br>hast geseufzt<br>hat geseufzt | haben geseufzt<br>habt geseufzt<br>haben geseufzt |
| | **Past** | | **Past Perfect** | |
| | seufzte<br>seufztest<br>seufzte | seufzten<br>seufztet<br>seufzten | hatte geseufzt<br>hattest geseufzt<br>hatte geseufzt | hatten geseufzt<br>hattet geseufzt<br>hatten geseufzt |
| | **Future** | | **Future Perfect** | |
| | werde seufzen<br>wirst seufzen<br>wird seufzen | werden seufzen<br>werdet seufzen<br>werden seufzen | werde geseufzt haben<br>wirst geseufzt haben<br>wird geseufzt haben | werden geseufzt haben<br>werdet geseufzt haben<br>werden geseufzt haben |
| Subjunctive | **Present** | | **Present Perfect** | |
| | seufze<br>seufzest<br>seufze | seufzen<br>seufzet<br>seufzen | habe geseufzt<br>habest geseufzt<br>habe geseufzt | haben geseufzt<br>habet geseufzt<br>haben geseufzt |
| | **Past** | | **Past Perfect** | |
| | seufzte<br>seufztest<br>seufzte | seufzten<br>seufztet<br>seufzten | hätte geseufzt<br>hättest geseufzt<br>hätte geseufzt | hätten geseufzt<br>hättet geseufzt<br>hätten geseufzt |
| | **Future** | | **Future Perfect** | |
| | werde seufzen<br>werdest seufzen<br>werde seufzen | werden seufzen<br>werdet seufzen<br>werden seufzen | werde geseufzt haben<br>werdest geseufzt haben<br>werde geseufzt haben | werden geseufzt haben<br>werdet geseufzt haben<br>werden geseufzt haben |
| | **Present and Future Conditional** | | **Past Conditional** | |
| | würde seufzen<br>würdest seufzen<br>würde seufzen | würden seufzen<br>würdet seufzen<br>würden seufzen | würde geseufzt haben<br>würdest geseufzt haben<br>würde geseufzt haben | würden geseufzt haben<br>würdet geseufzt haben<br>würden geseufzt haben |

## EXAMPLES

Der alte Graf seufzte leise und starb.
The old count sighed quietly and died.

Warum seufzen Sie immer, wenn ich versuche meine Schulden zu erklären?
Why do you always sigh whenever I try to explain my debts?

**siedeln**

to settle, to colonize

**Auxiliary verb:** haben **Past participle:** gesiedelt

**Imperative:** Siedele! Siedelt! Siedeln Sie!

| Mode | Simple Tenses | | Compound Tenses | |
|---|---|---|---|---|
| | *Singular* | *Plural* | *Singular* | *Plural* |
| Indicative | **Present** | | **Present Perfect** | |
| | siedele<br>siedelst<br>siedelt | siedeln<br>siedelt<br>siedeln | habe gesiedelt<br>hast gesiedelt<br>hat gesiedelt | haben gesiedelt<br>habt gesiedelt<br>haben gesiedelt |
| | **Past** | | **Past Perfect** | |
| | siedelte<br>siedeltest<br>siedelte | siedelten<br>siedeltet<br>siedelten | hatte gesiedelt<br>hattest gesiedelt<br>hatte gesiedelt | hatten gesiedelt<br>hattet gesiedelt<br>hatten gesiedelt |
| | **Future** | | **Future Perfect** | |
| | werde siedeln<br>wirst siedeln<br>wird siedeln | werden siedeln<br>werdet siedeln<br>werden siedeln | werde gesiedelt haben<br>wirst gesiedelt haben<br>wird gesiedelt haben | werden gesiedelt haben<br>werdet gesiedelt haben<br>werden gesiedelt haben |
| Subjunctive | **Present** | | **Present Perfect** | |
| | siedele<br>siedelst<br>siedele | siedeln<br>siedelt<br>siedeln | habe gesiedelt<br>habest gesiedelt<br>habe gesiedelt | haben gesiedelt<br>habet gesiedelt<br>haben gesiedelt |
| | **Past** | | **Past Perfect** | |
| | siedelte<br>siedeltest<br>siedelte | siedelten<br>siedeltet<br>siedelten | hätte gesiedelt<br>hättest gesiedelt<br>hätte gesiedelt | hätten gesiedelt<br>hättet gesiedelt<br>hätten gesiedelt |
| | **Future** | | **Future Perfect** | |
| | werde siedeln<br>werdest siedeln<br>werde siedeln | werden siedeln<br>werdet siedeln<br>werden siedeln | werde gesiedelt haben<br>werdest gesiedelt haben<br>werde gesiedelt haben | werden gesiedelt haben<br>werdet gesiedelt haben<br>werden gesiedelt haben |
| | **Present and Future Conditional** | | **Past Conditional** | |
| | würde siedeln<br>würdest siedeln<br>würde siedeln | würden siedeln<br>würdet siedeln<br>würden siedeln | würde gesiedelt haben<br>würdest gesiedelt haben<br>würde gesiedelt haben | würden gesiedelt haben<br>würdet gesiedelt haben<br>würden gesiedelt haben |

## EXAMPLES

Engländer, Franzosen und Spanier haben in Nordamerika gesiedelt.

People from England, France, and Spain settled in North America.

Wo siedelten die ersten englischen Kolonisten?

Where did the first English colonists settle?

**sieden**
to boil, to seethe
**Auxiliary verb:** haben **Past participle:** gesotten
**Imperative:** Siede! Siedet! Sieden Sie!

| Mode | Simple Tenses | | Compound Tenses | |
|---|---|---|---|---|
| | *Singular* | *Plural* | *Singular* | *Plural* |
| Indicative | **Present** | | **Present Perfect** | |
| | siede<br>siedest<br>siedet | sieden<br>siedet<br>sieden | habe gesotten<br>hast gesotten<br>hat gesotten | haben gesotten<br>habt gesotten<br>haben gesotten |
| | **Past** | | **Past Perfect** | |
| | sott<br>sottest<br>sott | sotten<br>sottet<br>sotten | hatte gesotten<br>hattest gesotten<br>hatte gesotten | hatten gesotten<br>hattet gesotten<br>hatten gesotten |
| | **Future** | | **Future Perfect** | |
| | werde sieden<br>wirst sieden<br>wird sieden | werden sieden<br>werdet sieden<br>werden sieden | werde gesotten haben<br>wirst gesotten haben<br>wird gesotten haben | werden gesotten haben<br>werdet gesotten haben<br>werden gesotten haben |
| Subjunctive | **Present** | | **Present Perfect** | |
| | siede<br>siedest<br>siede | sieden<br>siedet<br>sieden | habe gesotten<br>habest gesotten<br>habe gesotten | haben gesotten<br>habet gesotten<br>haben gesotten |
| | **Past** | | **Past Perfect** | |
| | sötte<br>söttest<br>sötte | sötten<br>söttet<br>sötten | hätte gesotten<br>hättest gesotten<br>hätte gesotten | hätten gesotten<br>hättet gesotten<br>hätten gesotten |
| | **Future** | | **Future Perfect** | |
| | werde sieden<br>werdest sieden<br>werde sieden | werden sieden<br>werdet sieden<br>werden sieden | werde gesotten haben<br>werdest gesotten haben<br>werde gesotten haben | werden gesotten haben<br>werdet gesotten haben<br>werden gesotten haben |
| | **Present and Future Conditional** | | **Past Conditional** | |
| | würde sieden<br>würdest sieden<br>würde sieden | würden sieden<br>würdet sieden<br>würden sieden | würde gesotten haben<br>würdest gesotten haben<br>würde gesotten haben | würden gesotten haben<br>würdet gesotten haben<br>würden gesotten haben |

**Note:** This verb is sometimes conjugated regularly: *siedet, siedete, hat gesiedet.*

## EXAMPLES

Wasser siedet bei 100 Grad Celsius. — Water boils at 100 degrees Celsius.
Auf der Burg gab es gesottenes Wildschwein. — At the castle they had boiled wild boar.

**siegen**
to be victorious
**Auxiliary verb:** haben **Past participle:** gesiegt
**Imperative:** Siege! Siegt! Siegen Sie!

| Mode | Simple Tenses | | Compound Tenses | |
|---|---|---|---|---|
| | *Singular* | *Plural* | *Singular* | *Plural* |
| Indicative | **Present** | | **Present Perfect** | |
| | siege<br>siegst<br>siegt | siegen<br>siegt<br>siegen | habe gesiegt<br>hast gesiegt<br>hat gesiegt | haben gesiegt<br>habt gesiegt<br>haben gesiegt |
| | **Past** | | **Past Perfect** | |
| | siegte<br>siegtest<br>siegte | siegten<br>siegtet<br>siegten | hatte gesiegt<br>hattest gesiegt<br>hatte gesiegt | hatten gesiegt<br>hattet gesiegt<br>hatten gesiegt |
| | **Future** | | **Future Perfect** | |
| | werde siegen<br>wirst siegen<br>wird siegen | werden siegen<br>werdet siegen<br>werden siegen | werde gesiegt haben<br>wirst gesiegt haben<br>wird gesiegt haben | werden gesiegt haben<br>werdet gesiegt haben<br>werden gesiegt haben |
| Subjunctive | **Present** | | **Present Perfect** | |
| | siege<br>siegest<br>siege | siegen<br>sieget<br>siegen | habe gesiegt<br>habest gesiegt<br>habe gesiegt | haben gesiegt<br>habet gesiegt<br>haben gesiegt |
| | **Past** | | **Past Perfect** | |
| | siegte<br>siegtest<br>siegte | siegten<br>siegtet<br>siegten | hätte gesiegt<br>hättest gesiegt<br>hätte gesiegt | hätten gesiegt<br>hättet gesiegt<br>hätten gesiegt |
| | **Future** | | **Future Perfect** | |
| | werde siegen<br>werdest siegen<br>werde siegen | werden siegen<br>werdet siegen<br>werden siegen | werde gesiegt haben<br>werdest gesiegt haben<br>werde gesiegt haben | werden gesiegt haben<br>werdet gesiegt haben<br>werden gesiegt haben |
| | **Present and Future Conditional** | | **Past Conditional** | |
| | würde siegen<br>würdest siegen<br>würde siegen | würden siegen<br>würdet siegen<br>würden siegen | würde gesiegt haben<br>würdest gesiegt haben<br>würde gesiegt haben | würden gesiegt haben<br>würdet gesiegt haben<br>würden gesiegt haben |

## EXAMPLES

Sie hat mit einer Rekordzeit von 11,3 Sekunden gesiegt.
She won with a record time of 11.3 seconds.

„Wir werden mit einem hölzernen Pferd siegen," erklärte der griechische König.
"We will be victorious with a wooden horse," declared the Greek king.

**singen**
to sing
**Auxiliary verb:** haben **Past participle:** gesungen
**Imperative:** Singe! Singt! Singen Sie!

| Mode | Simple Tenses | | Compound Tenses | |
|---|---|---|---|---|
| | *Singular* | *Plural* | *Singular* | *Plural* |
| Indicative | **Present** | | **Present Perfect** | |
| | singe<br>singst<br>singt | singen<br>singt<br>singen | habe gesungen<br>hast gesungen<br>hat gesungen | haben gesungen<br>habt gesungen<br>haben gesungen |
| | **Past** | | **Past Perfect** | |
| | sang<br>sangst<br>sang | sangen<br>sangt<br>sangen | hatte gesungen<br>hattest gesungen<br>hatte gesungen | hatten gesungen<br>hattet gesungen<br>hatten gesungen |
| | **Future** | | **Future Perfect** | |
| | werde singen<br>wirst singen<br>wird singen | werden singen<br>werdet singen<br>werden singen | werde gesungen haben<br>wirst gesungen haben<br>wird gesungen haben | werden gesungen haben<br>werdet gesungen haben<br>werden gesungen haben |
| Subjunctive | **Present** | | **Present Perfect** | |
| | singe<br>singest<br>singe | singen<br>singet<br>singen | habe gesungen<br>habest gesungen<br>habe gesungen | haben gesungen<br>habet gesungen<br>haben gesungen |
| | **Past** | | **Past Perfect** | |
| | sänge<br>sängest<br>sänge | sängen<br>sänget<br>sängen | hätte gesungen<br>hättest gesungen<br>hätte gesungen | hätten gesungen<br>hättet gesungen<br>hätten gesungen |
| | **Future** | | **Future Perfect** | |
| | werde singen<br>werdest singen<br>werde singen | werden singen<br>werdet singen<br>werden singen | werde gesungen haben<br>werdest gesungen haben<br>werde gesungen haben | werden gesungen haben<br>werdet gesungen haben<br>werden gesungen haben |
| | **Present and Future Conditional** | | **Past Conditional** | |
| | würde singen<br>würdest singen<br>würde singen | würden singen<br>würdet singen<br>würden singen | würde gesungen haben<br>würdest gesungen haben<br>würde gesungen haben | würden gesungen haben<br>würdet gesungen haben<br>würden gesungen haben |

**Note:** The verb *bedingen* follows the conjugational pattern illustrated above. However, the past tense can be said as *bedingte* and the past subjunctive is *bedünge*.

## EXAMPLES

Ich liebe die Musik, kann aber weder ein Instrument spielen noch singen.
I love music but can neither play an instrument nor sing.

Sie wollen ein paar Volkslieder singen.
They want to sing a few folksongs.

**sinken**
to sink, to drop
**Auxiliary verb:** sein **Past participle:** gesunken
**Imperative:** Sinke! Sinkt! Sinken Sie!

| Mode | Simple Tenses | | Compound Tenses | |
|---|---|---|---|---|
| | *Singular* | *Plural* | *Singular* | *Plural* |
| Indicative | **Present** | | **Present Perfect** | |
| | sinke<br>sinkst<br>sinkt | sinken<br>sinkt<br>sinken | bin gesunken<br>bist gesunken<br>ist gesunken | sind gesunken<br>seid gesunken<br>sind gesunken |
| | **Past** | | **Past Perfect** | |
| | sank<br>sankst<br>sank | sanken<br>sankt<br>sanken | war gesunken<br>warst gesunken<br>war gesunken | waren gesunken<br>wart gesunken<br>waren gesunken |
| | **Future** | | **Future Perfect** | |
| | werde sinken<br>wirst sinken<br>wird sinken | werden sinken<br>werdet sinken<br>werden sinken | werde gesunken sein<br>wirst gesunken sein<br>wird gesunken sein | werden gesunken sein<br>werdet gesunken sein<br>werden gesunken sein |
| Subjunctive | **Present** | | **Present Perfect** | |
| | sinke<br>sinkest<br>sinke | sinken<br>sinket<br>sinken | sei gesunken<br>seiest gesunken<br>sei gesunken | seien gesunken<br>seiet gesunken<br>seien gesunken |
| | **Past** | | **Past Perfect** | |
| | sänke<br>sänkest<br>sänke | sänken<br>sänket<br>sänken | wäre gesunken<br>wärest gesunken<br>wäre gesunken | wären gesunken<br>wäret gesunken<br>wären gesunken |
| | **Future** | | **Future Perfect** | |
| | werde sinken<br>werdest sinken<br>werde sinken | werden sinken<br>werdet sinken<br>werden sinken | werde gesunken sein<br>werdest gesunken sein<br>werde gesunken sein | werden gesunken sein<br>werdet gesunken sein<br>werden gesunken sein |
| | **Present and Future Conditional** | | **Past Conditional** | |
| | würde sinken<br>würdest sinken<br>würde sinken | würden sinken<br>würdet sinken<br>würden sinken | würde gesunken sein<br>würdest gesunken sein<br>würde gesunken sein | würden gesunken sein<br>würdet gesunken sein<br>würden gesunken sein |

## EXAMPLES

Kannst du schwimmen? Das Boot sinkt!
Can you swim? The boat's sinking!

Die Temperaturen sind wieder unter fünf Grad gesunken.
The temperature has dropped to less than five degrees again.

**sitzen**
to sit, to fit
**Auxiliary verb:** haben **Past participle:** gesessen
**Imperative:** Sitze! Sitzt! Sitzen Sie!

| Mode | Simple Tenses | | Compound Tenses | |
|---|---|---|---|---|
| | *Singular* | *Plural* | *Singular* | *Plural* |
| Indicative | **Present** | | **Present Perfect** | |
| | sitze<br>sitzt<br>sitzt | sitzen<br>sitzt<br>sitzen | habe gesessen<br>hast gesessen<br>hat gesessen | haben gesessen<br>habt gesessen<br>haben gesessen |
| | **Past** | | **Past Perfect** | |
| | saß<br>saßest<br>saß | saßen<br>saßt<br>saßen | hatte gesessen<br>hattest gesessen<br>hatte gesessen | hatten gesessen<br>hattet gesessen<br>hatten gesessen |
| | **Future** | | **Future Perfect** | |
| | werde sitzen<br>wirst sitzen<br>wird sitzen | werden sitzen<br>werdet sitzen<br>werden sitzen | werde gesessen haben<br>wirst gesessen haben<br>wird gesessen haben | werden gesessen haben<br>werdet gesessen haben<br>werden gesessen haben |
| Subjunctive | **Present** | | **Present Perfect** | |
| | sitze<br>sitzest<br>sitze | sitzen<br>sitzet<br>sitzen | habe gesessen<br>habest gesessen<br>habe gesessen | haben gesessen<br>habet gesessen<br>haben gesessen |
| | **Past** | | **Past Perfect** | |
| | säße<br>säßest<br>säße | säßen<br>säßet<br>säßen | hätte gesessen<br>hättest gesessen<br>hätte gesessen | hätten gesessen<br>hättet gesessen<br>hätten gesessen |
| | **Future** | | **Future Perfect** | |
| | werde sitzen<br>werdest sitzen<br>werde sitzen | werden sitzen<br>werdet sitzen<br>werden sitzen | werde gesessen haben<br>werdest gesessen haben<br>werde gesessen haben | werden gesessen haben<br>werdet gesessen haben<br>werden gesessen haben |
| | **Present and Future Conditional** | | **Past Conditional** | |
| | würde sitzen<br>würdest sitzen<br>würde sitzen | würden sitzen<br>würdet sitzen<br>würden sitzen | würde gesessen haben<br>würdest gesessen haben<br>würde gesessen haben | würden gesessen haben<br>würdet gesessen haben<br>würden gesessen haben |

**Note:** With inseparable prefixes, the principal parts of this verb are, for example, *besitzt, besaß, hat besessen.*

## EXAMPLES

Der neue Anzug sitzt gut. — The new suit fits you well.
Lena, wollen wir nicht im Garten sitzen? — Lena, why don't we sit in the garden?

**sollen**
should, supposed to, ought to
**Auxiliary verb:** haben **Past participle:** gesollt
**Imperative:** N/A

| Mode | Simple Tenses | | Compound Tenses | |
|---|---|---|---|---|
| | *Singular* | *Plural* | *Singular* | *Plural* |
| Indicative | **Present** | | **Present Perfect** | |
| | soll<br>sollst<br>soll | sollen<br>sollt<br>sollen | habe gesollt<br>hast gesollt<br>hat gesollt | haben gesollt<br>habt gesollt<br>haben gesollt |
| | **Past** | | **Past Perfect** | |
| | sollte<br>solltest<br>sollte | sollten<br>solltet<br>sollten | hatte gesollt<br>hattest gesollt<br>hatte gesollt | hatten gesollt<br>hattet gesollt<br>hatten gesollt |
| | **Future** | | **Future Perfect** | |
| | werde sollen<br>wirst sollen<br>wird sollen | werden sollen<br>werdet sollen<br>werden sollen | werde gesollt haben<br>wirst gesollt haben<br>wird gesollt haben | werden gesollt haben<br>werdet gesollt haben<br>werden gesollt haben |
| Subjunctive | **Present** | | **Present Perfect** | |
| | solle<br>sollest<br>solle | sollen<br>sollet<br>sollen | habe gesollt<br>habest gesollt<br>habe gesollt | haben gesollt<br>habet gesollt<br>haben gesollt |
| | **Past** | | **Past Perfect** | |
| | sollte<br>solltest<br>sollte | sollten<br>solltet<br>sollten | hätte gesollt<br>hättest gesollt<br>hätte gesollt | hätten gesollt<br>hättet gesollt<br>hätten gesollt |
| | **Future** | | **Future Perfect** | |
| | werde sollen<br>werdest sollen<br>werde sollen | werden sollen<br>werdet sollen<br>werden sollen | werde gesollt haben<br>werdest gesollt haben<br>werde gesollt haben | werden gesollt haben<br>werdet gesollt haben<br>werden gesollt haben |
| | **Present and Future Conditional** | | **Past Conditional** | |
| | würde sollen<br>würdest sollen<br>würde sollen | würden sollen<br>würdet sollen<br>würden sollen | würde gesollt haben<br>würdest gesollt haben<br>würde gesollt haben | würden gesollt haben<br>würdet gesollt haben<br>würden gesollt haben |

**Note:** This verb is a modal auxiliary. In the perfect and future tenses, when there is a second verb in the sentence, a double-infinitive structure is required: *Haben Sie mit ihm sprechen sollen?* ("Were you supposed to speak with him?")

## EXAMPLES

| | |
|---|---|
| Du sollst nicht fluchen. | You shouldn't swear. |
| Die Politiker hätten ihre Pflicht tun sollen. | The politicians should have done their duty. |
| Sie sollte Ärztin werden. | She should become a doctor. |

**sorgen (sich)**
to be concerned, to provide for
**Auxiliary verb:** haben **Past participle:** gesorgt
**Imperative:** Sorge! Sorgt! Sorgen Sie!

| Mode | Simple Tenses | | Compound Tenses | |
|---|---|---|---|---|
| | *Singular* | *Plural* | *Singular* | *Plural* |
| Indicative | **Present** | | **Present Perfect** | |
| | sorge<br>sorgst<br>sorgt | sorgen<br>sorgt<br>sorgen | habe gesorgt<br>hast gesorgt<br>hat gesorgt | haben gesorgt<br>habt gesorgt<br>haben gesorgt |
| | **Past** | | **Past Perfect** | |
| | sorgte<br>sorgtest<br>sorgte | sorgten<br>sorgtet<br>sorgten | hatte gesorgt<br>hattest gesorgt<br>hatte gesorgt | hatten gesorgt<br>hattet gesorgt<br>hatten gesorgt |
| | **Future** | | **Future Perfect** | |
| | werde sorgen<br>wirst sorgen<br>wird sorgen | werden sorgen<br>werdet sorgen<br>werden sorgen | werde gesorgt haben<br>wirst gesorgt haben<br>wird gesorgt haben | werden gesorgt haben<br>werdet gesorgt haben<br>werden gesorgt haben |
| Subjunctive | **Present** | | **Present Perfect** | |
| | sorge<br>sorgest<br>sorge | sorgen<br>sorget<br>sorgen | habe gesorgt<br>habest gesorgt<br>habe gesorgt | haben gesorgt<br>habet gesorgt<br>haben gesorgt |
| | **Past** | | **Past Perfect** | |
| | sorgte<br>sorgtest<br>sorgte | sorgten<br>sorgtet<br>sorgten | hätte gesorgt<br>hättest gesorgt<br>hätte gesorgt | hätten gesorgt<br>hättet gesorgt<br>hätten gesorgt |
| | **Future** | | **Future Perfect** | |
| | werde sorgen<br>werdest sorgen<br>werde sorgen | werden sorgen<br>werdet sorgen<br>werden sorgen | werde gesorgt haben<br>werdest gesorgt haben<br>werde gesorgt haben | werden gesorgt haben<br>werdet gesorgt haben<br>werden gesorgt haben |
| | **Present and Future Conditional** | | **Past Conditional** | |
| | würde sorgen<br>würdest sorgen<br>würde sorgen | würden sorgen<br>würdet sorgen<br>würden sorgen | würde gesorgt haben<br>würdest gesorgt haben<br>würde gesorgt haben | würden gesorgt haben<br>würdet gesorgt haben<br>würden gesorgt haben |

## EXAMPLES

Eine nette Krankenschwester sorgte für Peter, als er im Krankenhaus war.
A nice nurse took care of Peter when he was in the hospital.

Sorgen Sie sich nicht. Es geht Ihrem Kind schon wieder besser.
Don't be concerned. Your child is already doing better.

**spalten**

to split, to cleave, to cut open

**Auxiliary verb:** haben **Past participle:** gespalten

**Imperative:** Spalte! Spaltet! Spalten Sie!

| Mode | Simple Tenses | | Compound Tenses | |
|---|---|---|---|---|
| | *Singular* | *Plural* | *Singular* | *Plural* |
| Indicative | **Present** | | **Present Perfect** | |
| | spalte<br>spaltest<br>spaltet | spalten<br>spaltet<br>spalten | habe gespalten<br>hast gespalten<br>hat gespalten | haben gespalten<br>habt gespalten<br>haben gespalten |
| | **Past** | | **Past Perfect** | |
| | spaltete<br>spaltetest<br>spaltete | spalteten<br>spaltetet<br>spalteten | hatte gespalten<br>hattest gespalten<br>hatte gespalten | hatten gespalten<br>hattet gespalten<br>hatten gespalten |
| | **Future** | | **Future Perfect** | |
| | werde spalten<br>wirst spalten<br>wird spalten | werden spalten<br>werdet spalten<br>werden spalten | werde gespalten haben<br>wirst gespalten haben<br>wird gespalten haben | werden gespalten haben<br>werdet gespalten haben<br>werden gespalten haben |
| Subjunctive | **Present** | | **Present Perfect** | |
| | spalte<br>spaltest<br>spalte | spalten<br>spaltet<br>spalten | habe gespalten<br>habest gespalten<br>habe gespalten | haben gespalten<br>habet gespalten<br>haben gespalten |
| | **Past** | | **Past Perfect** | |
| | spaltete<br>spaltetest<br>spaltete | spalteten<br>spaltetet<br>spalteten | hätte gespalten<br>hättest gespalten<br>hätte gespalten | hätten gespalten<br>hättet gespalten<br>hätten gespalten |
| | **Future** | | **Future Perfect** | |
| | werde spalten<br>werdest spalten<br>werde spalten | werden spalten<br>werdet spalten<br>werden spalten | werde gespalten haben<br>werdest gespalten haben<br>werde gespalten haben | werden gespalten haben<br>werdet gespalten haben<br>werden gespalten haben |
| | **Present and Future Conditional** | | **Past Conditional** | |
| | würde spalten<br>würdest spalten<br>würde spalten | würden spalten<br>würdet spalten<br>würden spalten | würde gespalten haben<br>würdest gespalten haben<br>würde gespalten haben | würden gespalten haben<br>würdet gespalten haben<br>würden gespalten haben |

**Note:** The past participle *gespaltet* is sometimes used in the perfect tenses.

## EXAMPLES

| | |
|---|---|
| Wir wissen heute, dass man das Atom spalten kann. | Today we know that the atom can be split. |
| Die Partei ist in der Frage der EU-Mitgliedschaft tief gespalten. | The party is deeply divided on the question of membership in the European Union. |

**sparen**
to save, to be thrifty
**Auxiliary verb:** haben **Past participle:** gespart
**Imperative:** Spare! Spart! Sparen Sie!

| Mode | Simple Tenses | | Compound Tenses | |
|---|---|---|---|---|
| | *Singular* | *Plural* | *Singular* | *Plural* |
| Indicative | **Present** | | **Present Perfect** | |
| | spare<br>sparst<br>spart | sparen<br>spart<br>sparen | habe gespart<br>hast gespart<br>hat gespart | haben gespart<br>habt gespart<br>haben gespart |
| | **Past** | | **Past Perfect** | |
| | sparte<br>spartest<br>sparte | sparten<br>spartet<br>sparten | hatte gespart<br>hattest gespart<br>hatte gespart | hatten gespart<br>hattet gespart<br>hatten gespart |
| | **Future** | | **Future Perfect** | |
| | werde sparen<br>wirst sparen<br>wird sparen | werden sparen<br>werdet sparen<br>werden sparen | werde gespart haben<br>wirst gespart haben<br>wird gespart haben | werden gespart haben<br>werdet gespart haben<br>werden gespart haben |
| Subjunctive | **Present** | | **Present Perfect** | |
| | spare<br>sparest<br>spare | sparen<br>sparet<br>sparen | habe gespart<br>habest gespart<br>habe gespart | haben gespart<br>habet gespart<br>haben gespart |
| | **Past** | | **Past Perfect** | |
| | sparte<br>spartest<br>sparte | sparten<br>spartet<br>sparten | hätte gespart<br>hättest gespart<br>hätte gespart | hätten gespart<br>hättet gespart<br>hätten gespart |
| | **Future** | | **Future Perfect** | |
| | werde sparen<br>werdest sparen<br>werde sparen | werden sparen<br>werdet sparen<br>werden sparen | werde gespart haben<br>werdest gespart haben<br>werde gespart haben | werden gespart haben<br>werdet gespart haben<br>werden gespart haben |
| | **Present and Future Conditional** | | **Past Conditional** | |
| | würde sparen<br>würdest sparen<br>würde sparen | würden sparen<br>würdet sparen<br>würden sparen | würde gespart haben<br>würdest gespart haben<br>würde gespart haben | würden gespart haben<br>würdet gespart haben<br>würden gespart haben |

## EXAMPLES

Mein Sohn spart auf ein neues Fahrrad.
My son's saving for a new bike.

Wir haben noch nicht genug gespart, um ein neues Haus in einem Vorort zu kaufen.
We still haven't saved enough to buy a new house in a suburb.

**spazieren**
to stroll, to walk
**Auxiliary verb:** sein **Past participle:** spaziert
**Imperative:** Spaziere! Spaziert! Spazieren Sie!

| Mode | Simple Tenses | | Compound Tenses | |
|---|---|---|---|---|
| | *Singular* | *Plural* | *Singular* | *Plural* |
| Indicative | **Present** | | **Present Perfect** | |
| | spaziere<br>spazierst<br>spaziert | spazieren<br>spaziert<br>spazieren | bin spaziert<br>bist spaziert<br>ist spaziert | sind spaziert<br>seid spaziert<br>sind spaziert |
| | **Past** | | **Past Perfect** | |
| | spazierte<br>spaziertest<br>spazierte | spazierten<br>spaziertet<br>spazierten | war spaziert<br>warst spaziert<br>war spaziert | waren spaziert<br>wart spaziert<br>waren spaziert |
| | **Future** | | **Future Perfect** | |
| | werde spazieren<br>wirst spazieren<br>wird spazieren | werden spazieren<br>werdet spazieren<br>werden spazieren | werde spaziert sein<br>wirst spaziert sein<br>wird spaziert sein | werden spaziert sein<br>werdet spaziert sein<br>werden spaziert sein |
| Subjunctive | **Present** | | **Present Perfect** | |
| | spaziere<br>spazierest<br>spaziere | spazieren<br>spazieret<br>spazieren | sei spaziert<br>seiest spaziert<br>sei spaziert | seien spaziert<br>seiet spaziert<br>seien spaziert |
| | **Past** | | **Past Perfect** | |
| | spazierte<br>spaziertest<br>spazierte | spazierten<br>spaziertet<br>spazierten | wäre spaziert<br>wärest spaziert<br>wäre spaziert | wären spaziert<br>wäret spaziert<br>wären spaziert |
| | **Future** | | **Future Perfect** | |
| | werde spazieren<br>werdest spazieren<br>werde spazieren | werden spazieren<br>werdet spazieren<br>werden spazieren | werde spaziert sein<br>werdest spaziert sein<br>werde spaziert sein | werden spaziert sein<br>werdet spaziert sein<br>werden spaziert sein |
| | **Present and Future Conditional** | | **Past Conditional** | |
| | würde spazieren<br>würdest spazieren<br>würde spazieren | würden spazieren<br>würdet spazieren<br>würden spazieren | würde spaziert sein<br>würdest spaziert sein<br>würde spaziert sein | würden spaziert sein<br>würdet spaziert sein<br>würden spaziert sein |

## EXAMPLES

Wir spazieren gerne im Park.
Wollt ihr mit uns spazieren gehen?

We like strolling in the park.
Do you want to go for a walk with us?

**speichern**
to store, to warehouse, to save
**Auxiliary verb:** haben **Past participle:** gespeichert
**Imperative:** Speichere! Speichert! Speichern Sie!

| Mode | Simple Tenses | | Compound Tenses | |
|---|---|---|---|---|
| | *Singular* | *Plural* | *Singular* | *Plural* |
| Indicative | **Present** | | **Present Perfect** | |
| | speichere<br>speicherst<br>speichert | speichern<br>speichert<br>speichern | habe gespeichert<br>hast gespeichert<br>hat gespeichert | haben gespeichert<br>habt gespeichert<br>haben gespeichert |
| | **Past** | | **Past Perfect** | |
| | speicherte<br>speichertest<br>speicherte | speicherten<br>speichertet<br>speicherten | hatte gespeichert<br>hattest gespeichert<br>hatte gespeichert | hatten gespeichert<br>hattet gespeichert<br>hatten gespeichert |
| | **Future** | | **Future Perfect** | |
| | werde speichern<br>wirst speichern<br>wird speichern | werden speichern<br>werdet speichern<br>werden speichern | werde gespeichert haben<br>wirst gespeichert haben<br>wird gespeichert haben | werden gespeichert haben<br>werdet gespeichert haben<br>werden gespeichert haben |
| Subjunctive | **Present** | | **Present Perfect** | |
| | speichere<br>speicherst<br>speichere | speichern<br>speichert<br>speichern | habe gespeichert<br>habest gespeichert<br>habe gespeichert | haben gespeichert<br>habet gespeichert<br>haben gespeichert |
| | **Past** | | **Past Perfect** | |
| | speicherte<br>speichertest<br>speicherte | speicherten<br>speichertet<br>speicherten | hätte gespeichert<br>hättest gespeichert<br>hätte gespeichert | hätten gespeichert<br>hättet gespeichert<br>hätten gespeichert |
| | **Future** | | **Future Perfect** | |
| | werde speichern<br>werdest speichern<br>werde speichern | werden speichern<br>werdet speichern<br>werden speichern | werde gespeichert haben<br>werdest gespeichert haben<br>werde gespeichert haben | werden gespeichert haben<br>werdet gespeichert haben<br>werden gespeichert haben |
| | **Present and Future Conditional** | | **Past Conditional** | |
| | würde speichern<br>würdest speichern<br>würde speichern | würden speichern<br>würdet speichern<br>würden speichern | würde gespeichert haben<br>würdest gespeichert haben<br>würde gespeichert haben | würden gespeichert haben<br>würdet gespeichert haben<br>würden gespeichert haben |

## EXAMPLES

Ich habe alle Informationen auf meinem Computer gespeichert.
I've saved all the information on my computer.

Diese Talsperre speichert genug Wasser für eine ganze Stadt.
This dam stores enough water for a whole city.

**speisen**
to feed, to dine
**Auxiliary verb:** haben **Past participle:** gespeist
**Imperative:** Speise! Speist! Speisen Sie!

| Mode | Simple Tenses | | Compound Tenses | |
|---|---|---|---|---|
| | *Singular* | *Plural* | *Singular* | *Plural* |
| Indicative | **Present** | | **Present Perfect** | |
| | speise<br>speist<br>speist | speisen<br>speist<br>speisen | habe gespeist<br>hast gespeist<br>hat gespeist | haben gespeist<br>habt gespeist<br>haben gespeist |
| | **Past** | | **Past Perfect** | |
| | speiste<br>speistest<br>speiste | speisten<br>speistet<br>speisten | hatte gespeist<br>hattest gespeist<br>hatte gespeist | hatten gespeist<br>hattet gespeist<br>hatten gespeist |
| | **Future** | | **Future Perfect** | |
| | werde speisen<br>wirst speisen<br>wird speisen | werden speisen<br>werdet speisen<br>werden speisen | werde gespeist haben<br>wirst gespeist haben<br>wird gespeist haben | werden gespeist haben<br>werdet gespeist haben<br>werden gespeist haben |
| Subjunctive | **Present** | | **Present Perfect** | |
| | speise<br>speisest<br>speise | speisen<br>speiset<br>speisen | habe gespeist<br>habest gespeist<br>habe gespeist | haben gespeist<br>habet gespeist<br>haben gespeist |
| | **Past** | | **Past Perfect** | |
| | speiste<br>speistest<br>speiste | speisten<br>speistet<br>speisten | hätte gespeist<br>hättest gespeist<br>hätte gespeist | hätten gespeist<br>hättet gespeist<br>hätten gespeist |
| | **Future** | | **Future Perfect** | |
| | werde speisen<br>werdest speisen<br>werde speisen | werden speisen<br>werdet speisen<br>werden speisen | werde gespeist haben<br>werdest gespeist haben<br>werde gespeist haben | werden gespeist haben<br>werdet gespeist haben<br>werden gespeist haben |
| | **Present and Future Conditional** | | **Past Conditional** | |
| | würde speisen<br>würdest speisen<br>würde speisen | würden speisen<br>würdet speisen<br>würden speisen | würde gespeist haben<br>würdest gespeist haben<br>würde gespeist haben | würden gespeist haben<br>würdet gespeist haben<br>würden gespeist haben |

## EXAMPLES

Der Fluss wird durch zahlreiche Bäche gespeist. — The river is fed by numerous streams.
Wir haben gespeist wie die Könige. — We ate like kings.

**spenden**
to donate, to dispense
**Auxiliary verb:** haben **Past participle:** gespendet
**Imperative:** Spende! Spendet! Spenden Sie!

| Mode | Simple Tenses | | Compound Tenses | |
|---|---|---|---|---|
| | *Singular* | *Plural* | *Singular* | *Plural* |
| Indicative | **Present** | | **Present Perfect** | |
| | spende<br>spendest<br>spendet | spenden<br>spendet<br>spenden | habe gespendet<br>hast gespendet<br>hat gespendet | haben gespendet<br>habt gespendet<br>haben gespendet |
| | **Past** | | **Past Perfect** | |
| | spendete<br>spendetest<br>spendete | spendeten<br>spendetet<br>spendeten | hatte gespendet<br>hattest gespendet<br>hatte gespendet | hatten gespendet<br>hattet gespendet<br>hatten gespendet |
| | **Future** | | **Future Perfect** | |
| | werde spenden<br>wirst spenden<br>wird spenden | werden spenden<br>werdet spenden<br>werden spenden | werde gespendet haben<br>wirst gespendet haben<br>wird gespendet haben | werden gespendet haben<br>werdet gespendet haben<br>werden gespendet haben |
| Subjunctive | **Present** | | **Present Perfect** | |
| | spende<br>spendest<br>spende | spenden<br>spendet<br>spenden | habe gespendet<br>habest gespendet<br>habe gespendet | haben gespendet<br>habet gespendet<br>haben gespendet |
| | **Past** | | **Past Perfect** | |
| | spendete<br>spendetest<br>spendete | spendeten<br>spendetet<br>spendeten | hätte gespendet<br>hättest gespendet<br>hätte gespendet | hätten gespendet<br>hättet gespendet<br>hätten gespendet |
| | **Future** | | **Future Perfect** | |
| | werde spenden<br>werdest spenden<br>werde spenden | werden spenden<br>werdet spenden<br>werden spenden | werde gespendet haben<br>werdest gespendet haben<br>werde gespendet haben | werden gespendet haben<br>werdet gespendet haben<br>werden gespendet haben |
| | **Present and Future Conditional** | | **Past Conditional** | |
| | würde spenden<br>würdest spenden<br>würde spenden | würden spenden<br>würdet spenden<br>würden spenden | würde gespendet haben<br>würdest gespendet haben<br>würde gespendet haben | würden gespendet haben<br>würdet gespendet haben<br>würden gespendet haben |

## EXAMPLES

Wir werden 200 Euro für die Krebsforschung spenden.
We're going to donate 200 euros for cancer research.

Hast du auch für die Erdbebenopfer gespendet?
Did you also donate money for the earthquake victims?

**sperren**

to obstruct, to barricade, to blockade

**Auxiliary verb:** haben **Past participle:** gesperrt

**Imperative:** Sperre! Sperrt! Sperren Sie!

| Mode | Simple Tenses | | Compound Tenses | |
|---|---|---|---|---|
| | *Singular* | *Plural* | *Singular* | *Plural* |
| Indicative | **Present** | | **Present Perfect** | |
| | sperre<br>sperrst<br>sperrt | sperren<br>sperrt<br>sperren | habe gesperrt<br>hast gesperrt<br>hat gesperrt | haben gesperrt<br>habt gesperrt<br>haben gesperrt |
| | **Past** | | **Past Perfect** | |
| | sperrte<br>sperrtest<br>sperrte | sperrten<br>sperrtet<br>sperrten | hatte gesperrt<br>hattest gesperrt<br>hatte gesperrt | hatten gesperrt<br>hattet gesperrt<br>hatten gesperrt |
| | **Future** | | **Future Perfect** | |
| | werde sperren<br>wirst sperren<br>wird sperren | werden sperren<br>werdet sperren<br>werden sperren | werde gesperrt haben<br>wirst gesperrt haben<br>wird gesperrt haben | werden gesperrt haben<br>werdet gesperrt haben<br>werden gesperrt haben |
| Subjunctive | **Present** | | **Present Perfect** | |
| | sperre<br>sperrest<br>sperre | sperren<br>sperret<br>sperren | habe gesperrt<br>habest gesperrt<br>habe gesperrt | haben gesperrt<br>habet gesperrt<br>haben gesperrt |
| | **Past** | | **Past Perfect** | |
| | sperrte<br>sperrtest<br>sperrte | sperrten<br>sperrtet<br>sperrten | hätte gesperrt<br>hättest gesperrt<br>hätte gesperrt | hätten gesperrt<br>hättet gesperrt<br>hätten gesperrt |
| | **Future** | | **Future Perfect** | |
| | werde sperren<br>werdest sperren<br>werde sperren | werden sperren<br>werdet sperren<br>werden sperren | werde gesperrt haben<br>werdest gesperrt haben<br>werde gesperrt haben | werden gesperrt haben<br>werdet gesperrt haben<br>werden gesperrt haben |
| | **Present and Future Conditional** | | **Past Conditional** | |
| | würde sperren<br>würdest sperren<br>würde sperren | würden sperren<br>würdet sperren<br>würden sperren | würde gesperrt haben<br>würdest gesperrt haben<br>würde gesperrt haben | würden gesperrt haben<br>würdet gesperrt haben<br>würden gesperrt haben |

## EXAMPLES

Wegen der Demonstration muss die Hauptstraße gesperrt werden.

Because of the demonstration, Main Street has to be closed.

Der lang gesuchte Verbrecher ist endlich ins Gefängnis gesperrt worden.

The long-sought-after criminal was finally put in jail.

**spielen**
to play, to act
**Auxiliary verb:** haben **Past participle:** gespielt
**Imperative:** Spiele! Spielt! Spielen Sie!

| Mode | Simple Tenses | | Compound Tenses | |
|---|---|---|---|---|
| | *Singular* | *Plural* | *Singular* | *Plural* |
| Indicative | **Present** | | **Present Perfect** | |
| | spiele<br>spielst<br>spielt | spielen<br>spielt<br>spielen | habe gespielt<br>hast gespielt<br>hat gespielt | haben gespielt<br>habt gespielt<br>haben gespielt |
| | **Past** | | **Past Perfect** | |
| | spielte<br>spieltest<br>spielte | spielten<br>spieltet<br>spielten | hatte gespielt<br>hattest gespielt<br>hatte gespielt | hatten gespielt<br>hattet gespielt<br>hatten gespielt |
| | **Future** | | **Future Perfect** | |
| | werde spielen<br>wirst spielen<br>wird spielen | werden spielen<br>werdet spielen<br>werden spielen | werde gespielt haben<br>wirst gespielt haben<br>wird gespielt haben | werden gespielt haben<br>werdet gespielt haben<br>werden gespielt haben |
| Subjunctive | **Present** | | **Present Perfect** | |
| | spiele<br>spielest<br>spiele | spielen<br>spielet<br>spielen | habe gespielt<br>habest gespielt<br>habe gespielt | haben gespielt<br>habet gespielt<br>haben gespielt |
| | **Past** | | **Past Perfect** | |
| | spielte<br>spieltest<br>spielte | spielten<br>spieltet<br>spielten | hätte gespielt<br>hättest gespielt<br>hätte gespielt | hätten gespielt<br>hättet gespielt<br>hätten gespielt |
| | **Future** | | **Future Perfect** | |
| | werde spielen<br>werdest spielen<br>werde spielen | werden spielen<br>werdet spielen<br>werden spielen | werde gespielt haben<br>werdest gespielt haben<br>werde gespielt haben | werden gespielt haben<br>werdet gespielt haben<br>werden gespielt haben |
| | **Present and Future Conditional** | | **Past Conditional** | |
| | würde spielen<br>würdest spielen<br>würde spielen | würden spielen<br>würdet spielen<br>würden spielen | würde gespielt haben<br>würdest gespielt haben<br>würde gespielt haben | würden gespielt haben<br>würdet gespielt haben<br>würden gespielt haben |

## EXAMPLES

Spielst du gern Schach?
Do you like playing chess?

Ich habe neulich mit meiner Kusine Tennis gespielt.
I recently played tennis with my cousin.

**spinnen**
to spin, to be crazy
**Auxiliary verb:** haben **Past participle:** gesponnen
**Imperative:** Spinne! Spinnt! Spinnen Sie!

| Mode | Simple Tenses | | Compound Tenses | |
|---|---|---|---|---|
| | *Singular* | *Plural* | *Singular* | *Plural* |
| Indicative | **Present** | | **Present Perfect** | |
| | spinne<br>spinnst<br>spinnt | spinnen<br>spinnt<br>spinnen | habe gesponnen<br>hast gesponnen<br>hat gesponnen | haben gesponnen<br>habt gesponnen<br>haben gesponnen |
| | **Past** | | **Past Perfect** | |
| | spann<br>spannst<br>spann | spannen<br>spannt<br>spannen | hatte gesponnen<br>hattest gesponnen<br>hatte gesponnen | hatten gesponnen<br>hattet gesponnen<br>hatten gesponnen |
| | **Future** | | **Future Perfect** | |
| | werde spinnen<br>wirst spinnen<br>wird spinnen | werden spinnen<br>werdet spinnen<br>werden spinnen | werde gesponnen haben<br>wirst gesponnen haben<br>wird gesponnen haben | werden gesponnen haben<br>werdet gesponnen haben<br>werden gesponnen haben |
| Subjunctive | **Present** | | **Present Perfect** | |
| | spinne<br>spinnest<br>spinne | spinnen<br>spinnet<br>spinnen | habe gesponnen<br>habest gesponnen<br>habe gesponnen | haben gesponnen<br>habet gesponnen<br>haben gesponnen |
| | **Past** | | **Past Perfect** | |
| | spönne<br>spönnest<br>spönne | spönnen<br>spönnet<br>spönnen | hätte gesponnen<br>hättest gesponnen<br>hätte gesponnen | hätten gesponnen<br>hättet gesponnen<br>hätten gesponnen |
| | **Future** | | **Future Perfect** | |
| | werde spinnen<br>werdest spinnen<br>werde spinnen | werden spinnen<br>werdet spinnen<br>werden spinnen | werde gesponnen haben<br>werdest gesponnen haben<br>werde gesponnen haben | werden gesponnen haben<br>werdet gesponnen haben<br>werden gesponnen haben |
| | **Present and Future Conditional** | | **Past Conditional** | |
| | würde spinnen<br>würdest spinnen<br>würde spinnen | würden spinnen<br>würdet spinnen<br>würden spinnen | würde gesponnen haben<br>würdest gesponnen haben<br>würde gesponnen haben | würden gesponnen haben<br>würdet gesponnen haben<br>würden gesponnen haben |

## EXAMPLES

Die Spinne hat ein feines Netz in der Ecke der Küchentür gesponnen.
Mensch, du spinnst!

The spider spun a fine web in the corner of the kitchen door.
Man, you're nuts!

**spotten**
to mock, to scoff at
**Auxiliary verb:** haben **Past participle:** gespottet
**Imperative:** Spotte! Spottet! Spotten Sie!

| Mode | Simple Tenses | | Compound Tenses | |
|---|---|---|---|---|
| | *Singular* | *Plural* | *Singular* | *Plural* |
| Indicative | **Present** | | **Present Perfect** | |
| | spotte<br>spottest<br>spottet | spotten<br>spottet<br>spotten | habe gespottet<br>hast gespottet<br>hat gespottet | haben gespottet<br>habt gespottet<br>haben gespottet |
| | **Past** | | **Past Perfect** | |
| | spottete<br>spottetest<br>spottete | spotteten<br>spottetet<br>spotteten | hatte gespottet<br>hattest gespottet<br>hatte gespottet | hatten gespottet<br>hattet gespottet<br>hatten gespottet |
| | **Future** | | **Future Perfect** | |
| | werde spotten<br>wirst spotten<br>wird spotten | werden spotten<br>werdet spotten<br>werden spotten | werde gespottet haben<br>wirst gespottet haben<br>wird gespottet haben | werden gespottet haben<br>werdet gespottet haben<br>werden gespottet haben |
| Subjunctive | **Present** | | **Present Perfect** | |
| | spotte<br>spottest<br>spotte | spotten<br>spottet<br>spotten | habe gespottet<br>habest gespottet<br>habe gespottet | haben gespottet<br>habet gespottet<br>haben gespottet |
| | **Past** | | **Past Perfect** | |
| | spottete<br>spottetest<br>spottete | spotteten<br>spottetet<br>spotteten | hätte gespottet<br>hättest gespottet<br>hätte gespottet | hätten gespottet<br>hättet gespottet<br>hätten gespottet |
| | **Future** | | **Future Perfect** | |
| | werde spotten<br>werdest spotten<br>werde spotten | werden spotten<br>werdet spotten<br>werden spotten | werde gespottet haben<br>werdest gespottet haben<br>werde gespottet haben | werden gespottet haben<br>werdet gespottet haben<br>werden gespottet haben |
| | **Present and Future Conditional** | | **Past Conditional** | |
| | würde spotten<br>würdest spotten<br>würde spotten | würden spotten<br>würdet spotten<br>würden spotten | würde gespottet haben<br>würdest gespottet haben<br>würde gespottet haben | würden gespottet haben<br>würdet gespottet haben<br>würden gespottet haben |

**Note:** The verb *trotten* has the same conjugation as the one illustrated above, except that it requires *sein* as its auxiliary in the perfect tenses.

## EXAMPLES

| | |
|---|---|
| Warum musst du über mich spotten? | Why do you have to mock me? |
| Der Gräuel des Unfalls spottet jeder Beschreibung. | The horror of the accident defies description. |

**sprechen**
to speak
**Auxiliary verb:** haben **Past participle:** gesprochen
**Imperative:** Sprich! Sprecht! Sprechen Sie!

| Mode | Simple Tenses | | Compound Tenses | |
|---|---|---|---|---|
| | *Singular* | *Plural* | *Singular* | *Plural* |
| Indicative | **Present** | | **Present Perfect** | |
| | spreche<br>sprichst<br>spricht | sprechen<br>sprecht<br>sprechen | habe gesprochen<br>hast gesprochen<br>hat gesprochen | haben gesprochen<br>habt gesprochen<br>haben gesprochen |
| | **Past** | | **Past Perfect** | |
| | sprach<br>sprachst<br>sprach | sprachen<br>spracht<br>sprachen | hatte gesprochen<br>hattest gesprochen<br>hatte gesprochen | hatten gesprochen<br>hattet gesprochen<br>hatten gesprochen |
| | **Future** | | **Future Perfect** | |
| | werde sprechen<br>wirst sprechen<br>wird sprechen | werden sprechen<br>werdet sprechen<br>werden sprechen | werde gesprochen haben<br>wirst gesprochen haben<br>wird gesprochen haben | werden gesprochen haben<br>werdet gesprochen haben<br>werden gesprochen haben |
| Subjunctive | **Present** | | **Present Perfect** | |
| | spreche<br>sprechest<br>spreche | sprechen<br>sprechet<br>sprechen | habe gesprochen<br>habest gesprochen<br>habe gesprochen | haben gesprochen<br>habet gesprochen<br>haben gesprochen |
| | **Past** | | **Past Perfect** | |
| | spräche<br>sprächest<br>spräche | sprächen<br>sprächet<br>sprächen | hätte gesprochen<br>hättest gesprochen<br>hätte gesprochen | hätten gesprochen<br>hättet gesprochen<br>hätten gesprochen |
| | **Future** | | **Future Perfect** | |
| | werde sprechen<br>werdest sprechen<br>werde sprechen | werden sprechen<br>werdet sprechen<br>werden sprechen | werde gesprochen haben<br>werdest gesprochen haben<br>werde gesprochen haben | werden gesprochen haben<br>werdet gesprochen haben<br>werden gesprochen haben |
| | **Present and Future Conditional** | | **Past Conditional** | |
| | würde sprechen<br>würdest sprechen<br>würde sprechen | würden sprechen<br>würdet sprechen<br>würden sprechen | würde gesprochen haben<br>würdest gesprochen haben<br>würde gesprochen haben | würden gesprochen haben<br>würdet gesprochen haben<br>würden gesprochen haben |

**Note:** With inseparable prefixes, the principal parts of this verb are, for example, *verspricht, versprach, hat versprochen.* With separable prefixes, the principal parts are, for example, *spricht aus, sprach aus, hat ausgesprochen.*

## EXAMPLES

| | |
|---|---|
| Wir haben gerade über sein neuestes Schauspiel gesprochen. | We were just talking about his newest play. |
| Der Lehrer möchte mit den Eltern des unartigen Schülers sprechen. | The teacher wants to speak with the parents of the naughty pupil. |

**springen**
to jump, to leap, to bounce
**Auxiliary verb:** sein **Past participle:** gesprungen
**Imperative:** Springe! Springt! Springen Sie!

| Mode | Simple Tenses | | Compound Tenses | |
|---|---|---|---|---|
| | *Singular* | *Plural* | *Singular* | *Plural* |
| Indicative | **Present** | | **Present Perfect** | |
| | springe<br>springst<br>springt | springen<br>springt<br>springen | bin gesprungen<br>bist gesprungen<br>ist gesprungen | sind gesprungen<br>seid gesprungen<br>sind gesprungen |
| | **Past** | | **Past Perfect** | |
| | sprang<br>sprangst<br>sprang | sprangen<br>sprangt<br>sprangen | war gesprungen<br>warst gesprungen<br>war gesprungen | waren gesprungen<br>wart gesprungen<br>waren gesprungen |
| | **Future** | | **Future Perfect** | |
| | werde springen<br>wirst springen<br>wird springen | werden springen<br>werdet springen<br>werden springen | werde gesprungen sein<br>wirst gesprungen sein<br>wird gesprungen sein | werden gesprungen sein<br>werdet gesprungen sein<br>werden gesprungen sein |
| Subjunctive | **Present** | | **Present Perfect** | |
| | springe<br>springest<br>springe | springen<br>springet<br>springen | sei gesprungen<br>seiest gesprungen<br>sei gesprungen | seien gesprungen<br>seiet gesprungen<br>seien gesprungen |
| | **Past** | | **Past Perfect** | |
| | spränge<br>sprängest<br>spränge | sprängen<br>spränget<br>sprängen | wäre gesprungen<br>wärest gesprungen<br>wäre gesprungen | wären gesprungen<br>wäret gesprungen<br>wären gesprungen |
| | **Future** | | **Future Perfect** | |
| | werde springen<br>werdest springen<br>werde springen | werden springen<br>werdet springen<br>werden springen | werde gesprungen sein<br>werdest gesprungen sein<br>werde gesprungen sein | werden gesprungen sein<br>werdet gesprungen sein<br>werden gesprungen sein |
| | **Present and Future Conditional** | | **Past Conditional** | |
| | würde springen<br>würdest springen<br>würde springen | würden springen<br>würdet springen<br>würden springen | würde gesprungen sein<br>würdest gesprungen sein<br>würde gesprungen sein | würden gesprungen sein<br>würdet gesprungen sein<br>würden gesprungen sein |

## EXAMPLES

Mir macht es gar keinen Spaß aus solcher Höhe ins Wasser zu springen.
It's no fun at all for me to jump into the water from such a height.

Der Hund ist wieder über den Zaun gesprungen.
The dog jumped over the fence again.

**spritzen**

to spurt, to squirt, to inject

**Auxiliary verb:** haben **Past participle:** gespritzt

**Imperative:** Spritze! Spritzt! Spritzen Sie!

| Mode | Simple Tenses | | Compound Tenses | |
|---|---|---|---|---|
| | *Singular* | *Plural* | *Singular* | *Plural* |
| Indicative | **Present** | | **Present Perfect** | |
| | spritze<br>spritzt<br>spritzt | spritzen<br>spritzt<br>spritzen | habe gespritzt<br>hast gespritzt<br>hat gespritzt | haben gespritzt<br>habt gespritzt<br>haben gespritzt |
| | **Past** | | **Past Perfect** | |
| | spritzte<br>spritztest<br>spritzte | spritzten<br>spritztet<br>spritzten | hatte gespritzt<br>hattest gespritzt<br>hatte gespritzt | hatten gespritzt<br>hattet gespritzt<br>hatten gespritzt |
| | **Future** | | **Future Perfect** | |
| | werde spritzen<br>wirst spritzen<br>wird spritzen | werden spritzen<br>werdet spritzen<br>werden spritzen | werde gespritzt haben<br>wirst gespritzt haben<br>wird gespritzt haben | werden gespritzt haben<br>werdet gespritzt haben<br>werden gespritzt haben |
| Subjunctive | **Present** | | **Present Perfect** | |
| | spritze<br>spritzest<br>spritze | spritzen<br>spritzet<br>spritzen | habe gespritzt<br>habest gespritzt<br>habe gespritzt | haben gespritzt<br>habet gespritzt<br>haben gespritzt |
| | **Past** | | **Past Perfect** | |
| | spritzte<br>spritztest<br>spritzte | spritzten<br>spritztet<br>spritzten | hätte gespritzt<br>hättest gespritzt<br>hätte gespritzt | hätten gespritzt<br>hättet gespritzt<br>hätten gespritzt |
| | **Future** | | **Future Perfect** | |
| | werde spritzen<br>werdest spritzen<br>werde spritzen | werden spritzen<br>werdet spritzen<br>werden spritzen | werde gespritzt haben<br>werdest gespritzt haben<br>werde gespritzt haben | werden gespritzt haben<br>werdet gespritzt haben<br>werden gespritzt haben |
| | **Present and Future Conditional** | | **Past Conditional** | |
| | würde spritzen<br>würdest spritzen<br>würde spritzen | würden spritzen<br>würdet spritzen<br>würden spritzen | würde gespritzt haben<br>würdest gespritzt haben<br>würde gespritzt haben | würden gespritzt haben<br>würdet gespritzt haben<br>würden gespritzt haben |

## EXAMPLES

Meine kleine Schwester hat Wasser auf meine Hausarbeit gespritzt.

My little sister spurted water onto my homework.

Der Bus fuhr durch die Pfütze und das schmutzige Wasser spritzte auf meine Schuhe.

The bus drove through the puddle, and the dirty water splattered my shoes.

**spüren**
to feel, to perceive
**Auxiliary verb:** haben **Past participle:** gespürt
**Imperative:** Spüre ! Spürt! Spüren Sie!

| Mode | Simple Tenses | | Compound Tenses | |
|---|---|---|---|---|
| | *Singular* | *Plural* | *Singular* | *Plural* |
| Indicative | **Present** | | **Present Perfect** | |
| | spüre<br>spürst<br>spürt | spüren<br>spürt<br>spüren | habe gespürt<br>hast gespürt<br>hat gespürt | haben gespürt<br>habt gespürt<br>haben gespürt |
| | **Past** | | **Past Perfect** | |
| | spürte<br>spürtest<br>spürte | spürten<br>spürtet<br>spürten | hatte gespürt<br>hattest gespürt<br>hatte gespürt | hatten gespürt<br>hattet gespürt<br>hatten gespürt |
| | **Future** | | **Future Perfect** | |
| | werde spüren<br>wirst spüren<br>wird spüren | werden spüren<br>werdet spüren<br>werden spüren | werde gespürt haben<br>wirst gespürt haben<br>wird gespürt haben | werden gespürt haben<br>werdet gespürt haben<br>werden gespürt haben |
| Subjunctive | **Present** | | **Present Perfect** | |
| | spüre<br>spürest<br>spüre | spüren<br>spüret<br>spüren | habe gespürt<br>habest gespürt<br>habe gespürt | haben gespürt<br>habet gespürt<br>haben gespürt |
| | **Past** | | **Past Perfect** | |
| | spürte<br>spürtest<br>spürte | spürten<br>spürtet<br>spürten | hätte gespürt<br>hättest gespürt<br>hätte gespürt | hätten gespürt<br>hättet gespürt<br>hätten gespürt |
| | **Future** | | **Future Perfect** | |
| | werde spüren<br>werdest spüren<br>werde spüren | werden spüren<br>werdet spüren<br>werden spüren | werde gespürt haben<br>werdest gespürt haben<br>werde gespürt haben | werden gespürt haben<br>werdet gespürt haben<br>werden gespürt haben |
| | **Present and Future Conditional** | | **Past Conditional** | |
| | wurde spüren<br>würdest spüren<br>würde spüren | wurden spüren<br>würdet spüren<br>würden spüren | wurde gespürt haben<br>würdest gespürt haben<br>würde gespürt haben | wurden gespürt haben<br>würdet gespürt haben<br>würden gespürt haben |

## EXAMPLES

Er spürte den Alkohol schon nach einer Flasche Bier.
Nach dem Fitnesstraining spürte er alle Knochen.

He felt the effects of the alcohol after only one bottle of beer.
After the workout, he felt every bone in his body.

**stattfinden**
to take place
**Auxiliary verb:** haben **Past participle:** stattgefunden
**Imperative:** N/A

| Mode | Simple Tenses | | Compound Tenses | |
|---|---|---|---|---|
| | *Singular* | *Plural* | *Singular* | *Plural* |
| Indicative | **Present** | | **Present Perfect** | |
| | findet statt | finden statt | hat stattgefunden | haben stattgefunden |
| | **Past** | | **Past Perfect** | |
| | fand statt | fanden statt | hatte stattgefunden | hatten stattgefunden |
| | **Future** | | **Future Perfect** | |
| | wird stattfinden | werden stattfinden | wird stattgefunden haben | werden stattgefunden haben |
| Subjunctive | **Present** | | **Present Perfect** | |
| | finde statt | finden statt | habe stattgefunden | haben stattgefunden |
| | **Past** | | **Past Perfect** | |
| | fände statt | fänden statt | hätte stattgefunden | hätten stattgefunden |
| | **Future** | | **Future Perfect** | |
| | werde stattfinden | werden stattfinden | werde stattgefunden haben | werden stattgefunden haben |
| | **Present and Future Conditional** | | **Past Conditional** | |
| | würde stattfinden | würden stattfinden | würde stattgefunden haben | würden stattgefunden haben |

**Note:** This verb is used primarily in the third-person singular and plural.

## EXAMPLES

Wann findet das nächste Examen statt?
When does the next examination take place?

Die Beerdigung hat letzte Woche stattgefunden.
The burial took place last week.

**stechen**
to stab, to sting, to pierce
**Auxiliary verb:** haben **Past participle:** gestochen
**Imperative:** Stich! Stecht! Stechen Sie!

| Mode | Simple Tenses | | Compound Tenses | |
|---|---|---|---|---|
| | *Singular* | *Plural* | *Singular* | *Plural* |
| Indicative | **Present** | | **Present Perfect** | |
| | steche<br>stichst<br>sticht | stechen<br>stecht<br>stechen | habe gestochen<br>hast gestochen<br>hat gestochen | haben gestochen<br>habt gestochen<br>haben gestochen |
| | **Past** | | **Past Perfect** | |
| | stach<br>stachst<br>stach | stachen<br>stacht<br>stachen | hatte gestochen<br>hattest gestochen<br>hatte gestochen | hatten gestochen<br>hattet gestochen<br>hatten gestochen |
| | **Future** | | **Future Perfect** | |
| | werde stechen<br>wirst stechen<br>wird stechen | werden stechen<br>werdet stechen<br>werden stechen | werde gestochen haben<br>wirst gestochen haben<br>wird gestochen haben | werden gestochen haben<br>werdet gestochen haben<br>werden gestochen haben |
| Subjunctive | **Present** | | **Present Perfect** | |
| | stoche<br>stechest<br>steche | stechen<br>stechet<br>stechen | habe gestochen<br>habest gestochen<br>habe gestochen | haben gestochen<br>habet gestochen<br>haben gestochen |
| | **Past** | | **Past Perfect** | |
| | stäche<br>stächest<br>stäche | stächen<br>stächet<br>stächen | hätte gestochen<br>hättest gestochen<br>hätte gestochen | hätten gestochen<br>hättet gestochen<br>hätten gestochen |
| | **Future** | | **Future Perfect** | |
| | werde stechen<br>werdest stechen<br>werde stechen | werden stechen<br>werdet stechen<br>werden stechen | werde gestochen haben<br>werdest gestochen haben<br>werde gestochen haben | werden gestochen haben<br>werdet gestochen haben<br>werden gestochen haben |
| | **Present and Future Conditional** | | **Past Conditional** | |
| | würde stechen<br>würdest stechen<br>würde stechen | würden stechen<br>würdet stechen<br>würden stechen | würde gestochen haben<br>würdest gestochen haben<br>würde gestochen haben | würden gestochen haben<br>würdet gestochen haben<br>würden gestochen haben |

## EXAMPLES

| | |
|---|---|
| Das weinende Kind ist von einer Biene gestochen worden. | The crying child was stung by a bee. |
| Ich stach mir mit der Nadel in den Daumen. | I stuck my thumb with the needle. |

**stecken**

to put, to set, to stick

**Auxiliary verb:** haben **Past participle:** gesteckt

**Imperative:** Stecke! Steckt! Stecken Sie!

| Mode | Simple Tenses | | Compound Tenses | |
|---|---|---|---|---|
| | *Singular* | *Plural* | *Singular* | *Plural* |
| Indicative | **Present** | | **Present Perfect** | |
| | stecke<br>steckst<br>steckt | stecken<br>steckt<br>stecken | habe gesteckt<br>hast gesteckt<br>hat gesteckt | haben gesteckt<br>habt gesteckt<br>haben gesteckt |
| | **Past** | | **Past Perfect** | |
| | steckte<br>stecktest<br>steckte | steckten<br>stecktet<br>steckten | hatte gesteckt<br>hattest gesteckt<br>hatte gesteckt | hatten gesteckt<br>hattet gesteckt<br>hatten gesteckt |
| | **Future** | | **Future Perfect** | |
| | werde stecken<br>wirst stecken<br>wird stecken | werden stecken<br>werdet stecken<br>werden stecken | werde gesteckt haben<br>wirst gesteckt haben<br>wird gesteckt haben | werden gesteckt haben<br>werdet gesteckt haben<br>werden gesteckt haben |
| Subjunctive | **Present** | | **Present Perfect** | |
| | stecke<br>steckest<br>stecke | stecken<br>stecket<br>stecken | habe gesteckt<br>habest gesteckt<br>habe gesteckt | haben gesteckt<br>habet gesteckt<br>haben gesteckt |
| | **Past** | | **Past Perfect** | |
| | steckte<br>stecktest<br>steckte | steckten<br>stecktet<br>steckten | hätte gesteckt<br>hättest gesteckt<br>hätte gesteckt | hätten gesteckt<br>hättet gesteckt<br>hätten gesteckt |
| | **Future** | | **Future Perfect** | |
| | werde stecken<br>werdest stecken<br>werde stecken | werden stecken<br>werdet stecken<br>werden stecken | werde gesteckt haben<br>werdest gesteckt haben<br>werde gesteckt haben | werden gesteckt haben<br>werdet gesteckt haben<br>werden gesteckt haben |
| | **Present and Future Conditional** | | **Past Conditional** | |
| | würde stecken<br>würdest stecken<br>würde stecken | würden stecken<br>würdet stecken<br>würden stecken | würde gesteckt haben<br>würdest gesteckt haben<br>würde gesteckt haben | würden gesteckt haben<br>würdet gesteckt haben<br>würden gesteckt haben |

## EXAMPLES

Ich habe das Geld in die Tasche gesteckt. — I stuck the money in my pocket.

Herr Mayer steckt bis über beide Ohren in Schulden. — Mr. Mayer is up to his ears in debt.

**stehen**
to stand, to suit
**Auxiliary verb:** haben **Past participle:** gestanden
**Imperative:** Stehe! Steht! Stehen Sie!

| Mode | Simple Tenses | | Compound Tenses | |
|---|---|---|---|---|
| | *Singular* | *Plural* | *Singular* | *Plural* |
| Indicative | **Present** | | **Present Perfect** | |
| | stehe<br>stehst<br>steht | stehen<br>steht<br>stehen | habe gestanden<br>hast gestanden<br>hat gestanden | haben gestanden<br>habt gestanden<br>haben gestanden |
| | **Past** | | **Past Perfect** | |
| | stand<br>standest<br>stand | standen<br>standet<br>standen | hatte gestanden<br>hattest gestanden<br>hatte gestanden | hatten gestanden<br>hattet gestanden<br>hatten gestanden |
| | **Future** | | **Future Perfect** | |
| | werde stehen<br>wirst stehen<br>wird stehen | werden stehen<br>werdet stehen<br>werden stehen | werde gestanden haben<br>wirst gestanden haben<br>wird gestanden haben | werden gestanden haben<br>werdet gestanden haben<br>werden gestanden haben |
| Subjunctive | **Present** | | **Present Perfect** | |
| | stehe<br>stehest<br>stehe | stehen<br>stehet<br>stehen | habe gestanden<br>habest gestanden<br>habe gestanden | haben gestanden<br>habet gestanden<br>haben gestanden |
| | **Past** | | **Past Perfect** | |
| | stände<br>ständest<br>stände | ständen<br>ständet<br>ständen | hätte gestanden<br>hättest gestanden<br>hätte gestanden | hätten gestanden<br>hättet gestanden<br>hätten gestanden |
| | **Future** | | **Future Perfect** | |
| | werde stehen<br>werdest stehen<br>werde stehen | werden stehen<br>werdet stehen<br>werden stehen | werde gestanden haben<br>werdest gestanden haben<br>werde gestanden haben | werden gestanden haben<br>werdet gestanden haben<br>werden gestanden haben |
| | **Present and Future Conditional** | | **Past Conditional** | |
| | würde stehen<br>würdest stehen<br>würde stehen | würden stehen<br>würdet stehen<br>würden stehen | würde gestanden haben<br>würdest gestanden haben<br>würde gestanden haben | würden gestanden haben<br>würdet gestanden haben<br>würden gestanden haben |

**Note:** In the past subjunctive, you'll frequently encounter *stünde* in place of *stände*. With inseparable prefixes, the principal parts of this verb are, for example, *besteht, bestand, hat bestanden.* With separable prefixes, the principal parts are, for example, *steht auf, stand auf, ist aufgestanden.* Note that *aufstehen* and *entstehen* require *sein* as their auxiliary in the perfect tenses.

## EXAMPLES

| | |
|---|---|
| Warum steht mein Name auf der Liste der durchgefallenen Studenten? | Why is my name on the list of failed students? |
| Wie steht mir dieser Regenmantel? | How does this raincoat look on me? |
| Das Mädchen stand hinter ihrem Vater und weinte. | The girl stood behind her father and cried. |

**stehlen**
to steal
**Auxiliary verb:** haben **Past participle:** gestohlen
**Imperative:** Stiehl! Stehlt! Stehlen Sie!

| Mode | Simple Tenses | | Compound Tenses | |
|---|---|---|---|---|
| | *Singular* | *Plural* | *Singular* | *Plural* |
| Indicative | **Present** | | **Present Perfect** | |
| | stehle<br>stiehlst<br>stiehlt | stehlen<br>stehlt<br>stehlen | habe gestohlen<br>hast gestohlen<br>hat gestohlen | haben gestohlen<br>habt gestohlen<br>haben gestohlen |
| | **Past** | | **Past Perfect** | |
| | stahl<br>stahlst<br>stahl | stahlen<br>stahlt<br>stahlen | hatte gestohlen<br>hattest gestohlen<br>hatte gestohlen | hatten gestohlen<br>hattet gestohlen<br>hatten gestohlen |
| | **Future** | | **Future Perfect** | |
| | werde stehlen<br>wirst stehlen<br>wird stehlen | werden stehlen<br>werdet stehlen<br>werden stehlen | werde gestohlen haben<br>wirst gestohlen haben<br>wird gestohlen haben | werden gestohlen haben<br>werdet gestohlen haben<br>werden gestohlen haben |
| Subjunctive | **Present** | | **Present Perfect** | |
| | stehle<br>stehlest<br>stehle | stehlen<br>stehlet<br>stehlen | habe gestohlen<br>habest gestohlen<br>habe gestohlen | haben gestohlen<br>habet gestohlen<br>haben gestohlen |
| | **Past** | | **Past Perfect** | |
| | stöhle<br>stöhlest<br>stöhle | stöhlen<br>stöhlet<br>stöhlen | hätte gestohlen<br>hättest gestohlen<br>hätte gestohlen | hätten gestohlen<br>hättet gestohlen<br>hätten gestohlen |
| | **Future** | | **Future Perfect** | |
| | werde stehlen<br>werdest stehlen<br>werde stehlen | werden stehlen<br>werdet stehlen<br>werden stehlen | werde gestohlen haben<br>werdest gestohlen haben<br>werde gestohlen haben | werden gestohlen haben<br>werdet gestohlen haben<br>werden gestohlen haben |
| | **Present and Future Conditional** | | **Past Conditional** | |
| | würde stehlen<br>würdest stehlen<br>würde stehlen | würden stehlen<br>würdet stehlen<br>würden stehlen | würde gestohlen haben<br>würdest gestohlen haben<br>würde gestohlen haben | würden gestohlen haben<br>würdet gestohlen haben<br>würden gestohlen haben |

## EXAMPLES

Ihm wurde gestern Abend in der Bibliothek sein Regenschirm gestohlen.
His umbrella was stolen at the library last night.

Der Dieb stahl mir nicht nur mein Geld, sondern auch meine Zeit.
The thief didn't just steal my money but my time, too.

**steigen**
to climb, to go up, to increase
**Auxiliary verb:** sein **Past participle:** gestiegen
**Imperative:** Steige! Steigt! Steigen Sie!

| Mode | Simple Tenses | | Compound Tenses | |
|---|---|---|---|---|
| | *Singular* | *Plural* | *Singular* | *Plural* |
| Indicative | **Present** | | **Present Perfect** | |
| | steige<br>steigst<br>steigt | steigen<br>steigt<br>steigen | bin gestiegen<br>bist gestiegen<br>ist gestiegen | sind gestiegen<br>seid gestiegen<br>sind gestiegen |
| | **Past** | | **Past Perfect** | |
| | stieg<br>stiegst<br>stieg | stiegen<br>stiegt<br>stiegen | war gestiegen<br>warst gestiegen<br>war gestiegen | waren gestiegen<br>wart gestiegen<br>waren gestiegen |
| | **Future** | | **Future Perfect** | |
| | werde steigen<br>wirst steigen<br>wird steigen | werden steigen<br>werdet steigen<br>werden steigen | werde gestiegen sein<br>wirst gestiegen sein<br>wird gestiegen sein | werden gestiegen sein<br>werdet gestiegen sein<br>werden gestiegen sein |
| Subjunctive | **Present** | | **Present Perfect** | |
| | steige<br>steigest<br>steige | steigen<br>steiget<br>steigen | sei gestiegen<br>seiest gestiegen<br>sei gestiegen | seien gestiegen<br>seiet gestiegen<br>seien gestiegen |
| | **Past** | | **Past Perfect** | |
| | stiege<br>stiegest<br>stiege | stiegen<br>stieget<br>stiegen | wäre gestiegen<br>wärest gestiegen<br>wäre gestiegen | wären gestiegen<br>wäret gestiegen<br>wären gestiegen |
| | **Future** | | **Future Perfect** | |
| | werde steigen<br>werdest steigen<br>werde steigen | werden steigen<br>werdet steigen<br>werden steigen | werde gestiegen sein<br>werdest gestiegen sein<br>werde gestiegen sein | werden gestiegen sein<br>werdet gestiegen sein<br>werden gestiegen sein |
| | **Present and Future Conditional** | | **Past Conditional** | |
| | würde steigen<br>würdest steigen<br>würde steigen | würden steigen<br>würdet steigen<br>würden steigen | würde gestiegen sein<br>würdest gestiegen sein<br>würde gestiegen sein | würden gestiegen sein<br>würdet gestiegen sein<br>würden gestiegen sein |

**Note:** With separable prefixes, the principal parts of this verb are, for example, *steigt aus, stieg aus, ist ausgestiegen*

## EXAMPLES

Sebastian ist über das Skateboard gestiegen.
Sebastian stepped over the skateboard.

In den letzten vier Monaten sind die Benzinpreise um mehr als zehn Prozent gestiegen.
In the last four months, gas prices have increased by more than 10 percent.

**stellen**

to put, to place, to set

**Auxiliary verb:** haben **Past participle:** gestellt

**Imperative:** Stelle! Stellt! Stellen Sie!

| Mode | Simple Tenses | | Compound Tenses | |
|---|---|---|---|---|
| | *Singular* | *Plural* | *Singular* | *Plural* |
| Indicative | **Present** | | **Present Perfect** | |
| | stelle<br>stellst<br>stellt | stellen<br>stellt<br>stellen | habe gestellt<br>hast gestellt<br>hat gestellt | haben gestellt<br>habt gestellt<br>haben gestellt |
| | **Past** | | **Past Perfect** | |
| | stellte<br>stelltest<br>stellte | stellten<br>stelltet<br>stellten | hatte gestellt<br>hattest gestellt<br>hatte gestellt | hatten gestellt<br>hattet gestellt<br>hatten gestellt |
| | **Future** | | **Future Perfect** | |
| | werde stellen<br>wirst stellen<br>wird stellen | werden stellen<br>werdet stellen<br>werden stellen | werde gestellt haben<br>wirst gestellt haben<br>wird gestellt haben | werden gestellt haben<br>werdet gestellt haben<br>werden gestellt haben |
| Subjunctive | **Present** | | **Present Perfect** | |
| | stelle<br>stellest<br>stelle | stellen<br>stellet<br>stellen | habe gestellt<br>habest gestellt<br>habe gestellt | haben gestellt<br>habet gestellt<br>haben gestellt |
| | **Past** | | **Past Perfect** | |
| | stellte<br>stelltest<br>stellte | stellten<br>stelltet<br>stellten | hätte gestellt<br>hättest gestellt<br>hätte gestellt | hätten gestellt<br>hättet gestellt<br>hätten gestellt |
| | **Future** | | **Future Perfect** | |
| | werde stellen<br>werdest stellen<br>werde stellen | werden stellen<br>werdet stellen<br>werden stellen | werde gestellt haben<br>werdest gestellt haben<br>werde gestellt haben | werden gestellt haben<br>werdet gestellt haben<br>werden gestellt haben |
| | **Present and Future Conditional** | | **Past Conditional** | |
| | würde stellen<br>würdest stellen<br>würde stellen | würden stellen<br>würdet stellen<br>würden stellen | würde gestellt haben<br>würdest gestellt haben<br>würde gestellt haben | würden gestellt haben<br>würdet gestellt haben<br>würden gestellt haben |

**Note:** With inseparable prefixes, the principal parts of this verb are, for example, *bestellt, bestellte, hat bestellt.* With separable prefixes, the principal parts are, for example, *stellt vor, stellte vor, hat vorgestellt.*

## EXAMPLES

| | |
|---|---|
| Stellen Sie bitte das Radio auf den Schreibtisch. | Please put the radio on the desk. |
| Er hat die Frage gestellt, ob Erhardt noch in der Hauptstadt sei. | He asked whether Erhardt was still in the capital. |

**stemmen**

to stem, to stand firm, to lift weights

**Auxiliary verb:** haben **Past participle:** gestemmt

**Imperative:** Stemme! Stemmt! Stemmen Sie!

| Mode | Simple Tenses | | Compound Tenses | |
|---|---|---|---|---|
| | *Singular* | *Plural* | *Singular* | *Plural* |
| Indicative | **Present** | | **Present Perfect** | |
| | stemme<br>stemmst<br>stemmt | stemmen<br>stemmt<br>stemmen | habe gestemmt<br>hast gestemmt<br>hat gestemmt | haben gestemmt<br>habt gestemmt<br>haben gestemmt |
| | **Past** | | **Past Perfect** | |
| | stemmte<br>stemmtest<br>stemmte | stemmten<br>stemmtet<br>stemmten | hatte gestemmt<br>hattest gestemmt<br>hatte gestemmt | hatten gestemmt<br>hattet gestemmt<br>hatten gestemmt |
| | **Future** | | **Future Perfect** | |
| | werde stemmen<br>wirst stemmen<br>wird stemmen | werden stemmen<br>werdet stemmen<br>werden stemmen | werde gestemmt haben<br>wirst gestemmt haben<br>wird gestemmt haben | werden gestemmt haben<br>werdet gestemmt haben<br>werden gestemmt haben |
| Subjunctive | **Present** | | **Present Perfect** | |
| | stemme<br>stemmest<br>stemme | stemmen<br>stemmet<br>stemmen | habe gestemmt<br>habest gestemmt<br>habe gestemmt | haben gestemmt<br>habet gestemmt<br>haben gestemmt |
| | **Past** | | **Past Perfect** | |
| | stemmte<br>stemmtest<br>stemmte | stemmten<br>stemmtet<br>stemmten | hätte gestemmt<br>hättest gestemmt<br>hätte gestemmt | hätten gestemmt<br>hättet gestemmt<br>hätten gestemmt |
| | **Future** | | **Future Perfect** | |
| | werde stemmen<br>werdest stemmen<br>werde stemmen | werden stemmen<br>werdet stemmen<br>werden stemmen | werde gestemmt haben<br>werdest gestemmt haben<br>werde gestemmt haben | werden gestemmt haben<br>werdet gestemmt haben<br>werden gestemmt haben |
| | **Present and Future Conditional** | | **Past Conditional** | |
| | würde stemmen<br>würdest stemmen<br>würde stemmen | würden stemmen<br>würdet stemmen<br>würden stemmen | würde gestemmt haben<br>würdest gestemmt haben<br>würde gestemmt haben | würden gestemmt haben<br>würdet gestemmt haben<br>würden gestemmt haben |

## EXAMPLES

Sie stemmte die Arme in die Seiten und starrte mich wütend an.

She put her hands on her hips and stared at me angrily.

Der muskulöse Mann stemmt täglich Gewichte.

The muscular man lifts weights every day.

**stempeln**

to stamp, to mark, to cancel

**Auxiliary verb:** haben **Past participle:** gestempelt

**Imperative:** Stempele! Stempelt! Stempeln Sie!

| Mode | Simple Tenses | | Compound Tenses | |
|---|---|---|---|---|
| | *Singular* | *Plural* | *Singular* | *Plural* |
| Indicative | **Present** | | **Present Perfect** | |
| | stempele<br>stempelst<br>stempelt | stempeln<br>stempelt<br>stempeln | habe gestempelt<br>hast gestempelt<br>hat gestempelt | haben gestempelt<br>habt gestempelt<br>haben gestempelt |
| | **Past** | | **Past Perfect** | |
| | stempelte<br>stempeltest<br>stempelte | stempelten<br>stempeltet<br>stempelten | hatte gestempelt<br>hattest gestempelt<br>hatte gestempelt | hatten gestempelt<br>hattet gestempelt<br>hatten gestempelt |
| | **Future** | | **Future Perfect** | |
| | werde stempeln<br>wirst stempeln<br>wird stempeln | werden stempeln<br>werdet stempeln<br>werden stempeln | werde gestempelt haben<br>wirst gestempelt haben<br>wird gestempelt haben | werden gestempelt haben<br>werdet gestempelt haben<br>werden gestempelt haben |
| Subjunctive | **Present** | | **Present Perfect** | |
| | stempele<br>stempelst<br>stempele | stempeln<br>stempelt<br>stempeln | habe gestempelt<br>habest gestempelt<br>habe gestempelt | haben gestempelt<br>habet gestempelt<br>haben gestempelt |
| | **Past** | | **Past Perfect** | |
| | stempelte<br>stempeltest<br>stempelte | stempelten<br>stempeltet<br>stempelten | hätte gestempelt<br>hättest gestempelt<br>hätte gestempelt | hätten gestempelt<br>hättet gestempelt<br>hätten gestempelt |
| | **Future** | | **Future Perfect** | |
| | werde stempeln<br>werdest stempeln<br>werde stempeln | werden stempeln<br>werdet stempeln<br>werden stempeln | werde gestempelt haben<br>werdest gestempelt haben<br>werde gestempelt haben | werden gestempelt haben<br>werdet gestempelt haben<br>werden gestempelt haben |
| | **Present and Future Conditional** | | **Past Conditional** | |
| | würde stempeln<br>würdest stempeln<br>würde stempeln | würden stempeln<br>würdet stempeln<br>würden stempeln | würde gestempelt haben<br>würdest gestempelt haben<br>würde gestempelt haben | würden gestempelt haben<br>würdet gestempelt haben<br>würden gestempelt haben |

## EXAMPLES

Bevor Sie abreisen, müssen Sie das Visum stempeln lassen.

Before you depart, you have to have the visa stamped.

Diese Briefmarke ist noch nicht gestempelt worden und ist gültig.

This stamp hasn't been stamped yet and is valid.

**sterben**
to die
**Auxiliary verb:** sein **Past participle:** gestorben
**Imperative:** Stirb! Sterbt! Sterben Sie!

| Mode | Simple Tenses | | Compound Tenses | |
|---|---|---|---|---|
| | *Singular* | *Plural* | *Singular* | *Plural* |
| Indicative | **Present** | | **Present Perfect** | |
| | sterbe<br>stirbst<br>stirbt | sterben<br>sterbt<br>sterben | bin gestorben<br>bist gestorben<br>ist gestorben | sind gestorben<br>seid gestorben<br>sind gestorben |
| | **Past** | | **Past Perfect** | |
| | starb<br>starbst<br>starb | starben<br>starbt<br>starben | war gestorben<br>warst gestorben<br>war gestorben | waren gestorben<br>wart gestorben<br>waren gestorben |
| | **Future** | | **Future Perfect** | |
| | werde sterben<br>wirst sterben<br>wird sterben | werden sterben<br>werdet sterben<br>werden sterben | werde gestorben sein<br>wirst gestorben sein<br>wird gestorben sein | werden gestorben sein<br>werdet gestorben sein<br>werden gestorben sein |
| Subjunctive | **Present** | | **Present Perfect** | |
| | sterbe<br>sterbest<br>sterbe | sterben<br>sterbet<br>sterben | sei gestorben<br>seiest gestorben<br>sei gestorben | seien gestorben<br>seiet gestorben<br>seien gestorben |
| | **Past** | | **Past Perfect** | |
| | stürbe<br>stürbest<br>stürbe | stürben<br>stürbet<br>stürben | wäre gestorben<br>wärest gestorben<br>wäre gestorben | wären gestorben<br>wäret gestorben<br>wären gestorben |
| | **Future** | | **Future Perfect** | |
| | werde sterben<br>werdest sterben<br>werde sterben | werden sterben<br>werdet sterben<br>werden sterben | werde gestorben sein<br>werdest gestorben sein<br>werde gestorben sein | werden gestorben sein<br>werdet gestorben sein<br>werden gestorben sein |
| | **Present and Future Conditional** | | **Past Conditional** | |
| | würde sterben<br>würdest sterben<br>würde sterben | würden sterben<br>würdet sterben<br>würden sterben | würde gestorben sein<br>würdest gestorben sein<br>würde gestorben sein | würden gestorben sein<br>würdet gestorben sein<br>würden gestorben sein |

**Note:** With inseparable prefixes, the principal parts of this verb are, for example, *verstirbt, verstarb, ist verstorben.* With separable prefixes, the principal parts are, for example, *stirbt aus, starb aus, ist ausgestorben.*

## EXAMPLES

| | |
|---|---|
| Mein Onkel ist vor sechs Jahren an einer Lungenentzündung gestorben. | My uncle died six years ago from pneumonia. |
| Wann essen wir? Ich sterbe vor Hunger. | When will we eat? I'm dying of hunger. |

**steuern**

to steer, to pilot, to navigate

**Auxiliary verb:** haben **Past participle:** gesteuert

**Imperative:** Steuere! Steuert! Steuern Sie!

| Mode | Simple Tenses | | Compound Tenses | |
|---|---|---|---|---|
| | *Singular* | *Plural* | *Singular* | *Plural* |
| Indicative | **Present** | | **Present Perfect** | |
| | steuere<br>steuerst<br>steuert | steuern<br>steuert<br>steuern | habe gesteuert<br>hast gesteuert<br>hat gesteuert | haben gesteuert<br>habt gesteuert<br>haben gesteuert |
| | **Past** | | **Past Perfect** | |
| | steuerte<br>steuertest<br>steuerte | steuerten<br>steuertet<br>steuerten | hatte gesteuert<br>hattest gesteuert<br>hatte gesteuert | hatten gesteuert<br>hattet gesteuert<br>hatten gesteuert |
| | **Future** | | **Future Perfect** | |
| | werde steuern<br>wirst steuern<br>wird steuern | werden steuern<br>werdet steuern<br>werden steuern | werde gesteuert haben<br>wirst gesteuert haben<br>wird gesteuert haben | werden gesteuert haben<br>werdet gesteuert haben<br>werden gesteuert haben |
| Subjunctive | **Present** | | **Present Perfect** | |
| | steuere<br>steuerst<br>steuere | steuern<br>steuert<br>steuern | habe gesteuert<br>habest gesteuert<br>habe gesteuert | haben gesteuert<br>habet gesteuert<br>haben gesteuert |
| | **Past** | | **Past Perfect** | |
| | steuerte<br>steuertest<br>steuerte | steuerten<br>steuertet<br>steuerten | hätte gesteuert<br>hättest gesteuert<br>hätte gesteuert | hätten gesteuert<br>hättet gesteuert<br>hätten gesteuert |
| | **Future** | | **Future Perfect** | |
| | werde steuern<br>werdest steuern<br>werde steuern | werden steuern<br>werdet steuern<br>werden steuern | werde gesteuert haben<br>werdest gesteuert haben<br>werde gesteuert haben | werden gesteuert haben<br>werdet gesteuert haben<br>werden gesteuert haben |
| | **Present and Future Conditional** | | **Past Conditional** | |
| | würde steuern<br>würdest steuern<br>würde steuern | würden steuern<br>würdet steuern<br>würden steuern | würde gesteuert haben<br>würdest gesteuert haben<br>würde gesteuert haben | würden gesteuert haben<br>würdet gesteuert haben<br>würden gesteuert haben |

**Note:** This verb can act as a verb of motion. In such a case, it requires *sein* as its auxiliary in the perfect tenses.

## EXAMPLES

Ich verstehe nicht, wie man so ein riesiges Schiff steuern kann.

I don't understand how someone can pilot such a gigantic ship.

Mein Freund steuerte das Auto direkt in den Straßengraben.

My friend steered the car right into the ditch.

**stinken**
to stink
**Auxiliary verb:** haben **Past participle:** gestunken
**Imperative:** Stinke! Stinkt! Stinken Sie!

| Mode | Simple Tenses | | Compound Tenses | |
|---|---|---|---|---|
| | *Singular* | *Plural* | *Singular* | *Plural* |
| Indicative | **Present** | | **Present Perfect** | |
| | stinke<br>stinkst<br>stinkt | stinken<br>stinkt<br>stinken | habe gestunken<br>hast gestunken<br>hat gestunken | haben gestunken<br>habt gestunken<br>haben gestunken |
| | **Past** | | **Past Perfect** | |
| | stank<br>stankst<br>stank | stanken<br>stankt<br>stanken | hatte gestunken<br>hattest gestunken<br>hatte gestunken | hatten gestunken<br>hattet gestunken<br>hatten gestunken |
| | **Future** | | **Future Perfect** | |
| | werde stinken<br>wirst stinken<br>wird stinken | werden stinken<br>werdet stinken<br>werden stinken | werde gestunken haben<br>wirst gestunken haben<br>wird gestunken haben | werden gestunken haben<br>werdet gestunken haben<br>werden gestunken haben |
| Subjunctive | **Present** | | **Present Perfect** | |
| | stinke<br>stinkest<br>stinke | stinken<br>stinket<br>stinken | habe gestunken<br>habest gestunken<br>habe gestunken | haben gestunken<br>habet gestunken<br>haben gestunken |
| | **Past** | | **Past Perfect** | |
| | stänke<br>stänkest<br>stänke | stänken<br>stänket<br>stänken | hätte gestunken<br>hättest gestunken<br>hätte gestunken | hätten gestunken<br>hättet gestunken<br>hätten gestunken |
| | **Future** | | **Future Perfect** | |
| | werde stinken<br>werdest stinken<br>werde stinken | werden stinken<br>werdet stinken<br>werden stinken | werde gestunken haben<br>werdest gestunken haben<br>werde gestunken haben | werden gestunken haben<br>werdet gestunken haben<br>werden gestunken haben |
| | **Present and Future Conditional** | | **Past Conditional** | |
| | würde stinken<br>würdest stinken<br>würde stinken | würden stinken<br>würdet stinken<br>würden stinken | würde gestunken haben<br>würdest gestunken haben<br>würde gestunken haben | würden gestunken haben<br>würdet gestunken haben<br>würden gestunken haben |

## EXAMPLES

Gestern hat es in der Stadt nach Abgasen gestunken.
Yesterday in the city it reeked of automobile exhaust fumes.

In der Küche stinkt es nach Essig.
The kitchen stinks like vinegar.

**stören**
to disturb, to annoy
**Auxiliary verb:** haben **Past participle:** gestört
**Imperative:** Störe! Stört! Stören Sie!

| Mode | Simple Tenses | | Compound Tenses | |
|---|---|---|---|---|
| | *Singular* | *Plural* | *Singular* | *Plural* |
| Indicative | **Present** | | **Present Perfect** | |
| | störe<br>störst<br>stört | stören<br>stört<br>stören | habe gestört<br>hast gestört<br>hat gestört | haben gestört<br>habt gestört<br>haben gestört |
| | **Past** | | **Past Perfect** | |
| | störte<br>störtest<br>störte | störten<br>störtet<br>störten | hatte gestört<br>hattest gestört<br>hatte gestört | hatten gestört<br>hattet gestört<br>hatten gestört |
| | **Future** | | **Future Perfect** | |
| | werde stören<br>wirst stören<br>wird stören | werden stören<br>werdet stören<br>werden stören | werde gestört haben<br>wirst gestört haben<br>wird gestört haben | werden gestört haben<br>werdet gestört haben<br>werden gestört haben |
| Subjunctive | **Present** | | **Present Perfect** | |
| | störe<br>störest<br>störe | stören<br>störet<br>stören | habe gestört<br>habest gestört<br>habe gestört | haben gestört<br>habet gestört<br>haben gestört |
| | **Past** | | **Past Perfect** | |
| | störte<br>störtest<br>störte | störten<br>störtet<br>störten | hätte gestört<br>hättest gestört<br>hätte gestört | hätten gestört<br>hättet gestört<br>hätten gestört |
| | **Future** | | **Future Perfect** | |
| | werde stören<br>werdest stören<br>werde stören | werden stören<br>werdet stören<br>werden stören | werde gestört haben<br>werdest gestört haben<br>werde gestört haben | werden gestört haben<br>werdet gestört haben<br>werden gestört haben |
| | **Present and Future Conditional** | | **Past Conditional** | |
| | würde stören<br>würdest stören<br>würde stören | würden stören<br>würdet stören<br>würden stören | würde gestört haben<br>würdest gestört haben<br>würde gestört haben | würden gestört haben<br>würdet gestört haben<br>würden gestört haben |

## EXAMPLES

| | |
|---|---|
| Der Mann, der so laut flucht, ist geistig gestört. | The man who is cursing so loudly is mentally disturbed. |
| Bitte stören Sie mich nicht! | Please, don't interrupt me. |

**stoßen**
to push, to shove, to hit
**Auxiliary verb:** haben **Past participle:** gestoßen
**Imperative:** Stoße! Stoßt! Stoßen Sie!

| Mode | Simple Tenses | | Compound Tenses | |
|---|---|---|---|---|
| | *Singular* | *Plural* | *Singular* | *Plural* |
| Indicative | **Present** | | **Present Perfect** | |
| | stoße<br>stößt<br>stößt | stoßen<br>stoßt<br>stoßen | habe gestoßen<br>hast gestoßen<br>hat gestoßen | haben gestoßen<br>habt gestoßen<br>haben gestoßen |
| | **Past** | | **Past Perfect** | |
| | stieß<br>stießest<br>stieß | stießen<br>stießt<br>stießen | hatte gestoßen<br>hattest gestoßen<br>hatte gestoßen | hatten gestoßen<br>hattet gestoßen<br>hatten gestoßen |
| | **Future** | | **Future Perfect** | |
| | werde stoßen<br>wirst stoßen<br>wird stoßen | werden stoßen<br>werdet stoßen<br>werden stoßen | werde gestoßen haben<br>wirst gestoßen haben<br>wird gestoßen haben | werden gestoßen haben<br>werdet gestoßen haben<br>werden gestoßen haben |
| Subjunctive | **Present** | | **Present Perfect** | |
| | stoße<br>stoßest<br>stoße | stoßen<br>stoßet<br>stoßen | habe gestoßen<br>habest gestoßen<br>habe gestoßen | haben gestoßen<br>habet gestoßen<br>haben gestoßen |
| | **Past** | | **Past Perfect** | |
| | stieße<br>stießest<br>stieße | stießen<br>stießet<br>stießen | hätte gestoßen<br>hättest gestoßen<br>hätte gestoßen | hätten gestoßen<br>hättet gestoßen<br>hätten gestoßen |
| | **Future** | | **Future Perfect** | |
| | werde stoßen<br>werdest stoßen<br>werde stoßen | werden stoßen<br>werdet stoßen<br>werden stoßen | werde gestoßen haben<br>werdest gestoßen haben<br>werde gestoßen haben | werden gestoßen haben<br>werdet gestoßen haben<br>werden gestoßen haben |
| | **Present and Future Conditional** | | **Past Conditional** | |
| | würde stoßen<br>würdest stoßen<br>würde stoßen | würden stoßen<br>würdet stoßen<br>würden stoßen | würde gestoßen haben<br>würdest gestoßen haben<br>würde gestoßen haben | würden gestoßen haben<br>würdet gestoßen haben<br>würden gestoßen haben |

## EXAMPLES

| | |
|---|---|
| Er hat sich an dem niedrigen Türrahmen gestoßen. | He bumped his head on the low door frame. |
| Martin stößt seinen Bruder auf den Boden. | Martin pushes his brother onto the floor. |

**strafen**

to punish, to fine

**Auxiliary verb:** haben **Past participle:** gestraft

**Imperative:** Strafe! Straft! Strafen Sie!

| Mode | Simple Tenses | | Compound Tenses | |
|---|---|---|---|---|
| | *Singular* | *Plural* | *Singular* | *Plural* |
| Indicative | **Present** | | **Present Perfect** | |
| | strafe<br>strafst<br>straft | strafen<br>straft<br>strafen | habe gestraft<br>hast gestraft<br>hat gestraft | haben gestraft<br>habt gestraft<br>haben gestraft |
| | **Past** | | **Past Perfect** | |
| | strafte<br>strattest<br>strafte | straften<br>straftet<br>straften | hatte gestraft<br>hattest gestraft<br>hatte gestraft | hatten gestraft<br>hattet gestraft<br>hatten gestraft |
| | **Future** | | **Future Perfect** | |
| | werde strafen<br>wirst strafen<br>wird strafen | werden strafen<br>werdet strafen<br>werden strafen | werde gestraft haben<br>wirst gestraft haben<br>wird gestraft haben | werden gestraft haben<br>werdet gestraft haben<br>werden gestraft haben |
| Subjunctive | **Present** | | **Present Perfect** | |
| | strafe<br>strafest<br>strafe | strafen<br>strafet<br>strafen | habe gestraft<br>habest gestraft<br>habe gestraft | haben gestraft<br>habet gestraft<br>haben gestraft |
| | **Past** | | **Past Perfect** | |
| | strafte<br>straftest<br>strafte | straften<br>straftet<br>straften | hätte gestraft<br>hättest gestraft<br>hätte gestraft | hätten gestraft<br>hättet gestraft<br>hätten gestraft |
| | **Future** | | **Future Perfect** | |
| | werde strafen<br>werdest strafen<br>werde strafen | werden strafen<br>werdet strafen<br>werden strafen | werde gestraft haben<br>werdest gestraft haben<br>werde gestraft haben | werden gestraft haben<br>werdet gestraft haben<br>werden gestraft haben |
| | **Present and Future Conditional** | | **Past Conditional** | |
| | würde strafen<br>würdest strafen<br>würde strafen | würden strafen<br>würdet strafen<br>würden strafen | würde gestraft haben<br>würdest gestraft haben<br>würde gestraft haben | würden gestraft haben<br>würdet gestraft haben<br>würden gestraft haben |

**Note:** With inseparable prefixes, the principal parts of this verb are, for example, *bestraft, bestrafte, hat bestraft.*

## EXAMPLES

Die Frau strafte ihn mit einem verachtungsvollen Blick.
The woman punished him with a contemptuous look.

Der Lehrer wird den Schüler mit Nachsitzen strafen.
The teacher will punish the student with detention.

**streichen**
to strike, to erase, to paint
**Auxiliary verb:** haben **Past participle:** gestrichen
**Imperative:** Streiche! Streicht! Streichen Sie!

| Mode | Simple Tenses | | Compound Tenses | |
|---|---|---|---|---|
| | *Singular* | *Plural* | *Singular* | *Plural* |
| Indicative | **Present** | | **Present Perfect** | |
| | streiche<br>streichst<br>streicht | streichen<br>streicht<br>streichen | habe gestrichen<br>hast gestrichen<br>hat gestrichen | haben gestrichen<br>habt gestrichen<br>haben gestrichen |
| | **Past** | | **Past Perfect** | |
| | strich<br>strichst<br>strich | strichen<br>stricht<br>strichen | hatte gestrichen<br>hattest gestrichen<br>hatte gestrichen | hatten gestrichen<br>hattet gestrichen<br>hatten gestrichen |
| | **Future** | | **Future Perfect** | |
| | werde streichen<br>wirst streichen<br>wird streichen | werden streichen<br>werdet streichen<br>werden streichen | werde gestrichen haben<br>wirst gestrichen haben<br>wird gestrichen haben | werden gestrichen haben<br>werdet gestrichen haben<br>werden gestrichen haben |
| Subjunctive | **Present** | | **Present Perfect** | |
| | streiche<br>streichest<br>streiche | streichen<br>streichet<br>streichen | habe gestrichen<br>habest gestrichen<br>habe gestrichen | haben gestrichen<br>habet gestrichen<br>haben gestrichen |
| | **Past** | | **Past Perfect** | |
| | striche<br>strichest<br>striche | strichen<br>strichet<br>strichen | hätte gestrichen<br>hättest gestrichen<br>hätte gestrichen | hätten gestrichen<br>hättet gestrichen<br>hätten gestrichen |
| | **Future** | | **Future Perfect** | |
| | werde streichen<br>werdest streichen<br>werde streichen | werden streichen<br>werdet streichen<br>werden streichen | werde gestrichen haben<br>werdest gestrichen haben<br>werde gestrichen haben | werden gestrichen haben<br>werdet gestrichen haben<br>werden gestrichen haben |
| | **Present and Future Conditional** | | **Past Conditional** | |
| | würde streichen<br>würdest streichen<br>würde streichen | würden streichen<br>würdet streichen<br>würden streichen | würde gestrichen haben<br>würdest gestrichen haben<br>würde gestrichen haben | würden gestrichen haben<br>würdet gestrichen haben<br>würden gestrichen haben |

## EXAMPLES

Vorsicht! Frisch gestrichen!
Careful! Fresh paint!

Ich werde das letzte Wort in diesem Satz streichen.
I'm going to erase the last word in this sentence.

**streiten (sich)**
to dispute, to quarrel
**Auxiliary verb:** haben **Past participle:** gestritten
**Imperative:** Streite! Streitet! Streiten Sie!

| Mode | Simple Tenses | | Compound Tenses | |
|---|---|---|---|---|
| | *Singular* | *Plural* | *Singular* | *Plural* |
| Indicative | **Present** | | **Present Perfect** | |
| | streite<br>streitest<br>streitet | streiten<br>streitet<br>streiten | habe gestritten<br>hast gestritten<br>hat gestritten | haben gestritten<br>habt gestritten<br>haben gestritten |
| | **Past** | | **Past Perfect** | |
| | stritt<br>strittst<br>stritt | stritten<br>strittet<br>stritten | hatte gestritten<br>hattest gestritten<br>hatte gestritten | hatten gestritten<br>hattet gestritten<br>hatten gestritten |
| | **Future** | | **Future Perfect** | |
| | werde streiten<br>wirst streiten<br>wird streiten | werden streiten<br>werdet streiten<br>werden streiten | werde gestritten haben<br>wirst gestritten haben<br>wird gestritten haben | werden gestritten haben<br>werdet gestritten haben<br>werden gestritten haben |
| Subjunctive | **Present** | | **Present Perfect** | |
| | streite<br>streitest<br>streite | streiten<br>streitet<br>streiten | habe gestritten<br>habest gestritten<br>habe gestritten | haben gestritten<br>habet gestritten<br>haben gestritten |
| | **Past** | | **Past Perfect** | |
| | stritte<br>strittest<br>stritte | stritten<br>strittet<br>stritten | hätte gestritten<br>hättest gestritten<br>hätte gestritten | hätten gestritten<br>hättet gestritten<br>hätten gestritten |
| | **Future** | | **Future Perfect** | |
| | werde streiten<br>werdest streiten<br>werde streiten | werden streiten<br>werdet streiten<br>werden streiten | werde gestritten haben<br>werdest gestritten haben<br>werde gestritten haben | werden gestritten haben<br>werdet gestritten haben<br>werden gestritten haben |
| | **Present and Future Conditional** | | **Past Conditional** | |
| | würde streiten<br>würdest streiten<br>würde streiten | würden streiten<br>würdet streiten<br>würden streiten | würde gestritten haben<br>würdest gestritten haben<br>würde gestritten haben | würden gestritten haben<br>würdet gestritten haben<br>würden gestritten haben |

## EXAMPLES

Sie streiten sich immer über Politik und Religion. — They always argue about politics and religion.

Es lohnt sich nicht, darüber zu streiten. — It's not worth quarreling about.

**stricken**
to knit
**Auxiliary verb:** haben **Past participle:** gestrickt
**Imperative:** Stricke! Strickt! Stricken Sie!

| Mode | Simple Tenses | | Compound Tenses | |
|---|---|---|---|---|
| | *Singular* | *Plural* | *Singular* | *Plural* |
| Indicative | **Present** | | **Present Perfect** | |
| | stricke<br>strickst<br>strickt | stricken<br>strickt<br>stricken | habe gestrickt<br>hast gestrickt<br>hat gestrickt | haben gestrickt<br>habt gestrickt<br>haben gestrickt |
| | **Past** | | **Past Perfect** | |
| | strickte<br>stricktest<br>strickte | strickten<br>stricktet<br>strickten | hatte gestrickt<br>hattest gestrickt<br>hatte gestrickt | hatten gestrickt<br>hattet gestrickt<br>hatten gestrickt |
| | **Future** | | **Future Perfect** | |
| | werde stricken<br>wirst stricken<br>wird stricken | werden stricken<br>werdet stricken<br>werden stricken | werde gestrickt haben<br>wirst gestrickt haben<br>wird gestrickt haben | werden gestrickt haben<br>werdet gestrickt haben<br>werden gestrickt haben |
| Subjunctive | **Present** | | **Present Perfect** | |
| | stricke<br>strickest<br>stricke | stricken<br>stricket<br>stricken | habe gestrickt<br>habest gestrickt<br>habe gestrickt | haben gestrickt<br>habet gestrickt<br>haben gestrickt |
| | **Past** | | **Past Perfect** | |
| | strickte<br>stricktest<br>strickte | strickten<br>stricktet<br>strickten | hätte gestrickt<br>hättest gestrickt<br>hätte gestrickt | hätten gestrickt<br>hättet gestrickt<br>hätten gestrickt |
| | **Future** | | **Future Perfect** | |
| | werde stricken<br>werdest stricken<br>werde stricken | werden stricken<br>werdet stricken<br>werden stricken | werde gestrickt haben<br>werdest gestrickt haben<br>werde gestrickt haben | werden gestrickt haben<br>werdet gestrickt haben<br>werden gestrickt haben |
| | **Present and Future Conditional** | | **Past Conditional** | |
| | würde stricken<br>würdest stricken<br>würde stricken | würden stricken<br>würdet stricken<br>würden stricken | wurde gestrickt haben<br>würdest gestrickt haben<br>würde gestrickt haben | würden gestrickt haben<br>würdet gestrickt haben<br>würden gestrickt haben |

## EXAMPLES

Mein Bruder strickt besser als meine Mutter. — My brother knits better than my mother.
Ist dieser Pullover handgestrickt? — Is this sweater hand-knit?

**stürmen**

to storm, to be stormy

**Auxiliary verb:** haben **Past participle:** gestürmt

**Imperative:** Stürme! Stürmt! Stürmen Sie!

| Mode | Simple Tenses | | Compound Tenses | |
|---|---|---|---|---|
| | *Singular* | *Plural* | *Singular* | *Plural* |
| Indicative | **Present** | | **Present Perfect** | |
| | stürme<br>stürmst<br>stürmt | stürmen<br>stürmt<br>stürmen | habe gestürmt<br>hast gestürmt<br>hat gestürmt | haben gestürmt<br>habt gestürmt<br>haben gestürmt |
| | **Past** | | **Past Perfect** | |
| | stürmte<br>stürmtest<br>stürmte | stürmten<br>stürmtet<br>stürmten | hatte gestürmt<br>hattest gestürmt<br>hatte gestürmt | hatten gestürmt<br>hattet gestürmt<br>hatten gestürmt |
| | **Future** | | **Future Perfect** | |
| | werde stürmen<br>wirst stürmen<br>wird stürmen | werden stürmen<br>werdet stürmen<br>werden stürmen | werde gestürmt haben<br>wirst gestürmt haben<br>wird gestürmt haben | werden gestürmt haben<br>werdet gestürmt haben<br>werden gestürmt haben |
| Subjunctive | **Present** | | **Present Perfect** | |
| | stürme<br>stürmest<br>stürme | stürmen<br>stürmet<br>stürmen | habe gestürmt<br>habest gestürmt<br>habe gestürmt | haben gestürmt<br>habet gestürmt<br>haben gestürmt |
| | **Past** | | **Past Perfect** | |
| | stürmte<br>stürmtest<br>stürmte | stürmten<br>stürmtet<br>stürmten | hätte gestürmt<br>hättest gestürmt<br>hätte gestürmt | hätten gestürmt<br>hättet gestürmt<br>hätten gestürmt |
| | **Future** | | **Future Perfect** | |
| | werde stürmen<br>werdest stürmen<br>werde stürmen | werden stürmen<br>werdet stürmen<br>werden stürmen | werde gestürmt haben<br>werdest gestürmt haben<br>werde gestürmt haben | werden gestürmt haben<br>werdet gestürmt haben<br>werden gestürmt haben |
| | **Present and Future Conditional** | | **Past Conditional** | |
| | würde stürmen<br>würdest stürmen<br>würde stürmen | würden stürmen<br>würdet stürmen<br>würden stürmen | würde gestürmt haben<br>würdest gestürmt haben<br>würde gestürmt haben | würden gestürmt haben<br>würdet gestürmt haben<br>würden gestürmt haben |

**Note:** When this verb means "to dash" or "to hurry along," it becomes a verb of motion and requires the auxiliary *sein* in the perfect tenses.

## EXAMPLES

Als es anfing hell zu werden, stürmten die Ritter die Burg.

When it began to grow light, the knights stormed the castle.

Es hat die ganze Nacht durch gestürmt.

It stormed through the whole night.

**stürzen**

to plunge, to fall, to overthrow

**Auxiliary verb:** sein **Past participle:** gestürzt

**Imperative:** Stürze! Stürzt! Stürzen Sie!

| Mode | Simple Tenses | | Compound Tenses | |
|---|---|---|---|---|
| | *Singular* | *Plural* | *Singular* | *Plural* |
| Indicative | **Present** | | **Present Perfect** | |
| | stürze<br>stürzt<br>stürzt | stürzen<br>stürzt<br>stürzen | bin gestürzt<br>bist gestürzt<br>ist gestürzt | sind gestürzt<br>seid gestürzt<br>sind gestürzt |
| | **Past** | | **Past Perfect** | |
| | stürzte<br>stürztest<br>stürzte | stürzten<br>stürztet<br>stürzten | war gestürzt<br>warst gestürzt<br>war gestürzt | waren gestürzt<br>wart gestürzt<br>waren gestürzt |
| | **Future** | | **Future Perfect** | |
| | werde stürzen<br>wirst stürzen<br>wird stürzen | werden stürzen<br>werdet stürzen<br>werden stürzen | werde gestürzt sein<br>wirst gestürzt sein<br>wird gestürzt sein | werden gestürzt sein<br>werdet gestürzt sein<br>werden gestürzt sein |
| Subjunctive | **Present** | | **Present Perfect** | |
| | stürze<br>stürzest<br>stürze | stürzen<br>stürzet<br>stürzen | sei gestürzt<br>seiest gestürzt<br>sei gestürzt | seien gestürzt<br>seiet gestürzt<br>seien gestürzt |
| | **Past** | | **Past Perfect** | |
| | stürzte<br>stürztest<br>stürzte | stürzten<br>stürztet<br>stürzten | wäre gestürzt<br>wärest gestürzt<br>wäre gestürzt | wären gestürzt<br>wäret gestürzt<br>wären gestürzt |
| | **Future** | | **Future Perfect** | |
| | werde stürzen<br>werdest stürzen<br>werde stürzen | werden stürzen<br>werdet stürzen<br>werden stürzen | werde gestürzt sein<br>werdest gestürzt sein<br>werde gestürzt sein | werden gestürzt sein<br>werdet gestürzt sein<br>werden gestürzt sein |
| | **Present and Future Conditional** | | **Past Conditional** | |
| | würde stürzen<br>würdest stürzen<br>würde stürzen | würden stürzen<br>würdet stürzen<br>würden stürzen | würde gestürzt sein<br>würdest gestürzt sein<br>würde gestürzt sein | würden gestürzt sein<br>würdet gestürzt sein<br>würden gestürzt sein |

**Note:** With the meaning "to overthrow," *stürzen* becomes transitive and the auxiliary verb is *haben*.

## EXAMPLES

| | |
|---|---|
| Als der Krieg zu Ende ging, stürzten die Preise. | When the war ended, prices fell. |
| Die Revolutionäre versuchten die neue Regierung zu stürzen. | The revolutionaries tried to overthrow the new government. |

**stützen (sich)**

to prop, to support, to rely on

**Auxiliary verb:** haben **Past participle:** gestützt

**Imperative:** Stütze! Stützt! Stützen Sie!

| Mode | Simple Tenses | | Compound Tenses | |
|---|---|---|---|---|
| | *Singular* | *Plural* | *Singular* | *Plural* |
| Indicative | **Present** | | **Present Perfect** | |
| | stütze<br>stützt<br>stützt | stützen<br>stützt<br>stützen | habe gestützt<br>hast gestützt<br>hat gestützt | haben gestützt<br>habt gestützt<br>haben gestützt |
| | **Past** | | **Past Perfect** | |
| | stützte<br>stütztest<br>stützte | stützten<br>stütztet<br>stützten | hatte gestützt<br>hattest gestützt<br>hatte gestützt | hatten gestützt<br>hattet gestützt<br>hatten gestützt |
| | **Future** | | **Future Perfect** | |
| | werde stützen<br>wirst stützen<br>wird stützen | werden stützen<br>werdet stützen<br>werden stützen | werde gestützt haben<br>wirst gestützt haben<br>wird gestützt haben | werden gestützt haben<br>werdet gestützt haben<br>werden gestützt haben |
| Subjunctive | **Present** | | **Present Perfect** | |
| | stütze<br>stützest<br>stütze | stützen<br>stützet<br>stützen | habe gestützt<br>habest gestützt<br>habe gestützt | haben gestützt<br>habet gestützt<br>haben gestützt |
| | **Past** | | **Past Perfect** | |
| | stützte<br>stütztest<br>stützte | stützten<br>stütztet<br>stützten | hätte gestützt<br>hättest gestützt<br>hätte gestützt | hätten gestützt<br>hättet gestützt<br>hätten gestützt |
| | **Future** | | **Future Perfect** | |
| | werde stützen<br>werdest stützen<br>werde stützen | werden stützen<br>werdet stützen<br>werden stützen | werde gestützt haben<br>werdest gestützt haben<br>werde gestützt haben | werden gestützt haben<br>werdet gestützt haben<br>werden gestützt haben |
| | **Present and Future Conditional** | | **Past Conditional** | |
| | würde stützen<br>würdest stützen<br>würde stützen | würden stützen<br>würdet stützen<br>würden stützen | würde gestützt haben<br>würdest gestützt haben<br>würde gestützt haben | würden gestützt haben<br>würdet gestützt haben<br>würden gestützt haben |

## EXAMPLES

| | |
|---|---|
| Die alte Dame musste von ihrer Pflegerin gestützt werden. | The old lady had to be supported by her nurse. |
| Die Theorie des Professors stützt sich auf die neueste Forschung. | The professor's theory is based on the newest research. |

**suchen**
to seek, to look for
**Auxiliary verb:** haben **Past participle:** gesucht
**Imperative:** Suche! Sucht! Suchen Sie!

| Mode | Simple Tenses | | Compound Tenses | |
|---|---|---|---|---|
| | *Singular* | *Plural* | *Singular* | *Plural* |
| Indicative | **Present** | | **Present Perfect** | |
| | suche<br>suchst<br>sucht | suchen<br>sucht<br>suchen | habe gesucht<br>hast gesucht<br>hat gesucht | haben gesucht<br>habt gesucht<br>haben gesucht |
| | **Past** | | **Past Perfect** | |
| | suchte<br>suchtest<br>suchte | suchten<br>suchtet<br>suchten | hatte gesucht<br>hattest gesucht<br>hatte gesucht | hatten gesucht<br>hattet gesucht<br>hatten gesucht |
| | **Future** | | **Future Perfect** | |
| | werde suchen<br>wirst suchen<br>wird suchen | werden suchen<br>werdet suchen<br>werden suchen | werde gesucht haben<br>wirst gesucht haben<br>wird gesucht haben | werden gesucht haben<br>werdet gesucht haben<br>werden gesucht haben |
| Subjunctive | **Present** | | **Present Perfect** | |
| | suche<br>suchest<br>suche | suchen<br>suchet<br>suchen | habe gesucht<br>habest gesucht<br>habe gesucht | haben gesucht<br>habet gesucht<br>haben gesucht |
| | **Past** | | **Past Perfect** | |
| | suchte<br>suchtest<br>suchte | suchten<br>suchtet<br>suchten | hätte gesucht<br>hättest gesucht<br>hätte gesucht | hätten gesucht<br>hättet gesucht<br>hätten gesucht |
| | **Future** | | **Future Perfect** | |
| | werde suchen<br>werdest suchen<br>werde suchen | werden suchen<br>werdet suchen<br>werden suchen | werde gesucht haben<br>werdest gesucht haben<br>werde gesucht haben | werden gesucht haben<br>werdet gesucht haben<br>werden gesucht haben |
| | **Present and Future Conditional** | | **Past Conditional** | |
| | würde suchen<br>würdest suchen<br>würde suchen | würden suchen<br>würdet suchen<br>würden suchen | würde gesucht haben<br>würdest gesucht haben<br>würde gesucht haben | würden gesucht haben<br>würdet gesucht haben<br>würden gesucht haben |

**Note:** With inseparable prefixes, the principal parts of this verb are, for example, *besucht, besuchte, hat besucht.* With separable prefixes, the principal parts are, for example, *sucht aus, suchte aus, hat ausgesucht.*

## EXAMPLES

Ich suche die Bahnhofstraße. Ist sie weit von hier?
I'm looking for Bahnhof Street. Is it far from here?

Sie hat eine neue Wohnung in diesem Stadtviertel gesucht.
She looked for a new apartment in this area of the city.

**summen**
to hum, to buzz
**Auxiliary verb:** haben **Past participle:** gesummt
**Imperative:** Summe! Summt! Summen Sie!

| Mode | Simple Tenses | | Compound Tenses | |
|---|---|---|---|---|
| | *Singular* | *Plural* | *Singular* | *Plural* |
| Indicative | **Present** | | **Present Perfect** | |
| | summe<br>summst<br>summt | summen<br>summt<br>summen | habe gesummt<br>hast gesummt<br>hat gesummt | haben gesummt<br>habt gesummt<br>haben gesummt |
| | **Past** | | **Past Perfect** | |
| | summte<br>summtest<br>summte | summten<br>summtet<br>summten | hatte gesummt<br>hattest gesummt<br>hatte gesummt | hatten gesummt<br>hattet gesummt<br>hatten gesummt |
| | **Future** | | **Future Perfect** | |
| | werde summen<br>wirst summen<br>wird summen | werden summen<br>werdet summen<br>werden summen | werde gesummt haben<br>wirst gesummt haben<br>wird gesummt haben | werden gesummt haben<br>werdet gesummt haben<br>werden gesummt haben |
| Subjunctive | **Present** | | **Present Perfect** | |
| | summe<br>summest<br>summe | summen<br>summet<br>summen | habe gesummt<br>habest gesummt<br>habe gesummt | haben gesummt<br>habet gesummt<br>haben gesummt |
| | **Past** | | **Past Perfect** | |
| | summte<br>summtest<br>summte | summten<br>summtet<br>summten | hätte gesummt<br>hättest gesummt<br>hätte gesummt | hätten gesummt<br>hättet gesummt<br>hätten gesummt |
| | **Future** | | **Future Perfect** | |
| | werde summen<br>werdest summen<br>werde summen | werden summen<br>werdet summen<br>werden summen | werde gesummt haben<br>werdest gesummt haben<br>werde gesummt haben | werden gesummt haben<br>werdet gesummt haben<br>werden gesummt haben |
| | **Present and Future Conditional** | | **Past Conditional** | |
| | würde summen<br>würdest summen<br>würde summen | würden summen<br>würdet summen<br>würden summen | würde gesummt haben<br>würdest gesummt haben<br>würde gesummt haben | würden gesummt haben<br>würdet gesummt haben<br>würden gesummt haben |

## EXAMPLES

Es summt dem kleinen Jungen in den Ohren. — The little boy's ears are buzzing.
Hörst du dieses Summen? — Do you hear that buzzing?

**tanken**

to put gas in the tank, to refuel

**Auxiliary verb:** haben **Past participle:** getankt

**Imperative:** Tanke! Tankt! Tanken Sie!

| Mode | Simple Tenses | | Compound Tenses | |
|---|---|---|---|---|
| | *Singular* | *Plural* | *Singular* | *Plural* |
| Indicative | **Present** | | **Present Perfect** | |
| | tanke<br>tankst<br>tankt | tanken<br>tankt<br>tanken | habe getankt<br>hast getankt<br>hat getankt | haben getankt<br>habt getankt<br>haben getankt |
| | **Past** | | **Past Perfect** | |
| | tankte<br>tanktest<br>tankte | tankten<br>tanktet<br>tankten | hatte getankt<br>hattest getankt<br>hatte getankt | hatten getankt<br>hattet getankt<br>hatten getankt |
| | **Future** | | **Future Perfect** | |
| | werde tanken<br>wirst tanken<br>wird tanken | werden tanken<br>werdet tanken<br>werden tanken | werde getankt haben<br>wirst getankt haben<br>wird getankt haben | werden getankt haben<br>werdet getankt haben<br>werden getankt haben |
| Subjunctive | **Present** | | **Present Perfect** | |
| | tanke<br>tankest<br>tanke | tanken<br>tanket<br>tanken | habe getankt<br>habest getankt<br>habe getankt | haben getankt<br>habet getankt<br>haben getankt |
| | **Past** | | **Past Perfect** | |
| | tankte<br>tanktest<br>tankte | tankten<br>tanktet<br>tankten | hätte getankt<br>hättest getankt<br>hätte getankt | hätten getankt<br>hättet getankt<br>hätten getankt |
| | **Future** | | **Future Perfect** | |
| | werde tanken<br>werdest tanken<br>werde tanken | werden tanken<br>werdet tanken<br>werden tanken | werde getankt haben<br>werdest getankt haben<br>werde getankt haben | werden getankt haben<br>werdet getankt haben<br>werden getankt haben |
| | **Present and Future Conditional** | | **Past Conditional** | |
| | würde tanken<br>würdest tanken<br>würde tanken | würden tanken<br>würdet tanken<br>würden tanken | würde getankt haben<br>würdest getankt haben<br>würde getankt haben | würden getankt haben<br>würdet getankt haben<br>würden getankt haben |

## EXAMPLES

Siehst du eine Tankstelle? Ich muss tanken.

Do you see a gas station? I have to get gas.

Sein alter Wagen verbrauchte viel Benzin. Er hat oft tanken müssen.

His old car used a lot of gas. He had to refuel often.

**tanzen**
to dance
**Auxiliary verb:** haben **Past participle:** getanzt
**Imperative:** Tanze! Tanzt! Tanzen Sie!

| Mode | Simple Tenses | | Compound Tenses | |
|---|---|---|---|---|
| | *Singular* | *Plural* | *Singular* | *Plural* |
| Indicative | **Present** | | **Present Perfect** | |
| | tanze<br>tanzt<br>tanzt | tanzen<br>tanzt<br>tanzen | habe getanzt<br>hast getanzt<br>hat getanzt | haben getanzt<br>habt getanzt<br>haben getanzt |
| | **Past** | | **Past Perfect** | |
| | tanzte<br>tanztest<br>tanzte | tanzten<br>tanztet<br>tanzten | hatte getanzt<br>hattest getanzt<br>hatte getanzt | hatten getanzt<br>hattet getanzt<br>hatten getanzt |
| | **Future** | | **Future Perfect** | |
| | werde tanzen<br>wirst tanzen<br>wird tanzen | werden tanzen<br>werdet tanzen<br>werden tanzen | werde getanzt haben<br>wirst getanzt haben<br>wird getanzt haben | werden getanzt haben<br>werdet getanzt haben<br>werden getanzt haben |
| Subjunctive | **Present** | | **Present Perfect** | |
| | tanze<br>tanzest<br>tanze | tanzen<br>tanzet<br>tanzen | habe getanzt<br>habest getanzt<br>habe getanzt | haben getanzt<br>habet getanzt<br>haben getanzt |
| | **Past** | | **Past Perfect** | |
| | tanzte<br>tanztest<br>tanzte | tanzten<br>tanztet<br>tanzten | hätte getanzt<br>hättest getanzt<br>hätte getanzt | hätten getanzt<br>hättet getanzt<br>hätten getanzt |
| | **Future** | | **Future Perfect** | |
| | werde tanzen<br>werdest tanzen<br>werde tanzen | werden tanzen<br>werdet tanzen<br>werden tanzen | werde getanzt haben<br>werdest getanzt haben<br>werde getanzt haben | werden getanzt haben<br>werdet getanzt haben<br>werden getanzt haben |
| | **Present and Future Conditional** | | **Past Conditional** | |
| | würde tanzen<br>würdest tanzen<br>würde tanzen | würden tanzen<br>würdet tanzen<br>würden tanzen | würde getanzt haben<br>würdest getanzt haben<br>würde getanzt haben | würden getanzt haben<br>würdet getanzt haben<br>würden getanzt haben |

## EXAMPLES

Alex hat schon zum vierten Mal mit der Französin getanzt.
Alex already danced with the French girl four times.

Sie sagte, dass sie sehr gut tanzen könnte.
She said she could dance very well.

**tauchen**
to plunge, to dive, to stay underwater
**Auxiliary verb:** haben **Past participle:** getaucht
**Imperative:** Tauche! Taucht! Tauchen Sie!

| Mode | Simple Tenses | | Compound Tenses | |
|---|---|---|---|---|
| | *Singular* | *Plural* | *Singular* | *Plural* |
| Indicative | **Present** | | **Present Perfect** | |
| | tauche<br>tauchst<br>taucht | tauchen<br>taucht<br>tauchen | habe getaucht<br>hast getaucht<br>hat getaucht | haben getaucht<br>habt getaucht<br>haben getaucht |
| | **Past** | | **Past Perfect** | |
| | tauchte<br>tauchtest<br>tauchte | tauchten<br>tauchtet<br>tauchten | hatte getaucht<br>hattest getaucht<br>hatte getaucht | hatten getaucht<br>hattet getaucht<br>hatten getaucht |
| | **Future** | | **Future Perfect** | |
| | werde tauchen<br>wirst tauchen<br>wird tauchen | werden tauchen<br>werdet tauchen<br>werden tauchen | werde getaucht haben<br>wirst getaucht haben<br>wird getaucht haben | werden getaucht haben<br>werdet getaucht haben<br>werden getaucht haben |
| Subjunctive | **Present** | | **Present Perfect** | |
| | tauche<br>tauchest<br>tauche | tauchen<br>tauchet<br>tauchen | habe getaucht<br>habest getaucht<br>habe getaucht | haben getaucht<br>habet getaucht<br>haben getaucht |
| | **Past** | | **Past Perfect** | |
| | tauchte<br>tauchtest<br>tauchte | tauchten<br>tauchtet<br>tauchten | hätte getaucht<br>hättest getaucht<br>hätte getaucht | hätten getaucht<br>hättet getaucht<br>hätten getaucht |
| | **Future** | | **Future Perfect** | |
| | werde tauchen<br>werdest tauchen<br>werde tauchen | werden tauchen<br>werdet tauchen<br>werden tauchen | werde getaucht haben<br>werdest getaucht haben<br>werde getaucht haben | werden getaucht haben<br>werdet getaucht haben<br>werden getaucht haben |
| | **Present and Future Conditional** | | **Past Conditional** | |
| | würde tauchen<br>würdest tauchen<br>würde tauchen | würden tauchen<br>würdet tauchen<br>würden tauchen | würde getaucht haben<br>würdest getaucht haben<br>würde getaucht haben | würden getaucht haben<br>würdet getaucht haben<br>würden getaucht haben |

**Note:** When used as a verb of motion, this verb requires *sein* as its auxiliary in the perfect tenses.

## EXAMPLES

| | |
|---|---|
| Das riesige U-Boot taucht wieder auf. | The gigantic submarine returns to the surface. |
| Ich kann weder schwimmen noch tauchen. | I can neither swim nor dive. |

**tauen**

to thaw

**Auxiliary verb:** haben **Past participle:** getaut

**Imperative:** Taue! Taut! Tauen Sie!

| Mode | Simple Tenses | | Compound Tenses | |
|---|---|---|---|---|
| | *Singular* | *Plural* | *Singular* | *Plural* |
| Indicative | **Present** | | **Present Perfect** | |
| | taue<br>taust<br>taut | tauen<br>taut<br>tauen | habe getaut<br>hast getaut<br>hat getaut | haben getaut<br>habt getaut<br>haben getaut |
| | **Past** | | **Past Perfect** | |
| | taute<br>tautest<br>taute | tauten<br>tautet<br>tauten | hatte getaut<br>hattest getaut<br>hatte getaut | hatten getaut<br>hattet getaut<br>hatten getaut |
| | **Future** | | **Future Perfect** | |
| | werde tauen<br>wirst tauen<br>wird tauen | werden tauen<br>werdet tauen<br>werden tauen | werde getaut haben<br>wirst getaut haben<br>wird getaut haben | werden getaut haben<br>werdet getaut haben<br>werden getaut haben |
| Subjunctive | **Present** | | **Present Perfect** | |
| | taue<br>tauest<br>taue | tauen<br>tauet<br>tauen | habe getaut<br>habest getaut<br>habe getaut | haben getaut<br>habet getaut<br>haben getaut |
| | **Past** | | **Past Perfect** | |
| | taute<br>tautest<br>taute | tauten<br>tautet<br>tauten | hätte getaut<br>hättest getaut<br>hätte getaut | hätten getaut<br>hättet getaut<br>hätten getaut |
| | **Future** | | **Future Perfect** | |
| | werde tauen<br>werdest tauen<br>werde tauen | werden tauen<br>werdet tauen<br>werden tauen | werde getaut haben<br>werdest getaut haben<br>werde getaut haben | werden getaut haben<br>werdet getaut haben<br>werden getaut haben |
| | **Present and Future Conditional** | | **Past Conditional** | |
| | würde tauen<br>würdest tauen<br>würde tauen | würden tauen<br>würdet tauen<br>würden tauen | würde getaut haben<br>würdest getaut haben<br>würde getaut haben | würden getaut haben<br>würdet getaut haben<br>würden getaut haben |

## EXAMPLES

Es taut.
It's thawing.

Wenn die Temperaturen nicht steigen, wird der Schnee nie tauen.
If the temperature doesn't rise, the snow will never melt.

**taufen**
to baptize
**Auxiliary verb:** haben **Past participle:** getauft
**Imperative:** Taufe! Tauft! Taufen Sie!

| Mode | Simple Tenses | | Compound Tenses | |
|---|---|---|---|---|
| | *Singular* | *Plural* | *Singular* | *Plural* |
| Indicative | **Present** | | **Present Perfect** | |
| | taufe<br>taufst<br>tauft | taufen<br>tauft<br>taufen | habe getauft<br>hast getauft<br>hat getauft | haben getauft<br>habt getauft<br>haben getauft |
| | **Past** | | **Past Perfect** | |
| | taufte<br>tauftest<br>taufte | tauften<br>tauftet<br>tauften | hatte getauft<br>hattest getauft<br>hatte getauft | hatten getauft<br>hattet getauft<br>hatten getauft |
| | **Future** | | **Future Perfect** | |
| | werde taufen<br>wirst taufen<br>wird taufen | werden taufen<br>werdet taufen<br>werden taufen | werde getauft haben<br>wirst getauft haben<br>wird getauft haben | werden getauft haben<br>werdet getauft haben<br>werden getauft haben |
| Subjunctive | **Present** | | **Present Perfect** | |
| | taufe<br>taufest<br>taufe | taufen<br>taufet<br>taufen | habe getauft<br>habest getauft<br>habe getauft | haben getauft<br>habet getauft<br>haben getauft |
| | **Past** | | **Past Perfect** | |
| | taufte<br>tauftest<br>taufte | tauften<br>tauftet<br>tauften | hätte getauft<br>hättest getauft<br>hätte getauft | hätten getauft<br>hättet getauft<br>hätten getauft |
| | **Future** | | **Future Perfect** | |
| | werde taufen<br>werdest taufen<br>werde taufen | werden taufen<br>werdet taufen<br>werden taufen | werde getauft haben<br>werdest getauft haben<br>werde getauft haben | werden getauft haben<br>werdet getauft haben<br>werden getauft haben |
| | **Present and Future Conditional** | | **Past Conditional** | |
| | würde taufen<br>würdest taufen<br>würde taufen | würden taufen<br>würdet taufen<br>würden taufen | würde getauft haben<br>würdest getauft haben<br>würde getauft haben | würden getauft haben<br>würdet getauft haben<br>würden getauft haben |

## EXAMPLES

Ich taufe dieses Kind auf den Namen Niklas. — I baptize this child Niklas.

Mit achtzig Jahren will er sich endlich taufen lassen. — At 80 years of age, he finally wants to get baptized.

**teilen (sich)**
to divide, to share
**Auxiliary verb:** haben **Past participle:** geteilt
**Imperative:** Teile! Teilt! Teilen Sie!

| Mode | Simple Tenses | | Compound Tenses | |
|---|---|---|---|---|
| | *Singular* | *Plural* | *Singular* | *Plural* |
| Indicative | **Present** | | **Present Perfect** | |
| | teile<br>teilst<br>teilt | teilen<br>teilt<br>teilen | habe geteilt<br>hast geteilt<br>hat geteilt | haben geteilt<br>habt geteilt<br>haben geteilt |
| | **Past** | | **Past Perfect** | |
| | teilte<br>teiltest<br>teilte | teilten<br>telltet<br>teilten | hatte geteilt<br>hattest geteilt<br>hatte geteilt | hatten geteilt<br>hattet geteilt<br>hatten geteilt |
| | **Future** | | **Future Perfect** | |
| | werde teilen<br>wirst teilen<br>wird teilen | werden teilen<br>werdet teilen<br>werden teilen | werde geteilt haben<br>wirst geteilt haben<br>wird geteilt haben | werden geteilt haben<br>werdet geteilt haben<br>werden geteilt haben |
| Subjunctive | **Present** | | **Present Perfect** | |
| | teile<br>teilest<br>teile | teilen<br>teilet<br>teilen | habe geteilt<br>habest geteilt<br>habe geteilt | haben geteilt<br>habet geteilt<br>haben geteilt |
| | **Past** | | **Past Perfect** | |
| | teilte<br>teiltest<br>teilte | teilten<br>teiltet<br>teilten | hätte geteilt<br>hättest geteilt<br>hätte geteilt | hätten geteilt<br>hättet geteilt<br>hätten geteilt |
| | **Future** | | **Future Perfect** | |
| | werde teilen<br>werdest teilen<br>werde teilen | werden teilen<br>werdet teilen<br>werden teilen | werde geteilt haben<br>werdest geteilt haben<br>werde geteilt haben | werden geteilt haben<br>werdet geteilt haben<br>werden geteilt haben |
| | **Present and Future Conditional** | | **Past Conditional** | |
| | würde teilen<br>würdest teilen<br>würde teilen | würden teilen<br>würdet teilen<br>würden teilen | würde geteilt haben<br>würdest geteilt haben<br>würde geteilt haben | würden geteilt haben<br>würdet geteilt haben<br>würden geteilt haben |

## EXAMPLES

Teile die Summe durch vier.
Divide the sum by four.

Jan muss sich das Schlafzimmer und das Badezimmer mit seinen vier Brüdern teilen.
Jan has to share the bedroom and bathroom with his four brothers.

**tippen**
to type
**Auxiliary verb:** haben **Past participle:** getippt
**Imperative:** Tippe! Tippt! Tippen Sie!

| Mode | Simple Tenses | | Compound Tenses | |
|---|---|---|---|---|
| | *Singular* | *Plural* | *Singular* | *Plural* |
| Indicative | **Present** | | **Present Perfect** | |
| | tippe<br>tippst<br>tippt | tippen<br>tippt<br>tippen | habe getippt<br>hast getippt<br>hat getippt | haben getippt<br>habt getippt<br>haben getippt |
| | **Past** | | **Past Perfect** | |
| | tippte<br>tipptest<br>tippte | tippten<br>tipptet<br>tippten | hatte getippt<br>hattest getippt<br>hatte getippt | hatten getippt<br>hattet getippt<br>hatten getippt |
| | **Future** | | **Future Perfect** | |
| | werde tippen<br>wirst tippen<br>wird tippen | werden tippen<br>werdet tippen<br>werden tippen | werde getippt haben<br>wirst getippt haben<br>wird getippt haben | werden getippt haben<br>werdet getippt haben<br>werden getippt haben |
| Subjunctive | **Present** | | **Present Perfect** | |
| | tippe<br>tippest<br>tippe | tippen<br>tippet<br>tippen | habe getippt<br>habest getippt<br>habe getippt | haben getippt<br>habet getippt<br>haben getippt |
| | **Past** | | **Past Perfect** | |
| | tippte<br>tipptest<br>tippte | tippten<br>tipptet<br>tippten | hätte getippt<br>hättest getippt<br>hätte getippt | hätten getippt<br>hättet getippt<br>hätten getippt |
| | **Future** | | **Future Perfect** | |
| | werde tippen<br>werdest tippen<br>werde tippen | werden tippen<br>werdet tippen<br>werden tippen | werde getippt haben<br>werdest getippt haben<br>werde getippt haben | werden getippt haben<br>werdet getippt haben<br>werden getippt haben |
| | **Present and Future Conditional** | | **Past Conditional** | |
| | würde tippen<br>würdest tippen<br>würde tippen | würden tippen<br>würdet tippen<br>würden tippen | würde getippt haben<br>würdest getippt haben<br>würde getippt haben | würden getippt haben<br>würdet getippt haben<br>würden getippt haben |

## EXAMPLES

Können Sie tippen?
Er setzte sich an eine altmodische Schreibmaschine und fing an zu tippen.

Can you type?
He sat down at an old-fashioned typewriter and began to type.

**toben**

to rave, to rage

**Auxiliary verb:** haben **Past participle:** getobt

**Imperative:** Tobe! Tobt! Toben Sie!

| Mode | Simple Tenses | | Compound Tenses | |
|---|---|---|---|---|
| | *Singular* | *Plural* | *Singular* | *Plural* |
| Indicative | **Present** | | **Present Perfect** | |
| | tobe<br>tobst<br>tobt | toben<br>tobt<br>toben | habe getobt<br>hast getobt<br>hat getobt | haben getobt<br>habt getobt<br>haben getobt |
| | **Past** | | **Past Perfect** | |
| | tobte<br>tobtest<br>tobte | tobten<br>tobtet<br>tobten | hatte getobt<br>hattest getobt<br>hatte getobt | hatten getobt<br>hattet getobt<br>hatten getobt |
| | **Future** | | **Future Perfect** | |
| | werde toben<br>wirst toben<br>wird toben | werden toben<br>werdet toben<br>werden toben | werde getobt haben<br>wirst getobt haben<br>wird getobt haben | werden getobt haben<br>werdet getobt haben<br>werden getobt haben |
| Subjunctive | **Present** | | **Present Perfect** | |
| | tobe<br>tobest<br>tobe | toben<br>tobet<br>toben | habe getobt<br>habest getobt<br>habe getobt | haben getobt<br>habet getobt<br>haben getobt |
| | **Past** | | **Past Perfect** | |
| | tobte<br>tobtest<br>tobte | tobten<br>tobtet<br>tobten | hätte getobt<br>hättest getobt<br>hätte getobt | hätten getobt<br>hättet getobt<br>hätten getobt |
| | **Future** | | **Future Perfect** | |
| | werde toben<br>werdest toben<br>werde toben | werden toben<br>werdet toben<br>werden toben | werde getobt haben<br>werdest getobt haben<br>werde getobt haben | werden getobt haben<br>werdet getobt haben<br>werden getobt haben |
| | **Present and Future Conditional** | | **Past Conditional** | |
| | würde toben<br>würdest toben<br>würde toben | würden toben<br>würdet toben<br>würden toben | würde getobt haben<br>würdest getobt haben<br>würde getobt haben | würden getobt haben<br>würdet getobt haben<br>würden getobt haben |

## EXAMPLES

Der Sturm tobte die ganze Nacht hindurch. — The storm raged through the whole night.

Das verwöhnte Kind hat wie ein Wahnsinniger getobt. — The spoiled child raved like a lunatic.

**töten**
to kill
**Auxiliary verb:** haben **Past participle:** getötet
**Imperative:** Töte! Tötet! Töten Sie!

| Mode | Simple Tenses | | Compound Tenses | |
|---|---|---|---|---|
| | *Singular* | *Plural* | *Singular* | *Plural* |
| Indicative | **Present** | | **Present Perfect** | |
| | töte<br>tötest<br>tötet | töten<br>tötet<br>töten | habe getötet<br>hast getötet<br>hat getötet | haben getötet<br>habt getötet<br>haben getötet |
| | **Past** | | **Past Perfect** | |
| | tötete<br>tötetest<br>tötete | töteten<br>tötetet<br>töteten | hatte getötet<br>hattest getötet<br>hatte getötet | hatten getötet<br>hattet getötet<br>hatten getötet |
| | **Future** | | **Future Perfect** | |
| | werde töten<br>wirst töten<br>wird töten | werden töten<br>werdet töten<br>werden töten | werde getötet haben<br>wirst getötet haben<br>wird getötet haben | werden getötet haben<br>werdet getötet haben<br>werden getötet haben |
| Subjunctive | **Present** | | **Present Perfect** | |
| | töte<br>tötest<br>töte | töten<br>tötet<br>töten | habe getötet<br>habest getötet<br>habe getötet | haben getötet<br>habet getötet<br>haben getötet |
| | **Past** | | **Past Perfect** | |
| | tötete<br>tötetest<br>tötete | töteten<br>tötetet<br>töteten | hätte getötet<br>hättest getötet<br>hätte getötet | hätten getötet<br>hättet getötet<br>hätten getötet |
| | **Future** | | **Future Perfect** | |
| | werde töten<br>werdest töten<br>werde töten | werden töten<br>werdet töten<br>werden töten | werde getötet haben<br>werdest getötet haben<br>werde getötet haben | werden getötet haben<br>werdet getötet haben<br>werden getötet haben |
| | **Present and Future Conditional** | | **Past Conditional** | |
| | würde töten<br>würdest töten<br>würde töten | würden töten<br>würdet töten<br>würden töten | würde getötet haben<br>würdest getötet haben<br>würde getötet haben | würden getötet haben<br>würdet getötet haben<br>würden getötet haben |

## EXAMPLES

Der Jäger hat einen großen Bären getötet. — The hunter killed a large bear.
Das Kind schrie, als ob ich es töten würde. — The child screamed as if I were killing him.

**tragen**

to carry, to wear

**Auxiliary verb:** haben **Past participle:** getragen

**Imperative:** Trage! Tragt! Tragen Sie!

| Mode | Simple Tenses | | Compound Tenses | |
|---|---|---|---|---|
| | *Singular* | *Plural* | *Singular* | *Plural* |
| Indicative | **Present** | | **Present Perfect** | |
| | trage<br>trägst<br>trägt | tragen<br>tragt<br>tragen | habe getragen<br>hast getragen<br>hat getragen | haben getragen<br>habt getragen<br>haben getragen |
| | **Past** | | **Past Perfect** | |
| | trug<br>trugst<br>trug | trugen<br>trugt<br>trugen | hatte getragen<br>hattest getragen<br>hatte getragen | hatten getragen<br>hattet getragen<br>hatten getragen |
| | **Future** | | **Future Perfect** | |
| | werde tragen<br>wirst tragen<br>wird tragen | werden tragen<br>werdet tragen<br>werden tragen | werde getragen haben<br>wirst getragen haben<br>wird getragen haben | werden getragen haben<br>werdet getragen haben<br>werden getragen haben |
| Subjunctive | **Present** | | **Present Perfect** | |
| | trage<br>tragest<br>trage | tragen<br>traget<br>tragen | habe getragen<br>habest getragen<br>habe getragen | haben getragen<br>habet getragen<br>haben getragen |
| | **Past** | | **Past Perfect** | |
| | trüge<br>trügest<br>trüge | trügen<br>trüget<br>trügen | hätte getragen<br>hättest getragen<br>hätte getragen | hätten getragen<br>hättet getragen<br>hätten getragen |
| | **Future** | | **Future Perfect** | |
| | werde tragen<br>werdest tragen<br>werde tragen | werden tragen<br>werdet tragen<br>werden tragen | werde getragen haben<br>werdest getragen haben<br>werde getragen haben | werden getragen haben<br>werdet getragen haben<br>werden getragen haben |
| | **Present and Future Conditional** | | **Past Conditional** | |
| | würde tragen<br>würdest tragen<br>würde tragen | würden tragen<br>würdet tragen<br>würden tragen | würde getragen haben<br>würdest getragen haben<br>würde getragen haben | würden getragen haben<br>würdet getragen haben<br>würden getragen haben |

**Note:** With inseparable prefixes, the principal parts of this verb are, for example, *verträgt, vertrug, hat vertragen.* With separable prefixes, the principal parts are, for example, *trägt bei, trug bei, hat beigetragen.*

## EXAMPLES

| | |
|---|---|
| Du sollst nicht versuchen den schweren Koffer zu tragen. | You shouldn't try to carry the heavy suitcase. |
| Karin trägt eine blaue Bluse und einen schwarzen Rock. | Karin is wearing a blue blouse and a black skirt. |

**trauen**
to trust, to believe in
**Auxiliary verb:** haben **Past participle:** getraut
**Imperative:** Traue! Traut! Trauen Sie!

| Mode | Simple Tenses | | Compound Tenses | |
|---|---|---|---|---|
| | *Singular* | *Plural* | *Singular* | *Plural* |
| Indicative | **Present** | | **Present Perfect** | |
| | traue<br>traust<br>traut | trauen<br>traut<br>trauen | habe getraut<br>hast getraut<br>hat getraut | haben getraut<br>habt getraut<br>haben getraut |
| | **Past** | | **Past Perfect** | |
| | traute<br>trautest<br>traute | trauten<br>trautet<br>trauten | hatte getraut<br>hattest getraut<br>hatte getraut | hatten getraut<br>hattet getraut<br>hatten getraut |
| | **Future** | | **Future Perfect** | |
| | werde trauen<br>wirst trauen<br>wird trauen | werden trauen<br>werdet trauen<br>werden trauen | werde getraut haben<br>wirst getraut haben<br>wird getraut haben | werden getraut haben<br>werdet getraut haben<br>werden getraut haben |
| Subjunctive | **Present** | | **Present Perfect** | |
| | traue<br>trauest<br>traue | trauen<br>trauet<br>trauen | habe getraut<br>habest getraut<br>habe getraut | haben getraut<br>habet getraut<br>haben getraut |
| | **Past** | | **Past Perfect** | |
| | traute<br>trautest<br>traute | trauten<br>trautet<br>trauten | hätte getraut<br>hättest getraut<br>hätte getraut | hätten getraut<br>hättet getraut<br>hätten getraut |
| | **Future** | | **Future Perfect** | |
| | werde trauen<br>werdest trauen<br>werde trauen | werden trauen<br>werdet trauen<br>werden trauen | werde getraut haben<br>werdest getraut haben<br>werde getraut haben | werden getraut haben<br>werdet getraut haben<br>werden getraut haben |
| | **Present and Future Conditional** | | **Past Conditional** | |
| | würde trauen<br>würdest trauen<br>würde trauen | würden trauen<br>würdet trauen<br>würden trauen | würde getraut haben<br>würdest getraut haben<br>würde getraut haben | würden getraut haben<br>würdet getraut haben<br>würden getraut haben |

## EXAMPLES

Glaubst du, dass wir ihnen trauen können? — Do you think we can trust them?
Ich traue kaum meinen Augen. — I can hardly believe my eyes.

**trauern**

to grieve, to mourn

**Auxiliary verb:** haben **Past participle:** getrauert

**Imperative:** Trauere! Trauert! Trauern Sie!

| Mode | Simple Tenses | | Compound Tenses | |
|---|---|---|---|---|
| | *Singular* | *Plural* | *Singular* | *Plural* |
| Indicative | **Present** | | **Present Perfect** | |
| | trauere<br>trauerst<br>trauert | trauern<br>trauert<br>trauern | habe getrauert<br>hast getrauert<br>hat getrauert | haben getrauert<br>habt getrauert<br>haben getrauert |
| | **Past** | | **Past Perfect** | |
| | trauerte<br>trauertest<br>trauerte | trauerten<br>trauertet<br>trauerten | hatte getrauert<br>hattest getrauert<br>hatte getrauert | hatten getrauert<br>hattet getrauert<br>hatten getrauert |
| | **Future** | | **Future Perfect** | |
| | werde trauern<br>wirst trauern<br>wird trauern | werden trauern<br>werdet trauern<br>werden trauern | werde getrauert haben<br>wirst getrauert haben<br>wird getrauert haben | werden getrauert haben<br>werdet getrauert haben<br>werden getrauert haben |
| Subjunctive | **Present** | | **Present Perfect** | |
| | trauere<br>trauerst<br>trauere | trauern<br>trauert<br>trauern | habe getrauert<br>habest getrauert<br>habe getrauert | haben getrauert<br>habet getrauert<br>haben getrauert |
| | **Past** | | **Past Perfect** | |
| | trauerte<br>trauertest<br>trauerte | trauerten<br>trauertet<br>trauerten | hätte getrauert<br>hättest getrauert<br>hätte getrauert | hätten getrauert<br>hättet getrauert<br>hätten getrauert |
| | **Future** | | **Future Perfect** | |
| | werde trauern<br>werdest trauern<br>werde trauern | werden trauern<br>werdet trauern<br>werden trauern | werde getrauert haben<br>werdest getrauert haben<br>werde getrauert haben | werden getrauert haben<br>werdet getrauert haben<br>werden getrauert haben |
| | **Present and Future Conditional** | | **Past Conditional** | |
| | würde trauern<br>würdest trauern<br>würde trauern | würden trauern<br>würdet trauern<br>würden trauern | würde getrauert haben<br>würdest getrauert haben<br>würde getrauert haben | würden getrauert haben<br>würdet getrauert haben<br>würden getrauert haben |

## EXAMPLES

Sie trauern schon wochenlang. — They have been in mourning for weeks.

Die Eltern trauern um ihr gestorbene Kind. — The parents grieve for their dead child.

**träumen**
to dream
**Auxiliary verb:** haben **Past participle:** geträumt
**Imperative:** Träume! Träumt! Träumen Sie!

| Mode | Simple Tenses | | Compound Tenses | |
|---|---|---|---|---|
| | *Singular* | *Plural* | *Singular* | *Plural* |
| Indicative | **Present** | | **Present Perfect** | |
| | träume<br>träumst<br>träumt | träumen<br>träumt<br>träumen | habe geträumt<br>hast geträumt<br>hat geträumt | haben geträumt<br>habt geträumt<br>haben geträumt |
| | **Past** | | **Past Perfect** | |
| | träumte<br>träumtest<br>träumte | träumten<br>träumtet<br>träumten | hatte geträumt<br>hattest geträumt<br>hatte geträumt | hatten geträumt<br>hattet geträumt<br>hatten geträumt |
| | **Future** | | **Future Perfect** | |
| | werde träumen<br>wirst träumen<br>wird träumen | werden träumen<br>werdet träumen<br>werden träumen | werde geträumt haben<br>wirst geträumt haben<br>wird geträumt haben | werden geträumt haben<br>werdet geträumt haben<br>werden geträumt haben |
| Subjunctive | **Present** | | **Present Perfect** | |
| | träume<br>träumest<br>träume | träumen<br>träumet<br>träumen | habe geträumt<br>habest geträumt<br>habe geträumt | haben geträumt<br>habet geträumt<br>haben geträumt |
| | **Past** | | **Past Perfect** | |
| | träumte<br>träumtest<br>träumte | träumten<br>träumtet<br>träumten | hätte geträumt<br>hättest geträumt<br>hätte geträumt | hätten geträumt<br>hättet geträumt<br>hätten geträumt |
| | **Future** | | **Future Perfect** | |
| | werde träumen<br>werdest träumen<br>werde träumen | werden träumen<br>werdet träumen<br>werden träumen | werde geträumt haben<br>werdest geträumt haben<br>werde geträumt haben | werden geträumt haben<br>werdet geträumt haben<br>werden geträumt haben |
| | **Present and Future Conditional** | | **Past Conditional** | |
| | würde träumen<br>würdest träumen<br>würde träumen | würden träumen<br>würdet träumen<br>würden träumen | würde geträumt haben<br>würdest geträumt haben<br>würde geträumt haben | würden geträumt haben<br>würdet geträumt haben<br>würden geträumt haben |

## EXAMPLES

| | |
|---|---|
| Ich träume vom Wildwasserfahren in Österreich. | I dream of white-water rafting in Austria. |
| Er hat geträumt, dass er ein reicher Mann geworden ist. | He dreamed that he had become a rich man. |

**treffen**

to meet, to strike

**Auxiliary verb:** haben **Past participle:** getroffen

**Imperative:** Triff! Trefft! Treffen Sie!

| Mode | Simple Tenses | | Compound Tenses | |
|---|---|---|---|---|
| | *Singular* | *Plural* | *Singular* | *Plural* |
| Indicative | **Present** | | **Present Perfect** | |
| | treffe<br>triffst<br>trifft | treffen<br>trefft<br>treffen | habe getroffen<br>hast getroffen<br>hat getroffen | haben getroffen<br>habt getroffen<br>haben getroffen |
| | **Past** | | **Past Perfect** | |
| | traf<br>trafst<br>traf | trafen<br>traft<br>trafen | hatte getroffen<br>hattest getroffen<br>hatte getroffen | hatten getroffen<br>hattet getroffen<br>hatten getroffen |
| | **Future** | | **Future Perfect** | |
| | werde treffen<br>wirst treffen<br>wird treffen | werden treffen<br>werdet treffen<br>werden treffen | werde getroffen haben<br>wirst getroffen haben<br>wird getroffen haben | werden getroffen haben<br>werdet getroffen haben<br>werden getroffen haben |
| Subjunctive | **Present** | | **Present Perfect** | |
| | treffe<br>treffest<br>treffe | treffen<br>treffet<br>treffen | habe getroffen<br>habest getroffen<br>habe getroffen | haben getroffen<br>habet getroffen<br>haben getroffen |
| | **Past** | | **Past Perfect** | |
| | träfe<br>träfest<br>träfe | träfen<br>träfet<br>träfen | hätte getroffen<br>hättest getroffen<br>hätte getroffen | hätten getroffen<br>hättet getroffen<br>hätten getroffen |
| | **Future** | | **Future Perfect** | |
| | werde treffen<br>werdest treffen<br>werde treffen | werden treffen<br>werdet treffen<br>werden treffen | werde getroffen haben<br>werdest getroffen haben<br>werde getroffen haben | werden getroffen haben<br>werdet getroffen haben<br>werden getroffen haben |
| | **Present and Future Conditional** | | **Past Conditional** | |
| | würde treffen<br>würdest treffen<br>würde treffen | würden treffen<br>würdet treffen<br>würden treffen | würde getroffen haben<br>würdest getroffen haben<br>würde getroffen haben | würden getroffen haben<br>würdet getroffen haben<br>würden getroffen haben |

## EXAMPLES

Der Wolkenkratzer ist mehr als zwanzig mal vom Blitz getroffen worden.

The skyscraper has been struck by lightning more than 20 times.

Wir treffen uns jeden Freitag im Restaurant.

We meet every Friday at the restaurant.

**treiben**
to drive, to pursue
**Auxiliary verb:** haben **Past participle:** getrieben
**Imperative:** Treibe! Treibt! Treiben Sie!

| Mode | Simple Tenses | | Compound Tenses | |
|---|---|---|---|---|
| | *Singular* | *Plural* | *Singular* | *Plural* |
| Indicative | **Present** | | **Present Perfect** | |
| | treibe<br>treibst<br>treibt | treiben<br>treibt<br>treiben | habe getrieben<br>hast getrieben<br>hat getrieben | haben getrieben<br>habt getrieben<br>haben getrieben |
| | **Past** | | **Past Perfect** | |
| | trieb<br>triebst<br>trieb | trieben<br>triebt<br>trieben | hatte getrieben<br>hattest getrieben<br>hatte getrieben | hatten getrieben<br>hattet getrieben<br>hatten getrieben |
| | **Future** | | **Future Perfect** | |
| | werde treiben<br>wirst treiben<br>wird treiben | werden treiben<br>werdet treiben<br>werden treiben | werde getrieben haben<br>wirst getrieben haben<br>wird getrieben haben | werden getrieben haben<br>werdet getrieben haben<br>werden getrieben haben |
| Subjunctive | **Present** | | **Present Perfect** | |
| | treibe<br>treibest<br>treibe | treiben<br>treibet<br>treiben | habe getrieben<br>habest getrieben<br>habe getrieben | haben getrieben<br>habet getrieben<br>haben getrieben |
| | **Past** | | **Past Perfect** | |
| | triebe<br>triebest<br>triebe | trieben<br>triebet<br>trieben | hätte getrieben<br>hättest getrieben<br>hätte getrieben | hätten getrieben<br>hättet getrieben<br>hätten getrieben |
| | **Future** | | **Future Perfect** | |
| | werde treiben<br>werdest treiben<br>werde treiben | werden treiben<br>werdet treiben<br>werden treiben | werde getrieben haben<br>werdest getrieben haben<br>werde getrieben haben | werden getrieben haben<br>werdet getrieben haben<br>werden getrieben haben |
| | **Present and Future Conditional** | | **Past Conditional** | |
| | würde treiben<br>würdest treiben<br>würde treiben | würden treiben<br>würdet treiben<br>würden treiben | würde getrieben haben<br>würdest getrieben haben<br>würde getrieben haben | würden getrieben haben<br>würdet getrieben haben<br>würden getrieben haben |

## EXAMPLES

Karl und Martin treiben viel Sport.
Karl and Martin go in for a lot of sports.

Sie haben den korrupten Präsidenten aus dem Amt getrieben.
They drove the corrupt president out of office.

**trennen (sich)**
to separate, to part
**Auxiliary verb:** haben **Past participle:** getrennt
**Imperative:** Trenne! Trennt! Trennen Sie!

| Mode | Simple Tenses | | Compound Tenses | |
|---|---|---|---|---|
| | *Singular* | *Plural* | *Singular* | *Plural* |
| Indicative | **Present** | | **Present Perfect** | |
| | trenne<br>trennst<br>trennt | trennen<br>trennt<br>trennen | habe getrennt<br>hast getrennt<br>hat getrennt | haben getrennt<br>habt getrennt<br>haben getrennt |
| | **Past** | | **Past Perfect** | |
| | trennte<br>trenntest<br>trennte | trennten<br>trenntet<br>trennten | hatte getrennt<br>hattest getrennt<br>hatte getrennt | hatten getrennt<br>hattet getrennt<br>hatten getrennt |
| | **Future** | | **Future Perfect** | |
| | werde trennen<br>wirst trennen<br>wird trennen | werden trennen<br>werdet trennen<br>werden trennen | werde getrennt haben<br>wirst getrennt haben<br>wird getrennt haben | werden getrennt haben<br>werdet getrennt haben<br>werden getrennt haben |
| Subjunctive | **Present** | | **Present Perfect** | |
| | trenne<br>trennest<br>trenne | trennen<br>trennet<br>trennen | habe getrennt<br>habest getrennt<br>habe getrennt | haben getrennt<br>habet getrennt<br>haben getrennt |
| | **Past** | | **Past Perfect** | |
| | trennte<br>trenntest<br>trennte | trennten<br>trenntet<br>trennten | hätte getrennt<br>hättest getrennt<br>hätte getrennt | hätten getrennt<br>hättet getrennt<br>hätten getrennt |
| | **Future** | | **Future Perfect** | |
| | werde trennen<br>werdest trennen<br>werde trennen | werden trennen<br>werdet trennen<br>werden trennen | werde getrennt haben<br>werdest getrennt haben<br>werde getrennt haben | werden getrennt haben<br>werdet getrennt haben<br>werden getrennt haben |
| | **Present and Future Conditional** | | **Past Conditional** | |
| | würde trennen<br>würdest trennen<br>würde trennen | würden trennen<br>würdet trennen<br>würden trennen | würde getrennt haben<br>würdest getrennt haben<br>würde getrennt haben | würden getrennt haben<br>würdet getrennt haben<br>würden getrennt haben |

# EXAMPLES

Die Brüder raufen oft und müssen dann getrennt werden.
The brothers often fight and have to be separated.

Frau Behmann sagt, dass sie sich von ihrem Mann trennen will.
Ms. Behmann says that she wants to separate from her husband.

**treten**
to step, to tread
**Auxiliary verb:** sein **Past participle:** getreten
**Imperative:** Tritt! Tretet! Treten Sie!

| Mode | Simple Tenses | | Compound Tenses | |
|---|---|---|---|---|
| | *Singular* | *Plural* | *Singular* | *Plural* |
| Indicative | **Present** | | **Present Perfect** | |
| | trete<br>trittst<br>tritt | treten<br>tretet<br>treten | bin getreten<br>bist getreten<br>ist getreten | sind getreten<br>seid getreten<br>sind getreten |
| | **Past** | | **Past Perfect** | |
| | trat<br>tratest<br>trat | traten<br>tratet<br>traten | war getreten<br>warst getreten<br>war getreten | waren getreten<br>wart getreten<br>waren getreten |
| | **Future** | | **Future Perfect** | |
| | werde treten<br>wirst treten<br>wird treten | werden treten<br>werdet treten<br>werden treten | werde getreten sein<br>wirst getreten sein<br>wird getreten sein | werden getreten sein<br>werdet getreten sein<br>werden getreten sein |
| Subjunctive | **Present** | | **Present Perfect** | |
| | trete<br>tretest<br>trete | treten<br>tretet<br>treten | sei getreten<br>seiest getreten<br>sei getreten | seien getreten<br>seiet getreten<br>seien getreten |
| | **Past** | | **Past Perfect** | |
| | träte<br>trätest<br>träte | träten<br>trätet<br>träten | wäre getreten<br>wärest getreten<br>wäre getreten | wären getreten<br>wäret getreten<br>wären getreten |
| | **Future** | | **Future Perfect** | |
| | werde treten<br>werdest treten<br>werde treten | werden treten<br>werdet treten<br>werden treten | werde getreten sein<br>werdest getreten sein<br>werde getreten sein | werden getreten sein<br>werdet getreten sein<br>werden getreten sein |
| | **Present and Future Conditional** | | **Past Conditional** | |
| | würde treten<br>würdest treten<br>würde treten | würden treten<br>würdet treten<br>würden treten | würde getreten sein<br>würdest getreten sein<br>würde getreten sein | würden getreten sein<br>würdet getreten sein<br>würden getreten sein |

**Note:** With inseparable prefixes, the principal parts of this verb are, for example, *vertritt, vertrat, hat vertreten.* With separable prefixes, the principal parts are, for example, *tritt auf, trat auf, ist aufgetreten.*

## EXAMPLES

Sie sind mir auf den Fuß getreten!
You stepped on my foot!

Der Chef hat sich entschieden in den Hintergrund zu treten. Ein anderer kann die Firma leiten.
The boss decided to step into the background. Someone else can run the company.

**trinken**
to drink
**Auxiliary verb:** haben **Past participle:** getrunken
**Imperative:** Trinke! Trinkt! Trinken Sie!

| Mode | Simple Tenses | | Compound Tenses | |
|---|---|---|---|---|
| | *Singular* | *Plural* | *Singular* | *Plural* |
| Indicative | **Present** | | **Present Perfect** | |
| | trinke<br>trinkst<br>trinkt | trinken<br>trinkt<br>trinken | habe getrunken<br>hast getrunken<br>hat getrunken | haben getrunken<br>habt getrunken<br>haben getrunken |
| | **Past** | | **Past Perfect** | |
| | trank<br>trankst<br>trank | tranken<br>trankt<br>tranken | hatte getrunken<br>hattest getrunken<br>hatte getrunken | hatten getrunken<br>hattet getrunken<br>hatten getrunken |
| | **Future** | | **Future Perfect** | |
| | werde trinken<br>wirst trinken<br>wird trinken | werden trinken<br>werdet trinken<br>werden trinken | werde getrunken haben<br>wirst getrunken haben<br>wird getrunken haben | werden getrunken haben<br>werdet getrunken haben<br>werden getrunken haben |
| Subjunctive | **Present** | | **Present Perfect** | |
| | trinke<br>trinkest<br>trinke | trinken<br>trinket<br>trinken | habe getrunken<br>habest getrunken<br>habe getrunken | haben getrunken<br>habet getrunken<br>haben getrunken |
| | **Past** | | **Past Perfect** | |
| | tränke<br>tränkest<br>tränke | tränken<br>tränket<br>tränken | hätte getrunken<br>hättest getrunken<br>hätte getrunken | hätten getrunken<br>hättet getrunken<br>hätten getrunken |
| | **Future** | | **Future Perfect** | |
| | werde trinken<br>werdest trinken<br>werde trinken | werden trinken<br>werdet trinken<br>werden trinken | werde getrunken haben<br>werdest getrunken haben<br>werde getrunken haben | werden getrunken haben<br>werdet getrunken haben<br>werden getrunken haben |
| | **Present and Future Conditional** | | **Past Conditional** | |
| | würde trinken<br>würdest trinken<br>würde trinken | würden trinken<br>würdet trinken<br>würden trinken | würde getrunken haben<br>würdest getrunken haben<br>würde getrunken haben | würden getrunken haben<br>würdet getrunken haben<br>würden getrunken haben |

**Note:** With inseparable prefixes, the principal parts of this verb are, for example, *ertrinkt, ertrank, ist ertrunken.* With separable prefixes, the principal parts are, for example, *trinkt aus, trank aus, hat ausgetrunken.*

## EXAMPLES

Ich habe gestern Abend mit Erich Brüderschaft getrunken.

Last night, Erich and I drank to our friendship (and now address one another with *du*).

Er möchte gerne ein Bier trinken.

He'd like to drink a beer.

**trocknen**
to dry
**Auxiliary verb:** haben **Past participle:** getrocknet
**Imperative:** Trockne! Trocknet! Trocknen Sie!

| Mode | Simple Tenses | | Compound Tenses | |
|---|---|---|---|---|
| | *Singular* | *Plural* | *Singular* | *Plural* |
| Indicative | **Present** | | **Present Perfect** | |
| | trockne<br>trocknest<br>trocknet | trocknen<br>trocknet<br>trocknen | habe getrocknet<br>hast getrocknet<br>hat getrocknet | haben getrocknet<br>habt getrocknet<br>haben getrocknet |
| | **Past** | | **Past Perfect** | |
| | trocknete<br>trocknetest<br>trocknete | trockneten<br>trocknetet<br>trockneten | hatte getrocknet<br>hattest getrocknet<br>hatte getrocknet | hatten getrocknet<br>hattet getrocknet<br>hatten getrocknet |
| | **Future** | | **Future Perfect** | |
| | werde trocknen<br>wirst trocknen<br>wird trocknen | werden trocknen<br>werdet trocknen<br>werden trocknen | werde getrocknet haben<br>wirst getrocknet haben<br>wird getrocknet haben | werden getrocknet haben<br>werdet getrocknet haben<br>werden getrocknet haben |
| Subjunctive | **Present** | | **Present Perfect** | |
| | trockne<br>trocknest<br>trockne | trocknen<br>trocknet<br>trocknen | habe getrocknet<br>habest getrocknet<br>habe getrocknet | haben getrocknet<br>habet getrocknet<br>haben getrocknet |
| | **Past** | | **Past Perfect** | |
| | trocknete<br>trocknetest<br>trocknete | trockneten<br>trocknetet<br>trockneten | hätte getrocknet<br>hättest getrocknet<br>hätte getrocknet | hätten getrocknet<br>hättet getrocknet<br>hätten getrocknet |
| | **Future** | | **Future Perfect** | |
| | werde trocknen<br>werdest trocknen<br>werde trocknen | werden trocknen<br>werdet trocknen<br>werden trocknen | werde getrocknet haben<br>werdest getrocknet haben<br>werde getrocknet haben | werden getrocknet haben<br>werdet getrocknet haben<br>werden getrocknet haben |
| | **Present and Future Conditional** | | **Past Conditional** | |
| | würde trocknen<br>würdest trocknen<br>würde trocknen | würden trocknen<br>würdet trocknen<br>würden trocknen | würde getrocknet haben<br>würdest getrocknet haben<br>würde getrocknet haben | wurden getrocknet haben<br>würdet getrocknet haben<br>würden getrocknet haben |

## EXAMPLES

| | |
|---|---|
| Bei diesem regnerischen Wetter trocknet die Wäsche langsam. | The wash dries slowly in this rainy weather. |
| Wo kann ich dieses nasse Hemd trocknen? | Where can I dry this wet shirt? |

**trösten (sich)**
to console, to comfort
**Auxiliary verb:** haben **Past participle:** getröstet
**Imperative:** Tröste! Tröstet! Trösten Sie!

| Mode | Simple Tenses | | Compound Tenses | |
|---|---|---|---|---|
| | *Singular* | *Plural* | *Singular* | *Plural* |
| Indicative | **Present** | | **Present Perfect** | |
| | tröste<br>tröstest<br>tröstet | trösten<br>tröstet<br>trösten | habe getröstet<br>hast getröstet<br>hat getröstet | haben getröstet<br>habt getröstet<br>haben getröstet |
| | **Past** | | **Past Perfect** | |
| | tröstete<br>tröstetest<br>tröstete | trösteten<br>tröstetet<br>trösteten | hatte getröstet<br>hattest getröstet<br>hatte getröstet | hatten getröstet<br>hattet getröstet<br>hatten getröstet |
| | **Future** | | **Future Perfect** | |
| | werde trösten<br>wirst trösten<br>wird trösten | werden trösten<br>werdet trösten<br>werden trösten | werde getröstet haben<br>wirst getröstet haben<br>wird getröstet haben | werden getröstet haben<br>werdet getröstet haben<br>werden getröstet haben |
| Subjunctive | **Present** | | **Present Perfect** | |
| | tröste<br>tröstest<br>tröste | trösten<br>tröstet<br>trösten | habe getröstet<br>habest getröstet<br>habe getröstet | haben getröstet<br>habet getröstet<br>haben getröstet |
| | **Past** | | **Past Perfect** | |
| | tröstete<br>tröstetest<br>tröstete | trösteten<br>tröstetet<br>trösteten | hätte getröstet<br>hättest getröstet<br>hätte getröstet | hätten getröstet<br>hättet getröstet<br>hätten getröstet |
| | **Future** | | **Future Perfect** | |
| | werde trösten<br>werdest trösten<br>werde trösten | werden trösten<br>werdet trösten<br>werden trösten | werde getröstet haben<br>werdest getröstet haben<br>werde getröstet haben | werden getröstet haben<br>werdet getröstet haben<br>werden getröstet haben |
| | **Present and Future Conditional** | | **Past Conditional** | |
| | würde trösten<br>würdest trösten<br>würde trösten | würden trösten<br>würdet trösten<br>würden trösten | würde getröstet haben<br>würdest getröstet haben<br>würde getröstet haben | würden getröstet haben<br>würdet getröstet haben<br>würden getröstet haben |

# EXAMPLES

| | |
|---|---|
| Ich wünschte, ich könnte ihn an diesem traurigen Tag trösten. | I wish I could comfort him on this sad day. |
| Der arme Mann hat sich mit Schnaps getröstet. | The poor man consoled himself with schnapps. |
| Die Mutter tröstet das weinende Kind mit einem Kuss. | The mother comforts the crying child with a kiss. |

**tun**

to do, to make, to put

**Auxiliary verb:** haben **Past participle:** getan

**Imperative:** Tue! Tut! Tun Sie!

| Mode | Simple Tenses | | Compound Tenses | |
|---|---|---|---|---|
| | *Singular* | *Plural* | *Singular* | *Plural* |
| Indicative | **Present** | | **Present Perfect** | |
| | tue<br>tust<br>tut | tun<br>tut<br>tun | habe getan<br>hast getan<br>hat getan | haben getan<br>habt getan<br>haben getan |
| | **Past** | | **Past Perfect** | |
| | tat<br>tatest<br>tat | taten<br>tatet<br>taten | hatte getan<br>hattest getan<br>hatte getan | hatten getan<br>hattet getan<br>hatten getan |
| | **Future** | | **Future Perfect** | |
| | werde tun<br>wirst tun<br>wird tun | werden tun<br>werdet tun<br>werden tun | werde getan haben<br>wirst getan haben<br>wird getan haben | werden getan haben<br>werdet getan haben<br>werden getan haben |
| Subjunctive | **Present** | | **Present Perfect** | |
| | tue<br>tuest<br>tue | tuen<br>tuet<br>tuen | habe getan<br>habest getan<br>habe getan | haben getan<br>habet getan<br>haben getan |
| | **Past** | | **Past Perfect** | |
| | täte<br>tätest<br>täte | täten<br>tätet<br>täten | hätte getan<br>hättest getan<br>hätte getan | hätten getan<br>hättet getan<br>hätten getan |
| | **Future** | | **Future Perfect** | |
| | werde tun<br>werdest tun<br>werde tun | werden tun<br>werdet tun<br>werden tun | werde getan haben<br>werdest getan haben<br>werde getan haben | werden getan haben<br>werdet getan haben<br>werden getan haben |
| | **Present and Future Conditional** | | **Past Conditional** | |
| | würde tun<br>würdest tun<br>würde tun | würden tun<br>würdet tun<br>würden tun | würde getan haben<br>würdest getan haben<br>würde getan haben | würden getan haben<br>würdet getan haben<br>würden getan haben |

## EXAMPLES

Wer hat so viel Salz in die Suppe getan?
Who put so much salt in the soup?

Ich habe jeden Tag viel zu tun.
I have a lot to do every day.

**turnen**
to do gymnastics
**Auxiliary verb:** haben **Past participle:** geturnt
**Imperative:** Turne! Turnt! Turnen Sie!

| Mode | Simple Tenses | | Compound Tenses | |
|---|---|---|---|---|
| | *Singular* | *Plural* | *Singular* | *Plural* |
| Indicative | **Present** | | **Present Perfect** | |
| | turne<br>turnst<br>turnt | turnen<br>turnt<br>turnen | habe geturnt<br>hast geturnt<br>hat geturnt | haben geturnt<br>habt geturnt<br>haben geturnt |
| | **Past** | | **Past Perfect** | |
| | turnte<br>turntest<br>turnte | turnten<br>turntet<br>turnten | hatte geturnt<br>hattest geturnt<br>hatte geturnt | hatten geturnt<br>hattet geturnt<br>hatten geturnt |
| | **Future** | | **Future Perfect** | |
| | werde turnen<br>wirst turnen<br>wird turnen | werden turnen<br>werdet turnen<br>werden turnen | werde geturnt haben<br>wirst geturnt haben<br>wird geturnt haben | werden geturnt haben<br>werdet geturnt haben<br>werden geturnt haben |
| Subjunctive | **Present** | | **Present Perfect** | |
| | turne<br>turnest<br>turne | turnen<br>turnet<br>turnen | habe geturnt<br>habest geturnt<br>habe geturnt | haben geturnt<br>habet geturnt<br>haben geturnt |
| | **Past** | | **Past Perfect** | |
| | turnte<br>turntest<br>turnte | turnten<br>turntet<br>turnten | hätte geturnt<br>hättest geturnt<br>hätte geturnt | hätten geturnt<br>hättet geturnt<br>hätten geturnt |
| | **Future** | | **Future Perfect** | |
| | werde turnen<br>werdest turnen<br>werde turnen | werden turnen<br>werdet turnen<br>werden turnen | werde geturnt haben<br>werdest geturnt haben<br>werde geturnt haben | werden geturnt haben<br>werdet geturnt haben<br>werden geturnt haben |
| | **Present and Future Conditional** | | **Past Conditional** | |
| | würde turnen<br>würdest turnen<br>würde turnen | würden turnen<br>würdet turnen<br>würden turnen | würde geturnt haben<br>würdest geturnt haben<br>würde geturnt haben | würden geturnt haben<br>würdet geturnt haben<br>würden geturnt haben |

## EXAMPLE

Die junge Sportlerin turnt sehr gut.

The young athlete is a very good gymnast.

**üben**

to practice, to exercise

**Auxiliary verb:** haben **Past participle:** geübt

**Imperative:** Übe! Übt! Üben Sie!

| Mode | Simple Tenses | | Compound Tenses | |
|---|---|---|---|---|
| | *Singular* | *Plural* | *Singular* | *Plural* |
| Indicative | **Present** | | **Present Perfect** | |
| | übe<br>übst<br>übt | üben<br>übt<br>üben | habe geübt<br>hast geübt<br>hat geübt | haben geübt<br>habt geübt<br>haben geübt |
| | **Past** | | **Past Perfect** | |
| | übte<br>übtest<br>übte | übten<br>übtet<br>übten | hatte geübt<br>hattest geübt<br>hatte geübt | hatten geübt<br>hattet geübt<br>hatten geübt |
| | **Future** | | **Future Perfect** | |
| | werde üben<br>wirst üben<br>wird üben | werden üben<br>werdet üben<br>werden üben | werde geübt haben<br>wirst geübt haben<br>wird geübt haben | werden geübt haben<br>werdet geübt haben<br>werden geübt haben |
| Subjunctive | **Present** | | **Present Perfect** | |
| | übe<br>übest<br>übe | üben<br>übet<br>üben | habe geübt<br>habest geübt<br>habe geübt | haben geübt<br>habet geübt<br>haben geübt |
| | **Past** | | **Past Perfect** | |
| | übte<br>übtest<br>übte | übten<br>übtet<br>übten | hätte geübt<br>hättest geübt<br>hätte geübt | hätten geübt<br>hättet geübt<br>hätten geübt |
| | **Future** | | **Future Perfect** | |
| | werde üben<br>werdest üben<br>werde üben | werden üben<br>werdet üben<br>werden üben | werde geübt haben<br>werdest geübt haben<br>werde geübt haben | werden geübt haben<br>werdet geübt haben<br>werden geübt haben |
| | **Present and Future Conditional** | | **Past Conditional** | |
| | würde üben<br>würdest üben<br>würde üben | würden üben<br>würdet üben<br>würden üben | würde geübt haben<br>würdest geübt haben<br>würde geübt haben | würden geübt haben<br>würdet geübt haben<br>würden geübt haben |

## EXAMPLES

Ich spiele gern Klavier, aber ich übe nicht gern.

I like playing the piano, but I don't like to practice.

Sie hat täglich drei Stunden geübt, aber jonglieren kann sie immer noch nicht.

She practiced three hours a day, but she still can't juggle.

**überlégen (sich)**
to consider, to reflect on
**Auxiliary verb:** haben **Past participle:** überlegt
**Imperative:** Überlege! Überlegt! Überlegen Sie!

| Mode | Simple Tenses | | Compound Tenses | |
|---|---|---|---|---|
| | *Singular* | *Plural* | *Singular* | *Plural* |
| Indicative | **Present** | | **Present Perfect** | |
| | überlege<br>überlegst<br>überlegt | überlegen<br>überlegt<br>überlegen | habe überlegt<br>hast überlegt<br>hat überlegt | haben überlegt<br>habt überlegt<br>haben überlegt |
| | **Past** | | **Past Perfect** | |
| | überlegte<br>uberlegtest<br>überlegte | überlegten<br>überlegtet<br>überlegten | hatte überlegt<br>hattest überlegt<br>hatte überlegt | hatten überlegt<br>hattet überlegt<br>hatten überlegt |
| | **Future** | | **Future Perfect** | |
| | werde überlegen<br>wirst überlegen<br>wird überlegen | werden überlegen<br>werdet überlegen<br>werden überlegen | werde überlegt haben<br>wirst überlegt haben<br>wird überlegt haben | werden überlegt haben<br>werdet überlegt haben<br>werden überlegt haben |
| Subjunctive | **Present** | | **Present Perfect** | |
| | überlege<br>überlegest<br>überlege | überlegen<br>überleget<br>überlegen | habe überlegt<br>habest überlegt<br>habe überlegt | haben überlegt<br>habet überlegt<br>haben überlegt |
| | **Past** | | **Past Perfect** | |
| | überlegte<br>überlegtest<br>überlegte | überlegten<br>überlegtet<br>überlegten | hätte überlegt<br>hättest überlegt<br>hätte überlegt | hätten überlegt<br>hättet überlegt<br>hätten überlegt |
| | **Future** | | **Future Perfect** | |
| | werde überlegen<br>werdest überlegen<br>werde überlegen | werden überlegen<br>werdet überlegen<br>werden überlegen | werde überlegt haben<br>werdest überlegt haben<br>werde überlegt haben | werden überlegt haben<br>werdet überlegt haben<br>werden überlegt haben |
| | **Present and Future Conditional** | | **Past Conditional** | |
| | würde überlegen<br>würdest überlegen<br>würde überlegen | würden überlegen<br>würdet überlegen<br>würden überlegen | würde überlegt haben<br>würdest überlegt haben<br>würde überlegt haben | würden überlegt haben<br>würdet überlegt haben<br>würden überlegt haben |

## EXAMPLES

Ich werde mir die Sache überlegen.
I'll consider the matter.

Hanno überlegte sich, ob er Angela zum Tanz einladen soll oder nicht.
Hanno thought about whether or not he should invite Angela to the dance.

**überráschen**
to surprise
**Auxiliary verb:** haben **Past participle:** überrascht
**Imperative:** Überrasche! Überrascht! Überraschen Sie!

| Mode | Simple Tenses | | Compound Tenses | |
|---|---|---|---|---|
| | *Singular* | *Plural* | *Singular* | *Plural* |
| Indicative | **Present** | | **Present Perfect** | |
| | überrasche<br>überraschst<br>überrascht | überraschen<br>überrascht<br>überraschen | habe überrascht<br>hast überrascht<br>hat überrascht | haben überrascht<br>habt überrascht<br>haben überrascht |
| | **Past** | | **Past Perfect** | |
| | überraschte<br>überraschtest<br>überraschte | überraschten<br>überraschtet<br>überraschten | hatte überrascht<br>hattest überrascht<br>hatte überrascht | hatten überrascht<br>hattet überrascht<br>hatten überrascht |
| | **Future** | | **Future Perfect** | |
| | werde überraschen<br>wirst überraschen<br>wird überraschen | werden überraschen<br>werdet überraschen<br>werden überraschen | werde überrascht haben<br>wirst überrascht haben<br>wird überrascht haben | werden überrascht haben<br>werdet überrascht haben<br>werden überrascht haben |
| Subjunctive | **Present** | | **Present Perfect** | |
| | überrasche<br>überraschest<br>überrasche | überraschen<br>überraschet<br>überraschen | habe überrascht<br>habest überrascht<br>habe überrascht | haben überrascht<br>habet überrascht<br>haben überrascht |
| | **Past** | | **Past Perfect** | |
| | überraschte<br>überraschtest<br>überraschte | überraschten<br>überraschtet<br>überraschten | hätte überrascht<br>hättest überrascht<br>hätte überrascht | hätten überrascht<br>hättet überrascht<br>hätten überrascht |
| | **Future** | | **Future Perfect** | |
| | werde überraschen<br>werdest überraschen<br>werde überraschen | werden überraschen<br>werdet überraschen<br>werden überraschen | werde überrascht haben<br>werdest überrascht haben<br>werde überrascht haben | werden überrascht haben<br>werdet überrascht haben<br>werden überrascht haben |
| | **Present and Future Conditional** | | **Past Conditional** | |
| | würde überraschen<br>würdest überraschen<br>würde überraschen | würden überraschen<br>würdet überraschen<br>würden überraschen | würde überrascht haben<br>würdest überrascht haben<br>würde überrascht haben | würden überrascht haben<br>würdet überrascht haben<br>würden überrascht haben |

## EXAMPLES

Ich überraschte meine Freundin mit einem Blumenstrauß.
I surprised my girlfriend with a bouquet of flowers.

Das kleine Mädchen ist überraschend schnell gelaufen.
The little girl ran surprisingly fast.

**übersétzen**
to translate
**Auxiliary verb:** haben **Past participle:** übersetzt
**Imperative:** Übersetze! Übersetzt! Übersetzen Sie!

| Mode | Simple Tenses | | Compound Tenses | |
|---|---|---|---|---|
| | *Singular* | *Plural* | *Singular* | *Plural* |
| Indicative | **Present** | | **Present Perfect** | |
| | übersetze<br>übersetzt<br>übersetzt | übersetzen<br>übersetzt<br>übersetzen | habe übersetzt<br>hast übersetzt<br>hat übersetzt | haben übersetzt<br>habt übersetzt<br>haben übersetzt |
| | **Past** | | **Past Perfect** | |
| | übersetzte<br>übersetztest<br>übersetzte | übersetzten<br>übersetztet<br>übersetzten | hatte übersetzt<br>hattest übersetzt<br>hatte übersetzt | hatten übersetzt<br>hattet übersetzt<br>hatten übersetzt |
| | **Future** | | **Future Perfect** | |
| | werde übersetzen<br>wirst übersetzen<br>wird übersetzen | werden übersetzen<br>werdet übersetzen<br>werden übersetzen | werde übersetzt haben<br>wirst übersetzt haben<br>wird übersetzt haben | werden übersetzt haben<br>werdet übersetzt haben<br>werden übersetzt haben |
| Subjunctive | **Present** | | **Present Perfect** | |
| | übersetze<br>übersetzest<br>übersetze | übersetzen<br>übersetzet<br>übersetzen | habe übersetzt<br>habest übersetzt<br>habe übersetzt | haben übersetzt<br>habet übersetzt<br>haben übersetzt |
| | **Past** | | **Past Perfect** | |
| | übersetzte<br>übersetztest<br>übersetzte | übersetzten<br>übersetztet<br>übersetzten | hätte übersetzt<br>hättest übersetzt<br>hätte übersetzt | hätten übersetzt<br>hättet übersetzt<br>hätten übersetzt |
| | **Future** | | **Future Perfect** | |
| | werde übersetzen<br>werdest übersetzen<br>werde übersetzen | werden übersetzen<br>werdet übersetzen<br>werden übersetzen | werde übersetzt haben<br>werdest übersetzt haben<br>werde übersetzt haben | werden übersetzt haben<br>werdet übersetzt haben<br>werden übersetzt haben |
| | **Present and Future Conditional** | | **Past Conditional** | |
| | würde übersetzen<br>würdest übersetzen<br>würde übersetzen | würden übersetzen<br>würdet übersetzen<br>würden übersetzen | würde übersetzt haben<br>würdest übersetzt haben<br>würde übersetzt haben | würden übersetzt haben<br>würdet übersetzt haben<br>würden übersetzt haben |

## EXAMPLES

Sie versuchte den Text wortgetreu zu übersetzen.
She tried translating the text literally.

Wir haben mehrere Sätze ins Deutsche übersetzen müssen.
We had to translate several sentences into German.

**übertrágen**
to transfer, to transmit, to broadcast
**Auxiliary verb:** haben **Past participle:** übertragen
**Imperative:** Übertrage! Übertragt! Übertragen Sie!

| Mode | Simple Tenses | | Compound Tenses | |
|---|---|---|---|---|
| | *Singular* | *Plural* | *Singular* | *Plural* |
| Indicative | **Present** | | **Present Perfect** | |
| | übertrage<br>überträgst<br>überträgt | übertragen<br>übertragt<br>übertragen | habe übertragen<br>hast übertragen<br>hat übertragen | haben übertragen<br>habt übertragen<br>haben übertragen |
| | **Past** | | **Past Perfect** | |
| | übertrug<br>übertrugst<br>übertrug | übertrugen<br>übertrugt<br>übertrugen | hatte übertragen<br>hattest übertragen<br>hatte übertragen | hatten übertragen<br>hattet übertragen<br>hatten übertragen |
| | **Future** | | **Future Perfect** | |
| | werde übertragen<br>wirst übertragen<br>wird übertragen | werden übertragen<br>werdet übertragen<br>werden übertragen | werde übertragen haben<br>wirst übertragen haben<br>wird übertragen haben | werden übertragen haben<br>werdet übertragen haben<br>werden übertragen haben |
| Subjunctive | **Present** | | **Present Perfect** | |
| | übertrage<br>übertragest<br>übertrage | übertragen<br>übertraget<br>übertragen | habe übertragen<br>habest übertragen<br>habe übertragen | haben übertragen<br>habet übertragen<br>haben übertragen |
| | **Past** | | **Past Perfect** | |
| | übertrüge<br>übertrügest<br>übertrüge | übertrügen<br>übertrüget<br>übertrügen | hätte übertragen<br>hättest übertragen<br>hätte übertragen | hätten übertragen<br>hättet übertragen<br>hätten übertragen |
| | **Future** | | **Future Perfect** | |
| | werde übertragen<br>werdest übertragen<br>werde übertragen | werden übertragen<br>werdet übertragen<br>werden übertragen | werde übertragen haben<br>werdest übertragen haben<br>werde übertragen haben | werden übertragen haben<br>werdet übertragen haben<br>werden übertragen haben |
| | **Present and Future Conditional** | | **Past Conditional** | |
| | würde übertragen<br>würdest übertragen<br>würde übertragen | würden übertragen<br>würdet übertragen<br>würden übertragen | würde übertragen haben<br>würdest übertragen haben<br>würde übertragen haben | würden übertragen haben<br>würdet übertragen haben<br>würden übertragen haben |

# EXAMPLES

Das Konzert ist im Radio übertragen worden.
The concert was broadcast over the radio.

Die Krankheit kann nur durch Hautkontakt übertragen werden.
The disease can only be transmitted by contact with the skin.

**übertréiben**

to carry too far, to exaggerate

**Auxiliary verb:** haben **Past participle:** übertrieben

**Imperative:** Übertreibe! Übertreibt! Übertreiben Sie!

| Mode | Simple Tenses | | Compound Tenses | |
|---|---|---|---|---|
| | *Singular* | *Plural* | *Singular* | *Plural* |
| Indicative | **Present** | | **Present Perfect** | |
| | übertreibe<br>übertreibst<br>übertreibt | übertreiben<br>übertreibt<br>übertreiben | habe übertrieben<br>hast übertrieben<br>hat übertrieben | haben übertrieben<br>habt übertrieben<br>haben übertrieben |
| | **Past** | | **Past Perfect** | |
| | übertrieb<br>übertriebst<br>übertrieb | übertrieben<br>übertriebt<br>übertrieben | hatte übertrieben<br>hattest übertrieben<br>hatte übertrieben | hatten übertrieben<br>hattet übertrieben<br>hatten übertrieben |
| | **Future** | | **Future Perfect** | |
| | werde übertreiben<br>wirst übertreiben<br>wird übertreiben | werden übertreiben<br>werdet übertreiben<br>werden übertreiben | werde übertrieben haben<br>wirst übertrieben haben<br>wird übertrieben haben | werden übertrieben haben<br>werdet übertrieben haben<br>werden übertrieben haben |
| Subjunctive | **Present** | | **Present Perfect** | |
| | übertreibe<br>übertreibest<br>übertreibe | übertreiben<br>übertreibet<br>übertreiben | habe übertrieben<br>habest übertrieben<br>habe übertrieben | haben übertrieben<br>habet übertrieben<br>haben übertrieben |
| | **Past** | | **Past Perfect** | |
| | übertriebe<br>übertriebest<br>übertriebe | übertrieben<br>übertriebet<br>übertrieben | hätte übertrieben<br>hättest übertrieben<br>hätte übertrieben | hätten übertrieben<br>hättet übertrieben<br>hätten übertrieben |
| | **Future** | | **Future Perfect** | |
| | werde übertreiben<br>werdest übertreiben<br>werde übertreiben | werden übertreiben<br>werdet übertreiben<br>werden übertreiben | werde übertrieben haben<br>werdest übertrieben haben<br>werde übertrieben haben | werden übertrieben haben<br>werdet übertrieben haben<br>werden übertrieben haben |
| | **Present and Future Conditional** | | **Past Conditional** | |
| | würde übertreiben<br>würdest übertreiben<br>würde übertreiben | würden übertreiben<br>würdet übertreiben<br>würden übertreiben | würde übertrieben haben<br>würdest übertrieben haben<br>würde übertrieben haben | würden übertrieben haben<br>würdet übertrieben haben<br>würden übertrieben haben |

## EXAMPLES

Er kann nicht reden, ohne zu übertreiben. — He can't talk without exaggerating.

Der Schauspieler sprach mit einem übertriebenen Akzent. — The actor spoke with an exaggerated accent.

**überzéugen**
to convince
**Auxiliary verb:** haben **Past participle:** überzeugt
**Imperative:** Überzeuge! Überzeugt! Überzeugen Sie!

| Mode | Simple Tenses | | Compound Tenses | |
|---|---|---|---|---|
| | *Singular* | *Plural* | *Singular* | *Plural* |
| Indicative | **Present** | | **Present Perfect** | |
| | überzeuge<br>überzeugst<br>überzeugt | überzeugen<br>überzeugt<br>überzeugen | habe überzeugt<br>hast überzeugt<br>hat überzeugt | haben überzeugt<br>habt überzeugt<br>haben überzeugt |
| | **Past** | | **Past Perfect** | |
| | überzeugte<br>überzeugtest<br>überzeugte | überzeugten<br>überzeugtet<br>überzeugten | hatte überzeugt<br>hattest überzeugt<br>hatte überzeugt | hatten überzeugt<br>hattet überzeugt<br>hatten überzeugt |
| | **Future** | | **Future Perfect** | |
| | werde überzeugen<br>wirst überzeugen<br>wird überzeugen | werden überzeugen<br>werdet überzeugen<br>werden überzeugen | werde überzeugt haben<br>wirst überzeugt haben<br>wird überzeugt haben | werden überzeugt haben<br>werdet überzeugt haben<br>werden überzeugt haben |
| Subjunctive | **Present** | | **Present Perfect** | |
| | überzeuge<br>überzeugest<br>überzeuge | überzeugen<br>überzeuget<br>überzeugen | habe überzeugt<br>habest überzeugt<br>habe überzeugt | haben überzeugt<br>habet überzeugt<br>haben überzeugt |
| | **Past** | | **Past Perfect** | |
| | überzeugte<br>überzeugtest<br>überzeugte | überzeugten<br>überzeugtet<br>überzeugten | hätte überzeugt<br>hättest überzeugt<br>hätte überzeugt | hätten überzeugt<br>hättet überzeugt<br>hätten überzeugt |
| | **Future** | | **Future Perfect** | |
| | werde überzeugen<br>werdest überzeugen<br>werde überzeugen | werden überzeugen<br>werdet überzeugen<br>werden überzeugen | werde überzeugt haben<br>werdest überzeugt haben<br>werde überzeugt haben | werden überzeugt haben<br>werdet überzeugt haben<br>werden überzeugt haben |
| | **Present and Future Conditional** | | **Past Conditional** | |
| | würde überzeugen<br>würdest überzeugen<br>würde überzeugen | würden überzeugen<br>würdet überzeugen<br>würden überzeugen | würde überzeugt haben<br>würdest überzeugt haben<br>würde überzeugt haben | würden überzeugt haben<br>würdet überzeugt haben<br>würden überzeugt haben |

# EXAMPLES

Du wirst mich nie von dieser Idee überzeugen.
You'll never convince me of this idea.

Wenn Sie wollen, können Sie sich selbst davon überzeugen.
If you want, you can convince yourself of it.

**umármen (sich)**
to embrace
**Auxiliary verb:** haben **Past participle:** umarmt
**Imperative:** Umarme! Umarmt! Umarmen Sie!

| Mode | Simple Tenses | | Compound Tenses | |
|---|---|---|---|---|
| | *Singular* | *Plural* | *Singular* | *Plural* |
| Indicative | **Present** | | **Present Perfect** | |
| | umarme<br>umarmst<br>umarmt | umarmen<br>umarmt<br>umarmen | habe umarmt<br>hast umarmt<br>hat umarmt | haben umarmt<br>habt umarmt<br>haben umarmt |
| | **Past** | | **Past Perfect** | |
| | umarmte<br>umarmtest<br>umarmte | umarmten<br>umarmtet<br>umarmten | hatte umarmt<br>hattest umarmt<br>hatte umarmt | hatten umarmt<br>hattet umarmt<br>hatten umarmt |
| | **Future** | | **Future Perfect** | |
| | werde umarmen<br>wirst umarmen<br>wird umarmen | werden umarmen<br>werdet umarmen<br>werden umarmen | werde umarmt haben<br>wirst umarmt haben<br>wird umarmt haben | werden umarmt haben<br>werdet umarmt haben<br>werden umarmt haben |
| Subjunctive | **Present** | | **Present Perfect** | |
| | umarme<br>umarmest<br>umarme | umarmen<br>umarmet<br>umarmen | habe umarmt<br>habest umarmt<br>habe umarmt | haben umarmt<br>habet umarmt<br>haben umarmt |
| | **Past** | | **Past Perfect** | |
| | umarmte<br>umarmtest<br>umarmte | umarmten<br>umarmtet<br>umarmten | hätte umarmt<br>hättest umarmt<br>hätte umarmt | hätten umarmt<br>hättet umarmt<br>hätten umarmt |
| | **Future** | | **Future Perfect** | |
| | werde umarmen<br>werdest umarmen<br>werde umarmen | werden umarmen<br>werdet umarmen<br>werden umarmen | werde umarmt haben<br>werdest umarmt haben<br>werde umarmt haben | werden umarmt haben<br>werdet umarmt haben<br>werden umarmt haben |
| | **Present and Future Conditional** | | **Past Conditional** | |
| | würde umarmen<br>würdest umarmen<br>würde umarmen | würden umarmen<br>würdet umarmen<br>würden umarmen | würde umarmt haben<br>würdest umarmt haben<br>würde umarmt haben | würden umarmt haben<br>würdet umarmt haben<br>würden umarmt haben |

## EXAMPLES

Sie sitzen im Dunklen und umarmen sich.
They sit in the dark and embrace.

Kinder, lasst euch umarmen!
Children, let me give you all a hug.

**umdrehen (sich)**
to turn, to rotate
**Auxiliary verb:** haben **Past participle:** umgedreht
**Imperative:** Drehe um! Dreht um! Drehen Sie um!

| Mode | Simple Tenses | | Compound Tenses | |
|---|---|---|---|---|
| | *Singular* | *Plural* | *Singular* | *Plural* |
| Indicative | **Present** | | **Present Perfect** | |
| | drehe um<br>drehst um<br>dreht um | drehen um<br>dreht um<br>drehen um | habe umgedreht<br>hast umgedreht<br>hat umgedreht | haben umgedreht<br>habt umgedreht<br>haben umgedreht |
| | **Past** | | **Past Perfect** | |
| | drehte um<br>drehtest um<br>drehte um | drehten um<br>drehtet um<br>drehten um | hatte umgedreht<br>hattest umgedreht<br>hatte umgedreht | hatten umgedreht<br>hattet umgedreht<br>hatten umgedreht |
| | **Future** | | **Future Perfect** | |
| | werde umdrehen<br>wirst umdrehen<br>wird umdrehen | werden umdrehen<br>werdet umdrehen<br>werden umdrehen | werde umgedreht haben<br>wirst umgedreht haben<br>wird umgedreht haben | werden umgedreht haben<br>werdet umgedreht haben<br>werden umgedreht haben |
| Subjunctive | **Present** | | **Present Perfect** | |
| | drehe um<br>drehest um<br>drehe um | drehen um<br>drehet um<br>drehen um | habe umgedreht<br>habest umgedreht<br>habe umgedreht | haben umgedreht<br>habet umgedreht<br>haben umgedreht |
| | **Past** | | **Past Perfect** | |
| | drehte um<br>drehtest um<br>drehte um | drehten um<br>drehtet um<br>drehten um | hätte umgedreht<br>hättest umgedreht<br>hätte umgedreht | hätten umgedreht<br>hättet umgedreht<br>hätten umgedreht |
| | **Future** | | **Future Perfect** | |
| | werde umdrehen<br>werdest umdrehen<br>werde umdrehen | werden umdrehen<br>werdet umdrehen<br>werden umdrehen | werde umgedreht haben<br>werdest umgedreht haben<br>werde umgedreht haben | werden umgedreht haben<br>werdet umgedreht haben<br>werden umgedreht haben |
| | **Present and Future Conditional** | | **Past Conditional** | |
| | würde umdrehen<br>würdest umdrehen<br>würde umdrehen | würden umdrehen<br>würdet umdrehen<br>würden umdrehen | würde umgedreht haben<br>würdest umgedreht haben<br>würde umgedreht haben | würden umgedreht haben<br>würdet umgedreht haben<br>würden umgedreht haben |

## EXAMPLES

Was für ein hässliches Bild. Drehe es um!
Als ich mich umdrehte, sah ich ihr Gesicht.

What an ugly picture. Turn it over.
When I turned around, I saw her face.

**umkippen**
to tip over
**Auxiliary verb:** haben **Past participle:** umgekippt
**Imperative:** Kippe um! Kippt um! Kippen Sie um!

| Mode | Simple Tenses | | Compound Tenses | |
|---|---|---|---|---|
| | *Singular* | *Plural* | *Singular* | *Plural* |
| Indicative | **Present** | | **Present Perfect** | |
| | kippe um<br>kippst um<br>kippt um | kippen um<br>kippt um<br>kippen um | habe umgekippt<br>hast umgekippt<br>hat umgekippt | haben umgekippt<br>habt umgekippt<br>haben umgekippt |
| | **Past** | | **Past Perfect** | |
| | kippte um<br>kipptest um<br>kippte um | kippten um<br>kipptet um<br>kippten um | hatte umgekippt<br>hattest umgekippt<br>hatte umgekippt | hatten umgekippt<br>hattet umgekippt<br>hatten umgekippt |
| | **Future** | | **Future Perfect** | |
| | werde umkippen<br>wirst umkippen<br>wird umkippen | werden umkippen<br>werdet umkippen<br>werden umkippen | werde umgekippt haben<br>wirst umgekippt haben<br>wird umgekippt haben | werden umgekippt haben<br>werdet umgekippt haben<br>werden umgekippt haben |
| Subjunctive | **Present** | | **Present Perfect** | |
| | kippe um<br>kippest um<br>kippe um | kippen um<br>kippet um<br>kippen um | habe umgekippt<br>habest umgekippt<br>habe umgekippt | haben umgekippt<br>habet umgekippt<br>haben umgekippt |
| | **Past** | | **Past Perfect** | |
| | kippte um<br>kipptest um<br>kippte um | kippten um<br>kipptet um<br>kippten um | hätte umgekippt<br>hättest umgekippt<br>hätte umgekippt | hätten umgekippt<br>hättet umgekippt<br>hätten umgekippt |
| | **Future** | | **Future Perfect** | |
| | werde umkippen<br>werdest umkippen<br>werde umkippen | werden umkippen<br>werdet umkippen<br>werden umkippen | werde umgekippt haben<br>werdest umgekippt haben<br>werde umgekippt haben | werden umgekippt haben<br>werdet umgekippt haben<br>werden umgekippt haben |
| | **Present and Future Conditional** | | **Past Conditional** | |
| | würde umkippen<br>würdest umkippen<br>würde umkippen | würden umkippen<br>würdet umkippen<br>würden umkippen | würde umgekippt haben<br>würdest umgekippt haben<br>würde umgekippt haben | würden umgekippt haben<br>würdet umgekippt haben<br>würden umgekippt haben |

**Note:** When used as a verb of motion, this verb requires *sein* as its auxiliary in the perfect tenses.

## EXAMPLES

Johannes hat den Stuhl umgekippt. — Johannes tipped over the chair.
Der betrunkene Mann kippte zweimal um. — The drunken man fell over twice.

**umkommen**
to die, to perish
**Auxiliary verb:** sein **Past participle:** umgekommen
**Imperative:** Komme um! Kommt um! Kommen Sie um!

| Mode | Simple Tenses | | Compound Tenses | |
|---|---|---|---|---|
| | *Singular* | *Plural* | *Singular* | *Plural* |
| Indicative | **Present** | | **Present Perfect** | |
| | komme um<br>kommst um<br>kommt um | kommen um<br>kommt um<br>kommen um | bin umgekommen<br>bist umgekommen<br>ist umgekommen | sind umgekommen<br>seid umgekommen<br>sind umgekommen |
| | **Past** | | **Past Perfect** | |
| | kam um<br>kamst um<br>kam um | kamen um<br>kamt um<br>kamen um | war umgekommen<br>warst umgekommen<br>war umgekommen | waren umgekommen<br>wart umgekommen<br>waren umgekommen |
| | **Future** | | **Future Perfect** | |
| | werde umkommen<br>wirst umkommen<br>wird umkommen | werden umkommen<br>werdet umkommen<br>werden umkommen | werde umgekommen sein<br>wirst umgekommen sein<br>wird umgekommen sein | werden umgekommen sein<br>werdet umgekommen sein<br>werden umgekommen sein |
| Subjunctive | **Present** | | **Present Perfect** | |
| | komme um<br>kommest um<br>komme um | kommen um<br>kommet um<br>kommen um | sei umgekommen<br>seiest umgekommen<br>sei umgekommen | seien umgekommen<br>seiet umgekommen<br>seien umgekommen |
| | **Past** | | **Past Perfect** | |
| | käme um<br>kämest um<br>käme um | kämen um<br>kämet um<br>kämen um | wäre umgekommen<br>wärest umgekommen<br>wäre umgekommen | wären umgekommen<br>wäret umgekommen<br>wären umgekommen |
| | **Future** | | **Future Perfect** | |
| | werde umkommen<br>werdest umkommen<br>werde umkommen | werden umkommen<br>werdet umkommen<br>werden umkommen | werde umgekommen sein<br>werdest umgekommen sein<br>werde umgekommen sein | werden umgekommen sein<br>werdet umgekommen sein<br>werden umgekommen sein |
| | **Present and Future Conditional** | | **Past Conditional** | |
| | würde umkommen<br>würdest umkommen<br>würde umkommen | würden umkommen<br>würdet umkommen<br>würden umkommen | würde umgekommen sein<br>würdest umgekommen sein<br>würde umgekommen sein | würden umgekommen sein<br>würdet umgekommen sein<br>würden umgekommen sein |

**Note:** With inseparable prefixes, the principal parts of this verb are, for example, *verkommt, verkam, ist verkommen.* With separable prefixes, the principal parts are, for example, *kommt an, kam an, ist angekommen.*

## EXAMPLES

| | |
|---|---|
| Ach, ich komme vor Langeweile um. | Oh, I'm dying of boredom. |
| Der junge Offizier ist auf dem Schlachtfeld umgekommen. | The young officer died on the battlefield. |

**umsteigen**

to change (transportation), to transfer

**Auxiliary verb:** sein **Past participle:** umgestiegen

**Imperative:** Steige um! Steigt um! Steigen Sie um!

| Mode | Simple Tenses | | Compound Tenses | |
|---|---|---|---|---|
| | *Singular* | *Plural* | *Singular* | *Plural* |
| Indicative | **Present** | | **Present Perfect** | |
| | steige um<br>steigst um<br>steigt um | steigen um<br>steigt um<br>steigen um | bin umgestiegen<br>bist umgestiegen<br>ist umgestiegen | sind umgestiegen<br>seid umgestiegen<br>sind umgestiegen |
| | **Past** | | **Past Perfect** | |
| | stieg um<br>stiegst um<br>stieg um | stiegen um<br>stiegt um<br>stiegen um | war umgestiegen<br>warst umgestiegen<br>war umgestiegen | waren umgestiegen<br>wart umgestiegen<br>waren umgestiegen |
| | **Future** | | **Future Perfect** | |
| | werde umsteigen<br>wirst umsteigen<br>wird umsteigen | werden umsteigen<br>werdet umsteigen<br>werden umsteigen | werde umgestiegen sein<br>wirst umgestiegen sein<br>wird umgestiegen sein | werden umgestiegen sein<br>werdet umgestiegen sein<br>werden umgestiegen sein |
| Subjunctive | **Present** | | **Present Perfect** | |
| | steige um<br>steigest um<br>steige um | steigen um<br>steiget um<br>steigen um | sei umgestiegen<br>seiest umgestiegen<br>sei umgestiegen | seien umgestiegen<br>seiet umgestiegen<br>seien umgestiegen |
| | **Past** | | **Past Perfect** | |
| | stiege um<br>stiegest um<br>stiege um | stiegen um<br>stieget um<br>stiegen um | wäre umgestiegen<br>wärest umgestiegen<br>wäre umgestiegen | wären umgestiegen<br>wäret umgestiegen<br>wären umgestiegen |
| | **Future** | | **Future Perfect** | |
| | werde umsteigen<br>werdest umsteigen<br>werde umsteigen | werden umsteigen<br>werdet umsteigen<br>werden umsteigen | werde umgestiegen sein<br>werdest umgestiegen sein<br>werde umgestiegen sein | werden umgestiegen sein<br>werdet umgestiegen sein<br>werden umgestiegen sein |
| | **Present and Future Conditional** | | **Past Conditional** | |
| | würde umsteigen<br>würdest umsteigen<br>würde umsteigen | würden umsteigen<br>würdet umsteigen<br>würden umsteigen | würde umgestiegen sein<br>würdest umgestiegen sein<br>würde umgestiegen sein | würden umgestiegen sein<br>würdet umgestiegen sein<br>würden umgestiegen sein |

## EXAMPLES

| | |
|---|---|
| An der nächsten Haltestelle müssen wir umsteigen. | We have to transfer at the next stop. |
| Wir sind in München umgestiegen. | We changed trains/planes/buses in Munich. |

**unterdrücken**
to suppress, to oppress
**Auxiliary verb:** haben **Past participle:** unterdrückt
**Imperative:** Unterdrücke! Unterdrückt! Unterdrücken Sie!

| Mode | Simple Tenses | | Compound Tenses | |
|---|---|---|---|---|
| | *Singular* | *Plural* | *Singular* | *Plural* |
| Indicative | **Present** | | **Present Perfect** | |
| | unterdrücke<br>unterdrückst<br>unterdrückt | unterdrücken<br>unterdrückt<br>unterdrücken | habe unterdrückt<br>hast unterdrückt<br>hat unterdrückt | haben unterdrückt<br>habt unterdrückt<br>haben unterdrückt |
| | **Past** | | **Past Perfect** | |
| | unterdrückte<br>unterdrücktest<br>unterdrückte | unterdrückten<br>unterdrücktet<br>unterdrückten | hatte unterdrückt<br>hattest unterdrückt<br>hatte unterdrückt | hatten unterdrückt<br>hattet unterdrückt<br>hatten unterdrückt |
| | **Future** | | **Future Perfect** | |
| | werde unterdrücken<br>wirst unterdrücken<br>wird unterdrücken | werden unterdrücken<br>werdet unterdrücken<br>werden unterdrücken | werde unterdrückt haben<br>wirst unterdrückt haben<br>wird unterdrückt haben | werden unterdrückt haben<br>werdet unterdrückt haben<br>werden unterdrückt haben |
| Subjunctive | **Present** | | **Present Perfect** | |
| | unterdrücke<br>unterdrückest<br>unterdrücke | unterdrücken<br>unterdrücket<br>unterdrücken | habe unterdrückt<br>habest unterdrückt<br>habe unterdrückt | haben unterdrückt<br>habet unterdrückt<br>haben unterdrückt |
| | **Past** | | **Past Perfect** | |
| | unterdrückte<br>unterdrücktest<br>unterdrückte | unterdrückten<br>unterdrücktet<br>unterdrückten | hätte unterdrückt<br>hättest unterdrückt<br>hätte unterdrückt | hätten unterdrückt<br>hättet unterdrückt<br>hätten unterdrückt |
| | **Future** | | **Future Perfect** | |
| | werde unterdrücken<br>werdest unter-<br>drücken<br>werde unterdrücken | werden unterdrücken<br>werdet unterdrücken<br>werden unterdrücken | werde unterdrückt haben<br>werdest unterdrückt haben<br>werde unterdrückt haben | werden unterdrückt haben<br>werdet unterdrückt haben<br>werden unterdrückt haben |
| | **Present and Future Conditional** | | **Past Conditional** | |
| | würde unterdrücken<br>würdest unter-<br>drücken<br>würde unterdrücken | würden unterdrücken<br>würdet unterdrücken<br>würden unterdrücken | würde unterdrückt haben<br>würdest unterdrückt haben<br>würde unterdrückt haben | würden unterdrückt haben<br>würdet unterdrückt haben<br>würden unterdrückt haben |

# EXAMPLES

Die unterdrückte Bevölkerung rebellierte und stürzte die Regierung.
The oppressed population rose up and overthrew the government.

Sie haben die Sklaven unterdrückt.
They suppressed the slaves.

Ich unterdrückte ein Kichern.
I suppressed a giggle.

**unterněhmen**

to undertake, to attempt

**Auxiliary verb:** haben **Past participle:** unternommen

**Imperative:** Unternimm! Unternehmt! Unternehmen Sie!

| Mode | Simple Tenses | | Compound Tenses | |
|---|---|---|---|---|
| | *Singular* | *Plural* | *Singular* | *Plural* |
| Indicative | **Present** | | **Present Perfect** | |
| | unternehme<br>unternimmst<br>unternimmt | unternehmen<br>unternehmt<br>unternehmen | habe unternommen<br>hast unternommen<br>hat unternommen | haben unternommen<br>habt unternommen<br>haben unternommen |
| | **Past** | | **Past Perfect** | |
| | unternahm<br>unternahmst<br>unternahm | unternahmen<br>unternahmt<br>unternahmen | hatte unternommen<br>hattest unternommen<br>hatte unternommen | hatten unternommen<br>hattet unternommen<br>hatten unternommen |
| | **Future** | | **Future Perfect** | |
| | werde unternehmen<br>wirst unternehmen<br>wird unternehmen | werden unternehmen<br>werdet unternehmen<br>werden unternehmen | werde unternommen haben<br>wirst unternommen haben<br>wird unternommen haben | werden unternommen haben<br>werdet unternommen haben<br>werden unternommen haben |
| Subjunctive | **Present** | | **Present Perfect** | |
| | unternehme<br>unternehmest<br>unternehme | unternehmen<br>unternehmet<br>unternehmen | habe unternommen<br>habest unternommen<br>habe unternommen | haben unternommen<br>habet unternommen<br>haben unternommen |
| | **Past** | | **Past Perfect** | |
| | unternähme<br>unternähmest<br>unternähme | unternähmen<br>unternähmet<br>unternähmen | hätte unternommen<br>hättest unternommen<br>hätte unternommen | hätten unternommen<br>hättet unternommen<br>hätten unternommen |
| | **Future** | | **Future Perfect** | |
| | werde unternehmen<br>werdest unternehmen<br>werde unternehmen | werden unternehmen<br>werdet unternehmen<br>werden unternehmen | werde unternommen haben<br>werdest unternommen haben<br>werde unternommen haben | werden unternommen haben<br>werdet unternommen haben<br>werden unternommen haben |
| | **Present and Future Conditional** | | **Past Conditional** | |
| | würde unternehmen<br>würdest unternehmen<br>würde unternehmen | würden unternehmen<br>würdet unternehmen<br>würden unternehmen | würde unternommen haben<br>würdest unternommen haben<br>würde unternommen haben | würden unternommen haben<br>würdet unternommen haben<br>würden unternommen haben |

**Note:** Without a prefix, the principal parts of this verb are *nimmt, nahm, hat genommen.* With separable prefixes, the principal parts are, for example, *nimmt zu, nahm zu, hat zugenommen.*

## EXAMPLES

Die Regierung hat nichts gegen das wachsende Drogenproblem unternommen.

The government hasn't done anything about the mounting drug problem.

Sie werden endlich etwas gegen die Arbeitslosigkeit unternehmen.

They're finally going to do something about unemployment.

Wollen wir am Wochenende etwas zusammen unternehmen?

Would you like to do something together this weekend?

**verabschieden (sich)**
to say goodbye
**Auxiliary verb:** haben **Past participle:** verabschiedet
**Imperative:** Verabschiede! Verabschiedet! Verabschieden Sie!

| Mode | Simple Tenses | | Compound Tenses | |
|---|---|---|---|---|
| | *Singular* | *Plural* | *Singular* | *Plural* |
| Indicative | **Present** | | **Present Perfect** | |
| | verabschiede<br>verabschiedest<br>verabschiedet | verabschieden<br>verabschiedet<br>verabschieden | habe verabschiedet<br>hast verabschiedet<br>hat verabschiedet | haben verabschiedet<br>habt verabschiedet<br>haben verabschiedet |
| | **Past** | | **Past Perfect** | |
| | verabschiedete<br>verabschiedetest<br>verabschiedete | verabschiedeten<br>verabschiedetet<br>verabschiedeten | hatte verabschiedet<br>hattest verabschiedet<br>hatte verabschiedet | hatten verabschiedet<br>hattet verabschiedet<br>hatten verabschiedet |
| | **Future** | | **Future Perfect** | |
| | werde verabschieden<br>wirst verabschieden<br>wird verabschieden | werden verabschieden<br>werdet verabschieden<br>werden verabschieden | werde verabschiedet haben<br>wirst verabschiedet haben<br>wird verabschiedet haben | werden verabschiedet haben<br>werdet verabschiedet haben<br>werden verabschiedet haben |
| Subjunctive | **Present** | | **Present Perfect** | |
| | verabschiede<br>verabschiedest<br>verabschiede | verabschieden<br>verabschiedet<br>verabschieden | habe verabschiedet<br>habest verabschiedet<br>habe verabschiedet | haben verabschiedet<br>habet verabschiedet<br>haben verabschiedet |
| | **Past** | | **Past Perfect** | |
| | verabschiedete<br>verabschiedetest<br>verabschiedete | verabschiedeten<br>verabschiedetet<br>verabschiedeten | hätte verabschiedet<br>hättest verabschiedet<br>hätte verabschiedet | hätten verabschiedet<br>hättet verabschiedet<br>hätten verabschiedet |
| | **Future** | | **Future Perfect** | |
| | werde verabschieden<br>werdest verabschieden<br>werde verabschieden | werden verabschieden<br>werdet verabschieden<br>werden verabschieden | werde verabschiedet haben<br>werdest verabschiedet haben<br>werde verabschiedet haben | werden verabschiedet haben<br>werdet verabschiedet haben<br>werden verabschiedet haben |
| | **Present and Future Conditional** | | **Past Conditional** | |
| | würde verabschieden<br>würdest verabschieden<br>würde verabschieden | würden verabschieden<br>würdet verabschieden<br>würden verabschieden | würde verabschiedet haben<br>würdest verabschiedet haben<br>würde verabschiedet haben | würden verabschiedet haben<br>würdet verabschiedet haben<br>würden verabschiedet haben |

## EXAMPLES

Die Schule verabschiedete ihre Abschlussklasse.
The school said goodbye to its graduating class.

Sie haben sich noch nicht verabschiedet.
They still haven't said goodbye.

**verbieten**
to forbid, to prohibit
**Auxiliary verb:** haben **Past participle:** verboten
**Imperative:** Verbiete! Verbietet! Verbieten Sie!

| Mode | Simple Tenses | | Compound Tenses | |
|---|---|---|---|---|
| | *Singular* | *Plural* | *Singular* | *Plural* |
| Indicative | **Present** | | **Present Perfect** | |
| | verbiete<br>verbietest<br>verbietet | verbieten<br>verbietet<br>verbieten | habe verboten<br>hast verboten<br>hat verboten | haben verboten<br>habt verboten<br>haben verboten |
| | **Past** | | **Past Perfect** | |
| | verbot<br>verbotest<br>verbot | verboten<br>verbotet<br>verboten | hatte verboten<br>hattest verboten<br>hatte verboten | hatten verboten<br>hattet verboten<br>hatten verboten |
| | **Future** | | **Future Perfect** | |
| | werde verbieten<br>wirst verbieten<br>wird verbieten | werden verbieten<br>werdet verbieten<br>werden verbieten | werde verboten haben<br>wirst verboten haben<br>wird verboten haben | werden verboten haben<br>werdet verboten haben<br>werden verboten haben |
| Subjunctive | **Present** | | **Present Perfect** | |
| | verbiete<br>verbietest<br>verbiete | verbieten<br>verbietet<br>verbieten | habe verboten<br>habest verboten<br>habe verboten | haben verboten<br>habet verboten<br>haben verboten |
| | **Past** | | **Past Perfect** | |
| | verböte<br>verbötest<br>verböte | verböten<br>verbötet<br>verböten | hätte verboten<br>hättest verboten<br>hätte verboten | hätten verboten<br>hättet verboten<br>hätten verboten |
| | **Future** | | **Future Perfect** | |
| | werde verbieten<br>werdest verbieten<br>werde verbieten | werden verbieten<br>werdet verbieten<br>werden verbieten | werde verboten haben<br>werdest verboten haben<br>werde verboten haben | werden verboten haben<br>werdet verboten haben<br>werden verboten haben |
| | **Present and Future Conditional** | | **Past Conditional** | |
| | würde verbieten<br>würdest verbieten<br>würde verbieten | würden verbieten<br>würdet verbieten<br>würden verbieten | würde verboten haben<br>würdest verboten haben<br>würde verboten haben | würden verboten haben<br>würdet verboten haben<br>würden verboten haben |

**Note:** Without a prefix, the principal parts of this verb are *bietet, bot, hat geboten.* With separable prefixes, the principal parts are, for example, *bietet an, bot an, hat angeboten.*

## EXAMPLES

Die Eltern haben den Kindern verboten mit dem alten Hund zu spielen.
The parents have forbidden the children from playing with the old dog.

Rauchen verboten!
No smoking.

**verderben**
to spoil, to ruin, to drag down
**Auxiliary verb:** haben **Past participle:** verdorben
**Imperative:** Verdirb! Verderbt! Verderben Sie!

| Mode | Simple Tenses | | Compound Tenses | |
|---|---|---|---|---|
| | *Singular* | *Plural* | *Singular* | *Plural* |
| Indicative | **Present** | | **Present Perfect** | |
| | verderbe<br>verdirbst<br>verdirbt | verderben<br>verderbt<br>verderben | habe verdorben<br>hast verdorben<br>hat verdorben | haben verdorben<br>habt verdorben<br>haben verdorben |
| | **Past** | | **Past Perfect** | |
| | verdarb<br>verdarbst<br>verdarb | verdarben<br>verdarbt<br>verdarben | hatte verdorben<br>hattest verdorben<br>hatte verdorben | hatten verdorben<br>hattet verdorben<br>hatten verdorben |
| | **Future** | | **Future Perfect** | |
| | werde verderben<br>wirst verderben<br>wird verderben | werden verderben<br>werdet verderben<br>werden verderben | werde verdorben haben<br>wirst verdorben haben<br>wird verdorben haben | werden verdorben haben<br>werdet verdorben haben<br>werden verdorben haben |
| Subjunctive | **Present** | | **Present Perfect** | |
| | verderbe<br>verderbest<br>verderbe | verderben<br>verderbet<br>verderben | habe verdorben<br>habest verdorben<br>habe verdorben | haben verdorben<br>habet verdorben<br>haben verdorben |
| | **Past** | | **Past Perfect** | |
| | verdürbe<br>verdürbest<br>verdürbe | verdürben<br>verdürbet<br>verdürben | hätte verdorben<br>hättest verdorben<br>hätte verdorben | hätten verdorben<br>hättet verdorben<br>hätten verdorben |
| | **Future** | | **Future Perfect** | |
| | werde verderben<br>werdest verderben<br>werde verderben | werden verderben<br>werdet verderben<br>werden verderben | werde verdorben haben<br>werdest verdorben haben<br>werde verdorben haben | werden verdorben haben<br>werdet verdorben haben<br>werden verdorben haben |
| | **Present and Future Conditional** | | **Past Conditional** | |
| | würde verderben<br>würdest verderben<br>würde verderben | würden verderben<br>würdet verderben<br>würden verderben | würde verdorben haben<br>würdest verdorben haben<br>würde verdorben haben | würden verdorben haben<br>würdet verdorben haben<br>würden verdorben haben |

## EXAMPLES

Die Krankheit meiner Frau hat unsere Ferienreise verdorben.
My wife's illness ruined our vacation trip.

Seine Anwesenheit verdirbt mir die ganze Party.
His presence spoils the whole party for me.

**vergessen**
to forget
**Auxiliary verb:** haben **Past participle:** vergessen
**Imperative:** Vergiss! Vergesst! Vergessen Sie!

| Mode | Simple Tenses | | Compound Tenses | |
|---|---|---|---|---|
| | *Singular* | *Plural* | *Singular* | *Plural* |
| Indicative | **Present** | | **Present Perfect** | |
| | vergesse<br>vergisst<br>vergisst | vergessen<br>vergesst<br>vergessen | habe vergessen<br>hast vergessen<br>hat vergessen | haben vergessen<br>habt vergessen<br>haben vergessen |
| | **Past** | | **Past Perfect** | |
| | vergaß<br>vergaßest<br>vergaß | vergaßen<br>vergaßt<br>vergaßen | hatte vergessen<br>hattest vergessen<br>hatte vergessen | hatten vergessen<br>hattet vergessen<br>hatten vergessen |
| | **Future** | | **Future Perfect** | |
| | werde vergessen<br>wirst vergessen<br>wird vergessen | werden vergessen<br>werdet vergessen<br>werden vergessen | werde vergessen haben<br>wirst vergessen haben<br>wird vergessen haben | werden vergessen haben<br>werdet vergessen haben<br>werden vergessen haben |
| Subjunctive | **Present** | | **Present Perfect** | |
| | vergesse<br>vergessest<br>vergesse | vergessen<br>vergesset<br>vergessen | habe vergessen<br>habest vergessen<br>habe vergessen | haben vergessen<br>habet vergessen<br>haben vergessen |
| | **Past** | | **Past Perfect** | |
| | vergäße<br>vergäßest<br>vergäße | vergäßen<br>vergäßet<br>vergäßen | hätte vergessen<br>hättest vergessen<br>hätte vergessen | hätten vergessen<br>hättet vergessen<br>hätten vergessen |
| | **Future** | | **Future Perfect** | |
| | werde vergessen<br>werdest vergessen<br>werde vergessen | werden vergessen<br>werdet vergessen<br>werden vergessen | werde vergessen haben<br>werdest vergessen haben<br>werde vergessen haben | werden vergessen haben<br>werdet vergessen haben<br>werden vergessen haben |
| | **Present and Future Conditional** | | **Past Conditional** | |
| | würde vergessen<br>würdest vergessen<br>würde vergessen | würden vergessen<br>würdet vergessen<br>würden vergessen | würde vergessen haben<br>würdest vergessen haben<br>würde vergessen haben | würden vergessen haben<br>würdet vergessen haben<br>würden vergessen haben |

# EXAMPLES

Ich erkenne Ihr Gesicht, aber Ihren Namen habe ich vergessen.
I recognize your face, but I've forgotten your name.

Ich werde dich nie vergessen.
I'll never forget you.

**verhaften**
to arrest
**Auxiliary verb:** haben **Past participle:** verhaftet
**Imperative:** Verhafte! Verhaftet! Verhaften Sie!

| Mode | Simple Tenses | | Compound Tenses | |
|---|---|---|---|---|
| | *Singular* | *Plural* | *Singular* | *Plural* |
| Indicative | **Present** | | **Present Perfect** | |
| | verhafte<br>verhaftest<br>verhaftet | verhaften<br>verhaftet<br>verhaften | habe verhaftet<br>hast verhaftet<br>hat verhaftet | haben verhaftet<br>habt verhaftet<br>haben verhaftet |
| | **Past** | | **Past Perfect** | |
| | verhaftete<br>verhaftetest<br>verhaftete | verhafteten<br>verhaftetet<br>verhafteten | hatte verhaftet<br>hattest verhaftet<br>hatte verhaftet | hatten verhaftet<br>hattet verhaftet<br>hatten verhaftet |
| | **Future** | | **Future Perfect** | |
| | werde verhaften<br>wirst verhaften<br>wird verhaften | werden verhaften<br>werdet verhaften<br>werden verhaften | werde verhaftet haben<br>wirst verhaftet haben<br>wird verhaftet haben | werden verhaftet haben<br>werdet verhaftet haben<br>werden verhaftet haben |
| Subjunctive | **Present** | | **Present Perfect** | |
| | verhafte<br>verhaftest<br>verhafte | verhaften<br>verhaftet<br>verhaften | habe verhaftet<br>habest verhaftet<br>habe verhaftet | haben verhaftet<br>habet verhaftet<br>haben verhaftet |
| | **Past** | | **Past Perfect** | |
| | verhaftete<br>verhaftetest<br>verhaftete | verhafteten<br>verhaftetet<br>verhafteten | hätte verhaftet<br>hättest verhaftet<br>hätte verhaftet | hätten verhaftet<br>hättet verhaftet<br>hätten verhaftet |
| | **Future** | | **Future Perfect** | |
| | werde verhaften<br>werdest verhaften<br>werde verhaften | werden verhaften<br>werdet verhaften<br>werden verhaften | werde verhaftet haben<br>werdest verhaftet haben<br>werde verhaftet haben | werden verhaftet haben<br>werdet verhaftet haben<br>werden verhaftet haben |
| | **Present and Future Conditional** | | **Past Conditional** | |
| | würde verhaften<br>würdest verhaften<br>würde verhaften | würden verhaften<br>würdet verhaften<br>würden verhaften | würde verhaftet haben<br>würdest verhaftet haben<br>würde verhaftet haben | würden verhaftet haben<br>würdet verhaftet haben<br>würden verhaftet haben |

## EXAMPLES

Zwei verdächtige Männer wurden an der Grenze verhaftet.
Two suspicious men were arrested at the border.

Der Polizist verhaftet einen Taschendieb.
The policeman is arresting a pickpocket.

**verheiraten**

to marry, to give in marriage

**Auxiliary verb:** haben **Past participle:** verheiratet

**Imperative:** Verheirate! Verheiratet! Verheiraten Sie!

| Mode | Simple Tenses | | Compound Tenses | |
|---|---|---|---|---|
| | *Singular* | *Plural* | *Singular* | *Plural* |
| Indicative | **Present** | | **Present Perfect** | |
| | verheirate<br>verheiratest<br>verheiratet | verheiraten<br>verheiratet<br>verheiraten | habe verheiratet<br>hast verheiratet<br>hat verheiratet | haben verheiratet<br>habt verheiratet<br>haben verheiratet |
| | **Past** | | **Past Perfect** | |
| | verheiratete<br>verheiratetest<br>verheiratete | verheirateten<br>verheiratetet<br>verheirateten | hatte verheiratet<br>hattest verheiratet<br>hatte verheiratet | hatten verheiratet<br>hattet verheiratet<br>hatten verheiratet |
| | **Future** | | **Future Perfect** | |
| | werde verheiraten<br>wirst verheiraten<br>wird verheiraten | werden verheiraten<br>werdet verheiraten<br>werden verheiraten | werde verheiratet haben<br>wirst verheiratet haben<br>wird verheiratet haben | werden verheiratet haben<br>werdet verheiratet haben<br>werden verheiratet haben |
| Subjunctive | **Present** | | **Present Perfect** | |
| | verheirate<br>verheiratest<br>verheirate | verheiraten<br>verheiratet<br>verheiraten | habe verheiratet<br>habest verheiratet<br>habe verheiratet | haben verheiratet<br>habet verheiratet<br>haben verheiratet |
| | **Past** | | **Past Perfect** | |
| | verheiratete<br>verheiratetest<br>verheiratete | verheirateten<br>verheiratetet<br>verheirateten | hätte verheiratet<br>hättest verheiratet<br>hätte verheiratet | hätten verheiratet<br>hättet verheiratet<br>hätten verheiratet |
| | **Future** | | **Future Perfect** | |
| | werde verheiraten<br>werdest verheiraten<br>werde verheiraten | werden verheiraten<br>werdet verheiraten<br>werden verheiraten | werde verheiratet haben<br>werdest verheiratet haben<br>werde verheiratet haben | werden verheiratet haben<br>werdet verheiratet haben<br>werden verheiratet haben |
| | **Present and Future Conditional** | | **Past Conditional** | |
| | würde verheiraten<br>würdest verheiraten<br>würde verheiraten | würden verheiraten<br>würdet verheiraten<br>würden verheiraten | würde verheiratet haben<br>würdest verheiratet haben<br>würde verheiratet haben | würden verheiratet haben<br>würdet verheiratet haben<br>würden verheiratet haben |

**Note:** The verb *heiraten* is used to say that someone "is getting married." After the marriage ceremony, someone is *verheiratet*.

## EXAMPLES

Wie lange seid ihr schon verheiratet? — How long have you two been married?

Erik will sie heiraten. — Erik wants to marry her.

**verhungern**
to starve, to die from hunger
**Auxiliary verb:** sein **Past participle:** verhungert
**Imperative:** Verhungere! Verhungert! Verhungern Sie!

| Mode | Simple Tenses | | Compound Tenses | |
|---|---|---|---|---|
| | *Singular* | *Plural* | *Singular* | *Plural* |
| Indicative | **Present** | | **Present Perfect** | |
| | verhungere<br>verhungerst<br>verhungert | verhungern<br>verhungert<br>verhungern | bin verhungert<br>bist verhungert<br>ist verhungert | sind verhungert<br>seid verhungert<br>sind verhungert |
| | **Past** | | **Past Perfect** | |
| | verhungerte<br>verhungertest<br>verhungerte | verhungerten<br>verhungertet<br>verhungerten | war verhungert<br>warst verhungert<br>war verhungert | waren verhungert<br>wart verhungert<br>waren verhungert |
| | **Future** | | **Future Perfect** | |
| | werde verhungern<br>wirst verhungern<br>wird verhungern | werden verhungern<br>werdet verhungern<br>werden verhungern | werde verhungert sein<br>wirst verhungert sein<br>wird verhungert sein | werden verhungert sein<br>werdet verhungert sein<br>werden verhungert sein |
| Subjunctive | **Present** | | **Present Perfect** | |
| | verhungere<br>verhungerst<br>verhungere | verhungern<br>verhungert<br>verhungern | sei verhungert<br>seiest verhungert<br>sei verhungert | seien verhungert<br>seiet verhungert<br>seien verhungert |
| | **Past** | | **Past Perfect** | |
| | verhungerte<br>verhungertest<br>verhungerte | verhungerten<br>verhungertet<br>verhungerten | wäre verhungert<br>wärest verhungert<br>wäre verhungert | wären verhungert<br>wäret verhungert<br>wären verhungert |
| | **Future** | | **Future Perfect** | |
| | werde verhungern<br>werdest verhungern<br>werde verhungern | werden verhungern<br>werdet verhungern<br>werden verhungern | werde verhungert sein<br>werdest verhungert sein<br>werde verhungert sein | werden verhungert sein<br>werdet verhungert sein<br>werden verhungert sein |
| | **Present and Future Conditional** | | **Past Conditional** | |
| | würde verhungern<br>würdest verhungern<br>würde verhungern | würden verhungern<br>würdet verhungern<br>würden verhungern | würde verhungert sein<br>würdest verhungert sein<br>würde verhungert sein | würden verhungert sein<br>würdet verhungert sein<br>würden verhungert sein |

## EXAMPLES

Ohne Lebensmittelvorräte fingen die Soldaten an zu verhungern.
Without provisions, the soldiers began to starve.

In Afrika verhungern noch viele Menschen.
Many people still starve to death in Africa.

**verlangen**
to demand, to ask for
**Auxiliary verb:** haben **Past participle:** verlangt
**Imperative:** Verlange! Verlangt! Verlangen Sie!

| Mode | Simple Tenses | | Compound Tenses | |
|---|---|---|---|---|
| | *Singular* | *Plural* | *Singular* | *Plural* |
| Indicative | **Present** | | **Present Perfect** | |
| | verlange<br>verlangst<br>verlangt | verlangen<br>verlangt<br>verlangen | habe verlangt<br>hast verlangt<br>hat verlangt | haben verlangt<br>habt verlangt<br>haben verlangt |
| | **Past** | | **Past Perfect** | |
| | verlangte<br>verlangtest<br>verlangte | verlangten<br>verlangtet<br>verlangten | hatte verlangt<br>hattest verlangt<br>hatte verlangt | hatten verlangt<br>hattet verlangt<br>hatten verlangt |
| | **Future** | | **Future Perfect** | |
| | werde verlangen<br>wirst verlangen<br>wird verlangen | werden verlangen<br>werdet verlangen<br>werden verlangen | werde verlangt haben<br>wirst verlangt haben<br>wird verlangt haben | werden verlangt haben<br>werdet verlangt haben<br>werden verlangt haben |
| Subjunctive | **Present** | | **Present Perfect** | |
| | verlange<br>verlangest<br>verlange | verlangen<br>verlanget<br>verlangen | habe verlangt<br>habest verlangt<br>habe verlangt | haben verlangt<br>habet verlangt<br>haben verlangt |
| | **Past** | | **Past Perfect** | |
| | verlangte<br>verlangtest<br>verlangte | verlangten<br>verlangtet<br>verlangten | hätte verlangt<br>hättest verlangt<br>hätte verlangt | hätten verlangt<br>hättet verlangt<br>hätten verlangt |
| | **Future** | | **Future Perfect** | |
| | werde verlangen<br>werdest verlangen<br>werde verlangen | werden verlangen<br>werdet verlangen<br>werden verlangen | werde verlangt haben<br>werdest verlangt haben<br>werde verlangt haben | werden verlangt haben<br>werdet verlangt haben<br>werden verlangt haben |
| | **Present and Future Conditional** | | **Past Conditional** | |
| | würde verlangen<br>würdest verlangen<br>würde verlangen | würden verlangen<br>würdet verlangen<br>würden verlangen | würde verlangt haben<br>würdest verlangt haben<br>würde verlangt haben | würden verlangt haben<br>würdet verlangt haben<br>würden verlangt haben |

## EXAMPLES

Mein Vater verlangt von mir, mein Studium fortzusetzen.
My father demands that I continue my studies.

Wie viel verlangen Sie für den Wagen?
How much are you asking for the car?

**verletzen**
to hurt, to injure
**Auxiliary verb:** haben **Past participle:** verletzt
**Imperative:** Verletze! Verletzt! Verletzen Sie!

| Mode | Simple Tenses | | Compound Tenses | |
|---|---|---|---|---|
| | *Singular* | *Plural* | *Singular* | *Plural* |
| Indicative | **Present** | | **Present Perfect** | |
| | verletze<br>verletzt<br>verletzt | verletzen<br>verletzt<br>verletzen | habe verletzt<br>hast verletzt<br>hat verletzt | haben verletzt<br>habt verletzt<br>haben verletzt |
| | **Past** | | **Past Perfect** | |
| | verletzte<br>verletztest<br>verletzte | verletzten<br>verletztet<br>verletzten | hatte verletzt<br>hattest verletzt<br>hatte verletzt | hatten verletzt<br>hattet verletzt<br>hatten verletzt |
| | **Future** | | **Future Perfect** | |
| | werde verletzen<br>wirst verletzen<br>wird verletzen | werden verletzen<br>werdet verletzen<br>werden verletzen | werde verletzt haben<br>wirst verletzt haben<br>wird verletzt haben | werden verletzt haben<br>werdet verletzt haben<br>werden verletzt haben |
| Subjunctive | **Present** | | **Present Perfect** | |
| | verletze<br>verletzest<br>verletze | verletzen<br>verletzet<br>verletzen | habe verletzt<br>habest verletzt<br>habe verletzt | haben verletzt<br>habet verletzt<br>haben verletzt |
| | **Past** | | **Past Perfect** | |
| | verletzte<br>verletztest<br>verletzte | verletzten<br>verletztet<br>verletzten | hätte verletzt<br>hättest verletzt<br>hätte verletzt | hätten verletzt<br>hättet verletzt<br>hätten verletzt |
| | **Future** | | **Future Perfect** | |
| | werde verletzen<br>werdest verletzen<br>werde verletzen | werden verletzen<br>werdet verletzen<br>werden verletzen | werde verletzt haben<br>werdest verletzt haben<br>werde verletzt haben | werden verletzt haben<br>werdet verletzt haben<br>werden verletzt haben |
| | **Present and Future Conditional** | | **Past Conditional** | |
| | würde verletzen<br>würdest verletzen<br>würde verletzen | würden verletzen<br>würdet verletzen<br>würden verletzen | würde verletzt haben<br>würdest verletzt haben<br>würde verletzt haben | würden verletzt haben<br>würdet verletzt haben<br>würden verletzt haben |

## EXAMPLES

Die Frau scheint schwer verletzt zu sein.
The woman appears to be badly injured.

Sie haben den guten Namen des Richters verletzt.
They have damaged the judge's good name.

**verlieren**
to lose
**Auxiliary verb:** haben **Past participle:** verloren
**Imperative:** Verliere! Verliert! Verlieren Sie!

| Mode | Simple Tenses | | Compound Tenses | |
|---|---|---|---|---|
| | *Singular* | *Plural* | *Singular* | *Plural* |
| Indicative | **Present** | | **Present Perfect** | |
| | verliere<br>verlierst<br>verliert | verlieren<br>verliert<br>verlieren | habe verloren<br>hast verloren<br>hat verloren | haben verloren<br>habt verloren<br>haben verloren |
| | **Past** | | **Past Perfect** | |
| | verlor<br>verlorst<br>verlor | verloren<br>verlort<br>verloren | hatte verloren<br>hattest verloren<br>hatte verloren | hatten verloren<br>hattet verloren<br>hatten verloren |
| | **Future** | | **Future Perfect** | |
| | werde verlieren<br>wirst verlieren<br>wird verlieren | werden verlieren<br>werdet verlieren<br>werden verlieren | werde verloren haben<br>wirst verloren haben<br>wird verloren haben | werden verloren haben<br>werdet verloren haben<br>werden verloren haben |
| Subjunctive | **Present** | | **Present Perfect** | |
| | verliere<br>verlierest<br>verliere | verlieren<br>verlieret<br>verlieren | habe verloren<br>habest verloren<br>habe verloren | haben verloren<br>habet verloren<br>haben verloren |
| | **Past** | | **Past Perfect** | |
| | verlöre<br>verlörest<br>verlöre | verlören<br>verlöret<br>verlören | hätte verloren<br>hättest verloren<br>hätte verloren | hätten verloren<br>hättet verloren<br>hätten verloren |
| | **Future** | | **Future Perfect** | |
| | werde verlieren<br>werdest verlieren<br>werde verlieren | werden verlieren<br>werdet verlieren<br>werden verlieren | werde verloren haben<br>werdest verloren haben<br>werde verloren haben | werden verloren haben<br>werdet verloren haben<br>werden verloren haben |
| | **Present and Future Conditional** | | **Past Conditional** | |
| | würde verlieren<br>würdest verlieren<br>würde verlieren | würden verlieren<br>würdet verlieren<br>würden verlieren | würde verloren haben<br>würdest verloren haben<br>würde verloren haben | würden verloren haben<br>würdet verloren haben<br>würden verloren haben |

## EXAMPLES

Die beste Mannschaft hat überraschend verloren. — Surprisingly, the best team lost.
Er verliert andauernd seine Brille. — He loses his glasses all the time.

**vermehren**
to increase, to multiply
**Auxiliary verb:** haben **Past participle:** vermehrt
**Imperative:** Vermehre! Vermehrt! Vermehren Sie!

| Mode | Simple Tenses | | Compound Tenses | |
|---|---|---|---|---|
| | *Singular* | *Plural* | *Singular* | *Plural* |
| Indicative | **Present** | | **Present Perfect** | |
| | vermehre<br>vermehrst<br>vermehrt | vermehren<br>vermehrt<br>vermehren | habe vermehrt<br>hast vermehrt<br>hat vermehrt | haben vermehrt<br>habt vermehrt<br>haben vermehrt |
| | **Past** | | **Past Perfect** | |
| | vermehrte<br>vermehrtest<br>vermehrte | vermehrten<br>vermehrtet<br>vermehrten | hatte vermehrt<br>hattest vermehrt<br>hatte vermehrt | hatten vermehrt<br>hattet vermehrt<br>hatten vermehrt |
| | **Future** | | **Future Perfect** | |
| | werde vermehren<br>wirst vermehren<br>wird vermehren | werden vermehren<br>werdet vermehren<br>werden vermehren | werde vermehrt haben<br>wirst vermehrt haben<br>wird vermehrt haben | werden vermehrt haben<br>werdet vermehrt haben<br>werden vermehrt haben |
| Subjunctive | **Present** | | **Present Perfect** | |
| | vermehre<br>vermehrest<br>vermehre | vermehren<br>vermehret<br>vermehren | habe vermehrt<br>habest vermehrt<br>habe vermehrt | haben vermehrt<br>habet vermehrt<br>haben vermehrt |
| | **Past** | | **Past Perfect** | |
| | vermehrte<br>vermehrtest<br>vermehrte | vermehrten<br>vermehrtet<br>vermehrten | hätte vermehrt<br>hättest vermehrt<br>hätte vermehrt | hätten vermehrt<br>hättet vermehrt<br>hätten vermehrt |
| | **Future** | | **Future Perfect** | |
| | werde vermehren<br>werdest vermehren<br>werde vermehren | werden vermehren<br>werdet vermehren<br>werden vermehren | werde vermehrt haben<br>werdest vermehrt haben<br>werde vermehrt haben | werden vermehrt haben<br>werdet vermehrt haben<br>werden vermehrt haben |
| | **Present and Future Conditional** | | **Past Conditional** | |
| | würde vermehren<br>würdest vermehren<br>würde vermehren | würden vermehren<br>würdet vermehren<br>würden vermehren | würde vermehrt haben<br>würdest vermehrt haben<br>würde vermehrt haben | würden vermehrt haben<br>würdet vermehrt haben<br>würden vermehrt haben |

## EXAMPLES

Diese Tiere vermehren sich rasch.
These animals breed rapidly.

Anstatt Geld zu sparen, hat er seine Schulden vermehrt.
Instead of saving money, he increased his debts.

**vermieten**

to let, to rent out

**Auxiliary verb:** haben **Past participle:** vermietet

**Imperative:** Vermiete! Vermietet! Vermieten Sie!

| Mode | Simple Tenses | | Compound Tenses | |
|---|---|---|---|---|
| | *Singular* | *Plural* | *Singular* | *Plural* |
| Indicative | **Present** | | **Present Perfect** | |
| | vermiete<br>vermietest<br>vermietet | vermieten<br>vermietet<br>vermieten | habe vermietet<br>hast vermietet<br>hat vermietet | haben vermietet<br>habt vermietet<br>haben vermietet |
| | **Past** | | **Past Perfect** | |
| | vermietete<br>vermietetest<br>vermietete | vermieteten<br>vermietetet<br>vermieteten | hatte vermietet<br>hattest vermietet<br>hatte vermietet | hatten vermietet<br>hattet vermietet<br>hatten vermietet |
| | **Future** | | **Future Perfect** | |
| | werde vermieten<br>wirst vermieten<br>wird vermieten | werden vermieten<br>werdet vermieten<br>werden vermieten | werde vermietet haben<br>wirst vermietet haben<br>wird vermietet haben | werden vermietet haben<br>werdet vermietet haben<br>werden vermietet haben |
| Subjunctive | **Present** | | **Present Perfect** | |
| | vermiete<br>vermietest<br>vermiete | vermieten<br>vermietet<br>vermieten | habe vermietet<br>habest vermietet<br>habe vermietet | haben vermietet<br>habet vermietet<br>haben vermietet |
| | **Past** | | **Past Perfect** | |
| | vermietete<br>vermietetest<br>vermietete | vermieteten<br>vermietetet<br>vermieteten | hätte vermietet<br>hättest vermietet<br>hätte vermietet | hätten vermietet<br>hättet vermietet<br>hätten vermietet |
| | **Future** | | **Future Perfect** | |
| | werde vermieten<br>werdest vermieten<br>werde vermieten | werden vermieten<br>werdet vermieten<br>werden vermieten | werde vermietet haben<br>werdest vermietet haben<br>werde vermietet haben | werden vermietet haben<br>werdet vermietet haben<br>werden vermietet haben |
| | **Present and Future Conditional** | | **Past Conditional** | |
| | würde vermieten<br>würdest vermieten<br>würde vermieten | würden vermieten<br>würdet vermieten<br>würden vermieten | würde vermietet haben<br>würdest vermietet haben<br>würde vermietet haben | würden vermietet haben<br>würdet vermietet haben<br>würden vermietet haben |

## EXAMPLES

Es tut mir leid, aber das letzte Zimmer ist bereits vermietet.

I'm sorry, but the last room is already rented.

Solche große Häuser lassen sich nicht leicht vermieten.

Such large houses aren't rented easily.

**vernichten**
to annihilate, to destroy
**Auxiliary verb:** haben **Past participle:** vernichtet
**Imperative:** Vernichte! Vernichtet! Vernichten Sie!

| Mode | Simple Tenses | | Compound Tenses | |
|---|---|---|---|---|
| | *Singular* | *Plural* | *Singular* | *Plural* |
| Indicative | **Present** | | **Present Perfect** | |
| | vernichte<br>vernichtest<br>vernichtet | vernichten<br>vernichtet<br>vernichten | habe vernichtet<br>hast vernichtet<br>hat vernichtet | haben vernichtet<br>habt vernichtet<br>haben vernichtet |
| | **Past** | | **Past Perfect** | |
| | vernichtete<br>vernichtetest<br>vernichtete | vernichteten<br>vernichtetet<br>vernichteten | hatte vernichtet<br>hattest vernichtet<br>hatte vernichtet | hatten vernichtet<br>hattet vernichtet<br>hatten vernichtet |
| | **Future** | | **Future Perfect** | |
| | werde vernichten<br>wirst vernichten<br>wird vernichten | werden vernichten<br>werdet vernichten<br>werden vernichten | werde vernichtet haben<br>wirst vernichtet haben<br>wird vernichtet haben | werden vernichtet haben<br>werdet vernichtet haben<br>werden vernichtet haben |
| Subjunctive | **Present** | | **Present Perfect** | |
| | vernichte<br>vernichtest<br>vernichte | vernichten<br>vernichtet<br>vernichten | habe vernichtet<br>habest vernichtet<br>habe vernichtet | haben vernichtet<br>habet vernichtet<br>haben vernichtet |
| | **Past** | | **Past Perfect** | |
| | vernichtete<br>vernichtetest<br>vernichtete | vernichteten<br>vernichtetet<br>vernichteten | hätte vernichtet<br>hättest vernichtet<br>hätte vernichtet | hätten vernichtet<br>hättet vernichtet<br>hätten vernichtet |
| | **Future** | | **Future Perfect** | |
| | werde vernichten<br>werdest vernichten<br>werde vernichten | werden vernichten<br>werdet vernichten<br>werden vernichten | werde vernichtet haben<br>werdest vernichtet haben<br>werde vernichtet haben | werden vernichtet haben<br>werdet vernichtet haben<br>werden vernichtet haben |
| | **Present and Future Conditional** | | **Past Conditional** | |
| | würde vernichten<br>würdest vernichten<br>würde vernichten | würden vernichten<br>würdet vernichten<br>würden vernichten | würde vernichtet haben<br>würdest vernichtet haben<br>würde vernichtet haben | würden vernichtet haben<br>würdet vernichtet haben<br>würden vernichtet haben |

## EXAMPLES

Der Hagel hat die gesamte Ernte vernichtet.
The hail destroyed the entire crop.

Sie haben keine Hoffnung mehr, dass sie den Feind vernichten können.
They don't have any more hope that they can annihilate the enemy.

Das Feuer vernichtete alle Spuren des Verbrechens.
The fire destroyed all traces of the crime.

**verprügeln**
to thrash, to beat
**Auxiliary verb:** haben **Past participle:** verprügelt
**Imperative:** Verprügele! Verprügelt! Verprügeln Sie!

| Mode | Simple Tenses | | Compound Tenses | |
|---|---|---|---|---|
| | *Singular* | *Plural* | *Singular* | *Plural* |
| Indicative | **Present** | | **Present Perfect** | |
| | verprügele<br>verprügelst<br>verprügelt | verprügeln<br>verprügelt<br>verprügeln | habe verprügelt<br>hast verprügelt<br>hat verprügelt | haben verprügelt<br>habt verprügelt<br>haben verprügelt |
| | **Past** | | **Past Perfect** | |
| | verprügelte<br>verprügeltest<br>verprügelte | verprügelten<br>verprügeltet<br>verprügelten | hatte verprügelt<br>hattest verprügelt<br>hatte verprügelt | hatten verprügelt<br>hattet verprügelt<br>hatten verprügelt |
| | **Future** | | **Future Perfect** | |
| | werde verprügeln<br>wirst verprügeln<br>wird verprügeln | werden verprügeln<br>werdet verprügeln<br>werden verprügeln | werde verprügelt haben<br>wirst verprügelt haben<br>wird verprügelt haben | werden verprügelt haben<br>werdet verprügelt haben<br>werden verprügelt haben |
| Subjunctive | **Present** | | **Present Perfect** | |
| | verprügele<br>verprügelst<br>verprügele | verprügeln<br>verprügelt<br>verprügeln | habe verprügelt<br>habest verprügelt<br>habe verprügelt | haben verprügelt<br>habet verprügelt<br>haben verprügelt |
| | **Past** | | **Past Perfect** | |
| | verprügelte<br>verprügeltest<br>verprügelte | verprügelten<br>verprügeltet<br>verprügelten | hätte verprügelt<br>hättest verprügelt<br>hätte verprügelt | hätten verprügelt<br>hättet verprügelt<br>hätten verprügelt |
| | **Future** | | **Future Perfect** | |
| | werde verprügeln<br>werdest verprügeln<br>werde verprügeln | werden verprügeln<br>werdet verprügeln<br>werden verprügeln | werde verprügelt haben<br>werdest verprügelt haben<br>werde verprügelt haben | werden verprügelt haben<br>werdet verprügelt haben<br>werden verprügelt haben |
| | **Present and Future Conditional** | | **Past Conditional** | |
| | würde verprügeln<br>würdest verprügeln<br>würde verprügeln | würden verprügeln<br>würdet verprügeln<br>würden verprügeln | würde verprügelt haben<br>würdest verprügelt haben<br>würde verprügelt haben | würden verprügelt haben<br>würdet verprügelt haben<br>würden verprügelt haben |

## EXAMPLES

Die Räuber haben ihm das Geld gestohlen und ihn verprügelt.
The robbers stole his money and beat him up.

Der Vater war wütend und verprügelte den unartigen Jungen.
The father was furious and thrashed the naughty boy.

**verraten**
to betray
**Auxiliary verb:** haben **Past participle:** verraten
**Imperative:** Verrate! Verratet! Verraten Sie!

| Mode | Simple Tenses | | Compound Tenses | |
|---|---|---|---|---|
| | *Singular* | *Plural* | *Singular* | *Plural* |
| Indicative | **Present** | | **Present Perfect** | |
| | verrate<br>verrätst<br>verrät | verraten<br>verratet<br>verraten | habe verraten<br>hast verraten<br>hat verraten | haben verraten<br>habt verraten<br>haben verraten |
| | **Past** | | **Past Perfect** | |
| | verriet<br>verrietest<br>verriet | verrieten<br>verrrietet<br>verrieten | hatte verraten<br>hattest verraten<br>hatte verraten | hatten verraten<br>hattet verraten<br>hatten verraten |
| | **Future** | | **Future Perfect** | |
| | werde verraten<br>wirst verraten<br>wird verraten | werden verraten<br>werdet verraten<br>werden verraten | werde verraten haben<br>wirst verraten haben<br>wird verraten haben | werden verraten haben<br>werdet verraten haben<br>werden verraten haben |
| Subjunctive | **Present** | | **Present Perfect** | |
| | verrate<br>verratest<br>verrate | verraten<br>verratet<br>verraten | habe verraten<br>habest verraten<br>habe verraten | haben verraten<br>habet verraten<br>haben verraten |
| | **Past** | | **Past Perfect** | |
| | verriete<br>verrietest<br>verriete | verrieten<br>verrrietet<br>verrieten | hätte verraten<br>hättest verraten<br>hätte verraten | hätten verraten<br>hättet verraten<br>hätten verraten |
| | **Future** | | **Future Perfect** | |
| | werde verraten<br>werdest verraten<br>werde verraten | werden verraten<br>werdet verraten<br>werden verraten | werde verraten haben<br>werdest verraten haben<br>werde verraten haben | werden verraten haben<br>werdet verraten haben<br>werden verraten haben |
| | **Present and Future Conditional** | | **Past Conditional** | |
| | würde verraten<br>würdest verraten<br>würde verraten | würden verraten<br>würdet verraten<br>würden verraten | wurde verraten haben<br>würdest verraten haben<br>würde verraten haben | würden verraten haben<br>würdet verraten haben<br>würden verraten haben |

## EXAMPLES

Christoph hat seinem Freund verraten, wo er das Geld versteckt hat.
Christoph told his friend where he hid the money.

Der Verräter verriet die Geheimnisse an eine feindliche Regierung.
The traitor betrayed the secrets to an enemy government.

**versäumen**
to neglect, to miss
**Auxiliary verb:** haben **Past participle:** versäumt
**Imperative:** Versäume! Versäumt! Versäumen Sie!

| Mode | Simple Tenses | | Compound Tenses | |
|---|---|---|---|---|
| | *Singular* | *Plural* | *Singular* | *Plural* |
| Indicative | **Present** | | **Present Perfect** | |
| | versäume<br>versäumst<br>versäumt | versäumen<br>versäumt<br>versäumen | habe versäumt<br>hast versäumt<br>hat versäumt | haben versäumt<br>habt versäumt<br>haben versäumt |
| | **Past** | | **Past Perfect** | |
| | versäumte<br>versäumtest<br>versäumte | versäumten<br>versäumtet<br>versäumten | hatte versäumt<br>hattest versäumt<br>hatte versäumt | hatten versäumt<br>hattet versäumt<br>hatten versäumt |
| | **Future** | | **Future Perfect** | |
| | werde versäumen<br>wirst versäumen<br>wird versäumen | werden versäumen<br>werdet versäumen<br>werden versäumen | werde versäumt haben<br>wirst versäumt haben<br>wird versäumt haben | werden versäumt haben<br>werdet versäumt haben<br>werden versäumt haben |
| Subjunctive | **Present** | | **Present Perfect** | |
| | versäume<br>versäumest<br>versäume | versäumen<br>versäumet<br>versäumen | habe versäumt<br>habest versäumt<br>habe versäumt | haben versäumt<br>habet versäumt<br>haben versäumt |
| | **Past** | | **Past Perfect** | |
| | versäumte<br>versäumtest<br>versäumte | versäumten<br>versäumtet<br>versäumten | hätte versäumt<br>hättest versäumt<br>hätte versäumt | hätten versäumt<br>hättet versäumt<br>hätten versäumt |
| | **Future** | | **Future Perfect** | |
| | werde versäumen<br>werdest versäumen<br>werde versäumen | werden versäumen<br>werdet versäumen<br>werden versäumen | werde versäumt haben<br>werdest versäumt haben<br>werde versäumt haben | werden versäumt haben<br>werdet versäumt haben<br>werden versäumt haben |
| | **Present and Future Conditional** | | **Past Conditional** | |
| | würde versäumen<br>würdest versäumen<br>würde versäumen | würden versäumen<br>würdet versäumen<br>würden versäumen | würde versäumt haben<br>würdest versäumt haben<br>würde versäumt haben | würden versäumt haben<br>würdet versäumt haben<br>würden versäumt haben |

## EXAMPLES

Karl hat es versäumt, Abschied von seinen Gastgebern zu nehmen.
Karl neglected to say goodbye to his hosts.

Wegen seiner Krankheit hat der Schwimmer zwei Wettkämpfe versäumen müssen.
Because of his illness, the swimmer had to miss two competitions.

**verschwenden**
to waste, to squander
**Auxiliary verb:** haben **Past participle:** verschwendet
**Imperative:** Verschwende! Verschwendet! Verschwenden Sie!

| Mode | Simple Tenses | | Compound Tenses | |
|---|---|---|---|---|
| | *Singular* | *Plural* | *Singular* | *Plural* |
| Indicative | **Present** | | **Present Perfect** | |
| | verschwende<br>verschwendest<br>verschwendet | verschwenden<br>verschwendet<br>verschwenden | habe verschwendet<br>hast verschwendet<br>hat verschwendet | haben verschwendet<br>habt verschwendet<br>haben verschwendet |
| | **Past** | | **Past Perfect** | |
| | verschwendete<br>verschwendetest<br>verschwendete | verschwendeten<br>verschwendetet<br>verschwendeten | hatte verschwendet<br>hattest verschwendet<br>hatte verschwendet | hatten verschwendet<br>hattet verschwendet<br>hatten verschwendet |
| | **Future** | | **Future Perfect** | |
| | werde verschwenden<br>wirst verschwenden<br>wird verschwenden | werden verschwenden<br>werdet verschwenden<br>werden verschwenden | werde verschwendet haben<br>wirst verschwendet haben<br>wird verschwendet haben | werden verschwendet haben<br>werdet verschwendet haben<br>werden verschwendet haben |
| Subjunctive | **Present** | | **Present Perfect** | |
| | verschwende<br>verschwendest<br>verschwende | verschwenden<br>verschwendet<br>verschwenden | habe verschwendet<br>habest verschwendet<br>habe verschwendet | haben verschwendet<br>habet verschwendet<br>haben verschwendet |
| | **Past** | | **Past Perfect** | |
| | verschwendete<br>verschwendetest<br>verschwendete | verschwendeten<br>verschwendetet<br>verschwendeten | hätte verschwendet<br>hättest verschwendet<br>hätte verschwendet | hätten verschwendet<br>hättet verschwendet<br>hätten verschwendet |
| | **Future** | | **Future Perfect** | |
| | werde verschwenden<br>werdest verschwenden<br>werde verschwenden | werden verschwenden<br>werdet verschwenden<br>werden verschwenden | werde verschwendet haben<br>werdest verschwendet haben<br>werde verschwendet haben | werden verschwendet haben<br>werdet verschwendet haben<br>werden verschwendet haben |
| | **Present and Future Conditional** | | **Past Conditional** | |
| | würde verschwenden<br>würdest verschwenden<br>würde verschwenden | würden verschwenden<br>würdet verschwenden<br>würden verschwenden | würde verschwendet haben<br>würdest verschwendet haben<br>würde verschwendet haben | würden verschwendet haben<br>würdet verschwendet haben<br>würden verschwendet haben |

## EXAMPLES

Benzin ist sehr teuer und sollte nicht verschwendet werden.
Gas is expensive and shouldn't be wasted.

Ich verschwende an dich keine Mühe mehr.
I'm not wasting any more effort on you.

**verschwinden**
to disappear, to vanish
**Auxiliary verb:** sein **Past participle:** verschwunden
**Imperative:** Verschwinde! Verschwindet! Verschwinden Sie!

| Mode | Simple Tenses | | Compound Tenses | |
|---|---|---|---|---|
| | *Singular* | *Plural* | *Singular* | *Plural* |
| Indicative | **Present** | | **Present Perfect** | |
| | verschwinde<br>verschwindest<br>verschwindet | verschwinden<br>verschwindet<br>verschwinden | bin verschwunden<br>bist verschwunden<br>ist verschwunden | sind verschwunden<br>seid verschwunden<br>sind verschwunden |
| | **Past** | | **Past Perfect** | |
| | verschwand<br>verschwandest<br>verschwand | verschwanden<br>verschwandet<br>verschwanden | war verschwunden<br>warst verschwunden<br>war verschwunden | waren verschwunden<br>wart verschwunden<br>waren verschwunden |
| | **Future** | | **Future Perfect** | |
| | werde verschwinden<br>wirst verschwinden<br>wird verschwinden | werden verschwinden<br>werdet verschwinden<br>werden verschwinden | werde verschwunden sein<br>wirst verschwunden sein<br>wird verschwunden sein | werden verschwunden sein<br>werdet verschwunden sein<br>werden verschwunden sein |
| Subjunctive | **Present** | | **Present Perfect** | |
| | verschwinde<br>verschwindest<br>verschwinde | verschwinden<br>verschwindet<br>verschwinden | sei verschwunden<br>seiest verschwunden<br>sei verschwunden | seien verschwunden<br>seiet verschwunden<br>seien verschwunden |
| | **Past** | | **Past Perfect** | |
| | verschwände<br>verschwändest<br>verschwände | verschwänden<br>verschwändet<br>verschwänden | wäre verschwunden<br>wärest verschwunden<br>wäre verschwunden | wären verschwunden<br>wäret verschwunden<br>wären verschwunden |
| | **Future** | | **Future Perfect** | |
| | werde verschwinden<br>werdest verschwinden<br>werde verschwinden | werden verschwinden<br>werdet verschwinden<br>werden verschwinden | werde verschwunden sein<br>werdest verschwunden sein<br>werde verschwunden sein | werden verschwunden sein<br>werdet verschwunden sein<br>werden verschwunden sein |
| | **Present and Future Conditional** | | **Past Conditional** | |
| | würde verschwinden<br>würdest verschwinden<br>würde verschwinden | würden verschwinden<br>würdet verschwinden<br>würden verschwinden | würde verschwunden sein<br>würdest verschwunden sein<br>würde verschwunden sein | würden verschwunden sein<br>würdet verschwunden sein<br>würden verschwunden sein |

## EXAMPLES

Vor einer Minute hat sie an der Ecke gestanden. Jetzt ist sie verschwunden.
A minute ago, she was standing on the corner. Now she's vanished.

Verschwinde! Die Polizei kommt!
Get out of here. The police are coming.

**versichern**
to insure, to assure
**Auxiliary verb:** haben **Past participle:** versichert
**Imperative:** Versichere! Versichert! Versichern Sie!

| Mode | Simple Tenses | | Compound Tenses | |
|---|---|---|---|---|
| | *Singular* | *Plural* | *Singular* | *Plural* |
| Indicative | **Present** | | **Present Perfect** | |
| | versichere<br>versicherst<br>versichert | versichern<br>versichert<br>versichern | habe versichert<br>hast versichert<br>hat versichert | haben versichert<br>habt versichert<br>haben versichert |
| | **Past** | | **Past Perfect** | |
| | versicherte<br>versichertest<br>versicherte | versicherten<br>versichertet<br>versicherten | hatte versichert<br>hattest versichert<br>hatte versichert | hatten versichert<br>hattet versichert<br>hatten versichert |
| | **Future** | | **Future Perfect** | |
| | werde versichern<br>wirst versichern<br>wird versichern | werden versichern<br>werdet versichern<br>werden versichern | werde versichert haben<br>wirst versichert haben<br>wird versichert haben | werden versichert haben<br>werdet versichert haben<br>werden versichert haben |
| Subjunctive | **Present** | | **Present Perfect** | |
| | versichere<br>versicherst<br>versichere | versichern<br>versichert<br>versichern | habe versichert<br>habest versichert<br>habe versichert | haben versichert<br>habet versichert<br>haben versichert |
| | **Past** | | **Past Perfect** | |
| | versicherte<br>versichertest<br>versicherte | versicherten<br>versichertet<br>versicherten | hätte versichert<br>hättest versichert<br>hätte versichert | hätten versichert<br>hättet versichert<br>hätten versichert |
| | **Future** | | **Future Perfect** | |
| | werde versichern<br>werdest versichern<br>werde versichern | werden versichern<br>werdet versichern<br>werden versichern | werde versichert haben<br>werdest versichert haben<br>werde versichert haben | werden versichert haben<br>werdet versichert haben<br>werden versichert haben |
| | **Present and Future Conditional** | | **Past Conditional** | |
| | würde versichern<br>würdest versichern<br>würde versichern | würden versichern<br>würdet versichern<br>würden versichern | würde versichert haben<br>würdest versichert haben<br>würde versichert haben | würden versichert haben<br>würdet versichert haben<br>würden versichert haben |

## EXAMPLES

Er fährt einen neuen Wagen, ist aber nicht versichert.
He's driving a new car but isn't insured.

Ich versichere euch, dass ich mich gut um euer Kind kümmern werde.
I assure you that I'll take good care of your child.

**versprechen**
to promise
**Auxiliary verb:** haben **Past participle:** versprochen
**Imperative:** Versprich! Versprecht! Versprechen Sie!

| Mode | Simple Tenses | | Compound Tenses | |
|---|---|---|---|---|
| | *Singular* | *Plural* | *Singular* | *Plural* |
| Indicative | **Present** | | **Present Perfect** | |
| | verspreche<br>versprichst<br>verspricht | versprechen<br>versprecht<br>versprechen | habe versprochen<br>hast versprochen<br>hat versprochen | haben versprochen<br>habt versprochen<br>haben versprochen |
| | **Past** | | **Past Perfect** | |
| | versprach<br>versprachst<br>versprach | versprachen<br>verspracht<br>versprachen | hatte versprochen<br>hattest versprochen<br>hatte versprochen | hatten versprochen<br>hattet versprochen<br>hatten versprochen |
| | **Future** | | **Future Perfect** | |
| | werde versprechen<br>wirst versprechen<br>wird versprechen | werden versprechen<br>werdet versprechen<br>werden versprechen | werde versprochen haben<br>wirst versprochen haben<br>wird versprochen haben | werden versprochen haben<br>werdet versprochen haben<br>werden versprochen haben |
| Subjunctive | **Present** | | **Present Perfect** | |
| | verspreche<br>versprechest<br>verspreche | versprechen<br>versprechet<br>versprechen | habe versprochen<br>habest versprochen<br>habe versprochen | haben versprochen<br>habet versprochen<br>haben versprochen |
| | **Past** | | **Past Perfect** | |
| | verspräche<br>versprächest<br>verspräche | versprächen<br>versprächet<br>versprächen | hätte versprochen<br>hättest versprochen<br>hätte versprochen | hätten versprochen<br>hättet versprochen<br>hätten versprochen |
| | **Future** | | **Future Perfect** | |
| | werde versprechen<br>werdest versprechen<br>werde versprechen | werden versprechen<br>werdet versprechen<br>werden versprechen | werde versprochen haben<br>werdest versprochen haben<br>werde versprochen haben | werden versprochen haben<br>werdet versprochen haben<br>werden versprochen haben |
| | **Present and Future Conditional** | | **Past Conditional** | |
| | würde versprechen<br>würdest versprechen<br>würde versprechen | würden versprechen<br>würdet versprechen<br>würden versprechen | würde versprochen haben<br>würdest versprochen haben<br>würde versprochen haben | würden versprochen haben<br>würdet versprochen haben<br>würden versprochen haben |

**Note:** Without a prefix, the principal parts of this verb are *spricht, sprach, hat gesprochen.* With separable prefixes, the principal parts are, for example, *spricht aus, sprach aus, hat ausgesprochen.*

## EXAMPLES

Ich kann dir nicht versprechen, dass ich dein Haus kaufe.
I can't promise you that I'm going to buy your house.

Sie verspricht eine große Politikerin zu werden.
She promises to be a great politician.

**verstehen**
to understand
**Auxiliary verb:** haben **Past participle:** verstanden
**Imperative:** Verstehe! Versteht! Verstehen Sie!

| Mode | Simple Tenses | | Compound Tenses | |
|---|---|---|---|---|
| | *Singular* | *Plural* | *Singular* | *Plural* |
| Indicative | **Present** | | **Present Perfect** | |
| | verstehe<br>verstehst<br>versteht | verstehen<br>versteht<br>verstehen | habe verstanden<br>hast verstanden<br>hat verstanden | haben verstanden<br>habt verstanden<br>haben verstanden |
| | **Past** | | **Past Perfect** | |
| | verstand<br>verstandest<br>verstand | verstanden<br>verstandet<br>verstanden | hatte verstanden<br>hattest verstanden<br>hatte verstanden | hatten verstanden<br>hattet verstanden<br>hatten verstanden |
| | **Future** | | **Future Perfect** | |
| | werde verstehen<br>wirst verstehen<br>wird verstehen | werden verstehen<br>werdet verstehen<br>werden verstehen | werde verstanden haben<br>wirst verstanden haben<br>wird verstanden haben | werden verstanden haben<br>werdet verstanden haben<br>werden verstanden haben |
| Subjunctive | **Present** | | **Present Perfect** | |
| | verstehe<br>verstehest<br>verstehe | verstehen<br>verstehet<br>verstehen | habe verstanden<br>habest verstanden<br>habe verstanden | haben verstanden<br>habet verstanden<br>haben verstanden |
| | **Past** | | **Past Perfect** | |
| | verstände<br>verständest<br>verstände | verständen<br>verständet<br>verständen | hätte verstanden<br>hättest verstanden<br>hätte verstanden | hätten verstanden<br>hättet verstanden<br>hätten verstanden |
| | **Future** | | **Future Perfect** | |
| | werde verstehen<br>werdest verstehen<br>werde verstehen | werden verstehen<br>werdet verstehen<br>werden verstehen | werde verstanden haben<br>werdest verstanden haben<br>werde verstanden haben | werden verstanden haben<br>werdet verstanden haben<br>werden verstanden haben |
| | **Present and Future Conditional** | | **Past Conditional** | |
| | würde verstehen<br>würdest verstehen<br>würde verstehen | würden verstehen<br>würdet verstehen<br>würden verstehen | würde verstanden haben<br>würdest verstanden haben<br>würde verstanden haben | würden verstanden haben<br>würdet verstanden haben<br>würden verstanden haben |

**Note:** In the past subjunctive, this verb is also conjugated as *verstünde.* Without a prefix, the principal parts of this verb are *steht, stand, hat gestanden.* With separable prefixes, the principal parts are, for example, *steht auf, stand auf, ist aufgestanden.*

## EXAMPLES

Ich verstehe sie nicht, wenn sie Russisch sprechen.
I don't understand them when they speak Russian.

Ingrid hat gut zugehört, aber sie hat nichts verstanden.
Ingrid listened closely, but she didn't understand anything.

**verteidigen**
to defend
**Auxiliary verb:** haben **Past participle:** verteidigt
**Imperative:** Verteidige! Verteidigt! Verteidigen Sie!

| Mode | Simple Tenses | | Compound Tenses | |
|---|---|---|---|---|
| | *Singular* | *Plural* | *Singular* | *Plural* |
| Indicative | **Present** | | **Present Perfect** | |
| | verteidige<br>verteidigst<br>verteidigt | verteidigen<br>verteidigt<br>verteidigen | habe verteidigt<br>hast verteidigt<br>hat verteidigt | haben verteidigt<br>habt verteidigt<br>haben verteidigt |
| | **Past** | | **Past Perfect** | |
| | verteidigte<br>verteidigtest<br>verteidigte | verteidigten<br>verteidigtet<br>verteidigten | hatte verteidigt<br>hattest verteidigt<br>hatte verteidigt | hatten verteidigt<br>hattet verteidigt<br>hatten verteidigt |
| | **Future** | | **Future Perfect** | |
| | werde verteidigen<br>wirst verteidigen<br>wird verteidigen | werden verteidigen<br>werdet verteidigen<br>werden verteidigen | werde verteidigt haben<br>wirst verteidigt haben<br>wird verteidigt haben | werden verteidigt haben<br>werdet verteidigt haben<br>werden verteidigt haben |
| Subjunctive | **Present** | | **Present Perfect** | |
| | verteidige<br>verteidigest<br>verteidige | verteidigen<br>verteidiget<br>verteidigen | habe verteidigt<br>habest verteidigt<br>habe verteidigt | haben verteidigt<br>habet verteidigt<br>haben verteidigt |
| | **Past** | | **Past Perfect** | |
| | verteidigte<br>verteidigtest<br>verteidigte | verteidigten<br>verteidigtet<br>verteidigten | hätte verteidigt<br>hättest verteidigt<br>hätte verteidigt | hätten verteidigt<br>hättet verteidigt<br>hätten verteidigt |
| | **Future** | | **Future Perfect** | |
| | werde verteidigen<br>werdest verteidigen<br>werde verteidigen | werden verteidigen<br>werdet verteidigen<br>werden verteidigen | werde verteidigt haben<br>werdest verteidigt haben<br>werde verteidigt haben | werden verteidigt haben<br>werdet verteidigt haben<br>werden verteidigt haben |
| | **Present and Future Conditional** | | **Past Conditional** | |
| | würde verteidigen<br>würdest verteidigen<br>würde verteidigen | würden verteidigen<br>würdet verteidigen<br>würden verteidigen | würde verteidigt haben<br>würdest verteidigt haben<br>würde verteidigt haben | würden verteidigt haben<br>würdet verteidigt haben<br>würden verteidigt haben |

## EXAMPLES

| | |
|---|---|
| Ein paar Soldaten versuchen eine Brücke zu verteidigen. | A few soldiers are trying to defend a bridge. |
| Er verteidigt seine Schwester gegen die Vorwürfe ihres Freundes. | He defends his sister against her boyfriend's accusations. |

**vertragen (sich)**
to tolerate, to get along with
**Auxiliary verb:** haben **Past participle:** vertragen
**Imperative:** Vertrage! Vertragt! Vertragen Sie!

| Mode | Simple Tenses | | Compound Tenses | |
|---|---|---|---|---|
| | *Singular* | *Plural* | *Singular* | *Plural* |
| Indicative | **Present** | | **Present Perfect** | |
| | vertrage<br>verträgst<br>verträgt | vertragen<br>vertragt<br>vertragen | habe vertragen<br>hast vertragen<br>hat vertragen | haben vertragen<br>habt vertragen<br>haben vertragen |
| | **Past** | | **Past Perfect** | |
| | vertrug<br>vertrugst<br>vertrug | vertrugen<br>vertrugt<br>vertrugen | hatte vertragen<br>hattest vertragen<br>hatte vertragen | hatten vertragen<br>hattet vertragen<br>hatten vertragen |
| | **Future** | | **Future Perfect** | |
| | werde vertragen<br>wirst vertragen<br>wird vertragen | werden vertragen<br>werdet vertragen<br>werden vertragen | werde vertragen haben<br>wirst vertragen haben<br>wird vertragen haben | werden vertragen haben<br>werdet vertragen haben<br>werden vertragen haben |
| Subjunctive | **Present** | | **Present Perfect** | |
| | vertrage<br>vertragest<br>vertrage | vertragen<br>vertraget<br>vertragen | habe vertragen<br>habest vertragen<br>habe vertragen | haben vertragen<br>habet vertragen<br>haben vertragen |
| | **Past** | | **Past Perfect** | |
| | vertrüge<br>vertrügest<br>vertrüge | vertrügen<br>vertrüget<br>vertrügen | hätte vertragen<br>hättest vertragen<br>hätte vertragen | hätten vertragen<br>hättet vertragen<br>hätten vertragen |
| | **Future** | | **Future Perfect** | |
| | werde vertragen<br>werdest vertragen<br>werde vertragen | werden vertragen<br>werdet vertragen<br>werden vertragen | werde vertragen haben<br>werdest vertragen haben<br>werde vertragen haben | werden vertragen haben<br>werdet vertragen haben<br>werden vertragen haben |
| | **Present and Future Conditional** | | **Past Conditional** | |
| | würde vertragen<br>würdest vertragen<br>würde vertragen | würden vertragen<br>würdet vertragen<br>würden vertragen | würde vertragen haben<br>würdest vertragen haben<br>würde vertragen haben | würden vertragen haben<br>würdet vertragen haben<br>würden vertragen haben |

**Note:** Without a prefix, the principal parts of this verb are *trägt, trug, hat getragen.* With separable prefixes, the principal parts are, for example, *trägt bei, trug bei, hat beigetragen.*

## EXAMPLES

Dieses fette Fleisch können die Kinder nicht vertragen.
The children will get sick from this greasy meat.

Ich vertrage es nicht, wenn du so viel rauchst.
I feel sick when you smoke so much.

Die Kinder vertragen sich neuerdings sehr gut.
The children have been getting along very well lately.

**vertrauen (sich)**
to confide, to trust in
**Auxiliary verb:** haben **Past participle:** vertraut
**Imperative:** Vertraue! Vertraut! Vertrauen Sie!

| Mode | Simple Tenses | | Compound Tenses | |
|---|---|---|---|---|
| | *Singular* | *Plural* | *Singular* | *Plural* |
| Indicative | **Present** | | **Present Perfect** | |
| | vertraue<br>vertraust<br>vertraut | vertrauen<br>vertraut<br>vertrauen | habe vertraut<br>hast vertraut<br>hat vertraut | haben vertraut<br>habt vertraut<br>haben vertraut |
| | **Past** | | **Past Perfect** | |
| | vertraute<br>vertrautest<br>vertraute | vertrauten<br>vertrautet<br>vertrauten | hatte vertraut<br>hattest vertraut<br>hatte vertraut | hatten vertraut<br>hattet vertraut<br>hatten vertraut |
| | **Future** | | **Future Perfect** | |
| | werde vertrauen<br>wirst vertrauen<br>wird vertrauen | werden vertrauen<br>werdet vertrauen<br>werden vertrauen | werde vertraut haben<br>wirst vertraut haben<br>wird vertraut haben | werden vertraut haben<br>werdet vertraut haben<br>werden vertraut haben |
| Subjunctive | **Present** | | **Present Perfect** | |
| | vertraue<br>vertrauest<br>vertraue | vertrauen<br>vertrauet<br>vertrauen | habe vertraut<br>habest vertraut<br>habe vertraut | haben vertraut<br>habet vertraut<br>haben vertraut |
| | **Past** | | **Past Perfect** | |
| | vertraute<br>vertrautest<br>vertraute | vertrauten<br>vertrautet<br>vertrauten | hätte vertraut<br>hättest vertraut<br>hätte vertraut | hätten vertraut<br>hättet vertraut<br>hätten vertraut |
| | **Future** | | **Future Perfect** | |
| | werde vertrauen<br>werdest vertrauen<br>werde vertrauen | werden vertrauen<br>werdet vertrauen<br>werden vertrauen | werde vertraut haben<br>werdest vertraut haben<br>werde vertraut haben | werden vertraut haben<br>werdet vertraut haben<br>werden vertraut haben |
| | **Present and Future Conditional** | | **Past Conditional** | |
| | würde vertrauen<br>würdest vertrauen<br>würde vertrauen | würden vertrauen<br>würdet vertrauen<br>würden vertrauen | würde vertraut haben<br>würdest vertraut haben<br>würde vertraut haben | würden vertraut haben<br>würdet vertraut haben<br>würden vertraut haben |

## EXAMPLES

Vertraue mir! Ich weiß, wo Onkel Peter das Geld verborgen hat.
Trust me. I know where Uncle Peter hid the money.

Man kann Herrn Bauer leider nicht vertrauen.
Unfortunately, Mr. Bauer can't be trusted.

**vertreten**
to represent, to replace
**Auxiliary verb:** haben **Past participle:** vertreten
**Imperative:** Vertritt! Vertretet! Vertreten Sie!

| Mode | Simple Tenses | | Compound Tenses | |
|---|---|---|---|---|
| | *Singular* | *Plural* | *Singular* | *Plural* |
| Indicative | **Present** | | **Present Perfect** | |
| | vertrete<br>vertrittst<br>vertritt | vertreten<br>vertretet<br>vertreten | habe vertreten<br>hast vertreten<br>hat vertreten | haben vertreten<br>habt vertreten<br>haben vertreten |
| | **Past** | | **Past Perfect** | |
| | vertrat<br>vertratest<br>vertrat | vertraten<br>vertratet<br>vertraten | hatte vertreten<br>hattest vertreten<br>hatte vertreten | hatten vertreten<br>hattet vertreten<br>hatten vertreten |
| | **Future** | | **Future Perfect** | |
| | werde vertreten<br>wirst vertreten<br>wird vertreten | werden vertreten<br>werdet vertreten<br>werden vertreten | werde vertreten haben<br>wirst vertreten haben<br>wird vertreten haben | werden vertreten haben<br>werdet vertreten haben<br>werden vertreten haben |
| Subjunctive | **Present** | | **Present Perfect** | |
| | vertrete<br>vertretest<br>vertrete | vertreten<br>vertretet<br>vertreten | habe vertreten<br>habest vertreten<br>habe vertreten | haben vertreten<br>habet vertreten<br>haben vertreten |
| | **Past** | | **Past Perfect** | |
| | verträte<br>verträtest<br>verträte | verträten<br>verträtet<br>verträten | hätte vertreten<br>hättest vertreten<br>hätte vertreten | hätten vertreten<br>hättet vertreten<br>hätten vertreten |
| | **Future** | | **Future Perfect** | |
| | werde vertreten<br>werdest vertreten<br>werde vertreten | werden vertreten<br>werdet vertreten<br>werden vertreten | werde vertreten haben<br>werdest vertreten haben<br>werde vertreten haben | werden vertreten haben<br>werdet vertreten haben<br>werden vertreten haben |
| | **Present and Future Conditional** | | **Past Conditional** | |
| | würde vertreten<br>würdest vertreten<br>würde vertreten | würden vertreten<br>würdet vertreten<br>würden vertreten | würde vertreten haben<br>würdest vertreten haben<br>würde vertreten haben | würden vertreten haben<br>würdet vertreten haben<br>würden vertreten haben |

**Note:** Without a prefix, the principal parts of this verb are *tritt, trat, ist getreten.* With separable prefixes, the principal parts are, for example, *tritt ein, trat ein, ist eingetreten.*

## EXAMPLES

Glaubst du wirklich, dass du meine Meinung vertreten kannst?
Do you really believe that you can represent my opinion?

Herr Bauer wird die Firma in den USA vertreten.
Mr. Bauer is going to represent the company in the United States.

**verzeihen**

to pardon, to forgive

**Auxiliary verb:** haben **Past participle:** verziehen

**Imperative:** Verzeihe! Verzeiht! Verzeihen Sie!

| Mode | Simple Tenses | | Compound Tenses | |
|---|---|---|---|---|
| | *Singular* | *Plural* | *Singular* | *Plural* |
| Indicative | **Present** | | **Present Perfect** | |
| | verzeihe<br>verzeihst<br>verzeiht | verzeihen<br>verzeiht<br>verzeihen | habe verziehen<br>hast verziehen<br>hat verziehen | haben verziehen<br>habt verziehen<br>haben verziehen |
| | **Past** | | **Past Perfect** | |
| | verzieh<br>verziehst<br>verzieh | verziehen<br>verzieht<br>verziehen | hatte verziehen<br>hattest verziehen<br>hatte verziehen | hatten verziehen<br>hattet verziehen<br>hatten verziehen |
| | **Future** | | **Future Perfect** | |
| | werde verzeihen<br>wirst verzeihen<br>wird verzeihen | werden verzeihen<br>werdet verzeihen<br>werden verzeihen | werde verziehen haben<br>wirst verziehen haben<br>wird verziehen haben | werden verziehen haben<br>werdet verziehen haben<br>werden verziehen haben |
| Subjunctive | **Present** | | **Present Perfect** | |
| | verzeihe<br>verzeihest<br>verzeihe | verzeihen<br>verzeihet<br>verzeihen | habe verziehen<br>habest verziehen<br>habe verziehen | haben verziehen<br>habet verziehen<br>haben verziehen |
| | **Past** | | **Past Perfect** | |
| | verziehe<br>verziehest<br>verziehe | verziehen<br>verziehet<br>verziehen | hätte verziehen<br>hättest verziehen<br>hätte verziehen | hätten verziehen<br>hättet verziehen<br>hätten verziehen |
| | **Future** | | **Future Perfect** | |
| | werde verzeihen<br>werdest verzeihen<br>werde verzeihen | werden verzeihen<br>werdet verzeihen<br>werden verzeihen | werde verziehen haben<br>werdest verziehen haben<br>werde verziehen haben | werden verziehen haben<br>werdet verziehen haben<br>werden verziehen haben |
| | **Present and Future Conditional** | | **Past Conditional** | |
| | würde verzeihen<br>würdest verzeihen<br>würde verzeihen | würden verzeihen<br>würdet verzeihen<br>würden verzeihen | würde verziehen haben<br>würdest verziehen haben<br>würde verziehen haben | würden verziehen haben<br>würdet verziehen haben<br>würden verziehen haben |

## EXAMPLES

| | |
|---|---|
| Verzeihen Sie, dass ich Ihre Familie gestört habe. | Excuse me for having disturbed your family. |
| Wir werden euch nie wieder verzeihen. | We'll never forgive you again. |

**verzichten**
to renounce, to give up claim to
**Auxiliary verb:** haben **Past participle:** verzichtet
**Imperative:** Verzichte! Verzichtet! Verzichten Sie!

| Mode | Simple Tenses | | Compound Tenses | |
|---|---|---|---|---|
| | *Singular* | *Plural* | *Singular* | *Plural* |
| Indicative | **Present** | | **Present Perfect** | |
| | verzichte<br>verzichtest<br>verzichtet | verzichten<br>verzichtet<br>verzichten | habe verzichtet<br>hast verzichtet<br>hat verzichtet | haben verzichtet<br>habt verzichtet<br>haben verzichtet |
| | **Past** | | **Past Perfect** | |
| | verzichtete<br>verzichtetest<br>verzichtete | verzichteten<br>verzichtetet<br>verzichteten | hatte verzichtet<br>hattest verzichtet<br>hatte verzichtet | hatten verzichtet<br>hattet verzichtet<br>hatten verzichtet |
| | **Future** | | **Future Perfect** | |
| | werde verzichten<br>wirst verzichten<br>wird verzichten | werden verzichten<br>werdet verzichten<br>werden verzichten | werde verzichtet haben<br>wirst verzichtet haben<br>wird verzichtet haben | werden verzichtet haben<br>werdet verzichtet haben<br>werden verzichtet haben |
| Subjunctive | **Present** | | **Present Perfect** | |
| | verzichte<br>verzichtest<br>verzichte | verzichten<br>verzichtet<br>verzichten | habe verzichtet<br>habest verzichtet<br>habe verzichtet | haben verzichtet<br>habet verzichtet<br>haben verzichtet |
| | **Past** | | **Past Perfect** | |
| | verzichtete<br>verzichtetest<br>verzichtete | verzichteten<br>verzichtetet<br>verzichteten | hätte verzichtet<br>hättest verzichtet<br>hätte verzichtet | hätten verzichtet<br>hättet verzichtet<br>hätten verzichtet |
| | **Future** | | **Future Perfect** | |
| | werde verzichten<br>werdest verzichten<br>werde verzichten | werden verzichten<br>werdet verzichten<br>werden verzichten | werde verzichtet haben<br>werdest verzichtet haben<br>werde verzichtet haben | werden verzichtet haben<br>werdet verzichtet haben<br>werden verzichtet haben |
| | **Present and Future Conditional** | | **Past Conditional** | |
| | würde verzichten<br>würdest verzichten<br>würde verzichten | wurden verzichten<br>würdet verzichten<br>würden verzichten | würde verzichtet haben<br>würdest verzichtet haben<br>würde verzichtet haben | würden verzichtet haben<br>würdet verzichtet haben<br>würden verzichtet haben |

## EXAMPLES

Ein armer Student muss auf vieles verzichten.
A poor student has to give up a lot.

Wie kann ich auf das Haus meines eigenen Vaters verzichten?
How can I give up claim to my own father's house?

**vorbereiten**

to prepare, to make ready

**Auxiliary verb:** haben **Past participle:** vorbereitet

**Imperative:** Bereite vor! Bereitet vor! Bereiten Sie vor!

| Mode | Simple Tenses | | Compound Tenses | |
|---|---|---|---|---|
| | *Singular* | *Plural* | *Singular* | *Plural* |
| Indicative | **Present** | | **Present Perfect** | |
| | bereite vor<br>bereitest vor<br>bereitet vor | bereiten vor<br>bereitet vor<br>bereiten vor | habe vorbereitet<br>hast vorbereitet<br>hat vorbereitet | haben vorbereitet<br>habt vorbereitet<br>haben vorbereitet |
| | **Past** | | **Past Perfect** | |
| | bereitete vor<br>bereitetest vor<br>bereitete vor | bereiteten vor<br>bereitetet vor<br>bereiteten vor | hatte vorbereitet<br>hattest vorbereitet<br>hatte vorbereitet | hatten vorbereitet<br>hattet vorbereitet<br>hatten vorbereitet |
| | **Future** | | **Future Perfect** | |
| | werde vorbereiten<br>wirst vorbereiten<br>wird vorbereiten | werden vorbereiten<br>werdet vorbereiten<br>werden vorbereiten | werde vorbereitet haben<br>wirst vorbereitet haben<br>wird vorbereitet haben | werden vorbereitet haben<br>werdet vorbereitet haben<br>werden vorbereitet haben |
| Subjunctive | **Present** | | **Present Perfect** | |
| | bereite vor<br>bereitest vor<br>bereite vor | bereiten vor<br>bereitet vor<br>bereiten vor | habe vorbereitet<br>habest vorbereitet<br>habe vorbereitet | haben vorbereitet<br>habet vorbereitet<br>haben vorbereitet |
| | **Past** | | **Past Perfect** | |
| | bereitete vor<br>bereitetest vor<br>bereitete vor | bereiteten vor<br>bereitetet vor<br>bereiteten vor | hätte vorbereitet<br>hättest vorbereitet<br>hätte vorbereitet | hätten vorbereitet<br>hättet vorbereitet<br>hätten vorbereitet |
| | **Future** | | **Future Perfect** | |
| | werde vorbereiten<br>werdest vorbereiten<br>werde vorbereiten | werden vorbereiten<br>werdet vorbereiten<br>werden vorbereiten | werde vorbereitet haben<br>werdest vorbereitet haben<br>werde vorbereitet haben | werden vorbereitet haben<br>werdet vorbereitet haben<br>werden vorbereitet haben |
| | **Present and Future Conditional** | | **Past Conditional** | |
| | würde vorbereiten<br>würdest vorbereiten<br>würde vorbereiten | würden vorbereiten<br>würdet vorbereiten<br>würden vorbereiten | würde vorbereitet haben<br>würdest vorbereitet haben<br>würde vorbereitet haben | würden vorbereitet haben<br>würdet vorbereitet haben<br>würden vorbereitet haben |

## EXAMPLES

Ich habe heute keine Zeit die Party vorzubereiten.

I don't have time today to get ready for the party.

Die Studenten bereiten sich auf das Staatsexamen vor.

The students are getting ready for the state examination.

**vornehmen (sich)**
to undertake, to intend to do
**Auxiliary verb:** haben **Past participle:** vorgenommen
**Imperative:** Nimm vor! Nehmt vor! Nehmen Sie vor!

| Mode | Simple Tenses | | Compound Tenses | |
|---|---|---|---|---|
| | *Singular* | *Plural* | *Singular* | *Plural* |
| Indicative | **Present** | | **Present Perfect** | |
| | nehme vor<br>nimmst vor<br>nimmt vor | nehmen vor<br>nehmt vor<br>nehmen vor | habe vorgenommen<br>hast vorgenommen<br>hat vorgenommen | haben vorgenommen<br>habt vorgenommen<br>haben vorgenommen |
| | **Past** | | **Past Perfect** | |
| | nahm vor<br>nahmst vor<br>nahm vor | nahmen vor<br>nahmt vor<br>nahmen vor | hatte vorgenommen<br>hattest vorgenommen<br>hatte vorgenommen | hatten vorgenommen<br>hattet vorgenommen<br>hatten vorgenommen |
| | **Future** | | **Future Perfect** | |
| | werde vornehmen<br>wirst vornehmen<br>wird vornehmen | werden vornehmen<br>werdet vornehmen<br>werden vornehmen | werde vorgenommen haben<br>wirst vorgenommen haben<br>wird vorgenommen haben | werden vorgenommen haben<br>werdet vorgenommen haben<br>werden vorgenommen haben |
| Subjunctive | **Present** | | **Present Perfect** | |
| | nehme vor<br>nehmest vor<br>nehme vor | nehmen vor<br>nehmet vor<br>nehmen vor | habe vorgenommen<br>habest vorgenommen<br>habe vorgenommen | haben vorgenommen<br>habet vorgenommen<br>haben vorgenommen |
| | **Past** | | **Past Perfect** | |
| | nähme vor<br>nähmest vor<br>nähme vor | nähmen vor<br>nähmet vor<br>nähmen vor | hätte vorgenommen<br>hättest vorgenommen<br>hätte vorgenommen | hätten vorgenommen<br>hättet vorgenommen<br>hätten vorgenommen |
| | **Future** | | **Future Perfect** | |
| | werde vornehmen<br>werdest vornehmen<br>werde vornehmen | werden vornehmen<br>werdet vornehmen<br>werden vornehmen | werde vorgenommen haben<br>werdest vorgenommen haben<br>werde vorgenommen haben | werden vorgenommen haben<br>werdet vorgenommen haben<br>werden vorgenommen haben |
| | **Present and Future Conditional** | | **Past Conditional** | |
| | würde vornehmen<br>würdest vornehmen<br>würde vornehmen | würden vornehmen<br>würdet vornehmen<br>würden vornehmen | würde vorgenommen haben<br>würdest vorgenommen haben<br>würde vorgenommen haben | würden vorgenommen haben<br>würdet vorgenommen haben<br>würden vorgenommen haben |

**Note:** With inseparable prefixes, the principal parts of this verb are, for example, *unternimmt, unternahm, hat unternommen.* With separable prefixes, the principal parts are, for example, *nimmt zu, nahm zu, hat zugenommen.*

## EXAMPLES

| | |
|---|---|
| Sie hat sich vorgenommen Englisch zu lernen. | She intends to learn English. |
| Hattest du dir nicht vorgenommen weniger zu trinken und zu rauchen? | Didn't you make up your mind to drink and smoke less? |

**vorstellen (sich)**
to introduce, to imagine
**Auxiliary verb:** haben **Past participle:** vorgestellt
**Imperative:** Stelle vor! Stellt vor! Stellen Sie vor!

| Mode | Simple Tenses | | Compound Tenses | |
|---|---|---|---|---|
| | *Singular* | *Plural* | *Singular* | *Plural* |
| Indicative | **Present** | | **Present Perfect** | |
| | stelle vor<br>stellst vor<br>stellt vor | stellen vor<br>stellt vor<br>stellen vor | habe vorgestellt<br>hast vorgestellt<br>hat vorgestellt | haben vorgestellt<br>habt vorgestellt<br>haben vorgestellt |
| | **Past** | | **Past Perfect** | |
| | stellte vor<br>stelltest vor<br>stellte vor | stellten vor<br>stelltet vor<br>stellten vor | hatte vorgestellt<br>hattest vorgestellt<br>hatte vorgestellt | hatten vorgestellt<br>hattet vorgestellt<br>hatten vorgestellt |
| | **Future** | | **Future Perfect** | |
| | werde vorstellen<br>wirst vorstellen<br>wird vorstellen | werden vorstellen<br>werdet vorstellen<br>werden vorstellen | werde vorgestellt haben<br>wirst vorgestellt haben<br>wird vorgestellt haben | werden vorgestellt haben<br>werdet vorgestellt haben<br>werden vorgestellt haben |
| Subjunctive | **Present** | | **Present Perfect** | |
| | stelle vor<br>stellest vor<br>stelle vor | stellen vor<br>stellet vor<br>stellen vor | habe vorgestellt<br>habest vorgestellt<br>habe vorgestellt | haben vorgestellt<br>habet vorgestellt<br>haben vorgestellt |
| | **Past** | | **Past Perfect** | |
| | stellte vor<br>stelltest vor<br>stellte vor | stellten vor<br>stelltet vor<br>stellten vor | hätte vorgestellt<br>hättest vorgestellt<br>hätte vorgestellt | hätten vorgestellt<br>hättet vorgestellt<br>hätten vorgestellt |
| | **Future** | | **Future Perfect** | |
| | werde vorstellen<br>werdest vorstellen<br>werde vorstellen | werden vorstellen<br>werdet vorstellen<br>werden vorstellen | werde vorgestellt haben<br>werdest vorgestellt haben<br>werde vorgestellt haben | werden vorgestellt haben<br>werdet vorgestellt haben<br>werden vorgestellt haben |
| | **Present and Future Conditional** | | **Past Conditional** | |
| | würde vorstellen<br>würdest vorstellen<br>würde vorstellen | würden vorstellen<br>würdet vorstellen<br>würden vorstellen | würde vorgestellt haben<br>würdest vorgestellt haben<br>würde vorgestellt haben | würden vorgestellt haben<br>würdet vorgestellt haben<br>würden vorgestellt haben |

## EXAMPLES

Ich möchte euch meine Kinder vorstellen.
Kannst du dir vorstellen, wie anders das Leben in Asien ist?

I'd like to introduce my children to you.
Can you imagine how different life is in Asia?

**wachsen**
to grow
**Auxiliary verb:** sein **Past participle:** gewachsen
**Imperative:** Wachse! Wachst! Wachsen Sie!

| Mode | Simple Tenses | | Compound Tenses | |
|---|---|---|---|---|
| | *Singular* | *Plural* | *Singular* | *Plural* |
| Indicative | **Present** | | **Present Perfect** | |
| | wachse<br>wächst<br>wächst | wachsen<br>wachst<br>wachsen | bin gewachsen<br>bist gewachsen<br>ist gewachsen | sind gewachsen<br>seid gewachsen<br>sind gewachsen |
| | **Past** | | **Past Perfect** | |
| | wuchs<br>wuchsest<br>wuchs | wuchsen<br>wuchst<br>wuchsen | war gewachsen<br>warst gewachsen<br>war gewachsen | waren gewachsen<br>wart gewachsen<br>waren gewachsen |
| | **Future** | | **Future Perfect** | |
| | werde wachsen<br>wirst wachsen<br>wird wachsen | werden wachsen<br>werdet wachsen<br>werden wachsen | werde gewachsen sein<br>wirst gewachsen sein<br>wird gewachsen sein | werden gewachsen sein<br>werdet gewachsen sein<br>werden gewachsen sein |
| Subjunctive | **Present** | | **Present Perfect** | |
| | wachse<br>wachsest<br>wachse | wachsen<br>wachset<br>wachsen | sei gewachsen<br>seiest gewachsen<br>sei gewachsen | seien gewachsen<br>seiet gewachsen<br>seien gewachsen |
| | **Past** | | **Past Perfect** | |
| | wüchse<br>wüchsest<br>wüchse | wüchsen<br>wüchset<br>wüchsen | wäre gewachsen<br>wärest gewachsen<br>wäre gewachsen | wären gewachsen<br>wäret gewachsen<br>wären gewachsen |
| | **Future** | | **Future Perfect** | |
| | werde wachsen<br>werdest wachsen<br>werde wachsen | werden wachsen<br>werdet wachsen<br>werden wachsen | werde gewachsen sein<br>werdest gewachsen sein<br>werde gewachsen sein | werden gewachsen sein<br>werdet gewachsen sein<br>werden gewachsen sein |
| | **Present and Future Conditional** | | **Past Conditional** | |
| | würde wachsen<br>würdest wachsen<br>würde wachsen | würden wachsen<br>würdet wachsen<br>würden wachsen | würde gewachsen sein<br>würdest gewachsen sein<br>würde gewachsen sein | würden gewachsen sein<br>würdet gewachsen sein<br>würden gewachsen sein |

## EXAMPLES

Warum wachsen in Ihrem Garten keine Blumen?
Why don't flowers grow in your garden?

In den letzten sechs Monaten ist Sven acht Zentimeter gewachsen.
Sven has grown 8 centimeters in the last six months.

**wählen**

to choose, to elect, to vote

**Auxiliary verb:** haben **Past participle:** gewählt

**Imperative:** Wähle! Wählt! Wählen Sie!

| Mode | Simple Tenses | | Compound Tenses | |
|---|---|---|---|---|
| | *Singular* | *Plural* | *Singular* | *Plural* |
| Indicative | **Present** | | **Present Perfect** | |
| | wähle<br>wählst<br>wählt | wählen<br>wählt<br>wählen | habe gewählt<br>hast gewählt<br>hat gewählt | haben gewählt<br>habt gewählt<br>haben gewählt |
| | **Past** | | **Past Perfect** | |
| | wählte<br>wähltest<br>wählte | wählten<br>wähltet<br>wählten | hatte gewählt<br>hattest gewählt<br>hatte gewählt | hatten gewählt<br>hattet gewählt<br>hatten gewählt |
| | **Future** | | **Future Perfect** | |
| | werde wählen<br>wirst wählen<br>wird wählen | werden wählen<br>werdet wählen<br>werden wählen | werde gewählt haben<br>wirst gewählt haben<br>wird gewählt haben | werden gewählt haben<br>werdet gewählt haben<br>werden gewählt haben |
| Subjunctive | **Present** | | **Present Perfect** | |
| | wähle<br>wählest<br>wähle | wählen<br>wählet<br>wählen | habe gewählt<br>habest gewählt<br>habe gewählt | haben gewählt<br>habet gewählt<br>haben gewählt |
| | **Past** | | **Past Perfect** | |
| | wählte<br>wähltest<br>wählte | wählten<br>wähltet<br>wählten | hätte gewählt<br>hättest gewählt<br>hätte gewählt | hätten gewählt<br>hättet gewählt<br>hätten gewählt |
| | **Future** | | **Future Perfect** | |
| | werde wählen<br>werdest wählen<br>werde wählen | werden wählen<br>werdet wählen<br>werden wählen | werde gewählt haben<br>werdest gewählt haben<br>werde gewählt haben | werden gewählt haben<br>werdet gewählt haben<br>werden gewählt haben |
| | **Present and Future Conditional** | | **Past Conditional** | |
| | würde wählen<br>würdest wählen<br>würde wählen | würden wählen<br>würdet wählen<br>würden wählen | würde gewählt haben<br>würdest gewählt haben<br>würde gewählt haben | würden gewählt haben<br>würdet gewählt haben<br>würden gewählt haben |

## EXAMPLES

Welche Telefonnummer soll ich wählen? — What telephone number should I dial?

Mein Vater hat die Sozialdemokraten gewählt. — My father voted for the Social Democrats.

**wandern**
to roam, to wander, to hike
**Auxiliary verb:** sein **Past participle:** gewandert
**Imperative:** Wandere! Wandert! Wandern Sie!

| Mode | Simple Tenses | | Compound Tenses | |
|---|---|---|---|---|
| | *Singular* | *Plural* | *Singular* | *Plural* |
| Indicative | **Present** | | **Present Perfect** | |
| | wandere<br>wanderst<br>wandert | wandern<br>wandert<br>wandern | bin gewandert<br>bist gewandert<br>ist gewandert | sind gewandert<br>seid gewandert<br>sind gewandert |
| | **Past** | | **Past Perfect** | |
| | wanderte<br>wandertest<br>wanderte | wanderten<br>wandertet<br>wanderten | war gewandert<br>warst gewandert<br>war gewandert | waren gewandert<br>wart gewandert<br>waren gewandert |
| | **Future** | | **Future Perfect** | |
| | werde wandern<br>wirst wandern<br>wird wandern | werden wandern<br>werdet wandern<br>werden wandern | werde gewandert sein<br>wirst gewandert sein<br>wird gewandert sein | werden gewandert sein<br>werdet gewandert sein<br>werden gewandert sein |
| Subjunctive | **Present** | | **Present Perfect** | |
| | wandere<br>wanderst<br>wandere | wandern<br>wandert<br>wandern | sei gewandert<br>seiest gewandert<br>sei gewandert | seien gewandert<br>seiet gewandert<br>seien gewandert |
| | **Past** | | **Past Perfect** | |
| | wanderte<br>wandertest<br>wanderte | wanderten<br>wandertet<br>wanderten | wäre gewandert<br>wärest gewandert<br>wäre gewandert | wären gewandert<br>wäret gewandert<br>wären gewandert |
| | **Future** | | **Future Perfect** | |
| | werde wandern<br>werdest wandern<br>werde wandern | werden wandern<br>werdet wandern<br>werden wandern | werde gewandert sein<br>werdest gewandert sein<br>werde gewandert sein | werden gewandert sein<br>werdet gewandert sein<br>werden gewandert sein |
| | **Present and Future Conditional** | | **Past Conditional** | |
| | würde wandern<br>würdest wandern<br>würde wandern | würden wandern<br>würdet wandern<br>würden wandern | würde gewandert sein<br>würdest gewandert sein<br>würde gewandert sein | würden gewandert sein<br>würdet gewandert sein<br>würden gewandert sein |

## EXAMPLES

Wir sind in diesem Tal oft gewandert. — We often went hiking in this valley.
Beim Wandern hat er sich das Bein gebrochen. — He broke his leg while hiking.

**warnen**

to warn

**Auxiliary verb:** haben **Past participle:** gewarnt

**Imperative:** Warne! Warnt! Warnen Sie!

| Mode | Simple Tenses | | Compound Tenses | |
|---|---|---|---|---|
| | *Singular* | *Plural* | *Singular* | *Plural* |
| Indicative | **Present** | | **Present Perfect** | |
| | warne<br>warnst<br>warnt | warnen<br>warnt<br>warnen | habe gewarnt<br>hast gewarnt<br>hat gewarnt | haben gewarnt<br>habt gewarnt<br>haben gewarnt |
| | **Past** | | **Past Perfect** | |
| | warnte<br>warntest<br>warnte | warnten<br>warntet<br>warnten | hatte gewarnt<br>hattest gewarnt<br>hatte gewarnt | hatten gewarnt<br>hattet gewarnt<br>hatten gewarnt |
| | **Future** | | **Future Perfect** | |
| | werde warnen<br>wirst warnen<br>wird warnen | werden warnen<br>werdet warnen<br>werden warnen | werde gewarnt haben<br>wirst gewarnt haben<br>wird gewarnt haben | werden gewarnt haben<br>werdet gewarnt haben<br>werden gewarnt haben |
| Subjunctive | **Present** | | **Present Perfect** | |
| | warne<br>warnest<br>warne | warnen<br>warnet<br>warnen | habe gewarnt<br>habest gewarnt<br>habe gewarnt | haben gewarnt<br>habet gewarnt<br>haben gewarnt |
| | **Past** | | **Past Perfect** | |
| | warnte<br>warntest<br>warnte | warnten<br>warntet<br>warnten | hätte gewarnt<br>hättest gewarnt<br>hätte gewarnt | hätten gewarnt<br>hättet gewarnt<br>hätten gewarnt |
| | **Future** | | **Future Perfect** | |
| | werde warnen<br>werdest warnen<br>werde warnen | werden warnen<br>werdet warnen<br>werden warnen | werde gewarnt haben<br>werdest gewarnt haben<br>werde gewarnt haben | werden gewarnt haben<br>werdet gewarnt haben<br>werden gewarnt haben |
| | **Present and Future Conditional** | | **Past Conditional** | |
| | würde warnen<br>würdest warnen<br>würde warnen | würden warnen<br>würdet warnen<br>würden warnen | würde gewarnt haben<br>würdest gewarnt haben<br>würde gewarnt haben | würden gewarnt haben<br>würdet gewarnt haben<br>würden gewarnt haben |

## EXAMPLES

In seiner Rede hat der Außenminister vor einer drohenden Gefahr gewarnt.

The foreign minister warned against a threat of danger in his speech.

Ich warne dich. Solchen Leuten ist nicht zu trauen.

I'm warning you. Such people can't be trusted.

**warten**
to wait
**Auxiliary verb:** haben **Past participle:** gewartet
**Imperative:** Warte! Wartet! Warten Sie!

| Mode | Simple Tenses | | Compound Tenses | |
|---|---|---|---|---|
| | *Singular* | *Plural* | *Singular* | *Plural* |
| Indicative | **Present** | | **Present Perfect** | |
| | warte<br>wartest<br>wartet | warten<br>wartet<br>warten | habe gewartet<br>hast gewartet<br>hat gewartet | haben gewartet<br>habt gewartet<br>haben gewartet |
| | **Past** | | **Past Perfect** | |
| | wartete<br>wartetest<br>wartete | warteten<br>wartetet<br>warteten | hatte gewartet<br>hattest gewartet<br>hatte gewartet | hatten gewartet<br>hattet gewartet<br>hatten gewartet |
| | **Future** | | **Future Perfect** | |
| | werde warten<br>wirst warten<br>wird warten | werden warten<br>werdet warten<br>werden warten | werde gewartet haben<br>wirst gewartet haben<br>wird gewartet haben | werden gewartet haben<br>werdet gewartet haben<br>werden gewartet haben |
| Subjunctive | **Present** | | **Present Perfect** | |
| | warte<br>wartest<br>warte | warten<br>wartet<br>warten | habe gewartet<br>habest gewartet<br>habe gewartet | haben gewartet<br>habet gewartet<br>haben gewartet |
| | **Past** | | **Past Perfect** | |
| | wartete<br>wartetest<br>wartete | warteten<br>wartetet<br>warteten | hätte gewartet<br>hättest gewartet<br>hätte gewartet | hätten gewartet<br>hättet gewartet<br>hätten gewartet |
| | **Future** | | **Future Perfect** | |
| | werde warten<br>werdest warten<br>werde warten | werden warten<br>werdet warten<br>werden warten | werde gewartet haben<br>werdest gewartet haben<br>werde gewartet haben | werden gewartet haben<br>werdet gewartet haben<br>werden gewartet haben |
| | **Present and Future Conditional** | | **Past Conditional** | |
| | würde warten<br>würdest warten<br>würde warten | würden warten<br>würdet warten<br>würden warten | würde gewartet haben<br>würdest gewartet haben<br>würde gewartet haben | würden gewartet haben<br>würdet gewartet haben<br>würden gewartet haben |

## EXAMPLES

Wie lange muss ich noch warten?
How much longer do I have to wait?

Wir haben zwei Stunden auf Herrn Bauer gewartet.
We waited two hours for Mr. Bauer.

**waschen**
to wash
**Auxiliary verb:** haben **Past participle:** gewaschen
**Imperative:** Wasche! Wascht! Waschen Sie!

| Mode | Simple Tenses | | Compound Tenses | |
|---|---|---|---|---|
| | *Singular* | *Plural* | *Singular* | *Plural* |
| Incicative | **Present** | | **Present Perfect** | |
| | wasche<br>wäschst<br>wäscht | waschen<br>wascht<br>waschen | habe gewaschen<br>hast gewaschen<br>hat gewaschen | haben gewaschen<br>habt gewaschen<br>haben gewaschen |
| | **Past** | | **Past Perfect** | |
| | wusch<br>wuschest<br>wusch | wuschen<br>wuscht<br>wuschen | hatte gewaschen<br>hattest gewaschen<br>hatte gewaschen | hatten gewaschen<br>hattet gewaschen<br>hatten gewaschen |
| | **Future** | | **Future Perfect** | |
| | werde waschen<br>wirst waschen<br>wird waschen | werden waschen<br>werdet waschen<br>werden waschen | werde gewaschen haben<br>wirst gewaschen haben<br>wird gewaschen haben | werden gewaschen haben<br>werdet gewaschen haben<br>werden gewaschen haben |
| Subjunctive | **Present** | | **Present Perfect** | |
| | wasche<br>waschest<br>wasche | waschen<br>waschet<br>waschen | habe gewaschen<br>habest gewaschen<br>habe gewaschen | haben gewaschen<br>habet gewaschen<br>haben gewaschen |
| | **Past** | | **Past Perfect** | |
| | wüsche<br>wüschest<br>wüsche | wüschen<br>wüschet<br>wüschen | hätte gewaschen<br>hättest gewaschen<br>hätte gewaschen | hätten gewaschen<br>hättet gewaschen<br>hätten gewaschen |
| | **Future** | | **Future Perfect** | |
| | werde waschen<br>werdest waschen<br>werde waschen | werden waschen<br>werdet waschen<br>werden waschen | werde gewaschen haben<br>werdest gewaschen haben<br>werde gewaschen haben | werden gewaschen haben<br>werdet gewaschen haben<br>werden gewaschen haben |
| | **Present and Future Conditional** | | **Past Conditional** | |
| | würde waschen<br>würdest waschen<br>würde waschen | würden waschen<br>würdet waschen<br>würden waschen | würde gewaschen haben<br>würdest gewaschen haben<br>würde gewaschen haben | würden gewaschen haben<br>würdet gewaschen haben<br>würden gewaschen haben |

## EXAMPLES

Wo kann ich mir die Hände waschen? — Where can I wash my hands?
Dienstags waschen wir Wäsche. — On Tuesdays, we do the laundry.

**weben**

to weave

**Auxiliary verb:** haben **Past participle:** gewebt

**Imperative:** Webe! Webt! Weben Sie!

| Mode | Simple Tenses | | Compound Tenses | |
|---|---|---|---|---|
| | *Singular* | *Plural* | *Singular* | *Plural* |
| Indicative | **Present** | | **Present Perfect** | |
| | webe<br>webst<br>webt | weben<br>webt<br>weben | habe gewebt<br>hast gewebt<br>hat gewebt | haben gewebt<br>habt gewebt<br>haben gewebt |
| | **Past** | | **Past Perfect** | |
| | webte<br>webtest<br>webte | webten<br>webtet<br>webten | hatte gewebt<br>hattest gewebt<br>hatte gewebt | hatten gewebt<br>hattet gewebt<br>hatten gewebt |
| | **Future** | | **Future Perfect** | |
| | werde weben<br>wirst weben<br>wird weben | werden weben<br>werdet weben<br>werden weben | werde gewebt haben<br>wirst gewebt haben<br>wird gewebt haben | werden gewebt haben<br>werdet gewebt haben<br>werden gewebt haben |
| Subjunctive | **Present** | | **Present Perfect** | |
| | webe<br>webest<br>webe | weben<br>webet<br>weben | habe gewebt<br>habest gewebt<br>habe gewebt | haben gewebt<br>habet gewebt<br>haben gewebt |
| | **Past** | | **Past Perfect** | |
| | webte<br>webtest<br>webte | webten<br>webtet<br>webten | hätte gewebt<br>hättest gewebt<br>hätte gewebt | hätten gewebt<br>hättet gewebt<br>hätten gewebt |
| | **Future** | | **Future Perfect** | |
| | werde weben<br>werdest weben<br>werde weben | werden weben<br>werdet weben<br>werden weben | werde gewebt haben<br>werdest gewebt haben<br>werde gewebt haben | werden gewebt haben<br>werdet gewebt haben<br>werden gewebt haben |
| | **Present and Future Conditional** | | **Past Conditional** | |
| | würde weben<br>würdest weben<br>würde weben | würden weben<br>würdet weben<br>würden weben | würde gewebt haben<br>würdest gewebt haben<br>würde gewebt haben | würden gewebt haben<br>würdet gewebt haben<br>würden gewebt haben |

## EXAMPLES

In diesem Dorf wird der feinste Stoff gewebt. They weave the finest fabrics in this village.

Sein Hobby ist Weben. His hobby is weaving.

**wechseln**

to change, to exchange

**Auxiliary verb:** haben **Past participle:** gewechselt

**Imperative:** Wechs(e)le! Wechselt! Wechseln Sie!

| Mode | Simple Tenses | | Compound Tenses | |
|---|---|---|---|---|
| | *Singular* | *Plural* | *Singular* | *Plural* |
| Indicative | **Present** | | **Present Perfect** | |
| | wechsele<br>wechselst<br>wechselt | wechseln<br>wechselt<br>wechseln | habe gewechselt<br>hast gewechselt<br>hat gewechselt | haben gewechselt<br>habt gewechselt<br>haben gewechselt |
| | **Past** | | **Past Perfect** | |
| | wechselte<br>wechseltest<br>wechselte | wechselten<br>wechseltet<br>wechselten | hatte gewechselt<br>hattest gewechselt<br>hatte gewechselt | hatten gewechselt<br>hattet gewechselt<br>hatten gewechselt |
| | **Future** | | **Future Perfect** | |
| | werde wechseln<br>wirst wechseln<br>wird wechseln | werden wechseln<br>werdet wechseln<br>werden wechseln | werde gewechselt haben<br>wirst gewechselt haben<br>wird gewechselt haben | werden gewechselt haben<br>werdet gewechselt haben<br>werden gewechselt haben |
| Subjunctive | **Present** | | **Present Perfect** | |
| | wechsele<br>wechselst<br>wechsele | wechseln<br>wechselt<br>wechseln | habe gewechselt<br>habest gewechselt<br>habe gewechselt | haben gewechselt<br>habet gewechselt<br>haben gewechselt |
| | **Past** | | **Past Perfect** | |
| | wechselte<br>wechseltest<br>wechselte | wechselten<br>wechseltet<br>wechselten | hätte gewechselt<br>hättest gewechselt<br>hätte gewechselt | hätten gewechselt<br>hättet gewechselt<br>hätten gewechselt |
| | **Future** | | **Future Perfect** | |
| | werde wechseln<br>werdest wechseln<br>werde wechseln | werden wechseln<br>werdet wechseln<br>werden wechseln | werde gewechselt haben<br>werdest gewechselt haben<br>werde gewechselt haben | werden gewechselt haben<br>werdet gewechselt haben<br>werden gewechselt haben |
| | **Present and Future Conditional** | | **Past Conditional** | |
| | würde wechseln<br>würdest wechseln<br>würde wechseln | würden wechseln<br>würdet wechseln<br>würden wechseln | würde gewechselt haben<br>würdest gewechselt haben<br>würde gewechselt haben | würden gewechselt haben<br>würdet gewechselt haben<br>würden gewechselt haben |

## EXAMPLES

Die Touristen müssen mehr Geld wechseln. — The tourists have to exchange more money.

Warum hast du Schlösser gewechselt? — Why did you change the locks?

**wecken**

to waken, to rouse someone

**Auxiliary verb:** haben **Past participle:** geweckt

**Imperative:** Wecke! Weckt! Wecken Sie!

| Mode | Simple Tenses | | Compound Tenses | |
|---|---|---|---|---|
| | *Singular* | *Plural* | *Singular* | *Plural* |
| Indicative | **Present** | | **Present Perfect** | |
| | wecke<br>weckst<br>weckt | wecken<br>weckt<br>wecken | habe geweckt<br>hast geweckt<br>hat geweckt | haben geweckt<br>habt geweckt<br>haben geweckt |
| | **Past** | | **Past Perfect** | |
| | weckte<br>wecktest<br>weckte | weckten<br>wecktet<br>weckten | hatte geweckt<br>hattest geweckt<br>hatte geweckt | hatten geweckt<br>hattet geweckt<br>hatten geweckt |
| | **Future** | | **Future Perfect** | |
| | werde wecken<br>wirst wecken<br>wird wecken | werden wecken<br>werdet wecken<br>werden wecken | werde geweckt haben<br>wirst geweckt haben<br>wird geweckt haben | werden geweckt haben<br>werdet geweckt haben<br>werden geweckt haben |
| Subjunctive | **Present** | | **Present Perfect** | |
| | wecke<br>weckest<br>wecke | wecken<br>wecket<br>wecken | habe geweckt<br>habest geweckt<br>habe geweckt | haben geweckt<br>habet geweckt<br>haben geweckt |
| | **Past** | | **Past Perfect** | |
| | weckte<br>wecktest<br>weckte | weckten<br>wecktet<br>weckten | hätte geweckt<br>hättest geweckt<br>hätte geweckt | hätten geweckt<br>hättet geweckt<br>hätten geweckt |
| | **Future** | | **Future Perfect** | |
| | werde wecken<br>werdest wecken<br>werde wecken | werden wecken<br>werdet wecken<br>werden wecken | werde geweckt haben<br>werdest geweckt haben<br>werde geweckt haben | werden geweckt haben<br>werdet geweckt haben<br>werden geweckt haben |
| | **Present and Future Conditional** | | **Past Conditional** | |
| | würde wecken<br>würdest wecken<br>würde wecken | würden wecken<br>würdet wecken<br>würden wecken | würde geweckt haben<br>würdest geweckt haben<br>würde geweckt haben | würden geweckt haben<br>würdet geweckt haben<br>würden geweckt haben |

## EXAMPLES

Es ist schon zehn Uhr. Wecke deinen Vater!

It's ten o'clock. Wake your father.

Ich versuchte ihn zu wecken, aber der arme Kerl war bewusstlos.

I tried to waken him, but the poor fellow was unconscious.

**weinen**

to cry, to weep

**Auxiliary verb:** haben **Past participle:** geweint

**Imperative:** Weine! Weint! Weinen Sie!

| Mode | Simple Tenses | | Compound Tenses | |
|---|---|---|---|---|
| | *Singular* | *Plural* | *Singular* | *Plural* |
| Indicative | **Present** | | **Present Perfect** | |
| | weine<br>weinst<br>weint | weinen<br>weint<br>weinen | habe geweint<br>hast geweint<br>hat geweint | haben geweint<br>habt geweint<br>haben geweint |
| | **Past** | | **Past Perfect** | |
| | weinte<br>weintest<br>weinte | weinten<br>weintet<br>weinten | hatte geweint<br>hattest geweint<br>hatte geweint | hatten geweint<br>hattet geweint<br>hatten geweint |
| | **Future** | | **Future Perfect** | |
| | werde weinen<br>wirst weinen<br>wird weinen | werden weinen<br>werdet weinen<br>werden weinen | werde geweint haben<br>wirst geweint haben<br>wird geweint haben | werden geweint haben<br>werdet geweint haben<br>werden geweint haben |
| Subjunctive | **Present** | | **Present Perfect** | |
| | weine<br>weinest<br>weine | weinen<br>weinet<br>weinen | habe geweint<br>habest geweint<br>habe geweint | haben geweint<br>habet geweint<br>haben geweint |
| | **Past** | | **Past Perfect** | |
| | weinte<br>weintest<br>weinte | weinten<br>weintet<br>weinten | hätte geweint<br>hättest geweint<br>hätte geweint | hätten geweint<br>hättet geweint<br>hätten geweint |
| | **Future** | | **Future Perfect** | |
| | werde weinen<br>werdest weinen<br>werde weinen | werden weinen<br>werdet weinen<br>werden weinen | werde geweint haben<br>werdest geweint haben<br>werde geweint haben | werden geweint haben<br>werdet geweint haben<br>werden geweint haben |
| | **Present and Future Conditional** | | **Past Conditional** | |
| | würde weinen<br>würdest weinen<br>würde weinen | würden weinen<br>würdet weinen<br>würden weinen | würde geweint haben<br>würdest geweint haben<br>würde geweint haben | würden geweint haben<br>würdet geweint haben<br>würden geweint haben |

## EXAMPLES

| | |
|---|---|
| Sie weinte die ganze Nacht und konnte nicht schlafen. | She cried all night long and couldn't sleep. |
| Unser Vater hat vor Freude geweint. | Our father cried with joy. |

**weisen**
to show, to direct, to point
**Auxiliary verb:** haben **Past participle:** gewiesen
**Imperative:** Weise! Weist! Weisen Sie!

| Mode | Simple Tenses | | Compound Tenses | |
|---|---|---|---|---|
| | *Singular* | *Plural* | *Singular* | *Plural* |
| Indicative | **Present** | | **Present Perfect** | |
| | weise<br>weist<br>weist | weisen<br>weist<br>weisen | habe gewiesen<br>hast gewiesen<br>hat gewiesen | haben gewiesen<br>habt gewiesen<br>haben gewiesen |
| | **Past** | | **Past Perfect** | |
| | wies<br>wiesest<br>wies | wiesen<br>wiest<br>wiesen | hatte gewiesen<br>hattest gewiesen<br>hatte gewiesen | hatten gewiesen<br>hattet gewiesen<br>hatten gewiesen |
| | **Future** | | **Future Perfect** | |
| | werde weisen<br>wirst weisen<br>wird weisen | werden weisen<br>werdet weisen<br>werden weisen | werde gewiesen haben<br>wirst gewiesen haben<br>wird gewiesen haben | werden gewiesen haben<br>werdet gewiesen haben<br>werden gewiesen haben |
| Subjunctive | **Present** | | **Present Perfect** | |
| | weise<br>weisest<br>weise | weisen<br>weiset<br>weisen | habe gewiesen<br>habest gewiesen<br>habe gewiesen | haben gewiesen<br>habet gewiesen<br>haben gewiesen |
| | **Past** | | **Past Perfect** | |
| | wiese<br>wiesest<br>wiese | wiesen<br>wieset<br>wiesen | hätte gewiesen<br>hättest gewiesen<br>hätte gewiesen | hätten gewiesen<br>hättet gewiesen<br>hätten gewiesen |
| | **Future** | | **Future Perfect** | |
| | werde weisen<br>werdest weisen<br>werde weisen | werden weisen<br>werdet weisen<br>werden weisen | werde gewiesen haben<br>werdest gewiesen haben<br>werde gewiesen haben | werden gewiesen haben<br>werdet gewiesen haben<br>werden gewiesen haben |
| | **Present and Future Conditional** | | **Past Conditional** | |
| | würde weisen<br>würdest weisen<br>würde weisen | würden weisen<br>würdet weisen<br>würden weisen | würde gewiesen haben<br>würdest gewiesen haben<br>würde gewiesen haben | würden gewiesen haben<br>würdet gewiesen haben<br>würden gewiesen haben |

## EXAMPLES

Können Sie mir den Weg in die Berge weisen? — Can you show me the way to the mountains?

Onkel Heinrich hat dem unverschämten Mann die Tür gewiesen. — Uncle Heinrich showed the rude man the door.

**wenden (sich)**

to turn

**Auxiliary verb:** haben **Past participle:** gewandt

**Imperative:** Wende! Wendet! Wenden Sie!

| Mode | Simple Tenses | | Compound Tenses | |
|---|---|---|---|---|
| | *Singular* | *Plural* | *Singular* | *Plural* |
| Indicative | **Present** | | **Present Perfect** | |
| | wende<br>wendest<br>wendet | wenden<br>wendet<br>wenden | habe gewandt<br>hast gewandt<br>hat gewandt | haben gewandt<br>habt gewandt<br>haben gewandt |
| | **Past** | | **Past Perfect** | |
| | wandte<br>wandtest<br>wandte | wandten<br>wandtet<br>wandten | hatte gewandt<br>hattest gewandt<br>hatte gewandt | hatten gewandt<br>hattet gewandt<br>hatten gewandt |
| | **Future** | | **Future Perfect** | |
| | werde wenden<br>wirst wenden<br>wird wenden | werden wenden<br>werdet wenden<br>werden wenden | werde gewandt haben<br>wirst gewandt haben<br>wird gewandt haben | werden gewandt haben<br>werdet gewandt haben<br>werden gewandt haben |
| Subjunctive | **Present** | | **Present Perfect** | |
| | wende<br>wendest<br>wende | wenden<br>wendet<br>wenden | habe gewandt<br>habest gewandt<br>habe gewandt | haben gewandt<br>habet gewandt<br>haben gewandt |
| | **Past** | | **Past Perfect** | |
| | wendete<br>wendetest<br>wendete | wendeten<br>wendetet<br>wendeten | hätte gewandt<br>hättest gewandt<br>hätte gewandt | hätten gewandt<br>hättet gewandt<br>hätten gewandt |
| | **Future** | | **Future Perfect** | |
| | werde wenden<br>werdest wenden<br>werde wenden | werden wenden<br>werdet wenden<br>werden wenden | werde gewandt haben<br>werdest gewandt haben<br>werde gewandt haben | werden gewandt haben<br>werdet gewandt haben<br>werden gewandt haben |
| | **Present and Future Conditional** | | **Past Conditional** | |
| | würde wenden<br>würdest wenden<br>würde wenden | würden wenden<br>würdet wenden<br>würden wenden | würde gewandt haben<br>würdest gewandt haben<br>würde gewandt haben | würden gewandt haben<br>würdet gewandt haben<br>würden gewandt haben |

**Note:** This verb is sometimes treated as a regular verb with the following principal parts: *wendet, wendete, hat gewendet.*

## EXAMPLES

Bitte wenden Sie sich an die Verwaltung! — Please contact the management.

Das Gespräch wandte sich endlich auf den wichtigen Gegenstand. — The conversation finally turned to the important subject.

**werden**
to become, to get
**Auxiliary verb:** sein **Past participle:** geworden
**Imperative:** Werde! Werdet! Werden Sie!

| Mode | Simple Tenses | | Compound Tenses | |
|---|---|---|---|---|
| | *Singular* | *Plural* | *Singular* | *Plural* |
| Indicative | **Present** | | **Present Perfect** | |
| | werde<br>wirst<br>wird | werden<br>werdet<br>werden | bin geworden<br>bist geworden<br>ist geworden | sind geworden<br>seid geworden<br>sind geworden |
| | **Past** | | **Past Perfect** | |
| | wurde<br>wurdest<br>wurde | wurden<br>wurdet<br>wurden | war geworden<br>warst geworden<br>war geworden | waren geworden<br>wart geworden<br>waren geworden |
| | **Future** | | **Future Perfect** | |
| | werde werden<br>wirst werden<br>wird werden | werden werden<br>werdet werden<br>werden werden | werde geworden sein<br>wirst geworden sein<br>wird geworden sein | werden geworden sein<br>werdet geworden sein<br>werden geworden sein |
| Subjunctive | **Present** | | **Present Perfect** | |
| | werde<br>werdest<br>werde | werden<br>werdet<br>werden | sei geworden<br>seiest geworden<br>sei geworden | seien geworden<br>seiet geworden<br>seien geworden |
| | **Past** | | **Past Perfect** | |
| | würde<br>würdest<br>würde | würden<br>würdet<br>würden | wäre geworden<br>wärest geworden<br>wäre geworden | wären geworden<br>wäret geworden<br>wären geworden |
| | **Future** | | **Future Perfect** | |
| | werde werden<br>werdest werden<br>werde werden | werden werden<br>werdet werden<br>werden werden | werde geworden sein<br>werdest geworden sein<br>werde geworden sein | werden geworden sein<br>werdet geworden sein<br>werden geworden sein |
| | **Present and Future Conditional** | | **Past Conditional** | |
| | würde werden<br>würdest werden<br>würde werden | würden werden<br>würdet werden<br>würden werden | würde geworden sein<br>würdest geworden sein<br>würde geworden sein | würden geworden sein<br>würdet geworden sein<br>würden geworden sein |

## EXAMPLES

Meine Schwester ist Ärztin geworden. — My sister became a doctor.
Der alte Mann wird allmählich blind. — The old man is gradually going blind.

**werfen**
to throw
**Auxiliary verb:** haben **Past participle:** geworfen
**Imperative:** Wirf! Werft! Werfen Sie!

| Mode | Simple Tenses | | Compound Tenses | |
|---|---|---|---|---|
| | *Singular* | *Plural* | *Singular* | *Plural* |
| Indicative | **Present** | | **Present Perfect** | |
| | werfe<br>wirfst<br>wirft | werfen<br>werft<br>werfen | habe geworfen<br>hast geworfen<br>hat geworfen | haben geworfen<br>habt geworfen<br>haben geworfen |
| | **Past** | | **Past Perfect** | |
| | warf<br>warfst<br>warf | warfen<br>warft<br>warfen | hatte geworfen<br>hattest geworfen<br>hatte geworfen | hatten geworfen<br>hattet geworfen<br>hatten geworfen |
| | **Future** | | **Future Perfect** | |
| | werde werfen<br>wirst werfen<br>wird werfen | werden werfen<br>werdet werfen<br>werden werfen | werde geworfen haben<br>wirst geworfen haben<br>wird geworfen haben | werden geworfen haben<br>werdet geworfen haben<br>werden geworfen haben |
| Subjunctive | **Present** | | **Present Perfect** | |
| | werfe<br>werfest<br>werfe | werfen<br>werfet<br>werfen | habe geworfen<br>habest geworfen<br>habe geworfen | haben geworfen<br>habet geworfen<br>haben geworfen |
| | **Past** | | **Past Perfect** | |
| | würfe<br>würfest<br>würfe | würfen<br>würfet<br>würfen | hätte geworfen<br>hättest geworfen<br>hätte geworfen | hätten geworfen<br>hättet geworfen<br>hätten geworfen |
| | **Future** | | **Future Perfect** | |
| | werde werfen<br>werdest werfen<br>werde werfen | werden werfen<br>werdet werfen<br>werden werfen | werde geworfen haben<br>werdest geworfen haben<br>werde geworfen haben | werden geworfen haben<br>werdet geworfen haben<br>werden geworfen haben |
| | **Present and Future Conditional** | | **Past Conditional** | |
| | würde werfen<br>würdest werfen<br>würde werfen | würden werfen<br>würdet werfen<br>würden werfen | würde geworfen haben<br>würdest geworfen haben<br>würde geworfen haben | würden geworfen haben<br>würdet geworfen haben<br>würden geworfen haben |

## EXAMPLES

Marco hat den Ball über den Zaun geworfen. — Marco threw the ball over the fence.
Sie hat den langweiligen Roman beiseite geworfen. — She threw the boring novel aside.

**widerspiegeln (sich)**
to mirror, to reflect
**Auxiliary verb:** haben **Past participle:** widergespiegelt
**Imperative:** Spiegele wider! Spiegelt wider! Spiegeln Sie wider!

| Mode | Simple Tenses | | Compound Tenses | |
|---|---|---|---|---|
| | *Singular* | *Plural* | *Singular* | *Plural* |
| Indicative | **Present** | | **Present Perfect** | |
| | spiegele wider<br>spiegelst wider<br>spiegelt wider | spiegeln wider<br>spiegelt wider<br>spiegeln wider | habe widergespiegelt<br>hast widergespiegelt<br>hat widergespiegelt | haben widergespiegelt<br>habt widergespiegelt<br>haben widergespiegelt |
| | **Past** | | **Past Perfect** | |
| | spiegelte wider<br>spiegeltest wider<br>spiegelte wider | spiegelten wider<br>spiegeltet wider<br>spiegelten wider | hatte widergespiegelt<br>hattest widergespiegelt<br>hatte widergespiegelt | hatten widergespiegelt<br>hattet widergespiegelt<br>hatten widergespiegelt |
| | **Future** | | **Future Perfect** | |
| | werde widerspiegeln<br>wirst widerspiegeln<br>wird widerspiegeln | werden widerspiegeln<br>werdet widerspiegeln<br>werden widerspiegeln | werde widergespiegelt haben<br>wirst widergespiegelt haben<br>wird widergespiegelt haben | werden widergespiegelt haben<br>werdet widergespiegelt haben<br>werden widergespiegelt haben |
| Subjunctive | **Present** | | **Present Perfect** | |
| | spiegele wider<br>spiegelst wider<br>spiegele wider | spiegeln wider<br>spiegelt wider<br>spiegeln wider | habe widergespiegelt<br>habest widergespiegelt<br>habe widergespiegelt | haben widergespiegelt<br>habet widergespiegelt<br>haben widergespiegelt |
| | **Past** | | **Past Perfect** | |
| | spiegelte wider<br>spiegeltest wider<br>spiegelte wider | spiegelten wider<br>spiegeltet wider<br>spiegelten wider | hätte widergespiegelt<br>hättest widergespiegelt<br>hätte widergespiegelt | hätten widergespiegelt<br>hättet widergespiegelt<br>hätten widergespiegelt |
| | **Future** | | **Future Perfect** | |
| | werde widerspiegeln<br>werdest widerspiegeln<br>werde widerspiegeln | werden widerspiegeln<br>werdet widerspiegeln<br>werden widerspiegeln | werde widergespiegelt haben<br>werdest widergespiegelt haben<br>werde widergespiegelt haben | werden widergespiegelt haben<br>werdet widergespiegelt haben<br>werden widergespiegelt haben |
| | **Present and Future Conditional** | | **Past Conditional** | |
| | würde widerspiegeln<br>würdest widerspiegeln<br>würde widerspiegeln | würden widerspiegeln<br>würdet widerspiegeln<br>würden widerspiegeln | würde widergespiegelt haben<br>würdest widergespiegelt haben<br>würde widergespiegelt haben | würden widergespiegelt haben<br>würdet widergespiegelt haben<br>würden widergespiegelt haben |

## EXAMPLES

Seine harte Arbeit hat sich in guten Noten widergespiegelt. — His hard work was reflected in good grades.

Ihr Gesicht spiegelt sich im Wasser wider. — Her face is reflected in the water.

**wíederholen**
to bring back, to fetch
**Auxiliary verb:** haben **Past participle:** wiedergeholt
**Imperative:** Hole wieder! Holt wieder! Holen Sie wieder!

| Mode | Simple Tenses | | Compound Tenses | |
|---|---|---|---|---|
| | *Singular* | *Plural* | *Singular* | *Plural* |
| Indicative | **Present** | | **Present Perfect** | |
| | hole wieder<br>holst wieder<br>holt wieder | holen wieder<br>holt wieder<br>holen wieder | habe wiedergeholt<br>hast wiedergeholt<br>hat wiedergeholt | haben wiedergeholt<br>habt wiedergeholt<br>haben wiedergeholt |
| | **Past** | | **Past Perfect** | |
| | holte wieder<br>holtest wieder<br>holte wieder | holten wieder<br>holtet wieder<br>holten wieder | hatte wiedergeholt<br>hattest wiedergeholt<br>hatte wiedergeholt | hatten wiedergeholt<br>hattet wiedergeholt<br>hatten wiedergeholt |
| | **Future** | | **Future Perfect** | |
| | werde wiederholen<br>wirst wiederholen<br>wird wiederholen | werden wiederholen<br>werdet wiederholen<br>werden wiederholen | werde wiedergeholt haben<br>wirst wiedergeholt haben<br>wird wiedergeholt haben | werden wiedergeholt haben<br>werdet wiedergeholt haben<br>werden wiedergeholt haben |
| Subjunctive | **Present** | | **Present Perfect** | |
| | hole wieder<br>holest wieder<br>hole wieder | holen wieder<br>holet wieder<br>holen wieder | habe wiedergeholt<br>habest wiedergeholt<br>habe wiedergeholt | haben wiedergeholt<br>habet wiedergeholt<br>haben wiedergeholt |
| | **Past** | | **Past Perfect** | |
| | holte wieder<br>holtest wieder<br>holte wieder | holten wieder<br>holtet wieder<br>holten wieder | hätte wiedergeholt<br>hättest wiedergeholt<br>hätte wiedergeholt | hätten wiedergeholt<br>hättet wiedergeholt<br>hätten wiedergeholt |
| | **Future** | | **Future Perfect** | |
| | werde wiederholen<br>werdest wiederholen<br>werde wiederholen | werden wiederholen<br>werdet wiederholen<br>werden wiederholen | werde wiedergeholt haben<br>werdest wiedergeholt haben<br>werde wiedergeholt haben | werden wiedergeholt haben<br>werdet wiedergeholt haben<br>werden wiedergeholt haben |
| | **Present and Future Conditional** | | **Past Conditional** | |
| | würde wiederholen<br>würdest wiederholen<br>würde wiederholen | würden wiederholen<br>würdet wiederholen<br>würden wiederholen | würde wiedergeholt haben<br>würdest wiedergeholt haben<br>würde wiedergeholt haben | würden wiedergeholt haben<br>würdet wiedergeholt haben<br>würden wiedergeholt haben |

**Note:** This verb and the one that follows are spelled identically. This verb, however, has the accent on the prefix *wieder–*, which makes it a separable prefix.

## EXAMPLES

| | |
|---|---|
| Der Hund holte den Ball wieder. | The dog fetched the ball. |
| Ich habe mir dieses Buch wiedergeholt. | I got this book back. |

**wiederhólen**
to repeat
**Auxiliary verb:** haben **Past participle:** wiederholt
**Imperative:** Wiederhole! Wiederholt! Wiederholen Sie!

| Mode | Simple Tenses | | Compound Tenses | |
|---|---|---|---|---|
| | *Singular* | *Plural* | *Singular* | *Plural* |
| Indicative | **Present** | | **Present Perfect** | |
| | wiederhole<br>wiederholst<br>wiederholt | wiederholen<br>wiederholt<br>wiederholen | habe wiederholt<br>hast wiederholt<br>hat wiederholt | haben wiederholt<br>habt wiederholt<br>haben wiederholt |
| | **Past** | | **Past Perfect** | |
| | wiederholte<br>wiederholtest<br>wiederholte | wiederholten<br>wiederholtet<br>wiederholten | hatte wiederholt<br>hattest wiederholt<br>hatte wiederholt | hatten wiederholt<br>hattet wiederholt<br>hatten wiederholt |
| | **Future** | | **Future Perfect** | |
| | werde wiederholen<br>wirst wiederholen<br>wird wiederholen | werden wiederholen<br>werdet wiederholen<br>werden wiederholen | werde wiederholt haben<br>wirst wiederholt haben<br>wird wiederholt haben | werden wiederholt haben<br>werdet wiederholt haben<br>werden wiederholt haben |
| Subjunctive | **Present** | | **Present Perfect** | |
| | wiederhole<br>wiederholest<br>wiederhole | wiederholen<br>wiederholet<br>wiederholen | habe wiederholt<br>habest wiederholt<br>habe wiederholt | haben wiederholt<br>habet wiederholt<br>haben wiederholt |
| | **Past** | | **Past Perfect** | |
| | wiederholte<br>wiederholtest<br>wiederholte | wiederholten<br>wiederholtet<br>wiederholten | hätte wiederholt<br>hättest wiederholt<br>hätte wiederholt | hätten wiederholt<br>hättet wiederholt<br>hätten wiederholt |
| | **Future** | | **Future Perfect** | |
| | werde wiederholen<br>werdest wiederholen<br>werde wiederholen | werden wiederholen<br>werdet wiederholen<br>werden wiederholen | werde wiederholt haben<br>werdest wiederholt haben<br>werde wiederholt haben | werden wiederholt haben<br>werdet wiederholt haben<br>werden wiederholt haben |
| | **Present and Future Conditional** | | **Past Conditional** | |
| | würde wiederholen<br>würdest wiederholen<br>würde wiederholen | würden wiederholen<br>würdet wiederholen<br>würden wiederholen | würde wiederholt haben<br>würdest wiederholt haben<br>würde wiederholt haben | würden wiederholt haben<br>würdet wiederholt haben<br>würden wiederholt haben |

**Note:** This verb and the one that precedes it are spelled identically. This verb, however, has the accent on the stem of the verb, which makes the prefix *wieder–* an inseparable prefix.

## EXAMPLES

Bitte wiederholen Sie den letzten Satz! — Please repeat the last sentence.

Diese Klasse hat dieselbe Übung dreimal wiederholt. — This class repeated the same exercise three times.

**wirken**

to produce an effect, to work, to operate

**Auxiliary verb:** haben **Past participle:** gewirkt

**Imperative:** Wirke! Wirkt! Wirken Sie!

| Mode | Simple Tenses | | Compound Tenses | |
|---|---|---|---|---|
| | *Singular* | *Plural* | *Singular* | *Plural* |
| Indicative | **Present** | | **Present Perfect** | |
| | wirke<br>wirkst<br>wirkt | wirken<br>wirkt<br>wirken | habe gewirkt<br>hast gewirkt<br>hat gewirkt | haben gewirkt<br>habt gewirkt<br>haben gewirkt |
| | **Past** | | **Past Perfect** | |
| | wirkte<br>wirktest<br>wirkte | wirkten<br>wirktet<br>wirkten | hatte gewirkt<br>hattest gewirkt<br>hatte gewirkt | hatten gewirkt<br>hattet gewirkt<br>hatten gewirkt |
| | **Future** | | **Future Perfect** | |
| | werde wirken<br>wirst wirken<br>wird wirken | werden wirken<br>werdet wirken<br>werden wirken | werde gewirkt haben<br>wirst gewirkt haben<br>wird gewirkt haben | werden gewirkt haben<br>werdet gewirkt haben<br>werden gewirkt haben |
| Subjunctive | **Present** | | **Present Perfect** | |
| | wirke<br>wirkest<br>wirke | wirken<br>wirket<br>wirken | habe gewirkt<br>habest gewirkt<br>habe gewirkt | haben gewirkt<br>habet gewirkt<br>haben gewirkt |
| | **Past** | | **Past Perfect** | |
| | wirkte<br>wirktest<br>wirkte | wirkten<br>wirktet<br>wirkten | hätte gewirkt<br>hättest gewirkt<br>hätte gewirkt | hätten gewirkt<br>hättet gewirkt<br>hätten gewirkt |
| | **Future** | | **Future Perfect** | |
| | werde wirken<br>werdest wirken<br>werde wirken | werden wirken<br>werdet wirken<br>werden wirken | werde gewirkt haben<br>werdest gewirkt haben<br>werde gewirkt haben | werden gewirkt haben<br>werdet gewirkt haben<br>werden gewirkt haben |
| | **Present and Future Conditional** | | **Past Conditional** | |
| | würde wirken<br>würdest wirken<br>würde wirken | würden wirken<br>würdet wirken<br>würden wirken | würde gewirkt haben<br>würdest gewirkt haben<br>würde gewirkt haben | würden gewirkt haben<br>würdet gewirkt haben<br>würden gewirkt haben |

## EXAMPLES

Diese Tabletten wirken nicht mehr bei mir. — These pills aren't working on me anymore.

Jedes Wort, das er aussprach, wirkte. — Every word that he pronounced had an effect.

**wissen**
to know, to have knowledge
**Auxiliary verb:** haben **Past participle:** gewusst
**Imperative:** Wisse! Wisst! Wissen Sie!

| Mode | Simple Tenses | | Compound Tenses | |
|---|---|---|---|---|
| | *Singular* | *Plural* | *Singular* | *Plural* |
| Indicative | **Present** | | **Present Perfect** | |
| | weiß<br>weißt<br>weiß | wissen<br>wisst<br>wissen | habe gewusst<br>hast gewusst<br>hat gewusst | haben gewusst<br>habt gewusst<br>haben gewusst |
| | **Past** | | **Past Perfect** | |
| | wusste<br>wusstest<br>wusste | wussten<br>wusstet<br>wussten | hatte gewusst<br>hattest gewusst<br>hatte gewusst | hatten gewusst<br>hattet gewusst<br>hatten gewusst |
| | **Future** | | **Future Perfect** | |
| | werde wissen<br>wirst wissen<br>wird wissen | werden wissen<br>werdet wissen<br>werden wissen | werde gewusst haben<br>wirst gewusst haben<br>wird gewusst haben | werden gewusst haben<br>werdet gewusst haben<br>werden gewusst haben |
| Subjunctive | **Present** | | **Present Perfect** | |
| | wisse<br>wissest<br>wisse | wissen<br>wisset<br>wissen | habe gewusst<br>habest gewusst<br>habe gewusst | haben gewusst<br>habet gewusst<br>haben gewusst |
| | **Past** | | **Past Perfect** | |
| | wüsste<br>wüsstest<br>wüsste | wüssten<br>wüsstet<br>wüssten | hätte gewusst<br>hättest gewusst<br>hätte gewusst | hätten gewusst<br>hättet gewusst<br>hätten gewusst |
| | **Future** | | **Future Perfect** | |
| | werde wissen<br>werdest wissen<br>werde wissen | werden wissen<br>werdet wissen<br>werden wissen | werde gewusst haben<br>werdest gewusst haben<br>werde gewusst haben | werden gewusst haben<br>werdet gewusst haben<br>werden gewusst haben |
| | **Present and Future Conditional** | | **Past Conditional** | |
| | würde wissen<br>würdest wissen<br>würde wissen | würden wissen<br>würdet wissen<br>würden wissen | würde gewusst haben<br>würdest gewusst haben<br>würde gewusst haben | würden gewusst haben<br>würdet gewusst haben<br>würden gewusst haben |

## EXAMPLES

Wissen Sie, wo Herr Schneider wohnt?
Do you know where Mr. Schneider lives?

So viel ich weiß, wird Nils in der Hauptstadt bleiben.
As far as I know, Nils is going to stay in the capital.

**wohnen**
to live, to reside
**Auxiliary verb:** haben **Past participle:** gewohnt
**Imperative:** Wohne! Wohnt! Wohnen Sie!

| Mode | Simple Tenses | | Compound Tenses | |
|---|---|---|---|---|
| | *Singular* | *Plural* | *Singular* | *Plural* |
| Indicative | **Present** | | **Present Perfect** | |
| | wohne<br>wohnst<br>wohnt | wohnen<br>wohnt<br>wohnen | habe gewohnt<br>hast gewohnt<br>hat gewohnt | haben gewohnt<br>habt gewohnt<br>haben gewohnt |
| | **Past** | | **Past Perfect** | |
| | wohnte<br>wohntest<br>wohnte | wohnten<br>wohntet<br>wohnten | hatte gewohnt<br>hattest gewohnt<br>hatte gewohnt | hatten gewohnt<br>hattet gewohnt<br>hatten gewohnt |
| | **Future** | | **Future Perfect** | |
| | werde wohnen<br>wirst wohnen<br>wird wohnen | werden wohnen<br>werdet wohnen<br>werden wohnen | werde gewohnt haben<br>wirst gewohnt haben<br>wird gewohnt haben | werden gewohnt haben<br>werdet gewohnt haben<br>werden gewohnt haben |
| Subjunctive | **Present** | | **Present Perfect** | |
| | wohne<br>wohnest<br>wohne | wohnen<br>wohnet<br>wohnen | habe gewohnt<br>habest gewohnt<br>habe gewohnt | haben gewohnt<br>habet gewohnt<br>haben gewohnt |
| | **Past** | | **Past Perfect** | |
| | wohnte<br>wohntest<br>wohnte | wohnten<br>wohntet<br>wohnten | hätte gewohnt<br>hättest gewohnt<br>hätte gewohnt | hätten gewohnt<br>hättet gewohnt<br>hätten gewohnt |
| | **Future** | | **Future Perfect** | |
| | werde wohnen<br>werdest wohnen<br>werde wohnen | werden wohnen<br>werdet wohnen<br>werden wohnen | werde gewohnt haben<br>werdest gewohnt haben<br>werde gewohnt haben | werden gewohnt haben<br>werdet gewohnt haben<br>werden gewohnt haben |
| | **Present and Future Conditional** | | **Past Conditional** | |
| | würde wohnen<br>würdest wohnen<br>würde wohnen | würden wohnen<br>würdet wohnen<br>würden wohnen | würde gewohnt haben<br>würdest gewohnt haben<br>würde gewohnt haben | würden gewohnt haben<br>würdet gewohnt haben<br>würden gewohnt haben |

## EXAMPLES

Wie lange habt ihr in Oldenburg gewohnt? — How long did you live in Oldenburg?
Mein Neffe wohnt nicht weit von hier. — My nephew doesn't live far from here.

**wollen**
to want
**Auxiliary verb:** haben **Past participle:** gewollt
**Imperative:** Wolle! Wollt! Wollen Sie!

| Mode | Simple Tenses | | Compound Tenses | |
|---|---|---|---|---|
| | *Singular* | *Plural* | *Singular* | *Plural* |
| Indicative | **Present** | | **Present Perfect** | |
| | will<br>willst<br>will | wollen<br>wollt<br>wollen | habe gewollt<br>hast gewollt<br>hat gewollt | haben gewollt<br>habt gewollt<br>haben gewollt |
| | **Past** | | **Past Perfect** | |
| | wollte<br>wolltest<br>wollte | wollten<br>wolltet<br>wollten | hatte gewollt<br>hattest gewollt<br>hatte gewollt | hatten gewollt<br>hattet gewollt<br>hatten gewollt |
| | **Future** | | **Future Perfect** | |
| | werde wollen<br>wirst wollen<br>wird wollen | werden wollen<br>werdet wollen<br>werden wollen | werde gewollt haben<br>wirst gewollt haben<br>wird gewollt haben | werden gewollt haben<br>werdet gewollt haben<br>werden gewollt haben |
| Subjunctive | **Present** | | **Present Perfect** | |
| | wolle<br>wollest<br>wolle | wollen<br>wollet<br>wollen | habe gewollt<br>habest gewollt<br>habe gewollt | haben gewollt<br>habet gewollt<br>haben gewollt |
| | **Past** | | **Past Perfect** | |
| | wollte<br>wolltest<br>wollte | wollten<br>wolltet<br>wollten | hätte gewollt<br>hättest gewollt<br>hätte gewollt | hätten gewollt<br>hättet gewollt<br>hätten gewollt |
| | **Future** | | **Future Perfect** | |
| | werde wollen<br>werdest wollen<br>werde wollen | werden wollen<br>werdet wollen<br>werden wollen | werde gewollt haben<br>werdest gewollt haben<br>werde gewollt haben | werden gewollt haben<br>werdet gewollt haben<br>werden gewollt haben |
| | **Present and Future Conditional** | | **Past Conditional** | |
| | würde wollen<br>würdest wollen<br>würde wollen | würden wollen<br>würdet wollen<br>würden wollen | würde gewollt haben<br>würdest gewollt haben<br>würde gewollt haben | würden gewollt haben<br>würdet gewollt haben<br>würden gewollt haben |

**Note:** This verb is a modal auxiliary. In the perfect and future tenses, when there is a second verb in the sentence, a double-infinitive structure is required: *Haben Sie mit ihm sprechen wollen?* ("Did you want to speak with him?")

## EXAMPLES

| | |
|---|---|
| Er will, dass sein Sohn Professor wird. | He wants his son to become a professor. |
| Was wollen Sie hier? | What do you want here? |

**wünschen**

to wish, to desire

**Auxiliary verb:** haben **Past participle:** gewünscht

**Imperative:** Wünsche! Wünscht! Wünschen Sie!

| Mode | Simple Tenses | | Compound Tenses | |
|---|---|---|---|---|
| | *Singular* | *Plural* | *Singular* | *Plural* |
| Indicative | **Present** | | **Present Perfect** | |
| | wünsche<br>wünschst<br>wünscht | wünschen<br>wünscht<br>wünschen | habe gewünscht<br>hast gewünscht<br>hat gewünscht | haben gewünscht<br>habt gewünscht<br>haben gewünscht |
| | **Past** | | **Past Perfect** | |
| | wünschte<br>wünschtest<br>wünschte | wünschten<br>wünschtet<br>wünschten | hatte gewünscht<br>hattest gewünscht<br>hatte gewünscht | hatten gewünscht<br>hattet gewünscht<br>hatten gewünscht |
| | **Future** | | **Future Perfect** | |
| | werde wünschen<br>wirst wünschen<br>wird wünschen | werden wünschen<br>werdet wünschen<br>werden wünschen | werde gewünscht haben<br>wirst gewünscht haben<br>wird gewünscht haben | werden gewünscht haben<br>werdet gewünscht haben<br>werden gewünscht haben |
| Subjunctive | **Present** | | **Present Perfect** | |
| | wünsche<br>wünschest<br>wünsche | wünschen<br>wünschet<br>wünschen | habe gewünscht<br>habest gewünscht<br>habe gewünscht | haben gewünscht<br>habet gewünscht<br>haben gewünscht |
| | **Past** | | **Past Perfect** | |
| | wünschte<br>wünschtest<br>wünschte | wünschten<br>wünschtet<br>wünschten | hätte gewünscht<br>hättest gewünscht<br>hätte gewünscht | hätten gewünscht<br>hättet gewünscht<br>hätten gewünscht |
| | **Future** | | **Future Perfect** | |
| | werde wünschen<br>werdest wünschen<br>werde wünschen | werden wünschen<br>werdet wünschen<br>werden wünschen | werde gewünscht haben<br>werdest gewünscht haben<br>werde gewünscht haben | werden gewünscht haben<br>werdet gewünscht haben<br>werden gewünscht haben |
| | **Present and Future Conditional** | | **Past Conditional** | |
| | würde wünschen<br>würdest wünschen<br>würde wünschen | würden wünschen<br>würdet wünschen<br>würden wünschen | würde gewünscht haben<br>würdest gewünscht haben<br>würde gewünscht haben | würden gewünscht haben<br>würdet gewünscht haben<br>würden gewünscht haben |

## EXAMPLE

| | |
|---|---|
| Ich wünschte, ich könnte einen nagelneuen Wagen kaufen. | I wish I could buy a brand-new car. |

**zahlen**
to pay
**Auxiliary verb:** haben **Past participle:** gezahlt
**Imperative:** Zahle! Zahlt! Zahlen Sie!

| Mode | Simple Tenses | | Compound Tenses | |
|---|---|---|---|---|
| | *Singular* | *Plural* | *Singular* | *Plural* |
| Indicative | **Present** | | **Present Perfect** | |
| | zahle<br>zahlst<br>zahlt | zahlen<br>zahlt<br>zahlen | habe gezahlt<br>hast gezahlt<br>hat gezahlt | haben gezahlt<br>habt gezahlt<br>haben gezahlt |
| | **Past** | | **Past Perfect** | |
| | zahlte<br>zahltest<br>zahlte | zahlten<br>zahltet<br>zahlten | hatte gezahlt<br>hattest gezahlt<br>hatte gezahlt | hatten gezahlt<br>hattet gezahlt<br>hatten gezahlt |
| | **Future** | | **Future Perfect** | |
| | werde zahlen<br>wirst zahlen<br>wird zahlen | werden zahlen<br>werdet zahlen<br>werden zahlen | werde gezahlt haben<br>wirst gezahlt haben<br>wird gezahlt haben | werden gezahlt haben<br>werdet gezahlt haben<br>werden gezahlt haben |
| Subjunctive | **Present** | | **Present Perfect** | |
| | zahle<br>zahlest<br>zahle | zahlen<br>zahlet<br>zahlen | habe gezahlt<br>habest gezahlt<br>habe gezahlt | haben gezahlt<br>habet gezahlt<br>haben gezahlt |
| | **Past** | | **Past Perfect** | |
| | zahlte<br>zahltest<br>zahlte | zahlten<br>zahltet<br>zahlten | hätte gezahlt<br>hättest gezahlt<br>hätte gezahlt | hätten gezahlt<br>hättet gezahlt<br>hätten gezahlt |
| | **Future** | | **Future Perfect** | |
| | werde zahlen<br>werdest zahlen<br>werde zahlen | werden zahlen<br>werdet zahlen<br>werden zahlen | werde gezahlt haben<br>werdest gezahlt haben<br>werde gezahlt haben | werden gezahlt haben<br>werdet gezahlt haben<br>werden gezahlt haben |
| | **Present and Future Conditional** | | **Past Conditional** | |
| | würde zahlen<br>würdest zahlen<br>würde zahlen | würden zahlen<br>würdet zahlen<br>würden zahlen | würde gezahlt haben<br>würdest gezahlt haben<br>würde gezahlt haben | würden gezahlt haben<br>würdet gezahlt haben<br>würden gezahlt haben |

## EXAMPLES

Kann ich mit Kreditkarte zahlen? — May I pay by credit card?
Zahlen, bitte! — Check, please.

**zählen**

to count, to reckon

**Auxiliary verb:** haben **Past participle:** gezählt

**Imperative:** Zähle! Zählt! Zählen Sie!

| Mode | Simple Tenses | | Compound Tenses | |
|---|---|---|---|---|
| | *Singular* | *Plural* | *Singular* | *Plural* |
| Indicative | **Present** | | **Present Perfect** | |
| | zähle<br>zählst<br>zählt | zählen<br>zählt<br>zählen | habe gezählt<br>hast gezählt<br>hat gezählt | haben gezählt<br>habt gezählt<br>haben gezählt |
| | **Past** | | **Past Perfect** | |
| | zählte<br>zähltest<br>zählte | zählten<br>zähltet<br>zählten | hatte gezählt<br>hattest gezählt<br>hatte gezählt | hatten gezählt<br>hattet gezählt<br>hatten gezählt |
| | **Future** | | **Future Perfect** | |
| | werde zählen<br>wirst zählen<br>wird zählen | werden zählen<br>werdet zählen<br>werden zählen | werde gezählt haben<br>wirst gezählt haben<br>wird gezählt haben | werden gezählt haben<br>werdet gezählt haben<br>werden gezählt haben |
| Subjunctive | **Present** | | **Present Perfect** | |
| | zähle<br>zählest<br>zähle | zählen<br>zählet<br>zählen | habe gezählt<br>habest gezählt<br>habe gezählt | haben gezählt<br>habet gezählt<br>haben gezählt |
| | **Past** | | **Past Perfect** | |
| | zählte<br>zähltest<br>zählte | zählten<br>zähltet<br>zählten | hätte gezählt<br>hättest gezählt<br>hätte gezählt | hätten gezählt<br>hättet gezählt<br>hätten gezählt |
| | **Future** | | **Future Perfect** | |
| | werde zählen<br>werdest zählen<br>werde zählen | werden zählen<br>werdet zählen<br>werden zählen | werde gezählt haben<br>werdest gezählt haben<br>werde gezählt haben | werden gezählt haben<br>werdet gezählt haben<br>werden gezählt haben |
| | **Present and Future Conditional** | | **Past Conditional** | |
| | würde zählen<br>würdest zählen<br>würde zählen | würden zählen<br>würdet zählen<br>würden zählen | würde gezählt haben<br>würdest gezählt haben<br>würde gezählt haben | würden gezählt haben<br>würdet gezählt haben<br>würden gezählt haben |

## EXAMPLES

Der Dreijährige kann schon von eins bis zehn zählen.

The 3-year-old can already count from one to ten.

Der Kranke ist schwach. Seine Tage sind gezählt.

The patient is weak. His days are numbered.

**zeigen**
to show, to point out
**Auxiliary verb:** haben **Past participle:** gezeigt
**Imperative:** Zeige! Zeigt! Zeigen Sie!

| Mode | Simple Tenses | | Compound Tenses | |
|---|---|---|---|---|
| | *Singular* | *Plural* | *Singular* | *Plural* |
| Indicative | **Present** | | **Present Perfect** | |
| | zeige<br>zeigst<br>zeigt | zeigen<br>zeigt<br>zeigen | habe gezeigt<br>hast gezeigt<br>hat gezeigt | haben gezeigt<br>habt gezeigt<br>haben gezeigt |
| | **Past** | | **Past Perfect** | |
| | zeigte<br>zeigtest<br>zeigte | zeigten<br>zeigtet<br>zeigten | hatte gezeigt<br>hattest gezeigt<br>hatte gezeigt | hatten gezeigt<br>hattet gezeigt<br>hatten gezeigt |
| | **Future** | | **Future Perfect** | |
| | werde zeigen<br>wirst zeigen<br>wird zeigen | werden zeigen<br>werdet zeigen<br>werden zeigen | werde gezeigt haben<br>wirst gezeigt haben<br>wird gezeigt haben | werden gezeigt haben<br>werdet gezeigt haben<br>werden gezeigt haben |
| Subjunctive | **Present** | | **Present Perfect** | |
| | zeige<br>zeigest<br>zeige | zeigen<br>zeiget<br>zeigen | habe gezeigt<br>habest gezeigt<br>habe gezeigt | haben gezeigt<br>habet gezeigt<br>haben gezeigt |
| | **Past** | | **Past Perfect** | |
| | zeigte<br>zeigtest<br>zeigte | zeigten<br>zeigtet<br>zeigten | hätte gezeigt<br>hättest gezeigt<br>hätte gezeigt | hätten gezeigt<br>hättet gezeigt<br>hätten gezeigt |
| | **Future** | | **Future Perfect** | |
| | werde zeigen<br>werdest zeigen<br>werde zeigen | werden zeigen<br>werdet zeigen<br>werden zeigen | werde gezeigt haben<br>werdest gezeigt haben<br>werde gezeigt haben | werden gezeigt haben<br>werdet gezeigt haben<br>werden gezeigt haben |
| | **Present and Future Conditional** | | **Past Conditional** | |
| | würde zeigen<br>würdest zeigen<br>würde zeigen | würden zeigen<br>würdet zeigen<br>würden zeigen | würde gezeigt haben<br>würdest gezeigt haben<br>würde gezeigt haben | würden gezeigt haben<br>würdet gezeigt haben<br>würden gezeigt haben |

## EXAMPLES

Ich habe den Kindern auf der Landkarte gezeigt, wo Deutschland liegt.
Zeige uns, was du geschrieben hast!

I showed the children on the map where Germany is located.
Show us what you wrote.

**zerreißen**

to tear up, to rip to pieces

**Auxiliary verb:** haben **Past participle:** zerrissen

**Imperative:** Zerreiße! Zerreißt! Zerreißen Sie!

| Mode | Simple Tenses | | Compound Tenses | |
|---|---|---|---|---|
| | *Singular* | *Plural* | *Singular* | *Plural* |
| Indicative | **Present** | | **Present Perfect** | |
| | zerreiße<br>zerreißt<br>zerreißt | zerreißen<br>zerreißt<br>zerreißen | habe zerrissen<br>hast zerrissen<br>hat zerrissen | haben zerrissen<br>habt zerrissen<br>haben zerrissen |
| | **Past** | | **Past Perfect** | |
| | zerriss<br>zerrissest<br>zerriss | zerrissen<br>zerrisst<br>zerrissen | hatte zerrissen<br>hattest zerrissen<br>hatte zerrissen | hatten zerrissen<br>hattet zerrissen<br>hatten zerrissen |
| | **Future** | | **Future Perfect** | |
| | werde zerreißen<br>wirst zerreißen<br>wird zerreißen | werden zerreißen<br>werdet zerreißen<br>werden zerreißen | werde zerrissen haben<br>wirst zerrissen haben<br>wird zerrissen haben | werden zerrissen haben<br>werdet zerrissen haben<br>werden zerrissen haben |
| Subjunctive | **Present** | | **Present Perfect** | |
| | zerreiße<br>zerreißest<br>zerreiße | zerreißen<br>zerreißet<br>zerreißen | habe zerrissen<br>habest zerrissen<br>habe zerrissen | haben zerrissen<br>habet zerrissen<br>haben zerrissen |
| | **Past** | | **Past Perfect** | |
| | zerrisse<br>zerrissest<br>zerrisse | zerrissen<br>zerrisset<br>zerrissen | hätte zerrissen<br>hättest zerrissen<br>hätte zerrissen | hätten zerrissen<br>hättet zerrissen<br>hätten zerrissen |
| | **Future** | | **Future Perfect** | |
| | werde zerreißen<br>werdest zerreißen<br>werde zerreißen | werden zerreißen<br>werdet zerreißen<br>werden zerreißen | werde zerrissen haben<br>werdest zerrissen haben<br>werde zerrissen haben | werden zerrissen haben<br>werdet zerrissen haben<br>werden zerrissen haben |
| | **Present and Future Conditional** | | **Past Conditional** | |
| | würde zerreißen<br>würdest zerreißen<br>würde zerreißen | würden zerreißen<br>würdet zerreißen<br>würden zerreißen | würde zerrissen haben<br>würdest zerrissen haben<br>würde zerrissen haben | würden zerrissen haben<br>würdet zerrissen haben<br>würden zerrissen haben |

**Note:** Without a prefix, the principal parts of this verb are *reißt, riss, hat gerissen.* With separable prefixes, the principal parts are, for example, *reißt aus, riss aus, hat* or *ist ausgerissen.*

## EXAMPLES

Er schrieb ihr elf Liebesbriefe. Langsam zerriss sie sie.

He wrote her 11 love letters. She slowly tore them up.

Hilf mir! Ich kann mich schließlich nicht zerreißen.

Help me. I can't be in two places at one time, after all.

**zerschmettern**
to smash, to shatter
**Auxiliary verb:** haben **Past participle:** zerschmettert
**Imperative:** Zerschmettere! Zerschmettert! Zerschmettern Sie!

| Mode | Simple Tenses | | Compound Tenses | |
|---|---|---|---|---|
| | *Singular* | *Plural* | *Singular* | *Plural* |
| Indicative | **Present** | | **Present Perfect** | |
| | zerschmettere<br>zerschmetterst<br>zerschmettert | zerschmettern<br>zerschmettert<br>zerschmettern | habe zerschmettert<br>hast zerschmettert<br>hat zerschmettert | haben zerschmettert<br>habt zerschmettert<br>haben zerschmettert |
| | **Past** | | **Past Perfect** | |
| | zerschmetterte<br>zerschmettertest<br>zerschmetterte | zerschmetterten<br>zerschmettertet<br>zerschmetterten | hatte zerschmettert<br>hattest zerschmettert<br>hatte zerschmettert | hatten zerschmettert<br>hattet zerschmettert<br>hatten zerschmettert |
| | **Future** | | **Future Perfect** | |
| | werde zerschmettern<br>wirst zerschmettern<br>wird zerschmettern | werden zerschmettern<br>werdet zerschmettern<br>werden zerschmettern | werde zerschmettert haben<br>wirst zerschmettert haben<br>wird zerschmettert haben | werden zerschmettert haben<br>werdet zerschmettert haben<br>werden zerschmettert haben |
| Subjunctive | **Present** | | **Present Perfect** | |
| | zerschmettere<br>zerschmetterst<br>zerschmettere | zerschmettern<br>zerschmettert<br>zerschmettern | habe zerschmettert<br>habest zerschmettert<br>habe zerschmettert | haben zerschmettert<br>habet zerschmettert<br>haben zerschmettert |
| | **Past** | | **Past Perfect** | |
| | zerschmetterte<br>zerschmettertest<br>zerschmetterte | zerschmetterten<br>zerschmettertet<br>zerschmetterten | hätte zerschmettert<br>hättest zerschmettert<br>hätte zerschmettert | hätten zerschmettert<br>hättet zerschmettert<br>hätten zerschmettert |
| | **Future** | | **Future Perfect** | |
| | werde zerschmettern<br>werdest zerschmet-<br>tern<br>werde zerschmettern | werden zerschmettern<br>werdet zerschmettern<br>werden zerschmettern | werde zerschmettert haben<br>werdest zerschmettert haben<br>werde zerschmettert haben | werden zerschmettert haben<br>werdet zerschmettert haben<br>werden zerschmettert haben |
| | **Present and Future Conditional** | | **Past Conditional** | |
| | würde zerschmettern<br>würdest zerschmet-<br>tern<br>würde zerschmettern | würden zerschmettern<br>würdet zerschmettern<br>würden zerschmettern | würde zerschmettert haben<br>würdest zerschmettert haben<br>würde zerschmettert haben | würden zerschmettert haben<br>würdet zerschmettert haben<br>würden zerschmettert haben |

## EXAMPLES

Der zornige Riese zerschmetterte den Felsen. — The angry giant smashed the rock to pieces.
Überall auf dem Boden liegt zerschmettertes Glas. — There's shattered glass all over the floor.

**zerstören**
to destroy
**Auxiliary verb:** haben **Past participle:** zerstört
**Imperative:** Zerstöre! Zerstört! Zerstören Sie!

| Mode | Simple Tenses | | Compound Tenses | |
|---|---|---|---|---|
| | *Singular* | *Plural* | *Singular* | *Plural* |
| Indicative | **Present** | | **Present Perfect** | |
| | zerstöre<br>zerstörst<br>zerstört | zerstören<br>zerstört<br>zerstören | habe zerstört<br>hast zerstört<br>hat zerstört | haben zerstört<br>habt zerstört<br>haben zerstört |
| | **Past** | | **Past Perfect** | |
| | zerstörte<br>zerstörtest<br>zerstörte | zerstörten<br>zerstörtet<br>zerstörten | hatte zerstört<br>hattest zerstört<br>hatte zerstört | hatten zerstört<br>hattet zerstört<br>hatten zerstört |
| | **Future** | | **Future Perfect** | |
| | werde zerstören<br>wirst zerstören<br>wird zerstören | werden zerstören<br>werdet zerstören<br>werden zerstören | werde zerstört haben<br>wirst zerstört haben<br>wird zerstört haben | werden zerstört haben<br>werdet zerstört haben<br>werden zerstört haben |
| Subjunctive | **Present** | | **Present Perfect** | |
| | zerstöre<br>zerstörest<br>zerstöre | zerstören<br>zerstöret<br>zerstören | habe zerstört<br>habest zerstört<br>habe zerstört | haben zerstört<br>habet zerstört<br>haben zerstört |
| | **Past** | | **Past Perfect** | |
| | zerstörte<br>zerstörtest<br>zerstörte | zerstörten<br>zerstörtet<br>zerstörten | hätte zerstört<br>hättest zerstört<br>hätte zerstört | hätten zerstört<br>hättet zerstört<br>hätten zerstört |
| | **Future** | | **Future Perfect** | |
| | werde zerstören<br>werdest zerstören<br>werde zerstören | werden zerstören<br>werdet zerstören<br>werden zerstören | werde zerstört haben<br>werdest zerstört haben<br>werde zerstört haben | werden zerstört haben<br>werdet zerstört haben<br>werden zerstört haben |
| | **Present and Future Conditional** | | **Past Conditional** | |
| | würde zerstören<br>würdest zerstören<br>würde zerstören | würden zerstören<br>würdet zerstören<br>würden zerstören | würde zerstört haben<br>würdest zerstört haben<br>würde zerstört haben | würden zerstört haben<br>würdet zerstört haben<br>würden zerstört haben |

# EXAMPLES

Die Schule ist von einem Erdbeben zerstört worden.
The school was destroyed by an earthquake.

Das Feuer zerstörte ein Haus nach dem anderen.
The fire destroyed one house after another.

**ziehen**
to pull, to tow, to draw
**Auxiliary verb:** haben **Past participle:** gezogen
**Imperative:** Ziehe! Zieht! Ziehen Sie!

| Mode | Simple Tenses | | Compound Tenses | |
|---|---|---|---|---|
| | *Singular* | *Plural* | *Singular* | *Plural* |
| Indicative | **Present** | | **Present Perfect** | |
| | ziehe<br>ziehst<br>zieht | ziehen<br>zieht<br>ziehen | habe gezogen<br>hast gezogen<br>hat gezogen | haben gezogen<br>habt gezogen<br>haben gezogen |
| | **Past** | | **Past Perfect** | |
| | zog<br>zogst<br>zog | zogen<br>zogt<br>zogen | hatte gezogen<br>hattest gezogen<br>hatte gezogen | hatten gezogen<br>hattet gezogen<br>hatten gezogen |
| | **Future** | | **Future Perfect** | |
| | werde ziehen<br>wirst ziehen<br>wird ziehen | werden ziehen<br>werdet ziehen<br>werden ziehen | werde gezogen haben<br>wirst gezogen haben<br>wird gezogen haben | werden gezogen haben<br>werdet gezogen haben<br>werden gezogen haben |
| Subjunctive | **Present** | | **Present Perfect** | |
| | ziehe<br>ziehest<br>ziehe | ziehen<br>ziehet<br>ziehen | habe gezogen<br>habest gezogen<br>habe gezogen | haben gezogen<br>habet gezogen<br>haben gezogen |
| | **Past** | | **Past Perfect** | |
| | zöge<br>zögest<br>zöge | zögen<br>zöget<br>zöge | hätte gezogen<br>hättest gezogen<br>hätte gezogen | hätten gezogen<br>hättet gezogen<br>hätten gezogen |
| | **Future** | | **Future Perfect** | |
| | werde ziehen<br>werdest ziehen<br>werde ziehen | werden ziehen<br>werdet ziehen<br>werden ziehen | werde gezogen haben<br>werdest gezogen haben<br>werde gezogen haben | werden gezogen haben<br>werdet gezogen haben<br>werden gezogen haben |
| | **Present and Future Conditional** | | **Past Conditional** | |
| | würde ziehen<br>würdest ziehen<br>würde ziehen | würden ziehen<br>würdet ziehen<br>würden ziehen | würde gezogen haben<br>würdest gezogen haben<br>würde gezogen haben | würden gezogen haben<br>würdet gezogen haben<br>würden gezogen haben |

**Note:** With inseparable prefixes, the principal parts of this verb are, for example, *erzieht, erzog, hat erzogen.* With separable prefixes, the principal parts are, for example, *zieht zurück, zog zurück, hat zurückgezogen.*

## EXAMPLES

Der kleine Junge zog seine Schwester immer am Pferdeschwanz.
The little boy always pulled his sister's ponytail.

Vor einer Woche hat Opa seine letzten vier Zähne ziehen lassen.
A week ago, grandpa had his last four teeth pulled out.

**zugeben**

to add, to give into, to admit

**Auxiliary verb:** haben **Past participle:** zugegeben

**Imperative:** Gib zu! Gebt zu! Geben Sie zu!

| Mode | Simple Tenses | | Compound Tenses | |
|---|---|---|---|---|
| | *Singular* | *Plural* | *Singular* | *Plural* |
| Indicative | **Present** | | **Present Perfect** | |
| | gebe zu<br>gibst zu<br>gibt zu | geben zu<br>gebt zu<br>geben zu | habe zugegeben<br>hast zugegeben<br>hat zugegeben | haben zugegeben<br>habt zugegeben<br>haben zugegeben |
| | **Past** | | **Past Perfect** | |
| | gab zu<br>gabst zu<br>gab zu | gaben zu<br>gabt zu<br>gaben zu | hatte zugegeben<br>hattest zugegeben<br>hatte zugegeben | hatten zugegeben<br>hattet zugegeben<br>hatten zugegeben |
| | **Future** | | **Future Perfect** | |
| | werde zugeben<br>wirst zugeben<br>wird zugeben | werden zugeben<br>werdet zugeben<br>werden zugeben | werde zugegeben haben<br>wirst zugegeben haben<br>wird zugegeben haben | werden zugegeben haben<br>werdet zugegeben haben<br>werden zugegeben haben |
| Subjunctive | **Present** | | **Present Perfect** | |
| | gebe zu<br>gebest zu<br>gebe zu | geben zu<br>gebet zu<br>geben zu | habe zugegeben<br>habest zugegeben<br>habe zugegeben | haben zugegeben<br>habet zugegeben<br>haben zugegeben |
| | **Past** | | **Past Perfect** | |
| | gäbe zu<br>gäbest zu<br>gäbe zu | gäben zu<br>gäbet zu<br>gäben zu | hätte zugegeben<br>hättest zugegeben<br>hätte zugegeben | hätten zugegeben<br>hättet zugegeben<br>hätten zugegeben |
| | **Future** | | **Future Perfect** | |
| | werde zugeben<br>werdest zugeben<br>werde zugeben | werden zugeben<br>werdet zugeben<br>werden zugeben | werde zugegeben haben<br>werdest zugegeben haben<br>werde zugegeben haben | werden zugegeben haben<br>werdet zugegeben haben<br>werden zugegeben haben |
| | **Present and Future Conditional** | | **Past Conditional** | |
| | würde zugeben<br>würdest zugeben<br>würde zugeben | würden zugeben<br>würdet zugeben<br>würden zugeben | würde zugegeben haben<br>würdest zugegeben haben<br>würde zugegeben haben | würden zugegeben haben<br>würdet zugegeben haben<br>würden zugegeben haben |

**Note:** With inseparable prefixes, the principal parts of this verb are, for example, *vergibt, vergab, hat vergeben.* Without a prefix, the principal parts are *gibt, gab, hat gegeben.*

## EXAMPLES

Wir mussten zugeben, dass Anke und Martin viel mehr als wir gearbeitet hatten.
We had to admit that Anke and Martin worked a lot more than we did.

Ich gebe zu, du hast wie immer Recht.
I admit it—you're right as usual.

**zuhören**
to listen to, to pay attention to
**Auxiliary verb:** haben **Past participle:** zugehört
**Imperative:** Höre zu! Hört zu! Hören Sie zu!

| Mode | Simple Tenses | | Compound Tenses | |
|---|---|---|---|---|
| | *Singular* | *Plural* | *Singular* | *Plural* |
| Indicative | **Present** | | **Present Perfect** | |
| | höre zu<br>hörst zu<br>hört zu | hören zu<br>hört zu<br>hören zu | habe zugehört<br>hast zugehört<br>hat zugehört | haben zugehört<br>habt zugehört<br>haben zugehört |
| | **Past** | | **Past Perfect** | |
| | hörte zu<br>hörtest zu<br>hörte zu | hörten zu<br>hörtet zu<br>hörten zu | hatte zugehört<br>hattest zugehört<br>hatte zugehört | hatten zugehört<br>hattet zugehört<br>hatten zugehört |
| | **Future** | | **Future Perfect** | |
| | werde zuhören<br>wirst zuhören<br>wird zuhören | werden zuhören<br>werdet zuhören<br>werden zuhören | werde zugehört haben<br>wirst zugehört haben<br>wird zugehört haben | werden zugehört haben<br>werdet zugehört haben<br>werden zugehört haben |
| Subjunctive | **Present** | | **Present Perfect** | |
| | höre zu<br>hörest zu<br>höre zu | hören zu<br>höret zu<br>hören zu | habe zugehört<br>habest zugehört<br>habe zugehört | haben zugehört<br>habet zugehört<br>haben zugehört |
| | **Past** | | **Past Perfect** | |
| | hörte zu<br>hörtest zu<br>hörte zu | hörten zu<br>hörtet zu<br>hörten zu | hätte zugehört<br>hättest zugehört<br>hätte zugehört | hätten zugehört<br>hättet zugehört<br>hätten zugehört |
| | **Future** | | **Future Perfect** | |
| | werde zuhören<br>werdest zuhören<br>werde zuhören | werden zuhören<br>werdet zuhören<br>werden zuhören | werde zugehört haben<br>werdest zugehört haben<br>werde zugehört haben | werden zugehört haben<br>werdet zugehört haben<br>werden zugehört haben |
| | **Present and Future Conditional** | | **Past Conditional** | |
| | würde zuhören<br>würdest zuhören<br>würde zuhören | würden zuhören<br>würdet zuhören<br>würden zuhören | würde zugehört haben<br>würdest zugehört haben<br>würde zugehört haben | würden zugehört haben<br>würdet zugehört haben<br>würden zugehört haben |

## EXAMPLES

Kinder, hört genau zu!
Children, listen carefully.

Ich habe dem Redner zugehört, ohne ein einziges Wort verstanden zu haben.
I listened to the speaker without understanding a single word.

**zunehmen**

to take on, to increase, to put on weight

**Auxiliary verb:** haben **Past participle:** zugenommen

**Imperative:** Nimm zu! Nehmt zu! Nehmen Sie zu!

| Mode | Simple Tenses | | Compound Tenses | |
|---|---|---|---|---|
| | *Singular* | *Plural* | *Singular* | *Plural* |
| Indicative | **Present** | | **Present Perfect** | |
| | nehme zu<br>nimmst zu<br>nimmt zu | nehmen zu<br>nehmt zu<br>nehmen zu | habe zugenommen<br>hast zugenommen<br>hat zugenommen | haben zugenommen<br>habt zugenommen<br>haben zugenommen |
| | **Past** | | **Past Perfect** | |
| | nahm zu<br>nahmst zu<br>nahm zu | nahmen zu<br>nahmt zu<br>nahmen zu | hatte zugenommen<br>hattest zugenommen<br>hatte zugenommen | hatten zugenommen<br>hattet zugenommen<br>hatten zugenommen |
| | **Future** | | **Future Perfect** | |
| | werde zunehmen<br>wirst zunehmen<br>wird zunehmen | werden zunehmen<br>werdet zunehmen<br>werden zunehmen | werde zugenommen haben<br>wirst zugenommen haben<br>wird zugenommen haben | werden zugenommen haben<br>werdet zugenommen haben<br>werden zugenommen haben |
| Subjunctive | **Present** | | **Present Perfect** | |
| | nehme zu<br>nehmest zu<br>nehme zu | nehmen zu<br>nehmet zu<br>nehmen zu | habe zugenommen<br>habest zugenommen<br>habe zugenommen | haben zugenommen<br>habet zugenommen<br>haben zugenommen |
| | **Past** | | **Past Perfect** | |
| | nähme zu<br>nähmest zu<br>nähme zu | nähmen zu<br>nähmet zu<br>nähmen zu | hätte zugenommen<br>hättest zugenommen<br>hätte zugenommen | hätten zugenommen<br>hättet zugenommen<br>hätten zugenommen |
| | **Future** | | **Future Perfect** | |
| | werde zunehmen<br>werdest zunehmen<br>werde zunehmen | werden zunehmen<br>werdet zunehmen<br>werden zunehmen | werde zugenommen haben<br>werdest zugenommen haben<br>werde zugenommen haben | werden zugenommen haben<br>werdet zugenommen haben<br>werden zugenommen haben |
| | **Present and Future Conditional** | | **Past Conditional** | |
| | würde zunehmen<br>würdest zunehmen<br>würde zunehmen | würden zunehmen<br>würdet zunehmen<br>würden zunehmen | würde zugenommen haben<br>würdest zugenommen haben<br>würde zugenommen haben | würden zugenommen haben<br>würdet zugenommen haben<br>würden zugenommen haben |

**Note:** Without a prefix, the principal parts of this verb are *nimmt, nahm, hat genommen.* With inseparable prefixes, the principal parts of this verb are, for example, *benimmt, benahm, hat benommen.*

## EXAMPLES

Frau Bauer sieht aus, als ob sie mehr als fünfzehn Kilo zugenommen hätte.

Mrs. Bauer looks like she's put on more than 15 kilos.

Die Angriffe durch Computerviren nehmen in letzter Zeit zu.

Computer virus attacks have become more frequent recently.

**zurückgehen**
to go back, to return
**Auxiliary verb:** sein **Past participle:** zurückgegangen
**Imperative:** Gehe zurück! Geht zurück! Gehen Sie zurück!

| Mode | Simple Tenses | | Compound Tenses | |
|---|---|---|---|---|
| | *Singular* | *Plural* | *Singular* | *Plural* |
| Indicative | **Present** | | **Present Perfect** | |
| | gehe zurück<br>gehst zurück<br>geht zurück | gehen zurück<br>geht zurück<br>gehen zurück | bin zurückgegangen<br>bist zurückgegangen<br>ist zurückgegangen | sind zurückgegangen<br>seid zurückgegangen<br>sind zurückgegangen |
| | **Past** | | **Past Perfect** | |
| | ging zurück<br>gingst zurück<br>ging zurück | gingen zurück<br>gingt zurück<br>gingen zurück | war zurückgegangen<br>warst zurückgegangen<br>war zurückgegangen | waren zurückgegangen<br>wart zurückgegangen<br>waren zurückgegangen |
| | **Future** | | **Future Perfect** | |
| | werde zurückgehen<br>wirst zurückgehen<br>wird zurückgehen | werden zurückgehen<br>werdet zurückgehen<br>werden zurückgehen | werde zurückgegangen sein<br>wirst zurückgegangen sein<br>wird zurückgegangen sein | werden zurückgegangen sein<br>werdet zurückgegangen sein<br>werden zurückgegangen sein |
| Subjunctive | **Present** | | **Present Perfect** | |
| | gehe zurück<br>gehest zurück<br>gehe zurück | gehen zurück<br>gehet zurück<br>gehen zurück | sei zurückgegangen<br>seiest zurückgegangen<br>sei zurückgegangen | seien zurückgegangen<br>seiet zurückgegangen<br>seien zurückgegangen |
| | **Past** | | **Past Perfect** | |
| | ginge zurück<br>gingest zurück<br>ginge zurück | gingen zurück<br>ginget zurück<br>gingen zurück | wäre zurückgegangen<br>wärest zurückgegangen<br>wäre zurückgegangen | wären zurückgegangen<br>wäret zurückgegangen<br>wären zurückgegangen |
| | **Future** | | **Future Perfect** | |
| | werde zurückgehen<br>werdest zurückgehen<br>werde zurückgehen | werden zurückgehen<br>werdet zurückgehen<br>werden zurückgehen | werde zurückgegangen sein<br>werdest zurückgegangen sein<br>werde zurückgegangen sein | werden zurückgegangen sein<br>werdet zurückgegangen sein<br>werden zurückgegangen sein |
| | **Present and Future Conditional** | | **Past Conditional** | |
| | würde zurückgehen<br>würdest zurückgehen<br>würde zurückgehen | würden zurückgehen<br>würdet zurückgehen<br>würden zurückgehen | würde zurückgegangen sein<br>würdest zurückgegangen sein<br>würde zurückgegangen sein | würden zurückgegangen sein<br>würdet zurückgegangen sein<br>würden zurückgegangen sein |

**Note:** With inseparable prefixes, the principal parts of this verb are, for example, *begeht, beging, hat begangen.* Without a prefix, the principal parts are *geht, ging, ist gegangen.*

## EXAMPLES

Nach einem ganzen Jahr in Hamburg ging sie nach Bremen zurück.
After a whole year in Hamburg, she went back to Bremen.

Gehen wir den Fluss entlang zurück.
Let's go back along the river.

**zurückkehren**
to return
**Auxiliary verb:** sein **Past participle:** zurückgekehrt
**Imperative:** Kehre zurück! Kehrt zurück! Kehren Sie zurück!

| Mode | Simple Tenses | | Compound Tenses | |
|---|---|---|---|---|
| | *Singular* | *Plural* | *Singular* | *Plural* |
| Indicative | **Present** | | **Present Perfect** | |
| | kehre zurück<br>kehrst zurück<br>kehrt zurück | kehren zurück<br>kehrt zurück<br>kehren zurück | bin zurückgekehrt<br>bist zurückgekehrt<br>ist zurückgekehrt | sind zurückgekehrt<br>seid zurückgekehrt<br>sind zurückgekehrt |
| | **Past** | | **Past Perfect** | |
| | kehrte zurück<br>kehrtest zurück<br>kehrte zurück | kehrten zurück<br>kehrtet zurück<br>kehrten zurück | war zurückgekehrt<br>warst zurückgekehrt<br>war zurückgekehrt | waren zurückgekehrt<br>wart zurückgekehrt<br>waren zurückgekehrt |
| | **Future** | | **Future Perfect** | |
| | werde zurückkehren<br>wirst zurückkehren<br>wird zurückkehren | werden zurückkehren<br>werdet zurückkehren<br>werden zurückkehren | werde zurückgekehrt sein<br>wirst zurückgekehrt sein<br>wird zurückgekehrt sein | werden zurückgekehrt sein<br>werdet zurückgekehrt sein<br>werden zurückgekehrt sein |
| Subjunctive | **Present** | | **Present Perfect** | |
| | kehre zurück<br>kehrest zurück<br>kehre zurück | kehren zurück<br>kehret zurück<br>kehren zurück | sei zurückgekehrt<br>seiest zurückgekehrt<br>sei zurückgekehrt | seien zurückgekehrt<br>seiet zurückgekehrt<br>seien zurückgekehrt |
| | **Past** | | **Past Perfect** | |
| | kehrte zurück<br>kehrtest zurück<br>kehrte zurück | kehrten zurück<br>kehrtet zurück<br>kehrten zurück | wäre zurückgekehrt<br>wärest zurückgekehrt<br>wäre zurückgekehrt | wären zurückgekehrt<br>wäret zurückgekehrt<br>wären zurückgekehrt |
| | **Future** | | **Future Perfect** | |
| | werde zurückkehren<br>werdest zurückkehren<br>werde zurückkehren | werden zurückkehren<br>werdet zurückkehren<br>werden zurückkehren | werde zurückgekehrt sein<br>werdest zurückgekehrt sein<br>werde zurückgekehrt sein | werden zurückgekehrt sein<br>werdet zurückgekehrt sein<br>werden zurückgekehrt sein |
| | **Present and Future Conditional** | | **Past Conditional** | |
| | würde zurückkehren<br>würdest zurückkehren<br>würde zurückkehren | würden zurückkehren<br>würdet zurückkehren<br>würden zurückkehren | würde zurückgekehrt sein<br>würdest zurückgekehrt sein<br>würde zurückgekehrt sein | würden zurückgekehrt sein<br>würdet zurückgekehrt sein<br>würden zurückgekehrt sein |

## EXAMPLES

Ich möchte irgendwann nach Europa zurückkehren.
Someday I'd like to return to Europe.

Nach vier Wochen sind sie nach Hause zurückgekehrt.
After four weeks, they returned home.

**zurückziehen (sich)**
to withdraw, to retire, to retreat
**Auxiliary verb:** haben **Past participle:** zurückgezogen
**Imperative:** Ziehe zurück! Zieht zurück! Ziehen Sie zurück!

| Mode | Simple Tenses | | Compound Tenses | |
|---|---|---|---|---|
| | *Singular* | *Plural* | *Singular* | *Plural* |
| Indicative | **Present** | | **Present Perfect** | |
| | ziehe zurück<br>ziehst zurück<br>zieht zurück | ziehen zurück<br>zieht zurück<br>ziehen zurück | habe zurückgezogen<br>hast zurückgezogen<br>hat zurückgezogen | haben zurückgezogen<br>habt zurückgezogen<br>haben zurückgezogen |
| | **Past** | | **Past Perfect** | |
| | zog zurück<br>zogst zurück<br>zog zurück | zogen zurück<br>zogt zurück<br>zogen zurück | hatte zurückgezogen<br>hattest zurückgezogen<br>hatte zurückgezogen | hatten zurückgezogen<br>hattet zurückgezogen<br>hatten zurückgezogen |
| | **Future** | | **Future Perfect** | |
| | werde zurückziehen<br>wirst zurückziehen<br>wird zurückziehen | werden zurückziehen<br>werdet zurückziehen<br>werden zurückziehen | werde zurückgezogen haben<br>wirst zurückgezogen haben<br>wird zurückgezogen haben | werden zurückgezogen haben<br>werdet zurückgezogen haben<br>werden zurückgezogen haben |
| Subjunctive | **Present** | | **Present Perfect** | |
| | ziehe zurück<br>ziehest zurück<br>ziehe zurück | ziehen zurück<br>ziehet zurück<br>ziehen zurück | habe zurückgezogen<br>habest zurückgezogen<br>habe zurückgezogen | haben zurückgezogen<br>habet zurückgezogen<br>haben zurückgezogen |
| | **Past** | | **Past Perfect** | |
| | zöge zurück<br>zögest zurück<br>zöge zurück | zögen zurück<br>zöget zurück<br>zögen zurück | hätte zurückgezogen<br>hättest zurückgezogen<br>hätte zurückgezogen | hätten zurückgezogen<br>hättet zurückgezogen<br>hätten zurückgezogen |
| | **Future** | | **Future Perfect** | |
| | werde zurückziehen<br>werdest zurückziehen<br>werde zurückziehen | werden zurückziehen<br>werdet zurückziehen<br>werden zurückziehen | werde zurückgezogen haben<br>werdest zurückgezogen haben<br>werde zurückgezogen haben | werden zurückgezogen haben<br>werdet zurückgezogen haben<br>werden zurückgezogen haben |
| | **Present and Future Conditional** | | **Past Conditional** | |
| | würde zurückziehen<br>würdest zurückziehen<br>würde zurückziehen | würden zurückziehen<br>würdet zurückziehen<br>würden zurückziehen | würde zurückgezogen haben<br>würdest zurückgezogen haben<br>würde zurückgezogen haben | würden zurückgezogen haben<br>würdet zurückgezogen haben<br>würden zurückgezogen haben |

**Note:** When this verb is used as a verb of motion, it requires *sein* as its auxiliary in the perfect tenses.

## EXAMPLES

Der Käufer hat sein Angebot zurückgezogen. — The buyer withdrew his offer.
Ihnen wurde befohlen sich zurückzuziehen. — They were given the order to pull back.

**zuschauen**

to watch, to look on

**Auxiliary verb:** haben **Past participle:** zugeschaut

**Imperative:** Schaue zu! Schaut zu! Schauen Sie zu!

| Mode | Simple Tenses | | Compound Tenses | |
|---|---|---|---|---|
| | *Singular* | *Plural* | *Singular* | *Plural* |
| Indicative | **Present** | | **Present Perfect** | |
| | schaue zu<br>schaust zu<br>schaut zu | schauen zu<br>schaut zu<br>schauen zu | habe zugeschaut<br>hast zugeschaut<br>hat zugeschaut | haben zugeschaut<br>habt zugeschaut<br>haben zugeschaut |
| | **Past** | | **Past Perfect** | |
| | schaute zu<br>schautest zu<br>schaute zu | schauten zu<br>schautet zu<br>schauten zu | hatte zugeschaut<br>hattest zugeschaut<br>hatte zugeschaut | hatten zugeschaut<br>hattet zugeschaut<br>hatten zugeschaut |
| | **Future** | | **Future Perfect** | |
| | werde zuschauen<br>wirst zuschauen<br>wird zuschauen | werden zuschauen<br>werdet zuschauen<br>werden zuschauen | werde zugeschaut haben<br>wirst zugeschaut haben<br>wird zugeschaut haben | werden zugeschaut haben<br>werdet zugeschaut haben<br>werden zugeschaut haben |
| Subjunctive | **Present** | | **Present Perfect** | |
| | schaue zu<br>schauest zu<br>schaue zu | schauen zu<br>schauet zu<br>schauen zu | habe zugeschaut<br>habest zugeschaut<br>habe zugeschaut | haben zugeschaut<br>habet zugeschaut<br>haben zugeschaut |
| | **Past** | | **Past Perfect** | |
| | schaute zu<br>schautest zu<br>schaute zu | schauten zu<br>schautet zu<br>schauten zu | hätte zugeschaut<br>hättest zugeschaut<br>hätte zugeschaut | hätten zugeschaut<br>hättet zugeschaut<br>hätten zugeschaut |
| | **Future** | | **Future Perfect** | |
| | werde zuschauen<br>werdest zuschauen<br>werde zuschauen | werden zuschauen<br>werdet zuschauen<br>werden zuschauen | werde zugeschaut haben<br>werdest zugeschaut haben<br>werde zugeschaut haben | werden zugeschaut haben<br>werdet zugeschaut haben<br>werden zugeschaut haben |
| | **Present and Future Conditional** | | **Past Conditional** | |
| | würde zuschauen<br>würdest zuschauen<br>würde zuschauen | würden zuschauen<br>würdet zuschauen<br>würden zuschauen | würde zugeschaut haben<br>würdest zugeschaut haben<br>würde zugeschaut haben | würden zugeschaut haben<br>würdet zugeschaut haben<br>würden zugeschaut haben |

## EXAMPLES

Ich habe meinen Neffen beim Schwimmen zugeschaut.
I looked on as my nephews swam.

Schaut mir zu, wenn ich laufe.
Watch me when I run the race.

**zwingen**
to force, to compel
**Auxiliary verb:** haben **Past participle:** gezwungen
**Imperative:** Zwinge! Zwingt! Zwingen Sie!

| Mode | Simple Tenses | | Compound Tenses | |
|---|---|---|---|---|
| | *Singular* | *Plural* | *Singular* | *Plural* |
| Indicative | **Present** | | **Present Perfect** | |
| | zwinge<br>zwingst<br>zwingt | zwingen<br>zwingt<br>zwingen | habe gezwungen<br>hast gezwungen<br>hat gezwungen | haben gezwungen<br>habt gezwungen<br>haben gezwungen |
| | **Past** | | **Past Perfect** | |
| | zwang<br>zwangst<br>zwang | zwangen<br>zwangt<br>zwangen | hatte gezwungen<br>hattest gezwungen<br>hatte gezwungen | hatten gezwungen<br>hattet gezwungen<br>hatten gezwungen |
| | **Future** | | **Future Perfect** | |
| | werde zwingen<br>wirst zwingen<br>wird zwingen | werden zwingen<br>werdet zwingen<br>werden zwingen | werde gezwungen haben<br>wirst gezwungen haben<br>wird gezwungen haben | werden gezwungen haben<br>werdet gezwungen haben<br>werden gezwungen haben |
| Subjunctive | **Present** | | **Present Perfect** | |
| | zwinge<br>zwingest<br>zwinge | zwingen<br>zwinget<br>zwingen | habe gezwungen<br>habest gezwungen<br>habe gezwungen | haben gezwungen<br>habet gezwungen<br>haben gezwungen |
| | **Past** | | **Past Perfect** | |
| | zwänge<br>zwängest<br>zwänge | zwängen<br>zwänget<br>zwängen | hätte gezwungen<br>hättest gezwungen<br>hätte gezwungen | hätten gezwungen<br>hättet gezwungen<br>hätten gezwungen |
| | **Future** | | **Future Perfect** | |
| | werde zwingen<br>werdest zwingen<br>werde zwingen | werden zwingen<br>werdet zwingen<br>werden zwingen | werde gezwungen haben<br>werdest gezwungen haben<br>werde gezwungen haben | werden gezwungen haben<br>werdet gezwungen haben<br>werden gezwungen haben |
| | **Present and Future Conditional** | | **Past Conditional** | |
| | würde zwingen<br>würdest zwingen<br>würde zwingen | würden zwingen<br>würdet zwingen<br>würden zwingen | würde gezwungen haben<br>würdest gezwungen haben<br>würde gezwungen haben | würden gezwungen haben<br>würdet gezwungen haben<br>würden gezwungen haben |

## EXAMPLES

Ich wurde gezwungen das Gemälde zu stehlen. — I was forced to steal the painting.
Niemand wird dich dazu zwingen. — No one's going to force you to do it.

# APPENDIX OF ADDITIONAL VERBS

This appendix consists of over 1,500 additional verbs. Each verb in this appendix has a reference to a fully conjugated verb with a matching conjugation. For example, *abfahren* (to depart) will point you to page 173, where you'll find *fahren* (to drive), because both verbs are identically conjugated. This appendix provides many verbs with either separable or inseparable prefixes. Just as the preceding example illustrated, you may be directed from a verb with a prefix to one that has no prefix—from *abfahren* to *fahren*. Or you may be directed from a verb with a separable prefix to one with an inseparable prefix. This occurs, because prefixes are a matter of position with a verb and do not affect the conjugation.

| GERMAN VERB | ENGLISH VERB | PAGE NUMBER |
|---|---|---|
| **abbiegen** | to bend off, to turn off | 106 |
| **abfahren** | to depart by transport | 173 |
| **abfertigen** | to finish, to dispatch | 89 |
| **abfinden** | to settle | 184 |
| **abführen** | to lead away, to take into police custody | 203 |
| **abgewöhnen (sich)** | to break or give up a habit | 223 |
| **abhalten** | to hold off, to restrain | 236 |
| **abhängen von** | to depend on | 238 |
| **abholen** | to fetch, to call for, to pick up | 253 |
| **abhören** | to listen in, to wiretap | 255 |
| **ablassen** | to drain, to empty | 296 |
| **ablaufen** | to run down, to run off, to expire | 298 |
| **ablegen** | to put away, to take off | 301 |
| **ablehnen** | to decline | 43 |
| **abliefern** | to deliver, to drop off | 47 |
| **abmachen** | to undo, to detach, to settle | 317 |
| **abmelden** | to check out, to sign off, to announce a withdrawal | 324 |
| **abnehmen** | to take off, to decrease, to reduce | 612 |
| **abonnieren** | to subscribe | 57 |

| | | |
|---|---|---|
| **abräumen** | to clear, to remove | 59 |
| **abreisen** | to depart on a journey | 378 |
| **absagen** | to call off, to cancel | 394 |
| **abschaffen** | to abolish, to repeal | 43 |
| **abschalten** | to disconnect | 402 |
| **abschleppen** | to tow away, to drag away | 429 |
| **abschließen** | to lock up | 430 |
| **absehen** | to anticipate | 66 |
| **absieden** | to boil off | 471 |
| **absondern (sich)** | to isolate, to segregate | 354 |
| **abspannen** | to slacken, to relax | 43 |
| **absperren** | to shut off, to barricade | 43 |
| **absprengen** | to blow off | 43 |
| **abstammen** | to descend, to come from | 43 |
| **abstehen** | to stand off | 495 |
| **abstellen** | to put away, to turn off | 580 |
| **abstimmen** | to tune, to lower the sound, to take a vote | 95 |
| **abstöpseln** | to uncork, to unplug | 588 |
| **abstreichen** | to wipe off | 507 |
| **abstreifen** | to strip off | 43 |
| **abstreiten** | to dispute, to deny | 508 |
| **abstufen** | to terrace, to grade | 43 |
| **abstumpfen** | to dull, to blunt | 43 |
| **abstürzen** | to precipitate, to plunge | 511 |
| **abteilen** | to divide | 520 |
| **abtönen** | to tone down | 43 |
| **abtreiben** | to carry away, to have an abortion | 529 |
| **abtrocknen** | to wipe dry | 533 |
| **abwaschen** | to wash up | 586 |
| **abwechseln** | to exchange, to alternate | 588 |
| **ächzen** | to moan, to groan | 232 |
| **adoptieren** | to adopt | 57 |
| **ähneln** | to resemble, to take after | 71 |
| **akzeptieren** | to accept | 57 |
| **alarmieren** | to alarm | 57 |
| **alliieren** | to ally | 57 |

| | | |
|---|---|---|
| **amüsieren** | to amuse, to enjoy oneself | 57 |
| **analysieren** | to analyze | 57 |
| **anbauen** | to cultivate, to add to by building | 72 |
| **anbeißen** | to bite at | 82 |
| **anbeten** | to worship | 97 |
| **anbrennen** | to kindle, to scorch, to burn (food) | 119 |
| **andauern** | to continue, to last | 123 |
| **androhen** | to menace, to threaten | 131 |
| **anerkennen** | to acknowledge, to recognize | 267 |
| **anfahren** | to start moving (a car), to drive up to, to collide with | 173 |
| **anfallen** | to attack | 209 |
| **anfassen** | to take hold of, to seize | 178 |
| **anfeuchten** | to moisten, to dampen | 585 |
| **anfordern** | to demand, to claim | 193 |
| **anfressen** | to gnaw, to corrode | 198 |
| **anfühlen (sich)** | to feel | 202 |
| **angeben** | to declare, to indicate, to pretend, to boast | 63 |
| **angehören** | to belong to, to pertain to | 212 |
| **angeln** | to fish | 71 |
| **angewöhnen** | to accustom | 223 |
| **angreifen** | to attack | 230 |
| **angrenzen** | to border, to adjoin | 232 |
| **ängstigen** | to frighten, to alarm | 357 |
| **anhaben** | to have on, to wear | 235 |
| **anhalten** | to check, to restrain, to stop | 236 |
| **anhängen** | to hang on, to attach, to append | 238 |
| **anhören** | to listen | 255 |
| **animieren** | to animate | 57 |
| **anklagen** | to accuse | 269 |
| **ankleben** | to adhere, to stick to | 272 |
| **ankleiden** | to put clothes on | 273 |
| **anklicken** | to click on (a Web site icon) | 416 |
| **anklopfen** | to knock, to rap on | 277 |
| **ankündigen** | to announce, to proclaim | 357 |

| | | |
|---|---|---|
| **anlasten** | to accuse of a crime | 51 |
| **anlegen** | to lay on, to apply | 301 |
| **anlehnen** | to lean against | 43 |
| **anlocken** | to lure | 59 |
| **anmachen** | to fasten, to attach, to switch on | 317 |
| **anmalen** | to paint | 321 |
| **anmelden (sich)** | to announce, to report, to register | 324 |
| **anmerken** | to perceive, to remark, to write down | 326 |
| **annehmen** | to take, to accept, to suppose | 612 |
| **anordnen** | to order, to direct, to put in order | 342 |
| **anpassen** | to try on, to make fit | 346 |
| **anprobieren** | to try on | 57 |
| **anreden** | to speak to, to address | 372 |
| **anregen** | to stir up, to stimulate | 60 |
| **anreizen** | to incite, to induce | 88 |
| **anrichten** | to regulate, to prepare, to dish up | 383 |
| **anrühren** | to touch, to mix | 389 |
| **ansagen** | to announce, to notify | 394 |
| **anschalten** | to switch on | 402 |
| **anschauen** | to look at | 616 |
| **anschlagen** | to strike against, to ring | 425 |
| **anschnallen (sich)** | to buckle up | 580 |
| **anschreiben** | to write on a board, to note, to run a tab | 449 |
| **anschwärzen** | to slander, to blacken someone's name | 196 |
| **ansehen** | to look at | 66 |
| **ansein** | to be on | 466 |
| **anspannen** | to hitch, to harness | 149 |
| **ansprechen** | to speak to, to address | 488 |
| **ansteigen** | to rise, to ascend, to increase | 548 |
| **anstellen** | to place near, to arrange, to employ | 580 |
| **anstrengen (sich)** | to exert oneself | 60 |
| **antragen** | to propose, to offer | 524 |
| **anvertrauen** | to confide, to entrust to | 574 |
| **anweisen** | to direct, to point out, to assign | 591 |

| | | |
|---|---|---|
| **anzahlen** | to make a down payment | 603 |
| **anzeigen** | to announce, to advertise | 605 |
| **anzünden** | to kindle, to light | 231 |
| **aufatmen** | to breathe freely | 58 |
| **aufbauen** | to build up, to erect | 72 |
| **aufbessern** | to improve, to repair | 155 |
| **aufbewahren** | to store, to preserve | 59 |
| **aufbleiben** | to remain open, to remain up, to stay awake | 112 |
| **aufbrechen** | to break open | 118 |
| **aufbürden** | to burden, to impose upon | 134 |
| **aufdecken** | to uncover, to reveal | 124 |
| **aufeinander folgen** | to follow one another | 192 |
| **auffallen** | to attract attention, to strike | 137 |
| **auffassen** | to perceive, to comprehend | 178 |
| **auffordern** | to call upon, to summon, to ask to dance | 193 |
| **aufführen** | to perform | 203 |
| **aufgeben** | to give up, to surrender | 63 |
| **aufgehen** | to rise, to swell | 613 |
| **aufhaben** | to have on, to be open | 235 |
| **aufhalten** | to hold up, to delay, to hold open | 236 |
| **aufhängen** | to hang up, to suspend | 238 |
| **aufheben** | to lift, to raise, to pick up | 241 |
| **aufhellen** | to clear, to brighten | 580 |
| **aufhören** | to stop, to cease | 255 |
| **aufklappen** | to open, to unfold | 270 |
| **aufklären** | to clear up, to enlighten | 59 |
| **aufkleben** | to stick on, to affix | 272 |
| **aufladen** | to load, to charge up | 138 |
| **auflegen** | to lay on, to apply | 301 |
| **aufmachen** | to open, to unlock | 317 |
| **aufnehmen** | to take in, to take a picture, to record | 612 |
| **aufopfern** | to sacrifice | 354 |
| **aufpassen** | to pay attention to, to watch | 346 |
| **aufprobieren** | to try on | 57 |
| **aufrichten** | to set up, to erect | 383 |

| | | |
|---|---|---|
| **aufrufen** | to summon, to call up | 50 |
| **aufsagen** | to recite | 394 |
| **aufschlagen** | to break open, to open (a book) | 425 |
| **aufschließen** | to unlock | 430 |
| **aufschreiben** | to write down, to note, to enter | 449 |
| **aufsein** | to be awake, to be open | 466 |
| **aufsetzen** | to put on, to draw up | 196 |
| **aufsparen** | to save up | 479 |
| **aufsperren** | to open wide, to unlock | 59 |
| **aufspüren** | to track down | 59 |
| **aufstehen** | to get up, to stand up | 495 |
| **aufstellen** | to install, to set up | 580 |
| **aufsuchen** | to seek out, to search for | 513 |
| **auftauchen** | to emerge, to appear | 517 |
| **auftreffen** | to impact on, to strike | 528 |
| **auftreten** | to tread, to appear | 531 |
| **aufwecken** | to waken, to rouse | 589 |
| **aufweichen** | to soften | 61 |
| **aufwickeln** | to roll up, to wind up | 150 |
| **aufziehen** | to draw up, to bring up | 609 |
| **ausatmen** | to exhale | 58 |
| **ausbeuten** | to exploit | 51 |
| **ausbilden** | to educate, to develop | 108 |
| **ausblasen** | to blow out | 111 |
| **ausbleiben** | to stay away, to be absent | 112 |
| **ausblühen** | to stop blooming | 114 |
| **ausbrennen** | to burn out, to cease burning | 119 |
| **ausdehnen** | to extend | 59 |
| **ausdrücken** | to express | 132 |
| **auseinander bringen** | to separate | 120 |
| **auseinander fallen** | to fall to pieces | 137 |
| **auseinander falten** | to unfold | 175 |

| | | |
|---|---|---|
| **auseinander gehen** | to separate | 613 |
| **auseinander halten** | to distinguish between | 236 |
| **auserwählen** | to choose, to select | 582 |
| **ausfallen** | to drop out, to be omitted, to be cancelled | 137 |
| **ausfertigen** | to draw up, to execute | 572 |
| **ausfliegen** | to fly out, to escape | 186 |
| **ausfragen** | to interrogate | 197 |
| **ausführen** | to execute, to carry out, to walk a dog | 203 |
| **ausgleichen** | to make even, to equalize | 227 |
| **ausgraben** | to dig out | 228 |
| **aushalten** | to hold out, to endure | 236 |
| **aushelfen** | to help out, to aid | 246 |
| **auskaufen** | to buy out | 265 |
| **auskennen (sich)** | to know one's way around | 267 |
| **auskleiden** | to undress | 273 |
| **auskommen** | to come out, to get by with | 49 |
| **ausladen** | to unload, to disembark | 138 |
| **ausleihen** | to lend out | 304 |
| **auslernen** | to finish learning, to finish an apprenticeship | 308 |
| **auslesen** | to select, to finish reading | 309 |
| **auslöschen** | to put out, to extinguish | 314 |
| **ausmachen** | to open, to make up, to settle, to turn/switch off | 317 |
| **ausmessen** | to measure out | 327 |
| **ausnehmen** | to take out, to exclude | 612 |
| **ausnutzen** | to wear out, to utilize, to take advantage of | 88 |
| **auspacken** | to unpack | 345 |
| **ausprobieren** | to try out, to taste | 57 |
| **ausradieren** | to erase, to rub out | 57 |
| **ausreden** | to finish speaking | 372 |
| **ausreichen** | to suffice | 376 |
| **ausreißen** | to tear out | 379 |
| **ausrotten** | to exterminate | 51 |
| **ausruhen** | to rest | 62 |
| **ausrutschen** | to slip, to skid | 392 |

| | | |
|---|---|---|
| **ausschalten** | to eliminate, to switch off | 402 |
| **ausschenken** | to pour out | 413 |
| **ausschlafen** | to have a good night's sleep | 424 |
| **ausschließen** | to exclude, to lock out | 430 |
| **ausschreiben** | to write to the end, to advertise a job opening | 449 |
| **aussein** | to be out | 466 |
| **äußern (sich)** | to express an opinion | 56 |
| **aussetzen** | to expose, to pause, to take a break | 196 |
| **ausspielen** | to play out | 485 |
| **aussprechen** | to pronounce | 488 |
| **ausspülen** | to rinse out | 43 |
| **ausstatten** | to equip, to outfit | 51 |
| **ausstehen** | to be outstanding | 495 |
| **ausstellen** | to exhibit | 580 |
| **aussterben** | to die out, to become extinct | 501 |
| **ausstrecken** | to reach out, to extend | 494 |
| **aussuchen** | to search, to seek out | 513 |
| **austeilen** | to distribute | 520 |
| **austreiben** | to drive out, to expel | 529 |
| **austrinken** | to finish drinking | 532 |
| **ausüben** | to practice (a profession) | 537 |
| **ausverkaufen** | to sell off, to sell on sale | 265 |
| **auswählen** | to choose, to select | 582 |
| **auswandern** | to emigrate | 583 |
| **ausweichen** | to make way | 380 |
| **ausweinen** | to have a good cry | 590 |
| **ausweisen** | to turn out, to expel, to deport | 591 |
| **auswickeln** | to unroll, to unwrap | 150 |
| **auszahlen** | to pay out | 603 |
| **auszeichnen** | to mark out, to distinguish, to reward | 370 |
| **ausziehen** | to undress | 609 |
| **baumeln** | to dangle | 71 |
| **beabsichtigen** | to intend | 91 |
| **beachten** | to notice, to heed, to regard | 44 |

| | | |
|---|---|---|
| **beängstigen** | to alarm, to make anxious | 76 |
| **beanspruchen** | to lay claim to, to demand | 96 |
| **beantragen** | to propose, to move | 96 |
| **beantworten** | to answer a question | 52 |
| **bearbeiten** | to cultivate, to work, to treat | 55 |
| **bebauen** | to build on, to cultivate | 72 |
| **beben** | to quake, to shake, to tremble | 127 |
| **bedanken (sich)** | to thank | 86 |
| **bedauern** | to regret | 123 |
| **bedecken** | to cover, to protect | 124 |
| **bedeuten** | to mean | 87 |
| **bedingen** | to imply, to stipulate | 269 |
| **bedrohen** | to endanger, to threaten | 131 |
| **bedürfen** | to need, to be in want | 135 |
| **beeindrucken** | to impress | 86 |
| **beeinflussen** | to influence | 88 |
| **beendigen** | to end, to finish | 76 |
| **beerdigen** | to bury, to inter | 76 |
| **befallen** | to befall, to happen | 209 |
| **befeuchten** | to moisten, to dampen | 44 |
| **befinden (sich)** | to be located | 184 |
| **beflecken** | to spot, to stain | 141 |
| **befreien** | to free | 199 |
| **befreunden** | to befriend | 74 |
| **befürworten** | to recommend, to advocate | 52 |
| **begeben (sich)** | to proceed, to set out for | 207 |
| **begehen** | to commit, to celebrate | 210 |
| **begehren** | to desire, to long for | 557 |
| **begeistern** | to inspire | 557 |
| **beglücken** | to make happy | 86 |
| **beglückwünschen** | to congratulate | 602 |
| **begraben** | to bury | 228 |
| **begreifen** | to comprehend, to grasp | 230 |
| **begrenzen** | to border on, to limit | 154 |
| **begründen** | to found, to establish | 231 |
| **begrüßen** | to greet | 233 |

| | | |
|---|---|---|
| **behaupten** | to maintain | 145 |
| **beherrschen** | to rule, to control | 247 |
| **beherzigen** | to take to heart | 76 |
| **behüten** | to guard, to preserve | 97 |
| **beibringen** | to teach | 120 |
| **beistehen** | to stand by, to aid | 495 |
| **beitragen** | to contribute | 524 |
| **beiwohnen** | to be present at | 600 |
| **bejahen** | to assent to, to give consent | 96 |
| **bekannt geben** | to make known | 63 |
| **bekehren** | to convert, to change one's ways | 266 |
| **bekennen** | to confess, to own up | 267 |
| **beklagen (sich)** | to complain | 269 |
| **bekräftigen** | to strengthen, to confirm | 76 |
| **belasten** | to load, to burden | 219 |
| **belästigen** | to trouble, to bother, to harass | 76 |
| **beleben** | to enliven, to animate | 299 |
| **belegen** | to cover, to lay down, to prove | 301 |
| **beleidigen** | to insult, to offend | 572 |
| **belügen** | to lie to | 316 |
| **bemühen (sich)** | to take the trouble, to strive | 131 |
| **benachrichtigen** | to inform, to send word | 76 |
| **benehmen (sich)** | to behave | 337 |
| **benetzen** | to moisten, wet | 540 |
| **benötigen** | to require, to need | 76 |
| **beobachten** | to observe | 44 |
| **bereuen** | to regret | 199 |
| **bergen** | to save, to secure | 214 |
| **bergsteigen** | to go mountain climbing | 548 |
| **berichten** | to report | 383 |
| **bersten** | to burst, to explode | 214 |
| **beruhigen** | to quiet, to pacify | 76 |
| **beschießen** | to fire at, to bombard | 418 |
| **beschimpfen** | to insult, to abuse | 421 |
| **beschlagnahmen** | to seize, to confiscate | 95 |
| **beschließen** | to close, to conclude | 430 |

| | | |
|---|---|---|
| **beschränken** | to limit, to restrict | 141 |
| **beschuldigen** | to accuse, to charge with | 148 |
| **beschützen** | to guard, to protect | 454 |
| **beschweren (sich)** | to load, to burden, to complain | 94 |
| **beseelen** | to inspire, to animate | 94 |
| **besichtigen** | to view, to go sightseeing | 76 |
| **besitzen** | to own | 475 |
| **besorgen** | to get, to procure | 477 |
| **bestätigen** | to confirm | 76 |
| **bestehen** | to undergo, to get through, to pass an exam | 495 |
| **bestrafen** | to punish | 506 |
| **beteiligen** | to give a share, to participate in | 76 |
| **betonen** | to emphasize, to stress | 96 |
| **betrachten** | to consider, to observe | 44 |
| **betragen** | to amount to | 524 |
| **betreffen** | to befall, to affect, to concern | 528 |
| **betreiben** | to practice, to pursue (studies) | 529 |
| **bevölkern** | to populate | 557 |
| **bevorstehen** | to be imminent, to impend | 495 |
| **bevorzugen** | to favor, to prefer | 217 |
| **bewässern** | to water, to irrigate | 557 |
| **bewundern** | to admire | 557 |
| **bezeichnen** | to signify, to designate | 370 |
| **beziehen (sich)** | to refer, to relate | 609 |
| **bezweifeln** | to doubt, to question | 564 |
| **blättern** | to leaf through a book | 191 |
| **blenden** | to blind, to dazzle | 70 |
| **blicken** | to look, to glance | 124 |
| **bluten** | to bleed | 256 |
| **brauen** | to brew | 72 |
| **brausen** | to storm, to rage, to bluster | 315 |
| **bremsen** | to brake | 315 |
| **brühen** | to blanch, to brew | 318 |
| **brüllen** | to roar, to yell | 498 |
| **brummen** | to growl, to buzz | 499 |
| **brüsten (sich)** | to put on airs, to brag | 534 |

| | | |
|---|---|---|
| **buchstabieren** | to spell | 57 |
| **bücken (sich)** | to stoop, to bow | 416 |
| **bügeln** | to iron | 71 |
| **bummeln** | to loiter, to saunter, to stroll | 71 |
| **bürsten** | to brush | 534 |
| **büßen** | to atone for, to make amends | 233 |
| **chatten** | to chat (in an Internet chat room) | 44 |
| **dämmern** | to dawn, to become light | 237 |
| **dämpfen** | to damp, to smother, muffle | 421 |
| **darbieten** | to present, to offer | 46 |
| **datieren** | to date | 57 |
| **demonstrieren** | to demonstrate | 57 |
| **demütigen** | to humble, to humiliate | 76 |
| **desinfizieren** | to disinfect | 57 |
| **deuten** | to point, to indicate | 44 |
| **diktieren** | to dictate | 57 |
| **dirigieren** | to direct (an orchestra) | 57 |
| **diskriminieren** | to discriminate | 57 |
| **diskutieren** | to discuss | 57 |
| **dolmetschen** | to translate | 185 |
| **dosieren** | to measure a dose | 57 |
| **drängeln** | to urge, to press forward | 71 |
| **dreschen** | to thresh | 214 |
| **dressieren** | to train, to break in | 57 |
| **driften** | to float, to drift | 378 |
| **ducken (sich)** | to duck, to stoop | 416 |
| **duften** | to be fragrant | 555 |
| **düngen** | to fertilize | 394 |
| **durchblättern** | to turn pages, to skim through a book | 191 |
| **durchbóhren** | to bore through, to penetrate | 203 |
| **durchbrechen** | to break through | 118 |
| **durchdríngen** | to penetrate, to pierce | 130 |
| **durchfahren** | to drive through | 173 |
| **durchfallen** | to fall through, to fail | 137 |
| **durchführen** | to accomplish, to carry out | 203 |
| **durchgehen** | to go through, to be transmitted | 210 |

| | | |
|---|---|---|
| **durchhalten** | to hold out, to endure | 236 |
| **durchhelfen** | help through, to give support | 246 |
| **durchkämpfen (sich)** | to fight to the end | 262 |
| **durchkommen** | to get through, to succeed | 49 |
| **durchreisen** | to travel through, to traverse | 378 |
| **durchschláfen** | to sleep through | 424 |
| **durchschneiden** | to cut through | 443 |
| **durchsehen** | to see through, to see clearly, to understand | 66 |
| **durchsetzen (sich)** | to enforce, to push through, to prevail | 196 |
| **durchsickern** | to leak, to drip through | 47 |
| **durchsieben** | to sift, to sieve | 310 |
| **durchsprechen** | to discuss thoroughly | 488 |
| **durchstechen** | to pierce through, to stab | 493 |
| **durchstoßen** | to break through | 505 |
| **durchstreichen** | to cross out, to erase | 507 |
| **durchströmen** | to flow through, to perfuse | 510 |
| **durchsúchen** | to search thoroughly | 513 |
| **durchtreiben** | to force through, to effect | 529 |
| **durchwáchen** | to watch through, to lie awake | 294 |
| **durchwében** | to interweave | 587 |
| **durchwinden** | to wind through | 109 |
| **durchziehen** | to draw through | 609 |
| **dursten** | to be thirsty | 256 |
| **duschen** | to shower | 329 |
| **ebben** | to ebb | 115 |
| **ehren** | to honor | 203 |
| **eignen (sich)** | to be useful | 341 |
| **eilen** | to make haste, to hurry | 192 |
| **einatmen** | to inhale | 58 |
| **einbauen** | to install | 72 |
| **einbilden (sich)** | to imagine, to be conceited | 108 |
| **eindeutschen** | to translate into German | 602 |
| **eindringen** | to invade, to break in | 130 |
| **einheften** | to sew in, to file (papers) | 555 |

| | | |
|---|---|---|
| **einheiraten** | to marry into (a business) | 243 |
| **einigen (sich)** | to agree, to come to terms | 572 |
| **einkremen** | to use suntan cream | 43 |
| **einleiten** | to initiate, to introduce | 51 |
| **einlösen** | to ransom, to redeem | 315 |
| **einmischen (sich)** | to interfere, to meddle | 329 |
| **einnehmen** | to take in, to accept, to occupy | 612 |
| **einpacken** | to pack, to wrap up | 416 |
| **einquartieren** | to billet, to quarter | 57 |
| **einrichten** | to set right, to arrange, to adjust | 383 |
| **einschließen** | to include, to lock in | 430 |
| **einschränken** | to limit, to check, to reduce | 326 |
| **einschreiben (sich)** | to enroll, to matriculate | 449 |
| **einsetzen (sich)** | to insert, to place, to install, to promote, to support | 196 |
| **einstellen** | to tune in, to focus, to hire | 580 |
| **eintragen** | to introduce, to enter, to record | 524 |
| **eintreten** | to enter, to commence | 531 |
| **einwandern** | to immigrate | 583 |
| **einweichen** | to soak | 61 |
| **einwerfen** | to throw in, to smash | 594 |
| **einziehen** | to draw in, to retract, to move in | 609 |
| **elektrifizieren** | to electrify | 57 |
| **emigrieren** | to emigrate | 480 |
| **empfangen** | to receive, to welcome | 176 |
| **empfehlen** | to recommend | 75 |
| **empfinden** | to feel, to perceive | 152 |
| **empören** | to shock, to make indignant | 504 |
| **engagieren** | to engage | 57 |
| **entbehren** | to do without, to dispense with | 561 |
| **entbinden** | to set free, to release, to give birth | 109 |
| **entführen** | to abduct | 203 |
| **entgegenkommen** | to come to meet, to advance, to compromise | 49 |
| **entgegnen** | to answer, to respond | 463 |
| **entgiften** | to decontaminate | 562 |

| | | |
|---|---|---|
| **enthalten** | to contain | 80 |
| **enthüllen** | to expose, to reveal | 86 |
| **entkommen** | to escape | 281 |
| **entkräften** | to weaken, to debilitate | 156 |
| **entladen** | to unload | 138 |
| **entlassen** | to release, to fire | 296 |
| **entlaufen** | to run away | 298 |
| **entlausen** | to delouse | 315 |
| **entmutigen** | to discourage | 159 |
| **entreißen** | to tear away | 379 |
| **entscheiden (sich)** | to decide | 409 |
| **entschließen (sich)** | to make up one's mind | 430 |
| **entschulden** | to free from debts | 87 |
| **entsetzen** | to terrify | 468 |
| **entsprechen** | to correspond | 570 |
| **entstammen** | to originate | 142 |
| **entstehen** | to originate, to develop | 495 |
| **entstellen** | to disfigure, to deform | 94 |
| **entwaffnen** | to disarm | 162 |
| **entwässern** | to drain, to distill | 557 |
| **entweichen** | to leak | 380 |
| **entwerfen** | to sketch, to draft, to design | 594 |
| **entwerten** | to depreciate | 74 |
| **entzücken** | to charm, to delight | 416 |
| **entzünden** | to set fire to, to inflame | 74 |
| **erarbeiten** | to earn, to achieve through work | 55 |
| **erbarmen (sich)** | to be moved to pity | 95 |
| **erbauen** | to build up, to construct | 72 |
| **erbittern** | to embitter, to enrage | 557 |
| **erblicken** | to catch sight of | 416 |
| **erblinden** | to become blind | 74 |
| **erbosen** | to make angry | 315 |
| **erdulden** | to endure, to put up with | 134 |
| **ereignen (sich)** | to occur, to happen | 162 |

| | | |
|---|---|---|
| **erfahren** | to learn, to experience | 173 |
| **erfrieren** | to freeze to death | 200 |
| **erfüllen** | to fulfill | 62 |
| **ergeben** | to yield, to result in | 207 |
| **ergrauen** | to get gray hair | 378 |
| **ergreifen** | to take hold of, to seize | 230 |
| **erhalten** | to obtain, to receive | 236 |
| **erheben** | to elevate, to raise up | 241 |
| **erheitern** | to cheer up, to brighten | 557 |
| **erhöhen** | to heighten, to elevate | 114 |
| **erholen (sich)** | to recover, to get better | 253 |
| **erkennen** | to recognize | 267 |
| **erkranken** | to become ill | 413 |
| **erkundigen** | to inquire | 76 |
| **erleben** | to experience, to witness | 299 |
| **erlegen** | to slay, to hunt and kill an animal | 301 |
| **erleuchten** | to illuminate | 97 |
| **erlöschen** | to go out, to be extinguished | 314 |
| **ermächtigen** | to empower, to authorize | 76 |
| **ermäßigen** | to moderate, to reduce | 76 |
| **ermorden** | to murder | 70 |
| **ernennen** | to nominate, to call into office | 339 |
| **erneuern** | to renew, to renovate | 557 |
| **erniedrigen** | to lower, to humble, to degrade | 572 |
| **ernten** | to harvest | 44 |
| **erörtern** | to discuss, to debate | 557 |
| **erpressen** | to extort, to blackmail | 178 |
| **erraten** | to guess, to solve | 565 |
| **erregen** | to excite, to stir up | 60 |
| **errichten** | to erect, to set upright | 383 |
| **erschießen** | to shoot dead | 418 |
| **erschlagen** | to strike dead, to slay | 425 |
| **ersetzen** | to replace | 468 |
| **ersparen** | to economize, to save, to spare | 479 |
| **erstaunen** | to astonish | 142 |
| **ersticken** | to stifle, to suffocate | 509 |

| | | |
|---|---|---|
| **erwachsen** | to grow from, accrue | 581 |
| **erwägen** | to consider, to ponder | 106 |
| **erwählen** | to choose, to elect | 582 |
| **erwähnen** | to mention | 142 |
| **erweisen** | to prove, to show | 104 |
| **erweitern** | to expand, to widen | 160 |
| **erwidern** | to reply, to retort | 155 |
| **erwürgen** | to strangle, to choke | 217 |
| **erzeugen** | to beget, to breed, to cause | 543 |
| **erzielen** | to achieve, to attain | 520 |
| **evakuieren** | to evacuate | 57 |
| **existieren** | to exist | 57 |
| **experimentieren** | to experiment | 57 |
| **explodieren** | to explode | 57 |
| **exportieren** | to export | 57 |
| **fabrizieren** | to manufacture | 57 |
| **faulenzen** | to be lazy, to lounge | 516 |
| **fegen** | to sweep | 301 |
| **fernsehen** | to watch television | 66 |
| **festhalten** | to detain | 236 |
| **festmachen** | to fasten, to tighten | 317 |
| **festschnallen** | to tie to | 580 |
| **feuern** | to fire, to sack | 502 |
| **filtrieren** | to filter | 57 |
| **finanzieren** | to finance | 57 |
| **fischen** | to fish | 329 |
| **fixieren** | to fix, to stare | 57 |
| **flicken** | to mend, to patch | 509 |
| **flimmern** | to glitter, to glisten | 237 |
| **flirten** | to flirt | 44 |
| **fluten** | to flood, to flow, to surge | 44 |
| **foltern** | to torture, to torment | 502 |
| **fortarbeiten** | to continue working | 55 |
| **fortbewegen (sich)** | to propel, to continue moving | 102 |
| **fortbilden (sich)** | to continue one's education | 108 |

| | | |
|---|---|---|
| **fortbleiben** | to stay away | 112 |
| **fortbringen** | to take away | 120 |
| **fortfahren** | to drive off, to depart, to continue | 173 |
| **fortführen** | to lead forth, to go on with | 203 |
| **fortgehen** | to go away, to depart | 210 |
| **fortjagen** | to chase away | 257 |
| **fortkommen** | to get away, to prosper | 49 |
| **fortlaufen** | to run away, to run on | 298 |
| **fortleben** | to live on, to survive | 299 |
| **fortnehmen** | to take from, to remove from | 612 |
| **fortpflanzen (sich)** | to propagate, to spread | 349 |
| **fortreisen** | to set out on a journey | 378 |
| **fortreißen** | to tear away | 379 |
| **fortschaffen** | to get rid of, to dismiss | 43 |
| **fortschreiten** | to step forward, to advance | 451 |
| **fortschwemmen** | to wash away | 59 |
| **forttreiben** | to drive away, to force away | 529 |
| **fortwähren** | to last, to persist | 266 |
| **fortziehen** | to draw away, to move away | 615 |
| **frankieren** | to pay the postage | 57 |
| **freihaben** | to have time off | 235 |
| **freilassen** | to release, to liberate | 296 |
| **frömmeln** | to affect piety | 293 |
| **frösteln** | to feel chilled | 293 |
| **funkeln** | to sparkle, to twinkle | 71 |
| **funktionieren** | to function | 57 |
| **fürchten (sich)** | to be afraid | 44 |
| **galvanisieren** | to galvanize | 57 |
| **gären** | to ferment, to effervesce | 255 |
| **garnieren** | to trim, to garnish | 57 |
| **gebieten** | to command, to bid | 107 |
| **gedeihen** | to increase, to develop, to flourish | 112 |
| **gedenken** | to bear in mind, to remember | 125 |
| **gefährden** | to endanger | 70 |
| **Geige spielen** | to play the violin | 485 |

| | | |
|---|---|---|
| **gelangen** | to reach, to get to | 192 |
| **gellen** | to sound shrill | 498 |
| **geloben** | to vow, to promise solemnly | 312 |
| **genehmigen** | to approve of, to sanction | 76 |
| **genieren (sich)** | to be embarrassed | 389 |
| **geraten** | to get, to come upon, to manage | 367 |
| **gern haben** | to like | 235 |
| **geziemen** | to be suitable, to befit | 95 |
| **glattlegen** | to smooth out a fold | 301 |
| **gleiten** | to glide, to skid | 227 |
| **glotzen** | to gape, to stare | 353 |
| **glühen** | to glow | 114 |
| **gönnen** | to not to envy, to not to grudge | 499 |
| **gratulieren** | to congratulate | 57 |
| **grenzen** | to border | 232 |
| **grillen** | to grill, to barbeque | 498 |
| **grollen** | to resent, to rumble | 498 |
| **grübeln** | to ponder | 71 |
| **gruppieren** | to group, to classify | 57 |
| **gutmachen** | to make amends for | 317 |
| **hallen** | to resound, to echo | 242 |
| **hantieren** | to handle, to manipulate | 57 |
| **haschen** | to snatch, to seize | 329 |
| **heimbringen** | to bring home | 120 |
| **heimfahren** | to drive home | 173 |
| **heimgehen** | to go home | 613 |
| **heimkehren** | to return home | 614 |
| **heimkommen** | to come home | 49 |
| **hemmen** | to hem in, to inhibit, to check | 499 |
| **heraufblicken** | to glance up | 416 |
| **heraufkommen** | to come up | 49 |
| **heraufsteigen** | to mount, to ascend | 548 |
| **herausbringen** | to bring out, to issue | 120 |
| **herausfinden** | to find out, to discover | 184 |
| **herausfordern** | to challenge, to provoke | 193 |
| **herausgeben** | to publish | 63 |

| | | |
|---|---|---|
| **herauskommen** | to come out, to be issued | 49 |
| **herausstellen (sich)** | to turn out, to appear | 580 |
| **hereinfallen** | to fall into | 137 |
| **hereinlassen** | to let in | 296 |
| **herstellen** | to put here, to manufacture | 580 |
| **herumdrehen** | to turn around | 545 |
| **herumfragen** | to ask around | 197 |
| **herumkommen** | to travel about, to become known | 49 |
| **herumtasten** | to feel around | 51 |
| **herunterkommen** | to come down, to alight | 49 |
| **herunterschlucken** | to swallow, to gulp down | 416 |
| **herzen** | to embrace, to press to one's heart | 245 |
| **hetzen** | to pursue, to sic, to drive | 245 |
| **hinausgehen** | to go out | 613 |
| **hindeuten** | to point, to show | 44 |
| **hinfallen** | to fall down | 137 |
| **hinlegen (sich)** | to lay down, to lie down | 301 |
| **hinsetzen (sich)** | to sit down, to seat oneself | 196 |
| **hochgehen** | to rise, to soar, to go upstairs | 613 |
| **hochhalten** | to think highly of, hold up high | 236 |
| **hochschätzen** | to esteem highly | 405 |
| **höhnen** | to scoff, to sneer | 320 |
| **huldigen** | to pay one's respects, to pay homage to | 76 |
| **hüllen** | to wrap up, to envelop | 498 |
| **humpeln** | to hobble | 462 |
| **hüpfen** | to hop, to leap | 378 |
| **hüsteln** | to clear one's throat | 71 |
| **hüten (sich)** | be on one's guard | 44 |
| **hypnotisieren** | to hypnotize | 57 |
| **identifizieren** | to identify | 57 |
| **illustrieren** | to illustrate | 57 |
| **imitieren** | to imitate | 57 |
| **immatrikulieren (sich)** | to matriculate | 57 |
| **impfen** | to inoculate | 421 |

| | | |
|---|---|---|
| **imponieren** | to impress | 57 |
| **importieren** | to import | 57 |
| **imstande sein** | to be in a position | 466 |
| **industrialisieren** | to industrialize | 57 |
| **ineinander fügen** | to join | 250 |
| **ineinander greifen** | to mesh, to cooperate | 230 |
| **informieren** | to inform | 57 |
| **innehaben** | to occupy, to possess | 235 |
| **innewerden** | to perceive, to become aware | 593 |
| **installieren** | to install | 57 |
| **instandhalten** | to maintain, to keep repaired | 236 |
| **instandsetzen** | to make ready, to repair | 196 |
| **integrieren** | to integrate | 57 |
| **interessieren (sich)** | to interest | 57 |
| **interpretieren** | to interpret | 57 |
| **interpunktieren** | to punctuate | 57 |
| **interviewen** | to interview | 57 |
| **irren (sich)** | to go astray, to err | 255 |
| **isolieren** | to isolate, to insulate | 57 |
| **jäten** | to weed | 44 |
| **jaulen** | to whine, to howl | 253 |
| **jonglieren** | to juggle | 57 |
| **kalibrieren** | to calibrate | 57 |
| **kanten** | to edge as in skiing | 44 |
| **kaputt gehen** | to get broken (on its own) | 613 |
| **kaputt machen** | to break | 317 |
| **kaputt sein** | to be broken | 466 |
| **kassieren** | to cash, to receive money | 57 |
| **kauterisieren** | to cauterize | 57 |
| **kegeln** | to bowl | 71 |
| **keifen** | to scold, to chide | 265 |
| **keimen** | to germinate | 261 |
| **kennen lernen** | to become acquainted | 308 |
| **kerben** | to indent, to notch | 151 |
| **ketten** | to chain | 44 |

| | | |
|---|---|---|
| **kichern** | to giggle | 354 |
| **kitzeln** | to tickle | 71 |
| **kläffen** | to bark, to yelp | 265 |
| **klaffen** | to gape, to yawn | 265 |
| **klären** | to clear, to clarify | 157 |
| **klassifizieren** | to classify | 57 |
| **klauben** | to pick out, to sort | 226 |
| **klauen** | to steal, to pilfer | 406 |
| **kleben** | to adhere to | 44 |
| **klecksen** | to make a stain | 315 |
| **klemmen** | to squeeze, to pinch, to be stuck | 499 |
| **klimpern** | to jingle, to clink | 354 |
| **klirren** | to clink | 255 |
| **klittern** | to cheat, to change details | 191 |
| **klumpen** | to cake, to get lumpy | 521 |
| **knabbern** | to nibble, to gnaw | 47 |
| **knacken** | to crack | 416 |
| **knallen** | to burst, to pop | 253 |
| **knechten** | to subjugate, to enslave | 44 |
| **kneifen** | to pinch, to squeeze | 508 |
| **kneten** | to knead | 44 |
| **knicken** | to bend, to break | 416 |
| **knickern** | to be mean, to be stingy | 204 |
| **knien** | to kneel, to genuflect | 253 |
| **knipsen** | to punch (a hole), to take a picture | 390 |
| **knirschen** | to grind, to creak | 247 |
| **knistern** | to crackle | 191 |
| **knospen** | to bud, to sprout | 521 |
| **knuffen** | to cuff, to pommel | 265 |
| **knuspern** | to crunch | 191 |
| **ködern** | to bait, to lure | 193 |
| **kombinieren** | to combine | 57 |
| **kommandieren** | to command | 57 |
| **kompilieren** | to compile | 57 |
| **komponieren** | to compose | 57 |
| **konkurrieren** | to compete | 57 |

| | | |
|---|---|---|
| **kontrollieren** | to control | 57 |
| **konzentrieren** | to concentrate | 57 |
| **kooperieren** | to cooperate | 57 |
| **köpfen** | to behead | 421 |
| **kopieren** | to copy | 57 |
| **koppeln** | to tie together | 71 |
| **korrigieren** | to correct | 57 |
| **kotzen** | to vomit (colloquial) | 468 |
| **krachen** | to crack, to crash | 294 |
| **krallen** | to claw, to pilfer | 253 |
| **krampfen** | to cramp | 262 |
| **kränken** | to offend, to hurt | 598 |
| **kräuseln** | to curl | 191 |
| **kreischen** | to shriek | 443 |
| **kreisen** | to circle | 315 |
| **kreuzen** | to cross | 468 |
| **kreuzigen** | to crucify | 76 |
| **kritisieren** | to criticize | 57 |
| **kritteln** | to find fault | 289 |
| **kröpfen** | to bend at a right angle | 421 |
| **krümeln** | to crumble | 71 |
| **krümmen** | to bend, to curve | 514 |
| **kühlen** | to cool, to chill | 202 |
| **kultivieren** | to cultivate | 57 |
| **kümmern (sich)** | to take care of | 47 |
| **kundgeben** | to make known, to announce | 63 |
| **kündigen** | to give notice | 159 |
| **künsteln** | to elaborate, to overrefine | 71 |
| **kuppeln** | to couple, to connect | 71 |
| **küren** | to select, to inspect | 255 |
| **kurven** | to curve | 310 |
| **kürzen** | to shorten | 468 |
| **laben** | to refresh | 310 |
| **lackieren** | to lacquer, to varnish | 57 |
| **lallen** | to stammer | 498 |
| **landen** | to land | 189 |

| | | |
|---|---|---|
| **langen** | to hand, to reach, to be enough | 558 |
| **lärmen** | to make noise | 295 |
| **lästern** | to slander | 297 |
| **lauschen** | to listen in, to eavesdrop | 247 |
| **läuten** | to ring, to toll | 97 |
| **lauten** | to sound, to read as | 97 |
| **läutern** | to refine, to purify | 297 |
| **leeren** | to empty | 302 |
| **lehnen** | to lean | 308 |
| **Leid tun** | to be sorry | 535 |
| **leuchten** | to shine, to illuminate | 44 |
| **leugnen** | to deny | 463 |
| **liberalisieren** | to liberalize, to relax | 57 |
| **lichten** | to thin out | 383 |
| **liebäugeln** | to ogle | 71 |
| **liebhaben** | to love, to be fond of | 235 |
| **liefern** | to deliver | 481 |
| **lispeln** | to lisp | 71 |
| **locken** | to attract, to entice | 124 |
| **lodern** | to blaze, to flare up | 47 |
| **löhnen** | to pay | 313 |
| **losarbeiten** | to loosen, to work free | 55 |
| **losbinden** | to untie, to loosen | 109 |
| **losbrechen** | to break loose | 118 |
| **losfahren** | to set off, to leave | 173 |
| **losgehen** | to set out, to leave, to start | 613 |
| **loshaken** | to unhook | 43 |
| **loshauen** | to cut loose | 406 |
| **loslassen** | to let loose, to let go | 296 |
| **löten** | to solder | 97 |
| **lotsen** | to pilot | 315 |
| **lullen** | to lull, to sing | 498 |
| **lüsten** | to covet | 256 |
| **lutschen** | to suck | 271 |
| **magnetisieren** | to magnetize | 57 |
| **maischen** | to mash (as in beer production) | 329 |

| | | |
|---|---|---|
| **mäkeln** | to find fault with | 71 |
| **mampfen** | to eat with the mouth full | 421 |
| **mangeln** | to lack, to be deficient | 275 |
| **maniküren** | to manicure | 480 |
| **manipulieren** | to manipulate | 57 |
| **manövrieren** | to manoeuver | 57 |
| **marmorieren** | to marble, to grain | 57 |
| **marschieren** | to march | 347 |
| **martern** | to torment, to inflict martyrdom | 481 |
| **massieren** | to massage | 57 |
| **maßregeln** | to reprimand | 564 |
| **mästen** | to fatten, to cram | 283 |
| **mauen** | to mew | 518 |
| **meckern** | to bleat, to grumble | 47 |
| **mehren** | to increase, to augment | 561 |
| **mengen** | to mix, to mingle | 394 |
| **meutern** | to mutiny | 481 |
| **miauen** | to mew | 518 |
| **mimen** | to act, to pretend | 45 |
| **missachten** | to disregard, to slight | 44 |
| **missen** | to do without, to miss | 292 |
| **misshandeln** | to abuse, to mistreat | 81 |
| **missstimmen** | to put in bad temper, to upset | 95 |
| **misstönen** | to be out of tune | 162 |
| **misstrauen** | to mistrust | 574 |
| **missverstehen** | to misunderstand | 571 |
| **mitarbeiten** | to cooperate | 55 |
| **mitbringen** | to bring along | 120 |
| **miterben** | to inherit jointly | 151 |
| **miterleben** | to experience firsthand | 299 |
| **mitessen** | to dine with | 172 |
| **mitführen** | to bring along | 203 |
| **mitgeben** | to give to a departing guest, to impart | 63 |
| **mithalten** | to share, to hold jointly | 236 |
| **mithelfen** | to cooperate with, to help | 246 |
| **mitkommen** | to come along | 49 |

| | | |
|---|---|---|
| **mitnehmen** | to take along | 612 |
| **mitreisen** | to travel with | 378 |
| **mitschreiben** | to take notes | 449 |
| **mitspielen** | to play with | 485 |
| **mitsprechen** | to join in a conversation | 488 |
| **mitstimmen** | to add one's vote | 95 |
| **mobilisieren** | to mobilize | 57 |
| **monieren** | to criticize | 57 |
| **moralisieren** | to moralize | 57 |
| **murmeln** | to mumble, to mutter | 71 |
| **murren** | to murmur, to grumble | 255 |
| **nachäffen** | to mimic | 252 |
| **nachahmen** | to imitate | 59 |
| **nachbestellen** | to order anew, to reorder | 94 |
| **nachbezahlen** | to pay later, to pay extra (later) charges | 105 |
| **nachbilden** | to reproduce, to copy | 108 |
| **nachbleiben** | to remain behind | 112 |
| **nachdenken** | to reflect, to ponder | 125 |
| **nachdrängen** | to crowd, to push | 129 |
| **nachdringen** | to be in hot pursuit | 130 |
| **nachdrucken** | to reprint, to republish | 132 |
| **nacheifern** | to emulate | 481 |
| **nachempfinden** | to empathize | 492 |
| **nacherzählen** | to retell | 170 |
| **nachfolgen** | to follow, to pursue | 192 |
| **nachforschen** | to search after, to investigate | 195 |
| **nachfragen** | to inquire about | 197 |
| **nachgeben** | to give in, to yield | 63 |
| **nachgehen** | to be behind, to follow, to investigate | 613 |
| **nachhallen** | to echo | 580 |
| **nachhalten** | to hold out | 236 |
| **nachholen** | to retrieve, to recover | 253 |
| **nachjagen** | to chase after | 257 |
| **nachkommen** | to come after | 49 |
| **nachleuchten** | to be luminous | 44 |
| **nachliefern** | to deliver subsequently | 481 |

| | | |
|---|---|---|
| **nachprüfen** | to verify | 358 |
| **nachschauen** | to gaze after, to check | 616 |
| **nachschieben** | to push along | 417 |
| **nachschlagen** | to consult a book, to look up in a book | 425 |
| **nachsehen** | to look after, to follow with the eyes, to check | 66 |
| **nachsenden** | to send after, to forward | 467 |
| **nachsetzen** | to set behind, to add | 196 |
| **nachstellen** | to lie in wait | 580 |
| **nachsuchen** | to search for | 513 |
| **nachweinen** | to mourn, to lament | 590 |
| **nachwirken** | to produce an after-effect | 598 |
| **nageln** | to nail | 71 |
| **nagen** | to gnaw | 338 |
| **nähern (sich)** | to approach, to draw near | 47 |
| **narren** | to make a fool of someone | 480 |
| **naschen** | to eat sweets | 247 |
| **neiden** | to envy | 87 |
| **nesteln** | to fiddle with | 71 |
| **neutralisieren** | to neutralize | 57 |
| **nicken** | to nod | 124 |
| **niederbeugen** | to bend down | 100 |
| **niederbrechen** | to break down | 118 |
| **niederbrennen** | to burn down | 119 |
| **niederhalten** | to hold down | 236 |
| **niederkämpfen** | to overpower | 262 |
| **niederlegen** | to lay down | 301 |
| **niedermetzeln** | to cut down, to massacre | 71 |
| **niederrollen** | to roll down | 192 |
| **niederschießen** | to shoot down | 418 |
| **niederschlagen** | to knock down | 425 |
| **niederschmettern** | to strike down | 607 |
| **niederschreien** | to shout down | 450 |
| **niedersinken** | to sink down | 474 |
| **niedertreten** | to trample down | 531 |
| **niederwerfen** | to throw down | 594 |
| **nieseln** | to drizzle | 71 |

| | | |
|---|---|---|
| **nieten** | to rivet | 97 |
| **nisten** | to nest | 44 |
| **nötigen** | to necessitate, to oblige | 159 |
| **nullifizieren** | to nullify | 57 |
| **numerieren** | to number | 57 |
| **offenhalten** | to keep open | 236 |
| **offenlassen** | to leave open | 296 |
| **offenstehen** | to be at liberty, to remain unsettled | 495 |
| **operieren** | to operate | 57 |
| **opfern** | to sacrifice | 47 |
| **organisieren** | to organize | 57 |
| **packen** | to pack, to seize, to grasp | 345 |
| **patschen** | to clap, to smack | 271 |
| **pauken** | to beat a drum | 124 |
| **peitschen** | to whip | 271 |
| **pendeln** | to swing, to oscillate | 71 |
| **pfänden** | to seize, to take in pledge | 44 |
| **pflügen** | to plow | 350 |
| **pfuschen** | to cheat on an exam | 247 |
| **photographieren** | to photograph | 57 |
| **pinseln** | to brush, to paint | 71 |
| **planen** | to plan | 308 |
| **platschen** | to splash | 271 |
| **plombieren** | to seal with lead, to plug, to put in a tooth filling | 57 |
| **prangen** | to be resplendent | 394 |
| **preisen** | to praise, to extol | 409 |
| **produzieren** | to produce | 57 |
| **programmieren** | to program | 57 |
| **protestieren** | to protest | 57 |
| **Rad fahren** | to go bike riding | 173 |
| **rasieren (sich)** | to shave | 57 |
| **räuchern** | to smoke, to cure | 481 |
| **raufen (sich)** | to scuffle | 265 |
| **räumen** | to clear away, to forcibly remove | 59 |
| **raunen** | to whisper | 308 |
| **rauschen** | to rustle, to roar | 247 |

| | | |
|---|---|---|
| **reagieren** | to react | 373 |
| **realisieren** | to realize | 57 |
| **Rechte verletzen** | to violate the law | 559 |
| **reduzieren** | to reduce | 57 |
| **regeln** | to regulate | 71 |
| **regen** | to move, to stir | 60 |
| **reimen** | to rhyme | 295 |
| **reinmachen** | to clean | 317 |
| **renovieren** | to renovate | 57 |
| **reparieren** | to repair | 57 |
| **reservieren** | to reserve | 57 |
| **restaurieren** | to restore | 57 |
| **ringen** | to wrestle, to grapple, to wring | 473 |
| **rinnen** | to drip, to trickle | 486 |
| **riskieren** | to risk | 57 |
| **rollen** | to roll | 498 |
| **röntgen** | to x-ray | 394 |
| **rösten** | to roast | 44 |
| **rücken** | to move, to shove | 336 |
| **ruinieren** | to ruin | 57 |
| **rüsten** | to equip, to fit out | 65 |
| **sägen** | to saw | 301 |
| **saubermachen** | to clean | 317 |
| **säubern** | to cleanse, to purge | 481 |
| **säumen** | to hem, to linger | 566 |
| **sausen** | to bluster, to howl | 394 |
| **schallen** | to sound, to peal | 498 |
| **schäumen** | to foam, to froth | 403 |
| **schelten** | to scold, to reproach | 214 |
| **schichten** | to layer | 383 |
| **schlendern** | to saunter | 583 |
| **schlichten** | to arbitrate | 383 |
| **schlingen** | to wind, to twist, to entwine | 473 |
| **Schlittschuh laufen** | to go iceskating | 298 |
| **schlitzen** | to slit | 468 |

| | | |
|---|---|---|
| **schlurfen** | to drag one's feet | 277 |
| **Schluß machen** | to end, to stop | 317 |
| **schmachten** | to pine, to long for | 44 |
| **schnallen** | to buckle, to fasten | 498 |
| **schockieren** | to shock | 57 |
| **schrecken** | to be frightened, to be startled | 598 |
| **schwächen** | to weaken | 294 |
| **schwanken** | to shake, to roll, to sway | 598 |
| **schwänzen** | to play hooky | 468 |
| **schwarzfahren** | to travel without a ticket | 173 |
| **schwatzen** | to chat, to chatter | 468 |
| **schwenken** | to swing, to swivel | 326 |
| **schwerfallen** | to be difficult or burdensome | 137 |
| **schwindeln** | to swindle | 71 |
| **schwinden** | to become less, to shrink, to fade | 568 |
| **schwingen** | to swing, to brandish | 473 |
| **seekrank sein** | to be seasick | 466 |
| **seekrank werden** | to become seasick | 593 |
| **servieren** | to serve | 57 |
| **sichten** | to sight (in the distance) | 383 |
| **siezen** | to address with *Sie* | 245 |
| **sitzen bleiben** | to remain sitting, to repeat a year (in school) | 112 |
| **Ski fahren** | to go skiing | 173 |
| **sondern** | to separate | 47 |
| **sonnen (sich)** | to sunbathe, to bask in the sun | 308 |
| **sortieren** | to sort | 57 |
| **spazieren gehen** | to go for a stroll | 613 |
| **spazieren** | to stroll | 347 |
| **spekulieren** | to speculate | 57 |
| **spendieren** | to treat, to pay for | 57 |
| **spiegeln** | to sparkle, to reflect | 71 |
| **spionieren** | to spy | 57 |
| **sprengen** | to burst, to explode | 394 |
| **sprießen** | to sprout, to bud | 188 |
| **sprühen** | to spray, to sprinkle | 114 |
| **spucken** | to spit, to vomit | 124 |

| | | |
|---|---|---|
| **spülen** | to wash, to rinse | 43 |
| **stammen** | to originate | 499 |
| **starten** | to start | 44 |
| **Staub saugen** | to vacuum | 398 |
| **staunen** | to be astonished | 308 |
| **stehen bleiben** | to remain standing | 112 |
| **stehen lassen** | to leave behind, to leave in place | 296 |
| **steigern** | to raise, to heighten | 481 |
| **stiften** | to found, to establish | 44 |
| **stöhnen** | to groan | 45 |
| **stolpern** | to stumble | 583 |
| **stopfen** | to cram, to fill, to mend | 277 |
| **stoppen** | to stop | 521 |
| **stornieren** | to annul, to cancel | 57 |
| **strahlen** | to beam, to shine | 253 |
| **strecken** | to stretch, to extend | 494 |
| **streicheln** | to stroke, to caress | 71 |
| **streiken** | to strike | 124 |
| **streuen** | to strew, to spread | 525 |
| **strömen** | to stream, to flow | 378 |
| **strotzen** | to be puffed up | 468 |
| **studieren** | to study | 57 |
| **stutzen** | to stop short, to hesitate, to crop | 512 |
| **surfen** | to surf | 277 |
| **tänzeln** | to skip, to hop | 462 |
| **taugen** | to be of value, to be worth | 301 |
| **täuschen (sich)** | to deceive, to be mistaken | 247 |
| **teilnehmen** | to participate | 612 |
| **telefonieren** | to telephone | 57 |
| **telegrafieren** | to telegraph | 57 |
| **tilgen** | to extinguish, to erase | 472 |
| **tönen** | to resound, to ring | 308 |
| **töpfern** | to make pottery | 277 |
| **trachten** | to strive for | 44 |
| **trainieren** | to train | 57 |
| **transportieren** | to transport | 57 |

| | | |
|---|---|---|
| **trappeln** | to trot, to patter | 462 |
| **triefen** | to drip, to secrete | 107 |
| **trillern** | to trill, to warble | 481 |
| **trommeln** | to drum | 71 |
| **tröpfeln** | to drip | 71 |
| **trotten** | to jog along | 189 |
| **trotzen** | to defy, to be obstinate | 468 |
| **trüben** | to make muddy, to cloud | 310 |
| **trügen** | to deceive, to delude | 98 |
| **überfáhren** | to pass over, to run over | 173 |
| **überfállen** | to fall upon, to attack | 209 |
| **überfórdern** | to overcharge | 193 |
| **übergében** | to deliver, to hand over | 207 |
| **überhólen** | to overhaul, to overtake | 253 |
| **überhören** | to ignore, to miss | 86 |
| **überlaufen** | to run, to flow over | 298 |
| **überlében** | to outlive, to survive | 299 |
| **übermüden** | to overtire | 144 |
| **übernáchten** | to spend the night | 44 |
| **überméhmen** | to take possession of, to take charge | 550 |
| **überquéren** | to cross | 538 |
| **überréden** | to persuade | 372 |
| **überréichen** | to hand over | 376 |
| **überschätzen** | to overestimate | 405 |
| **überséhen** | to miss, to overlook | 464 |
| **überwéisen** | to remit, to transfer, to give a referral | 591 |
| **überwínden** | to overcome, to prevail | 109 |
| **überziehen** | to cover, to spread over | 615 |
| **umändern** | to alter, to transform | 47 |
| **umbiegen** | to bend back, to turn back | 106 |
| **umbringen** | to kill | 120 |
| **umfáhren** | to drive round | 173 |
| **úmfahren** | to run over | 173 |
| **umfassen** | to embrace, to clasp | 178 |
| **umgestalten** | to transform | 219 |
| **umleiten** | to divert | 306 |

| | | |
|---|---|---|
| **umrühren** | to stir, to agitate | 389 |
| **umschalten** | to switch over, to switch channels | 402 |
| **umschauen (sich)** | to look around | 616 |
| **umschnallen** | to strap on | 580 |
| **umstellen (sich)** | to rearrange, to adapt | 580 |
| **umtauschen** | to exchange | 68 |
| **umwandeln** | to change, to alter | 395 |
| **umziehen (sich)** | to change clothes | 615 |
| **unterbréchen** | to interrupt | 118 |
| **unterbringen** | to shelter, to quarter | 120 |
| **untergehen** | to set (as of the sun), to founder | 613 |
| **unterhálten (sich)** | to converse | 80 |
| **unterkommen** | to find shelter | 49 |
| **unterordnen** | to subordinate | 342 |
| **unterríchten** | to teach, to instruct | 383 |
| **unterschätzen** | to undervalue | 88 |
| **unterschréiben** | to sign | 90 |
| **untersúchen** | to investigate, to analyze, to examine | 96 |
| **untervermieten** | to sublet | 328 |
| **urteilen** | to judge, to form an opinion | 520 |
| **verabreden (sich)** | to make a date | 372 |
| **verabreichen** | to hand over, to give medicine | 376 |
| **verabscheuen** | to abhor | 574 |
| **verachten** | to despise | 44 |
| **veralbern** | to ridicule | 569 |
| **veralten** | to grow old, to turn stale | 189 |
| **verändern** | to alter, to change | 47 |
| **verankern** | to anchor, to moor | 569 |
| **veranlassen** | to cause | 315 |
| **veranstalten** | to arrange, to organize | 562 |
| **verantworten** | to answer for, to be responsible | 52 |
| **verarbeiten** | to use as a material, to process | 55 |
| **verarmen** | to become poor | 544 |
| **verbauen** | to obstruct, to block out | 72 |
| **verbergen** | to hide | 214 |
| **verbessern** | to improve | 569 |

| | | |
|---|---|---|
| **verbinden** | to bind, to connect, to put on a bandage | 109 |
| **verbleiben** | to remain | 112 |
| **verbleichen** | to grow pale, to fade | 380 |
| **verbleien** | to coat with lead | 574 |
| **verblenden** | to blind | 567 |
| **verblüffen** | to startle, to bewilder | 558 |
| **verblühen** | to fade, to wither | 378 |
| **verbluten** | to bleed to death | 562 |
| **verbrauchen** | to use up, to consume | 208 |
| **verbrechen** | to commit a crime | 118 |
| **verbrennen** | to burn, to scorch | 119 |
| **verbringen** | to spend time | 120 |
| **verdächtigen** | to be suspicious | 89 |
| **verdeutschen** | to translate into German | 539 |
| **verdichten** | to thicken, to condense | 126 |
| **verdicken** | to thicken, to swell | 558 |
| **verdienen** | to earn, to deserve | 127 |
| **verdunkeln** | to darken | 150 |
| **verdünnen** | to thin | 558 |
| **verdunsten** | to evaporate | 146 |
| **verdüstern (sich)** | to darken | 569 |
| **verdutzen** | to bewilder, to startle | 559 |
| **verebben** | to die down | 558 |
| **verehelichen (sich)** | to marry | 96 |
| **verehren** | to honor, to revere | 561 |
| **vereidigen** | to swear in | 572 |
| **vereinbaren** | to come to an understanding | 608 |
| **vereinfachen** | to simplify | 558 |
| **vereinheitlichen** | to standardize | 96 |
| **vereinigen** | to unite | 558 |
| **vereinsamen** | to grow lonely | 558 |
| **vereinzeln** | to isolate | 564 |
| **vereiteln** | to frustrate, to thwart | 564 |
| **verelenden** | to fall into poverty | 189 |

| | | |
|---|---|---|
| **verenden** | to die | 74 |
| **verengen** | to narrow | 569 |
| **vererben** | to bequeath | 151 |
| **verewigen** | to immortalize | 558 |
| **verfahren** | to act, to handle, to manage | 173 |
| **verfallen** | to decay, to deteriorate | 174 |
| **verfälschen** | to adulterate, to counterfeit | 539 |
| **verfärben** | to discolor | 177 |
| **verfassen** | to compose | 178 |
| **verfaulen** | to rot | 566 |
| **verfeinden (sich)** | to make an enemy of | 74 |
| **verfließen** | to flow away, to blend | 188 |
| **verfluchen** | to curse, to damn | 189 |
| **verfolgen** | to persecute | 558 |
| **verfrühen (sich)** | to come early | 574 |
| **verfügen** | to order, to arrange | 250 |
| **verführen** | to lead astray | 203 |
| **verfüttern** | to use as fodder | 204 |
| **vergasen** | to vaporize, to gas | 315 |
| **vergattern** | to enclose with grating | 569 |
| **vergeben** | to award, to forgive | 207 |
| **vergegenwärtigen** | to bring to mind | 572 |
| **vergehen** | to pass, to elapse, to vanish | 210 |
| **vergelten** | to pay back | 214 |
| **vergeuden** | to squander | 74 |
| **vergewaltigen** | to rape | 76 |
| **vergewissern** | to confirm | 569 |
| **vergießen** | to spill | 224 |
| **vergiften** | to poison | 562 |
| **verglasen** | to glaze | 88 |
| **vergleichen** | to compare | 227 |
| **verglühen** | to burn out, to stop glowing | 192 |
| **vergnügen (sich)** | to amuse | 217 |
| **vergolden** | to gild | 74 |
| **vergönnen** | to permit, to grant | 566 |
| **vergöttern** | to idolize | 569 |

| | | |
|---|---|---|
| **vergraben** | to bury, to hide | 228 |
| **vergreifen (sich)** | to make a mistake, to assault | 230 |
| **vergreisen** | to age, to become old | 232 |
| **vergrößern (sich)** | to enlarge, to increase | 569 |
| **vergüten** | to make amends, to pay | 562 |
| **verhallen** | to fade away | 378 |
| **verhalten (sich)** | to behave, to have a relation to | 236 |
| **verhalten** | to hold back | 80 |
| **verhandeln** | to negotiate | 81 |
| **verhärten** | to harden | 74 |
| **verhauen** | to beat, to beat up | 240 |
| **verheeren** | to ravage | 561 |
| **verhehlen** | to conceal from | 325 |
| **verheilen** | to heal up | 378 |
| **verheimlichen** | to conceal | 96 |
| **verherrlichen** | to glorify | 96 |
| **verhindern** | to hinder, to prevent | 569 |
| **verhöhnen** | to mock | 85 |
| **verhören** | to examine, to question | 255 |
| **verhüllen** | to veil, to wrap up | 94 |
| **verhüten** | to prevent, to use contraception | 74 |
| **verkalken** | to calcify | 141 |
| **verkaufen** | to sell | 265 |
| **verkehren** | to frequent, to transform into the opposite | 266 |
| **verkennen** | to fail to recognize | 267 |
| **verklagen** | to accuse, to sue | 269 |
| **verklären** | to make radiant | 157 |
| **verkleiden** | to cover, to disguise | 273 |
| **verkommen** | to decay, to go bad | 281 |
| **verkörpern** | to embody | 569 |
| **verkürzen** | to shorten | 154 |
| **verlachen** | to deride | 294 |
| **verlängern** | to lengthen | 569 |
| **verlaufen (sich)** | to elapse, to turn out, to get lost | 298 |
| **verlegen** | to transfer, to put off, to reschedule | 538 |
| **verlesen** | to read out, to call off | 309 |

| | | |
|---|---|---|
| **verleugnen** | to deny | 463 |
| **verlieben (sich)** | to fall in love | 310 |
| **verloben (sich)** | to become engaged | 312 |
| **vermeiden** | to avoid | 322 |
| **vermischen** | to mix, to blend | 329 |
| **vermissen** | to miss | 559 |
| **vermitteln** | to mediate, to adjust | 150 |
| **vermummen** | to wrap up | 514 |
| **vermurchsen** | to mess up, to bungle | 247 |
| **vermuten** | to suppose | 562 |
| **vernehmen** | to perceive, to question a witness/suspect | 550 |
| **verneinen** | to deny, to disavow | 566 |
| **veröffentlichen** | to publish | 96 |
| **verpachten** | to lease, to farm out | 343 |
| **verpassen** | to miss | 346 |
| **verpesten** | to pollute, to contaminate | 146 |
| **verpflegen** | to feed, to provide for | 350 |
| **verpflichten** | to oblige, to bind | 44 |
| **verpfuschen** | to blunder, to bungle | 558 |
| **verrecken** | to kick the bucket | 192 |
| **verreißen** | to criticize harshly | 379 |
| **verrichten** | to perform, to execute | 383 |
| **verriegeln** | to bolt | 81 |
| **verringern** | to diminish | 155 |
| **versagen** | to deny, to refuse, to fail | 394 |
| **versammeln (sich)** | to assemble, to convene | 395 |
| **verschärfen** | to sharpen, to intensify | 404 |
| **verschieben** | to move out of place, to reschedule | 417 |
| **verschießen** | to discharge, to fire | 418 |
| **verschlechtern** | to make worse | 160 |
| **verschonen** | to spare | 558 |
| **verschreiben (sich)** | to prescribe, to write wrong, to make a typo | 90 |
| **verschweigen** | to keep secret | 457 |
| **versehen** | to furnish, to supply with | 464 |

| | | |
|---|---|---|
| **versetzen** | to transfer, to (double) promote | 468 |
| **versilbern** | to silver-plate | 569 |
| **versklaven** | to enslave | 558 |
| **versorgen** | to provide, to attend to | 477 |
| **verspäten (sich)** | to be delayed | 74 |
| **verspotten** | to mock | 487 |
| **verständigen (sich)** | to come to an understanding, to communicate | 76 |
| **versterben** | to expire | 501 |
| **verstimmen** | to put in a bad mood | 95 |
| **verstricken** | to entangle | 509 |
| **versuchen** | to try | 96 |
| **verteilen** | to distribute | 520 |
| **vertilgen** | to annihilate | 558 |
| **verunglücken** | to have an accident | 141 |
| **verursachen** | to cause | 96 |
| **verwahren** | to keep, to secure | 558 |
| **verwalten** | to administer | 74 |
| **verwandeln** | to transform | 150 |
| **verwässern** | to water down, to dilute | 160 |
| **verwechseln** | to confuse, to mix up | 588 |
| **verwehren** | to deny somebody something | 558 |
| **verweigern** | to refuse, to reject | 354 |
| **verweilen** | to linger | 520 |
| **verweisen** | to reprimand | 104 |
| **verwelken** | to wilt | 192 |
| **verwesen** | to decompose | 192 |
| **verwickeln** | to implicate | 150 |
| **verwirklichen** | to realize | 96 |
| **verwirren** | to tangle, to confuse | 161 |
| **verzehren** | to consume | 161 |
| **verzieren** | to adorn | 161 |
| **verzollen** | to pay duty | 94 |
| **verzweifeln** | to despair | 81 |
| **vollbríngen** | to accomplish | 120 |
| **vollmachen** | to fill up, to complete | 317 |

| | | |
|---|---|---|
| **vollpfropfen** | to stuff | 421 |
| **vollzíehen (sich)** | to accomplish, to take place | 615 |
| **vorangehen** | to precede, to progress | 613 |
| **vorankommen** | to make progress | 49 |
| **voranschicken** | to send ahead | 416 |
| **vorarbeiten** | to prepare work, to work ahead | 55 |
| **vorausbedingen** | to stipulate | 473 |
| **vorausbestellen** | to order in advance | 94 |
| **vorausbezahlen** | to prepay | 105 |
| **vorausdatieren** | to antedate | 57 |
| **vorauseilen** | to hurry ahead | 192 |
| **vorausgehen** | to go on ahead | 613 |
| **voraushaben** | to have an advantage | 235 |
| **vorausnehmen** | to anticipate | 612 |
| **voraussagen** | to predict | 394 |
| **vorausschauen** | to look forward | 616 |
| **vorausschicken** | to send in advance | 416 |
| **voraussehen** | to foresee | 66 |
| **voraussetzen** | to assume | 196 |
| **vorbedingen** | to stipulate in advance | 473 |
| **vorbehalten** | to withhold, to reserve | 236 |
| **vorbeifahren** | to drive by | 173 |
| **vorbeigehen** | to go by | 613 |
| **vorbeikommen** | to come by | 49 |
| **vorbeimarschieren** | to march by | 347 |
| **vorbeischießen** | to shoot past | 418 |
| **vorbeten** | to recite in prayer | 97 |
| **vorbeugen (sich)** | to bend forward | 100 |
| **vorbringen** | to bring forward | 120 |
| **vordatieren** | to antedate | 57 |
| **vordrängen** | to push forward | 129 |
| **vordringen** | to push on | 489 |
| **vorenthalten** | to withhold | 80 |
| **vorfahren** | to drive up to | 173 |
| **vorfallen** | to happen | 137 |
| **vorfinden** | to come upon | 184 |

| | | |
|---|---|---|
| **vorfühlen** | to have a foreboding | 202 |
| **vorführen** | to bring to the front, to parade, to show | 203 |
| **vorgaukeln** | to lead someone to believe something | 293 |
| **vorgeben** | to give a handicap, to pretend | 63 |
| **vorgehen** | to go before, to proceed | 613 |
| **vorgreifen** | to forestall | 230 |
| **vorhaben** | to intend | 235 |
| **vorhalten** | to hold before, to reproach | 236 |
| **vorherbestimmen** | to settle beforehand, to preordain | 95 |
| **vorhergeschehen** | to happen previously | 218 |
| **vorherrschen** | to prevail | 247 |
| **vorhersehen** | to foresee | 464 |
| **vorherwissen** | to know beforehand | 599 |
| **vorknöpfen** | to take to task | 421 |
| **vorkommen** | to come forth, to occur | 49 |
| **vorlassen** | to let come forward | 296 |
| **vorlegen** | to lay before, to present | 301 |
| **vorlesen** | to read to | 309 |
| **vorliegen** | to be in front of, to be present | 311 |
| **vorlügen** | to tell lies to someone | 316 |
| **vornehmen (sich)** | to put on, to undertake, to plan | 612 |
| **vorragen** | to jut out, to project | 394 |
| **vorrechnen** | to demonstrate a calculation | 370 |
| **vorrichten** | to prepare | 383 |
| **vorrücken** | to move forward | 124 |
| **vorsagen** | to prompt | 394 |
| **vorschicken** | to send forward | 416 |
| **vorschieben** | to push forward | 417 |
| **vorschlagen** | to suggest | 425 |
| **vorschreiben** | to prescribe, to order | 449 |
| **vorschreiten** | to step forward | 451 |
| **vorsetzen** | to set before | 196 |
| **vorsingen** | to sing to | 473 |
| **vorspielen** | to play to | 485 |
| **vorspringen** | to leap forward | 489 |
| **vorstehen** | to jut out, to lead | 495 |

| | | |
|---|---|---|
| **vorstrecken** | to stretch forward, to loan money | 509 |
| **vorübergehen** | to pass by | 613 |
| **vorwärmen** | to preheat | 59 |
| **vorwärtsgehen** | to go forward | 613 |
| **vorwärtskommen** | to come forward | 49 |
| **vorweisen** | to display | 591 |
| **vorwerfen** | to cast before, to accuse of | 594 |
| **vorziehen** | to draw forward | 615 |
| **wabern** | to flicker | 193 |
| **wachsen** | to coat with wax | 315 |
| **wägen** | to ponder | 106 |
| **wagen** | to wager, to bet | 301 |
| **währen** | to last | 302 |
| **wahrnehmen** | to perceive, to be aware of | 612 |
| **walten** | to rule | 44 |
| **wälzen (sich)** | to roll, to rotate | 245 |
| **wegbleiben** | to stay away | 112 |
| **wegbrennen** | to burn away | 119 |
| **wegbringen** | to take away | 120 |
| **wegeilen** | to hurry off | 192 |
| **wegfahren** | to drive away | 173 |
| **wegfallen** | to fall off, to disappear | 137 |
| **wegführen** | to lead away | 203 |
| **weggeben** | to give away | 63 |
| **weggehen** | to go away | 613 |
| **weghaben** | to have the knack of | 235 |
| **weghelfen** | to help get away | 246 |
| **wegjagen** | to chase away | 257 |
| **wegkommen** | to get away | 49 |
| **weglassen** | to leave out | 296 |
| **weglegen** | to put aside | 301 |
| **wegnehmen** | to take away | 612 |
| **wegpacken** | to pack away, to put away | 124 |
| **wegreisen** | to depart | 378 |
| **wegreißen** | to tear down, to tear away | 379 |
| **wegschicken** | to send away | 416 |

| | | |
|---|---|---|
| **wegsehen** | to look away | 66 |
| **wegsetzen (sich)** | to put aside, to change seats | 196 |
| **wegtreiben** | to drive away | 529 |
| **wegtun** | to set aside | 535 |
| **wegwerfen** | to throw away | 594 |
| **wegwischen** | to wipe away | 329 |
| **wegziehen** | to pull away, to move away | 615 |
| **wehen** | to blow, to flutter | 114 |
| **wehren (sich)** | to defend | 203 |
| **weichen** | to yield | 380 |
| **weigern (sich)** | to refuse | 47 |
| **weihen** | to dedicate | 114 |
| **weilen** | to stay, to tarry | 520 |
| **weismachen** | to make believe, to pull a hoax | 317 |
| **weiten** | to widen | 44 |
| **weiterbefördern** | to send on | 193 |
| **weiterbestehen** | to go on | 495 |
| **weiterbewegen** | to move forward | 102 |
| **weiterbringen** | to promote | 120 |
| **weiterführen** | to continue | 203 |
| **weitergeben** | to pass on | 63 |
| **weitergehen** | to walk on | 613 |
| **weiterhelfen** | to help to continue | 246 |
| **weiterlesen** | to read on | 309 |
| **weitersagen** | to tell others | 394 |
| **weiterschicken** | to send on | 416 |
| **weiterspielen** | to continue playing | 485 |
| **welken** | to wilt | 192 |
| **werben** | to recruit, to solicit, to advertise | 214 |
| **wetten** | to bet, to wager | 97 |
| **wetzen** | to grind, to sharpen | 245 |
| **wickeln** | to wind | 71 |
| **widerlégen** | to refute | 538 |
| **widerspréchen** | to contradict | 570 |
| **widersténen** | to resist, to oppose | 571 |
| **widmen** | to dedicate, to devote | 58 |

| | | |
|---|---|---|
| **wiederkommen** | to come back | 49 |
| **wiederverkaufen** | to resell | 265 |
| **wiegen** | to weigh | 106 |
| **winken** | to wave | 598 |
| **wühlen** | to dig, to burrow | 202 |
| **wundern (sich)** | to astonish, to wonder | 354 |
| **würzen** | to spice | 468 |
| **zanken (sich)** | to quarrel | 124 |
| **zelten** | to camp out | 44 |
| **zerbrechen** | to break to pieces | 118 |
| **zerfallen** | to fall apart | 174 |
| **zerlegen** | to take apart | 538 |
| **zerplatzen** | to burst into pieces | 353 |
| **zerquetschen** | to crush | 271 |
| **zerren** | to pull, to tug | 302 |
| **zerschießen** | to shoot to pieces | 418 |
| **zerstampfen** | to mash, to trample | 262 |
| **zerstreuen** | to disperse | 85 |
| **zeugen** | to beget | 100 |
| **zielen** | to aim | 520 |
| **zitieren** | to quote | 57 |
| **zittern** | to tremble | 47 |
| **zögern** | to hesitate | 47 |
| **zubereiten** | to prepare, to cook | 578 |
| **zubinden** | to tie up | 109 |
| **züchten** | to breed | 44 |
| **zudecken** | to cover up | 124 |
| **zuhaben** | to be closed, to stay closed | 235 |
| **zuheilen** | to heal up | 378 |
| **zuknöpfen** | to button up | 277 |
| **zukommen** | to come up to, to approach | 49 |
| **zulächeln** | to smile at | 293 |
| **zulassen** | to leave closed | 296 |
| **zumachen** | to close | 317 |
| **zureden** | to advise, to urge | 372 |
| **zureichen** | to suffice, to pass to | 376 |

| | | |
|---|---|---|
| **zürnen** | to be annoyed | 308 |
| **zurückbekommen** | to recover | 83 |
| **zurückbezahlen** | to pay back | 105 |
| **zurückbleiben** | to remain behind | 112 |
| **zurückblicken** | to look back | 416 |
| **zurückbringen** | to bring back | 120 |
| **zurückfahren** | to drive back | 173 |
| **zurückfallen** | to fall back | 137 |
| **zurückfinden** | to find the way back | 492 |
| **zurückführen** | to lead back | 203 |
| **zurückgeben** | to give back | 63 |
| **zurückhalten** | to hold back | 236 |
| **zurückkommen** | to come back | 49 |
| **zurücklassen** | to leave behind | 296 |
| **zurücklaufen** | to run back | 298 |
| **zurückleiten** | to lead back | 306 |
| **zurücklenken** | to guide back | 307 |
| **zurückrufen** | to call back | 50 |
| **zurückschicken** | to send back | 416 |
| **zurückschlagen** | to beat back, to hit back | 425 |
| **zurückspringen** | to jump back | 489 |
| **zurückstellen** | to put back | 580 |
| **zurückstoßen** | to push back | 505 |
| **zurücktreiben** | to drive back | 529 |
| **zurücktreten** | to step back, to resign | 531 |
| **zurückweichen** | to give way | 380 |
| **zurückweisen** | to reject, to rebuff | 591 |
| **zurückwerfen** | to throw back | 594 |
| **zusammenarbeiten** | to cooperate | 55 |
| **zusammenbeißen** | to clench the teeth | 82 |
| **zusammenbrechen** | to collapse | 118 |
| **zusammenfassen** | to summarize | 178 |
| **zusammenleben** | to live together | 299 |
| **zusammenpassen** | to go well together | 346 |
| **zuschlagen** | to slam | 425 |
| **zuschreiben** | to assign, to attribute | 449 |

| | | |
|---|---|---|
| **zusein** | to be closed | 466 |
| **zusprechen** | to impart by word of mouth | 488 |
| **zussammnbinden** | to tie together | 109 |
| **zustimmen** | to agree to | 95 |
| **zuwerfen** | to throw to | 594 |
| **zuwinken** | to wave to | 616 |
| **zuziehen** | to draw together, to draw tight | 615 |
| **zweifeln** | to doubt | 71 |
| **zwicken** | to pinch | 336 |
| **zwirbeln** | to twirl | 71 |
| **zwitschern** | to chirp | 419 |

# APPENDIX OF IRREGULAR VERB FORMS

If a verb has an irregularity in the present tense, in the past tense, or as a past participle, those forms are shown here in the third-person singular *(er, sie, es)*. I've provided the infinitive of the irregular verb, as well as the page number where you can find the equivalent conjugation of the verb.

**B**

bäckt, buk or backte, gebacken **backen 69**

band, gebunden **binden 109**

band los, losgebunden **binden 109**

band zu, zugebunden **binden 109**

bat, gebeten **bitten 110**

bedarf, bedurfte, bedurft **dürfen 135**

befällt, befiel, befallen **befallen 80**

befand, befunden **befinden 184**

befiehlt, befahl, befohlen **befehlen 75**

begann, begonnen **beginnen 78**

begibt, begab, begeben **begeben 207**

beging, begangen **begehen 210**

begriff, begriffen **begreifen 230**

behält, behielt, behalten **behalten 80**

behält vor, behielt vor, vorbehalten **vorbehalten 80**

bekam, bekommen **bekommen 83**

bekam zurück, zurückbekommen **zurückbekommen 83**

bekannte, bekannt **bekennen 267**

belog, belogen **belügen 316**

benimmt, benahm, benommen **benehmen 550**

berggestiegen **bergsteigen 548**

besaß, besessen **besitzen 475**

beschloss, beschlossen **beschließen 430**

beschoss, beschossen **beschießen 418**

beschrieb, beschrieben **beschreiben 90**

bestand, bestanden **bestehen 571**

bestand weiter, weiterbestanden **weiterbestehen 571**

beträgt, betrug, betragen **betragen 573**

betrieb, betrieben **betreiben 529**

betrifft, betraf, betroffen **betreffen 528**

betrog, betrogen **betrügen 98**

bewies, bewiesen **beweisen 104**

bewog, bewogen **bewegen 103**

bezog, bezogen **beziehen 171**

birst, barst, geborsten **bersten 488**

biss, gebissen **beißen 82**

biss an, angebissen **anbeißen 82**

biss zusammen, zusammengebissen **zusammenbeißen 82**

bläst, blies, geblasen **blasen 111**

bläst auf, blies auf, aufgeblasen **aufblasen 111**

blieb, geblieben **bleiben 112**

blieb auf, aufgeblieben **aufbleiben 112**

blieb aus, ausgeblieben **ausbleiben 112**

blieb fort, fortgeblieben **fortbleiben 112**

blieb sitzen, sitzen geblieben **sitzen bleiben 112**

blieb stehen, stehen geblieben **stehen bleiben 112**

blieb zurück, zurückgeblieben **zurückbleiben 112**

bog, gebogen **biegen 106**

bog ab, abgebogen **abbiegen 106**

bog um, umgebogen **umbiegen 106**

bot, geboten **bieten 46**

bot an, angeboten **anbieten 46**

bot dar, dargeboten **darbieten 46**

brachte, gebracht **bringen 120**

brachte auseinander, auseinander gebracht **auseinander bringen 120**

brachte bei, beigebracht **beibringen 120**

brachte fort, fortgebracht **fortbringen 120**

brachte heim, heimgebracht **heimbringen 120**

brachte heraus, herausgebracht **herausbringen 120**

brachte mit, mitgebracht **mitbringen 120**

brachte um, umgebracht **umbringen 120**

brachte unter, untergebracht **unterbringen 120**

brachte vor, vorgebracht **vorbringen 120**

brachte vorwärts, vorwärts gebracht **vorwärts bringen 120**

brachte weiter, weitergebracht **weiterbringen 120**

brachte zurück, zurückgebracht **zurückbringen 120**

brannte, gebrannt **brennen 119**

brannte an, angebrannt **anbrennen 119**

brannte aus, ausgebrannt **ausbrennen 119**

brannte nieder, niedergebrannt **niederbrennen 119**

brät, briet, gebraten **braten 116**

bricht, brach, gebrochen **brechen 118**

bricht auf, brach auf, aufgebrochen **aufbrechen 118**

bricht durch, brach durch, durchgebrochen **durchbrechen 118**

bricht los, brach los, losgebrochen **losbrechen 118**

bricht nieder, brach nieder, niedergebrochen **niederbrechen 118**

bricht zusammen, brach zusammen, zusammengebrochen **zusammenbrechen 118**

## D

dachte, gedacht **denken 125**

dachte nach, nachgedacht **nachdenken 125**

darf, durfte, gedurft **dürfen 135**

drang, gedrungen **dringen 130**

drang durch, durchgedrungen **durchdringen 130**

drang ein, eingedrungen **eindringen 489**

drischt, drosch, gedroschen **dreschen 214**

durchschläft, durchschlief, durchschlafen **durchschlafen 424**

## E

empfand, empfunden **empfinden 152**

empfand nach, nachempfunden **nachempfinden 492**

empfängt, empfing, empfangen **empfangen 176**

empfiehlt, empfahl, empfohlen **empfehlen 75**

entfloh, entflohen **entfliehen 143**

enthält, enthielt, enthalten **enthalten 80**

entkam, entkommen **entkommen 281**

entlädt, entlud, entladen **entladen 138**

entlässt, entließ, entlassen **entlassen 296**

entläuft, entlief, entlaufen **entlaufen 298**

entriss, entrissen **entreißen 379**

entschied, entschieden **entscheiden 147**

entschloss, entschlossen **entschließen 430**

entstand, entstanden **entstehen 495**

entwirft, entwarf, entworfen **entwerfen 594**

erfährt, erfuhr, erfahren **erfahren 173**

erfand, erfunden **erfinden 152**

erfror, erfroren **erfrieren 200**

ergibt, ergab, ergeben **ergeben 207**

ergriff, ergriffen **ergreifen 230**

erhält, erhielt, erhalten **erhalten 80**

erhob, erhoben **erheben 241**

erkannte, erkannt **erkennen 267**

erkannte an, anerkannt **anerkennen 267**

erlosch, erloschen **erlöschen 314**

ernannte, ernannt **ernennen 339**

errät, erriet, erraten **erraten 565**

erschien, erschienen **erscheinen 164**

erschlägt, erschlug, erschlagen **erschlagen 425**

erschoss, erschossen **erschießen 418**

erschrickt, erschrak, erschrocken **erschrecken 166**

erträgt, ertrug, ertragen **ertragen 167**

ertrank, ertrunken **ertrinken 168**

erwächst, erwuchs, erwachsen **erwachsen 581**

erwies, erwiesen **erweisen 104**

erzog, erzogen **erziehen 171**

## F

fährt, fuhr, gefahren **fahren 173**

fährt ab, fuhr ab, abgefahren **abfahren 173**

fährt an, fuhr an, angefahren **anfahren 173**

fährt durch, fuhr durch, durchgefahren **durchfahren 173**

fährt fort, fuhr fort, fortgefahren **fortfahren 173**

fährt heim, fuhr heim, heimgefahren **heimfahren 173**

fährt los, fuhr los, losgefahren **losfahren 173**

fährt Rad, fuhr Rad, Rad gefahren **Rad fahren 173**

fährt schwarz, fuhr schwarz, schwarzgefahren **schwarzfahren 173**

fährt Ski, fuhr Ski, Ski gefahren **Ski fahren 173**

fährt um, fuhr um, umgefahren **umfahren 173**

fährt vor, fuhr vor, vorgefahren **vorfahren 173**

fährt vorbei, fuhr vorbei, vorbeigefahren **vorbeifahren 173**

fährt weg, fuhr weg, weggefahren **wegfahren 173**

fährt weiter, fuhr weiter, weitergefahren **weiterfahren 173**

fährt zurück, fuhr zurück, zurückgefahren **zurückfahren 173**

fällt, fiel, gefallen **fallen 174**

fällt an, fiel an, angefallen **anfallen 137**

fällt auf, fiel auf, aufgefallen **auffallen 137**

fällt aus, fiel aus, ausgefallen **ausfallen 137**

fällt durch, fiel durch, durchgefallen **durchfallen 137**

fällt ein, fiel ein, eingefallen **einfallen 137**

fällt herein, fiel herein, hereingefallen **hereinfallen 137**

fällt hin, fiel hin, hingefallen **hinfallen 137**

fällt leicht, fiel leicht, leichtgefallen **leichtfallen 137**

fällt schwer, fiel schwer, schwergefallen **schwerfallen 137**

fällt vor, fiel vor, vorgefallen **vorfallen 137**

fällt zurück, fiel zurück, zurückgefallen **zurückfallen 137**

fand, gefunden **finden 184**

fand ab, abgefunden **abfinden 492**

fand heraus, herausgefunden **herausfinden 492**

fand statt, stattgefunden **stattfinden 492**

fand vor, vorgefunden **vorfinden 492**

fand zurück, zurückgefunden **zurückfinden 492**

fängt, fing, gefangen **fangen 176**

fängt an, fing an, angefangen **anfangen 48**

ficht, focht, gefochten **fechten 180**

flog, geflogen **fliegen 186**

flog aus, ausgeflogen **ausfliegen 186**

floh, geflohen **fliehen 187**

floss, geflossen **fließen 188**

frisst, fraß, gefressen **fressen 198**

frisst an, fraß an, angefressen **anfressen 198**

fror, gefroren **frieren 200**

## G

gebärt or gebiert, gebar, geboren **gebären 206**

gebot, geboten **gebieten 107**

gedachte, gedacht **gedenken 125**

gedieh, gediehen **gedeihen 112**

gefällt, gefiel, gefallen **gefallen 209**

gelang, gelungen **gelingen 213**

gemahlen **mahlen 319**

genoss, genossen **genießen 216**

gerät, geriet, geraten **geraten 367**

geschieht, geschah, geschehen **geschehen 218**

gespalten **spalten 478**

gestand, gestanden **gestehen 221**

gewann, gewonnen **gewinnen 222**

gibt, gab, gegeben **geben 207**

gibt an, gab an, angegeben **angeben 63**

gibt auf, gab auf, aufgegeben **aufgeben 63**

gibt aus, gab aus, ausgegeben **ausgeben 63**

gibt bekannt, gab bekannt, bekannt gegeben **bekannt geben 63**

gibt heraus, gab heraus, herausgegeben **herausgeben 63**

gibt kund, gab kund, kundgegeben **kundgeben 63**

gibt mit, gab mit, mitgegeben **mitgeben 63**

gibt nach, gab nach, nachgegeben **nachgeben 63**

gibt vor, gab vor, vorgegeben **vorgeben 63**

gibt weiter, gab weiter, weitergegeben **weitergeben 63**

gibt zu, gab zu, zugegeben **zugeben 63**

gibt zurück, gab zurück, zurückgegeben **zurückgeben 63**

gilt, galt, gegolten **gelten 214**

ging, gegangen **gehen 210**

ging auf, aufgegangen **aufgehen 613**

ging auseinander, auseinander gegangen **auseinander gehen 613**

ging durch, durchgegangen **durchgehen 613**

ging fort, fortgegangen **fortgehen 613**

ging heim, heimgegangen **heimgehen 613**

ging hinaus, hinausgegangen **hinausgehen 613**

ging hoch, hochgegangen **hochgehen 613**

ging kaputt, kaputt gegangen **kaputt gehen 613**

ging los, losgegangen **losgehen 613**

ging nach, nachgegangen **nachgehen 613**

ging spazieren, spazieren gegangen **spazieren gehen 613**

ging unter, untergegangen **untergehen 613**

ging vor, vorgegangen **vorgehen 613**

ging voran, vorangegangen **vorangehen 613**

ging voraus, vorausgegangen **vorausgehen 613**

ging vorbei, vorbeigegangen **vorbeigehen 613**

ging vorüber, vorübergegangen **vorübergehen 613**

ging vorwärts, vorwärts gegangen **vorwärts gehen 613**

ging weiter, weitergegangen **weitergehen 613**

ging zurück, zurückgegangen **zurückgehen 613**

glich, geglichen **gleichen 227**

glitt, geglitten **gleiten 380**

goss, gegossen **gießen 224**

gräbt, grub, gegraben **graben 228**

gräbt aus, grub aus, ausgegraben **ausgraben 228**

griff, gegriffen **greifen 230**

griff an, angegriffen **angreifen 230**

griff ineinander, ineinander gegriffen **ineinander greifen 230**

griff vor, vorgegriffen **vorgreifen 230**

## H

hält, hielt, gehalten **halten 236**

hält ab, hielt ab, abgehalten **abhalten 236**

hält an, hielt an, angehalten **anhalten 236**

hält auf, hielt auf, aufgehalten **aufhalten 236**

hält aus, hielt aus, ausgehalten **aushalten 236**

hält auseinander, hielt auseinander, auseinander gehalten **auseinander halten 236**

hält durch, hielt durch, durchgehalten **durchhalten 236**

hält fest, hielt fest, festgehalten **festhalten 236**

hält hoch, hielt hoch, hochgehalten **hochhalten 236**

hält instand, hielt instand, instandgehalten **instandhalten 236**

hält mit, hielt mit, mitgehalten **mithalten 236**

hält nieder, hielt nieder, niedergehalten **niederhalten 236**

hält offen, hielt offen, offengehalten **offenhalten 236**

hält vor, hielt vor, vorgehalten **vorhalten 236**

hält zurück, hielt zurück, zurückgehalten **zurückhalten 236**

hängt an, hing an, angehangen **anhängen 238**

hat, hatte, gehabt **haben 235**

hat an, hatte an, angehabt **anhaben 235**

hat auf, hatte auf, aufgehabt **aufhaben 235**

hat frei, hatte frei, freigehabt **freihaben 235**

hat gern, hatte gern, gern gehabt **gern haben 235**

hat inne, hatte inne, innegehabt **innehaben 235**

hat lieb, hatte lieb, lieb gehabt **lieb haben 235**

hat vor, hatte vor, vorgehabt **vorhaben 235**

hat voraus, hatte voraus, vorausgehabt **voraushaben 235**

hat zu, hatte zu, zugehabt **zuhaben 235**

hieb, gehauen **hauen 240**

hieß, geheißen **heißen 244**

hilft, half, geholfen **helfen 246**

hilft aus, half aus, ausgeholfen **aushelfen 246**

hilft durch, half durch, durchgeholfen **durchhelfen 246**

hilft mit, half mit, mitgeholfen **mithelfen 246**

hilft weiter, half weiter, weitergeholfen **weiterhelfen 246**

hob, gehoben **heben 241**

hob auf, aufgehoben **aufheben 241**

## I

isst, aß, gegessen **essen 172**

isst auf, aß auf, aufgegessen **aufessen 172**

isst mit, aß mit, mitgegessen **mitessen 172**

ist, war, gewesen **sein 466**

ist an, war an, angewesen **ansein 466**

ist auf, war auf, aufgewesen **aufsein 466**

ist aus, war aus, ausgewesen **aussein 466**

ist imstande, war imstande, imstande gewesen **imstande sein 466**

ist seekrank, war seekrank, seekrank gewesen **seekrank sein 466** ist zu, war zu, zugewesen **zusein 466**

## K

kam, gekommen **kommen 281**

kam an, angekommen **ankommen 49**

kam aus, ausgekommen **auskommen 49**

kam durch, durchgekommen **durchkommen 49**

kam entgegen, entgegengekommen **entgegenkommen 49**

kam fort, fortgekommen **fortkommen 49**

kam heim, heimgekommen **heimkommen 49**

kam herauf, heraufgekommen **heraufkommen 49**

kam heraus, herausgekommen **herauskommen 49**

kam herum, herumgekommen **herumkommen 49**

kam herunter, heruntergekommen **herunterkommen 49**

kam mit, mitgekommen **mitkommen 49**

kam nach, nachgekommen **nachkommen 49**

kam um, umgekommen **umkommen 547**

kam unter, untergekommen **unterkommen 49**

kam vor, vorgekommen **vorkommen 49**

kam voran, vorangekommen **vorankommen 49**

kam vorbei, vorbeigekommen **vorbeikommen 49**

kam vorwärts, vorwärts gekommen **vorwärts kommen 49**

kam wieder, wiedergekommen **wiederkommen 49**

kam zu, zugekommen **zukommen 49**

kam zurück, zurückgekommen **zurückkommen 49**

kann, konnte, gekonnt **können 282**

kannte, gekannt **kennen 267**

kannte aus, ausgekannt **auskennen 267**

klang, geklungen **klingen 276**

kroch, gekrochen **kriechen 287**

## L

lädt aus, lud aus, ausgeladen **ausladen 138**

lädt ein, lud ein, eingeladen **einladen 138**

lag, gelegen **liegen 311**

lag nebeneinander, nebeneinander gelegen **nebeneinander liegen 311**

lag vor, vorgelegen **vorliegen 311**

lässt, ließ, gelassen **lassen 296**

lässt ab, ließ ab, abgelassen **ablassen 296**

lässt frei, ließ frei, freigelassen **freilassen 296**

lässt herein, ließ herein, hereingelassen **hereinlassen 296**

lässt los, ließ los, losgelassen **loslassen 296**

lässt nach, ließ nach, nachgelassen **nachlassen 296**

lässt offen, ließ offen, offengelassen **offenlassen 296**

lässt stehen, ließ stehen, stehen gelassen **stehen lassen 296**

lässt vor, ließ vor, vorgelassen **vorlassen 296**

lässt zu, ließ zu, zugelassen **zulassen 296**

läuft ab, lief ab, abgelaufen **ablaufen 298**

läuft fort, lief fort, fortgelaufen **fortlaufen 298**

läuft Schlittschuh, lief Schlittschuh, Schlittschuh gelaufen **Schlittschuh laufen 298**

läuft über, lief über, übergelaufen **überlaufen 298**

läuft zurück, lief zurück, zurückgelaufen **zurücklaufen 298**

lieh, geliehen **leihen 304**

lieh aus, ausgeliehen **ausleihen 304**

liest, las, gelesen **lesen 309**

liest aus, las aus, ausgelesen **auslesen 309**

liest vor, las vor, vorgelesen **vorlesen 309**

liest weiter, las weiter, weitergelesen **weiterlesen 309**

litt, gelitten **leiden 303**

log, gelogen **lügen 316**

log vor, vorgelogen **vorlügen 316**

## M

mag, mochte, gemocht **mögen 332**

melkte or molk, gemelkt or gemolken **melken 325**

mied, gemieden **meiden 322**

misst, maß, gemessen **messen 327**

misst aus, maß aus, ausgemessen **ausmessen 327**

missverstand, missverstanden **missverstehen 571**

muss, musste, gemusst **müssen 334**

## N

nannte, genannt **nennen 339**

nimmt, nahm, genommen **nehmen 337**

nimmt ab, nahm ab, abgenommen **abnehmen 612**

nimmt an, nahm an, angenommen **annehmen 612**

nimmt auf, nahm auf, aufgenommen **aufnehmen 612**

nimmt aus, nahm aus, ausgenommen **ausnehmen 612**

nimmt ein, nahm ein, eingenommen **einnehmen 612**

nimmt fort, nahm fort, fortgenommen **fortnehmen 612**

nimmt mit, nahm mit, mitgenommen **mitnehmen 612**

nimmt teil, nahm teil, teilgenommen **teilnehmen 612**

nimmt vor, nahm vor, vorgenommen **vornehmen 612**

nimmt voraus, nahm voraus, vorausgenommen **vorausnehmen 612**

nimmt weg, nahm weg, weggenommen **wegnehmen 612**

nimmt zu, nahm zu, zugenommen **zunehmen 612**

## P

pfiff, gepfiffen **pfeifen 348**

pries, gepriesen **preisen 409**

## Q

quillt, quoll, gequollen **quellen 364**

## R

rang, gerungen **ringen 473**

rann, geronnen **rinnen 501**

rannte, gerannt **rennen 381**

rät, riet, geraten **raten 367**

rieb, gerieben **reiben 375**

rief, gerufen **rufen 386**

rief an, angerufen **anrufen 50**

rief auf, aufgerufen **aufrufen 50**

rief zurück, zurückgerufen **zurückrufen 50**

riss, gerissen **reißen 379**

riss aus, ausgerissen **ausreißen 379**

riss fort, fortgerissen **fortreißen 379**

ritt, geritten **reiten 380**

roch, gerochen **riechen 384**

## S

sandte, gesandt **senden 467**

sandte nach, nachgesandt **nachsenden 467**

sang, gesungen **singen 473**

sang vor, vorgesungen **vorsingen 473**

sank, gesunken **sinken 474**

sank nieder, niedergesunken **niedersinken 474**

saß, gesessen **sitzen 475**

säuft, soff, gesoffen **saufen 397**

schied, geschieden **scheiden 409**

schien, geschienen **scheinen 410**

schilt, schalt, gescholten **schelten 412**

schläft, schlief, geschlafen **schlafen 424**

schläft aus, schlief aus, ausgeschlafen **ausschlafen 424**

schläft ein, schlief ein, eingeschlafen **einschlafen 139**

schlägt, schlug, geschlagen **schlagen 425**

schlägt an, schlug an, angeschlagen **anschlagen 425**

schlägt auf, schlug auf, aufgeschlagen **aufschlagen 425**

schlägt nach, schlug nach, nachgeschlagen **nachschlagen 425**

schlägt nieder, schlug nieder, niedergeschlagen **niederschlagen 425**

schlägt vor, schlug vor, vorgeschlagen **vorschlagen 425**

schlägt zurück, schlug zurück, zurückgeschlagen **zurückschlagen 425**

schlang, geschlungen **schlingen 473**

schlich, geschlichen **schleichen 380**

schliff, geschliffen **schleifen 428**

schloss, geschlossen **schließen 430**

schloss ab, abgeschlossen **abschließen 430**

schloss auf, aufgeschlossen **aufschließen 430**

schloss aus, ausgeschlossen **ausschließen 430**

schloss ein, eingeschlossen **einschließen 430**

schmilzt, schmolz, geschmolzen **schmelzen 436**

schmiss, geschmissen **schmeißen 435**

schnitt, geschnitten **schneiden 443**

schnitt durch, durchgeschnitten **durchschneiden 443**

schob, geschoben **schieben 417**

schob nach, nachgeschoben **nachschieben 417**

schob vor, vorgeschoben **vorschieben 417**

schor, geschoren **scheren 414**

schoss, geschossen **schießen 418**

schoss nieder, niedergeschossen **niederschießen 418**

schoss vorbei, vorbeigeschossen **vorbeischießen 418**

schrie, geschrien **schreien 450**

schrie nieder, niedergeschrien **niederschreien 450**

schrieb, geschrieben **schreiben 449**

schrieb an, angeschrieben **anschreiben 449**

schrieb auf, aufgeschrieben **aufschreiben 449**

schrieb aus, ausgeschrieben **ausschreiben 449**

schrieb ein, eingeschrieben **einschreiben 449**

schrieb nach, nachgeschrieben **nachschreiben 449**

schrieb vor, vorgeschrieben **vorschreiben 449**

schrieb zu, zugeschrieben **zuschreiben 449**

schritt, geschritten **schreiten 451**

schritt fort, fortgeschritten **fortschreiten 451**

schritt voran, vorangeschritten **voranschreiten 451**

schuf, geschaffen **schaffen 400**

schund, geschunden **schinden 422**

schwamm, geschwommen **schwimmen 459**

schwand, geschwunden **schwinden 568**

schwang, geschwungen **schwingen 473**

schwieg, geschwiegen **schweigen 457**

schwillt, schwoll, geschwollen **schwellen 458**

schwor, geschworen **schwören 461**

sieht, sah, gesehen **sehen 464**

sieht an, sah an, angesehen **ansehen 66**

sieht aus, sah aus, ausgesehen **aussehen 66**

sieht durch, sah durch, durchgesehen **durchsehen 66**

sieht fern, sah fern, fern gesehen **fern sehen 66**

sieht nach, sah nach, nachgesehen **nachsehen 66**

sieht voraus, sah voraus, vorausgesehen **voraussehen 66**

sieht vorher, sah vorher, vorhergesehen **vorhersehen 66**

sog, gesogen **saugen 398**

soll, sollte, gesollt **sollen 476**

sott, gesotten **sieden 471**

spann, gesponnen **spinnen 486**

sprang, gesprungen **springen 489**

sprang vor, vorgesprungen **vorspringen 489**

sprang zurück, zurückgesprungen **zurückspringen 489**

spricht, sprach, gesprochen **sprechen 488**

spricht an, sprach an, angesprochen **ansprechen 488**

spricht aus, sprach aus, ausgesprochen **aussprechen 488**

spricht durch, sprach durch, durchgesprochen **durchsprechen 488**

spricht mit, sprach mit, mitgesprochen **mitsprechen 488**

spross, gesprossen **sprießen 188**

stand, gestanden **stehen 495**

stand auf, aufgestanden **aufstehen 495**

stand aus, ausgestanden **ausstehen 495**

stand bei, beigestanden **beistehen 495**

stand bevor, bevorgestanden **bevorstehen 495**

stand nebeneinander, nebeneinander gestanden **nebeneinander stehen 495**

stand offen, offengestanden **offenstehen 495**

stand vor, vorgestanden **vorstehen 495**

stank, gestunken **stinken 503**

sticht, stach, gestochen **stechen 493**

sticht durch, stach durch, durchgestochen **durchstechen 493**

stieg, gestiegen **steigen 497**

stieg an, angestiegen **ansteigen 548**

stieg aus, ausgestiegen **aussteigen 67**

stieg ein, eingestiegen **einsteigen 140**

stieg heraus, herausgestiegen **heraussteigen 548**

stieg um, umgestiegen **umsteigen 548**

stiehlt, stahl, gestohlen **stehlen 496**

stirbt, starb, gestorben **sterben 501**

stirbt aus, starb aus, ausgestorben **aussterben 501**

stößt, stieß, gestoßen **stoßen 505**

stößt durch, stieß durch, durchgestoßen **durchstoßen 505**

stößt zurück, stieß zurück, zurückgestoßen **zurückstoßen 505**

strich, gestrichen **streichen 507**

strich durch, durchgestrichen **durchstreichen 507**

stritt, gestritten **streiten 508**

## T

tat, getan **tun 535**

tat Leid, Leid getan **Leid tun 535**

trägt, trug, getragen **tragen 524**

trägt auf, trug auf, aufgetragen **auftragen 524**

trägt bei, trug bei, beigetragen **beitragen 524**

trägt ein, trug ein, eingetragen **eintragen 524**

trank, getrunken **trinken 532**

trank aus, ausgetrunken **austrinken 532**

trieb, getrieben **treiben 529**

trieb ab, abgetrieben **abtreiben 529**

trieb aus, ausgetrieben **austreiben 529**

trieb durch, durchgetrieben **durchtreiben 529**

trieb fort, fortgetrieben **forttreiben 529**

trieb vorwärts, vorwärts getrieben **vorwärts treiben 529**

trieb zurück, zurückgetrieben **zurücktreiben 529**

trifft, traf, getroffen **treffen 528**

tritt, trat, getreten **treten 531**

tritt auf, trat auf, aufgetreten **auftreten 531**

tritt ein, trat ein, eingetreten **eintreten 531**

tritt in Kraft, trat in Kraft, in Kraft getreten **in Kraft treten 531**

tritt nieder, trat nieder, niedergetreten **niedertreten 531**

tritt zurück, trat zurück, zurückgetreten **zurücktreten 531**

troff, getroffen **triefen 188**

## U

überfährt, überfuhr, überfahren **überfahren 173**

überfällt, überfiel, überfallen **überfallen 174**

übergibt, übergab, übergeben **übergeben 207**

übernimmt, übernahm, übernommen **übernehmen 550**

übersieht, übersah, übersehen **übersehen 464**

überträgt, übertrug, übertragen **übertragen 573**

übertrieb, übertrieben **übertreiben 542**

überwand, überwunden **überwinden 109**

überwies, überwiesen **überweisen 104**

unterbricht, unterbrach, unterbrochen **unterbrechen 118**

unterhält, unterhielt, unterhalten **unterhalten 80**

unternimmt, unternahm, unternommen **unternehmen 550**

unterschrieb, unterschrieben **unterschreiben 90**

## V

verband, verbunden **verbinden 109**

verbirgt, verbarg, verborgen **verbergen 214**

verblich, verblichen **verbleichen 380**

verblieb, verblieben **verbleiben 112**

verbot, verboten **verbieten 552**

verbrachte, verbracht **v erbringen 120**

verbrannte, verbrannt **verbrennen 119**

verbricht, verbrach, verbrochen **verbrechen 118**

verdirbt, verdarb, verdorben **verderben 553**

verfährt, verfuhr, verfahren **verfahren 173**

verfällt, verfiel, verfallen **verfallen 174**

verfloss, verflossen **verfließen 188**

vergibt, vergab, vergeben **vergeben 207**

verging, vergangen **vergehen 210**

vergisst, vergaß, vergessen **vergessen 554**

verglich, verglichen **vergleichen 227**

vergoss, vergossen **vergießen 224**

vergräbt, vergrub, vergraben **vergraben 228**

vergriff, vergriffen **vergreifen 230**

verhält, verhielt, verhalten **verhalten 80**

verhohlen **verhehlen 325**

verkam, verkommen **verkommen 281**

verläuft, verlief, verlaufen **verlaufen 298**

verlor, verloren **verlieren 560**

vermied, vermieden **vermeiden 322**

verrät, verriet, verraten **verraten 565**

verriss, verrissen **verreißen 606**

verschob, verschoben **verschieben 417**

verschoss, verschossen **verschießen 418**

verschrieb, verschrieben **verschreiben 90**

verschwand, verschwunden **verschwinden 568**

verschwieg, verschwiegen **verschweigen 457**

versieht, versah, versehen **versehen 464**

verspricht, versprach, versprochen **versprechen 570**

verstand, verstanden **verstehen 571**

verstirbt, verstarb, verstorben **versterben 501**

verträgt, vertrug, vertragen **vertragen 573**

vertritt, vertrat, vertreten **vertreten 575**

verwies, verwiesen **verweisen 104**

verzieh, verziehen **verzeihen 576**

vollbrachte, vollbracht **vollbringen 120**

vollzog, vollzogen **vollziehen 609**

## W

wächst, wuchs, gewachsen **wachsen 581**

wächst auf, wuchs auf, aufgewachsen **aufwachsen 581**

wand, gewunden **winden 184**

wand durch, durchgewunden **durchwinden 109**

wandte an, angewandt **anwenden 592**

wäscht, wusch, gewaschen **waschen 586**

wäscht ab, wusch ab, abgewaschen **abwaschen 586**

weiß, wusste, gewusst **wissen 599**

weiß vorher, wusste vorher, vorhergewusst **vorherwissen 599**

wich, gewichen **weichen 303**

wich zurück, zurückgewichen **zurückweichen 303**

widerspricht, widersprach, widersprochen **widersprechen 570**

widerstand, widerstanden **widerstehen 571**

wies, gewiesen **weisen 591**

wies an, angewiesen **anweisen 591**

wies aus, ausgewiesen **ausweisen 591**

wies ein, eingewiesen **einweisen 591**

wies vor, vorgewiesen **vorweisen 591**

wies zurück, zurückgewiesen **zurückweisen 591**

will, wollte, gewollt **wollen 601**

wirbt, warb, geworben **werben 214**

wird, wurde, geworden **werden 593**

wird inne, wurde inne, innegeworden **innewerden 593**

wird seekrank, wurde seekrank, seekrank geworden **seekrank werden 593**

wirft, warf, geworfen **werfen 594**

wirft nieder, warf nieder, niedergeworfen **niederwerfen 594**

wirft vor, warf vor, vorgeworfen **vorwerfen 594**

wirft weg, warf weg, weggeworfen **wegwerfen 594**

wirft zurück, warf zurück, zurückgeworfen **zurückwerfen 594**

wog, gewogen **wiegen 106**

## Z

zerbricht, zerbrach, zerbrochen **zerbrechen 118**

zerfällt, zerfiel, zerfallen **zerfallen 174**

zerriss, zerrissen **zerreißen 606**

zerschoss, zerschossen **zerschießen 418**

zog, gezogen **ziehen 609**

zog auf, aufgezogen **aufziehen 615**

zog aus, ausgezogen **ausziehen 615**

zog durch, durchgezogen **durchziehen 615**

zog ein, eingezogen **einziehen 615**

zog fort, fortgezogen **fortziehen 615**

zog über, übergezogen **überziehen 615**

zog um, umgezogen **umziehen 615**

zog vor, vorgezogen **vorziehen 615**

zog zu, zugezogen **zuziehen 615**

zog zurück, zurückgezogen **zurückziehen 615**

zwang, gezwungen **zwingen 617**

# ENGLISH-GERMAN VERB INDEX

This appendix consists of the verbs illustrated in the verb charts as well as the verbs found in the Appendix of Additional Verbs. They are listed by their English meaning. The German translation follows the English verb, and the translation is followed by the page number where the equivalent verb can be found.


abduct **entführen 203**

abhor **verabscheuen 558**

abolish **abschaffen 43**

abuse, despise **schmähen 114**

abuse, mistreat **misshandeln 81**

accept **akzeptieren 57**

accept, admit, suppose **annehmen 612**

accompany, escort **begleiten 79**

accomplish **leisten 305**

accomplish **vollbringen 120**

accomplish, carry out **durchführen 203**

accomplish, take place **vollziehen (sich) 615**

accuse **anklagen 269**

accuse **verklagen 269**

accuse, charge with **beschuldigen 148**

accuse of a crime **anlasten 51**

accustom **gewöhnen 223**

achieve, attain **erzielen 520**

acknowledge, recognize **anerkennen 267**

act, handle, manage **verfahren 173**

act, pretend **mimen 45**

add one's vote **mitstimmen 95**

add to, append **hinzufügen 250**

address, speak to **ansprechen 488**

address someone with *du* **duzen 512**

address someone with *Sie* **siezen 245**

adhere, stick to **ankleben 43**

adhere to **kleben 43**

adjoin, border upon **angrenzen 468**

adjust, set right, direct **richten 383**

administer **verwalten 562**

admire **bewundern 354**

admit **hereinlassen 296**

admit **zugeben 63**

admit, confess **gestehen 221**

adopt **adoptieren 57**

adore, worship **anbeten 97**

adorn **verzieren 161**

adulterate, counterfeit **verfälschen 153**

advise **raten 367**

advise, urge **zureden 372**

affect piety **frömmeln 293**

age, become old **vergreisen 468**
agree, come to terms **einigen (sich) 357**
agree to **zustimmen 95**
aid, stand by **beistehen 495**
aim **zielen 520**
air out, ventilate **auslüften 64**
alarm **alarmieren 57**
alarm, frighten **ängstigen 357**
alarm, make anxious **beängstigen 159**
alienate, estrange **entfremden 144**
alleviate, lighten **erleichtern 160**
allow **erlauben 158**
allow, permit **gestatten 220**
ally **alliieren 57**
alter, change **verändern 47**
alter, transform **umändern 47**
amount to **betragen 573**
amuse **vergnügen 217**
amuse, enjoy oneself **amüsieren (sich) 57**
analyze **analysieren 57**
anchor, moor **verankern 569**
animate **animieren 57**
animate, enliven **beleben 299**
annihilate **vertilgen 558**
announce **ankündigen 159**
announce **ansagen 394**
announce, advertise **anzeigen 605**
annoy, vex **ärgern 56**
annul, cancel **stornieren 57**
answer **beantworten 52**
answer, reply **antworten 52**
answer, respond **entgegnen 463**
answer for, be responsible **verantworten 52**
antedate **vorausdatieren 57**
antedate **vordatieren 57**
anticipate **absehen 66**
anticipate **vorausnehmen 612**
appear **erscheinen 164**
apply, lay on **anlegen 301, auflegen 301**
approach, draw near **nähern (sich) 47**
approve of, sanction **genehmigen 159**
arbitrate **schlichten 423**
argue **streiten 508**
arrange **arrangieren 57**
arrange, order **ordnen 342**
arrange, organize **veranstalten 562**
arrest **verhaften 555**
arrive **ankommen 49**
ask **fragen 197**
ask, call upon, request **auffordern 193**
ask, request **bitten 110**
ask around **herumfragen 197**
assemble **versammeln (sich) 395**
assent to, give consent **bejahen 157**
assign, attribute **zuschreiben 449**
assume **voraussetzen 468**
astonish **erstaunen 158**
astonish, wonder **wundern (sich) 354**
atone for, make amends **büßen 292**
attach, fasten **anmachen 317**
attach, fasten, fix **befestigen 76**
attract attention, strike **auffallen 137**

attract, entice **locken 124**
attract, lure **anlocken 124**
avenge, revenge **rächen 365**
avoid **vermeiden 322**
avoid, shun **meiden 322**
bait, lure **ködern 193**
bake **backen 69**
baptize **taufen 519**
bar, barricade **sperren 484**
bark **bellen 485**
bark, yelp **kläffen 252**
bathe **baden 70**
battle, struggle **kämpfen 262**
be **sein 466**
be afraid **fürchten (sich) 44**
be annoyed **zürnen 308**
be ashamed **schämen (sich) 403**
be astonished **staunen 308**
be at liberty, remain unsettled **offenstehen 495**
be behind, follow **nachgehen 613**
be broken **kaputt sein 466**
be closed **zusein 466**
be descended, originate **stammen 499**
be difficult or burdensome **schwerfallen 137**
be embarrassed **genieren (sich) 57**
be fragrant **duften 134**
be imminent, impend **bevorstehen 495**
be in a position **imstande sein 466**
be in front of **vorliegen 311**
be lazy, lounge **faulenzen 468**
be luminous **nachleuchten 44**
be mean, be stingy **knickern 354**
be moved to pity **erbarmen (sich) 158**
be of value, be worth **taugen 301**
be on **ansein 466**
be on one's guard **hüten (sich) 44**
be open, be awake **aufsein 466**
be out **aussein 466**
be out of tune **misstönen 162**
be outstanding, stand out **ausstehen 495**
be parched with thirst **lechzen 284**
be present at **beiwohnen 600**
be puffed up **strotzen 512**
be resentful **grollen 498**
be seasick **seekrank sein 466**
be sickly **kränkeln 285**
be silent **schweigen 457**
be sorry **Leid tun 535**
be suitable, befit **geziemen (sich) 208**
be suspicious **verdächtigen 89**
be thirsty **dursten 283**
be useful **eignen (sich) 463**
be valid, be current **gelten 214**
be worried **sorgen (sich) 477**
be wrecked **scheitern 411**
beam, shine **strahlen 253**
bear (young) **gebären 206**
bear, endure **dulden 134, ertragen 573**
bear, tolerate **vertragen 573**
bear in mind **gedenken 125**
beat a drum **pauken 124**
beat back **zurückschlagen 425**
become, get **werden 593**
become acquainted **kennen lernen 308**

become blind **erblinden 169**

become engaged **verloben (sich) 561**

become ill **erkranken 141**

become less, shrink, fade **schwinden 568**

become poor **verarmen 544**

become seasick **seekrank werden 593**

befall, affect, concern **betreffen 528**

befall, happen **befallen 209**

befriend **befreunden 74**

beg **betteln 99**

beget **zeugen 301**

beget, breed **erzeugen 301**

begin, start **beginnen 78**

behave **benehmen (sich) 550**

behave, have a relation to **verhalten (sich) 80**

behead **enthaupten 145, köpfen 421**

belch **rülpsen 390**

believe **glauben 226**

belong to **gehören 212**

belong to, pertain to **angehören 212**

bend, break **knicken 124**

bend, curve **biegen 106, krümmen 527**

bend at a right angle **kröpfen 421**

bend back, turn back **umbiegen 106**

bend down **niederbeugen 100**

bend forward **vorbeugen 100**

bequeath **vererben 151**

bet, wager **wetten 44**

betray **verraten 565**

bewilder, startle **verdutzen 559**

bid, command **gebieten 107**

bid farewell **verabschieden (sich) 562**

billet, quarter **einquartieren 57**

bind, connect **verbinden 109**

bind, tie **binden 109**

bite **beißen 82**

bite at, take a bite **anbeißen 82**

blanch, brew **brühen 114**

blaze, flare up **lodern 47**

bleat, grumble **meckern 47**

bleed **bluten 44**

bleed to death **verbluten 189**

bless **segnen 463**

blind **blenden 483, verblenden 567**

bloom, flower **blühen 114**

blow **blasen 111**

blow, flutter **wehen 335**

blow out **ausblasen 111**

blunder, bungle **verpfuschen 558**

blush, turn red **erröten 163**

bluster, howl **sausen 315**

bolt **verriegeln 564**

border **grenzen 468**

border on **begrenzen 468**

bore through, penetrate **durchbohren 161**

borrow, lend **borgen 115**

bowl **kegeln 99**

brag **prahlen 356**

brake **bremsen 315**

break **brechen 118**

break **kaputt machen 317**

break down **niederbrechen 118**

break loose **losbrechen 118**

break open **aufbrechen 118**

break open, open (a book) **aufschlagen 425**

break or give up a habit **abgewöhnen (sich) 223**

break through **durchbrechen 118, durchstoßen 505**

break to pieces **zerbrechen 118**

breathe **atmen 58**

breathe freely **aufatmen 58**

breed **züchten 343**

brew **brauen 72**

bring **bringen 120**

bring along **mitbringen 120, mitführen 203**

bring back **zurückbringen 120**

bring back, fetch **wiederholen (wiederholen)**

bring forward **vorbringen 120**

bring out, issue **herausbringen 120**

bring to a close **vollenden 74**

bring to mind **vergegenwärtigen 76**

bring to the front **vorführen 203**

bring up, educate **erziehen 171**

brush **bürsten 283**

brush, paint **pinseln 71**

buckle **schnallen 498**

buckle up **anschnallen 580**

bud, sprout **knospen 521**

build **bauen 72**

build on, cultivate **bebauen 72**

build up, construct **erbauen 72**

bungle , mess up **vermurksen 315**

burden, impose **aufbürden 51**

burn **brennen 119**

burn, scorch **verbrennen 381**

burn away **wegbrennen 119**

burn down **niederbrennen 381**

burn out **verglühen 192**

burn out, scorch **ausbrennen 119**

burst **platzen 353**

burst, explode **bersten 214, sprengen 558**

burst, pop **knallen 253**

burst into pieces **zerplatzen 353**

bury **begraben 228**

bury, hide **vergraben 228**

bury, inter **beerdigen 76**

button up **zuknöpfen 277**

buy up, ransom **auskaufen 265**

cake, get lumpy **klumpen 521**

calcify **verkalken 141**

calibrate **kalibrieren 57**

call **rufen 386**

call, name **heißen 244**

call back **zurückrufen 50**

call off, cancel **absagen 394**

call to mind, remember **besinnen (sich) 93**

call up, summon **aufrufen 50**

call up, telephone **anrufen 50**

camp out **zelten 585**

can, be able to **können 282**

carry, wear **tragen 524**

carry away, have an abortion **abtreiben 529**

carry off, lead away, mislead **abführen 203**

carry on, continue **fortsetzen 196**

cast before **vorwerfen 594**

catch **fangen 176**

catch cold **erkälten (sich) 156**

catch sight of **erblicken 416**

cause **veranlassen 315, verursachen 294**

cauterize **kauterisieren 57**

celebrate **feiern 182**

chain **ketten 97**

challenge, provoke **herausfordern 193**

change **ändern 47, wechseln 588**

change, alter **umwandeln 395**

change, exchange **austauschen 68**

change clothes **umziehen 615**

change details, cheat **klittern 191**

charm, delight **entzücken 141**

chase after **nachjagen 257**

chase away **wegjagen 257**

chase away, dismiss **fortjagen 257**

chat **plaudern 354**

chat (in an Internet chat room) **chatten 382**

chatter, chat **schwatzen 468**

check out, sign off, announce a withdrawal **abmelden 324**

cheer up, brighten **erheitern 160**

chew **kauen 72**

chill, cause to shiver **frösteln 293**

chirp **zwitschern 481**

choke, strangle **erwürgen 217**

choose, elect **erwählen 582**

choose, select **auserwählen 582, auswählen 582, wählen 582**

circle, revolve **kreisen 378**

claim, demand, exact **anfordern 193**

clap **klatschen 271**

clap, smack **platschen 271**

classify **klassifizieren 57**

claw, pilfer **krallen 253**

clean **reinmachen 317, saubermachen 317**

clean, purge **säubern 47**

clean, purify **reinigen 377**

clean, remove, clear away **abräumen 59**

clean, scour **putzen 360**

clean up, tidy up **aufräumen 59**

clear, clarify **klären 157**

clear away **räumen 527**

clear one's throat **hüsteln 71**

clear up, enlighten **aufklären 157**

clench the teeth **zusammenbeißen 82**

click on (Web site icon) **anklicken 416**

climb **klettern 274**

climb, go up **steigen 497**

clink **klirren 255**

clip, shear **scheren 414**

close **schließen 430, zumachen 317**

close, conclude **beschließen 430**

clothe **kleiden 273**

coat with lead **verbleien 450**

coat with wax **wächsen 581**

coin, stamp **prägen 355**

collapse **zusammenbrechen (sein) 118**

collect **sammeln 395**

comb **kämmen 261**

combine **kombinieren 57**

come **kommen 281**

come after **nachkommen 49**

come along **mitkommen 49**

come back **wiederkommen 49, zurückkommen 49**

come by **vorbeikommen 49**

come down, alight **herunterkommen 49**

come early **verfrühen (sich) 574**

come forth, occur **vorkommen 49**

come forward **vorwärtskommen 49**

come home **heimkommen 49**

come out, be issued **herauskommen 49**

come out, get by **auskommen 49**

come to an understanding **vereinbaren 608, verständigen (sich) 76**

come to meet, advance **entgegenkommen 49**

come up **heraufkommen 49**

come up to, reach **zukommen 49**

come upon **vorfinden 492**

comfort **trösten 534**

command **kommandieren 57**

command, direct, put in order **anordnen 342**

command, order **befehlen 75**

commit **begehen 210**

commit a crime **verbrechen 118**

compare **vergleichen 227**

compete **konkurrieren 57**

compile **kompilieren 57**

complain **beklagen (sich) 269, klagen 269**

complete **ergänzen 154**

compose **komponieren 57, verfassen 178**

compose poetry **dichten 126**

comprehend, grasp **begreifen 230**

conceal **verheimlichen 96**

conceal from **verhehlen 325**

concentrate **konzentrieren 57**

confess, own up **bekennen 267**

confirm **bestätigen 76, vergewissern 569**

confuse, mix up **verwechseln 588**

congratulate **beglückwünschen 602, gratulieren 57**

conquer **besiegen 472**

consider **betrachten 44**

consider, ponder **erwägen 106**

consult a book, look up in a book **nachschlagen 425**

consume **verzehren 561**

contain **enthalten 80**

continue **weiterführen 203**

continue one's education **fortbilden (sich) 108**

continue playing **weiterspielen 485**

continue working **fortarbeiten 55**

contradict **widersprechen 570**

contribute **beitragen 524**

control **kontrollieren 57**

control, govern **beherrschen 247**

converse **unterhalten (sich) 80**

convert, change one's ways **bekehren (sich) 266**

convince **überzeugen 543**

cook, boil **kochen 280**

cool, chill **kühlen 202**

cooperate **kooperieren 57, mitarbeiten 55, zusammenarbeiten 55**

cooperate with, help **mithelfen 246**

copy **kopieren 57**

correct **korrigieren 57**

correspond **entsprechen 570**

corrode, gnaw at **anfressen 198**
cost **kosten 283**
cough **husten 256**
count **zählen 604**
count, reckon **rechnen 370**
couple **kuppeln 71**
cover **decken 124**
cover, conceal **verdecken 141**
cover, disguise **verkleiden 273**
cover, lay down **belegen 301**
cover, protect **bedecken 141**
cover, spread over **überziehen 615**
cover up **zudecken 124**
covet **lüsten 256**
crack **knacken 416**
crack, crash **krachen 294**
crackle **knistern 191**
cram, fill, mend **stopfen 277**
cramp **krampfen 262**
crawl, creep, sneak **schleichen 427**
create, accomplish **schaffen 400**
create, scoop up **schöpfen 447**
creep, crawl **kriechen 287**
criticize **kritisieren 57, monieren 57**
criticize harshly **verreißen 379**
croak, caw **krächzen 284**
cross **kreuzen 468, überquéren 538**
cross out, erase **durchstreichen 507**
crouch, squat **hocken 251**
crowd, push **nachdrängen 129**
crown **krönen 290**
crucify **kreuzigen 76**
crumble **krümeln 71**
crunch **knuspern 47**
crush **zerquetschen 539**
cry **weinen 590**
cuff, pommel **knuffen 279**
cultivate **kultivieren 57**
cultivate, add on by building **anbauen 72**
cultivate, work, treat **bearbeiten 55**
curl **kräuseln 191**
curse **verfluchen 189**
curse, swear **fluchen 189**
curve **kurven 310**
cut **schneiden 443**
cut down, massacre **niedermetzeln 71**
cut loose **loshauen 406**
cut out, eliminate **ausschalten 402**
cut through **durchschneiden 443**
damp, smother, muffle **dämpfen 262**
dampen, moisten **anfeuchten 51**
dance **tanzen (tanzen)**
dangle **baumeln 71**
darken **verdunkeln 569, verdüstern 569**
date **datieren 57**
dawn, grow light **dämmern 47**
decay, deteriorate **verfallen 174**
decay, go bad **verkommen 281**
deceive **betrügen 98, täuschen (sich) 247, trügen 98**
decide **entscheiden (sich) 147**
decline, refuse **ablehnen 43**
decompose **verwesen 192**
decontaminate **entgiften 144**
dedicate **weihen 590**
dedicate, devote **widmen 58**

defend **verteidigen 159**

defend oneself **wehren (sich) 302**

defy, be obstinate **trotzen 468**

delay **verspäten 74**

deliver **abliefern 481, liefern 481**

deliver, hand over **übergében 207**

deliver subsequently **nachliefern 481**

delouse **entlausen 88**

demand **verlangen 558**

demand, claim **fordern 193**

demonstrate **demonstrieren 57**

demonstrate a calculation **vorrechnen 370**

deny **leugnen 463, verleugnen 463**

deny, disavow **verneinen 558**

deny, refuse **versagen 394**

deny somebody something **verwehren 558**

depart **abfahren 173, abreisen 378, wegfahren 173, wegreisen 378**

depreciate **entwerten 169**

deride **verlachen 558**

descend, come from **abstammen 43**

describe **beschreiben 90**

desire, long for **begehren 302**

despair **verzweifeln 81**

despise **verachten 44**

destroy **vernichten 563, zerstören 608**

determine, decide **bestimmen 95**

determine, establish **feststellen 183**

develop **entwickeln 150**

dictate **diktieren 57**

die **sterben 501, umkommen 547, verenden 74**

die down **verebben 558**

die out, become extinct **aussterben 501**

differ, diverge **auseinander gehen 613**

dig **graben 228**

dig, burrow **wühlen 582**

dig out **ausgraben 228**

diminish **verringern 569**

dine with **mitessen 172**

direct (an orchestra) **dirigieren 57**

direct, connect, switch **schalten 402**

direct, send **weisen 591**

disappear **verschwinden 568**

disarm **entwaffnen 162**

discharge, fire **verschießen 418**

discolor **verfärben 177**

disconnect, break contact **abschalten 402**

discourage **entmutigen 159**

discover **entdecken 141**

discriminate **diskriminieren 57**

discuss **diskutieren 57**

discuss, debate **erörtern 160**

discuss thoroughly **durchsprechen 488**

disfigure, deform **entstellen 94**

disinfect **desinfizieren 57**

dispense, bestow **spenden 483**

disperse **zerstreuen 608**

display **vorweisen 591**

dispute, contest **abstreiten 508**

disregard, slight **missachten 44**

distinguish **auseinander halten 236**

distribute **austeilen 520, verteilen 101**

disturb **stören 504**

dive, dip **tauchen 517**

divert **umleiten 306**

do **tun 535**

do gymnastics **turnen 536**

do handicrafts, tinker **basteln 71**

do without, dispense with **entbehren 302**

do without, miss **missen 292**

doubt **zweifeln 71**

doubt, question **bezweifeln 564**

drag, haul **schleppen 429**

drag off, tow away **abschleppen 429**

drag one's feet **schlurfen 277**

drain, distill **entwässern 569**

draw, pull **ziehen 609**

draw away, move away **fortziehen 615**

draw forward **vorziehen 615**

draw in, retract, move in **einziehen 615**

draw through **durchziehen 615**

draw together, draw tight **zuziehen 615**

draw up **ausfertigen 76**

dream **träumen 527**

drink **trinken 532**

drink, tipple **saufen 397**

drink up, finish drinking **austrinken 532**

drip **tröpfeln 71**

drip, secrete **triefen 397**

drip, trickle **rinnen 486**

drive, push **treiben 529**

drive, travel **fahren 173**

drive away **wegtreiben 529**

drive away, force away **forttreiben 529**

drive back **zurückfahren 173, zurücktreiben 529**

drive by **vorbeifahren 173**

drive home **heimfahren 173**

drive off, depart **fortfahren 173**

drive out, eject **austreiben 529**

drive round **úmfáhren 173**

drive through **durchfahren 173**

drive up to **vorfahren 173**

drizzle **nieseln 71**

drop out, be omitted **ausfallen 137**

drown **ertrinken 168**

dry **trocknen 533**

dry, wipe dry **abtrocknen 533**

duck, stoop **ducken (sich) 124**

dye, color **färben 177**

earn, achieve through work **erarbeiten 55**

earn, deserve **verdienen 127**

eat **essen 172**

eat, take a meal **speisen 482**

eat (of animals) **fressen 198**

eat sweets **naschen 247**

eat with the mouth full **mampfen 262**

ebb **ebben 299**

echo **nachhallen 580**

economize, save **ersparen 479**

edge, border **kanten 44**

educate **ausbilden 108**

elaborate, overrefine **künsteln 71**

elapse, turn out **verlaufen 298**
electrify **elektrifizieren 57**
elevate, raise up **erheben 241**
embitter, exasperate **erbittern 155**
embody **verkörpern 569**
embrace **umármen 544**
embrace, clasp **umfassen 178**
embrace, press to one's heart **herzen 245**
emerge, show up **auftauchen 517**
emigrate **auswandern 583, emigrieren 347**
empathize **nachempfinden 492**
emphasize, stress **betonen 85**
employ, make use of **anwenden 592**
empower, authorize **ermächtigen 89**
empty **leeren 255**
empty, decant, reduce **ablassen 296**
emulate **nacheifern 481**
enclose with grating **vergattern 569**
encounter, meet **begegnen 77**
end, finish **beenden 74, beendigen 76**
end, stop **Schluß machen 317**
endanger **gefährden 74**
endanger, threaten **bedrohen 131**
endure, suffer, hold out **aushalten 236**
enforce, push through **durchsetzen 196**
engage **engagieren 57**
enjoy **genießen 216**
enlarge, increase **vergrößern 569**
enroll, matriculate **einschreiben (sich) 449**
enslave **versklaven 558**
enter, commence **eintreten 531**
entrust, confide **anvertrauen 574**
envy **beneiden 87, neiden 87**
equal, match **gleichen 227**
equalize **ausgleichen 227**
equip, fit out **rüsten 146**
equip, outfit **ausrüsten 65**
equip, provide with **ausstatten 65**
erase, rub out **ausradieren 57**
erect, build up **aufbauen 72**
erect, set up **aufrichten 383**
erect, set upright **errichten 383**
escape **entkommen 281**
establish, found **gründen 231**
esteem highly **hochschätzen 405**
evacuate **evakuieren 57**
evaporate **verdunsten 146**
exaggerate **übertréiben 542**
except, exclude **ausnehmen 612**
exchange **umtauschen 68**
exchange, vary **abwechseln 588**
excite, stir up **erregen 60**
exclude, lock out **ausschließen 430**
excuse **verzeihen (verzeihen)**
excuse, pardon **entschuldigen 148**
execute, carry out **ausführen 203**
exert, strain oneself **anstrengen (sich) 60**
exhale **ausatmen 58**
exhaust **erschöpfen 165**
exhibit **ausstellen 580**
exist **existieren 57**
expand, widen **erweitern 160**
expect, await **erwarten 169**

experience, witness **erleben 299**
experience first hand **miterleben 299**
experiment **experimentieren 57**
expire **versterben 501**
explain **erklären 157**
explode **explodieren 57**
exploit **ausbeuten 65**
export **exportieren 57**
expose, pause **aussetzen 468**
expose, reveal **enthüllen 142**
express **ausdrücken 132**
extend **ausdehnen 62**
extend, reach out **ausstrecken 509**
exterminate, root out **ausrotten 65**
extinguish **tilgen 472**
extinguish, put out **auslöschen 314, löschen 314**
extort, blackmail **erpressen 178**
fade, wither **verblühen 378**
fade away **verhallen 378**
fail to recognize **verkennen 267**
fall **fallen 174**
fall apart **zerfallen 174**
fall asleep **einschlafen 139**
fall away **wegfallen 137**
fall back **zurückfallen 137**
fall down **hinfallen 137**
fall in love **vergaffen 566, verlieben (sich) 310**
fall into **hereinfallen 137**
fall through, fail **durchfallen 137**
fall to pieces **auseinander fallen 137**
fall upon, attack **anfallen 209, überfällen 209**
fast **fasten 179**
fasten, join **knüpfen 279**
fasten, paste on **aufkleben 272**
fasten, tighten **festmachen 317**
fatten, cram **mästen 283**
favor **bevorzugen 217**
feed **füttern 204**
feed, provide for **verpflegen 350**
feel **fühlen 202, spüren 491**
feel, perceive **empfinden 152**
feel, touch **anfühlen 202**
feel about **herumtasten 51**
ferment, effervesce **gären 203**
fertilize **düngen 472**
fetch, call for **abholen 253**
fiddle with, fumble **nesteln 71**
fight, fence **fechten 180**
fight to the end **durchkämpfen (sich) 262**
fill out **ausfüllen 62**
filter **filtrieren 57**
finance **finanzieren 57**
find **finden 184**
find, be located **befinden (sich) 152**
find fault **kritteln 289**
find fault with **mäkeln 71**
find out, discover **herausfinden 492**
find shelter **unterkommen 49**
find the way back **zurückfinden 492**
finish, dismiss without ceremony **abfertigen 76**
finish blooming **ausblühen 114**
finish learning, finish an apprenticeship **auslernen 308**

finish speaking **ausreden 372**
fire, sack **feuern 481**
fire at, bombard **beschießen 418**
fish **angeln 71, fischen 247**
fit **passen 346**
fix, stare **fixieren 57**
flap, work out **klappen 270**
flatter **schmeicheln 434**
flee **fliehen 187**
flee, take flight **flüchten (sich) 189**
flicker **wabern 354**
fling, hurl **schmeißen 435**
flirt **flirten 97**
float, drift **driften 97**
flood, flow, surge **fluten 189**
flow **fließen 188**
flow, empty **münden 333**
flow away, blend **verfließen 188**
flow through, perfuse **durchströmen 510**
fly **fliegen 186**
fly out, escape **ausfliegen 186**
foam, froth **schäumen 403**
fold **falten 175**
follow, pursue **nachfolgen 192**
follow one another **aufeinander folgen 192**
forbid **verbieten 552**
force, compel **zwingen 617**
force through, effect **durchtreiben 529**
foresee **voraussehen 66, vorhersehen 66**
forestall **vorgreifen 230**
forget **vergessen 554**
forgive **vergeben 207**
form **bilden 108**
form, shape **gestalten 219**
found, establish **begründen 231, stiften 44**
free **befreien 94**
free from debts **entschulden 452**
freeze **frieren 200**
freeze to death **erfrieren 200**
frequent, transform **verkehren 266**
frighten **schrecken 598**
frighten, terrify **erschrecken 166**
frustrate, thwart **vereiteln 569**
fulfill **erfüllen 62**
fume, rage **toben 522**
function **funktionieren 57**
furnish **möblieren 331**
furnish, supply with **versehen 464**
further, promote **fördern 193**
galvanize **galvanisieren 57**
gape, stare **glotzen 468**
gape, yawn **klaffen 252**
gaze after **nachschauen 616**
Germanize **eindeutschen 68**
get, catch **kriegen 288**
get, come upon **geraten 367**
get, fetch **holen 253**
get accustomed to **angewöhnen 223**
get away **wegkommen 49**
get away, prosper **fortkommen 49**
get back **zurückbekommen 83**
get broken **kaputt gehen 613**
get carried away, sweep away **fortreißen 379**
get dark, become gloomy **düstern 191**

get gray hair **ergrauen 229**
get on, get in **einsteigen 67**
get out, get off **aussteigen 67**
get rid of, dismiss **fortschaffen 43**
get through, succeed **durchkommen 49**
get well, recover **genesen 215**
giggle **kichern 481**
gild **vergolden 74**
give **geben 207**
give, present **schenken 416**
give a handicap **vorgeben 63**
give a share, participate in **beteiligen 76**
give away **weggeben 63**
give back **zurückgeben 63**
give notice **kündigen 159**
give to a departing guest, impart **mitgeben 63**
give up, hand in **aufgeben 63**
give way **zurückweichen 380**
give way, yield **nachgeben 63**
glance up **heraufblicken 59**
glaze **verglasen 559**
gleam, shine **glänzen 225**
glitter, gleam **schimmern 420**
glitter, glisten **flimmern 420**
glorify **verherrlichen 208**
glow **glühen 114**
glue, stick **kleben 272**
gnaw **nagen 338**
go **gehen 210**
go astray, err **irren (sich) 504**
go away **weggehen 613**
go away, depart **fortgehen 613**
go back **zurückgehen 613**
go before **vorgehen 613**
go bike riding **Rad fahren 173**
go by **vorbeigehen 613**
go forward **vorwärtsgehen 613**
go home **heimgehen 613**
go iceskating **Schlittschuh laufen 298**
go mountain climbing **bergsteigen 497**
go on **weiterbestehen 495**
go on ahead **voranschreiten 451, vorausgehen 613**
go out **hinausgehen 613**
go out, be extinguished **erlöschen 314**
go skiing **Ski fahren 173**
go strolling **spazieren gehen 613**
go through, be transmitted **durchgehen 613**
go well together **zusammenpassen 346**
grasp, seize **fassen 178, greifen 230**
grease, lubricate **schmieren 438**
greet **begrüßen 233, grüßen 233**
grieve **trauern 526**
grill, barbeque **grillen 498**
grind, creak **knirschen 247**
grind, sharpen **wetzen 468**
groan **stöhnen 45**
group, classify **gruppieren 57**
grow **wachsen 581**
grow from, accrue **erwachsen 581**
grow lonely **vereinsamen 566**
grow old, stale **veralten 189**
grow pale **verbleichen 380**
grow up **aufwachsen 581**

growl **brummen 514**
guard, preserve **behüten 562**
guard, protect **beschützen 454**
guess, solve **erraten 565**
guide **leiten 306**
guide back **zurücklenken 307**
gush, well up **quellen 364**
hammer **hämmern 237**
hand, reach **langen 558**
hand over **überreichen 376, verabreichen 376**
handle, manipulate **hantieren 57**
handle, seize **angreifen 230**
hang **hängen 238**
hang on, attach, append **anhängen 238**
hang up, suspend **aufhängen 238**
happen **geschehen 218, vorfallen 137**
happen, occur **passieren 347**
harden **verhärten 562**
harm **schaden 399**
harvest **ernten 44**
hate **hassen 239**
have **haben 235**
have a feeling about, suspect **ahnen 45**
have a foreboding **vorfühlen 202**
have a good sleep **ausschlafen 424**
have an accident **verunglücken 141**
have an advantage **voraushaben 235**
have an aversion to **grauen 229**
have breakfast **frühstücken 201**
have on, wear **anhaben 235**
have on (clothing) **aufhaben 235**
have the knack of **weghaben 235**
have the opinion, mean **meinen 323**
have time off **freihaben 235**
have to, must **müssen 334**
heal **heilen 242**
heal up **verheilen 378, zuheilen 378**
hear **hören 255**
heat **heizen 245**
heighten, elevate **erhöhen 561**
help **helfen 246**
help get away **weghelfen 246**
help out, assist **aushelfen 246**
help out, give support **durchhelfen 246**
help to continue **weiterhelfen 246**
hem, linger **säumen 566**
hem in, inhibit, check **hemmen 514**
hesitate **zögern 193**
hew, chop, strike **hauen 240**
hide **verbergen 214**
hinder **verhindern 557**
hit, strike **schlagen 425**
hitch, harness up **anspannen 59**
hobble **humpeln 462**
hold **halten 236**
hold back **verhalten 80, zurückhalten 236**
hold before **vorhalten 236**
hold down **niederhalten 236**
hold fast, detain **festhalten 236**
hold out **nachhalten 236**
hold out, endure **durchhalten 236**
hold up, delay **aufhalten 236**

honor **ehren 302**

honor, revere **verehren 302**

hop, leap **hüpfen 378**

hope **hoffen 252**

hover, soar **schweben 456**

howl **heulen 248**

hum **summen 514**

humble, humiliate **demütigen 159**

hunt, chase **jagen 257**

hunt, seek out **aufsuchen 513**

hurl, plunge **stürzen 511**

hurry ahead **vorauseilen 192**

hurry **beeilen (sich) 73, eilen 192**

hurry off **wegeilen 192**

hurt **verletzen 559**

hypnotize **hypnotisieren 57**

identify **identifizieren 57**

idolize **vergöttern 569**

ignore, miss **überhören 538**

illuminate **erleuchten 74**

illustrate **illustrieren 57**

imagine, be conceited **einbilden (sich) 108**

imitate **imitieren 57, nachahmen 59**

immigrate **einwandern 583**

immortalize **verewigen 572**

impart by word of mouth **zusprechen 488**

impinge **auftreffen (sein) 528**

implicate **verwickeln 150**

imply, stipulate **bedingen 269**

import **importieren 57**

impose **auferlegen 301**

impress **beeindrucken 141, imponieren 57**

improve **verbessern 569**

improve, repair, increase **aufbessern 569**

incite, instigate **anreizen 245**

incite, stir up **anregen 60**

include, lock in **einschließen 430**

increase **zunehmen 612**

increase, augment **mehren 561**

increase, develop, flourish **gedeihen 112**

increase, multiply **vermehren 561**

indent, notch **kerben 151**

induce, persuade **bewegen (2) 103**

industrialize **industrialisieren 57**

influence **beeinflussen 292**

inform **informieren 57, mitteilen 330**

inform, notify **melden 324**

inform, send word **benachrichtigen 558**

inhale **einatmen 58**

inherit **erben 151**

inherit jointly **miterben 151**

initiate, introduce **einleiten 306**

inoculate **impfen 421**

inquire **erkundigen 159**

inquire about **nachfragen 197**

insert, place, install **einsetzen (sich) 196**

inspire **begeistern 569**

inspire, animate **beseelen 73**

install **installieren 57**

install, fit **einbauen 72**

install, set up **aufstellen 580**

instruct, point out **anweisen 591**

insult, abuse **beschimpfen 421**

insult, offend **beleidigen 159**

insult, scold **schimpfen 421**
insure **versichern 569**
integrate **integrieren 57**
intend **beabsichtigen 91, vorhaben 235**
interest **interessieren (sich) 57**
interfere, meddle **einmischen (sich) 329**
interpret **interpretieren 57**
interrogate **ausfragen 197**
interrupt **unterbrechen 118**
interview **interviewen 57**
interweave **durchweben 587**
introduce, enter, record **eintragen 524**
invade, break in **eindringen 130**
invent **erfinden 152**
investigate **untersuchen 96**
invite **einladen 138**
iron **bügeln 71**
isolate **absondern (sich) 47, vereinzeln 564**
isolate, insulate **isolieren 57**
jingle, clink **klimpern 193**
jog along **trotten 189**
join **ineinander fügen 250**
join in conversation **mitsprechen 488**
joke **scherzen 415**
judge **beurteilen 101**
judge, give an opinion **urteilen 101**
juggle **jonglieren 57**
jump **springen 489**
jump back **zurückspringen 489**
justify **rechtfertigen 371**
jut out **vorstehen 495**
keep, maintain **behalten 80**
keep, secure **verwahren 558**
keep open **offenhalten 236**
keep secret **verschweigen 457**
kick open, come forward **auftreten 531**
kick the bucket **verrecken 192**
kill **töten 523, umbringen 120**
kiss **küssen 292**
knead **kneten 283**
knit **stricken 509**
knock **klopfen 277**
knock, rap on **anklopfen 277**
knock down **niederschlagen 425**
know **wissen 599**
know, be acquainted **kennen 267**
know beforehand **vorherwissen 599**
know one's way around **auskennen (sich) 267**
lack, be deficient **mangeln 275**
lack, be in the wrong **fehlen 181**
lacquer, varnish **lackieren 57**
land **landen 189**
last, continue **andauern 123, dauern 123, währen 582**
last, persist **fortwähren 302**
laugh **lachen 294**
lay **legen 301**
lay before **vorlegen 301**
lay claim to, demand **beanspruchen 96**
lay down **niederlegen 301**
lay down, lie down **hinlegen (sich) 301**
layer **schichten 44**
lead **führen 203**
lead astray **verführen 203**

lead away **wegführen 203**

lead away, take into police custody **abführen 203**

lead back **zurückführen 203, zurückleiten 306**

lead forth, go on with **fortführen 203**

lead someone to believe **vorgaukeln 293**

leak **entweichen 380**

leak, drip through **durchsickern 583**

lean **lehnen 308**

lean against **anlehnen 308**

leap forward **vorspringen 489**

learn **lernen 308**

learn, experience **erfahren 173**

lease, farm out **verpachten 343**

leave behind **zurücklassen 296**

leave behind, in place **stehen lassen 296**

leave closed **zulassen 296**

leave open **offenlassen 296**

leave out **weglassen 296**

lend **leihen 304**

lend out, hire out **ausleihen 304**

lengthen **verlängern 569**

let, allow **lassen 296**

let come forward **vorlassen 296**

let loose **loslassen 296**

liberalize, relax **liberalisieren 57**

lick, leak **lecken 300**

lie down, crouch **kuschen (sich) 247**

lie in wait **nachstellen 580**

lie, fib **lügen 316**

lie, recline **liegen 311**

lie to **belügen 316**

lift, raise **heben 241**

light, kindle **anzünden 65**

light up, brighten up **aufhellen 580**

lightning **blitzen 113**

like **gern haben 235**

limit, check, reduce **einschränken 413**

limit, restrict **beschränken 413**

limp **hinken 598**

linger **verweilen 558**

lisp **lispeln 71**

listen **anhören 611, horchen 254**

listen, eavesdrop **lauschen 247**

listen to **zuhören 611**

live **leben 299**

live, reside **wohnen 600**

live on, survive **fortleben 299**

live together **zusammenleben 299**

load, burden **belasten 146**

load, burden with **aufladen 138**

load, burden, complain **beschweren (sich) 86**

lock up, seclude **abschließen 430**

loiter, saunter, stroll **bummeln 71**

long, yearn **sehnen 465**

look **blicken 416, gucken 234, schauen 406**

look after, follow with the eyes **nachsehen 66**

look around **umschauen 616**

look at **anschauen 616, ansehen 66**

look at, watch **zuschauen 616**

look away **wegsehen 66**

look back **zurückblicken 416**

look for, seek **suchen 513**

look forward **vorausschauen 616**
look like **aussehen 66**
look through (a book) **nachblättern 191**
loosen, work free **losarbeiten 55**
lose **verlieren (verlieren)**
love **lieben 310**
love, be fond of **lieb haben 235**
lower, humble, degrade **erniedrigen 159**
lull, sing **lullen 498**
lurk **lauern 297**
magnetize **magnetisieren 57**
maintain, assert **behaupten 145**
maintain, keep repaired **instandhalten 236**
make, do **machen 317**
make a date **verabreden (sich) 372**
make a down payment **anzahlen 603**
make a fool of someone **narren 504**
make a mistake, assault **vergreifen (sich) 230**
make a show, look resplendent **prangen 558**
make a stain **klecksen 315**
make amends **vergüten 562**
make amends for **gutmachen 317**
make an enemy of **verfeinden 74**
make angry **erbosen 315**
make believe, hoax **weismachen 317**
make glad, delight **freuen 199**
make happy **beglücken 141**
make known **bekannt geben 63**
make known, announce **kundgeben 63**
make muddy, cloud **trüben 522**
make noise **lärmen 295**
make pottery **töpfern 47**
make progress **vorankommen 49**
make radiant **verklären 157**
make ready **instandsetzen 196**
make up one's mind **entschließen (sich) 430**
make way **ausweichen 380**
make worse **verschlechtern 160**
manicure **manikürен 504**
manipulate **manipulieren 57**
maneuver **manövrieren 57**
manufacture **fabrizieren 57**
marble, grain **marmorieren 57**
march **marschieren 347**
march by **vorbeimarschieren 347**
mark out, distinguish **auszeichnen 600**
marry **heiraten 243, verehelichen 96, verheiraten 556**
marry into (a business) **einheiraten 243**
mash, trample **zerstampfen 262**
massage **massieren 57**
matriculate **immatrikulieren (sich) 57**
may **mögen 332**
may, be allowed **dürfen 135**
mean **bedeuten 74**
measure **messen 327**
measure a dose **dosieren 57**
mediate, adjust **vermitteln 564**
meet **treffen 528**
melt **schmelzen 436**

menace, threaten **androhen 131**
mend, patch **flicken 509**
mention **erwähnen 158**
mesh, cooperate **ineinander greifen 230**
mew **mauen 518**
milk **melken 325**
mill, grind **mahlen 319**
mimic **nachäffen 252**
miss **vermissen 559, verpassen 346**
miss, overlook **überséhen 464**
miss out **versäumen 566**
mistrust **misstrauen 574**
misunderstand **missverstehen 571**
mix **mischen 329**
mix, blend **vermischen 329**
mix, mingle **mengen 558**
moan, groan **ächzen 468**
mobilize **mobilisieren 57**
mock **spotten 487, verhöhnen 85, verspotten 487**
moderate, reduce **ermäßigen 159**
moisten, dampen **befeuchten 87**
moralize **moralisieren 57**
mount, ascend **heraufsteigen 67**
mourn, lament **nachweinen 590**
move **bewegen (1) 102**
move, shove **rücken 336**
move, stir **regen 60**
move forward **vorrücken 336, weiterbewegen 102**
move out of place **verschieben 417**
move quickly, sweep over **streichen 507**
mumble, mutter **murmeln 71**
murder **ermorden 74**
murmur **murmeln 71**
murmur, grumble **murren 255**
mutilate **verhauen 240**
mutiny **meutern 481**
nail **nageln 71**
name **nennen 339**
narrow **verengern 569**
necessitate, oblige **nötigen 159**
need **brauchen 117**
need, be in want **bedürfen 135**
negotiate **verhandeln 81**
nest **nisten 44**
neutralize **neutralisieren 57**
nibble, crunch **knuspern 47**
nibble, gnaw **knabbern 191**
nod **nicken 336**
nominate **ernennen 339**
not envy, not grudge **gönnen 308**
note, mark **merken 326**
notice, heed, regard **beachten 44**
notice, remark **bemerken 86**
nourish, feed **ernähren 161**
nullify **nullifizieren 57**
number **numerieren 57**
obey **gehorchen (gehorchen)**
oblige, bind **verpflichten 577**
observe **beobachten 577**
observe, remark, note **anmerken 326**
obstruct, block out **verbauen 72**
obtain, receive **erhalten 80**
occupy, make busy **beschäftigen 89**
occupy, possess **innehaben 235**
occur, happen **ereignen (sich) 162**

occur to a person **einfallen (sich) 137**
offend, hurt **kränken 598**
offer **anbieten 46, bieten 107**
offer, propose **antragen 524**
ogle **liebäugeln 71**
open **öffnen 341**
open, inaugurate **eröffnen 162**
open, unfold **aufklappen 270**
open, untie **aufmachen 317**
operate **operieren 57**
oppose **widerstéhen 495**
order **bestellen 94**
order, arrange **verfügen 250**
order anew, reorder **nachbestellen 580**
order in advance **vorausbestellen 580**
organize **organisieren 57**
originate **entstammen 378, entstehen 495**
outlive, survive **überlében 538**
overcharge **überfórdern 193**
overcome, prevail **überwínden 109**
overestimate **überschätzen 405**
overhaul, overtake **überhólen 253**
overpower **niederkämpfen 262**
overtire **übermüden 144**
owe **schulden 452**
own **besitzen 475**
pack, seize, grasp **packen 416**
pack, wrap up **einpacken 345**
pack away **wegpacken 345**
paddle, row **paddeln 344**
pain, hurt **schmerzen 437**
paint **anmalen 321, malen 321**
pant, gasp **keuchen 189**
paralyze, cripple **lähmen 295**
park **parken 345**
participate **teilnehmen 612**
pass, elapse, vanish **vergehen 210**
pass by **vorübergehen 613**
pass on **weitergeben 63**
pass over, run over **überfáhren 173**
pay **bezahlen 105, löhnen 313, zahlen 603**
pay back **vergelten 214, zurückbezahlen 105**
pay duty **verzollen 558**
pay later **nachbezahlen 105**
pay one's respects, pay homage **huldigen 159**
pay out **auszahlen 603**
pay the postage cost **frankieren 57**
peel, pare **schälen 401**
penetrate, pierce **durchdríngen 130**
perceive **vernehmen 550**
perceive, be aware of **wahrnehmen 612**
perceive, become aware **innewerden 593**
perceive, understand **auffassen 178**
perform **aufführen 203**
perform, execute **verrichten 383**
permit, grant **vergönnen 308**
persecute **verfolgen 192**
persuade **überréden 372**
photograph **photographieren 57**
pick, pluck **pflücken 351**
pick out, sort **klauben 226**
pick up, call for, collect **abholen 253**

pierce through, stab **durchstechen 493**

pilot **lotsen 315**

pinch **zwicken 416**

pinch, squeeze **kneifen 508**

pine, long for **schmachten 423**

place, put **stellen 498**

place before **vorsetzen 196**

place before, introduce **vorstellen 580**

plague **plagen 352**

plan **planen 308**

plant **pflanzen 349**

play **spielen 485**

play a drum **trommeln 71**

play hooky **schwänzen 455**

play out, play to the end **ausspielen 485**

play the violin **Geige spielen 485**

play to **vorspielen 485**

play with **mitspielen 485**

please, like **gefallen 209**

plow **pflügen 350**

pluck, pull **rupfen 391**

point, indicate **deuten 97**

point, show **hindeuten 51**

poison **vergiften 562**

pollute, contaminate **verpesten 562**

ponder **grübeln 71, wägen 106**

populate **bevölkern 160**

portray **schildern 419**

pour **gießen 224**

pour out **ausschenken 413**

pout, sulk **schmollen 440**

powder **pudern 385**

practice **üben 537**

practice, pursue studies **betreiben 529**

practice (a profession) **ausüben 537**

praise **loben 312**

praise, extol **preisen 409, rühmen 295**

pray **beten 97**

preach **predigen 357**

precede **vorangehen 613**

precipitate, plunge, crash **abstürzen 511**

predict **voraussagen 394**

preheat **vorwärmen 59**

prepare **vorbereiten 578, vorrichten 383**

prepare, cook **zubereiten 578**

prepare work **vorarbeiten 55**

prepay **vorausbezahlen 105**

prescribe **verschreiben 90**

present, offer **darbieten 46**

press **drücken 132**

prevail **vorherrschen 247**

prevent **verhindern 47**

print **drucken 132**

proceed, set out for **begeben (sich) 207**

process **verarbeiten 55**

procure **besorgen 477**

produce **produzieren 57**

produce an after-effect **nachwirken 598**

program **programmieren 57**

promise **versprechen 570**

promote **weiterbringen 120**

pronounce **aussprechen 488**

prop, support **stützen 512**

propagate, spread **fortpflanzen (sich) 349**
propel, continue moving **fortbewegen (sich) 102**
propose, move **beantragen 92**
protect **schützen 454**
protest **protestieren 57**
prove **beweisen 104**
prove, show **erweisen 104**
provide **versorgen 477**
provoke, irritate **entrüsten 146**
publish **herausgeben 63, veröffentlichen 96**
pull, tug **zerren 302**
pull away **wegziehen 615**
pull out, undress **ausziehen 615**
punch (a hole), take a picture **knipsen 315**
punctuate **interpunktieren 57**
punish **bestrafen 506**
punish, fine **strafen 506**
pursue, sic **hetzen 245**
push along **nachschieben 417**
push back **zurückstoßen 505**
push forward **vordrängen 129**
push on **vordringen 489**
push, shove **drängeln 71, stoßen 505**
push, urge **drängen 129**
put, stick **stecken 494**
put aside **weglegen 301, wegsetzen 196**
put away, turn off, abolish **abstellen 580**
put back **zurückstellen 580**
put gas in the tank **tanken 515**
put here, manufacture **herstellen 580**
put in a bad mood **verstimmen 509**
put in a bad temper, upset **missstimmen 95**
put near, employ, engage **anstellen 580**
put on, compose **aufsetzen 196**
put on, undertake **vornehmen (sich) 612**
put on airs, brag **brüsten (sich) 283**
put on clothes **ankleiden 273**
quake, shake, tremble **beben 299**
quarrel **zanken 598**
quiet, pacify **beruhigen 159**
quote **zitieren 57**
rain **regnen (regnen)**
raise, draw up **aufziehen 615**
raise, heighten **steigern 481**
raise up, lift **aufheben 241**
ransom, redeem **einlösen 315**
rape **vergewaltigen 159**
rattle, clatter **knattern 278**
ravage **verheeren 561**
rave, be mad **rasen 366**
reach, get to **gelangen 192**
reach, pass **reichen 376**
react **reagieren 373**
read **lesen 309**
read off, call off **verlesen 309**
read on **weiterlesen 309**
read to **vorlesen 309**
realize **realisieren 57, verwirklichen 96**
rearrange **umstellen 580**
receive, get **bekommen 83**
receive, welcome **empfangen 176**
receive money, cash **kassieren 57**

recite **aufsagen 394, vorsagen 394**

recite in prayer **vorbeten 97**

recognize **erkennen 267**

recommend **empfehlen 75**

recommend, advocate **befürworten 52**

recover, get better **erholen (sich) 253**

recruit, solicit **werben 214**

reduce **reduzieren 57**

refer, relate **beziehen (sich) 171**

refine, purify **läutern 297**

reflect **widerspiegeln 595**

reflect, ponder **nachdenken 125**

reflect on, consider **überlégen 538**

refresh **erfrischen 153, laben 312**

refuse **weigern (sich) 47, 481**

refuse, reject **verweigern 569**

refute **widerlégen 538**

regard, respect **achten 44**

regret **bedauern 569, bereuen 574**

regulate **regeln 395**

regulate, prepare, dish up **anrichten 383**

reject **zurückweisen 591**

relax **entspannen 149**

release, fire **entlassen 296**

release, liberate **freilassen 296**

remain **verbleiben 112**

remain, stay **bleiben 112**

remain behind **nachbleiben 112, zurückbleiben 112**

remain open, remain up **aufbleiben 112**

remain sitting **sitzen bleiben 112**

remain standing **stehen bleiben 112**

remember **erinnern (sich) 155**

remind, warn **mahnen 320**

remit **überwéisen 591**

remove **entfernen 142**

renew, renovate **erneuern 155**

renounce **verzichten 577**

renovate **renovieren 57**

rent **mieten (mieten), pachten 343, vermieten (vermieten)**

repair **reparieren 57**

repeat **wiederhólen 596**

repeat what was heard, retell **nacherzählen 170**

replace **ersetzen 540**

reply, retort **erwidern 155**

report **berichten 383**

report, notify **anmelden (sich) 324**

represent **vertreten 575**

represent, state **darstellen 580**

reprimand **maßregeln 564, verweisen 104**

reprint, republish **nachdrücken 132**

reproduce, copy **nachbilden 108**

require, need **benötigen 89**

resell **wiederverkaufen 265**

resemble, take after **ähneln 71**

reserve **reservieren 57, vorbehalten 80**

resound, echo **hallen 498**

resound, peal **schallen 498**

rest **ausruhen 59, ruhen 114**

restore **restaurieren 57**

restrain, prevent, deter **abhalten 236**

retrieve, recover **nachholen 253**

return home **heimkehren 614**

reward **belohnen 85**

reward, be worth **lohnen 85**

rhyme **reimen 295**
ride **reiten 380**
ridicule **veralbern 569**
ring, toll **läuten 97**
rinse out **ausspülen 43**
rip **reißen 379**
rip to pieces **zerreißen 379**
rise, ascend, increase **ansteigen 67**
rise, soar **hochgehen 613**
rise, swell **aufgehen 613**
risk **riskieren 57**
rivet **nieten 97**
roar **brüllen 498**
roast **braten 116, rösten 283**
roll **rollen 498**
roll, rotate **wälzen 468**
roll down **niederrollen 192**
roll up **aufwickeln 150**
rot **verfaulen 192**
rouse, excite **aufregen 60**
row **rudern 385**
rub **reiben 375**
ruin **ruinieren 57**
rule **walten 585**
rule, govern **regieren 373**
rule, reign **herrschen 247**
run **laufen 298, rennen 381**
run, flow over **überläufen 298**
run away **entlaufen 298**
run away, escape **entfliehen 143**
run away, run on **fortlaufen 298**
run back **zurücklaufen 298**
run off, expire **ablaufen 298**
run over **umfahren 173**
rustle, roar **rauschen 369**
sacrifice **aufopfern 47, opfern 47**
sail **segeln 462**
satisfy, pay off, make a settlement **abfinden 492**
satisfy, sate **sättigen 100**
saunter **schlendern 583**
save **sparen 479**
save, rescue **retten 382**
save, secure **bergen 214**
save up **aufsparen 479**
saw **sägen 301**
say **sagen 394**
scoff, sneer **höhnen 308**
scold, chide **keifen 506**
scold, reproach **schelten 214**
scratch **kratzen 286**
screw **schrauben 448**
scribble **kritzeln 289**
scuffle **raufen (sich) 368**
seal with lead, plug **plombieren 57**
search, investigate **forschen 195**
search after, investigate **nachforschen 195**
search for **nachsuchen 513**
search thoroughly **durchsuchen 513**
seat oneself, sit down **hinsetzen (sich) 196**
see **sehen 464**
see through, see clearly **durchsehen 66**
seek, search out **aussuchen 513**
seem **scheinen 410**
seize, confiscate **beschlagnahmen 85**
seize, take in pledge **pfänden 44**
select, inspect **küren 255**
select, pick out, read to the end **auslesen 309**

sell **verkaufen 265**

sell off, sell on sale **ausverkaufen 265**

send **schicken 416, senden 467**

send after, forward **nachsenden 467**

send away **wegschicken 416**

send back **zurückschicken 416**

send forward **vorschicken 416**

send in advance **vorausschicken 416**

send on **weiterbefördern 193, weiterschicken 416**

send on ahead **voranschicken 416**

separate **auseinander bringen 120, sondern 47, trennen 530**

separate, divorce **scheiden (sich) 409**

serve **dienen 127, servieren 57**

set, put **setzen 468**

set (as of the sun), founder **untergehen 613**

set aside **wegtun 535**

set behind **nachsetzen 196**

set fire to, inflame **entzünden 144**

set fire to, kindle **anbrennen 119**

set free, release **entbinden 109**

set off **losfahren 173**

set out **losgehen 613**

set out on a journey **fortreisen 378**

set right, arrange, adjust **einrichten 383**

settle, bring to a close **erledigen 159**

settle, colonize **siedeln 71**

settle beforehand **vorherbestimmen 95**

sew **nähen 335**

sew in, file (papers) **einheften 51**

shake **schütteln 453**

shake, roll, sway **schwanken 598**

share, divide **teilen 520**

share, hold jointly **mithalten 236**

sharpen **schärfen 404**

sharpen, intensify **verschärfen 404**

shave **rasieren 57**

shelter, quarter **unterbringen 120**

shine, illuminate **leuchten 44**

shine through **durchstrahlen 43**

shock **schockieren 57**

shock, make indignant **empören 142**

shoot **schießen 418**

shoot dead **erschießen 418**

shoot down **niederschießen 418**

shoot past **vorbeischießen 418**

shoot to pieces **zerschießen 418**

shorten **kürzen 468, verkürzen 540**

should **sollen 476**

shout **schreien 450**

shout down **niederschreien 450**

shout with joy **jubeln 259**

shove **schieben 417**

shove or push forward **vorschieben 417**

shovel **schaufeln 407**

show, point out **zeigen 605**

shower **duschen 247**

shriek **kreischen 443**

shut off, barricade **absperren 484**

sift, sieve **durchsieben 43**

sigh **seufzen 469**

sight (in the distance) **sichten 383**

sign **unterschréiben 90**

signify, designate **bezeichnen 85**

silver-plate **versilbern 569**
simplify **vereinfachen 558**
sing **singen 473**
sing to **vorsingen 473**
sink **sinken 474**
sink down **niedersinken 474**
sink into poverty **verelenden 189**
sip, lap **schlürfen 262**
sit **sitzen 475**
sketch, draft, design **entwerfen 594**
skin, flay **schinden 184**
skip, hop **tänzeln 462**
slam **zuschlagen 425**
slander **lästern 297**
slander, blacken one's name **anschwärzen 196**
slaughter **schlachten 423**
slay, kill animals **erlegen 301**
sleep **schlafen 424**
sleep through **durchschläfen 424**
slide, glide **schleifen 428**
slide, skid **gleiten 380**
slide, slip **rutschen 392**
slip, skid **ausrutschen 392**
slip, slide **schlüpfen 431**
slit, slash **schlitzen 468**
smash **zerschmettern 607**
smell **riechen 384**
smile **lächeln 293**
smile at **zulächeln 293**
smoke **rauchen 369**
smoke, cure **räuchern 481**
smooth out a fold **glattlegen 301**
smuggle **schmuggeln 441**
snarl **fletschen 185**
snatch, seize **haschen 247**
sneeze **niesen 340**
snore **schnarchen 442**
snow **schneien 444**
snuggle up **kuscheln (sich) 291**
soak **einweichen 61**
soften **aufweichen 61**
solder **löten 97**
solve, dissolve **lösen 315**
sort, sort out **sortieren 57**
sound **klingen 276**
sound shrill **gellen 498**
sound, read as **lauten 44**
sound, resound **tönen 45**
sow **säen 393**
spare **verschonen 446**
spare, treat with consideration **schonen 446**
sparkle, reflect **spiegeln 71**
sparkle, twinkle **funkeln 204**
speak **sprechen 488**
speak to, address **anreden 372**
speculate **spekulieren 57**
spell **buchstabieren 57**
spend **ausgeben 63**
spend the night **übernächten 74**
spend time **verbringen 120**
spice **würzen 512**
spill **vergießen 224**
spin, twist **spinnen 486**
spit **spucken 234**
splash **platschen 271**
split **spalten 478**
spoil **verderben 553**
spot, stain **beflecken 141**
spray, sprinkle **sprühen 114**

sprout, bud **sprießen 188**

spy **spionieren 57**

squander **vergeuden 74, verschwenden 567**

squat, crouch **kauern 291**

squeeze, pinch **klemmen 514**

squirt, splash **spritzen 490**

stab, pierce **stechen 493**

stammer **lallen 498**

stamp **stempeln 500**

stand **stehen 495**

stand up, get up **aufstehen 495**

standardize **vereinheitlichen 96**

start **starten 44**

start, begin **anfangen 48**

start moving a car **anfahren 173**

startle, bewilder **verblüffen 558**

starve **verhungern 557**

state, indicate, give in advance **angeben 63**

stay, tarry **weilen 520**

stay away **fortbleiben 112, wegbleiben 112**

stay away, be absent **ausbleiben 112**

stay shut **zuhaben 235**

steal **stehlen 496**

steal, pilfer **klauen 72**

steal, plunder **rauben 368**

steal away **wegstehlen 496**

steer **steuern 502**

stem, lift weights **stemmen 499**

step, proceed **schreiten 451**

step, walk **treten 531**

step back **zurücktreten 531**

step forward **vorschreiten 451**

step forward, advance **fortschreiten 451**

stifle, suffocate **ersticken 156**

stink **stinken 503**

stipulate **vorausbedingen 473**

stipulate in advance **vorbedingen 473**

stir, agitate **umrühren 389**

stir, touch **rühren 389**

stoop, bow **bücken (sich) 494**

stop **stoppen 252**

stop, cease **aufhören 611**

stop, check, restrain **anhalten 236**

stop short, hesitate **stutzen 512**

store **speichern 481**

store away, preserve **aufbewahren 105**

storm **stürmen 510**

storm, rage, bluster **brausen 315**

strap on **umschnallen 580**

stream, flow **strömen 378**

strengthen, confirm **bekräftigen 89**

stretch, extend **strecken 494**

stretch forward **vorstrecken 59**

strew, spread **streuen 525**

strike **streiken 124**

strike against, ring **anschlagen 425**

strike dead, slay **erschlagen 425**

strike down **niederschmettern 607**

strive for **trachten 383**

stroke, caress **streicheln 71**

stroll **spazieren 347**

study **studieren 57**

stuff **vollpfropfen 262**

stumble **stolpern 583**

subjugate, enslave **knechten 44**

sublet **untervermieten 562**
subordinate **unterordnen 342**
subscribe **abonnieren 57**
succeed, manage to do **gelingen 213**
suck **lutschen 271, saugen 398**
suffer, bear **leiden 303**
suffice **zureichen 376**
suffice, be adequate **ausreichen 376**
suffice, be enough **genügen 217**
suggest **vorschlagen 425**
summarize **zusammenfassen 178**
sun, bask in the sun **sonnen (sich) 308**
suppose **vermuten 562**
suppress **unterdrücken 132**
surf **surfen 277**
surprise **überräschen 539**
survey, overlook **überséhen 464**
swallow, gulp down **herunterschlucken 59**
swear, take an oath **schwören 461**
swear in **vereidigen 572**
sweat **schwitzen 460**
sweep **kehren 266**
sweep, wipe **fegen 301**
swell, rise **schwellen 458**
swim **schwimmen 459**
swindle **schwindeln 71**
swing **schaukeln 408**
swing, brandish **schwingen 473**
swing, oscillate **pendeln 99**
swing, swivel **schwenken 598**
switch on **anschalten 402**
switch over **umschalten 402**
take **nehmen 337**
take along **mitnehmen 612**
take apart **zerlegen 538**
take away **fortbringen 120, wegbringen 120, wegnehmen 612**
take care of **kümmern (sich) 47**
take dimensions **ausmessen 327**
take down, depend on **abhängen 238**
take from, remove from **fortnehmen 612**
take hold of **anfassen 178**
take hold of, seize **ergreifen 230**
take home **heimbringen 120**
take in, accept, occupy **einnehmen 612**
take in, take a photograph **aufnehmen 612**
take notes **mitschreiben 449**
take off, lay down, undress **ablegen 301**
take off, reduce, diminish **abnehmen 612**
take place **stattfinden 492**
take place previously **vorhergeschehen 218**
take possession of, take charge **übernéhmen 550**
take the trouble, strive **bemühen (sich) 85**
take to heart **beherzigen 89**
take to task **vorknöpfen 277**
talk **reden 372**
talk nonsense **quatschen 363**
tangle **verwirren 558**
taste **schmecken 433**
teach **beibringen 120, lehren 302**
teach, instruct **unterríchten 383**
tear away **entreißen 379**
tear down **wegreißen 379**

tear out **ausreißen 379**

tease **necken 336**

telegraph **telegrafieren 57**

telephone **telefonieren 57**

tell, relate, narrate **erzählen 170**

tell lies to someone **vorlügen 316**

tell others **weitersagen 394**

tend, care for **pflegen 350**

terrify **entsetzen 468**

test **prüfen 358**

thank **bedanken (sich) 141, danken 121**

thaw **tauen 518**

thicken, condense **verdichten 126**

thicken, swell **verdicken 558**

thin **verdünnen 558**

thin out **lichten 383**

think **denken 125**

think highly of **hochhalten 236**

thrash **verprügeln 564**

threaten **drohen 131**

thresh **dreschen 214**

throw **werfen 594**

throw away **wegwerfen 594**

throw back **zurückwerfen 594**

throw down **niederwerfen 594**

throw in, smash **einwerfen 594**

throw to **zuwerfen 594**

thunder **donnern 128**

tickle **kitzeln 289**

tie to **festschnallen 580**

tie together **koppeln 71, zusammenbinden 109**

tie up **zubinden 109**

tie up with string **schnüren 445**

tilt, bend **neigen 338**

tinkle, ring **klingeln 275**

tip **kippen 268**

tip over **umkippen 546**

torment, inflict martyrdom **martern 481**

torture **quälen 361**

torture, torment **foltern 191**

touch, handle, attack **antasten 51**

touch, mix, stir **anrühren 389**

track down **aufspüren 59**

train **trainieren 57**

train, break in **dressieren 57**

trample down **niedertreten 531**

transfer **versetzen 540**

transfer, change transportation **umsteigen 67**

transfer, put off **verlegen 301**

transfer, transmit **übertrágen 573**

transform **verwandeln 150**

translate **dolmetschen 271, übersétzen 540**

translate into German **verdeutschen 539**

transport **transportieren 57**

travel **reisen 378**

travel about, become known **herumkommen 49**

travel through, traverse **durchreisen 378**

travel with **mitreisen 378**

travel without a ticket **schwarzfahren 173**

treat, handle **behandeln 81**

treat, pay for **spendieren 57**

tremble **zittern 481**

trim, garnish **garnieren 57**

trot, patter **trappeln 462**

trouble, bother **belästigen 89**

trust **trauen 525, vertrauen 574**
try **versuchen 96**
try, examine **verhören 255**
try, taste **probieren 57**
try on **anprobieren 57**
try on, make fit **anpassen 346**
try on (headgear) **aufprobieren 57**
try out, taste **ausprobieren 57**
tunc, adjust **abstimmcn 95**
tune in, focus **einstellen 580**
turn **wenden 592**
turn, guide **lenken 307**
turn around **herumdrehen 545, umdrehen 545**
turn into **wandeln 395**
turn off **ausmachen 317**
turn off, branch off, deflect **abbiegen 106**
turn out, appear **herausstellen (sich) 580**
turn out, expel **ausweisen 591**
turn pages, skim through a book **durchblättern 160**
twirl **zwirbeln 71**
type **tippen 521**
uncover, reveal **aufdecken 124**
undergo, get through **bestehen 571**
understand **verstehen 571**
undertake **unternehmen 550**
undervalue **unterschätzen 540**
undo, settle, arrange **abmachen 317**
undress **auskleiden 273**
unfold **auseinander falten 175**
unhook **loshaken 43**
unite **vereinigen 558**
unload **entladen 138**
unload, disembark **ausladen 138**
unlock **aufschließen 430**
unlock, open up **aufsperren 484**
unpack **auspacken 345**
unroll, unwrap **auswickeln 150**
untie, loosen **losbinden 109**
upset, put in a bad mood **verstimmen 95**
urge, press, penetrate **dringen 130**
use **benutzen 88, gebrauchen 208**
use as fodder **verfüttern 204**
use cream or lotion **einkremen 59**
use makeup **schminken 439**
use up, consume **verbrauchen 208**
utilize, wear out **ausnutzen 88**
utter, express **äußern 481**
vacuum **Staub saugen 398**
value, esteem, respect **schätzen 405**
vaporize, gas **vergasen 315**
veil, wrap up **verhüllen 94**
venture, risk **wagen 584**
verify **nachprüfen 358**
view, go sightseeing **besichtigen 91**
violate the law **Rechte verletzen 559**
visit **besuchen 96**
vomit (colloquial) **kotzen 468**
vow, promise solemnly **geloben 312**
wait **warten 585**
wake up **aufwachen 61**
waken, rouse **aufwecken 59, wecken 589**
walk on **weitergehen 613**
wander, hike **wandern 583**
want **wollen 601**

warn **warnen 584**
wash **waschen 586**
wash, rinse **spülen 43**
wash away **fortschwemmen 43**
wash off, rinse **abspülen 43**
wash up **abwaschen 586**
watch over, pay attention **auf passen 346**
watch television **fernsehen 66**
watch through, lie awake **durchwáchen 538**
water, irrigate **bewässern 569**
water down, dilute **verwässern 569**
wave **winken 598**
wave to **zuwinken 598**
weaken **schwächen 294**
weaken, debilitate **entkräften 562**
weave **weben 587**
weed **jäten 97**
weep, have a good cry **ausweinen 590**
weigh **wiegen 106**
wet, moisten **benetzen 468**
whine, howl **jaulen 253**
whip **peitschen 271**
whisper **flüstern 191, raunen 465**
whistle **pfeifen 348**
widen **weiten 585**
wilt **verwelken 192, welken 192**
win **gewinnen 222**
wind **wickeln 71**
wind, twist **schlängeln 426**
wind, twist, entwine **schlingen 473**
wind through **durchwinden 184**
wipe away **wegwischen 329**
wiretap **abhören 255**
wish, desire **wünschen 602**
withdraw **zurückziehen 615**
withhold **vorenthalten 80**
work **arbeiten 55**
work, operate, function **wirken 598**
wrap up **vermummen 514**
wrap up, envelop **hüllen 498**
wrestle, grapple **ringen 473**
write **schreiben 449**
write down, ascribe to **anschreiben 449**
write down, enter **aufschreiben 449**
write out, finish writing **ausschreiben 449**
x-ray **röntgen 558**
yawn **gähnen 205**
yield **weichen 380**
yield, result in **ergeben 207**
yodel **jodeln 258**